SEVENTH EDITION

AMERICA'S HISTORY

James A. Henretta
University of Maryland

Rebecca Edwards
Vassar College

Robert O. Self
Brown University

BEDFORD / ST. MARTIN'S

Boston • New York

For Bedford/St.Martin's
Publisher for History: Mary Dougherty
Executive Editor for History: William J. Lombardo
Director of Development for History: Jane Knetzger
Developmental Editor: Danielle Slevens
Senior Production Editor: Deborah Baker
Production Supervisor: Andrew Ensor
Executive Marketing Manager: Jenna Bookin Barry
Editorial Assistant: Robin Soule
Production Assistant: David Ayers
Copyeditor: Janet Renard
Indexer: Ed Prucha, EdIndex
Photo Researcher: Pembroke Herbert and Sandi Rygiel/Picture Research Consultants & Archives
Permissions Manager: Kalina Ingham Hintz
Senior Art Director: Anna Palchik
Cover Designer: Marine Miller
Cover Photo: Looking Across the valley to Yosemite Falls, USA (1917). Underwood & Underwood/© Royal
 Geographical Society, London/Bridgeman Art Library
Cartography: Mapping Specialists Limited
Composition: NK Graphics
Printing and Binding: RR Donnelley and Sons

President: Joan E. Feinberg
Editorial Director: Denise B. Wydra
Director of Marketing: Karen R. Soeltz
Director of Production: Susan W. Brown
Associate Director, Editorial Production: Elise S. Kaiser
Managing Editor: Elizabeth M. Schaaf

Library of Congress Control Number: 2010928991

Manufactured in the United States of America.

2   3   4   5   6   15   14   13   12   11

For information, write: Bedford/St. Martin's, 75 Arlington Street, Boston, MA 02116 (617-399-4000)
ISBN: 978-0-312-38789-1   (combined edition)
ISBN: 978-0-312-38791-4   (Vol. 1)
ISBN: 978-0-312-38792-1   (Vol. 2)
ISBN: 978-0-312-38793-8   (high school edition)

Acknowledgments

Preface for Instructors

How do we teach our students to think like historians? How do we give them a basic understanding of key events and facts, while also helping them engage the past, not as a rote list of names and dates, but as the fascinating, conflicted prelude to their lives today? In the seventh edition of *America's History*, we aim to help instructors meet those challenges. *America's History* has long been known for its breadth, balance, and ability to explain to students not just what happened, but *why*. The latest edition both preserves and substantially builds upon those strengths.

The extensive changes in this edition begin with the author team. All three of us—James Henretta, who has guided the book from the start, and new authors Rebecca Edwards and Robert Self—have spent our careers working to integrate top-down narratives of politics and economic affairs with bottom-up narratives of lived experience. Using the findings of the new social history and details of the experiences of ordinary people, James Henretta has in his work offered new ways of looking at the lives of early Americans, both free and enslaved. Rebecca Edwards has used insights from women's and gender history to reinterpret nineteenth-century electoral politics. Robert Self has explored the relationship between urban and suburban politics, social movements, and the state. In *America's History*, we bring those perspectives to bear on the full sweep of America's past. Our goal is to help students achieve a richer understanding of politics, diplomacy, war, economics, intellectual and cultural life, and gender, class, and race relations, by exploring how developments in all these areas were interconnected.

The core of a textbook is its narrative, and we have endeavored to make ours clear, accessible, and lively. In it, we focus not only on the marvelous diversity of peoples who came to call themselves Americans, but also on the institutions that have forged a common national identity. Without losing our central focus on U.S. history, we call attention to connections with the histories of Canada, Latin America, Europe, Africa, and Asia. Many of today's students were born outside the United States; those who were not may one day live or do business abroad (and they may, as we write, be conversing over the Internet with people on other conti-

nents). Meanwhile, we confront political problems of global scope, ranging from financial crises and oil spills to terrorist attacks. As it has since its inception, *America's History* helps students understand the world in which we live, by drawing links between events in the United States and those elsewhere.

New Parts and New Scholarship

One of the greatest strengths of *America's History* is its part structure, which helps students identify the key forces and major developments that shaped each era. A four-page Part Opener begins each part, using analysis, striking images, and a detailed timeline to orient students to the major themes of each era and the ways in which those themes were manifest in society, culture, politics, and the economy. By organizing U.S. history into seven distinct periods, rather than just thirty-one successive chapters, we encourage students to trace changes and continuities over time and grasp connections between political, economic, social, and cultural events.

While retaining a seven-part framework, the latest edition significantly reshapes it, offering instructors a bold reconceptualization of U.S. history that reflects the latest, most exciting scholarship in the field. Throughout the book, we have given increased attention to political culture and political economy, using this analysis to help students understand how society, culture, politics, and the economy informed one another. A sharpened continental perspective, in this edition, is based on expanded coverage of Native American history, environmental history, and the trans-Mississippi West. Religion receives new attention throughout the text, particularly in the late nineteenth and twentieth centuries. Enhanced coverage of gender, ethnicity, and race includes greater emphasis on gay and lesbian history, Asian and Latino immigration, and the Civil Rights Movement, the last of which now receives a complete chapter of its own.

Part 1, "The Creation of American Society," focuses on the period 1450–1763. This part explores the impact of men and women of European origin on Native American cultures, and the creation of new kinds of social, political, economic, and cultural life in the English mainland colonies. **Part 2, "The New Republic"**—spanning the years 1763–1820—explores the evolving values and institutions of the colonial social order and the fundamental changes Americans made in their economic, religious, and cultural practices. **Part 3, "Overlapping Revolutions,"** now focuses on the period 1820–1860 and the political, economic, and social and cultural revolutions that shaped it: the creation of a democratic polity, the shift from a predominantly agricultural to a booming industrial economy, and the advent of the Second Great Awakening, as well as a host of social reforms and a complex intellectual culture.

Three fields of scholarship contribute many of the additions to Parts 1–3. New research on Native Americans informs and deepens our treatment of Bacon's Rebellion in Virginia in the 1670s, the interaction between Lewis and Clark and the Mandans of the Upper Missouri River Valley in the 1800s, and the character of the buffalo-hunting peoples of the Great Plains between 1820 and 1870. New findings in African American history likewise enhance our discussion of the transition to slavery in Virginia, the repercussions of the Haitian Revolution, and many other aspects of the black experience. Finally, using new scholarship on the building of early modern empires, we have sharpened our analysis of Britain's purposeful pursuit of trade and imperial power in the period between 1650 and 1750.

Part 4, "Creating and Preserving a Continental Nation"—now covering the period from 1844 to 1877—traces the rise of America's continental empire. It places the shattering events of the Civil War in the context of other wars that textbooks too often underemphasize: the Mexican American War, and the final conquest of North America's native peoples. Part 4 treats these as three interrelated conflicts, showing how all of them contributed to confirmation of the nation's modern borders and to the consolidation of federal authority. This analysis helps students situate North-South sectionalism and the Civil War in broad contexts, and to compare the end of slavery and the emergence of the modern American nation with similar projects in other countries. Part 4 also provides expanded coverage of the California Gold Rush and development of the Pacific coast; Native American history during and after the Civil War; and Reconstruction as it was experienced by ordinary southerners, both black and white.

The reorganization of Part 4 also offers instructors expanded options as they decide where to draw the dividing line between the first and second halves of the U.S. survey. The entirety of Part 4—including not only the chapter on Reconstruction (Chapter 15) but also a substantially revised chapter on post–Civil War diplomacy, economic development, and the trans-Mississippi West (Chapter 16)—is included in Volume 1 of *America's History*. First-half instructors can thus either choose the Civil War or Reconstruction as the end point for their classes, or they can include Chapter 16 and invite students to explore additional long-term consequences of Union victory, with special attention to the West. As Volume 2 begins with Chapter 15, those teaching the second half of the survey can, likewise, choose the chapter and context in which they wish to begin their course.

Part 5, "Bold Experiments in an Era of Industrialization," now covers the years between 1877 and 1929 as a single, unified era. In doing so, it offers a streamlined and innovative treatment of the decades when the United States became a global industrial power. Reflecting recent scholarship, we locate the origins of modern America in the post-Reconstruction years, rather than after 1900. Revising older views of progressivism as primarily an elite and middle-class, urban phenomenon, we also emphasize the significant roles played by rural and working-class Americans in demanding stronger government to combat the ills of industrialization. This approach allows students to receive a more inclusive and coherent picture of state-building from the era of Reconstruction to the New Deal.

Part 5 also gives more attention to such topics as the rise of high school and college education and women's political activism in the post–Civil War decades. All students will enjoy new material on the emergence of college and professional sports. In keeping with the urgent economic issues that confront the United States today, such as the "Great Recession" that began in 2008, a reorganized chapter on the 1920s connects the "boom" of that decade more clearly to the "bust" of the Great Depression that followed. And the United States' military and diplomatic involvement in World War I, formerly covered in a distinct chapter, is now folded into broader treatment of America's rise to global diplomatic power. The result is a clearer, more compelling analysis of the ways in which Americans both contributed to and critiqued imperialism, extending through the catastrophic legacies of the Great War. As a happy side effect of Part 5's new integrated narrative, a chapter has also been trimmed from this section, enabling instructors to move ahead briskly and devote more attention to later events.

Part 6, "The Modern State and the Age of Liberalism," has been reconceptualized to include the period between the beginning of the Great Depression in 1929 and the economic turmoil that began in 1973. This broader canvas places the New Deal, World War II, and the 1960s into a single interpretation of the growth, flowering, and retreat of political liberalism. Students can view the depression-era welfare state and the rights-based politics of the 1960s as part of a continuum in twentieth-century American politics. Taking the narrative into the early 1970s brings the women's movement, the later antiwar movement, and the Chicano and Native American movements into this structure, rather than arbitrarily breaking apart those histories at 1968.

In Part 6, we have devoted an entire chapter to the civil rights movement, which covers the full period between World War II and the early 1970s — what many historians have called the "long Civil Rights Movement." We have also expanded our coverage of women, gay and lesbian communities, suburbanization, and the rise of the Sunbelt. Finally, a major theme of Part 6 remains the emergence of the United States as a major force in global geopolitics during and after World War II. A largely reluctant international power outside of the Western Hemisphere before 1941, the United States came to project its military power and economic might into the far corners of the globe during and after the Second World War. We have retained the traditional focus on the Cold War at home and abroad, while revising themes and topics to reflect new scholarly interpretations. Our aim is for students to see the close connections between developments at home and abroad in this turbulent era.

In Part 7, "Global Capitalism and the End of the American Century," we have sought a delicate balance between the historian's scholarly distance and the immediacy of recent events. For instance, we treat globalization as a unique force reshaping American society and its economy, but we stress that global economic networks have always been intimately linked to national history. Students will find that our approach to the recent past helps them connect developments in their own lives with deeper, more long-term historical patterns. American involvement in the Middle East, the nation's increasing racial and ethnic diversity, and the role of digital technology, to name just three examples, have each been contextualized in terms of developments across much of the twentieth century.

Part 7 includes a new emphasis on how ordinary Americans experienced and tried to make sense of the sexual revolution, economic malaise, and changing family structure in the 1970s. This includes treatment of religious fundamentalism and the extraordinary growth of evangelical churches in recent decades. Of special interest in Part 7 is our enhanced treatment of domestic political events in the era after 1973, a year of profound domestic and international shifts. Drawing from recent work in gender and sexuality studies, the history of race, women's history, and political economy, we offer a synthetic treatment of the complex movement known as the New Right. And while it is still too early to offer definitive historical interpretations of the election of Barack Obama to the presidency and the passage of major health-care legislation, we encourage students to assess the significance of these events with the knowledge they've gained from Part 7 as a whole.

Primary-Source Features and Study Aids

To offer further entry points into this appealing narrative, each chapter provides aids to student comprehension and study. An opening **chapter outline** and **thematic introduction** orient readers to the central themes of each chapter. At the end of each chapter, we use a **timeline** to remind students of important events and reiterate the themes in an **analytic summary**. We append **focus questions** to the major subsections of each chapter and close with a set of **review questions** for the chapter as a whole. Where students are likely to stumble over a key concept, we boldface it in the text wherever it is first mentioned and provide a **glossary** that defines each term. Brief end-of-chapter essays entitled **"For Further Exploration"** direct students to resources for additional reading. To assist instructors and advanced students, a **full bibliography** is available online at **bedfordstmartins.com/henretta**.

America's History has long emphasized primary sources. In addition to weaving lively quotations throughout the narrative, we offer students substantial excerpts from historical documents — letters, diaries, autobiographies, public testimony, and even poems and novels. These documents allow students to experience the past through the words and perspectives of those who lived it and, equally important, to gain skill in interpreting historical evidence. Each chapter contains three primary-source features. **Comparing American Voices**, a two-page feature in each chapter, helps students learn to think critically by comparing texts written from two or more perspectives. **Reading American Pictures** helps students learn to interpret paintings, cartoons, and other visual images from the past.

Voices from Abroad uses commentary from foreign observers—and occasionally from Americans who traveled overseas—to situate U.S. history in its global context. Many instructors rely on these rich and varied features to introduce beginning students to primary-source analysis.

For the Seventh Edition we have revised one-third of the primary-source features, choosing topics that will engage students' interest and sharpen their understanding of the past. "Comparing American Voices," for example, now includes selections that contrast the beliefs and outlooks of advocates of evangelical religion and Enlightenment rationalism; documents from the Reconstruction-era debate over Mormon plural marriage; and a debate between Phyllis Schlafly and her feminist opponents. In "Voices from Abroad," we have incorporated more non-European documents for a truly global perspective. In the Sixth Edition, no Asian perspectives appeared in this feature before Chapter 25; now students can read the demand of merchant Norman Assing (Yuan Sheng) for equal treatment of Chinese migrants in California in 1852 (Chapter 13); a Chinese official's poetic protest over the treatment of his countrymen during the era of Exclusion (Chapter 17); and a Japanese Buddhist's 1893 assessment of Christian missions in his country (Chapter 18). African voices also receive their due. In Chapter 27, students can read an Ethiopian journalist's account of American race relations. In keeping with the growing economic strength of East Asia in the twentieth century, we have included the perspectives of a Japanese commentator on the American economy in Chapter 30.

As in past editions, an outstanding **visual program** engages students' attention. The Seventh Edition features over 450 paintings, cartoons, illustrations, photographs, and charts, most of them in full color and many new to this edition. We also provide informative captions that set the illustrations in context. Keenly aware that students lack geographic literacy, we have included dozens of **maps** and cross-referenced them in the narrative text; map captions help students interpret what they see.

Taken together, these documents, maps, and illustrations provide instructors with a trove of teaching materials, so that *America's History* offers not only a compelling narrative, but also—right in the text—the ancillary materials that instructors need to bring the past alive. We also believe this edition will appeal to your students. Whatever their backgrounds, interests, and concerns may be, *America's History* will help students link the complex events of U.S. history to their experiences today, in ways that increase their understanding of the world around them and provoke critical engagement with the American past.

Acknowledgments

We are grateful to the following scholars and teachers who reported on their experiences with the Sixth Edition or reviewed chapters of this Seventh Edition. Their comments often challenged us to rethink or justify our interpretations and always provided a check on accuracy down to the smallest detail.

Paul C. Anderson, Clemson University
Alexis Antracoli, Saint Francis University
Charles Pete Banner-Haley, Colgate University
Heather Barry, St. Joseph's College
Ken Bridges, South Arkansas Community College
Jennifer Brooks, Auburn University
Jared S. Burkholder, Grace College
Laurie Chin, California State University–Long Beach
Stephen Cresswell, West Virginia Wesleyan College
Paul Doucette, Frederica Academy
Elisa Guernsey, Monroe Community College
Dixie Haggard, Valdosta State University
Michael Harkins, William Rainey Harper College
Andrew Johns, Brigham Young University
David Johnson, University of South Florida
Jon Timothy Kelly, West Valley College
Jeff Kleiman, University of Wisconsin–Marshfield
Rebecca Kosary, Texas Lutheran University
Derek Maxfield, Capital Community College
Ryan McMillen, Santa Monica College
Michelle Morgan, University of Wisconsin–Whitewater
Scott Newman, Loyola University Chicago
Robert Owens, Wichita State University
Ronnie Peacock, Community College of Aurora
Donald Rogers, Central Connecticut State University
Mary Ellen Rowe, University of Central Missouri
Matthew Schaffer, Florence-Darlington Technical College
Lois Scozzari, Holyoke Community College
Aaron Shapiro, Auburn University
David Sicilia, University of Maryland, College Park
John Simpson, Pierce College
E. Timothy Smith, Barry University
Nikki Taylor, University of Cincinnati
Jennifer Terry, American River College
Ruth Terry, Johnson County Community College and Lee's Summit Community Christian School

David Thompson, Illinois Central College
Russell Tremayne, College of Southern Idaho
Jere Vincent, Great Bay Community College
Cheryl Waite, Community College of Aurora
Eddie Weller, San Jacinto College
Jennifer Williams, Firelands College

As the authors of *America's History*, we know better than anyone else how much this book is the work of other hands and minds. We are grateful to departing author David Brody, who extended a welcoming hand and wise guidance to his successors. We are indebted to Mary Dougherty, William J. Lombardo, and Jane Knetzger, who oversaw this edition, and Danielle Slevens, who asked the right questions, suggested a multitude of improvements, and expertly guided the manuscript to completion. As usual, Joan E. Feinberg generously provided the resources we needed to produce an outstanding volume. Deborah Baker did a masterful job consulting with the authors and implementing a bold and powerful new design. Karen Melton Soeltz and Jenna Bookin Barry in the marketing department understood how to communicate our vision to teachers; they and the members of the college and high school sales force did wonderful work in helping this edition reach the classroom. We also thank the rest of our editorial and production team for their dedicated efforts: Robin Soule; Janet Renard, who copyedited the manuscript; Pembroke Herbert and Sandi Rygiel at Picture Research Consultants and Archives; and Kalina Ingham Hintz and Diane Kraut. Finally, we want to express our appreciation for the invaluable assistance of Rebecca Henretta, who redesigned many of the charts and graphs; Michelle Cantos and Mark Seidl, for invaluable research aid; and Linglan Edwards and Hiraku Shimoda, for assistance with translations. Many thanks to all of you for your contributions to this new edition of *America's History*.

James A. Henretta
Rebecca Edwards
Robert O. Self

Versions and Supplements

America's History is supported by loads of resources — study tools for students, instructor materials, and many options for packaging the book with documents readers, trade books, atlases, and other guides — for free or at a substantial discount. Descriptions follow, but for more information, visit this book's catalog site at **bedfordstmartins.com/henretta/catalog** or contact your local Bedford/St. Martin's sales representative.

Available Versions of This Book

To accommodate different course lengths and course budgets, this title is available in several different formats. The three-hole punched loose-leaf Budget Books versions and the e-books are available at a substantial discount.

Combined Volume (Chapters 1–31) — available in hardcover, loose-leaf, and e-book formats
Volume 1: To 1877 (Chapters 1–16) — available in paperback, loose-leaf, and e-book formats
Volume 2: Since 1865 (Chapters 15–31) — available in paperback, loose-leaf, and e-book formats

With our innovative e-books your students get the content you want in a convenient format — for about half the cost of a print book. **Bedford/St. Martin's e-Books** have been optimized for reading and studying online. **CourseSmart e-Books** can be downloaded or used online, whichever is more convenient for your students.

Companion Site at bedfordstmartins.com/henretta

Our new companion sites gather free and premium resources, giving students a way to extend their Bedford book, online. These book-specific sites provide one destination to practice, read, write, and study — and to find and access quizzes and activities, study aids, and history research and writing help.

FREE **Online Study Guide.** Available at the companion site, this popular resource provides students with self-review quizzes and activities for each chapter, including a multiple-choice self-test that focuses on important concepts; an identification quiz that helps students remember key people, places, and events; a flashcard activity that tests students' knowledge of key terms; and map activities to strengthen students' geography skills. Instructors can monitor students' progress through an online Quiz Gradebook or receive e-mail updates.

FREE **History Research and Writing Help.** Also available on the companion site, this resource includes the textbook authors' **Suggested References** organized by chapter; **History Research and Reference Sources**, with links to history-related databases, indexes, and journals; **More Sources and How to Format a History Paper**, with clear advice on how to integrate primary and secondary sources into research papers and how to cite and format sources correctly; **Build a Bibliography**, a simple Web-based tool that generates bibliographies in four commonly used documentation styles; and **Tips on Avoiding Plagiarism**, an online tutorial that reviews the consequences of plagiarism and features exercises to help students practice integrating sources and recognize acceptable summaries.

Instructor Resources

Bedford/St. Martin's has developed a wide range of teaching resources for this book and for this course. They range from lecture and presentation materials to assessment tools and course management options. Most can be downloaded or ordered at **bedfordstmartins .com/henretta/catalog**.

HistoryClass for America's History. HistoryClass, a Bedford/St. Martin's Online Course Space, puts the online resources available with this textbook in one convenient place — an interactive e-book and primary sources reader; maps, images, documents, and links; chapter review quizzes; interactive multimedia exercises; and research and writing help. Get into *HistoryClass* and get all our premium content and tools in one completely customizable course space; then assign, rearrange, and mix our resources with yours. For more information visit **yourhistoryclass.com**.

Bedford/St. Martin's Course Cartridges. Whether you use Blackboard, WebCT, Desire2Learn, Angel, Sakai, or Moodle, we have free content and support available for you to plug our content into your course management system. Registered instructors can download cartridges with no hassle, no strings attached. Content includes our most popular free resources and book-specific content for *America's History*. Visit **bedfordstmartins .com/cms** to get a demo, find your version, or download your cartridge.

Instructor's Resource Manual. The instructor's manual offers both experienced and first-time instructors tools for presenting material in engaging ways. It includes chapter review, teaching strategies, and a guide to chapter-specific supplements available for the text.

Guide to Changing Editions. Designed to facilitate an instructor's transition to the Seventh Edition of *America's History*, this guide presents an overview of major changes as well as changes in each chapter.

Computerized Test Bank. The test bank includes a mix of fresh, carefully crafted multiple-choice, fill-in-the-blank, short-answer, and essay questions for each chapter. Questions appear in Microsoft Word format and in easy-to-use test bank software that allows instructors to easily add, edit, re-sequence, and print questions and answers. Questions can also be exported into a variety of formats, including WebCT and Blackboard.

PowerPoint Maps, Images, Lecture Outlines, and i>clicker Content. Look good and save time with *The Bedford Lecture Kit*. These presentation materials are downloadable individually from the Media and Supplements tab at **bedfordstmartins.com/henretta/ catalog**, and they are available on *The Bedford Lecture Kit Instructor's Resource* CD-ROM. They include ready-made and fully customizable PowerPoint multimedia presentations built around lecture outlines that are embedded with maps, figures, and selected images from the textbook and are supplemented by more detailed instructor notes on key points. Also available are maps and selected images in JPEG and PowerPoint format; content for i>clicker, a classroom response system, in Microsoft Word and PowerPoint formats; and outline maps in PDF format for quizzing or handouts.

All files are suitable for copying onto transparency acetates.

Make History — **Free Documents, Maps, Images, and Web Sites**. *Make History* combines the best Web resources with hundreds of maps and images, to make it simple to find the source material you need. Browse the collection of thousands of resources by course or by topic, date, and type. Each item has been carefully chosen and helpfully annotated to make it easy to find exactly what you need. Available at **bedfordstmartins .com/makehistory**.

NEW *America in Motion: Videoclips for U.S. History*. Set history in motion with *America in Motion*, an instructor DVD containing dozens of digital movie files of events in twentieth-century American history. From the wreckage of the battleship *Maine*, to FDR's Fireside Chats, to Oliver North testifying before Congress, *America in Motion* engages your students with dynamic scenes from key events and challenges them to think critically. All files are classroom-ready, edited for brevity, and easily integrated with PowerPoint or other presentation software for electronic lectures or assignments. An accompanying guide provides each clip's historical context, ideas for use, and suggested questions.

Videos and Multimedia. A wide assortment of videos and multimedia CD-ROMs on various topics in U.S. history is available to qualified adopters through your Bedford/St. Martin's sales representative.

Packaging Opportunities

Save your students money and package your favorite text with more! For information on free packages and discounts up to 50%, visit **bedfordstmartins.com/ henretta/catalog** or contact your local Bedford/St. Martin's sales representative.

e-Book. The e-book for this title can be packaged with the print text at no additional cost.

Documents for America's History. Edited by Melvin Yazawa, University of New Mexico (Vol. 1), and Kevin Fernlund, University of Missouri, St. Louis (Vol. 2), this primary-source reader offers a chorus of voices from the past to enrich the study of U.S. history. Both celebrated figures and ordinary people, from Frederick Douglass to mill workers, demonstrate the diversity of America's history while putting a human face on historical experience. Brief introductions set each document in context, while questions for analysis help link the individual source to larger themes. Available free when packaged with the text.

E-Documents for America's History. The documents reader is also available as an e-book, and is free when packaged with the print or electronic textbook.

Rand McNally Atlas of American History. This collection of more than eighty full-color maps illustrates key events and eras from early exploration, settlement, expansion, and immigration to U.S. involvement in wars abroad and on U.S. soil. Introductory pages for each section include brief overviews, timelines, graphs, and photographs to establish a historical context. Available for $3.00 when packaged with the text.

Maps in Context: A Workbook for American History. Written by historical cartography expert Gerald A. Danzer (University of Illinois at Chicago), this skill-building workbook helps students comprehend essential connections between geographic literacy and historical understanding. Organized to correspond to the U.S. history survey course, *Maps in Context* presents a wealth of projects and convenient quizzes to give students hands-on experience working with maps. Available free when packaged with the text.

The Bedford Glossary for U.S. History. This handy supplement gives students historically contextualized definitions for terms — from *abolitionism* to *zoot suit* — that students will encounter in the survey course. Available free when packaged with the text.

U.S. History Matters: A Student Guide to U.S. History Online. This resource, written by Kelly Schrum, Alan Gevinson, and the late Roy Rosenzweig (all of George Mason University), provides an illustrated and annotated guide to 250 of the most useful Web sites for student research in U.S. history as well as advice on evaluating and using Internet sources. This essential guide is based on the acclaimed "History Matters" Web site developed by the American Social History Project and the Center for History and New Media. Available free when packaged with the text.

The Bedford Series in History and Culture. The more than one hundred titles in this highly praised series combine first-rate scholarship, historical narrative, and important primary documents for undergraduate courses.

Each book is brief, inexpensive, and focused on a specific topic or period. For a list of titles, visit **bedford stmartins.com/bshc**. Package discounts are available.

Trade Books. Titles published by sister companies Hill & Wang; Farrar, Straus and Giroux; Henry Holt and Company; St. Martin's Press; Picador; and Palgrave Macmillan are available at a 50% discount when packaged with Bedford/St. Martin's textbooks. For information, visit **bedfordstmartins.com/tradeup**.

Going to the Source: The Bedford Reader in American History. Developed by Victoria Bissell Brown and Timothy J. Shannon, this reader's strong pedagogical framework helps students learn to ask fruitful questions to evaluate documents effectively and develop critical reading skills. This reader's wide variety of chapter topics complements the survey course and its rich diversity of sources — from personal letters to political cartoons — provoking students' interest as it teaches them the skills they need to successfully interrogate sources. Package discounts are available.

America Firsthand. With its distinctive focus on ordinary people, this primary documents reader, by Robert D. Marcus, David Burner, and Anthony Marcus, offers a wide range of perspectives on U.S. history from those who lived it. Popular "Points of View" sections expose students to different views on an event or topic, and "Visual Portfolios" features invite analysis of the visual record. Package discounts are available.

A Pocket Guide to Writing in History. This portable and affordable reference tool by Mary Lynn Rampolla provides reading, writing, and research advice useful to students in all history courses. Concise yet comprehensive advice on approaching typical assignments, developing critical reading skills, writing effective papers, conducting research, using and documenting sources, and avoiding plagiarism — enhanced with tips and examples — have made this slim reference a best-seller. Package discounts are available.

A Student's Guide to History. This complete guide to success in any history course provides the practical help students need. In addition to introducing students to the nature of the discipline, author Jules Benjamin teaches skills from preparing for exams to approaching common writing assignments, and explains the research and documentation process with plentiful examples. Package discounts are available.

Brief Contents

Contents

PART 1 The Creation of American Society, 1450–1763   *3*

CHAPTER 1
The New Global World, 1450–1620   *7*

CHAPTER 2
The Invasion and Settlement of North America, 1550–1700   *41*

CHAPTER 3

Creating a British Empire in America, 1660–1750   *73*

CHAPTER 4

Growth and Crisis in Colonial Society, 1720–1765   *105*

PART 4   Creating and Preserving a Continental Nation, 1844–1877   *393*

PART **5**   **Bold Experiments in an Era of Industrialization, 1877–1929**   *525*

CHAPTER 21
An Emerging World Power, 1877–1918   *653*

CHAPTER 22
Wrestling with Modernity, 1918–1929   *685*

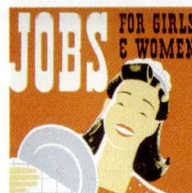

CHAPTER 31

National Dilemmas in a Global Society, 1989–2011   *977*

Maps

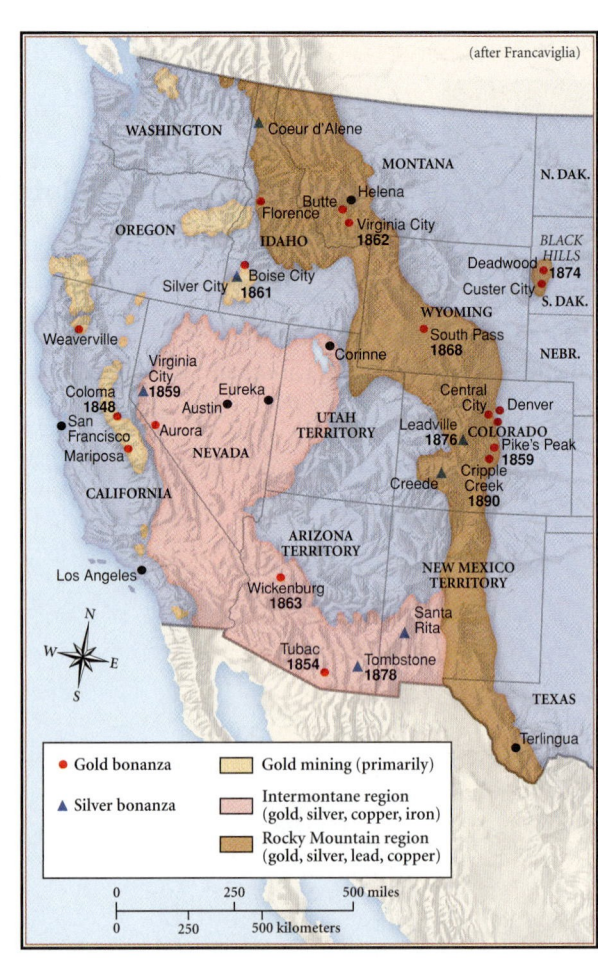

Figures
and Tables

Special Features

VOICES FROM ABROAD

America's History

PART

1

THE CREATION OF AMERICAN SOCIETY, 1450–1763

Historians know that societies are the creation of decades, even centuries, of human endeavor and experience. Historians also know that the first Americans were hunters and gatherers who migrated to the Western Hemisphere from Asia. Over many generations, these migrants—the Native Americans—came to live in a wide variety of environments and cultures. In much of North America, they developed kinship-based societies that relied on farming and hunting. But in the lower Mississippi River Valley around A.D. 900, Native Americans fashioned a hierarchical social order similar to those of the impressive civilizations of the Aztecs, Mayas, and Incas.

In Part 1, we describe how Europeans, with their steel weapons, attractive trade goods, and diseases, shredded the fabric of many Native American cultures. These settlers—the Spanish in Mesoamerica and South America, the French in Canada, and the English along the Atlantic coast of North America—gradually came to dominate the native peoples.

Our story focuses on the Europeans who settled in the English mainland colonies, expecting to transplant their traditional societies, cultures, and religious beliefs into the soil of the New World. But things did not work out exactly as planned. In learning to live in the new land, English, German, and Scots-Irish settlers created societies that differed from those of their homelands in their economic life, social character, political systems, religions, and cultures. Here, in brief, is the story of that transformation as we explain it in Part 1.

ECONOMY

... the settlers in North America created a bustling economy

From Subsistence to Staple Crops to Diversification

Britain's American colonies were a great economic success, as part of an expanding commercial empire. Traditional Europe consisted of poor, overcrowded, and unequal societies that periodically suffered devastating famines. But with few people and bountiful resources, the settlers in North America created a bustling economy in what British and German migrants called "the best poor man's country." Communities of independent farm families produced crops to be sold in Europe and the West Indies, the sugar islands that were the driving force of the Atlantic economy.

SOCIETY

... some European settlements became places of oppressive captivity for Africans

Changing Class, Racial, and Ethnic Conflicts

Simultaneously, some European settlements became places of oppressive captivity for Africans, with profound consequences for America's social development. As the supply of white indentured servants from Europe dwindled after 1680, planters in the Chesapeake region imported enslaved Africans to work in their tobacco fields. Spurred by profits in the sugar trade, British slave traders also procured hundreds of thousands of African slaves and transported them to West Indian sugar plantations. Slowly and with great effort, these slaves and their descendants created a variety of African American cultures within the European-dominated societies in which they labored.

GOVERNMENT

... white settlers ... devised an increasingly free and competitive political system

From Imperial Control to Local Autonomy

The first English migrants transplanted authoritarian institutions to America and, beginning around 1650, the home government intervened frequently in their affairs. But after the Glorious Revolution of 1688, white settlers in the English mainland colonies devised an increasingly free and competitive political system. Thereafter, local governments and representative assemblies became more powerful and created a tradition of self-rule that would spark demands for political autonomy after the Great War for Empire ended in 1763.

RELIGION

American Protestant Christianity became ... tolerant, democratic, and optimistic

From Established Churches to Pluralism

The American experience profoundly changed religious institutions and values. Many migrants fled Europe because of government persecution and conflicts among rival Christian churches. For the most part, they practiced their religions in America without interference. Religion became more prominent in colonial life after the evangelical revivals of the 1740s, and the churches less dogmatic. Americans increasingly rejected the harshest tenets of Calvinism (a strict version of Protestantism), and a significant minority of educated colonists embraced the rational outlook of the European Enlightenment. As a result, American Protestant Christianity became increasingly tolerant, democratic, and optimistic.

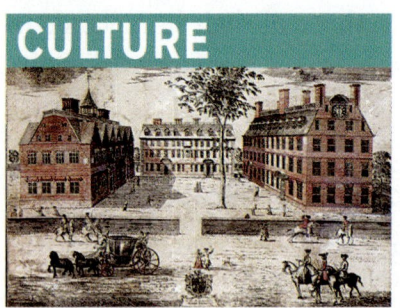

CULTURE

This new American society was pluralistic

The Creation of American Identities

Life in America changed traditional family and community life. The first English settlers lived in families ruled by dominant fathers, in communities controlled by men of high status. However, by 1750, many American fathers no longer strictly managed their children's lives and, because of widespread property ownership, many men and some women enjoyed greater personal independence. This new American society was pluralistic, being composed of migrants from many European ethnic groups—English, Scots, Scots-Irish, Dutch, and Germans—as well as enslaved Africans and generally subordinated Native American peoples. Distinct regional cultures developed in New England, the Middle Atlantic colonies, the Chesapeake, and the Carolinas. Consequently, an overarching American identity based on the English language, English legal and political institutions, and shared experiences emerged very slowly.

The multifaceted story of the colonial experience is both depressing and uplifting. European acquisitiveness and diseases destroyed many Native American peoples, and European planters held tens of thousands of Africans in bondage. However, white migrants enjoyed unprecedented opportunities for economic security, political freedom, and spiritual fulfillment. This contradictory experience—of native decline, black bondage, and white opportunity—would continue far into the American future.

THE CREATION OF AMERICAN SOCIETY, 1450–1763

	ECONOMY	SOCIETY	GOVERNMENT	RELIGION	CULTURE
1450	• Native American subsistence economy • Europeans fish off North American coast	• Sporadic warfare among Indian peoples • Spanish conquest of Mexico and Peru (1519–1535)	• Rise of monarchical nation-states in Europe • English monarchs adopt mercantilist policies	• Protestant Reformation (1517) sparks century of religious warfare • Henry VIII creates Church of England	• Diverse Native American cultures in eastern woodlands
1600	• First staple export crops: furs and tobacco • Subsistence farms in New England	• First set of English-Indian wars • African servitude begins in Virginia (1619)	• James I claims divine right to rule England • Virginia House of Burgesses (1619)	• Persecuted English Puritans and Catholics migrate to America	• Puritans embed Calvinism, education, and freehold ideal in New England
1640	• South Atlantic System on sugar islands • Mercantilist regulation: first Navigation Act (1651)	• White indentured servitude shapes Chesapeake society • Indians retreat inland; Africans lose rights (1670s)	• English Puritan Revolution • Stuart restoration (1660) • Bacon's Rebellion in Virginia (1675)	• Established churches set up in Puritan New England and Anglican Virginia • Dissenters settle in Rhode Island	• Aristocratic aspirations in Chesapeake region
1680	• Tobacco trade stagnates • Rice cultivation in South Carolina • Britain dominates slave trade	• Indian wars and slavery grow in the Carolinas • Major influx of Africans creates "slave societies"	• Central control: dominion of New England • Revolutions in England and colonies (1688–1689)	• Rise of tolerance among colonial Protestants • Wars with Catholic France in Europe and America	• Quaker influence in Pennsylvania • Africans create new African American languages and cultures
1720	• Mature yeoman farm economy in northern colonies • 1740s: imports from Britain increase	• Large-scale Scots-Irish and German migration • Inequality grows among whites in rural and urban areas	• Salutary Neglect allows rise of the colonial assemblies • British state supports commercial expansion in Atlantic and India	• German and Scots-Irish Pietists in Middle Atlantic colonies • Great Awakening revives religion and splits churches	• Expansion of colleges, newspapers, and magazines • Franklin and the American Enlightenment
1760	• End of British military aid sparks postwar recession	• Uprisings by tenants and backcountry farmers	• Britain vanquishes France in Great War for Empire (1757–1763)	• Rise of evangelical Baptists in Virginia	• First signs of a distinct American identity within the Atlantic world

The New Global World, 1450–1620

"Before the French came among us," an elder of the Natchez people of Mississippi complained, "we were men . . . and we walked with boldness every road, but now we walk like slaves, which we shall soon be, since the French already treat us . . . as they do their black slaves." Before the 1490s, the Natchez and other Native American peoples knew nothing of the light-skinned inhabitants of Europe and the dark-complexioned peoples of Africa. But when Christopher Columbus, a European searching for a sea route to Asia, encountered the peoples of the Western Hemisphere in 1492, the destinies of four continents quickly became intertwined. In 1502, when Nicolás de Ovando replaced Columbus as governor of Hispaniola, his fleet of thirty ships carried both Spanish adventurers and enslaved Africans, initiating the centuries-long process that would produce a diaspora of Africans and Europeans and the creation of tri-racial societies in the Americas.

These new societies were based on exploitation, not equality. As early as 1494 Columbus, frustrated by his inability to govern the native peoples of Hispaniola, decided to "subjugate by force of arms." To terrorize the natives he unleashed 200 troops, twenty on horseback, and (according to Bartolomé de las Casas) "the other most terrible and frightful weapon for the Indians, after the horses and this was twenty greyhound catch-dogs, whom after being set loose . . . in one hour each tore 100 Indians to pieces." Two centuries later, the Natchez suffered a similar fate. Helped by Indian allies, the French savagely killed hundreds of Natchez and sold the survivors into slavery in the West Indies, where tens of thousands of forced migrants from Africa already toiled on European-run sugar plantations. In the centuries following Columbus's first voyage, many native peoples came under the domination of Europeans—Spanish, Portuguese, French, English, and Dutch—who seized their lands and often worked them with enslaved Africans.

How did this happen? What made Native Americans vulnerable to conquest by European adventurers? What led to the transatlantic trade in African slaves? And how did Europeans become leaders in world trade and create an economically integrated Atlantic world? In the answers to these questions lie the origins of the United States.

Astronomers at Istanbul (Constantinople), 1581

As the heirs of Byzantine civilization, Arab and Turkish scholars transmitted ancient Greek and Roman texts and learning to Europeans during the Middle Ages and the Renaissance. Their works, and practical classical inventions such as the globe and the astrolabe shown in this painting, provided much of the geographical and astronomical knowledge used by European explorers between 1450 and 1600, the great Age of Discovery. ©University Library, Istanbul, Turkey/The Bridgeman Art Library.

The Native American Experience

When the Europeans arrived, about 7 million Native Americans resided in what is now the United States and Canada. These northern peoples mostly lived in hunter-gatherer or agricultural communities governed by kin ties. However, most native people—about 40 million, scholars estimate—lived in Mesoamerica (present-day Mexico and Guatemala) and along the western coast of South America (present-day Peru). The Mayas and Aztecs in Mesoamerica and the Incas in Peru fashioned societies ruled by warrior-kings and priests, and created civilizations whose art, religion, and economy were as complex as those of Europe and the Mediterranean world.

The First Americans

Every people has a creation story. In the Mayan version, the god of lightning, K'awiil, hurled a bolt that split a great mountain and revealed two life-giving plants: maize and cacao. The Kiowa entered the world from a hollow log. For Judeo-Christians, God created Adam and Eve. But the first Iroquois fell from the sky; Algonquians descended from ash trees.

Inca Cup

This painted wooden *q'iru* (drinking cup) shows how the Incas, who ruled a great sixteenth-century empire in present-day Peru (see Map 1.5), made use of history. Around A.D. 1000, the Tiwanaku people ruled an empire in the highlands of Peru. A central motif of their culture was a sacred staircase symbolizing heavens, earth, and the underworld. By placing that Tiwanaku motif on the central band of this cup and adding a symbol of their own—the man with the staff, shield, and headdress—the Incas grounded their claim of royal authority in the prestige of the Tiwanaku.
Courtesy, National Museum of American Indian, Smithsonian Institution.

According to modern scientists, migrants from Asia crossed a 100-mile-wide land bridge connecting Siberia and Alaska during the last Ice Age and thus became the first Americans. An oral history of the Tuscarora Indians, who settled in present-day North Carolina, tells of a famine in the old world and a journey over ice toward where "the sun rises," bringing their ancestors to a lush forest with abundant food and game. But the most compelling evidence is a genetic marker on the male Y chromosome, shared by Asians and Native Americans. This migratory stream from Asia lasted from about fifteen thousand to nine thousand years ago. Then the glaciers melted, and the rising ocean waters submerged the land bridge and created the Bering Strait (Map 1.1). Around eight thousand years ago, a second movement of peoples, traveling by water across the narrow strait, brought the ancestors of the Navajos and the Apaches to North America. The forebears of the Aleut and Inuit peoples, the "Eskimos," came in a third migration around five thousand years ago. Then, for three hundred generations, the peoples of the Western Hemisphere were largely cut off from the rest of the world.

During this long era, hunting and gathering became the economic basis for a remarkably variegated and complex tribal world. Everywhere, the first Americans proved highly adaptive and inventive. In the most favorable spots, such as the Pacific Northwest and along the California coast, Native Americans lived in permanent villages, sometimes of a thousand or more inhabitants. On the Great Plains, after hunting mastodons and other Paleolithic mammals to extinction, they adopted new weapons—the *atlatl* (a spear thrower) and later the bow and arrow—for bringing down swifter prey. Against the bison, these horseless hunters organized drives that were marvels of intricate planning. In the eastern woodlands, Algonquians engaged in controlled burning, creating parklike forests that, in the eyes of the first Europeans, were "very beautiful and commodious." Simple kin-based groupings evolved into complex tribal structures, cemented by rituals, founding myths, and distinctive crafts.

By about 6000 B.C., some Native American peoples in present-day Mexico and Peru were raising domesticated crops. They gradually bred maize into a nutritious plant that had a higher yield per acre than did wheat, barley, or rye, the staple cereals of Europe. They learned to plant beans and squash with the maize, a mix of crops that provided a diet rich in amino acids and kept the soil fertile. The resulting agricultural surplus encouraged population growth and eventually laid the economic foundation for wealthy, urban societies in Mexico, Peru, and the Mississippi River Valley (Map 1.2).

Using a global projection, the cartographer has placed North America in the center of the map, but parts of four other continents appear.

Evidence indicates that peoples came from Asia to the Americas during the Ice Age, when the sea level was much lower than today and a large land bridge-labeled Beringia on the map-connected the continents.

As scholars learn more about the advances and retreats of the ice sheets, the camping sites of the migrating peoples, and changes in vegetation zones, a more complete picture of the peopling of the Americas will emerge.

Current scholarship holds that the migrating peoples initially traveled on a narrow strip of ice-free land along the Pacific coast. As the area between the Cordilleran and Laurentide ice sheets lost its cover of ice, probably between 14,000 and 12,000 B.C., migrants may also have used the inland routes from present-day Alaska to the American interior.

Many groups, accustomed to living at the ocean's edge, probably continued along this route, pushing ever southward into South America.

ASIA
SIBERIA
JAPAN
KURIL IS.
25,000–12,000 B.C. Land bridge open
BERINGIA
Bering Sea
ALASKA
Cordilleran ice sheet
PACIFIC OCEAN
ROCKY MOUNTAINS
NORTH AMERICA
Laurentide ice sheet
Pack ice
Greenland ice sheet
Scandinavian ice sheet
EUROPE
AFRICA
ATLANTIC OCEAN
approximate ice-age coastline
FLORIDA
Gulf of Mexico
Caribbean Sea
SOUTH AMERICA

Migration Routes into America, c. 16,000–10,000 B.C.

Ice sheets, c. 16,000 B.C.
Ice sheets, c. 12,000 B.C.
Vegetation zones:
- Tundra
- Conifer forest
- Deciduous forest
- Prairie
- Desert
- Migration route

(after Tanner)

0   500   1,000 miles
0   500   1,000 kilometers

MAP 1.1

The Ice Age and the Settling of the Americas

Some sixteen thousand years ago, a sheet of ice covered much of Europe and North America. The ice lowered the level of the world's oceans, which created a broad bridge of land between Siberia and Alaska. Using that land bridge, hunting peoples from Asia migrated to North America as they pursued woolly mammoths and other large game animals and sought ice-free habitats. By 10,000 B.C., the descendants of these migrant peoples had moved south to present-day Florida and central Mexico. In time, they would settle as far south as the tip of South America and as far east as the Atlantic coast of North America.

MAP 1.2

Native American Peoples, 1492

Having learned to live in many environments, Native Americans populated the entire Western Hemisphere. They created cultures that ranged from centralized agriculture-based societies (the Mayas and Aztecs), to societies that combined farming and hunting (the Iroquois and Algonquians), to seminomadic tribes of hunter-gatherers (the Micmacs and Ottowas). The great diversity of Native American peoples — in language, tribal identity, and ways of life — and the long-standing rivalries among neighboring peoples usually prevented them from uniting to resist the European invaders.

The Mayas and the Aztecs

The flowering of Mesoamerican civilization began around 700 B.C. among the Olmec people, who lived along the Gulf of Mexico. Subsequently, the Mayas of the Yucatán Peninsula of Mexico and the neighboring rain forests of Guatemala built large urban centers that relied on elaborate systems of irrigation. By A.D. 300, more than 20,000 people were living in the Mayan city of Tikal [*TEE-kall*]. Most were farmers, whose labor built the city's huge stone temples. An elite class claiming descent from the gods ruled Mayan society and lived

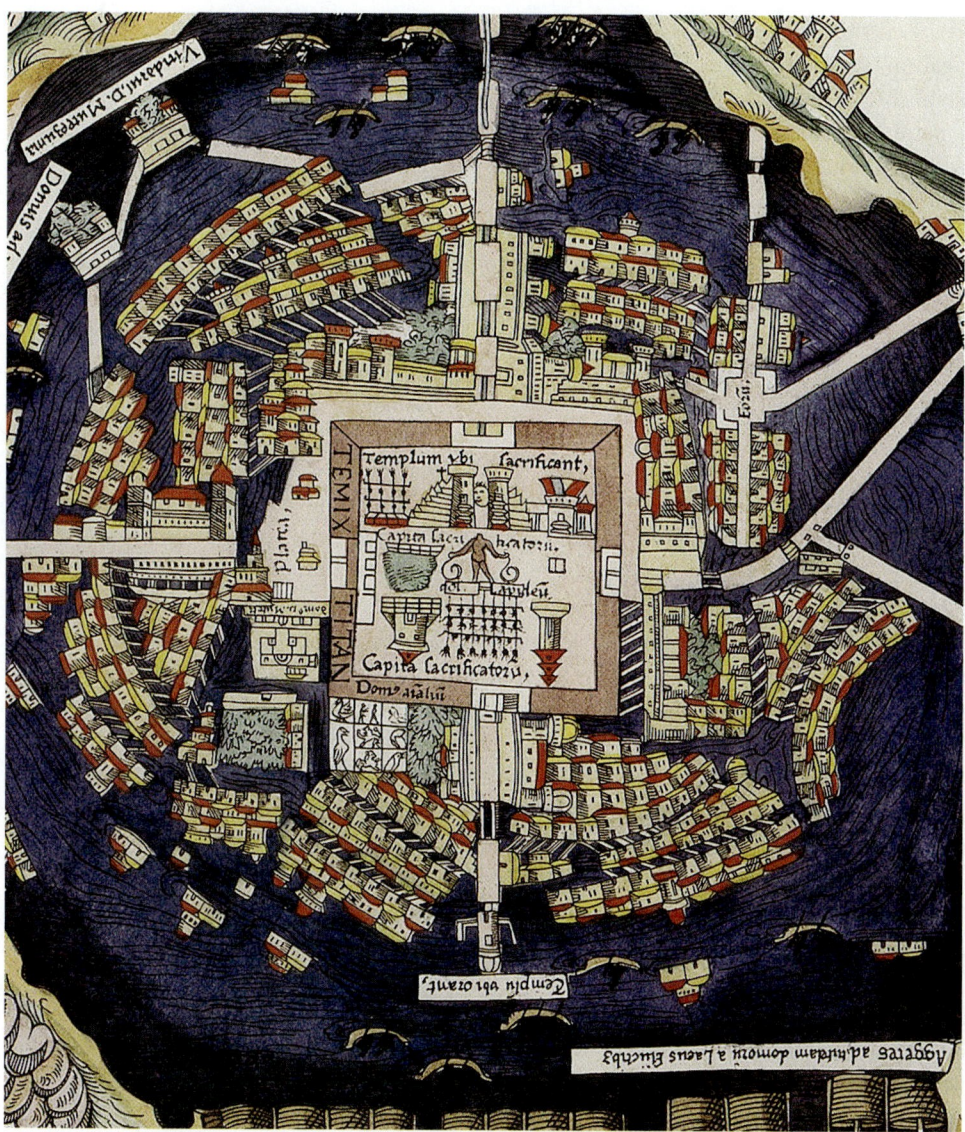

Understanding the Cosmos of the Aztecs

Using Aztec sources, German geographers drew this map of Tenochtitlán in 1524. Recent scholarship suggests that the Aztecs viewed their city as a cosmic linchpin, where the human world brushed up against the divine. In the center of the city stand two elevated temples that represent Coatepec, the Serpent Mountain and the mythic birthplace of the Aztecs' tribal god Huitzilopochtli. Priests sacrificed thousands of men and women here, a ritual the Aztecs believed transformed the temples into the Sacred Mountain and sustained the cosmos. Bildarchiv Preussischer Kulturbesitz/Art Resource, NY.

in splendor on goods and taxes extracted from peasant families. Drawing on the religious and artistic traditions of the Olmecs, Mayan artisans decorated temples and palaces with depictions of jaguars and warrior-gods. Mayan astronomers accurately predicted eclipses of the sun and the moon, and scholars developed hieroglyphic writing to record royal lineages and wars. Aside from boosting the authority of the ruling class of warriors and priests, these intellectual skills provided the Mayans with a sense of history and a complex, prosperous culture.

But between A.D. 800 and 900, Mayan civilization went into decline. Evidence suggests that a two-century-long drought led overtaxed peasants to desert the temple cities and retreat to the countryside. Consequently, when the Spanish invaders arrived in the 1520s, there were few strong Mayan city-states to resist them.

A second Mesoamerican civilization developed among the peoples who lived in the fertile valleys in the highlands of Mexico. A major center was the city of Teotihuacán [*tay-o-tee-wa-KAHN*]. At its zenith, about A.D. 500, Teotihuacán had more than one hundred temples, including the magnificent Pyramid of the Sun; some four thousand apartment buildings; and a population of at least 100,000. By 800, the city was in decline, the victim of long-term drought and recurrent invasions by seminomadic warrior peoples. Some of these invaders, such as the Toltecs and the Aztecs, established even more extensive empires.

The Aztecs settled on an island in Lake Texcoco, not far from the great pyramid. There, in 1325, they built a new city, Tenochtitlán [*teh-noch-teet-LAN*] — Mexico City today — that was designed to reflect their understanding of the divine cosmos. The Aztecs mastered the complex irrigation systems of the long-resident peoples and established a hierarchical social order. Priests and warrior-nobles ruled over free Aztec commoners who farmed communal land. The nobles also used huge numbers of non-Aztec Indians to labor as slaves or serfs on their private estates.

An aggressive people, the Aztecs soon subjugated most of central Mexico. Their rulers demanded both economic and human tribute from subject peoples, and their priests brutally sacrificed thousands of men and women; they believed that these ritual murders sustained the cosmos, ensuring fertile fields and the daily return of the sun.

Aztec merchants forged trading routes that crisscrossed the empire, importing furs, gold, textiles, food, and obsidian from as far north as the Rio Grande and as far south as present-day Panama. By 1500, Tenochtitlán was a magnificent metropolis with more than 200,000 inhabitants — far more populous than most European cities. Its splendor and wealth dazzled Spanish soldiers. "These great towns and pyramids and buildings arising from the water, all made of stone, seemed like an enchanted vision," marveled one Spaniard. The Aztecs' strong political institutions and military power posed a formidable challenge to the Spanish intruders.

The Indians of the North

North of the Rio Grande, as the practice of agriculture spread, so did the urban, trade-oriented Mesoamerican way of life. But apart from a few exceptions — such as the Hopewell, Pueblo, and Mississippian peoples — northern Indian societies were far less populous, wealthy, and culturally complex than those of the Aztecs and the Mayas. Consequently, when Europeans intruded into North America after 1500, there were neither powerful Indian empires to confront them nor densely settled and rich societies for them to exploit.

The Hopewell Culture | Indeed, by 1500 the great periods of northern Indian economic and cultural creativity lay mostly in the past. Around A.D. 100, the vigorous Hopewell people of present-day Ohio had domesticated plants, organized themselves into large villages, and set up a trading network that stretched from present-day Louisiana to Wisconsin (see Reading American Pictures, "Maize for Blankets: Indian Trading Networks on the Great Plains," p. 13). They imported obsidian from the Yellowstone region of the Rocky Mountains, copper from the Great Lakes, and pottery and marine shells from the Gulf of Mexico. The Hopewells built large burial mounds in extensive earthworks that still survive, and skilled artisans fashioned striking ornaments that were buried with the dead. For unknown reasons, the Hopewells' elaborate trading network collapsed around 400.

The Peoples of the Southwest | Another complex culture densely settled, with highly developed crafts and governing institutions — appeared among the Pueblo peoples of southwestern North America: the Hohokams, Mogollons, and Anasazis. By A.D. 600, the Hohokam [*ho-HO-kam*] people in the high country of present-day Arizona and New Mexico were using irrigation to grow two crops a year, fashioning fine pottery with red-on-buff designs, and worshipping their gods on platform mounds; by 1000, they had built elaborate multistory, multiroom stone or mud-brick structures called **pueblos** and had adopted the Mayan ritual of drinking chocolate on sacred occasions. To the east, in the Mimbres Valley of present-day New Mexico, the Mogollon [*mog-ga-YON*] people developed a distinctive black-on-white pottery. And by A.D. 900, the Anasazi people had become master architects. They built residential-ceremonial villages in steep cliffs, a pueblo in Chaco Canyon that housed 1,000 people, and 400 miles of straight roads. But as soil exhaustion and extended droughts disrupted maize production, the Pueblo peoples' expansive urban culture gradually declined after 1150 and they abandoned Chaco Canyon and other large pueblos. Their descendants — including the Acomas, Zunis, and Hopis — built smaller village societies that were better suited to the dry and unpredictable climate of the Southwest.

Mississippian Civilization | The Mississippi River Valley was home to the last large-scale northern Indian culture. Beginning about A.D. 800, the Mississippian peoples planted new strains of maize imported from Mesoamerica — the northern flint variety — and produced an agricultural surplus. They built small, fortified temple cities with a robust religious culture. By 1150, the largest city, Cahokia [*ka-HO-kee-ah*], near present-day St. Louis, boasted a population of 15,000 to 20,000 and more than one hundred temple mounds. As in the Mayan city-states in Mesoamerica, the tribute paid by peasant farmers supported a privileged class of nobles and priests who claimed descent from the sun god, patronized artisans, and waged war against neighboring chiefdoms. But none of the Mississippian peoples had the military or civil skills of the Toltecs or the Aztecs, and so there were no great Indian empires in the Mississippi Valley.

Maize for Blankets: Indian Trading Networks on the Great Plains

In most Native American societies, there were no merchants, storekeepers, or traders. Yet many Indian peoples exchanged goods with their neighbors and often acquired wares produced in distant lands. They also acquired captives taken in raids, mostly women and children, who were put to work as household slaves or integrated into the host society though marriage or adoption. This 1973 painting by Tom Lovell offers a historical reconstruction of the commerce in goods at the fortified Towa pueblo of Cicúye (in what today is Pecos, New Mexico). The pueblo, which stands on a high mountain pass between the Rio Grande Valley and the Great Plains, looms in the background to the left.

Tom Lovell, *Trading at the Pecos Pueblo*. Courtesy of Abell-Hanger Foundation and of the Permian Basin Petroleum Museum, Library and Hall of Fame of Midland, Texas, where the painting is on permanent display.

ANALYZING THE EVIDENCE

• Why did the location of the Towa pueblo at Pecos make it a major trading post? One clue comes from a Spanish explorer who visited the pueblo in 1541 with Francisco Vásquez de Coronado's expedition. He reported that Indians from the Great Plains exchanged "*cueros de Cíbola* [bison hides] and deer skins" for the "maize and blankets" produced by the Pueblo peoples. Do you see any other pueblo products in this painting?

• What do the clothing, material goods, and lodgings of the two peoples—the Towas and the Apaches—tell us about their respective ways of life?

• How have the Apaches transported their goods to the pueblo? Based on what you have read in the text, can you explain why no horses appear in this painting, which is set in A.D. 1500?

• Look closely at what the men and women are doing. What does the painting suggest about gender roles among native peoples of the region?

The Great Serpent Mound

Scholars long believed that this mound was the work of the Adena peoples (500 B.C.–A.D. 200) because of its proximity to an Adena burial site in present-day southern Ohio. Recent research places the mound at a much later date (A.D. 950–1200) and, because of the serpent imagery, ties it to the culture of Mississippian peoples. The head of the serpent is aligned with the sunset of the summer solstice (June 20 or 21 in the Northern Hemisphere), an event of great religious significance to a sun-worshipping culture.
© Richard Cooke/Corbis.

As the climate cooled after 1300, crop yields declined, undermining the economic basis of urban life. By 1350, Mississippian civilization was in rapid decline. Tuberculosis and other urban diseases took the lives of many Indians, and relatively dense populations overburdened the environment, depleting nearby forests and herds of deer. Still, Mississippian institutions and practices endured for centuries. When Spanish conquistador Hernán de Soto invaded the region in the 1539, he found the Calusa, Apalachee [*ap-a-LAH-chee*], Timucua [*TEE-moo-KOO-wa*], and other Mississippian peoples living in permanent settlements under the command of powerful chiefs (see Voices from Abroad, "De Soto's March of Destruction," p. 16). "If you desire to see me, come where I am," a chief told de Soto. "Neither for you, nor for any man, will I set back one foot." A century and a half later, French traders and priests reported that the Natchez people were rigidly divided

among hereditary chiefs, nobles and honored people, and a bottom class of peasants. "Their chiefs possess all authority and distribute their favors and presents at will," a Frenchman noted. Influenced by Mesoamerican rituals, the Natchez marked the death of a chief by sacrificing his wives and burying their remains in a ceremonial mound.

Eastern Woodland Peoples Most native peoples east of the Mississippi lived in self-governing tribes made up of **clans**, groups of families that traced their lineage to a real or legendary common ancestor. These kin-based societies looked inward; the names they called themselves—Innu, Lenape, and dozens of others—mean "human beings" or "real people"; all others were aliens. Clan elders and village chiefs conducted ceremonies, resolved personal feuds, set war policy, and enforced customs such as a ban

Timucua Raid, 1560s

In 1564, French Protestants founded Fort Caroline, near present-day Jacksonville, Florida. Soon, the Spanish governor of Florida wiped it out and executed hundreds of those he called "Lutheran heretics." The artist Jacque Le Moyne de Morgues was among the few survivors. His watercolors inspired a series of beautiful engravings by Theodor de Bry. Here, Timucua warriors attack a neighboring people, shooting burning arrows into a fortified village and seizing those who flee. Library of Congress.

on marriage between members of the same clan. But they lacked the spiritual authority and coercive institutions of Mesoamerican priests and elites, and relied on kin ties to govern. "When you command, all the French obey and go to war," the Chippewa chief Chigabe [*chi-GAH-bee*] told the governor of Canada, the Comte de Frontenac, "[but] I shall not be heeded and obeyed by my nation [except by] those immediately allied to me."

The culture of these lineage-based societies discouraged accumulation; individual ownership of goods and land was virtually unknown. "[They] possess hardly anything except in common," noted a French missionary among the Iroquois. Strong customs dictated that members would share food and other scarce goods, fostering an ethic of reciprocity rather than one of self-interest. "You are covetous, and neither generous nor kind," the Micmac Indians of Nova Scotia told acquisitive French fur traders. "As for us, if we have a morsel of bread, we share it with our neighbor."

In other respects, the cultures of the native peoples of eastern North America were diverse. Like the Natchez, the Creeks, Choctaws, and Chickasaws who lived in present-day Alabama and Mississippi had once been organized in powerful chiefdoms. However, the European epidemic diseases carried by members of de Soto's expedition killed thousands of Indians in the 1540s and destroyed their traditional institutions. The survivors intermarried and settled in smaller, less disciplined agricultural communities.

In these Muskogean-speaking societies—and among the Algonquian-speaking and Iroquoian peoples

to the north and east—the men hunted and fished while the women, using flint hoes, raised corn, squash, and beans. Because of the importance of farming, a **matrilineal** system of kinship and inheritance developed among some eastern Indian peoples, such as the Five Nations of the Iroquois, who resided in present-day New York State. In these matrilineal societies, fathers stood outside the main lines of descent and authority. Women passed use-rights to cultivated fields to their daughters, and mothers and their brothers took principal responsibility for child rearing. Emotional intimacy between spouses was muted: "My wife is not my friend," explained a Delaware man. "[T]hat is, she is not related to me, . . . she is only my wife." Religious rituals centered on the agricultural cycle. For example, the Iroquois celebrated green corn and strawberry festivals. Although eastern woodland peoples enjoyed an adequate diet, they had a sparse, uncertain material life and their populations grew slowly.

It was these relatively small and weak lineage-based societies that confronted the English, Dutch, and French adventurers in eastern North America around 1600. Lacking numbers, valuable manufactured goods, and gold, they could provide the invaders with only furs from the forests and the land on which they lived.

- What were the main characteristics of the Indian civilizations of Mesoamerica?

- How were eastern woodland Indian societies organized and governed?

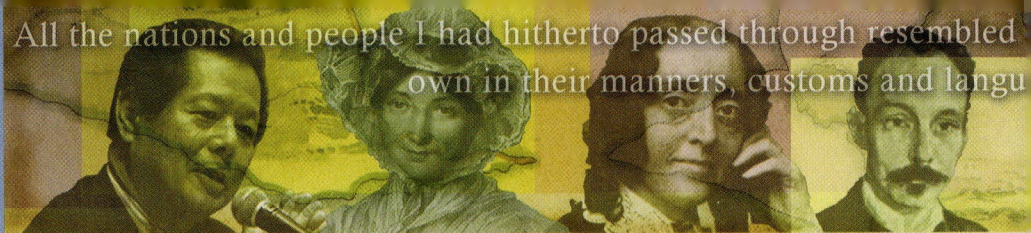

All the nations and people I had hitherto passed through resembled
own in their manners, customs and langu

Hernán de Soto
De Soto's March of Destruction

From 1539 to 1542, Hernán de Soto and an army of 600 Spaniards roamed through northern Florida and the southeastern part of the present-day United States. They killed, raped, and enslaved hundreds of Indians from many different peoples, and inadvertently introduced smallpox, measles, and other viruses that took the lives of tens of thousands more. All to no avail: The Spanish found no gold, de Soto died of a fever in 1542, and only a few hundred of his soldiers survived the ordeal. One was Rodrigo Rangel, de Soto's private secretary, whose diary provided the material for this account, composed in 1546 by royal historian Gonzalo Fernandez de Oviedo.

On Sunday, the tenth of October [1540], the Governor [de Soto] entered in the town of Tascalua, which was called Athahachi, a new town; and the cacique [the Calusa chieftain] was on a balcony that was made on a mound to one side of the plaza, about his head a certain headdress like an almaizar [turban] worn like a Moor, which gave him an appearance of authority, and a pelote or blanket of feathers down to his feet, very authoritative, seated upon some high cushions, and many principals of his Indians with him. He was of as tall a stature as that Antonico of the guard of the Emperor our lord, and of very good proportions, a very well built and noble man; he had a young son as tall as he, but he was more slender. Always in front of this cacique was a very graceful Indian on foot, with a sunshade, on a pole, which was like a round and very large fly-flap. . . . And although the Governor entered in the plaza and dismounted and went up to him, he did not rise but rather was quiet and composed, as if he were a king, and with much gravity. The Governor sat with him a bit, and after a little while he [de Soto] rose and said that they should go to eat and took him with him, and Indians came to dance; and they danced very well in the way of the peasants of Spain, in such a manner that it was a pleasure to see.

At night he [the chieftain] wished to go [from our camp], but the adelantado [de Soto] told him that he had to sleep there; and he understood it and showed that he scoffed at such a decision, being lord, to give him so suddenly a restraint or impediment to his liberty. . . . The next day the Governor [de Soto] asked for tamemes [carriers] and one hundred Indian women, and the cacique gave them four hundred tamemes and said that he would give them the rest of the tamemes and the women in Mabila, the province of a principal vassal of his, and the Governor was content that the rest of his unjust demand would be satisfied in Mabila. . . .

On Saturday, the sixteenth of October, they departed from there and went to a forest, where one of the two Christians that the Governor had sent to Mabila came; and he said that there was a great gathering of armed people in Mabila. . . . On Monday, the eighteenth of October, the day of St. Luke, the Governor arrived at Mabila. . . . The Indians then did an areito, which is their kind of ball with dancing and singing.

While watching this, some soldiers saw them [the Indians] placing bundles of bows and arrows secretively in some palm leaves, and other Christians saw that the huts were filled high and low with concealed people. The Governor was warned, and he placed his helmet on his head and commanded that all should mount their horses. . . . And all the Spaniards fought like men of great spirit, and twenty-two of them died, and they wounded another one hundred and forty-eight [Spaniards] with six hundred and eighty-eight arrow wounds, and they killed seven horses and wounded twenty-nine others. The women and even boys of four years struggled against the Christians, and many Indians hanged themselves in order not to fall into their hands. . . .

The battle having taken place in the manner stated above, they rested there until Sunday, the fourteenth of November, treating the wounded and the horses, and they burned a great part of the land. From the time that this Governor and his armies entered in the land of Florida up to the time that they left from there, all the dead were one hundred and two Christians, and not all, to my way of thinking, in true penitence.

Source: "Account of the Northern Conquest and Discovery of Hernando de Soto by Rodrigo Rangel," trans. John E. Worth, in *The De Soto Chronicles: The Expedition of Hernando de Soto to North America in 1539–1543*, 2 vols., eds., Lawrence A. Clayton, Vernon James Knight Jr., and Edward C. Moore (Tuscaloosa: University of Alabama Press, 1993), 1:288–294.

ANALYZING THE EVIDENCE

- What were the causes of this particular battle?
- What do the results of the battle suggest about the relative strength of the Spaniards and the Indians?
- What is the stance of the author toward these events? How can you tell?

Tradition-Bound Europe

In 1450, no one would have predicted that Europeans would become overlords of the Western Hemisphere. A thousand years after the fall of the Roman Empire, Europe remained a mosaic of small and relatively weak kingdoms with populations that relied on subsistence agriculture. Moreover, around 1350, a deadly plague that was introduced from the subcontinent of India — the Black Death — had killed one-third of Europe's population. The future looked as difficult and dark as the past.

European Peasant Society

In 1450, most Europeans were **peasants** who lived in small, compact agricultural villages surrounded by open fields. Because the fields were divided into narrow strips cultivated by different families, cooperative farming was a necessity. The community decided which crops to grow, and every family followed the community's dictates. On manorial lands, tillage rights came in exchange for weekly labor on the lord's estate, an arrangement that turned peasants into serfs. Gradually, obligatory manorial services gave way to paying rent; or, as in France, customary tillage rights became, for practical purposes, land ownership. Once freed from their obligation to labor for their farming rights, serfs had fresh incentives to work. The peasants' output, once inferior to the corn culture of Native Americans, produced surpluses and created a local market economy.

The Peasantry For European peasants, as for Native Americans, the rhythm of life followed the seasons. The agricultural year began in late March, when the ground thawed and dried and the villagers began the exhausting work of plowing and then planting wheat, rye, and oats. During the busy spring months, the men sheared the thick winter wool of their sheep, which the women washed and spun into yarn. In June, peasants cut the first crop of hay and stored it as winter fodder for their livestock. During the summer, life was more relaxed, and families repaired their houses and barns. Fall brought the strenuous harvest, followed by solemn feasts of thanksgiving and riotous bouts of merrymaking. As winter approached, peasants slaughtered excess livestock and salted or smoked the meat. During the cold months, they threshed grain and wove textiles, visited friends and relatives, and celebrated the winter solstice or the birth of Christ. Just before the farming cycle began again in the spring, they held carnivals, celebrating with drink and dance the end of the long winter night. Even births and deaths followed the seasons: For reasons not yet fully understood, more successful conceptions took place in early summer than at any other time of the year. And many rural people died either in January and February, victims of viral diseases, or in August and September in epidemics of fly-borne dysentery (Figure 1.1).

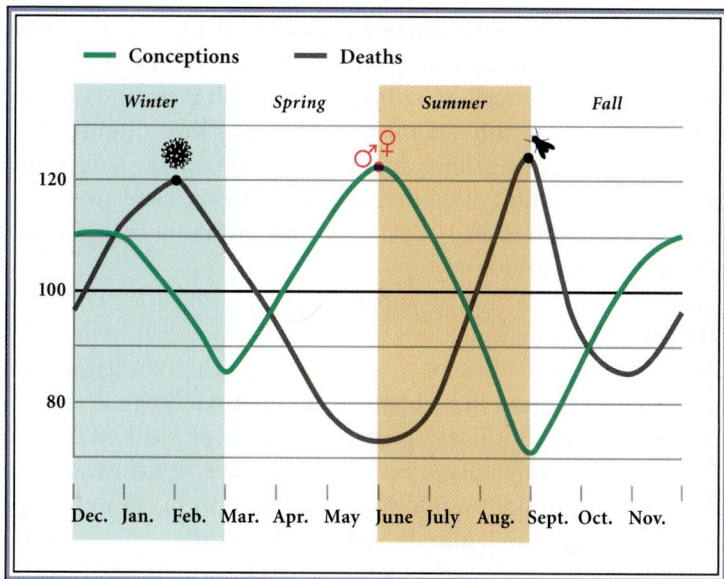

FIGURE 1.1

The Yearly Rhythm of Rural Life and Death

The annual cycle of nature profoundly affected life in the traditional agricultural world. The death rate soared by 20 percent in February (from viruses) and September (from fly-borne dysentery). Summer was the healthiest season, with the fewest deaths and the most successful conceptions (as measured by births nine months later). A value of 100 indicates an equal number of deaths and conceptions.

The Peasant's Fate For most peasants, survival meant constant labor, breaking the soil with primitive wooden plows and harvesting hay and grain with small hand sickles. In the absence of today's high-quality seeds, chemical fertilizers, and pesticides, output was pitifully small — less than one-twelfth of present-day yields. The margin of existence was small, and poverty corroded family relationships. Malnourished mothers fed their babies sparingly, calling them "greedy and gluttonous," and many newborn girls were "helped to die" so that their brothers would have enough to eat. Half of all peasant children died before the age of twenty-one, victims of malnourishment and disease. "I have seen the latest epoch of misery," a French doctor reported as famine struck. "The inhabitants . . . lie down in a meadow to eat grass, and share the food of wild beasts." Often destitute, usually exploited by landlords and nobles, many peasants drew on strong religious beliefs, "counting blessings" and accepting their harsh existence. Others, however, hoped for a better life for themselves and their children. It was the peasants of Spain, Germany, and Britain who would supply the majority of white migrants to the Western Hemisphere.

Hierarchy and Authority

In traditional hierarchical societies — Mesoamerican or European — authority came from above. In Europe, kings and princes owned vast tracts of land, forcibly conscripted men for military service, and lived in splendor off the peasantry's labor. Yet monarchs were far from supreme: Local nobles also owned large estates and controlled hundreds of peasant families. Collectively, these nobles challenged royal authority with both their military power and their legislative institutions, such as the French *parlements* and the English House of Lords.

Just as kings and nobles ruled society, so men governed families. Rich or poor, the man was the head of the house, his power justified by the teachings of the Christian church. As one English clergyman put it: "The woman is a weak creature not embued with like strength and constancy of mind"; law and custom "subjected her to the power of man." Once married, an Englishwoman assumed her husband's surname, submitted to his orders, and surrendered the legal right to all her property. Her sole protection: When he died, she received a **dower**, usually the use during her lifetime of one-third of the family's land and goods.

Men also controlled the lives of their children, who usually worked for their father into their middle or late

Artisan Family

Work was slow and output limited in the preindustrial world, and survival required the efforts of all family members. Here a fifteenth-century French woodworker planes a panel of wood while his wife twists flax fibers into linen yarn for the family's clothes. Their young son cleans up wood shavings to use later to start fires.   Giraudon/Art Resource, New York.

twenties. Then landowning peasants would give land to their sons and dowries to their daughters and choose marriage partners of appropriate wealth and status. In many regions, fathers bestowed all their land on their eldest son — a practice known as **primogeniture** — forcing many younger children to join the ranks of the roaming poor. In this society, few men and even fewer women had much personal freedom or individual identity.

Hierarchy and authority prevailed in traditional European society because of the power held by established institutions — nobility, church, and village — and because, in a violent and unpredictable world, they offered ordinary people a measure of security. Carried by migrants to America, these security-conscious institutions would shape the character of family and society well into the eighteenth century.

The Last Judgment, 1467–1471

Death—and their fate in the afterlife—loomed large in the minds of fifteenth-century Christians, and artists depicted their hopes and fears in vividly rendered scenes. In this painting by the German-Flemish artist Hans Memling (c. 1433–1494), Christ and his apostles sit in judgment as the world ends and the dead rise from their graves. The archangel Michael weighs the souls of the dead in a balance to determine their final fate; either eternal life with God in heaven or everlasting punishment in hell. Erich Lessing / Art Resource, NY.

The Power of Religion

For centuries, the Roman Catholic Church was the great unifying institution in Western Europe. The pope in Rome headed a vast hierarchy of cardinals, bishops, and priests. Catholic theologians preserved Latin, the great language of classical scholarship, and Christian dogma provided a common understanding of God and human history. Every village had a church, and holy shrines served as points of contact with the sacred world.

Christian doctrine penetrated deeply into the everyday lives of peasants. Originally, most Europeans were **pagans** who, like the Indians of North America, were animists; that is, they believed that the natural world—the sun, wind, stones, animals—was animated by spiritual forces that had to be heeded. However,

Christian priests taught that spiritual power came from outside nature, from a supernatural God who had sent his divine son, Jesus Christ, into the world to save humanity from its sins. The Christian Church devised a religious calendar that transformed animist festivals into holy days. The winter solstice, which for pagans marked the return of the sun, became the feast of Christmas, to celebrate the birth of Christ. Christianized peasants no longer made ritual offerings to nature in hopes of averting famine and plague; instead, they offered prayers to Christ.

The Church also taught that Satan, a lesser and wicked supernatural being, was constantly challenging God by tempting people to sin. If a devout Christian fell mysteriously ill, the cause might be an evil spell cast by a witch in league with Satan. Prophets who spread

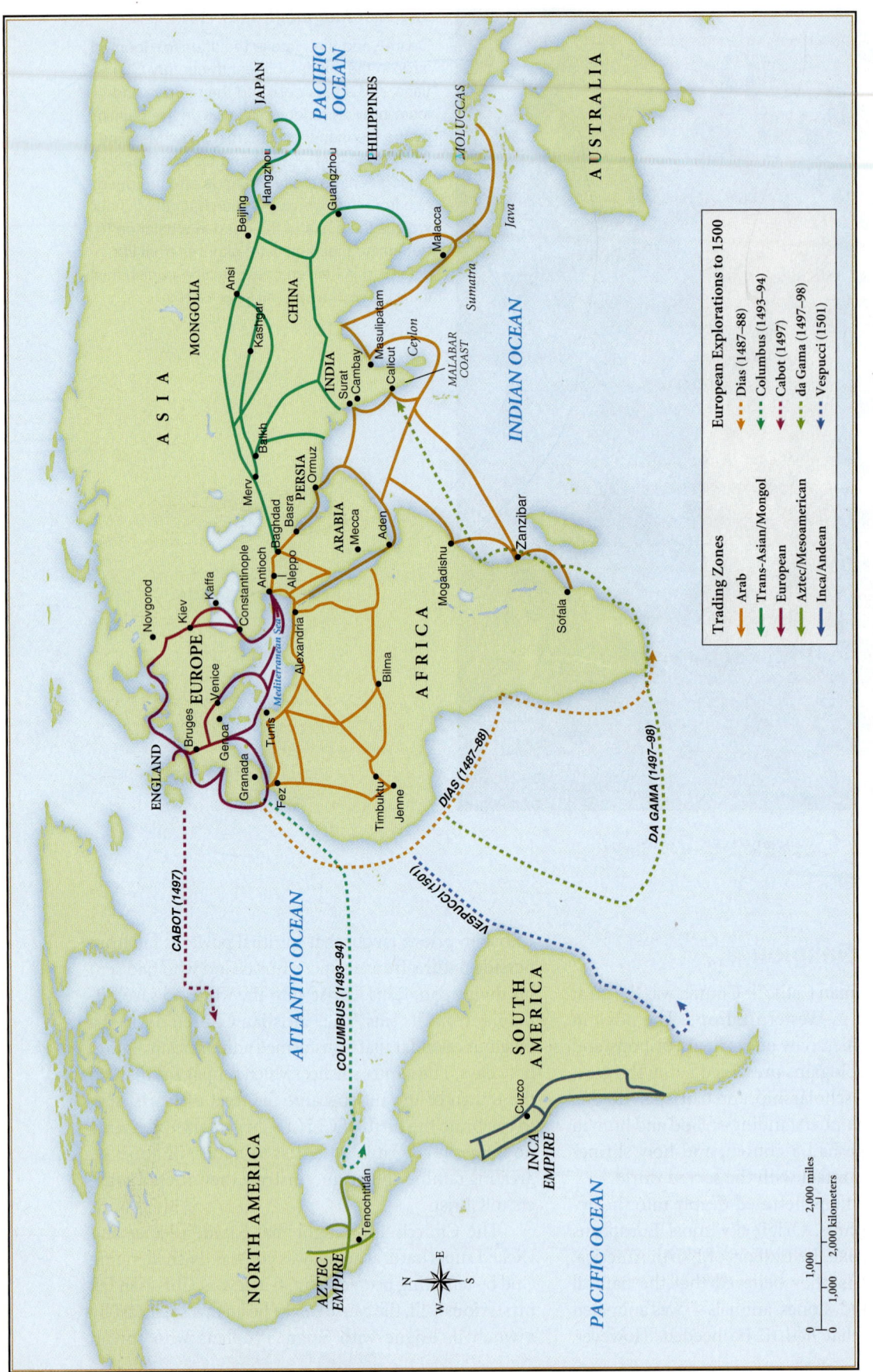

MAP 1.3

The Eurasian Trade System and European Maritime Ventures, c. 1500

For centuries, the Mediterranean Sea was the meeting point for the commerce of Europe, North Africa, and Asia – via the Silk Road from China and the Spice Route from India. Beginning in the 1490s, Portuguese, Spanish, and Dutch rulers and merchants subsidized Christian maritime explorers who discovered new trade routes around Africa and new sources of wealth in the Americas. These initiatives undermined the commercial primacy of the Arab Muslim–dominated Mediterranean.

heresies—doctrines that were inconsistent with the teachings of the Church—were seen as the tools of Satan. Suppressing false doctrines became an obligation of Christian rulers. So did combating Islam, a religion that, like Christianity, proclaimed a single god. Following the death in A.D. 632 of the prophet Muhammad, the founder of Islam, the newly converted Arab peoples of North Africa used force and fervor to spread the Muslim faith into sub-Saharan Africa, India, and Indonesia, as well as deep into Spain and the Balkan regions of Europe. Between 1096 and 1291, Christian armies undertook a series of Crusades to reverse the Muslim advance into Europe and win back the holy lands where Christ had lived.

The crusaders had some military successes, but their most profound impact was on European society. Religious warfare intensified Europe's Christian identity and prompted the persecution of Jews and their expulsion from many European countries. The Crusades also broadened the horizons of Western European merchants, who became aware of the trade routes that stretched from Constantinople to China along the Silk Road and from the Mediterranean Sea through the Persian Gulf to the Indian Ocean (Map 1.3).

- **Compare and contrast the main features of the traditional agricultural society of Europe with those of Mesoamerica and the eastern woodlands of North America.**

Europeans Create a Global World, 1450–1600

Whatever the hopes of European merchants, they faced formidable odds. Arabs controlled trade in the Mediterranean region, Africa, and the Near East. Moreover, China—a vast empire of 75 million people—seemed about to seize control of world commerce. Between 1405 and 1433, Ming emperors dispatched seven mammoth maritime expeditions to the Indian Ocean. Commanded by Admiral Zheng He, fleets of 300 ships and 28,000 men subdued pirates in the South China Sea, set up a major port at Malacca on the Malaysian peninsula, and exchanged silk and porcelain for spices and jewels in India and East Africa. Then, abruptly, China-centered bureaucrats at the imperial court halted these voyages to Southwest Asia. Two generations later, explorer Vasco da Gama's puny fleet of four ships and 170 men would seize the trade of the vast Indian Ocean for Portugal.

The Renaissance Changes Europe, 1300–1500

The Crusades exposed educated Europeans to Arab learning and Eastern luxuries. Arab merchants had access to spices from India and silks, magnetic compasses, water-powered mills, and mechanical clocks from China. Arab scholars carried on the legacy of Byzantine civilization, which had preserved the great achievements of the Greeks and Romans in medicine, philosophy, mathematics, astronomy, and geography. Stimulated by this knowledge, first Italy and then the countries of northern Europe experienced a rebirth of cultural life, scientific progress, and economic energy.

Innovations in Economics, Art, and Politics | The Renaissance had its greatest impact on the upper classes. Merchants from the Italian city-states of Genoa, Florence, Pisa, and especially Venice dispatched ships to Alexandria, Beirut, and other eastern Mediterranean ports, where they purchased goods from China, India, Persia, and Arabia to be sold throughout Europe. This enormously profitable commerce created wealthy merchants, bankers, and textile manufacturers who expanded trade, lent vast sums of money, and spurred technological innovation in silk and wool production. Italian moneyed elites ruled their city-states as **republics**, with no prince or king. They celebrated **civic humanism**, an **ideology** that praised public virtue and service to the state and in time profoundly influenced European and American conceptions of government.

Perhaps no other age in European history has produced such a flowering of artistic genius. Michelangelo, Andrea Palladio, and Filippo Brunelleschi designed and built great architectural masterpieces. Leonardo da Vinci, Jacopo Bellini, and Raphael produced magnificent religious paintings, setting styles and standards that have endured into the modern era. This creative energy inspired Renaissance rulers as well: In *The Prince* (1513), Niccolò Machiavelli summed up a century of monarchical experience in accumulating political power. The kings of Western Europe had created royal law courts and bureaucracies to reduce the power of the landed nobility and had forged alliances with merchants and urban artisans. Monarchs allowed merchants to trade throughout their realms, granted privileges to the artisan organizations called **guilds**, and safeguarded commercial transactions in royal law courts, thereby encouraging domestic manufacturing and foreign trade. In return, kings and princes extracted taxes from towns and loans from merchants to support their armies and officials.

Maritime Exploration | Around 1400, the Portuguese monarchy propelled Europe into overseas expansion, initially by confronting Muslim states in North Africa. As a young soldier of the Crusading Order of Christ, Prince Henry of Portugal (1394–1460) learned of Arab merchants' rich trade in gold and slaves across the Sahara. Seeking a maritime route to the source of this trade in West Africa, Henry drew on the work of Renaissance thinkers and Arab and Italian geographers. In 1420, he founded a center for oceanic navigation in southern Portugal. He urged his captains to find a way around Cape Bojador in North Africa, a region of fierce winds and treacherous currents, and to explore the "Sea of Darkness" to the south. Eventually, Henry's mariners designed a better-handling vessel, the caravel, rigged with a lateen (triangular) sail that enabled the ship to tack into the wind. This innovation allowed them to sail far into the Atlantic, where they discovered and colonized the Madeira and Azore islands. From there, they sailed in 1435 to sub-Saharan Sierra Leone, where they exchanged salt, wine, and fish for African ivory and gold. By the 1440s, the Portuguese were trading in humans as well, the first Europeans to engage in the long-established African trade in slaves. Henry's mission of enhancing Portugal's wealth through trade with West Africa had succeeded.

West African Society and Slavery

Vast and diverse, West Africa stretches from present-day Senegal to the Democratic Republic of Congo. In the 1400s, tropical rain forests covered much of the coast, but a series of great rivers — the Senegal, Gambia, Volta, Niger, and Congo — provided relatively easy access to the woodlands and savannas of the interior, where most people lived. There were few coastal cities because there was little seaborne trade (Map 1.4).

West African Life | West Africa was in general a hard place to live, with a thin soil and daunting diseases. Most West Africans lived in small villages and farmed modest plots. Normally, the men cleared the land and the women planted and harvested the crops. Tsetse flies, carriers of sleeping sickness to humans and disease deadly to cattle, wiped out livestock in wooded and low-lying areas, leaving people with a diet deficient in protein and milk. To secure meat, forest dwellers exchanged palm oil and kola nuts (which contained a highly valued stimulant), for the livestock, leather goods, and cotton textiles that savanna dwellers produced. Merchants collected valuable salt, which was gathered along the coast and mined in great de-posits in the Sahara, and traded it for iron, gold, and manufactures along the Niger and other rivers.

West Africans lived in diverse ethnic groups and spoke four basic languages, each with many dialects. Among West Atlantic–speakers, the Fulani and Wolof peoples were most numerous. Mande-speakers in the upper Niger region included the Malinke and Bambara peoples; the Yorubas and the Ibos of southern Nigeria spoke varieties of the Kwa language. Finally, the Mossis and other Voltaic-speakers inhabited the area along the upper Volta River. Most West Africans lived in societies similar to those of the Mayans and Aztecs: socially stratified states ruled by kings and princes. Some lived in city-states that produced high-quality metal, leather, textiles, and pottery. Other West African societies were stateless, organized by household and lineage, much like those of the eastern woodland Indians in North America.

Spiritual beliefs varied greatly. Some West Africans who lived immediately south of the Sahara — the Fulanis in Senegal, Mande-speakers in Mali, and Hausas in northern Nigeria — learned about Islam from Arab merchants and imams, knew the Koran, and worshipped only a single God. But most West Africans acknowledged the presence of multiple gods, as well as spirits that lived in the earth, animals, and plants. Many people believed that their kings had divine attributes and could contact the spirit world. They treated their ancestors with great respect, believing that the dead resided in a nearby spiritual realm and interceded in their lives. Most West African peoples had secret societies, such as the Poro for men and the Sande for women, which united people from different lineages and clans. These societies educated their members in sexual practices and conducted tribal rituals that celebrated male virility and female fecundity. "Without children you are naked," said a Yoruba proverb. Happy was the man with a big household, many wives, many children, and many relatives — and, in a not very different vein, many slaves.

Portuguese Trade | European traders initially had a positive impact on West Africa by introducing new plants and animals and expanding African trade networks. Portuguese merchants brought coconuts from East Africa; oranges and lemons from the Mediterranean; pigs from Western Europe; and, after 1492, maize, manioc, and tomatoes from the Americas. From small, fortified trading posts on the coast, merchants shipped metal products and manufactures to inland regions and took gold, ivory, and pepper in return. To handle the inland trade, the Portuguese relied on Africans, since Portuguese ships could travel no

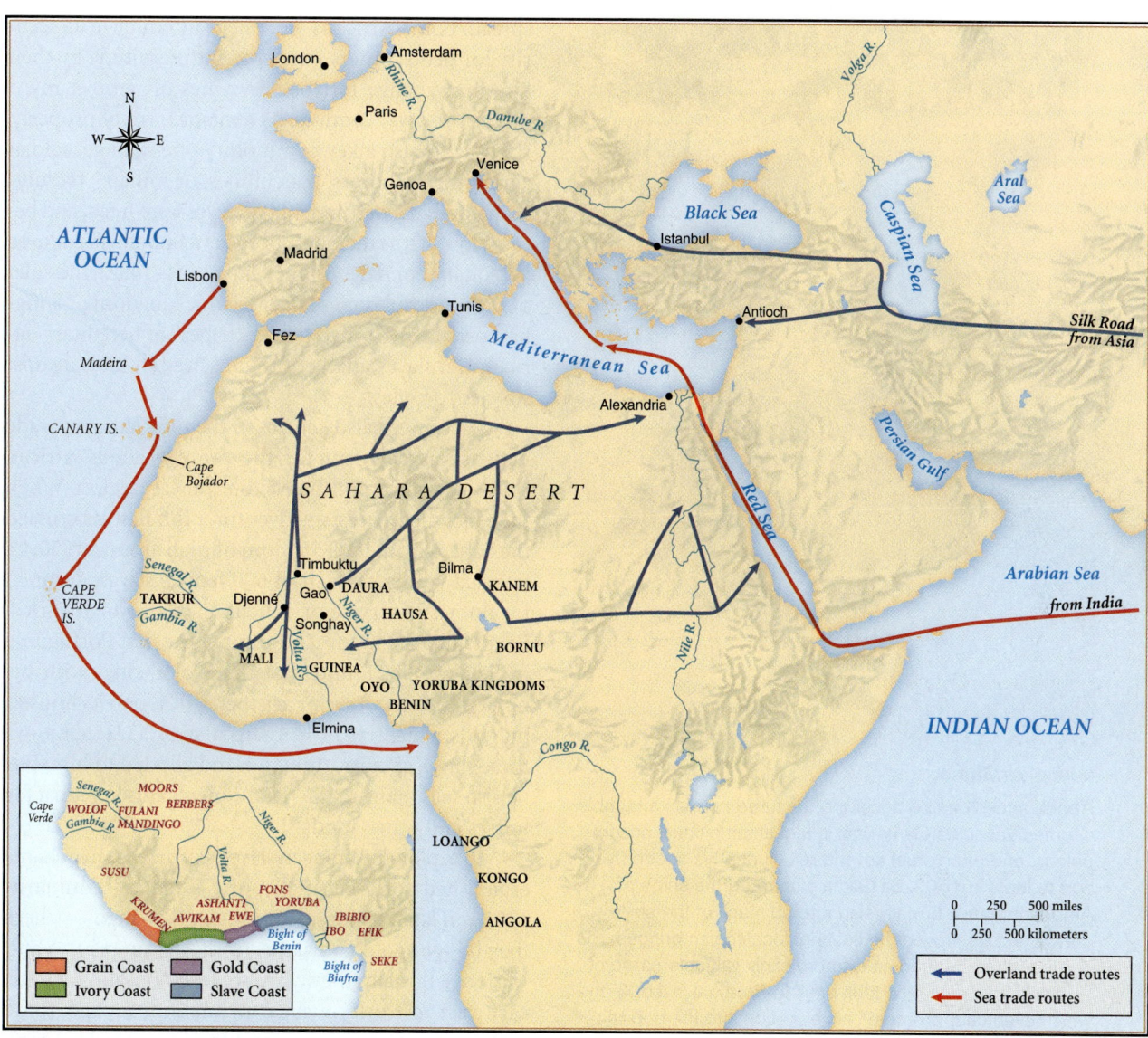

MAP 1.4

West Africa and the Mediterranean in the Fifteenth Century

Trade routes across the Sahara had long connected West Africa with the Mediterranean region. Gold, ivory, and slaves moved north and east; fine textiles, spices, and the Muslim faith traveled south. Beginning in the 1430s, the Portuguese opened up maritime trade with the coastal regions of West Africa, which were home to many peoples and dozens of large and small states. Over the next century, the transatlantic movement of gold and slaves would surpass that across the Sahara.

more than 150 miles up the slow-flowing Gambia and lesser distances on the other rivers. Moreover, yellow fever, malaria, and dysentery quickly struck down Europeans who spent time in the interior of West Africa, often killing as many as half of them each year.

From West Africa, Portuguese adventurers looked for an ocean route to Asia. In 1488, Bartholomeu Dias rounded the Cape of Good Hope, the southern tip of Africa. Ten years later, Vasco da Gama reached East Af-

rica and India; his ships were mistaken for those of Chinese traders, the last pale-skinned men to arrive by sea. Although da Gama's inferior goods—tin basins, coarse cloth, honey, and coral beads—were snubbed by the Arab and Indian merchants along India's Malabar Coast, he managed to acquire a highly profitable cargo of cinnamon and pepper. To acquire more spices and Indian textiles, da Gama returned to India in 1502 with twenty-one fighting vessels, which outmaneuvered

Vasco da Gama

Appearances can be deceiving. Pictured here as a humble courtier, Vasco da Gama was in fact an ambitious, unscrupulous, and often cruel adventurer. During his second voyage to India in 1502, da Gama plundered the ships of Arab merchants, brutally slaughtered many of the ships' crews, and destroyed the fleets of local Indian princes. His depredations secured an extraordinarily valuable cargo of silks and spices that he took back to Portugal in 1503 and which eventually prompted his elevation into the nobility, as the Count of Vidigueira.   The Pierpoint Morgan Library/Art Resource, NY.

and outgunned the Arab fleets. That expedition netted 1,700 tons of spices, as much as flowed through Venice in an entire year. Soon the Portuguese government set up fortified trading posts for its merchants at key points around the Indian Ocean, in Indonesia, and along the coast of China. In a transition that sparked the momentous growth of European wealth and power, the Portuguese and then the Dutch replaced the Arabs as the leaders in Asian commerce.

The Slave Trade | Portuguese traders likewise ousted Arab merchants as the prime purveyors of African slaves. Coerced labor—slavery, serfdom, or indentured servitude—was the norm in most premodern societies, and in Africa, slavery was wide-spread. Some Africans were held in bondage as security for debts; others were sold into servitude by their kin, in exchange for food in times of famine; many others were war captives. As a major form of property, slaves were also a key commodity of exchange, sold as agricultural laborers, concubines, or military recruits. Sometimes the descendants of slaves were freed, and became low-status members of society, but others endured hereditary bondage. Sonni Ali (r. 1464–1492), the ruler of the powerful upper Niger Islamic kingdom of Songhay, personally owned twelve "tribes" of hereditary agricultural slaves, many of them seized in raids against stateless peoples.

Slaves were also central to the international trade network as payment for the prestige goods African rulers coveted from the Mediterranean region. When the renowned Tunisian adventurer Ibn Battuta crossed the Sahara from the Kingdom of Mali around 1350, he traveled with a caravan of 600 female slaves, destined for domestic service or concubinage in North Africa, Egypt, and the Ottoman Empire. The first Portuguese in Senegambia found that the Wolof king, with his horse-mounted warrior aristocracy, "supports himself by raids which result in many slaves. . . . He employs these slaves in cultivating the land allotted to him; but he also sells many to the [Arab] merchants in return for horses and other goods."

To exploit this trade in slaves, Portuguese merchants established forts at small ports—first at Elmina in 1482 and later at Gorée, Mpinda, and Loango—where they bought gold and slaves from African princes and warlords. Initially, they carried a few thousand Africans each year to work on sugar plantations on São Tomé (off the coast of Gabon), and the Cape Verde, Azore, and Madeira islands; they also sold slaves in Lisbon, which soon had an African population of 9,000. After 1550, the maritime slave trade—a forced diaspora of African peoples—expanded enormously as Europeans set up sugar plantations in Brazil and the West Indies.

Europeans Explore America

As Portuguese traders sailed south and east, the Spanish monarchs Ferdinand II of Aragon and Isabel I of Castile financed an explorer who looked to the west. As Renaissance rulers, Ferdinand (r. 1474–1516) and Isabel (r. 1474–1504) saw national unity and foreign commerce as the keys to power and prosperity. Married in an arranged match to combine their Christian kingdoms, the young rulers completed the centuries-long *reconquista* by capturing Granada, the last Islamic territory in Western Europe, in 1492. Using Catholicism to build a sense of

The Arab Saharan Slave Trade
Long before the Atlantic slave trade began around 1500, Arab merchants had been driving Africans across the Sahara to the Mediterranean region, where they sold them as domestic servants and concubines. Between 1000 and 1900, some 9 million enslaved Africans endured the walk across the desert from Timbuktu to Marrakesh or from Bilma to Tripoli. They usually traveled shackled together in large coffles, like that pictured in this engraving of unknown date.
© Bettmann/Corbis.

"Spanishness," they launched the brutal Inquisition against suspected Christian heretics and expelled or forcibly converted thousands of Jews and Muslims.

Columbus and America Simultaneously, Ferdinand and Isabel sought trade and empire by subsidizing the voyages of Christopher Columbus, an ambitious and daring mariner from Genoa. Misinterpreting the findings of Italian geographers, Columbus believed that the Atlantic Ocean, long feared by Arab merchants as a 10,000-mile-wide "green sea of darkness," was a much narrower channel of water separating Europe from Asia. After cajoling and lobbying for six years, Columbus persuaded Genoese investors in Seville; influential courtiers; and, finally, Ferdinand and Isabel to accept his dubious theories and finance a western voyage to Asia.

Columbus set sail in three small ships in August 1492. Six weeks later, after a perilous voyage of 3,000 miles, he disembarked on an island in the present-day Bahamas. Believing that he had reached Asia — "the Indies," in fifteenth-century parlance — Columbus called the native inhabitants Indians and the islands the West Indies. He was surprised by the crude living conditions but expected the native peoples "easily [to] be made Christians." He claimed the islands for Spain and for Christendom by naming them after the Spanish royal family and Catholic holy days. Columbus then explored the neighboring Caribbean islands and demanded tribute from the local Taino [*TIE-no*], Arawak [*air-a-WAK*], and Carib peoples. Buoyed by stories of rivers of gold lying "to the west," Columbus left 40 men on the island of Hispaniola (present-day Haiti and the Dominican Republic) and returned triumphantly to Spain.

Although Columbus brought back no gold, the Spanish monarchs supported three more of his voyages. Columbus colonized the West Indies with more than 1,000 Spanish settlers — all men — and hundreds of domestic animals. But he failed to find either golden treasures or great kingdoms, and his death in 1506 went virtually unnoticed.

A German geographer soon labeled the newly found continents "America" in honor of a Florentine explorer, Amerigo Vespucci. Vespucci, who had explored the coast of present-day South America around 1500, denied that the region was part of Asia. He called it a *nuevo mundo*, a "new world." The Spanish crown called the two continents *Las Indias* ("the Indies") and wanted to make them a new Spanish world.

The Spanish Conquest

Spanish adventurers ruled the Caribbean with an iron hand. After subduing the Arawaks and Tainos on Hispaniola, the Spanish probed the mainland for gold and slaves. In 1513, Juan Ponce de León explored the coast of Florida and gave that peninsula its name. In the same year, Vasco Núñez de Balboa crossed the Isthmus of Darién (Panama) and became the first European to see the Pacific Ocean. Rumors of rich Indian kingdoms encouraged other Spaniards, including hardened veterans of the *reconquista*, to invade the mainland. The Spanish monarchs offered successful conquistadors noble titles, vast estates, and Indian laborers.

The Map Behind Columbus's Voyage

In 1489, Henricus Martellus, a German cartographer living in Florence, produced this huge (4 feet by 6 feet) view of the known world, probably working from a map devised by Christopher Columbus's brother, Bartholomew. The map uses the spatial projection of the ancient Greek philosopher Claudius Ptolemy (A.D. 90–168) and incorporates information from Marco Polo's explorations in Asia and Bartolomeu Dias's recent voyage around the tip of Africa. Most important, it greatly exaggerates the width of Eurasia, thereby suggesting that Asia lies only 5,000 miles west of Europe (rather than the actual distance of 15,000 miles). Using Martellus's map, Columbus persuaded the Spanish monarchs to support his westward voyage.   Bildarchiv Preussischer Kulturbesitz/Art Resource, NY.

The Fall of the Aztecs | Hernán Cortés (1485–1547) conquered the Aztec empire and destroyed its civilization. Cortés came from a family of minor gentry; seeking military adventure and material gain, he sailed to Santo Domingo, the capital of Hispaniola, in 1506. Ambitious and charismatic, he distinguished himself in battle, putting down a revolt and helping to conquer Cuba. These exploits and his marriage to a well-connected Spanish woman won Cortés an extensive Cuban estate and a series of administrative appointments.

Eager to increase his fortune, Cortés jumped at a chance in 1519 to lead an expedition to the mainland. He landed with 600 men near the Mayan settlement of Potonchan, which he quickly overpowered. Then Cortés got lucky. The defeated Mayans presented him with slave women to serve as servants and concubines. Among them was Malinali, a young woman of noble birth and, a Spanish soldier noted, "of pleasing appearance and sharp-witted and outward-going." Malinali spoke Nahuatl, the Aztecs' language. Cortés took her as his mistress and interpreter, and soon she became his guide. When the Spanish leader learned from Malinali the extent of the Aztec empire, his goal became power rather than plunder. He would depose its king, Moctezuma [*mok-tah-ZOO-mah*], and take over his realm.

Of Malinali's motives for helping Cortés, there is no record. Like his Spanish followers, she may have

been dazzled by his powerful personality. Or perhaps she calculated that Cortés was her best hope for escaping slavery and reclaiming her noble status. Whatever her reasons, Malinali's loyalty was complete. As the Spanish marched on the Aztec capital of Tenochtitlán, she warned Cortés of a surprise attack in the city of Cholula and negotiated his way into the Aztec capital. "Without her," concluded Bernal Díaz del Castillo, the Spanish chronicler of the conquest, Cortés would "have been unable to surmount many difficulties."

Awed by the Spanish invaders, Moctezuma received Cortés with great ceremony (see Comparing American Voices, "The Spanish Conquest of Mexico," pp. 28–29). However, Cortés soon held the emperor captive, and when Moctezuma's supporters tried to expel the invaders, they faced superior European military technology. The sight of the Spaniards in full metal armor, with guns that shook the heavens and inflicted devastating wounds, made a deep impression on the Aztecs, who knew how to purify gold but not how to produce iron tools or weapons. Moreover, the Aztecs had no wheeled carts or cavalry, and their warriors, fighting on foot with flint- or obsidian-tipped spears and arrows, were no match for Spanish horsemen wielding steel swords and aided by vicious attack dogs. Although suffering great losses, Cortés and his men fought their way out of the Aztec capital.

Winning a battle was one thing; conquering an empire was another. Had Moctezuma ruled a united empire, he could have overwhelmed the 600 Spanish invaders. But many Indian peoples hated the Aztecs, and Cortés deftly exploited their anger. With the help of Malinali, he formed military alliances with the Tlaxcaltecs and other subject groups whose wealth had been seized by Aztec nobles and whose people had been sacrificed to the Aztec sun god. Moctezuma's empire collapsed, the victim of a vast Indian rebellion instigated by the wily Cortés.

The Impact of Diseases The Spanish also had a silent ally: disease. Having been separated from Eurasia for thousands of years, the inhabitants of the Americas had no immunities to common European diseases. After the Spanish exodus, a massive smallpox epidemic ravaged Tenochtitlán, "striking everywhere in the city," according to an Aztec source, and killing Moctezuma's brother and thousands more. "They could not move, they could not stir. . . . Covered, mantled with pustules, very many people died of them." Subsequent outbreaks of smallpox, influenza, and measles killed hundreds of thousands of Indians and sapped the survivors' morale. Exploiting this demographic weakness, Cortés quickly extended Spanish rule over the Aztec empire. His lieutenants then moved against the Mayan city-states of the Yucatán Peninsula, eventually conquering them as well.

In 1524, Francisco Pizarro set out to accomplish the same feat in Peru. There the rich and powerful

Thus I have given you, I think, the Substance of the Arguments o ... both sides of that great and important Questic ...

The Spanish Conquest of Mexico

How could a Spanish force of 600 men take control of an empire of 20 million people? That the Spanish had steel swords and armor and some guns, horses and attack dogs certainly gave them a military advantage. Still, concerted attack by the armies of the Aztecs and their allies would have overwhelmed the invaders before they reached the Mexican capital of Tenochtitlán. Why was there no such attack? One reason was that Cortés's force was bolstered by a sizable army of Tlaxcaltecs, from the independent coastal kingdom of Tlaxcala. The combined forces had shown their might by massacring thousands of residents of the city of Cholula, an Aztec ally. Also, some influential Aztecs, including Moctezuma, thought that Cortés might be an emissary of their god Quetzalcoatl.

These documents, which describe Cortés's initial entry, come from the memoir of a participant and an oral history. Consider them first as *sources*: How trustworthy are they? Are they biased in any way? Then think about their *contents*: Do their accounts agree? Do they identify key events? Do they explain why the Spaniards reached the city unmolested?

Bernal Díaz del Castillo

Cortés and Moctezuma Meet

Bernal Díaz was an unlikely chronicler of great events. Born poor, he went to America as a common soldier in 1514 and served under conquistadors in Panama and Cuba. In 1519, he joined Cortés's expedition, fought in many battles, and as a reward received an estate in present-day Guatemala. In his old age, Díaz wrote *The True History of the Conquest of New Spain*, a compelling memoir written from the perspective of a common soldier. In fresh and straightforward prose, it depicts the conquest as a divinely blessed event that saved the non-Aztec peoples of Mexico from a barbarous regime.

The Great Moctezuma had sent these great Caciques in advance to receive us, and when they came before Cortés they bade us welcome in their language, and as a sign of peace, they touched their hands against the ground. . . .

When we arrived near to [Tenochtitlán], . . . the Great Moctezuma got down from his litter, and those great Caciques supported him with their arms beneath a marvelously rich canopy of green coloured feathers with much gold and silver embroidery . . . which was wonderful to look at. The Great Moctezuma was richly attired according to his usage, and he was shod with sandals, the soles were of gold and the upper part adorned with precious stones. . . .

Many other Lords walked before the Great Moctezuma, sweeping the ground where he would tread and spreading cloths on it, so that he should not tread on the earth. Not one of these chieftains dared even to think of looking him in the face, but kept their eyes lowered with great reverence. . . .

When Cortés was told that the Great Moctezuma was approaching, and he saw him coming, he dismounted from his horse, and when he was near Moctezuma, they simultaneously paid great reverence to one another. Moctezuma bade him welcome and our Cortés replied through Doña Marina [Malinali, also called Malinche, Cortés's Indian mistress and interpreter] wishing him very good health. . . . And then Cortés brought out a necklace which he had ready at hand, made of glass stones, . . . which have within them many patterns of diverse colours, these were strung on a cord of gold and with musk so that it should have a sweet scent, and he placed it round the neck of the Great Moctezuma. . . . Then Cortés through the mouth of Doña Marina told him that now his heart rejoiced having seen such a great Prince, and that he took it as a great honour that he had come in person to meet him. . . .

Thus space was made for us to enter the streets of Mexico, without being so much crowded. But who could now count the multitude of men and women and boys who were in the streets and in canoes on the canals, who had come out to see us. It was indeed wonderful. . . . Coming to think it over it seems to be a great mercy that our Lord Jesus Christ was pleased to give us grace and courage to dare to enter into such a city; and for the many times He has saved me from danger of death . . . I give Him sincere thanks. . . .

They took us to lodge in some large houses, where there were apartments for all of us, for they had belonged to the father of the Great Moctezuma, who was named Axayaca. . . .

Cortés thanked Moctezuma through our interpreters, and Moctezuma replied, "Malinche, you and your brethren are in your own house, rest awhile," and then he went to his palaces, which were not far away, and we divided our lodgings by companies, and placed the artillery pointing in a convenient direction, and the order which we had to keep was clearly explained to us, and that we were to be much on the alert, both the cavalry and all of us soldiers. A sumptuous dinner was provided for us according to their use and custom, and we ate it at once. So this was our lucky and daring entry into the great city of Tenochtitlan Mexico on the 8th day of November the year of our Saviour Jesus Christ, 1519.

Source: Bernal Díaz del Castillo, *The True History of the Conquest of New Spain*, trans. A. P. Maudslay (1632; London: Routledge, 1928), pp. 272–275.

Friar Bernardino de Sahagún

Aztec Elders Describe the Behavior of Moctezuma

During the 1550s, Friar Bernardino de Sahagún published *General History of the Things of New Spain*. According to Sahagún, the authors of the *History* were Aztec elders who lived through the Conquest. They told their stories to Sahagún in a repetitive style, according to the conventions of Aztec oral histories, and he translated them into Spanish.

Moctezuma enjoyed no sleep, no food, no one spoke to him. Whatsoever he did, it was as if he were in torment. Ofttimes it was as if he sighed, became weak, felt weak. . . . Wherefore he said, "What will now befall us? Who indeed stands [in charge]? Alas, until now, I. In great torment is my heart; as if it were washed in chili water it indeed burns." And when he had so heard what the messengers reported, he was terrified, he was astounded. . . . Especially did it cause him to faint away when he heard how the gun, at [the Spaniards'] command, discharged: how it resounded as if it thundered when it went off. It indeed bereft one of strength; it shut off one's ears. And when it discharged, something like a round pebble came forth from within. Fire went showering forth; sparks went blazing forth. And its smoke smelled very foul; it had a fetid odor which verily wounded the head. And when [the shot] struck a mountain, it was as if it were destroyed, dissolved . . . as if someone blew it away.

All iron was their war array. In iron they clothed themselves. With iron they covered their heads. Iron were their swords. Iron were their crossbows. Iron were their shields. Iron were their lances. And those which bore them upon their backs, their deer [horses], were as tall as roof terraces.

And their bodies were everywhere covered; only their faces appeared. They were very white; they had chalky faces; they had yellow hair, though the hair of some was black. . . . And when Moctezuma so heard, he was much terrified. It was as if he fainted away. His heart saddened; his heart failed him. . . . [but] he made himself resolute; he put forth great effort; he quieted, he controlled his heart; he submitted himself entirely to whatsoever he was to see, at which he was to marvel. . . . [He then greeted Cortés, as described above.]

And when [the Spaniards] were well settled, they thereupon inquired of Moctezuma as to all the city's treasure . . . the devices, the shields. Much did they importune him; with great zeal they sought gold. . . . Thereupon were brought forth all the brilliant things; the shields, the golden discs, the devils' necklaces, the golden nose crescents, the golden leg bands, the golden arm bands, the golden forehead bands.

Source: Friar Bernardino de Sahagún, *Florentine Codex: General History of the Things of New Spain*, trans. Arthur J. O. Anderson and Charles E. Dibble (Santa Fe, NM, and Salt Lake City: The School of American Research and University of Utah Press, 1975), book 12: pp. 17–20, 26.

ANALYZING THE EVIDENCE

- Díaz's account is a memoir, written in retrospect. What effect does that have on the structure and tone of the account? How is the Aztec selection different in those respects?

- Why does Moctezuma pay "great reverence" to Cortés? Why does Cortés return the honor? What is the strategy of each leader?

- What is Díaz's explanation for the easy entry of the Spanish into the city? What explanation is suggested by the elders' account?

Inca empire stretched 2,000 miles along the Pacific coast of South America. To govern this far-flung empire (and avert local famines), the Inca rulers had laid 24,000 miles of roads and built dozens of administrative centers, filled with finely crafted stone buildings. An Inca king, claiming divine status, ruled the empire through a bureaucracy of nobles. By the time Pizarro and his small force of 168 men and 67 horses finally reached Peru in 1532, half of the Inca population had already died from European diseases spread by Indian traders. Weakened militarily and divided between rival claimants to the throne, the Inca nobility was easy prey. Pizarro killed Atahualpa, the last Inca emperor, and seized his enormous wealth. Although Inca resistance continued for a generation (and the dream of an "Inca Return" persisted until a failed rebellion in 1781), Spain was now the master of the wealthiest and most populous regions of the Western Hemisphere (Map 1.5).

The Spanish invasion changed life forever in the Americas. Disease and warfare wiped out virtually all of the Indians of Hispaniola—at least 300,000 people. In Peru, the population of 9 million in 1530 plummeted to fewer than 500,000 a century later. Mesoamerica suffered the greatest losses: In one of the great demographic disasters in world history, its population of 30 million Native Americans in 1500 had dwindled to just 3 million in 1650.

The Legacy of the Conquest Once the conquistadors had triumphed, the Spanish monarchs quickly transferred Iberian institutions—municipal councils, the legal code, the Catholic Church—to America, creating a bureaucratic empire. From its headquarters in Madrid, the Council of the Indies issued laws and decrees to viceroys, governors, judges, and other Spanish officials. But the conquistadors and their descendants remained powerful because they held many

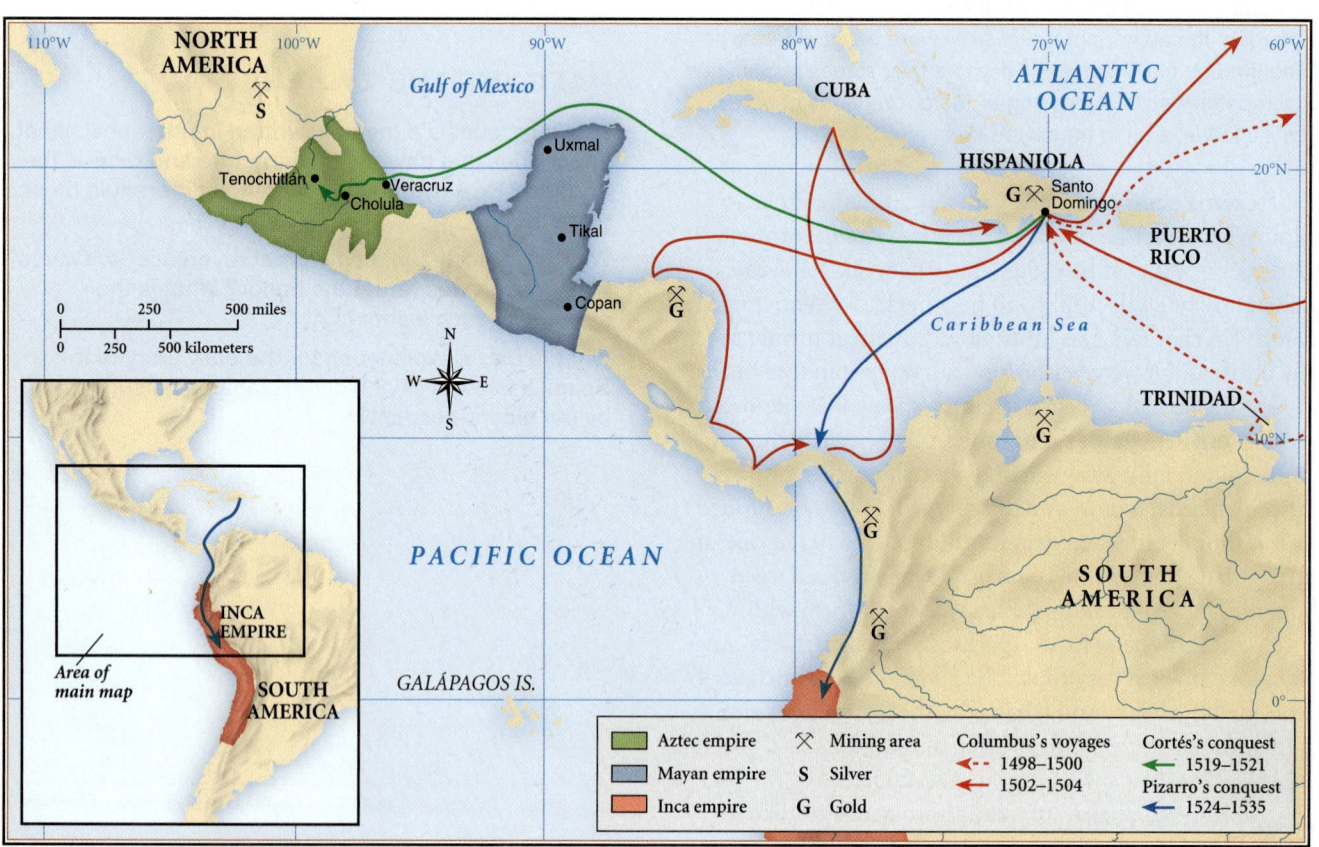

MAP 1.5

The Spanish Conquest of the Great Indian Civilizations

The Spanish first invaded the islands of the Caribbean, largely wiping out the native peoples. Rumors of a gold-rich civilization led to Cortés's invasion of the Aztec empire in 1519. By 1535, other Spanish conquistadors had conquered the Mayan temple cities and the Inca empire in Peru, completing one of the great conquests in world history.

positions in the colonial bureaucracy and owned **encomiendas**, royal grants giving them legal control over land and Native American workers. They ruthlessly exploited their laborers, forcing them to raise crops and cattle for local consumption and for export to Europe. The Spanish invasion permanently altered the natural as well as the human environment: Eurasian and African livestock (horses, cattle, sheep, and goats), grain crops (wheat, barley, and rice), and diseases (smallpox, measles, chickenpox, influenza, malaria, and yellow fever) now became part of life in the Americas.

The Spanish conquest changed the ecology of Europe, Africa, and Asia as well. In a process that historians call the **Columbian Exchange**, the food products of the Western Hemisphere—especially maize, potatoes, manioc, sweet potatoes, and tomatoes—significantly increased agricultural yields and population growth in other continents (Map 1.6). Maize and potatoes, for example, reached China around 1700; in the following century, the Chinese population tripled from 100 million to 300 million. Vast amounts of silver poured across the Pacific Ocean to China, where it was minted into money. In exchange, Spain received valuable Chinese silks, spices, and ceramics. In Europe, the gold that had formerly honored Aztec and Inca gods now flowed into the countinghouses of Spain and gilded the Catholic churches of Europe. A less welcome transfer was the virulent strain of syphilis Columbus's sailors took back with them. The American wealth that flowed around the globe between 1540 and 1640 made Spain the richest and most powerful nation in Europe. Indeed, Spanish rulers now claimed a "lordship of all the world."

Meanwhile, the once magnificent civilizations of Mexico and Peru lay in ruins. "Of all these wonders"—

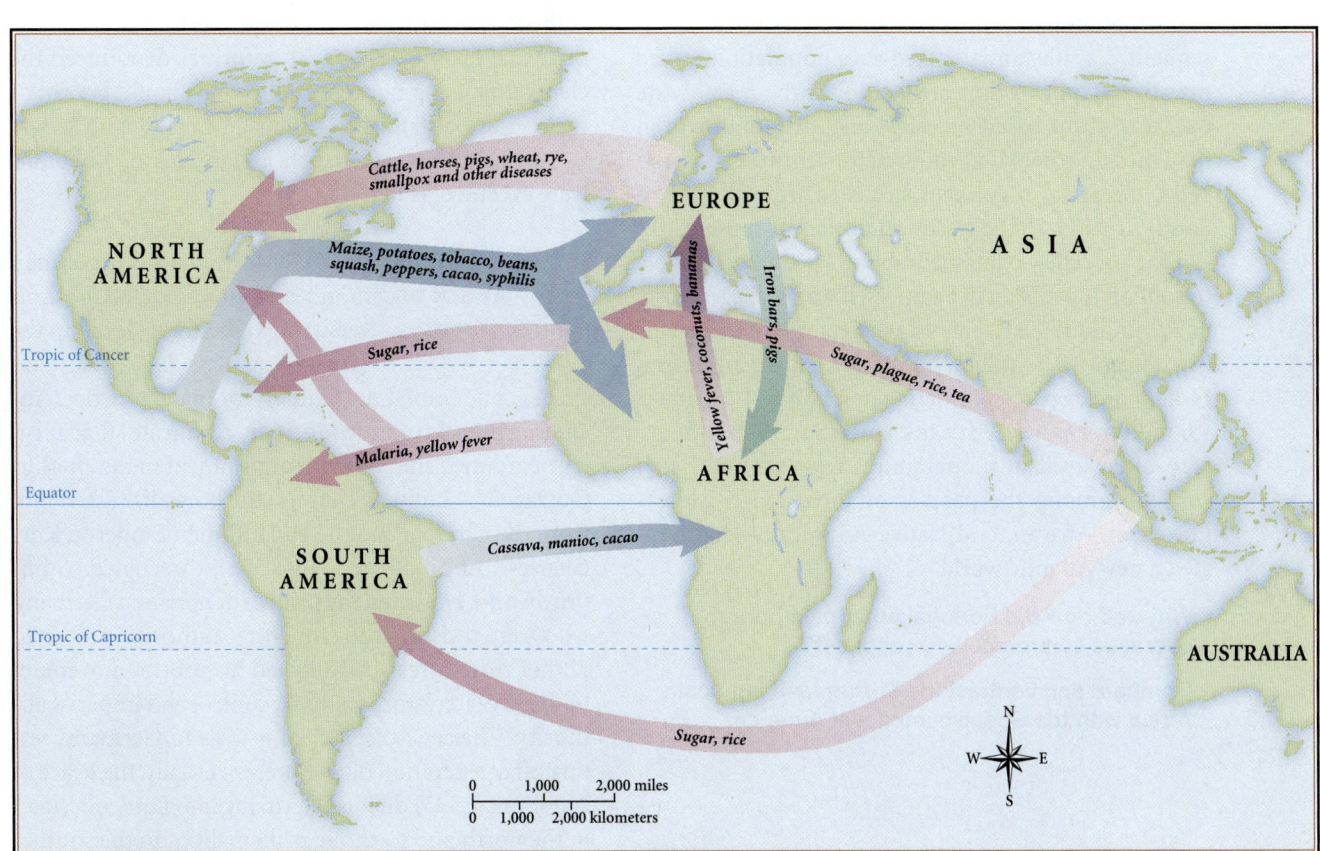

MAP 1.6

The Columbian Exchange

As European traders and adventurers traversed the world between 1430 and 1600, they began what historians call the Columbian Exchange, a vast intercontinental movement of the plants, animals, and diseases that changed the course of historical development. The nutritious, high-yielding American crops of corn and potatoes enriched the diets of Europeans, Africans, and Asians. However, the Eurasian and African diseases of smallpox, diphtheria, malaria, and yellow fever nearly wiped out the native inhabitants of the Western Hemisphere and virtually ensured that they would lose control of their lands.

the great city of Tenochtitlán, the bountiful irrigated fields, the rich orchards, the overflowing markets—"all is overthrown and lost, nothing left standing," recalled Bernal Díaz, who had been a young soldier in Cortés's army. So, too, with native religion and culture: Cortés built a grand cathedral with the stones from Moctezuma's palace, while Spanish priests suppressed traditional religious ceremonies and gave Catholic identities to Indian gods. As early as 1531, an Indian convert reported a vision of a dark-skinned Virgin Mary, later known as the Virgin of Guadalupe, a Christian version of the "corn mother" who traditionally protected the maize crop.

A new society took shape on the lands emptied by disease and exploitation. Between 1500 and 1650, at least 350,000 Spaniards migrated to Mesoamerica and western South America. More than 75 percent were men—poor, unmarried, and unskilled refugees from Andalusia and later a broader mix of Castilians—and many took Indian women as wives or mistresses. Consequently, a substantial mixed-race population, called **mestizos**, quickly appeared, along with an elaborate **caste system** based on racial ancestry (and, within that, on skin color) that endured for centuries. Around 1800, the Spanish colonies stretched from the tip of South America to the northern border of present-day California. They contained about 16 million people (6 million more than in Spain itself): a privileged caste of 3.2 million, the Españols, who claimed pure Spanish descent; 5.5 million mestizos, people of mixed Indian and Spanish genetic and cultural heritage; 1.0 million enslaved Africans; and 6.5 million Indians, who often lived in mountainous regions. The harsh collision among the peoples of three old worlds—European, African, and Native American—had created a new Atlantic world.

- Why and how did Portugal and Spain pursue overseas commerce and conquest?
- Compare and contrast the Portuguese impact in Africa with the Spanish impact in America.

The Rise of Protestant England, 1500–1620

On the basis of Columbus's discovery, Pope Alexander VI (r. 1492–1503) issued an edict declaring Spain's absolute dominion over the New World: Any intruder "even imperial and royal, . . . will incur the wrath of Almighty God." Soon, however, Roman Catholicism ceased to be a unifying force in European society. During the 1520s, religious doctrines preached by Martin Luther and other reformers divided Europe between Catholic and Protestant states and plunged the continent into a century of religious warfare. During these conflicts, France replaced Spain as the most powerful Catholic state and, along with the Protestant states of Holland and England, colonized North America in defiance of the papal edict.

The Protestant Movement

Over the centuries, the Catholic Church had become a large and wealthy institution. Renaissance popes and cardinals used the Church's wealth to patronize the arts and enrich themselves. Pope Leo X (r. 1513–1521) received half a million ducats a year (about $20 million in 2009 dollars) by selling religious offices. Corruption at the top encouraged ordinary priests to seek economic or sexual favors. An English reformer denounced the clergy as a "gang of scoundrels" who should be "rid of their vices or stripped of their authority," but he was ignored. Other critics, such as Jan Hus of Bohemia, were executed as heretics.

Martin Luther's Attack on Church Doctrine In 1517, Martin Luther, a German monk and professor at the university in Wittenberg, took up the cause of reform. His *Ninety-five Theses* condemned the Church for many practices, including the sale of **indulgences**, certificates that allegedly pardoned sinners from punishment in the afterlife. Outraged by Luther's charges, the pope dismissed him from the Church, and the Holy Roman Emperor, King Charles I of Spain (r. 1516–1556), threatened to imprison him. However, the princes of northern Germany, who were resisting the emperor's authority, protected Luther from arrest and allowed his protest movement to survive. To restore Catholic control and imperial authority, Charles I dispatched armies to Germany, setting off a generation of warfare. Eventually, the Peace of Augsburg (1555) divided Germany into Lutheran states in the north and Catholic principalities in the south.

Luther took issue with Roman Catholic doctrine in three major respects. First, he argued that humans were innately depraved and could not secure salvation through good deeds or the purchase of indulgences; instead, they could be saved only by grace, which came as a free gift from God. Second, Luther downplayed the role of the clergy as mediators between God and believers: "Our baptism consecrates us all without exception and makes us all priests." Third, he said that Christians must look to the Bible — not to the Church — as the ultimate authority in matters of faith. So that every literate German could read the Bible, previously available only in Latin, Luther translated it into German.

The Doctrines of John Calvin | Meanwhile, in Geneva, Switzerland, French theologian John Calvin established a rigorous Protestant regime. Even more than Luther, Calvin stressed human weakness and God's omnipotence. His *Institutes of the Christian Religion* (1536) depicted God as an absolute sovereign who governed the "wills of men so as to move precisely to that end directed by him." Calvin preached the doctrine of **predestination**, the idea that God chooses certain people for salvation before they are born and condemns the rest to eternal damnation. In Geneva, he set up a model Christian community, eliminating bishops and placing spiritual authority in ministers chosen by their congregations. Ministers and pious laymen ruled the city, prohibiting frivolity and luxury. "We know," wrote Calvin, "that man is of so perverse and crooked a nature, that everyone would scratch out his neighbor's eyes if there were no bridle to hold them in." Calvin's authoritarian doctrine won converts all over Europe, becoming the theology of the Huguenots in France, the Reformed Dutch Church, and the Presbyterians and Puritans in Scotland and England (Map 1.7).

English Protestantism | The English King Henry VIII (r. 1509–1547) had initially opposed Protestantism. However, when the pope refused to annul his marriage to the Spanish princess Catherine of Aragon in 1534, Henry broke with Rome and placed himself at the head of the new Church of England, which promptly granted an annulment. Although Henry's new church maintained most Catholic doctrines and practices, Protestant teachings continued to spread. Faced with popular pressure for reform, Henry's daughter and successor, Queen Elizabeth I

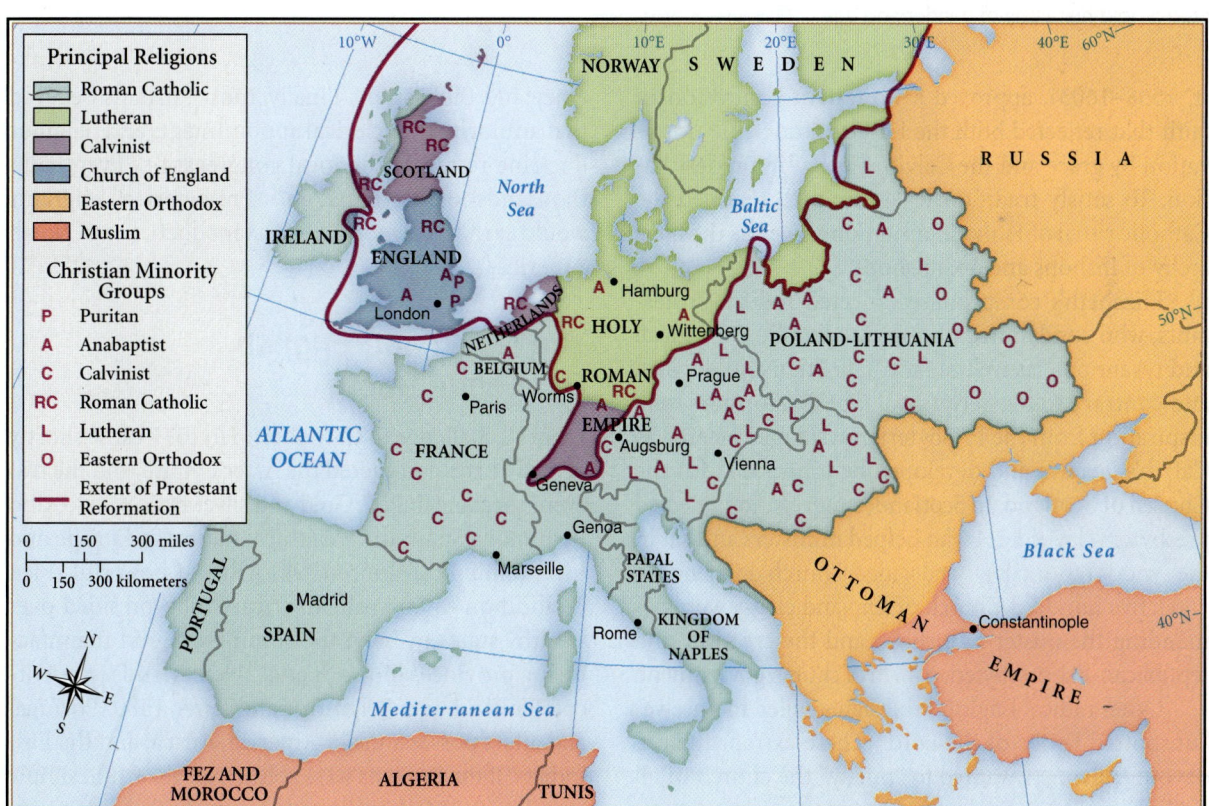

MAP 1.7

Religious Diversity in Europe, 1600

By 1600, Europe was permanently divided among rival Christian churches. Catholicism remained dominant in the south; Lutheran princes and monarchs ruled northern Europe; and Calvinism had strongholds in Switzerland, Holland, and Scotland. By persecuting radical Christian sects, the legally established churches — both Protestant and Catholic — encouraged the migration of sect members to America.

A Dutch Merchant Family

This 1563 painting of Antwerp wine merchant Pierre de Moucheron and his family by artist Cornelius de Zeeuw captures both the prosperity of the Dutch merchant class and the severe Calvinist ethos of sixteenth-century Holland. It also illustrates the character of the traditional patriarchal family, in which status reflected a rigid hierarchy of gender and age.   Rijksmuseum, Amsterdam.

(r. 1558–1603), approved a Protestant confession of faith that reflected both the Lutheran doctrine of salvation by grace and the Calvinist belief in predestination. To satisfy traditionalists, Elizabeth retained the Catholic ritual of Holy Communion as well as the hierarchy of bishops and archbishops.

Elizabeth's compromises angered radical Protestants, who condemned bishops as "proude, pontificall and tyrannous" as well as "anti-Christian and devilish and contrary to the Scriptures." These reformers took inspiration from the Presbyterian system pioneered in Calvin's Geneva and developed by John Knox for the Church of Scotland. In Scotland, congregations elected presbyters (lay elders) who helped ministers and sat in the synods (councils) that decided Church doctrine. By 1600, five hundred Church of England clergy were demanding the ouster of bishops and the creation of a republican-like presbyterian form of church government.

Other radical English Protestants called themselves "unspotted lambs of the Lord." These extraordinarily devout Calvinists wanted to "purify" the church of all Catholic teachings and magical or idolatrous practices, such as burning incense and praying to dead saints. Labeled Puritans, they sought inspiration from carefully argued sermons and placed emphasis on the "conversion experience," the felt infusion of God's grace. To ensure that all men and women had direct access to God's commands in the Bible, Puritans promoted lit-

eracy and Bible study. Finally, most Puritans believed that authority over clerical appointments and religious doctrine rested in the local congregation. Eventually, thousands of Puritans and Presbyterian migrants would carry their radical Protestant doctrines to North America.

The Dutch and English Challenge Spain

Luther's challenge to Catholicism in 1517 came shortly before Cortés conquered the Aztec empire, and the two events became linked. Gold and silver from Mexico and Peru made Spain the wealthiest nation in Europe and King Philip II (r. 1556–1598) its most powerful ruler. In addition to Spanish America, Philip presided over wealthy states in Italy; the commercial and manufacturing provinces of the Spanish Netherlands (present-day Holland and Belgium); and, after 1580, Portugal and all its possessions in America, Africa, and the East Indies. "If the Romans were able to rule the world simply by ruling the Mediterranean," boasted a Spanish priest, "what of the man who rules the Atlantic and Pacific oceans, since they surround the world?"

An ardent Catholic, Philip tried to root out Islam in North Africa and Protestantism in England and the Netherlands. He failed to do either. A massive Spanish fleet defeated a Turkish armada at Lepanto in the east-

Elizabeth I (r. 1558–1603)

Dressed in richly decorated clothes that symbolize her power, Queen Elizabeth I celebrates the destruction of the Spanish Armada (pictured in the background) and proclaims her nation's imperial ambitions. The queen's hand rests on a globe, asserting England's claims in the Western Hemisphere.   © The Gallery Collection/Corbis.

ern Mediterranean in 1571, freeing 15,000 Christian galley slaves, but Muslims continued to rule all of North Africa. Moreover, the Spanish Netherlands remained a hotbed of Calvinism. These Dutch- and Flemish-speaking provinces had grown wealthy from textile manufacturing and trade with Portuguese outposts in Africa and Asia. To protect their Calvinist faith and political liberties, they revolted against Spanish rule in 1566. After fifteen years of war, the seven northern provinces declared their independence, becoming the Dutch Republic (or Holland) in 1581.

Elizabeth I of England aided the Dutch cause by dispatching 6,000 troops to Holland. She also supported military expeditions that imposed English rule over Gaelic-speaking Catholic Ireland. Calling the Irish "wild savages" who were "more barbarous and more brutish in their customs . . . than in any other part of the world," English soldiers brutally massacred thousands, prefiguring the treatment of Indians in North America. To meet Elizabeth's challenge to Catholicism, Philip sent a Spanish Armada—130 ships and 30,000 men—against England in 1588. Philip intended to restore the Roman Church in England and then to wipe out Calvinism in Holland. But he failed utterly: A fierce storm and English ships destroyed the Spanish fleet.

Philip continued to spend his American gold and silver on religious wars, an ill-advised policy that diverted workers and resources from Spain's fledgling industries. The gold was like a "shewer of Raine," complained one critic, that left "no benefite behind." Oppressed by high taxes on agriculture and fearful of

military service, more than 200,000 residents of Castile, once the most prosperous region of Spain, migrated to America. By the time of Philip's death in 1598, Spain was in serious economic decline.

As mighty Spain faltered, tiny Holland prospered. Dutch warships sacked Spain's Caribbean ports and in 1628 captured the entire Spanish bullion fleet. This booty financed the capture of Portuguese trading posts in the Indian Ocean and its valuable sugar colony in Brazil. Amsterdam emerged as the financial capital of northern Europe, and the Dutch East India Company became the dominant trader from West Africa to Indonesia, China, and Japan. Dutch merchants also created the West India Company (1621), which invested in Brazilian sugar and established the fur-trading colony of New Netherland along the Hudson River.

Like Holland, England grew significantly during the sixteenth century, its economy stimulated, as colonial advocate Richard Hakluyt noted, by a "wounderful increase of our people." As England's population soared from 3 million in 1500 to 5 million in 1630, its monarchs supported the expansion of commerce and manufacturing. English merchants had long supplied European weavers with high-quality wool; around 1500, they created their own **outwork** textile industry. Merchants bought wool from the owners of great estates and sent it "out" to landless peasants in small cottages to spin and weave into cloth. The government aided textile entrepreneurs by setting low wage rates, and helped merchants by giving them monopolies in foreign markets. Queen Elizabeth granted exclusive licenses to the

Levant Company (to trade tin for silk and spices in Turkey) in 1581, the Guinea Company (to exchange manufactures for slaves in Africa) in 1588, and the East India Company (to import cotton cloth and spices from India) in 1600.

This system of state-assisted manufacturing and trade became known as **mercantilism**. By encouraging textile production, Elizabeth reduced imports and increased exports. The resulting favorable balance of trade caused gold and silver to flow into England and stimulated further economic expansion. Increased trade with Turkey and India also boosted import duties, which swelled the royal treasury and the monarch's power. By 1600, Elizabeth's mercantile policies had laid the foundations for overseas colonization. Now the English, as well as the Dutch, had the merchant fleets and wealth needed to challenge Spain's control of the Western Hemisphere.

The Social Causes of English Expansion

England sent people as well as merchant fleets and manufactures to America. Rapid population growth after 1550 provided a large body of potential settlers, and economic hardship put them in motion. Their troubles stemmed in part from the massive influx of American gold and silver, which doubled the money supply of Europe and sparked a major inflation—an upheaval known today as the **Price Revolution** (Figure 1.2).

The Decline of the Nobility England's landed nobility was the first casualty of the Price Revolution. Aristocrats customarily rented out their estates on long leases for fixed rents, which provided a secure income and plenty of leisure. As one English nobleman put it, "We eat and drink and rise up to play and this is to live like a gentleman." Then inflation struck. In less than two generations, the price of goods tripled while the nobility's income from rents barely increased. As the purchasing power of the aristocracy fell, that of the gentry and the yeomen rose. The **gentry**, nonnoble landholders with substantial estates, kept pace with inflation by renting land on short leases at higher rates. **Yeomen**, described by a European traveler as "middle people of a condition between gentlemen and peasants," owned small farms that they worked with family labor. As wheat prices tripled, yeomen used the profits to build larger houses and provide their children with land.

Economics influenced politics. As nobles lost wealth, the House of Lords, their branch of Parliament, lost power. Simultaneously, members of the rising gentry entered the House of Commons, the political voice of the propertied classes, and demanded greater authority over taxation and other policies. In this way, the Price Revolution enhanced the influence of representative institutions in which rich commoners and property-owning yeomen had a voice. And it encouraged the spread of republican principles that

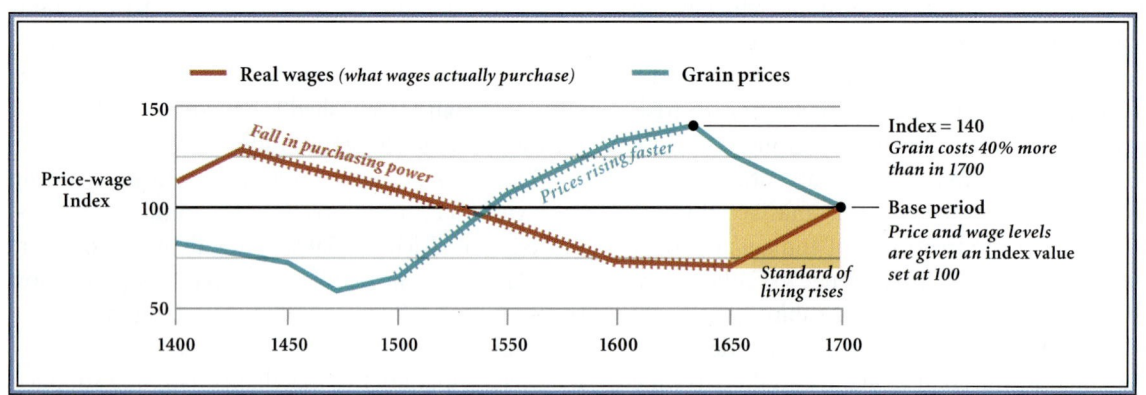

FIGURE 1.2

Price Inflation and Living Standards in Europe

American gold and silver poured into Europe after 1520, and the metals were minted into money. People then used that money to bid up the price of grain, which was in short supply. As the number of Europeans rose from 68 million in 1500 to 120 million in 1700, the scarcity of food and other goods caused a century-long decline in living standards. Along with the enhanced supply of money, scarcity of goods also created the great Price Inflation, which altered the relations among social classes. (See Figure 1.1 for another example of an indexed figure.)

changed the course of English—and American—political history.

The Dispossession of the Peasantry The Price Revolution likewise transformed the lives of peasants, who made up three-fourths of the English population (Figure 1.3). As Spanish gold and silver spurred the expansion of the textile industry, profit-minded landlords and wool merchants persuaded Parliament to pass **enclosure acts**. These laws allowed owners to kick peasants off their lands, fence in their fields, and put sheep to graze there. Dispossessed peasant families lived on the brink of poverty, spinning and weaving wool or working as agricultural wage laborers. Wealthy men had "taken farms into their hands," an observer noted with disgust in 1600, "whereby the peasantry of England is decayed and become servants to gentlemen."

These social changes were magnified by the coldest decades of "the Little Ice Age," an era of low global temperatures (c. 1350–c. 1850). Throughout Europe between 1620 and 1660, crop yields fell and grain prices soared, bringing famine and social unrest. "Thieves and rogues do swarm the highways," warned one justice of the peace. Beset by an onslaught of "necessitous people, the fuel of dangerous insurrections," the Virginia Company persuaded thousands of poor young men and women to migrate to America. By signing contracts known as **indentures**, the migrants sold their labor (and freedom) for four or five years. In return, they received passage across the Atlantic and a promise of land at the end of their service. Dispossessed peasants and weavers threatened by a recession in the English cloth trade were likewise ready to try their luck elsewhere. Thousands of yeomen families were also on the move, looking for affordable land on which to settle

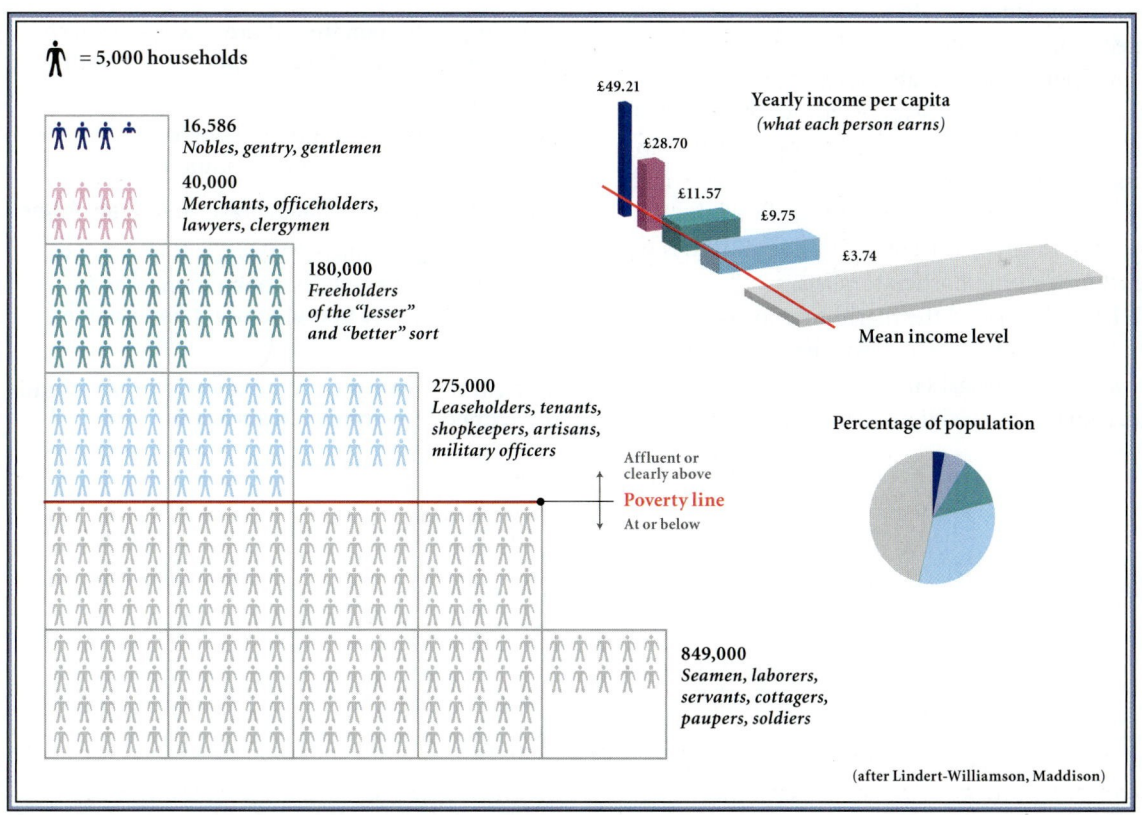

FIGURE 1.3

The Hierarchy of English Society, 1688

The graphic on the left was created from a famous table devised by Gregory King, a seventeenth-century statistician. According to King, the majority of English families (some 849,000) lived below the poverty line and were "Decreasing the Wealth of the Kingdom." In fact, the labor of the poor produced much of the wealth owned by the 511,586 families on the higher rungs of the social scale. Historians continue to revise King's data and have arranged them to show the wealth of individuals in each of King's social groups, as shown in the two graphs to the right.

their children. By 1640, more than 100,000 English and Scots had migrated to Ulster in Ireland, and 50,000 more had moved to North America and the Caribbean Islands. As Puritans looked for religious freedom and peasants for economic security, they formed a powerful migratory movement.

- How did Protestant religious doctrine differ from that of Roman Catholicism?

- What was the impact of the Columbian Exchange in food, people, diseases, and gold on the Americas, Europe, and Africa?

- What factors prompted the large-scale migration from England to America?

SUMMARY

In this chapter, we have seen that the first human inhabitants of the Western Hemisphere were hunter-gatherers from Asia. Their descendants would form many cultures and speak many languages. In Mesoamerica, the Mayan and Aztec peoples developed populous agricultural societies and highly sophisticated religious and political systems; so, too, did the Incas along the western coast of South America. In North America, the Hopewell, Pueblo, and Mississippian peoples created complex societies and cultures; but in 1500, most Indians north of the Rio Grande lived in small self-governing communities of foragers, hunters, and horticulturalists.

We have also traced the maritime expansion that brought Europeans to the Americas. The Spanish crown, eager to share in Portugal's mercantile success in Africa and India, financed expeditions to find new trade routes to Asia. When Christopher Columbus revealed the "new world" of the Western Hemisphere to Europeans in 1492, Spanish adventurers undertook to conquer it. By 1535, conquistadors had destroyed the civilizations of Mesoamerica and Peru and inadvertently introduced diseases that would kill millions of Native Americans. Through the Columbian Exchange in crops, animals, plants, and diseases, there was a significant alteration in the ecology of much of the world.

Population growth, religious warfare, and American gold and silver transformed European society in the sixteenth century. As religious warfare sapped Spain's strength, the rise of strong governments in Holland, France, and England, along with a class of increasingly powerful merchants, enhanced the economies of those countries and whetted their peoples' appetites for overseas expansion.

CHAPTER REVIEW QUESTIONS

- How do you explain the different ways in which the Indian peoples of Mesoamerica and North America developed?

- What made Native American peoples vulnerable to conquest by European adventurers?

- What led to the transatlantic trade in African slaves?

- What was mercantilism? How did this doctrine shape the policies of European monarchs to promote domestic manufacturing and foreign trade?

- How did Europeans become leaders in world trade and extend their influence across the Atlantic?

FOR FURTHER EXPLORATION

Kenneth Pomeranz, *The Great Divergence: China, Europe, and the Making of the Modern World Economy* (2000), examines the impact of the Americas on world history. Brian M. Fagan, *The Great Journey: The Peopling of Ancient America* (1987), and Alvin M. Josephy Jr., ed., *America in 1492: The World of the Indian Peoples Before the Arrival of Columbus* (1991), are reliable and vividly written studies. Visit "1492: An Ongoing Voyage" (**www.loc.gov/exhibits/1492/intro.html**) for images and analysis of the native cultures of the Western Hemisphere.

For the European background of colonization, consult George Huppert's highly readable study, *After the Black Death*, 2nd ed. (1998); see also the engaging biography by William D. Phillips Jr. and Carla Rahn Phillips, *The Worlds of Christopher Columbus* (1992). A fine comparative study is J. H. Elliott, *Empires of the Atlantic World: Britain and Spain in America, 1492–1830* (2006). Giles Milton, *Nathaniel's Nutmeg* (1999), tells the rousing tale of European competition for the spice trade and, subsequently, the New World.

Geoffrey Parker, *The World Crisis, 1635–1665* (2010), sets the context for events in England, which are directly addressed in Andrew McRae, *God Speed the Plough* (2002), and Alison Games, *The Web of Empire: English Cosmopolitans in an Age of Expansion, 1560–1660* (2008). The "Martin Luther" Web site (**www.luther.de/en**) offers biographies and striking images of the era of the Protestant Reformation.

TEST YOUR KNOWLEDGE

To assess your command of the material in this chapter, see the Online Study Guide at **bedfordstmartins.com/henretta**.

For Web sites, images, and documents related to topics and places in this chapter, visit **bedfordstmartins.com/makehistory**.

TIMELINE

13,000–3000 B.C.	Asian migrants reach North America
3000 B.C.	Horticulture begins in Mesoamerica
A.D. 100–400	Flourishing of Hopewell culture
300	Rise of Mayan civilization
500	Zenith of Teotihuacán civilization
600	Pueblo cultures emerge
632–1100	Arab people adopt Islam and spread its influence
800–1350	Development of Mississippian culture
1096–1291	Crusades link Europe with Arab learning
1300–1450	Italian Renaissance
1325	Aztecs establish capital at Tenochtitlán
1430 on	Portugal trades along West and Central African coasts
1492	Christopher Columbus makes first voyage to America
1498	Portugal's Vasco da Gama reaches India
1513	Juan Ponce de León explores Florida
1517	Martin Luther sparks Protestant Reformation
1519–1521	Hernán Cortés conquers Aztec empire
1520–1650	Price Revolution in Europe
1532–1535	Francisco Pizarro vanquishes Incas
1534	Henry VIII establishes Church of England
1536	John Calvin publishes *Institutes of the Christian Religion*
1550–1630	English crown supports mercantilism Parliament passes enclosure acts
1556–1598	Reign of Philip II, king of Spain
1558–1603	Reign of Elizabeth I, queen of England
1560–1620	Growth of English Puritan movement
1588	Storms and English ships destroy Spanish Armada

The manner of their attire and
painting them selues when
they goe to their generall
huntings, or at theire
Solemne feasts.

The Invasion and Settlement of North America, 1550–1700

Establishing colonies in North America was not for the faint of heart. First came a long voyage over stormy, dangerous waters, where shipwrecks, spoiled food, and disease claimed many lives. Of 300 migrants to New France in 1663, seventy died en route. On arrival, the settlers had to build shelters, quickly plant crops, and survive an often dangerous climate. Two French Huguenots who migrated to Carolina in the 1670s protested they had "never before seen so miserable a country, nor an atmosphere so unhealthy. Fevers prevail all the year, from which those who are attacked seldom recover." Many other migrants faced hostile Indian peoples. "We neither fear them nor trust them but rely on our musketeers," declared Francis Higginson, a Puritan settler in the Massachusetts Bay Colony. Still, despite great risks and uncertain rewards, thousands of English, French, and Spanish migrants crossed the Atlantic, driven from their homelands by wars, epidemics, and poverty. To escape the life that English political philosopher Thomas Hobbes famously described in 1650 as "solitary, poor, nasty, brutish, and short," Europeans looked to America. There, an early explorer assured them, "every man may be master of his own labour and land . . . and by industry grow rich."

For Native Americans, however, the intrusion of thousands of Europeans ended the world as they had long known it. Whether they came as settlers, fur traders, or missionaries, the Christian peoples and their African slaves brought new diseases and beliefs that threatened the Indians' lives and cultures. "Our fathers had plenty of deer and skins, . . . and our coves were full of fish and fowl," Narragansett chief Miantonomi recalled in 1642 of his peoples' lands (in what is now Connecticut and Rhode Island), "but these English having gotten our land . . . their cows and horses eat the grass, and their hogs spoil our clam banks, and we shall all be starved." Indeed, hogs brought to North America by the new arrivals and left to forage for their own food became a dynamic vehicle of English expansion, destroying traditional food sources such as corn fields as well as clam beds, and disrupting Indian communities. Miantonomi went to Long Island seeking other tribes to join together

A Carolina Indian, 1585

The artist John White was one of the English settlers in Sir Walter Raleigh's colony on Roanoke Island. Fortunately, he returned to England before the colony met its mysterious fate (see p. 50), as his watercolors provide a rich visual record of Native American life. As White explains, the Secotan and Pomeiooc warriors appeared this way—carrying their bow and quiver full of arrows, and painted and dressed in deerskin and feathers, as well as beaded ornaments—"when they goe to their generall huntings, or at theire Solemne Feasts." © Trustees of the British Museum/Art Resource, NY.

in a united resistance: "We [are] all Indians [and must] say brother to one another, . . . otherwise we shall all be gone shortly." The chief's fate — murdered in 1643 at the behest of officials of the Massachusetts Bay Colony — and his plea foretold the course of North American history: The European invaders would advance, enslaved Africans would endure, and Indian peoples would decline.

Rival Imperial Models: Spain, France, and Holland

In Mesoamerica and South America, the Spanish had seized the Indians' lands, converted many Indians to Catholicism, and forced them to mine gold and farm large estates. In the sparsely populated eastern regions of North America, by contrast, the newly arrived French and Dutch merchants created fur-trading colonies, and the native peoples retained their lands and political autonomy (Figure 2.1). Whatever the Europeans' colonial goals, Indian peoples diminished in numbers and those who remained soon sought to expel the invaders.

New Spain: Colonization and Conversion

In their ceaseless quest for gold, Spanish explorers penetrated deep into the present-day United States. In the 1540s, Francisco Vásquez de Coronado searched in vain for the legendary seven golden cities of Cíbola;

what he discovered was the Grand Canyon, the Pueblo peoples of the Southwest, and the grasslands of Kansas. Meanwhile, Hernán de Soto and a force of 600 Spaniards were cutting a bloody swath across what is now northern Florida and Alabama, battling the Apalachee and the Coosa peoples but finding no gold (Map 2.1).

By the 1560s, Spanish officials had given up the search for gold and now began to focus on defending their empire. Roving English "sea dogs" were plundering Spanish treasure ships, and French Protestants were settling Florida. Following King Philip II's order to cast out the Frenchmen "by the best means," Spanish troops massacred 300 members of the "evil Lutheran sect" near the St. Johns River. To safeguard the route of its treasure fleet, Spain established a fort at St. Augustine in 1565, making it the first permanent European settlement in the future United States. However, raids by the Calusas and Timucuas wiped out a dozen other Spanish military outposts in Florida, and Algonquians destroyed Jesuit religious missions further north along the Atlantic coast, including one near the Chesapeake Bay.

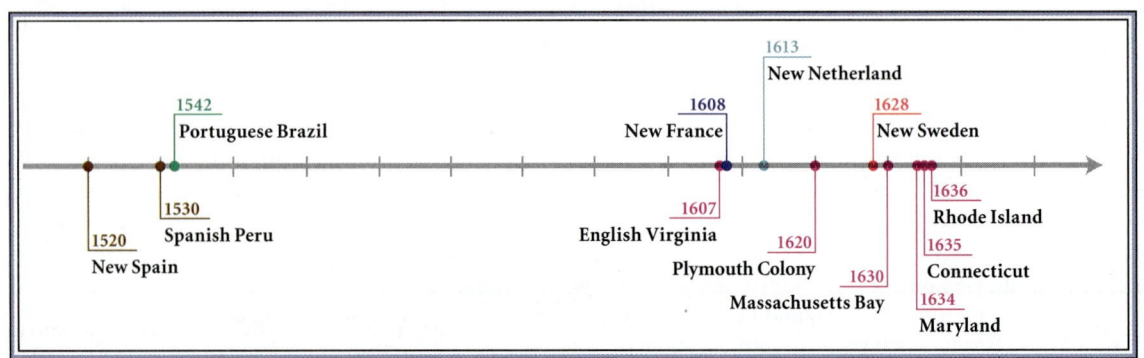

FIGURE 2.1

Chronology of European Colonies in the Americas

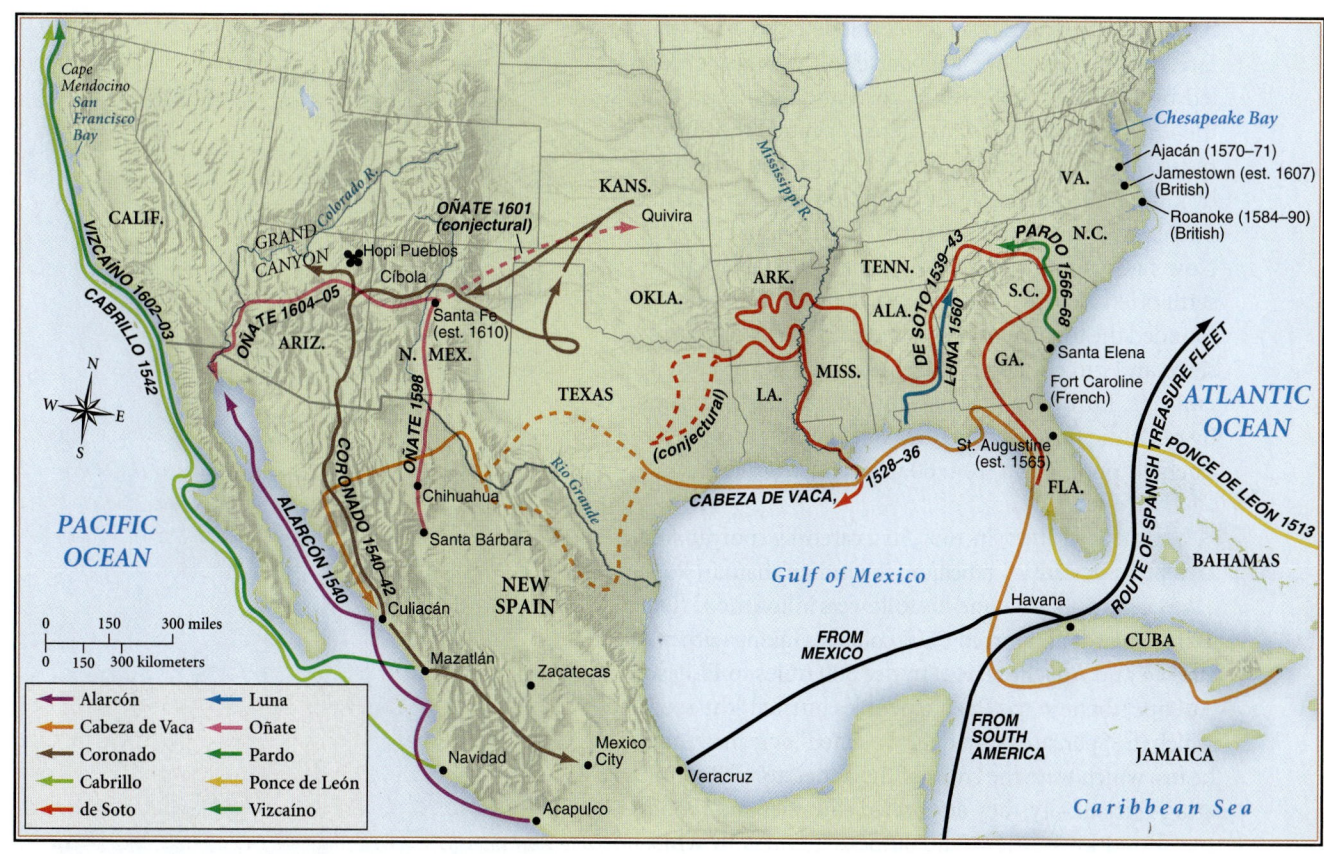

MAP 2.1

New Spain Looks North, 1513–1610

The search for gold drew Spanish explorers first to the Florida peninsula and then deep into the present-day United States. When the wide-ranging expeditions of Hernán de Soto and Francisco Vásquez de Coronado failed to find gold or flourishing Indian civilizations, authorities in New Spain limited settlements in the northern territories to St. Augustine in Florida (to protect the treasure fleet) and Santa Fe in the upper Rio Grande Valley.

Franciscan Missions and Indian Revolts

These military setbacks and the urgings of Franciscan friars prompted Spanish leaders to adopt a new policy of Christianizing the Indian peoples. The Comprehensive Orders for New Discoveries (1573) placed the task of pacification primarily in the hands of missionaries, not conquistadors. Over the next century, Franciscan friars set up missions among the Apalachees in Florida and the Pueblo peoples in the lands the Spanish named Nuevo México. The friars often learned Indian languages, but they also systematically attacked the natives' culture. And their methods were anything but peaceful. Protected by Spanish soldiers, missionaries whipped Indians who continued to practice **polygamy**, smashed the Indians' religious idols, and punished those who worshipped traditional gods. On one occasion, forty-seven "sorcerers" in Nuevo México were sold into slavery.

Religious conversion, cultural assimilation, and forced labor went hand in hand. The Franciscans encouraged the Indians to talk, cook, and dress like Spaniards. They ignored laws that protected the native peoples and allowed privileged Spanish landowners (*encomenderos*) to extract goods and forced labor. The missions themselves depended on Indian workers to grow crops and carry them to market.

Native Americans initially tolerated the Franciscans because they feared military reprisals and hoped to learn the friars' spiritual secrets. But when Christian prayers failed to protect their communities from European diseases, droughts, and raids by nomadic Apaches and Pawnees, many Pueblos returned to their ancestral gods. As an Indian explained, the people of the Zuni pueblo of Hawikuh refused to become "wet-heads" (as they called baptized Christians) "because with the water of baptism they would have to die." In 1598, the tense relations between Indians and Spaniards exploded into open warfare. An expedition of 500 Spanish soldiers and settlers led by Juan de Oñate seized corn and clothing from the Pueblo peoples and murdered or raped those who resisted. When Indians of the Acoma pueblo retaliated by killing 11 soldiers, the Spanish troops destroyed the pueblo and murdered 800 men, women, and children. Now faced with bitterly hostile native peoples, most settlers left New Mexico. In 1610, the Spanish returned, founded the town of Santa Fe, and reestablished the missions and forced-labor system. Over the next two generations, European diseases, forced tribute, and raids by nomadic Indians from the Great Plains reduced the Pueblos' population from 60,000 to just 17,000.

Popé and the Uprising of 1680   In 1680, in a carefully coordinated rebellion, the Indian shaman Popé and his followers killed more than 400 Spaniards and forced 1,500 colonists (along with 500 Pueblo and Apache slaves) to flee 300 miles to El Paso. At Popé's behest, the Pueblo peoples burned "the seeds which the Spaniards sowed" and planted "only maize and beans, which were the crops of their ancestors." Repudiating Christianity, they desecrated churches and rebuilt the sacred kivas, the round stone structures in which they had long worshipped. Like many later Native American rebels, Popé marched forward while looking backward, seeking to restore the traditional way of life.

It was not to be. A decade later, Spain reasserted control over most of the Pueblo peoples. The oppressed natives rebelled again in 1696 and were again subdued. Exhausted by a generation of warfare, the Pueblos agreed to a compromise that reduced the amount of forced labor. In return, they spoke Spanish, accepted a patrilineal kinship system, and helped defend Nuevo México against nomadic Apaches and Comanches. Some Pueblo women married Spaniards, and their offspring formed a bicultural mestizo population. But most Pueblos continued to practice the old ways, worshipping the Corn Mother as well as Jesus. As a Franciscan friar admitted, "They are still drawn more by their idolatry and infidelity than by the Christian doctrine." Spain had maintained its northern empire, but had done so without assimilating the Indian peoples.

Spain experienced similar disappointment in Florida. In the early 1700s, English raiders from Carolina destroyed most of the Franciscan missions and killed or enslaved most Catholic converts. These setbacks persuaded imperial officials not to settle the distant northern province of California. Santa Fe and St. Augustine stood alone as the northern outposts of Spain's American empire.

Madonna on Buffalo Hide, c. 1675

Even as the shaman Popé was successfully urging the Pueblo peoples to rebel against Spanish rule and revive traditional religious rituals, some Indians were embracing Christianity. A native artist painted the image of Christ's mother on tanned bison hide, and, in a sign of religious syncretism, gave the Virgin Mary the facial features of a Pueblo woman.   Elisabeth Waldo-Denzel Art Collection.

New France: Fur Traders and Missionaries

Far to the northeast, the French were confronting the 250,000 native peoples of eastern Canada — Cree-speaking Montagnais; Algonquian-speaking Micmacs, Ottawas, and Ojibwas; and Iroquois-speaking Hurons. In the 1530s, Jacques Cartier had claimed the lands bordering the Gulf of St. Lawrence for France.

The first permanent settlement came in 1608, when Samuel de Champlain founded the fur-trading post of Quebec. But the colony languished until 1662, when King Louis XIV (r. 1643–1714) turned New France into a royal colony and subsidized the migration of indentured servants. French servants labored under contract for three years, received a salary, and could eventually lease a farm — far more generous terms than those for indentured servants in the English colonies.

Nonetheless, few people moved to New France, a cold and forbidding country "at the end of the world," as one migrant put it. Also, state policies discouraged migration. More intent on expanding France's boundaries in Europe than on encouraging overseas settlements, Louis XIV drafted tens of thousands of men into military service. The Catholic monarch also barred Huguenots (French Calvinist Protestants) from migrating to New France, fearing they might win converts and take control of the colony. Moreover, the French legal system gave peasants strong rights to their village lands, whereas migrants to New France faced an oppressive, aristocracy- and church-dominated feudal system. In the village of Saint Ours in Quebec's fertile Richelieu Valley, for example, peasants paid 45 percent of their wheat crop to nobles and the Catholic Church. By 1698, only 15,200 Europeans lived in New France, compared to 100,000 in England's North American colonies.

Lacking settlers to farm the land, New France developed as a vast enterprise for acquiring furs. Furs — mink, otter, and beaver — were in great demand in Europe to make felt hats and fur garments. To secure plush beaver pelts from the Hurons, who controlled trade north of the Great Lakes, Champlain provided them with manufactures. Selling pelts, an Indian told a French priest, "makes kettles, hatchets, swords, knives, bread." It also made guns, which Champlain sold to the Hurons to fight the expansionist-minded Five Nations of New York (see Voices from Abroad, "Samuel de Champlain: Going to War with the Hurons," p. 46). Searching for more furs, explorer Jacques Marquette reached the Mississippi River in present-day Wisconsin in 1673 and floated south on the river as far as Arkansas. Then, in 1681, Robert de La Salle traveled down the majestic river to the Gulf of Mexico, trading as he went. As a French priest noted with disgust, La Salle and his associates hoped "to buy all the Furs and Skins of the remotest Savages, who, as they thought, did not know their Value; and so enrich themselves in one single voyage." To honor Louis XIV, La Salle named the region Louisiana; by 1718, French merchants had founded the port of New Orleans where the Mississippi empties into the Gulf of Mexico.

The Rise of the Iroquois | Despite their small numbers, the French settlers had a disastrous impact. Unwittingly introducing European diseases, they triggered epidemics that killed from 25 to 90 percent of many Indian peoples. Moreover, by bartering guns for furs, the French (and Dutch) sparked a series of deadly wars. The Five Nations of the Iroquois were the prime aggressors. From their strategic location in central New York, the Iroquois obtained guns and goods from Dutch merchants at Albany and attacked other Indian peoples. Iroquois warriors moved east along the Mohawk River as far as New England and south along the Delaware and Susquehanna rivers as far as the Carolinas. They traveled north via Lake Champlain and the Richelieu River to Quebec. And they journeyed west via the Great Lakes to exploit the rich fur-bearing lands of the upper Mississippi River Valley.

The rise of the Iroquois was breathtakingly rapid. In 1600, the Iroquois numbered about 30,000 and lived in large towns of 500 to 2,000 inhabitants. Over the next two decades, they organized themselves into a confederation of five nations: Senecas, Cayugas, Onondagas, Oneidas, and Mohawks. Partly in response to a virulent smallpox epidemic in 1633, which cut their number by one-third, the Iroquois waged a series of devastating wars against the Hurons (1649), Neutrals (1651), Eries (1657), and Susquehannocks (1660) — all Iroquoian-speaking peoples. They razed villages and killed most of the men, cooking and eating their flesh to gain access to their spiritual powers. They took thousands of women and children captive and ritually adopted them into Iroquois lineages. The conquered Hurons simply ceased to exist as a distinct people; survivors trekked westward with displaced Algonquian peoples and formed a new tribe, the Wyandots.

The Jesuit Missions | Between 1625 and 1763, hundreds of French priests lived among the Huron, Iroquois, and other Great Lakes peoples. Most were members of the Society of Jesus (or Jesuits), a Catholic religious order founded to combat the Protestant Reformation. The Jesuits — unlike the Spanish Franciscan monks — came to understand and respect the Indians' values. One priest noted the Hurons' belief that "our souls have desires which are inborn and concealed, yet are made known by means of dreams." Many Indian peoples initially welcomed the French "Black Robes" as powerful spiritual beings with magical secrets, including the ability to forge iron. But when prayers to the Christian god did not protect them from disease, the Indians grew skeptical. A Peoria

VOICES FROM ABROAD

Samuel de Champlain
Going to War with the Hurons

Samuel de Champlain is best known as the founder of Quebec, but he was primarily a soldier and an adventurer. After fighting in the religious wars within France, Champlain joined the Company of New France and set out to create an empire in North America. In 1603, he traveled down the St. Lawrence River as far as Quebec. He then lived for several years in the company's failing settlement in Maine and returned to Quebec in 1608. To ensure French access to the western fur trade, Champlain joined the Hurons in a raid against the Iroquois in 1609, which he later described in a book of his American adventures.

Pursuing our route, I met some two or three hundred savages, who were encamped in huts near a little island called St. Eloi. . . . We made a reconnaissance, and found that they were tribes of savages called Ochasteguins I [Hurons] and Algonquins, on their way to Quebec to assist us in exploring the territory of the Iroquois, with whom they are in deadly hostility. . . . [We joined with them and] went to the mouth of the River of the Iroquois [the Richelieu River, where it joins the St. Lawrence River], where we stayed two days, refreshing ourselves with good venison, birds, and fish, which the savages gave us.

In all their encampments, they have their Pilotois, or Ostemoy, a class of persons who play the part of soothsayers, in whom these people have faith. One of these builds a cabin, surrounds it with small pieces of wood and covers it with his robe: after it is built, he places himself inside, so as not to be seen at all, when he seizes and shakes one of the posts of his cabin, muttering some words between his teeth, by which he says he invokes the devil, who appears to him in the form of a stone, and tells them whether they will meet their enemies and kill many of them. . . . They frequently told me that the shaking of the cabin, which I saw, proceeded from the devil, who made it move, and not the man inside, although I could see the contrary. . . . They told me also that I should see fire come out from the top, which I did not see at all.

Now, as we began to approach within two or three days' journey of the abode of our enemies, we advanced only at night. . . . By day, they withdraw into the interior of the woods, where they rest, without straying off, neither making any noise, even for the sake of cooking, so as not to be noticed in case their enemies should by accident pass by. They make no fire, except in smoking, which amounts to almost nothing. They eat baked Indian meal, which they soak in water, when it becomes a kind of porridge. . . .

In order to ascertain what was to be the result of their undertaking, they often asked me if I had had a dream, and seen their enemies, to which I replied in the negative. . . . [Then one night] while sleeping, I dreamed that I saw our enemies, the Iroquois, drowning near a mountain, within sight. When I expressed a wish to help them, our allies, the savages, told me we must let them all die. . . . This, upon being related [to our allies], gave them so much confidence that they did not doubt any longer that good was to happen to them. . . .

[After our victory over the Iroquois] they took one of the prisoners, to whom they made a harangue, enumerating the cruelties which he and his men had already practiced toward them without any mercy, and that, in like manner, he ought to make up his mind to receive as much. They commanded him to sing, if he had courage, which he did; but it was a very sad song.

Meanwhile, our men kindled a fire; and, when it was well burning, they each took a brand, and burned this poor creature gradually, so as to make him suffer greater torment. Sometimes they stopped, and threw water on his back. Then they tore out his nails, and applied fire to the extremities of his fingers and private member. Afterwards, they flayed the top of his head, and had a kind of gum poured all hot upon it.

Source: Samuel de Champlain, *Voyages of Samuel de Champlain, 1604–1618*, ed. W. L. Grant (New York: Charles Scribner's Sons, 1907), 79–86.

ANALYZING THE EVIDENCE

- How do you account for the differences between the Hurons' and Champlain's perceptions of the soothsayer's hut? What do the differences suggest about their respective views of the world?

- Having read this passage, what would you say was the role of dreams in Huron culture?

- At the beginning of this passage, Champlain refers to the Indians as savages. Would the torture he describes help to explain that characterization? How might a modern anthropologist, sensitive to differences among cultures, explain the Indians' custom of torturing war captives?

chief charged that a priest's "fables are good only in his own country; we have our own [beliefs], which do not make us die as his do." When a drought struck, Indians blamed the missionaries. "If you cannot make rain, they speak of nothing less than making away with you," lamented one Jesuit.

Whatever the limits of their powers, the French Jesuits did not exploit Indian labor. Moreover, they tried to keep brandy, which wreaked havoc among the natives, from becoming a bargaining chip in the French fur trade. And the Jesuits won converts by adapting Christian beliefs to the Indians' needs. In the 1690s, for example, the Jesuits introduced the cult of the Virgin Mary to the young women of the Illinois people. Its emphasis on chastity reinforced the existing Illinois belief that unmarried women were "masters of their own body."

Despite the Jesuits' efforts, however, the French fur trade brought cultural devastation. Epidemics killed tens of thousands of Indians, and pelt-hungry Iroquois warriors murdered thousands more. Nor did the Iroquois escape unscathed. Although they forged an alliance—the so-called Covenant Chain—with the English in New York in the 1670s, the French and their Algonquian allies invaded Iroquois lands in the 1690s, burned villages and cornfields, and killed many warriors. "Everywhere there was peril and everywhere mourning," recalled an oral Iroquois legend.

New Netherland: Commerce

By every measure—wealth, trade, art, scholarship, naval prowess—the Dutch Republic was a powerhouse of seventeenth-century Europe. No small nation ever cast a bigger shadow. By 1600, Amsterdam had become the financial and commercial hub of northern Europe. Strategically located near the Baltic Sea and the mouth of the great Rhine River, the city boasted an enterprising class of merchants and entrepreneurs. Dutch financiers dominated the European banking, insurance, and textile industries; Dutch merchants owned more ships and employed more sailors than did the combined fleets of England, France, and Spain. Indeed, the Dutch managed much of the world's commerce. During their struggle for independence from Spain and Portugal (ruled by Spanish monarchs, 1580–1640), the Dutch seized Portuguese forts in Africa and Indonesia and sugar plantations in Brazil. These conquests gave the Dutch control of the Atlantic trade in slaves and sugar and the Indian Ocean commerce in East Indian spices and Chinese silks and ceramics (Map 2.2).

In 1609, Dutch merchants dispatched the English mariner Henry Hudson to locate a navigable route to the riches of the East Indies. What he found as he probed the rivers of northeast America was a fur bonanza. Following Hudson's exploration of the river that now bears his name, the merchants built Fort Orange (Albany) in 1614 to trade for furs with the Munsee and Iroquois Indians. Then, in 1621, the Dutch government chartered the West India Company, which founded the colony of New Netherland, set up New Amsterdam (on Manhattan Island) as its capital, and brought in farmers and artisans to make the enterprise self-sustaining. The new colony did not thrive. The population of the Dutch Republic was too small to support much emigration—just 1.5 million people, compared to 5 million in Britain and 20 million in France—and its migrants sought riches in Southeast Asia rather than fur-trading profits in America. To protect its colony from rival European nations, the West India Company granted huge estates along the Hudson River to wealthy Dutchmen who promised to populate them. But by 1664, New Netherland had only 5,000 residents, and fewer than half of them were Dutch.

Like New France, New Netherland flourished as a fur-trading enterprise. Trade with the powerful Iroquois, though rocky at first, rose by 1635 to 16,300 pelts, a tidy business at 8 guilders a pelt in Amsterdam. Dutch settlers had less respect for their Algonquian-speaking neighbors. They seized prime farming land from the Algonquian peoples and took over their trading network, which exchanged corn and wampum from Long Island for furs from Maine. In response, in 1643 the Algonquians launched attacks that nearly destroyed the colony. "Almost every place is abandoned," a settler lamented, "whilst the Indians daily threaten to overwhelm us." To defeat the Algonquians, the Dutch waged vicious warfare—maiming, burning, and killing hundreds of men, women, and children—and formed an alliance with the Mohawks, who were no less brutal. The grim progression of Euro-Indian relations—an uneasy welcome, followed by rising tensions and war—afflicted even the Dutch, who had few designs on Indian lands or on their "unregenerate" souls and were only looking to do business.

After the crippling Indian war, the West India Company ignored New Netherland, and expanded its profitable trade in African slaves and Brazilian sugar. In New Amsterdam, Governor Peter Stuyvesant ruled in an authoritarian fashion. He rejected the demands of English Puritans on Long Island for a representative system of government and alienated the colony's diverse

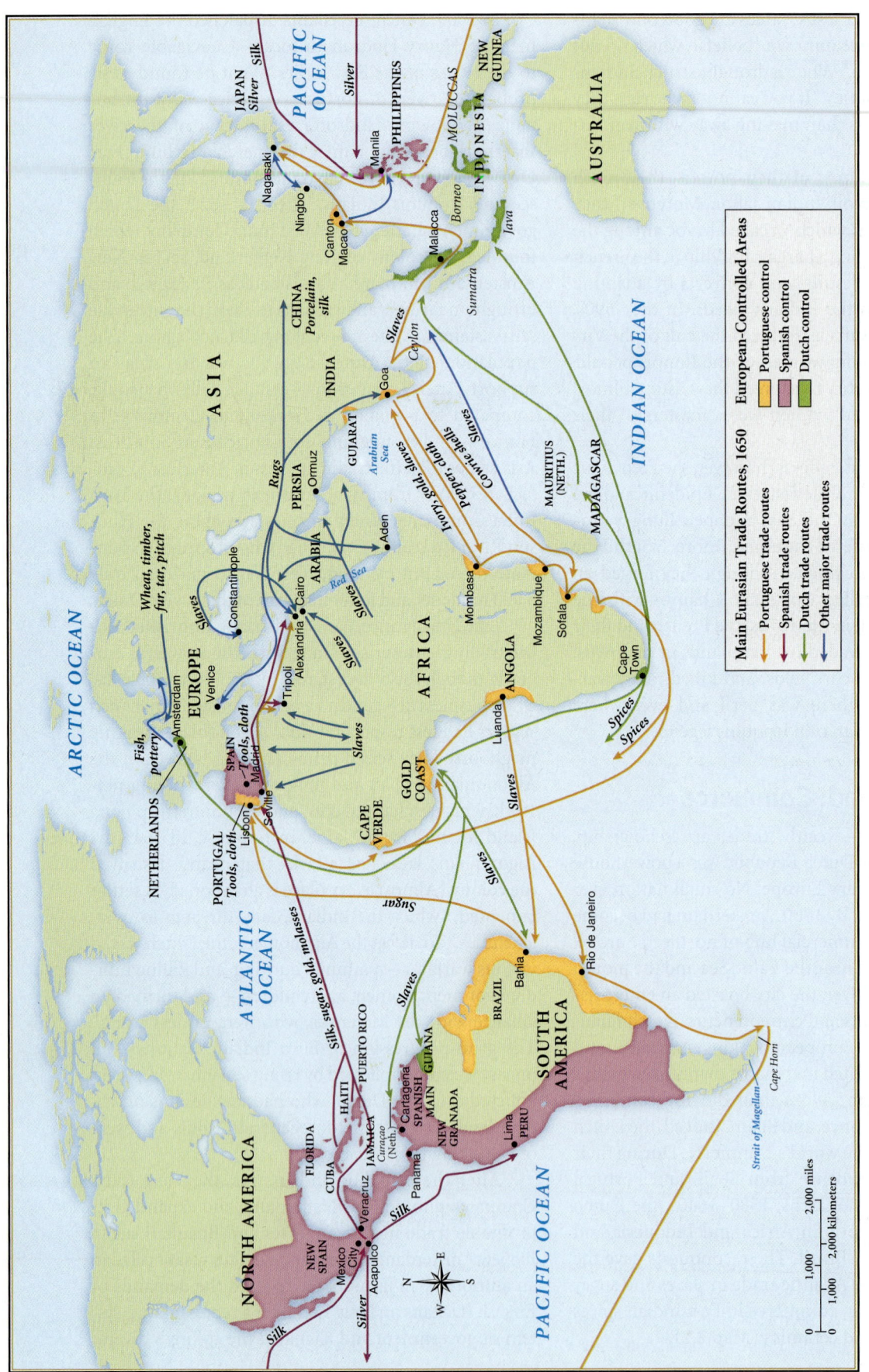

MAP 2.2

The Eurasian Trade System and European Spheres of Influence, 1650

Between 1550 and 1650, Spanish, Portuguese, and Dutch merchants took control of the maritime trade routes between Europe, and India, Indonesia, and China. They also created two new trading connections. The South Atlantic System carried slaves, sugar, and manufactured goods between Europe, Africa, and the valuable plantation settlements in Brazil and the Caribbean Islands. And a trans-Pacific trade carried Spanish American silver to China in exchange for silks, ceramics, and other manufactures. (To trace long-term changes in trade and empires, see Map 1.3 on p. 20 and Map 5.1 on p. 143.)

New Amsterdam, c. 1640

As the wooden palisade suggests, New Amsterdam was a fortlike trading post at the edge of a vast land populated by alien Indian peoples feared by the Dutch. The city was also a pale miniature imitation of Amsterdam, with its many canals. The first settlers built their houses in the Dutch style, with gable ends facing the street (note the two middle houses), and excavated a canal across lower Manhattan Island (New York City's Canal Street today).   Library of Congress.

Dutch, English, and Swedish residents. Consequently, the residents of New Netherland offered little resistance when England invaded the colony in 1664.

The Duke of York, the overlord of the new English colony of New York, initially ruled with a mild hand, allowing the Dutch residents to retain their property, legal system, and religious institutions. However, after the Dutch briefly recaptured the colony in 1673, the duke's governor, Edmund Andros, shut down the Dutch courts, imposed English law, and demanded an oath of allegiance. Thereafter, Dutch residents largely avoided the English courts and resisted cultural assimilation: They spoke Dutch, married among themselves, and worshipped at the Dutch Reformed Church. Once dominant over the Algonquians, the Dutch had themselves become a subject people. As an English resident noted in 1699, New York "seemed rather like a conquered Foreign Province held by the terror of a Garrison, than an English colony."

- What were the colonial goals of the Spanish, French, and Dutch? How successful were they in achieving those goals?

- What happened to the Five Nations of the Iroquois between 1600 and 1700? Were the Iroquois better off at the beginning of the period or at the end? Why?

The English Arrive in the Chesapeake

Unlike the Dutch and the French, the English founded colonies in North America that attracted thousands of settlers. But that was not the plan of the London investors who financed an expedition to Virginia in 1607. They expected to establish a trading outpost, like those recently set up in India, Sierra Leone, and Morocco, to buy gold or other valuable goods from the native peoples. Not finding such goods, the adventurers gradually created a tobacco-growing economy based on the labor of indentured English servants and enslaved Africans.

Settling the Tobacco Colonies

The first English ventures in North America were private enterprises, organized by minor nobles, merchants, and religious dissidents. Although the English monarch and ministry approved these ventures, they did not control them. Consequently, the English settlements, unlike the state-supervised Spanish and French colonies, enjoyed considerable autonomy and developed in markedly different ways.

The private ventures organized by the nobles were abject failures. In the 1580s, Sir Humphrey Gilbert's settlement in Newfoundland collapsed for lack of financing, and Sir Ferdinando Gorges's colony along the coast of Maine floundered in the harsh climate. Sir Walter Raleigh's three expeditions to North Carolina likewise ended in disaster when 117 settlers on Roanoke Island vanished without a trace. (Roanoke is still known as the "lost colony.")

The Jamestown Settlement Merchants then took charge of English expansion. In 1606, King James I (r. 1603–1625) granted to the Virginia Company of London all the lands stretching from present-day North Carolina to southern New York. To honor the memory of Elizabeth I, the never-married "Virgin Queen," the company's directors named

Carolina Indians Fishing, 1585

Though maize was a mainstay of the Indian diet, native peoples along the Atlantic coast also harvested protein-rich fish, crabs, and oysters. In this watercolor by the English adventurer John White, Indians gather fish (in their "cannow," or dugout canoe) in the shallow waters of the Albemarle Sound, off present-day North Carolina. On the left, note the weir used both to catch fish and to store them live for later consumption.
© Trustees of the British Museum/Art Resource, NY.

the region Virginia (Map 2.3). For the Virginia Company, trade with the native population was the primary goal. So in 1607, it dispatched a group of male traders—no women, farmers, or ministers—who were employees of the company. They were to procure their own food and to ship gold, exotic crops, and Indian goods to England. Some traders were young gentlemen with personal ties to the company's shareholders: a bunch of "unruly Sparks, packed off by their Friends to escape worse Destinies at home." Others were cynical men looking for a quick profit: All they wanted, one of them said, was to "dig gold, refine gold, load gold."

But there was no gold, and the traders fared poorly in their new environment. Arriving in Virginia after an exhausting four-month voyage, they settled on a swampy peninsula, which they named Jamestown to honor the king. There the adventurers lacked access to fresh water, refused to plant crops, and quickly died off; only 38 of the 120 men were alive nine months later. Death rates remained high: By 1611, the Virginia Company had dispatched 1,200 settlers to Jamestown, but fewer than half remained alive. "Our men were destroyed with cruell diseases, as Swellings, Fluxes, Burning Fevers, and by warres," reported one of the settlement's leaders, "but for the most part they died of meere famine."

Powhatan, the paramount chief of the thirty tribal chiefdoms between the James and Potomac rivers, treated the English traders as potential allies and a source of valuable goods. The Powhatan chief spared the life of Captain John Smith, who had been taken captive by his brother Opechancanough, and provided the hungry English adventurers with corn. In return, he demanded that the English offer him tribute of "hatchets . . . bells, beads, and copper" as well as "two great guns" and become a dependent community within his chiefdom of Tsenacommacah. Subsequently, Powhatan arranged a marriage between his daughter Pocahontas and John Rolfe, an English colonist. But these tactics failed. Rolfe had imported tobacco seed from the West Indies and produced a crop of "pleasant, sweet, and strong Tobacco," which fetched a high price in England and spurred the migration of thousands of English settlers. Now Powhatan accused the English of coming "not to trade but to invade my people and possess my country."

To foster the flow of migrants, the Virginia Company allowed individual settlers to own land, granting 100 acres to every freeman and more to those who imported servants. The company also issued a "greate Charter" that created a system of representative government: The House of Burgesses, first convened in 1619, could make laws and levy taxes, although the governor and the company council in England could veto its acts. By

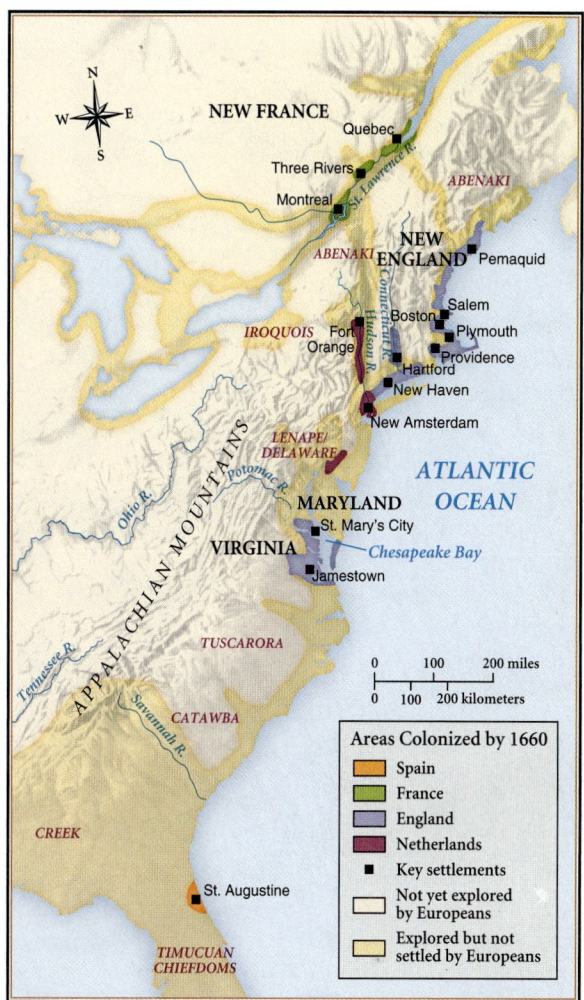

MAP 2.3

Eastern North America, 1650

By 1650, four European nations had permanent settlements along the eastern coast of North America, but only England had substantial numbers of settlers, some 25,000 in New England and another 15,000 in the Chesapeake region. Europeans also had a small presence in the interior, as French and Dutch fur traders carried European goods—and diseases—to distant tribes.

1622, land ownership, self-government, and a judicial system based on "the lawes of the realme of England" had attracted some 4,500 new recruits. To encourage a transition to a settler colony, the Virginia Company recruited dozens of "Maides young and uncorrupt to make wifes to the Inhabitants."

The Indian War of 1622   The influx of land-hungry migrants and conversion-minded ministers into Virginia sparked an all-out conflict with the Indian peoples. The struggle began with an assault led by Opechancanough [*O-pee-chan-KA-no*],

C.Smith taketh the King of Pamavnkee prisoner 1608

John Smith and Opechancanough

The powerful Indian warrior Opechancanough towers over English explorer John Smith in this engraving showing the two men in confrontation over English access to Indian food supplies in 1607. Never having seen an Indian, the engraver apparently relied on John White's watercolor of a Carolina Indian (see p. 40) in depicting the future chief of the Powhatan confederacy. The note at the bottom of the engraving is doubly mistaken, as it was Opechancanough (not Powhatan) who took Smith captive.   Library of Congress.

Powhatan's younger brother and successor. In 1607, Opechancanough had attacked some of the first English invaders, killing many of them and capturing Captain John Smith. Subsequently, the Indian chief "stood aloof" from the English settlers and "would not be drawn to any Treaty." In particular, he resisted English proposals to place Indian children in schools to be "brought upp in Christianytie." Upon becoming the main chief in 1621, Opechancanough told the leader of the Potomacks: "Before the end of two moons, there should not be an Englishman in all their Countries."

Opechancanough almost succeeded. In 1622, he coordinated a surprise attack by twelve Indian chiefdoms that killed 347 English settlers, nearly one-third of the white population. The English fought back by seizing the fields and food of those they now called "naked, tanned, deformed Savages," and declared "a perpetual war without peace or truce" that lasted for a decade. They sold captured warriors into slavery, "destroy[ing] them who sought to destroy us" and taking control of "their cultivated places."

Shocked by the Indian uprising, James I revoked the Virginia Company's charter and, in 1624, made Virginia a royal colony. Now the king and his ministers appointed the governor and a small advisory council, retaining the House of Burgesses but stipulating that the king's Privy Council (a committee of political advisers), must ratify all legislation. The king also decreed the legal establishment of the Church of England in the colony, which meant that residents had to pay taxes to support its clergy. These institutions — an appointed governor, an elected assembly, a formal legal system, and an established Anglican church — became the model for royal colonies throughout English America.

Lord Baltimore Settles Catholics in Maryland A second tobacco-growing colony, with a very different set of institutions, developed in neighboring Maryland. King Charles I (r. 1625–1649), James's successor, was secretly sympathetic toward Catholicism. So in 1632, he granted the lands bordering the vast Chesapeake Bay to Catholic

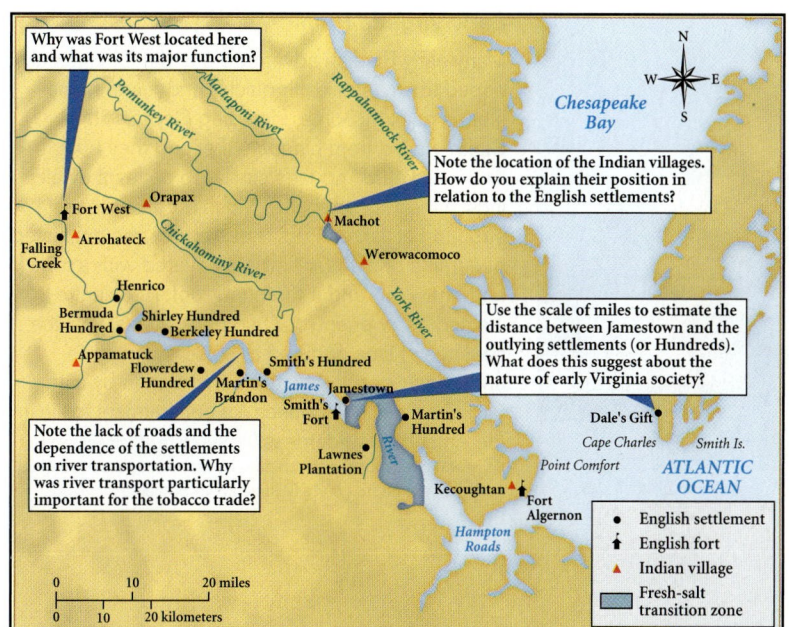

Why was Fort West located here and what was its major function?

Note the location of the Indian villages. How do you explain their position in relation to the English settlements?

Use the scale of miles to estimate the distance between Jamestown and the outlying settlements (or Hundreds). What does this suggest about the nature of early Virginia society?

Note the lack of roads and the dependence of the settlements on river transportation. Why was river transport particularly important for the tobacco trade?

- English settlement
- English fort
- Indian village
- Fresh-salt transition zone

MAP 2.4

River Plantations in Virginia, c. 1640

The first migrants settled in widely dispersed plantations along the James River, a settlement pattern promoted by the tobacco economy. From their riverfront plantations wealthy planter-merchants could easily load heavy hogsheads of tobacco onto oceangoing ships, and offload supplies that they then sold to smallholding planters. Consequently, few substantial towns or trading centers developed in the Chesapeake region.

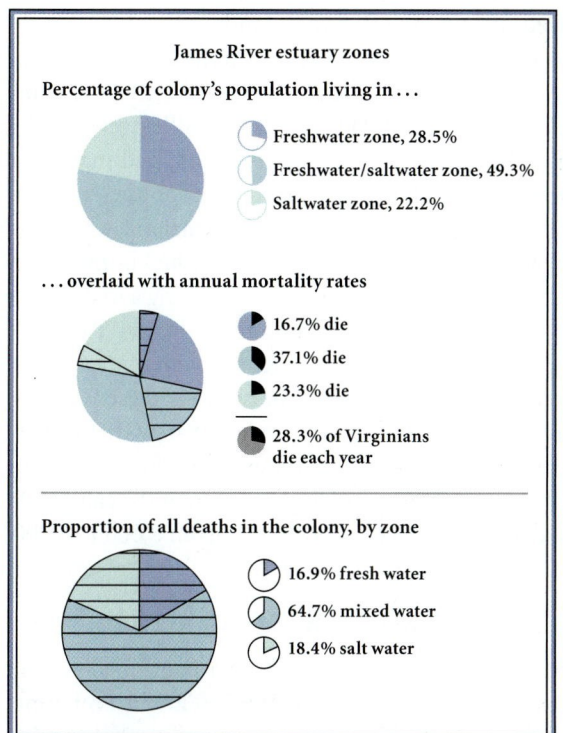

James River estuary zones

Percentage of colony's population living in . . .

- Freshwater zone, 28.5%
- Freshwater/saltwater zone, 49.3%
- Saltwater zone, 22.2%

. . . overlaid with annual mortality rates

- 16.7% die
- 37.1% die
- 23.3% die
- 28.3% of Virginians die each year

Proportion of all deaths in the colony, by zone

- 16.9% fresh water
- 64.7% mixed water
- 18.4% salt water

FIGURE 2.2

Environment and Death in Virginia, 1618–1624

Virginia was a deadly place for the English during the settlement's first decades. About 28 percent of the residents died each year; the colony grew only because of a constant stream of migrants. Most settlers lived along the James River estuary and, as Map 2.4 and this figure show, their location along the river determined their chances of survival. Those who lived in the zone with a mix of freshwater and saltwater had the highest death rates by far. The inflow of salt water during the dry summer months (when the river's freshwater volume decreased) trapped human and animal waste from upriver. That fecal matter contaminated the water and its fish, oysters, and crabs, leading to epidemics of typhoid and dysentery (which residents called "the bloody flux"). Source: Adapted from Carville V. Earle, "Environment, Disease, and Mortality in Early Virginia," in *The Chesapeake in the Seventeenth Century*, ed. Thad W. Tate and David L. Ammerman (New York: W.W. Norton, 1979), table 3.

aristocrat Cecilius Calvert, who carried the title Lord Baltimore. As the territorial lord (or proprietor) of Maryland, Baltimore could sell, lease, or give away the land as he pleased. He also had the authority to appoint public officials and to found churches.

Lord Baltimore wanted Maryland to become a refuge for Catholics, who were subject to persecution in England. In 1634, twenty gentlemen, mostly Catho-lics, and 200 artisans and laborers, mostly Protestants, established St. Mary's City at the point where the Po-tomac River flows into Chesapeake Bay. To minimize religious confrontations, the proprietor instructed the governor (his brother, Leonard Calvert) to allow "no scandall nor offence to be given to any of the Protes-tants" and to "cause All Acts of Romane Catholicque Religion to be done as privately as may be."

Early Virginia House

Many early English adventurers to the Chesapeake hoped to amass wealth quickly and return home just as quickly. Some, including Captain John Smith, hailed from Lincolnshire, and they built "mud and stud" houses similar to peasant dwellings in their home county. Much like this reconstruction at James Fort, these structures consisted of a frame of slender timbers covered with a mud and straw mix and a thatched roof. Housing remained a low priority for two generations, until the passage of time nurtured a "settler mentality" and—as evidenced by the construction by elite Virginians of brick houses—a commitment to life in the American "wilderness." Structure at Jamestown Settlement history museum re-created by archaeologists at Historic Jamestowne; photo courtesy Jamestown Settlement.

Maryland's population grew quickly because the Calverts imported many artisans and offered ample lands to wealthy migrants. But political conflict threatened the colony's stability. Disputing Baltimore's lordly powers, settlers demanded that he govern in accordance with the "Advice, Assent, and Approbation" of the freemen. They elected a representative assembly and insisted on the right to initiate legislation, which Baltimore grudgingly granted. Anti-Catholic agitation by Protestants also threatened the Calverts' religious goals. To protect his coreligionists, who remained a minority, Lord Baltimore persuaded the assembly to enact the Toleration Act (1649), which granted all Christians the right to follow their beliefs and hold church services.

In Maryland, as in Virginia, tobacco quickly became the main crop. Indians had long used tobacco as a medicine and a stimulant, and the English came to crave the nicotine it contained. By the 1620s, they were smoking, chewing, and snorting tobacco with abandon. James I initially condemned the plant as a "vile Weed" whose "black stinking fumes" were "baleful to the nose, harmful to the brain, and dangerous to the lungs." But the king's attitude changed as taxes on imported tobacco bolstered the royal treasury.

European demand for tobacco set off a forty-year economic boom in the Chesapeake region. "All our riches for the present do consist in tobacco," a planter remarked in 1630. Exports rose from 3 million pounds in 1640 to 10 million pounds in 1660. Initially, most plantations were small **freeholds**, owned and farmed by families or male partners. But after 1650, wealthy migrants from gentry or noble families established large estates along the coastal rivers. Coming primarily from southern England, where tenants and wage laborers farmed large manors, they copied that hierarchical system by buying English indentured servants and enslaved Africans to work their lands.

For rich and poor alike, life in the Chesapeake was harsh. The scarcity of towns deprived settlers of community (Map 2.4 and Figure 2.2). Families were equally scarce because there were few women, and marriages often ended with the early death of a spouse. Pregnant women were especially vulnerable to malaria, which was spread by the mosquitoes that flourished in the warm climate. Many mothers died after bearing a first or second child, so orphaned children (along with unmarried young men) formed a large segment of the society. Sixty percent of the children born in Middlesex County, Virginia, before 1680 lost one or both parents before they were thirteen. Death was pervasive. Although 15,000 English migrants arrived in Virginia between 1622 and 1640, the colony's population rose only from 2,000 to 8,000.

Masters, Servants, and Slaves

Still, the prospect of owning land continued to lure settlers. By 1700, more than 100,000 English migrants had come to Virginia and Maryland, mostly as indentured servants. Shipping registers from the English port of Bristol reveal the backgrounds of 5,000 embarking servants. Three-quarters were young men, many of them displaced by the enclosure of their village lands (see Chapter 1). They came to Bristol searching for work; once there, merchants persuaded them to sign contracts to labor in America. The indenture contracts bound the men—and the quarter who were women—to work for a master for four or five years, after which they would be free to marry and work for themselves.

Indentured Servitude For merchants, servants were valuable cargo: Their contracts fetched high prices from Chesapeake (and West Indian) planters (Figure 2.3). For the plantation owners, indentured servants were an incredible bargain. During the tobacco boom, a male servant could produce five times his purchase price in a single year. To maximize their gains, most masters ruthlessly exploited servants, forcing them to work long hours, beating them without cause, and withholding permission to marry. If servants ran away or became pregnant, masters went to court to increase the term of their service. Female servants were especially vulnerable to abuse. A Virginia law of 1692 stated that "dissolute masters have gotten their maids with child; and yet claim the benefit of their service." Planters got rid of uncooperative servants by selling their contracts. In Virginia, an Englishman remarked in disgust that "servants were sold up and down like horses."

Most indentured servants in the Chesapeake colonies did not escape poverty. Half the men died before completing the term of their contract, and another quarter remained landless. Only one-quarter achieved their quest for property and respectability. Female servants generally fared better. Men had grown "very sensible of the Misfortune of Wanting Wives," so many propertied planters married female servants. Thus, by migrating to the Chesapeake, a few—very fortunate—men and women escaped a life of landless poverty.

African Laborers The first African workers in North America faced even worse prospects than indentured servants did. In 1619, John Rolfe noted that "a Dutch man of warre . . . sold us twenty Negars"—slaves originally shipped by the Portuguese from the port of Luanda in Angola. For a generation, the number of Africans remained small. About 400 Africans lived in the Chesapeake colonies in 1649, just 2 percent of the population. By 1670, that figure had reached 5 percent and, significantly, the growing numbers of Africans labored primarily for powerful men: members of the Virginia council and wealthy officers of county governments. Although most of these early African workers served their English masters for life, they were not legally enslaved. English **common law** did not acknowledge **chattel slavery**, the ownership of a human being as property. Also, some of these Africans came from the Kingdom of Kongo, where Portuguese missionaries had converted the king and some of his subjects to Christianity. Knowing the customs of Europeans, a few of these workers found ways to escape their bondage. Once free, some ambitious Africans even purchased slaves, bought the labor contracts of English servants, or married Englishwomen.

Social mobility for Africans ended in the 1660s with the collapse of the tobacco boom and the increasing political power of the gentry. Tobacco had once sold for 30 pence a pound; now it fetched less than one-tenth of that. The "low price of Tobacco requires it should bee made as cheap as possible," declared Virginia planter-politician Nicholas Spencer, and "blacks can make it cheaper than whites." As they imported more African workers, the English-born political elite grew more race-conscious. Increasingly, Spencer and other leading legislators distinguished English from African residents by color (white-black) rather than by religion (Christian-pagan). By 1671, the Virginia House of Burgesses had forbidden Africans to own guns or

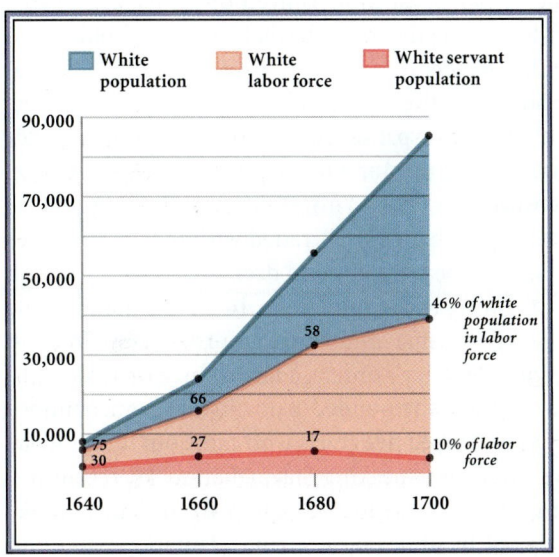

FIGURE 2.3

Chesapeake Whites: Workers, Dependents, and Indentured Servants, 1640–1700

The Chesapeake's white population grew tenfold in the years after 1640, and changed significantly in character. As more women migrated to Virginia and Maryland and bore children, the percentage of the population who worked in the fields daily fell dramatically, from 75 percent to 46 percent. The proportion of indentured servants in the labor force likewise declined, from 30 percent to 10 percent. Source: Adapted from Carville V. Earle, "Environment, Disease, and Mortality in Early Virginia," in *The Chesapeake in the Seventeenth Century,* ed. Thad W. Tate and David L. Ammerman (New York: W. W. Norton, 1979), table 3.

join the militia. It also barred them—"tho baptized and enjoying their own Freedom"—from owning English servants. Being black was increasingly a mark of inferior legal status, and slavery was fast becoming a permanent and hereditary condition. As an English clergyman observed, "These two words, Negro and Slave had by custom grown Homogeneous and convertible."

Bacon's Rebellion

As the tobacco boom went bust, long-standing social conflicts flared into political turmoil. Falling tobacco prices signaled an imbalanced market; exports doubled between 1670 and 1700, outstripping European demand. But the falling prices also reflected Parliament's passage of Acts of Trade and Navigation in 1651, 1660, and 1663. The Navigation Acts allowed only English or colonial-owned ships to enter American ports, thereby excluding Dutch merchants, who paid the highest prices for tobacco, sold the best goods, and provided the cheapest shipping services. The legislation also required colonists to ship tobacco, sugar, and other "enumerated articles" only to England, where monarchs continually raised import duties, stifling market demand. By the 1670s, tobacco planters were getting just a penny a pound for their crop; one Virginian grumbled that the planters had become mere "beneficial Slaves" to England's merchants and monarch.

The Seeds of Social Revolt | Despite the low prices, Virginians continued to plant tobacco because there was no other cash crop. To preserve soil fertility without costly manuring, yeomen adopted a long-fallow system (rotating fields over a twenty-year cycle) and pocketed just enough income to scrape by. Worse off were newly freed indentured servants, who could not earn enough to buy tools and seed or to pay the fees required to exercise their right to 50 acres of land. Many ex-servants had to sell their labor again, either signing new indentures or becoming wage workers or tenant farmers.

Consequently, after 1670, a planter-merchant elite dominated the Chesapeake colonies. By securing grants from royal governors, they owned nearly half of all settled land in Virginia. Like the English gentry, the planter-merchants leased these large estates to the ever-more-numerous group of former servants. Other well-to-do planters became commercial middlemen and moneylenders, setting up stores that sold imported goods and charging commissions for shipping tobacco grown by smallholding farmers. In Maryland, well-connected Catholic planters were equally powerful; by

1720, one of those planters, Charles Carroll, owned 47,000 acres of land, which was farmed by scores of tenants, indentured servants, and slaves.

William Berkeley, governor of Virginia between 1642 and 1652 and again after 1660, set the stage for conflict. A corrupt man with equally corrupt allies, Berkeley bestowed large land grants on members of his council. The councilors promptly exempted these lands from taxation and appointed friends as local justices of the peace and county judges. To win support in the House of Burgesses, Berkeley bought off legislators with land grants and lucrative appointments as sheriffs and tax collectors. But social unrest erupted when the Burgesses took the vote away from landless freemen, who by now constituted half the adult white men. Property-holding yeomen retained their voting rights, but were angered by falling tobacco prices, political corruption, and "grievous taxations" that threatened the "utter ruin of us the poor commonalty." Berkeley and his gentry allies were living on borrowed time.

Indians and Frontiersmen | As the aggressive planter-entrepreneurs of Virginia confronted a multitude of free, young, and landless laborers, armed political conflict broke out during the 1670s. This struggle would leave a complex legacy: a decrease in class conflict among whites, violent campaigns against neighboring Indians, and increasing racial divisions because of massive imports of enslaved Africans.

An Indian conflict ignited the flame of social rebellion. In 1607, when the English intruded, 30,000 Native Americans resided in Virginia; by 1675, the native population had dwindled to only 3,500. By then, Europeans numbered some 38,000 and Africans another 2,500. Most Indians lived on treaty-guaranteed territory along the frontier, where poor freeholders and landless former servants now wanted to settle. They demanded that the natives be expelled or exterminated. Opposition to expansion came from wealthy river-valley planters, who wanted a ready supply of tenant farmers and wage laborers, and from Governor Berkeley and the planter-merchants, who traded with the Occaneechee Indians for beaver pelts and deerskins.

Fighting broke out late in 1675, when a vigilante band of Virginia militiamen murdered 30 Indians. Defying Berkeley's orders, a larger force of 1,000 militiamen then surrounded a fortified Susquehannock village and killed five chiefs who came out to negotiate. The Iroquoian-speaking Susquehannocks, recent migrants to the Chesapeake region from Pennsylvania, retaliated by attacking outlying plantations and killing 300 whites. In response, Berkeley proposed a defensive military strategy: a series of frontier forts to deter Indian intrusions. The settlers dismissed this scheme as a militarily useless plot by planter-merchants to impose high taxes and take "all our tobacco into their own hands."

Nathaniel Bacon, Rebel Leader | Nathaniel Bacon, a young, well-connected migrant from England, emerged as the leader of the rebels. Bacon held a position on the governor's council, but as the owner of a frontier estate, he differed with Berkeley on Indian policy. When the governor refused to grant him a military commission, Bacon mobilized his neighbors and attacked any Indians he could find. Condemning the frontiersmen as "rebels and mutineers," Berkeley expelled Bacon from the council and had him arrested. But Bacon's army forced the governor to release their leader and to hold legislative elections. The newly elected House of Burgesses enacted far-reaching political reforms that not only curbed the powers of the governor and council but also restored voting rights to landless freemen.

These much-needed reforms came too late. Bacon remained bitter toward Berkeley, and poor farmers and servants resented years of exploitation by wealthy planters, arrogant justices of the peace, and "wicked & pernicious Counsellors." As one yeoman rebel complained, "A poor man who has only his labour to maintain himself and his family pays as much [in taxes] as a man who has 20,000 acres." Backed by 400 armed men, Bacon issued a "Manifesto and Declaration of the People" that demanded the death or removal of the Indians and an end to the rule of wealthy "parasites." "All the power and sway is got into the hands of the rich," Bacon proclaimed as his army burned Jamestown to the ground and plundered the plantations of Berkeley's allies. When Bacon died suddenly of dysentery in October 1676, the governor took revenge, dispersing the rebel army, seizing the estates of well-to-do rebels, and hanging 23 men.

Bacon's Rebellion was a pivotal event in the history of the Chesapeake colonies. Thereafter, landed planters retained their dominance by curbing corruption and appointing ambitious yeomen to public office. They appeased yeomen and tenants by cutting taxes and expelling the Susquehannocks, Piscataways, and other Indian peoples from the region. Most important, planters forestalled another rebellion by poor whites by cutting the use of indentured servants and instead importing thousands of African laborers; the Burgesses explicitly legalized chattel slavery in 1705. Those fateful decisions

Nathaniel Bacon

Condemned as a rebel and a traitor in his own time, Nathaniel Bacon emerged in the late nineteenth century as a Southern hero, a harbinger of the Confederate rebels of 1860–1865. The Association for the Preservation of Virginia Antiquities, founded in 1888, commissioned this stained-glass window depicting Bacon in dual guises of a well-dressed gentleman and a rebel in body armor. Installing Bacon's portrait in a window of the Powder Magazine in Williamsburg (built by Governor Alexander Spotswood in 1715) explained a leading member of the association, would connect "present Virginia with her great and noble past" and commemorate those who shed their "blood for Virginia and the South." The Association for the Preservation of Virginia Antiquities.

committed subsequent generations of Americans to a social system based on racial exploitation.

- **What were the various systems of bound labor that took hold in the Chesapeake colonies? What accounts for their appearance?**

- **Compare the Indian uprising in Virginia in 1622 with Bacon's Rebellion in 1675. What were the consequences of each for Virginia's development?**

Puritan New England

As people scrambled for wealth in the Chesapeake, Puritans created colonies in New England that had strong spiritual goals. Between 1620 and 1640, thousands of Puritans fled to America seeking land and religious freedom. By distributing land broadly, they built a society of independent farm families. And by establishing a "holy commonwealth," Puritans tried to preserve a "pure" Christian faith. Their "errand into the wilderness" gave a moral dimension to American history that survives today.

The Puritan Migration

New England differed from other European colonies. Unruly male adventurers founded New Spain and Jamestown, and male traders dominated life in New France and New Netherland. By contrast, the leaders of the Plymouth and Massachusetts Bay colonies were pious Protestants, and the settlers included women and children as well as men (Map 2.5).

The Pilgrims The Pilgrims were religious separatists—Puritans who had left the Church of England. When King James I threatened to drive Puritans "out of the land, or else do worse," some Puritans chose to live among Dutch Calvinists in Holland. Subsequently, 35 of these exiles resolved to maintain their English identity by moving to America. Led by William Bradford and joined by 67 migrants from England, the Pilgrims sailed to America in 1620 aboard the *Mayflower* and settled in Plymouth, near Cape Cod in southeastern Massachusetts. Because they lacked a royal charter, their leader explained, we "combine[d] ourselves together into a civill body politick." This Mayflower Compact used the Puritans' self-governing religious congregation as the model for their political structure.

The first winter in Plymouth tested the Pilgrims. Of the 102 migrants who arrived in November, only half survived until spring. Thereafter Plymouth became a healthy and thriving community, as the cold climate inhibited the spread of mosquito-borne disease, and the Pilgrims' religious discipline encouraged a strong work ethic. Moreover, a smallpox epidemic in 1618 had killed most of the local Wampanoag people, so the migrants faced few external threats. The Pilgrims built solid houses and planted ample crops, and their numbers grew rapidly. By 1640, there were 3,000 settlers in Plymouth. To ensure political stability, they issued a written legal code that provided for representative self-government, broad political rights, property ownership, and religious freedom of conscience.

Meanwhile, England plunged deeper into religious turmoil. When King Charles I repudiated certain Protestant doctrines, including the role of grace in salvation, English Puritans, now powerful in Parliament, accused the king of "popery"—of holding Catholic beliefs. In 1629, Charles dissolved Parliament, claimed the authority to rule by "divine right," and raised money through royal edicts and the sale of monopolies. When Archbishop William Laud, whom Charles chose to head the Church of England, dismissed hundreds of dissident ministers, thousands of Puritan families fled to America.

John Winthrop and Massachusetts Bay The Puritan exodus began in 1630 with the departure of 900 migrants led by John Winthrop, a well-educated country squire who became the first governor of the Massachusetts Bay Colony. Calling England morally corrupt and "overburdened with people," Winthrop sought land for his children and a place in Christian history for his people. "We must consider that we shall be as a City upon a Hill," Winthrop told the migrants. "The eyes of all people are upon us." Like the Pilgrims, the Puritans envisioned a reformed Christian society with "authority in magistrates, liberty in people, purity in the church," as minister John Cotton put it. By creating a genuinely "New" England, they hoped to inspire religious reform throughout Christendom.

Winthrop and his associates governed the Massachusetts Bay Colony from the town of Boston. They transformed their **joint-stock corporation**, the General Court of shareholders, into a representative political system with a governor, council, and assembly. To ensure rule by the godly, the Puritans limited the right to vote and hold office to men who were church members. Rejecting the Plymouth Colony's policy of religious tolerance, the Massachusetts Bay Colony established Puritanism as the state-supported religion, barred other faiths from conducting services, and used the Bible as a legal guide. "Where there is no Law," they said, magistrates should rule "as near the law of God as they can." Over the next decade, about 10,000 Puritans migrated to the colony, along with 10,000 others fleeing hard times in England.

The New England Puritans sought to emulate the simplicity of the first Christians. Seeing bishops as "traitours unto God," they placed power in the congregation of members—hence the name *Congregationalist* for their churches. Inspired by John Calvin,

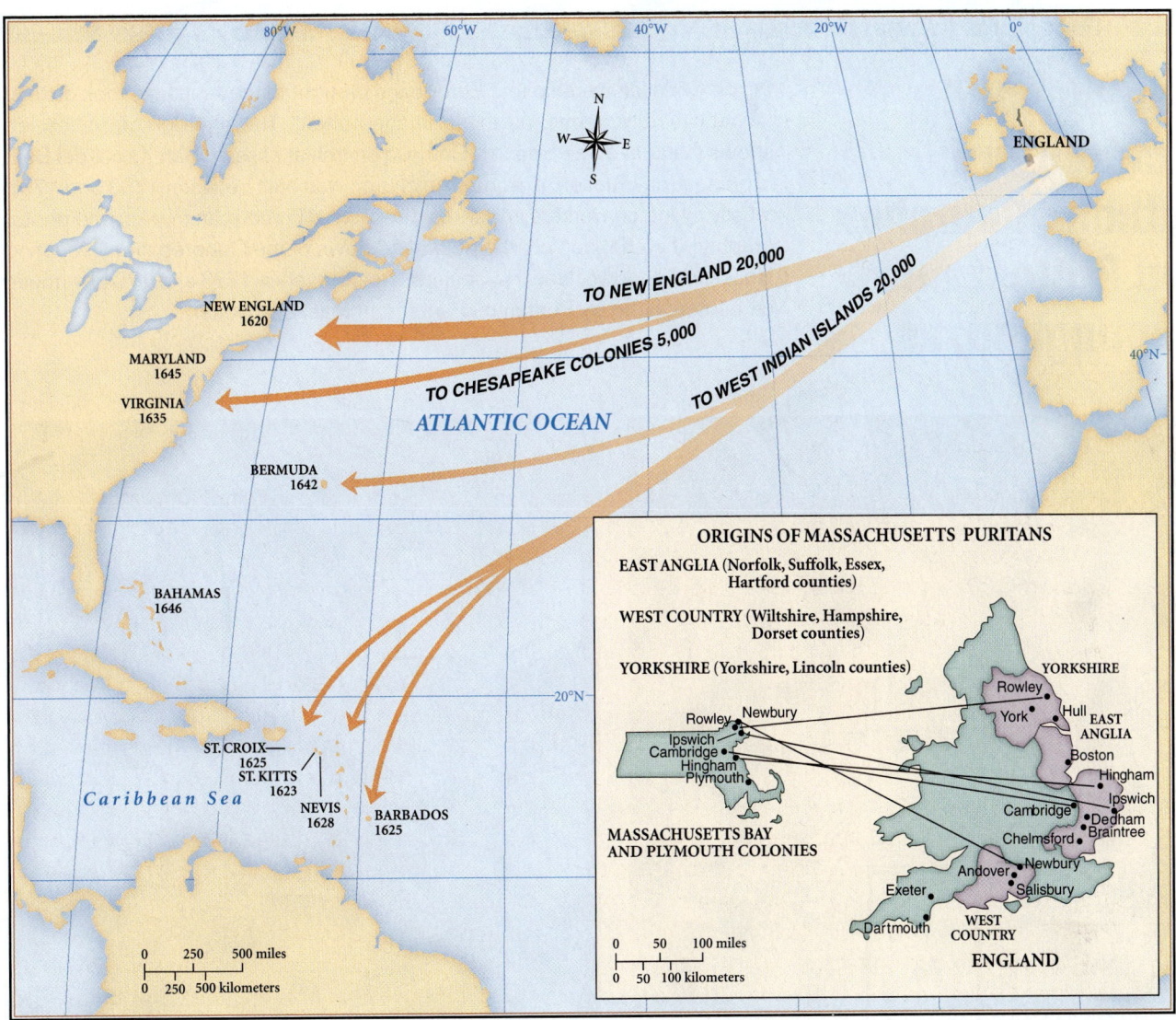

MAP 2.5

The Puritan Migration to America, 1620–1640

Forty-five thousand Puritans left England for America and the West Indies between 1620 and 1640, but they created religion-based colonies only in New England—at Plymouth, Massachusetts Bay, and Connecticut. Migrants from the three major centers of Puritanism in England—Yorkshire, East Anglia, and the West Country—commonly settled among those from their own region. Often they named American communities after their English towns of origin and tried to live as they had in Old England. For example, settlers from Rowley in Yorkshire transplanted their customary system of open-field agriculture to Rowley in Massachusetts Bay.

many Puritans embraced predestination, the doctrine that God chose (before their birth) only a few men and women for salvation. Church members often lived in great anxiety, worried that God had not placed them among these "elect." Some hoped for a conversion experience, the intense sensation of receiving God's grace and being "born again." Other Puritans relied on "prep-

aration," the confidence in salvation that came from spiritual guidance by their ministers. Still others believed that they were God's chosen people, the new Israelites, and would be saved if they obeyed his laws (see Reading American Pictures, "Ideology and Architecture: Catholic Churches and Protestant Meetinghouses," p. 60).

Ideology and Architecture: Catholic Churches and Protestant Meetinghouses

The Christian worship that Europeans brought to the Americas took distinct architectural forms, as these images attest. The photograph to the left shows the altar of the Spanish Catholic church at Mission San Xavier del Bac, in present-day Tucson, Arizona. The church was built between 1783 and 1797, mostly by Indian workers under the direction of Franciscan monks. The photograph to the right depicts the pulpit and pews of the Congregational Meeting House in Sandown, New Hampshire, constructed in 1773 and 1774 by house carpenters hired by Puritan migrants from Massachusetts.

Altar of the Spanish Catholic Mission San Xavier del Bac. Geremia.

Pulpit of the Congregational Meeting House, Sandown, New Hampshire. Image copyright William Owens www.wwowens.com.

ANALYZING THE EVIDENCE

- How would you describe the look or the feel of each house of worship? What is the central visual focus of each image? Why is that important?

- The great English Puritan poet John Milton argued that Catholics made God "earthy and fleshy because they could not make themselves heavenly and spiritual." Are there any features of the altar of the Mission San Xavier del Bac that give credence to Milton's claim?

- Puritans were sometimes called "people of the Word" because of their reliance on the Bible and their attention to carefully argued sermons. How does the interior design of the New Hampshire meetinghouse express their religious outlook?

- The purpose of the Mission San Xavier del Bac was to convert the Tohono O'odham (Papago) Indians to Catholicism. Would the altar aid that effort? If so, how? Protestant clergy in New England likewise sought to convert native peoples to their religion. Given Puritan practices and doctrines, how might they approach that task and what role, if any, would the meetinghouse play?

Roger Williams and Rhode Island   To maintain God's favor, the Massachusetts Bay magistrates purged their society of religious dissidents. One target was Roger Williams, the Puritan minister in Salem, a coastal town north of Boston. Williams opposed the decision to establish Congregationalism as the official religion and praised the Pilgrims' separation of church and state. He advocated toleration, arguing that political magistrates had authority over only the "bodies, goods, and outward estates of men," not their spiritual lives. Williams also questioned the Puritans' seizure of Indian lands. The magistrates banished him from the colony in 1636.

Williams and his followers settled 50 miles south of Boston, founding the town of Providence on land purchased from the Narragansett Indians. Other religious dissidents settled nearby at Portsmouth and Newport. In 1644, these settlers obtained a corporate charter from Parliament for a new colony—Rhode Island—with full authority to rule themselves. In Rhode Island, as in Plymouth, there was no legally established church, and individuals could worship God as they pleased.

Anne Hutchinson   The Massachusetts Bay magistrates saw a second threat to their authority in Anne Hutchinson. The wife of a merchant and mother of seven, Hutchinson held weekly prayer meetings for women and accused various Boston clergymen of placing undue emphasis on good behavior. Like Martin Luther, Hutchinson denied that salvation could be earned through good deeds: There was no "covenant of works"; God bestowed salvation only through the "covenant of grace." Hutchinson likewise declared that God "revealed" divine truth directly to individual believers, a controversial doctrine that the Puritan magistrates denounced as heretical.

The magistrates also resented Hutchinson because of her sex. Like other Christians, Puritans believed that both men and women could be saved. But gender equality stopped there. Women were inferior to men in earthly affairs, said leading Puritan divines, who told married women: "Thy desires shall bee subject to thy husband, and he shall rule over thee." Puritan women could not be ministers or lay preachers, nor could they vote in church affairs. As Pilgrim minister John Robinson put it, women "are debarred by their sex from ordinary prophesying, and from any other dealing in the church wherein they take authority over the man." In 1637, the magistrates accused Hutchinson of teaching that inward grace freed an individual from the rules of the church and found her guilty of holding heretical views.

Banished, she followed Roger Williams into exile in Rhode Island.

Such coercive policies and a quest for better farming land prompted some Puritans to move to the Connecticut River Valley. In 1636, pastor Thomas Hooker and his congregation established the town of Hartford, and other Puritans settled along the river at Wethersfield and Windsor. In 1660, they secured a charter from King Charles II (r. 1660–1685) for the self-governing colony of Connecticut. Like Massachusetts Bay, Connecticut had a legally established church and an elected governor and assembly; however, it granted voting rights to most property-owning men, not just to church members as in the original Puritan colony.

The Puritan Revolution in England   Meanwhile, a religious civil war had engulfed England. Archbishop Laud had imposed the Church of England prayer book on Presbyterian Scotland in 1637; five years later, a rebel Scottish army invaded England. Thousands of English Puritans (and hundreds of American Puritans) joined the Scots, demanding religious reform and parliamentary power. After years of civil war, parliamentary forces led by Oliver Cromwell emerged victorious. In 1649, Parliament executed King Charles I, proclaimed a republican commonwealth, and banished bishops and elaborate rituals from the Church of England.

The Puritan triumph in England was short-lived. Popular support for the Commonwealth ebbed after Cromwell took dictatorial control in 1653. Following his death in 1658, moderate Protestants and a resurgent aristocracy restored the monarchy and the hierarchy of bishops. For many Puritans, Charles II's accession to the throne in 1660 represented the coming of Antichrist, the false prophesying "beast" described in the biblical Book of Revelation.

For the Puritans in America, the restoration of the monarchy began a new phase of their "errand into the wilderness." They had come to New England to preserve the "pure" Christian church, expecting to return to Europe in triumph. When the failure of the English Revolution dashed that sacred mission, ministers exhorted congregations to create a godly republican society in America. The Puritan colonies now stood as outposts of Calvinism and the Atlantic republican tradition.

Puritanism and Witchcraft

Like Native Americans, Puritans believed that the physical world was full of supernatural forces. Devout Christians saw signs of God's (or Satan's) power in blazing

The Reverend Increase Mather, 1688

Increase Mather (the father of Cotton Mather) was an influential Massachusetts minister; the president of Harvard College (1692–1701); and, as the portrait suggests, a prolific author (of 125 sermons and books). Jan van der Spriett executed this painting in London, where Mather persuaded King William to approve the Massachusetts Charter of 1692 and thereby preserved Puritan power in the colony. In *Cases of Conscience Concerning Evil Spirits* (1693), Mather criticized the use of "spectral evidence" in the Salem witchcraft trials but, to uphold the colony's fragile new government, defended the verdict of the judges and execution of the alleged witches.   Bridgeman Art Library Ltd.

The Protestant Almanack, 1700

The conflict between Protestants and Catholics took many forms. To reinforce the religious identity of English Protestants, a writer using the pseudonym "Philopretes" published this almanac that charted not only the passage of the seasons (and the influence of the pagan signs of the "Zodiack") but also the "Pernicious Revolutions of the Papacy against the Lord and his Anointed."   By permission of the Syndics of Cambridge University Library.

stars, birth defects, and other unusual events. Noting after a storm that the houses of many ministers "had been smitten with Lightning," Cotton Mather, a prominent Puritan theologian, wondered "what the meaning of God should be in it."

Belief in "forces" and "spirits" stemmed in part from Christian teachings—the Catholic belief in miracles, for example, and the Protestant faith in grace. It also reflected pagan influence. Samuel Sewall, a well-educated Puritan merchant and judge, fended off evil spirits by driving a metal pin into his new house. And thousands of farmers—Puritan saints as well as non–church members—followed pagan astrological charts printed in almanacs to determine the best times to plant crops, marry off their children, and take other important actions.

Zealous Puritan ministers and laypeople attacked these practices as "superstition" and condemned "cunning" individuals who claimed powers as healers or prophets. Indeed, many believed such conjurers were Satan's "wizards" or "witches." People in the town of Andover "were much addicted to sorcery," claimed one observer, and "there were forty men in it that could raise the Devil as well as any astrologer." Between 1647 and 1662, civil authorities in New England hanged 14 people for witchcraft, most of them older women accused of being "double-tongued" or of having "an unruly spirit."

The most dramatic episode of witch-hunting occurred in Salem in 1692. Several girls who had experienced strange seizures accused neighbors of bewitching them. When judges at the accused witches' trials allowed the use of "spectral" evidence — visions of evil beings and marks seen only by the girls — the accusations spun out of control. Eventually, Massachusetts Bay authorities tried 175 people for witchcraft and executed 19 of them. The causes of this mass hysteria were complex and are still debated. Some historians point to group rivalries: Many accusers were the daughters or servants of poor farmers, whereas many of the alleged witches were wealthier church members or their friends. Because 18 of those put to death were women, other historians see the episode as part of a broader Puritan effort to subordinate women. Still others focus on political instability in Massachusetts Bay in the early 1690s and on fears raised by recent Indian attacks in nearby Maine, which had killed the parents of some of the young accusers. It is likely that all of these causes played some role in the executions.

Whatever the cause, the Salem episode marked a major turning point. Shaken by the number of deaths, government officials now discouraged legal prosecutions for witchcraft. Moreover, many influential people embraced the outlook of the European Enlightenment, a major intellectual movement that began around 1675 and promoted a rational, scientific view of the world. Increasingly, educated men and women explained strange happenings and sudden deaths by reference to "natural causes," not witchcraft. Unlike Cotton Mather (1663–1728), who believed that lightning was a supernatural sign, Benjamin Franklin (1706–1790) and other well-read men of his generation would investigate it as a natural phenomenon.

A Yeoman Society, 1630–1700

In building their communities, New England Puritans consciously rejected the feudal practices of English society. Many Puritans came from middling families in East Anglia, a region of pasture lands and few manors, and had no desire to live as tenants of wealthy aristocrats or submit to oppressive taxation by a distant government. They had "escaped out of the pollutions of the world," the settlers of Watertown in Massachu-

An Affluent Puritan Woman of the 1670s
This well-known painting of Elizabeth Clarke Freake and her daughter, Mary (the youngest of her eight children), is perhaps the finest portrait we have of a seventeenth-century American. The unknown artist gives most attention to the finery of Mrs. Freake's silk dress, with its elaborate lace collar and its red underskirt embroidered with gold and silver. The painting testifies to the prosperity of Boston's Puritan merchants and their embrace of a cosmopolitan outlook. As minister Samuel Torrey complained at the time, "a spirit of worldliness, a spirit of sensuality" had asserted itself among the younger generation of Puritans.   Worcester Art Museum.

setts Bay declared, and vowed to live "close togither" in self-governing communities. Accordingly, the General Courts of Massachusetts Bay and Connecticut bestowed land on groups of settlers, or **proprietors**, who then distributed it among the male heads of families.

Widespread ownership of land did not mean equality of wealth or status. "God had Ordained different degrees and orders of men," proclaimed Boston merchant John Saffin, "some to be Masters and Commanders, others to be Subjects, and to be commanded." Town proprietors normally awarded the largest plots to men of high social status who often became selectmen and justices of the peace. However, all families received some land, and most adult men had a vote in the **town meeting**, the main institution of local government (Map 2.6).

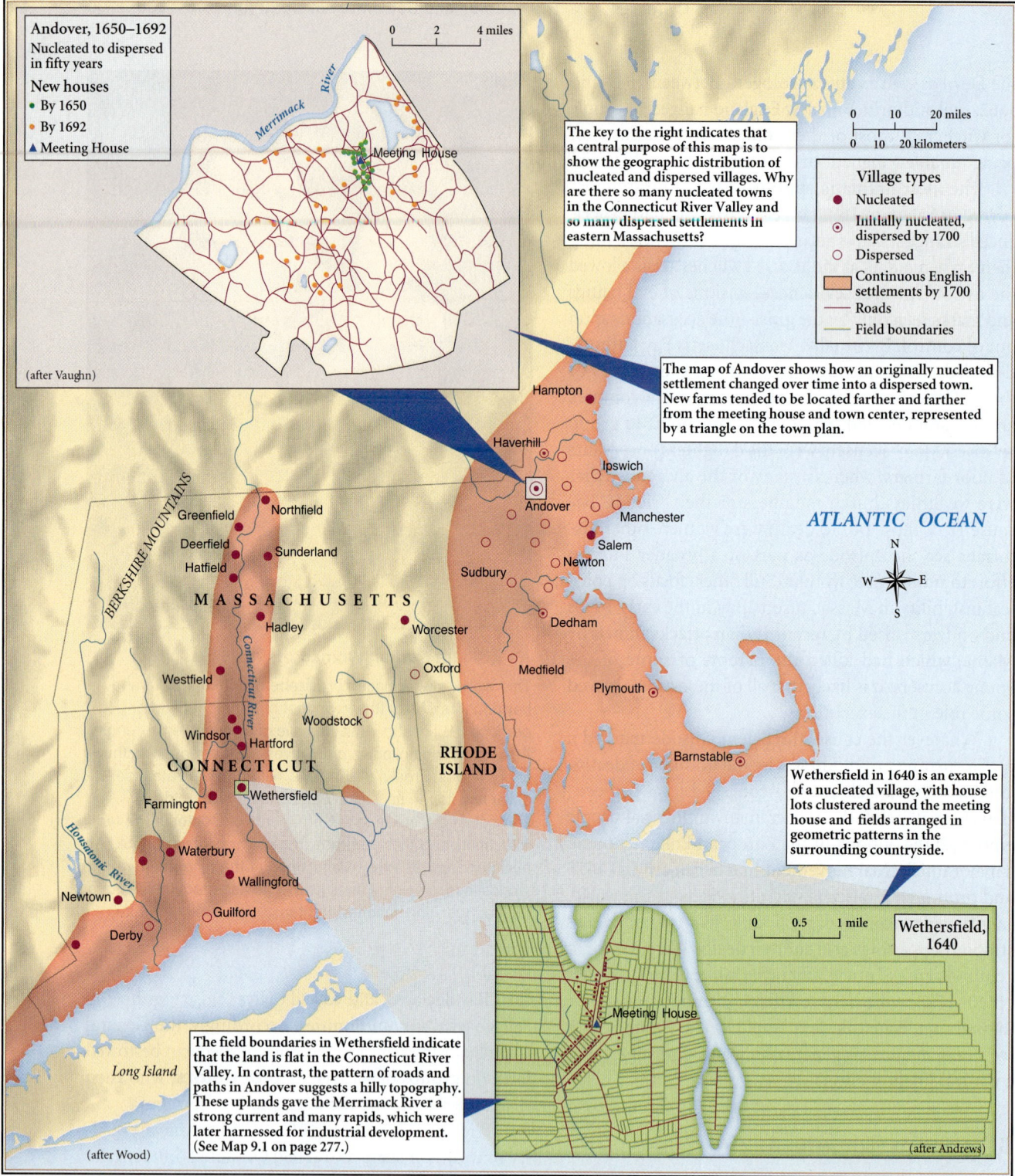

Andover, 1650–1692
Nucleated to dispersed in fifty years

New houses
- By 1650
- By 1692
- ▲ Meeting House

(after Vaughn)

The key to the right indicates that a central purpose of this map is to show the geographic distribution of nucleated and dispersed villages. Why are there so many nucleated towns in the Connecticut River Valley and so many dispersed settlements in eastern Massachusetts?

Village types
- Nucleated
- Initially nucleated, dispersed by 1700
- Dispersed
- Continuous English settlements by 1700
- Roads
- Field boundaries

The map of Andover shows how an originally nucleated settlement changed over time into a dispersed town. New farms tended to be located farther and farther from the meeting house and town center, represented by a triangle on the town plan.

ATLANTIC OCEAN

Hampton
Haverhill
Ipswich
Andover
Manchester
Salem
Newton
Sudbury
Dedham
Medfield
Plymouth
Barnstable
Oxford
Worcester

MASSACHUSETTS

Greenfield
Northfield
Deerfield
Sunderland
Hatfield
Hadley
Westfield
Windsor
Woodstock
Hartford
CONNECTICUT
Wethersfield
Farmington
Waterbury
Wallingford
Newtown
Guilford
Derby

BERKSHIRE MOUNTAINS
Connecticut River
Housatonic River
Merrimack River

RHODE ISLAND

Long Island

Wethersfield in 1640 is an example of a nucleated village, with house lots clustered around the meeting house and fields arranged in geometric patterns in the surrounding countryside.

The field boundaries in Wethersfield indicate that the land is flat in the Connecticut River Valley. In contrast, the pattern of roads and paths in Andover suggests a hilly topography. These uplands gave the Merrimack River a strong current and many rapids, which were later harnessed for industrial development. (See Map 9.1 on page 277.)

(after Wood)

Meeting House

Wethersfield, 1640

(after Andrews)

MAP 2.6

Settlement Patterns in New England Towns, 1630–1700

Initially, most Puritan towns were compact: Regardless of the local topography — hills or plains — families lived close to one another in village centers and traveled daily to work in the surrounding fields. This 1640 map of Wethersfield, Connecticut, a town situated on the broad plains of the Connecticut River Valley, shows this pattern clearly. The first settlers in Andover, Massachusetts, also chose to live in the village center. However, the rugged topography of eastern Massachusetts encouraged the townspeople to disperse. By 1692 (as the varied location of new houses shows), many Andover residents were living on farms distant from the village center.

In this society of independent households and self-governing communities, ordinary farmers had much more political power than Chesapeake yeomen and European peasants did. Although Nathaniel Fish was one of the poorest men in the town of Barnstable—he owned just a two-room cottage, 8 acres of land, an ox, and a cow—he was a voting member of the town meeting. Each year, Fish and other Barnstable farmers levied taxes; enacted ordinances governing fencing, road building, and the use of common fields; and chose the selectmen who managed town affairs. The farmers also selected the town's representatives to the General Court, which gradually displaced the governor as the center of political authority. For Fish and thousands of other ordinary settlers, New England had proved to be a new world of opportunity.

- Why did the Puritans of Massachusetts Bay create an established church and persecute dissenters when they had fled England to escape those things?

- What was the social and political structure of the New England colonies? Why did they develop in that fashion?

The Eastern Indians' New World

Native Americans also lived in a new world, but for them, it was a bleak and dangerous place. In New England, an observer reported, so many Indians were stricken in a smallpox epidemic that they were "not able to help one another, no not to make a fire nor fetch a little water to drink, nor any to bury the dead." Those Indians who survived lacked the numbers to retain their ancestral lands. However, some Indian peoples, most prominently the Iroquois, used European weapons to resist the intruders and dominate other tribes. Other native peoples retreated into the mountains or moved westward to preserve their traditional cultures.

Puritans and Pequots

As the Puritans embarked for New England, they pondered the morality of acquiring Native American lands. "By what right or warrant can we enter into the land of the Savages?" they asked themselves. Responding to such concerns, John Winthrop detected God's hand in a recent smallpox epidemic: "If God were not pleased with our inheriting these parts," he asked, "why doth he still make roome for us by diminishing them as we increase?" Citing the Book of Genesis, the Massachusetts Bay magistrates argued that the Indians had not "subdued" their land and therefore had no "just right" to it. Decades later, political philosopher John Locke would offer the same justification.

Believing they were God's chosen people, the Puritans often treated Native Americans with a brutality equal to that of the Spanish conquistadors and Nathaniel Bacon's frontiersmen. When Pequot warriors resisted English encroachment onto their Connecticut River Valley lands in 1636, a Puritan militia attacked a Pequot village and massacred some 500 men, women, and children. "God laughed at the Enemies of his People," one soldier boasted, "filling the Place with Dead Bodies."

English Puritans saw the Indians as "savages" who were culturally, though not racially, inferior. To their minds, Europeans and Native Americans were genetically the same; sin, not race, accounted for their degeneracy. "Probably the devil" delivered these "miserable savages" to America, Cotton Mather suggested, "in hopes that the gospel of the Lord Jesus Christ would never come here." To convert Indians to Christianity, Puritan minister John Eliot translated the Bible into Algonquian. Only a few Native Americans became full members of Puritan congregations, because of the rigorous admission standards. However, Eliot and other ministers turned fourteen Indian villages, such as Natick (Massachusetts) and Maanexit (Connecticut), into **praying towns**. Like the Franciscan missions in New Mexico, these towns were intended as intensely Christian communities. By 1670, more than 1,000 Indians lived in these settlements, losing their independence and traditional culture but, by infusing their churches with traditional spiritual beliefs, creating new native forms of Christianity.

Metacom's War of 1675–1676

By the 1670s, Europeans in New England outnumbered Indians by three to one. The English population had multiplied to 55,000, while native peoples had diminished—from an estimated 120,000 in 1570 to 70,000 in 1620, to barely 16,000. To the Wampanoag leader Metacom (also known as King Philip) the prospects for coexistence looked dim. When his people copied English ways by raising hogs and selling pork in Boston, Puritan officials accused them of selling at "an under rate" and restricted their trade. When Indians killed wandering hogs that devastated their cornfields,

Metacom (King Philip), Chief of the Wampanoags
The Indian War of 1675–1676 left an indelible mark on the history of New England. This painting from the 1850s, done on semitransparent cloth and lit from behind for effect, was used by traveling performers to tell the story of King Philip's War. Notice that Metacom is pictured not as a savage but as a dignified man. No longer in danger of Indian attack, nineteenth-century whites in New England adopted a romanticized version of their region's often brutal history.
© Shelburne Museum, Shelburne Vermont.

authorities prosecuted them for violating English property rights (see Comparing American Voices, "The Causes of the War of 1675–1676," pp. 68–69).

Like Opechancanough in Virginia and Popé in New Mexico, Metacom concluded that the Europeans had to be expelled. In 1675, the Wampanoags' leader forged a military alliance with the Narragansetts and Nipmucks and attacked white settlements throughout New England. Almost every day, settler William Harris fearfully reported, he heard new reports of the Indians' "burneing houses, takeing cattell, killing men & women & Children: & carrying others captive." Bitter fighting continued into 1676, as the Indians exploited their strategic control of large tracts of territory and most of the rivers. It ended only when the Indian warriors ran short of gunpowder and the Massachusetts Bay government hired Mohegan and Mohawk warriors, who killed Metacom.

Metacom's War of 1675–1676 (which English settlers also called King Philip's War) was a deadly affair. Indians destroyed one-fifth of the English towns in Massachusetts and Rhode Island and killed 1,000 settlers, nearly 5 percent of the adult population. The Puritan experiment hung in the balance. Had "the Indeans not been divided," remarked one settler, "they might have forced us [to evacuate] to Som Islands: & there to have planted a little Corne, & fished for our liveings." But the natives' losses—from famine and disease, death in battle, and sale into slavery—were much larger: About 4,500 Indians died, one-quarter of an already-diminished population. Many of the surviving Wampanoag, Narragansett, and Nipmuck peoples migrated into the backcountry, where they intermarried with Algonquian tribes allied to the French. Over the next century, these displaced Indian peoples would take their revenge, joining with French Catholics to attack their Puritan enemies.

The Destructive Impact of the Fur Trade

As English towns filled the river valleys along the Atlantic coast, the Indians in the great forested areas beyond the Appalachian Mountains remained independent. Yet the distant Indian peoples—the Iroquois, Ottawas, Crees, Illinois, and many others—felt the European presence through the fur trade. As they bargained for woolen blankets, iron cookware, knives, and guns, Indians avoided the French at Montreal, who demanded two beaver skins for a woolen blanket. Instead, they dealt with the Dutch and English merchants at Albany, who asked for only one pelt and could be played off against one another. "They are marvailous subtle in their bargains to save a penny," an English trader complained. "They will beate all markets and try all places . . . to save six pence." Still, because the Indians did not know the value of their pelts in Europe, they rarely secured the highest possible price.

Nor could they stop European diseases, guns, and rum from sapping the vitality of their society. In South Carolina, a smallpox epidemic killed nearly half of the Catawbas, and "strong spirits" took a toll among the survivors: "Many of our people has Lately Died by

The Hurons' Feast of the Dead

Hurons buried their dead in temporary raised tombs so they could easily care for their spirits. When they moved their villages in search of fertile soil and better hunting, the Hurons held a Feast of the Dead and reburied the bones of their own deceased and often bones from other villages in a common pit lined with beaver robes. This solemn ceremony united living as well as dead clan members, strengthening the bonds of the Huron Confederacy. It also was believed to release the spirits of the dead, allowing them to travel to the land where the first Huron, Aataentsic, fell from the sky, "made earth and man," and lived with her son and assistant, Iouskeha.   Library of Congress.

the Effects of that Strong Drink," a Catawba lamented. Most native societies also lost their economic independence. As they exchanged furs for European-made iron utensils and woolen blankets, Indians neglected their traditional artisan skills, making fewer flint hoes, clay pots, and skin garments. "Every necessity of life we must have from the white people," a Cherokee chief complained. Religious autonomy vanished as well. When French missionaries won converts among the Hurons, Iroquois, and Illinois, they divided Indian communities into hostile religious factions.

Likewise, constant warfare for furs altered the dynamics of tribal politics by shifting power from cautious elders to headstrong young warriors. The sachems (chiefs), a group of young Seneca warriors said scornfully, "were a parcell of Old People who say much but who Mean or Act very little." The status of Indian women changed in especially complex ways. Traditionally, eastern woodland women had a voice in political councils because they were the chief providers of food and handcrafted goods. As a French Jesuit noted of the Iroquois, "The women are always the first to deliberate. . . . They hold their councils apart and . . . advise the chiefs . . . so that the latter may deliberate on them in their turn." The disruption of farming by warfare and the influx of

European goods undermined women's economic power. Yet, paradoxically, among victorious warring tribes such as the Iroquois, the influence of women probably increased in other respects, because they managed the cultural assimilation of hundreds of captives.

There is no doubt that the sheer extent of the fur industry—the slaughter of hundreds of thousands of beaver, deer, otter, and other animals—profoundly altered the environment. As early as the 1630s, a French Jesuit worried that the Montagnais people, who lived north of the St. Lawrence, were killing so many beaver that they would "exterminate the species in this Region, as has happened among the Hurons." As the animal populations died off, streams ran faster (there were fewer beaver dams) and the underbrush grew denser (there were fewer deer to trim the vegetation). The native environment, as well as its animals and peoples, were now part of a new American world of relentless exploitation and little civility.

- Compare the causes of the uprisings led by Popé in New Mexico and Metacom in New England. Which rebellion was more successful? Why?

- What were the major social and environmental changes that made America a new world for Indians?

Thus I have given you, I think, the Substance of the Arguments or both sides of that great and important Questio

The Causes of the War of 1675–1676

The causes of — and responsibility for — every American war are much debated, and the war of 1675–1676 between Puritans and Native Americans is no exception. The English settlers called it King Philip's War, suggesting that the Wampanoag chief Metacom (King Philip) instigated it. Was that the case? We have no firsthand Indian accounts of its origins, but three English accounts offer different versions of events. Given the variation among the accounts and their fragmentary character, how can historians reconstruct what "really happened"? Moreover, should the story be told from the Indian or the English point of view?

John Easton

A Relacion of the Indyan Warre

John Easton was the deputy governor of Rhode Island and a Quaker. Like many Quakers, Easton was a pacifist and tried to prevent the war. He wrote this "Relacion" shortly after the conflict ended.

In [January 1675], an Indian was found dead; and by a coroner inquest of Plymouth Colony judged murdered. . . . The dead Indian was called Sassamon, and a Christian that could read and write. . . .

The report came that . . . three Indians had confessed and accused Philip [of employing them to kill Sassamon, and that consequently] . . . the English would hang Philip. So the Indians were afraid, and reported that . . . Philip [believed that the English] . . . might kill him to have his land. . . . So Philip kept his men in arms.

Plymouth governor [Josiah Winslow] required him to disband his men, and informed him his jealousy [his worry about land seizure] was false. Philip answered he would do no harm, and thanked the Governor for his information. The three Indians were hung [on June 8, 1675]. . . . And it was reported [that] Sassamon, before his death had informed [the English] of the Indian plot, and that if the Indians knew it they would kill him, and that the heathen might destroy the English for their wickedness as God had permitted the heathen to destroy the Israelites of old.

So the English were afraid and Philip was afraid and both increased in arms; but for forty years' time reports and jealousies of war had been very frequent that we did not think that now a war was breaking forth. But about a week before it did we had cause to think it would; then to endeavor to prevent it, we sent a man to Philip. . . .

He called his council and agreed to come to us; [Philip] came himself, unarmed, and about forty of his men, armed. Then five of us went over [to speak to the Indians]. Three were magistrates. We sat very friendly together [June 14–18]. We told him our business was to endeavor

that they might not . . . do wrong. They said that was well; they had done no wrong; the English wronged them. We said we knew the English said that the Indians wronged them, and the Indians said the English wronged them, but our desire was the quarrel might rightly be decided in the best way, and not as dogs decide their quarrels.

The Indians owned that fighting was the worst way; then they propounded how right might take place; we said by arbitration. They said all English agreed against them; and so by arbitration they had had much wrong, many square miles of land so taken from them, for the English would have English arbitrators. . . .

Another grievance [of the Indians]: the English cattle and horses still increased [and that] . . . they could not keep their corn from being spoiled [by the English livestock]. . . .

So we departed without any discourtesies; and suddenly [c. June 25] had [a] letter from [the] Plymouth governor, [that] they intended in arms to [subjugate] Philip . . . and in a week's time after we had been with the Indians the war thus begun.

Source: John Easton, "A Relacion of the Indyan Warre, by Mr. Easton, of Roade Isld., 1675," in *Narratives of the Indian Wars, 1675–1699*, ed. Charles H. Lincoln (New York: Charles Scribner's Sons, 1913), 7–17.

Edward Randolph

Short Narrative of My Proceedings

Edward Randolph, an English customs official in Boston, denounced the independent policies of the Puritan colonies and tried to subject them to English control. His "Short Narrative," written in 1675, was a report to his superiors in London.

Various are the reports and conjectures of the causes of the present Indian war. Some impute it to an impudent zeal in the magistrates of Boston to Christianize those heathen before they were civilized and enjoining them the strict observation of their laws, which, to a people so rude and licentious, hath proved even intolerable. . . . While the magistrates, for their profit, put the laws severely in execution against the Indians, the people, on the other side, for lucre and gain, entice and provoke the Indians . . . to drunkenness, to which those people are so generally addicted that they will strip themselves to their skin to have their fill of rum and brandy. . . .

Some believe there have been vagrant and jesuitical [French] priests, who have made it their business, for some years past, to go from Sachem to Sachem [chief to chief], to exasperate the Indians against the English and to bring them into a confederacy, and that they were promised supplies from France and other parts to extirpate the English nation out of the continent of America. . . . Others impute the cause to some injuries offered to the Sachem Philip; for he being possessed of a tract of land called Mount Hope . . . some English had a mind to dispossess him thereof, who never wanting one pretence or other to attain their end, complained of injuries done by Philip and his Indians to their stock and cattle, whereupon Philip was often summoned before the magistrate, sometimes imprisoned, and never released but upon parting with a considerable part of his land.

But the government of the Massachusetts . . . do declare [that because of the sins of the people] . . . God hath given the heathen commission to rise against them. . . . For men wearing long hair and periwigs made of women's hair; for women . . . cutting, curling and laying out the hair. . . . For profaneness in the people not frequenting their [church] meetings.

Source: Albert B. Hart, ed., *American History Told by Contemporaries* (New York: Macmillan, 1897), 1: 458–460.

Benjamin Church
Entertaining Passages

Captain Benjamin Church fought in the war and helped end it by capturing Metacom's wife and son and leading the expedition that killed the Indian chieftain. Forty years later, in 1716, Church's son Thomas wrote an account of the war based on his father's notes and recollections.

While Mr. Church was diligently settling his new farm . . . Behold! The rumor of a war between the English and the natives gave a check to his projects. . . . Philip, according to his promise to his people, permitted them to march out of the neck [of the Mount Hope peninsula, where they lived]. . . . They plundered the nearest houses that the inhabitants had deserted [on the rumor of a war], but as yet offered no violence to the people, at least none were killed. . . . However, the alarm was given by their numbers, and hostile equipage, and by the prey they made of what they could find in the forsaken houses.

An express came the same day to the governor [c. June 25], who immediately gave orders to the captains of the towns to march the greatest part of their companies [of militia], and to rendezvous at Taunton. . . .

The enemy, who began their hostilities with plundering and destroying cattle, did not long content themselves with that game. They thirsted for English blood, and they soon broached it; killing two men in the way not far from Mr. Miles's garrison. And soon after, eight more at Mattapoisett, upon whose bodies they exercised more than brutish barbarities. . . .

These provocations drew out the resentment of some of Capt. Prentice's troop, who desired they might have liberty to go out and seek the enemy in their own quarters [c. June 26].

Source: Benjamin Church, *Entertaining Passages Relating to Philip's War Which Began in the Month of June, 1675*, ed. Thomas Church (Boston: B. Green, 1716).

ANALYZING THE EVIDENCE

- **What event or set of events led to the war?**
- **Where do the documents agree and disagree about the causes of the war? Given what you know from the discussion in the text, how might the war have been prevented?**
- **According to Randolph, what did the magistrates of Massachusetts Bay believe to be a major cause of the war? Could historians verify or disprove their explanation? How? What additional sources of evidence might be useful?**
- **Who was the prime instigator of the war? Which documents provide the most compelling evidence for your conclusion? Why?**

SUMMARY

We have seen that Spain created a permanent settlement in North America in 1565 and that England, France, and the Dutch Republic did likewise between 1607 and 1614. All of these European incursions inadvertently spread devastating diseases among the native residents and reduced some Indians to subject peoples. But there were important differences among the groups of settlers. The French and the Dutch established fur-trading colonies, while the Spanish and the English created settler colonies. Spanish settlers frequently intermarried with the Indians, but the English did not. Alone among the colonizers, the Dutch did not seek to convert the Indians to Christianity.

We also saw major differences between England's Chesapeake colonies, in which bound laborers raised tobacco for export to Europe, and those in New England, where pious Puritan yeomen lived in self-governing farming communities. Still, both regions boasted representative political institutions. Both experienced Indian wars in the first decades of settlement (1622 in Virginia and 1636 in New England) and again in 1675–1676. Indeed, the simultaneous eruption of Bacon's Rebellion and Metacom's War suggests that the histories of the two English regions had begun to converge.

CHAPTER REVIEW QUESTIONS

- Outline the goals of the directors of the Virginia Company and the leaders of the Massachusetts Bay Company. Where did they succeed? In what ways did they fall short?

- Why were there no major witchcraft scares in the Chesapeake colonies and no uprising like Bacon's Rebellion in New England? Consider the possible social, economic, and religious causes of both phenomena.

FOR FURTHER EXPLORATION

A fine narrative of Spanish activities north of the Rio Grande is David Weber's *The Spanish Frontier in North America* (1992). Alison Games, *Migration and the Origins of the English Atlantic World* (2001), sets English settlement in context. In *American Slavery, American Freedom* (1975), Edmund Morgan offers a compelling portrait of white servitude and black slavery in early Virginia. Colin Calloway, *New Worlds for All: Indians, Europeans, and the Remaking of Early America* (1997), is a broad overview, while John Demos, *The Unredeemed Captive* (1994), relates the gripping tale of Eunice Williams, a captured Puritan girl who lived her life among the Mohawks. Three recent books are Francis J. Bremer, *John Winthrop: America's Forgotten Founding Father* (2003); James D. Rice, *Nature & History in the Potomac Country* (2009); and Virginia DeJohn Anderson, *Creatures of Empire: How Domestic Animals Transformed Early America* (2004).

Two fine Web sites focus on the Pilgrims at Plymouth: "Caleb Johnson's Mayflower History" (**www.mayflowerhistory.com**) and "The Plymouth Colony Archive Project" (**www.histarch.uiuc.edu/plymouth/index.html**). For insight into early New England life, see the excellent eight-part PBS series *Colonial House* and its Web site (**www.pbs.org/wnet/colonialhouse**). Extensive materials on the Salem witchcraft trials can be viewed at **etext.virginia .edu/salem/witchcraft**.

TEST YOUR KNOWLEDGE

To assess your command of the material in this chapter, see the Online Study Guide at **bedfordstmartins.com/henretta**.

For Web sites, images, and documents related to topics and places in this chapter, visit **bedfordstmartins.com/makehistory**.

TIMELINE

1539–1543	Coronado and de Soto lead gold-seeking expeditions
1565	Spain establishes fort at St. Augustine
1598	Acomas rebel in New Mexico
1603–1625	Reign of James I, king of England
1607	English traders settle Jamestown (Virginia)
1608	Samuel de Champlain founds Quebec
1613	Dutch set up fur-trading post on Manhattan Island
1619	First Africans arrive in Chesapeake region House of Burgesses convenes in Virginia
1620	Pilgrims found Plymouth Colony
1620–1660	Chesapeake colonies enjoy tobacco boom
1621	Dutch West India Company chartered
1622	Opechancanough's uprising
1624	Virginia becomes royal colony
1625–1649	Reign of Charles I, king of England
1630	Puritans found Massachusetts Bay Colony
1634	Settlers arrive in Maryland
1636	Puritan-Pequot War Roger Williams founds Providence
1637	Anne Hutchinson banished from Massachusetts Bay
1640s	Iroquois initiate wars over fur trade
1642–1659	Puritan Revolution in England
1651	First Navigation Act
1660	Restoration of English monarchy Tobacco prices fall and remain low
1664	English conquer New Netherland
1675	Bacon's Rebellion in Virginia
1675–1676	Metacom's War in New England
1680	Popé's rebellion in New Mexico
1692	Salem witchcraft trials
1705	Virginia enacts law defining slavery

CHAPTER 3

Creating a British Empire in America, 1660-1750

When Charles II came to the throne in 1660, England was a second-class commercial power, its merchants picking up the crumbs left by the worldwide maritime empire of the Dutch. "What we want is more of the trade the Dutch now have," declared the Duke of Albemarle, a trusted minister of the king and a proprietor of Carolina. To get it, the English government embarked on a century-long quest for trade and empire in America and Asia. It passed the Navigation Acts, which prohibited "Ships of any Foreign Nation whatsoever to come to, Trade in, or Traffice with any of the English Plantations in America." Then, the English went to war to destroy Holland's maritime dominance. By the 1720s, Great Britain (the recently unified kingdoms of England and Scotland) had seized control of the transatlantic trade in American sugar, and the Royal African Company—and subsequently Liverpool merchants—had taken over the Atlantic slave trade. The emerging British Empire, boasted the ardent imperialist Malachy Postlethwayt, "was a magnificent superstructure of American commerce and naval power on an African foundation."

That was only the half of it. Great Britain's commerce now spanned the world: Its merchants exported woolen and iron manufactures to Europe, America, and Africa. From its trading posts in India, the British East India Company sent home cotton, indigo, and tea—15 percent of all British imports in 1720—and company ships carried silver to China to exchange for tea, ceramics, and silks. To protect the empire's valuable sugar colonies and trade routes and to force entry into the commerce of other empires, British ministers repeatedly waged war, first against the Dutch and then against the French. Boasted one English pamphleteer: "We are, of any nation, the best situated for trade, . . . capable of giving maritime laws to the world."

That dictum included Britain's North American and West Indian colonies, which were becoming increasingly valuable parts of the empire. By 1685 Charles II was earning £100,000 a year on excise taxes on tobacco from Virginia and even more from duties on sugar from the Caribbean. So when imperial official Edward Randolph reported that "there is no notice taken of the act of navigation," the home government decided to impose its political will on the American settlements.

Power and Race in the Chesapeake

In this 1670 painting by Gerard Soest, proprietor Lord Baltimore holds a map of Maryland, the colony he owned, and which would soon belong to his grandson Cecil Calvert, shown in the painting as already grasping his magnificent inheritance. The presence of a young African servant foretells the importance of slave labor in the post-1700 economy of the Chesapeake colonies. Enoch Pratt Free Library of Baltimore.

The Politics of Empire, 1660–1713

Before 1660, England governed its New England and Chesapeake colonies haphazardly. Taking advantage of that laxness and the English civil war, local "big men" (Puritan magistrates and tobacco planters) ran their societies as they wished. Following the restoration of the monarchy in 1660, royal bureaucrats tried to impose order on the unruly settlements and, enlisting the aid of Indian allies, warred with rival European powers.

Imperial Expansion and Aristocratic Power

Charles II (r. 1660–1685) expanded English power in Asia and America. In 1662, he married the Portuguese princess Catherine of Braganza, whose dowry included the islands of Bombay (present-day Mumbai). The following year, Charles initiated new outposts in America by authorizing eight loyal noblemen to settle Carolina, an area that had long been claimed by Spain and populated by thousands of Indians. Subsequently, he awarded the just-conquered Dutch colony of New Netherland to his brother James, the Duke of York (who renamed the colony New York). In a great land grab, England had ousted the Dutch from North America and intruded into Spain's northern empire.

The Carolinas   Like Lord Baltimore's Maryland, the new settlements—the Restoration Colonies, as historians call them—were proprietorships: The Duke of York and his fellow aristocrats in Carolina owned all the land and could rule their colonies as they wished, provided that their laws conformed broadly to those of England (Table 3.1). Indeed, in New York, James II refused to allow an elective assembly and ruled by decree. The Carolina proprietors envisioned a traditional European society; the Fundamental Constitutions of Carolina (1669) legally established the Church of England and prescribed a **manorial system**, with a mass of serfs governed by a handful of powerful nobles.

The manorial system proved a fantasy. The first North Carolina settlers were a mixture of poor families and runaway servants from Virginia and English Quakers, an equality-minded Protestant sect (also known as the Society of Friends). Quakers "think there is no difference between a Gentleman and a labourer," complained an Anglican clergyman. Refusing to work on large manors, the settlers raised corn, hogs, and tobacco on modest family farms. Inspired by Bacon's Rebellion in Virginia, the residents of Albemarle County staged an uprising in 1677 against taxes on tobacco and rebelled again in 1708, this time against taxes to support the Anglican Church. The residents were "stubborn and disobedient," a wealthy Anglican landowner charged; nonetheless, and by resisting a series of governors, they

---

TABLE 3.1

English Colonies Established in North America, 1660–1750

Colony	Date	Original Colony Type	Religion	Status in 1775	Chief Export/ Economic Activity
Carolina	1663	Proprietary	Church of England	Royal	
North	1691				Farming, naval stores
South	1691				Rice, indigo
New Jersey	1664	Proprietary	Church of England	Royal	Wheat
New York	1664	Proprietary	Church of England	Royal	Wheat
Pennsylvania	1681	Proprietary	Quaker	Proprietary	Wheat
Georgia	1732	Trustees	Church of England	Royal	Rice
New Hampshire (separated from Massachusetts)	1741	Royal	Congregationalist	Royal	Mixed farming, lumber, naval stores
Nova Scotia	1749	Royal	Church of England	Royal	Fishing, mixed farming, naval stores

forced the proprietors to abandon their dreams of a feudal society.

In South Carolina, the colonists also went their own way. The leading white settlers there were migrants from the overcrowded sugar-producing island of Barbados, and wanted to re-create that island's hierarchical slave society. They used enslaved workers—both Africans and Native Americans—to raise cattle and food crops for export to the West Indies. Carolina merchants opened a lucrative trade in deerskins with neighboring Indian peoples. In exchange for rum and guns, the Carolinians' Indian trading partners also provided slaves—captives from other Native American peoples. By 1708, white Carolinians were working their coastal plantations with 1,400 Indian and 2,900 African slaves, and brutal Indian warfare continued in the backcountry. South Car-olina would remain a violent frontier settlement until the 1720s.

William Penn and Pennsylvania | In dramatic contrast to the Caro-linians, the 15,000 migrants who settled in Pennsylvania in the late seventeenth century pursued a pacifistic policy toward Native Americans and quickly became prosperous. In 1681, Charles II bestowed Pennsylvania (which included present-day Delaware) on William Penn as payment for a large debt owed to Penn's father. The younger Penn, though born to wealth—he owned substantial estates in Ireland and England, and lived lavishly—joined the Quakers, who condemned extravagance. Penn designed Pennsylvania as a refuge for his fellow Quakers, who were persecuted in England because they refused to

William Penn's Treaty with the Indians, 1683
Benjamin West executed this famous picture of William Penn's meeting with the Lenni-Lenapes, who called themselves the Common People. A Quaker pacifist, Penn refused to seize Indian lands by force and negotiated their purchase. But his son, Thomas Penn, probably had a political purpose when he commissioned the painting in 1771. By evoking a peaceful past, West's work reinforced the Penn family's proprietary claims, which were under strong attack by the Pennsylvania assembly.   Courtesy of the Pennsylvania Academy of Fine Arts, Philadelphia (Gift of Mrs. Sarah Harrison; the Joseph Harrison Jr. Collection).

serve in the military or pay taxes to support the Church of England. Penn himself had spent more than two years in jail in England for preaching his beliefs.

Like the Puritans, the Quakers sought to restore Christianity to its early simple spirituality. But they rejected the Puritans' pessimistic Calvinist doctrines, which restricted salvation to a small elect. The Quakers followed the teachings of two English visionaries, George Fox and Margaret Fell, who argued that God had imbued all men—and women—with an "inner light" of grace or understanding. Reflecting the sect's emphasis on gender equality, 350 Quaker women would serve as ministers in the colonies.

Penn's Frame of Government (1681) applied the Quakers' radical beliefs to politics. It ensured religious freedom by prohibiting a legally established church, and it promoted political equality by allowing all property-owning men to vote and hold office. Cheered by these provisions, thousands of Quakers—mostly yeoman families from the northwest Midland region of England—flocked to Pennsylvania. Initially, they settled along the Delaware River near the city of Philadelphia, which Penn himself laid out in a grid with wide main streets and many parks. To attract European Protestants, Penn published pamphlets in Germany promising cheap land and religious toleration. In 1683, migrants from Saxony founded Germantown (just outside Philadelphia), and thousands of other Germans soon followed. Ethnic diversity, pacifism, and freedom of conscience made Pennsylvania the most open and democratic of the Restoration Colonies.

From Mercantilism to Imperial Dominion

As Charles II distributed his American lands, his ministers devised policies to keep their trade—and that of other colonies—in English hands. Since the 1560s, the English crown had pursued mercantilist policies, using government subsidies and charters to stimulate English manufacturing and foreign trade. Now it extended these mercantilist strategies to the American settlements through the Navigation Acts (Table 3.2).

The Navigation Acts | English ministers wanted the colonies to produce agricultural goods and raw materials for English merchants to carry to England. Certain products would then be exported immediately to Europe in return for gold or goods; other imports would be manufactured into finished products and then exported. The Navigation Act of 1651 attempted to keep colonial trade in English hands by excluding Dutch and French vessels from American ports; the act also required that goods be carried only on ships owned by English or colonial merchants. New parliamentary acts in 1660 and 1663 strengthened the ban on foreign traders, requiring colonists to export sugar and tobacco only to England, and mandating that colonists import European goods only through England. To pay the customs officials who enforced these mercantilist laws, the Revenue Act of 1673 imposed a "plantation duty" on American exports of sugar and tobacco.

TABLE 3.2		
Navigation Acts, 1651–1751		
	Purpose	**Compliance**
Act of 1651	Cut Dutch trade	Mostly ignored
Act of 1660	Ban foreign shipping; enumerate goods that go only to England	*Partially obeyed*
Act of 1663	Allow European imports only through England	*Partially obeyed*
Staple Act (1673)	Ensure enumerated goods go only to England	Mostly obeyed
Act of 1696	Prevent frauds; create vice-admiralty courts	Mostly obeyed
Woolen Act (1699)	Prevent export or intercolonial sale of textiles	*Partially obeyed*
Hat Act (1732)	Prevent export or intercolonial sale of hats	*Partially obeyed*
Molasses Act (1733)	Cut American imports of molasses from French West Indies	**Extensively violated**
Iron Act (1750)	Prevent manufacture of finished iron products	**Extensively violated**
Currency Act (1751)	End use of paper currency as legal tender in New England	Mostly obeyed

The English government backed these policies with military force. In three commercial wars between 1652 and 1674, the English navy drove the Dutch from New Netherland and contested Holland's control of the Atlantic slave trade by attacking Dutch forts and ships along the West African coast. Meanwhile, English merchants expanded their fleets, which increased in capacity from 150,000 tons in 1640 to 340,000 tons in 1690.

Many colonists ignored the mercantilist laws and, until the wars of the 1690s, continued to trade with Dutch merchants. They also imported sugar and molasses from the French West Indies. The Massachusetts Bay assembly boldly declared: "The laws of England are bounded within the seas [surrounding it] and do not reach America." Outraged by this insolence, customs official Edward Randolph called for troops to "reduce Massachusetts to obedience." Instead, the Lords of Trade—the administrative body charged with colonial affairs—opted for a punitive legal strategy. In 1679, it denied the claim of Massachusetts Bay to New Hampshire and eventually established a separate royal colony there. Then, in 1684, the Lords of Trade persuaded an English court to annul the Massachusetts Bay charter by charging the Puritan government with violating the Navigation Acts and virtually outlawing the Church of England.

The Dominion of New England

The Puritans' troubles had only begun, thanks to the accession of King James II (r. 1685–1688), an aggressive and inflexible ruler. During the reign of Oliver Cromwell, James had grown up in exile in France, and he admired its authoritarian king, Louis XIV. Believing that monarchs had a "divine right" to rule, James instructed the Lords of Trade to impose strict royal control on the American colonies. In 1686, the Lords revoked the corporate charters of Connecticut and Rhode Island and merged them with the Massachusetts Bay and Plymouth colonies to form a new royal province, the Dominion of New England. As governor of the Dominion, James II appointed Sir Edmund Andros, a hard-edged former military officer. Two years later, James II added New York and New Jersey to the Dominion, creating a vast colony that stretched from Maine to Pennsylvania (Map 3.1).

The Dominion extended to America the authoritarian model of colonial rule that the English government had imposed on Catholic Ireland. James II ordered Governor Andros to abolish the existing legislative assemblies. In Massachusetts, Andros immediately banned town meetings, angering villagers who prized local self-rule; and advocated public worship in the Church of England, offending Puritan Congregationalists. Even worse,

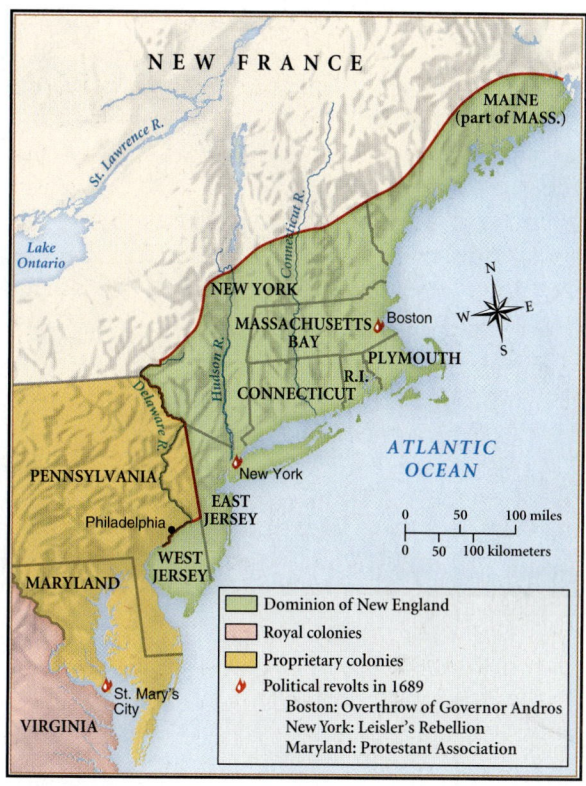

MAP 3.1

The Dominion of New England, 1686–1689

In the Dominion, James II created a vast royal colony that stretched nearly 500 miles along the Atlantic coast. During the Glorious Revolution in England, politicians and ministers in Boston and New York City led revolts that ousted Dominion officials and repudiated their authority. King William and Queen Mary replaced the Dominion with governments that balanced the power held by imperial authorities and local political institutions.

from the colonists' perspective, the governor challenged all land titles granted under the original Massachusetts Bay charter. Andros offered to provide new deeds, but only if the colonists would agree to pay an annual fee.

The Glorious Revolution in England and America

Fortunately for the colonists, James II angered English political leaders as much as Andros alienated American settlers. The king revoked the charters of English towns, rejected the advice of Parliament, and aroused popular opposition by openly practicing Roman Catholicism. Then, in 1688, James's Spanish Catholic wife gave birth to a son, raising the prospect of a Catholic heir to the throne. To forestall that outcome, Protestant bishops and parliamentary leaders in the **Whig** Party led

The Leviathan Absolutist State

This detail from the title-page engraving of Thomas Hobbes's *Leviathan* (1651) conveys Hobbes's belief that peace and security required submission to a powerful sovereign. In this image, a giant king looms over his domain, his staff and sword symbolizing his civil and religious powers. He is the head of a body made up of the multitudes of his faceless and voiceless subjects, as they carry out his commands. What Hobbes celebrated, a majority of English politicians and people rejected. Fearing the claims of absolute power by Stuart kings, they revolted twice, executing Charles I in 1642 and deposing James II in 1688.   Library of Congress.

a quick and bloodless coup known as the Glorious Revolution. Backed by the populace and the military, the bishops and Whigs forced James into exile and in 1689 enthroned Mary, his Protestant daughter by his first wife, and her Dutch Protestant husband, William of Orange. Whig politicians forced King William and Queen Mary to accept the Declaration of Rights, creating a constitutional monarchy that enhanced the powers of the House of Commons at the expense of the crown. The Whigs wanted political power—especially the power to levy taxes—to reside in the hands of the gentry, merchants, and other substantial property owners.

To justify their coup, the members of Parliament relied on political philosopher John Locke. In his *Two Treatises on Government* (1690), Locke rejected the divine-right monarchy celebrated by James II, arguing that the legitimacy of government rests on the consent of the governed and that individuals have inalienable natural rights to life, liberty, and property. Locke's celebration of individual rights and representative government had a lasting influence in America, where many political leaders wanted to expand the powers of the colonial assemblies.

Rebellions in America The Glorious Revolution sparked rebellions by Protestant colonists in Massachusetts, Maryland, and New York. When news of the coup reached Boston in April 1689, Puritan leaders and 2,000 militiamen seized Governor Andros,

accused him of Catholic sympathies, and shipped him back to England. Heeding American complaints of authoritarian rule, the new monarchs broke up the Dominion of New England. However, they refused to restore the old Puritan-dominated government of Massachusetts Bay, instead creating in 1692 a new royal colony (which included Plymouth and Maine). The new charter empowered the king to appoint the governor and customs officials, gave the vote to all male property owners (not just Puritan church members), and eliminated Puritan restrictions on the Church of England.

The uprising in Maryland had economic as well as religious causes. Since 1660, falling prices had hurt tobacco-growing smallholders, tenant farmers, and former indentured servants. These poorer farmers were overwhelmingly Protestant, and they resented the rising taxes and fees imposed by wealthy proprietary officials, who were mostly Catholic. When Parliament ousted James II, a Protestant association mustered 700 men and forcibly removed the Catholic governor. The Lords of Trade supported this Protestant initiative: They suspended Lord Baltimore's proprietorship, imposed royal government, and made the Church of England the legal religion in the colony. This arrangement lasted until 1715, when Benedict Calvert, the fourth Lord Baltimore, converted to the Anglican faith and the king restored the proprietorship to the Calvert family.

In New York, Jacob Leisler led the rebellion against the Dominion of New England. Leisler, once a German

A Prosperous Dutch Farmstead

Dutch farmers in the Hudson River Valley prospered because of their easy access to markets downstream at New York, and their exploitation of black slaves (three of whom can be seen in this painting), which they owned in far greater numbers than did their English neighbors. To record his good fortune, Martin Van Bergen of Leeds, New York, had this mural painted over his mantelpiece. New-York State Historical Association.

soldier for the Dutch West India Company, had become a merchant and married into a prominent Dutch family in New York. He was a militant Calvinist, rigid and hot-tempered; but he quickly emerged as a leader of the Dutch Protestant artisans in New York City, who welcomed the succession of Queen Mary and her Dutch husband. Led by Leisler, the Dutch militia ousted Lieutenant Governor Nicholson, an Andros appointee and an alleged Catholic sympathizer.

Initially, all classes and ethnic groups rallied behind Leisler, who headed a temporary government. However, Leisler's denunciations of political rivals as "popish dogs" and "Roages, Rascalls, and Devills" soon alienated many English-speaking New Yorkers. When Leisler imprisoned 40 of his political opponents, imposed new taxes, and championed the artisans' cause, the prominent Dutch merchants who had traditionally controlled the city's government also condemned his rule. In 1691, the merchants found an ally in Colonel Henry Sloughter, the newly appointed governor, who had Leisler indicted for treason. Convicted by an English jury, Leisler was hanged and then decapitated, an act of ethnic vengeance that corrupted New York politics for a generation.

The Glorious Revolution of 1688–1689 began a new, nonauthoritarian political era in both England and America. In England, William and Mary ruled as constitutional monarchs and promoted an empire based on commerce. Because the new Protestant monarchs wanted American support for a war against Catholic France, they accepted the overthrow of the Dominion of New England and allowed the restoration of self-government in Massachusetts and New York. Parliament created a Board of Trade in 1696 to supervise the American settlements, but it had limited success. Settlers and proprietors resisted the board's attempt to install royal governments, as did many English political leaders, who feared an increase in monarchical power. The result was another period of lax political administration. The home government imposed only a few laws and taxes on the North American settlements, allowed rule by local elites, and encouraged English merchants to develop them as sources of trade.

Imperial Wars and Native Peoples

In a world of commercial competition, Britain's success depended on both mercantile skills and military power. Between 1689 and 1815, Britain fought a series of increasingly intense wars with France (Table 3.3). To win wars in Western Europe, the Caribbean, and far-flung oceans, British leaders created a powerful central state that spent three-quarters of its revenue on military and naval expenses. As the conflicts spread to the North American mainland, they drew in Native American peoples, who tried to turn the fighting to their own advantage.

The first significant battles in North America occurred during the War of the Spanish Succession

TABLE 3.3

English Wars, 1650–1750

War	Date	Purpose	Result
Anglo-Dutch	1652–1654	Control markets and African slave trade	Stalemate
Anglo-Dutch	1664	Markets; conquest	England takes New Amsterdam
Anglo-Dutch	1673	Commercial markets	England makes maritime gains
King William's	1689–1697	Maintain European balance of power	Stalemate in North America
Queen Anne's	1702–1713	Maintain European balance of power	British acquire Hudson Bay and Nova Scotia
Jenkins's Ear	1739–1741	Expand markets in Spanish America	English merchants expand influence
King George's	1740–1748	Maintain European balance of power	Capture and return of Louisbourg

(1702–1713), which pitted Britain against France and Spain. English settlers in the Carolinas armed the Creeks, whose 15,000 members farmed the fertile lands along the present-day border of Georgia and Alabama. A joint English-Creek expedition attacked Spanish Florida, burning the town of St. Augustine but failing to capture the nearby fort. To protect Havana in nearby Cuba, the Spanish reinforced St. Augustine and unsuccessfully attacked Charleston, South Carolina.

Indian Goals The Creeks had their own agenda: To become the dominant tribe in the region, they needed to vanquish their longtime enemies, the pro-French Choctaws to the west and the Spanish-allied Apalachees to the south. Beginning in 1704, a force of Creek and Yamasee warriors destroyed the remaining Franciscan missions in northern Florida, attacked the Spanish settlement at Pensacola, and captured a thousand Apalachees, whom they sold to South Carolinian slave traders for sale in the West Indies. Simultaneously, a Carolina-supported Creek expedition attacked the Iroquois-speaking Tuscarora people of North Carolina, killing hundreds, executing 160 male captives, and sending 400 women and children into slavery. The surviving Tuscaroras joined the Iroquois in New York (who now became the Six Nations of the Iroquois). The Carolinians, having used the Creeks to kill Spaniards, now died at the hands of their former allies. When English traders demanded payment for trade debts in 1715, the Creeks and Yamasees revolted. They killed 400 colonists before being overwhelmed by the Carolinians and their new Indian allies, the Cherokees.

Native Americans also joined in the warfare between French Catholics in Canada and English Protestants in New England. With French aid, Catholic Mohawk and Abenaki warriors took revenge on their Puritan enemies. They destroyed English settlements in Maine and, in 1704, attacked the western Massachusetts town of Deerfield, where they killed 48 residents and carried 112 into captivity. In response, New England militia attacked French settlements and, in 1710, joined with British naval forces to seize Port Royal in French Acadia (Nova Scotia). However, a major British–New England expedition against the French stronghold at Quebec, inspired in part by the visit of four Indian "kings" to London, failed miserably.

The New York frontier remained quiet. French and English merchants did not want to disrupt the lucrative fur trade, and the Earl of Bellomont, governor of New York, counseled caution: A "general defection of the Indians," he warned in 1700, would "drive us quite out of this Continent." However, the Iroquois, tired of war, had adopted a policy of "aggressive neutrality." In 1701, they concluded a peace treaty with France and its Indian allies and renewed the Covenant Chain, a quasi-alliance with the English government in New York and various Indian peoples who were their dependents (see Chapter 2). For the next half century, the Iroquois exploited their strategic location by trading with both the English and the French colonies but refusing to fight for either. Their strategy, according to their Delaware ally Teedyuscung, was "to defend our land against both."

Stalemated militarily in America, Britain won major territorial and commercial concessions through its

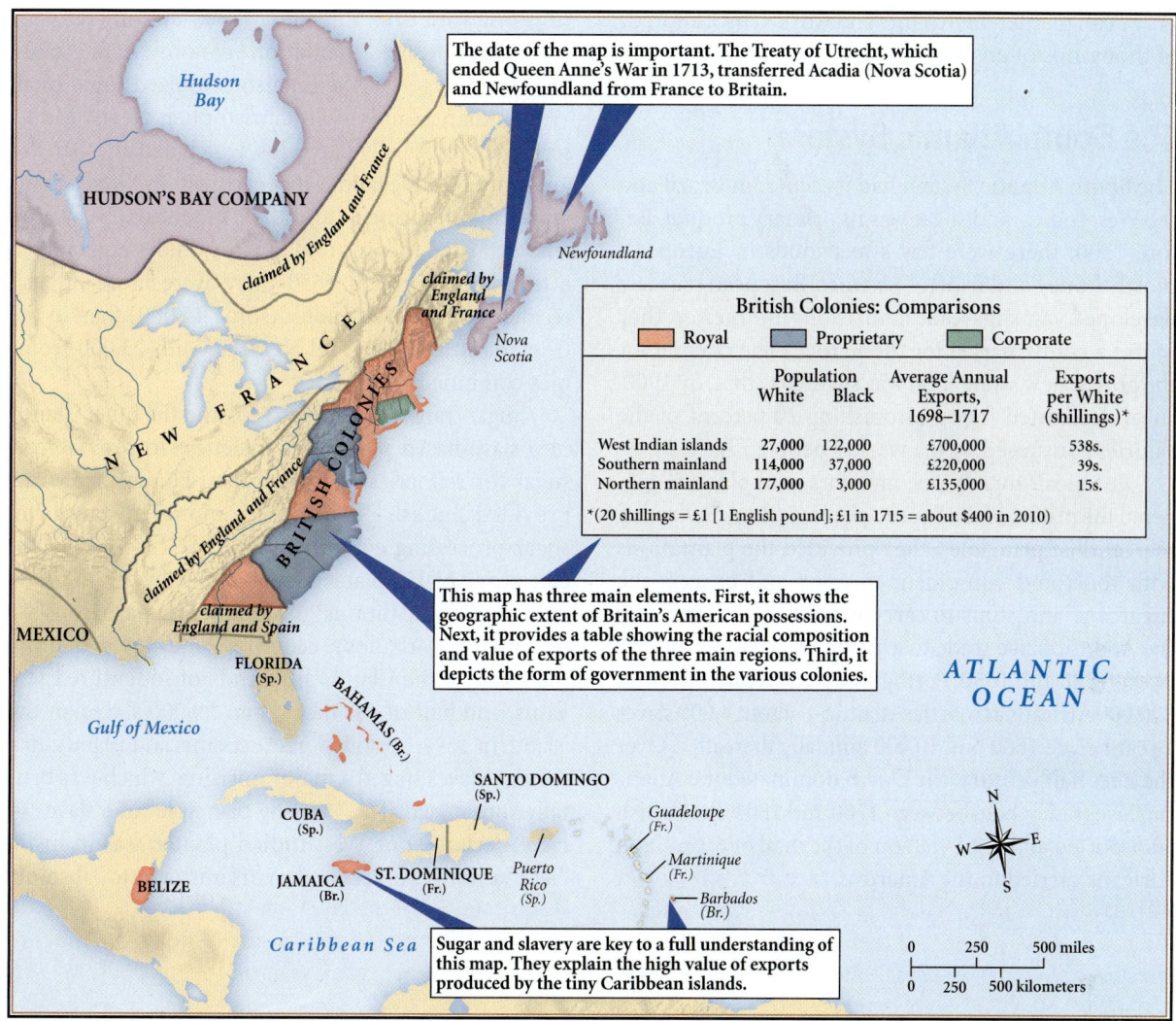

The date of the map is important. The Treaty of Utrecht, which ended Queen Anne's War in 1713, transferred Acadia (Nova Scotia) and Newfoundland from France to Britain.

This map has three main elements. First, it shows the geographic extent of Britain's American possessions. Next, it provides a table showing the racial composition and value of exports of the three main regions. Third, it depicts the form of government in the various colonies.

Sugar and slavery are key to a full understanding of this map. They explain the high value of exports produced by the tiny Caribbean islands.

British Colonies: Comparisons

Royal Proprietary Corporate

	Population White	Black	Average Annual Exports, 1698–1717	Exports per White (shillings)*
West Indian islands	27,000	122,000	£700,000	538s.
Southern mainland	114,000	37,000	£220,000	39s.
Northern mainland	177,000	3,000	£135,000	15s.

*(20 shillings = £1 [1 English pound]; £1 in 1715 = about $400 in 2010)

MAP 3.2

Britain's American Empire, 1713

Many of Britain's possessions in the West Indies were tiny islands, mere dots on the Caribbean Sea. However, in 1713, these small pieces of land were by far the most valuable parts of the empire. Their sugar crops brought wealth to English merchants, commerce to the northern colonies, and a brutal life and early death to the hundreds of thousands of African slaves working on the plantations.

victories in Europe. In the Treaty of Utrecht (1713), Britain obtained Newfoundland, Acadia, and the Hudson Bay region of northern Canada from France, as well as access through Albany to the western Indian trade. From Spain, Britain acquired the strategic fortress of Gibraltar at the entrance to the Mediterranean and a thirty-year contract to supply slaves to Spanish America. These gains advanced Britain's quest for commercial supremacy and brought peace to eastern North America for a generation (Map 3.2).

- **What was the role of the colonies in the British mercantilist system?**

- **Explain the causes and the results of the Glorious Revolution in England and America.**

The Imperial Slave Economy

Britain's focus on America reflected the growth of a new agricultural and commercial order—the South Atlantic System—that produced sugar, tobacco, rice, and other subtropical products for an international market. At its center stood plantation societies ruled by

European planter-merchants and worked by hundreds of thousands of enslaved Africans (Figure 3.1).

The South Atlantic System

The South Atlantic System had its center in Brazil and the West Indies, and sugar was its primary product. Before 1500, there were few sweet foods in Europe — mostly honey and fruits — so when European planters developed vast sugarcane plantations in America, they found a ready market for their crop. (The craving for the potent new sweet food was so intense that, by 1900, sugar accounted for an astonishing 20 percent of the calories consumed by the world's people.)

European merchants, investors, and planters garnered the profits of the South Atlantic System. Following mercantilist principles, they provided the plantations with tools and equipment to grow and process the sugarcane and ships to carry it to Europe. But it was the Atlantic slave trade that made the system run. Between 1520 and 1650, Portuguese traders carried about 820,000 Africans across the Atlantic — about 4,000 slaves a year before 1600 and 10,000 annually thereafter. Over the next half century, the Dutch dominated the Atlantic slave trade; then, between 1700 and 1800, the British transported about 2.5 million of the total of 6.1 million Africans carried to the Americas.

England and the West Indies England was a latecomer to the plantation economy. In the 1620s, the English colonized some small West Indian islands — St. Christopher, Nevis, Montserrat, and especially Barbados, which had an extensive amount of arable land. Most early settlers were small-scale English farmers (and their indentured servants) who exported tobacco and livestock hides and created a thriving colony. In 1650 there were more English residents in the West Indies (some 44,000) than in the Chesapeake (20,000) and New England (23,000) colonies combined.

Sugar transformed Barbados and the other islands into slave-based plantation societies. To provide raw sugar for refineries in Amsterdam, Dutch merchants provided English planters with money to buy land, sugar-processing equipment, and slaves. By 1680, an elite group of 175 planters — described by one antislavery writer of the time as "inhumane and barbarous" — dominated Barbados's economy; they owned more than half of the island, thousands of indentured servants, and half of the more than 50,000 slaves on the island. In 1692, exploited Irish servants and island-born African slaves staged a major uprising, which was brutally suppressed. The "leading principle" in a slave society, declared one West Indian planter, was to instill "fear" among workers and a commitment to "absolute

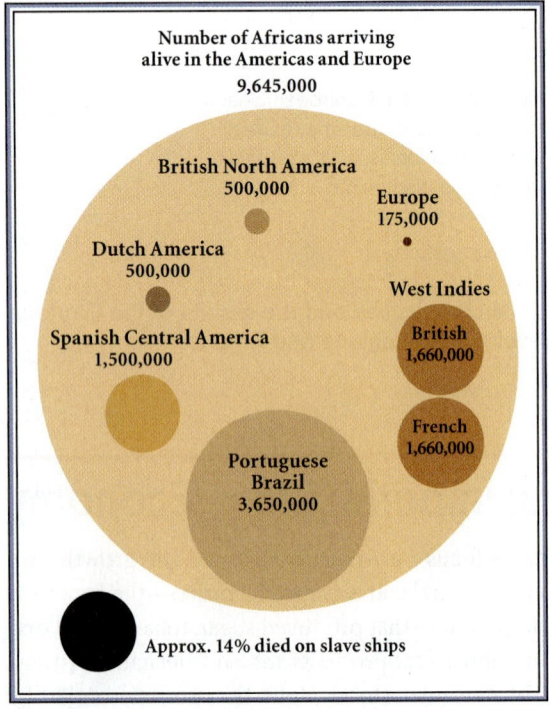

FIGURE 3.1

The Transit of Africans to the Americas

Though approximately 11 million enslaved Africans boarded ships to the Americas, about 1.5 million (14 percent) of them died en route. Two-thirds of the survivors ended up in Brazil (3.65 million) and the West Indies (3.32 million), where they worked primarily on sugar plantations. Only 0.5 million landed in the present-day United States.

A Sugar Mill in the French West Indies, 1655
Making sugar required both hard labor and considerable expertise. Field slaves labored strenuously in the hot tropical sun to cut the sugarcane and carry or cart it to an oxen- or wind-powered mill, where it was pressed to yield the juice. Then skilled slave artisans took over. They carefully heated the juice and, at the proper moment, added ingredients that granulated the sugar and separated it from the molasses, which was later distilled into rum.   The Granger Collection, New York.

coercive" force among masters. As social inequality and racial conflict increased, hundreds of English farmers fled to South Carolina and the large island of Jamaica, which England had seized from Spain in 1655. But the days of Caribbean smallholders were numbered. English sugar merchants soon invested heavily in Jamaica; by 1750, it had seven hundred large sugar plantations—worked by more than 105,000 slaves—and had become the wealthiest British colony.

Sugar was a rich man's crop because it could be produced most efficiently on large plantations. Scores of slaves planted and cut the sugarcane, which was then processed by expensive equipment—crushing mills, boiling houses, distilling apparatus—into raw sugar, molasses, and rum. The affluent planter-merchants who controlled the sugar industry drew annual profits of more than 10 percent on their investment. As Scottish economist Adam Smith noted in his famous treatise *The Wealth of Nations* (1776), sugar was the most profitable crop grown in America or Europe.

The Impact on Britain | The South Atlantic System brought wealth to the entire British—and European—economy, and helped Europeans achieve world economic leadership. Most British West Indian plantations belonged to absentee owners who lived in England, where they spent their profits and formed a powerful "sugar lobby." The Navigation

Acts kept the British sugar trade in the hands of British merchants, who exported it to foreign markets. By 1750, reshipments of American sugar and tobacco to Europe accounted for half of British exports. Enormous profits also flowed into Britain from the slave trade. The value of the guns, iron, rum, and cloth that were used to buy slaves was only about one-tenth (in the 1680s) to one-third (by the 1780s) of the value of the crops those slaves produced in America. This substantial differential allowed the Royal African Company and other English traders to sell slaves in the West Indies for three to five times what they paid for them in Africa.

These massive profits drove the slave trade. At its height in the 1790s, Britain annually exported three hundred thousand guns to Africa, and a British ship carrying 300 to 350 slaves left an African port every other day. This commerce stimulated the entire British economy. English and Scottish shipyards built hundreds of vessels, and thousands of people worked in trade-related industries: building port facilities and warehouses, refining sugar and tobacco, distilling rum from molasses, and manufacturing textiles and iron products for the growing markets in Africa and America. More than one thousand British merchant ships were plying the Atlantic by 1750, providing a supply of experienced sailors and laying the foundation for the supremacy of the Royal Navy.

Africa, Africans, and the Slave Trade

As the South Atlantic System enhanced European prosperity, it imposed enormous costs on West and Central Africa. Between 1550 and 1870, the Atlantic slave trade uprooted eleven million Africans, draining lands south of the Sahara of people and wealth and changing African society (Map 3.3). By directing commerce away from the savannas and the Islamic world on the other side of the Sahara, the Atlantic slave trade changed the economic and religious dynamics of the African interior. It also fostered militaristic, centralized states in the coastal areas.

Africans and the Slave Trade | Warfare and slaving had been part of African life for centuries, driven by conflicts among numerous states and ethnic groups. But the South Atlantic System made slaving a favorite tactic of ambitious kings and plundering warlords. "Whenever the King of Barsally wants Goods or Brandy," an observer noted, "the King goes and ransacks some of his enemies' towns, seizing the people and selling them." Supplying slaves became a way of life in the West African state of Dahomey, where the royal house monopolized the sale of slaves and used European guns to create a military despotism. Dahomey's army, which included a contingent of 5,000 women, raided the interior for captives; between 1680 and 1730, Dahomey annually exported 20,000 slaves exported from the ports of Allada and Whydah. The Asante kings likewise used slaving to conquer states along the Gold Coast as well as Muslim kingdoms in the savanna. By the 1720s, they had created a prosperous empire of 3 to 5 million people. Yet participation in Atlantic trade remained a choice for Africans, not a necessity. The powerful kingdom of Benin, famous for its cast bronzes and carved ivory, prohibited for decades the export of all slaves, male and female. Other Africans expiated their guilt for selling neighbors into slavery by building hidden shrines, often in the household granary.

The trade in humans produced untold misery. Hundreds of thousands of young Africans died, and millions more endured a brutal life in the Americas. In Africa itself, class divisions hardened as people of noble birth enslaved and sold those of lesser status. Gender relations shifted as well. Two-thirds of the slaves sent across the Atlantic were men, because European planters paid more for men and "stout men boys" and because Africans sold enslaved women locally and across the Sahara as agricultural workers, house servants, and concubines. The resulting sexual imbalance prompted African men to take several wives, changing the meaning of marriage. Finally, the expansion of the Atlantic trade increased the extent of slavery in Africa. Sultan Mawlay Ismail of Morocco (r. 1672–1727) owned 150,000 black slaves, obtained by trade in Timbuktu and in wars he waged in Senegal. In Africa, as in the Americas, slavery eroded the dignity of human life.

The Middle Passage | Africans sold into the South Atlantic System suffered the bleakest fate. Torn from their villages, they were marched in chains to coastal ports, their first passage in slavery. Then, they endured the perilous **Middle Passage** to the New World in hideously overcrowded ships. The captives had little to eat or drink, and some died from dehydration. The feces, urine, and vomit below-decks prompted outbreaks of dysentery, which took more lives. "I was so overcome by the heat, stench, and foul air that I nearly fainted," reported a European doctor. Some slaves jumped overboard, choosing to drown rather than endure more suffering (see Voices from Abroad, "Olaudah Equiano: The Brutal 'Middle Passage,'" p. 88). Others staged violent shipboard revolts. Slave uprisings occurred on two thousand voyages, roughly one of every ten Atlantic passages. Nearly 100,000 slaves died in these

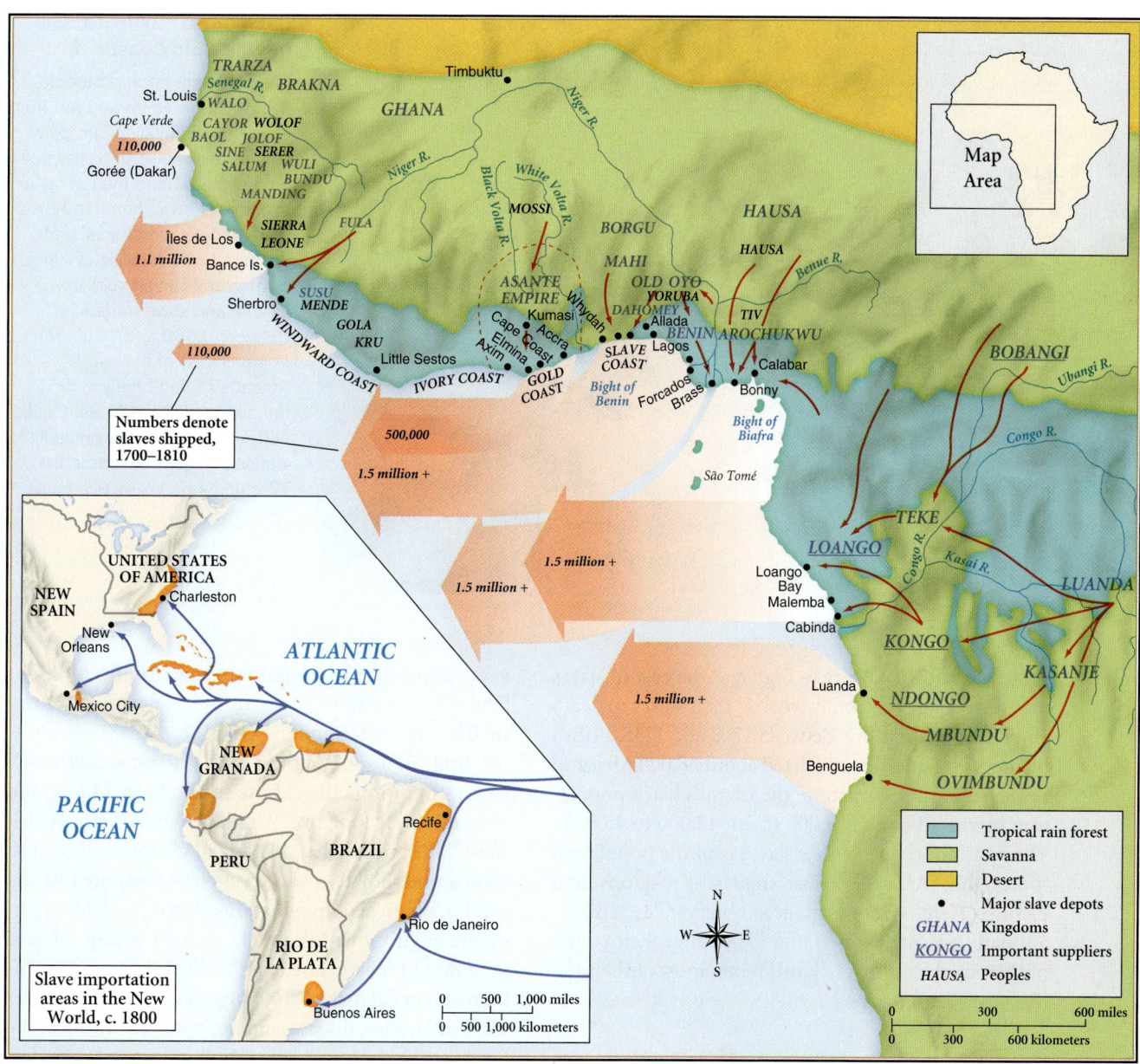

MAP 3.3

Africa and the Atlantic Slave Trade, 1700–1810

The tropical rain forest of West Africa was home to scores of peoples and dozens of kingdoms. With the rise of the slave trade, some of these kingdoms became aggressive slavers. Dahomey's army, for example, seized tens of thousands of captives in wars with neighboring peoples and sold them to European traders. About 14 percent of the captives died during the grueling Middle Passage, the transatlantic voyage between Africa and the Americas. Most of the survivors labored on sugar plantations in Brazil and the British and French West Indies (see Table 3.4).

insurrections, and nearly 1.5 million others—about 14 percent of those who were transported—died of disease or illness on the month-long journey.

For those who survived the Atlantic crossing, things only got worse as they passed into endless slavery. Life on the sugar plantations of northwestern Brazil and the

West Indies was one of relentless exploitation. Slaves worked ten hours a day under the hot semitropical sun; slept in flimsy huts; and lived on a starchy diet of corn, yams, and dried fish. They were subjected to brutal discipline: "The fear of punishment is the principle [we use] . . . to keep them in awe and order," one planter

Cape Coast Castle, Ghana (on the Gold Coast)

The guns that once protected this British slave-trading fort from naval attacks by rival European nations and pirate ships still point out to sea. Behind the fort lay a substantial town, home to African slave traders, merchants, and the mixed-race families of African women and British soldiers, sailors, and slave traders. Between 1660 and 1800, tens of thousands of enslaved Africans stayed briefly in the dungeons of Cape Coast Castle before being shipped primarily to Britain's sugar colonies in the West Indies.   Werner Foreman/Art Resource, NY.

declared. With sugar prices high and the cost of slaves low, many planters simply worked their slaves to death and then bought more: Between 1708 and 1735, British planters on Barbados imported about 85,000 Africans; however, in that same time the island's black population increased by only 4,000 (from 42,000 to 46,000). The constant influx of new slaves kept the population thoroughly "African" in its languages, religions, and culture. "Here," wrote a Jamaican observer, "each different nation of Africa meet and dance after the manner of their own country . . . [and] retain most of their native customs."

Slavery in the Chesapeake and South Carolina

West Indian–type slavery came to Virginia and Maryland following Bacon's Rebellion as elite planter-politicians led a "tobacco revolution." They took advantage of the expansion of the British slave trade (following the end of the Royal African Company's monopoly in 1698) and bought more Africans, putting these slaves to work on ever-larger plantations. By 1720, Africans made up 20 percent of the Chesapeake population; by 1740, nearly 40 percent. Slavery had become a core institution, no longer just one of several forms of unfree labor. Moreover, slavery was now defined in racial terms. Virginia legislators prohibited sexual intercourse between English and Africans and defined virtually all resident Africans as slaves: "All ser-

vants imported or brought into this country by sea or land who were not Christians in their native country shall be accounted and be slaves."

Still, slaves in Virginia and Maryland had much better conditions than those in the West Indies, and lived relatively long lives. Unlike sugar and rice, which were "killer crops" that demanded strenuous labor in a subtropical climate, tobacco cultivation required steady, careful, physically undemanding labor in a more temperate environment. Workers planted young tobacco seedlings in spring, hoed and weeded the crop in summer, and in fall picked and hung the leaves to cure over the winter. Also, diseases did not spread as easily in the Chesapeake, because plantation quarters were less crowded and more dispersed than those in the West Indies. Finally, because tobacco profits were lower than those from sugar, planters treated their slaves less harshly than West Indian planters did.

Many tobacco planters increased their workforce by buying female slaves and encouraging them to have children. In 1720, women made up more than one-third of the Africans in Maryland and the black population had begun to increase naturally. "Be kind and indulgent to the breeding wenches," one slave owner told his overseer, "[and do not] force them when with child upon any service or hardship that will be injurious to them." By midcentury, more than three-quarters of the enslaved workers in the Chesapeake were American-born.

Slaves in South Carolina labored under much more oppressive conditions. The colony grew slowly

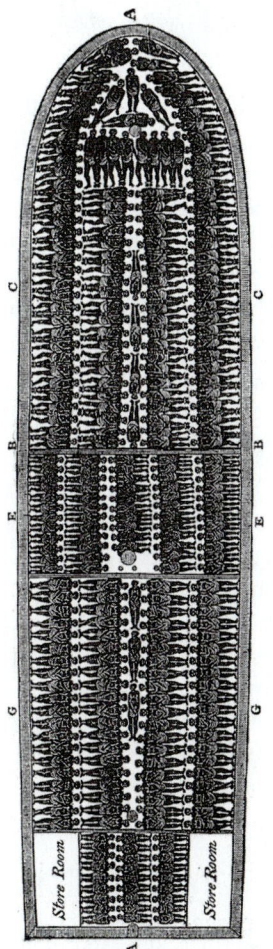

Two Views of the Middle Passage

An 1846 watercolor (on the right) shows the cargo hold of a slave ship en route to Brazil, which imported large numbers of African slaves until the 1860s. Painted by a ship's officer, the work minimizes the brutality of the Middle Passage—none of the slaves are in chains—and captures the Africans' humanity and dignity. A layout of the hold (on the left) captures the reality of the slave trade, in which the human cargo was packed in with no more respect than that given to hogsheads of sugar and tobacco.   Private Collection/© Michael Graham-Stewart/The Bridgeman Art Library. / © National Maritime Museum, London.

until 1700, when planters began to plant and export rice to southern Europe, where it was in great demand. To expand production, planters imported thousands of Africans—some of them from rice-growing societies. By 1705, Africans formed a majority of the total population, rising to 80 percent in rice-growing areas (Figure 3.2).

Most rice plantations lay in inland swamps, and the work of cultivation was dangerous and exhausting. Slaves planted, weeded, and harvested the rice in ankle-deep mud. Pools of stagnant water bred mosquitoes, which transmitted diseases that claimed hundreds of African lives. Other slaves, forced to move tons of dirt to build irrigation works, died from exhaustion. "The labour required [for growing rice] is only fit for slaves,"

a Scottish traveler remarked, "and I think the hardest work I have seen them engaged in." In South Carolina, as in the West Indies and Brazil, there were many slave deaths and few births, and the arrival of new slaves continually "re-Africanized" the black population.

An African American Community Emerges

Slaves came from many peoples in West Africa and the Central African regions of Kongo and Angola (Table 3.4). White planters welcomed ethnic diversity to deter slave revolts. "The safety of the Plantations," declared a widely read English pamphlet, "depends upon having Negroes from all parts of Guiny, who do not understand each

All the nations and people I had hitherto passed through resembled
own in their manners, customs and langua

Olaudah Equiano
The Brutal "Middle Passage"

Olaudah Equiano claimed to have been born in Igboland (present-day south-ern Nigeria). But Vincent Carretta of the University of Maryland has recently discovered strong evidence that Equiano was born in South Carolina and lived on an American plantation as a boy. He suggests that Equiano drew on conver-sations with African-born slaves to create a fictitious history of an idyllic childhood in West Africa, his kidnapping at the age of eleven, and a traumatic passage across the Atlantic. After being purchased by an English sea captain, Equiano bought his freedom in 1766. In London, he became an antislavery activist, and in 1789 published the memoir from which the following selections are drawn.

My father, besides many slaves, had a numerous family of which seven lived to grow up, including myself and a sister who was the only daughter. . . . I was trained up from my earliest years in the art of war, my daily exercise was shoot-ing and throwing javelins, and my mother adorned me with emblems after the manner of our greatest warriors. One day, when all our people were gone out to their works as usual and only I and my dear sister were left to mind the house, two men and a woman got over our walls, and in a moment seized us both, and without giving us time to cry out or make resistance they stopped our mouths and ran off with us into the nearest wood. . . .

At length, after many days' travelling, during which I had often changed masters, I got into the hands of a chieftain in a very pleasant country. This man had two wives and some children, and they all used me extremely well and did all they could to comfort me, particularly the first wife, who was something like my mother. Although I was a great many days' journey from my father's house, yet these people spoke exactly the same language with us. This first master of mine, as I may call him, was a [blacksmith], and my principal employment was working his bellows.

I was again sold and carried through a number of places till . . . at the end of six or seven months after I had been kidnapped I arrived at the sea coast.

The first object which saluted my eyes when I arrived on the coast was the sea, and a slave ship which was then riding at anchor and waiting for its cargo. I now saw myself deprived of all chance of returning to my native country . . . ; and I even wished for my former slavery in preference to my present situation, which was filled with horrors of every kind. . . . I was soon put down under the decks, and there I received such a salutation in my nostrils as I had never ex-perienced in my life; so that with the loathsomeness of the stench and crying together, I became so sick and low that I was not able to eat, nor had I the least desire to taste any thing. I now wished for the last friend, death, to relieve me; but soon, to my grief, two of the white men offered me

eatables, and on my refusing to eat, one of them held me fast by the hands and laid me across I think the windlass, and tied my feet while the other flogged me severely. I had never experienced anything of this kind before, and although, not being used to the water, I naturally feared that element the first time I saw it, yet nevertheless could I have got over the nettings, I would have jumped over the side, but I could not. . . . One day, when we had a smooth sea and moderate wind, two of my wearied countrymen who were chained together (I was near them at the time), preferring death to such a life of misery, somehow made it through the nettings and jumped into the sea. . . .

At last we came in sight of the island of Barbados; the white people got some old slaves from the land to pacify us. They told us we were not to be eaten but to work, and were soon to go on land where we should see many of our country people. This report eased us much; and sure enough soon after we were landed there came to us Africans of all languages.

Source: *The Interesting Narrative of the Life of Olaudah Equiano, or Gustavus Vassa, the African, Written by Himself* (London, 1789), 15, 22–23, 28–29.

ANALYZING THE EVIDENCE

- In what ways is Equiano's evocation of slavery in Africa consistent with the analysis in this text?

- What evidence does Equiano offer in his description of the Middle Passage that explains the average slave mortality rate of about 14 percent during the Atlantic crossing?

- Assuming that Carretta is correct, and Equiano was not born in Africa, why do you think he composed this fictitious narrative of his childhood instead of describing the facts of his own life in slavery?

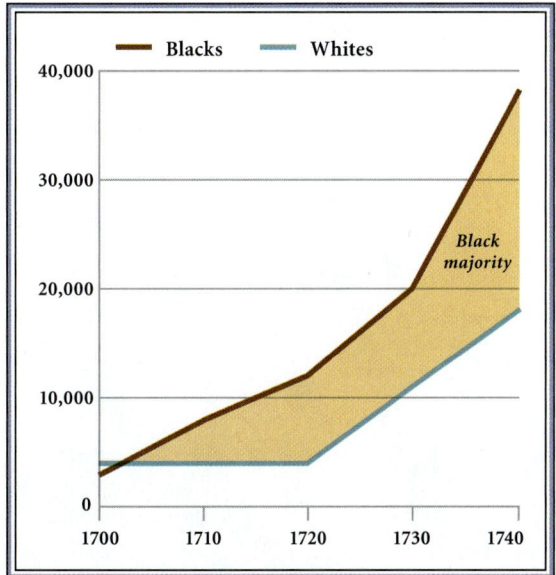

FIGURE 3.2

A Black Majority Emerges in South Carolina, 1700–1740

Between disease and the toll taken by the Indian wars, South Carolina's white population hardly grew at all between 1690 and 1720. But white planters imported thousands of enslaved Africans to grow rice, an extremely profitable plantation crop. As early as 1705, the colony had a black majority, which allowed the development among slaves of a strong Afrocentric language and culture.

other's languages and Customs and cannot agree to Rebel." By accident or design, most plantations drew laborers of many languages, including Kwa, Mande, and Kikongo. Among Africans imported after 1730 into the upper James River region of Virginia, 41 percent came from ethnic groups in present-day Nigeria, and another 25 percent from West-Central Africa. The rest hailed from the Windward and Gold coasts, Senegambia, and Sierra Leone. In South Carolina, plantation owners preferred laborers from the Gold Coast and Gambia, who had a reputation as hardworking farmers. But as African sources of slaves shifted southward after 1730, more than 30 percent of the colony's workers later came from Kongo and Angola.

Initially, the slaves did not think of themselves as Africans or blacks but as members of a specific family, clan, or people—Wolof, Hausa, Ibo, Yoruba, Teke, Ngola—and they sought out those who shared their language and customs. In the upper James River region, Ibo men and women arrived in equal numbers, married each other, and maintained their Ibo culture.

Building Community | Over time, slaves made friendships and married across ethnic lines, in the process creating new common languages. Thus, the Gullah dialect of the South Carolina lowlands combined words from English and a variety of African languages in an African grammatical

---

TABLE 3.4

African Slaves Imported into North America by Region of Departure and Ethnicity, 1700–1775

Region of Departure	Ethnicity	Number	Percentage of Imported Slaves
Senegambia	Mandinka, Fulbe, Serer, Jola, Wolof, Bambara	47,300	17
Sierra Leone	Vai, Mende, Kpelle, Kru	33,400	12
Gold Coast	Ashanti, Fanti	19,500	7
Bight of Benin, Bight of Biafra	Ibo, Ibibio	47,300	17
West Central Africa	Kongo, Tio, Matamba	44,600	16
Southeast Africa	Unknown	2,800	1
Other or unknown		83,500	30
Total		**278,400**	**100**

NOTE: The numbers are extrapolated from known voyages involving 195,000 Africans. The ethnic origins of the slaves are tentative because peoples from different regions often left from the same port and because the regions of departure of 83,500 Africans (30 percent) are not known.

SOURCE: Aaron S. Fogleman, "From Slaves, Convicts, and Servants to Free Passengers: The Transformation of Immigration in the Era of the American Revolution," *Journal of American History* 85 (June 1998), table A.4.

Hulling Rice in West Africa and Georgia

Cultural practices often extend over time and space. The eighteenth-century engraving on the left shows West African women using huge wooden mortars and pestles to strip the tough outer hull from rice kernels. In the photo on the right, taken a century and a half later, African American women in Georgia use similar tools to prepare rice for their families.   Library of Congress. / Georgia Division of Archives and History, Office of Secretary of State.

structure. "They have a language peculiar to themselves," a missionary reported, "a wild confused medley of Negro and corrupt English." In the Chesapeake region, where there were more American-born slaves, most people of African descent gradually lost their native tongues. In the 1760s, a European visitor reported with surprise that in Virginia "all the blacks spoke very good English."

A common language—Gullah or English or French (in Louisiana and the French West Indies)—was one key to the emergence of an African American community. Nearly equal numbers of men and women—which encouraged marriage, stable families, and continuity between generations—was another. In South Carolina, the high death rate among slaves undermined ties of family and kinship; but after 1725, Chesapeake-area blacks created strong nuclear families and extended kin relations. On one of Charles Carroll's estates in Maryland, 98 of the 128 slaves were members of two extended families. These African American kin groups passed on family names, traditions, and knowledge to the next generation, and thus a distinct culture gradually developed. As one observer suggested, blacks had created a separate world, "a Nation within a Nation."

As the slaves forged a new identity, they carried on certain African practices but let others go. Many Africans arrived in America with ritual scars that white planters called "country markings"; these signs of ethnic identity fell into disuse on culturally diverse plantations. But the slaves' African heritage took some tangible forms, including hairstyles, motifs used in wood carvings and pottery, the large wooden mortars and pestles used to hull rice, and the design of houses, in which rooms were arranged from front to back in a distinctive "I" pattern, not side by side as was common in English dwellings.

African values also persisted (see Reading American Pictures, "Jumping the Broomstick: An African Marriage Ceremony," p. 91). Some slaves passed down Muslim beliefs, and many more told their children of the spiritual powers of conjurers, known as *obeah* or *ifa*, who knew the ways of the African gods. Enslaved Yorubas consulted Orunmila, the god of fate, and other Africans (a Jamaican planter noted) relied on *obeah*

Jumping the Broomstick: An African Marriage Ceremony

Enslaved Africans carried their customs to the Americas, where they created a variety of new cultures that combined the traditions of many African and European peoples. How can we better understand this cultural synthesis? Slaves left few written records; but we do have visual evidence, such as this painting of a dance on a South Carolina plantation—probably a wedding ceremony—by an unknown artist.

The Old Plantation, c. 1800. Abby Aldrich Rockefeller Folk Art Museum, Williamsburg, VA.

ANALYZING THE EVIDENCE

- The painting depicts a scene on a South Carolina plantation. What clues can you see in the image suggesting that the location is a rice plantation in the low country of that colony?

- Does the evidence in the picture suggest that these people are recent arrivals from Africa? What artifacts might be African in origin? What have you learned from the text about the conditions on rice plantations that would account for a steady stream of African-born slaves?

- African peoples from different ethnic groups mingled on large plantations. Do you see any evidence in the painting that suggests different ethnic identities? Look carefully at the clothes of the two dancers—perhaps the bride and groom—at the left-center of the painting; what might indicate that they come from different African peoples?

- Around 1860, a Virginia slave recounted the story of her parents' marriage: "Ant Lucky read sumpin from de Bible, an' den she put de broomstick down an' dey locked dey arms together an' jumped over it. Den dey was married." In the scene depicted in this painting from around 1800, the man in the red breeches is holding a long stick, similar to a broomstick. If this is a wedding, is there any evidence of Christianity in the ceremony as there was in the marriage described above?

- Look closely at the men's and women's clothes. Do they reveal signs of European cultural influence?

"to revenge injuries and insults, discover and punish thieves and adulterers; [and] to predict the future."

Resistance and Accommodation

There were drastic limits on creativity among African Americans. Most slaves were denied opportunities to gain an education, accumulate material possessions, or create associations. Slaves who challenged these boundaries did so at their peril. Planters whipped slaves who refused to work; some turned to greater cruelties. Declaring the chronic runaway Ballazore an "incorrigeble rogue," a Virginia planter ordered all his toes cut off: "Nothing less than dismembering will reclaim him," the planter reasoned. Thomas Jefferson, who witnessed such punishments on his father's Virginia plantation, noted that each generation of whites was "nursed, educated, and daily exercised in tyranny," and concluded that the relationship "between master and slave is a perpetual exercise of the most unremitting despotism on the one part, and degrading submission on the other." A fellow Virginian, planter George Mason, agreed: "Every Master is born a petty tyrant."

The extent of white violence often depended on the size and density of the slave population. As Virginia planter William Byrd II complained of his slaves in 1736, "Numbers make them insolent." In the northern colonies, where slaves were few, white violence was sporadic. But plantation owners and overseers in the sugar- and rice-growing areas, where Africans outnumbered Europeans eight to one, routinely whipped assertive slaves. They also prohibited their workers from leaving the plantation without special passes and called on their poor white neighbors to patrol the countryside at night, a duty that (authorities regularly reported) was "almost totally neglected."

Slaves dealt with their plight in several ways. Some newly arrived Africans fled to the frontier, establishing traditional villages or marrying into Indian tribes. American-born blacks who were fluent in English fled to towns, and tried to pass as free. Those who remained enslaved bargained continually with their masters over the terms of their bondage. Some blacks bartered extra work for better food and clothes; others seized a small privilege and dared the master to revoke it. In this way, Sundays gradually became a day of rest — asserted as a right, rather than granted as a privilege. When bargaining failed, slaves protested silently by working slowly or stealing. Others, provoked beyond endurance, killed their owners or overseers. In the 1760s, in Amherst County, Virginia, a slave killed four whites; in Elizabeth City County, eight slaves strangled their master in bed.

A few blacks even plotted rebellion, despite white superiority in guns and, in many regions, numbers.

The Stono Rebellion Predictably, South Carolina witnessed the largest slave uprising: the Stono Rebellion of 1739. The Catholic governor of the Spanish colony of Florida instigated the revolt by promising freedom to fugitive slaves. By February 1739, at least 69 slaves had escaped to St. Augustine, and rumors circulated "that a Conspiracy was formed by Negroes in Carolina to rise and make their way out of the province." When war between England and Spain broke out in September (see p. 98), 75 Africans rose in revolt and killed a number of whites near the Stono River. According to one account, some of the rebels were Portuguese-speaking Catholics from the Kingdom of Kongo who had been attracted by the prospect of life in Catholic Florida. Displaying their skills as soldiers — decades of brutal slave raiding in Kongo had militarized the society there — the rebels marched toward Florida "with Colours displayed and two Drums beating." White militia killed many of the Stono rebels, preventing a general uprising; after this, frightened whites cut slave imports and tightened plantation discipline.

William Byrd and the Rise of the Southern Gentry

As the southern colonies became full-fledged slave societies, life changed for whites as well as for blacks. Consider the career of William Byrd II (1674–1744). Byrd's father, a successful planter-merchant in Virginia, hoped to marry his children into the English gentry. To smooth his son's entry into landed society, Byrd sent him to England for his education. But his status-conscious classmates at the Felsted School shunned young Byrd, calling him a "colonial," a first bitter taste of the gradations of rank in English society.

Other English rejections followed. Lacking aristocratic connections, Byrd was denied a post with the Board of Trade, passed over three times for the royal governorship of Virginia, and rejected as a suitor by a rich Englishwoman. In 1726, at age fifty-two, Byrd finally gave up and moved back to Virginia, where he sometimes felt he was "being buried alive." Accepting his lesser destiny as a member of the colony's elite, Byrd built an elegant brick mansion on the family's estate at Westover, sat in "the best pew in the church," and won an appointment to the governor's council.

William Byrd II's experience mirrored that of many planter-merchants, trapped in Virginia and South Carolina by their inferior colonial status. They not only

***Virginian Luxuries*, c. 1810**
This painting by an unknown artist depicts the physical and sexual exploitation inherent in a slave society. On the right, an owner chastises a male slave by beating him with a cane; on the left, ignoring the cultural and legal rules prohibiting sexual intercourse between the races, a white master prepares to bed his black mistress. Abby Aldrich Rockefeller Folk Art Museum, Williamsburg, VA.

used their wealth to rule over white yeomen families and tenant farmers but also relied on violence to exploit enslaved blacks, the American equivalent of the oppressed peasants of Europe. Planters used Africans to grow food, as well as tobacco; to build houses, wagons, and tobacco casks; and to make shoes and clothes. By making their plantations self-sufficient, the Chesapeake elite survived the depressed tobacco market between 1670 and 1720.

White Identity and Inequality To prevent uprisings like Bacon's Rebellion, the Chesapeake gentry found ways to assist middling and poor whites (see Chapter 2). They gradually lowered taxes; in Virginia, for example, the annual head tax (on each adult man) fell from 45 pounds of tobacco in 1675 to just 5 pounds in 1750. They also encouraged smallholders to improve their economic lot by using slave labor, and many did so. By 1770, 60 percent of English families in the Chesapeake owned at least one slave. On the political front, planters now allowed poor yeomen and some tenants to vote. The strategy of the leading families — the Carters, Lees, Randolphs, and Robinsons — was to bribe these voters with rum, money, and the promise of minor offices in county governments. In return, they expected the yeomen and tenants to elect them to office and defer to their rule. This horse-trading solidified the authority of the planter elite, which used its control of the House of Burgesses to limit the power of the royal governor. Hundreds of yeomen farmers benefited as well, tasting political power and garnering substantial fees and salaries as deputy sheriffs, road surveyors, estate appraisers, and grand jurymen.

Even as wealthy Chesapeake gentlemen formed political ties with smallholders, they took measures to set themselves apart culturally. As late as the 1720s, leading planters were boisterous, aggressive men who lived much like the common folk — hunting, drinking, gambling on horse races, and demonstrating their manly prowess by forcing themselves on female servants and slaves. As time passed, however, the planters began — like William Byrd II — to model themselves on the English aristocracy, remaining sexual predators but learning from advice books how to act like gentlemen in other regards: "I must not sit in others' places; Nor sneeze, nor cough in people's faces. Nor with my fingers pick my nose, Nor wipe my hands upon my clothes." Cultivating **gentility** — a refined but elaborate lifestyle — they replaced their modest wooden houses with mansions of brick and mortar. Robert "King" Carter, who owned hundreds of slaves, filled his house — 75 feet long, 44 feet wide, and 40 feet high — with fine furniture and rugs. Planters educated their sons in London as lawyers and gentlemen. But unlike Byrd's father, they expected them to return to America, marry local heiresses, and assume their fathers' roles: managing plantations, socializing with fellow gentry, and running the political system.

Wealthy Chesapeake and South Carolina women likewise emulated the English elite. They read English newspapers and fashionable magazines, wore the finest English clothes, and dined in the English fashion, including an elaborate afternoon tea. To enhance their daughters' gentility (and improve their marriage prospects), parents hired English tutors. Once married, planter women deferred to their husbands, reared pious

Captain Thomas Smith, *Self-Portrait*, c. 1680
As the background of this painting suggests, Thomas Smith had military experience, though the details are sketchy (it's thought that he fought under Oliver Cromwell during the Puritan Revolution of the 1640s). An artist as well as a sea captain, Smith moved to Boston and carried with him the Baroque style of painting, which uses light and shadows to create the illusion of forms in space (for example, note the dark shadow that sets off the bottom part of the fort in the background). The last line of the poem visible under the skull shows that Smith, though contemplating death in his advancing years, remained a devout Puritan committed to the Covenant of Grace, hopeful that God would "Crowne me (after Grace) with Glory." The Worcester Art Museum.

children, and maintained elaborate social networks, in time creating a new ideal: the southern gentlewoman. Using the profits generated by enslaved Africans in the South Atlantic System of commerce, wealthy planters formed an increasingly well-educated, refined, and stable ruling class.

The Northern Maritime Economy

The South Atlantic System had a broad geographical reach. As early as the 1640s, New England farmers supplied the sugar islands with bread, lumber, fish, and meat. As a West Indian explained, planters "had rather buy foode at very deare rates than produce it by labour, soe infinite is the profitt of sugar works." By 1700, the economies of the West Indies and New England were closely interwoven. Soon farmers and merchants in New York, New Jersey, and Pennsylvania were also ship-

ping wheat, corn, and bread to the Caribbean. By the 1750s, about two-thirds of New England's exports and half of those from the Middle colonies went to the British and French sugar islands.

The sugar economy linked Britain's entire Atlantic empire. In return for the sugar they sent to England, West Indian planters received credit—in the form of **bills of exchange**—from London merchants. The planters used these bills to buy slaves from Africa and to pay North American farmers and merchants for their provisions and shipping services. The mainland colonists then exchanged the bills for British manufactures, primarily textiles and iron goods.

The Urban Economy | The West Indian trade created the first American merchant fortunes and the first urban industries (Map 3.4). Merchants in Boston, Newport, Providence, Philadelphia, and New York invested their profits in new ships; some set up manufacturing enterprises, including twenty-six refineries that processed raw sugar into finished loaves. Mainland distilleries turned West Indian molasses into rum—producing more than 2.5 million gallons in Massachusetts alone by the 1770s. Merchants in Salem, Marblehead, and smaller New England ports built a major fishing industry by selling salted mackerel and cod to the sugar islands and to southern Europe. Baltimore merchants transformed their town into a major port by developing a bustling export business in wheat, while traders in Charleston shipped deerskins, indigo, and rice to European markets.

As transatlantic commerce expanded—from five hundred voyages a year in the 1680s to fifteen hundred annually in the 1730s—American port cities grew in size and complexity. Seeking jobs and excitement, British and German migrants and young people from the country-side (servant girls, male laborers, and apprentice artisans) flocked to urban areas. By 1750, the populations of Newport and Charleston were nearly 10,000; Boston had 15,000 residents; and New York had almost 18,000. The largest port was Philadelphia, whose population by 1776 had reached 30,000, the size of a large European provincial city. Smaller coastal towns emerged as centers of the lumber and shipbuilding industries. Seventy sawmills lined the Piscataqua River in New Hampshire, providing low-cost wood for homes, warehouses, and especially shipbuilding. Taking advantage of the Navigation Acts, which allowed colonists to build and own trading vessels, hundreds of shipwrights turned out oceangoing vessels, while other artisans made ropes, sails, and metal fittings for the new fleet. By the 1770s, colonial-built ships made up one-third of the British merchant fleet.

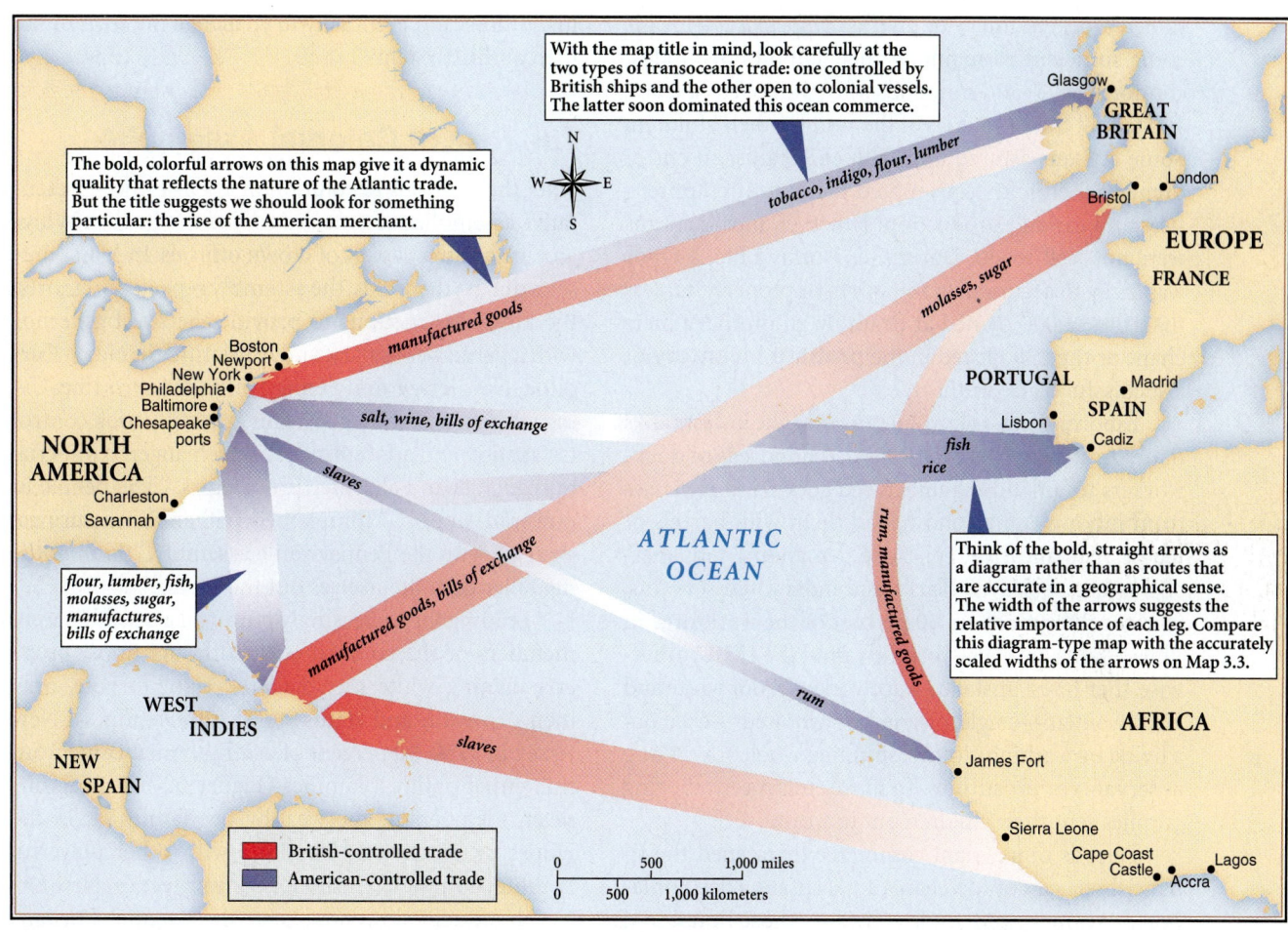

MAP 3.4

The Rise of the American Merchant, 1750

Throughout the colonial era, British merchant houses dominated the transatlantic trade in manufactures, sugar, tobacco, and slaves. However, by 1750, American-born merchants in Boston, New York, and Philadelphia had seized control of the commerce between the mainland and the West Indies. In addition, Newport traders played a small role in the slave trade from Africa, and Boston and Charleston merchants grew rich carrying fish and rice to southern Europe.

The South Atlantic System extended far into the interior. A fleet of small vessels sailed back and forth on the Hudson and Delaware rivers, delivering cargoes of European manufactures and picking up barrels of flour and wheat to carry to New York and Philadelphia for export to the West Indies and Europe. By the 1750s, hundreds of professional teamsters in Maryland were transporting 370,000 bushels of wheat and corn and 16,000 barrels of flour to urban markets each year — more than 10,000 wagon trips. To service this traffic, entrepreneurs and artisans set up taverns, horse stables, and barrel-making shops in towns along the wagon roads. Lancaster, in a prosperous wheat-growing area of Pennsylvania, boasted more than 200 German and English artisans and a dozen merchants.

Urban Society Wealthy merchants dominated the social life of seaport cities. In 1750, about 40 merchants controlled more than 50 percent of Philadelphia's trade; they had taxable assets averaging £10,000, a huge sum at the time. Like the Chesapeake gentry, urban merchants imitated the British upper classes, importing architectural design books from England and building Georgian-style mansions to display their wealth. Their wives strove to create a genteel culture by buying fine furniture and entertaining guests at elegant dinners.

Artisan and shopkeeper families, the middle ranks of seaport society, made up nearly half the population. Innkeepers, butchers, seamstresses, shoemakers, weavers, bakers, carpenters, masons, and dozens of other skilled workers toiled to gain a *competency*—an income sufficient to maintain their families in modest comfort. Wives and husbands often worked as a team, and taught the "mysteries of the craft" to their children. Some artisans aspired to wealth and status, an entrepreneurial ethic that prompted them to hire apprentices and expand production. However, most artisans were not well-to-do. During his working life, a tailor was lucky to accumulate £30 worth of property, far less than the £2,000 owned at death by an ordinary merchant or the £300 listed in the **probate inventory** of a successful blacksmith.

Laboring men and women formed the lowest ranks of urban society. Merchants needed hundreds of dockworkers to unload manufactured goods and molasses from inbound ships and reload them with barrels of wheat, fish, and rice. For these demanding jobs merchants used enslaved blacks and indentured servants, who together made up 30 percent of the workforce in Philadelphia and New York City until the 1750s; otherwise, they hired unskilled wageworkers. Poor white and black women—single, married, or widowed—eked out a living by washing clothes, spinning wool, or working as servants or prostitutes. To make ends meet, laboring families sent their children out to work.

Periods of stagnant commerce threatened the financial security of merchants and artisans alike. For laborers, seamen, and seamstresses—whose household budgets left no margin for sickness or unemployment—depressed trade meant hunger, dependence on public charity, and (for the most desperate) petty thievery or prostitution. The sugar- and slave-based South Atlantic System brought economic uncertainty as well as opportunity to the people of the northern colonies.

- How did the South Atlantic System work, and what were its major elements? How did it shape the development of the various colonies?

- What role did Africans play in the expansion of the Atlantic slave trade? What was the role of Europeans?

The New Politics of Empire, 1713–1750

The South Atlantic System changed the politics of empire. British ministers, pleased with the wealth produced by the trade in slaves, sugar, rice, and tobacco, ruled the colonies with a gentle hand. The colonists took advantage of that leniency to strengthen their political institutions and eventually to challenge the rules of the mercantilist system.

The Rise of Colonial Assemblies

After the Glorious Revolution of 1688–1689, representative assemblies in America copied the English Whigs and limited the powers of crown officials. In Massachusetts during the 1720s, the assembly repeatedly ignored the king's instructions to provide the royal governor with a permanent salary, and legislatures in North Carolina, New Jersey, and Pennsylvania did the same. Using such tactics, the legislatures gradually took control of taxation and appointments, which angered imperial bureaucrats and absentee proprietors. "The people in power in America," complained William Penn during a struggle with the Pennsylvania assembly, "think nothing taller than themselves but the Trees."

Leading the increasingly powerful assemblies were members of the colonial elite. Although most property-owning white men had the right to vote, only men of wealth and status stood for election. In New Jersey in 1750, 90 percent of assemblymen came from influential political families (Figure 3.3). In Virginia, seven members of the wealthy Lee family sat in the House of Burgesses and, along with other powerful families, dominated its major committees. In New England, affluent descendants of the original Puritans formed a core of political leaders. "Go into every village in New England," John Adams wrote in 1765, "and you will find that the office of justice of the peace, and even the place of representative, have generally descended from generation to generation, in three or four families at most."

However, neither elitist assemblies nor wealthy property owners could impose unpopular edicts on the people. Purposeful crowd actions were a fact of colonial life. An uprising of ordinary citizens overthrew the Dominion of New England in 1689. In New York, mobs closed houses of prostitution; in Salem, Massachusetts, they ran people with infectious diseases out of town; and in New Jersey, in the 1730s and 1740s, mobs of farmers battled with proprietors who were forcing tenants off disputed lands. When officials in Boston restricted the sale of farm produce to a single public market, a crowd destroyed the building, and its members defied the authorities to arrest them. "If you touch One you shall touch All," an anonymous letter warned the sheriff, "and we will show you a Hundred Men where you can show one." These expressions of popular discontent, combined with the growing authority of the assemblies, created a political system that was broadly

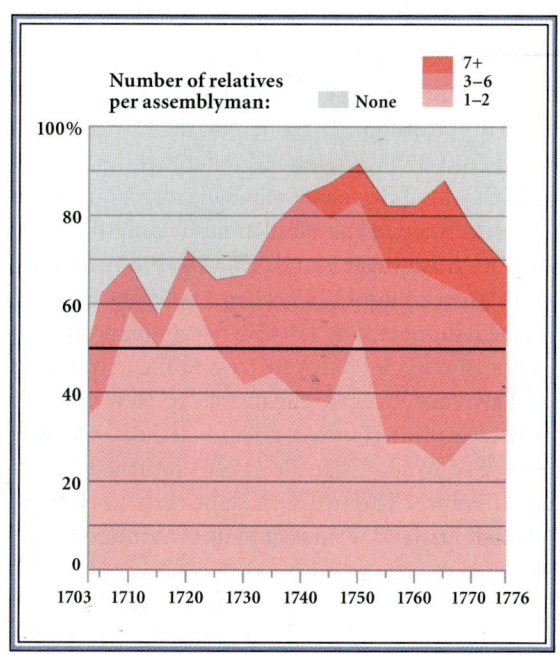

FIGURE 3.3

Family Connections and Political Power, New Jersey, 1700–1776

As early as 1700, more than 50 percent of the members of the New Jersey assembly came from families with a history of political leadership. By 1750, the percentage whose fathers or other relatives had served in the assembly reached 90 percent; indeed, some members had seven relatives who were (or had been) political leaders, clear testimony of the emergence of powerful political families and an experienced governing elite. However, as the conflict with Britain increased after 1765, voters in New Jersey and elsewhere ousted lukewarm patriots, and new families entered the political ranks.

responsive to popular pressure and increasingly resistant to British control.

Salutary Neglect

British colonial policy during the reigns of George I (r. 1714–1727) and George II (r. 1727–1760) allowed the rise of American self-government. Royal bureaucrats, pleased by growing trade and import duties, relaxed their supervision of internal colonial affairs. In 1775, British political philosopher Edmund Burke would praise this strategy as **salutary neglect**.

Salutary neglect was a by-product of the political system developed by Sir Robert Walpole, the Whig leader in the House of Commons from 1720 to 1742. By providing supporters with appointments and pensions, Walpole won parliamentary approval for his policies. However, his patronage appointments filled the British government, including the Board of Trade and the colonial bureaucracy, with do-nothing political hacks. When Governor Gabriel Johnson arrived in North Carolina in the 1730s, he vowed to curb the powers of the assembly and "make a mighty change in the face of affairs." Receiving little support from the Board of Trade, Johnson renounced reform and decided "to do nothing which can be reasonably blamed, and leave the rest to time, and a new set of inhabitants."

Walpole's tactics also weakened the empire by undermining the legitimacy of the political system. **Radical Whigs** protested that Walpole had betrayed the Glorious Revolution by using patronage and bribery

Sir Robert Walpole, the King's Minister

All eyes are on the secretary of the treasury, Sir Robert Walpole (left), as he offers advice to the Speaker of the House of Commons. A brilliant politician, Walpole used patronage to command a majority in the Commons and also won the confidence of George I and George II, the German-speaking monarchs from the duchy of Hanover. Walpole's personal motto, "Let sleeping dogs lie," helps explain his colonial policy of salutary neglect.   National Trust Photographic Library/Hawksley Studios/The Bridgeman Art Library.

to create a strong Court (or Kingly) Party. The Country Party—whose members were landed gentlemen—likewise warned that Walpole's policies of high taxes and a bloated royal bureaucracy threatened British liberties. Heeding these arguments, colonial legislators complained that royal governors abused their patronage powers. To preserve American liberty, the colonists strengthened the powers of the representative assemblies, unintentionally laying the foundation for the American independence movement (see Comparing American Voices, "The Rise of Colonial Self-Government," pp. 100–101).

Protecting the Mercantile System

Apart from patronage, Walpole focused on protecting British commercial interests. Initially, Walpole pursued a cautious foreign policy to allow Britain to recover from a generation of war (1689–1713) against Louis XIV of France. But in 1732, he provided a parliamentary subsidy for the new colony of Georgia. Georgia's reform-minded trustees envisioned the colony as a refuge for Britain's poor. To create a society of independent family farmers, the trustees limited most land grants to 500 acres and outlawed slavery.

Walpole had little interest in social reform; he subsidized Georgia to protect the valuable rice-growing colony of South Carolina. The subsidy, however, did exactly the opposite. Britain's expansion into Georgia outraged Spanish officials, who were already angry over British trade tactics in New Spain. British merchants had silently taken over the Andalusian firms that held a monopoly on Spanish-American trade, and now—violating Spanish law—provided many of the slaves and manufactures imported by the Spanish colonies. To counter Britain's commercial imperialism, Spanish naval forces stepped up their seizure of illegal traders, including mutilation of an English sea captain, Robert Jenkins.

Commercial Aggression Yielding to parliamentary pressure, Walpole declared war on Spain in 1739. However, the so-called War of Jenkins's Ear (1739–1741) did nothing to undermine Spain's American empire. In 1740, British regulars failed to capture St. Augustine because South Carolina whites, still shaken by the Stono Rebellion, refused to commit militia units to the expedition. A year later, a major British and American assault on the prosperous seaport of Cartagena (in present-day Colombia) also failed. Instead of enriching themselves with Spanish booty, hundreds of troops from the mainland colonies died in the attack, mostly from tropical diseases.

The War of Jenkins's Ear quickly became part of a general European conflict, the War of the Austrian Succession (1740–1748). Massive French armies battled British-subsidized German forces in Europe, and French naval forces roamed the West Indies, vainly trying to conquer a British sugar island. There was little fighting in North America until 1745, when 3,000 New England militiamen, supported by a British naval squadron, captured Louisbourg, a French fortress at the entrance to the St. Lawrence River. To the dismay of New England Puritans, who feared invasion from Catholic Quebec, the Treaty of Aix-la-Chapelle (1748) returned Louisbourg to France. The treaty made it clear to colonial leaders that England would act in its own interests, not theirs.

The American Economic Challenge

The Walpole ministry had its own complaints about American economic activities. The Navigation Acts stipulated that the colonies were to produce staple crops and to consume British manufactured goods. To enforce the British trade monopoly, Parliament prohibited Americans from selling colonial-made textiles (Woolen Act, 1699), hats (Hat Act, 1732), and iron products such as plows, axes, and skillets (Iron Act, 1750).

The Politics of Mercantilism However, the Navigation Acts had a major loophole: They allowed Americans to own ships and transport goods. Colonial merchants exploited those provisions to take control of 75 percent of the transatlantic trade in manufactures and 95 percent of the commerce between the mainland and the British West Indies. Moreover, by the 1720s, the British sugar islands could not absorb all the flour, fish, and meat produced by mainland settlers. So, ignoring Britain's intense rivalry with France, colonial merchants sold their produce to the French sugar islands. Soon French planters were producing low-cost sugar that drove British products off the European market. When American rum distillers began to buy cheap molasses from the French islands, the West Indian "sugar lobby" in London intervened, persuading Parliament to pass the Molasses Act of 1733. The act allowed mainland colonies to export fish and flour to the French islands but—to give a price advantage to British sugar planters—placed a high tariff on French molasses. American merchants and legislators protested that the Molasses Act would cut off molasses

The Siege and Capture of Louisbourg, 1745

In 1760, as British and colonial troops moved toward victory in the French and Indian War (1754–1763), the London artist J. Stevens sought to bolster imperial pride by celebrating an earlier Anglo-American triumph. In 1745, a British naval squadron led a flotilla of colonial ships and thousands of New England militiamen in an attack on the French fort at Louisbourg, on Cape Breton Island, near the mouth of the St. Lawrence River. After a siege of forty days, the Anglo-American force captured the fort, long considered impregnable. The victory was bittersweet because the Treaty of Aix-la-Chapelle (1748) returned the island to France. Courtesy of the John Carter Brown Library at Brown University.

imports, which would cripple the distilling industry; cut farm exports; and, by slashing colonial income, reduce the mainland's purchases of British goods. When Parliament ignored these arguments, American merchants smuggled in French molasses by bribing customs officials. Luckily for the Americans, sugar prices in Britain rose sharply in the late 1730s, so the act was not rigorously enforced.

The lack of currency in the colonies prompted another conflict with British officials. To pay for British manufactures, American merchants used the bills of exchange and the gold and silver coins earned in the West Indian trade. These payments drained the colonial economy of money, making it difficult for Americans to borrow funds or to buy and sell goods among themselves. To remedy the problem, ten colonial assemblies established public **land banks**, which lent paper money to farmers who pledged their land as collateral for the loans. Farmers used the currency to buy tools or livestock or to pay creditors, thereby stimulating trade. However, some assemblies, particularly the legislature in Rhode Island, issued huge quantities of paper money (which consequently decreased in value) and required merchants to accept it as legal tender. English merchants and other creditors rightly complained about being forced to accept devalued money. So in 1751, Parliament passed the Currency Act, which barred the New England colonies from establishing new land banks and

prohibited the use of publicly issued paper money to pay private debts.

These conflicts over trade and paper money angered a new generation of English political leaders. In 1749, Charles Townshend of the Board of Trade charged that the American assemblies had assumed many of the "ancient and established prerogatives wisely preserved in the Crown"; he vowed to replace salutary neglect with more rigorous imperial control.

The wheel of empire had come full circle. In the 1650s, England had set out to create a centrally managed Atlantic empire and, over the course of a century, achieved the military and economic aspects of that goal. Mercantilist legislation, maritime warfare, commercial expansion, and the forced labor of a million African slaves brought prosperity to Britain. However, internal unrest (the Glorious Revolution) and a policy of salutary neglect had weakened Britain's political authority over its American colonies. Recognizing the threat self-government posed to the empire, British officials in the late 1740s vowed to reassert their power in America — an initiative with disastrous results.

- **How did the ideas and policies of the English Whigs affect British and colonial politics between 1700 and 1760?**

- **What was the British policy of salutary neglect? Why did the British follow this policy and what were its consequences?**

The Rise of Colonial Self-Government

Between 1700 and 1760, members of the representative assemblies in British North America gradually expanded their authority and power. Their success was the result of greater popular participation in politics and their own political skills. However, the shift in power from imperial appointees to colonial legislators occurred in a piecemeal fashion, as the almost unconscious product of a series of small, seemingly inconsequential struggles. As you read the following correspondence among legislators, governors, and the British officials, look closely at the character of the disputes and how they were resolved.

Alexander Spotswood

Confronting the House of Burgesses

As a reward for his military service fighting the forces of Louis XIV of France, Alexander Spotswood became governor of Virginia in 1710. A contentious man, Spotswood was a controversial governor. He told the House of Burgesses to its face that the voters had mistakenly chosen "a set of representatives whom heaven has not generally endowed with the ordinary [intellectual or social] qualifications requisite to legislators." Spotswood set out to reform the voting system that, in his judgment, produced such mediocre representatives. His efforts to oust popular members of the gentry from the House of Burgesses created few friends; in 1722, his enemies in Virginia used their influence in London to have him removed from office.

To ye Council of Trade, Virginia, October 15, 1712
MY LORDS:
. . . The Indians continue their Incursions in North Carolina, and the Death of Colo. Hyde, their Gov'r, which happened the beginning of last Month, increases the misery of that province. . . .

This Unhappy State of her Maj't's Subjects in my Neighbourhood is ye more Affecting to me because I have very little hopes of being enabled to relieve them by our Assembly, which I have called to meet next Week; for the Mob of this Country, having tried their Strength in the late Election and finding themselves able to carry whom they please, have generally chosen representatives of their own Class, who as their principal Recommendation have declared their resolution to raise no Tax on the people, let the occasion be what it will. This is owing to a defect in the Constitution, which allows to every one, tho' but just out of the Condition of a Servant, and that can but purchase half an acre of Land, an equal Vote with the Man of the best Estate in the Country.

The Militia of this Colony is perfectly useless without Arms or ammunition, and by an unaccountable infatuation, no arguments I have used can prevail on these people to make their Militia more Serviceable, or to fall into any other measures for the Defence of their Country.

[From the Journal of the Virginia Council]
December the 17th, 1714
The Governor this day laying before the Council a letter from the Right Honorable the Lords Commissioners for Trade dated the 23d of April 1713 directing him to advise with the Council & to recommend to the Generall Assembly to pass a law for qualifying the Electors & the persons Elected Burgesses to serve in the Generall Assembly of this Colony in a more just & equal manner than the Laws now in force do direct. . . . The Council declare that they cannot advise the Governor to move for any alteration in the present method of Electing of Burgesses, some being of opinion that this is not a proper time, & others that the present manner of electing of Burgesses & the qualifications of the elected is sufficiently provided for by the Laws now in force.

To Mr. Secretary James Stanhope, July 15, 1715
. . . I cannot forbear regretting yt I must always have to do with ye Representatives of ye Vulgar People, and mostly with such members as are of their Stamp and Understanding, for so long as half an Acre of Land (which is of small value in this Country) qualifys a man to be an Elector, the meaner sort of People will ever carry ye Elections, and the humour generally runs to choose such men as are their most familiar Companions, who very eagerly seek to be Burgesses merely for the lucre of the Salary, and who, for fear of not being chosen again, dare in Assembly do nothing that may be disrelished [disapproved] out of the House by ye Common People. Hence it often happens yt what appears prudent and feasible to his Majesty's Governors and Council here will not pass with the House of Burgesses, upon whom they must depend for the means of putting their designs in Execution.

To the Lords Commissioners of Trade, May 23, 1716

… The behaviour of this Gentleman [Philip Ludwell Jr., the colony's Auditor] in constantly opposing whatever I have offered for ye due collecting the Quitt rents [annual feudal dues on land] and regulating the Acc'ts; his stirring up ye humours of the people before the last election of Burgesses; tampering with the most mutinous of that house, and betraying to them the measures resolved on in Council for his Majesty's Service, would have made me likewise suspend him from ye Council, but I find by the late Instructions I have received from his Majesty that Power is taken from ye Governor and transferred upon the majority of that Board [of Councilors], and while there are no less than seven of his Relations there, it is impossible to get a Majority to consent to the Suspension of him.

Sources: R. A. Brock, ed., *The Official Letters of Alexander Spotswood* (Richmond: Virginia Historical Society, 1885), 2: 1–2, 124, 154–155; H. R. MacIlwaine, ed., *Executive Journals of the Council of Colonial Virginia* (Richmond: Virginia State Library, 1928), 3: 392.

George Clinton
A Plea for Assistance

George Clinton served as governor of New York from 1744 to 1752. Like many governors during the era of salutary neglect, Clinton owed his appointment to political connections in England. As the second son of the seventh Earl of Lincoln, he would inherit neither the family's estate nor his father's position in the House of Lords; those went to his elder brother. To provide an income for Clinton, his family traded its votes in Parliament for patronage appointments. However, once Clinton was installed as governor of New York, he found himself dependent on the assembly for the payment of his salary—and the salaries of all members of his administration.

My Lords,

I have in my former letters inform'd Your Lordships what Incroachments the Assemblys of this province have from time to time made on His Majesty's Prerogative & Authority in this Province in drawing an absolute dependence of all the Officers upon them for their Saleries & Reward of their services, & by their taking in effect the Nomination to all Officers. …

1stly, That the Assembly refuse to admit of any amendment to any money bill, in any part of the Bill; so that the Bill must pass as it comes from the Assembly, or all the Supplies granted for the support of Government, & the most urgent services must be lost.

2ndly, It appears that they take the Payment of the [military] Forces, passing of Muster Rolls into their own hands by naming the Commissaries for those purposes in the Act.

3rdly, They by granting the Saleries to the Officers personally by name & not to the Officer for the time being, intimate that if any person be appointed to any Office his Salery must depend upon their approbation of the Appointment. …

I must now refer it to Your Lordships' consideration whether it be not high time to put a stop to these usurpations of the Assembly on His Majesty's Authority in this Province and for that purpose may it not be proper that His Majesty signify his Disallowance of the Act at least for the payment of Saleries.

Source: E. B. O'Callaghan, ed., *Documents Relative to the Colonial History of the State of New York* (Albany, 1860–), 2: 211.

ANALYZING THE EVIDENCE

- What policies does Spotswood wish to pursue? Why can't he persuade the House of Burgesses to implement them? According to Spotswood, what is wrong with Virginia's political system? How does he propose to reform it?

- Unlike the House of Burgesses, which was elected by qualified voters, the members of the Governor's Council in Virginia were appointed by the king, usually on the governor's recommendation. What is the council's response to the plan to reform the political system? Given Spotswood's description of the incident involving Philip Ludwell, where did the political sympathies of the council lie?

- What were Clinton's complaints about the actions of the New York assembly? Did these actions represent a more or less serious threat to imperial power than the activities of the Virginia Burgesses? Based on their correspondence with the Board of Trade, which governor—Spotswood or Clinton—was the stronger representative of the interests of the crown?

Bristol Docks and Quay
Bristol, in southwest England, served as a hub for the trade with Africa, the West Indies, and the American mainland. This detail from an eighteenth-century painting of the bustling seaport shows horses drawing large hogsheads of West Indian sugar to local factories and workers readying smaller barrels of rum and other goods for export to Africa.   Bristol City Museum and Art Gallery/UK Bridgeman Art Library.

SUMMARY

In this chapter, we examined processes of change in politics and society. The political story began in the 1660s as Britain imposed controls on its American possessions. Parliament passed the Acts of Trade and Navigation to keep colonial products and trade in English hands. Then King James II abolished representative institutions in the northern colonies and created the authoritarian Dominion of New England. Following the Glorious Revolution, the Navigation Acts remained in place and tied the American economy to that of Britain. But the uprisings of 1688–1689 did overturn James II's policy of strict imperial control, restore American self-government, and usher in an era of salutary political neglect.

The social story centers on the development of the South Atlantic System of production and trade, which involved an enormous expansion in African slave raiding; the Atlantic slave trade; and the cultivation of sugar, rice, and tobacco in America. This complex system created an exploited African American labor force in the southern mainland and West Indian colonies and also prosperous communities of European American farmers, merchants, and artisans on the North American mainland. How would the two stories play out? In 1750, slavery and the South Atlantic System seemed firmly entrenched, but the days of salutary neglect appeared numbered.

CHAPTER REVIEW QUESTIONS

• Describe the dramatic expansion of the British empire in North America in the late seventeenth and early eighteenth centuries. What role did the South Atlantic System play?

• In what ways did politics in the British empire change in the decades following the Glorious Revolution? How do you explain those changes?

FOR FURTHER EXPLORATION

Atlantic history stands at the center of recent scholarship. See *The Creation of the British Atlantic World* (2005), eds. Elizabeth Mancke and Carole Shammas; *The British Atlantic World, 1500–1800*, 2nd ed. (2009), eds. David Armitage and Michael J. Braddick; and *Atlantic History: A Critical Appraisal* (2009), eds. Jack P. Greene and Philip D. Morgan. Richard Bushman, *King and People in Provincial Massachusetts* (1985), and Brendan McConville, *The King's Three Faces* (2007), explore the decline of British authority.

Betty Wood, *The Origins of American Slavery* (1998), and David Eltis, *The Rise of African Slavery in the Americas* (2000), offer fine surveys. For the diversity and evolution of African bondage, see Ira Berlin, *Many Thousands Gone: The First Two Centuries of Slavery in North America* (1999), and Trevor Burnard, *Mastery, Tyranny, and Desire: Thomas Thistlewood and His Slaves in the Anglo-Jamaican World* (2004). Olaudah Equiano, *The Interesting Narrative of the Life of Olaudah Equiano* (1789, reprint 1995), sketches the emergence of an "African" identity. See also John Thornton, *Africa and Africans in the Making of the Atlantic World, 1400–1800* (1998).

The PBS video *Africans in America, Part 1: Terrible Transformation, 1450–1750,* and the related Web site (**www.pbs.org/wgbh/aia/part1/title.html**) cover the early African American experience. A visual record of the slave experience appears at **hitchcock.itc.virginia .edu/Slavery**. Also see the Library of Congress online exhibit "African American Odyssey" (**memory.loc.gov/ ammem/aaohtml**) and the wide-ranging material on the British slave trade (1600–1807) at **slavetrade .parliament.uk/slavetrade/index.html**.

TEST YOUR KNOWLEDGE

To assess your command of the material in this chapter, see the Online Study Guide at **bedfordstmartins.com/henretta**.

For Web sites, images, and documents related to topics and places in this chapter, visit **bedfordstmartins.com/makehistory**.

TIMELINE

1651	First Navigation Act
1660–1685	Reign of Charles II, king of England
1663	Charles II grants Carolina proprietorship
1664	English capture New Netherland; rename it New York
1681	William Penn founds Pennsylvania
1685–1688	Reign of James II, king of England
1686–1689	Dominion of New England
1688–1689	Glorious Revolution in England
1689	William and Mary ascend throne in England Revolts in Massachusetts, Maryland, and New York
1689–1713	England, France, and Spain at war
1696	Parliament creates Board of Trade
1705	Virginia enacts slavery legislation
1714–1750	British policy of salutary neglect; American assemblies gain power
1720–1742	Robert Walpole leads Parliament
1720–1750	African American community forms Rice exports from South Carolina soar Planter aristocracy emerges Seaport cities expand
1732	Parliament charters Georgia, challenging Spain Hat Act limits colonial enterprise
1733	Molasses Act threatens distillers
1739	Stono Rebellion in South Carolina
1739–1748	War with Spain in the Caribbean and France in Canada and Europe
1750	Iron Act restricts colonial iron production
1751	Currency Act prohibits land banks and paper money

CHAPTER 4

Growth and Crisis in Colonial Society, 1720–1765

In 1736, Alexander MacAllister left the Highlands of Scotland for the backcountry of North Carolina, where his wife and three sisters soon joined him. MacAllister prospered as a landowner and mill proprietor and had only praise for his new home. Carolina was "the best poor man's country," he wrote to his brother Hector, urging him to "advise all poor people . . . to take courage and come." In North Carolina, there were no landlords to keep "the face of the poor . . . to the grinding stone," and so many Highlanders were arriving that "it will soon be a new Scotland." Here, on the far margins of the British empire, people could "breathe the air of liberty, and not want the necessarys of life." Some 300,000 European migrants—primarily Highland Scots, Scots-Irish, and Germans—heeded MacAllister's advice and helped swell the population of Britain's North American settlements from 400,000 in 1720 to almost 2 million by 1765.

The rapid increase in white settlers and the arrival of nearly 300,000 enslaved Africans transformed life throughout British North America. Long-settled towns in New England became overcrowded. Antagonistic ethnic and religious communities jostled uneasily with one another in the Middle Atlantic colonies; in 1742 there were more than fifty German Lutheran and Reformed congregations in Quaker-led Pennsylvania, and by 1748 more than one hundred. By then, the MacAllisters and thousands of other Celtic and German migrants altered the social landscape and introduced religious conflict into the southern backcountry. "Live like Brethren in Unity," Anglican minister Charles Woodhouse advised a Scots-Irish Presbyterian congregation.

Everywhere, two European cultural movements—the Enlightenment and Pietism—changed the tone of intellectual and spiritual life. Advocates of "rational thought" viewed human beings as agents of moral self-determination and urged Americans to fashion a better social order. However, religious pietists outnumbered them and had more influence. Convinced of the weakness of human nature, evangelical ministers told their followers to seek regeneration through divine grace. Amidst this intellectual and religious ferment, migrants and the landless children of long-settled families moved inland and sparked wars with the native peoples and with France and Spain. A generation of dynamic growth produced a decade of deadly warfare that would set the stage for a new era in American history.

John Collet, *George Whitefield Preaching*

No painting could capture English minister George Whitefield's magical appeal, although this image conveys his open demeanor and religious intensity, as well as his effect on his audiences. When Whitefield spoke to a crowd near Philadelphia, an observer noted that his words were "sharper than a two-edged sword. . . . Some of the people were pale as death; others were wringing their hands . . . and most lifting their eyes to heaven and crying to God for mercy." An astute businessman as well as a charismatic preacher, Whitefield tirelessly promoted the sale of his sermons and books. © Private Collection/The Bridgeman Art Library.

New England's Freehold Society

In the 1630s, the Puritans had fled England, where a small elite of nobles and gentry owned 75 percent of the arable land and used **leaseholding** tenants and propertyless workers to farm it. In New England, the Puritans created a yeoman society of relatively equal landowning farm families. But by 1750, the migrants' numerous descendants had parceled out the best farmland, threatening the future of the freehold ideal.

Farm Families: Women in the Household Economy

The Puritans' vision of social equality did not extend to women, and their ideology placed the husband firmly at the head of the household. In *The Well-Ordered Family* (1712), Reverend Benjamin Wadsworth of Boston advised women that being richer, more intelligent, or of higher social status than their husbands mattered little: "Since he is thy Husband, God has made him the head and set him above thee." It was a wife's duty "to love and reverence" her husband.

Women learned this subordinate role throughout their lives. Small girls watched their mothers defer to their fathers, and as young women, they were told to be "silent in company," and saw the courts prosecute many women and few men for the crime of fornication (having sexual intercourse outside of marriage). Soon they found that their marriage portions would be inferior to those of their brothers. Thus, Ebenezer Chittendon of Guilford, Connecticut, left his land to his sons, decreeing that "Each Daughter [shall] have half so much as Each Son, one half in money and the other half in Cattle." Because English law had eliminated most customary restrictions on inheritances, fathers could divide their property as they pleased.

In rural New England, and throughout the colonies, women assumed the role of dutiful helpmeets (helpmates) to their husbands. Farmwives tended gardens that provided fresh vegetables and herbs, and spun thread and yarn from flax and wool and then wove it into cloth for shirts and gowns. They knitted sweaters and stockings, made candles and soap, churned milk into butter and pressed curds into cheese, fermented malt for beer, preserved meats, and mastered dozens of other household tasks. "Notable women"—those who excelled at domestic arts—won praise and high status.

Bearing and rearing children were equally important tasks. Most women in New England married in their early twenties and by their early forties had given birth to six or seven children, delivered with the help of a female neighbor or a midwife. Such large families sapped the physical and emotional strength of most mothers for twenty of their most active years. One Massachusetts mother confessed that she had little time for religious activities because "the care of my Babes takes up so large a portion of my time and attention." Yet most Puritan congregations were filled with women: "In a Church of between *Three* and *Four* Hundred *Communicants*," the eminent minister Cotton Mather noted, "there are but few more than *One* Hundred *Men*; all

The First, Second, and Last Scene of Mortality.   Prudence Punderson.

Prudence Punderson (1758–1784), *The First, Second and Last Scenes of Mortality*

This powerful image reveals both the artistic skills of colonial women in the traditional medium of needlework and the Puritans' continuing cultural concern with the inevitability of death. Prudence Punderson, the Connecticut woman who embroidered this scene, rejected a marriage proposal and followed her Loyalist father into exile on Long Island in 1778. Sometime later, she married a cousin, Timothy Rossiter, and bore a daughter, Sophia, who may well be the baby in the cradle being rocked by "Jenny," a slave owned by Prudence's father. Long worried by "my ill state of health" and perhaps now anticipating her own death, Prudence has inscribed her initials on the coffin—and, in creating this embroidery, transformed her personal experience into a broader mediation on the progression from birth, to motherhood, to death.   Connecticut Historical Society.

the Rest are Women." Many women claimed a conversion experience and became full members, revivalist minister Jonathan Edwards suggested, because they feared death during childbirth and because that status meant that "their children may be baptized."

As the size of farms shrank in long-settled communities, many couples chose to have fewer children. After 1750, women in the typical Massachusetts farm village of Andover bore an average of only four children and had time and energy for other tasks. Women in farming families now could make yarn, cloth, or cheese to exchange with neighbors or sell to shopkeepers, raising their families' standard of living. Or, like Susan Huntington of Boston, the wife of a prosperous merchant, they spent more time in "the care & culture of children, and the perusal of necessary books, including the scriptures."

Still, women's lives remained tightly bound by a web of legal and cultural restrictions. Ministers praised women for their piety but excluded them from an equal role in the church. When Hannah Heaton, a Connecticut farmwife, grew dissatisfied with her Congregationalist minister, thinking him unconverted and a "blind guide," she sought out equality-minded Quaker and evangelist Baptist churches that welcomed questioning women such as herself and treated "saved" women equally with men. However, by the 1760s, many evangelical congregations had lost some of their religious zeal and had reinstituted men's dominance over women. "The government of Church and State must be . . . family government" controlled by its "king," declared the Danbury (Connecticut) Baptist Association. Willingly or not, most colonial women abided by the custom that, as essayist Timothy Dwight put it, they should be subservient to their husbands and "employed only in and about the house."

Farm Property: Inheritance

By contrast, European men who migrated to the colonies escaped many traditional constraints, including the curse of landlessness. "The hope of having land of their own & becoming independent of Landlords is what chiefly induces people into America," an official noted in the 1730s. Owning property gave formerly dependent peasants a new social identity.

Property ownership and family authority were closely related. Most migrating Europeans wanted farms that would provide a living for themselves and ample land for their children. Parents who could not give their offspring land placed these children as indentured servants in more prosperous households. When the inden-

tures ended at age eighteen or twenty-one, propertyless sons faced a decades-long climb up the agricultural ladder, from laborer to tenant and finally to freeholder.

Sons and daughters in well-to-do farm families were luckier: They received a marriage portion when they were between the ages of twenty-three and twenty-five. That portion — land, livestock, or farm equipment — repaid children for their past labor and allowed parents to choose their children's partners, which they did not hesitate to do. Parents' security during old age depended on a wise choice of son- or daughter-in-law. Although the young people could refuse an unacceptable match, they did not have the luxury of falling in love with and marrying whomever they pleased.

Marriage under eighteenth-century English common law was not a contract between equals. A bride relinquished to her husband the legal ownership of all her property. After his death, she received a dower right — the right to use (though not sell), one-third of the family's property; on this widow's death or remarriage, her portion was divided among the children. Thus the widow's property rights were subordinate to those of the family line, which stretched across the generations.

A father's duty was to provide inheritances for his children so that one day they could "be for themselves." Men who failed to do so lost status in the community. Some fathers willed the family farm to a single son and either provided other children with money, an apprenticeship, or uncleared frontier tracts, or required the inheriting son to do so. Other yeomen moved their families to the frontier, where life was hard but land was cheap and abundant. "The Squire's House stands on the Bank of the Susquehannah," traveler Philip Fithian reported from the Pennsylvania backcountry in the early 1760s. "He tells me that he will be able to settle all his sons and his fair Daughter Betsy on the Fat of the Earth."

These farmers' historic achievement was the creation of many communities of independent property owners. A French visitor noted the sense of personal dignity in this rural world, which contrasted sharply with that of European peasants. He found "men and women whose features are not marked by poverty . . . or by a feeling that they are insignificant subjects and subservient members of society."

Freehold Society in Crisis

How long would this happy circumstance last? Because of rapid natural increase, New England's population doubled each generation, from 100,000 in 1700, to nearly 200,000 in 1725, to almost 400,000 in 1750. Farms had been divided and then subdivided, making them so small—50 acres or less—that parents could provide only one child with an adequate inheritance. In the 1740s, Reverend Samuel Chandler of Andover, Massachusetts, was "much distressed for land for his children," seven of them young boys. A decade later, in nearby Concord, about 60 percent of the farmers owned less land than their fathers had. And overfishing meant that the region's rivers, once overflowing with nutritious fish, had been severely depleted.

Because parents had less to give their sons and daughters, they had less control over their children's lives. The traditional system of arranged marriages broke down, as young people engaged in premarital sex and then used the urgency of pregnancy to win permission to marry. Throughout New England, premarital conceptions rose dramatically, from about 10 percent of firstborn children in the 1710s to more than 30 percent in the 1740s. Given another chance, young people "would do the same again," an Anglican minister observed, "because otherwise they could not obtain their parents' consent to marry."

Even as New England families changed, they maintained the freeholder ideal. Some parents chose to have smaller families and used birth control to do so: abstention, coitus interruptus, or primitive condoms. Other families petitioned the provincial government for frontier land grants and hacked new farms out of the forests of central Massachusetts, western Connecticut, and eventually New Hampshire and Vermont. Still others improved their farms' productivity by replacing the traditional English crops of wheat and barley with high-yielding potatoes and maize (Indian corn). Corn was an especially wise choice: It yielded a hearty food crop for human consumption, and its stalk and leaves furnished feed for cattle and pigs, which provided milk and meat. Gradually, New England changed from a grain to a livestock economy, becoming a major exporter of salted meat to the plantations of the West Indies.

Finally, New England farmers developed the full potential of what one historian has called the "household mode of production." In this system of community exchange, families swapped labor and goods. Women and children worked in groups to spin yarn, sew quilts, and shuck corn. Men loaned neighbors tools, draft animals, and grazing land. Farmers plowed fields owned by artisans and shopkeepers, who repaid them with shoes, furniture, or store credit. Partly because currency was in short supply, no cash changed hands. Instead, farmers, artisans, and shopkeepers recorded debits and credits and "balanced" the books every few years by transferring small amounts of cash. This system allowed households—and the region's economy—to maximize agricultural output and so preserve the freehold ideal.

- In what ways were the lives of women and men in New England similar? In what ways were they different?

- What was the threat to the freehold ideal in midcentury New England, and what strategies did farming families use to preserve this ideal?

Toward a New Society: The Middle Colonies, 1720–1765

The Middle colonies—New York, New Jersey, and Pennsylvania—became home to peoples of differing origins, languages, and religions. Scots-Irish Presbyterians, English and Welsh Quakers, German Lutherans and Moravians, and Dutch Reformed Protestants formed ethnic and religious communities that coexisted uneasily.

Economic Growth and Social Inequality

Ample fertile land attracted migrants to the Middle colonies, and grain exports to Europe and the West Indies financed the colonies' rapid settlement. Between 1720 and 1770, a growing demand for wheat, corn, and flour doubled their prices and brought people and prosperity to the region: The region's population surged from 120,000 in 1720 to 450,000 in 1765 (Figure 4.1).

Tenancy in New York   Many migrants refused to settle in New York's fertile Hudson River Valley—and with good reason. There, wealthy Dutch and English families—the Van Rensselaers, Philipses, Livingstons, and Clarks—presided over the huge manors created by the Dutch West India Company and English governors (Map 4.1). Like Chesapeake planters, the New York landlords aspired to live in the same manner as did the European gentry, but they found that few migrants wanted to labor as peasants. To attract tenants, the manorial lords granted long leases, with the right to sell improvements—houses and barns, for example—to the next tenant. Still, the number of tenants rose slowly; the vast 100,000-acre Van Rensselaer estate had only 82 in 1714 and 345 in 1752, with a jump to 700 by 1765.

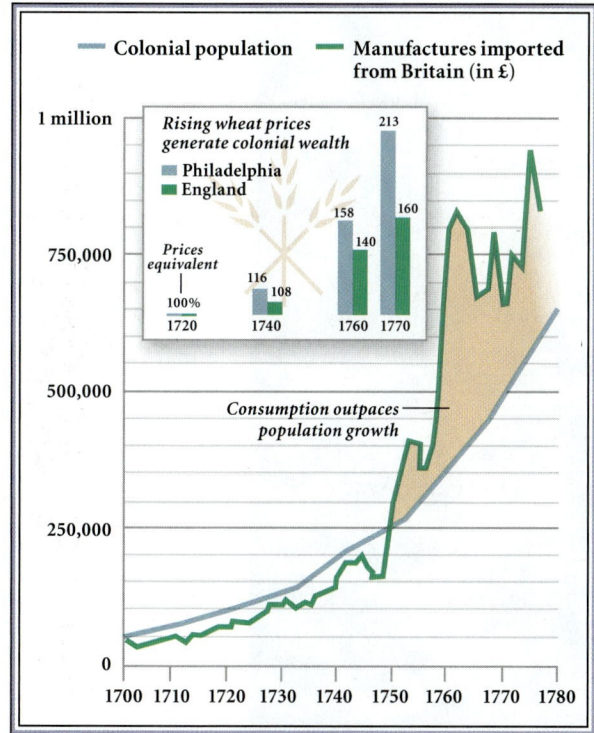

FIGURE 4.1

Population Growth, Wheat Prices, and British Imports in the Middle Atlantic Colonies

Wheat prices doubled in Philadelphia between 1720 and 1770 as demand swelled both in Europe and the West Indies. The income earned from the exports of grain and flour paid for English manufactures, which the settlers in the Middle Colonies imported in large quantities after 1750.

Most tenant families hoped that with hard work and ample sales they could eventually buy their own farmsteads. But preindustrial technology during the crucial harvest season limited output. Wheat had to be harvested when it was ripe, but before it sprouted and became useless, yet a worker with a hand sickle could reap only half an acre of wheat, rye, or oats a day. The cradle scythe, a tool introduced during the 1750s, doubled or tripled the amount of grain one worker could cut. Even so, a family with two adult workers could reap only about 12 acres of grain, or roughly 150 to 180 bushels of wheat. After saving enough grain for food and seed, the surplus might be worth £15 — enough to buy salt and sugar, tools, and cloth, but little else. The road to landownership was not an easy one.

Conflict in Pennsylvania | In Quaker-dominated Pennsylvania and New Jersey, wealth was initially distributed more evenly than in New York. The first migrants arrived with few resources and lived simply in small, one- or two-room houses

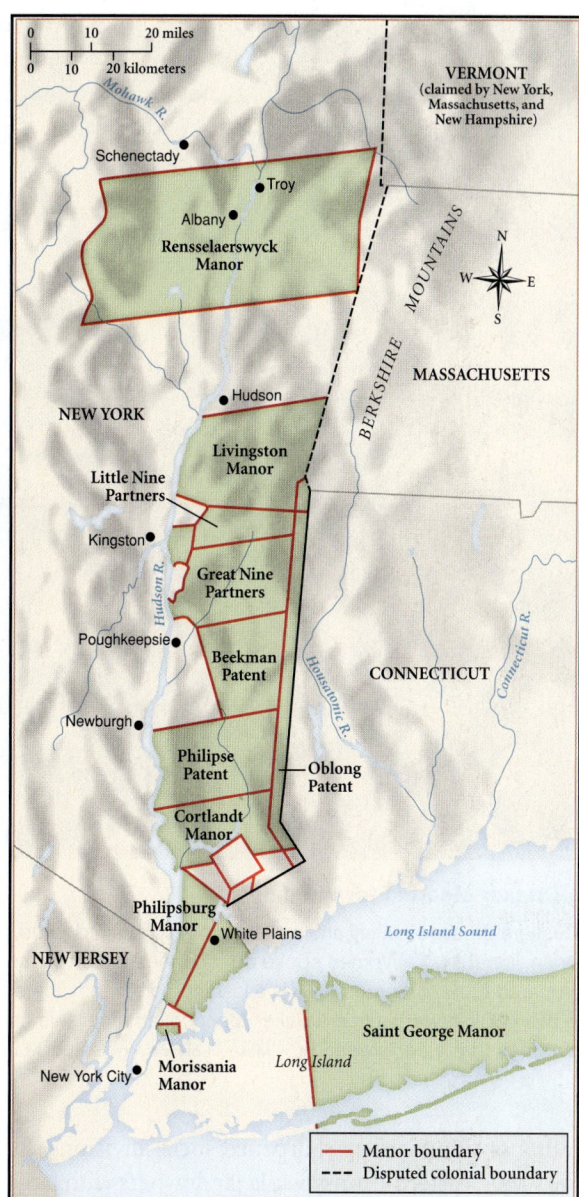

MAP 4.1

The Hudson River Manors

Dutch and English manorial lords owned much of the fertile east bank of the Hudson River, where they leased farms on perpetual contracts to German tenants and refused to sell land to freehold-seeking migrants from overcrowded New England. This powerful landed elite produced aristocratic-minded Patriot leaders such as Gouverneur Morris and Robert Livingston, as well as prominent American families such as the Roosevelts.

with a sleeping loft, a few benches or stools, and some wooden platters and cups. Only a few wealthy families ate off pewter or ceramic plates imported from England or Holland.

However, the expanding trade in wheat and an

A Quaker Meeting for Worship

Quakers dressed plainly and met for worship in unadorned buildings, sitting in silence until inspired by an "inner light." Women spoke during meetings on terms of near-equality to men, a tradition that prepared Quaker women to take a leading part in the nineteenth-century women's rights movement. In this English work, titled *Quaker Meeting*, an elder (his hat on a peg above his head) conveys his thoughts to the congregation.   Museum of Fine Arts, Boston. M. and M. Karolik Collection.

influx of poor settlers sharpened social divisions. By the 1760s, eastern Pennsylvania landowners with large farms were using slaves and poor Scots-Irish migrants to grow wheat. Other ambitious men were buying up land and dividing it into small tenancies, which they let out on profitable leases. Still others were accumulating wealth by providing new settlers with farming equipment, sugar and rum from the West Indies, and financial services. These large-scale farmers, rural landlords, speculators, storekeepers, and gristmill operators formed a distinct class of agricultural capitalists. They built large stone houses for their families, furnishing them with four-poster beds and expensive mahogany tables, on which they laid elegant linen and handsomely decorated Dutch dinnerware.

In contrast, one-half of the Middle colonies' white men owned no land and little personal property. A few propertyless men were the sons of smallholding farmers and would eventually inherit some land. But most were Scots-Irish or German "inmates"—single men or families, explained a tax assessor, "such as live in small cottages and have no taxable property, except a cow." In the predominantly German township of Lancaster, Pennsylvania, a merchant noted an "abundance of Poor people" who "maintain their Families with great difficulty by day Labour." Although these workers hoped eventually to become landowners, an abrupt and steep rise in land prices prevented many from realizing their dreams.

Some hard-pressed migrants turned to crime, which rose sharply after 1720. Previously, merchant Isaac Norris recalled, "we could Safely go to bed with our doors open but now Robberies, housebreaking, Rapes, & other crimes are become Common." In 1732, the Philadelphia Society of Friends publicly identified the criminals as "the vicious and scandalous Refuse of other Countries," a charge confirmed by recent scholarship. Pennsylvania's religious peoples—Quakers, Mennonites, Amish, Moravians, and Lutherans—broke relatively few laws; those who committed crimes were usually either propertyless individuals, indentured servants, or Scots-Irish (or often all three).

Merchants and artisans took advantage of the ample labor supply to set up an outwork system. They bought wool or flax from farmers and paid propertyless workers and land-poor farm families to spin it into yarn or weave it into cloth. In the 1760s, an English traveler reported that hundreds of Pennsylvanians had turned "to manufacture, and live upon a small farm, as in many parts of England." In the Middle Atlantic as in New England, many communities were now as crowded and socially divided as those in rural England, with many families fearing they were fated to return to the lowly status of the European peasant.

Cultural Diversity

The Middle Atlantic colonies were not a melting pot. Most European migrants held tightly to their traditions, creating a patchwork of ethnically and religiously diverse communities (Figure 4.2). In 1748, Swedish traveler Peter Kalm counted no fewer than twelve religious denominations in Philadelphia, including Anglicans, Baptists, Quakers, Swedish and German Lutherans, Mennonites, Scots-Irish Presbyterians, and Roman Catholics.

Migrants preserved their cultural identity by marrying within their ethnic groups and maintaining Old World customs. A major exception was the Huguenots, Calvinists who had been expelled from Catholic France in the 1680s and resettled in Holland, England, and the British colonies. Huguenots in American port cities—such as Boston, New York, and Charleston—quickly lost their French identities by intermarrying with other Protestants. More typical were the Welsh Quakers in Chester County, Pennsylvania: Seventy percent of the children of the original Welsh migrants married other Welsh Quakers, as did 60 percent of the third generation.

In Pennsylvania and western New Jersey, Quakers shaped the culture because of their numbers, wealth, and social cohesion. Most Quakers came from English counties with few landlords and brought with them traditions of local village governance, popular participation in politics, and social equality. Because Quakers were also pacifists, Pennsylvania officials bought the land they settled from Native Americans rather than seizing it. However, in 1737, Governor Thomas Penn used sharp tactics to oust the Lenni-Lenape (or Delaware) Indians from a vast area, creating a bitterness that led to war in the 1750s. By that time, Quakers had extended their belief in equality to African Americans. Many Quaker meetings (congregations) condemned slavery, and some expelled members who continued to keep slaves.

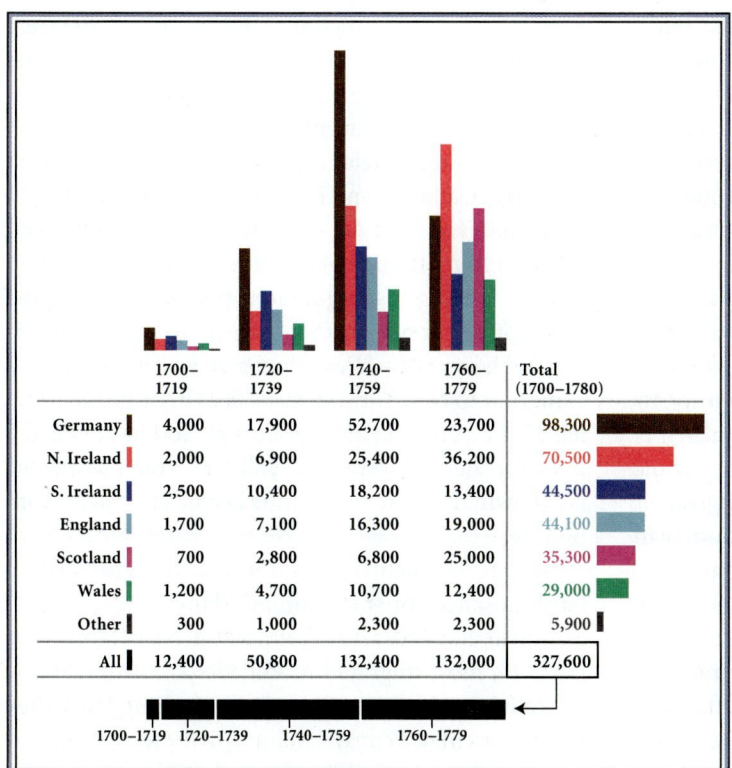

FIGURE 4.2

Estimated European Migration to the British Mainland Colonies, 1700–1780

After 1720, European migration to British North America increased dramatically, peaking between 1740 and 1780, when more than 264,000 settlers arrived in the mainland colonies. Emigration from Germany peaked in the 1740s, but the number of migrants from Ireland, Scotland, England, and Wales continued to increase during the 1760s and early 1770s. Most migrants, including those from Ireland, were Protestants. Source: Adapted from Aaron Fogelman, "Migrations to the Thirteen British North American Colonies, 1700–1775: New Estimates," *Journal of Interdisciplinary History* 22 (1992).

	1700–1719	1720–1739	1740–1759	1760–1779	Total (1700–1780)
Germany	4,000	17,900	52,700	23,700	98,300
N. Ireland	2,000	6,900	25,400	36,200	70,500
S. Ireland	2,500	10,400	18,200	13,400	44,500
England	1,700	7,100	16,300	19,000	44,100
Scotland	700	2,800	6,800	25,000	35,300
Wales	1,200	4,700	10,700	12,400	29,000
Other	300	1,000	2,300	2,300	5,900
All	12,400	50,800	132,400	132,000	327,600

The Demory House, c. 1780

The Demory House lies near the Shenandoah Valley in northwestern Virginia, and was probably built by a migrant from Pennsylvania according to a German design used by both German and Scots-Irish settlers. The house is small but sturdy. It measures 20 feet by 14 feet deep, and has one and a half stories. The two first-floor rooms, a kitchen and a parlor, are separated by an 18 x 18–inch square chimney set in the center of the house, as well as the stairs leading up to the sleeping chamber. Clay and small stones fill the gaps in the exterior walls, which consist of timber planking about 12 inches tall and 6 to 8 inches wide.   © 2003 Copyright and All Rights Reserved by Christopher C. Fennell.

The German Influx

The Quaker vision of a "peaceable kingdom" attracted 100,000 German migrants who had fled their homelands because of military conscription, religious persecution, and high taxes. First to arrive, in 1683, were the Mennonites, religious dissenters drawn by the promise of freedom of worship. In the 1720s, a larger wave of German migrants arrived from the overcrowded villages of southwestern Germany and Switzerland. "Wages were far better" in Pennsylvania, Heinrich Schneebeli reported to his friends in Zurich, and "one also enjoyed there a free unhindered exercise of religion." A third wave of Germans and Swiss—nearly 40,000 strong—landed in Philadelphia between 1749 and 1756. Some were redemptioners (indentured servants who migrated as individuals or families) but many more were propertied farmers and artisans in search of better opportunities.

Germans soon dominated many districts in eastern Pennsylvania, and thousands more moved down the fertile Shenandoah Valley into the western backcountry of Maryland, Virginia, and the Carolinas (Map 4.2). Many migrants preserved their cultural identity by settling in Lutheran and Reformed communities. A minister in North Carolina admonished young people "not to contract any marriages with the English or Irish," arguing that "we owe it to our native country to do our part that German blood and the German language be preserved in America." Well beyond 1800, many settlers spoke German, read German-language newspapers, and preserved German farming practices, among which was sending women into the fields to plow and reap.

These settlers were willing colonial subjects of Britain's German-born and German-speaking Protestant monarchs, George I (r. 1714–1727) and George II (r. 1727–1760). They generally avoided politics except to protect their cultural practices; for example, they insisted that married women have the legal right to hold property and write wills, as they did in Germany.

Scots-Irish Settlers

Migrants from Ireland, who numbered about 115,000, were the most numerous of the incoming Europeans. Some were Irish and Catholic but most were Scots and Presbyterian, the descendants of the Calvinist Protestants sent to Ireland during the seventeenth century to solidify English rule there. Once in Ireland, the Scots faced hostility from both Irish Catholics and English officials and landlords. Thus, the Irish Test Act of 1704 restricted voting and office-holding to members of the Church of England, English mercantilist regulations placed heavy import duties on linens made by Scots-Irish weavers, and farmers paid heavy taxes. "Read this letter, Rev. Baptist Boyd," a migrant to New York wrote back to his minister, "and tell all the poor folk of ye place that God has opened a door for their deliverance . . . all that a man works for is his own; there are no revenue hounds to take it from us here."

Lured by such reports, thousands of Scots-Irish families sailed for the colonies. Many who landed in Boston in the 1710s settled primarily in New Hampshire. By 1720, most migrated to Philadelphia, attracted by the religious tolerance there. Seeking cheap land, they moved to central Pennsylvania and to the fertile Shenan-

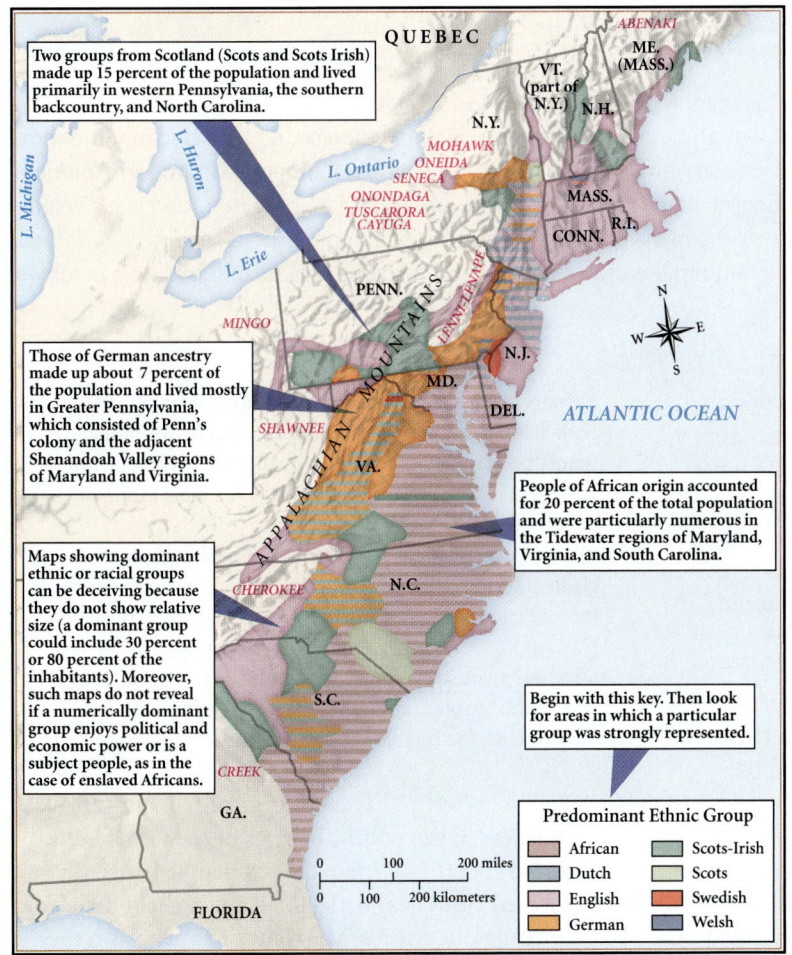

Two groups from Scotland (Scots and Scots Irish) made up 15 percent of the population and lived primarily in western Pennsylvania, the southern backcountry, and North Carolina.

Those of German ancestry made up about 7 percent of the population and lived mostly in Greater Pennsylvania, which consisted of Penn's colony and the adjacent Shenandoah Valley regions of Maryland and Virginia.

Maps showing dominant ethnic or racial groups can be deceiving because they do not show relative size (a dominant group could include 30 percent or 80 percent of the inhabitants). Moreover, such maps do not reveal if a numerically dominant group enjoys political and economic power or is a subject people, as in the case of enslaved Africans.

People of African origin accounted for 20 percent of the total population and were particularly numerous in the Tidewater regions of Maryland, Virginia, and South Carolina.

Begin with this key. Then look for areas in which a particular group was strongly represented.

Predominant Ethnic Group

- African
- Dutch
- English
- German
- Scots-Irish
- Scots
- Swedish
- Welsh

MAP 4.2

Ethnic and Racial Diversity in the British Colonies, 1775

In 1700, most colonists in British North America were of English origin; by 1775, settlers of English descent constituted only about 50 percent of the total population. African Americans now accounted for one-third of the residents of the South, while tens of thousands of German and Scots-Irish migrants added ethnic and religious diversity in the Middle colonies, the southern backcountry, and northern New England (see Figure 4.2).

---

doah Valley to the south. Governor William Gooch of Virginia welcomed the Scots-Irish presence to secure "the Country against the Indians." An Anglican planter, however, thought them as dangerous as "the Goths and Vandals of old" had been to the Roman Empire. Like the Germans, the Scots-Irish retained their culture, living in ethnic communities and holding firm to the Presbyterian Church.

Religious Identity and Political Conflict

In Western Europe, the leaders of church and state condemned religious diversity. "To tolerate all [religions] without controul is the way to have none at all," declared an Anglican clergyman. Orthodox church officials carried such sentiments to Pennsylvania. "The preachers do not have the power to punish anyone, or to force anyone to go to church," complained Gottlieb Mittelberger, an influential German minister. As a re-

sult, "Sunday is very badly kept. Many people plough, reap, thresh, hew or split wood and the like." He concluded: "Liberty in Pennsylvania does more harm than good to many people, both in soul and body."

Mittelberger was mistaken. Although ministers in Pennsylvania could not invoke government authority to uphold religious values, the result was not social anarchy. Instead, religious sects enforced moral behavior through communal self-discipline. Among Quakers, families attended a weekly meeting for worship and a monthly meeting for business, and every three months, a committee reminded parents to provide proper religious instruction. Parents took the committee's words to heart. "If thou refuse to be obedient to God's teachings," Walter Faucit of Chester County admonished his son, "thou will be a fool and a vagabond." The committee also supervised adult behavior; a Chester County meeting, for example, disciplined a member "to reclaim him from drinking to excess and keeping vain company." Significantly, Quaker meetings allowed couples

Henry Melchior Muhlenberg
Cultural Conflict in Pennsylvania

Henry Melchior Muhlenberg (1711–1787) arrived in Pennsylvania in 1742. The first German Lutheran minister in British colonies, he also became the most influential and is known as "the Patriarch of the Lutheran Church in America." Fluent in English and Dutch as well as German, Muhlenberg recorded in his voluminous journals the many conflicts – over religious dogma, Indian affairs, and political allegiance – among the diverse ethnic and religious groups of the Middle colonies.

JULY 17 [1753]. . . . Since the justice of the peace, who is a member of the Presbyterian Church, shares the secret prejudice of his fellow Presbyterians that the German Lutherans retain too much of the papistical [Catholic] leaven, he wrote into the deed of conveyance a derogatory [limiting] clause, stating that the church site is to remain the property of the Lutherans only until a further reformation takes place in our church.

JULY 21 [1753]. . . . Mr. Rose told me that a German married couple lived on this road, in service with a Dutch Reformed man, and that these people had a child to be baptized. Several weeks before, they had walked ten miles to have their child baptized in Neshaminy because it was said that I was going to preach there. But since I had not come, they had asked the Dutch Reformed preacher to baptize their child; but he would not baptize it unless they promised to rear the child in the Reformed religion. And since they neither would nor could promise such a thing, they had returned without having gained their end. . . . I baptized the child to the joy and comfort of the parents.

FEBRUARY 1 [1764]. This afternoon all citizens were summoned to the state house by the governor [who] made a public proclamation:

1) That it had been learned that a large mob of frontier settlers [the Scots-Irish Paxton Boys], who had killed several Indians in Lancaster, were coming to Philadelphia to kill the Indian families . . . under the protection of the government. . . .

3) That the governor and *counsel* called upon citizens who were willing to lend armed assistance and resist the rebellion to band themselves together. . . .

As far as I can learn, the opinion and sentiment of various ones of our German citizens is as follows:

1) They were of the opinion that it could be proved that the Indians who had lived among the so-called Moravian Brethren had secretly killed several settlers.

2) That the Quakers and Bethlehemites [Moravians] had only used some of the aforesaid Indians as spies and that they had in view only their own selfish interests, without considering at all that they had murdered their fellow Christians.

3) Indeed, [this] . . . explained why the Quakers, etc. in Philadelphia did not exhibit the least evidence of human sympathy, etc. when Germans and other settlers on the frontiers were massacred and destroyed in the most inhuman manner by the Indians. . .

4) Our German citizens . . . would unhesitatingly and gladly pour out their possessions and their blood for our most gracious king [George II, who was also the Prince of Hanover in Germany] and his officers, but they would not wage war against their own suffering fellow citizens for the sake of the Quakers and Moravians and their creatures or instruments, the double-dealing Indians.

OCTOBER 3 [1764]. . . . There was great rejoicing and great bitterness in the political circles of the city, since it was reported that the German church people [the Lutheran and Reformed churches] had gained a victory in the election by putting our *trustee*, Mr. Henry Keppele, into the *assembly*. . . . The English and German Quakers, the Moravians, Mennonites, and Schwenkfelders formed one party, and the English of the High Church and the Presbyterian Church, the German Lutherans, and the German Reformed joined the other party and gained the upper hand—a thing heretofore unheard of.

Source: Henry Melchior Muhlenberg, *The Notebook of a Colonial Clergyman*, trans. and ed. Theodore G. Tappert and John W. Doberstein (Philadelphia: Muhlenberg Press, 1959), 46–47, 50–51, 95–97, 111.

ANALYZING THE EVIDENCE

- Why were Germans reluctant to take up arms against the Paxton Boys?

- One line of religious division separated sects based primarily on congregations (Quakers, Moravians, Mennonites) from churches with hierarchies and bishops (Anglicans, Presbyterians, Lutherans, Reformed). What else separated these Christians? Why would a Reformed minister refuse to baptize a Lutheran child? Why would a Presbyterian justice of the peace limit the property rights of German Lutherans?

to marry only if they had land and livestock sufficient to support a family. As a result, the children of well-to-do Friends usually married within the sect, while poor Quakers remained unmarried, wed later in life, or married without permission—in which case they were often ousted from the meeting. These marriage rules helped the Quakers build a self-contained and prosperous community.

In the 1740s, Quaker dominance in Pennsylvania was threatened: The flood of new migrants reduced Quakers to a minority—a mere 30 percent of Pennsylvanians. Moreover, Scots-Irish settlers in central Penn-

sylvania were demanding an aggressive Indian policy, challenging the pacifism of the assembly. To retain power, Quaker politicians sought an alliance with German religious groups who also embraced pacifism and voluntary (not compulsory) militia service (see Voices from Abroad, "Henry Melchior Muhlenberg: Cultural Conflict in Pennsylvania," p. 114). But German leaders demanded more seats in the assembly, in which Quakers were overrepresented, and laws that respected their inheritance customs. Other Germans—Lutherans and Baptists—tried to seize control of the assembly by forming a "general confederacy" with Scots-Irish Presbyterians. An observer, noting that "religious zeal is secretly burning," predicted that the scheme was doomed to failure because of "mutual jealousy" (Map 4.3).

By the 1750s, politics throughout the Middle colonies had become a roiling cauldron of such conflicts. In New York, a Dutchman declared that he "Valued English Law no more than a Turd," while in Pennsylvania, Benjamin Franklin disparaged the "boorish" character and "swarthy complexion" of German migrants. The Middle Atlantic's experiment in social diversity prefigured the bitter ethnic and religious tensions that would pervade American society in the centuries to come.

- Who were the new migrants to the Middle colonies? Why did they leave Europe? What were their goals in British North America?

- What were the main issues that divided the ethnic and religious groups of the Middle colonies?

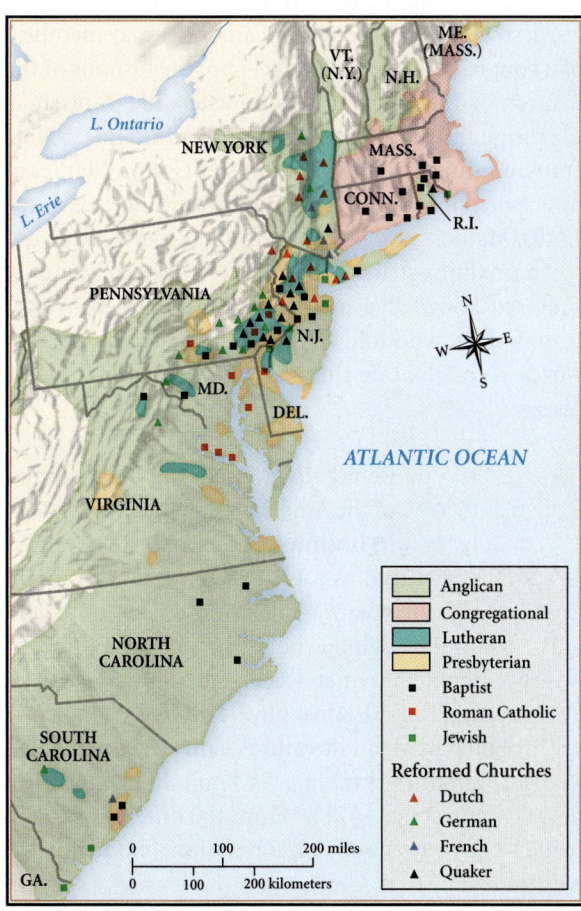

MAP 4.3

Religious Diversity in 1750

By 1750, religious diversity was on the rise, not only in the multiethnic Middle colonies but in all of British North America. Baptists had increased their numbers in New England, long the stronghold of Congregationalists, and would soon become important in Virginia. Already there were considerable numbers of Presbyterians, Lutherans, and German Reformed in the South, where Anglicanism was the established religion.

The Enlightenment and the Great Awakening, 1720–1765

Two great European cultural movements reached America between the 1720s and the 1760s: the Enlightenment and Pietism. The Enlightenment, which emphasized the power of human reason to understand and shape the world, appealed especially to urban artisans and well-educated men and women from merchant or planter families. Pietism, an evangelical Christian movement that stressed the individual's personal relationship with God, attracted many more adherents, primarily farmers and urban laborers. Together, the two movements transformed American intellectual and cultural life.

The Enlightenment in America

To explain the workings of the natural world, some settlers relied on folk wisdom. Swedish migrants in Pennsylvania, for example, attributed magical powers to the great white mullein, a common wildflower, and treated fevers by tying the plant's leaves around their feet and arms. Other settlers relied on religion. As most Christians believed that the earth stood at the center of the universe and that God (and Satan) intervened directly and continuously in human affairs, they were constantly on the watch for signs of God's favor and Satan's wiles.

The European Enlightenment   The scientific revolution of the sixteenth and seventeenth centuries challenged both folk and traditional Christian worldviews. In 1543, the Polish astronomer Copernicus published his observation that the earth traveled around the sun, not vice versa. Copernicus's discovery suggested that humans occupied a more modest place in the universe than Christian theology assumed. In the next century Sir Isaac Newton, in his *Principia Mathematica* (1687), used the sciences of mathematics and physics to explain the movement of the planets around the sun. Newton's laws of motion and gravity described how the universe operated by means of natural forces. By accounting for the movement of the planets without recourse to a supernatural being, Newton's work undermined the traditional Christian understanding of the cosmos.

In the century between the *Principia Mathematica* and the French Revolution of 1789, the philosophers of the European Enlightenment used empirical research and scientific reasoning to study all aspects of life, including social institutions and human behavior. Enlightenment thinkers advanced four fundamental principles: the lawlike order of the natural world, the power of human reason, the "natural rights" of individuals (including the right to self-government), and the progressive improvement of society.

English philosopher John Locke was a major contributor to the Enlightenment. In his *Essay Concerning Human Understanding* (1690), Locke stressed the impact of environment and experience on human behavior and beliefs. He argued that the character of individuals and societies was not fixed but could be changed through education, rational thought, and purposeful action. Locke's *Two Treatises of Government* (1690) advanced the revolutionary theory that political authority was not given by God to monarchs, as James II had insisted (see Chapter 3). Instead, it derived from social compacts that people made to preserve their "natural rights" to life, liberty, and property. In Locke's view, the people should have the power to change government policies—or even their form of government.

Locke's ideas and those of other Enlightenment thinkers (arriving in America by way of books and educated migrants) caused some clergymen to respond by devising a rational form of Christianity. Rejecting supernatural interventions and a vengeful Calvinist God, Congregationalist minister Andrew Eliot maintained that "there is nothing in Christianity that is contrary to reason." Reverend John Wise of Ipswich, Massachusetts, used Locke's philosophy to defend the vesting of power in ordinary church members. Just as the social compact formed the basis of political society, Wise argued, so the religious covenant among the lay members of a congregation made them—not the bishops of the Church of England or even ministers like himself— the proper interpreters of religious truth. The Enlightenment influenced Puritan minister Cotton Mather as well. When a measles epidemic ravaged Boston in the 1710s, Mather thought that only God could end it; but when smallpox struck a decade later, he used his newly acquired knowledge of inoculation—gained in part from a slave, who told him of the practice's success in Africa—to advocate this scientific preventive for the disease.

Franklin's Contributions   Benjamin Franklin was the exemplar of the American Enlightenment. Born in Boston in 1706 to devout Calvinists and apprenticed as a youth to a printer, Franklin was a self-educated man. While working as a printer and journalist in Philadelphia, he formed a "club of mutual improvement" that met weekly to discuss "Morals, Politics, or Natural Philosophy." These discussions, as well as Enlightenment literature (rather than the Bible), shaped Franklin's thinking. As Franklin explained in his *Autobiography* (1771), "From the different books I read, I began to doubt of Revelation [God-revealed truth]."

Like many urban artisans, wealthy Virginia planters, and affluent seaport merchants, Franklin became a deist. **Deism** was a way of thinking, not an established religion. "My own mind is my own church," said deist Thomas Paine. "I am of a sect by myself," added Thomas Jefferson. Influenced by Enlightenment science, deists such as Jefferson believed that a Supreme Being (or Grand Architect) created the world, then allowed it to operate by natural laws, and did not intervene in history or in people's lives. Rejecting the divinity of Christ and the authority of the Bible, deists relied on "natural

Benjamin Franklin's Influence

Benjamin Franklin's work as a scientist and inventor not only won the admiration of eighteenth-century European scientists but also captivated subsequent generations of Americans. This painted panel (c. 1830) from a fire engine of the Franklin Volunteer Fire Company of Philadelphia depicts Franklin's 1752 experiment in which he demonstrated the presence of electricity in lightning.   National Museum of American History, Smithsonian Institution.

reason," their innate moral sense, to define right and wrong (see Comparing American Voices, "Evangelical Religion and Enlightenment Rationalism," pp. 118–119). Thus Franklin, a onetime slave owner, came to question the morality of slavery, repudiating it once he recognized the parallels between racial bondage and the colonies' political bondage to Britain.

Franklin popularized the practical outlook of the Enlightenment in *Poor Richard's Almanack* (1732–1757), an annual publication that was read by thousands. He also founded the American Philosophical Society (1743–present) to promote "useful knowledge." Adopting this goal in his own life, Franklin invented bifocal lenses for eyeglasses, the Franklin stove, and the lightning rod. His book on electricity, published in England in 1751, won praise as the greatest contribution to science since Newton's discoveries. Inspired by Franklin, ambitious printers in America's seaport cities published newspapers and gentlemen's magazines, the first significant

nonreligious periodicals to appear in the colonies. The European Enlightenment, then, added a secular dimension to colonial cultural life, foreshadowing the great contributions to republican political theory by American intellectuals of the revolutionary era: John Adams, James Madison, and Thomas Jefferson.

American Pietism and the Great Awakening

As educated Americans turned to deism, thousands of other colonists embraced Pietism, a Christian movement originating in Germany around 1700 and emphasizing pious behavior (hence the name). In its emotional worship services and individual striving for a mystical union with God, Pietism appealed to believers' hearts rather than their minds. In the 1720s, German migrants carried Pietism to America, sparking a religious **revival** in Pennsylvania and New Jersey, where Dutch minister

Thus I have given you, I think, the Substance of the Arguments on both sides of that great and important Question

Evangelical Religion and Enlightenment Rationalism

Two great historical movements—Enlightenment thought and pietistic religion—swept across British North America in the eighteenth century and offered radically different—indeed, almost completely contradictory—worldviews. Pietism sparked religious revivals based on passion and emotion, while Enlightenment rationalism encouraged personal restraint and intellectual logic. Both movements shaped American cultural development: Pietism transformed American religious life, and Enlightenment thinking influenced the principles of the American government.

Sarah Lippet
Death as a Passage to Life

Sarah Lippet was a longtime member of the Baptist church of Middletown in eastern New Jersey. She died in October 1767, at the age of sixty-one; fellow parishioners reported her sentiments as she lay, for four days, on her deathbed.

All my lifetime I have been in fears and doubts, but now am delivered. He hath delivered them who through fear of death were all their lifetime subject to bondage. For the love I have for Christ I am willing to part with all my friends to be with Him, for I love Him above all; yet it is nothing in me, for I know if I had my desert I should be in Hell. I believe in Christ, and I know that I put my whole trust in Him, and he that believeth in Him shall not be ashamed nor be confounded. . . .

Why do you mourn when I rejoice? You should not; it is no more for me to die and leave my friends for the great love I have for Christ than for me to go to sleep. I have no fears of death in my mind. Christ has the keys of death and hell, and blessed are the dead that die in the Lord. I can't bear to see a tear shed. You should not mourn. . . .

Source: "The Triumphant Christian," in John E. Stillwell, ed., *Historical and Genealogical Miscellany* (New York, 1964), 3: 465–466.

Nathan Cole
The Struggle for Salvation

Connecticut farmer Nathan Cole found God after listening to a sermon by George Whitefield, the great English evangelist. But Cole's spiritual quest was not easy. He struggled for two years before coming to believe that he was saved.

[After hearing Whitefield] I began to think I was not Elected, and that God made some for heaven and me for hell. And I thought God was not Just in so doing. . . . My heart then rose against God exceedingly, for his making me for hell;

Now this distress lasted Almost two years—Poor Me—Miserable me. . . . I was loaded with the guilt of Sin. . . .

Hell fire was most always in my mind; and I have hundreds of times put my fingers into my pipe when I have been smoking to feel how fire felt: And to see how my Body could bear to lye in Hell fire for ever and ever. . . . And while these thoughts were in my mind God appeared unto me and made me Skringe: before whose face the heavens and the earth fled away; and I was Shrinked into nothing; I knew not whether I was in the body or out, I seemed to hang in open Air before God, and he seemed to Speak to me in an angry and Sovereign way[:] what won't you trust your Soul with God; My heart answered O yes, yes, yes. . . .

When God disappeared or in some measure withdrew, every thing was in its place again and I was on my Bed. . . . I was set free, my distress was gone, and I was filled with a pineing desire to see Christs own words in the bible; . . . I got the bible up under my Chin and hugged it; it was sweet and lovely; the word was nigh [near] me in my hand, then I began to pray and to praise God.

Source: "The Spiritual Travels of Nathan Cole, 1741" in *The Great Awakening: Documents on the Revival of Religion, 1740–1745*, ed. Richard L. Bushman (New York: Atheneum, 1970), 68–70.

Benjamin Franklin
The Importance of a Virtuous Life

Franklin stood at the center of the American Enlightenment. In his *Autobiography*, he outlined his religious views and his human-centered moral principles.

My Parents had early given me religious Impressions, and brought me through my Childhood piously in the Dissenting Way. But I was scarce 15 when, after doubting by turns of several Points as I found them disputed in the different Books I read, I began to doubt of Revelation itself. Some Books against Deism fell into my Hands. . . . It happened that they wrought an Effect on me quite contrary to what was intended by them: For the Arguments of the Deists [that were quoted in those books] appeared to me much Stronger than the Refutations. In short I soon became a thorough Deist. . . .

I grew convinc'd that Truth, Sincerity & Integrity in Dealings between Man & Man, were of the utmost Importance to the Felicity of Life, and I form'd written Resolutions, (which still remain in my Journal Book) to practice them ever while I lived. . . .

About the Year 1734. There arrived among us from Ireland, a young Presbyterian Preacher named Hemphill, who delivered with a good Voice, & apparently extempore, most excellent Discourses, which drew together considerable Numbers of different Persuasions, who join'd in admiring them. Among the rest I became one of his constant Hearers, his Sermons pleasing me as they had little of the dogmatical kind, but inculcated strongly the Practice of Virtue, or what in the religious Stile are called Good Works. Those however, of our Congregation, who considered themselves as orthodox Presbyterians, disapprov'd his Doctrine, and were join'd by most of the old Clergy, who arraign'd him of Heterodoxy before the Synod, in order to have him silenc'd. I became his zealous Partisan. . . .

I never was without some religious Principles; I never doubted, for instance, the Existance of the Deity, that he made the World, & govern'd it by his Providence; that the most acceptable Service of God was the doing Good to Man; that our Souls are immortal; and that all Crime will be punished & Virtue rewarded either here or hereafter; these I esteem'd the Essentials of every Religion.

Source: Louis P. Masur, ed., *The Autobiography of Benjamin Franklin, with Related Documents*, 2nd ed. (Boston: Bedford/St. Martin's, 2003), 73–74, 93–94, 108.

John Wise

The Primacy of Human Reason and Natural Laws

Reverend John Wise (1652–1725) served for many years as a pastor in Ipswich, Massachusetts. A graduate of Harvard College, Wise used the Enlightenment doctrines of John Locke and Samuel von Pufendorf to justify the democratic structure of New England Congregational churches.

I Shall disclose several Principles of Natural Knowledge; plainly discovering the Law of Nature; or the true sentiments of Natural Reason, with Respect to Mans Being and Government. . . . I shall consider Man in a state of Natural Being, as a Free-Born Subject under the Crown of Heaven, and owing Homage to none but God himself. It is certain Civil Government in General, is a very Admirable Result of Providence, and an Incomparable Benefit to Mankind, yet must needs be acknowledged to be the Effect of Humane Free-Compacts and not of Divine Institution; it is the Produce of Mans Reason, of Humane and Rational Combinations, and not from any direct Orders of Infinite Wisdom. . . .

The Prime Immunity in Mans State, is that he is most properly the Subject of the Law of Nature. He is the Favourite Animal on Earth; in that this Part of Gods Image, viz. Reason is Congenate with his Nature, wherein by a Law Immutable, Instampt upon his Frame, God has provided a Rule for Men in all their Actions; obliging each one to the performance of that which is Right, not only as to Justice, but likewise as to all other Moral Vertues, which is nothing but the Dictate of Right Reason founded in the Soul of Man. . . .

The Second Great Immunity of Man is an Original Liberty Instampt upon his Rational Nature. He that intrudes upon this Liberty, Violates the Law of Nature. . . .

The Third Capital Immunity belonging to Mans Nature, is an equality amongst Men; Which is not to be denied by the Law of Nature, till Man has Resigned himself with all his Rights for the sake of a Civil State; and then his Personal Liberty and Equality is to be cherished, and preserved to the highest degree.

Source: John Wise, *A Vindication of the Government of New England Churches* (Boston: J. Allen, for N. Boone, 1717), 32–40.

ANALYZING THE EVIDENCE

- All of these writers declare a belief in God. How, then, do their beliefs and outlooks differ?
- According to these authors, what is the role of "faith" and of "reason" in their religious lives?
- How would the various writers determine what was "right," or morally correct? What are the sources on which they would rely?
- John Wise asserts that civil government (political institutions) is the "Produce of Mans Reason . . . and not from any direct Orders of Infinite Wisdom." Would Nathan Cole and Sarah Lippet agree?

Enlightenment Philanthropy: Pennsylvania Hospital, Philadelphia

Using public funds and private donations, Philadelphia reformers built this imposing structure in 1753. The new hospital embodied two principles of the Enlightenment: that purposeful actions could improve society, and that the products of these actions should express reason and order, exhibited here in the building's symmetrical facade. Etchings like this one from the 1760s (*A Perspective View of the Pennsylvania Hospital*, by John Streeper and Henry Dawkins) circulated widely and bolstered Philadelphia's reputation as the center of the American Enlightenment.   Historical Society of Pennsylvania, Philadelphia.

Theodore Jacob Frelinghuysen preached passionate sermons to German settlers and encouraged church members to spread the message of spiritual urgency. A decade later, William Tennent and his son Gilbert copied Frelinghuysen's approach and led revivals among Scots-Irish Presbyterians throughout the Middle Atlantic region.

Jonathan Edwards's Calvinism | Simultaneously, an American-born Pietist movement appeared in New England. The original Puritans were intensely pious Christians, but their spiritual zeal had faded over the decades. In the 1730s, Jonathan Edwards restored that zeal to Congregational churches in the Connecticut River Valley. Edwards was born in 1703, the only son among the eleven children of Timothy and Esther Stoddard Edwards. His father was a poorly paid rural minister, but his mother was the daughter of Solomon Stoddard, a famous Puritan preacher who

taught that a compassionate God would give sainthood to more than a select few.

As a young man, Edwards rejected Stoddard's thinking. Inspired by the harsh theology of John Calvin, he preached that men and women were helpless creatures, completely dependent on the mercy of God. In his most famous sermon, "Sinners in the Hands of an Angry God" (1741), Edwards declared: "There is Hell's wide gaping mouth open; and you have nothing to stand upon, nor any thing to take hold of: there is nothing between you and Hell but the air; 'tis only the power and mere pleasure of God that holds you up." According to one observer, the response was electric: "There was a great moaning and crying through the whole house. What shall I do to be saved—oh, I am going to Hell."

Surprisingly, Edwards contributed to Enlightenment thought, accepting Locke's argument in the *Essay Concerning Human Understanding* (1690) that

Jonathan Edwards (1703–1758)
From this engraving, based on a picture by Charles Willson Peale, it is easy to imagine that Edwards's direct gaze at the viewer was the same one experienced by the preacher's congregation in Northampton, Massachusetts, as he urged them to be "born again and made new creatures." Edwards was then in his late-forties and at the height of his powers as a scholar—but not as a pastor. When Edwards restricted full church membership to "Saints"—the Calvinist "elect"—his congregation voted 200 to 23 in 1750 to dismiss the great preacher and philosopher. Impoverished, Edwards moved to the frontier town of Stockbridge, where he ministered, without great success, to the Housatonic Indians.   © Bettmann/Corbis.

ideas are the product of experience as conveyed by the senses. However, Edwards also argued that people's beliefs depended on their passions. Edwards used his theory of knowledge to justify his preaching: Vivid words would "fright persons away from Hell" and promote conversions. News of Edwards's success stimulated religious fervor up and down the Connecticut River Valley.

Whitefield's Great Awakening | English minister George Whitefield transformed the local revivals of Edwards and the Tennents into a Great Awakening. After Whitefield had his personal awakening upon reading the German Pietists, he became a follower of John Wesley, the founder of English Methodism. In 1739, Whitefield carried Wesley's fervent message to America, where he attracted huge crowds of "enthusiasts" (as conservative ministers contemptuously labeled them) from Georgia to Massachusetts. "Religion is become the Subject of most Conversations," the *Pennsylvania Gazette* reported. "No books are in Request but those of Piety and Devotion." Whitefield's preaching so impressed Benjamin Franklin that when the revivalist asked for contributions, Franklin emptied the coins in his pockets "wholly into the collector's dish, gold and all." By the time Whitefield reached Boston, Reverend Benjamin Colman reported, the people were "ready to receive him as an angel of God."

Whitefield had a compelling presence. "He looked almost angelical; a young, slim, slender youth . . . cloathed with authority from the Great God," wrote a Connecticut farmer. Like most evangelical preachers, Whitefield did not read his sermons but spoke from memory. He gestured eloquently, raised his voice for dramatic effect, and at times assumed a female persona—as a woman in labor struggling to deliver the word of God. When the young preacher told his spellbound listeners that they had sinned and must seek salvation, some suddenly felt a "new light" within them. As "the power of god come down," Hannah Heaton recalled, "my knees smote together . . . [and] it seemed to me I was a sinking down into hell . . . but then I resigned my distress and was perfectly easy quiet and calm . . . [and] it seemed as if I had a new soul & body both." Strengthened and self-confident, the so-called New Lights were eager to spread Whitefield's message.

Religious Upheaval in the North

Like all cultural explosions, the Great Awakening was controversial. Conservative ministers—passionless Old Lights, according to the evangelists—condemned the "cryings out, faintings and convulsions" in revivalist meetings and the New Lights' claims of "working Miracles or speaking with Tongues." Boston minister Charles Chauncy attacked the New Lights for allowing women to speak in public: It was "a plain breach of that commandment of the LORD, where it is said, Let your WOMEN keep silence in the churches." In Connecticut, Old Lights persuaded the legislature to prohibit evangelists from speaking to a congregation without the minister's permission. Although Whitefield insisted, "I am no *Enthusiast*," he found many pulpits closed to him when he returned to Connecticut in 1744. But the New Lights refused to be silenced. Dozens of farmers, women, and artisans roamed the countryside, condemning the Old Lights as "unconverted" and willingly accepting imprisonment: "I shall bring glory to God in my bonds," a dissident preacher wrote from jail.

The Great Awakening undermined legally established churches and their tax-supported ministers. In New England, New Lights left the Congregational Church and founded 125 "separatist" churches that supported their ministers through voluntary contributions (Figure 4.3). Other religious dissidents joined Baptist congregations, which also condemned government support of churches: "God never allowed any civil state upon earth to impose religious taxes," declared Baptist preacher Isaac Backus. In New York and New Jersey, the Dutch Reformed Church split in two as New Lights refused to accept doctrines imposed by conservative church authorities in Holland.

Indeed, the Great Awakening challenged the authority of all ministers, whose status rested on respect for their education and knowledge of the Bible. In an influential pamphlet, *The Dangers of an Unconverted Ministry* (1740), Gilbert Tennent asserted that ministers' authority should come not from theological knowledge but from the conversion experience. Reaffirming Martin Luther's belief in the priesthood of all Christians, Tennent suggested that anyone who had felt God's redeeming grace could speak with min-

isterial authority. Isaac Backus likewise celebrated a spiritual democracy, noting with approval that "the common people now claim as good a right to judge and act in matters of religion as civil rulers or the learned clergy." Proving his point were revivalists like Sarah Harrah Osborne, a New Light "exhorter" in Rhode Island, who refused "to shut up my mouth . . . and creep into obscurity" when silenced by her minister. This subversive, critical spirit soon found other targets. Jonathan Edwards spoke for many farm families when he charged that the money-grubbing practices of merchants and land speculators were more suitable "for wolves and other beasts of prey, than for human beings."

As religious enthusiasm spread, churches founded new colleges to educate their young men and to train ministers. New Light Presbyterians established the College of New Jersey (Princeton) in 1746, and New York Anglicans founded King's College (Columbia) in 1754. Baptists set up the College of Rhode Island (Brown) in 1764; two years later, the Dutch Reformed Church subsidized Queen's College (Rutgers) in New Jersey. However, the main intellectual legacy of the Great Awakening was not education for the privileged few but a new sense of authority among the many. A European visi-

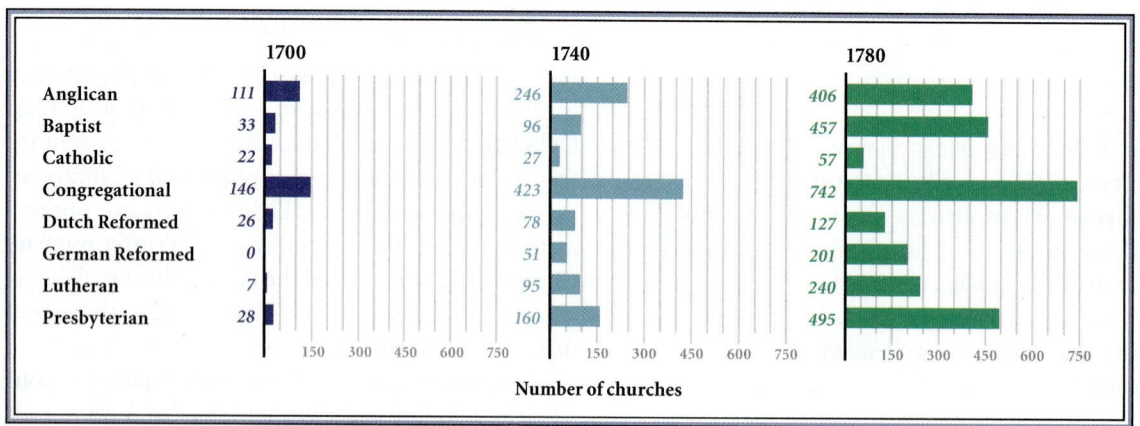

FIGURE 4.3

Church Growth by Denomination, 1700–1780

In 1700, and again in 1740, the Congregationalist and Anglican churches had the most members. By 1780, however, largely because of their enthusiastic evangelical message, Presbyterian and Baptist congregations outnumbered those of the Anglicans. The growth of immigrant denominations, such as the German Reformed and Lutheran, was equally impressive.

tor to Philadelphia remarked in surprise, "The poorest day-laborer . . . holds it his right to advance his opinion, in religious as well as political matters, with as much freedom as the gentleman."

Social and Religious Conflict in the South

In the southern colonies, where the Church of England was legally established, religious enthusiasm triggered social conflict. Anglican ministers generally ignored the spiritual needs of African Americans and landless whites, who numbered 40 percent and 20 percent of the population, respectively. Middling white freeholders (35 percent of the residents) formed the core of most Church of England congregations. But prominent planters (just 5 percent) held the real power, using their control of parish finances to discipline ministers. One clergyman complained that dismissal awaited any minister who "had the courage to preach against any Vices taken into favor by the leading Men of his Parish."

The Presbyterian Revival | Soon, a democratization of religion challenged the dominance of both the Anglican Church and the planter elite. In 1743, bricklayer Samuel Morris, inspired by reading George Whitefield's sermons, led a group of Virginia Anglicans out of their congregation. Seeking a deeper religious experience, Morris invited New Light Presbyterian Samuel Davies to lead their prayer meetings. Davies's sermons, filled with erotic devotional imagery and urging Christians to feel "ardent Passion," sparked Presbyterian revivals across the Tidewater region, threatening the social authority of the Virginia gentry. Traditionally, planters and their well-dressed families arrived at Anglican services in fancy carriages drawn by well-bred horses, and flaunted their power by marching in a body to their honored places in the front pews. Such ritual displays of the gentry's superiority were meaningless if freeholders attended other churches. Moreover, religious pluralism threatened the tax-supported status of the Anglican Church.

To halt the spread of New Light ideas, Virginia governor William Gooch denounced them as "false teachings," and Anglican justices of the peace closed Presbyterian churches. This harassment kept most white yeomen and poor tenant families in the Church of England; so did the fact that many well-educated Presbyterian ministers did not preach in the "enthusiastic" style preferred by illiterate farmers.

The Baptist Insurgency | New Light Baptist ministers did not hesitate to reach out to ordinary folk. During the 1760s, their vigorous preaching and democratic message converted thousands of white farm families. The Baptists were radical Protestants whose central ritual was adult (rather than infant) baptism. Once men and women had experienced the infusion of grace — had been "born again" — they were baptized in an emotional public ceremony, often involving complete immersion in water.

Even slaves were welcome at Baptist revivals. During the 1740s, George Whitefield had urged Carolina planters to bring their slaves into the Christian fold, but white opposition and the Africans' commitment to their ancestral religions kept the number of converts low. However, in the 1760s, native-born African Americans in Virginia welcomed the Baptists' message that all people were equal in God's eyes. Sensing a threat to the system of racial slavery, the House of Burgesses imposed heavy fines on Baptists who preached to slaves without their owners' permission.

The Baptists' insurgency posed other threats to gentry authority. Baptist preachers repudiated social distinctions and urged followers to call one another "brother" and "sister." They also condemned the planters' dissolute lifestyle. As planter Landon Carter complained, the Baptists were "destroying pleasure in the Country; for they encourage ardent Prayer . . . & an intire Banishment of *Gaming, Dancing,* & Sabbath-Day Diversions." The gentry responded with violence. Hearing Baptist Dutton Lane condemn "the vileness and danger" of drunkenness and whoring, planter John Giles took the charge personally: "I know who you mean! and by God I'll demolish you." In Caroline County, an Anglican posse attacked Brother John Waller at a prayer meeting. Waller "was violently jerked off the stage; they caught him by the back part of his neck, beat his head against the ground, and a gentleman gave him twenty lashes with his horsewhip."

Despite these attacks, Baptist congregations multiplied. By 1775, about 15 percent of Virginia's whites and hundreds of enslaved blacks had joined Baptist churches. To signify their state of grace, some Baptist men "cut off their hair, like Cromwell's round-headed chaplains." Others forged a new evangelical masculinity — "crying, weeping, lifting up the eyes, groaning" when touched by the Holy Spirit but defending themselves with vigor.

"Not able to bear the insults" of a heckler, a group of Baptists "took [him] by the neck and heels and threw him out of doors," setting off a bloody brawl.

The Baptist revival in the Chesapeake challenged customary authority in families and society but did not overturn it. Rejecting the pleas of evangelical women, Baptist men kept church authority in the hands of "free born male members"; and Anglican slaveholders retained control of the political system. Still, the Baptist insurgency infused the lives of poor tenant families with spiritual meaning and empowered yeomen to defend their economic interests. Moreover, as Baptist ministers spread Christianity among slaves, the cultural gulf between blacks and whites shrank, undermining one justification for slavery and giving some blacks a new religious identity. Within a generation, African Americans would develop distinctive versions of Protestant Christianity.

- In what ways did the Enlightenment and the Great Awakening prompt Americans to challenge traditional sources of authority?

- How did the Baptist insurgency in Virginia challenge conventional assumptions about race, gender, and class?

The Midcentury Challenge: War, Trade, and Social Conflict, 1750–1765

Between 1750 and 1765, three significant events transformed colonial life. First, Britain went to war against the French in America, sparking a worldwide conflict: the Great War for Empire. Second, a surge in trade boosted colonial consumption but caused Americans to become deeply indebted to British creditors. Third, westward migration sparked warfare with Indian peoples, violent disputes between settlers and land speculators, and backcountry rebellions against eastern-controlled governments.

The French and Indian War

By 1754, France and Britain had laid claim to the vast area between the Appalachian Mountains and the Mississippi River, but few Europeans had moved there (Map 4.4). Though terrain prevented easy access from Britain's seaboard colonies, the Iroquois and their native allies actively expelled white intruders.

However, the strategy the Indians had been using to obtain guns and other goods—playing off the French against the British—was breaking down. The Europeans resented the rising cost of the play-off "gifts," and the Indians faced increasing Anglo-American demands for their lands. In the late 1740s, the Mohawks rebuffed attempts by Sir William Johnson, a British agent and land speculator, to settle Scottish migrants west of Albany. The Iroquois also responded angrily when Virginia governor Robert Dinwiddie, in partnership with Virginia speculators and London merchants, formed the Ohio Company in 1749 and successfully petitioned the king for a grant of 200,000 acres. The land lay in the upper Ohio River Valley, an area the Iroquois controlled through alliances with the Delaware and Shawnee peoples. "We don't know what you Christians, English and French intend," the outraged Iroquois complained. "[W]e are so hemmed in by both, that we have hardly a hunting place left."

The Albany Congress | To mend relations with the Iroquois, the British Board of Trade called a meeting at Albany in June 1754. At the Albany Congress, British colonial delegates denied having designs on Iroquois lands and sought the Indians' aid against New France. Though small in numbers, the French colony had a broad reach. In the 1750s, the 15,000 French farm families along the St. Lawrence River supplied the fur-trading settlements of Montreal and Quebec and the hundreds of fur traders, missionaries, and soldiers who lived among the western Indian peoples.

To counter French expansion, Benjamin Franklin proposed a "Plan of Union," calling for a continental assembly to manage trade, Indian policy, and defense in the West. But neither Franklin's scheme nor a Board of Trade proposal for a political "union between ye Royal, Proprietary, & Charter Governments" was in the cards. The British ministry worried that union would spark demands for independence; the Americans, warned one official, felt themselves "intitled to a greater measure of Liberty than is enjoyed by the people of England." For their part, colonial leaders feared that a consolidated government would undermine the authority of their assemblies.

French authorities, alarmed as the Iroquois were by the Ohio Company's land grant, sought to stop Anglo-American settlers from pouring into the Ohio River Valley by building a series of forts. One of these, Fort Duquesne, stood where the Monongahela and Allegheny rivers join to form the Ohio River at present-day Pittsburgh. To reassert British claims, Governor

MAP 4.4

European Spheres of Influence in North America, 1754

In the mid-eighteenth century, France, Spain, and the British-owned Hudson Bay Company laid claim to the vast areas of North America still inhabited primarily by Indian peoples. British settlers had already occupied much of the land east of the Appalachian Mountains. To safeguard their lands west of the mountains, Native Americans played off one European power against another. As a British official remarked: "To preserve the Ballance between us and the French is the great ruling Principle of Modern Indian Politics." When Britain expelled France from North America in 1763, Indians had to face encroaching Anglo-American settlers on their own.

Dinwiddie dispatched an expedition led by Colonel George Washington, a young Virginia planter and Ohio Company stockholder. In July 1754, French troops seized Washington and his men, prompting Virginian and British expansionists to demand war. Henry Pelham, the British prime minister, urged calm: "There is such a load of debt, and such heavy taxes already laid upon the people, that nothing but an absolute necessity can justifie our engaging in a new War."

The War Hawks Win Pelham could not control the march of events. In Parliament, two expansionist-minded war hawks—rising British statesman William Pitt and Lord Halifax, the new head of the Board of Trade—persuaded Pelham to launch an American war. In June 1755, British and New England troops captured Fort Beauséjour in the disputed territory of Nova Scotia (which the French called Acadia). Soldiers from Puritan Massachusetts then forced nearly

Braddock's Defeat and Death, July 1755

In May 1755 General Edward Braddock led a force of 1,500 British regulars and Virginia militiamen out of Fort Cumberland in western Maryland, intending to oust the French from Fort Duquesne, 50 miles to the west. As Braddock neared the fort, the French garrison of 200 troops and about 600 Indian allies— mostly Potawotomis, Ottawas, Shawnees, and Delawares—set out to ambush his force. Instead, they unexpectedly met the British along a narrow roadway. As the French and Indians fanned out to attack from the woods, the British troops (George Washington reported) "were struck with such a panic that they behaved with more cowardice than it is possible to conceive. The officers behaved gallantly, in order to encourage their men, for which they suffered greatly." The British casualties—450 killed, 500 wounded— included General Braddock, pictured above, who later died from his wounds. © Chicago History Museum, USA/The Bridgeman Art Library International.

10,000 French settlers from their lands, arguing they were "rebels" without property rights, and deported them to France, the West Indies, and Louisiana (where "Acadians" was turned into "Cajuns"). English and Scottish Protestants took over the farms the French Catholics left behind.

This Anglo-American triumph was quickly offset by a stunning defeat. In July 1755, a French and Indian force attacked and routed 1,500 British regulars and Virginia militiamen advancing on Fort Duquesne. The attackers slew the British commander, General Edward Braddock, and killed or wounded more than half of his troops. "We have been beaten, most shamefully beaten, by a handfull of Men," George Washington complained bitterly as he led the survivors back to Virginia.

The Great War for Empire

By 1756, the American conflict had spread to Europe, where it was known as the Seven Years' War, and pitted Britain and Prussia against France, Spain, and Austria. When Britain mounted major offensives in India, West Africa, and the West Indies as well as in North America, the conflict became the Great War for Empire. Since 1700, Britain had reaped huge profits from its overseas trading empire; now it vowed to crush France, the main obstacle to further British expansion.

William Pitt emerged as the architect of the British war effort. Pitt, the grandson of the East Indies merchant Thomas "Diamond" Pitt, was a committed expansionist with a touch of arrogance. "I know that I can save this country and that I alone can," he boasted. In fact, Pitt was a master of both commercial and military strategy, and planned to cripple France by seizing its colonies. In designing the campaign against New France, Pitt exploited a demographic advantage: In North America, George II's 2 million subjects outnumbered the French 14 to 1. To mobilize the colonists, Pitt paid half the cost of their troops and supplied them with arms and equipment, at a cost of £1 million a year. He also committed a fleet of British ships and 30,000 British soldiers to the conflict in America.

Beginning in 1758, the powerful Anglo-American forces moved from one triumph to the next. They forced the French to abandon Fort Duquesne (renamed Fort Pitt) and then captured Fort Louisbourg, a stronghold at the mouth of the St. Lawrence. In 1759, an armada led by British general James Wolfe sailed down the St. Lawrence and took Quebec, the heart of France's American empire. The Royal Navy prevented French reinforcements from crossing the Atlantic, allowing British forces to complete the conquest of Canada in 1760 by capturing Montreal (Map 4.5).

Elsewhere, the British likewise had great success. From Spain, the British won Cuba and the Philippine Islands. Fulfilling Pitt's dream, the East India Company ousted French traders from India, and British forces seized French Senegal in West Africa. They also captured the rich sugar islands of Martinique and Guadeloupe in the French West Indies, but at the insistence of the West Indian sugar lobby (which wanted to protect its monopoly), the ministry returned the islands to France. In vain, William Burke (cousin to writer and philosopher Edmund Burke) argued that it was "by Means of the *West Indian* Trade that a great Part of *North America* is at all enable to trade with us." Despite the controversial decision to retain Canada rather than the sugar islands, the Treaty of Paris of 1763 confirmed Britain's triumph. It granted Britain sovereignty over half the continent of North America, including French Canada, all French territory east of the Mississippi River, Spanish Florida, and the recent conquests in Africa and India. Britain had forged a commercial and colonial empire that was nearly worldwide.

Britain's territorial acquisitions alarmed Indian peoples from New York to the Mississippi, who preferred the presence of a few French fur traders to an influx of thousands of Anglo-American settlers. To encourage the French to return, the Ottawa chief Pontiac declared, "I am French, and I want to die French." Neolin, a Delaware prophet, went further; he taught that the Indians' decline stemmed from their dependence on European goods, guns, and rum. He called for the expulsion of all white-skinned invaders: "If you suffer the English among you, you are dead men. Sickness, smallpox, and their poison [rum] will destroy you entirely." In 1763, inspired by Neolin's nativist vision, Pontiac led a major uprising by a group of loosely confederated tribes (stretching geographically from the New York Senecas to the Minnesota Chippewas). Indian forces seized nearly every British military garrison west of Fort Niagara, besieged the fort at Detroit, and killed or captured more than 2,000 settlers. But the Indian alliance gradually weakened, and British military expeditions defeated the Delawares near Fort Pitt and broke the siege of Detroit. In the peace settlement, Pontiac and his allies accepted the British as their new political "fathers." In return, the British issued the Proclamation of 1763, which prohibited white settlements west of the Appalachians. It was an edict that the colonists would ignore.

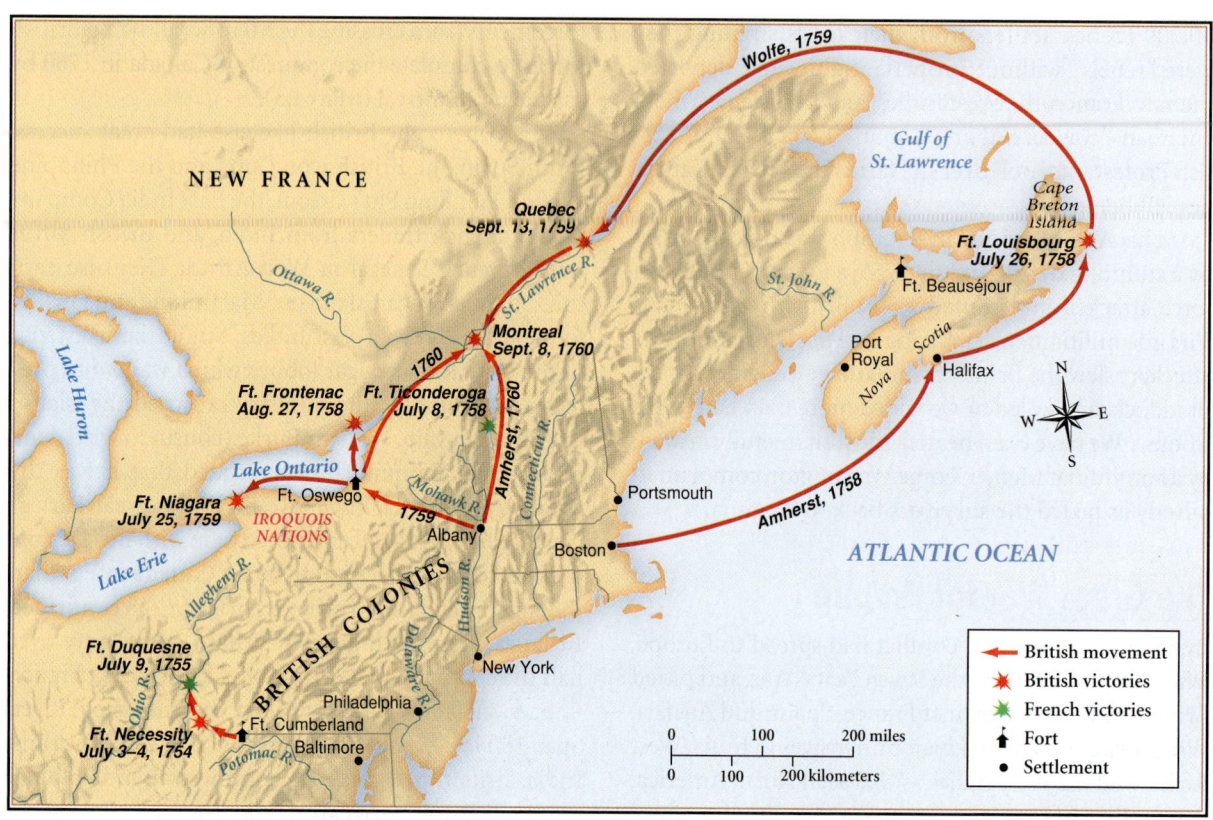

MAP 4.5

The Anglo-American Conquest of New France

After full-scale war with France began in 1756, it took almost three years for the British ministry to equip colonial forces and dispatch a sizable army to far-off America. In 1758, British and colonial troops attacked the heartland of New France, capturing Quebec in 1759 and Montreal in 1760. This conquest both united and divided the allies. Colonists celebrated the great victory: "The Illuminations and Fireworks exceeded any that had been exhibited before," reported the *South Carolina Gazette*. However, British officers had little respect for colonial soldiers. Said one, "[They are] the dirtiest, most contemptible, cowardly dogs you can conceive."

British Industrial Growth and the Consumer Revolution

Britain owed its military and diplomatic success to its unprecedented economic resources. Since 1700, when it had wrested control of many oceanic trade routes from the Dutch, Britain had become the dominant commercial power in the Atlantic and Indian oceans. By 1750, it was also becoming the first country to use new manufacturing technology and work discipline to expand output. This combination of commerce and industry would soon make Britain the most powerful nation in the world.

Mechanical power was key to Britain's Industrial Revolution. British artisans designed and built water mills and steam engines that efficiently powered a wide array of machines: lathes for shaping wood, jennies and

looms for spinning and weaving textiles, and hammers for forging iron. Compared with traditional manufacturing methods, the new power-driven machinery produced woolen and linen textiles, iron tools, furniture, and chinaware in greater quantities—and at lower cost. Moreover, the entrepreneurs running the new workshops drove their employees hard, forcing them to keep pace with the machines and work long hours. To market the abundant factory-produced goods, English and Scottish merchants extended credit to colonial shopkeepers for a full year instead of the traditional six months. Americans soon were purchasing 30 percent of all British exports.

To pay for British manufactures, mainland colonists increased their exports of tobacco, rice, indigo, and wheat. In Virginia, farmers moved into the Piedmont, the region of plains and rolling hills inland from the flat

Tidewater counties. Using credit advanced by Scottish merchants, planters bought land, slaves, and equipment to grow tobacco, which they exported to expanding markets in France and central Europe (see Reading American Pictures, "Selling Virginia Tobacco in Britain," p. 130). In South Carolina, rice planters enhanced their luxurious lifestyle by using British government subsidies to develop indigo plantations. By the 1760s, they were exporting the deep blue dye to English textile factories and 65 million pounds of rice a year to Holland and southern Europe. Simultaneously, New York, Pennsylvania, Maryland, and Virginia became the breadbasket of the Atlantic world, supplying Europe's exploding population with wheat. In Philadelphia, export prices for wheat jumped almost 50 percent between 1740 and 1765.

Americans used profits from agriculture to buy English manufactures, often on credit. Although this "consumer revolution" raised living standards, it landed many consumers—and the colonies as a whole—in debt (Figure 4.4). Even during the wartime boom of the 1750s, exports paid for only 80 percent of British imports. Britain financed the remaining 20 percent—the Americans' trade deficit—through the extension of credit and Pitt's military expenditures. When the military subsidies ended in 1763, the colonies fell into an economic recession. Merchants looked anxiously at their overstocked warehouses and feared bankruptcy. "I think we have a gloomy prospect before us," a Philadelphia trader noted in 1765, "as there are of late some

Persons failed, who were in no way suspected." The increase in transatlantic trade had made Americans more dependent on overseas credit and markets.

The Struggle for Land in the East

In good times and bad, the population continued to grow, intensifying the demand for arable land. Consider the experience of Kent, Connecticut, founded in 1738 by descendants of the original Puritan migrants. Like earlier generations, they had moved inland to establish new farms, but Kent stood at the colony's western boundary. To provide for the next generation, many Kent families joined the Susquehanna Company (1749), which speculated in lands in the Wyoming Valley in present-day northeastern Pennsylvania. As settlers took up farmsteads there, the company urged the Connecticut legislature to claim the region on the basis of Connecticut's "sea-to-sea" royal charter of 1662. However, Charles II had also granted the Wyoming Valley to William Penn, and the Penn family had sold farms there to Pennsylvania residents. By the late 1750s, settlers from Connecticut and Pennsylvania were at war, burning down their rivals' houses and barns.

Simultaneously, three distinct but related land disputes broke out in the Hudson River Valley (Map 4.6). Dutch tenant farmers, Wappinger Indians, and migrants from Massachusetts asserted ownership rights to lands long claimed by manorial families such as the Van

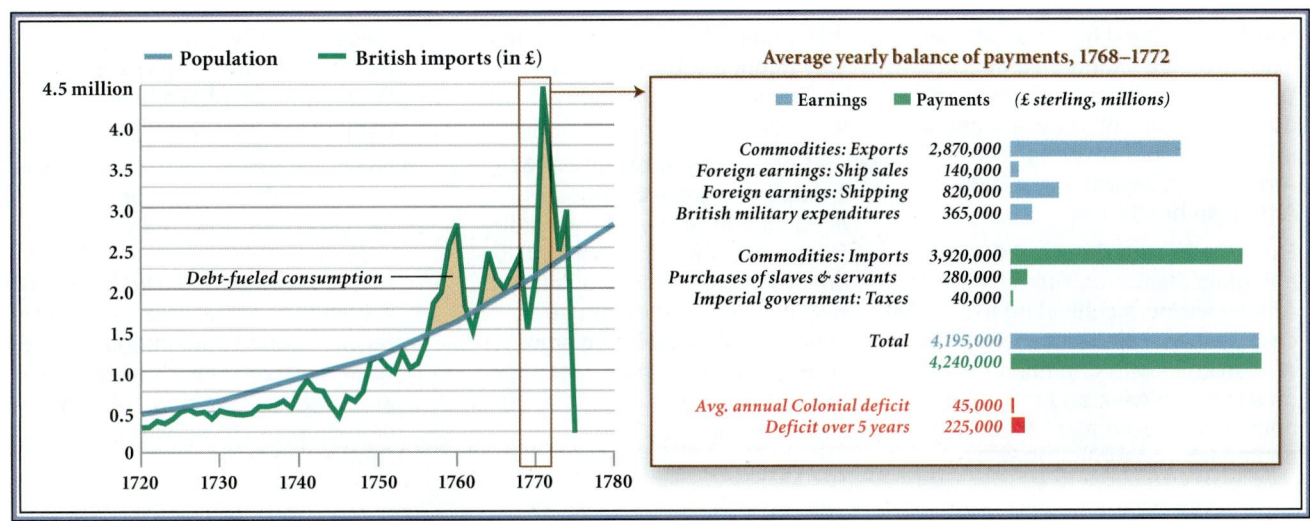

FIGURE 4.4

Mainland Population and British Imports

Around 1750, British imports were growing at a faster rate than the American population, indicating that the colonists were consuming more per capita. But Americans went into debt to pay for these goods, running an annual trade deficit with their British suppliers that by 1772 created a cumulative debt of £2 million.

Selling Virginia Tobacco in Britain

Tobacco was a big business in England in the 1760s, and the competition among tobacco sellers was keen. To attract customers to his shop, London grocer George Farr commissioned an engraver to create this advertising card, which wittily made a pun on his name. Other tobacco shops issued similar trade cards for their brands of "sweet-scented Virginia tobacco." Even more interesting than the explosion of commercial advertising in the mid-eighteenth century is the imagery used by Farr and other sellers, which both shows and conceals a great deal about the origins of the tobacco sold in Britain.

The Finest Tobacco by Farr, London, c. 1750–1770.
Library of Congress.

ANALYZING THE EVIDENCE

- Why is the central figure an African king or prince sitting on a throne? What would such a figure have to do with the sale of Virginia tobacco in London? And why might an African man be wearing a Native American headdress?

- Farr's trade card does not depict a Virginia plantation with enslaved African workers cultivating the crop. Rather, it shows a cherub-like African child with one hand resting on a tobacco cask and the other holding a tobacco plant. How might an English consumer interpret

this image of tobacco production? Why might a tobacco seller such as Farr choose to include a child in his advertisement?

- An English street ballad of 1676 condemned tobacco smoke, alleging that "cursed Pagans did, Devise this stinke," which for a long time had been "from Christians hid." Why did the ballad use religion to attack tobacco smokers? How does this advertisement of the 1760s, with its exotic imagery, address that issue?

- Observe the two ships in the background with flags waving. Why might they have been depicted in this advertisement?

- Neither African in Farr's advertisement is clothed. Another trade card shows a powerfully built, semi-naked African man pointing to a tobacco ad and a well-dressed British man smoking a pipe. What power relations are suggested by such interracial images of dress and undress? What might they convey about the ideology of the British empire?

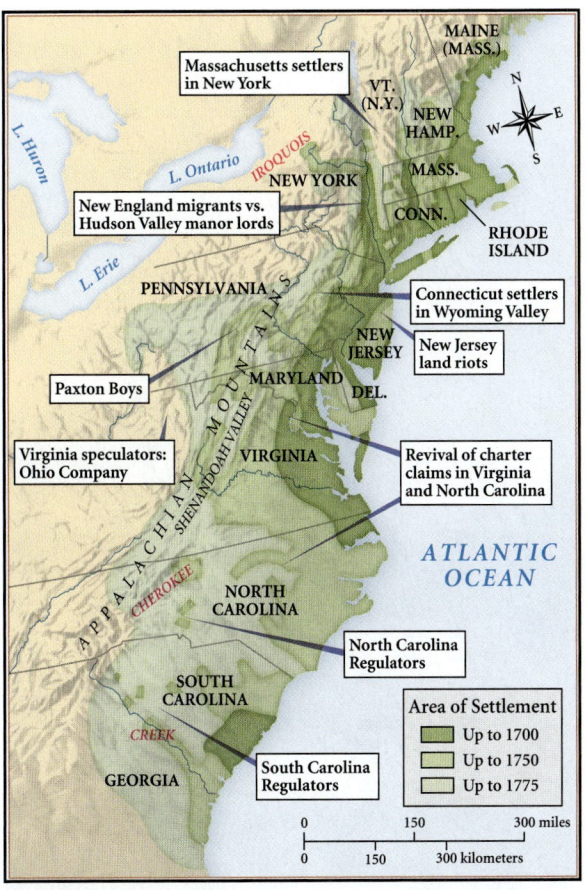

MAP 4.6

Westward Expansion and Land Conflicts, 1750–1775

Between 1750 and 1775, the mainland colonial population more than doubled—from 1.2 million to 2.5 million—triggering westward migrations and legal battles over land, which had become increasingly valuable. Violence broke out in eastern areas, where tenant farmers and smallholders contested landlords' property claims based on ancient titles; and in the backcountry, where migrating settlers fought with Indians, rival claimants, and the officials of eastern-dominated governments.

Rensselaers and the Livingstons. When the manorial lords turned to the legal system to uphold their claims, Dutch and English farmers in Westchester, Dutchess, and Albany counties rioted to close the courts. In response, New York's royal governor ordered British general Thomas Gage and two regiments of troops to assist local sheriffs and manorial bailiffs: They suppressed the tenant uprisings, intimidated the Wappingers, and evicted the Massachusetts squatters.

Other land disputes erupted in New Jersey and the southern colonies, where landlords and English aristocrats had successfully revived legal claims based on long-dormant seventeenth-century charters. One court decision allowed Lord Granville, the heir of an original

Carolina proprietor, to collect an annual tax on land in North Carolina; another decision awarded ownership of the entire northern neck of Virginia (along the Potomac River) to Lord Fairfax.

The revival of these proprietary claims by manorial lords and English nobles testified to the rising value of land along the Atlantic coastal plain. It also reflected the maturity of the colonial courts, which now had enough authority to uphold property rights. And it underscored the increasing similarities between rural societies in Europe and America. To avoid the status of European peasants, native-born yeomen and tenant families joined the stream of European migrants searching for cheap land near the Appalachian Mountains.

Western Rebels and Regulators

As would-be landowners moved westward, they sparked conflicts over Indian policy, political representation, and debts. During the war with France, Delaware and Shawnee warriors had exacted revenge for Thomas Penn's land swindle of 1737 by destroying frontier farms in Pennsylvania and killing hundreds of residents. Scots-Irish settlers demanded the expulsion of all Indians, but Quaker leaders refused. So in 1763, a group of Scots-Irish frontiersmen called the Paxton Boys massacred 20 members of the peaceful Conestoga tribe. When Governor John Penn tried to bring the murderers to justice, 250 armed Scots-Irish advanced on Philadelphia. Benjamin Franklin intercepted the angry mob at Lancaster and arranged a truce, averting a battle with the militia. Prosecution of the Paxton Boys failed for lack of witnesses, and the Scots-Irish dropped their demands that the Indians be expelled; but the episode left a legacy of racial hatred and political resentment.

The South Carolina Regulators | Violence also broke out in the backcountry of South Carolina, where land-hungry Scottish and Anglo-American settlers clashed repeatedly with Cherokees during the war with France. After the fighting ended in 1763, a group of landowning vigilantes known as the Regulators tried to suppress outlaw bands of whites that were stealing cattle. The Regulators also had political demands: that the eastern-controlled government provide western districts with more courts, fairer taxation, and greater representation in the assembly. "We are *Free-Men*—British Subjects—Not Born *Slaves*," declared a Regulator manifesto. Fearing slave revolts, the lowland rice planters who ran the South Carolina assembly compromised with the vigilantes rather than fighting them. In 1767, the assembly created western

A Hudson River Manor

Philipse Manor (just up the Hudson from present-day New York City) encompassed 90,000 acres, and included mills and warehouses as well as a grand house. In this unattributed painting dated 1783, the artist has dressed the women in the foreground in classical costumes, thereby linking the Philipses to the noble families of the Roman republic. To preserve their aristocratic lifestyle and the quasi-feudal leasehold system of agriculture, the Philipses joined with other Hudson River manorial lords to suppress tenant uprisings in the 1760s. During the American Revolution, the family remained loyal to the king and Patriot tenants took control of the manor.   Historic Hudson Valley, Tarrytown, New York.

courts and reduced the fees for legal documents; but it refused to reapportion the legislature or lower western taxes. Like the Paxton Boys in Pennsylvania, the South Carolina Regulators won attention to backcountry needs but failed to wrest power from the eastern elite.

Civil Strife in North Carolina In 1766, a more radical Regulator movement arose in North Carolina. When the economic recession of the early 1760s brought a sharp fall in tobacco prices, many farmers could not pay their debts. When creditors sued these farmers for payment, judges directed sheriffs to seize the debtors' property and sell it to pay debts and court costs. Many backcountry farmers—including evangelical Baptist, German pietist, and Scots-Irish Pres-

byterian migrants—denounced the merchants' lawsuits, both because they generated high fees for lawyers and court officials and because they violated rural customs, which allowed loans to remain unpaid in hard times. Others ended up in jail for resisting court orders.

To save their farms from grasping creditors and tax-hungry officials, North Carolina's debtors defied the government's authority. Disciplined mobs of farmers intimidated judges, closed courts, and freed their comrades from jail. Significantly, the Regulators proposed a coherent set of reforms, including lower legal fees and tax payments in the "produce of the country" rather than in cash. In addition, they demanded greater representation in the assembly and a just revenue system that would tax each person "in proportion to the profits aris-

Governor Tryon and the Regulators Meet at Hillsborough, 1768

Orange County, North Carolina, was home to the Sandy Creek Association, led by Herman Husband, a powerful advocate of social justice and the Regulator movement. Accused of corruption by the Associators, Orange County Sheriff Edmund Fanning assailed its members as "Rebels, Insurgents . . . [who should] be shot, hang'd, &c. as mad Dogs," and arrested Husband and two other leaders. To preserve order at Husband's trial, Governor William Tryon led a militia force of 1,400 to Hillsborough, where they confronted 800 Regulators. Only a set of judicious, politically driven decisions defused the potentially violent confrontation shown in the engraving. The judges acquitted Husband of "inciting to riot" but convicted his two associates (whose fines were promptly suspended by the governor). The court also convicted Sheriff Fanning of extortion, while fining him only 3 pennies. With each side claiming victory, the crisis eased but its underlying causes remained. In 1771, Tryon and the Regulators engaged in a pitched battle near the Alamance River, twenty miles west of Hillsborough.   Picture Research Consultants and Archives.

ing from his estate." All to no avail. In May 1771, Royal Governor William Tryon moved to suppress the Regulators. Mobilizing British troops and the eastern militia, Tryon defeated a large Regulator force at the Alamance River. When the fighting ended, 30 men lay dead, and Tryon summarily executed seven insurgent leaders. Not since Bacon's Rebellion in Virginia in 1675 and the colonial uprisings during the Glorious Revolution of 1688 (see Chapter 2) had an American domestic dispute caused so much bloodshed and political agitation.

In 1771, as in 1675 and 1688, colonial conflicts became linked with imperial politics. In Connecticut, Reverend Ezra Stiles defended the North Carolina Regulators. "What shall an injured & oppressed people do,"

he asked, "[when faced with] Oppression and tyranny?" Stiles's remarks reflected growing resistance to recently imposed British policies of taxation and control. The American colonies still depended primarily on Britain for their trade and military defense. However, by the 1760s, the mainland settlements had evolved into complex societies with the potential to exist independently. British policies would determine the direction the maturing colonies would take.

- What impact did the Industrial Revolution in England have on the American colonies?

- What were the causes of unrest in the American backcountry in the mid-eighteenth century?

SUMMARY

In this chapter, we observed dramatic changes in British North America between 1720 and 1765. An astonishing surge in population—from 400,000 to almost 2 million—was the combined result of natural increase, European migration, and the African slave trade. Three other transatlantic influences were equally important: The European Enlightenment, European Pietism, and British consumer goods altered the cultural landscape.

We watched the colonists confront three major regional challenges. In New England, crowded towns and ever-smaller farms threatened the yeoman ideal of independent farming, prompting families to limit births, move to the frontier, or participate in an "exchange" economy. In the Middle Atlantic colonies, Dutch, English, German, and Scots-Irish residents maintained their religious and cultural identities, leading to bruising ethnic conflicts. Finally, westward migration into the backcountry and the Ohio River Valley set off battles with Indian peoples, civil unrest among whites, and, ultimately, the Great War for Empire. In the aftermath of the fighting, Britain stood triumphant in Europe and America.

CHAPTER REVIEW QUESTIONS

- How did the three mainland regions in British North America—New England, the Middle colonies, and the South—become more like one another between 1720 and 1750? In what ways did they become increasingly different? From these comparisons, what conclusions can you draw about the character of American society in the mid-eighteenth century?

- Compare and contrast the ethnic complexity of the Middle colonies with the racial (and, in the backcountry, the ethnic) diversity of the southern colonies. What conflicts did this diversity cause?

FOR FURTHER EXPLORATION

Individual lives illuminate the social history of early America. In *A Midwife's Tale: The Life of Martha Ballard* (1990), Laurel Thatcher Ulrich vividly pictures women's experiences on the Maine frontier. See also the PBS video *A Midwife's Tale* and the related Web site (**www.pbs.org/amex/midwife**) as well as **www.DoHistory.org**. Benjamin Franklin's *Autobiography* (1771) describes his Enlightenment sensibilities. See also the Library of Congress exhibit, "Benjamin Franklin . . . in His Own Words" (**www.loc.gov/exhibits/treasures/franklin-home.html**), and "The Electric Franklin" site (**www.ushistory.org/franklin**). A failed quest for self-betterment is recounted in *The Infortunate: The Voyage and Adventures of William Moraley* (1992), edited by Susan E. Klepp and Billy G. Smith.

Fine studies of religious leaders are Harry S. Stout's *The Divine Dramatist: George Whitefield* (1991) and George M. Marsden's *Jonathan Edwards* (2003). The Web site of Yale's Jonathan Edwards Center has many resources (**edwards.yale.edu**).

For more information on the Scots-Irish, see Patrick Griffin, *The People with No Name* (2001); on migrant Germans, read Aaron Spencer Fogleman, *Hopeful Journeys* (1996); and on Highland Scots, consult Colin G. Calloway, *White People, Indians, and Highlanders* (2008).

Other important studies include Jane T. Merritt, *At the Crossroads: Indians & Empires on a Mid-Atlantic Frontier* (2003); John Oliphant, *Peace and War on the Anglo-Cherokee Frontier, 1756–63* (2001); and Richard Middleton, *Pontiac's War* (2007). Also see *The War That Made America*, a PBS series on the French and Indian War, and the related Web site (**www.thewarthatmadeamerica.org**).

TEST YOUR KNOWLEDGE

To assess your command of the material in this chapter, see the Online Study Guide at **bedfordstmartins.com/henretta**.

For Web sites, images, and documents related to topics and places in this chapter, visit **bedfordstmartins.com/makehistory**.

TIMELINE

1710s–1730s	Enlightenment ideas spread from Europe to America
	Germans and Scots-Irish settle in Middle Colonies
	Theodore Jacob Frelinghuysen preaches Pietism to German migrants
1730s	William and Gilbert Tennent lead Presbyterian revivals among Scots-Irish
	Jonathan Edwards preaches in New England
1739	George Whitefield sparks Great Awakening
1740s–1760s	Conflict between Old Lights and New Lights
	Shortage of farmland in New England threatens freehold ideal
	Growing ethnic and religious pluralism in Middle Atlantic colonies
	Religious denominations establish colleges
1743	Benjamin Franklin founds American Philosophical Society
	Samuel Morris starts Presbyterian revivals in Virginia
1749	Virginia speculators create Ohio Company; Connecticut farmers form Susquehanna Company
1750s	Industrial Revolution begins in England
	Consumer purchases increase American imports and debt
1754	French and Indian War begins
	Iroquois and colonists meet at Albany Congress; Franklin's Plan of Union
1756	Britain begins Great War for Empire
1759–1760	Britain completes conquest of Canada
1760s	Land conflict along New York and New England border
	Baptist revivals win converts in Virginia
1763	Pontiac's Rebellion leads to Proclamation of 1763
	Treaty of Paris ends Great War for Empire
	Scots-Irish Paxton Boys massacre Indians in Pennsylvania
1771	Royal governor puts down Regulator revolt in North Carolina

THE NEW REPUBLIC, 1763–1820

"The American war is over," Philadelphia Patriot Benjamin Rush declared in 1787, "but this is far from being the case with the American Revolution. On the contrary, nothing but the first act of the great drama is closed. It remains yet to establish and perfect our new forms of government." As will be seen in Part 2, the job was even greater than Rush imagined. The republican revolution—which began with the Patriot resistance movement of 1765 and took shape with the Declaration of Independence in 1776—reached far beyond politics. It challenged many of the values and institutions of the colonial social order and forced Americans to consider fundamental changes in their economic, religious, and cultural practices. Here, in summary, are the main themes of our discussion of America's emerging political and social order.

GOVERNMENT

... [political] experiments ... stretched over an entire generation

DIPLOMACY

... wars against Britain divided the new nation's white citizens into bitter factions

Creating Republican Institutions

Once Americans had repudiated their allegiance to Britain and its monarch, they had to create new systems of government. In 1776, no one knew how the states should go about setting up republican institutions. Nor did Patriot leaders know if there should be a permanent central authority along the lines of the Continental Congress. It would take experiments that stretched over an entire generation to find out. It would take even longer to assimilate a new American institution—the political party—into the workings of the new government. However, by 1820, difficult years of political conflict, compromise, and constitutional revision had resulted in republican national and state governments that commanded the allegiance of their citizens.

Contending with Foreign Entanglements

To create and preserve their new republic, Americans of European descent fought two wars against Great Britain, an undeclared war against France, and many battles with Indian peoples. The expansion of American sovereignty and settlements into the trans-Appalachian west was a cultural disaster for Indian peoples, who were brutally displaced from their lands. The wars against Britain divided the new nation's white citizens into bitter factions—Patriots against Loyalists in the War of Independence, and prowar Republicans versus antiwar Federalists in the War of 1812—and expended much blood and treasure. Despite these wars, by 1820, the United States had emerged as a strong independent state with internationally accepted boundaries. Freed from a half century of entanglement in European wars and diplomacy, its people began to exploit the riches of the continent.

ECONOMY

... merchants financed a banking system and ... manufacturing

Expanding Commerce and Manufacturing

By the 1760s, the expansion of farming and commerce had established the foundation for a vigorous national economy. Beginning in the 1780s, northern merchants financed a banking system and organized a rural system of manufacturing. Simultaneously, state governments used charters and other privileges to assist businesses and to improve roads, bridges, and waterways. Meanwhile, southern planters continued to use enslaved African Americans and exported a new staple crop—cotton—to markets in the North and in Europe. Many yeomen farm families migrated westward to grow grain; while workers in the East turned out raw materials such as leather and wool for burgeoning manufacturing enterprises, and made shoes, textiles, tinware, and other handicrafts for market sale. By 1820, the young American republic was on the verge of achieving economic as well as political independence.

SOCIETY

Americans confronted ... divisions of gender, race, religion, and class

Defining Liberty and Equality

As Americans confronted the challenges of creating and sustaining a republican society, they became increasingly conscious of long-standing (but previously little-examined) divisions of gender, race, religion, and class. They disagreed over fundamental issues such as legal equality for women, the status of slaves, the meaning of free speech and religious liberty, and the extent of public responsibility for social inequality. As we shall see, political leaders managed to resolve some of these disputes. Legislatures abolished slavery in the North, broadened religious liberty by allowing freedom of conscience, and, except in New England, ended the system of legally established churches. However, Americans continued to argue over social equality, in part because their republican creed placed family authority in the hands of men and political power in the hands of propertied individuals: This arrangement denied power and status not only to slaves but also to free blacks, women, and middling and poor white men.

CULTURE

... an American [was] ... a republican, a Protestant, and an enterprising individual

Forging Pluralism and National Identity

The British colonies in North America contained a diversity of peoples and ways of life. This complexity inhibited the effort to define an American culture and identity. Native Americans still lived in their own clans and nations; and black Americans, one-fifth of the enumerated population, were developing a distinct African American culture. White Americans were enmeshed in vigorous regional cultures—New England, Middle Atlantic, and Southern—and in strong ethnic communities—English, Scottish, Scots-Irish, German, and Dutch. However, over time, political institutions began to unite Americans of diverse backgrounds, as did increasing participation in the market economy and in evangelical Protestant churches. By 1820, to be an American meant, for many members of the dominant white population, to be a republican, a Protestant, and an enterprising individual in a capitalist-run market system.

THE NEW REPUBLIC, 1763–1820

	GOVERNMENT	DIPLOMACY	ECONOMY	SOCIETY	CULTURE
1763	• Stamp Act Congress (1765) • Committees of correspondence • First Continental Congress (1774)	• Treaty of Paris (1763) gives Britain control of Canada, Florida, and parts of India	• Merchants defy Sugar and Stamp Acts • Boycotts spur Patriot women to make textiles	• Artisans win political influence • Quebec Act (1774) allows Catholicism	• Patriots call for American unity • Concept of popular sovereignty takes hold
1775	• Second Continental Congress (1775) • States institute republican constitutions	• Independence declared (1776) • French provide secret aid to Patriots • Treaty of Alliance with France (1778)	• Manufacturing expands during war • Cutoff of trade and severe inflation threaten economy • War debt grows	• Judith Sargent Murray writes *On the Equality of the Sexes* (1779) • Emancipation of slaves begins in the North	• Thomas Paine's *Common Sense* (1776) calls for a republic • Fall in European migration (1775–1820) enhances American identity
1780	• Articles of Confederation ratified (1781) • Legislatures emerge as supreme in states • Philadelphia convention drafts U.S. Constitution (1787)	• Treaty of Paris (1783) • Britain restricts U.S. trade with West Indies • U.S. government signs treaties with Indian peoples	• Bank of North America founded (1781) • Commercial recession (1783–1789) • Land speculation increases in West	• Virginia enacts religious freedom legislation (1786) • Politicians and ministers deny vote to women; praise republican motherhood	• Noah Webster defines American English • State cessions and land ordinances create national domain in West • Many German settlers keep own language
1790	• Conflict over Alexander Hamilton's economic policies • First national parties: Federalists and Republicans	• Wars between France and Britain • Jay Treaty, Pinckney Treaty (both 1795) • Undeclared war with France (1798)	• First Bank of the United States (1792–1811) • States charter business corporations • Outwork system grows	• Bill of Rights ratified (1791) • Creation of French Republic (1793) sparks ideological debate • Sedition Act limits freedom of press	• Indians form Western Confederacy (1790) • Second Great Awakening (1790–1860) • Political divisions emerge between South and North
1800	• Jefferson's "Revolution of 1800" reduces activism of national government • Chief Justice Marshall asserts federal judicial powers	• Napoleonic Wars (1802–1815) • Haitian rebellion and independence • Louisiana Purchase (1803) • Embargo Act (1807)	• Cotton output and demand for African labor expands • Farm productivity improves • Embargo encourages U.S. manufacturing	• New Jersey retracts suffrage for propertied women (1807) • Atlantic slave trade legally ends (1808)	• Tenskwatawa and Tecumseh revive Western Indian Confederacy • Free blacks enhance sense of African American identity
1810	• Triumph of Republican Party and end of Federalist Party • State constitutions democratized	• War of 1812 (1812–1815) • John Quincy Adams makes border treaties • Monroe Doctrine (1823)	• Second Bank of the United States chartered (1816–1836) • Supreme Court guards property • Emergence of a national economy	• Suffrage for white men expands • American Colonization Society (1817) • Missouri Compromise (1819–1821)	• War of 1812 tests national unity • Religious benevolence engenders social reform movements

CHAPTER 5

Toward Independence: Years of Decision, 1763-1776

As the Great War for Empire ended in 1763, Massachusetts soldier Seth Metcalf celebrated the triumph of British arms. Metcalf thanked "the Great Goodness of God" for the "General Peace" that was so "perculary Advantageous to the English Nation." Just two years later, Metcalf was less optimistic. "God is angry with us of this land," the pious Calvinist wrote in his journal, "and is now Smiting [us] with his Rod Especially by the hands of our Rulers."

The rapid disintegration of the bonds uniting Britain and America—an event that Metcalf ascribed to Divine Providence—mystified many Americans. How had it happened, asked the president of King's College in New York, that such a "happily situated" people were ready to "hazard their Fortunes, their Lives, and their Souls, in a Rebellion"? White Americans lived in a prosperous, self-governing society, with little to gain and much to lose by rebelling. Or so it seemed before the British government began to reform the imperial system. As Metcalf noted apprehensively in 1765: "This year Came an act from England Called the Stamp Act . . . which is thought will be very oppressive."

Inspired by the great gains of the wars in India, Africa, and the Americas, British leaders envisioned a new type of empire. In place of the existing loosely governed commercial system, they advocated centralized administration by Parliament and authoritarian regimes in their far-flung colonies. And they were especially concerned about the settlers in America, who, according to former Georgia governor Henry Ellis, and now an adviser to the ministry, felt themselves "entitled to a greater measure of Liberty than is enjoyed by the people of England."

Ireland had been closely ruled for decades, and recently the East India Company set up dominion over millions of non-British peoples. Britain's American possessions were likewise filled with aliens and "undesirables": "French, Dutch, Germans innumerable, Indians, Africans, and a multitude of felons from this country," as one member of Parliament put it. Consequently, declared Lord Halifax, "The people of England" considered Americans "as foreigners."

Contesting that status, Pennsylvanian John Dickinson argued that his fellow colonists were "not [East Indian] Sea Poys, nor Marattas, but *British subjects* who are born to liberty, who know its worth, and who prize it high." Thus was the stage set for a struggle between the conceptions of identity—and empire—held by British ministers and American Patriots.

British Troops Occupy Concord, 1775

On the night of April 18, 1775, hundreds of British troops marched out of Boston in search of Patriot arms and munitions, and by morning they had reached the nearby towns of Lexington and Concord. The raid led to violent and deadly confrontations with the Patriot militia, an outcome indicated by the unknown artist's depiction of a graveyard in the foreground of this painting. Courtesy, Concord Museum.

Imperial Reform, 1763–1765

The Great War for Empire of 1754–1763 spurred movements for reform throughout the Atlantic world (Map 5.1). Charles III (r. 1759–1788) of Spain created disciplined military forces in his American possessions, imposed higher taxes on his colonial subjects, and dispatched imperial bureaucrats to rule them. In Britain, the war created an enormous debt, prompting George III (r. 1760–1820) and his ministers to expand the British fiscal-military state to America. Parliament quickly replaced salutary neglect (which had emphasized trade and colonial self-government) with imperial administration (which focused on regulation and taxation).

The Legacy of War

The war strained the ties between Britain and its North American colonies. British generals and American leaders disagreed on military strategy, and the presence of 30,000 British troops revealed sharp cultural differences. The arrogance of British officers shocked many Americans: British soldiers "are but little better than slaves to their officers," declared a Massachusetts militiaman. The hostility was mutual. British general James Wolfe complained that colonial troops came from the dregs of society and that "there was no depending on them in action."

Disputes over Trade and Troops The war also exposed the ineffectiveness of the royal governors. In theory, the governors had extensive political powers, including command of the provincial militia; in reality, they shared power with the colonial assemblies, which outraged British officials. The Board of Trade complained that in Massachusetts "almost every act of executive and legislative power is ordered and directed by votes and resolves of the General Court." To enforce the collection of trade duties, which colonial merchants had evaded for decades by bribing customs officials, Parliament passed the Revenue Act of 1762. The ministry also instructed the Royal Navy to seize American vessels carrying food crops from the mainland colonies to the French West Indies. It was absurd, declared a British politician, that French armies attempting "to Destroy one English province . . . are actually supported by Bread raised in another."

Britain's military victory brought a fundamental shift in policy: a new peacetime deployment of a 10,000-man army in North America. King George III wanted military commands for his friends, and the king's ministers feared a possible rebellion by the 60,000 French residents of Canada, Britain's newly conquered colony. Native Americans were also a concern: Pontiac's Rebellion had nearly overwhelmed Britain's frontier forts. Moreover, only a substantial military force would deter land-hungry whites from defying the Proclamation of 1763 and settling west of the Appalachian Mountains (see Chapter 4). Finally, British politicians worried about the colonists' loyalty now that they no longer faced a threat from French Canada. "The main purpose of Stationing a large Body of Troops in America," declared treasury official William Knox, "is to secure the Dependence of the Colonys on Great Britain." By stationing an army in America, the British ministry signaled its readiness to subdue restless Frenchmen, unruly Indians, or rebellious colonists.

The National Debt But troops cost money, which was in short supply. Britain's national debt had soared from £75 million in 1756 to £133 million in 1763 and was, an observer noted, "becoming the alarming object of every British subject." And with good reason: Interest on the war debt consumed 60 percent of the nation's budget. To restore fiscal stability, British prime minister Lord Bute decided to raise taxes. The Treasury opposed a higher tax on land, which would primarily affect the gentry and aristocracy, who had great influence in Parliament. So Bute taxed those with little political power—the poor and middling classes—by imposing higher import duties on tobacco and sugar, thus raising their cost to consumers. The ministry likewise increased excise levies—essentially sales taxes—on salt, beer, and distilled spirits, placing more war costs on the king's ordinary subjects. Left unresolved was the question of taxing the American colonists, who, like Britain's poor, had little influence in Parliament.

To collect the taxes—old and new—the government doubled the size of the tax bureaucracy (Figure 5.1). Customs agents patrolled the coasts of southern Britain, seizing tons of contraband French wines and Flemish textiles. Convicted smugglers faced heavy penalties, including death or forced "transportation" to America as indentured servants. (Despite protests by the colonial assemblies, nearly fifty thousand English criminals of all descriptions had already been shipped to America to be sold as indentured servants.)

The price of empire abroad had turned out to be a larger government and higher taxes at home, an outcome that confirmed the worst fears of the British opposition parties, the Radical Whigs and the Country Party.

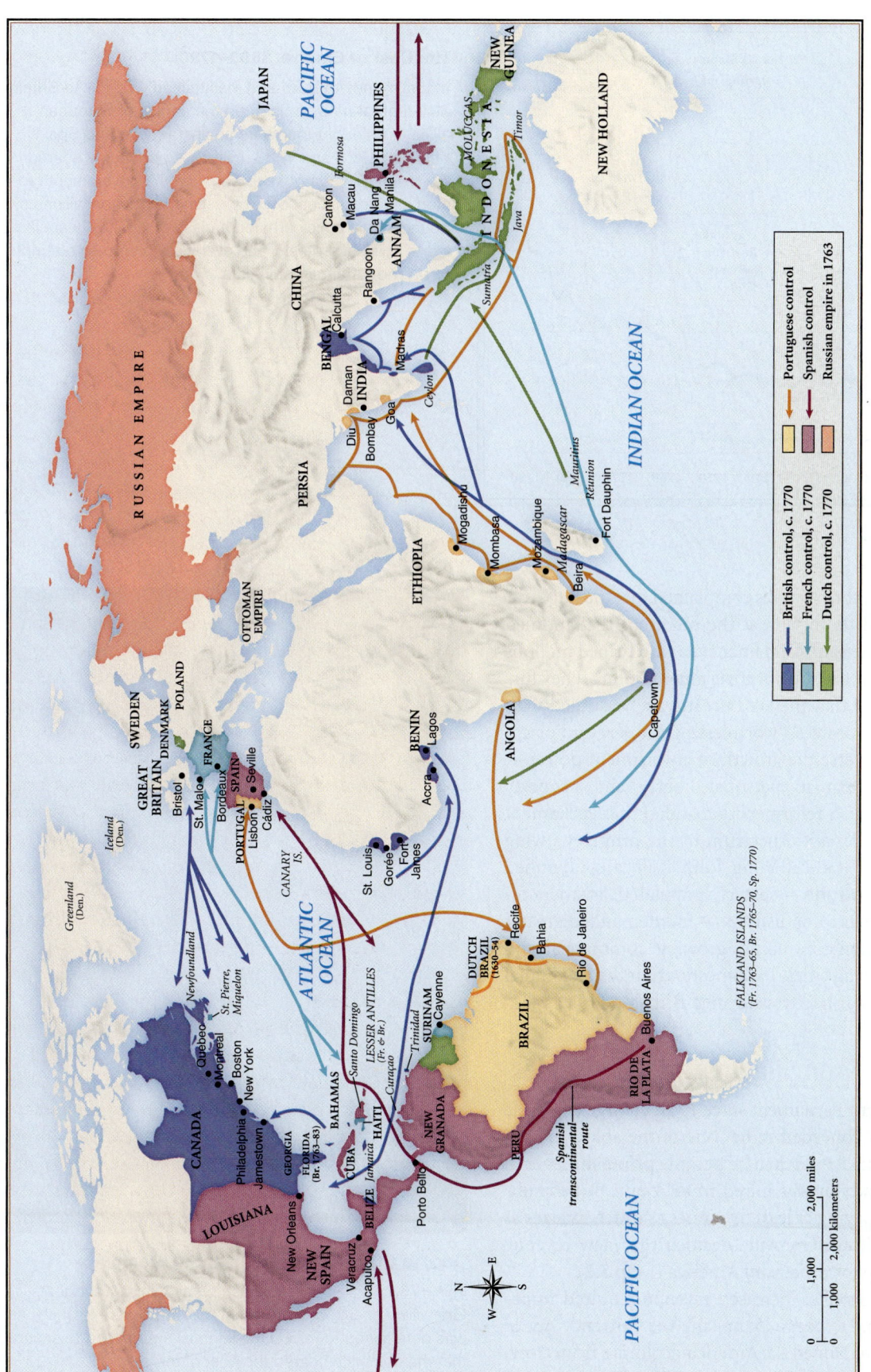

MAP 5.1

Eurasian Trade and European Colonies, c. 1770

By 1770, the Western European nations that had long dominated maritime trade had created vast colonial empires and spheres of influence. Spain controlled the western halves of North and South America, Portugal owned Brazil, and Holland ruled Indonesia. Britain, a newer imperial power, boasted settler societies in North America, rich sugar islands in the West Indies, slave ports in West Africa, and a growing presence on the Indian subcontinent. Only France had failed to acquire and hold on to a significant colonial empire. (To trace changes in empire and trade routes, see Map 1.3 on p. 20 and Map 2.2 on p. 48.)

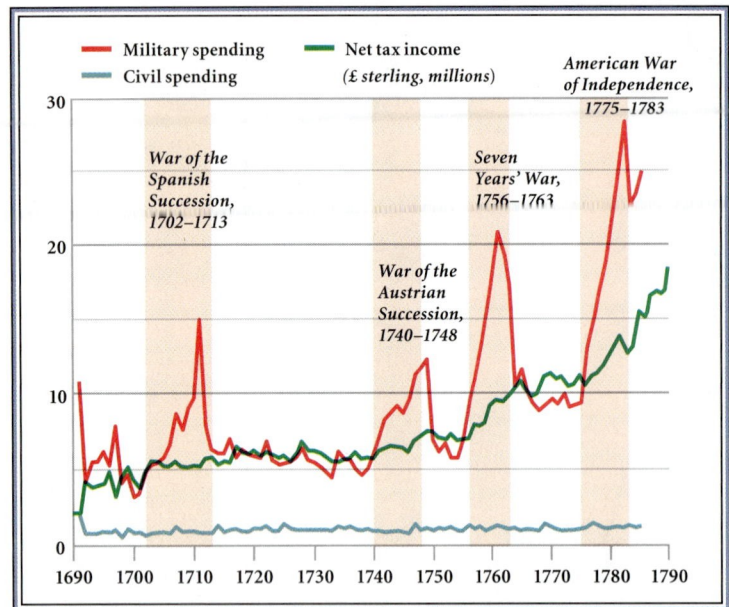

FIGURE 5.1

The Cost of Empire, 1690–1790

It cost money to build and maintain an empire. As Britain built a great navy, subsidized the armies of European allies, and fought four wars against France and Spain between 1702 and 1783, military expenditures soared. Tax revenues did not keep pace, so the government created a large national debt by issuing bonds for millions of pounds. This policy created a class of wealthy financiers, led to political protests, and eventually prompted attempts to tax the American colonists.

Members of those parties complained that the huge war debt placed the nation at the mercy of the "monied interests," the banks and financiers who reaped millions of pounds' interest from government bonds. They further charged that the tax bureaucracy was filled with political appointees, "worthless pensioners and placemen." To reverse the growth of government power — and the threat to personal liberty and property rights — British reformers demanded that Parliament represent a broader spectrum of the property-owing classes. The Radical Whig John Wilkes condemned **rotten boroughs** — sparsely populated, aristocratic-controlled electoral districts — and demanded greater representation for rapidly growing commercial and manufacturing cities. In domestic affairs as in colonial policy, the war had transformed British political life.

George Grenville: Imperial Reformer

A member of Parliament since 1741, George Grenville was widely conceded to be "one of the ablest men in Great Britain." But when he became prime minister in 1763, the nation was mired in debt and British subjects were paying at least five times as much in taxes as free Americans. Grenville decided that new revenue would have to come from America (Map 5.2).

For Grenville, increased revenue required imperial reform. He began by passing the Currency Act of 1764, which banned the American colonies from treating paper money as legal tender. Colonial shopkeepers,

George Grenville, Architect of the Stamp Act

This 1763 portrait of the British prime minister suggests Grenville's energy and ambition. As events were to show, he was determined to reform the imperial system and to ensure that the colonists shared the cost of the empire.   The Earl of Halifax, Garrowby, Yorkshire.

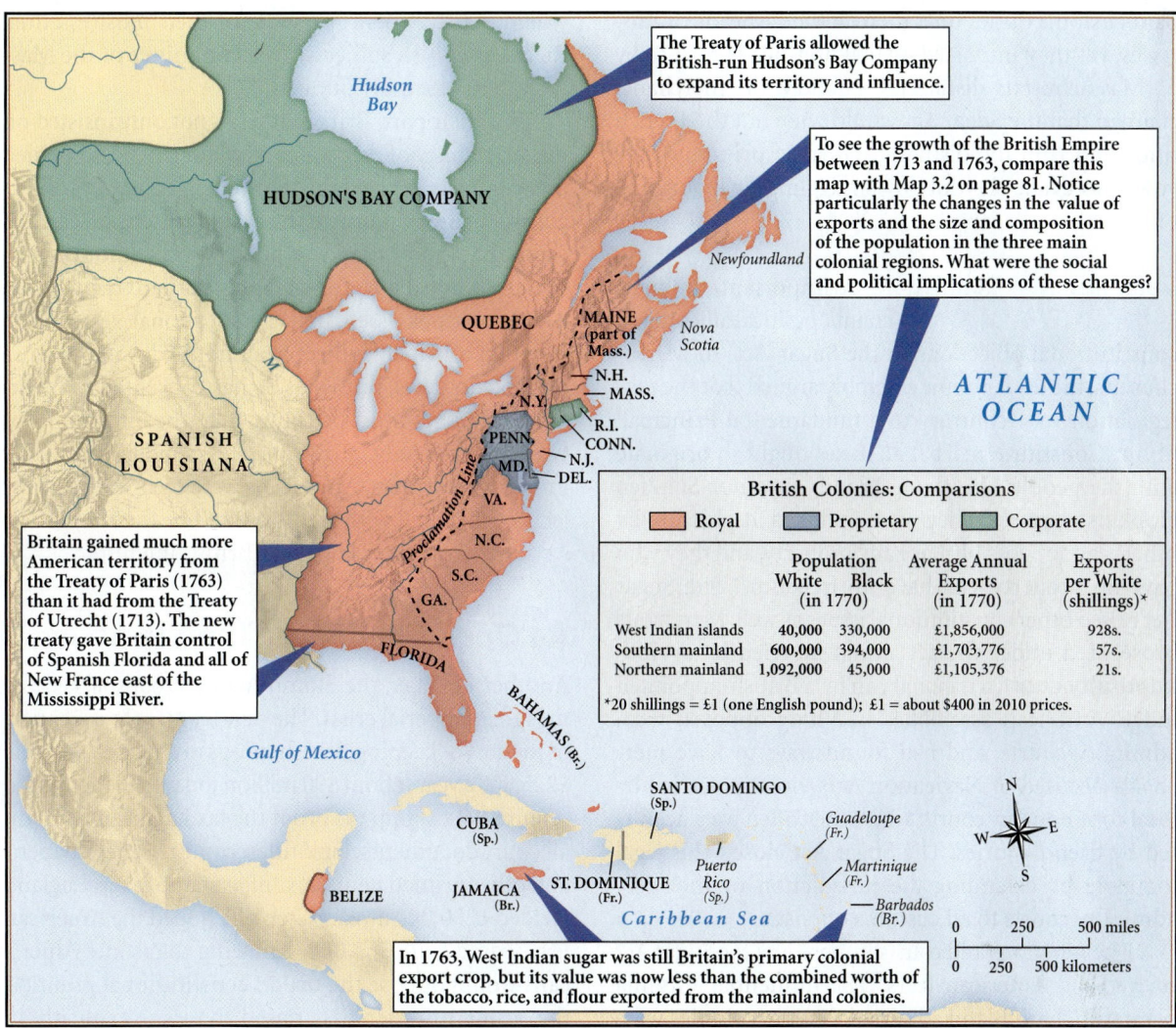

The Treaty of Paris allowed the British-run Hudson's Bay Company to expand its territory and influence.

To see the growth of the British Empire between 1713 and 1763, compare this map with Map 3.2 on page 81. Notice particularly the changes in the value of exports and the size and composition of the population in the three main colonial regions. What were the social and political implications of these changes?

Britain gained much more American territory from the Treaty of Paris (1763) than it had from the Treaty of Utrecht (1713). The new treaty gave Britain control of Spanish Florida and all of New France east of the Mississippi River.

British Colonies: Comparisons

	Royal	Proprietary	Corporate

	Population White Black (in 1770)		Average Annual Exports (in 1770)	Exports per White (shillings)*
West Indian islands	40,000	330,000	£1,856,000	928s.
Southern mainland	600,000	394,000	£1,703,776	57s.
Northern mainland	1,092,000	45,000	£1,105,376	21s.

*20 shillings = £1 (one English pound); £1 = about $400 in 2010 prices.

In 1763, West Indian sugar was still Britain's primary colonial export crop, but its value was now less than the combined worth of the tobacco, rice, and flour exported from the mainland colonies.

MAP 5.2

Britain's American Empire in 1763

The Treaty of Paris gave Britain control of the eastern half of North America and returned a few captured sugar islands in the West Indies to France. To protect the empire's new mainland territories, British ministers dispatched troops to Florida and Quebec. They also sent troops to uphold the terms of the Proclamation of 1763, which prohibited Anglo-American settlement west of the Appalachian Mountains.

planters, and farmers had used local currency—which had the same face value as gold or silver coins but was worth less—to pay their debts to British merchants. The Currency Act ensured that merchants would be paid in good money, boosting their profits and British wealth.

The Sugar Act | Grenville also won parliamentary approval of the Sugar Act of 1764 to replace the widely ignored Molasses Act of 1733 (see Chapter 3). The prime minister understood the pattern of colonial trade: He knew that mainland settlers had

to sell at least some of their wheat, fish, and lumber in the French sugar islands to accumulate funds to buy British manufactures. He therefore resisted demands from British sugar planters, who wanted to stop this trade by levying a heavy duty of 6 pence per gallon on French molasses; instead, he settled on a duty of 3 pence per gallon and tightened customs enforcement.

This carefully crafted policy garnered little support in America. New England merchants—among them John Hancock of Boston—had made their fortunes smuggling French molasses. In 1754, Boston merchants paid customs duties on a mere 400 hogsheads of molasses, yet they imported 40,000 hogsheads for use by 63 Massachusetts distilleries. Publicly, the merchants claimed that the Sugar Act would wipe out the French trade and ruin the distilling industry; privately, they vowed to evade the duty by smuggling or by bribing officials.

Constitutional Conflict More important, the merchants' political allies raised constitutional objections to the Sugar Act. In Massachusetts, the leader of the assembly argued that the new legislation was "contrary to a fundamental Principall of our Constitution: That all Taxes ought to originate with the people." In Rhode Island, governor Stephen Hopkins warned: "They who are taxed at pleasure by others cannot possibly have any property, and they who have no property, can have no freedom." The Sugar Act raised other constitutional issues as well. Merchants prosecuted under the act would be tried by a **vice-admiralty court**, a tribunal run by a British-appointed judge. American assemblies had long opposed vice-admiralty courts, and had found ways to have merchants accused of Navigation Acts violations tried by local common-law courts, where they often were acquitted by friendly juries. The Sugar Act closed this legal loophole by extending the jurisdiction of the vice-admiralty courts to all customs offenses.

The new taxes and courts imposed by the Sugar Act revived old American fears. The influential Virginia planter Richard Bland admitted that the colonies were subject to the Navigation Acts, which restricted their manufactures and commerce. But he also believed that the American settlers "were not sent out to be the Slaves but to be the Equals of those that remained behind." John Adams, the young Massachusetts lawyer defending John Hancock on a charge of smuggling, argued that the vice-admiralty courts diminished this equality by "degrad[ing] every American . . . below the rank of an Englishman."

While the logic of the Americans' arguments appeared compelling, some of their facts were wrong. The Navigation Acts certainly favored British merchants and manufacturers. However, accused smugglers in Britain were also tried in vice-admiralty courts, so there was no discrimination against Americans. The real issue was the exercise of the growing power of the British state. Americans had lived for decades under an administrative policy of salutary neglect and benefited from an "unwritten constitution" that assumed the king's officials would seek political compromises with colonial leaders. Now they saw that the new imperial regime would deprive them "of some of their most essential Rights as British subjects," as a committee of the Massachusetts assembly put it.

For their part, British officials not only insisted on the supremacy of parliamentary laws, they also denied that colonists enjoyed the traditional legal rights of Englishmen. Responding to the Massachusetts assembly's claim that there should be no taxation without representation, royal governor Francis Bernard denied that Americans possessed that constitutional right: "The rule that a British subject shall not be bound by laws or liable to taxes, but what he has consented to by his representatives must be confined to the inhabitants of Great Britain only." To Bernard, Grenville, and other imperial reformers, Americans were second-class subjects of the king, with rights limited by the Navigation Acts, parliamentary laws, and British interests.

An Open Challenge: The Stamp Act

Another new tax, the Stamp Act of 1765, sparked the first great imperial crisis. The new levy was to cover part of the cost of keeping British troops in America — some £225,000 a year (about $90 million today). The act would require a tax stamp (as proof the tax had been paid) on all court documents, land titles, contracts, newspapers, and other printed items. A similar stamp tax in England yielded £290,000 a year; Grenville hoped the American levy would raise £60,000. Knowing that some Americans would oppose the tax on constitutional grounds, the prime minister first raised the issue explicitly in the House of Commons: Did any member doubt "the power and sovereignty of Parliament over every part of the British dominions, for the purpose of raising or collecting any tax?" No one rose to object.

Confident of Parliament's support, Grenville then threatened to impose the stamp tax unless colonists paid the troops' expenses, which were for the colonists' own defense. London merchants — serving as agents for the colonial legislatures — protested that Americans lacked a continent-wide body to raise such funds. Colonial representatives had met officially only once, at the Albany Congress of 1754, and not a single assembly had accepted the Congress's proposal for a continental union (see Chapter 4). Benjamin Franklin, in Britain as the agent of the Pennsylvania assembly, proposed another solution to Grenville's challenge: American representation in Parliament. "If you chuse to tax us," he wrote, "give us Members in your Legislature, and let us be one People."

With the exception of William Pitt, British politicians rejected Franklin's idea as too radical. They argued that the colonists already had **virtual representation** in Parliament because some of its members were transatlantic merchants and West Indian sugar planters. Colonial leaders were equally skeptical of Franklin's plan. Americans were "situate at a great Distance from their Mother Country," the Connecticut assembly declared, and therefore "cannot participate in the general Legislature of the Nation."

Grenville then urged adoption of the Stamp Act, both to raise revenue and to assert a constitutional principle: "the Right of Parliament to lay an internal Tax upon the Colonies." The House of Commons ignored American opposition and passed the act by an overwhelming majority of 205 to 49. At the request of General Thomas Gage, the British military commander in America, Parliament also passed the Quartering Act, which required colonial governments to provide barracks and food for British troops. Finally, Parliament approved Grenville's proposal that violations of the Stamp Act be tried in vice-admiralty courts.

The design for reform was complete. Using the doctrine of parliamentary supremacy, Grenville had begun to fashion a centralized imperial system in America much like that already in place in Ireland: British officials would govern the colonies with little regard for the local assemblies. Consequently, the prime minister's plan provoked a constitutional confrontation on both the specific issues of taxation, jury trials, and military quartering as well as the general question of representative self-government.

- What were the goals of British imperial reformers?

- Why did the colonists object to the new taxes in 1764 and again in 1765? What arguments did they use? How did these conflicts turn into a constitutional crisis?

The Dynamics of Rebellion, 1765–1770

In the name of reform, Grenville had thrown down the gauntlet to the Americans. The colonists had often resisted unpopular laws and aggressive governors, but they had faced an all-out attack on their institutions only once before—in 1686, when James II had unilaterally imposed the Dominion of New England. Now the danger to colonial autonomy was even greater because both the king and Parliament backed reform. But the Patriots, as the defenders of American rights came to be called, met the challenge posed by Grenville and

The Intensity of Patrick Henry

This portrait, painted when Patrick Henry was in his sixties, captures the Patriot's enduring seriousness and intensity. As an orator, Henry drew on evangelical Protestantism to create a new mode of political oratory. "His figures of speech . . . were often borrowed from the Scriptures," a contemporary noted, and his speeches mirrored "the earnestness depicted in his own features."   Mead Art Museum, Amherst College. Bequest of Herbert L. Pratt.

his successor, Charles Townshend. They organized protests, violent as well as peaceful, and fashioned a compelling ideology of resistance.

Politicians Protest and the Crowd Rebels

Virginians took the lead. In May 1765, Patrick Henry, a hotheaded young member of the House of Burgesses, condemned Grenville's legislation and attacked George III for supporting it. Comparing the king to Charles I, whose tyranny had led to his overthrow and execution in the 1640s, Henry seemed to call for a new republican revolution. These remarks, which bordered on treason, frightened the burgesses; nonetheless, they condemned the Stamp Act as "a manifest Tendency to Destroy American freedom." In Massachusetts, James Otis, another republican-minded firebrand, persuaded the House of Representatives to call a meeting of all the mainland colonies "to implore Relief" from the act.

Protesting the Stamp Act in Portsmouth, New Hampshire
Throughout the colonies, disciplined mobs protesting the Stamp Act forced stamp distributors to resign their offices. In this engraving, protesters in the small city of Portsmouth, New Hampshire, stone an effigy of the distributor as other members of the mob carry off a coffin representing the death of American "Liberty." Picture Research Consultants & Archives.

The Stamp Act Congress Nine assemblies sent delegates to the Stamp Act Congress, which met in New York City in October 1765. The congress protested the loss of American "rights and liberties," especially the right to trial by jury. And it challenged the constitutionality of both the Stamp and Sugar Acts by declaring that only the colonists' elected representatives could tax them. Still, moderate-minded delegates wanted compromise, not confrontation. They assured Parliament that Americans "glory in being subjects of the best of Kings" and humbly petitioned for repeal of the Stamp Act. Other influential Americans favored active (but peaceful) resistance; they organized a boycott of British goods.

Popular opposition took a violent form, however. When the Stamp Act went into effect on November 1, 1765, disciplined mobs demanded the resignation of stamp-tax collectors. In Boston, a group calling itself the **Sons of Liberty** burned an effigy of collector Andrew Oliver and then destroyed Oliver's new brick warehouse. Two weeks later, Bostonians attacked the house of Lieutenant Governor Thomas Hutchinson, long known as a defender of social privilege and imperial authority, breaking his furniture, looting his wine cellar, and setting fire to his library.

Wealthy merchants and Patriot lawyers, such as John Hancock and John Adams, encouraged the mobs, which were usually led by middling artisans and minor merchants. "Spent the evening with the Sons of Liberty," Adams wrote in his diary, "John Smith, the brazier [metalworker], Thomas Crafts, the painter, Edes, the printer, Stephen Cleverly, the brazier; Chase, the dis-

tiller; [and] Joseph Field, Master of a vessel." Some of these men knew one another through their work; others were drinking buddies at the taverns that became centers of Patriot agitation.

In New York City, nearly three thousand shopkeepers, artisans, laborers, and seamen marched through the streets breaking windows and crying "Liberty!" Resistance to the Stamp Act spread far beyond the port cities: In nearly every colony, angry crowds—the "rabble," their detractors called them—intimidated royal officials. Near Wethersfield, Connecticut, 500 farmers seized tax collector Jared Ingersoll and forced him to resign his office in "the Cause of the People."

The Motives of the Crowd Such crowd actions were common in both Britain and America. Every November 5, Protestant mobs on both sides of the Atlantic celebrated Guy Fawkes Day, marking the anniversary of the failure of a 1605 Catholic plot to blow up the Houses of Parliament. Colonial crowds also regularly destroyed brothels and rioted against the impressment (forced service) of merchant seamen by the Royal Navy. Governments tolerated the mobs because they usually did little damage and because, short of calling out the militia, they had no means of stopping them.

But if rioting was traditional, its political goals were new. In New York City, for example, the leaders of the Sons of Liberty were Isaac Sears and Alexander McDougall, minor merchants who were also Radical Whigs. They feared that imperial reform would undermine political liberty. But many artisans and their journeymen joined the protests because low-priced imports of British shoes and other manufactures (like low-priced Chinese imports today) threatened their livelihoods. Other rioters feared new taxes and a parasitic British governing elite. One knowledgeable colonist observed that "the people of America . . . never would submit to be taxed that a few may be loaded with palaces and Pensions . . . while they cannot support themselves and their needy offspring with Bread."

Beliefs of many sorts—as well as a simple quest for excitement—motivated other protesters. Roused by the Great Awakening, evangelical Protestants resented arrogant British military officers and corrupt royal bureaucrats. In New England, where people and memories had long lives, rioters invoked the antimonarchy sentiments of their great-grandparents. An anonymous letter sent to a Boston newspaper promising to save "all the Freeborn Sons of America" was signed "Oliver Cromwell," the English republican revolutionary of the 1650s. Finally, the mobs also included apprentices, day laborers, and unemployed sailors—young men looking for excitement and, when fortified by drink, eager to resort to violence.

Nearly everywhere popular resistance nullified the Stamp Act. Fearing an assault on Fort George, New York lieutenant governor Cadwallader Colden called on General Gage to use his small military force to protect the stamps. Gage refused. "Fire from the Fort might disperse the Mob, but it would not quell them," he told Colden, and the result would be "an Insurrection, the Commencement of Civil War." Frightened collectors gave up their tax stamps, and angry Americans forced officials to accept legal documents without the stamp. This popular insurrection gave a democratic cast to the emerging Patriot movement. "Nothing is wanting but your own Resolution," declared a New York rioter, "for great is the Authority and Power of the People."

Because transatlantic communication took months, the British response to the Stamp Act Congress, the economic boycott, and the riots would not be known until the spring of 1766. However, royal officials in America already sensed the loss of the popular support that had sustained the empire for three generations. Lamented a customs collector in Philadelphia: "What can a Governor do without the assistance of the Governed?"

The Ideological Roots of Resistance

American resistance began in the seaports because British policies directly affected the economic lives of the residents. The Sugar Act raised the cost of molasses

for urban distillers; the Stamp Act taxed the newspapers and legal documents created by urban printers, lawyers, and merchants; and the flood of British manufactures threatened the jobs of seaport artisans. According to one pamphleteer, Americans were being compelled to give the British "our money, as oft and in what quantity they please to demand it."

But some Americans couched their resistance in constitutional terms. Many were lawyers or well-educated merchants and planters. Composing pamphlets of remarkable political sophistication, they gave the resistance movement its rationale, its political agenda, and its leaders.

Patriot writers drew on three intellectual traditions. The first was English common law, the centuries-old body of legal rules and procedures that protected the lives and property of the monarch's subjects. In the famous *Writs of Assistance* case of 1761, Boston lawyer James Otis invoked English legal precedents to challenge a general search warrant allowing customs officials to conduct wide-ranging inspections. As practitioners of English common law, Otis and his colleagues believed in trial by jury and generally opposed the judge-run vice-admiralty courts. In demanding a jury trial for John Hancock in the late 1760s, John Adams made reference to the Magna Carta (1215), the ancient document that, said Adams, "has for many Centuries been esteemed by Englishmen, as one of the . . . firmest Bulwarks of their Liberties." Other lawyers protested that new strictures violated specific "liberties and privileges" embodied in colonial charters and in Britain's "ancient constitution." They objected as well when the ministry declared that colonial judges served "at the pleasure" of royal governors, claiming that tenure would undermine the independence of the judiciary.

A second major intellectual resource for Patriot authors was the rationalist thought of the Enlightenment. Virginia planter Thomas Jefferson invoked David Hume and Francis Hutcheson, Enlightenment philosophers who applied reason in their critiques of traditional political practices and social ills. Jefferson and other Patriots also drew on the writings of John Locke, who had argued that all individuals possessed certain "natural rights"—life, liberty, and property—which governments must protect (see Chapter 4). And they turned as well to the works of French philosopher Montesquieu, who had maintained that a "separation of powers" among government departments prevented arbitrary rule.

The republican and Whig strands of the English political tradition provided a third ideological source for American Patriots. Puritan New England had long venerated the Commonwealth era (1649–1660), when England had been a republic (see Chapter 2). After the Glorious Revolution of 1688–1689, many colonists praised the English Whigs for creating a constitutional monarchy that prevented the king from imposing taxes and other measures. Beginning in the 1750s, Samuel Adams and other colonial leaders also applauded Britain's Radical Whigs for denouncing political corruption and the scheming of royal officials. Joseph Warren, a physician and a Radical Whig Patriot, suggested that the Stamp Act was part of a ministerial plot "to force the colonies into rebellion," and justify the use of "military power to reduce them to servitude."

Such arguments—widely publicized in newspapers and pamphlets—gave intellectual substance to the Patriot movement and turned a series of impromptu riots, tax protests, and boycotts of British manufactures into a formidable political force.

Parliament Compromises, 1766

When news of the Stamp Act riots and the boycott reached Britain, Parliament was already in turmoil. Disputes over domestic policy had led George III to dismiss Grenville as prime minister (Table 5.1). However, Grenville's allies demanded that imperial reform continue, if necessary at gunpoint. They wanted to uphold the constitutional supremacy of Parliament and its status as one of the few powerful representative bodies in eighteenth-century Europe. "The British legislature," declared Chief Justice Sir James Mansfield, "has authority to bind every part and every subject, whether such subjects have a right to vote or not."

Three other parliamentary factions pushed for repeal of the Stamp Act. The Old Whigs, now led by Lord Rockingham, the new prime minister, had long maintained that America was more important for its "flourishing and increasing trade" than its tax revenues. A

second group—acting at the behest of a committee of merchants in Liverpool, Bristol, and Glasgow—protested that the American trade boycott was cutting deeply into British exports. "The Avenues of Trade are all shut up," a Bristol merchant told Parliament: "We have no Remittances and are at our Witts End for want of Money to fulfill our Engagements with our Tradesmen." Finally, former prime minister William Pitt and his allies in Parliament argued that the Stamp Act was a mistake and insisted it "be repealed absolutely, totally, and immediately." Pitt tried to draw a subtle distinction between taxation and legislation: Parliament lacked the authority to tax the colonies, he said, but its power over America was "sovereign and supreme, in every circumstance of government and legislation whatsoever." As Pitt's ambiguous formula suggested, the Stamp Act raised the difficult constitutional question of the extent of Parliament's sovereign powers.

Rockingham, a young and inexperienced minister facing complex issues, decided on compromise. To mollify the colonists and help British merchants, he repealed the Stamp Act and reduced the duty on molasses imposed by the Sugar Act to a penny a gallon. Then he pacified imperial reformers and hard-liners with the Declaratory Act of 1766, which explicitly reaffirmed Parliament's "full power and authority to make laws and statutes . . . to bind the colonies and people of America . . . in all cases whatsoever." By swiftly ending the Stamp Act crisis, Rockingham hoped it would be forgotten just as quickly.

Charles Townshend Steps In

Often the course of history is changed by a small event—an illness, a personal grudge, a chance remark. That was the case in 1767, when Rockingham's ministry collapsed over domestic issues and George III named William Pitt to head a new government. Pitt, chronically ill with gout (a painful disease of the joints) and often absent from parliamentary debates, left chancellor of the exchequer Charles Townshend in command. Pitt was sympathetic toward America; Townshend was not. As a member of the Board of Trade, Townshend had sought restrictions on the colonial assemblies and strongly supported the Stamp Act. So, in 1767, when former prime minister Grenville demanded in Parliament that the colonists pay the costs of the British troops in America, Townshend made an unplanned and fateful decision. He promised to find a new source of revenue in America.

The new tax legislation, the Townshend Act of 1767, had both fiscal and political goals. The duties the

TABLE 5.1		
Ministerial Instability in Britain, 1760–1782		
Leading Minister	**Dates of Ministry**	**American Policy**
Lord Bute	1760–1763	*Mildly reformist*
George Grenville	1763–1765	**Ardently reformist**
Lord Rockingham	1765–1766	Accommodationist
William Pitt / Charles Townshend	1766–1770	**Ardently reformist**
Lord North	1770–1782	**Coercive**

THE REPEAL. — or the Funeral Procession, of MISS AMERIC-STAMP.

Celebrating Repeal

This British cartoon mocking supporters of the Stamp Act – "The Repeal, or the Funeral Procession of Miss Americ-Stamp" – was probably commissioned by merchants trading with America. Preceded by two flag bearers, George Grenville, the author of the legislation, carries a miniature coffin (representing the act) to a tomb, as a dog urinates on the leader of the procession. Two bales on the wharf, labeled "Stamps from America" and "Black cloth return'd from America," testify to the failure of the act.   The Granger Collection, New York.

statute imposed on colonial imports of paper, paint, glass, and tea, would raise about £40,000 a year. Though Townshend did allocate some of this revenue for American military expenses, he earmarked most of it to pay the salaries of royal governors, judges, and other imperial officials. Once freed from financial dependence on the American assemblies (that had previously paid them), royal appointees could enforce parliamentary laws and carry out the king's instructions. To strengthen imperial power further, Townshend devised the Revenue Act of 1767, which created a board of customs commissioners in Boston and vice-admiralty courts in Halifax, Boston, Philadelphia, and Charleston. By using parliamentary taxes to finance imperial administration, Townshend intended to undermine American political institutions.

The full implications of Townshend's policies became clear when the New York assembly refused to comply with the Quartering Act of 1765. Fearing an unlimited drain on its treasury, the assembly first denied General Gage's requests for barracks and supplies, then offered limited assistance. Townshend demanded full compliance and Parliament threatened to raise the funds by placing a special duty on New York's imports and exports. The Earl of Shelburne, the new secretary of state, went even further: He wanted to appoint a military governor authorized to seize funds from New York's treasury and "to act with Force or Gentleness as circumstances might make necessary." Townshend decided on a less provocative, but equally coercive measure: the Restraining Act of 1767, which suspended the New York assembly. Faced with the loss of self-government, New Yorkers reluctantly appropriated funds to quarter the troops.

The Restraining Act raised the stakes of the contest. Previously, the British Privy Council had invalidated about 5 percent of laws enacted by colonial legislatures, such as those establishing land banks. Townshend's Restraining Act went much further, declaring that the very existence of American representative assemblies depended on the will of Parliament.

America Debates and Resists Again

The Townshend duties revived the constitutional debate over taxation. During the Stamp Act crisis, some Americans, including Benjamin Franklin, distinguished between external and internal taxes. They suggested that external duties on trade (such as those long mandated by the Navigation Acts) were acceptable to Americans, but that direct, or internal, taxes were not. Townshend thought this distinction was "perfect nonsense," but he indulged the Americans and laid duties only on trade.

A Second Boycott and the Daughters of Liberty   Even so, most colonial leaders rejected the legitimacy of Townshend's measures. They agreed with lawyer John Dickinson, author of *Letters from a Farmer in Pennsylvania* (1768), that the real issue was the *intention* of the legislation. Because the Townshend duties were designed to raise revenue (not to regulate trade), they were taxes imposed without consent. In February 1768, the Massachusetts assembly circulated a letter condemning the Townshend Act, and Boston and New York merchants began a new boycott of British goods. Throughout Puritan New

England, ministers and public officials discouraged the purchase of "foreign superfluities" and promoted the domestic manufacture of cloth and other necessities.

American women, ordinarily excluded from public affairs, became crucial to the nonimportation movement through their production of **homespun** cloth. During the Stamp Act boycott of 1765, the wives and daughters of Patriot leaders had made more yarn and cloth, but the Townshend boycott mobilized women of other social groups. Pious farmwives spun yarn at the homes of their ministers. In Berwick, Maine, "true Daughters of Liberty" celebrated American products by "drinking rye coffee and dining on bear venison." Other women's groups supported the boycott with charitable work, spinning flax and wool for the needy. Just as Patriot men followed tradition by joining crowd actions, so women's protests reflected their customary concern for the well-being of the community.

Newspapers celebrated these exploits of the Daughters of Liberty. One Massachusetts town proudly claimed an annual output of 30,000 yards of cloth; East Hartford, Connecticut, reported 17,000 yards. This surge in domestic production did not offset the loss of British imports, which had averaged about 10 million yards of cloth annually, but it brought thousands of women into the public arena.

The boycott mobilized many American men as well. In the seaport cities, the Sons of Liberty published the names of merchants who imported British goods and harassed their employees and customers. By March 1769, the nonimportation movement had spread to Philadelphia; two months later, the members of the Virginia House of Burgesses vowed not to buy duted articles, luxury goods, or imported slaves. Reflecting colonial self-confidence, Benjamin Franklin called for a return to the pre-1763 mercantilist system: "Repeal the laws, renounce the right, recall the troops, refund the money, and return to the old method of requisition."

Britain Threatens Coercion | American resistance only increased British determination. When the Massachusetts assembly's letter opposing the Townshend duties reached London, Lord Hillsborough, the secretary of state for American affairs, branded it "unjustifiable opposition to the constitutional authority of Parliament." To strengthen the "Hand of Government" in Massachusetts, Hillsborough dispatched General Thomas Gage and 4,000 British troops to Boston (Map 5.3). Once in Massachusetts, Gage accused its leaders of "Treasonable and desperate Resolves" and advised the ministry to "Quash this Spirit at a Blow." In 1765, American resistance to the Stamp Act had sparked a parliamentary debate; in 1768, it provoked a plan for military coercion.

Lord North Compromises, 1770

At this critical moment, the ministry's resolve faltered. A series of harsh winters and dry summers in Great Britain had cut grain output and raised food prices. In Scotland and northern England, thousands of tenants deserted their farms and boarded ships for America. Food riots spread across the English countryside; there were riots in British-occupied Ireland, too, over its growing military budget.

Adding to the ministry's difficulties was Radical Whig John Wilkes. Supported by associations of mer-

John Wilkes, British Radical

Wilkes won fame on both sides of the Atlantic as the author of *North Briton, Number 45* (depicted on the left), which called for major reforms in the British political system. At a dinner in Boston, Radical Whigs raised their wineglasses to Wilkes, toasting him forty-five times! But Wilkes had many enemies in Britain, including the artist who created this image. Wilkes is depicted (in this 1763 caricature by artist William Hogarth) as a cunning demagogue, brandishing the cap of Liberty to curry favor with the mob.   Miriam and Ira D. Wallach Division of Art, Prints and Photographs, The New York Public Library. Astor, Lenox and Tilden Foundations.

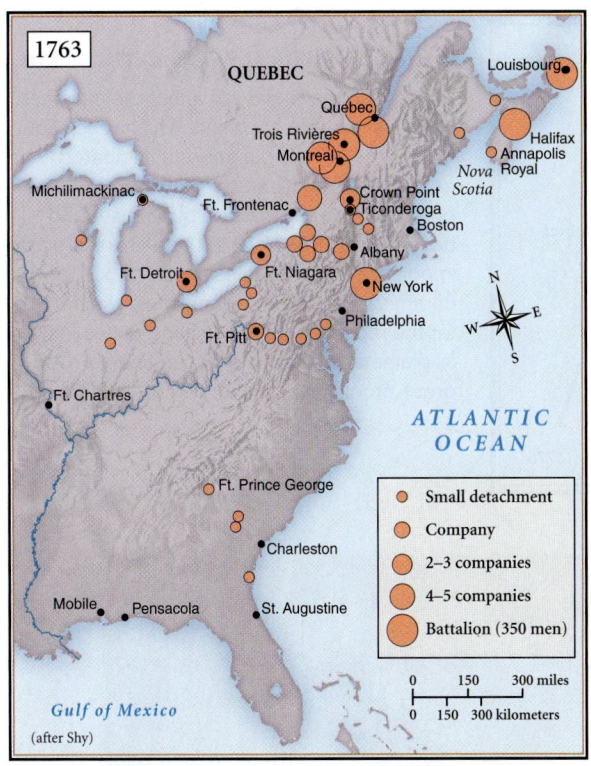

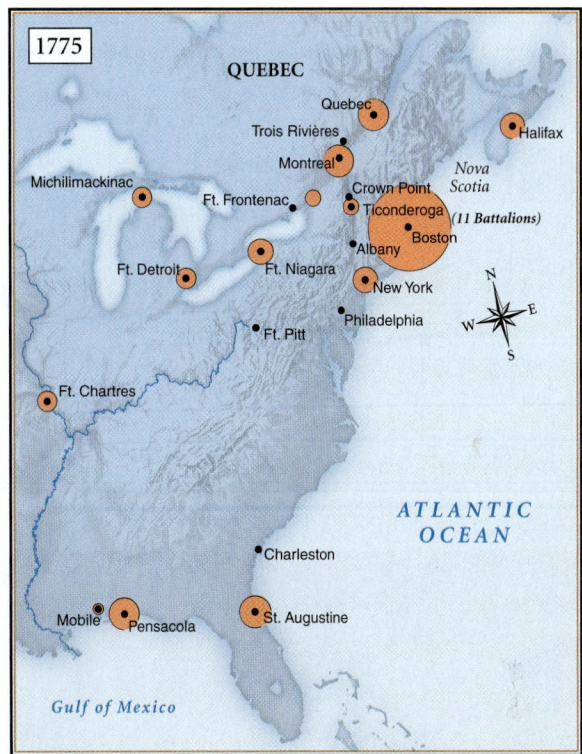

MAP 5.3

British Troop Deployments, 1763 and 1775

As the imperial crisis deepened, British military priorities changed. In 1763, most British battalions were stationed in Canada to deter Indian uprisings and French Canadian revolts. After the Stamp Act riots of 1765, the British placed large garrisons in New York and Philadelphia. By 1775, eleven battalions of British regulars occupied Boston, the center of the Patriot movement.

chants and artisans, Wilkes attacked government corruption and won election to Parliament. His radical politics endeared him to the American Patriots, who drank toasts to his name and bought teapots and mugs emblazoned with his picture. When Wilkes was imprisoned for libel against Parliament, seven members of an angry London crowd protesting his arrest were killed by troops in the highly publicized Massacre of Saint George's Field.

Nonimportation Succeeds | The American trade boycott also bit deeply into the British economy. In 1768, the colonies had cut imports of British manufactures, reducing their trade deficit from £500,000 to £230,000. By 1769, the boycott along with increases in American exports and shipping services gave the mainland colonies a balance-of-payments surplus of £816,000. Hard-hit by these developments, British merchants and manufacturers petitioned Parliament to repeal the Townshend duties. By late 1769, some

ministers felt that the duties were a mistake; also, the king no longer supported Hillsborough's plan to use military force against Massachusetts.

Early in 1770, Lord North became prime minister. A witty man and a skillful politician, North designed a new compromise. Arguing that it was foolish to tax British exports to America (thereby raising their price and decreasing consumption), he persuaded Parliament to repeal most of the Townshend duties. However, North retained the tax on tea as a symbol of Parliament's supremacy. Gratified by the partial repeal, colonial merchants called off the boycott (Figure 5.2).

Even outbreaks of violence did not destroy North's compromise. During the boycott, New York artisans and workers had taunted British troops, mostly with words but occasionally with stones and fists. In retaliation, the soldiers tore down a Liberty Pole (a Patriot flagpole), setting off a week of street fighting. In Boston, friction over constitutional principles and competition between residents and off-duty British soldiers

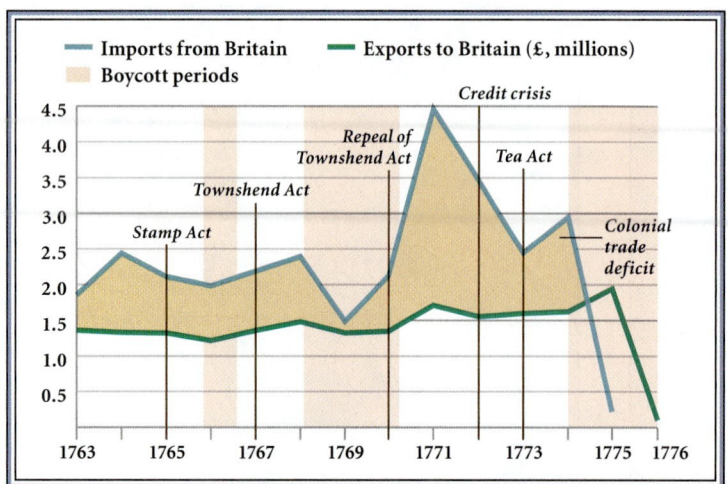

FIGURE 5.2

Trade as a Political Weapon, 1763–1776

Political upheaval did not affect the mainland colonies' exports to Britain, which rose slightly over the period, but imports fluctuated greatly. The American boycott of 1765–1766 prompted a dip in imports but the second boycott of 1768–1770 led to a sharp drop in imports of British textiles, metal goods, and ceramics. Imports of manufactures soared after the repeal of the Townshend duties, only to plummet when the First Continental Congress proclaimed a third boycott in 1774.

Patriot Propaganda

Silversmith Paul Revere issued this engraving of the confrontation between British redcoats and snowball-throwing Bostonians in the days after it occurred. To whip up opposition to the military occupation of their town, Revere and other Patriots labeled the incident "The Boston Massacre." The shooting confirmed their Radical Whig belief that "standing armies" were instruments of tyranny.   Library of Congress.

for jobs triggered a deadly conflict in March 1770, when a group of soldiers fired into a crowd of rowdy demonstrators, killing five men. Convinced of a ministerial conspiracy against liberty, Radical Whigs labeled the incident a "massacre" and filled the popular press with accusations that the British had planned the killings.

Sovereignty Debated | Although most Americans remained loyal to the empire, five years of conflict over taxes and constitutional principles had taken their toll. In 1765, American leaders had accepted Parliament's authority; the Stamp Act Resolves had opposed only certain "unconstitutional" legislation. By 1770, the most outspoken Patriots — Benjamin Franklin in Pennsylvania, Patrick Henry in Virginia, and Samuel Adams in Massachusetts — had concluded that the British ruling elite was determined to exploit the colonies for its own benefit. So they repudiated parliamentary supremacy and claimed equality for the American assemblies within the empire. Perhaps thinking of various European "composite monarchies," in which kings ruled far-distant provinces acquired by inheritance or conquest, Franklin suggested that the colonies were now "distinct and separate states" with the "the same Head, or Sovereign, the King."

Franklin's suggestion outraged Thomas Hutchinson, the American-born royal governor of Massachusetts. Hutchinson emphatically rejected the idea of "two independent legislatures in one and the same state." He told the Massachusetts assembly, "I know of no line that can be drawn between the supreme authority of Parliament and the total independence of the colonies."

There the matter rested. The British had twice imposed revenue acts on the colonies, and American Patriots had twice forced a retreat. If Parliament insisted on a policy of constitutional absolutism by imposing taxes a third time, some Americans were prepared to pursue violent resistance. Nor did they flinch when reminded that George III condemned their agitation. As the Massachusetts House replied to Hutchinson, "There is more reason to dread the consequences of absolute uncontrolled supreme power, whether of a nation or a monarch, than those of total independence." Fearful of civil war, Lord North's ministry hesitated to force the issue.

- If Grenville's and Townshend's initiatives had succeeded, how might the character of the British imperial system have changed?

- Weigh the relative importance of economic and ideological motives in promoting the colonial resistance movement. Which was more important? Why?

The Road to Independence, 1771–1776

Repeal of the Townshend duties in 1770 restored harmony to the British empire, but strong feelings and mutual distrust lay just below the surface. In 1773, those emotions erupted, destroying any hope of compromise. Within two years, the Americans and the British clashed in armed conflict, and Patriot legislators created provisional governments and military forces, the two essentials for independence.

A Compromise Repudiated

Once aroused, political passions are not easily quieted. In Boston, Samuel Adams and other radical Patriots continued to warn Americans of imperial domination and, late in 1772, persuaded the town meeting to set up a committee of correspondence "to state the Rights of the Colonists of this Province." Soon, eighty Massachusetts towns had similar committees. When British officials threatened to seize the Americans responsible for the burning of the customs vessel *Gaspée* and prosecute them in Britain, the Virginia House of Burgesses and several other assemblies set up their own committees of correspondence.

The East India Company and the Tea Act | These committees sprang into action when Parliament passed the Tea Act in May 1773. The act provided financial relief for the East India Company, a royally chartered private corporation that served as the instrument of Britain imperialism. The company was deeply in debt because of military expeditions in India and because high import duties had cut tea consumption in Britain, leaving it with a huge surplus. The Tea Act gave the company a government loan and, to boost its revenue, canceled the import duties on tea the company exported to Ireland and the American colonies. Now even with the Townshend duty of 3 pence a pound on tea, high-quality East India Company tea would cost less than the Dutch tea smuggled into the colonies by American merchants.

Events in far-off Asia thus directly influenced the course of American history. Radical Patriots accused the British ministry of bribing Americans with the cheaper East India Company's tea so they would give up their principled opposition to the tea tax. As an anonymous woman wrote to the *Massachusetts Spy*, "The use of [British] tea is considered not as a private but as a public evil . . . a handle to introduce a variety

The Boston Tea Party

Led by radical Patriots disguised as Mohawk Indians, Bostonians dumped the East India Company's taxed tea into the harbor. The rioters made clear their "pure" political motives by punishing those who sought personal gain: One Son of Liberty who stole some of the tea was "stripped of his booty and his clothes together, and sent home naked."   Library of Congress.

of . . . oppressions amongst us." Merchants joined the protest because the East India Company planned to distribute its tea directly to shopkeepers, excluding American wholesalers from the trade's profits. "The fear of an Introduction of a Monopoly in this Country," British general Frederick Haldimand reported from New York, "has induced the mercantile part of the Inhabitants to be very industrious in opposing this Step and added Strength to a Spirit of Independence already too prevalent."

The Tea Party and the Coercive Acts   The committees of correspondence organized resistance. They sponsored public bonfires and persuaded their fellow townspeople—sometimes gently, sometimes not—to consign British tea to the flames. When the Sons of Liberty prevented East India Company ships from delivering their cargoes, Royal Governor Hutchinson hatched a scheme to land the tea and collect the tax. When a tea shipment arrived in Boston Harbor on the *Dartmouth*, Hutchinson immediately passed the ship through customs. He intended to order British troops to unload the tea and supervise its sale by auction. To foil the governor's plan, artisans and laborers disguised as Indians boarded the *Dartmouth* on December 16, 1773, broke open 342 chests of tea (valued at about £10,000, or about $900,000 today), and threw them into the harbor. "This destruction of the Tea . . . must have so important Consequences," John Adams wrote in his diary, "that I cannot but consider it as an Epoch in History."

The British Privy Council was outraged, as was the king. "Concessions have made matters worse," George III declared. "The time has come for compulsion." Early in 1774, Parliament refused to repeal the American duty on tea; instead, it passed four Coercive Acts to force Massachusetts to pay for the tea and to submit to imperial authority. The Boston Port Bill closed Boston Harbor to shipping; the Massachusetts Government Act annulled the colony's charter and prohibited most town meetings; a new Quartering Act mandated new barracks for British troops; and the Justice Act allowed trials for capital crimes to be transferred to other colonies or to Britain (see Reading American Pictures, "A Political Cartoonist Sounds Off on the Crisis in the Colonies," p. 157).

Patriot leaders throughout the colonies branded the measures "Intolerable" and rallied support for Massachusetts. In Georgia, a Patriot warned the "Freemen

A Political Cartoonist Sounds Off on the Crisis in the Colonies

Britain's colonial policy between 1763 and 1775 created controversy in Britain as well as in America. George Grenville's ministry enacted the Stamp Act in 1765 only for it to be repealed the next year by Lord Rockingham's government. The conflict over colonial policy split hard-liners who favored coercing the colonies into paying taxes and quartering troops from Old Whigs who favored compromise. The debates roiled the halls of Parliament and spilled onto the pages of London's newspapers, where they took the form of controversial essays and political cartoons, like the one shown here. People of the time immediately understood the meaning — and the political bias — of these cartoons; more than two centuries later, we have to work a bit harder to understand what they are "saying."

"An Attempt to Land a Bishop in America," 1768.
Library of Congress.

ANALYZING THE EVIDENCE

- "An Attempt to Land a Bishop in America" addressed the proposal (never carried out) to dispatch a bishop of the Church of England to North America to supervise the clergy there. The bishop's jurisdiction would extend not only over Anglican ministers but also over Congregational (Puritan) and Presbyterian clergy. What is the cartoonist's position on the proposal?

- Read the signs and banners carefully. They invoke the name of John Locke, the famed advocate of self-government, and call for "Liberty & Freedom of Conscience." To interpret the words of protest in the balloon on the left — "No Lords Spiritual or Temporal in New England" — think back to the New England Puritans' opinions of bishops (see Chapter 2). What other aspects of the cartoon point to the artist's stance on the proposal to send a bishop to America?

- The name of the vessel being pushed away from the dock is *The Hillsborough*. When this cartoon was published in 1768, what was the significance of that name to those interested in American affairs?

of the Province" that "every privilege you at present claim as a birthright, may be wrested from you by the same authority that blockades the town of Boston." "The cause of Boston," George Washington declared in Virginia, "now is and ever will be considered as the cause of America." The committees of correspondence had created a firm sense of Patriot unity.

In 1774, Parliament also passed the Quebec Act, which allowed the practice of Roman Catholicism in Quebec. This concession to Quebec's predominantly Catholic population reignited religious passions in New England, where Protestants associated Catholicism with arbitrary royal government and "popish" superstition. Because the act extended Quebec's boundaries into the Ohio River Valley, it likewise angered influential land speculators in Virginia (Map 5.4). Although the ministry did not intend the Quebec Act as a coercive measure, many colonial leaders saw it as further proof of Parliament's intention to control American domestic affairs.

The Continental Congress Responds

In response to the Coercive Acts, Patriot leaders convened a new continent-wide body, the Continental Congress.

Twelve mainland colonies sent representatives. Four recently acquired colonies—Florida, Quebec, Nova Scotia, and Newfoundland—refused to send delegates, as did Georgia, where the royal governor controlled the legislature. The assemblies of Barbados, Jamaica, and the other sugar islands, although wary of British domination, were even more fearful of revolts by their predominantly African populations and therefore declined to attend.

The delegates who met in Philadelphia in September 1774 had different agendas. Southern representatives, fearing a British plot "to overturn the constitution and introduce a system of arbitrary government," advocated a new economic boycott. Independence-minded representatives from New England demanded political union and defensive military preparations. However, many delegates from the Middle Atlantic colonies favored a political compromise.

Led by Joseph Galloway of Pennsylvania, these men of "loyal principles" proposed a new political system similar to Benjamin Franklin's proposal at the Albany Congress of 1754: Each colony would retain its assembly to legislate on local matters, and a new continent-wide body would handle general American affairs. The king would appoint a president-general to preside over

MAP 5.4

British Western Policy, 1763–1774

The Proclamation of 1763 prohibited white settlement west of the Appalachian Mountains. Nonetheless, Anglo-American settlers and land speculators proposed the new colonies of Vandalia and Transylvania to the west of Virginia and North Carolina. When the Quebec Act of 1774 designated most western lands as Indian reserves and vastly enlarged the boundaries of Quebec, this dashed speculators' hopes and eliminated the old sea-to-sea land claims of many seaboard colonies. The act especially angered New England Protestants, who condemned it for allowing French residents to practice Catholicism; and colonial political leaders, who protested its failure to provide Quebec with a representative assembly.

a legislative council selected by the colonial assemblies. Although Galloway's plan gave the council veto power over parliamentary legislation affecting America, the delegates refused to endorse it. With British troops occupying Boston, most thought it was too conciliatory (see Comparing American Voices, "The Debate over Representation and Sovereignty," pp. 160–161).

Instead, a majority of the delegates passed a Declaration of Rights and Grievances, which demanded the repeal of the Coercive Acts. They repudiated the Declaratory Act of 1766, which had proclaimed Parliament's supremacy over the colonies, and stipulated that British control be limited to matters of trade. Finally, the Congress approved a program of economic retaliation: Americans would stop importing British goods in December 1774. If Parliament did not repeal the Coercive Acts by September 1775, the Congress vowed to cut off virtually all colonial exports to Britain, Ireland, and the British West Indies. Ten years of constitutional conflict had culminated in a threat of all-out commercial warfare.

A few British leaders still hoped for compromise. In January 1775, William Pitt, now sitting in the House of Lords as the Earl of Chatham, asked Parliament to renounce its power to tax the colonies and to recognize the Continental Congress as a lawful body. In return for these concessions, he suggested, the Congress should acknowledge parliamentary supremacy and provide a permanent source of revenue to help defray the national debt.

The British ministry rejected Pitt's plan. Twice it had backed down in the face of colonial resistance; a third retreat was impossible. Branding the Continental Congress an illegal assembly, the ministry rejected Lord Dartmouth's proposal to send commissioners to negotiate a settlement. Instead, Lord North set stringent terms: Americans must pay for their own defense and administration and acknowledge Parliament's authority to tax them. To put teeth in these demands, North imposed a naval blockade on American trade with foreign nations and ordered General Gage to suppress dissent in Massachusetts. "Now the case seemed desperate," the prime minister told Thomas Hutchinson, whom the Patriots had forced into exile in London. "Parliament would not—could not—concede. For aught he could see it must come to violence."

The Rising of the Countryside

The fate of the urban-led Patriot movement would depend on the colonies' large rural population. Most farmers had little interest in imperial affairs. Their lives were deeply rooted in the soil, and their prime allegiance was to family and community. But imperial policies had increasingly intruded into the lives of farm families by sending their sons to war and raising their taxes. In 1754 farmers on Long Island, New York, had paid an average tax of 10 shillings; by 1756, thanks to the Great War for Empire, their taxes had jumped to 30 shillings. Peace brought little relief: The British-imposed Quartering Act kept taxes high, an average of 20 shillings a year, angering farmers in New York and elsewhere.

The urban-led Patriot boycotts of 1765 and 1768 had also raised the political consciousness of rural Americans. When the First Continental Congress called for a new boycott of British goods in 1774, it easily set up a rural network of committees to enforce it. In Concord, Massachusetts, 80 percent of the male heads of families and a number of single women signed a "Solemn League and Covenant" supporting nonimportation. In other farm towns, men blacked their faces, disguised themselves in blankets "like Indians," and threatened violence against shopkeepers who traded "in rum, molasses, & Sugar, &c." in violation of the boycott.

Patriots likewise warned that British measures threatened the yeoman tradition of landownership. In Petersham, Massachusetts, the town meeting worried that new British taxes would drain "this People of the Fruits of their Toil." Arable land was now scarce and expensive in older communities, and in new settlements merchants were seizing farmsteads for delinquent debts. By the 1770s, many northern yeomen felt personally threatened by British policies which, a Patriot pamphlet warned, were "paving the way for reducing the country to lordships" (Table 5.2).

Despite their higher standard of living, southern slave owners had similar fears. Many Virginia Patriots—including Patrick Henry, George Washington, and Thomas Jefferson—speculated in western lands, and they reacted angrily when first the Proclamation of 1763 and then the Quebec Act of 1774 restricted their economic ambitions. Moreover, thanks to their extravagant lifestyle, many Chesapeake planters were deeply in debt to British merchants. Even so, George Washington noted, they lived "genteely and hospitably" and were "ashamed" to adopt frugal ways. Accustomed to being absolute masters on their slave-labor plantations and seeing themselves as guardians of English liberties, planters resented their financial dependence on British creditors and dreaded the prospect of political subservience to British officials.

That danger now seemed real. If Parliament used the Coercive Acts to subdue Massachusetts, then it might turn next to Virginia, dissolving its representative assembly and judicial institutions and assisting British

The Debate over Representation and Sovereignty

Speaking before the House of Commons, Benjamin Franklin declared that before 1763, Americans had paid little attention to the question of Parliament's "right to lay taxes and duties" in the colonies. The reason was simple, Franklin said: "A right to lay internal taxes was never supposed to be in Parliament, as we are not represented there." Franklin recognized that representation was central to the imperial debate. As the following selections show, the failure to solve the problem of representation — and the closely related issue of parliamentary sovereignty — led to the American rebellion.

Jared Ingersoll

Report on the Debates in Parliament (1765)

Connecticut lawyer Jared Ingersoll (1722–1781) served as his colony's agent, or lobbyist, in Britain. In this 1765 letter to the governor of Connecticut, Ingersoll summarizes the debate then underway in Parliament over the Stamp Act. When the act passed, he returned home to become the stamp distributor in Connecticut. A mob forced him to resign that post. Ingersoll later served as a vice-admiralty judge in Philadelphia and, during the revolution, remained loyal to Britain.

The principal Attention has been to the Stamp bill that has been preparing to Lay before Parliament for taxing America. The Point of the Authority of Parliament to impose such Tax I found on my Arrival here was so fully and Universally yielded [accepted], that there was not the least hopes of making any impressions that way. . . .

I beg leave to give you a Summary of the Arguments which are made use of in favour of such Authority. The House of Commons, say they, is a branch of the supreme legislature of the Nation, and which in its Nature is supposed to represent, or rather to stand in the place of, the Commons, that is, of the great body of the people. . . .

That this house of Commons, therefore, is now . . . a part of the Supreme unlimited power of the Nation, as in every State there must be some unlimited Power and Authority. . . .

They say a Power to tax is a necessary part of every Supreme Legislative Authority, and that if they have not that Power over America, they have none, and then America is at once a Kingdom of itself.

On the other hand those who oppose the bill say, it is true the Parliament have a supreme unlimited Authority over every Part and Branch of the Kings dominions and as well over Ireland as any other place.

Yet [they say] we believe a British parliament will never think it prudent to tax Ireland [or America]. Tis true they

say, that the Commons of England and of the British Empire are all represented in and by the house of Commons, but this representation is confessedly on all hands by Construction and Virtual [because most British subjects] . . . have no hand in choosing the representatives. . . .

[They say further] that the Effects of this implied Representation here and in America must be infinitely different in the Article of Taxation. . . . By any Mistake an act of Parliament is made that prove injurious and hard the Member of Parliament here [in Britain] sees with his own Eyes and is moreover very accessible to the people. . . . [Also,] the taxes are laid equally by one Rule and fall as well on the Member himself as on the people. But as to America, from the great distance in point of Situation [they are not represented in the same way]. . . .

[Finally, the opponents of the Act say] we already by the Regulations upon their trade draw from the Americans all that they can spare. . . . This Step [of taxation] should not take place until or unless the Americans are allowed to send Members to Parliament. . . .

Thus I have given you, I think, the Substance of the Arguments on both sides of that great and important Question of the right and also of the Expediency of taxing America by Authority of Parliament. . . . [But] upon a Division of the house upon the Question, there was about 250 to about 50 in favour of the Bill.

Source: New Haven Colony Historical Society, *Papers* (1918), 9: 306–315.

Joseph Galloway

Plan of Union (1775)

Speaker of the Pennsylvania assembly Joseph Galloway was a delegate to the First Continental Congress, where he proposed a plan that addressed the issue of representation. The colonies would remain British, but operate under a continental government with the power to veto parliamentary laws that affected America. Radical Patriots in the Congress, who favored independence, prevented a vote on Galloway's plan and suppressed mention of it in the records. Galloway remained loyal to the Crown, fought on the British side in the War for Independence, and moved to England in 1778.

If we sincerely mean to accommodate the difference between the two countries, . . . we must take into consideration a number of facts which led the Parliament to pass the acts complained of. . . . [You will recall] the dangerous situation of the Colonies from the intrigues of France, and the incursions of the Canadians and their Indian allies, at the commencement of the last war. . . . Great-Britain sent over her fleets and armies for their protection. . . .

In this state of the Colonies, it was not unreasonable to expect that Parliament would have levied a tax on them proportionate to their wealth, . . . Parliament was naturally led to exercise the power which had been, by its predecessors, so often exercised over the Colonies, and to pass the Stamp Act. Against this act, the Colonies petitioned Parliament, and denied its authority . . . [declaring] that the Colonies could not be represented in that body. This justly alarmed the British Senate. It was thought and called by the ablest men and Britain, a clear and explicit declaration of the American Independence, and compelled the Parliament to pass the Declaratory Act, in order to save its ancient and incontrovertible right of supremacy over all the parts of the empire. . . .

Having thus briefly stated the arguments in favour of parliamentary authority, . . . I am free to confess that the exercise of that authority is not perfectly constitutional in respect to the Colonies. We know that the whole landed interest of Britain is represented in that body, while neither the land nor the people of America hold the least participation in the legislative authority of the State. Representation, or a participation in the supreme councils of the State, is the great principle upon which the freedom of the British Government is established and secured.

I wish to see . . . the right to participate in the supreme councils of the State extended, in some form . . . to America . . . [and therefore] have prepared the draught of a plan for uniting America more intimately, in constitutional policy, with Great-Britain. . . . I am certain when dispassionately considered, it will be found to be the most perfect union in power and liberty with the Parent State, next to a representation in Parliament, and I trust it will be approved of by both countries.

The Plan
That the several [colonial] assemblies shall [form an American union and] choose members for the grand council. . . .

That the Grand Council . . . shall hold and exercise all the like rights, liberties and privileges, as are held and exercised by and in the House of Commons of Great-Britain. . . .

That the President-General shall hold his office during the pleasure of the King, and his assent shall be requisite to all acts of the Grand Council, and it shall be his office and duty to cause them to be carried into execution. . . .

That the President-General, by and with the advice and consent of the Grand-Council, hold and exercise all the legislative rights, powers, and authorities, necessary for regulating and administering all the general police and affairs of the colonies. . . .

That the said President-General and the Grand Council, be an inferior and distinct branch of the British legislature, united and incorporated with it, . . . and that the assent of both [Parliament and the Grand Council] shall be requisite to the validity of all such general acts or statutes [that affect the colonies].

Source: Joseph Galloway, *Historical and Political Reflections on the Rise and Progress of the American Rebellion* (London, 1780), 70.

ANALYZING THE EVIDENCE

- According to Ingersoll, what were the main arguments of those in Parliament who opposed the Stamp Act? Did those opposing the Stamp Act agree with the act's supporters that Parliament had the right to tax the colonies?

- How did Galloway's plan solve the problem of colonial representation in Parliament? How would the British ministers who advocated parliamentary supremacy have reacted to the plan?

- The framers of the U.S. Constitution addressed the problem of dividing authority between state governments and the national government by allowing the states to retain legal authority over most matters and delegating limited powers to the national government. Could such a solution have been implemented in the British empire? Why or why not?

TABLE 5.2

Patriot Resistance, 1762–1776

Date	British Action	Patriot Response
1762	Revenue Act	Merchants complain privately
1763	Proclamation Line	Land speculators voice discontent
1764	Sugar Act	Merchants and Massachusetts legislature protest
1765	Stamp Act	Sons of Liberty riot; Stamp Act Congress; first boycott of British goods
1765	Quartering Act	New York assembly refuses to fund until 1767
1767–1768	Townshend Act; military occupation of Boston	Second boycott of British goods; harassment of pro-British merchants
1772	Royal commission to investigate *Gaspée* affair	Committees of correspondence form
1773	Tea Act	Widespread resistance; Boston Tea Party
1774	Coercive Acts; Quebec Act	First Continental Congress; third boycott of British goods
1775	British raids near Boston; king's Proclamation for Suppressing Rebellion and Sedition	Armed resistance; Second Continental Congress; invasion of Canada; cutoff of colonial exports
1776	Military attacks led by royal governors in South	Paine's *Common Sense*; Declaration of Independence

merchants to seize debt-burdened properties. Consequently, the Virginia gentry supported demands by indebted yeomen farmers to close the law courts, so that they could bargain with merchants over debts without the threat of legal action. "The spark of liberty is not yet extinct among our people," declared one planter, "and if properly fanned by the Gentlemen of influence will, I make no doubt, burst out again into a flame."

Loyalist Americans

Other "Gentlemen of influence" worried that resistance to Britain would undermine all political institutions and "introduce Anarchy and disorder and render life and property here precarious." Their fears increased when the Sons of Liberty used intimidation and violence to uphold the boycotts. One well-to-do New Yorker complained, "No man can be in a more abject state of bondage than he whose Reputation, Property and Life are exposed to the discretionary violence . . . of the community." As the crisis deepened, such men became Loyalists—so called because they remained loyal to the British crown.

Less affluent Americans also refused to endorse the Patriot cause. In New Jersey and Pennsylvania, thousands of pacifist Quakers and Germans tried to remain neutral. In areas where wealthy landowners became Patriots—the Hudson River Valley of New York, for example—many tenant farmers supported the king because they hated their landlords. Similar social conflicts prompted some Regulators in the North Carolina backcountry and many farmers in eastern Maryland to oppose the Patriots there. Enslaved blacks had little reason to support the cause of their Patriot masters. In November 1774, James Madison reported that some Virginia slaves were planning to escape "when the English troops should arrive."

Prominent Loyalists—royal officials, merchants with military contracts, clergy of the Church of England, and well-established lawyers—tried to mobilize support for the king. Relying on their high status and rhetorical skills, they denounced Patriot leaders as troublemakers and accused them of working toward independence. But Loyalist leaders found relatively few active followers. A Tory association started by the governor of New Hampshire enrolled just fifty-nine members, including fourteen of his relatives. At this crucial juncture, Americans who supported resistance to British rule commanded the allegiance—or at least the acquiescence—of the majority of white Americans.

Armed Resistance Begins

When the Continental Congress had met in September 1774, Massachusetts was already defying British authority. In August, 150 delegates to an extralegal

Middlesex County Congress had urged Patriots to close the existing royal courts and to transfer their political allegiance to the popularly elected House of Representatives. Subsequently, armed crowds harassed Loyalists and ensured Patriot rule in most of New England.

General Thomas Gage, now the military governor of Massachusetts, tried desperately to maintain imperial power. In September 1774, he ordered British troops in Boston to seize Patriot armories in nearby Charlestown and Cambridge. Following that raid, 20,000 militiamen mobilized to safeguard other Massachusetts military depots. The Concord town meeting raised a defensive force, the famous **Minutemen**, to "Stand at a minutes warning in Case of alarm." Increasingly, Gage's authority was limited to Boston, where it rested on the bayonets of his 3,500 troops. Meanwhile, the Patriot-controlled Massachusetts assembly met in nearby Salem in open defiance of Parliament, collecting taxes, bolstering the militia, and assuming the responsibilities of government.

In London, the colonial secretary, Lord Dartmouth, proclaimed Massachusetts to be in "open rebellion" and ordered Gage to march against the "rude rabble." On the night of April 18, 1775, Gage dispatched seven hundred soldiers to capture colonial leaders and supplies at Concord. Paul Revere and a series of other riders warned Patriots in many towns; at dawn, militiamen confronted the British regulars first at Lexington and then at Concord. Those first skirmishes took a handful of lives, but as the British retreated to Boston, militia from neighboring towns repeatedly ambushed them. By the end of the day, 73 British soldiers were dead, 174 wounded, and 26 missing. British fire had killed 49 Massachusetts militiamen and wounded 39. Too much blood had been spilled to allow another compromise. Twelve years of economic and constitutional conflict had ended in civil violence.

The Second Continental Congress Organizes for War

A month later, in May 1775, Patriot leaders gathered in Philadelphia for the Second Continental Congress. As the Congress opened, 3,000 British troops attacked American fortifications on Breed's Hill and Bunker Hill overlooking Boston. After three assaults and 1,000 casualties, they finally dislodged the Patriot militia. Inspired by his countrymen's valor, John Adams exhorted the Congress to rise to the "defense of American liberty" by creating a continental army. He nominated George Washington to lead it. After bitter debate, the Congress

approved the proposals, but, Adams lamented, only "by bare majorities."

Congress versus King George | Despite the bloodshed in Massachusetts, a majority in the Congress still hoped for reconciliation. Led by John Dickinson of Pennsylvania, these moderates won approval of a petition expressing loyalty to George III and asking for repeal of oppressive parliamentary legislation. But Samuel Adams, Patrick Henry, and other zealous Patriots drummed up support for a Declaration of the Causes and Necessities of Taking Up Arms. Americans dreaded the "calamities of civil war," the declaration asserted, but were "resolved to die Freemen rather than to live [as] slaves." George III failed to exploit the divisions among the Patriots; instead, in August 1775, he issued a Proclamation for Suppressing Rebellion and Sedition.

Before the king's proclamation reached America, the radicals in the Congress had won support for an invasion of Canada. Patriot forces easily defeated the British forces at Montreal; but in December 1775, they failed to capture Quebec City and withdrew. Meanwhile, American merchants waged the financial warfare promised at the First Continental Congress by cutting off exports to Britain and its West Indian sugar islands, which were recovering from a series of major El Niño–caused hurricanes. Parliament retaliated with the Prohibitory Act, which outlawed all trade with the rebellious colonies.

Fighting in the South | Skirmishes between Patriot and Loyalist forces now broke out in the southern colonies. In Virginia, Patriots forced the royal governor, Lord Dunmore, to take refuge on a British warship in Chesapeake Bay. Branding the rebels "traitors," the governor organized two military forces: one white, the Queen's Own Loyal Virginians; and one black, the Ethiopian Regiment, which enlisted 1,000 slaves who had fled their Patriot owners. In November 1775, Dunmore issued a controversial proclamation promising freedom to black slaves and white indentured servants who joined the Loyalist cause. White planters denounced this "Diabolical scheme," claiming it "point[ed] a dagger to their Throats." A new rising of the black and white underclasses, as in Bacon's Rebellion in the 1670s, seemed a possibility. In Fincastle County in southwestern Virginia, Loyalist planter John Hiell urged workers to support the king, promising "a Servant man" that soon "he and all the negroes would get their freedom." Frightened by Dunmore's aggressive tactics, Patriot yeomen and tenants called for a final break with Britain.

Tryon's Palace in New Bern, North Carolina

William Tryon, appointed as the royal governor of North Carolina in 1764, was accustomed to living well. Born into a substantial landed-gentry family, he married a London heiress, the daughter of the East India Company's governor of Bombay. Upon his arrival in North Carolina, Tryon persuaded the colony's assembly to appropriate the princely sum of £10,000 to build a mansion for his use. Completed in 1770, the "palace," as critics called it, served as Tryon's home for only a year. After harshly suppressing the Regulator movement in 1771, Tryon was appointed royal governor of New York (he would be the colony's last). Though Tryon's North Carolina mansion burned to the ground in 1798, it was restored in the 1950s, using the original plans.   Tryon's Palace, New Bern, N.C.

In North Carolina, too, military clashes prompted demands for independence. Early in 1776, Josiah Martin, the colony's royal governor, raised a Loyalist force of 1,500 Scottish Highlanders in the backcountry. In response, Patriots mobilized the low-country militia and, in February, defeated Martin's army at the Battle of Moore's Creek Bridge, capturing more than 800 Highlanders. Following this victory, radical Patriots in the North Carolina assembly told its representatives to the Continental Congress to join with "other Colonies in declaring Independence, and forming foreign alliances." In May, the Virginia gentry followed suit: Led by James Madison, Edmund Pendleton, and Patrick Henry, the Patriots met in convention and resolved unanimously to support independence.

Thomas Paine's *Common Sense*

As radical Patriots edged toward independence, many colonists still retained an affection for the king. Joyous crowds had toasted the health of George III when he ascended the throne in 1760 and again in 1766, when his ministers repealed the Stamp Act. Their loyalty stemmed in part from the character of authority in a patriarchal society. Just as people followed the dictates of elders in town meetings and ministers in churches, so they should obey the king, their imperial "father." Every father was "a king, and governor in his family," as one group of Baptists put it. To deny the king's legitimacy would disrupt the entire social order.

But by late 1775, many Americans were turning against the monarch. As military conflicts escalated, they accused George III of supporting oppressive legislation and ordering armed retaliation. Agitation was especially intense in Philadelphia, where many Quaker and Anglican merchants were either "neutrals" or Loyalists. Artisans, including many Scots-Irish immigrants, became a major force in the city's Patriot movement. Angered by the merchants' passivity and worried that British imports threatened their small-scale manufacturing enterprises, they organized a Mechanics Association to protect America's "just Rights and Privileges." By February 1776, forty artisans sat with forty-seven merchants on the Philadelphia Committee of Resistance.

Cultural and religious motives prompted many Scots-Irish artisans and laborers to become Patriots. They came from Presbyterian families who had fled economic and religious discrimination in British-controlled Ireland, and many had embraced the egalitarian message preached by Gilbert Tennent and other New Light ministers (see Chapter 4). As pastor of Philadelphia's Second Presbyterian Church, Tennent had preached that all men and women were equal before God. Applying this idea to politics, New Light Presbyterians shouted in street demonstrations that they had "no king but King Jesus." Republican philosophy derived from the European Enlightenment also circulated freely among Pennsylvania artisans. Consequently, Patriot leaders Benjamin Franklin and Dr. Benjamin Rush found a receptive audience when they questioned not only the wisdom of George III but the very idea of monarchy.

With popular sentiment in flux, a single brief pamphlet tipped the balance. In January 1776, Thomas Paine published *Common Sense*, a rousing call for independence and a republican form of government. Paine had served as a minor customs official in England until he was fired for joining a protest against low wages. In 1774, Paine, migrated to Philadelphia, where he met Rush and other Patriots who shared his republican sentiments.

In *Common Sense*, Paine launched an assault on the traditional monarchical order in language that stirred popular emotions. "Monarchy and hereditary succession have laid the world in blood and ashes," Paine proclaimed, leveling a personal attack at George III, "the hard hearted sullen Pharaoh of England." Mixing insults with biblical quotations, Paine blasted the British system of "mixed government" among the three estates of king, lords, and commoners. Paine granted that the system "was noble for the dark and slavish times" of the past, but now it yielded only "monarchical tyranny in the person of the king" and "aristocratical tyranny in the persons of the peers."

Paine made a compelling case for American independence by turning the traditional metaphor of patriarchal authority on its head: "Is it the interest of a man to be a boy all his life?" he asked. Within six months, *Common Sense* had gone through twenty-five editions and reached hundreds of thousands of people throughout the colonies. "There is great talk of independence," a worried New York Loyalist noted, "the unthinking multitude are mad for it. . . . A pamphlet called Com-

Thomas Paine

Tom Paine was many things: a failed husband, businessman, and customs agent; a creative inventor and bridge designer; and, most important, a lifelong radical and the author of provocative works that helped change the course of history. In 1776, his pamphlet *Common Sense* sparked Americans to declare independence from Britain. Paine's defense of the French Revolution and attack on monarchy, *The Rights of Man* (1791), won him election to the National Convention, which created the First French Republic. And his *Age of Reason* (1794, 1796), a defense of deism and rational inquiry and a sustained assault on "revealed" religion and Christianity, won him the enmity of devout believers and political conservatives. *Thomas Paine* (oil on canvas), Otis, Bass (1784–1861) / Huntington Library ©The Huntington Library, Art Collections & Botanical Gardens / The Bridgeman Art Library.

mon Sense has carried off . . . thousands." Paine urged Americans to create independent republican states: "A government of our own is our natural right, 'TIS TIME TO PART" (see Voices from Abroad, "Thomas Paine: *Common Sense*," p. 166).

Independence Declared

Inspired by Paine's arguments and beset by armed Loyalists, Patriot conventions urged a break from Britain. In June 1776, Richard Henry Lee presented Virginia's resolution to the Continental Congress: "That these United Colonies are, and of right ought to be,

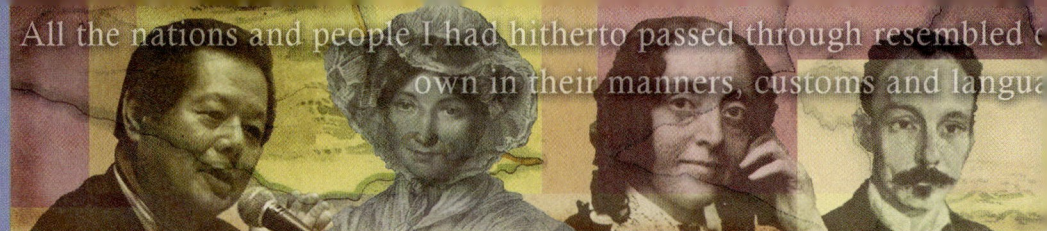
Thomas Paine
Common Sense

Thomas Paine was a sharp critic and an acute observer. Before arriving in Philadelphia from his native England in mid-1774, Paine had rejected the legitimacy of monarchy. He quickly came to understand the republican spirit of American politics and how this spirit could easily be tapped to create independent governments that might change the course of history. In his widely read political pamphlet *Common Sense* (1776), he showed the colonists that American independence was "natural" and simply "common sense."

In the following pages I offer nothing more than simple facts, plain arguments, and common sense.... The sun never shined on a cause of greater worth. 'Tis not the affair of a city, a country, a province, or a kingdom, but of a continent—of at least one eighth part of the habitable globe. 'Tis not the concern of a day, a year, or an age; posterity are virtually involved in the contest, and will be more or less affected, even to the end of time....

We have boasted the protection of Great-Britain, without considering, that her motive was *interest* not *attachment*; that she did not protect us from *our enemies* on *our account*, but from *her enemies* on *her own account*.... Our plan is commerce, and that, well attended to, will secure us the peace and friendship of all Europe; because, it is the interest of all Europe to have America a *free port*. Her trade will always be a protection, and her barrenness of gold and silver secure her from invaders. I challenge the warmest advocate for reconciliation, to shew, a single advantage that this continent can reap, by being connected with Great Britain.... Our corn will fetch its price in any market in Europe, and our imported goods must be paid for buy them where we will.

Every thing that is right or natural pleads for separation. The blood of the slain, the weeping voice of nature cries, 'TIS TIME TO PART. Even the distance at which the Almighty hath placed England and America, is a strong and natural proof, that the authority of the one, over the other, was never the design of Heaven.... There is something very absurd, in supposing a continent to be perpetually governed by an island. In no instance hath nature made the satellite larger than its primary planet, and as England and America, with respect to each other, reverses the common order of nature, it is evident they belong to different systems: England to Europe, America to itself.

But the most powerful of all arguments, is, that nothing but independence, i.e. a continental form of government, can keep the peace of the continent and preserve it inviolate from civil wars.... If there is any true cause of fear respecting independence, it is because no plan is yet laid down. Men do not see their way out—Wherefore,... I offer the following hints....

Let the assemblies [of the former colonies] be annual, with a President only . . . their business wholly domestic, and subject to the authority of a Continental Congress.

Let each colony be divided into six, eight, or ten convenient districts, each district to send a proper number of delegates to Congress, so that each colony send at least thirty. The whole number in Congress will be at least 390....

But where, say some, is the King of America? I'll tell you. Friend, . . . in America THE LAW IS KING. For as in absolute governments the King is law, so in free countries the law ought to be King; and there ought to be no other.... Let the crown at the conclusion of the ceremony, be demolished, and scattered among the people whose right it is. A government of our own is our natural right....

O ye that love mankind! Ye that dare oppose, not only the tyranny, but the tyrant, stand forth! Every spot of the old world is overrun with oppression. Freedom hath been hunted round the globe. Asia, and Africa, have long expelled her.—Europe regards her like a stranger, and England hath given her warning to depart. O! receive the fugitive, and prepare in time an asylum for mankind.

Source: Thomas Paine, *Common Sense* (Philadelphia, 1776).

ANALYZING THE EVIDENCE

- On what grounds does Paine argue for American independence? Where do you see the influence of Enlightenment thinking in his argument?
- Given that all European nations pursued mercantilist policies, was Paine correct in thinking they would welcome America as a "free port"? How were Europe's monarchies likely to respond to an independent American republic?
- How could Paine celebrate America as a land of freedom and an "asylum for mankind" given the importance of slavery and indentured servitude to its economy? What sort of liberty was Paine championing?
- Why do you think *Common Sense* struck such a chord with Americans throughout the colonies?

George III, 1771

King George III was a young man of twenty-seven when the American troubles began in 1765. Six years later, as this portrait by Johann Zoffany suggests, the king had aged. Initially, George had been headstrong and tried to impose his will on Parliament, but he succeeded only in generating political confusion and inept policy. He strongly supported Parliament's attempts to tax the colonies and continued the war in America long after most of his ministers agreed that it had been lost.   The Royal Collection © 2003 Her Majesty Queen Elizabeth II.

free and independent states." Faced with certain defeat, staunch Loyalists and anti-independence moderates withdrew from the Congress, leaving committed Patriots to take the fateful step. On July 4, 1776, the Congress approved the Declaration of Independence (see Documents, p. D-1).

The Declaration's main author, Thomas Jefferson of Virginia, had mobilized resistance to the Coercive Acts with the pamphlet *A Summary View of the Rights of British America* (1774). Now, in the Declaration, he justified independence and republicanism to Americans and the world, by vilifying George III: "He has plundered our seas, ravaged our coasts, burned our towns, and destroyed the lives of our people." Such a prince was a "tyrant," Jefferson concluded, and "is unfit to be the ruler of a free people."

Employing the ideas of the European Enlightenment, Jefferson proclaimed a series of "self-evident" truths: "that all men are created equal"; that they possess the "unalienable rights" of "Life, Liberty, and the pursuit of Happiness"; that government derives its "just powers from the consent of the governed" and can rightly be overthrown if it "becomes destructive of these ends." By linking these doctrines of individual liberty, **popular sovereignty**, and republican government with American independence, Jefferson established them as the defining political values of the new nation.

For Jefferson, as for Paine, the pen proved mightier than the sword. The Declaration won wide readership and support in France and Germany; at home, it sparked celebrations in rural hamlets and seaport cities, as crowds burned effigies and toppled statues of the king. On July 8, 1776, in Easton, Pennsylvania, a "great number of spectators" heard a reading of the Declaration, "gave their hearty assent with three loud huzzahs, and cried out, 'May God long preserve and unite the Free and Independent States of America.'"

- Why did the Patriot movement wane in the early 1770s? Why did the Tea Act reignite colonial resistance?

- Why did colonial and British leaders fail to reach a political compromise to save the empire?

SUMMARY

In this chapter we focused on a short span of time—a mere decade and a half—and outlined the plot of a political drama in three acts. In Act I, the Great War for Empire prompts British political leaders to implement a program of imperial reform and taxation. Act II is full of dramatic action, as colonial mobs riot, Patriot pamphleteers articulate ideologies of resistance, and British ministers search for compromise between claims of parliamentary sovereignty and assertions of colonial autonomy. Act III takes the form of tragedy: The once-proud British empire dissolves into civil war, an imminent nightmare of death and destruction.

Why did this happen? More than two centuries later, the answers still are not clear. Certainly, the lack of astute leadership in Britain was a major factor. But British leaders faced circumstances that limited their actions: a huge national debt and deep commitments to both a powerful fiscal-military state and the absolute supremacy of Parliament. Moreover, in America, decades of salutary neglect strengthened Patriots' demands for political autonomy, as did the fears and aspirations of artisans and farmers. The trajectories of their conflicting intentions and ideas placed Britain and its American possessions on course for a disastrous—and fatal—collision.

Independence Declared

In this painting by John Trumbull, Thomas Jefferson and the other drafters of the Declaration (John Adams of Massachusetts, Roger Sherman of Connecticut, Robert Livingston of New York, and Benjamin Franklin of Pennsylvania) present the document to John Hancock, the president of the Second Continental Congress. One Patriot observer reported that when the Declaration was read at a public meeting in New York City on July 10, a massive statue of George III was "pulled down by the Populace" and its four thousand pounds of lead melted down to make "Musquet balls" for use against the British troops massed on Staten Island.   Yale University Art Gallery/Art Resource, NY.

CHAPTER REVIEW QUESTIONS

- Trace the key events in both Britain and America from 1763 to 1776 that forged the Patriot movement. Why did those in Parliament believe that the arguments of the rebellious colonists were not justified? How did the Patriots gain the widespread support of the colonists?

- The narrative suggests that the war for American independence was not inevitable, that the British empire could have been saved. Do you agree? Was there a point during the imperial crisis at which peaceful compromise was possible?

FOR FURTHER EXPLORATION

Jack P. Greene and J. R. Pole, eds., *The Blackwell Encyclopedia of the American Revolution* (1991), and Barbara DeWolfe, *Discoveries of America: Personal Accounts of British Emigrants* (1997), illuminate the lives and events of the era. A. J. Langguth's *Patriots: The Men Who Started the American Revolution* (1988) should be read in conjunction with Gary B. Nash's *The Unknown American Revolution* (2005).

Edmund Morgan and Helen Morgan explore The *Stamp Act Crisis* (1953), and Philip Lawson's *George Grenville* (1984) examines the man who provoked it. Benjamin Labaree's *The Boston Tea Party* (1979) shows how a "small" event altered the course of history, while David Hackett Fischer explains the rise of the radical Patriots in *Paul Revere's Ride* (1994). For events in Virginia, see Woody Holton, *Forced Founders* (1999), and Michael A. McDonnell, *The Politics of War* (2007).

Liberty! The American Revolution (6 hours), a PBS video, has a fine Web site (**www.pbs.org/ktca/liberty/**). For a British perspective, see "This Sceptred Isle: Empire" (**www.bbc.co.uk/radio4/history/empire/regions/americas.shtml**). For links to many document collections, visit **userpages.umbc.edu/~bouton/Revolution.links.htm**. The National Gallery of Art (**www.nga.gov**) has paintings of the period. In *Angel in the Whirlwind: The Triumph of the American Revolution* (1997), Benson Bobrick narrates a grand epic; for more complex analyses, read John Ferling, *A Leap in the Dark: The Struggle to Create the American Republic* (2003), and David Armitage, *The Declaration of Independence: A Global History* (2007).

TEST YOUR KNOWLEDGE

To assess your command of the material in this chapter, see the Online Study Guide at **bedfordstmartins.com/henretta**.

For Web sites, images, and documents related to topics and places in this chapter, visit **bedfordstmartins.com/makehistory**.

TIMELINE

1756–1763	Great War for Empire British national debt doubles
1762	Revenue Act reforms customs service Royal Navy arrests colonial smugglers
1763	Treaty of Paris ends war Proclamation Line limits white settlement George Grenville becomes prime minister
1764	Sugar Act and Currency Act Colonists oppose vice-admiralty courts
1765	Stamp Act imposes direct tax Quartering Act requires barracks for British troops Sons of Liberty riot Stamp Act Congress meets First American boycott of British goods
1766	First compromise: Stamp Act repealed; Declaratory Act passed
1767	Townshend duties Restraining Act suspends New York assembly
1768	Second American boycott
1769	Daughters of Liberty make cloth British army occupies Boston
1770	Second compromise: Partial repeal of Townshend Act Boston "Massacre"
1772	Committees of correspondence form
1773	Tea Act assists British East India Company Boston Tea Party
1774	Coercive Acts punish Massachusetts Quebec Act angers Patriots First Continental Congress meets Third American boycott
1775	General Gage marches to Lexington and Concord Second Continental Congress creates Continental army Lord Dunmore recruits Loyalist slaves Patriots invade Canada and skirmish with Loyalists in South
1776	Thomas Paine's *Common Sense* Declaration of Independence

BOSTON

CHARLES TOWN

CHAPTER 6

Making War and Republican Governments, 1776–1789

When Patriots in Frederick County, Maryland, demanded his allegiance to their cause in 1776, Robert Gassaway would have none of it. "It was better for the poor people to lay down their arms and pay the duties and taxes laid upon them by King and Parliament than to be brought into slavery and commanded and ordered about [by you]," he told them. The story was much the same in Farmington, Connecticut, where Patriot officials imprisoned Nathaniel Jones and seventeen other men for "remaining neutral." In Pennsylvania, Quakers accused of Loyalism were rounded up, jailed, and charged with treason, and some were hung for aiding the British cause. Everywhere, the outbreak of fighting in 1776 forced families to choose the Loyalist or the Patriot side.

The Patriots' control of most local governments gave them an edge in this battle. Patriot leaders organized militia units and recruited volunteers for the Continental army, a ragtag force that surprisingly held its own on the battlefield. "I admire the American troops tremendously!" exclaimed a French officer. "It is incredible that soldiers composed of every age, even children of fifteen, of whites and blacks, almost naked, unpaid, and rather poorly fed, can march so well and withstand fire so steadfastly."

Military service created political commitment — and vice versa. Patriot leaders encouraged Americans not only to support the war but also to take an active role in government. As the common people entered into politics, the character of political identity changed. Previously, Americans had lived within a social world dominated by the links of family, kinship, and locality; now, republican citizenship emphasized the vertical ties connecting each individual with the state. "From subjects to citizens the difference is immense," remarked South Carolina Patriot David Ramsay. By repudiating monarchical rule and raising a democratic army, the Patriots launched the age of republican revolutions.

Soon republicanism would throw France into turmoil and inspire revolutionaries in Spain's American colonies. The independence of the Anglo-American colonies, remarked the Venezuelan political leader, Francisco de Miranda, who had been in New York and Philadelphia at the end of the American Revolution, "was bound to be . . . the infallible preliminary to our own [independence movement]." The Patriot uprising of 1776 had set in motion a process that by 1826 had replaced an Atlantic colonial system with an American system of new nations.

The Battle of Bunker Hill

As British warships and artillery lob cannon balls at Patriot positions, British redcoats advance up the steep slope of Bunker Hill (to the right). It took three assaults and a thousand casualties before they finally dislodged the Patriot militia. The British bombardment ignited fires in nearby Charlestown, which burns in the background. "*Attack on Bunker's Hill, with the Burning of Charles Town*," American Eighteenth Century. Gift of Edgar Williams and Bernice Chrysler Garbisch. Image © 2005 Board of Trustees, National Gallery of Art, Washington, D.C.

The Trials of War, 1776–1778

The Declaration of Independence appeared just as the British launched a full-scale military assault. For two years, British troops manhandled the Continental army. A few inspiring American victories kept the rebellion alive, but during the winters of 1776 and 1777, the Patriot cause hung in the balance.

War in the North

Once the British resorted to military force, few Europeans gave the rebels a chance. The population of Great Britain was 11 million; the colonies, 2.5 million— 20 percent of whom were enslaved Africans. Moreover, the British government had access to the immense wealth generated by the South Atlantic System and the emerging Industrial Revolution. Its military budget paid for the most powerful navy in the world, a standing army of 48,000 Britons (with an experienced officer corps), and thousands of German (Hessian) soldiers. Britain also had the support of thousands of American Loyalists and powerful Indian tribes: In the Carolinas, the Cherokees resisted colonists' demands for their lands by allying with the British, as did four of the six Iroquois nations of New York (Map 6.1).

By contrast, the Americans were economically and militarily weak. They lacked a strong central government and a reliable source of tax revenue. Their new Continental army, commanded by General George Washington, consisted of 18,000 poorly trained recruits. The Patriot militia would not march to distant battles, and American officers had never faced a disciplined European army.

To demonstrate Britain's military superiority, the prime minister, Lord North, ordered General William Howe to capture New York City. His strategy was to seize control of the Hudson River and thereby isolate the radical Patriots in New England from the colonies to the south. As the Second Continental Congress declared independence in Philadelphia in July 1776, Howe landed 32,000 troops—British regulars and German mercenaries—outside New York City. In August 1776, Howe defeated the Americans in the Battle of Long Island and forced their retreat to Manhattan Island. There, Howe outflanked Washington's troops and nearly trapped them. Outgunned and outmaneuvered, the Continental army again retreated, eventually crossing the Hudson River to New Jersey. By December, the British army had pushed the rebels across New Jersey and over the Delaware River into Pennsylvania.

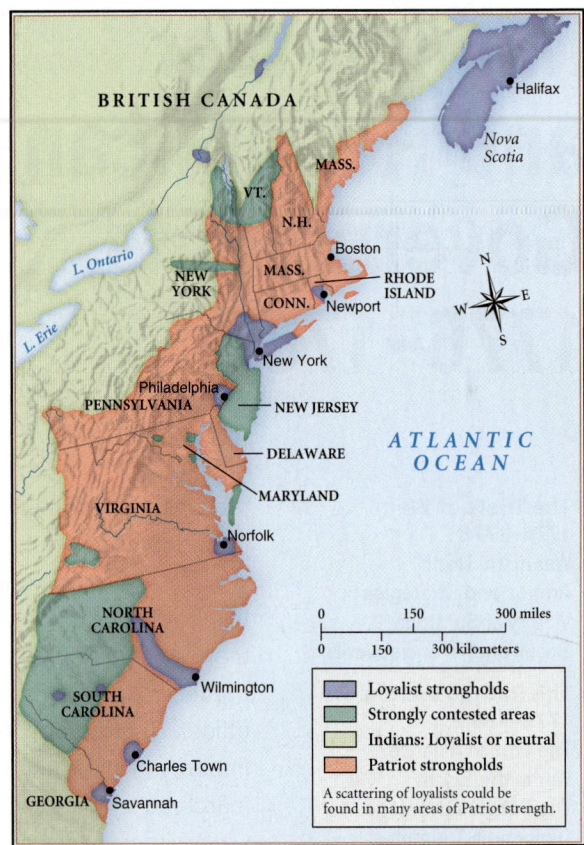

MAP 6.1

Patriot and Loyalist Strongholds

Patriots were in the majority in most of the thirteen mainland colonies and used their control of local governments to funnel men, money, and supplies to the rebel cause. Although Loyalists could be found in every colony, their strongholds were limited to Nova Scotia, eastern New York, New Jersey, and certain areas in the South. However, most Native American peoples favored the British cause and bolstered the power of Loyalist militias in central New York (see Map 6.3) and in the Carolina backcountry.

From the Patriots' perspective, winter came just in time. Following eighteenth-century custom, the British halted their military campaign for the cold months, allowing the Americans to catch them off guard. On Christmas night 1776, Washington crossed the Delaware River and staged a successful surprise attack on Trenton, New Jersey, where he forced the surrender of 1,000 German soldiers. In early January 1777, the Continental army won a small victory at nearby Princeton (Map 6.2). But like bright stars in a dark sky, these minor triumphs could not mask British military superiority. "These are the times," wrote Thomas Paine, "that try men's souls."

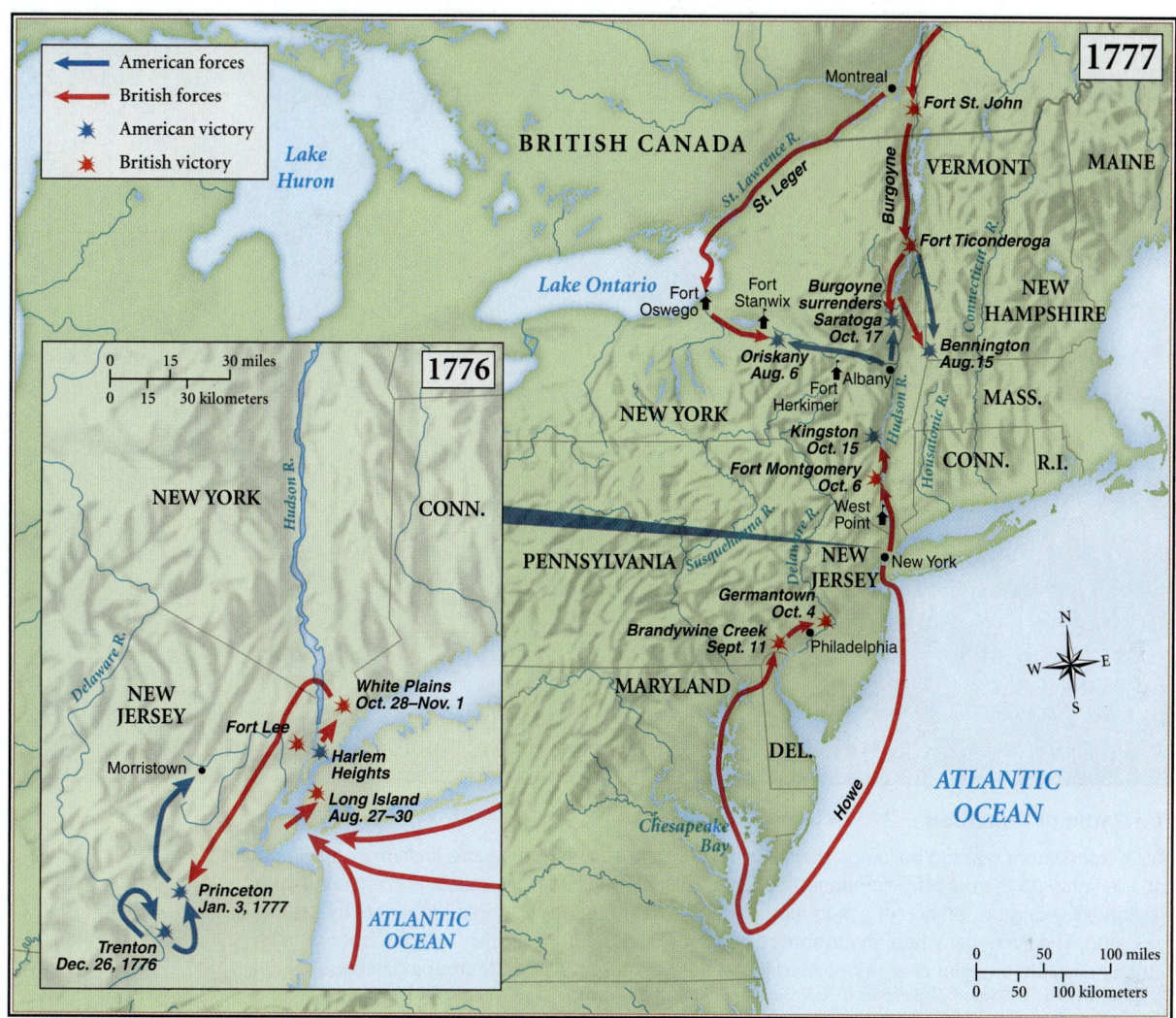

MAP 6.2

The War in the North, 1776–1777

In 1776, the British army drove Washington's forces across New Jersey into Pennsylvania. The Americans counterattacked successfully at Trenton and Princeton and then set up winter headquarters in Morristown. In 1777, British forces stayed on the offensive. General Howe attacked the Patriot capital, Philadelphia, from the south and captured it in early October. Meanwhile, General Burgoyne and Colonel St. Leger launched simultaneous invasions from Canada. With the help of thousands of New England militiamen, American troops commanded by General Horatio Gates defeated Burgoyne in August at Bennington, Vermont, and in October at Saratoga, New York, the military turning point in the war.

Armies and Strategies

Thanks in part to General Howe, the rebellion survived. Howe had opposed the Coercive Acts of 1774 and still hoped for a political compromise. So he did not try to destroy the American army but simply to show its weakness and persuade the Continental Congress to give up the struggle. Howe's restrained tactics cost Britain the opportunity to nip the rebellion in the bud.

For his part, Washington acted cautiously to avoid a major defeat: "On our Side the War should be defensive," he told Congress. His strategy was to draw the British away from the seacoast, extend their lines of supply, and sap their morale.

Congress had promised Washington a regular force of 75,000 men, but the Continental army never reached even a third of that number. Yeomen refused to be "Haras'd with callouts" that took them away from

The Battle of Princeton

Black smoke from burning buildings partially obscures the sun, as the muzzle flash from an American cannon lights up the battlefield. Pursued by Cornwallis after his surprise attack and victory at nearby Trenton, Washington (on horseback to the right of the flag) confronted three regiments of redcoats at Princeton. The Americans had an advantage in numbers and put the British to flight, but only after withstanding the bayonet charge depicted in the right-center of William Mercer's painting.   Library of Congress Manuscript Division. Department of Rare Books and Special Collections.

their families and farms, and would serve only in local militias. When the Virginia gentry imposed a military draft and three years of service on propertyless men — the "Lazy fellows who lurk about and are pests to Society"—they resisted so fiercely that the legislature had to pay them substantial bounties and agree to shorter terms of service. The Continental soldiers recruited in Maryland by General William Smallwood were poor American youths and older foreign-born men, often British ex-convicts and former indentured servants. Most enlisted for the $20 cash bonus (about $2,000 today) and the promise of 100 acres of land.

Molding such recruits into an effective fighting force was nearly impossible. Inexperienced soldiers panicked in the face of a British artillery bombardment or flank attack; and hundreds deserted, unwilling to submit to the discipline of military life. The soldiers who stayed resented the contempt their officers had for the "camp followers," the women who made do with the meager supplies provided to feed and care for the troops.

General Philip Schuyler of New York complained that his troops were "destitute of provisions, without camp equipage, with little ammunition, and not a single piece of cannon."

The Continental army was not only poorly supplied, but held in suspicion by Radical Whig Patriots, who believed that a standing army was a threat to liberty. Even in wartime, they preferred militias to a professional fighting force. Given these handicaps, Washington and his army were fortunate to have escaped an overwhelming defeat.

Victory at Saratoga

After Howe's dismaying failure to achieve an overwhelming victory, Lord North and his colonial secretary, Lord George Germain launched another major military campaign in 1777. Isolating New England remained the primary goal. To achieve it, Germain planned a three-pronged attack converging on Albany, New York. General John Burgoyne would lead a large contingent of regulars south from Quebec, Colonel Barry St. Leger and a force of Iroquois warriors would attack from the west, and General Howe would lead troops northward from New York City.

Howe had a different plan, which though carried out effectively, led to a disastrous result. He decided to attack Philadelphia, the home of the Continental Congress, hoping to end the rebellion with a single decisive blow. But instead of marching quickly across New Jersey, Howe loaded his troops onto boats and sailed up the Chesapeake Bay to attack Philadelphia from the south. The plan worked. Howe's troops easily outflanked the American positions along Brandywine Creek in Delaware and, in late September, marched triumphantly into Philadelphia. However, the capture of the rebels' capital did not end the uprising; the Continental Congress, determined to continue the struggle, fled into the interior.

Howe's slow campaign against Philadelphia contributed to the defeat of Burgoyne's army at Saratoga. Burgoyne's troops had at first advanced quickly (and successfully) from Quebec, crossing Lake Champlain, overwhelming the American defenses at Fort Ticonderoga in early July, and driving south toward the Hudson River. Then they stalled. Burgoyne—nicknamed "Gentleman Johnny"—was used to high living and had fought in Europe in a leisurely fashion; believing his large army would easily dominate the rebels, he stopped early each day to pitch comfortable tents and eat elaborate dinners with his officers. The American troops led by General Horatio Gates also slowed Burgoyne's progress by felling huge trees in the path of the British force, and by raiding British supply lines to Canada.

At summer's end, Burgoyne's army of 6,000 British and German troops and 600 Loyalists and Indians was stuck near Saratoga, New York. Desperate for food and horses, in August the British raided nearby Bennington, Vermont, but were beaten back by 2,000 American militiamen. Patriot forces to the west in the Mohawk Valley also threw St. Leger and the Iroquois into retreat. Making matters worse, the British commander in New York City recalled 4,000 troops he had sent toward Albany and ordered them to Philadelphia to bolster Howe's force. While Burgoyne waited in vain for help, thousands of Patriot militiamen from Massachusetts, New Hampshire, and New York joined Gates's forces, blocking his advance and retreat in a series of skirmishes that finally gave the British no avenue of escape. They "swarmed around the army like birds of prey," reported an English sergeant, and in October 1777, they forced Burgoyne to surrender.

Joseph Brant

Mohawk chief Thayendanegea, known to whites as Joseph Brant, was a devout member of the Church of England and helped to translate the Bible into the Iroquois language. Brant persuaded four of the six Iroquois nations to support Britain in the war. In 1778 and 1779, he led Iroquois warriors and Tory rangers in devastating attacks on American settlements in the Wyoming Valley of Pennsylvania and Cherry Valley in New York. In this 1797 portrait, artist Charles Willson Peale has portrayed Brant with European features. Independence National Historic Park, Philadelphia.

The victory at Saratoga was the turning point of the war. The Patriots captured more than 5,000 British troops, and ensured the diplomatic success of American representatives in Paris, who won a military alliance with France.

Social and Financial Perils

The Patriots' triumph at Saratoga was tempered by wartime difficulties. A British naval blockade cut off supplies of European manufactures and disrupted the New England fishing industry; meanwhile, the British occupation of Boston, New York, and Philadelphia reduced trade. As unemployed artisans and laborers moved to the countryside, New York City's population declined from 21,000 to 10,000. The British blockade cut tobacco exports in the Chesapeake, so planters grew grain to sell to the contending armies. All across the land, farmers and artisans adapted to a war economy.

With goods now scarce, governments requisitioned military supplies directly from the people. In 1776,

Wahrhafte Abbildung der Soldaten des Congreßes in Nordamerica, nach der Zeich‑ nung eines Deutschen Officiers. Die Mütze ist von Leder, mit der Aufschrift Congreß. Die ganße Kleidung von Zwillich überall mit weißen Franßen beseßt, die Beinkleider gehen bis auf die Knöchel herunter. Die Meisten laufen barfuß. Ihre Feuer‑gewehr sind mit sehr langen Payonets versehen, welche sie auch stat eines Seiten gewehrs gebrauchen.

American Militiamen

Beset by continuing shortages of cloth, the Patriot army dressed in a variety of uniforms and fabrics. This German engraving, taken from a drawing by a Hessian officer, shows two American militiamen (one of them barefoot) wearing hunting shirts and trousers made of ticking, the strong linen fabric often used to cover mattresses and pillows. Anne S. K. Brown Military Collection, Brown University.

Connecticut officials asked the citizens of Hartford to provide 1,000 coats and 1,600 shirts, and soldiers echoed their pleas. After losing all his shirts "except the one on my back" in the Battle of Long Island, Captain Edward Rogers told his wife that "the making of Cloath . . . must go on." Patriot women responded; in Elizabeth, New Jersey, they promised "upwards of 100,000 yards of lin‑nen and woolen cloth." Other women assumed the bur‑dens of farm work while their men were away at war and acquired a taste for decision-making. "We have sow'd our oats as you desired," Sarah Cobb Paine wrote to her absent husband. "Had I been master I should have planted it to Corn." Their self-esteem boosted by war‑time activities, some women expected greater legal rights in the new republican society.

Still, goods remained scarce and pricey. Hard-pressed consumers assailed shopkeepers as "enemies, extortioners, and monopolizers" and called for gov‑ernment regulation. But when the New England states imposed price ceilings in 1777, many farmers and ar‑tisans refused to sell their goods. Ultimately, a govern‑ment official admitted, consumers had to pay the higher market prices "or submit to starving."

Even more frightening, the fighting exposed tens of thousands of civilians to deprivation and death. A British officer, Lord Rawdon, favored giving "free lib‑erty to the soldiers to ravage [the country] at will, that these infatuated creatures may feel what a calamity war is." As British and American armies marched back and forth across New Jersey, they forced Patriot and Loyal‑ist families to flee their homes to escape arrest—or worse. Soldiers and partisans looted farms, and disor‑derly troops harassed and raped women and girls. "An army, even a friendly one, are a dreadful scourge to any people," wrote one Connecticut soldier. "You cannot imagine what devastation and distress mark their steps."

The war divided many farm communities. Patri‑ots formed committees of safety to collect taxes and seized the property of those who refused to pay. "Every Body submitted to our Sovereign Lord the Mob," la‑mented a Loyalist preacher. In parts of Maryland, the number of "nonassociators"—those who refused to join either side—was so large that they successfully defied Patriot mobs. "Stand off you dammed rebel sons of bitches," shouted Robert Davis of Anne Arundel County, "I will shoot you if you come any nearer."

Financial Crisis | Such defiance exposed the weakness of Patriot governments. Most states were afraid to raise taxes, so officials issued bonds to secure gold or silver from wealthy individuals. When those funds ran out, individual states financed the war by issuing so much paper money—some $260 million all told—that it lost worth, and most people refused to accept it at face value. In North Carolina, even tax collectors eventually rejected the state's currency.

The finances of the Continental Congress collapsed, too, despite the efforts of Philadelphia merchant Robert Morris, the government's chief treasury official. Be‑cause Congress lacked the authority to impose taxes, Morris relied on funds requisitioned from the states, but the states paid late or not at all. So Morris secured loans from France and Holland and sold Continental loan certificates to some 13,000 firms and individuals, many of them obscure. Isaac Vanbibber of Maryland bought $116,400 in bonds; Nehemiah Dunham of New Jersey acquired $127,000. All the while, the Congress was is‑suing paper money—some $200 million between 1776 and 1779—which, like state currencies, quickly fell in value. In 1778, a family needed $7 in Continental bills to buy goods worth $1 in gold or silver. As the exchange

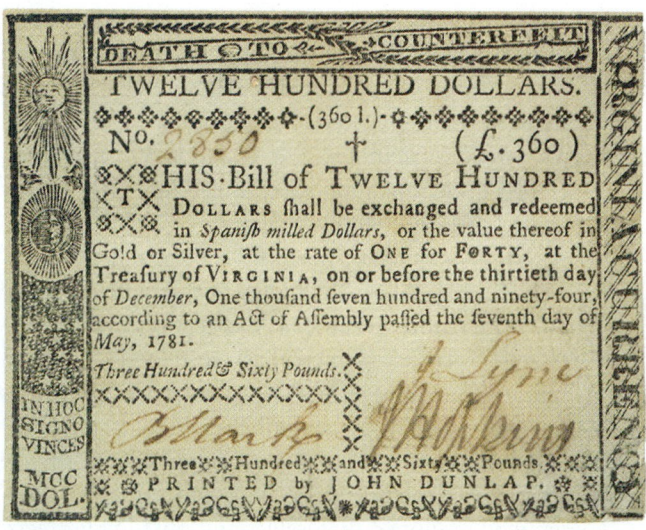

Paper Currency

Testifying to their independent status, the new state governments printed their own currencies. Rejecting the English system of pounds and shillings, Virginia used the Spanish gold dollar as its basic unit of currency, although the equivalent in English pounds is also shown. Initially, $1,200 was equal to £360 — a ratio of 3.3 to 1. By 1781, Virginia had printed so much paper money to pay its soldiers and wartime expenses that the value of its currency had depreciated. It now took $40 in Virginia currency to buy the same amount of goods as £1 sterling.   American Numismatic Society, New York City.

rate deteriorated—to 42 to 1 in 1779, 100 to 1 in 1780, and 146 to 1 in 1781—it sparked social upheaval. In Boston, a mob of women accosted merchant Thomas Boyleston, "seazd him by his Neck," and forced him to sell his wares at traditional prices. In rural Ulster County, New York, women told the committee of safety to lower food prices or "their husbands and sons shall fight no more." As morale crumbled, Patriot leaders feared the rebellion would collapse.

Valley Forge Fears reached their peak during the winter of 1777. While Howe's army lived comfortably in Philadelphia, Washington's army retreated 20 miles to Valley Forge, where 12,000 soldiers and hundreds of camp followers suffered horribly. "The army . . . now begins to grow sickly," a surgeon con-

fided to his diary. "Poor food—hard lodging—cold weather—fatigue—nasty clothes—nasty cookery. . . . Why are we sent here to starve and freeze?" Nearby farmers refused to help. Some were pacifists, Quakers and German sectarians unwilling to support either side. Others looked out for their own families, selling grain for gold from British quartermasters but refusing depreciated Continental currency. "Such a dearth of public spirit, and want of public virtue," lamented Washington. By spring, 1,000 hungry soldiers had deserted, and another 3,000 had died from malnutrition and disease. That winter at Valley Forge took as many American lives as had two years of fighting.

In this dark hour, Baron von Steuben raised the readiness of the American army. A former Prussian military officer, von Steuben was one of a handful of

A British Camp, c. 1778

While American troops at Valley Forge took shelter from the cold in tents, British troops stationed just outside New York City (on upper Manhattan Island) lived in simple but well-constructed and warm log cabins. Each hut, built into a slope but including a chimney for indoor heat, housed either a few officers or eight to ten soldiers of the 17th Regiment of Foot. John Ward Dunsmore executed this painting in 1915, basing it on the careful fieldwork of a team of archaeologists.
© Collection of the New-York Historical Society.

republican-minded foreign aristocrats who joined the American cause. Appointed as inspector general of the Continental Army, he instituted a strict drill system and encouraged officers to become more professional. Thanks to von Steuben, the smaller army that emerged from Valley Forge in the spring of 1778 was a much tougher and better-disciplined force.

- What accounted for British military superiority in the first years of the war? How did the Americans sustain their military effort between 1776 and 1778?

- Who was to blame for Britain's failure to win a quick victory over the American rebels: General Howe, General Burgoyne, or the ministers in London? Explain your answer.

The Path to Victory, 1778–1783

Wars are often won by astute diplomacy, and so it was with the War of Independence. The Patriots' prospects improved dramatically in 1778, when the Continental Congress concluded a military alliance with France, the most powerful nation in Europe. The alliance gave the Americans desperately needed money, supplies, and, eventually, troops. And it confronted Britain with an international war that challenged its domination of the Atlantic and Indian oceans.

The French Alliance

France and America were unlikely partners. France was Catholic and a monarchy; the United States was Protestant and a federation of republics. From 1689 to 1763, the two peoples had been enemies: New Englanders had brutally uprooted the French population from Acadia (Nova Scotia) in 1755, and the French and their Indian allies had raided British settlements. But the Comte de Vergennes, the French foreign minister, was determined to avenge the loss of Canada during the Great War for Empire and persuaded King Louis XVI to provide the rebellious colonies with a secret loan and much-needed gunpowder. When news of the rebel victory at Saratoga reached Paris in December 1777, Vergennes sought a formal alliance.

Benjamin Franklin and other American diplomats craftily exploited France's rivalry with Britain to win an explicit commitment to American independence. The Treaty of Alliance of February 1778 specified that once

France entered the war, neither partner would sign a separate peace without the "liberty, sovereignty, and independence" of the United States. In return, the Continental Congress agreed to recognize any French conquests in the West Indies. "France and America," warned Britain's Lord Stormont, "were indissolubly leagued for our destruction."

The alliance gave new life to the Patriots' cause. "There has been a great change in this state since the news from France," a Patriot soldier reported from Pennsylvania. Farmers—"mercenary wretches," he called them—"were as eager for Continental Money now as they were a few weeks ago for British gold." Its confidence bolstered, the Continental Congress addressed the demands of the officer corps. Most officers were gentlemen who equipped themselves and raised volunteers; in return, they insisted on lifetime military pensions at half pay. John Adams condemned the officers for "scrambling for rank and pay like apes for nuts," but General Washington urged Congress to grant the pensions: "The salvation of the cause depends upon it." Congress reluctantly granted the officers half pay, but only for seven years.

Meanwhile, the war had become unpopular in Britain. The gentry protested increases in the land tax, and merchants condemned new levies on carriages, wine, and imported goods. "It seemed we were to be taxed and stamped ourselves instead of inflicting taxes and stamps on others," a British politician complained.

At first, George III was determined to crush the rebellion. If America won independence, he warned Lord North, "the West Indies must follow them. Ireland would soon follow the same plan and be a separate state, then this island would be reduced to itself, and soon would be a poor island indeed." Stunned by the defeat at Saratoga, however, the king changed his mind. To thwart an American alliance with France, he authorized North to seek a negotiated settlement. In February 1778, North persuaded Parliament to repeal the Tea and Prohibitory acts and, amazingly, to renounce its power to tax the colonies. But the Patriots, now allied with France and committed to independence, rejected North's overture.

War in the South

The French alliance did not bring a rapid end to the war. When France entered the conflict in June 1778, it hoped to seize all of Britain's sugar islands. Spain, which joined the war against Britain in 1779, aimed to regain Florida and the fortress of Gibraltar at the entrance to the Mediterranean Sea.

Britain's Southern Strategy

For its part, the British government revised its military strategy to defend the West Indies and capture the rich tobacco- and rice-growing colonies: Virginia, the Carolinas, and Georgia. Once conquered, the ministry planned to use the Scottish Highlanders in the Carolinas and other Loyalists to hold them. It had already mobilized the Cherokees and Delawares against the land-hungry Americans and knew that the Patriots' fears of slave uprisings weakened them militarily (Map 6.3). As South Carolina Patriots admitted to the Continental Congress, they could raise only a few recruits "by reason of the great proportion of citizens necessary to remain at home to prevent insurrection among the Negroes."

It fell to Sir Henry Clinton to implement Britain's southern strategy. From the British army's main base in New York City, Clinton launched a seaborne attack on Savannah, Georgia. Troops commanded by Colonel Archibald Campbell captured the town in December 1778. Mobilizing hundreds of blacks to transport supplies, Campbell moved inland and captured Augusta early in 1779. By year's end, Clinton's forces and local Loyalists controlled coastal Georgia, and had 10,000 troops poised for an assault on South Carolina.

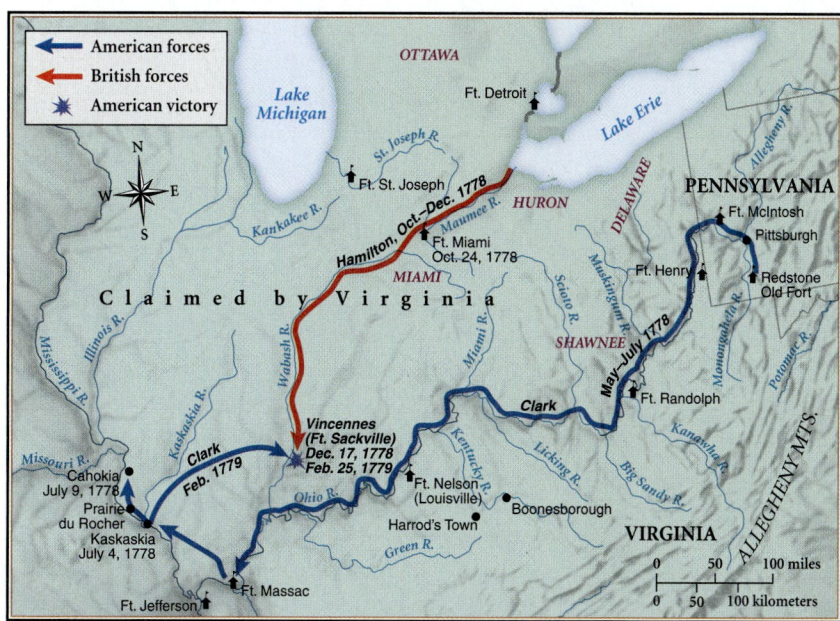

MAP 6.3

Native Americans and the War in the West, 1778–1779

Many Indian peoples remained neutral, but others, fearing land-hungry Patriot farmers, used British-supplied guns to raid American settlements. To thwart attacks by militant Shawnees, Cherokees, and Delawares, a Patriot militia led by George Rogers Clark captured the British fort and supply depot at Vincennes on the Wabash River in February 1779. To the north, Patriot generals John Sullivan and James Clinton defeated pro-British Indian forces near Tioga (on the New York–Pennsylvania border) in August 1779 and then systematically destroyed villages and crops throughout the lands of the Iroquois.

In 1780, British forces marched from victory to victory (Map 6.4). In May, Clinton forced the surrender of Charleston, South Carolina, and its garrison of 5,000 troops. Then Lord Charles Cornwallis assumed control of the British forces and, at Camden, defeated an American force commanded by General Horatio Gates, the hero of Saratoga. Only 1,200 Patriot militiamen joined Gates at Camden—a fifth of the number at Saratoga. Cornwallis took control of South Carolina, and hundreds of African Americans fled to freedom behind British lines. The southern strategy was working.

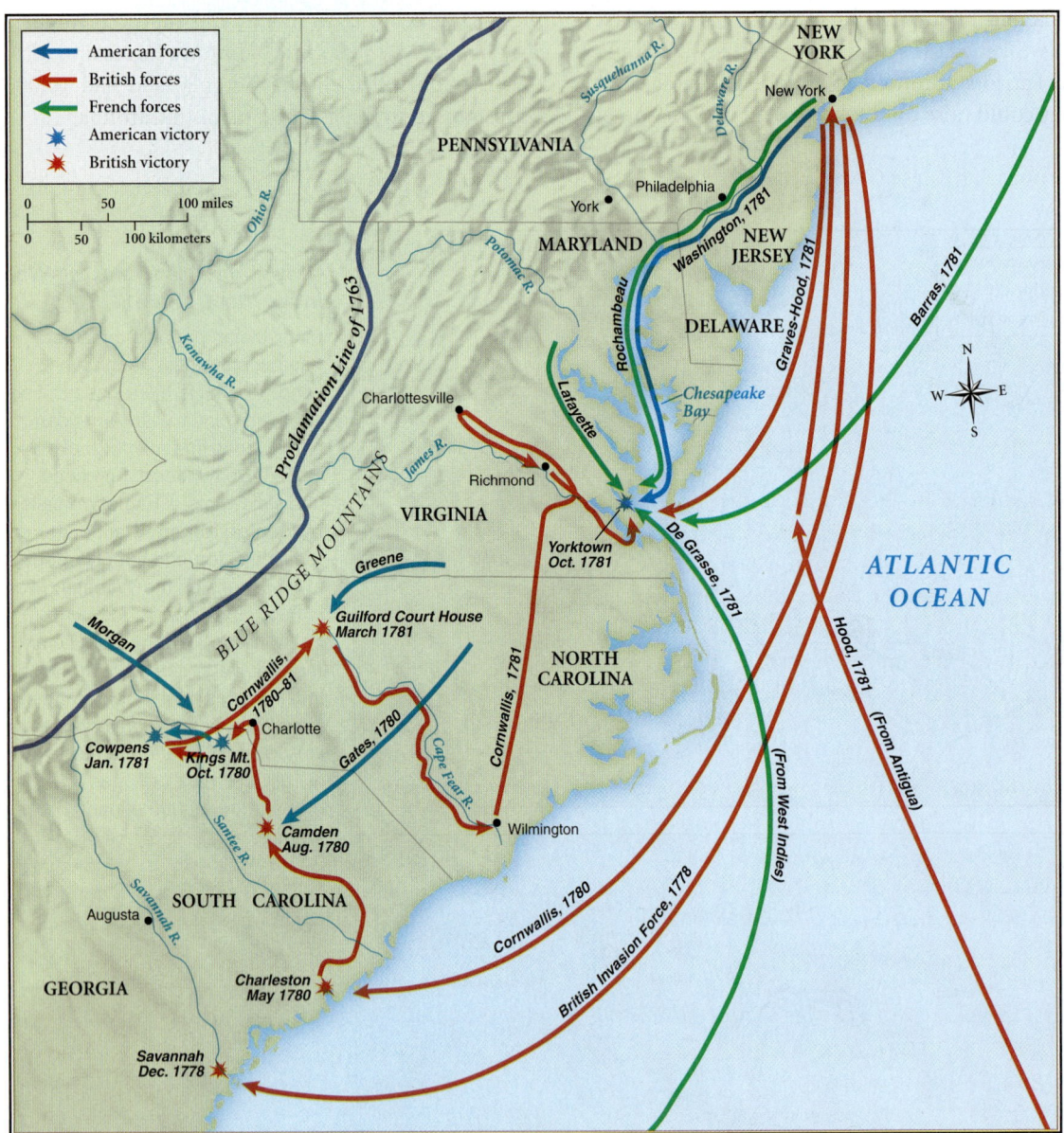

MAP 6.4

The War in the South, 1778–1781

Britain's southern military strategy started well. British forces captured Savannah in December 1778, took control of Georgia during 1779, and vanquished Charleston in May 1780. Over the next eighteen months, brutal warfare between the British troops and Loyalist units and the Continental army and militia raged in the interior of the Carolinas and ended in a stalemate. Hoping to break the deadlock, British general Charles Cornwallis carried the battle into Virginia in 1781. A Franco-American army led by Washington and Lafayette, with the help of the French fleet under Admiral de Grasse, surrounded Cornwallis's forces on the Yorktown Peninsula and forced their surrender.

Admiral Pierre Suffren in India

The American War for Independence became a worldwide conflict in 1778 when France entered the fight. French and British naval forces and troops clashed in West Africa over control of the slave trade, and in India over access to goods such as textiles, tea, and spices. Here French Admiral Suffren, who spent years in Asia campaigning against the British, exchanges greetings with his Indian ally, Hyder Ali. The ruler of the Indian kingdom of Mysore, Ali led a 1783 revolt against the British.   Bridgeman Art Library Ltd.

Then the tide of battle turned. Thanks to another republican-minded European aristocrat, the Marquis de Lafayette, France finally dispatched troops to the American mainland. A longtime supporter of the American cause, Lafayette persuaded King Louis XVI to send General Comte de Rochambeau and 5,500 men to Newport, Rhode Island. There, they threatened the British forces holding New York City.

Guerrilla Warfare in the Carolinas   Meanwhile, Washington dispatched General Nathanael Greene to recapture the Carolinas, where he found "a country that has been ravaged and plundered by both friends and enemies." Greene put local militiamen, who had been "without discipline and addicted to plundering," under strong leaders and unleashed them on less-mobile British forces. In October 1780, Patriot militia defeated a regiment of Loyalists at King's Mountain, South Carolina, taking about 1,000 prisoners. American guerrillas commanded by the "Swamp Fox," General Francis Marion, also won a series of small but fierce battles. Then, in January 1781, General Daniel Morgan led an American force to a bloody victory at Cowpens, South Carolina. But Loyalist garrisons, helped by the well-organized Cherokees, remained powerful. "We fight, get beaten, and fight again," General Greene declared doggedly. In March 1781, Greene's soldiers fought Cornwallis's seasoned army to a draw at North Carolina's Guilford Court House. Weakened by this **war**

of attrition, the British general decided to concede the Carolinas to Greene and seek a decisive victory in Virginia. There, many Patriot militiamen had refused to take up arms, claiming that "the Rich wanted the Poor to fight for them."

Exploiting these social divisions, Cornwallis moved easily through the Tidewater region of Virginia in the early summer of 1781. Reinforcements sent from New York and commanded by General Benedict Arnold, the infamous Patriot traitor, bolstered his ranks. As Arnold and Cornwallis sparred with an American force led by Lafayette near the York Peninsula, Washington was informed that France had finally sent its powerful West Indian fleet to North America, and devised an audacious plan. Feigning an assault on New York City, he secretly marched General Rochambeau's army from Rhode Island to Virginia. Simultaneously, the French fleet took control of Chesapeake Bay. By the time the British discovered Washington's scheme, Cornwallis was surrounded, and his 9,500-man army outnumbered 2 to 1 on land and cut off from reinforcement or retreat by sea. In a hopeless position, Cornwallis surrendered at Yorktown in October 1781.

The Franco-American victory broke the resolve of the British government. "Oh God! It is all over!" Lord North exclaimed. Isolated diplomatically in Europe, stymied militarily in America, and lacking public support at home, the British ministry gave up active prosecution of the war on the American mainland.

The Patriot Advantage

Angry members of Parliament demanded an explanation. How could mighty Britain, victorious in the Great War for Empire, lose to a motley rebel army? The ministry pointed to a series of blunders by the military leadership. Why had Howe not ruthlessly pursued Washington's army in 1776? Why had Howe and Burgoyne failed to coordinate their attacks in 1777? Why had Cornwallis marched deep into the Patriot-dominated state of Virginia in 1781?

Historians acknowledge British mistakes, but they also attribute the rebels' victory to French aid and the inspired leadership of George Washington. Astutely deferring to elected officials, Washington won the support of the Continental Congress and the state governments. Confident of his military abilities, he pursued a defensive strategy that minimized casualties and maintained the morale of his officers and soldiers through five difficult years of war. Moreover, the Patriots' control of local governments gave Washington a greater margin for error than the British generals had. Local militiamen provided the edge in the 1777 victory at Saratoga, and forced Cornwallis from the Carolinas in 1781.

In the end, it was the American people who decided the outcome, especially the one-third of the white colonists who were zealous Patriots. Tens of thousands of these farmers and artisans accepted Continental bills in payment for supplies, and thousands of soldiers took them as pay—even as the currency literally depreciated in their pockets. Rampant inflation meant that every paper dollar held for a week lost value, imposing a hidden "currency tax" on those who accepted the paper currency. Each individual tax was small—a few pennies on each dollar. But as millions of dollars changed hands multiple times, the currency taxes paid by ordinary citizens financed the American military victory.

Diplomatic Triumph

After Yorktown, diplomats took two years to conclude a peace treaty. Talks began in Paris in April 1782, but the French and Spanish, still hoping to seize a West Indian island or Gibraltar, stalled for time. Their tactics infuriated American diplomats Benjamin Franklin, John Adams, and John Jay. So the Americans negotiated secretly with the British, prepared if necessary to ignore the Treaty of Alliance and sign a separate peace. British ministers were equally eager: Parliament wanted peace, and they feared the loss of a rich sugar island.

Consequently, the American diplomats secured extremely favorable terms. In the Treaty of Paris, signed in September 1783, Great Britain formally recognized American independence and relinquished its claims to lands south of the Great Lakes and east of the Mississippi River. The British negotiators did not insist on a separate territory for their Indian allies. "In endeavouring to assist you," a Wea Indian complained to a British general, "it seems we have wrought our own ruin." The Cherokees were forced to relinquish claims to 5 million acres—three-quarters of their territory—in treaties with Georgia, the Carolinas, and Virginia.

The Paris treaty also granted Americans fishing rights off Newfoundland and Nova Scotia, prohibited the British from "carrying away any negroes or other property," and guaranteed freedom of navigation on the Mississippi to American citizens "forever." In return, the American government allowed British merchants to pursue legal claims for prewar debts and encouraged the state legislatures to return confiscated property to Loyalists and grant them citizenship.

In the Treaty of Versailles, signed simultaneously, Britain made peace with France and Spain. Neither American ally gained very much. Spain reclaimed Florida from Britain (Map 6.5), but not the strategic fortress at Gibraltar. France received the Caribbean island of Tobago, small consolation for a war that had sharply raised taxes and quadrupled France's national debt. Just six years later, cries for tax relief and political liberty would spark the French Revolution. Only Americans profited handsomely; the treaties gave them independence and access to the trans-Appalachian west.

- **Why did Britain switch to a southern military strategy? Why did that strategy ultimately fail?**

- **Without the French alliance, would the American rebellion have succeeded? Why or why not?**

Creating Republican Institutions, 1776–1787

When the Patriots declared independence, they confronted the issue of political authority. "Which of us shall be the rulers?" asked a Philadelphia newspaper. The question was multifaceted. Would power reside in the national government or the states? Who would control the new republican institutions: traditional elites or average citizens? Would women have greater political and

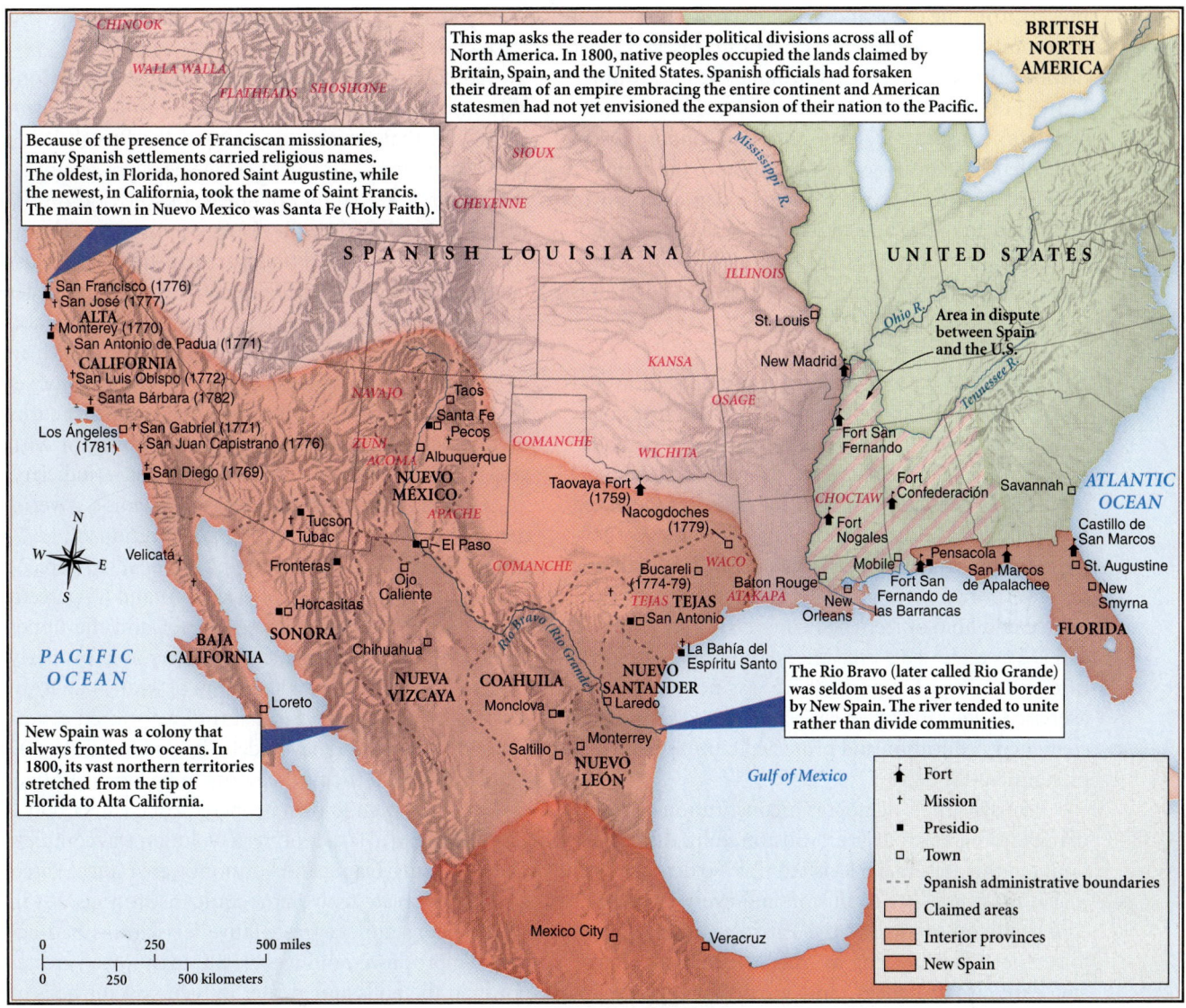

This map asks the reader to consider political divisions across all of North America. In 1800, native peoples occupied the lands claimed by Britain, Spain, and the United States. Spanish officials had forsaken their dream of an empire embracing the entire continent and American statesmen had not yet envisioned the expansion of their nation to the Pacific.

Because of the presence of Franciscan missionaries, many Spanish settlements carried religious names. The oldest, in Florida, honored Saint Augustine, while the newest, in California, took the name of Saint Francis. The main town in Nuevo Mexico was Santa Fe (Holy Faith).

The Rio Bravo (later called Rio Grande) was seldom used as a provincial border by New Spain. The river tended to unite rather than divide communities.

New Spain was a colony that always fronted two oceans. In 1800, its vast northern territories stretched from the tip of Florida to Alta California.

- ⬆ Fort
- ✝ Mission
- ■ Presidio
- ◻ Town
- – – – Spanish administrative boundaries
- Claimed areas
- Interior provinces
- New Spain

MAP 6.5

New Spain's Northern Empire, 1763–1800

After Spain acquired Louisiana from France in 1763, Spanish officials tried to create a northern empire. They established missions and forts (presidios) in California, expanded settlements in New Mexico, and (by allying with France during the War of Independence) won Florida back from Britain. However, by the early 1800s Spain's dream of a northern empire had been shattered by Indian uprisings in California and Texas, Napoleon's demand for the return of Louisiana, and the U.S. takeover of Florida.

legal rights? What would be the status of the slaves in the new republic?

The State Constitutions: How Much Democracy?

In May 1776, the Second Continental Congress urged Americans to reject royal authority and establish republican governments. Most states quickly complied. "Constitutions employ every pen," an observer noted. Within six months, Virginia, Maryland, North Carolina, New Jersey, Delaware, and Pennsylvania had all ratified new constitutions, and Connecticut and Rhode Island had revised their colonial charters to delete references to the king.

Republicanism meant more than ousting the king. The Declaration of Independence stated the principle of popular sovereignty: Governments derive "their just powers from the consent of the governed." In the heat of revolution, many Patriots gave this clause a further democratic twist. In North Carolina, the backcountry farmers of Mecklenburg County told their delegates to the state's constitutional convention to "oppose everything that leans to aristocracy or power in the hands of the rich." In Virginia, voters elected a new assembly in 1776 that, an eyewitness remarked, "was composed of men not quite so well dressed, nor so politely educated, nor so highly born" as colonial-era legislatures (Figure 6.1).

Pennsylvania's Controversial Constitution This democratic impulse flowered in Pennsylvania, thanks to a coalition of Scots-Irish farmers, Philadelphia artisans, and Enlightenment-influenced intellectuals. In 1776, these insurgents ousted every officeholder of the Penn family's proprietary government, abolished property ownership as a qualification for voting, and granted all taxpaying men the right to vote and hold office. The Pennsylvania constitution of 1776 also created a unicameral (one-house) legislature with complete power; there was no governor to exercise a veto. Other provisions mandated a system of elementary education and protected citizens from imprisonment for debt.

Pennsylvania's democratic constitution alarmed many leading Patriots. From Boston, John Adams denounced the unicameral legislature as "so democratical that it must produce confusion and every evil work." Along with other conservative Patriots, Adams wanted to restrict office holding to "men of learning, leisure and easy circumstances" and warned of oppression under majority rule: "If you give [ordinary citizens] the command or preponderance in the . . . legislature,

they will vote all property out of the hands of you aristocrats."

To counter the appeal of the Pennsylvania Constitution, Adams published *Thoughts on Government* (1776). In that treatise, he adapted the British Whig theory of mixed government (a sharing of power among the monarch, the Houses of Lords, and the Commons) to a republican society. To disperse authority and preserve liberty, he insisted on separate institutions: Legislatures would make laws, the executive would administer them, and the judiciary would enforce them. Adams also demanded a bicameral (two-house) legislature with an upper house of substantial property owners to offset the popular majorities in the lower one. As further curbs on democracy, he proposed an elected governor with veto power and an appointed—not elected—judiciary.

Conservative Patriots endorsed Adams's governmental system. In New York's Constitution of 1777, property qualifications for voting excluded 20 percent of white men from assembly elections and 60 percent from casting ballots for the governor and the upper house. In South Carolina, elite planters used property rules to disqualify about 90 percent of white men from office holding. The 1778 constitution required candidates for governor to have a debt-free estate of £10,000 (about $700,000 today), senators to be worth £2,000, and assemblymen to own property valued at £1,000.

The political legacy of the Revolution was complex. Only in Pennsylvania and Vermont were radical Patriots able to create truly democratic institutions. Yet in all the new states, representative legislatures had acquired more power, and average citizens now had greater power at the polls and greater influence in the halls of government (see Voices from Abroad, "A French Aristocrat Views Republican Manners," p. 185).

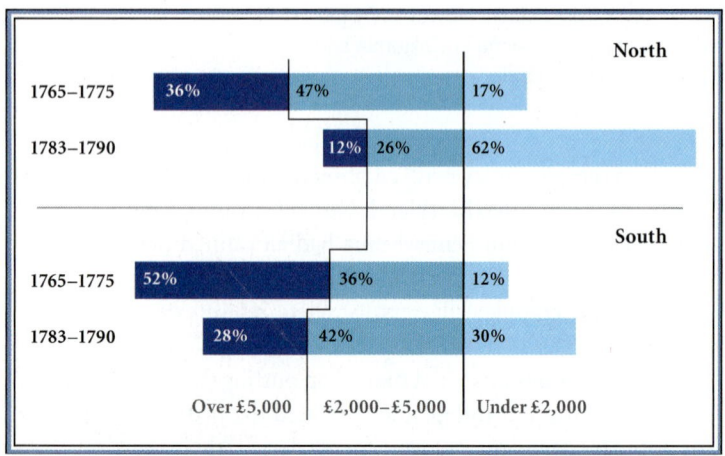

FIGURE 6.1

Middling Men Enter the Halls of Government, 1765–1790

Before the Revolution, wealthy men (with assets of £2,000 or more, as measured by tax lists and probate records) dominated most colonial assemblies. The power of money was especially apparent in the southern colonies, where representatives worth at least £5,000 formed a majority of the legislators. However, in the new American republic, the proportion of middling legislators (yeomen farmers and others worth less than £2,000) increased dramatically, especially in the northern states. Adapted from Jackson T. Main, "Government by the People: The American Revolution and the Democratization of the Legislatures," *William and Mary Quarterly*, 3rd ser., vol. 23 (1966).

VOICES FROM ABROAD

François Alexandre Frédéric

A French Aristocrat Views Republican Manners

When the French Revolution broke out in 1789, forty-two-year-old François Alexandre Frédéric, duc de la Rochefoucauld-Liancourt, won election to the National Constituent Assembly and served a term as its president. A reformer and a constitutionalist, he was also a monarchist and a confidant of King Louis XVI, who would be executed in 1793. Fearing for his safety, Rochefoucauld fled to England in 1792 and then moved to Philadelphia in 1794. The following year, he and five friends traveled through much of the northern United States and Upper Canada. He published a report of that journey and his speculations on American and Canadian affairs upon his return to Paris in 1799.

We overtook the stage-coach again at the White Horse, where the passengers breakfasted. It appears somewhat strange to Europeans, to see the coachman eat at the same table with the passengers; but it would seem equally strange to Americans, to see the coachman eating by himself. It is futile to argue against the customs of a country; we must submit. Equality, pretended equality, which widely differs from true freedom, is the foundation of this custom, which, in fact, injures nobody. . . .

A spirit, or rather habit of equality, is diffused among this people, as far as it possibly can go. In several inns, especially such as are situate on less frequented roads, the circumstance of our servant not dining with us at the same table excited general astonishment. . . .

The spirit of equality is carried as far as is consistent with order in a great society. The man who is possessed of the greatest wealth, and the most happily circumstanced in every respect, shakes hands with the workman whom he met on his way, converses with him, not under the idea of doing him an honour, as is often the notion elsewhere but from a consciousness, in the first instance, that he may at some future time stand in need of his assistance afterward, without any such interested consideration, but merely through habit, and the force of education, and because he sees in him his fellow-man, only placed in a different situation, to whom he is the less tempted to think himself superior, as it often happens that the now rich man has himself once been in a less enviable situation. . . .

The inferior classes of workmen, down to those who labour in the ports, do not appear to me to be so rustic [unsophisticated, subservient] in America as they generally do in the old world. The reason of this is, without doubt, that they are treated with more civility, and considered by those who employ them as free men with whom they have contracted, rather than as workmen, whom they compel to labour. They are like the workmen of every class, both in town and country, much better paid than in Europe, by which they are enabled to live well. There is not a family, even in the most miserable hut in the midst of the woods, who does not eat meat twice a day at least, and drink tea and coffee; . . . The shopkeeper and the artisan live much better here than in Europe. . . .

Though there be no distinctions acknowledged by law in the United States, fortune and the nature of professions form different classes. The merchants, the lawyers, the land-owners, who do not cultivate their land themselves (and the number, which is small from the state of Delaware to the north, is great in the states of the south), the physicians, and the clergy, form the first class. The inferior merchants, the farmers, and the artisans, may be included in the second; and the third class is composed of workmen, who let [hire out] themselves by the day, by the month, &c.

In balls, concerts, and public amusements, these classes do not mix; and yet, except the labourer in ports, and the common sailor, every one calls himself, and is called by others, a gentleman; a small fortune is sufficient for the assumption of this title, as it carries men from one class to another. They deceive themselves very much who think that pure republican manners prevail in America.

Source: François Alexandre Frédéric, Duc de la Rochefoucauld-Liancourt, *Travels through the United States of America . . . in the Years 1795, 1796, and 1797 . . .*, 2 vols., trans. H. Neuman (London: T. Davison, 1799), 1: 23–24, 68; 2: 215, 671–672.

ANALYZING THE EVIDENCE

- What is the source of the custom or "habit of equality" that Rochefoucauld finds in the United States?
- How does this French aristocrat explain the paradox of a "spirit of equality" in the midst a society of "different classes" who mostly "do not mix"? How would you explain it?
- What would a society with "pure republican manners" look like?

John and Abigail Adams
Both Adamses had strong personalities and often disagreed in private about political and social issues. In 1794, John playfully accused his wife of being a "Disciple of Wollstonecraft," but Abigail's commitment to legal equality for women long predated Mary Wollstonecraft's 1792 treatise, *A Vindication of the Rights of Woman.*   National Portrait Gallery, Smithsonian Institution/Art Resource, NY. / New York State Historical Association.

Women Seek a Public Voice

The extraordinary excitement of the Revolutionary era tested the dictum that only men could engage in politics. Men controlled all public institutions—legislatures, juries, government offices—but upper-class women engaged in political debate and, defying men's scorn, filled their letters, diaries, and conversations with opinions on public issues. "The men say we have no business [with politics]," Eliza Wilkinson of South Carolina complained in 1783. "They won't even allow us liberty of thought, and that is all I want."

As Wilkinson's remark suggests, women did not insist on civic equality with men; they sought only an end to restrictive customs and laws. Abigail Adams demanded equal legal rights for married women, who under common law could not own property, enter into contracts, or initiate lawsuits. The war bonds she purchased had to be held in a trust run by a male relative. "Men would be tyrants" if they continued to hold such power over women, Adams declared to her husband John, criticizing him and other Patriots for "emanci-pating all nations" from monarchical despotism while "retaining absolute power over Wives."

Most politicians ignored women's requests, and most men insisted on the traditional sexual and political prerogatives of their sex. Long-married husbands remained patriarchs who dominated their households, and even young men who embraced the republican ideal of "companionate marriage" did not support legal equality for their wives and daughters. Except in New Jersey, which until 1807 allowed unmarried and widowed female property holders to vote, women remained disenfranchised. In the new American republic, only white men enjoyed full citizenship.

Nevertheless, the republican belief in an educated citizenry created opportunities for some women. In her 1779 essay "On the Equality of the Sexes," Judith Sargent Murray argued that men and women had equal capacities for memory and that women had superior imaginations. She conceded that most women were inferior to men in judgment and reasoning, but only from lack of training: "We can only reason from what we know," she argued, and most women had been de-

Mrs. Mercy Otis Warren

Dressed in fine silks and lace for this 1763 portrait by John Singleton Copley, Mercy Otis Warren was a woman of means from a highly political family. The sister of one Patriot (the mercurial James Otis) and the wife of another (Dr. James Warren), Mercy demonstrated her Patriot credentials by authoring propaganda plays in the early 1770s, and her Antifederalist beliefs by opposing the Constitution and publishing a three-volume *History of the Rise, Progress, and Termination of the American Revolution* (1805).   Museum of Fine Arts. Bequest of Winslow Warren, 1931. Acc. No. 31.212.

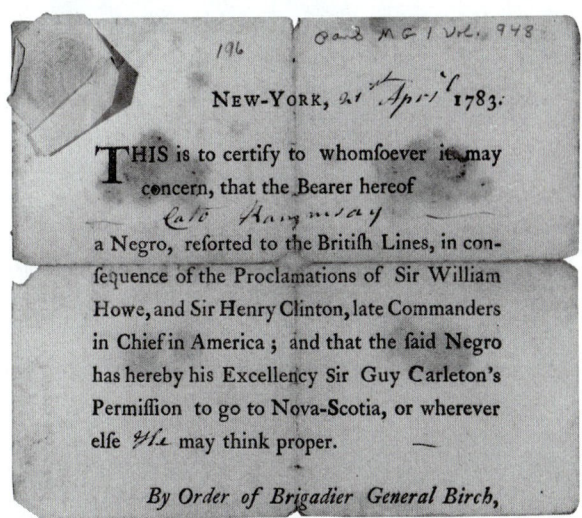

A Black Loyalist Pass, 1783

White Patriots claimed their freedom by fighting *against* the British; thousands of black slaves won their liberty by fighting *for* them. This pass certifies that Cato Rammsay (actually Ramsey), "a Negro, resorted to the British Lines" in search of the freedom promised by Virginia Royal Governor Dunmore and British Commander Henry Clinton to slaves who escaped from Patriot owners. Now age forty-five and a "slim fellow," Ramsey had escaped from his owner, John Ramsey of Norfolk, Virginia, in 1776, probably fleeing to Dunmore's ships. Seven years later, he ended up in New York, reunited with his wife, China Godfrey (thirty-five) and their three children: James (twenty), Betsey (fifteen), and Nelly Ramsey (ten), who had fled subsequently from other owners. As the British evacuated New York in 1783, Ramsey and his family were free "to go to Nova-Scotia," where they worked as farmers.   Nova Scotia Archives and Record Management, Halifax.

nied "the opportunity of acquiring knowledge." That situation changed in the 1790s, when the attorney general of Massachusetts declared that girls had an equal right to schooling under the state constitution. By 1850, the literacy rates of women and men in the northeastern states were equal, and educated women again challenged their subordinate legal and political status (see Reading American Pictures, "Did the Revolution Promote Women's Rights?" p. 188).

The Loyalist Exodus

The success of republican institutions was assisted by the departure of 100,000 monarchists, many of whom suffered severe financial losses. John Tabor Kempe, the last royal attorney general of New York, sought compensation of £65,000 sterling (about $4.5 million today) from the British government for lands seized by Patriots,

but only received a mere £5,000. Refugees also suffered psychologically. Loyalists who fled to England complained of "their uneasy abode in this country of aliens," as did many of the evacuees who settled in Canada or the West Indies. An exiled Loyalist woman in Nova Scotia confessed: "[I had] such a feeling of loneliness . . . [that] I sat down on the damp moss with my baby on my lap and cried bitterly."

Some Patriots demanded revolutionary justice: the seizure of all Loyalist property and its distribution to needy Americans. While every state seized some Loyalists' property, American leaders worried that wholesale confiscation would impair the nation's commercial credit and violate its republican principles. In Massachusetts, officials cited the state's constitution of 1780, which protected every citizen "in the enjoyment of his life, liberty, and property, according to the standing laws." When state governments did seize Loyalist property, they

Did the Revolution Promote Women's Rights?

As the text explains, the republican revolution forced Americans to address the scope of political rights. One question centered on women's claim to equal treatment: Did the doctrines of popular sovereignty and political equality apply to women as well as to men? These two engravings, both published in American magazines, offer evidence that the question was the subject of public debate. Pictures like these pose a twofold challenge to historians – to see them as contemporaries did, and, with the power of hindsight, to place them in a larger historical context. How do these pictures help us understand the status of women in the young republic, both in their own eyes and those of men?

Frontispiece from *Lady's Magazine*, 1792.
The Library Company of Philadelphia.

"Keep Within Compass," c. 1785. Henry Francis du Pont
Winterthur Museum, Winterthur, Delaware.

ANALYZING THE EVIDENCE

- The illustration on the left appeared at the front of *The Lady's Magazine and Repository of Entertaining*, published in Philadelphia in 1792. The magazine contained excerpts from Mary Wollstonecraft's *A Vindication of the Rights of Woman* (1792), which explicitly linked women's rights to the republican ideology of the American and French revolutions. What sort of clothing are the women wearing? Why? What does this sort of dress mean ideologically? Do you think this imagery was empowering to women at the time? Why or why not?

- In the engraving on the right, "Keep Within Compass," the first line of the small couplet at the top reads: "How blest the Maid whose bosom no headstrong passion knows." What do the smaller pictures on the lower left and lower right suggest might happen to women who are passionate? What is this engraving urging American women to do? What does it suggest about the thinking and emotions of American men in the new republican era?

often auctioned it to the highest bidders, who were usually wealthy Patriots rather than ambitious yeoman farmers or propertyless foot soldiers. In a few cases, confiscation did produce a democratic result: In North Carolina, about half the new owners of Loyalist lands were small-scale farmers, and in New York, the state government sold farmsteads on the Philipse manor to longtime tenants. When Frederick Philipse III tried to reclaim his estate, the new owners declared they had "purchased it with the price of their best blood," and added, "[We] will never become your vassals again." In general, though, the Revolution did not drastically alter the structure of rural society.

Social turmoil was greater in the cities, where Patriot merchants replaced Tories at the top of the economic ladder. In Massachusetts, the Lowell, Higginson, Jackson, and Cabot families moved their trading enterprises to Boston to fill the vacuum created by the departure of the Loyalist Hutchinson and Apthorp clans. In Philadelphia, small-scale Patriot traders stepped into the void left by the collapse of Anglican and Quaker mercantile firms. The war replaced a traditional economic elite—who invested profits from trade in real estate—with a group of republican entrepreneurs who promoted new trading ventures and domestic manufacturing. This shift facilitated America's economic development in the years to come.

The Articles of Confederation

As Patriots embraced independence in 1776, they envisioned a central government with limited powers. Carter Braxton of Virginia thought the Continental Congress should "regulate the affairs of trade, war, peace, alliances, &c." but "should by no means have authority to interfere with the internal police [governance] or domestic concerns of any Colony."

That thinking—of a limited central government—informed the Articles of Confederation, which were approved by the Continental Congress in November 1777. The Articles provided for a loose union in which "each state retains its sovereignty, freedom, and independence." As an association of equals, each state had one vote regardless of its size, population, or wealth. Important laws needed the approval of nine of the thirteen states, and changes in the Articles required unanimous consent. Though the Confederation had neither a chief executive nor a judiciary, the government still enjoyed considerable power. The Congress could declare war, make treaties with foreign nations, adjudicate disputes between the states, borrow and print money, and requi-

sition funds from the states "for the common defense or general welfare."

Although the Congress exercised authority from 1776—raising the Continental army, negotiating the treaty with France, and financing the war—the Articles won formal ratification only in 1781. The delay stemmed from conflicts over western lands. The royal charters of Virginia, Massachusetts, Connecticut, and other states set boundaries stretching to the Pacific Ocean. States without western lands—Maryland and Pennsylvania—refused to accept the Articles until the land-rich states relinquished these claims to the Confederation. Threatened by Cornwallis's army in 1781, Virginia gave up its claims, and Maryland, the last holdout, finally ratified the Articles (Map 6.6).

Continuing Fiscal Crisis The Confederation had a major weakness: It lacked the power to tax either the states or the people. By 1780, the central government was nearly bankrupt, and General Washington called urgently for a national tax system; without one, he warned, "our cause is lost." Led by Robert Morris, who became superintendent of finance in 1781, nationalist-minded Patriots tried to expand the Confederation's authority. They persuaded Congress to charter the Bank of North America, a private institution in Philadelphia, arguing that its notes would stabilize the inflated Continental currency. Morris also created a central bureaucracy that paid army expenses, apportioned war costs among the states, and assumed responsibility for the Confederation's debts. He hoped that the existence of a "national" debt would prompt Congress to enact an import duty to pay it off. However, Rhode Island and New York rejected Morris's proposal for an import tax of 5 percent. His state had opposed British import duties, New York's representative declared, and it would not accept them from Congress. To raise revenue, Congress looked to the sale of western lands. In 1783, it asserted that the recently signed Treaty of Paris had extinguished the Indians' rights to those lands and made them the property of the United States.

The Northwest Ordinance Settlers had already moved to the frontier. In 1784, the residents of what is now eastern Tennessee organized a new state, called it Franklin, and sought admission to the Confederation. To preserve its authority over the West, Congress refused to recognize Franklin. Subsequently, Congress created the Southwest and Mississippi Territories (the future states of Tennessee, Alabama, and Mississippi) from lands ceded by North

MAP 6.6

The Confederation and Western Land Claims, 1781–1802

The Congress formed by the Articles of Confederation had to resolve conflicting state claims to western lands. For example, the territories claimed by New York and Virginia on the basis of their royal charters overlapped extensively. Beginning in 1781, the Confederation Congress and, after 1789, the U.S. Congress persuaded all of the states to cede their western claims, creating a "national domain" open to all citizens. In the Northwest Ordinances, the Congress divided the domain north of the Ohio River into territories and set up democratic procedures by which they could eventually join the Union as states. South of the Ohio River, the Congress allowed the existing southern states to play a substantial role in the settling of the ceded lands.

Carolina and Georgia. Because these cessions carried the stipulation that "no regulation . . . shall tend to emancipate slaves," these states and all those south of the Ohio River allowed human bondage.

However, the Confederation Congress banned slavery north of the Ohio River. Between 1784 and 1787, it

issued three important ordinances organizing the "Old Northwest." The Ordinance of 1784, written by Thomas Jefferson, established the principle that territories could become states as their populations grew. The Land Ordinance of 1785 mandated a rectangular-grid system of surveying and specified a minimum price of $1 an acre. It also required that half of the townships be sold in single blocks of 23,040 acres each, which only large-scale speculators could afford, and the rest in parcels of 640 acres each, which restricted their sale to well-to-do farmers (Map 6.7).

Finally, the Northwest Ordinance of 1787 created the territories that would eventually become the states of Ohio, Indiana, Illinois, Michigan, and Wisconsin. The ordinance prohibited slavery and earmarked funds from land sales for the support of schools. It also specified that Congress would appoint a governor and judges to administer each new territory until the population reached 5,000 free adult men, at which point the citizens could elect a territorial legislature. When the population reached 60,000, the legislature could devise a republican constitution and apply to join the Confederation.

The land ordinances of the 1780s were a great and enduring achievement of the Confederation Congress. They provided for orderly settlement and the admission of new states on the basis of equality; there would be no politically dependent "colonies" in the West. But they also extended the geographical division between slave and free areas that would haunt the nation in the coming decades.

Shays's Rebellion

If the future of the West was bright, postwar conditions in the East were grim. The war had crippled American shipping and cut exports of tobacco, rice, and wheat. The British Navigation Acts, which had nurtured colonial commerce, now barred Americans from legal trade with the British West Indies. Moreover, low-priced British manufactures (and some from India as well) were flooding American markets, driving urban artisans and wartime textile firms out of business. Not until 1800 would white Americans again reach the levels of income and wealth they had enjoyed in 1775.

The fiscal condition of the state governments was dire, primarily because of war debts. Well-to-do merchants and landowners (including Abigail Adams) had invested in state bonds during the war; others had speculated in debt certificates, buying them on the cheap from hard-pressed farmers and soldiers. Now creditors and speculators demanded that the state governments redeem the bonds and certificates quickly and at full value, a policy that would require tax increases and a decrease in the amount of paper currency. Most legislatures refused. The new state constitutions apportioned seats on the basis of population, so many legislators were men of "middling circumstances" from rural com-

munities. By the mid-1780s, such middling farmers and artisans controlled the lower houses of most northern legislatures and formed a sizable minority in southern assemblies. They refused to levy higher taxes to redeem war bonds, instead authorizing new issues of paper currency and allowing debtors to pay private creditors in installments. Although wealthy men deplored these measures as "intoxicating Draughts of Liberty" that destroyed "the just rights of creditors," such political intervention prevented social upheaval.

A case in point was Massachusetts, where lawmakers refused to enact debtor-relief legislation, imposed high taxes to pay off the state's war debt, and cut the supply of paper currency. When cash-strapped farmers could not pay both their taxes and their debts, creditors threatened lawsuits. Debtor Ephraim Wetmore heard a rumor that merchant Stephan Salisbury "would have my Body Dead or Alive in case I did not pay." To protect their livelihoods, farmers called extralegal conventions to protest high taxes and property seizures. Then mobs of angry farmers—including men of high status—closed the courts by force. "[I] had no Intensions to Destroy the Publick Government," declared Captain Adam Wheeler, a former town selectman; his goal was simply to prevent "Valuable and Industrious members of Society [being] dragged from their families to prison" because of their debts. These crowd actions grew into a full-scale revolt led by Captain Daniel Shays, a Continental army veteran.

As a revolt against taxes imposed by a distant government, Shays's Rebellion resembled American resistance to the British Stamp Act. Consciously linking themselves to the Patriot movement, Shays's men placed pine twigs in their hats just as Continental troops had done. "The people have turned against their teachers the doctrines which were inculcated to effect the late revolution," complained Fisher Ames, a conservative Massachusetts lawmaker. Some of the radical Patriots of 1776 likewise condemned the Shaysites: "[Men who] would lessen the Weight of Government lawfully exercised must be Enemies to our happy Revolution and Common Liberty," charged Samuel Adams. To put down the rebellion, the Massachusetts legislature passed the Riot Act and wealthy bondholders equipped a formidable fighting force, which Governor James Bowdoin used to disperse Shays's ragtag army during the winter of 1786–1787.

Although Shays's Rebellion failed, it showed that many middling Patriot families felt that American oppressors had replaced British tyrants. Massachusetts voters turned Governor Bowdoin out of office, and debt-ridden farmers in New York, northern Pennsylvania,

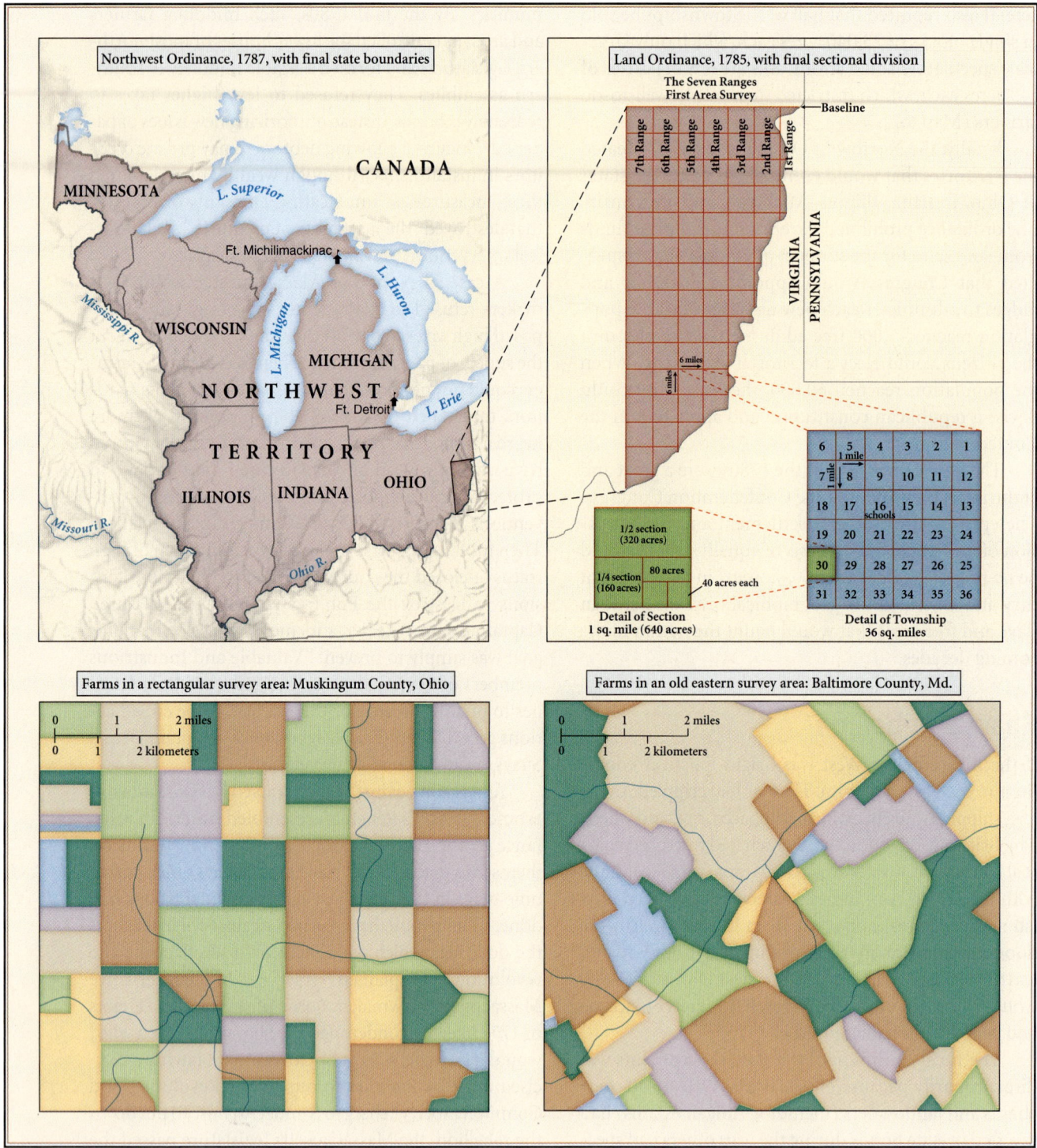

MAP 6.7

Land Division in the Northwest Territory

Throughout the Northwest Territory, government surveyors imposed a rectangular grid on the landscape, regardless of the local topography, so that farmers bought neatly defined tracts of land. The right-angled property lines in Muskingum County, Ohio (lower left), contrasted sharply with those in Baltimore County, Maryland (lower right), where—as in most of the eastern and southern states—boundaries followed the contours of the land.

Connecticut, and New Hampshire closed courthouses and forced their governments to provide economic relief. British officials in Canada predicted the imminent demise of the United States; and American leaders urged purposeful action to save their republican experiment. Events in Massachusetts, declared nationalist Henry Knox, formed "the strongest arguments possible" for the creation of "a strong general government."

- **What were the main differences between conservative state constitutions, such as those of Massachusetts and New York, and more democratic constitutions, such as Pennsylvania's?**

- **What were the causes of Shays's Rebellion, and what does it tell us about postwar America?**

The Constitution of 1787

From its creation, the U.S. Constitution was a controversial document, both acclaimed for solving the nation's woes and condemned for perverting its republican principles. Critics charged that republican institutions worked only in small political units—the states. Advocates replied that the Constitution extended republicanism by adding another level of government elected by the people. In the new two-level political federation created by the Constitution, the national government would exercise limited, delegated powers, and the existing state governments would retain authority over all other matters.

The Rise of a Nationalist Faction

Money questions—debts, taxes, and tariffs—dominated the postwar political agenda. Americans who had served the Confederation as military officers, officials, and diplomats viewed these issues from a national perspective and advocated a stronger central government. George Washington, Robert Morris, Benjamin Franklin, John Jay, and John Adams wanted Congress to control foreign commerce and tariff policy. However, lawmakers in Massachusetts, New York, and Pennsylvania—states with strong commercial traditions—insisted on controlling their own tariffs, both to protect their artisans from low-cost imports and to assist their merchants. Most southern states opposed tariffs because planters wanted to import British textiles and ironware at the lowest possible prices.

Nonetheless, some southern leaders became nationalists because their state legislatures had cut taxes and refused to redeem state war bonds. Such policies, lamented wealthy bondholder Charles Lee of Virginia, led taxpayers to believe they would "never be compelled to pay" the public debt. Creditors also condemned state laws that "stayed" (delayed) the payment of mortgages and other private debts. "While men are madly accumulating enormous debts, their legislators are making provisions for their nonpayment," complained a South Carolina merchant. To undercut the democratic majorities in the state legislatures, creditors joined the movement for a stronger central government.

In 1786, James Madison and other nationalists persuaded the Virginia legislature to call a convention in Annapolis, Maryland, to discuss tariff and taxation policies. When only five state governments sent representatives, the delegates called for another convention in Philadelphia. Spurred on by Shays's Rebellion, nationalists in Congress secured a resolution calling for the convention to revise the Articles of Confederation. Only an "efficient plan from the Convention," a fellow nationalist wrote to James Madison, "can prevent anarchy first & civil convulsions afterwards."

The Philadelphia Convention

In May 1787, fifty-five delegates arrived in Philadelphia. They came from every state except Rhode Island, where the legislature opposed increasing central authority. Most were strong nationalists; forty-two had served in the Confederation Congress. They were also educated and propertied: merchants, slaveholding planters, and "monied men." There were no artisans, backcountry settlers, or tenants, and only a single yeoman farmer.

Some influential Patriots missed the convention. John Adams and Thomas Jefferson were serving as American ministers to Britain and France, respectively. The Massachusetts General Court rejected Sam Adams as a delegate because he opposed a stronger national government, and his fellow firebrand from Virginia, Patrick Henry, refused to attend because he "smelt a rat."

The absence of experienced leaders and contrary-minded delegates allowed capable younger nationalists to set the agenda. Declaring that the convention would "decide for ever the fate of Republican Government," James Madison insisted on increased national authority. Alexander Hamilton of New York likewise demanded a strong central government to protect the republic from "the imprudence of democracy."

The Virginia and New Jersey Plans | The delegates elected Washington as their presiding officer and voted to meet behind closed doors. Then—momentously—they decided not to revise the Articles of Confederation but rather to consider the so-called Virginia Plan, a scheme for a powerful national government devised by James Madison. Just thirty-six years old, Madison was determined to fashion national political institutions run by men of high character. A graduate of Princeton, he had read classical and modern political theory and served in both the Confederation Congress and the Virginia assembly. Once an optimistic Patriot, Madison had grown discouraged because of the "narrow ambition" and outlook of state legislators.

Madison's Virginia Plan differed from the Articles of Confederation in three crucial respects. First, the plan rejected state sovereignty in favor of the "supremacy of national authority," including the power to overturn state laws. Second, it called for the national government to be established by the people (not the states) and for national laws to operate directly on citizens of the various states. Third, the plan proposed a three-tier election system in which ordinary voters would elect only the lower house of the national legislature. This lower house would then select the upper house, and both houses would appoint the executive and judiciary.

From a political perspective, Madison's plan had two fatal flaws. First, most state politicians and citizens resolutely opposed allowing the national government to veto state laws. Second, the plan based representation in the lower house on population; this provision, a Delaware delegate warned, would allow the populous states to "crush the small ones whenever they stand in the way of their ambitious or interested views."

So delegates from Delaware and other small states rallied behind a plan devised by William Paterson of New Jersey. The New Jersey Plan gave the Confederation the power to raise revenue, control commerce, and make binding requisitions on the states. But it preserved the states' control of their own laws and guaranteed their equality: As in the Confederation Congress, each state would have one vote in a unicameral legislature. Delegates from the more populous states vigorously opposed this provision. After a month-long debate on the two plans, a bare majority of the states agreed to use Madison's Virginia Plan as the basis of discussion.

This decision raised the odds that the convention would create a more powerful national government. Outraged by this prospect, two New York delegates accused their colleagues of exceeding their mandate to revise the Articles and left the convention. The remaining delegates met six days a week during the summer of 1787, debating both high principles and practical details. Experienced politicians, they looked for a plan that would be acceptable to most citizens and existing political interests. Pierce Butler of South Carolina invoked a classical Greek precedent: "We must follow the example of Solon, who gave the Athenians not the best government he could devise but the best they would receive."

James Madison, Statesman

Throughout his long public life, Madison kept the details of his private life to himself. His biography, he believed, should be a record of his public accomplishments, not his private affairs. Future generations celebrated him not as a great man (like Hamilton or Jefferson) or as a great president (like Washington), but as an original and incisive political thinker. The chief architect of the U.S. Constitution and the Bill of Rights, Madison was the preeminent republican political theorist of his generation.   Mead Art Museum, Amherst College.

The Great Compromise | As the convention grappled with the central problem of the representation of large and small states, the Connecticut delegates suggested a possible solution. They proposed that the national legislature's upper chamber (the Senate) have two members from each state, while seats in the lower chamber (the House of Representatives) be apportioned by population (determined every ten years by a national census). After bitter debate, delegates from the populous states reluctantly accepted this "Great Compromise."

Other state-related issues were quickly settled by restricting (or leaving ambiguous) the extent of central authority. Some delegates opposed a national system of courts, predicting that "the states will revolt at such encroachments" on their judicial authority. This danger led the convention to define the judicial power of the United States in broad terms, vesting it "in one supreme Court" and leaving the new national legislature to decide whether to establish lower courts within the states. The convention also refused to set a property requirement for voting in national elections. "Eight or nine states have extended the right of suffrage beyond the freeholders," George Mason of Virginia pointed out. "What will people there say if they should be disfranchised?" Finally, the convention specified that state legislatures would elect members of the upper house, or Senate, and the states would select the electors who would choose the president. By allowing states to have important roles in the new constitutional system, the delegates hoped that their citizens would accept limits on state sovereignty.

Negotiations over Slavery

The shadow of slavery hovered over many debates, and Gouverneur Morris of New York brought it into view. Born into the New York aristocracy, Morris had initially opposed independence because he feared the "domination of a riotous mob." Now a Patriot and a nationalist, he came to Philadelphia convinced that the protection of "property was the sole or primary object of Government & Society." To safeguard property rights, Morris wanted life terms for senators, a property qualification for voting in national elections, and a strong president with veto power. Nonetheless, he rejected the legitimacy of two traditional types of property: the feudal dues claimed by aristocratic landowners and the ownership of slaves. An advocate of **free markets** and personal liberty, Morris condemned slavery as "a nefarious institution."

Many slave-owning delegates from the Chesapeake region—including Madison and George Mason—recognized that slavery contradicted republican principles and hoped for its eventual demise. But these Upper South planters, who owned many slaves, only supported an end to American participation in the Atlantic slave trade—a proposal the South Carolina and Georgia delegates angrily rejected. Unless the importation of African slaves continued, these rice planters and merchants declared, their states "shall not be parties to the Union."

Gouverneur Morris, Federalist Statesman
When the war with Britain broke out, Morris had debated joining the Loyalist cause; he was a snob who liked privilege and feared the common people. ("The mob begins to think and reason. Poor reptiles!" he once noted with disdain.) He became a Federalist for much the same reasons. He helped write the Philadelphia constitution and strongly supported the Federalist Party. As American minister to France (1792–1794), Morris took as his mistress the young wife of an aging aristocrat and joined an unsuccessful aristocrat plot to smuggle King Louis XVI out of Paris.
National Portrait Gallery, Smithsonian Institution/Art Resource, New York.

At their insistence, the convention denied Congress the power to regulate immigration—and so the slave trade—until 1808 (see Comparing American Voices, "The First National Debate over Slavery," pp. 196–197).

To preserve national unity, the delegates devised other slavery-related compromises. To mollify southern planters, they devised a "fugitive clause" that allowed masters to reclaim enslaved blacks (or white indentured servants) who fled to other states. But in acknowledgment of the antislavery sentiments of Morris and other northerners, the delegates excluded the words *slavery* and *slave* from the Constitution; it spoke only of citizens and "all other Persons." Because slaves lacked the vote, antislavery delegates wanted their census numbers excluded when apportioning seats in Congress. For their part, Southerners—ironically, given that they

The First National Debate over Slavery

I n this part of the text, we trace the impact of republican ideology on American politics and society. What happened when republicanism collided head-on with the well-established practice of slavery? After the Revolution, the Massachusetts courts abolished slavery, but in 1787, slavery was legal in the rest of the Union and was the bedrock of social order and agricultural production in the southern states. A look at the debates on the issue of the African slave trade at the Philadelphia convention and in a state ratifying convention shows that slavery was an extremely divisive issue at the birth of the nation—a dark cloud threatening the bright future of the young republic.

The Constitutional Convention

Slavery was not a major topic of discussion at the Philadelphia convention, but it surfaced a number of times, notably in the important debate over representation (which produced the three-fifths clause). A discussion of the Atlantic slave trade began when Luther Martin, a delegate from Maryland, proposed a clause allowing Congress to impose a tax on or prohibit the importation of slaves.

Mr. Martin proposed to vary article 7, sect. 4 so as to allow a prohibition or tax on the importation of slaves.... [He believed] it was inconsistent with the principles of the Revolution, and dishonorable to the American character, to have such a feature [promoting the slave trade] in the Constitution.

Mr. [John] Rutledge [of South Carolina declared that] religion and humanity had nothing to do with this question. Interest alone is the governing principle with nations. The true question at present is whether the Southern states shall or shall not be parties to the Union....

Mr. [Oliver] Ellsworth [of Connecticut] was for leaving the clause as it stands. Let every state import what it pleases. The morality or wisdom of slavery are considerations belonging to the states themselves.... The old Confederation had not meddled with this point, and he did not see any greater necessity for bringing it within the policy of the new one.

Mr. [Charles C.] Pinckney [said] South Carolina can never receive the plan [for a new constitution] if it prohibits the slave trade. In every proposed extension of the powers of Congress, that state has expressly and watchfully excepted that of meddling with the importation of Negroes....

Mr. [Roger] Sherman [of Connecticut] was for leaving the clause as it stands. He disapproved of the slave trade; yet, as the states were now possessed of the right to import slaves, ... and as it was expedient to have as few objections as possible to the proposed scheme of government, he thought it best to leave the matter as we find it.

Col. [George] Mason [of Virginia stated that] this infernal trade originated in the avarice of British merchants. The British government constantly checked the attempts of Virginia to put a stop to it. The present question concerns not the importing states alone, but the whole Union.... Maryland and Virginia, he said, had already prohibited the importation of slaves expressly. North Carolina had done the same in substance. All this would be in vain if South Carolina and Georgia be at liberty to import. The Western people are already calling out for slaves for their new lands, and will fill that country with slaves, if they can be got through South Carolina and Georgia. Slavery discourages arts and manufactures. The poor despise labor when performed by slaves. They prevent the immigration of whites, who really enrich and strengthen a country....

Every master of slaves is born a petty tyrant. They bring the judgment of Heaven on a country. As nations cannot be rewarded or punished in the next world, they must be in this. By an inevitable chain of causes and effects, Providence punishes national sins by national calamities.... He held it essential, in every point of view, that the general government should have power to prevent the increase of slavery.

Mr. Ellsworth, as he had never owned a slave, could not judge of the effects of slavery on character. He said, however, that if it was to be considered in a moral light, we ought to go further, and free those already in the country.... Let us not intermeddle. As population increases, poor laborers will be so plenty as to render slaves useless. Slavery, in time, will not be a speck in our country....

Gen. [Charles C.] Pinckney [argued that] South Carolina and Georgia cannot do without slaves. As to Virginia, she will gain by stopping the importations. Her slaves will rise in value, and she has more than she wants. It would be unequal to require South Carolina and Georgia to confederate on such unequal terms.... He contended that the importation of slaves would be for the interest of the whole Union. The more slaves, the more produce to employ the carrying trade; the more consumption also; and the more of this, the more revenue for the common treasury. . . . [He] should consider a rejection of the [present] clause as an exclusion of South Carolina from the Union.

Source: Max Farrand, ed., *The Records of the Federal Convention of 1787* (New Haven: Yale University Press, 1911), 2: 364–365, 369–372.

The Massachusetts Ratifying Convention

In Philadelphia, the delegates agreed on a compromise: They gave Congress the power to tax or prohibit slave imports, as Luther Martin had proposed, but withheld that power for twenty years. In the Massachusetts convention, the delegates split on this issue and on many others. They ratified the Constitution by a narrow margin, 187 to 168.

Mr. Neal (from Kittery) [an Antifederalist] went over the ground of objection to . . . the idea that slave trade was allowed to be continued for 20 years. His profession, he said, obliged him to bear witness against any thing that should favor the making merchandize of the bodies of men, and unless his objection was removed, he could not put his hand to the constitution. Other gentlemen said, in addition to this idea, that there was not even a proposition that the negroes ever shall be free: and Gen. Thompson exclaimed— "Mr. President, shall it be said, that after we have established our own independence and freedom, we make slaves of others? Oh! Washington . . . he has immortalized himself! but he holds those in slavery who have a good right to be free as he is. . . ."

On the other side, gentlemen said, that the step taken in this article, towards the abolition of slavery, was one of the beauties of the constitution. They observed, that in the confederation there was no provision whatever for its ever being abolished; but this constitution provides, that Congress may after twenty years, totally annihilate the slave trade. . . .

Mr. Heath (Federalist): . . . I apprehend that it is not in our power to do any thing for or against those who are in slavery in the southern states. No gentleman within these walls detests every idea of slavery more than I do: it is generally detested by the people of this commonwealth, and I ardently hope that the time will soon come, when our brethren in the southern states will view it as we do, and put a stop to it; but to this we have no right to compel them.

Two questions naturally arise: if we ratify the Constitution, shall we do any thing by our act to hold the blacks in slavery or shall we become the partakers of other men's sins? I think neither of them: each state is sovereign and independent to a certain degree, and they have a right, and will regulate their own internal affairs, as to themselves appears proper. . . . We are not in this case partakers of other men's sins. . . .

The federal convention went as far as they could; the migration or immigration &c. is confined to the states, now existing only, new states cannot claim it. Congress, by their ordnance for erecting new states, some time since, declared that there shall be no slavery in them. But whether those in slavery in the southern states, will be emancipated after the year 1808, I do not pretend to determine: I rather doubt it.

Source: Jonathan Elliot, ed., *The Debates . . . on the Adoption of the Federal Constitution* (Philadelphia: J. B. Lippincott, 1836), 1: 103–105, 107, 112, 117.

ANALYZING THE EVIDENCE

- **At the constitutional convention in Philadelphia, what were the main arguments for and against federal restrictions on the Atlantic slave trade? How do you explain the position taken by the Connecticut delegates in Philadelphia and Mr. Heath in the Massachusetts debate?**

- **Why did George Mason, a Virginia slave owner, demand a prohibition of the Atlantic slave trade?**

- **What evidence of regional tensions appears in the documents? Several men from different states— Mason from Virginia, Ellsworth from Connecticut, and Heath from Massachusetts—offered predictions about the future of slavery. How accurate were they?**

considered slaves property—demanded that slaves be counted in the census the same as full citizens, so as to increase the South's representation. Ultimately, the delegates agreed that each slave would count as three-fifths of a free person for purposes of representation and taxation, a compromise that helped southern planters dominate the national government until 1860.

National Authority | Having addressed the concerns of small states and slave states, the convention created a powerful—and procreditor—national government. The Constitution declared that congressional legislation was the "supreme" law of the land. The national government was provided with broad powers of taxation, military defense, and external commerce and the authority to make all laws "necessary and proper" to implement those and other provisions. To assist creditors and establish the new government's fiscal integrity, the Constitution required the United States to honor the existing national debt and prohibited the states from issuing paper money or enacting "any Law impairing the Obligation of Contracts."

The proposed constitution was not a "perfect production," Benjamin Franklin admitted, as he urged the delegates to sign it in September 1787. But the great statesman confessed his astonishment at finding "this system approaching so near to perfection." His colleagues apparently agreed; all but three signed the document.

The People Debate Ratification

The procedure for ratifying the new constitution was as controversial as its contents. Knowing that Rhode Island (and perhaps other states) would reject it, the delegates did not submit the Constitution to the state legislatures for their unanimous consent, as required by the Articles of Confederation. Instead, they arbitrarily declared that it would take effect when ratified by conventions in nine of the thirteen states. Because of its nationalist sympathies, the Confederation Congress winked at this extralegal procedure; surprisingly, most state legislatures also winked and called ratification conventions.

As the constitutional debate began in early 1788, the nationalists seized the initiative with two bold moves. First, they called themselves **Federalists**, suggesting that they supported a federal union—a loose, decentralized system—and obscuring their commitment to a strong national government. Second, they launched a coordinated campaign in pamphlets and newspapers to explain and justify the Philadelphia constitution.

The Antifederalists | The opponents of the Constitution, the Antifederalists, had diverse backgrounds and motives. Some, like Governor George Clinton of New York, feared that state governments would lose power. Rural democrats protested that the proposed document, unlike most state constitutions, lacked a declaration of individual rights; they also feared that the central government would be run by wealthy men. "Lawyers and men of learning and monied men expect to be managers of this Constitution," worried a Massachusetts farmer. "[T]hey will swallow up all of us little folks . . . just as the whale swallowed up Jonah." Giving political substance to these fears, Melancton Smith of New York argued that the large electoral districts prescribed by the Constitution would restrict office-holding to wealthy men, whereas the smaller districts used in state elections usually produced legislatures "composed principally of respectable yeomanry." John Quincy Adams agreed: If only "*eight* men" would represent Massachusetts, "they will infallibly be chosen from the aristocratic part of the community."

Smith summed up the views of Americans who held traditional republican values. To keep government "close to the people," they wanted the states to remain small sovereign republics tied together only for trade and defense—not the "United States" but the "States United." Citing the French political philosopher Montesquieu, Antifederalists argued that republican institutions were best suited to small polities, a localist perspective that shaped American thinking well into the twentieth century. "No extensive empire can be governed on republican principles," declared James Winthrop of Massachusetts. Patrick Henry worried that the Constitution would re-create British rule: high taxes, an oppressive bureaucracy, a standing army, and a "great and mighty President . . . supported in extravagant munificence." As another Antifederalist put it, "I had rather be a free citizen of the small republic of Massachusetts than an oppressed subject of the great American empire."

In New York, where ratification was hotly contested, James Madison, John Jay, and Alexander Hamilton defended the proposed constitution in a series of eighty-five essays, collectively titled *The Federalist*. This work influenced political leaders throughout the country and subsequently won acclaim as an important treatise of practical republicanism. Its authors denied that a centralized government would lead to domestic tyranny. Drawing on Montesquieu's theories and John Adams's *Thoughts on Government*, Madison, Jay, and Hamilton pointed out that authority would be divided among the president, a bicameral legislature, and a judiciary. Each branch of government would "check and balance" the others and so preserve liberty.

In "Federalist No. 10," Madison challenged the view that republican governments only worked in small polities, arguing that a large state would better protect republican liberty. It was "sown in the nature of man," Madison wrote, for individuals to seek power and form factions. Indeed, "a landed interest, a manufacturing interest, a mercantile interest, a moneyed interest, with many lesser interests, grow up of necessity in civilized nations." A free society should welcome all factions but keep any one of them from becoming dominant — something best achieved in a large republic. "Extend the sphere and you take in a greater variety of parties and interests," Madison concluded, inhibiting the formation of a majority eager "to invade the rights of other citizens."

The Constitution Ratified

The delegates debating these issues in the state ratification conventions included untutored farmers and middling artisans as well as educated gentlemen. Generally, backcountry delegates were Antifederalists, while those from coastal areas were Federalists. In Pennsylvania, Philadelphia merchants and artisans joined commercial farmers to ratify the Constitution. Other early Federalist successes came in four less-populous states — Delaware, New Jersey, Georgia, and Connecticut — where delegates hoped that a strong national government would offset the power of large neighboring states (Map 6.8).

The Constitution's first real test came in January 1788 in Massachusetts, a hotbed of Antifederalist sentiment. Influential Patriots, including Samuel Adams and Governor John Hancock, opposed the new constitution, as did many followers of Daniel Shays. But Boston artisans, who wanted tariff protection from British imports, supported ratification. To win over other delegates, Federalist leaders assured the convention that they would enact a national bill of rights. By a close vote of 187 to 168, the Federalists carried the day.

Spring brought Federalist victories in Maryland, South Carolina, and New Hampshire, reaching the nine-state quota required for ratification. But it took the powerful arguments advanced in *The Federalist* and more promises of a bill of rights to secure the Constitution's adoption in the essential states of Virginia and New York. The votes were again close: 89 to 79 in Virginia and 30 to 27 in New York.

Testifying to their respect for popular sovereignty and majority rule, most Americans accepted the verdict of the ratifying conventions. "A decided majority" of the New Hampshire assembly had opposed the "new system," reported Joshua Atherton, but now they said, "It is adopted, let us try it." In Virginia, Patrick Henry vowed to "submit as a quiet citizen" and fight for amendments "in a constitutional way."

Unlike France, where the Revolution of 1789 divided the society into irreconcilable factions for generations, the American Constitutional Revolution of 1787 created a national republic based on broad popular support. Federalists celebrated their triumph by organizing great processions in the seaport cities. By marching in an orderly fashion — in conscious contrast to the riotous Revolutionary mobs — Federalist-minded citizens affirmed their allegiance to a self-governing but elite-ruled republican nation.

- According to the nationalists, what were the central problems of the Articles of Confederation? How did the delegates to the Philadelphia convention address them?

- How did the Philadelphia convention resolve the three controversial issues of the representation of large and small states, state power, and slavery?

- Who were the Antifederalists and why did they oppose the Constitution?

SUMMARY

In this chapter, we examined the unfolding of two related sets of events. The first was the war between Britain and its rebellious colonies that began in 1776 and ended in 1783. The two great battles of Saratoga (1777) and Yorktown (1781) determined the outcome of that conflict. Surprisingly, given the military might of the British empire, both were American victories. These triumphs testify to the determination of George Washington, the resilience of the Continental army, and support for the Patriot cause from hundreds of local militias and tens of thousands of taxpaying citizens.

This popular support reflected the Patriots' second success: building effective institutions of republican government. These elected institutions of local and state governance evolved naturally out of colonial-era town meetings and representative assemblies. They were defined in the state constitutions written between 1776 and 1781 and their principles informed the first national constitution, the Articles of Confederation. Despite the challenges posed by conflicts over suffrage, women's rights, and fiscal policy, these self-governing political institutions carried the new republic successfully though the war-torn era and laid the foundation for the Constitution of 1787, the national charter that endures today.

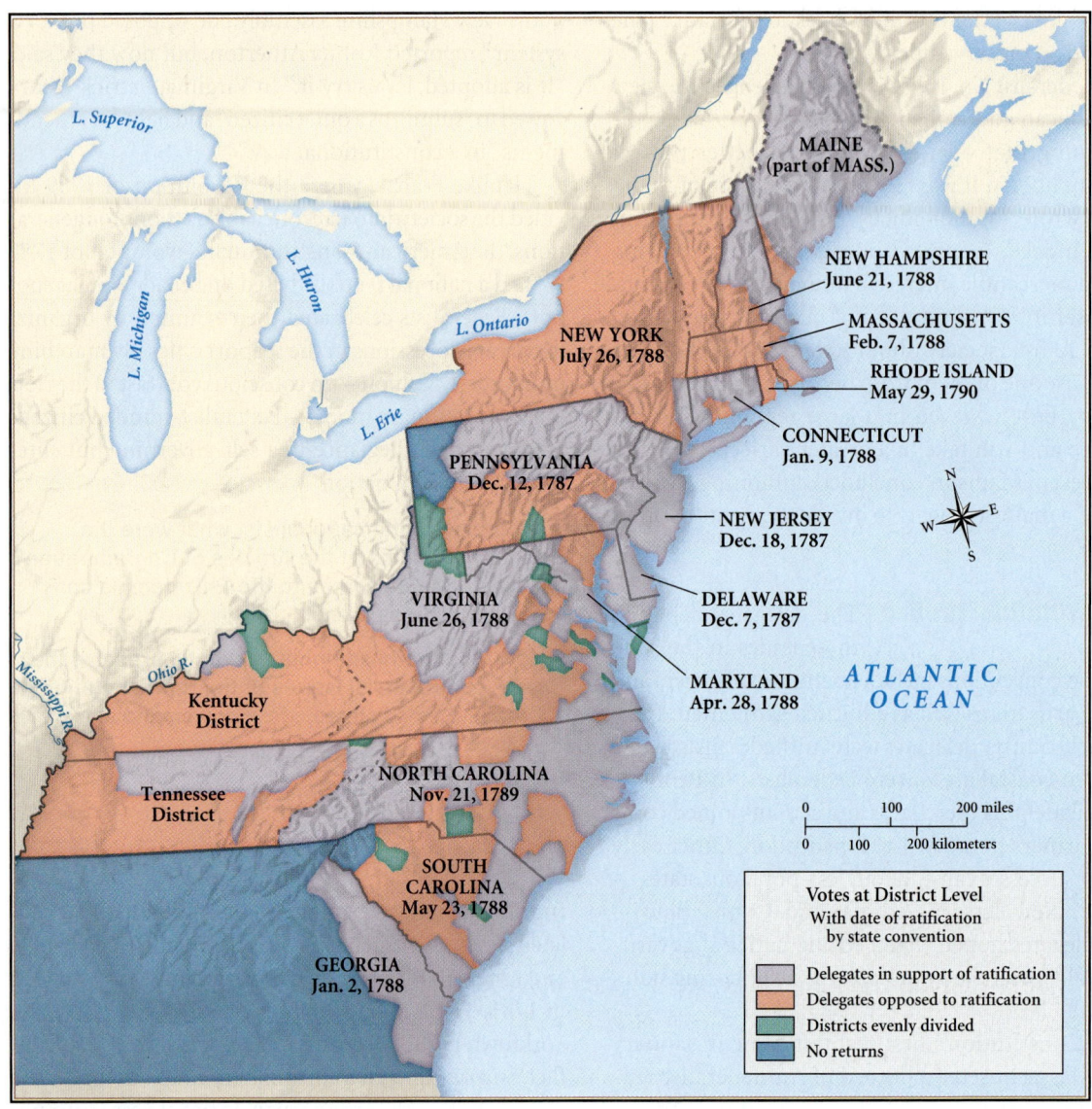

MAP 6.8

Ratifying the Constitution of 1787

In 1907, geographer Owen Libby mapped the votes of members of the state conventions that ratified the Constitution. His map showed that most delegates from seaboard or commercial farming districts (which sent many delegates to the conventions) supported the Constitution, while those from sparsely represented, subsistence-oriented backcountry areas opposed it. Subsequent research has confirmed Libby's socioeconomic interpretation of the voting patterns in North and South Carolina and in Massachusetts. However, other states' delegates were influenced by different factors. For example, in Georgia, delegates from all regions voted for ratification.

CHAPTER REVIEW QUESTIONS

- The text states that Saratoga was the turning point of the War of Independence. Do you agree? Explain your answer.

- How revolutionary was the American Revolution? What political, social, and economic changes did it produce? What stayed the same?

- Why was the Constitution a controversial document even as it was being written?

- Both the Federalists and the Antifederalists claimed to represent the true spirit of the Revolution. Which group do you think was right? Why?

FOR FURTHER EXPLORATION

The essays in *Empire and Nation: The American Revolution in the Atlantic World* (2005), edited by Eliga H. Gould and Peter S. Onuf, assess the impact of the revolution. For vivid accounts of the war, see John C. Dann, ed., *The Revolution Remembered: Eyewitness Accounts of the War for Independence* (1980).

Colin G. Calloway, *The American Revolution in Indian Country* (1995); Sylvia R. Frey, *Water from the Rock* (1991); and *Paths to Freedom: Manumission in the Atlantic World* (2009), edited by Rosemary Brana-Shute and Randy J. Sparks, study the revolution's impact on Native and African peoples. A data-rich source is "Africans in America: Revolution" (**www.pbs.org/wgbh/aia/part2/title.html**).

Three studies of women are Carol Berkin, *Revolutionary Mothers* (2005); Clare A. Lyons, *Sex Among the Rabble* (2006); and Cynthia Kierner, *Southern Women in Revolution, 1776–1800* (1998). For an intriguing portrait of "Deborah Sampson, Continental Soldier," go to **forum-network.org/lecture/masquerade-deborah-sampson-continental-soldier.**

Woody Holton, *Unruly Americans and the Origins of the Constitution* (2007), explores the events of the 1780s, while Catherine Drinker Bowen's *Miracle at Philadelphia* (1966) offers a dramatic portrayal of the convention. Jack Rakove's *Original Meanings: Politics and Ideas in the Making of the Constitution* (1996) and Saul Cornell's *The Other Founders* (1999) explore the ideologies of the Framers and their Antifederalist opponents. Also see the online exhibit "Religion and the Founding of the American Republic" (**www.loc.gov/exhibits/religion/rel03.html**), and Susan Juster, *Doomsayers: Anglo-American Prophecy in the Age of Revolution* (2003).

TEST YOUR KNOWLEDGE

To assess your command of the material in this chapter, see the Online Study Guide at **bedfordstmartins.com/henretta.**

For Web sites, images, and documents related to topics and places in this chapter, visit **bedfordstmartins.com/makehistory.**

TIMELINE

1776	Second Continental Congress declares independence
	Howe forces Washington to retreat from New York and New Jersey
	Pennsylvania approves democratic state constitution
	John Adams publishes *Thoughts on Government*
1777	Articles of Confederation create central government
	Patriot women contribute to war economy
	Howe occupies Philadelphia (September)
	Gates defeats Burgoyne at Saratoga (October)
	Severe inflation of paper currency begins
1778	Franco-American alliance (February)
	Lord North seeks political settlement; Congress rejects negotiations
	British adopt southern strategy; capture Savannah (December)
1779	British and American forces battle in Georgia
1780	Clinton seizes Charleston (May)
	French troops land in Rhode Island
1781	Cornwallis invades Virginia (April); surrenders at Yorktown (October)
	States finally ratify Articles of Confederation
	Substantial Loyalist emigration
1783	Treaty of Paris (September 3) officially ends war
1784–1785	Congress enacts political and land ordinances for new states
1786	Nationalists hold convention in Annapolis, Maryland
	Shays's Rebellion roils Massachusetts
1787	Congress passes Northwest Ordinance
	Constitutional convention in Philadelphia
1787–1788	Jay, Madison, and Hamilton write *The Federalist*
	Eleven states ratify U.S. Constitution

An EMBLEM of AMERICA.

CHAPTER 7

Politics and Society in the New Republic, 1787–1820

Like an earthquake, the American Revolution shook the European monarchical order, and its aftershocks reverberated for decades. By "creating a new republic based on the rights of the individual, the North Americans introduced a new force into the world," the eminent German historian Leopold von Ranke warned the king of Bavaria in 1854, a force that might cost the monarch his throne. Before 1776, "a king who ruled by the grace of God had been the center around which everything turned. Now the idea emerged that power should come from below [from the people]."

Other republican-inspired upheavals—England's Puritan Revolution of the 1640s and the French Revolution of 1789—ended in political chaos and military rule. Similar fates befell many Latin American republics that won independence from Spain in the early nineteenth century. But the American states escaped both social anarchy and military dictatorship. Having been raised in a Radical Whig political culture that viewed standing armies and powerful generals as instruments of tyranny, General George Washington left public life in 1783 to manage his plantation, astonishing European observers but bolstering the authority of elected Patriot leaders. "'Tis a Conduct so novel," American painter John Trumbull reported from London, that it is "inconceivable to People [here]."

The great task of fashioning representative republican governments absorbed the energy and intellect of an entire generation and was rife with conflict. Seeking to perpetuate the elite-led polity of the colonial era, Federalists celebrated "natural aristocrats" such as Washington and condemned the radical republicanism of the French Revolution. In response, Jefferson and his Republican followers claimed the Fourth of July as their holiday and "we the people" as their political language. "There was a grand democrat procession in Town on the 4th of July," came a report from Baltimore: "All the farmers, tanners, black-smiths, shoemakers, etc. were there . . . and afterwards they went to a grand feast."

Many people of high status worried that the new state governments were too attentive to the demands of such ordinary workers and their families. When considering a bill, Connecticut conservative Ezra Stiles grumbled, every elected official "instantly thinks how it will affect his constituents" rather than how it would enhance the general welfare. What Stiles criticized as irresponsible, however, most Americans welcomed. The concerns of ordinary citizens were now paramount, and traditional elites trembled.

An Emblem of America, 1800

In the first years of independence, citizens of the United States searched for a symbolic representation of their new nation. This engraving shows many of the choices: Should the symbol of "America" have an ideological meaning, as in the Goddess of Liberty? Or should it be represented by national heroes, as in the stone Memorial to Washington? Or should America's symbol be found among its unique features, such as Niagara Falls (pictured in the background) or the presence of Africans and Indians (as represented by the black youth to the right and the spear-brandishing figure in front of the falls)? Or, finally, should its symbol be the national flag? Courtesy of the John Carter Brown Library at Brown University.

The Political Crisis of the 1790s

The final decade of the eighteenth century brought fresh challenges for American politics. The Federalists split into two factions over financial policy and the French Revolution, and their leaders, Alexander Hamilton and Thomas Jefferson, offered contrasting visions of the future. Would the United States remain an agricultural nation governed by local officials, as Jefferson hoped? Or would Hamilton's vision of a strong national government and an economy based on manufacturing become reality?

The Federalists Implement the Constitution

The Constitution expanded the dimensions of political life by allowing voters to choose national leaders as well as local and state officials. The Federalists swept the election of 1788, winning forty-four seats in the House of Representatives; only eight Antifederalists won election. As expected, members of the Electoral College chose George Washington as president (see Reading American Pictures, "Creating a National Political Tradition," p. 205). John Adams received the second-highest number of electoral votes and became vice president.

Devising the New Government | Once the military savior of his country, Washington now became its political father. At age fifty-seven, the first president possessed great personal dignity and a cautious personality. To maintain continuity, he adopted many of the administrative practices of the Confederation and asked Congress to reestablish the existing executive departments: Foreign Affairs (State), Finance (Treasury), and War. He initiated one important practice: The Constitution required the Senate's approval for the appointment of major officials, but Washington insisted that the president had sole authority to remove them, thereby ensuring the executive's control of the bureaucracy. To head the Department of State, Washington chose Thomas Jefferson, a fellow Virginian and an experienced diplomat. For secretary of the treasury, he turned to Alexander Hamilton, a lawyer and his former military aide. The president designated Jefferson, Hamilton, and Secretary of War Henry Knox as his cabinet, or advisory body.

The Constitution mandated a supreme court, but the Philadelphia convention gave Congress the task of creating a national court system. The Federalists wanted strong national institutions, and the Judiciary Act of 1789 reflected their vision. The act established a federal district court in each state and three circuit courts to hear appeals from the districts, with the Supreme Court having the final say. The Judiciary Act also specified that cases arising in state courts that involved federal laws could be appealed to the Supreme Court. This provision ensured that federal judges would have the final say on the meaning of the Constitution.

The Bill of Rights | The Federalists kept their promise to add a declaration of rights to the Constitution. James Madison, now a member of the House of Representatives, submitted nineteen amendments to the First Congress; by 1791, ten had been approved by Congress and ratified by the states. These ten amendments, known as the Bill of Rights, safeguard fundamental personal rights, including freedom of speech and religion, and mandate legal procedures, such as trial by jury. By protecting individual citizens, the amendments eased Antifederalists' fears of an oppressive national government and secured the legitimacy of the Constitution. They also addressed the issue of federalism: the proper balance between the authority of the national and state governments. But that question was constantly contested until the Civil War and remains important today.

Hamilton's Financial Program

George Washington's most important decision was choosing Alexander Hamilton as secretary of the treasury. An ambitious self-made man of great intelligence, Hamilton married into the Schuyler family, influential Hudson River Valley landowners, and was a prominent lawyer in New York City. At the Philadelphia convention, he condemned the "democratic spirit" and called for an authoritarian government and a president with near-monarchical powers.

As treasury secretary, Hamilton devised bold policies to enhance national authority and to assist financiers and merchants. He outlined his plans in three path-breaking reports to Congress: on public credit (January 1790), on a national bank (December 1790), and on manufactures (December 1791). These reports outlined a coherent program of national mercantilism—government-assisted economic development.

Creating a National Political Tradition

"Four score and seven years ago our fathers brought forth, upon this continent, a new nation. . . ." So Abraham Lincoln began his famous address at Gettysburg in 1863. In fact, although the American Patriots founded a new republic in 1776, it became a *nation*, with a sense of national consciousness, only in subsequent decades. How did America's nationhood develop? The sheer act of living together and addressing common problems created a foundation for nationhood. But graphic representations such as these engravings shaped the national identity and created a sense of political continuity.

Washington's Journey from Mount Vernon.
Library of Congress.

"Independence Declared 1776. The Union Must Be Preserved." Library of Congress.

ANALYZING THE EVIDENCE

- George Washington—as myth and symbol—had a lot to do with creating America's sense of nationhood. How is Washington portrayed in the image on the left? It depicts his journey from Virginia to New York in 1789 to assume the presidency. Pay attention to the symbols in the engraving—the laurel wreaths, the American flags, the eagle—and to the fact that Washington is riding a horse, long a symbol of authority and aristocratic power. What do these symbols suggest about Washington? About the presidency? How might

they conflict with America's republican self-image?

- In the Gettysburg Address, Lincoln speaks reverently of "our fathers" bringing forth a new nation. The banner in the engraving of Washington, which was created in 1845, reads: "THE DEFENDER OF THE MOTHERS WILL BE THE PROTECTOR OF THE DAUGHTERS." What is the significance of the use of family imagery by Lincoln and the engraver? How does this imagery "make personal" the concept of the nation?

- The engraving on the right, from 1839, supports the incumbent president, Martin Van Buren (center left). He firmly clasps the hand of Andrew Jackson, his predecessor, political ally, and the author of the famous toast "The Union Must Be Preserved," which was directed against John C. Calhoun and his writings on nullification. What use does the engraver make of Washington and the presidents (arrayed at the top) who followed him? How might this imagery have helped to create a national political tradition?

Public Credit: Redemption and Assumption The financial and social implications of Hamilton's "Report on the Public Credit" made it instantly controversial. Hamilton asked Congress to redeem at face value the $55 million in Confederation securities held by foreign and domestic investors (Figure 7.1). His reasons were simple: As an underdeveloped nation, the United States needed good credit to secure loans from Dutch and British financiers. However, Hamilton's redemption plan would give enormous profits to speculators, who had bought up depreciated securities. For example, the Massachusetts firm of Burrell & Burrell had paid $600 for Confederation notes with a face value of $2,500; it stood to reap a profit of $1,900. Such windfall gains offended a majority of Americans, who condemned the speculative practices of capitalist financiers. Equally controversial was Hamilton's proposal to pay the Burrells and other note holders with new interest-bearing securities, thereby creating a permanent **national debt**.

Hamilton's plan for a national debt owned mostly by the wealthy reawakened the fears of Radical Whigs and "Old Republicans." Speaking for the Virginia House of Burgesses, Patrick Henry condemned this plan "to erect, and concentrate, and perpetuate a large monied interest" and warned that it would prove "fatal to the existence of American liberty." James Madison challenged the morality of Hamilton's plan. He demanded that Congress recompense those who originally owned Confederation securities: the thousands of shopkeepers, farmers, and soldiers who had bought or accepted them during the dark days of the war. However, it would have been difficult to trace the original owners; moreover, nearly half the members of the House of Representatives owned Confederation securities and would profit personally from Hamilton's plan. Melding practicality with self-interest, the House rejected Madison's suggestion.

Hamilton then proposed that the national government further enhance public credit by assuming the war debts of the states. This assumption plan, costing $22 million, also favored well-to-do creditors such as Abigail Adams, who had bought depreciated Massachusetts government bonds with a face value of $2,400 for only a few hundred dollars and would reap a windfall profit. Still, Adams was a long-term investor, not a speculator like Assistant Secretary of the Treasury William Duer. Knowing Hamilton's intentions in advance, Duer and his associates secretly bought up $4.6 million of the war bonds of southern states at bargain rates. Congressional critics condemned Duer's speculation. They also pointed out that some states had already paid off their war debts; in response, Hamilton promised to

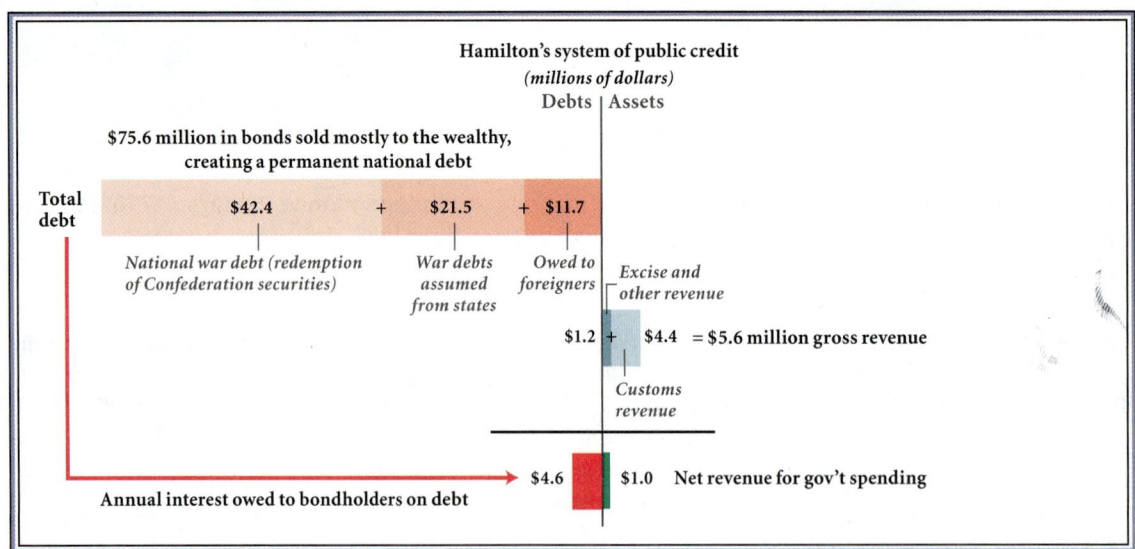

FIGURE 7.1

Hamilton's Fiscal Structure, 1792

As treasury secretary, Alexander Hamilton established a national debt by issuing government bonds and using the proceeds to redeem Confederation securities and assume the war debts of the states. To pay the annual interest due on the bonds, he used the revenue from excise taxes and customs duties. Hamilton deliberately did not attempt to redeem the bonds because he wanted to tie the interests of the wealthy Americans who owned them to the new national government.

reimburse those states. To win the votes of congressmen from Virginia and Maryland, the treasury chief arranged another deal: He agreed that the permanent national capital would be built along the Potomac River, where suspicious southerners could easily watch its operations. Such astute bargaining gave Hamilton the votes he needed to enact his redemption and assumption plans.

Creating a National Bank In December 1790, Hamilton issued a second report asking Congress to charter the Bank of the United States, which would be jointly owned by private stockholders and the national government. Hamilton argued that the bank would provide stability to the specie-starved American economy by making loans to merchants, handling government funds, and issuing bills of credit. These potential benefits persuaded Congress to grant Hamilton's bank a twenty-year charter and send the legislation to the president for his approval.

At this critical juncture, Secretary of State Thomas Jefferson joined with James Madison to oppose Hamilton's financial initiatives. Jefferson had already condemned Duer and the "corrupt squadron of paper dealers" who speculated in southern war bonds. Now he charged that Hamilton's national bank was unconstitutional. "The incorporation of a Bank," Jefferson told President Washington, was not a power expressly "delegated to the United States by the Constitution." Jefferson's argument rested on a *strict* interpretation of the national charter. Hamilton preferred a *loose* interpretation; he told Washington that Article 1, Section 8, empowered Congress to make "all Laws which shall be necessary and proper" to carry out the provisions of the Constitution. Agreeing with Hamilton, the president signed the legislation.

Raising Revenue through Tariffs Hamilton now sought revenue to pay the annual interest on the national debt. At his insistence, Congress imposed excise taxes, including a duty on whiskey distilled in the United States. These taxes would yield $1 million a year. To raise another $4 million to $5 million, the treasury secretary proposed higher tariffs on foreign imports. Although Hamilton's "Report on Manufactures" (1791) urged the expansion of American manufacturing, he did not support high **protective tariffs** that would exclude foreign products. Rather, he advocated moderate **revenue tariffs** that would pay the interest on the debt and other government expenses. To counter objections that "national tax collectors" would impair the "sovereignty" of the states, Hamilton selected respected state officials, including some Anti-federalists, for many customhouse positions.

Hamilton's scheme worked brilliantly. As American trade increased, customs revenue rose steadily and paid down the national debt. Because import duties covered federal government expenses, they also encouraged rapid settlement of the West. Congress sold land in the national domain at ever-lower prices, an outcome opposed by Hamilton and favored by his Jeffersonian opponents. Regardless, the treasury secretary had devised a strikingly modern and successful fiscal system. Since the "commencement of the funding system," entrepreneur Samuel Blodget Jr. declared in 1801, "the country prospered beyond all former example."

Jefferson's Agrarian Vision

Hamilton paid a high political price for his success. As Washington began his second four-year term in 1793, Hamilton's financial measures had split the Federalists into bitterly opposed factions. Most northern Federalists supported the treasury secretary, while most southern Federalists joined a group headed by Madison and Jefferson. By 1794, the two factions had acquired names. Hamiltonians remained Federalists; the allies of Madison and Jefferson called themselves Democratic Republicans or simply Republicans.

Thomas Jefferson spoke for southern planters and western farmers. Well-read in architecture, natural history, agricultural science, and political theory, Jefferson embraced the optimism of the Enlightenment. He believed in the "improvability of the human race" and deplored the corruption and social divisions that threatened its progress. Having seen the poverty of laborers in British factories, Jefferson doubted that wageworkers had the economic and political independence needed to sustain a republican polity.

Jefferson therefore set his democratic vision of America in a society of independent yeoman farm families. "Those who labor in the earth are the chosen people of God," he wrote in *Notes on the State of Virginia* (1785). The grain and meat from their homesteads would feed European nations, which "would manufacture and send us in exchange our clothes and other comforts." Jefferson's notion of an international division of labor resembled that proposed by Scottish economist Adam Smith in *The Wealth of Nations* (1776).

Turmoil in Europe brought Jefferson's vision closer to reality. The French Revolution began in 1789; four years later, the First French Republic (1792–1804) went to war against a British-led coalition of monarchies. As fighting disrupted European farming, wheat prices

Two Visions of America

Thomas Jefferson (left) and Alexander Hamilton confront each other in these portraits, as they did in the political battles of the 1790s. Jefferson was pro-French, Hamilton pro-British. Jefferson favored farmers and artisans; Hamilton supported merchants and financiers. Jefferson believed in democracy and rule by legislative majorities; Hamilton argued for strong exec utives and judges. Still, in the contested presidential election of 1800, Hamilton (who detested candidate Aaron Burr) threw his support to Jefferson and secured the presidency for his longtime political foe.   The White House Historical Association (White House Collection). / Yale University Art Gallery/Art Resource, NY.

leaped from 5 to 8 shillings a bushel and remained high for twenty years, bringing substantial profits to Chesapeake and Middle Atlantic farmers. "Our farmers have never experienced such prosperity," remarked one observer. Simultaneously, a boom in the export of raw cotton, fueled by the invention of the cotton gin and the mechanization of cloth production in Britain, boosted the economies of Georgia and South Carolina. As Jefferson had hoped, European markets brought prosperity to American agriculture.

The French Revolution Divides Americans

American merchants profited even more handsomely from the European war. In 1793, President Washington issued a Proclamation of Neutrality, allowing U.S. citizens to trade with all belligerents. As neutral carriers, American merchant ships claimed a right to pass through Britain's naval blockade of French ports, and American firms quickly took over the lucrative sugar trade between France and its West Indian islands. Commercial earnings rose spectacularly, averaging $20 million annually in the 1790s — twice the value of cotton and tobacco exports. As the American merchant fleet increased from 355,000 tons in 1790 to 1.1 million tons in 1808, northern shipbuilders and merchants provided work for thousands of shipwrights, sailmakers, dockhands, and seamen. Carpenters, masons, and cabinetmakers in Boston, New York, and Philadelphia easily found work building warehouses and fashionable "Federal-style" town houses for newly affluent merchants. In Philadelphia, a European visitor reported, "a great number of private houses have marble steps to the street door, and in other respects are finished in a style of elegance."

Ideological Politics   As Americans profited from Europe's struggles, they argued passionately over its ideologies. Most Americans had welcomed the French Revolution of 1789 because it abolished feudalism and established a constitutional monarchy. The creation of the First French Republic was more controversial. Urban artisans applauded the end of the monarchy and embraced the democratic, socially egalitarian ideology of the radical Jacobins. Like the Jacobins, they formed political clubs and began to address one another as "citizen." However, Americans with strong religious beliefs condemned the new French government for closing Christian churches and promoting a rational religion based on "natural morality." Fearing social revolution at home, wealthy Americans condemned Robespierre and his vengeance-minded followers for executing King Louis XVI and 3,000 aristocrats (see Voices from Abroad, "Peter Porcupine Attacks Pro-French Americans," p. 209).

Their fears were well founded, because Hamilton's economic policies quickly sparked a domestic insurgency. In 1794, western Pennsylvania farmers, already angered by the state's conservative fiscal policies, mounted the so-called Whiskey Rebellion to protest Hamilton's excise tax on spirits. This tax had cut demand for the corn whiskey the farmers distilled and bartered for eastern manufactures. Like the Sons of Liberty in 1765 and the Shaysites in 1786, the Whiskey Rebels assailed the tax collectors who sent the farmers' hard-earned money to a distant government. But the protesters also waved banners proclaiming the French revolutionary slogan "Liberty, Equality, Fraternity!" To deter popular rebellion and uphold national authority, President Washington raised an army of 12,000 troops and dispersed the Whiskey Rebels.

William Cobbett
Peter Porcupine Attacks Pro-French Americans

The Democratic Republican followers of Thomas Jefferson declared that "he who is an enemy to the French Revolution, cannot be a firm republican." William Cobbett, a British journalist who settled in Philadelphia and wrote under the pen name "Peter Porcupine," contested this definition of republicanism. A strong supporter of the Federalist Party, Cobbett regularly attacked its Republican opponents in caustic and widely read pamphlets and newspaper articles. Here he evokes the horrors of the Terror in France, which took the lives of thousands of aristocrats and their supporters, and warns that the triumph of doctrinaire republicans would bring the same fate to the United States.

France is a republic, and the decrees of the Legislators were necessary to maintain it a republic. This word outweighs, in the estimation of some persons (I wish I could say they were few in number), all the horrors that have been and that can be committed in that country. One of these modern republicans will tell you that he does not deny that hundreds of thousands of innocent persons have been murdered in France; that the people have neither religion nor morals; that all the ties of nature are rent asunder; . . . that its riches, along with millions of the best of the people, are gone to enrich and aggrandize its enemies; that its commerce, its manufactures, its sciences, its arts, and its honour, are no more; but at the end of all this, he will tell you that it must be happy, because it is a republic. I have heard more than one of these republican zealots declare, that he would sooner see the last of the French exterminated, than see them adopt any other form of government. Such a sentiment is characteristic of a mind locked up in a savage ignorance.

Shall we say that these things never can take place among us? . . . We are not what we were before the French revolution. Political projectors from every corner of Europe, troublers of society of every description, from the whining philosophical hypocrite to the daring rebel, and more daring blasphemer, have taken shelter in these States.

We have seen the guillotine toasted to three times three cheers. . . . And what would the reader say, were I to tell him of a Member of Congress, who wished to see one of these murderous machines employed for lopping off the heads of the French, permanent in the State-house yard of the city of Philadelphia?

If these men of blood had succeeded in plunging us into a war; if they had once got the sword into their hands, they would have mowed us down like stubble. The word Aristocrat would have been employed to as good account here, as ever it had been in France. We might, ere this, have seen our places of worship turned into stables; we might have seen the banks of the Delaware, like those of the Loire, covered with human carcasses, and its waters tinged with

blood: ere this we might have seen our parents butchered, and even the head of our admired and beloved President rolling on a scaffold.

I know the reader will start back with horror. His heart will tell him that it is impossible. But, once more, let him look at the example before us. The attacks on the character and conduct of the aged Washington, have been as bold, if not bolder, than those which led to the downfall of the unfortunate French Monarch [Louis XVI, executed in 1793]. Can it then be imagined, that, had they possessed the power, they wanted the will to dip their hands in his blood?

Source: William Cobbett, *Peter Porcupine in America*, ed. David A. Wilson (Ithaca: Cornell University Press, 1994), 150–154.

ANALYZING THE EVIDENCE

- **What horrors does Cobbett describe? Why does he believe a similar fate could befall the United States? What has happened to the republicanism embraced by Americans in 1776?**

- **By 1796, Americans had a long tradition of political violence, including Indian massacres, bitter fighting among Patriots and Loyalists during the American Revolution, and Shays's Rebellion. Do those episodes give credence to Cobbett's warning that a bloodbath might "take place among us"? Or was he exaggerating the danger?**

- **Why were Americans generally able to resolve their political disputes peacefully, while the French took up arms to do so? If 100,000 diehard Loyalists had not fled the United States, would the outcome have been different?**

Federalist Gentry

A prominent New England Federalist, Oliver Ellsworth served as chief justice of the United States from 1796 to 1800. His wife, Abigail Wolcott Ellsworth, was a member of a well-connected Connecticut family. In 1792, portraitist Ralph Earl captured the aspirations of the Ellsworths by painting them in fine clothes and prominently displaying their mansion (it can be seen through the window). Like other Federalists who tried to reconcile their wealth and social authority with republican values, Ellsworth dressed with restraint and his manners, remarked Timothy Dwight, were "wholly destitute of haughtiness and arrogance."   Wadsworth Athenaeum/Art Resource, NY.

Jay's Treaty Britain's maritime strategy intensified political divisions in America. Beginning in late 1793, the British navy seized 250 American ships carrying French sugar and other goods. Hoping to protect merchant property through diplomacy, Washington dispatched John Jay to Britain. But Jay returned with a controversial treaty that ignored the American claim that "free ships make free goods" and accepted Britain's right to stop neutral ships. The treaty also required the U.S. government to make "full and complete compensation" to British merchants for pre–Revolutionary War debts owed by American citizens. In return, the agreement allowed Americans to submit claims for illegal seizures and required the British to remove their troops and Indian agents from the Northwest Territory. Despite Republican charges that Jay's Treaty was too conciliatory, the Senate ratified it in 1795, but only by the two-thirds majority required by the Constitution. As long as the Federalists were in power, the United States would have a pro-British foreign policy.

The Rise of Political Parties

The appearance of Federalists and Republicans marked a new stage in American politics — what historians call the First Party System. Colonial legislatures had factions based on family, ethnicity, or region, but they did not have organized political parties. Nor did the new state and national constitutions make any provision for political societies. Indeed, most Americans believed that parties were dangerous because they looked out for themselves rather than serving the public interest. Thus, Senator Pierce Butler of South Carolina criticized his congressional colleagues as "men scrambling for partial advantage, State interests, and, in short, a train of narrow, impolitic measures."

But pursuit of the public interest collapsed in the face of sharp conflicts over Hamilton's fiscal policies. Most merchants and creditors supported the Federalist party, as did wheat-exporting slaveholders in the Tidewater districts of the Chesapeake. The emerging Republican coalition was more diverse. It included southern tobacco and rice planters, debt-conscious western farmers, Germans and Scots-Irish in the southern backcountry, and subsistence farmers in the Northeast.

Party identity crystallized in 1796. To prepare for the presidential election, Federalist and Republican leaders called caucuses in Congress and conventions in the states. They mobilized popular support by organizing public festivals and processions: The Federalists held banquets in February to celebrate Washington's birthday, and the Republicans marched through the streets on July 4 to honor the Declaration of Independence.

In the election, voters gave Federalists a majority in Congress and made John Adams president. Adams continued Hamilton's pro-British foreign policy and strongly criticized French seizures of American merchant ships. When the French foreign minister Talleyrand solicited a loan and a bribe from American diplomats to stop the seizures, Adams charged that Talleyrand's agents, whom he dubbed X, Y, and Z, had insulted America's honor. In response to the XYZ Affair, Congress cut off trade with France in 1798 and authorized American privateering (licensing private ships to seize French vessels). This undeclared maritime war cut off American trade with the French West Indies and resulted in the capture of nearly 200 French and American merchant vessels.

Constitutional Crisis and the "Revolution of 1800"

Ominously, the Federalists' attacks against the French Republic prompted domestic protests and governmental repression. When Republican-minded immigrants from Ireland vehemently attacked Adams's policies, a Federalist pamphleteer responded in kind: "Were I president, I would hang them for otherwise they would murder me." To silence the critics, the Federalists enacted three coercive laws limiting individual rights and threatening the fledgling party system. The Naturalization Act lengthened the residency requirement for American citizenship from five to fourteen years, the Alien Act authorized the deportation of foreigners, and the Sedition Act prohibited the publication of insults or malicious attacks on the president or members of Congress. "He that is not for us is against us," thundered the Federalist *Gazette of the United States*. Using the Sedition Act, Federalist prosecutors arrested more than twenty Republican newspaper editors and politicians, accused them of sedition, and convicted and jailed a number of them.

This repression sparked a constitutional crisis. Republicans charged that the Sedition Act violated the First Amendment's prohibition against "abridging the freedom of speech, or of the press." However, they did not appeal to the Supreme Court because the Court's power to review congressional legislation was uncertain and because most of the justices were Federalists. Instead, Madison and Jefferson looked to the state legislatures. At their urging, the Kentucky and Virginia legislatures issued resolutions in 1798 declaring the Alien and Sedition Acts to be "unauthoritative, void, and of no force." The resolutions set forth a **states' rights** interpretation of the Constitution, asserting that the states had a "right to judge" the legitimacy of national laws.

The conflict over the Sedition Act set the stage for the presidential election of 1800. Jefferson, once opposed on principle to political parties, now asserted that they

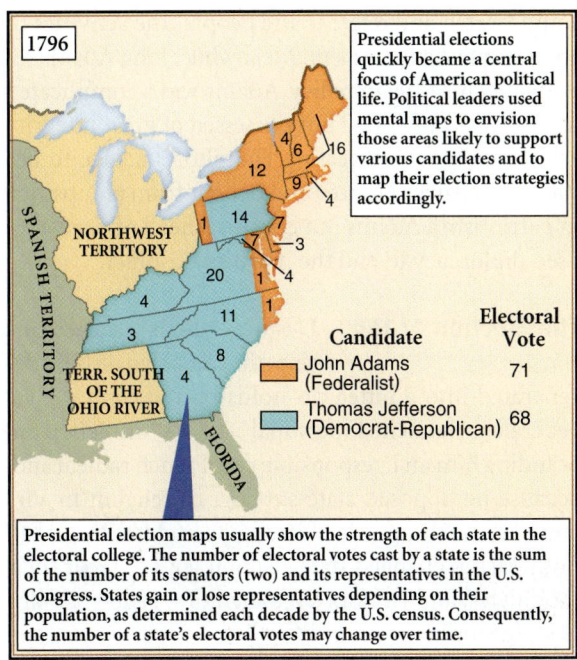

Presidential elections quickly became a central focus of American political life. Political leaders used mental maps to envision those areas likely to support various candidates and to map their election strategies accordingly.

Candidate	Electoral Vote
John Adams (Federalist)	71
Thomas Jefferson (Democrat-Republican)	68

Presidential election maps usually show the strength of each state in the electoral college. The number of electoral votes cast by a state is the sum of the number of its senators (two) and its representatives in the U.S. Congress. States gain or lose representatives depending on their population, as determined each decade by the U.S. census. Consequently, the number of a state's electoral votes may change over time.

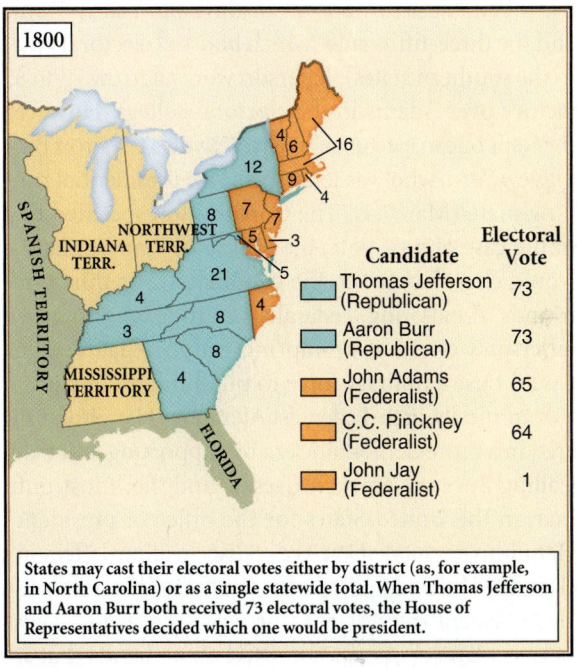

Candidate	Electoral Vote
Thomas Jefferson (Republican)	73
Aaron Burr (Republican)	73
John Adams (Federalist)	65
C.C. Pinckney (Federalist)	64
John Jay (Federalist)	1

States may cast their electoral votes either by district (as, for example, in North Carolina) or as a single statewide total. When Thomas Jefferson and Aaron Burr both received 73 electoral votes, the House of Representatives decided which one would be president.

MAP 7.1

The Presidential Elections of 1796 and 1800

Both elections pitted Federalist John Adams of Massachusetts against Republican Thomas Jefferson of Virginia, and both saw voters split along regional lines. Adams carried every New England state and, reflecting Federalist strength in maritime and commercial areas, the eastern districts of the Middle Atlantic states; Jefferson won most of the agricultural-based states of the south and west (Kentucky and Tennessee). New York was the pivotal swing state. It gave its twelve electoral votes to Adams in 1796 and, thanks to the presence of Aaron Burr on the Republican ticket, bestowed them on Jefferson in 1800.

could "watch and relate to the people" the activities of an oppressive government. Meanwhile, John Adams re-evaluated his foreign policy. Adams was a complicated man—easily offended but possessed of great integrity and a strong will. Rejecting Hamilton's advice to declare war against France (and benefit from an upsurge in patriotism), Adams put country ahead of party and used diplomacy to end the maritime conflict.

The Election of 1800 Despite Adams's statesmanship, the campaign of 1800 degenerated into a bitter, no-holds-barred contest. The Federalists launched personal attacks on Jefferson, branding him an irresponsible pro-French radical and, because he opposed state support of religion in Virginia, "the arch-apostle of irreligion and free thought." Both parties changed state election laws to favor their candidates, and rumors circulated of a Federalist plot to stage a military coup.

The election did not end these worries. Thanks to a low Federalist turnout in Virginia and Pennsylvania and the three-fifths rule (which boosted electoral votes in the southern states), Jefferson won a narrow 73 to 65 victory over Adams in the electoral college. However, the Republican electors also gave 73 votes to Aaron Burr of New York, who was Jefferson's vice presidential running mate (Map 7.1). The Constitution specified that in the case of a tie vote, the House of Representatives would choose between the candidates. For thirty-five rounds of balloting, Federalists in the House blocked Jefferson's election, prompting rumors that Virginia would raise a military force to put him into office.

Ironically, arch-Federalist Alexander Hamilton ushered in a more democratic era by supporting Jefferson. Calling Burr an "embryo Caesar" and the "most unfit man in the United States for the office of president," Hamilton persuaded key Federalists to allow Jefferson's election. The Federalists' concern for political stability also played a role. As Senator James Bayard of Delaware explained, "It was admitted on all hands that we must risk the Constitution and a Civil War or take Mr. Jefferson."

Jefferson called the election the "Revolution of 1800," and so it was. The bloodless transfer of power showed that popularly elected governments could be changed in an orderly way, even in times of bitter partisan conflict. In his inaugural address in 1801, Jefferson praised this achievement, declaring, "We are all Republicans, we are all Federalists." Defying the predictions (and hopes) of European conservatives, the American republican experiment of 1776 had survived a quarter century of economic and political turmoil.

- What was Hamilton's vision of the future? What policies did he implement to achieve it? How was Jefferson's vision different?

- What were the consequences of the French Revolution in American life and politics?

The Westward Movement and the Jeffersonian Revolution

The United States "is a country in flux," a visiting French aristocrat observed in 1799, and "that which is true today as regards its population, its establishments, its prices, its commerce will not be true six months from now." Indeed, the American republic was beginning a period of dynamic expansion, much of it to the west. Between 1790 and 1810, farm families settled as much land as they had during the entire colonial period. George Washington, himself a speculator in western lands, noted approvingly that the Sons of Liberty were quickly becoming "the lords and proprietors of a vast tract of continent." And the *New-York Evening Post* declared: "It belongs of right to the United States to regulate the future destiny of North America."

The Expanding Republic and Native American Resistance

In the Treaty of Paris of 1783, Great Britain gave up its claims to the trans-Appalachian region and, said one British diplomat, left the Indian nations "to the care of their [American] neighbours." *Care* was hardly the right word: Many white Americans wanted to destroy native communities. "Cut up every Indian Cornfield and burn every Indian town," proclaimed Congressman William Henry Drayton of South Carolina, so that their "nation be extirpated and the lands become the property of the public." Other leaders, including Henry Knox, Washington's first secretary of war, favored assimilating native peoples into Euro-American society. Knox proposed the division of tribal lands among individual Indian families, who would become citizens of the various states.

Conflict over Land Rights As in the past, the major struggle between natives and Europeans centered on land rights. Invoking the Paris treaty and regarding Britain's Indian allies as conquered peoples, the U.S. government asserted both sovereignty over and ownership of the trans-Appalachian west. Indian nations rejected both claims, pointing out they had not been conquered and had not signed the Paris treaty. "Our lands are our life and our breath," declared Creek chief Hallowing King, "if we part with them, we part with our blood." Brushing aside such objections and threatening military action, U.S. commissioners forced the pro-British Iroquois peoples—Mohawks, Onondagas, Cayugas, and Senecas—to cede huge tracts in New York and Pennsylvania in the Treaty of Fort Stanwix (1784). New York land speculators used liquor and bribes to take a million more acres, confining the once powerful Iroquois to reservations—essentially colonies of subordinate peoples.

American negotiators used similar tactics to grab western lands. In 1785, they persuaded the Chippewas, Delawares, Ottawas, and Wyandots to sign treaties giving away most of the future state of Ohio. The tribes quickly repudiated the agreements, justifiably claiming they were made under duress. To defend their lands, they joined with the Shawnee, Miami, and Potawatomi peoples in the Western Confederacy. Led by Miami chief Little Turtle, confederacy warriors crushed American

expeditionary forces sent by President Washington in 1790 and 1791.

Fearing an alliance between the Western Confederacy and the British in Canada, Washington doubled the size of the U.S. Army and ordered General "Mad Anthony" Wayne to lead a new expedition. In August 1794, Wayne defeated the Confederacy in the Battle of Fallen Timbers (near present-day Toledo, Ohio). However, continuing Indian resistance forced a compromise. In the Treaty of Greenville (1795), American negotiators acknowledged Indian ownership of the land and, in return for various payments, the Western Confederacy ceded most of Ohio (Map 7.2). The Indian peoples also agreed to accept American sovereignty, placing themselves "under the protection of the United States, and no other Power whatever." These American advances caused Britain to agree, in Jay's Treaty (1795), to reduce its trade and military aid to Indians in the trans-Appalachian region.

The Greenville Treaty sparked a wave of white migration. By 1805, the new state of Ohio had more than 100,000 residents. Thousands more farm families moved into the future states of Indiana and Illinois, sparking new conflicts with native peoples over land

MAP 7.2

Indian Cessions and State Formation, 1776–1840

By virtue of the Treaty of Paris (1783) with Britain, the United States claimed sovereignty over the entire trans-Appalachian west. The Western Confederacy contested this claim, but the U.S. government upheld it with military force. By 1840, armed diplomacy had forced most Native American peoples to move west of the Mississippi River. White settlers occupied their lands, formed territorial governments, and eventually entered the Union as members of separate—and equal—states. By 1860, the trans-Appalachian region constituted an important economic and political force in American national life.

Treaty Negotiations at Greenville, 1795

In 1785, Indian tribes in the Northwest Territory formed the Western Confederacy to prevent white settlement north of the Ohio River. After Indian triumphs in battles in the early 1790s, an American victory at the Battle of Fallen Timbers (1794) and the subsequent Treaty of Greenville (1795) opened up the region for white farmers. However, the treaty recognized many Indian rights because it was negotiated between relative equals on the battlefield. The artist suggests this equality: Notice the height and stately bearing of the Indian leaders—ninety of whom signed the document—and their placement slightly in front of the General Anthony Wayne and his officers.   Unknown, *Treaty of Greenville*, n.d., Chicago Historical Society.

and hunting rights. Declared one Delaware Indian: "The Elks are our horses, the buffaloes are our cows, the deer are our sheep, & the whites shan't have them."

Assimilation Rejected To prevent such conflicts, the U.S. government had encouraged Native Americans to assimilate into white society. The goal, as one Kentucky Protestant minister put it, was to make the Indian "a farmer, a citizen of the United States, and a Christian." Most Indians rejected wholesale assimilation; even those who joined Christian churches retained many ancestral values and religious beliefs. To think of themselves as individuals or members of a nuclear family, as white Americans were demanding, meant

repudiating the clan, the very essence of Indian life. To preserve "the old Indian way," many native communities expelled white missionaries and forced Christianized Indians to participate in tribal rites. As a Munsee prophet declared, "There are two ways to God, one for the whites and one for the Indians."

A few Indian leaders sought a middle path in which new beliefs overlapped with old practices. Among the Senecas, the prophet Handsome Lake encouraged traditional animistic rituals that gave thanks to the sun, the earth, water, plants, and animals. But he included Christian elements in his teachings—the concepts of heaven and hell, and an emphasis on personal morality—to deter his followers from alcohol, gambling, and witchcraft. Handsome Lake's teachings divided the Senecas into hostile factions. Led by Chief Red Jacket, traditionalists condemned European culture as evil and demanded a complete return to ancestral ways.

Most Indians also rejected the efforts of American missionaries to turn warriors into farmers and women into domestic helpmates. Among eastern woodland peoples, women grew corn, beans, and squash—the mainstays of the Indians' diet—and land cultivation rights passed through the female line. Consequently, women exercised considerable political influence, which they were eager to retain. Nor were Indian men interested in becoming farmers. When war raiding and hunting were no longer possible, they turned to grazing cattle and sheep.

Migration and the Changing Farm Economy

Native American resistance slowed the advance of white settlers but did not stop it. Nothing "short of a Chinese Wall, or a line of Troops," Washington declared, "will restrain . . . the Incroachment of Settlers, upon the In-dian Territory." During the 1790s, two great streams of migrants moved out of the southern states (Map 7.3).

Southern Migrants | One stream, composed primarily of white tenant farmers and struggling yeomen families, flocked through the Cumberland Gap into Kentucky and Tennessee. "Boundless settlements open a door for our citizens to run off and leave us," a worried Maryland landlord lamented, "depreciating all our landed property and disabling us from paying taxes." In fact, many migrants were fleeing from this planter-controlled society. They wanted more freedom and hoped to prosper by growing cotton and hemp, which were in great demand.

Many settlers in Kentucky and Tennessee lacked ready cash to buy land. Like the North Carolina Regulators in the 1770s, poorer migrants claimed a customary right to occupy "back waste vacant Lands" sufficient "to provide a subsistence to themselves and their Posterity." Virginia legislators, who administered the Kentucky Territory, had a more elitist vision. Although they allowed poor settlers to buy up to 1,400 acres of land at reduced prices, they sold or granted huge tracts of

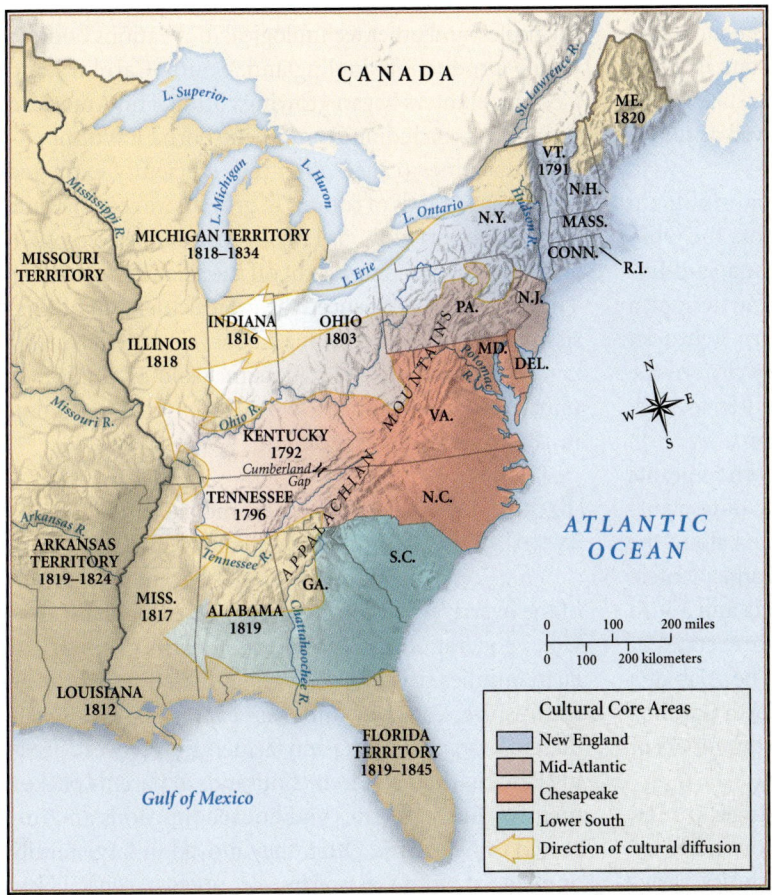

MAP 7.3

Regional Cultures Move West, 1790–1820

By 1790, four core cultures had developed in the long-settled states along the Atlantic seaboard. Between 1790 and 1820, migrants from these four regions carried their cultures into the trans-Appalachian west. New England customs and institutions were a dominant influence in upstate New York and along the Great Lakes, while the Lower South's hierarchical system of slavery and heavy concentration of African Americans shaped the character of the new states along the Gulf of Mexico. The pattern of cultural diffusion was more complex in the Ohio and Tennessee river valleys, which were settled by migrants from various core regions.

An Indian Log House in Georgia, 1791

The Indian peoples of the southeastern United States—the Cherokees, Creeks, Choctaws, and Chickasaws—quickly adopted European practices that fit easily into their relatively settled, agricultural-based way of life. This sturdy Creek log cabin was based on a Scots-Irish or German design and sat adjacent to the family's cornfields, visible in the background.   Library of Congress Prints and Photographs Division.

100,000 acres to twenty-one groups of speculators and leading men. When Kentucky became a state in 1792, this landed elite owned one-fourth of the state, while half the white men owned no land and lived as quasi-legal squatters or tenant farmers.

Widespread landlessness—and opposition to slavery—prompted a new migration across the Ohio River into the future states of Ohio, Indiana, and Illinois. In a free community, thought Peter Cartwright, a Methodist lay preacher from southwestern Kentucky who moved to Illinois, "I would be entirely clear of the evil of slavery . . . [and] could raise my children to work where work was not thought a degradation."

Meanwhile, a second stream of southern migrants from the Carolinas, composed of slave-owning planters and enslaved African Americans, moved along the coastal plain toward the Gulf of Mexico. Some planters set up new estates in the interior of Georgia and South Carolina, while others moved into the future states of Alabama, Mississippi, and Louisiana. "The Alabama Feaver rages here with great violence," a North Carolina planter remarked, "and has carried off vast numbers of our Citizens."

Cotton was the key to this migratory surge. Around 1750, the demand for raw wool and cotton increased dramatically as water-powered spinning jennies, weav-ing mules, and other technological innovations boosted textile production in England. South Carolina and Georgia planters began growing cotton, and American inventors—including Connecticut-born Eli Whitney—built machines (called gins) that efficiently extracted seeds from strands of cotton. To grow more cotton, white planters imported about 115,000 Africans between 1776 and 1808, when Congress cut off the Atlantic slave trade. The cotton boom financed the rapid settlement of Mississippi and Alabama—in a single year, a government land office in Huntsville, Alabama, sold $7 million of uncleared land—and the two states entered the Union in 1817 and 1819, respectively.

Exodus from New England   As southerners moved across the Appalachians and along the Gulf Coast, a third stream of migrants flowed out of the overcrowded communities of New England. Previous generations of Massachusetts and Connecticut farm families had moved north and east, settling New Hampshire, Vermont, and Maine. Now, in a vast self-directed surge, New England farmers moved west. Seeking land for their children, thousands of parents packed their wagons with tools and household goods and migrated to New York. Often they moved in large family or religious groups, as one traveler noted in central New

York: "The town of Herkimer is entirely populated by families come from Connecticut. We stayed at Mr. Snow's who came from New London with about ten male and female cousins." By 1820, almost 800,000 New Englanders lived in a string of settlements stretching from Albany to Buffalo, and many others had traveled on to Ohio and Indiana. Soon, much of the Northwest Territory consisted of New England communities that had moved inland.

In New York, as in Kentucky, well-connected speculators snapped up much of the best land. In the 1780s, financier Robert Morris acquired 1.3 million acres of central New York. The Wadsworth family bought thousands of acres in the Genesee region, hoping to re-create the leasehold manorial system of the Hudson River Valley. To attract tenants, the Wadsworths leased farms rent-free for the first seven years, after which they charged rents. Imbued with the "homestead" ethic, many New England families preferred to buy farms. They signed contracts with the Holland Land Company, a Dutch-owned syndicate of speculators, which allowed settlers to pay for their farms as they worked them.

Innovation on Eastern Farms The new farm economy in New York, Ohio, and Kentucky forced major changes in eastern agriculture. Unable to compete with lower-priced western grains, farmers in New England switched to potatoes, which were high yielding and nutritious. To make up for the labor of sons and daughters who had moved inland, Middle Atlantic farmers bought more efficient farm equipment. They replaced metal-tipped wooden plows with cast-iron models that dug deeper and required a single yoke of oxen instead of two. Such changes in crop mix and technology kept production high.

Easterners also adopted the progressive farming methods touted by British agricultural reformers. "Improvers" in Pennsylvania doubled their average yield per acre by rotating their crops and planting nitrogen-rich clover to offset nutrient-hungry wheat and corn. Yeomen farmers diversified production by raising sheep and selling the wool to textile manufacturers. Many farmers adopted a year-round planting cycle, sowing corn in the spring for animal fodder and then planting winter wheat in September for market sale. Women and girls milked the family cows and made butter and cheese to sell in the growing towns and cities.

Whether hacking fields out of western forests or carting manure to replenish eastern soils, farmers now worked harder and longer, but their increased productivity brought them a better standard of living. Westward migration—the settlement and exploitation of Indian lands—boosted the farming economy throughout the country.

The Jeffersonian Presidency

From 1801 to 1825, three Republicans from Virginia—Thomas Jefferson, James Madison, and James Monroe—each served two terms as president. Supported by farmers in the South and West and strong Republican majorities in Congress, this "Virginia Dynasty" completed what Jefferson had called the Revolution of 1800. It reversed many Federalist policies and actively supported westward expansion.

When Jefferson took office in 1801, he inherited an old international conflict. Beginning in the 1780s, the Barbary States of North Africa had raided merchant ships in the Mediterranean, and like many European nations, the United States had paid an annual bribe to protect its vessels. Initially Jefferson refused to pay this "tribute" and ordered the U.S. Navy to attack the pirates' home ports. However, to avoid an all-out war, which would have increased taxes and the national debt, Jefferson agreed to pay tribute at a lower rate.

At home, Jefferson inherited a national judiciary filled with Federalist appointees, including the formidable John Marshall of Virginia, the new chief justice of the Supreme Court. To add more Federalist judges, the outgoing Federalist Congress had passed the Judiciary Act of 1801. The act created sixteen new judgeships and various other positions, which President Adams filled at the last moment with "midnight appointees." The Federalists "have retired into the judiciary as a stronghold," Jefferson complained, "and from that battery all the works of Republicanism are to be beaten down and destroyed."

Jefferson's fears were soon realized. When Republican legislatures in Kentucky and Virginia repudiated the Alien and Sedition Acts as unconstitutional, Marshall declared that only the Supreme Court held the power of constitutional review. The Court claimed this authority for itself when James Madison, the new secretary of state, refused to deliver the commission of William Marbury, one of Adams's midnight appointees. In *Marbury v. Madison* (1803), Marshall asserted that Marbury had the right to the appointment but that the Court did not have the constitutional power to enforce it. In defining the Court's powers, Marshall voided a section of the Judiciary Act of 1789, in effect asserting the Court's authority to review congressional legislation and interpret the constitution. "It is emphatically the province and duty of the judicial department to

THE RESIDENCE OF DAVID TWINING. 1787.

Edward Hicks, *The Residence of David Twining*

Hicks painted this farm around 1845, as he remembered it from his childhood in the 1780s (he is the young lad standing next to Elizabeth Twining). By the 1780s, Bucks County in Pennsylvania had been settled by Europeans for more than a century. The county's prosperous Quaker farmers had built large and comfortable clapboard-covered houses, commodious barns, and solid fences. They hired workers, such as the black plowman in the painting, to cultivate their spacious well-manured fields and tend their cattle and sheep. Like many other rural easterners, they had become commercial farmers who sold their grain, meat, hides, and wool into the market economy.   Courtesy of the Abby Aldrich Rockefeller Folk Art Museum, Williamsburg, VA.

say what the law is," the chief justice declared, directly challenging the Republican view that the state legislatures had that power.

Ignoring this setback, Jefferson and the Republicans reversed other Federalist policies. When the Alien and Sedition Acts expired in 1801, Congress branded them unconstitutional political repression and refused to extend them. It also amended the Naturalization Act, restoring the original waiting period of five years for resident aliens to become citizens. Charging the Federalists with grossly expanding the national government's size and power, Jefferson had the Republican Congress

shrink it. He abolished all internal taxes, including the excise tax that had sparked the Whiskey Rebellion of 1794. To quiet Republican fears of a military coup, Jefferson reduced the size of the permanent army. He also secured repeal of the Judiciary Act of 1801, ousting forty of Adams's midnight appointees. Still, Jefferson retained competent Federalist officeholders, removing only 69 of 433 properly appointed Federalists during his eight years as president.

Jefferson likewise governed tactfully in fiscal affairs. He tolerated the economically important Bank of the United States, which he had once condemned as

America in the Middle East, 1804

To protect American merchants from capture and captivity in the Barbary States, President Thomas Jefferson sent in the U.S. Navy. This 1846 lithograph, created by the famous firm of Currier & Ives, depicts one of the three attacks on the North African port of Tripoli by Commodore Edward Preble in August 1804. As the USS *Constitution* and other large warships lob shells into the city, small American gunboats defend the fleet from Tripolitan gunboats. "Our loss in Killed & Wounded has been considerable," Preble reported, and "the Enemy must have suffered very much . . . among their Shipping and on shore."
The Granger Collection, New York.

unconstitutional. But he chose as his secretary of the treasury Albert Gallatin, a fiscal conservative who believed that the national debt was "an evil of the first magnitude." By limiting expenditures and using customs revenue to redeem government bonds, Gallatin reduced the debt from $83 million in 1801 to $45 million in 1812. With Jefferson and Gallatin at the helm, the nation's fiscal affairs were no longer run in the interests of northeastern creditors and merchants.

Jefferson and the West

Jefferson had long championed settlement of the West. He celebrated the yeoman farmer in *Notes on the State of Virginia*; wrote one of the Confederation's western land

ordinances; and supported Pinckney's Treaty (1795), the agreement between the United States and Spain that reopened the Mississippi River to American trade and allowed settlers to export crops via the Spanish-held port of New Orleans.

As president, Jefferson pursued policies that made it easier for farm families to acquire land. In 1796, a Federalist-dominated Congress had set the price of land in the national domain to $2 per acre; by the 1830s, Jefferson-inspired Republican Congresses had enacted more than three hundred laws that cut the cost to $1.25, eased credit terms, and allowed illegal squatters to buy their farms. Eventually, in the Homestead Act of 1862, Congress gave farmsteads to settlers for free.

Toussaint L'Ouverture, Haitian Revolutionary and Statesman

The American Revolution of 1776 constituted a victory for republicanism; the Haitian revolt of the 1790s represented a triumph of liberty over slavery and a demand for racial equality. After leading the black army that ousted French planters and British invaders from Haiti, Toussaint formed a constitutional government in 1801. A year later, when French troops invaded the island, he negotiated a treaty that halted Haitian resistance in exchange for a pledge that the French would not reinstate slavery. Subsequently, the French seized Toussaint and imprisoned him in France, where he died in 1803.   Snark/Art Resource, New York.

The Louisiana Purchase | International events challenged Jefferson's vision of westward expansion. In 1799, Napoleon Bonaparte seized power in France and sought to reestablish France's American empire. In 1801, he coerced Spain into signing a secret treaty that returned Louisiana to France and restricted American access to New Orleans, violating Pinckney's Treaty. Napoleon also launched an invasion to restore French rule in Haiti (then called Saint-Domingue), once the richest sugar colony in the Americas. After a massive slave revolt had convulsed the island in 1791, touching off years of civil war and Spanish and British invasions, black Haitians led by Toussaint L'Ouverture — himself a former slave-owning planter — seized control of the country in 1798. Now Napoleon wanted it back, to profit from its wealth and "to destroy the new Algiers that has been growing up in the middle of America."

Napoleon's actions in Haiti and Louisiana prompted Jefferson to question his pro-French foreign policy. "The day that France takes possession of New Orleans, we must marry ourselves to the British fleet and nation," the president warned, dispatching James Monroe to Britain to negotiate an alliance. To keep the Mississippi River open to western farmers, Jefferson told Robert Livingston, the American minister in Paris, to negotiate the purchase of New Orleans.

Jefferson's diplomacy yielded a magnificent prize: the entire territory of Louisiana. By 1802, the French invasion of Haiti was faltering in the face of disease and determined black resistance, a new war threatened in Europe, and Napoleon feared an American invasion of Louisiana. Acting with characteristic decisiveness, the French ruler offered to sell the entire territory of Louisiana for $15 million (about $500 million today). "We have lived long," Livingston remarked to Monroe as they concluded the Louisiana Purchase in 1803, "but this is the noblest work of our lives."

The Louisiana Purchase forced Jefferson to reconsider his strict interpretation of the Constitution. He had long believed that the national government possessed only the powers expressly delegated to it in the Constitution, but there was no provision for adding new territory. So Jefferson pragmatically accepted a loose interpretation of the Constitution and used its treaty-making powers to complete the deal with France. The new western lands, Jefferson wrote, would be "a means of tempting all our Indians on the East side of the Mississippi to remove to the West."

Secessionist Schemes | The acquisition of Louisiana brought new political problems. Some New England Federalists, fearing that western expansion would hurt their region and party, talked openly of leaving the Union and forming a confederacy of northeastern states. The secessionists won the support of Aaron Burr, the ambitious vice president. After Alexander Hamilton accused Burr of planning to destroy the Union, the two fought an illegal pistol duel that led to Hamilton's death.

This tragedy propelled Burr into another secessionist scheme, this time in the southwest. When his term as vice president ended in 1805, Burr moved west to avoid prosecution. There, he conspired with General James Wilkinson, the military governor of the Louisiana Territory, either to seize territory in New Spain or

A Mandan Village

This Mandan settlement in North Dakota, painted by George Catlin around 1837, resembled those in which the Lewis and Clark expedition spent the winter of 1804–1805. Note the palisade of logs that surrounds the village, as protection from the Sioux and other marauding Plains peoples, and the solidly built mud lodges that provided warm shelter from the bitter cold of winter. Smithsonian American Art Museum, Washington, D.C./Art Resource.

establish Louisiana as a separate nation. But Wilkinson, himself a Spanish spy and incipient traitor, betrayed Burr and arrested him. In a highly politicized trial presided over by Chief Justice John Marshall, the jury acquitted Burr of treason.

The Louisiana Purchase had increased party conflict and generated secessionist schemes in both New England and the southwest. Such sectional differences would continue, challenging Madison's argument in "Federalist No. 10" that a large and diverse republic was more stable than a small one.

Lewis and Clark Meet the Mandan and Sioux   A scientist as well as a statesman, Jefferson wanted information about Louisiana: its physical features, plant and animal life, and native peoples. He was also worried about intruders: The British-run Hudson's Bay Company and Northwest Company were actively trading for furs on the Upper Missouri River. So in 1804, Jefferson sent his personal secretary, Meriwether Lewis, to explore the region with William Clark, an army officer. From St. Louis, Lewis, Clark, and their party of American soldiers and frontiersmen traveled up the Missouri for 1,000 miles to the fortified, earth-lodge towns of the Mandan and Hidatsa peoples (near present-day Bismarck, North Dakota), where they spent the winter.

The Mandans lived primarily by horticulture, growing corn, beans, and squash. They had acquired horses by supplying food to nomadic Plains Indians and se-

cured guns, iron goods, and textiles by selling buffalo hides and dried meat to European traders. However, the Mandans (and neighboring Arikaras) had been hit hard by the smallpox epidemics that swept across the Great Plains in 1779–1781 and 1801–1802. Now they were threatened by Sioux peoples: Teton, Yanktonai, and Oglala. Originally, the Sioux had lived in the prairie and lake region of northern Minnesota. As their numbers rose and fish and game grew scarce, the Sioux moved westward, acquired horses, and hunted buffalo, living as nomads in portable skin tepees. The Sioux became ferocious fighters who tried to reduce the Mandans and other farming tribes to subject peoples. According to Lewis and Clark, they were the "pirates of the Missouri." Soon the Sioux would dominate the buffalo trade throughout the Upper Missouri region.

In the spring of 1805, Lewis and Clark began an epic 1,300-mile trek into unknown country. Their party now included Toussaint Charbonneau, a French Canadian fur trader, and his Shoshone wife, Sacagawea, who served as a guide and translator. After following the Missouri River to its source on the Idaho-Montana border, they crossed the Rocky Mountains, and—venturing far beyond the Louisiana Purchase—traveled down the Columbia River to the Pacific Ocean. Nearly everywhere, Indian peoples asked for guns so they could defend themselves from other armed tribes. In 1806, Lewis and Clark capped off their pathbreaking expedition by providing Jefferson with the first maps of the immense wilderness and a detailed account of its natural resources

MAP 7.4

U.S. Population Density in 1803 and the Louisiana Purchase

When the United States purchased Louisiana from France in 1803, much of the land to its east—the vast territory between the Appalachian Mountains and the Mississippi River—remained in Indian hands. The equally vast lands beyond the Mississippi were virtually unknown to Anglo-Americans, even after the epic explorations of Meriwether Lewis and William Clark, and Zebulon Pike. Still, President Jefferson predicted quite accurately that the huge Mississippi River Valley "from its fertility . . . will ere long yield half of our whole produce, and contain half of our whole population."

and inhabitants (Map 7.4). Their report prompted some Americans to envision a nation that would span the continent.

- Was there anything the Western Indian Confederacy could have done to limit white expansion and preserve Indian lands? Explain your position.

- Why did Jefferson support westward expansion? Why did eastern farm families leave their communities to go west? Were their reasons the same as Jefferson's?

The War of 1812 and the Transformation of Politics

The Napoleonic Wars that ravaged Europe after 1802 brought new attacks on American merchant ships. American leaders struggled desperately to protect the nation's commerce while avoiding war. When this effort finally failed, it sparked dramatic political changes that destroyed the Federalist Party and split the Republicans into National and Jeffersonian factions.

Conflict in the Atlantic and the West

As Napoleon conquered European countries, he cut off their commerce with Britain and seized American merchant ships that stopped in British ports. The British ministry responded with a naval blockade and seized American vessels carrying sugar and molasses from the French West Indies. The British navy also searched American merchant ships for British deserters and used these raids to replenish its crews, a practice known as impressment. Between 1802 and 1811, British naval officers impressed nearly 8,000 sailors, including many U.S. citizens. In 1807, American anger boiled over when a British warship attacked the U.S. Navy vessel *Chesapeake*, killing three, wounding eighteen, and seizing four alleged deserters. "Never since the battle of Lexington have I seen this country in such a state of exasperation as at present," Jefferson declared.

The Embargo of 1807 To protect American interests, Jefferson pursued a policy of peaceful coercion. Working closely with his secretary of state, James Madison, he devised the Embargo Act of 1807, which prohibited American ships from leaving their home ports until Britain and France stopped restricting U.S. trade. The embargo was a creative diplomatic measure, probably inspired by the boycotts of the 1760s and 1770s. But it overestimated the reliance of Britain and France on American shipping, and it underestimated the resistance of merchants, who feared the embargo would ruin them. "All is astonishment and alarm," exclaimed Virginia merchant Robert Gamble, "and God knows when the evil is to subside."

In fact, the embargo cut the American gross national product by 5 percent and weakened the entire economy. Exports plunged from $108 million in 1806 to $22 million in 1808, hurting farmers as well as merchants. "All was noise and bustle" in New York City before the embargo, one visitor remarked; afterward, everything was closed up as if "a malignant fever was raging in the place."

Despite popular discontent over the embargo, voters elected Republican James Madison to the presidency in 1808. A powerful advocate for the Constitution, the architect of the Bill of Rights, and a prominent congressman and party leader, Madison had served the nation well. But John Beckley, a loyal Republican, worried that Madison would be "too timid and indecisive as a statesman," and events proved him right. Acknowledging the embargo's failure, Madison replaced it with new economic restrictions, which also failed to protect American commerce. "The Devil himself could not tell which government, England or France, is the most wicked," an exasperated congressman declared.

Western War Hawks Republican congressmen from the West were certain that Britain was the primary offender. They pointed to its trade with Indians in the Ohio River Valley in violation of the Treaty of Paris and Jay's Treaty. Bolstered by British guns and supplies, the Shawnee war chief Tecumseh [*ta-KUM-sa*] revived the Western Confederacy in 1809. His brother, the prophet Tenskwatawa [*tens-QUA-ta-wa*], provided the confederacy with a powerful nativist ideology. He urged Indian peoples to shun Americans, "the children of the Evil Spirit . . . who have taken away your lands"; renounce alcohol; and return to traditional ways. The Shawnee leaders found their greatest support among Kickapoo, Potawatomi, Winnebago, Ottawa, and Chippewa warriors, westerners who lacked knowledge of the strength and numbers of the advancing Americans. They flocked to Tenskwatawa's holy village, Prophetstown, near the juncture of the Tippecanoe and Wabash rivers in the Indiana Territory.

As Tecumseh mobilized the western Indian peoples for war, William Henry Harrison, the governor of the Indiana territory, decided on a preemptive strike. In November 1811, when Tecumseh went south to seek support from the Chickasaws, Choctaws, and Creeks, Harrison took advantage of his absence and attacked Prophetstown. The governor's 1,000 troops and militiamen traded heavy casualties with the confederacy's warriors at the Battle of Tippecanoe and then destroyed the holy village.

With Britain assisting Indians in the western territories and seizing American ships in the Atlantic, Henry Clay of Kentucky, the new Speaker of the House of Representatives, and John C. Calhoun, a rising young congressman from South Carolina, pushed Madison toward war. Like other Republican "war hawks" from the West and South, they wanted to seize territory in British Canada and Spanish Florida. With national elections approaching, Madison issued an ultimatum to Britain. When Britain failed to respond quickly, the president asked Congress for a declaration of war. In June 1812, a sharply divided Senate voted 19 to 13 for war, and the House of Representatives concurred, 79 to 49.

The causes of the War of 1812 have been much debated. Officially, the United States went to war because Britain had violated its commercial rights as a neutral

Tenskwatawa, "The Prophet," 1830

Tenskwatawa added a spiritual dimension to Native American resistance by urging a holy war against the invading whites and calling for a return to sacred ancestral ways. His dress reflects his teachings: Note the animal-skin shirt and the heavily ornamented ears. However, some of Tenskwatawa's religious rituals reflected the influence of French Jesuits; he urged his followers to finger a sacred string of beads (such as those in his left hand) that were similar to the Catholic rosary, thereby "shaking hands with the Prophet." Whatever its origins, Tenskwatawa's message transcended the cultural differences among Indian peoples and helped his brother Tecumseh create a formidable political and military alliance.   Smithsonian American Art Museum, Washington, D.C./ Art Resource.

nation. But the Federalists in Congress who represented the New England and Middle Atlantic merchants voted against the war; and in the election of 1812, those regions cast their 89 electoral votes for the Federalist presidential candidate, De Witt Clinton of New York. Madison amassed most of his 128 electoral votes in the South and West, where voters and congressmen strongly supported the war. Many historians therefore argue that the conflict was actually "a western war with eastern labels" (see Comparing American Voices, "Factional Politics and the War of 1812," pp. 226–227).

The War of 1812

The War of 1812 was a near disaster for the United States, both militarily and politically. An invasion of British Canada in 1812 quickly ended in a retreat to Detroit. Nonetheless, the United States stayed on the offensive in the West. In 1813, American raiders burned the Canadian capital of York (present-day Toronto), Commodore Oliver Hazard Perry defeated a small British flotilla on Lake Erie, and General William Henry Harrison overcame a British and Indian force at the Battle of the Thames, taking the life of Tecumseh, now a British general.

In the East, political divisions prevented a major invasion of Canada. New England Federalists opposed the war and prohibited their states' militias from attacking Canada. Boston merchants and banks refused to lend money to the federal government, making the war difficult to finance. In Congress, Daniel Webster, a dynamic young politician from New Hampshire, led Federalists opposed to higher tariffs and national conscription of state militiamen.

Gradually, the tide of battle turned in Britain's favor. When the war began, American privateers had captured scores of British merchant vessels, but the Royal Navy soon seized the initiative. By 1813, a flotilla of Brit-

Counting Scalps

Effective propaganda usually contains a grain of truth, in this case the Indian warriors' practice of scalping their wartime victims. Entitled "A scene on the frontiers as practiced by the humane British and their worthy allies!", this cartoon by Philadelphia artist William Charles accuses the British of paying Indians to kill — and then mutilate — American soldiers. "Bring me the scalps, and the King our master will reward you," says the British officer in the cartoon. The verse at the bottom urges "Columbia's Sons" to press forward their attacks; otherwise, "The Savage Indian with his Scalping knife, / Or Tomahawk may seek to take your life."   Library of Congress.

ish warships was disrupting American commerce and threatening seaports along the Atlantic coast. In 1814, a British fleet sailed up the Chesapeake Bay, and troops stormed ashore to attack Washington City. Retaliating for the destruction of York, the invaders burned the U.S. Capitol and government buildings. After two years of fighting, the United States was stalemated along the Canadian frontier, on the defensive in the Atlantic, and its new capital city lay in ruins. The only U.S. victories came in the Southwest. There, a rugged slave-owning planter named Andrew Jackson and a force of Tennessee militiamen defeated British- and Spanish-supported Creek Indians in the Battle of Horseshoe Bend (1814) and forced the Indians to cede 23 million acres of land (Map 7.5).

Federalists Oppose the War | American military setbacks increased opposition to the war in New England. In 1814, Massachusetts Federalists called for a convention "to lay the foundation for a radical reform in the National Compact." When New England Federalists met in Hartford, Connecticut, some delegates proposed secession, but most wanted to revise the Constitution. To end Virginia's domination of the presidency, the Hartford Convention proposed a constitutional amendment limiting the office to a single four-year term and rotating it among citizens from different states. The convention also suggested amendments restricting commercial embargoes to sixty days and requiring a two-thirds majority in Congress to declare war, prohibit trade, or admit a new state to the Union.

As a minority party in Congress and the nation, the Federalists could prevail only if the war continued to go badly — a very real prospect. The war had cost $88 million, raising the national debt to $127 million. And now, as Albert Gallatin warned Henry Clay in May 1814, Britain's triumph over Napoleon in Europe meant that a "well organized and large army is [now ready] . . . to act immediately against us." When an attack from Canada came in the late summer of 1814, only an American naval victory on Lake Champlain stopped the British from marching down the Hudson River Valley. A few months later, thousands of seasoned British troops landed outside New Orleans, threatening

Thus I have given you, I think, the Substance of the Arguments o... both sides of that great and important Questio...

Factional Politics and the War of 1812

In the quarter-century following the ratification of the U.S. Constitution, American leaders had to deal with the wars of the French Revolution and Napoleon. These European conflicts posed two dangers to the United States. First, the naval blockades imposed by the British and the French hurt American commerce and prompted calls for a military response. Second, European ideological and political struggles intensified party conflicts in the United States. On three occasions, the American republic faced danger from the combination of an external military threat and internal political turmoil. In 1798, the Federalist administration of John Adams almost went to war with France to help American merchants and to undermine the Republican Party. In 1807, Thomas Jefferson's embargo on American commerce shocked Federalists and sharply increased political tensions. And, as the following selections show, these political divisions during the War of 1812 threatened the very existence of the American republic.

George Washington
Farewell Address, 1796

Washington's support for Alexander Hamilton's economic policies promoted political factionalism. Ignoring his own role in creating that political divide, Washington condemned factionalism and, as his presidency proceeded, tried to stand above party conflicts. In his farewell address, Washington warned Americans to stand united and avoid the "Spirit of Party."

A solicitude for your welfare [prompts me] . . . to offer . . . the disinterested warnings of a parting friend, who can possibly have no personal motive to bias his counsels. . . .

The Unity of Government which constitutes you one people . . . is a main Pillar in the Edifice of your real independence . . . your tranquility at home; your peace abroad. . . . But it is easy to foresee, that, from different causes, and from different quarters, much pains will be taken, many artifices employed, to weaken in your minds the conviction of this truth. . . .

I have already intimated to you the danger of parties in the State, with particular reference to founding them on geographical discriminations. Let me now take a more comprehensive view, and warn you, in the most solemn manner, against the baneful effects of the Spirit of Party, generally.

This spirit, unfortunately, is inseparable from our nature, having its root in the strongest passions of the human mind. It exists under different shapes, in all governments, more or less stifled, controlled or repressed; but in those of the popular form, it is seen in its greatest rankness, and is truly their worst enemy.

The alternate dominion of one faction over another, sharpened by the spirit of revenge . . . , is itself a frightful despotism; but this leads at length to a more formal and permanent despotism.

Source: James D. Richardson, ed., *A Compilation of the Messages and Papers of the Presidents, 1789–1896* (Washington, D.C.: U.S. Government Printing Office, 1896), 1: 213–215.

Josiah Quincy et al.
Federalists Protest "Mr. Madison's War"

Washington's warning was to no avail. The parties – and the nation – divided sharply over the War of 1812. As Congress debated the issue of going to war against Great Britain, Josiah Quincy and other antiwar Federalist congressmen published a manifesto that questioned the justifications for the war offered by President Madison and the military strategy proposed by Republican war hawks.

How will war upon the land [an invasion of British Canada] protect commerce upon the ocean? What balm has Canada for wounded honor? How are our mariners benefited by a war which exposes those who are free, without promising release to those who are impressed?

But it is said that war is demanded by honor. Is national honor a principle which thirsts after vengeance, and is appeased only by blood? . . . If honor demands a war with England, what opiate lulls that honor to sleep over the wrongs done us by France? On land, robberies, seizures, imprisonments, by French authority; at sea, pillage, sinkings, burnings, under French orders. These are notorious. Are they unfelt because they are French? . . .

There is . . . a headlong rushing into difficulties, with little calculation about the means, and little concern about the consequences. With a navy comparatively [small], we are about to enter into the lists against the greatest marine [power] on the globe. With a commerce unprotected and spread over every ocean, we propose to make a profit by privateering, and for this endanger the wealth of which we are honest proprietors. An invasion is threatened of the [British colonies in Canada, but Britain] . . . without putting a new ship into commission, or taking another soldier into pay, can spread alarm or desolation along the extensive range of our seaboard. . . .

What are the United States to gain by this war? Will the gratification of some privateersmen compensate the nation for that sweep of our legitimate commerce by the extended marine of our enemy which this desperate act invites? Will Canada compensate the Middle states for [the loss of] New York; or the Western states for [the loss of] New Orleans?

Let us not be deceived. A war of invasion may invite a retort of invasion. When we visit the peaceable, and as to us innocent, colonies of Great Britain with the horrors of war, can we be assured that our own coast will not be visited with like horrors?

Source: *Annals of Congress*, 12th Cong., 1st sess., vol. 2, cols. 2219–2221.

Hezekiah Niles

A Republican Defends the War

In 1814, what the Federalists feared had come to pass: British ships blockaded American ports, and British troops invaded American territory. In January 1815, Republican editor Hezekiah Niles used the pages of his influential Baltimore newspaper, *Niles' Weekly Register*, to explain current Republican policies and blame the Federalists for American reverses.

It is universally known that the causes for which we declared war are no obstruction to peace. The practice of blockade and impressment having ceased by the general pacification of Europe, our government is content to leave the principle as it was. . . .

We have no further business in hostility, than such as is purely defensive; while that of Great Britain is to humble or subdue us. The war, on our part, has become a contest for life, liberty and property—on the part of our enemy, of revenge or ambition. . . .

What then are we to do? Are we to encourage him by divisions among ourselves—to hold out the hope of a separation of the states and a civil war—to refuse to bring forth the resources of the country against him? . . . I did think that in a defensive war—a struggle for all that is valuable—that all parties would have united. But it is not so—every measure calculated to replenish the treasury or raise men is opposed [by Federalists] as though it were determined to strike the "star spangled banner" and exalt

the bloody cross. Look at the votes and proceedings of congress—and mark the late spirit [to secede from the Union] . . . that existed in Massachusetts, and see with what unity of action every thing has been done [by New England Federalists] to harass and embarrass the government. Our loans have failed; and our soldiers have wanted their pay, because those [New England merchants] who had the greater part of the monied capital covenanted with each other to refuse its aid to the country. They had a right, legally, to do this; and perhaps, also, by all the artifices of trade or power that money gave them, to oppress others not of their "stamp" and depress the national credit—but history will shock posterity by detailing the length to which they went to bankrupt the republic. . . .

To conclude—why does the war continue? It is not the fault of the government—we demand no extravagant thing. I answer the question, and say—*it lasts because Great Britain depends on the exertions of her "party" in this country to destroy our resources, and compel "unconditional submission."*

Thus the war began, and is continued, by our divisions.

Source: *Niles' Weekly Register*, January 28, 1815.

ANALYZING THE EVIDENCE

- **According to Washington, what is the ultimate cause of political factionalism? Why does Washington believe that factionalism is most dangerous in "popular"—that is, republican—governments?**

- **What specific dangers did Josiah Quincy and the Federalists foresee with regard to Republican war policies? Read the section on the War of 1812 in the text, and then discuss the accuracy of their predictions.**

- **According to Hezekiah Niles, by 1815, what were the war goals of the Republican administration? How had those goals changed since the start of the war? Niles charged the Federalists and their supporters with impeding the American war effort. What were his specific charges? Did they have any merit? How might the Federalists have defended their stance with respect to the war?**

MAP 7.5

The War of 1812

Unlike the War of Independence, the War of 1812 had few large-scale military campaigns. In 1812 and 1813, most of the fighting took place along the Canadian border, as small American military forces attacked British targets with mixed success (nos. 1–4). The British took the offensive in 1814, launching a successful raid on Washington, but their attack on Baltimore failed, and they suffered heavy losses when they invaded the United States along Lake Champlain (nos. 5–7). Near the Gulf of Mexico, American forces moved from one success to another: General Andrew Jackson defeated the pro-British Creek Indians at the Battle of Horseshoe Bend, won a victory in Pensacola, and, in the single major battle of the war, routed an invading British army at New Orleans (nos. 8–10).

***Battle of New Orleans*, by Jean-Hyacinthe de Laclotte (detail)**
As their artillery (right center) bombarded the American lines, British infantry attacked the center of
General Andrew Jackson's line of troops. At the same time, a column of redcoats (foreground) tried to
breach the right flank of the American fortifications. Secure behind their battlements, Jackson's forces
repelled the assaults, taking thousands of prisoners and leaving the ground littered with British casualties.
New Orleans Museum of Art, gift of Edgar William and Bernice Chrysler Garbisch.

American control of the Mississippi River. With the
nation politically divided and under attack from north
and south, Gallatin feared that "the war might prove
vitally fatal to the United States."

Fortunately for the young American republic, by
1815 Britain wanted peace. The twenty-year war with
France had sapped its wealth and energy, so it began
negotiations with the United States in Ghent, Belgium.
At first, the American commissioners—John Quincy

Adams, Gallatin, and Clay—demanded territory in
Canada and Florida, while British diplomats sought
an Indian buffer state between the United States and
Canada. Both sides quickly realized that these objectives were not worth the cost of prolonged warfare. The
Treaty of Ghent, signed on Christmas Eve 1814, retained
the prewar borders of the United States.

That result hardly justified three years of warfare,
but before news of the treaty reached the United States,

a final military victory lifted Americans' morale. On January 8, 1815, General Jackson's troops crushed the British forces attacking New Orleans. Fighting from carefully constructed breastworks, the Americans rained "grapeshot and cannister bombs" on the massed British formations. The British lost 700 men, and 2,000 more were wounded or taken prisoner; just 13 Americans died, and only 58 suffered wounds. A newspaper headline proclaimed: "Almost Incredible Victory!! Glorious News." The victory made Jackson a national hero, redeemed the nation's battered pride, and undercut the Hartford convention's demands for constitutional revision.

The Federalist Legacy

The War of 1812 ushered in a new phase of the Republican political revolution. Before the conflict, Federalists had strongly supported Alexander Hamilton's program of national mercantilism—a funded debt, a central bank, and tariffs—while Jeffersonian Republicans had opposed it. After the war, the Republicans split into two camps. Led by Henry Clay, National Republicans pursued Federalist-like policies. In 1816, Clay pushed legislation through Congress creating the Second Bank of the United States and persuaded President Madison to sign it. In 1817, Clay won passage of the Bonus Bill, which created a national fund for roads and other internal improvements. Madison vetoed it. Reaffirming traditional Jeffersonian Republican principles, he argued that the national government lacked the constitutional authority to fund internal improvements.

Meanwhile, the Federalist Party crumbled. As one supporter explained, the National Republicans in the eastern states had "destroyed the Federalist party by the adoption of its principles" while the favorable farm policies of Jeffersonians maintained the Republican Party's dominance in the South and West. "No Federal character can run with success," Gouverneur Morris of New York lamented, and the election of 1818 proved him right: Republicans outnumbered Federalists 37 to 7 in the Senate and 156 to 27 in the House. Westward expansion and the success of Jefferson's Revolution of 1800 had shattered the First Party System.

Marshall's Federalist Law   However, the Federalists' nationalist policies lived on thanks to John Marshall's long tenure on the Supreme Court. Appointed chief justice by President John Adams in January 1801, Marshall had a personality and intellect that allowed him to dominate the Court until 1822 and strongly influence its decisions until his death in 1835. Winning the support of Joseph Story and other National Republican justices, Marshall shaped the evolution of the Constitution.

Three principles informed Marshall's jurisprudence: judicial authority, the supremacy of national laws, and traditional property rights (Table 7.1). Marshall claimed the right of judicial review for the Supreme Court in *Marbury v. Madison* (1803), and the Court frequently used that power to overturn state laws that, in its judgment, violated the Constitution.

Asserting National Supremacy   The important case of *McCulloch v. Maryland* (1819) involved one such law. When Congress created the Second Bank of the United States in 1816, it allowed the bank to set up state branches that competed with state-chartered banks. To enhance the competitiveness

TABLE 7.1			
Marshall's Principles and the Major Decisions of the Marshall Court			
	Date	**Case**	**Significance of Decision**
Judicial Authority	1803	*Marbury v. Madison*	Asserts principle of judicial review
Property Rights	1810	*Fletcher v. Peck*	Protects property rights through broad reading of Constitution's contract clause
	1819	*Dartmouth College v. Woodward*	Safeguards property rights, especially of chartered corporations
Supremacy of National Law	1819	*McCulloch v. Maryland*	Interprets Constitution to give broad powers to national government
	1824	*Gibbons v. Ogden*	Gives national government jurisdiction over interstate commerce

John Marshall, by Chester Harding, c. 1830

Even at the age of seventy-five, John Marshall (1755–1835) had a commanding personal presence. After he became chief justice of the U.S. Supreme Court in 1801, Marshall elevated the Court from a minor department of the national government to a major institution in American legal and political life. His decisions on judicial review, contract rights, the regulation of commerce, and national banking permanently shaped the character of American constitutional law. *John Marshall*, 1830 (oil on canvas), Chester Harding (1792–1866). The Bridgeman Art Library.

of Maryland's banks, the state legislature imposed a tax on notes issued by the Baltimore branch of the Second Bank. The Second Bank refused to pay, claiming that the tax infringed on national powers and was therefore unconstitutional. The state's lawyers then invoked Jefferson's argument: that Congress lacked the constitutional authority to charter a national bank. Even if a national bank was legitimate, the lawyers argued, Maryland could tax its activities within the state.

Marshall and the nationalist-minded Republicans on the Court firmly rejected both arguments. The Second Bank was constitutional, said the chief justice, because it was "necessary and proper," given the national government's control over currency and credit. Like Alexander Hamilton, Marshall was a loose constructionist: If the goal of a law is "within the scope of the Constitution," he believed, then "all means which are appropriate" to secure that goal are also constitutional.

The Marshall Court again asserted the dominance of national over state statutes in *Gibbons v. Ogden* (1824). The decision struck down a New York law granting a monopoly to Aaron Ogden for steamboat passenger service across the Hudson River to New Jersey. Asserting that the Constitution gave the federal government authority over interstate commerce, the chief justice sided with Thomas Gibbons, who held a federal license to run steamboats between the two states.

Upholding Vested Property Rights

Finally, Marshall used the Constitution to uphold Federalist notions of property rights. During the 1790s, Jefferson Republicans had celebrated "the will of THE PEOPLE," prompting Federalists to worry that popular sovereignty would result in a "tyranny of the majority." If state legislatures enacted statutes infringing on the property rights of wealthy citizens, Federalist judges vowed to void them.

Marshall was no exception. Determined to protect individual property rights, he invoked the contract clause of the Constitution to do it. The contract clause (in Article I, Section 10) prohibits the states from passing any law "impairing the obligation of contracts." Economic conservatives at the Philadelphia convention had inserted the clause to prevent "stay" laws, which kept creditors from seizing the lands and goods of delinquent debtors. In *Fletcher v. Peck* (1810), Marshall greatly expanded its scope. The Georgia legislature had granted a huge tract of land to the Yazoo Land Company. When a new legislature canceled the grant, alleging fraud and bribery, speculators who had purchased Yazoo lands appealed to the Supreme Court to uphold their titles. Marshall did so by ruling that the legislative grant was a contract that could not revoked. His decision was controversial and far-reaching. It limited state power; bolstered vested property rights; and, by protecting out-of-state investors, promoted the development of a national capitalist economy.

The Court extended its defense of vested property rights in *Dartmouth College v. Woodward* (1819). Dartmouth College was a private institution created by a royal charter issued by King George III. In 1816, New Hampshire's Republican legislature enacted a statute converting the school into a public university. The Dartmouth trustees opposed the legislation and hired Daniel Webster to plead their case. A renowned constitutional lawyer and a leading Federalist, Webster cited the Court's decision in *Fletcher v. Peck* and argued that the royal charter was an unalterable contract. The Marshall Court agreed and upheld Dartmouth's claims.

The Diplomacy of John Quincy Adams

Even as John Marshall incorporated important Federalist principles into the American legal system, voting citizens and political leaders embraced the outlook of the Republican Party. The political career of John Quincy Adams was a case in point. Although he was the son of Federalist president John Adams, John Quincy Adams had joined the Republican Party before the War of 1812. He came to national attention for his role in negotiating the Treaty of Ghent, which ended the war.

Adams then served brilliantly as secretary of state for two terms under James Monroe (1817–1825). Ignoring Republican antagonism toward Great Britain, in 1817 Adams negotiated the Rush-Bagot Treaty, which limited American and British naval forces on the Great Lakes. In 1818, he concluded another agreement with Britain setting the forty-ninth parallel as the border between Canada and the lands of the Louisiana Purchase. Then, in the Adams-Onís Treaty of 1819, Adams persuaded Spain to cede the Florida territory to the United States (Map 7.6). In return, the American government accepted Spain's claim to Texas and agreed to a compromise on the western boundary for the state of Louisiana, which had entered the Union in 1812.

Finally, Adams persuaded President Monroe to declare American national policy with respect to the Western Hemisphere. At Adams's behest, Monroe warned Spain and other European powers to keep their hands off the newly independent republics in Latin America. The American continents were not "subject for further colonization," the president declared in 1823—a policy that thirty years later became known as the Monroe Doctrine. In return, Monroe pledged that the United States would not "interfere in the internal concerns" of European nations. Thanks to John Quincy Adams, the United States had successfully asserted its diplomatic leadership in the Western Hemisphere and won international acceptance of its northern and western boundaries.

The appearance of political consensus after two decades of bitter party conflict prompted observers to dub James Monroe's presidency the "Era of Good Feeling." This harmony was real but transitory. The Republican Party was now split between the National faction, led by Clay and Adams, and the Jeffersonian faction, soon to be led by Martin Van Buren and Andrew Jackson. The two groups differed sharply over federal support for roads and canals and many other issues. As the aging Jefferson himself complained, "You see so many of these new [National] republicans maintaining in Congress the rankest doctrines of the old federalists." This divi-

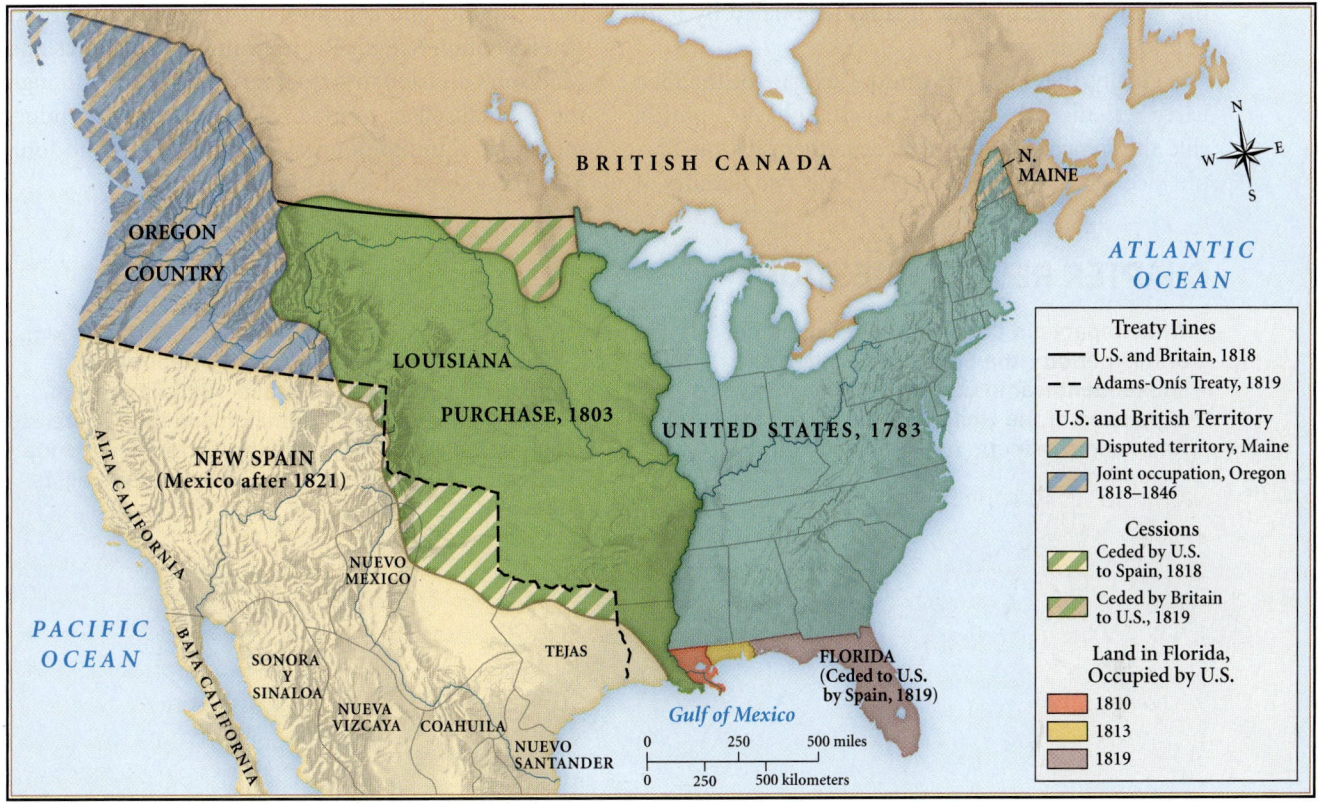

MAP 7.6

Defining the National Boundaries, 1800–1820

After the War of 1812, American diplomats negotiated treaties with Great Britain and Spain that defined the boundaries of the Louisiana Purchase, with British Canada to the north and New Spain (which in 1821 became the independent nation of Mexico) to the south and west. These treaties eliminated the threat of border wars with neighboring states for a generation, giving the United States a much-needed period of peace and security.

sion in the Republican Party would soon produce the Second Party System, in which national-minded Whigs and state-focused Democrats would confront each other. By the early 1820s, one cycle of American politics and economic debate had ended, and another was about to begin.

- Was the War of 1812 "necessary"? If so, why? If not, why did it occur?

- How did the decisions of the Supreme Court between 1801 and 1820 alter the nation's understanding of the Constitution? How did they change American society?

- Explain the causes of the rise and fall of the Federalist Party. Why was the Republican triumph so complete?

SUMMARY

In this chapter, we traced three interrelated themes: public policy, westward expansion, and party politics. We began by examining the contrasting public policies advocated by Alexander Hamilton and Thomas Jefferson. A Federalist, Hamilton supported a strong national government and created a fiscal infrastructure (the national debt, tariffs, and a national bank) to spur trade and manufacturing. By contrast, Jefferson wanted to preserve the authority of state governments, and he envisioned an America enriched by farming rather than industry.

Jefferson and the Republicans promoted a westward movement that transformed the agricultural economy and sparked new wars with the Indian peoples. Expansion westward also shaped American diplomatic and military policy, leading to the Louisiana Purchase, the War of 1812, and the treaties negotiated by John Quincy Adams.

Finally, there was the unexpected rise of the First Party System. As Hamilton's policies split the political elite, the French Revolution divided Americans into hostile ideological groups. The result was two decades of bitter conflict and controversial measures: the Federalists' Sedition Act, the Republicans' Embargo Act, and Madison's decision to go to war with Britain. Although the Federalist Party faded away, it left as its enduring legacy Hamilton's financial innovations and John Marshall's constitutional jurisprudence.

CHAPTER REVIEW QUESTIONS

- What impact did the two great developments of this period — the French Revolution and subsequent war in Europe, and the westward expansion of the United States across the North American continent — have on each other?

- Explain the rise and fall of the First Party System. How did the policies pursued by Republican presidents between 1801 and 1825 differ from those implemented by Hamilton and the Federalists during the 1790s? Why did the Federalist agenda fall out of favor? What legacy did the Federalists leave?

FOR FURTHER EXPLORATION

James Roger Sharp, *American Politics in the Early Republic* (1993), and Thomas P. Slaughter, *The Whiskey Rebellion* (1986), describe the perils of the 1790s. For the impact of the French Revolution, see "Liberty, Equality, Fraternity" (**chnm.gmu.edu/revolution**). Rosemarie Zagarri, *A Woman's Dilemma* (1995), and Linda Kerber, *No Constitutional Right to Be Ladies* (1999), discuss women's political lives.

For the writings of Washington and Jefferson, go to **www.virginia.edu/gwpapers** and **etext.virginia .edu/jefferson/quotations**. See also Annette Gordon-Reed, *Thomas Jefferson and Sally Hemings* (1997), and Ron Chernow, *Alexander Hamilton* (2004). David McCullough's *John Adams* (2001) draws material from the Adams Papers (**www.masshist.org/digitaladams /aea**). On the election of 1800, consult John Ferling, *Adams vs. Jefferson* (2004), and James Horn et al., eds., *The Revolution of 1800* (2002).

Gregory Evans Dowd, *A Spirited Resistance* (1992), and the "Chickasaw Historical Research Page" (**www .chickasawhistory.com**) survey Native Americans. Colin G. Calloway, *One Vast Winter Count* (2003), and Douglas Seefeldt et al., eds., *Across the Continent* (2005), cover the latest Lewis and Clark scholarship. See also **www.pbs.org/lewisandclark**. Theda Perdue, *Cherokee Women* (1998), and William G. McLoughlin, *Cherokee Renascence in the New Republic* (1986), explore cultural interaction.

Ralph Ketcham's *Presidents Above Party* (1984) probes the political world. For the War of 1812, see Donald R. Hickey, *The War of 1812* (1989), and "The War of 1812" site at **www.warof1812.ca/index.html**. R. Kent Newmyer, *The Supreme Court Under Marshall and Taney* (1968), concisely analyzes constitutional change.

TEST YOUR KNOWLEDGE

To assess your command of the material in this chapter, see the Online Study Guide at **bedfordstmartins.com/henretta**.

For Web sites, images, and documents related to topics and places in this chapter, visit **bedfordstmartins.com/makehistory**.

TIMELINE

1783	Treaty of Paris allows settlement of west
1784	Iroquois peoples cede lands in New York
1787	Northwest Ordinance
1789	Judiciary Act establishes federal courts French Revolution begins
1790	Hamilton's public credit system approved
1790–1791	Western Confederacy defeats U.S. armies
1791	Bill of Rights ratified Bank of the United States chartered
1792, 1796	Kentucky joins Union; Tennessee follows French Republic formed
1793	Madison and Jefferson found Republican Party War between Britain and France
1794	Whiskey Rebellion Battle of Fallen Timbers
1795	Jay's Treaty with Great Britain Pinckney's Treaty with Spain Greenville Treaty accepts Indian land rights
1798	XYZ Affair Alien, Sedition, and Naturalization Acts Kentucky and Virginia resolutions
1800	Jefferson elected president 1801 John Marshall becomes chief justice
1801–1807	Gallatin reduces national debt
1802–1807	France and Britain seize American ships
1803	Louisiana Purchase *Marbury v. Madison* asserts judicial review
1804–1806	Lewis and Clark explore West
1807	Embargo Act cripples American shipping
1808	Madison elected president
1809	Tecumseh and Tenskwatawa revive Western Confederacy
1812–1815	War of 1812
1817–1825	Era of Good Feeling
1819	Adams-Onís Treaty *McCulloch v. Maryland*; *Dartmouth College v. Woodward*

Creating a Republican Culture, 1790–1820

By the 1820s, a sense of optimism pervaded America's white citizenry. The new nation, a Kentucky judge declared in a Fourth of July speech, "already exhibits many signs that it is the promised land of civil liberty, and of institutions designed to liberate and exalt the human race." White Americans had good reason to feel fortunate. They lived under a representative republican government, free from arbitrary taxation and from domination by an established church. The deaths of former presidents John Adams and Thomas Jefferson on July 4, 1826 — the fiftieth anniversary of the Declaration of Independence — seemed to many Americans a sure sign that God looked with favor on their experiment in self-government.

Inspired by their political freedom, many citizens sought to extend republican principles throughout their society. But what *were* those principles? For entrepreneurial-minded merchants, farmers, and political leaders, republicanism meant the advance of **capitalism**: They wanted governments to solidify capitalist cultural values and create a dynamic market economy. Using their influence in state legislatures, they secured mercantilist policies that assisted private businesses and, they claimed, enhanced the "common wealth." Other Americans celebrated republican social values. In the North, they championed democratic republicanism: equality in family and social relationships. In the South, where class and race sharply divided society, politicians and pamphleteers endorsed an aristocratic republicanism that stressed liberty for whites rather than equality for all.

Yet another vision of American republicanism emerged during the massive religious revival that swept the nation between 1790 and 1850. The document that founded the national republic, the U.S. Constitution of 1787, is thoroughly secular, containing no reference to God and only mentioning religion to prohibit religious tests for holding federal office. But, as Alexis de Tocqueville reported in *Democracy in America* (1835), the Second Great Awakening gave "the Christian religion . . . a greater influence over the souls of men" than in any other country. The resulting religious enthusiasm — what Methodist Bishop McIlvaine praised as "the quickening of the people of God to a spirit and walk becoming the gospel" — prompted political activism on many fronts, from abolitionism, to temperance, to a condemnation of Sunday mail delivery. For those who embraced the Awakening, the United States was both a great experiment in republican government and a Christian civilization that would redeem the world — a moral mission that, for better or worse, would inform American diplomacy in the centuries to come.

The Fourth of July in Philadelphia, c. 1811

By the early nineteenth century, the Fourth of July celebration of American independence had become a popular holiday, especially among Jeffersonian Republicans. (Federalists commemorated Washington's birthday.) This detail from a painting by John Lewis Krimmel links the new nation to the Greek and Roman republics through architecture (the building and the statue), notes its social diversity (by including blacks as well as whites), and hints at the tenor of its social life. The young man buying an alcoholic drink and flirting with the young mother may well engage in some rowdy behavior before Independence Day is over. Pennsylvania Academy of the Fine Arts, Philadelphia. (detail) From the estate of Paul Beck Jr.

The Capitalist Commonwealth

If "the quick succession of sensations and ideas constitute life," observed a French visitor to the United States, "here one lives a hundred fold more than elsewhere; here, all is circulation, motion, and boiling agitation." Boiling agitation was especially evident in the Northeast, where republican state legislatures actively promoted banking and commerce. "Experiment follows experiment; enterprise follows enterprise," another European traveler noted, and "riches and poverty follow." Of the two, riches were readily apparent. Beginning around 1800, the average per capita income of Americans increased by more than 1 percent a year — more than 30 percent in a single generation.

Banks, Manufacturing, and Markets

America was "a Nation of Merchants," a British visitor reported from Philadelphia in 1798, "keen in the pursuit of wealth in all the various modes of acquiring it." And acquire it they did, making spectacular profits as the wars triggered by the French Revolution (1793–1815) crippled European merchant firms. Fur trader John Jacob Astor and merchant Robert Oliver became the nation's first millionaires. Oliver first worked for an Irish-owned linen firm in Baltimore and then achieved affluence by trading West Indian coffee and sugar. Astor, who migrated from Germany to New York in 1784, became wealthy carrying furs from the Pacific Northwest to markets in China.

Banking and Credit To finance such mercantile ventures, Americans needed banks. Before the Revolution, farmers relied on government-sponsored land banks for loans, while merchants arranged partnerships or obtained credit from British suppliers. During the War for Independence, Philadelphia merchants persuaded the Confederation Congress to charter the Bank of North America in 1781, and traders in Boston and New York soon founded similar lending institutions. "Our monied capital has so much increased from the Introduction of Banks, & the Circulation of the Funds," Philadelphia merchant William Bingham boasted in 1791, "that the Necessity of Soliciting Credits from England will no longer exist."

That same year, Federalists in Congress chartered the First Bank of the United States to issue notes and make commercial loans. The bank's profits averaged a handsome 8 percent annually; by 1805, it had branches

A Cloth Merchant, 1789

Originally a prosperous storekeeper in New Milford, Connecticut, Elijah Boardman (1760–1832) eventually became a U.S. senator. Like other American traders, he had imported huge quantities of cloth from Britain. When the wars of the 1790s cut off trade, some merchants financed the domestic production of textiles. Others, including Boardman, turned to land speculation. In 1795, he joined the Connecticut Land Company and bought huge tracts in Connecticut's Western Reserve, including the present towns of Medina, Palmyra, and Boardman, Ohio. Ralph Earl painted this portrait in 1789. Elijah Boardman, the Metropolitan Museum of Art, New York, Bequest of Susan W. Tyler, 1979.

in eight seaport cities. However, Jeffersonians attacked the bank as unconstitutional and claimed that it promoted "a consolidated, energetic government supported by public creditors, speculators, and other insidious men lacking in public spirit of any kind." When the bank's twenty-year charter expired in 1811, Jeffersonian Republicans refused to renew it. To provide credit, merchants, artisans, and farmers persuaded state legislatures to charter banks. By 1816, when Congress (now run by National Republicans) chartered the Second Bank of

The China Trade

Following the Revolution, New England merchants traded actively with the major Asian manufacturing centers of China and India. In this painting by George Chinnery (1774–1852), the American flag flies prominently, alongside other national banners, in front of the warehouse district in Canton (modern Guangzhou). There, merchants exchanged bundles of American furs for cargoes of Chinese tea, silks, and porcelain plates, cups, and serving dishes.   Bridgeman Art Library Ltd.

the United States, there were 246 state-chartered banks with tens of thousands of stockholders and $68 million in banknotes in circulation. But these state banks were often shady operations that issued notes without adequate specie reserves and made ill-advised loans to insiders.

Dubious banking policies helped bring on the Panic of 1819 (just as they caused the financial crisis of 2008). But the most important cause was an abrupt 30 percent drop in world agricultural prices after the Napoleonic Wars. In Charleston, South Carolina, in 1818, the price for a pound of raw cotton fell from 34 cents to 15 cents. As their income plummeted, planters and farmers could not pay their debts to their suppliers and banks. Many state banks went bust; those that were still solvent in 1821 had just $45 million in circulation. The panic gave Americans their first taste of a **business cycle**, the periodic expansion and contraction of output and jobs inherent to an unregulated market economy.

Rural Manufacturing The Panic of 1819 revealed that artisans and yeomen were now part of the market economy. Before 1800, many artisans worked part-time and sold their handicrafts locally; thus, a French traveler in central Massachusetts found many houses "inhabited by men who are both cultivators and artisans." Other artisans bartered products with neighbors. Clockmaker John Hoff of Lancaster, Pennsylvania, exchanged his fine, wooden-cased instruments for a dining table, a bedstead, and labor on his small farm. By 1820, many artisans — shipbuilders in seacoast towns, ironworkers in Pennsylvania and Maryland, and shoemakers in Massachusetts — had expanded their output and were selling their products throughout the nation.

The Yankee Peddler, c. 1830

Even in 1830, most Americans lived too far from a market town to go there regularly to buy goods. Instead, they purchased their tinware, clocks, textiles, and other manufactures from peddlers, often from New England, who traveled far and wide in small horse-drawn vans like the one visible through the doorway in this painting.   Courtesy IBM Corporation, Armonk, New York.

American entrepreneurs encouraged this expansion by developing rural manufacturing networks like those in Europe (see Chapter 1). Enterprising merchants bought raw materials, hired workers in farm families to process them, and sold the finished manufactures in regional or national markets. "Straw hats and Bonnets are manufactured by many families," an official in Maine noted in the 1810s. Merchants shipped these products — shoes, brooms, and palm-leaf hats as well as cups, baking pans, and other tin utensils — to stores in seaport cities. And New England peddlers, who quickly acquired the dubious reputation of being hard-bargaining "Yankees," sold them throughout the rural South.

This business expansion resulted from innovations in organizing production and in marketing; new technology played only a minor role. During the 1780s, New England and Middle Atlantic merchants built water-powered mills to run machines that combed wool — and later cotton — into long strands. But until the 1820s, they used the household-based outwork system for the next steps in the process: Farm women and children spun the machine-combed strands into thread and yarn on foot-driven spinning wheels, and men in other households used foot-powered looms to weave the yarn into cloth. In 1820, more than 12,000 household workers labored full-time weaving woolen cloth, which was then pounded flat and given a smooth finish in water-powered fulling mills. However, the transfer of spinning and weaving to factories was already in full swing; the number of water-driven cotton spindles soared from 8,000 in 1809 to 333,000 in 1817.

The growth of manufacturing offered farm families new opportunities — and new risks. Ambitious New

England farmers switched from growing crops for subsistence to raising livestock for sale. They sold meat, butter, and cheese to city markets and cattle hides to the booming shoe industry. "Along the whole road from Boston, we saw women engaged in making cheese," a Polish traveler reported. Other farm families raised sheep and sold raw wool to textile manufacturers. Processing these raw materials invigorated many farming towns. In 1792, Concord, Massachusetts, had one slaughterhouse and five small tanneries; a decade later, the town boasted eleven slaughterhouses and six large tanneries.

As the rural economy churned out more goods, it altered the environment. Foul odors from stockyards and tanning pits wafted over Concord and many other leather-producing towns. To secure hemlock bark to process stiff hides into pliable leather, tanners cut down thousands of acres of trees each year. More trees fell to the ax to create pasturelands for huge herds of livestock—dairy cows, cattle, and especially sheep. By 1850, most of the forests in southern New England and eastern New York were gone: "The hills had been stripped of their timber," New York's *Catskill Messenger* reported, "so as to present their huge, rocky projections." Scores of textile milldams dotted New England's rivers, altering their flow and preventing fish—already severely depleted from decades of overfishing—from reaching upriver spawning grounds. Even as the income of many farmers rose, the quality of their natural environment deteriorated.

In the new capitalist-run market economy, rural parents and their children worked longer and harder. They made yarn, hats, and brooms during the winter and then turned to their regular farming chores during the warmer seasons. More important, these farm families now depended on their wage labor and market sales to purchase the textiles, shoes, and hats they had once made for themselves. The new productive system made families and communities more efficient and prosperous—and more dependent on a market they could not control.

Building a Transportation Infrastructure

The expansion of the market depended on improvements in transportation. Between 1793 and 1812, the Massachusetts legislature granted charters to more than one hundred private turnpike companies. These charters gave the companies special legal status and often included monopoly rights to a transportation route.

Pennsylvania issued fifty-five charters, including one to the Lancaster Turnpike Company. The company built a 65-mile graded and graveled road between Lancaster and Philadelphia, which quickly boosted the regional economy. Although turnpike investors received only about "three percent annually," Henry Clay estimated, society as a whole "actually reap[ed] fifteen or twenty percent." A farm woman knew what Clay meant: "The turnpike is finished and we can now go to town at all times and in all weather." New turnpikes soon connected dozens of inland market centers to seaport cities.

Water transport was the quickest and cheapest way to get goods to market, so state governments and private entrepreneurs improved water transport by dredging shallow rivers and constructing canals to bypass waterfalls or rapids. Settlers took matters into their own hands. In the rapidly growing states of Kentucky and Tennessee and in southern Ohio, Indiana, and Illinois, settlers paid premium prices for farmland near the great Ohio and Mississippi rivers and their tributaries. And speculators bought up property in the cities along their banks: Cincinnati, Louisville, Chattanooga, and St. Louis. Farmers and merchants built barges to carry cotton, surplus grain, and meat downstream to New Orleans, which by 1815 was handling about $5 million in agricultural products yearly.

Public Enterprise: The Commonwealth System

Legislative support for road and canal companies reflected the ideology of mercantilism: government-assisted economic development. Just as the British Parliament had used the Navigation Acts to spur prosperity, so American legislatures enacted laws "of great public utility" that would increase the "common wealth." These statutes generally took the form of special charters that bestowed legal privileges. For example, most transportation charters included the power of eminent domain, which allowed turnpike, bridge, and canal corporations to force the sale of privately owned land along their routes. State legislatures also aided capitalist flour millers and textile manufacturers, who flooded adjacent farmland as they built dams to power their water-driven machinery. In Massachusetts, the Mill Dam Act of 1795 deprived farmers of their traditional right under common law to stop the flooding and forced them to accept "fair compensation" for their lost acreage. Judges approved this state-ordered shift in property rights. "The establishment of a great mill-power for manufacturing purposes," Justice Lemuel Shaw

View of Cincinnati, **by John Caspar Wild, c. 1835**

Thanks to its location on the Ohio River (a tributary of the Mississippi), Cincinnati quickly became one of the major processing centers for grain and hogs in the trans-Appalachian west. By the 1820s, passenger steamboats and freight barges connected the city with Pittsburgh to the north and the ocean port of New Orleans far to the south.   Museum of Fine Arts, Boston, M. and M. Karolik Collection.

intoned, was "one of the great industrial pursuits of the commonwealth."

Critics condemned the privileges given to private enterprises as "Scheme[s] of an evident antirepublican tendency," as some "freeholder citizens" in Putney, Vermont, put it. The award of "peculiar privileges" to corporations, they argued, not only violated the "equal rights" of all citizens but also lessened the power of the government. As a Pennsylvanian explained, "Whatever power is given to a corporation, is just so much power taken from the State." Nonetheless, judges in state courts, following the lead of John Marshall's Supreme Court (see Chapter 7), consistently upheld corporate charters and grants of eminent domain to private transportation companies. "The opening of good and easy internal communications is one of the highest duties of government," declared a New Jersey judge.

State mercantilism soon spread beyond transportation. Following Jefferson's embargo of 1807, which cut off goods and credit from Europe, the New England states awarded charters to two hundred iron-mining, textile-manufacturing, and banking companies, and Pennsylvania granted more than eleven hundred. By 1820, innovative state governments had created a republican political economy: a commonwealth system that funneled state aid to private businesses whose projects would improve the general welfare.

- How did promoters of mercantilism (the commonwealth system) use state and national governments to promote economic growth?

- Why did many Americans believe that the granting of special privileges and charters to private businesses violated republican principles?

Toward a Democratic Republican Culture

After independence, many Americans in the northern states embraced a democratic republicanism that celebrated political equality and social mobility. These citizens, primarily members of the emerging **middle class**, redefined the nature of the family and of education by seeking more egalitarian marriages and more affectionate ways of rearing their children.

Opportunity and Equality – for White Men

Between 1780 and 1820, hundreds of well-educated visitors agreed, almost unanimously, that the American social order was genuinely different from that of Europe. In his famous *Letters from an American Farmer* (1782), French-born essayist J. Hector St. Jean de Crèvecoeur wrote that European society was composed "of great lords who possess everything, and of a herd of people who have nothing." By contrast, the United States had "no aristocratical families, no courts, no kings, no bishops."

The absence of a hereditary aristocracy encouraged Americans to condemn inherited social privilege and to extol legal equality. "The law is the same for everyone [in America,]" noted one European traveler. Yet citizens of the new republic willingly accepted social divisions that reflected personal achievement. As individuals used their "talents, integrity, and virtue" to amass wealth, their social standing rose — a phenomenon that astounded many Europeans. "In Europe to say of someone that he rose from nothing is a disgrace and a reproach," remarked a Polish aristocrat. "It is the opposite here. To be the architect of your own fortune is honorable. It is the highest recommendation."

Some Americans from long-distinguished families felt threatened by the *nouveau riche* and their ideology of wealth-driven social mobility. "Man is estimated by dollars," complained Nathaniel Booth, whose high-status family had once dominated the small Hudson River port town of Kingston, New York. However, for most white men, a merit-based system meant the opportunity to better themselves (Map 8.1).

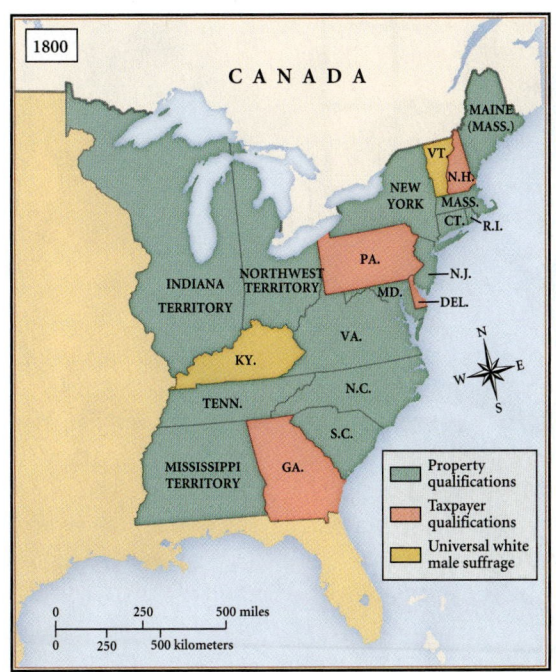

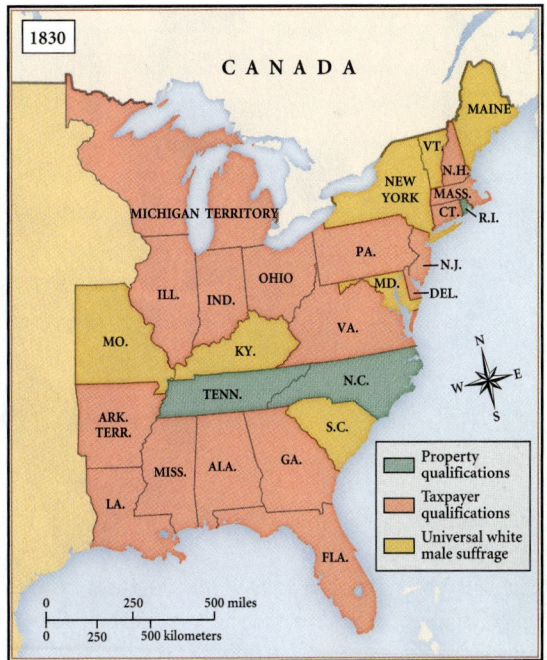

MAP 8.1

The Expansion of Voting Rights for White Men, 1800 and 1830

Between 1800 and 1830, the United States moved steadily toward political equality for white men. Many existing states revised their constitutions and replaced a property qualification for voting with a less-restrictive criterion (the voter must have paid taxes or have served in the militia). Some new states in the West extended the suffrage to all adult white men. As parties sought votes from a broader electorate, the tone of politics became more open and competitive — swayed by the interests and values of ordinary people.

Old cultural rules—and new laws—denied such chances to most women and African American men. When women and free blacks invoked the republican principle of equality and asked for voting rights, male legislators wrote explicit race and gender restrictions into the law. In 1802, Ohio disenfranchised African Americans, and the New York constitution of 1821 imposed a property-holding requirement on black voters. A striking case of sexual discrimination occurred in New Jersey, where the state constitution of 1776 had granted **suffrage** to all property holders. As Federalists and Republicans competed for power, they ignored customary gender rules and urged property-owning single women and widows to vote. Sensing a threat to men's monopoly on politics, the New Jersey legislature in 1807 limited voting rights to white men only. To justify the exclusion of women, legislators invoked both biology and custom: "Women, generally, are neither by nature, nor habit, nor education, nor by their necessary condition in society fitted to perform this duty with credit to themselves or advantage to the public."

Toward a Republican Marriage System

The controversy over women's political rights mirrored a debate over authority within the household. British and American husbands had long claimed patriarchal power and firm legal control of the family's property. But as John Adams lamented in 1776, the republican principle of equality had "spread where it was not intended," encouraging his wife and other women to speak out on politics and to demand legal and financial rights. Patriot author and historian Mercy Otis Warren maintained that patriarchy was not a "natural" rule but a social contrivance and could be justified only "for the sake of order in families."

Economic and cultural changes also eroded customary paternal authority. In colonial America, most property-owning parents had arranged their children's marriages to protect the family's welfare. They looked for a son- or daughter-in-law with moral values and financial resources; physical attraction and emotional

The Wedding, 1805

Bride and groom stare intently into each other's eyes as they exchange vows, suggesting that their union was a love match, not a marriage based on economic calculation. The plain costumes of the guests and the sparse furnishings of the room suggest that the unknown artist may have provided us with a picture of a rural Quaker wedding. Philadelphia Museum of Art.

A Tragedy Sentimentalized in Art

When the infant daughter of artist Charles Willson Peale died in 1772, he captured his wife's emotions in this painting, *Mrs. Rachel Brewer Peale with Daughter (Rachel Weeping)*. Although Rachel Peale looks toward heaven, she is not praying; the emphasis is on her emotional state, her intense feelings of sorrow over the loss of her child. This focus on personal experience was a hallmark of sentimentalism.   Philadelphia Museum of Art.

compatibility between the young people were secondary considerations. But as landholdings shrank in long-settled communities, many yeomen fathers lost control over their children's marriages because they had no farms to hand down. Young men and women chose their own partners, influenced by a new cultural attitude: **sentimentalism**.

The Impact of Sentimentalism   Sentimentalism originated in Europe as part of the Romantic movement and, after 1800, spread quickly through all classes of American society. Rejecting the Enlightenment's emphasis on rational thought, sentimentalism celebrated the importance of "feeling"—a physical, sensuous appreciation of God, nature, and fellow humans. This new emphasis on deep emotional feelings infused German and English literary works, pop-

ular theatrical melodramas, and the emotional rhetoric of revivalist preachers.

As the hot sentimental passions of the heart overwhelmed the cool rational logic of the mind, a new consent-based marriage system appeared. Magazines praised marriages "contracted from motives of affection, rather than of interest," and many young people looked for a relationship based on intimacy and a spouse who was, as Eliza Southgate of Maine put it, "calculated to promote my happiness." As young people fell in love and married, many fathers saw their roles change from authoritarian patriarchs to watchful paternalists. To guard against free-spending sons-in-law, wealthy fathers often placed their daughters' inheritance in a legal trust. Wrote one Virginia planter to his lawyer: "I rely on you to see the property settlement properly drawn before the marriage, for I by no means consent that Polly shall be left to the Vicissitudes of Life."

As voluntary agreements between individuals, love marriages conformed more closely to republican principles than did arranged matches. In theory, such **companionate marriages** gave wives and husbands "true equality, both of rank and fortune," as one Boston man suggested. In practice, though, husbands continued to dominate most marriages, both because male authority was deeply ingrained in cultural mores and because under American common law, as Abigail Adams complained, husbands had "sovereign authority" over the family's property. Moreover, the new love-based marriage system discouraged parents from protecting young wives, and governments refused to prevent domestic tyranny. As one lawyer noted, women who would rather "starve than submit" to their husbands were left to their fate. The marriage contract "is so much more important in its consequences to females than to males," a young man at the Litchfield Law School in Connecticut astutely observed in 1820, for "they subject themselves to his authority. He is their all—their only relative—their only hope" (see Comparing American Voices, "The Trials of Married Life," pp. 248–249).

Young adults who chose partners unwisely were severely disappointed when their spouses failed as providers or faithful companions. Before 1800, little could be done; officials granted divorces only in cases of neglect, abandonment, or adultery—serious offenses against the moral order of society. After 1800, most divorce petitions cited emotional problems. One woman complained that her husband had "ceased to cherish her," while a man grieved that his wife had "almost broke his heart." Responding to changing cultural values, several states expanded the legal grounds for divorce to include drunkenness and personal cruelty.

Republican Motherhood

Traditionally, American women had spent their active adult years working as farm wives and bearing and nurturing children. But by the 1790s, the birthrate in the northern states was dropping dramatically. In the farming village of Sturbridge in central Massachusetts, women who married before 1750 usually had eight or nine children; by contrast, those who married around 1810 had an average of six children. In the growing seaport cities, native-born white women bore an average of only four children.

The United States was among the first nations to experience this sharp decline in the birthrate—what

historians call the demographic transition. There were several causes. Beginning in the 1790s, thousands of young men migrated to the trans-Appalachian west, which increased the number of never-married women in the East and delayed marriage for many more. Women who married in their late twenties had fewer children. In addition, white couples in the urban middle classes deliberately limited the size of their families. Fathers wanted to leave their children an adequate inheritance; mothers, influenced by new ideas of individualism and self-achievement, did not want to spend their entire adulthood rearing children. After having four or five children, these couples used birth control or abstained from sexual intercourse.

Women's lives also changed because of new currents in Christian social thought. Traditionally, many religious writers had suggested that women were morally inferior to men and often were sexual temptresses. But by 1800, Protestant ministers were blaming men for sexual misconduct and claiming that purity and spirituality were part of women's nature. Influential laymen echoed that thinking. In his *Thoughts on Female Education* (1787), Philadelphia physician Benjamin Rush argued that a young woman should ensure her husband's "perseverance in the paths of rectitude" and receive intellectual training so that she would be "an agreeable companion." Rush called for loyal "republican mothers" who would instruct "their sons in the principles of liberty and government."

Christian ministers readily embraced the idea of **republican motherhood**. "Preserving virtue and instructing the young are not the fancied, but the real 'Rights of Women,'" Reverend Thomas Bernard told the Female Charitable Society of Salem, Massachusetts. He urged his audience to dismiss the public roles for women, such as voting or serving on juries, that English feminist Mary Wollstonecraft had advocated in *A Vindication of the Rights of Woman* (1792). Instead, women should care for their children, a responsibility that gave them "an extensive power over the fortunes of man in every generation."

Raising Republican Children

Republican values changed assumptions about inheritance and child rearing. English common law encouraged primogeniture, the inheritance of the family's property by the eldest son (see Chapter 1). After the Revolution, most state legislatures enacted statutes that required that the estates of fathers who died without wills be divided equally among all the offspring. Most American parents applauded these statutes be-

The Battle over Education

Here an unknown artist pokes fun at a tyrannical schoolmaster and, indirectly, at the strict approach to child rearing taken by evangelical authors, parents, and teachers. The students' faces reflect the artist's own rationalist outlook. One minister who had been influenced by the Enlightenment suggested that we see in young children's eyes "the first dawn of reason, beaming forth its immortal rays." Copyright The Frick Collection, New York City.

cause they had already begun to treat their children equally and respectfully.

Two Modes of Parenting Indeed, many European visitors believed that republican parents gave their children too much respect and freedom. Because of the "general ideas of Liberty and Equality engraved on their hearts," a Polish aristocrat suggested around 1800, American children had "scant respect" for their parents. Several decades later, a British traveler stood dumbfounded as an American father excused his son's "resolute disobedience" with a smile and the remark "A sturdy republican, sir." The traveler guessed that American parents encouraged such independence to prepare youth to "go their own way" in the world.

Permissive child rearing was not universal. Foreign visitors interacted primarily with well-to-do members of Episcopal or Presbyterian churches. Such parents often followed the teachings of rationalist religious writers influenced by John Locke and other Enlightenment thinkers. According to these authors, children were "rational creatures" who should be encouraged to act appropriately by means of advice and praise. The parents' role was to develop their child's conscience, self-discipline, and sense of responsibility. This rationalist method of child rearing was widely adopted by families in the rapidly expanding middle class.

By contrast, many yeomen and tenant farmers, influenced by the Second Great Awakening, raised their children in an authoritarian fashion. Evangelical Baptist and Methodist writers insisted that children were "full of the stains and pollution of sin" and needed strict rules and harsh discipline. Fear was a "useful and necessary principle in family government," John Abbott, a minister, advised parents; a child "should submit to your authority, not to your arguments or persuasions." Abbott told parents to instill humility in children and to teach them to subordinate their personal desires to God's will (see Reading American Pictures, "Changing Middle-Class Families: Assessing the Visual Record," p. 250).

Debates over Education Although families provided most moral and intellectual training, independence prompted a greater emphasis on schooling. Bostonian Caleb Bingham, an influential textbook author, called for "an equal distribution of knowledge to make us emphatically a 'republic of

COMPARING AMERICAN VOICES

The Trials of Married Life

As the text explains, the ideal American marriage of the early nineteenth century was republican (a contract between equals) and romantic (a match in which mutual love was foremost). Were these ideals attainable, given the social authority of men and the volatility of human passions? Letters, memoirs, and diaries are excellent sources for answering these questions. These selections from the personal writings of a variety of American women offer insights into the new system of marriage and how changes in cultural values intersected with individual lives.

Emma Hart Willard

The Danger of High Expectations

Born in Connecticut in 1787, Emma Hart married John Willard in 1809. An early proponent of advanced education for women, she founded female academies in Middlebury, Vermont (1814), and Waterford and Troy, New York (1821). She wrote this letter to her sister, Almira Hart, in 1815.

You think it strange that I should consider a period of happiness as more likely than any other to produce future misery. I know I did not sufficiently explain myself. Those tender and delicious sensations which accompany successful love, while they soothe and soften the mind, diminish its strength to bear or to conquer difficulties. It is the luxury of the soul; and luxury always enervates. . . . This life is a life of vicissitude. . . .

[Suppose] you are secured to each other for life. It will be natural that, at first, he should be much devoted to you; but, after a while, his business must occupy his attention. While absorbed in that he will perhaps neglect some of those little tokens of affection which have become necessary to your happiness. His affairs will sometimes go wrong, . . . and he may sometimes hastily give you a harsh word or a frown.

But where is the use, say you, of diminishing my present enjoyment by such gloomy apprehensions? Its use is this, that, if you enter the marriage state believing such things to be absolutely impossible, if you should meet them, they would come upon you with double force.

The planter's bride, who leaves a numerous and cheerful family in her paternal home, little imagines the change which awaits her in her own retired residence. She dreams of an independent sway over her household, devoted love and unbroken intercourse with her husband, and indeed longs to be released from the eyes of others, that she may dwell only beneath the sunbeam of his. And so it was with me. . . .

There we were together, asking for nothing but each other's presence and love. At length it was necessary for him to tear himself away to superintend his interests. . . . But the period of absence was gradually protracted; then a friend sometimes came home with him, and their talk was of crops and politics, draining the fields and draining the revenue. . . . A growing discomfort began to work upon my mind. I had undefined forebodings; I mused about past days; my views of life became slowly disorganized; my physical powers enfeebled; a nervous excitement followed: I nursed a moody discontent. . . .

If the reign of romance was really waning, I resolved not to chill his noble confidence, but to make a steadier light rise on his affections. . . . This task of self-government was not easy. To repress a harsh answer, to confess a fault . . . in gentle submission, sometimes requires a struggle like life and death; but these . . . efforts are the golden threads with which domestic happiness is woven. . . . How clear is it, then, that woman loses by petulance and recrimination! Her first study must be self-control, almost to hypocrisy. A good wife must smile amid a thousand perplexities.

Caroline Howard Gilman

Female Submission in Marriage

Born in Boston in 1794, Caroline Howard married in 1819 and moved to Charleston, South Carolina, with her husband, Samuel Gilman, a Unitarian minister. A novelist, she published *Recollections of a Housekeeper* (1835), a portrait of domestic life in New England, and *Recollections of a Southern Matron* (1838), a fictional account from which this selection is taken.

Martha Hunter Hitchcock

Isolation, Unmentionable Sorrows, and Suffering

Martha Hunter Hitchcock married a doctor in the U.S. Army. These excerpts from letters to her cousins Martha and Sarah Hunter describe her emotional dependence on her husband and her unhappy life. The letters are in the collection of the Virginia Historical Society.

To Martha Hunter, 1840:

If I had never married how much of pain, and dissatisfaction, should I have escaped—at all events I should never have known what jealousy is. You must not betray me, dear cousin, for despite all my good resolutions, I find it impossible always to struggle against my nature—the school of indulgence, in which I was educated, was little calculated to teach me, those lessons of forbearance, which I have had to practice so frequently, since my marriage—it is ungrateful in me to murmur, if perchance a little bitter is mingled in my cup of life.

To Sarah Hunter, 1841:

I have lived so long among strangers since my marriage, that when I contrast it with the old warm affection, in which I was nurtured, the contrast is so terrible, that I cannot refrain from weeping at the thought of it—I hope my dear cousin, that yours, will be a happier destiny than mine, in that respect—only think of it! Nearly a year and a half have passed away, since I have seen, a single relation!

To Martha Hunter, 1845:

Uneasiness about [my daughter] Lillie, and very great sorrows of my own, which I cannot commit to paper, have almost weighed me down to the grave; and indeed, without any affectation, I look forward to that, as the only real rest, I shall ever know.

To Martha Hunter, 1846:

Lillie had the scarlet fever, during our visit to Alabama, and she has never recovered from the effects of it—My life is a constant vigil—and there is nothing which wearies mind, and body, so much, as watching a sickly child.... All this I have to endure, and may have to suffer more for I know not, what Fate may have in store for me.

Elizabeth Scott Neblett

My Seasons of Gloom and Despondency

Elizabeth Scott Neblett lived with her husband and children in Navarro County, Texas. In 1860, she reflected in her diary on her bouts of depression and the difficulties of wives and husbands in understanding each other's inner lives.

It has now been almost eight years since I became a married woman. Eight years of checkered good and ill, and yet thro' all it seems the most of the ill has fallen to my lot, until now my poor weak cowardly heart sighs only for its final resting place, where sorrow grief nor pain can never reach it more.

I feel that I have faithfully discharged my duty towards you and my children, but for this I know that I deserve no credit nor aspire to none; my affection has been my prompter, and the task has proven a labor of love. You have not rightly understood me at all times, and being naturally very hopeful you could in no measure sympathize with me during my seasons of gloom and despondency.... But marriage is a lottery and that your draw proved an unfortunate one on your part is not less a subject of regret with me than you....

It is useless to say that during these eight years I have suffered ten times more than you have and ten times more than I can begin to make you conceive of, but of course you can not help the past, nor by knowing my suffering relieve it, but it might induce you to look with more kindness upon [my] faults.... The 17th of this month I was 27 years old and I think my face looks older than that, perhaps I'll never see an other birth day and I don't grieve at the idea.

Source: All of the selections are abridged versions of materials in Anya Jabour, ed., *Major Problems in the History of American Families and Children* (Boston: Houghton Mifflin, 2005), 108–113.

ANALYZING THE EVIDENCE

- **What problems do these women share? How might their problems reflect larger social and economic changes in nineteenth-century America?**

- **Was Emma Willard correct? Did the emotional problems experienced by these women stem, at least in part, from their overly optimistic expectations of love-based marriage? Or was something else the cause of their unhappiness?**

- **What was Caroline Gilman's advice to wives? Did the other women follow her advice?**

- **Do these selections suggest that most American women had unfulfilled marriages? Or were these isolated cases? Would you expect to find more records of unhappy marriages than happy ones?**

Changing Middle-Class Families: Assessing the Visual Record

Throughout the text, we have discussed and analyzed American families—white yeomen families, enslaved African American families, and now republican families. These two images allow us to compare two families of similar status: the Cheneys (top), a well-to-do family typical of the colonial era; and the Caverlys (bottom), a nineteenth-century middle-class family. Families being the basic social unit of society, comparing depictions of them allows us to see change over time and understand how shifts in personal relationships alter the nature of society.

ANALYZING THE EVIDENCE

• Count the number of children in each painting and look closely at their mothers. What impact would multiple pregnancies have on a mother's health? Given the data on birthrates discussed in the text, how many more children is Mrs. Caverly likely to bear? Why might she, like many other white nineteenth-century women, have had fewer children than Mrs. Cheney had?

• How are the children posed in each painting? What do their poses reveal about adults' perceptions of children? In the paintings, is there evidence of change in that thinking from the colonial era to the nineteenth century?

• Though Mrs. Caverly is shown looking toward her husband, there is a Bible on the table next to her; her husband is shown reading a newspaper. What do these clues suggest about women's and men's roles in the 1830s? From your reading of the text, how do these symbolic actions reflect important social and cultural values of the time?

• Whom do you see first when you look at the painting of the Cheneys? Is there a similar visual center in the image of the Caverlys? Notice the differences in the physical settings and in the placement of the family members, and compare the two backgrounds: Why is one plain and gray, and the other decorated and filled with objects? What do the differences tell you about the changing values of the middle class?

The Cheneys, c. 1795. National Gallery of Art, Washington, Gift of Edgar Williams and Bernice Chrysler Garbisch.

The Caverlys, 1836. Fenimore House Museum, New-York State Historical Association.

Women's Education
Even in education-conscious New England, during the colonial era few girls attended free public primary schools for more than a few years. After 1800, as this detail from *Scenes from a Seminary for Young Ladies* (c. 1810–1820) indicates, some girls stayed in school into their teenage years and studied a wide variety of subjects, including geography. Many graduates of these female academies became teachers, a new field of employment for women.   The St. Louis Art Museum, Purchase Funds Given by Decorative Arts Society.

letters.'" Both Thomas Jefferson and Benjamin Rush proposed ambitious schemes for a comprehensive system of primary and secondary schooling, followed by college training for bright young men. They also envisioned a university in which distinguished scholars would lecture on law, medicine, theology, and political economy.

To ordinary citizens, whose teenage children had to work, talk of secondary and college education smacked of elitism. Farmers, artisans, and laborers wanted elementary schools that would instruct their children in the "three Rs": reading, 'riting, and 'rithmetic. In New England, locally funded public schools offered most boys and some girls basic instruction in reading and writing. In other regions, there were few publicly funded schools, and only 25 percent of the boys and perhaps 10 percent of the girls attended private institutions or had personal tutors. Even in New England, only a small percentage of young men and almost no young women went on to grammar school (high school), and less than 1 percent of men attended college. "Let anybody show what advantage the poor man receives from colleges," an anonymous "Old Soldier" wrote to the *Maryland Gazette*. "Why should they support them, unless it is to serve those who are in affluent circumstances, whose children can be spared from labor, and receive the benefits?"

Although many state constitutions encouraged support for education, few legislatures acted until the 1820s. Then a new generation of reformers, primarily merchants and manufacturers, raised educational standards by certifying qualified teachers and appointing statewide superintendents of schools. To encourage self-discipline and individual enterprise in students, the reformers chose textbooks such as *The Life of George Washington* (c. 1800). Its author, Parson Mason Weems,

used examples of events from Washington's life to praise honesty and hard work and to condemn gambling, drinking, and laziness. Believing that patriotic instruction would foster shared cultural ideals, reformers required the study of American history. Thomas Low recalled his days as a New Hampshire schoolboy: "We were taught every day and in every way that ours was the freest, the happiest, and soon to be the greatest and most powerful country of the world."

Promoting Cultural Independence Like Caleb Bingham, writer Noah Webster believed that education should raise the nation's intellectual reputation. Asserting that "America must be as independent in *literature* as she is in politics," he called on his fellow citizens to free themselves "from the dependence on foreign opinions and manners, which is fatal to the efforts of genius in this country." Webster's *Dissertation on the English Language* (1789) helpfully defined words according to American usage. With less success, it proposed that words be spelled as they were pronounced, that *labour* (British spelling), for example, be spelled *labur*. Still, Webster's famous "blue-back speller," a compact textbook first published in 1783, sold 60 million copies over the next half-century and served the needs of Americans of all backgrounds. "None of us was 'lowed to see a book," an enslaved African American recalled, "but we gits hold of that Webster's old blue-back speller and we . . . studies [it]."

Despite Webster's efforts, a republican literary culture developed slowly. Ironically, the most successful writer in the new republic was Washington Irving, an elitist-minded Federalist. His whimsical essay and story collections—for example, *Salmagundi* (1807) and *The Sketch Book of Geoffrey Crayon* (1819–1820), which included "Rip Van Winkle" and "The Legend of Sleepy Hollow"—sold well in America and won praise abroad. Frustrated by the immaturity of American cultural life, Irving lived for seventeen years in Europe, reveling in its aristocratic culture and intense intellectuality.

Apart from Irving, no American author was well known in Europe or, indeed, in the United States. "Literature is not yet a distinct profession with us," Thomas Jefferson told an English friend. "Now and then a strong mind arises, and at its intervals from business emits a flash of light. But the first object of young societies is bread and covering." Not until the 1830s and 1840s would American authors achieve a professional identity and make a significant contribution to Western literature (see Chapter 11).

- Did American culture become more democratic—for men and for women—in the early nineteenth century? If so, why? If not, why not?

- How did republican ideas shape parent-child interactions, marriage relationships, and intellectual life?

Aristocratic Republicanism and Slavery

Republicanism in the South differed significantly from that in the North. Enslaved Africans constituted one-third of the South's population and exposed an enormous contradiction in white Americans' ideology of freedom and equality. "How is it that we hear the loudest yelps for liberty among the drivers of Negroes?" British author Samuel Johnson had chided the American rebels in 1775, a point that some Patriots took to heart. "I wish most sincerely there was not a Slave in the province," Abigail Adams confessed to her husband, John. "It always appeared a most iniquitous Scheme to me—to fight ourselves for what we are daily robbing and plundering from those who have as good a right to freedom as we have."

The Revolution and Slavery, 1776–1800

In fact, the whites' struggle for independence had raised the prospect of freedom for blacks. As the Revolutionary War began, a black preacher in Georgia told his fellow slaves that King George III "came up with the Book [the Bible], and was about to alter the World, and set the Negroes free." Similar rumors, probably prompted by

royal governor Lord Dunmore's proclamation of 1775 (see Chapter 5), circulated among slaves in Virginia and the Carolinas, prompting thousands of African Americans to flee behind British lines. Two neighbors of Richard Henry Lee, a Virginia Patriot, lost "every slave they had in the world," as did many other planters. In 1781, when the British army evacuated Charleston, more than 6,000 former slaves went with them; another 4,000 left from Savannah. All told, 30,000 blacks may have fled their owners. Hundreds of freed black Loyalists settled permanently in Canada. More than 1,000 others, poorly treated in British Nova Scotia, sought a better life in Sierra Leone, West Africa, a settlement founded by English antislavery organizations.

Manumission and Gradual Emancipation | Yet thousands of African Americans supported the Patriot cause. Eager to raise their social status, free blacks in New England volunteered for military service in the First Rhode Island Company and the Massachusetts "Bucks." In Maryland, a significant number of slaves took up arms for the rebels in return for the promise of freedom. Enslaved Virginians struck informal bargains with their Patriot owners, trading loyalty in wartime for the hope of liberty. In 1782, the Virginia assembly passed a **manumission** act, which allowed individual owners to free their slaves; within a decade, planters had released 10,000 slaves.

Quakers took the lead in condemning slavery. Beginning in the 1750s, Quaker evangelist John Woolman urged Friends to free their slaves, and many did so. Rapidly growing evangelical churches, especially Methodists and Baptists, initially advocated emancipation and admitted both enslaved and free blacks to their congregations. In 1784, a conference of Virginia Methodists declared that slavery was "contrary to the Golden Law of God on which hang all the Law and Prophets."

Enlightenment philosophy challenged the widespread belief among whites that Africans were inherently inferior to Europeans. John Locke had argued that ideas were not innate but stemmed from a person's experiences in the world. Accordingly, Enlightenment-influenced Americans suggested that the debased condition of blacks reflected their oppressive captivity: "A state of slavery has a mighty tendency to shrink and contract the minds of men." Defying popular opinion, Quaker philanthropist Anthony Benezet declared that African Americans were "as capable of improvement as White People" and funded a Philadelphia school for their education.

These religious and intellectual currents encouraged legal change. In 1784, judicial rulings abolished

Republican Families . . . and Servants

Around 1828, an unidentified artist painted this York, Pennsylvania, family with an African American servant. The husband and wife embody a republican companionate-style marriage (the artist gives equal emphasis to the wife and the husband) in which the mother takes the leading role in rearing and educating the children. Befitting its upper-middle-class status, the family employs an African American woman as a domestic servant and nanny—common occupations among free black women of the time.   Courtesy of The St. Louis Art Museum.

slavery in Massachusetts; over the next twenty years, every state north of Delaware enacted gradual emancipation legislation (Map 8.2). These laws recognized white property rights by requiring slaves to buy their freedom by years—even decades—of additional labor. For example, the New York Emancipation Act of 1799 allowed slavery to continue until 1828 and freed slave children only at the age of twenty-five. Subsequent legislation allowed enslaved people to marry and live where they pleased. Still, as late as 1810, almost 30,000 blacks in the northern states—nearly one-fourth of the African Americans living there—were still enslaved. Those blacks who were free faced severe prejudice from whites

who feared job competition and racial melding. Even as Massachusetts ended slavery, the legislature reenacted an old law that prohibited whites from marrying blacks, mulattos, or Indians.

Slavery Defended | The contradiction in American republican ideology between liberty and property rights was greatest in the South, where enslaved African Americans represented a huge financial investment. Some Chesapeake tobacco planters, moved by evangelical religion or an oversupply of workers, manumitted their slaves or allowed them to buy their freedom by working as artisans or laborers. Such measures gradually brought freedom to one-third of the African Americans in Maryland. Farther south, slavery remained ascendant. When the Virginia legislature allowed manumission in 1782, planters feared it would lead to emancipation. Hundreds of slave owners signed petitions demanding protection of "the most valuable and indispensible Article of our Property, our Slaves," and legislators forbade further manumissions. Following the lead of Thomas Jefferson, who owned more than a hundred slaves, they now argued that slavery was a "necessary evil" required to maintain white supremacy and the luxurious planter lifestyle. In North Carolina, legislators condemned private Quaker manumissions as "highly criminal and reprehensible." And the slave-hungry rice- and cotton-growing states of South Carolina and Georgia reopened the Atlantic slave trade. Between 1790 and 1808, merchants in Charleston and Savannah imported about 115,000 Africans, selling thousands to French and American planters in Louisiana (Table 8.1).

All debate in the South over emancipation ended in 1800, when Virginia authorities thwarted an uprising planned by Gabriel Prosser, an enslaved artisan, and hanged him and thirty of his followers. "Liberty and equality have brought the evil upon us," a letter to the *Virginia Herald* proclaimed, denouncing such doctrines as "dangerous and extremely wicked." To preserve their privileged social position, southern leaders redefined republicanism by limiting its principles of individual liberty and legal equality to whites, creating what historians call a *herrenvolk* ("master race") republic.

The North and South Grow Apart

European visitors to the United States agreed that North and South had distinct characters. A British observer said that New England was home to religious "fanaticism" but that "the lower orders of citizens" there had "a better education, [and were] more intelligent, and

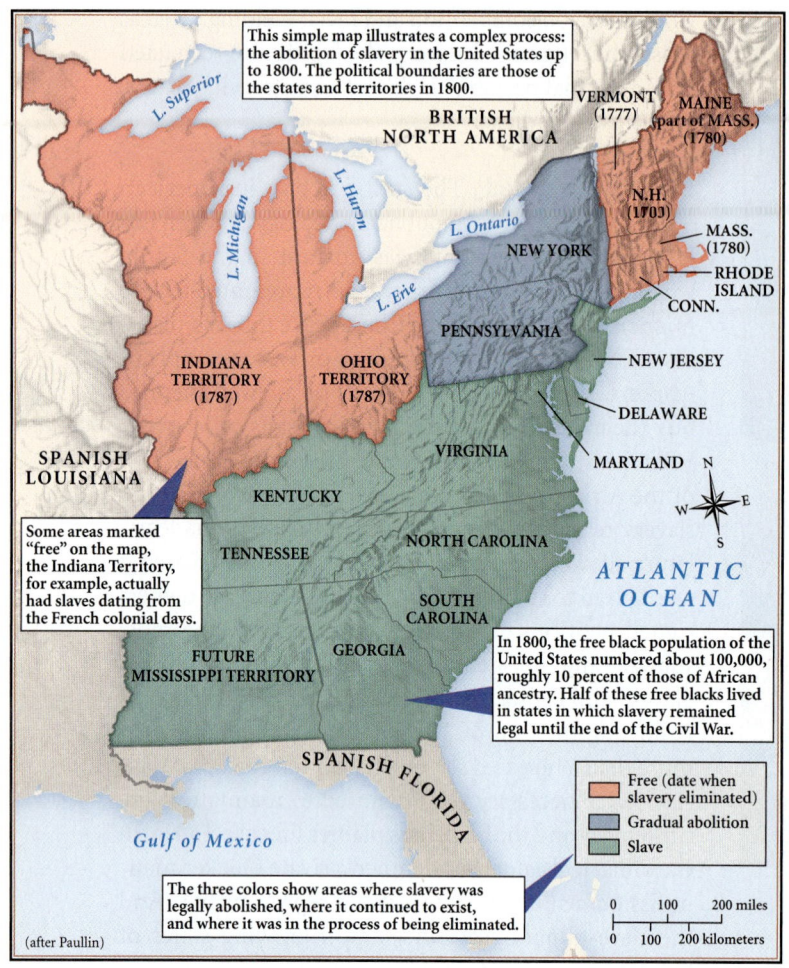

This simple map illustrates a complex process: the abolition of slavery in the United States up to 1800. The political boundaries are those of the states and territories in 1800.

Some areas marked "free" on the map, the Indiana Territory, for example, actually had slaves dating from the French colonial days.

In 1800, the free black population of the United States numbered about 100,000, roughly 10 percent of those of African ancestry. Half of these free blacks lived in states in which slavery remained legal until the end of the Civil War.

The three colors show areas where slavery was legally abolished, where it continued to exist, and where it was in the process of being eliminated.

Free (date when slavery eliminated)
Gradual abolition
Slave

(after Paullin)

MAP 8.2

The Status of Slavery, 1800

In 1775, racial slavery was legal in all of the British colonies in North America. By the time the states achieved their independence in 1783, most African Americans in New England had also been freed. By 1800, all of the states north of Maryland had provided for the gradual abolition of slavery, but the process was slow and not completed until the 1830s. Some slave owners in the Chesapeake region also manumitted their slaves, leaving only the whites of the Lower South firmly committed to racial bondage.

TABLE 8.1

African Slaves Imported into the United States, by Region of Departure and Ethnicity, 1776–1809

Region of Departure	Ethnicity	Number	Percentage of Imported Slaves
Senegambia	Mandinka, Fulbe, Serer, Jola, Wolof, Bambara	8,000	7
Sierra Leone	Vai, Mende, Kpelle, Kru	18,300	16
Gold Coast	Ashanti, Fanti	15,000	13
Bight of Benin, Bight of Biafra	Ibo, Ibibio	5,700	5
West Central Africa	Kongo, Tio, Matamba	37,800	33
Southeast Africa	Unknown	1,100	1
Other or unknown		28,700	25
Total		**114,600**	**100**

NOTE: Recent research suggests that 433,000 enslaved Africans arrived in British North America and the United States between 1607 and 1820: 33,200 before 1700; 278,400 from 1700 to 1775; 114,600 from 1776 to 1809; and 7,000 from 1810 to 1819. The numbers are extrapolated from known voyages of 65,000 Africans. Ethnicity should be considered very tentative because slaves from many regions left from the same port and because the regional and ethnic origins of 28,700 slaves (25 percent) are not known.

SOURCE: Aaron S. Fogleman, "From Slaves, Convicts, and Servants to Free Passengers: The Transformation of Immigration in the Era of the American Revolution," *Journal of American History* 85 (June 1998), table 1 and table A.6.

Aristocratic Republicanism in South Carolina

The money that paid for Drayton Hall came originally from raising cattle in South Carolina for sale in the West Indies. At his death in 1717, Thomas Drayton left an estate that included 1,300 cattle and 46 slaves (both Native American and African). His third son, John (1715–1779), used his inheritance to buy slaves, and create a rice-growing plantation along the Ashley River. The design of the home he erected on the site, Drayton Hall (built 1738–1742), was inspired by Andrea Palladio, the Italian Renaissance architect who celebrated the concepts of classical Roman proportion and decoration in his widely read *The Four Books of Architecture* (1516).   Photo courtesy of Drayton Hall.

better informed" than those he met in the South. "The state of poverty in which a great number of white people live in Virginia" surprised the Marquis de Chastellux. Other visitors to the South commented on the rude manners, heavy drinking, and weak work ethic of its residents. White tenants and smallholding farmers seemed only to have a "passion for gaming at the billiard table, a cock-fight or cards," and planters squandered their wealth on extravagant lifestyles while their slaves endured bitter poverty.

Some southerners worried that human bondage corrupted their society by encouraging ignorance and poverty among whites. A South Carolina merchant observed, "Where there are Negroes a White Man despises to work, saying what, will you have me a Slave and work like a Negroe?" Meanwhile, wealthy planters wanted a compliant labor force content with the drudgery of agricultural work. Consequently, they trained most of their slaves as field hands, allowing only a few to learn the arts of the blacksmith, carpenter, or bricklayer. Able

to hire tutors for their own children, well-to-do planters did little to provide other whites with elementary schooling. In 1800, elected officials in Essex County, Virginia, spent about 25 cents per person for local government, including schools, while their counterparts in Acton, Massachusetts, allocated about $1 per person. This difference in support for education mattered: By the 1820s, nearly all native-born men and women in New England could read and write, while more than one-third of white southerners could not.

Slavery and National Politics As the northern states ended human bondage, the South's commitment to slavery became a political issue. At the Philadelphia convention in 1787, northern delegates had reluctantly accepted clauses allowing slave imports for twenty years and guaranteeing the return of fugitive slaves (see Chapter 6). Seeking even more protection for their "peculiar institution," southerners in the new national legislature won approval of

James Madison's resolution that "Congress have no authority to interfere in the emancipation of slaves, or in the treatment of them within any of the States."

Nonetheless, slavery remained a contested issue. The black slave revolt in Haiti brought 6,000 white and free mulatto refugees to the United States in 1793, and their stories of atrocities frightened American slave owners. Meanwhile, northern politicians assailed the British impressment of American sailors as just "as oppressive and tyrannical as the slave trade" and demanded the end of both. When Congress outlawed the Atlantic slave trade in 1808, some northern representatives demanded an end to the trade in slaves between states. In response, southern leaders defended their labor system. "A large majority of people in the Southern states do not consider slavery as even an evil," declared one congressman. The South's political clout—its domination of the presidency and the Senate—ensured that the national government would protect slavery. American diplomats vigorously demanded compensation for slaves freed by British troops during the War of 1812, and Congress enacted legislation upholding slavery in the District of Columbia.

African Americans Speak Out   Heartened by the end of the Atlantic slave trade, black abolitionists spoke out. In speeches and pamphlets Henry Sipkins and Henry Johnson condemned slavery as "relentless tyranny." In their view, slavery—not freedom—was the central legacy of American colonial and revolutionary history. For inspiration, they looked to the Haitian Revolution, which overthrew slavery; for collective support, they joined together in secret societies, such as Prince Hall's African Lodge of Freemasons in Boston and affiliated lodges in other northern cities. Along with white antislavery advocates, black abolitionists hoped that slavery would die out naturally as the tobacco economy declined. Their hopes quickly faded as the cotton boom increased the demand for slaves, and Louisiana (1812), Mississippi (1817), and Alabama (1819) joined the Union with state constitutions that permitted slavery.

These events prompted a group of influential white Americans to found the American Colonization Society in 1817. According to Henry Clay—a society member, Speaker of the House of Representatives, and a slave owner—racial bondage had placed his state of Kentucky "in the rear of our neighbors . . . in the state of agriculture, the progress of manufactures, the advance of improvement, and the general prosperity of society." Slaves had to be freed, Clay and other colonizationists argued, and sent back to Africa. Clay feared that

emancipation without removal would prompt racial chaos—"a civil war that would end in the extermination or subjugation of the one race or the other." But few planters responded to the society's plea and, from among the 1.5 million African Americans in the United States in 1820, it resettled only about 6,000 in Liberia, the society's colony on the west coast of Africa.

Most free blacks strongly opposed such colonization schemes. As Bishop Richard Allen of the African Methodist Episcopal Church put it, "[T]his land which we have watered with our tears and our blood is now our mother country." Allen spoke from experience. Born into slavery in Philadelphia in 1760 and sold to a farmer in Delaware, Allen grew up in bondage. In 1777, Freeborn Garretson, an itinerant preacher, converted Allen to Methodism and convinced Allen's owner that on Judgment Day, slaveholders would be "weighted in the balance, and . . . found wanting." Allowed to buy his freedom, Allen enlisted in the Methodist cause, becoming a "licensed exhorter" and then a regular minister in Philadelphia. In 1795, Allen formed a separate black congregation, the Bethel Church; in 1816, he became the first bishop of a new denomination: the African Methodist Episcopal Church. Two years later, 3,000 African Americans met in Allen's church to condemn colonization and to claim American citizenship. Sounding the principles of democratic republicanism, they vowed to defy racial prejudice and advance in American society using "those opportunities . . . which the Constitution and the laws allow to all."

The Missouri Crisis, 1819–1821

The failure of colonization set the stage for a major battle over slavery. In 1818, Congressman Nathaniel Macon of North Carolina warned slave owners that radical members of the "bible and peace societies" hoped to use the national government to raise "the question of emancipation." And so they did. When Missouri applied for admission to the Union in 1819 with a constitution that allowed slavery, Congressman James Tallmadge of New York intervened: He would support Missouri's constitution only if it banned the entry of new slaves and provided for the emancipation of existing bondspeople. Missouri whites rejected Tallmadge's proposals, and the northern majority in the House of Representatives blocked the territory's admission.

White southerners were horrified. "It is believed by some, & feared by others," Alabama senator John Walker reported from Washington, that Tallmadge's amendment was "merely the entering wedge and that it points already to a total emancipation of the blacks." Mis-

Reverend Richard Allen and the African Methodist Episcopal Church

One of the best-known African Americans in the early republic, Richard Allen founded a separate congregation for Philadelphia's black Methodists, the Bethel Church. Working with other ministers in 1816, he created the first independent black religious domination in the United States—the African Methodist Episcopal (AME) Church—and became its first bishop.   Library of Congress. / The Mount Bethel African Methodist Episcopal Church.

sissippi congressman Christopher Rankin accused his northern colleagues of coercion: "You conduct us to an awful precipice, and hold us over it." To underline their commitment to slavery, southerners used their power in the Senate — where they held half the seats — to withhold statehood from Maine, which was seeking to separate itself from Massachusetts.

Constitutional Issues   In the ensuing debate, southerners advanced three constitutional arguments. First, invoking the principle of "equal rights," they argued that Congress could not impose conditions on Missouri that it had not imposed on other territories seeking statehood. Second, they maintained that the Constitution guaranteed a state's sovereignty with respect to its internal affairs and domestic institutions, such as slavery and marriage. Finally, they insisted that Congress had no authority to infringe on the property rights of individual slaveholders. In their view, the United States was a confederation of semi-sovereign states with limited national powers. Beyond that, southern leaders reaffirmed their commitment to human bondage. Abandoning the argument that slavery was a "necessary evil," they now invoked religion to champion it as a "positive good." "Christ himself gave a sanction to slavery," declared Senator William Smith of South Carolina. "If it be offensive and sinful to own slaves," a prominent Mississippi Methodist added, "I wish someone would just put his finger on the place in Holy Writ."

Controversy raged in Congress and the press for two years before Henry Clay put together a series of political agreements known collectively as the Missouri Compromise. Faced with unwavering southern opposition to Tallmadge's amendment, a group of northern congressmen deserted the antislavery coalition. They accepted a deal that allowed Maine to enter the Union as a free state in 1820 and Missouri to follow as a slave state in 1821. This agreement preserved a balance in the Senate between North and South and set a precedent for future admissions to the Union. For their part, southern senators accepted the prohibition of slavery in the vast northern section of the Louisiana Purchase, the lands north of latitude 36°30' outside the boundaries of Missouri (Map 8.3).

As they had in the Philadelphia Convention of 1787, white politicians had preserved the Union by compromising over slavery. Now the task was more difficult. The delegates in Philadelphia had resolved their sectional differences in two months; it took Congress two years to work out the Missouri Compromise, which even then did not command universal support. "If we yield now, beware," the *Richmond Enquirer* warned as southern congressmen agreed to exclude slavery from most of the Louisiana Purchase. "What is a *territorial* restriction to-day becomes a *state* restriction tomorrow." The fates of the western lands, enslaved blacks, and the Union itself were now inextricably intertwined, raising the specter of civil war and the end of the American republican experiment. As the aging Thomas

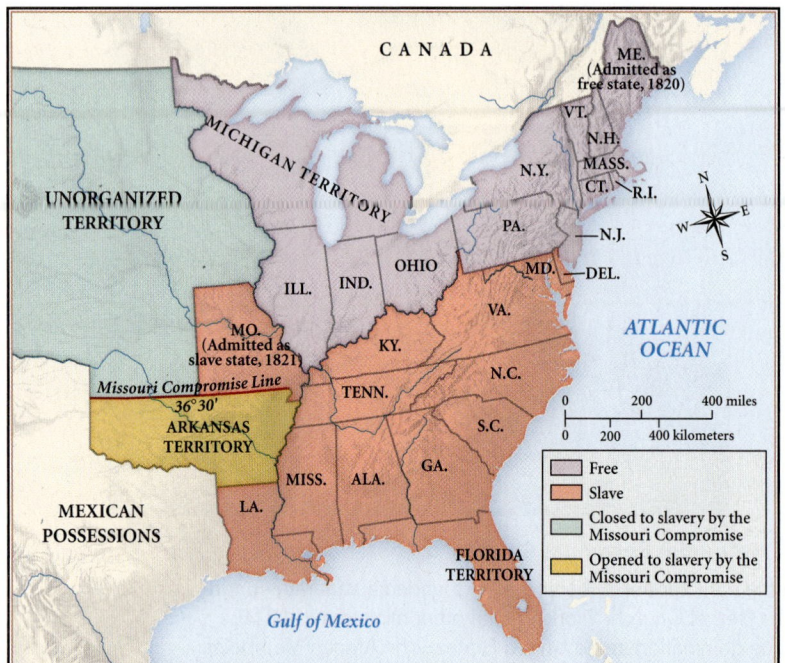

MAP 8.3

The Missouri Compromise, 1820–1821

The Missouri Compromise resolved for a generation the issue of slavery in the lands of the Louisiana Purchase. The agreement prohibited slavery north of the Missouri Compromise line (36°30' north latitude), with the exception of the state of Missouri. To maintain an equal number of senators from free and slave states in the U.S. Congress, the compromise provided for the nearly simultaneous admission to the Union of Missouri and Maine.

Jefferson exclaimed during the Missouri crisis, "This momentous question, like a fire-bell in the night, awakened and filled me with terror."

- **How did the aristocratic republicanism of the South differ from the democratic republicanism of the North?**

- **What compromises over slavery did the members of Congress make to settle the Missouri crisis? Who benefited most from the agreement?**

Protestant Christianity as a Social Force

Throughout the colonial era, religion played a role in American life that was significant but not overwhelming. Then, beginning around 1790, religious revivals planted the values of Protestant Christianity deep in the national character and gave a spiritual dimension to American republicanism. These revivals especially changed the lives of blacks and of women. Thousands of African Americans became Baptists and Methodists and created a powerful institution: the black Christian church. Evangelical Christianity also gave rise to new public roles for white women, especially in the North, and set in motion long-lasting movements for social reform.

A Republican Religious Order

The demand for greater liberty unleashed by the republican revolution of 1776 forced American lawmakers to devise new relationships between church and state. Previously, only the Quaker- and Baptist-controlled governments of Pennsylvania and Rhode Island had rejected a legally **established church** and compulsory religious taxes. Then, a convergence of factors—Enlightenment principles, wartime needs, and Baptist ideology—eliminated most state support for religion and encouraged voluntary church membership.

Religious Freedom Events in Virginia revealed the dynamics of change. In 1776, James Madison and George Mason advanced Enlightenment ideas of religious toleration as they sought to persuade the state's constitutional convention to guarantee all Christians the "free exercise of religion." This measure would end the privileged legal status of the Anglican Church. The delegates, many of whom were Anglicans, accepted this provision in part because they needed the support of Presbyterians and Baptists in the independence struggle. The Baptists also opposed the use of taxes to support religion, even their own. They convinced lawmakers to reject a tax bill (which was supported by George Washington and Patrick Henry) that would have funded all Christian churches. Instead, in 1786, the Virginia legislature enacted Thomas Jefferson's Bill for Establishing Religious Freedom, which made all churches equal in the eyes of the law and granted direct financial support to none.

Elsewhere, the old order of a single established church crumbled away. In New York and New Jersey, the sheer number of denominations—Episcopalian, Presbyterian, Dutch Reformed, Lutheran, and Quaker, among others—prevented lawmakers from agreeing on an established church or compulsory religious taxes. Congregationalism remained the official church in the New England states until the 1830s, but members of other denominations could now pay taxes to their own churches.

Church-State Relations | Few influential Americans wanted a complete separation of church and state because they believed that religious institutions promoted morality and respect for governmental authority. "Pure religion and civil liberty are inseparable companions," a group of North Carolinians advised their minister. "It is your particular duty to enlighten mankind with the unerring principles of truth and justice, the main props of all civil government." Accepting this premise, most state governments indirectly supported churches by exempting their property and ministers from taxation.

Freedom of conscience also came with sharp cultural limits. In Virginia, Jefferson's Bill for Establishing Religious Freedom prohibited religious requirements for holding public office, but other states discriminated against those who were not Protestant Christians. The North Carolina Constitution of 1776 disqualified from public employment any citizen "who shall deny the being of God, or the Truth of the Protestant Religion,

or the Divine Authority of the Old or New Testament." No Catholics or Jews need apply. New Hampshire's constitution contained a similar provision until 1868.

Americans influenced by Enlightenment deism and by evangelical Protestantism condemned these religious restrictions. Jefferson, Franklin, and other American intellectuals maintained that God had given humans the power of reason so that they could determine moral truths for themselves. To protect society from "ecclesiastical tyranny," they demanded complete freedom of conscience. Many evangelical Protestants also demanded religious liberty; their goal was to protect their churches from an oppressive government. Isaac Backus, a New England minister, warned Baptists not to incorporate their churches or accept public funds because that might lead to state control. In Connecticut, a devout Congregationalist welcomed "voluntarism," the uncoerced funding of churches by their members; it allowed the laity to control the clergy, he said, thereby supporting self-government and "the principles of republicanism."

The Second Great Awakening

Overshadowing such debates, a decades-long series of religious revivals—the Second Great Awakening—made the United States a genuinely Christian society. The most successful churches were those that preached spiritual equality and governed themselves democratically. Because bishops and priests controlled it, the Roman Catholic Church attracted few Protestants, who preferred Luther's doctrine of the priesthood of all believers. When some Catholics in Norfolk, Virginia, proposed in 1818 that "all Pastors should be appointed by

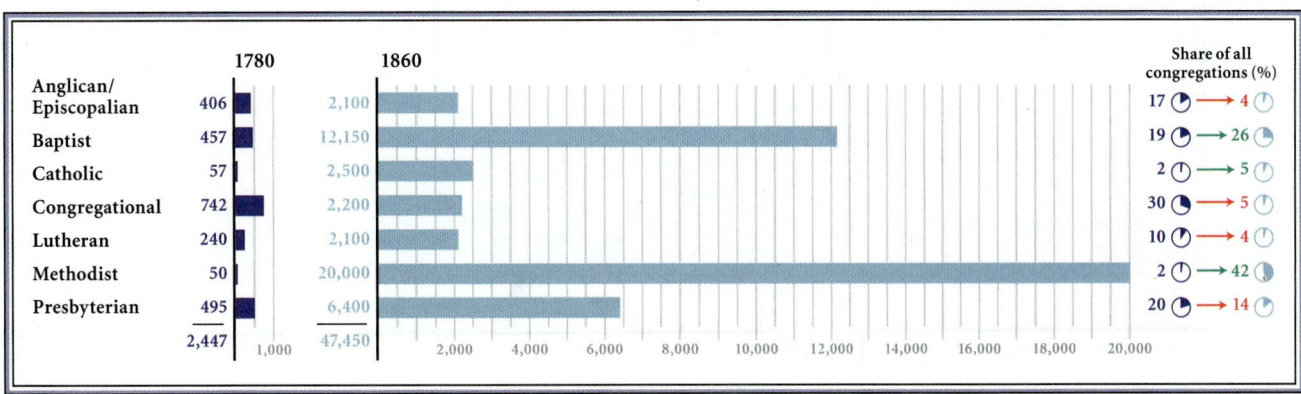

FIGURE 8.1

Number of Church Congregations by Denomination, 1780 and 1860

The growth of evangelical churches, Methodist and Baptist, transformed American Christianity during the first half of the nineteenth century. Also noteworthy was the surge in the number of Catholic congregations, the result of immigration from Ireland and Germany after 1830.

their respective congregations," they were denounced by church authorities. Nor did the Catholic Church appeal to the unchurched—the great number of Americans who simply ignored religious institutions. Likewise, few Americans joined the Protestant Episcopal Church, the successor to the Church of England, because wealthy lay members dominated many congregations and it, too, had a hierarchy of bishops (Figure 8.1). The Presbyterian Church attracted more adherents, in part because its churches elected laymen to the synods, the congresses that determined doctrine and practice.

Evangelical Churches | Evangelical Methodist and Baptist churches were by far the most popular. The Baptists boasted a republican church organization, with self-governing congregations.

Both Baptists and Methodists developed an egalitarian religious culture marked by communal singing and emotional services (see Voices from Abroad, "Frances Trollope: A Camp Meeting in Indiana," p. 261). These denominations came to the fore in the 1790s, as they evangelized the cities and the backcountry of New England. A new sect of Universalists, who repudiated the Calvinist doctrine of predestination and preached universal salvation, also gained tens of thousands of converts, especially in Massachusetts and northern New England. After 1800, enthusiastic camp meetings swept the frontier regions of South Carolina, Tennessee, Ohio, and Kentucky. The largest gathering, at Cane Ridge in Kentucky in 1801, lasted for nine electrifying days and nights and attracted almost 20,000 people (Map 8.4). With these revivals, Baptist and Methodist preachers

MAP 8.4

The Second Great Awakening, 1790–1860

The Second Great Awakening lasted for decades and invigorated churches in every part of the nation. The revivals in Kentucky and New York State, though, were particularly influential. As thousands of farm families migrated to the west, they carried with them the religious excitement generated by the Cane Ridge revival in Kentucky in 1801. And, between 1825 and 1835, the area along the Erie Canal in New York witnessed such fervor that it came to be known as the Burned-over District.

All the nations and people I had hitherto passed through resembl...
own in their manners, customs and ...

Frances Trollope
A Camp Meeting in Indiana

Frances Trollope, a successful English author and the mother of novelist Anthony Trollope, lived for a time in Cincinnati, where she owned a bazaar that sold imported goods from Europe. Unsuccessful as a storekeeper, she won great acclaim as a social commentator. Her critical-minded study, *Domestic Manners of the Americans* (1832), was a bestseller in Europe and the United States. Here Trollope provides a vivid description of a revivalist meeting in Indiana around 1830.

The prospect of passing a night in the back-woods of Indiana was by no means agreeable, but I screwed my courage to the proper pitch, determined to see with my own eyes, and hear with my own ears, what a camp meeting really was. . . . We reached the ground about an hour before midnight, and the approach to it was highly picturesque. The spot chosen was the verge of an unbroken forest, where a space of about twenty acres appeared to have been partially cleared for the purpose. Tents of different sizes were pitched very near together in a circle round the cleared space. . . .

Four high frames, constructed in the form of altars, were placed at the four corners of the inclosure; on these were supported layers of earth and sod, on which burned immense fires of blazing pine-wood. On one side a rude platform was erected to accommodate the preachers, fifteen of whom attended this meeting, and with very short intervals for necessary refreshment and private devotion, preached in rotation, day and night, from Tuesday to Saturday.

When we arrived, the preachers were silent; but we heard issuing from nearly every tent mingled sounds of praying, preaching, singing, and lamentation. . . . The floor [of one tent] was covered with straw, which round the sides was heaped in masses, that might serve as seats, but which at that moment were used to support the heads and arms of the close-packed circle of men and women who kneeled on the floor.

Out of about thirty persons thus placed, perhaps half a dozen were men. One of these [was] a handsome-looking youth of eighteen or twenty. . . . His arm was encircling the neck of a young girl who knelt beside him, with her hair hanging dishevelled upon her shoulders, and her features working with the most violent agitation; soon after they both fell forward on the straw, as if unable to endure in any other attitude the burning eloquence of a tall grim figure in black, who, standing erect in the center, was uttering with incredible vehemence an oration that seemed to hover between praying and preaching; his arms hung stiff and immoveable by his side, and he looked like an ill-constructed machine, set in action by a movement so violent as to threaten its own destruction, so jerkingly, painfully, yet rapidly, did his words tumble out; the kneel-

ing circle ceasing not to call, in every variety of tone, on the name of Jesus. . . .

One tent was occupied exclusively by Negroes. They were all full-dressed, and looked exactly as if they were performing a scene on a stage. One woman wore a dress of pink gauze trimmed with silver lace; another was dressed in pale yellow silk; one or two had splendid turbans; and all wore a profusion of ornaments. The men were in snow-white pantaloons, with gay colored linen jackets. One of these, a youth of coal–black comeliness, was preaching with the most violent gesticulations. . . .

At midnight, a horn sounded through the camp . . . to call the people from private to public worship; and we presently saw them flocking from all sides to the front of the preacher's stand. . . . about two thousand persons. . . .

One of the preachers began in a low nasal tone, and, like all other Methodist preachers, assured us of the enormous depravity of man. . . . Above a hundred persons, nearly all females, came forward, uttering howlings and groans so terrible that I shall never cease to shudder when I recall them. They appeared to drag each other forward, and on the word being given, "let us pray," they fell on their knees . . . and they were soon all lying on the ground in an indescribable confusion of heads and legs.

Source: Frances Trollope, *Domestic Manners of the Americans* (London: Whittaker, Treacher, 1832), 139–142.

ANALYZING THE EVIDENCE

- What is Trollope's opinion about what she witnessed? Did she see what she expected to see? What clues does the narrative provide?

- Who attended the camp meeting? How would you explain the different dress and deportment of the African American believers?

- How did the worship at this nineteenth-century camp meeting differ from that in a New England Congregational church in the eighteenth century? How do you explain the difference?

- How does Trollope characterize the theology of the Methodist preacher? How did it differ from that of earlier Calvinists who believed in predestination?

reshaped the spiritual landscape throughout the South. Offering a powerful emotional message and the promise of religious fellowship, revivalists attracted both unchurched individuals and pious families searching for social ties as they migrated to new communities.

The Second Great Awakening transformed the denominational makeup of American religion. The important churches of the colonial period — the Congregationalists, Episcopalians, and Quakers — grew slowly through natural increase, while Methodist and Baptist churches expanded spectacularly by winning converts. In rural areas, their preachers followed a circuit, "riding a hardy pony or horse" with their "Bible, hymn-book, and Discipline" to visit existing congregations on a regular schedule. They began new churches by searching out devout families, bringing them together for worship, and then appointing lay elders to lead the congregation and enforce moral discipline. Soon, they were the largest denominations.

To attract converts, evangelical ministers copied the "practical preaching" techniques of George Whitefield and other eighteenth-century revivalists (see Chapter 4). They spoke from memory in plain language and often with a flamboyant style and theatrical gestures. "Preach without papers," advised one minister. "[S]eem earnest & serious; & you will be listened to with Patience, & Wonder."

In the South, evangelical religion was initially a disruptive force because many ministers spoke of spiritual equality and criticized slavery. Husbands and planters grew angry when their wives became more assertive and when blacks joined their congregations. To retain white men in their churches, Methodist and Baptist preachers gradually adapted their religious message to justify the authority of yeomen patriarchs and slave-owning planters. One Baptist minister declared that a man was naturally at "the head of the woman," and a Methodist conference proclaimed "that a Christian slave must be submissive, faithful, and obedient."

Black Christianity Other evangelists persuaded planters to spread Protestant Christianity among their African American slaves. During the eighteenth century, most blacks had maintained the religious practices of their African homelands, giving homage to African gods and spirits or practicing Islam. "At the time I first went to Carolina," remembered Charles Ball, a former slave, "there were a great many African slaves in the country. . . . Many of them believed there were several gods [and] I knew several . . . Mohamedans [Muslims]." Beginning in the mid-1780s, Protestant evangelists converted hundreds of African Americans along the James River in Virginia and throughout the Chesapeake and the Carolinas.

Subsequently, black Christians adapted Protestant teachings to their own needs. They generally ignored the doctrines of original sin and Calvinist predestination as well as biblical passages that encouraged unthinking obedience to authority. Some African American converts envisioned the Christian God as a warrior who had liberated the Jews. Their own "cause was similar to the Israelites," preacher Martin Prosser told his fellow slaves as he and his brother Gabriel plotted rebellion in Virginia in 1800. "I have read in my Bible where God says, if we worship him, . . . five of you shall conquer a hundred and a hundred of you a hundred thousand of our enemies." Confident of a special relationship with God, Christian slaves prepared themselves spiritually for emancipation, the first step in their journey to the Promised Land.

Religion and Reform

Influenced by republican ideology, many whites also rejected the Calvinists' emphasis on human depravity and weakness; instead, they celebrated human reason and free will. In New England, many educated Congregationalists discarded the mysterious concept of the Trinity — Father, Son, and Holy Spirit — and, taking the name Unitarians, worshipped a "united" God and promoted rational thought. "The ultimate reliance of a human being is, and must be, on his own mind," argued William Ellery Channing, a famous Unitarian minister. A children's catechism conveyed the denomination's optimistic message: "If I am good, God will love me, and make me happy."

Other New England Congregationalists softened Calvinist doctrines. Lyman Beecher, the preeminent Congregationalist clergyman of the early nineteenth century, accepted the traditional Christian belief that people had a natural tendency to sin; but, rejecting predestination, he affirmed the capacity of all men and women to choose God. By embracing the doctrine of free will, Beecher testified to the growing belief that people could shape their destiny. "Free Will" Baptists held similar views.

Benevolence and Reform Reflecting this optimism, Reverend Samuel Hopkins linked individual salvation to religious benevolence — the practice of disinterested virtue. As the Presbyterian minister John Rodgers explained, fortunate individuals who had received God's grace had a duty "to dole out charity to their poorer brothers and sisters." Heed-

Women in the Awakening

The Second Great Awakening was a pivotal moment in the history of American women. In this detail from *Religious Camp Meeting*, painted by J. Maze Burbank in 1839, all the preachers are men, but women fill the audience and form the majority of those visibly "awakened." By transforming millions of women into devout Christians, the revival movement filled Protestant churches with dedicated workers, teachers, and morality-minded mothers. When tens of thousands of these women also joined movements for temperance, abolition, and women's rights, they spurred a great wave of social reform.   Old Dartmouth Historical Society/New Bedford Whaling Museum, New Bedford, Massachusetts.

ing this message, pious merchants in New York City founded the Humane Society and other charitable organizations. Devout women aided their ministers by holding prayer meetings and providing material aid to members and potential converts. By the 1820s, so many Protestant men and women had embraced benevolent reform that conservative church leaders warned them not to neglect spiritual matters. Still, improving society was a key element of the new religious sensibility. Said Lydia Maria Child, a devout Christian social reformer: "The only true church organization [is] when

heads and hearts unite in working for the welfare of the human-race."

By the 1820s, Protestant Christians were well positioned to undertake that task. Unlike the First Great Awakening, which split churches into warring factions, the Second Great Awakening fostered cooperation among denominations. Religious leaders founded five interdenominational societies: the American Education Society (1815), the Bible Society (1816), the Sunday School Union (1824), the Tract Society (1825), and the Home Missionary Society (1826). Based in eastern cities—New York, Boston, and Philadelphia—these societies ministered to the nation, dispatching hundreds of missionaries to the West and distributing thousands of religious pamphlets.

Increasingly, Protestant ministers and laypeople saw themselves as part of a united religious movement that could change the course of history. "I want to see our state evangelized," declared a churchgoer near the Erie Canal (where the fires of revivalism were so hot that it was known as the "Burned-over District"): "Suppose the great State of New York in all its physical, political, moral, commercial, and pecuniary resources should come over to the Lord's side. Why it would turn the scale and could convert the world. I shall have no rest until it is done."

Because the Second Great Awakening aroused such enthusiasm, religion became an important new force in political life. On July 4, 1827, Reverend Ezra Stiles Ely called on the members of the Seventh Presbyterian Church in Philadelphia to begin a "Christian party in politics." Ely's sermon that day, "The Duty of Christian Freemen to Elect Christian Rulers," proclaimed a religious goal for the American republic—an objective that Thomas Jefferson and John Adams would have found strange and troubling. The two founders had both died precisely a year before, on July 4, 1826, the fiftieth anniversary of the Declaration of Independence. They had gone to their graves believing that America's mission was to spread political republicanism. In contrast, Ely urged the United States to become an evangelical Christian nation dedicated to religious conversion at home and abroad: "All our rulers ought in their official capacity to serve the Lord Jesus Christ." Similar calls for a union of church and state would again be made by evangelical Christians during the Third (1880–1900) and Fourth (1970–present) Great Awakenings.

Women's New Religious Roles

The upsurge in religious enthusiasm prompted women to demonstrate their piety and even to found new sects. Mother Ann Lee organized the Shakers in Britain and then, in 1774, migrated to America, where she attracted numerous recruits; by the 1820s, Shaker communities dotted the American countryside from New Hampshire to Indiana. Jemima Wilkinson, a young Quaker woman in Rhode Island, found inspiration by reading George Whitefield's sermons. After experiencing a vision that she had died and been reincarnated as Christ, Wilkinson declared herself the "Publick Universal Friend," dressed in masculine attire, and preached a new gospel. Her

Mrs. Juliann Jane Tillman, 1844

In 1837, Mrs. Tillman explained in a newspaper article that she "was strangely wrought upon" and "went to God" for help. Soon, "what seemed to be an angel made his sudden appearance, and in his hand was a roll . . . on which was written, 'Thee I have chosen to preach my gospel without delay.'" After much anguish and more supernatural visitations, Mrs. Tillman overcame strong personal doubts – and the equally strong opposition of male ministers and laity – and began to preach in the African Methodist Episcopal Church. Library of Congress Prints and Photographs Division. Reproduction Number: LC-USZ62-54596 (2-21).

teachings blended the Calvinist warning of "a lost and guilty, gossiping, dying World" with Quaker-inspired plain dress, pacifism, and abolitionism. Wilkinson's charisma initially won scores of converts, but her radical lifestyle and ambiguous gender aroused hostility, and her sect dwindled away.

A Growing Public Presence The few female-led sects had less impact than the activities of thousands of women in mainstream churches. For example, women in New Hampshire managed more than fifty local "cent" societies to raise funds for the Society for Promoting Christian Knowledge, New York City women founded the Society for the Relief of Poor Widows, and young Quaker women in Philadelphia ran the Society for the Free Instruction of African Females.

Women took charge of religious and charitable enterprises because they were excluded from other public roles and because of their numbers. After 1800, more than 70 percent of the members of New England Congregational churches were women. The predominance of women prompted Congregational ministers to end traditional gender-segregated prayer meetings, and evangelical Methodist and Baptist preachers actively promoted mixed-sex praying. "Our prayer meetings have been one of the greatest means of the conversion of souls," a minister in central New York reported in the 1820s, "especially those in which brothers and sisters have prayed together."

Far from leading to sexual promiscuity, as critics feared, mixing men and women promoted greater self-discipline. Believing in female virtue, many young women and the men who courted them now postponed sexual intercourse until after marriage — previously a much rarer form of self-restraint. In Hingham, Massachusetts, and many other New England towns, more than 30 percent of the women who married between 1750 and 1800 bore a child within eight months of their wedding day; by the 1820s, the rate had dropped to 15 percent.

As women claimed more spiritual authority, men tried to curb their power. In the North as in the South, evangelical Baptist churches that had once advocated spiritual equality now prevented women from voting on church matters or offering public testimonies of faith. These activities, one layman declared, were "directly opposite to the apostolic command in [Corinthians] xiv, 34, 35, 'Let your women learn to keep silence in the churches.'" Another man claimed, "Women have a different *calling*. That they *be chaste, keepers at home* is the Apostle's direction." But such injunctions merely changed the focus of women's religious activism. Embracing the idea of republican motherhood, Christian women throughout the United States founded maternal associations to encourage proper child rearing. By the 1820s, *Mother's Magazine* and other newsletters, widely read in hundreds of small towns and villages, were giving women a sense of shared purpose and identity.

Religious activism also advanced female education, as churches sponsored academies where girls from the middling classes received intellectual and moral instruction. Emma Willard, the first American advocate of higher education for women, opened the Middlebury Female Seminary in Vermont in 1814 and later founded girls' academies in Waterford and Troy, New York. Beginning in the 1820s, women educated in these seminaries and academies displaced men as public-school teachers, in part because they accepted lower pay

than men would. Female schoolteachers earned from $12 to $14 a month with room and board — less than a farm laborer. But as schoolteachers, women had an acknowledged place in public life — a status that previously had been beyond their reach.

Just as the ideology of democratic republicanism had expanded voting rights and the political influence of ordinary white men in the North, so the values of Christian republicanism had bolstered the public authority of middling women. The Second Great Awakening made Americans a fervently Protestant people. Along with the values of republicanism and capitalism, this religious impulse formed the core of an emerging national identity.

- Which American churches were the most republican in their institutions and ideology?
- Why did Protestant Christianity and Protestant women emerge as forces for social change?

SUMMARY

Like all important ideologies, republicanism has many facets. We have explored three of them in this chapter. We saw how state legislatures created capitalist commonwealths in which governments actively supported private businesses that contributed to the public welfare. This republican-inspired policy of state mercantilism remained dominant until the 1840s, when it was replaced by classical liberal doctrines.

We also saw how republicanism influenced social and family values. The principle of legal equality encouraged social mobility among white men and prompted men and women to seek companionate marriages. Republicanism likewise encouraged parents to provide their children with equal inheritances and to allow them to choose their marriage partners. In the South, republican doctrines of liberty and equality coexisted uneasily with slavery and ultimately applied only to the white population.

Finally, we observed the complex interaction of republicanism and religion. Stirred by republican principles, many citizens joined democratic and egalitarian denominations, particularly Methodist and Baptist churches. Inspired by "benevolent" ideas and the enthusiastic preachers of the Second Great Awakening, many women devoted their energies to religious purposes and social reform organizations. The result of all these initiatives — in economic policy, social relations, and religious institutions — was the creation of a distinctive American republican culture.

CHAPTER REVIEW QUESTIONS

- Explain how the republican ideas of the Revolutionary era shaped American society and culture in the late eighteenth and early nineteenth centuries. What regional differences in the social development of republicanism emerged? How can we account for these differences?

- Trace the relationship between America's republican culture and the surge of evangelism called the Second Great Awakening. In what ways are the goals of the two movements similar? How are they different?

- The text argues that a distinct American identity had begun to emerge by 1820. How would you describe this identity? What were the forces that helped create unity? And what were the points of contention?

FOR FURTHER EXPLORATION

Jeffrey L. Pasley et al., eds., *Beyond the Founders* (2004), shows how ordinary citizens promoted a democratic polity. Rosemarie Zagarri, *Revolutionary Backlash* (2007), demonstrates its limited inclusion of women. Jack Larkin, *The Reshaping of Everyday Life, 1790–1840* (1997), and **memorialhall.mass.edu/collection/index.html** explore changes in material culture. See also Patrick Griffin, *American Leviathan: Empire, Nation, and Revolutionary Frontier* (2007).

Nancy Cott analyzes cultural shifts in *Public Vows: A History of Marriage and the Nation* (2000). For family life on the Maine frontier, see Laurel Thatcher Ulrich, *A Midwife's Tale: The Life of Martha Ballard* (1990), as well as the related Web sites, **www.pbs.org/wgbh/amex/midwife** and **www.DoHistory.org**.

Jan Lewis's *The Pursuit of Happiness* (1983) discusses the paternalistic slave-owning gentry of the Upper South; James David Miller, *South by Southwest: Planter Emigration and Identity in the Slave South* (2002), explores their move to the Mississippi Valley. For slavery, consult Douglas R. Egerton, *Gabriel's Rebellion: The Virginia Slave Conspiracies of 1800 and 1802* (1995); Randolph Ferguson Scully, *Religion and the Making of Nat Turner's Virginia* (2008); and the Web site at **www.disc.wisc.edu/slavedata**.

In *The Democratization of American Christianity* (1987), Nathan Hatch traces the impact of evangelical Protestantism. Other fine studies include Mark A. Noll, *America's God: From Jonathan Edwards to Abraham Lincoln* (2003), and Bernard Weisberger, *They Gathered at the River* (1958).

TEST YOUR KNOWLEDGE

To assess your command of the material in this chapter, see the Online Study Guide at **bedfordstmartins.com/henretta**.

For Web sites, images, and documents related to topics and places in this chapter, visit **bedfordstmartins.com/makehistory**.

TIMELINE

1782	St. Jean de Crèvecoeur publishes *Letters from an American Farmer* Virginia manumission law (repealed 1792)
1783	Noah Webster publishes his "blue-back" speller
1784	Slavery abolished in Massachusetts; other northern states begin gradual emancipation
1787	Benjamin Rush writes *Thoughts on Female Education*
1790s	States grant corporations charters and special privileges Private companies build roads and canals to facilitate trade Merchants develop rural outwork system Chesapeake blacks adopt Protestant beliefs Parents limit family size as farms shrink Second Great Awakening expands church membership
1791	Congress charters First Bank of the United States
1792	Mary Wollstonecraft, *A Vindication of the Rights of Woman*
1795	Massachusetts Mill Dam Act
1800	Gabriel Prosser plots slave rebellion in Virginia
1800s	Rise of sentimentalism and of companionate marriages Women's religious activism; founding of female academies Religious benevolence sparks social reform
1801	Cane Ridge revival in Kentucky
1807	New Jersey ends voting by propertied women
1816	Congress charters Second Bank of the United States
1817	Prominent whites create American Colonization Society
1819	Plummeting agricultural prices set off financial panic
1819–1821	Missouri Compromise
1820s	States reform public education Women become schoolteachers

PART

3

OVERLAPPING REVOLUTIONS, 1820-1860

"The procession was nearly a mile long . . . [and] the democrats marched in good order to the glare of torches," a French visitor remarked in amazement during the election of 1832. "These scenes belong to history . . . the wondrous epic of the coming of democracy." As we will see in Part 3, history was being made in many ways between 1820 and 1850. A series of overlapping revolutions were transforming American society. One was political: the creation of a genuinely democratic polity. The second was economic: In 1820, the United States was predominantly an agricultural nation; by 1850, the northern states boasted one of the world's foremost industrial economies. Third, there was far-reaching social and cultural change, including the Second Great Awakening, great movements of social reform, and the advent of a complex intellectual culture. These transformations affected every aspect of life in the North and Midwest and brought important changes in the South as well. Here, in brief, is an outline of that story.

ECONOMY

Advances in . . . production, transportation, and trade transformed the nation's economy

Making an Economic Revolution

Impressive advances in industrial production, transportation, and trade transformed the nation's economy. Factory owners used high-speed machines and a new system of labor discipline to boost the output of goods dramatically. Manufacturers produced 5 percent of the country's wealth in 1820 and nearly 20 percent by 1850. And thanks to enterprising merchants and entrepreneurs, who developed a network of canals and an integrated system of markets, they now sold their products throughout an expanding nation.

SOCIETY

The new economy created a class-based society

Forging a New Class Structure

The new economy created a class-based society in the North and Midwest. A wealthy elite of merchants, manufacturers, bankers, and entrepreneurs rose to the top of the social order. To maintain social stability, they adopted a paternalistic program of benevolent reform. But an expanding urban middle class created a distinct material and religious culture and lent support to movements for radical social reform. A mass of propertyless workers, including impoverished immigrants from Germany and Ireland, joined enslaved African Americans at the bottom of the social order. The growth of large cities, primarily in the North, fostered the emergence of new urban and popular cultures. Meanwhile, slavery expanded in numbers and scope as planters created new plantations as far south and west as Texas.

GOVERNMENT

... party competition engaged the energies of the electorate

Creating a Democratic Polity

The rapid growth of white male suffrage and political parties sparked the creation of a competitive and responsive democratic polity. Interest groups created various short-lived organizations, notably the Anti-Masonic, Workingmen's, and Liberty parties. Farmers, workers, and entrepreneurs persuaded governments to improve transportation, shorten workdays, and award valuable corporate charters. Catholic immigrants from Ireland and Germany entered local and state politics to protect their cultures from restrictive legislation advocated by Protestant nativists and reformers.

With Andrew Jackson at its head, the Democratic Party led a political and constitutional revolution that cut government aid to financiers, merchants, and corporations. To contend with the Democrats, the Whig Party devised a competing program that stressed economic development, moral reform, and individual social mobility. This party competition engaged the energies of the electorate and helped to unify a fragmented social order.

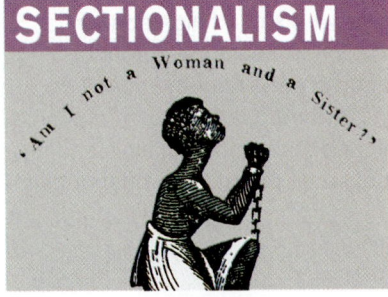

CULTURE

... a series of reform movements ... swept across America

Reforming People and Institutions

Between 1820 and 1850, a series of reform movements, many with religious roots and goals, swept across America. Ministers and pious church members embarked upon a program of Benevolent Reform, preaching the gospel of temperance, Sunday observance, prison reform, and many other causes. A few Americans pursued their social dreams in utopian communities, but most reformers worked within the existing society. Then, abolitionists and women's rights activists demanded radical social changes: the immediate end of slavery and the overthrow of the patriarchal legal order. However, southern planters increasingly defended slavery as a "positive good" and restated their commitment to a society based on white supremacy and forced labor.

SECTIONALISM

Slavery ... increasingly divided the nation

Compromising over Slavery

The economic revolution and social reform sharpened sectional divisions: The North developed into an urban industrial society based on free labor, whereas the South remained a rural agricultural society dependent on slavery. Beginning in the 1820s, the two sections fought over economic policy. Northern manufacturers, workers, and farmers won protective tariffs, which southern planters bitterly opposed. Eventually, there was a sectional compromise, as the North accepted tariff reductions. The sections clashed again over the expansion of slavery into Missouri and once again political leaders devised a compromise solution. But slavery—and the social and economic differences it symbolized—increasingly divided the nation.

The economic and cultural transformation of the North and, to a lesser extent, of the Midwest made those regions increasingly different from the South. And the democratic political revolution that affected all sections injected greater volatility and potential for conflict into the political system.

OVERLAPPING REVOLUTIONS, 1820–1860

	ECONOMY	SOCIETY	GOVERNMENT	CULTURE	SECTIONALISM
1820	• Waltham textile factory opens (1814) • Erie Canal completed (1825) • Market economy expands nationwide • Cotton belt emerges in South	• Business class develops • Rural women and girls recruited as factory workers • Mechanics form craft unions • Waged work increases	• Spread of universal white male suffrage • Rise of Andrew Jackson and Democratic Party • Anti-Masonic Party rises and declines	• American Colonization Society (1817) • Benevolent reform movements • Revivalist Charles G. Finney • Emerson and transcendentalism	• Missouri crisis and compromise (1819–1821) • David Walker's *Appeal . . . to the Colored Citizens of the World* (1829) • Domestic slave trade moves African Americans west
1830	• Protective tariffs (1828, 1832) trigger nullification crisis • Boom in cotton output • Panic of 1837 • U.S. textiles compete with British • Canal systems link eastern United States	• Charles G. Finney leads revivals • Depression (1837–1843) shatters labor movement • New urban popular culture appears	• Indian Removal Act (1830) • Whig Party forms (1834) • Second Party System emerges • Jackson destroys Second Bank and expands executive power	• Joseph Smith founds Mormonism • Temperance crusade expands • Middle-class culture spreads • Female Moral Reform Society (1834)	• Ordinance of Nullification (1832) and Force Bill (1833) • W. L. Garrison forms American Anti-Slavery Society (1833) • Texas independence
1840	• Irish immigrants join labor force • *Commonwealth v. Hunt* (1842) assists unions, but workers remain "servants" • Machine tool industry expands	• Working-class districts emerge in cities • Irish and German inflow sparks nativist movement	• Log cabin campaign (1840) mobilizes voters • Tyler's policies disrupt Whig agenda	• Fourierist and other communal settlements founded • Mormons resettle in Utah • Seneca Falls women's convention (1848)	• Slavery defended as a "positive good" • Anti-Slavery Liberty Party (1840) • Abolitionist movement splinters
1850	• Cincinnati emerges as hog processing center • McCormick, Deere, and other manufacturers set up in Midwest • Severe financial panic shakes economy (1857)	• Immigrants replace women in textile industry • Free labor ideology justifies growing inequality • New York City leads urban growth	• Ethnocultural issues shape politics • Conflict over polygamy in Utah Territory • Laws expand property rights of married women	• Minstrelsy rules popular culture • Public education expands with women as teachers	• Majority of enslaved African Americans live in Deep South • South remains rural and agricultural; North urbanizes and industrializes

ART IS THE HANDMAID OF HUMAN GOOD. · LOWELL ·

Economic Transformation, 1820–1860

In 1804, life turned grim for eleven-year-old Chauncey Jerome of Connecticut. His father died suddenly, and Jerome faced indentured servitude on a nearby farm. Knowing that few farmers "would treat a poor boy like a human being," Jerome bought out his indenture by making dials for clocks and then worked as a clockmaker for Eli Terry. A manufacturing wizard, Terry used water power to drive precision saws and woodworking lathes. Soon his shop was turning out thousands of tall case clocks with wooden works. Then, in 1816, Terry patented an enormously popular desk clock with brass parts; his business turned Litchfield, Connecticut, into the clock-making center of the United States. In 1816, Jerome set up his own clock factory. By organizing work more efficiently and using new machines that made interchangeable metal parts, he drove down the price of a simple clock from $20 to $5 and then to less than $2. By the 1840s, he was selling his clocks in England, the hub of the Industrial Revolution; two decades later, his workers were turning out 200,000 clocks a year, clear testimony to American industrial enterprise. By 1860, the United States was not only the world's leading exporter of cotton and wheat but also the third-ranked manufacturing nation behind Britain and France.

"Business is the very soul of an American: the fountain of all human felicity," author Francis Grund observed shortly after arriving from Europe. "It is as if all America were but one gigantic workshop, over the entrance of which there is the blazing inscription, 'No admission here, except on business.'" Stimulated by the entrepreneurial culture of early nineteenth-century America, thousands of artisan-inventors like Chauncey Jerome and thousands of merchants propelled the country into a new economic era. Two great changes defined that era: the **Industrial Revolution** (the growth and mechanization of industry) and the **Market Revolution** (the expansion and integration of markets).

Not all Americans embraced the new ethic of enterprise, and many did not share in the new prosperity. The increase in manufacturing, commerce, and finance created a class-divided society that challenged the founders' vision of an agricultural republic with few distinctions of wealth. As the philosopher Ralph Waldo Emerson warned in 1839: "The invasion of Nature by Trade with its Money, its Credit, its Steam, [and] its Railroad threatens to . . . establish a new, universal Monarchy."

Technology Celebrated

Artists joined manufacturers in praising the new industrial age. In this 1836 painting of the city seal of Lowell, Massachusetts, a cornucopia (horn of plenty) spreads its bounty over the symbols of the city's economic wealth. The artist implies that the bales of raw cotton in the foreground will be transformed in the water-powered textile factories into smooth cloth, for shipment to far-flung markets via the new railroad system. The image of technologically driven prosperity was deceptive. Two years earlier, 2,000 women textile workers had gone on strike in Lowell, claiming that their wages failed to provide a decent standard of living. Private Collection/Picture Research Consultants & Archives.

The American Industrial Revolution

Industrialization came to the United States between 1790 and 1860, as merchants and manufacturers reorganized work routines, built factories, and exploited an ever-wider range of natural resources. Thanks to **mass production**, goods that once had been luxury items became part of everyday life (Figure 9.1). The rapid construction of turnpikes, canals, and railroads by state governments and private entrepreneurs, working together in the Commonwealth System (see Chapter 8), allowed manufactures to be sold throughout the land.

The Division of Labor and the Factory

The increase of production stemmed initially from changes in the organization of work. Consider the shoe industry: Traditionally, New England shoemakers had turned leather hides into finished shoes and boots in small wooden shacks called "ten-footers," where they worked at their own pace. During the 1820s and 1830s, merchants in Lynn, Massachusetts, undermined the businesses of these independent artisans by introducing an outwork system and a **division of labor**. The merchants hired semiskilled journeymen and set them up in large shops cutting leather into soles and uppers. They sent out the upper sections to dozens of rural Massachusetts towns, where women binders sewed in fabric linings. The manufacturers then had other journeymen attach the uppers to the soles and return the shoes to the central shop for inspection, packing, and sale. The new system turned employers into powerful "shoe bosses" and eroded workers' wages and independence. But the expansion of shoe production created jobs, and the division of labor both increased output and cut prices.

For products not suited to the outwork system, manufacturers created the modern **factory**, which concentrated production under one roof. For example, in the 1830s, Cincinnati merchants built large slaughterhouses that processed thousands of hogs every month. The technology remained simple: A system of overhead rails moved the hog carcasses past workers. The division of labor made the difference. One worker split the animals, another removed the organs, and others trimmed the carcasses into pieces. Packers then stuffed the pork into barrels and pickled it to prevent spoilage. Reported journalist and landscape architect Frederick Law Olmsted:

> We entered an immense low-ceiling room and followed a vista of dead swine, upon their backs, their paws stretching mutely toward heaven. Walking down to the vanishing point, we found there a sort of human chopping-machine where the hogs were converted into commercial pork.... Plump falls the hog upon the table, chop, chop; chop, chop; chop, chop,

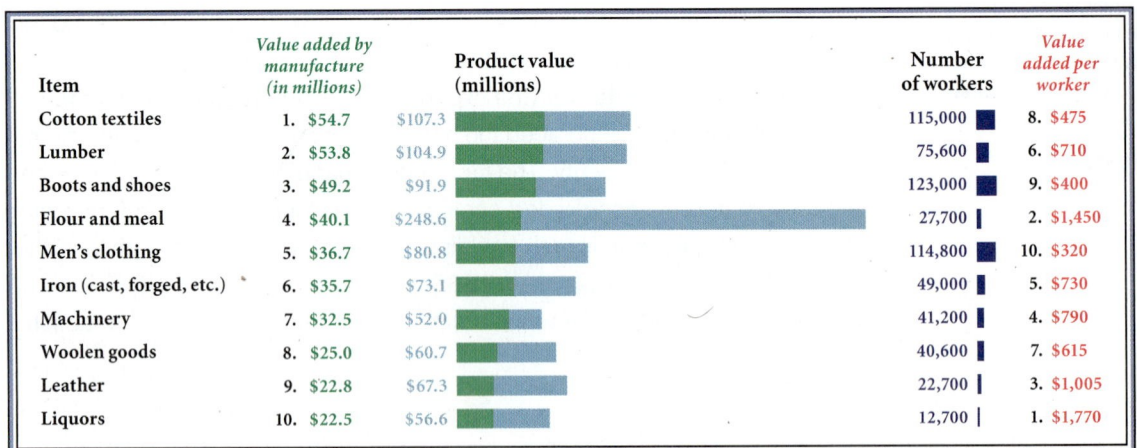

Item	Value added by manufacture (in millions)		Product value (millions)	Number of workers	Value added per worker
Cotton textiles	1. $54.7	$107.3		115,000	8. $475
Lumber	2. $53.8	$104.9		75,600	6. $710
Boots and shoes	3. $49.2	$91.9		123,000	9. $400
Flour and meal	4. $40.1	$248.6		27,700	2. $1,450
Men's clothing	5. $36.7	$80.8		114,800	10. $320
Iron (cast, forged, etc.)	6. $35.7	$73.1		49,000	5. $730
Machinery	7. $32.5	$52.0		41,200	4. $790
Woolen goods	8. $25.0	$60.7		40,600	7. $615
Leather	9. $22.8	$67.3		22,700	3. $1,005
Liquors	10. $22.5	$56.6		12,700	1. $1,770

FIGURE 9.1

Leading Branches of Manufacture, 1860

In 1860, three industries—boots and shoes, cotton textiles, and men's clothing—each employed more than 100,000 workers. However, three other industries with fewer employees—those engaged in the distilling of liquor, the tanning of leather, and the milling of flour—had the highest productivity, with each worker adding more than $1,000 in value to the finished goods. Source: Adapted from Douglass C. North, *Growth and Welfare in the American Past*, 2nd ed. (Paramus, NJ: Prentice Hall, 1974), table 6.1.

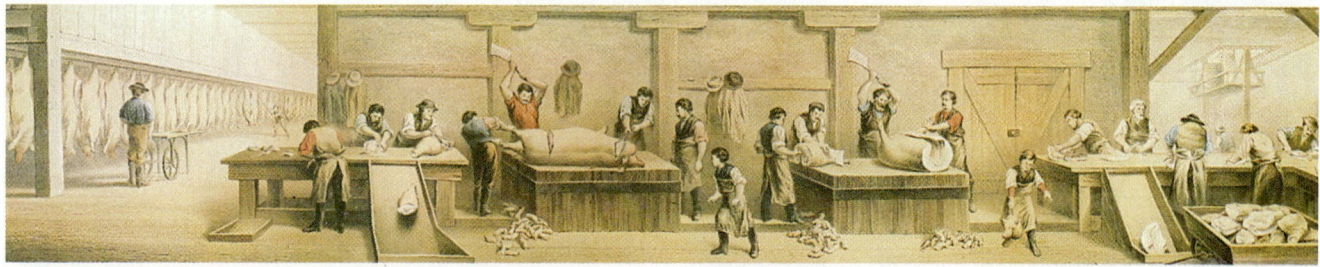

Pork Packing in Cincinnati

The only modern technology in this Cincinnati pork-packing plant was the overhead pulley that carried hog carcasses past the workers. The plant's efficiency came from its organization, a division of labor in which each worker performed a specific task. Plants such as this one pioneered the development of the moving assembly line, which would reach a high level of sophistication in the early twentieth century, in Henry Ford's automobile factories.   Cincinnati Museum Center.

fall the cleavers.... We took out our watches and counted thirty-five seconds, from the moment when one hog touched the table until the next occupied its place.

The Cincinnati system was so efficient—with "disassembly" lines processing sixty hogs an hour—that by the 1840s the city was known as "Porkopolis." By 1850, factories were slaughtering 334,000 hogs a year.

Other factories boasted impressive new technology. In the 1780s, Oliver Evans, a prolific Delaware inventor, built a highly automated flour mill driven by waterpower. His machinery lifted the wheat to the top of the mill, cleaned the grain as it fell into hoppers, ground it into flour, and then cooled the flour as it was poured into barrels. Evans's factory, remarked one observer, "was as full of machinery as the case of a watch." It needed only six men to mill 100,000 bushels of wheat

a year—perhaps ten times as much as they could grind in a traditional mill.

By the 1830s, a new "mineral" economy began to emerge. Manufacturers increasingly ran their machinery with coal-burning stationary steam engines rather than with water power. And they now fabricated metal products—iron, brass, and copper—as well as pork, leather, wool, cotton, and other agricultural goods. In Chicago, Cyrus McCormick used power-driven machines to make parts for farm reapers, which workers assembled on a conveyor belt (see Reading American Pictures, "American Technology Dramatically Increases Farm Productivity," p. 276). In Hartford, Connecticut, Samuel Colt built an assembly line to produce his invention, the six-shooter revolver. These advances in technology and factory organization alarmed British observers: "The contriving and making of machinery has become so common in this country . . . [that] it is

American Technology Dramatically Increases Farm Productivity

A central aspect of the economic transformation of the mid-nineteenth century was the increased productivity brought about by replacing human muscles with power-driven machinery. As factories installed waterwheels and steam engines to provide power to spinning and weaving machines, the output of woolen and cotton cloth increased dramatically. But what impact did machines have on farming, the dominant occupation in the United States at the time? How did farmers' productivity improve?

Wheat Farming at Bishop Hill, Illinois. Bishop Hill Historic Site/Illinois Historic Preservation Agency.

Diagram of McCormick's Reaper from *The Cultivator*, May 1846. Wisconsin Historical Society.

ANALYZING THE EVIDENCE

- The picture at the top shows the wheat harvest at Bishop Hill, a religious community founded in Illinois in 1848 by Swedish Pietists. What tools are the men using to cut the wheat? What are the women's tasks? These communalists certainly harvested more wheat than an individual farm family would reap, but did they do it more efficiently?

- Now look at the picture of McCormick's reaper, taken from an advertisement in a farm journal. Using this machine, the farmer and his son could cut as much grain in a day as the seven men with scythes at Bishop Hill (though the farmer would still have to hire workers to collect it). How did the reaper achieve such a dramatic increase in productivity? What costs did it add to the farm budget?

- Look closely at the reaper in the advertisement. What is the purpose of the letters inscribed on each part of the machine? What does this tell you about the standardization of parts that was crucial to the Industrial Revolution? Why do you think the McCormick Company provided this information to potential buyers?

to be feared that American manufacturers will become exporters not only to foreign countries, but even to England."

The Textile Industry and British Competition

British textile manufacturers were particularly worried about American competition. They persuaded the British government to prohibit the export of textile machinery and the emigration of **mechanics** (skilled craftsmen who invented and improved tools for industry). Lured by the prospect of higher wages, though, thousands of British mechanics disguised themselves as ordinary laborers and sailed to the United States. By 1812, at least three hundred British mechanics worked in the Philadelphia area alone.

Samuel Slater, the most important émigré mechanic, came to America in 1789 after working for Richard Arkwright, who had invented the most advanced British machinery for spinning cotton. A year later, Slater reproduced Arkwright's innovations in merchant Moses Brown's cotton mill in Providence, Rhode Island, beginning the American Industrial Revolution.

In competing with British mills, American manufacturers had the advantage of an abundance of natural resources. The nation's farmers produced huge amounts of cotton and wool, and the fast-flowing rivers that cascaded down from the Appalachian foothills to the Atlantic coastal plain provided a cheap source of energy. From Massachusetts to Delaware, these waterways were soon lined with industrial villages and textile mills as large as 150 feet long, 40 feet wide, and four stories high (Map 9.1).

American and British Advantages Still, British producers easily undersold their American competitors. Thanks to cheap transatlantic shipping and low interest rates in Britain, they could import raw cotton from the United States, manufacture it into cloth, and sell it in America at a bargain price. Moreover, thriving British companies could slash prices to drive fledgling American firms out of business. The most important British advantage was cheap labor: Britain had a larger population—about 12.6 million in 1810 compared to 7.3 million Americans—and thousands of landless laborers willing to take low-paying factory jobs. To offset these advantages, American entrepreneurs won help from the federal government: In 1816, 1824, and 1828, Congress passed tariff bills that taxed imported cotton and woolen cloth. But in the 1830s, Congress reduced the tariffs because southern planters, western farmers, and urban consumers demanded access to inexpensive imports.

MAP 9.1

New England's Dominance in Cotton Spinning, 1840

Although the South grew the nation's cotton, it did not process it in the years before the Civil War. Entrepreneurs in Massachusetts and Rhode Island built most of the factories that spun and wove raw cotton into cloth. The new factories made use of the abundant waterpower available in New England and the region's surplus labor force. Initially, factory managers hired young farm women to work the machines; later, they would rely on immigrants from Ireland and the French-speaking province of Quebec in Canada.

A Textile Operative at Work

Powered by water or steam driving a system of leather belts, the looms of the mid-nineteenth century wove cloth much faster and with far less effort than traditional treadle-driven handlooms. However, these new looms required constant attention to repair broken threads, reload shuttles, and prevent imperfections. In this rare daguerreotype of 1850, the young, frail-looking operative moves a lever that will tighten the weave, a task she will repeat many times over the course of her twelve-hour workday.   American Textile History Museum.

Better Machines, Cheaper Workers   American producers used two other strategies to compete with their British rivals. First, they improved on British technology. In 1811, Francis Cabot Lowell, a wealthy Boston merchant, toured British textile mills, secretly making detailed drawings of their power machinery. Paul Moody, an experienced American mechanic, then copied the machines and improved their design. In 1814, Lowell joined with merchants Nathan Appleton and Patrick Tracy Jackson to form the Boston Manufacturing Company. Having raised the staggering sum of $400,000, they built a textile plant in Waltham, Massachusetts — the first American factory to perform all the operations of clothmaking under one roof. Thanks to Moody's improvements, Waltham's power looms operated at higher speeds than British looms and needed fewer workers.

The second strategy was to tap a cheaper source of labor. In the 1820s, the Boston Manufacturing Company recruited thousands of young women from farm families, appealing to the women by providing them with rooms in boardinghouses and with evening lectures and other cultural activities. To reassure parents about their daughters' moral welfare, the mill owners enforced strict curfews, prohibited alcoholic beverages, and required regular church attendance. At Lowell (1822), Chicopee (1823), and other sites in Massachusetts and New Hampshire, the company built new cotton factories that used this labor system, known as the Waltham Plan.

By the early 1830s, more than 40,000 New England women were working in textile mills. As an observer noted, the wages were "more than could be obtained by the hitherto ordinary occupation of housework," the living conditions were better than those in crowded farmhouses, and the women had greater independence. Lucy Larcom became a Lowell textile operative at age eleven to support herself and not be "a trouble or burden or expense" to her widowed mother. Other women operatives used wages to pay off their father's farm mortgages, send brothers to school, or accumulate a marriage dowry for themselves.

Some operatives just had a good time. Susan Brown, who worked as a Lowell weaver for eight months, spent half her earnings on food and lodging and the rest on plays, concerts, lectures, and a two-day excursion to Boston. Like most textile workers, Brown soon tired of the rigors of factory work and the never-ceasing clatter of the machinery, which ran twelve hours a day, six days a week. After she quit, she lived at home for a time and then moved to another mill. Whatever the hardships, waged work gave young women a sense of freedom. "Don't I feel independent!" a woman mill worker wrote to her sister. "The thought that I am living on no one is a happy one indeed to me." The owners of the Boston Manufacturing Company were even happier. By combining tariff protection with improved technology and cheap female labor, they could undersell their British rivals. Their textiles were also cheaper than those made in New York and Pennsylvania, where farmworkers were better paid than in New England and textile wages consequently were higher. Manufacturers in those states garnered profits by using advanced technology to produce higher-quality cloth. Even Thomas Jefferson, the great champion of yeoman farming, was impressed. "Our manufacturers are now very nearly on a footing with those of England," he boasted in 1825.

American Mechanics and Technological Innovation

By the 1820s, American-born artisans had replaced British immigrants at the cutting edge of technological innovation. Though few mechanics had a formal education, they nevertheless commanded respect as "men professing an ingenious art." In the Philadelphia region, the remarkable Sellars family produced the most important inventors. Samuel Sellars Jr. invented a machine for twisting worsted woolen yarn to give it an especially smooth surface. His son John improved the efficiency of the waterwheels powering the family's sawmills and built a machine to weave wire sieves. John's sons and grandsons ran machine shops that turned out riveted leather fire hoses, papermaking equipment, and eventually locomotives. In 1824, the Sellars family and other mechanics founded the Franklin Institute in Philadelphia. Named after Benjamin Franklin, whom the mechanics admired for his work ethic and scientific accomplishments, the institute published a journal; provided high-school-level instruction in chemistry, mathematics, and mechanical design; and organized exhibits of new products. Craftsmen in Ohio and other states established similar institutes to disseminate technical knowledge and encourage innovation. Between 1820 and 1860, the number of patents issued by the U.S. Patent Office rose from two hundred to four thousand a year.

American craftsmen pioneered in the development of **machine tools**—machines that made parts for other machines. A key innovator was Eli Whitney (1765–1825), the son of a middling New England farm family. At the age of fourteen, Whitney began fashioning nails and knife blades; later, he made women's hatpins. Aspiring to wealth and status, Whitney won admission to Yale College and subsequently worked as a tutor on a Georgia cotton plantation. Using his expertise in making hatpins, he built a simple machine that separated the seeds in a cotton boll from the delicate fibers, work

Eli Whitney

Eli Whitney posed for this portrait in the 1820s, when he had achieved prosperity and social standing as the inventor of the cotton gin and other machines. Whitney's success prompted the artist—his young New Haven, Connecticut, neighbor Samuel F. B. Morse—to turn his creative energies from painting to industrial technology. By the 1840s, Morse had devised the first successful commercial telegraph.
Yale University Art Gallery/Art Resource, NY.

previously done by hand in a labor-intensive process. Although Whitney patented his cotton engine (or "gin," as it became known), other manufacturers improved on his design and captured the market.

Still seeking his fortune, Whitney decided in 1798 to manufacture military weapons. He eventually designed and built machine tools that could rapidly produce interchangeable musket parts, bringing him the wealth and fame that he had long craved. After Whitney's death in 1825, his partner John H. Hall built an array of metalworking machine tools, such as turret lathes, milling machines, and precision grinders.

Technological innovation now swept through American manufacturing. Mechanics in the textile industry invented lathes, planers, and boring machines that turned out standardized parts for new spinning jennies and weaving looms. Despite being mass-produced, these jennies and looms were precisely made and operated at higher speeds than British equipment. The leading inventor was Richard Garsed: He nearly doubled the

A New England Mill, 1850
This five-story woolen mill towers over the small houses of a New England village and assumed an equally dominant role in the lives of its people. As the population grew and farms shrank in size, rural folk took up work as artisans, out-workers, and factory laborers.

speed of the power looms in his father's Delaware factory and patented a cam-and-harness device making it possible for damask and other elaborately designed fabrics to be machine-woven. Meanwhile, the mechanics employed by Samuel W. Collins built a machine for pressing and hammering hot metal into dies, or cutting forms. Using this machine, a worker could make three hundred ax heads a day—compared to twelve using traditional methods. In Richmond, Virginia, Welsh- and American-born mechanics at the Tredegar Iron Works produced great quantities of low-cost parts for complicated manufacturing equipment at a rapid rate. As a group of British observers noted admiringly, many American products were made "with machinery applied to almost every process . . . all reduced to an almost perfect system of manufacture."

As mass production spread, the American Industrial Revolution came of age. The sheer volume of output elevated products such as Remington rifles, Singer sewing machines, and Yale locks into household names in the United States and abroad. After winning praise at the Crystal Palace Exhibition in London in 1851—the first major international display of industrial goods—Remington, Singer, and other American firms became multinational businesses, building factories in Great Britain and dominating some European markets. By 1877, the Singer Manufacturing Company controlled 75 percent of the world market for sewing machines.

Wageworkers and the Labor Movement

As the Industrial Revolution gathered momentum, it changed the nature of work and of workers' lives. From the early to the mid-nineteenth century, many American **craft workers** espoused **artisan republicanism**, an ideology based on liberty and equality. They saw themselves as a group of small-scale producers, equal to one another and free to work for themselves. The poet Walt Whitman summed up their outlook: "Men must be masters, under themselves."

Free Workers Form Unions However, as the outwork and factory systems spread, more and more workers became wage earners who labored under the direction of an employer. Unlike young women, who embraced factory work because it freed them from parental control and domestic service, men bridled at their status as supervised wage workers. To assert their independent status, male wage workers rejected the traditional terms of *master* and *servant*; instead, they used the Dutch word *boss* to refer to their employer. And lowly apprentices refused to allow their masters to control their private (nonwork) lives. Still, as hired hands, apprentices and journeymen received meager wages and had little job security. The artisan-republican ideal, a by-product of the American Revolution, found itself

Woodworker, c. 1850

Skilled furniture makers took great pride in their work, which was often intricately designed and beautifully executed. To underline the dignity of his occupation, this woodworker poses in formal dress and proudly displays the tools of his craft. A belief in the value of their labor was an important ingredient of the artisan-republican ideology held by many workers. Library of Congress.

challenged by the harsh reality of waged work—labor as a commodity—in an industrializing capitalist society.

Some journeymen wage earners worked in carpentry, stonecutting, masonry, and cabinetmaking—traditional crafts that required specialized skills. Their strong sense of identity, or trade consciousness, enabled these workers to form unions and bargain with their master-artisan employers over low wages and long hours, which restricted their family life and educational opportunities. Before 1800, the building trades' workday was twelve hours—6:00 A.M. to 6:00 P.M.—with an hour each for breakfast and lunch. By the 1820s, masters were demanding shorter meal breaks and longer workdays during the summer (when it stayed light longer), while offering the old daily pay rate. In response, 600 carpenters in Boston went on strike in 1825. The Boston protest failed, but by the mid-1830s, many building-trades workers had won a ten-hour workday. In 1840, craft workers in St. Louis secured a ten-hour day, and President Van Buren issued an executive order setting a similar workday for federal workers.

Artisans in other occupations were less successful in preserving their pay and working conditions. As aggressive entrepreneurs and machine technology changed the nature of production, shoemakers, hatters, printers, furniture makers, and weavers faced falling income, unemployment, and loss of status. To avoid the regimentation of factory work, some artisans in these trades moved to small towns or set up specialized shops. In New York City, 800 highly skilled cabinetmakers owned small shops that made fashionable or custom-made furniture. In status and income, they outranked a much larger group of 3,200 semitrained, wage-earning workers—disparagingly called "botches"—who made cheaper factory-produced tables and chairs. The new industrial system had divided the traditional artisan class into self-employed craftsmen and wage-earning workers.

When wage earners banded together to form unions, they faced a legal hurdle: English and American common law branded such organizations as illegal "combinations." As a Philadelphia judge put it, unions were "a government unto themselves" and unlawfully interfered with a "master's" authority over his "servant." Between 1806 and 1847, there were at least twenty-three legal cases accusing unions of "conspiring" to raise wages and thereby injuring employers. In 1835, the New York Supreme Court found that a shoemakers' union had illegally caused "an industrious man" to be "driven out of employment" because he would not join the union. "It is important to the best interests of society that the price of labor be left to regulate itself," the court declared. The following year, clothing manufacturers in New York City agreed to dismiss workers who belonged to the Society of Journeymen Tailors and circulated a list—a so-called **blacklist**—of the society's members.

Labor Ideology Despite such obstacles, journeymen shoemakers founded a mutual benefit society in Lynn, Massachusetts, in 1830, and similar organizations soon appeared in other shoemaking centers. "The division of society into the producing and non-producing classes," the journeymen explained, had made workers like themselves into a mere "commodity." As another group of workers explained, "The capitalist has no other interest in us, than to get as much labor out of us as possible. We are hired men, and hired men, like hired horses, have no souls." Indeed, workers were "slaves in the strictest sense of the word," declared Lowell textile workers. Still, they admitted: "We are not a quarter as bad off as the slaves of the south. . . . They can't vote nor complain and we can." To exert more pressure on their capitalist employers, in

1834, local unions from Boston to Philadelphia formed the National Trades Union, the first regional union of different trades.

Workers found considerable popular support for their cause. When a court in New York City upheld a conspiracy verdict against a tailors' union, tailors circulated handbills warning that the "Freemen of the North are now on a level with the slaves of the South," and a mass meeting of 27,000 people denounced the decision. In 1836, local juries hearing conspiracy cases acquitted shoemakers in Hudson, New York; carpet makers in Thompsonville, Connecticut; and plasterers in Philadelphia. Even when workers were convicted, judges refrained from handing out jail sentences and imposed only light fines; thus, labor organizers were not deterred. Then, in *Commonwealth v. Hunt* (1842), Chief Justice Lemuel Shaw of the Massachusetts Supreme Judicial Court upheld the right of workers to form unions. Shaw's decision overturned common-law precedents by ruling that a union was not an inherently illegal organization and could strike to enforce a **closed-shop** agreement that limited employment to union members. But many judges continued to resist unions by issuing **injunctions** forbidding strikes.

Union leaders took the artisan republicanism of craft workers and expanded it to include wage workers. Arguing that wage earners were becoming "slaves to a monied aristocracy," they condemned the new factory system in which "capital and labor stand opposed." To create a just society in which workers could "live as comfortably as others," they advanced a **labor theory of value**. Under this theory, the price of goods should reflect the labor required to make them, and the income from the goods' sale should go primarily to the producers, not to factory owners, middlemen, or storekeepers. "All who sell ought to have lawful gain," conceded minister Ezra Stiles Ely, but not at the expense of a widowed mother of ten unable to support herself by making "common shirts." Ely added that "the poor who perform the work, ought to receive at least half of that sum which is charged" to the consumer. Union activists agreed. Appealing to the spirit of the American Revolution, which had destroyed the aristocracy of birth, they called for a new revolution to demolish the aristocracy of capital. Union men organized nearly fifty strikes for higher wages in 1836.

Women textile operatives were equally active. Competition in the woolen and cotton textile industries was fierce because the mechanization of production caused output to grow faster than demand. As prices fell, manufacturers' revenues declined. To maintain profits, employers reduced workers' wages and imposed tougher work rules. In 1828, women mill workers in Dover, New Hampshire, struck against new rules and won some relief; six years later, 800 Dover women walked out again, to protest wage cuts. In Lowell, 2,000 women operatives backed a strike by withdrawing their savings from an employer-owned bank. "One of the leaders mounted a pump," the *Boston Transcript* reported, "and made a flaming . . . speech on the rights of women and the iniquities of the 'monied aristocracy.'" When conditions did not improve, young New England women refused to enter the mills. Impoverished Irish (and later French Canadian) immigrants took their places.

By the 1850s, workers in many mechanized industries faced unemployment as the supply of manufactures exceeded the demand for them. In 1857, industrial overproduction coincided with a financial panic sparked by the bankruptcies of several railroads. As the economy went into a recession, unemployment rose to 10 percent and reminded Americans of the social costs of the new—and otherwise very successful—system of industrial production.

- How did American textile manufacturers compete with British manufacturers? How successful were they?

- In what ways did the emerging industrial economy conflict with artisan republicanism? How did wage laborers respond to the new economy?

The Market Revolution

As American factories and farms turned out more goods, legislators and businessmen created faster and cheaper ways to get those products to consumers. Beginning in the late 1810s, they constructed a massive system of canals and roads that linked the states along the Atlantic coast with the new states in the trans-Appalachian west. This transportation system set in motion both a crucial market revolution and a great migration of people. By 1860, nearly one-third of the nation's citizens lived in the Midwest (the five states carved out of the Northwest Territory—Ohio, Indiana, Illinois, Michigan, and Wisconsin—along with Missouri, Iowa, and Minnesota), where they created both a complex economy and a society that increasingly resembled those of the Northeast.

The Erie Canal
This pastoral view of the Erie Canal near Lockport, New York, painted by artist John William Hill, only hints at this waterway's profound impact on American life. Without the canal, the town in the background would not exist and farmers such as the man in the foreground would only have local markets for their cattle and grain. By 1860, the success of the Erie Canal had resulted in the construction of a vast system of canals. This infrastructure was as important to the nation as the railroad network of the late nineteenth century and the interstate highway and airport transportation systems of the late twentieth century.
© Bettmann/Corbis

Canals and Steamboats Shrink Distance Even on well-built gravel roads, overland travel was slow and expensive. To carry people, crops, and manufactures to and from the Midwest, public money and private businesses developed a water-borne transportation system of unprecedented size, complexity, and cost. The key event was the New York legislature's 1817 decision to build the Erie Canal, a 364-mile waterway to connect the Hudson River and Lake Erie. At the time, the longest artificial waterway in the United States was just 28 miles long—a reflection of the huge capital cost of canals and the lack of American engineering expertise. But New York's ambitious project had three things working in its favor: the vigorous support of New York City's merchants, who wanted access to western markets; the backing of New York's governor, De Witt Clinton, who persuaded the legislature to finance the waterway from tax revenues, tolls, and bond sales to foreign investors; and the relatively gentle terrain west of Albany. Even so, the task was enormous. Workers—many of them Irish immigrants—had to dig out millions of cubic yards of soil, quarry thousands of tons of rock to build the huge locks that raised and lowered the boats, and construct vast reservoirs to ensure a steady supply of water.

The first great engineering project in American history, the Erie Canal altered the ecology of an entire region. As farming communities and market towns sprang up along the waterway, settlers cut down millions of trees to provide wood for houses and barns and to open the land for growing crops and grazing animals. Cows and sheep foraged in pastures that had recently been forests occupied by deer and bears, and spring rains caused massive erosion of the denuded landscape.

Whatever its environmental consequences, the Erie Canal was an instant economic success. The first 75-mile section opened in 1819 and quickly yielded enough revenue to repay its construction cost. When workers finished the canal in 1825, a 40-foot-wide ribbon of water stretched from Buffalo, on the eastern shore of Lake Erie, to Albany, where it joined the Hudson River for the 150-mile trip to New York City. The canal's water "must be the most fertilizing of all fluids," suggested novelist Nathaniel Hawthorne, "for it causes towns with their masses of brick and stone, their churches and theaters, their business and hubbub, their luxury and refinement, their gay dames and polished citizens, to spring up."

The Erie Canal brought prosperity to the farmers of central and western New York and the entire Great Lakes basin. Northeastern manufacturers shipped clothing, boots, and agricultural equipment to farm families; in return, farmers sent grain, cattle, and hogs as well as raw materials (leather, wool, and hemp, for example) to eastern cities and foreign markets. One-hundred-ton freight barges, each pulled by two horses, moved along the canal at a steady 30 miles a day, cutting transportation costs and accelerating the flow of goods. In 1818, the mills in Rochester, New York, processed 26,000 barrels of flour for export east; ten years later, their output soared to 200,000 barrels; and by 1840, it was at 500,000 barrels.

The spectacular benefits of the Erie Canal prompted a national canal boom. Civic and business leaders in Philadelphia and Baltimore proposed waterways to link their cities to the Midwest. Copying New York's fiscal innovations, they persuaded their state governments to invest directly in canal companies or to force state-chartered banks to do so. They also won state guarantees that encouraged British and Dutch investors; as one observer noted in 1844, "The prosperity of America, her railroads, canals, steam navigation, and banks, are the fruit of English capital." Soon, artificial waterways connected the farms and towns of the Great Lakes region with the great port cities of New York, Philadelphia, and Baltimore (via the Erie, Pennsylvania, and Chesapeake and Ohio canals). And every year, 25,000 farmer-built flatboats carried produce to New Orleans, via the Ohio and Mississippi rivers. In 1848, the completion of the Michigan and Illinois Canal, which linked Chicago to the Mississippi River, completed an inland all-water route from New York City to New Orleans (Map 9.3).

The steamboat, another product of the industrial age, ensured the economic success of the Midwest's river-borne transportation system. In 1807, engineer-inventor Robert Fulton built the first American steamboat, the *Clermont*, which he piloted up the Hudson River. To navigate shallow western rivers, engineers broadened steamboats' hulls to reduce their draft and enlarge their cargo capacity. These improved vessels halved the cost of upstream river transport and, along with the canals, dramatically increased the flow of goods, people, and news. In 1830, a traveler or a letter from New York could reach Buffalo or Pittsburgh by water in less than a week and Detroit or St. Louis in two weeks. In 1800, the same journeys had taken twice as long.

The state and national governments played key roles in developing interregional transportation and communication systems. State legislatures subsidized canals, while the national government created a vast postal system, the first network for the exchange of information. Thanks to the Post Office Act of 1792, there were more than eight thousand post offices by 1830, and the mails safely delivered thousands of letters and

MAP 9.3

The Transportation Revolution: Roads and Canals, 1820–1850

By 1850, the United States had an efficient system of water-borne transportation composed of three distinct parts. A system of short canals and navigable rivers carried cotton, tobacco, and other products from the countryside of the southern seaboard states into the Atlantic commercial system. A second system, centered on the Erie, Chesapeake and Ohio, and Pennsylvania Mainline canals, linked the major seaport cities of the Northeast to the vast trans-Appalachian region. Finally, a set of regional canals in the Old Northwest connected most of the Great Lakes region to the Ohio and Mississippi rivers and the port of New Orleans.

banknotes worth millions of dollars. The U.S. Supreme Court, headed by John Marshall, likewise encouraged interstate trade by striking down state restrictions on commerce. In *Gibbons v. Ogden* (1824), the Court voided a New York law that created a monopoly on steamboat travel into New York City and established federal authority over interstate commerce (see Chapter 7). That decision meant that no local or state monopolies—or tariffs—would impede the flow of goods, services, and news across the nation.

Railroads Foster Regional Ties By the 1850s, railroads—another technological innovation—were on their way to replacing canals as the core of the national transportation system (Map 9.4). In 1852, canals carried twice the tonnage transported by railroads. Then, capitalists in Boston, New York, and London invested heavily in railroad routes; by 1860, railroads were the main carriers of wheat and freight from the Midwest to the Northeast. Serviced by a vast network of locomotive and freight-car repair shops,

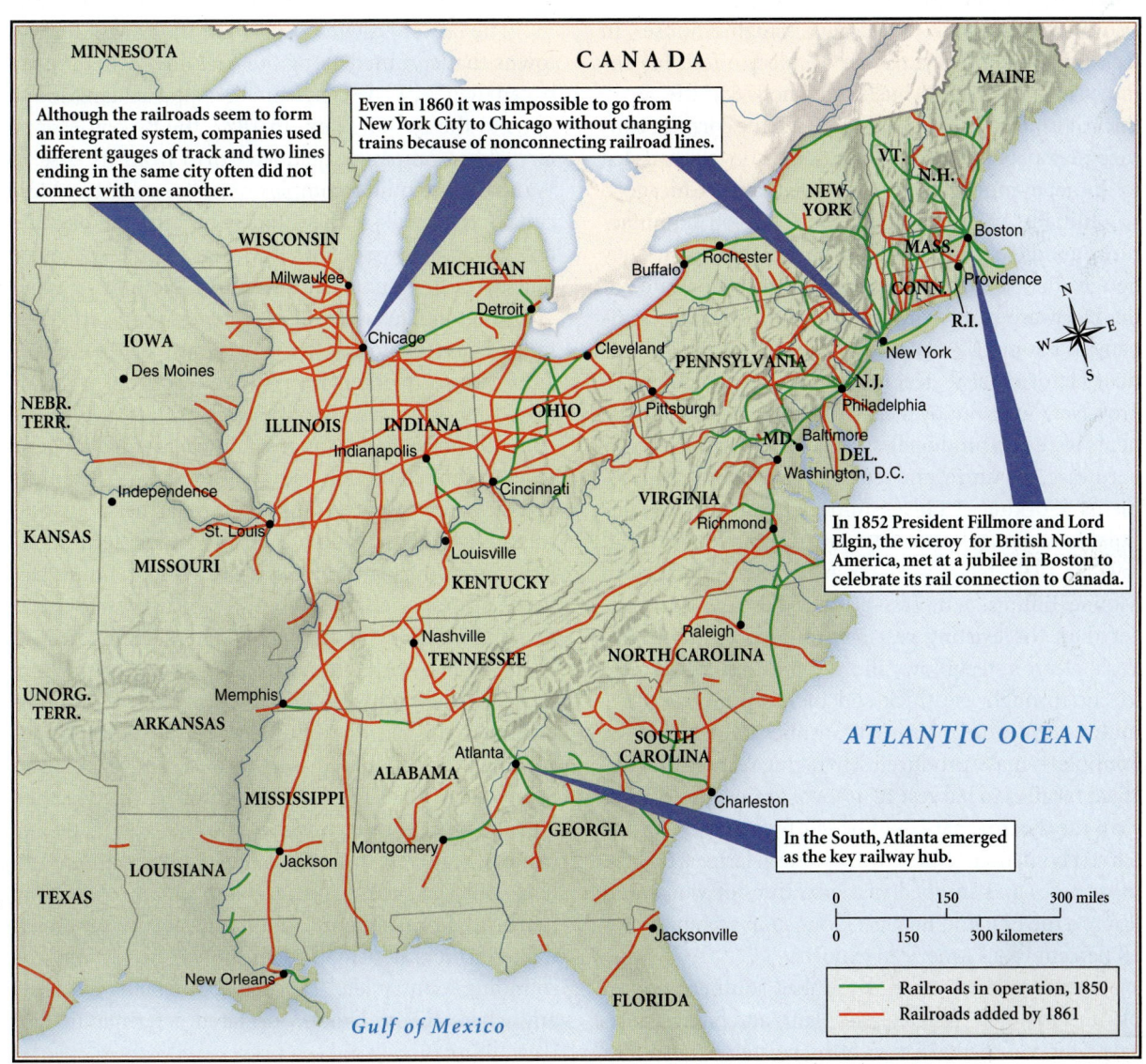

MAP 9.4

Railroads of the North and South, 1850 and 1861

In the decade before the Civil War, entrepreneurs in the Northeast and the Midwest financed thousands of miles of new railroad lines, creating an extensive and dense transportation system that stimulated economic development. The South built a more limited system of railroads. In all regions, railroad companies used different track gauges, which prevented the efficient flow of traffic.

the Erie Railroad, the Pennsylvania Railroad, the New York Central Railroad, and the Baltimore and Ohio Railroad connected the Atlantic ports—New York, Philadelphia, and Baltimore—with the rapidly expanding Great Lakes cities of Cleveland and Chicago.

The railroad boom of the 1850s expanded commerce into a vast territory around Chicago. Trains carried huge quantities of lumber from Michigan to the treeless prairies of Indiana, Illinois, Iowa, and Missouri, where settlers built 250,000 new farms (covering 19 million acres) and hundreds of small towns. The rail lines moved millions of bushels of wheat to Chicago for transport by boat or rail to eastern markets. Increasingly, they also carried livestock to Chicago's slaughterhouses. In Jacksonville, Illinois, a farmer decided to feed his entire corn crop of 1,500 bushels "to hogs & cattle, as we think it is more profitable than to sell the corn." A Chicago newspaper boasted, "In ancient times all roads led to Rome; in modern times all roads lead to Chicago."

Initially, midwestern settlers relied on manufactured goods made in Britain or in the Northeast. They bought high-quality shovels and spades fabricated at the Delaware Iron Works and the Oliver Ames Company in Easton, Massachusetts; axes forged in Connecticut factories; and steel horseshoes manufactured in Troy, New York. But by the 1840s, midwestern entrepreneurs were also producing such goods as machine tools, hardware, furniture, and especially agricultural implements. Working as a blacksmith in Grand Detour, Illinois, John Deere made his first steel plow out of old saws in 1837; ten years later, he opened a factory in Moline, Illinois, that mass-produced the plows. Stronger than the existing cast-iron models built in New York, Deere's steel plows allowed midwestern farmers to cut through the thick sod of the prairies. Other midwestern companies—McCormick and Hussey, for example—mass-produced self-raking reapers that enabled farmers to harvest 12 acres of grain a day (rather than the 2 acres that could be cut by hand). With the harvest bottleneck removed, midwestern farmers planted more acres and shipped vast quantities of wheat and flour to the East and Europe. Flour soon accounted for 10 percent of all American exports.

Extra-regional trade also linked southern cotton planters to northeastern textile plants and foreign markets. This commerce in raw cotton bolstered the wealth of the South but did not transform the economic and social order there as it did in the Midwest. With the exception of Richmond, Virginia, and a few other places, southern planters did not invest their cotton profits in manufacturing. Lacking cities, factories, and highly trained workers, the South remained tied to agriculture, even as the commerce in wheat, corn, and livestock promoted diversified economies in the Northeast and Midwest.

The Growth of Cities and Towns

The expansion of industry and trade dramatically increased America's urban population. In 1820, there were only 58 towns with more than 2,500 inhabitants in the United States; by 1840, there were 126 such towns, located mostly in the Northeast and Midwest. During those two decades, the total number of city dwellers grew more than fourfold, from 443,000 to 1,844,000.

The fastest growth occurred in the new industrial towns that sprouted along the "fall line," where rivers began their rapid descent from the Appalachian Mountains to the coastal plain. In 1822, the Boston Manufacturing Company expanded north from its base in Waltham and built a complex of mills in a sleepy Merrimack River village that quickly became the bustling textile factory town of Lowell, Massachusetts. The towns of Hartford, Connecticut; Trenton, New Jersey; and Wilmington, Delaware, also became urban centers as mill owners exploited the waterpower of their rivers and recruited workers from the countryside.

Western commercial cities such as Pittsburgh, Cincinnati, and New Orleans grew almost as rapidly. These cities expanded initially as transit centers—the points at which goods were transferred from farmers' rafts and wagons to boats or railroads. As the midwestern population grew during the 1830s and 1840s, St. Louis, Detroit, and especially Buffalo and Chicago emerged as dynamic centers of commerce. "There can be no two places in the world," journalist Margaret Fuller wrote from Chicago in 1843, "more completely thoroughfares than this place and Buffalo. . . . The life-blood [of commerce] rushes from east to west, and back again from west to east." To a German visitor, Chicago seemed "for the most part to consist of shops . . . [as if] people came here merely to trade, to make money, and not to live." Chicago's merchants and bankers developed the marketing, provisioning, and financial services essential to farmers and small-town shopkeepers in the surrounding countryside. "There can be no better [market] any where in the Union," declared a farmer in Paw Paw, Illinois.

These midwestern commercial hubs quickly became manufacturing centers as well. Capitalizing on the cities' locations as key junctions for railroad lines and steamboats, entrepreneurs built warehouses, flour mills, packing plants, and machine shops, creating work for hundreds of artisans and factory laborers. In 1846,

Cyrus McCormick moved his reaper factory from western Virginia to Chicago to be closer to his midwestern customers. By 1860, St. Louis and Chicago had become the nation's third and fourth largest cities, respectively, after New York and Philadelphia (Map 9.5).

The old Atlantic seaports—Boston, Philadelphia, Baltimore, Charleston, and especially New York City—remained important for their foreign commerce and, increasingly, as centers of finance and manufacturing. New York City and nearby Brooklyn grew at a phenomenal rate: Between 1820 and 1860, their combined populations increased nearly tenfold to 1 million people, thanks to the arrival of tens of thousands of German and Irish immigrants. Drawing on this abundant labor, New York became a center of small-scale manufacturing and the ready-made clothing industry, which relied on thousands of low-paid seamstresses. "The wholesale clothing establishments are . . . absorbing the business of the country," a "Country Tailor" complained to the *New York Tribune*, "casting many an honest and hardworking man out of employment [and helping] . . . the large cities to swallow up the small towns."

New York's growth stemmed primarily from its dominant position in foreign and domestic trade. It had the best harbor in the United States and, thanks to the Erie Canal, was the best gateway to the Midwest and the best outlet for western grain. Exploiting the city's prime location, in 1818 four Quaker merchants founded the Black Ball Line to carry cargo, people, and mail between New York and the European ports of Liverpool, London, and Le Havre, establishing the first transatlantic shipping service to run on a regular schedule. New York merchants likewise dominated trade with the newly independent South American nations of Brazil, Peru, and Venezuela. New York–based traders took over the cotton trade by offering finance, insurance, and shipping to export merchants in southern ports. By 1840, the port of New York handled almost two-thirds of foreign imports into the United States, almost half of all foreign trade, and much of the immigrant traffic.

- What roles did state and national government play in the development of America's transportation networks?

- Describe the different types of cities that emerged in the United States in the first half of the nineteenth century. How do you explain the differences in their development?

(after Conzen and Pred)

MAP 9.5

The Nation's Major Cities, 1840

By 1840, the United States boasted three major conglomerations of cities. The long-settled ports on the Atlantic—from Boston to Baltimore—served as centers for import merchants, banks, insurance companies, and manufacturers of ready-made clothing, and their reach extended far into the interior—nationwide in the case of New York City. A second group of cities stretched along the Great Lakes and included the wholesale distribution hubs of Buffalo, Detroit, and Chicago, as well as the manufacturing center of Cleveland. A third urban system extended along the Ohio River, comprising the industrial cities of Pittsburgh and Cincinnati and the wholesale centers of Louisville and St. Louis.

Hartford Family

Completely at home in their elegant drawing room, this elite family in Hartford, Connecticut, enjoys the fruits of the father's business success. As the father lounges in his silk robe, his eldest son (and presumptive heir) adopts an air of studied nonchalance and his daughter fingers a piano, signaling her musical accomplishments. A diminutive African American servant (her size suggesting her status) serves fruit to the lavishly attired woman of the house. The drawing room in such houses was usually sumptuously appointed, with a decor reflecting both the owners' prosperity and their aesthetic and cultural interests.   © White House Historical Association/ Photo by National Geographic Society.

New Social Classes and Cultures

The Industrial Revolution and the Market Revolution improved the lives of many Americans by enabling them to live in larger houses, cook on iron stoves, and wear better-made clothes. But especially in the cities, the new economic order spawned distinct social classes: a small but wealthy industrial and commercial elite, a substantial middle class, and a mass of propertyless wage earners. By creating a class-divided society, industrialization posed a momentous challenge to America's republican ideals.

The Business Elite

Before industrialization, white Americans thought of their society in terms of rank: "Notable" families had higher status than families of the "lower orders." Yet in many rural areas, people of different ranks shared a common culture. Gentlemen farmers talked easily with yeomen about crop yields, while their wives conversed about the art of quilting. In the South, humble tenants and aristocratic slave owners enjoyed the same amusements: gambling, cockfighting, and horse racing. Rich and poor attended the same Quaker meetinghouse or Presbyterian church. "Almost everyone eats, drinks, and dresses in the same way," a European visitor to Hartford, Connecticut, reported in 1798, "and one can see the most obvious inequality only in the dwellings."

The Industrial Revolution shattered this agrarian social order and fragmented society into distinct classes and cultures. As millions of Americans moved to large cities, they accentuated the differences between rural and urban life. Moreover, the urban economy made a few city residents—the merchants, manufacturers, bankers, and landlords who made up the business elite—very rich. In 1800, the top 10 percent of the nation's families owned about 40 percent of the wealth; by 1860, the richest 10 percent held nearly 70 percent of the wealth. In New York, Chicago, Baltimore, and New Orleans, the superrich—the top 1 percent—owned more than 40 percent of all tangible property (land and buildings, for example) and an even higher share of intangible property (stocks and bonds).

Government tax policies facilitated the accumulation of wealth. In an era before federal taxes on individual and corporate income, the U.S. Treasury raised most of its revenue from tariffs—regressive taxes on textiles and other imported goods purchased mostly by ordinary citizens. State and local governments also favored the wealthier classes. They taxed real estate (farms, city lots, and buildings) and tangible personal property (furniture, tools, and machinery), but almost never taxed stocks and bonds or the inheritances the rich passed on to their children.

As cities expanded in size and wealth, affluent families consciously set themselves apart. They dressed in well-tailored clothes, rode in fancy carriages, and bought expensively furnished houses tended by butlers, cooks, and other servants. The women no longer socialized with those of lesser wealth, and the men no longer labored side by side with their employees. Instead, they became managers and directors and relied on trusted subordinates to supervise hundreds of factory operatives. Increasingly, merchants, manufacturers, and bankers placed a premium on privacy and lived in separate neighborhoods, often at the edge of the city. The geographic isolation of privileged families and the massive flow of immigrants into separate districts divided cities spatially along lines of class, race, and ethnicity.

The Middle Class

Standing between wealthy owners and propertyless wage earners was a growing middle class—the social product of the economic revolution. The "middling class," a Boston printer explained, was made up of "the farmers, the mechanics, the manufacturers, the traders, who carry on professionally the ordinary operations of buying, selling, and exchanging merchandize." Other members of this new social group—building contractors, lawyers, surveyors, and so on—suddenly found their services in great demand and financially profitable. Middling business owners, white-collar clerks, and professionals were most numerous in the Northeast, where in the 1840s they numbered about 30 percent of the population. But they also could be found in the agrarian South. The cotton boomtown of Oglethorpe, Georgia (population 2,500), boasted eighty "business houses" and eight hotels in 1854.

The emergence of the middle class reflected a dramatic rise in urban prosperity. Between 1830 and 1857, the per capita income of Americans increased by about 2.5 percent a year, a remarkable rate that has never since been matched. This surge in income, along with an abundance of inexpensive mass-produced goods, fostered a distinct middle-class urban culture. Middle-class husbands earned enough to save about 15 percent of their income, which they used to buy well-built houses in a "respectable part of town." They purchased handsome clothes and drove to work and play in smart carriages. Middle-class wives became purveyors of genteel culture, buying books, pianos, lithographs, and comfortable furniture for their front parlors. Upper-middle-class families hired Irish or African American domestic servants, while less prosperous ones enjoyed the comforts provided by new industrial goods. The middle class outfitted their residences with furnaces (both to warm the entire house and heat water for bathing), cooking stoves with ovens, and Singer's treadle-operated sewing machines. Some urban families now kept their perishable food in iceboxes, which ice-company wagons periodically refilled, and bought many varieties of packaged goods. As early as 1825, the Underwood Company of Boston was marketing jars of well-preserved Atlantic salmon.

If material comfort was one distinguishing mark of the middle class, moral and mental discipline was another. Middle-class writers denounced carnivals and festivals as a "chaos of sin and folly, of misery and fun" and, by the 1830s, had managed to suppress them. Ambitious parents were equally concerned with their children's moral and intellectual development. To help their

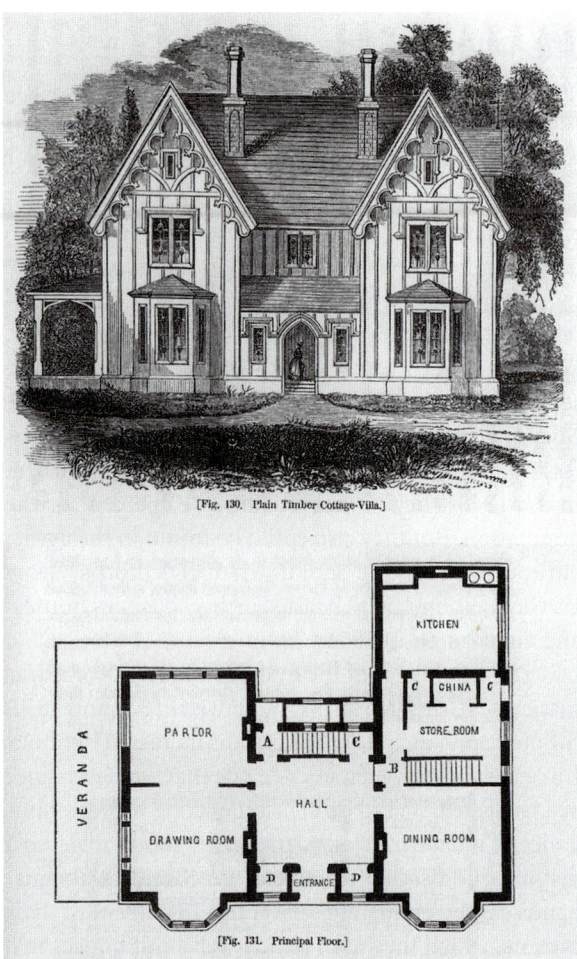

[Fig. 130. Plain Timber Cottage-Villa.]

[Fig. 131. Principal Floor.]

Architecture for the Emergent Middle Class

This dwelling was well suited for a "farmer of wealth" or a middle-class suburbanite, according to Alexander Downing, author of *The Architecture of Country Houses* (1850). The exterior of the house exhibited "a considerable degree of elegance," while the interior boasted a substantial drawing room and dining room, for the entertainment of guests, and a parlor for more intimate conversations among family and friends. Downing's books and similar style manuals by other authors helped define the culture of the growing middle class and diffuse it across the nation. Andrew J. Downing, *The Architecture of Country Houses*, 1850.

offspring succeed in life, middle-class parents often provided them with a high school education (in an era when most white children received only five years of schooling), and stressed the importance of discipline and hard work. American Protestants had long believed that diligent work in an earthly "calling" was a duty owed to God. Now the business elite and the middle class gave this idea a secular twist by celebrating work as the key to individual social mobility and national prosperity.

Benjamin Franklin gave classical expression to the secular work ethic in his *Autobiography*, which was published in full in 1818 (thirty years after his death) and immediately found a huge audience. Heeding Franklin's suggestion that an industrious man would become a rich one, tens of thousands of young American men saved their money, adopted temperate habits, and aimed to rise in the world. There was an "almost universal ambition to get forward," observed Hezekiah Niles, editor of *Niles' Weekly Register*. Warner Myers, a Philadelphia housepainter, raised funds from family, friends, and personal loans and became a builder, constructing sixty houses and garnering ample profits. Countless magazines, children's books, self-help manuals, and novels recounted the stories of similar individuals. The **self-made man** became a central theme of American popular culture and inspired many men (and a few women) to seek wealth. Just as the yeoman ethic had united the social ranks in pre-1800 America, the gospel of personal achievement linked the upper and middle classes of the new industrializing society.

Urban Workers and the Poor

As thoughtful business leaders surveyed society, they concluded that the yeoman farmer and artisan-republican ideal—a social order of independent producers—was no longer possible. "Entire independence ought not to be wished for," Ithamar A. Beard, the paymaster of the Hamilton Manufacturing Company (in Lowell, Massachusetts), told a mechanics' association in 1827. "In large manufacturing towns, many more must fill subordinate stations and must be under the immediate direction and control of a master or superintendent, than in the farming towns."

Beard had a point. In 1840, all of the nation's slaves and about half of its white workers were laboring for others. The bottom 10 percent of wage earners consisted of casual workers, who were hired on a short-term basis for the most arduous jobs. Poor women washed clothes; their husbands and sons carried lumber and bricks for construction projects, loaded ships, and dug out dirt and stones to build canals. When they could find jobs, these men earned "their dollar per diem," a longtime resident told readers of the *Baltimore American*, but he cautioned that they could never save enough "to pay rent, buy fire wood and eatables" when the harbor or the job market froze up. During business depressions, casual laborers bore the brunt of unemployment; even in good times, their jobs were temporary and dangerous.

Other laborers had greater security of employment, but few were prospering. In Massachusetts in 1825, an unskilled worker earned about two-thirds as much as a mechanic did; two decades later, it was less than half as much. A journeyman carpenter in Philadelphia reported that he was about "even with the World" after several years of work but that many of his coworkers were in debt. The 18,000 women who made men's clothing in New York City in the 1850s earned just a few pennies a day, less than $80 a year. Such meager wages barely paid for food and rent, so poorer workers could not take advantage of the rapidly falling prices of manufactured goods. Only the most fortunate working-class families could afford to educate their children, buy apprenticeships for their sons, or accumulate small dowries for their daughters. Most families sent ten-year-old children out to work, and the death of a parent often threw the survivors into dire poverty. As a charity worker noted, "What can a bereaved widow do, with 5 or 6 little children, destitute of every means of support but what her own hands can furnish (which in a general way does not amount to more than 25 cents a day)?"

Impoverished workers congregated in dilapidated housing in bad neighborhoods. Single men and women lived in crowded boardinghouses, while families jammed themselves into tiny apartments in the basements and attics of small houses. As immigrants poured in after 1840, urban populations soared, and developers squeezed more and more dwellings and foul-smelling outhouses onto a single lot. Venturing into the New York City slums in the 1850s, shocked state legislators found gaunt, shivering people with "wild ghastly faces" living amid "hideous squalor and deadly effluvia, the dim, undrained courts oozing with pollution, the dark, narrow stairways, decayed with age, reeking with filth, overrun with vermin."

Many wage earners sought solace in alcohol. Beer and rum had long been standard fare in American rituals: patriotic ceremonies, work breaks, barn raisings, and games. But during the 1820s and 1830s, the consumption of intoxicating beverages reached new heights, even among the elite; alcoholism killed Daniel Tompkins, vice president under James Monroe, and undermined Henry Clay's bid for the presidency. Heavy drinking was especially devastating for wage earners, who could ill afford its costs. Although Methodist artisans and ambitious craft workers swore off liquor to protect their work skills, health, and finances, other workers drank heavily on the job — and not just during the traditional 11 A.M. and 4 P.M. "refreshers." A baker recalled how "one man was stationed at the window to watch, while the rest drank." Long before the arrival of spirit-drinking Irish and beer-drinking German immigrants, grogshops dotted almost every block in working-class districts and were centers of disorder. Unrestrained drinking by young men led to fistfights, brawls, and robberies. The urban police, mostly low-paid watchmen and untrained constables, were unable to contain the lawlessness.

The Benevolent Empire

The disorder among wage earners alarmed the rising middle classes, who wanted safe cities and a disciplined workforce. To improve the world around them, many upwardly mobile men and women embraced religious benevolence. Led by Congregational and Presbyterian ministers, they created organizations of conservative social reform that historians call the **Benevolent Empire**. The reformers' goal was to restore "the moral government of God" by reducing intemperance and poverty, explained Presbyterian minister Lyman Beecher. Reform-minded individuals first regulated their own behavior and then tried to control the lives of working people. They would regulate popular behavior — by persuasion if possible, by law if necessary.

The Benevolent Empire targeted age-old evils such as drunkenness, adultery, prostitution, and crime, but its methods were new. Instead of relying on church sermons and persuasion by community leaders, the reformers created large-scale organizations to combat evil: the Prison Discipline Society and the American Society for the Promotion of Temperance, among many others. Each organization had a managing staff, a network of hundreds of chapters, thousands of volunteer members, and a newspaper.

Often acting in concert, these benevolent groups worked to improve society. First, they encouraged people to lead well-disciplined lives and acquire "regular habits." They persuaded local governments to ban carnivals of drink and dancing, such as Negro Election Day (festivities in which African Americans symbolically took over the government), which had been enjoyed by whites as well as blacks. Second, they devised new institutions to help the needy and control the unruly. Reformers provided homes of refuge for abandoned children and asylums for the insane, who previously had been confined by their families in attics and cellars. They campaigned to end corporal punishment of criminals and to rehabilitate them in new, specially designed penitentiaries.

Women formed a crucial part of the Benevolent Empire. Since the 1790s, upper-class women had sponsored charitable organizations such as the Society for

An Inside View of the Benevolent Empire

Early-nineteenth-century reformers condemned corporal punishment. So they built prisons designed to rehabilitate criminals and turn them into responsible citizens. As this folk painting by a Massachusetts penitentiary inmate suggests, prison officials imposed tight discipline. The inmates marched in silence: In line with the latest penal theories, prisoners were not allowed to speak with one another, the silence key to encouraging them to reflect on their crimes and express repentance.   Courtesy David A. Schorsch.

the Relief of Poor Widows with Small Children, which was founded in 1797 in New York by Isabella Graham, a devout Presbyterian widow. Her daughter Joanna Bethune set up other charitable institutions, including the Orphan Asylum Society and the Society for the Promotion of Industry, which found jobs for hundreds of poor women as spinners and seamstresses.

Some reformers believed that the decline of the traditional Christian observation of the Sabbath (Sunday) as a day of rest was the greatest threat to the "moral government of God." As the market revolution spread, merchants and storekeepers conducted business on Sundays, and urban saloons provided drink and entertainment. To halt these activities, Lyman Beecher and other ministers founded the General Union for Promoting the Observance of the Christian Sabbath in 1828. General Union chapters, replete with women's auxiliaries, sprang up from Maine to Cincinnati and beyond. To rally Chris-

tians, the General Union demanded Congress repeal an 1810 law allowing mail to be transported—though not delivered—on Sundays. Members boycotted shipping companies that did business on the Sabbath and campaigned for municipal laws forbidding games and festivals on the Lord's day.

The Benevolent Empire's efforts to impose its Sabbatarian values provoked opposition from workers and freethinkers. Men who labored twelve to fourteen hours a day, six days a week wanted the freedom to spend their one day of leisure as they wished. To keep goods moving, shipping company managers demanded that the Erie Canal provide lockkeepers on Sundays; using laws to enforce a particular set of moral beliefs was "contrary to the free spirit of our institutions," they said. When evangelical reformers proposed teaching Christianity to slaves, they aroused hostility among white southerners. This popular resistance by workers and planters limited the success of the initiatives of the Benevolent Empire.

Charles Grandison Finney: Revivalism and Reform

Presbyterian minister Charles Grandison Finney found a new way to propagate religious values. Finney was not part of the traditional religious elite. Born into a poor farming family in Connecticut, he had planned to become a lawyer and rise into the middle class. But in 1823, Finney underwent an intense conversion experience and chose the ministry as his career. Beginning in towns along the Erie Canal, the young minister conducted emotional revival meetings that stressed conversion rather than doctrine. Repudiating Calvinist beliefs, he preached that God would welcome any sinner who submitted to the Holy Spirit. Finney's ministry drew on—and greatly accelerated—the Second Great Awakening, the wave of Protestant revivalism that had begun after the Revolution (see Chapter 8).

Evangelical Beliefs Finney's central message was that "God has made man a moral free agent" who could choose salvation. This doctrine of free will was particularly attractive to members of the new middle class, who had already chosen to improve their material lives. But Finney also had great success in converting people at both ends of the social spectrum, from the haughty rich who had placed themselves above God, to the abject poor who seemed lost to drink and sloth. Finney celebrated their common fellowship in Christ and identified them spiritually with pious middle-class respectability.

Finney's most spectacular triumph came in 1830, when he moved his revivals from small towns to Rochester, New York, now a major milling and commercial city on the Erie Canal. Preaching every day for six months and promoting group prayer meetings in family homes, Finney won over the influential merchants and manufacturers of Rochester, who pledged to reform their lives and those of their workers. They promised to attend church, give up intoxicating beverages, and work hard. To encourage their employees to do the same, wealthy businessmen founded a Free Presbyterian church—"free" because members did not have to pay for pew space. Other Evangelical Protestants founded churches to serve transient canal laborers, and pious businessmen set up a savings bank to encourage thrift among the working classes. Meanwhile, Finney's wife, Lydia, and other middle-class women carried the Chris-

Charles Grandison Finney, Evangelist (1792–1875)
When an unknown artist painted this flattering portrait in 1834, Finney was forty-two years old and at the height of his career as an evangelist. Handsome and charismatic, Finney had just led a series of enormously successful revivals in Rochester, New York, and other cities along the Erie Canal. In 1835, he established a theology department at newly founded Oberlin College in Ohio, where he trained a generation of ministers and served as president from 1851 to 1866.   Oberlin College Archives.

tian message to the wives of the unconverted, set up Sunday schools for poor children, and formed the Female Charitable Society to assist the unemployed.

Finney's efforts to create a community of morally disciplined Christians were not completely successful. Skilled workers who belonged to strong craft organizations—boot makers, carpenters, stonemasons, and boatbuilders—protested that they needed higher wages and better schools more urgently than sermons and prayers. Poor people ignored Finney's revival, as did the Irish Catholic immigrants who had recently begun arriving in Rochester and other northeastern cities, bringing with them a hatred of Protestants as religious heretics and political oppressors.

Nonetheless, revivalists from New England to the Midwest copied Finney's evangelical message and techniques. In New York City, wealthy silk merchants Arthur and Lewis Tappan founded a magazine, *The Christian Evangelist*, which promoted Finney's ideas. The revivals swept through Pennsylvania, North Carolina, Tennessee, and Indiana, where, a convert reported, "you could not go upon the street and hear any conversation, except upon religion." The success of the revivals "has been so general and thorough," concluded a Presbyterian general assembly, "that the whole customs of society have changed."

Temperance | The **temperance movement** proved to be the most successful evangelical social reform. Soon after evangelical Protestants took over the American Temperance Society in 1832, the organization boasted two thousand chapters and more than 200,000 members. The society employed the methods of the revivals—group confession and prayer, a focus on the family and the spiritual role of women, and sudden emotional conversion—and took them to northern towns and southern villages. On one day in New York City in 1841, more than 4,000 people took the temperance "pledge." Throughout America, the annual consumption of spirits fell dramatically, from an average of 5 gallons per person in 1830 to 2 gallons in 1845.

Evangelical reformers celebrated religion as the key to moral improvement. Laziness and drinking might be cured by self-discipline, as Benjamin Franklin had argued, but people would certainly experience a profound change of heart through religious conversion. Religious discipline and the ideology of social mobility thus served as powerful cements, bonding middle-class Americans and wage-earning citizens to one another in the face of economic divisions created by industrialization, market expansion, and increasing cultural diversity.

Immigration and Cultural Conflict

Cultural diversity was the result of vast waves of immigrants. Between 1840 and 1860, about 2 million Irish, 1.5 million Germans, and 750,000 Britons poured into the United States. The British migrants were primarily Protestants and relatively prosperous; their ranks included trained professionals, propertied farmers, and skilled workers. Many German immigrants also came from property-owning farming and artisan families and had sufficient resources to move to the midwestern states of Wisconsin, Iowa, and Missouri. Other Germans and most of the Irish settled in the Northeast, where by 1860, they accounted for nearly one-third of white adults. Most immigrants avoided the South because they opposed slavery, feared competition from enslaved workers, and preferred jobs in the northern manufacturing centers.

Irish Poverty | The poorest migrants, the Irish peasants and laborers, were fleeing a famine caused by severe overpopulation and a devastating blight that destroyed much of the Irish potato crop. Arriving in dire poverty, the Irish settled mostly in the cities of New England and New York. The men took low-paying jobs as factory hands, construction workers, and canal diggers, while the women became washerwomen and domestic servants. Irish families crowded into cheap tenement buildings with primitive sanitation systems and were the first to die when disease struck a city. In the summer of 1849, a cholera epidemic took the lives of thousands of poor immigrants in St. Louis and New York City.

In times of hardship and sorrow, immigrants turned to their churches. Many Germans and virtually all the Irish were Catholics, and they fueled the growth of the American Catholic Church. In 1840, there were sixteen Catholic dioceses and seven hundred churches; by 1860, there were forty-five dioceses and twenty-five hundred churches. Under the guidance of their priests and bishops, Catholics built an impressive network of institutions—charitable societies, orphanages, militia companies, parochial schools, and political organizations—that helped them maintain both their religion and their German or Irish identity.

Nativism | The Protestant fervor stirred up by the Second Great Awakening meant that a barrage of anti-Catholic publications greeted these new immigrants (see Comparing American Voices, "A Debate over Catholic Immigration," pp. 298–299). The artist and inventor Samuel F. B. Morse was a militant critic of Catholicism. In 1834, Morse published *Foreign Conspiracy Against the Liberties of the United States*, which warned of a Catholic threat to American republican institutions. Morse believed that Catholic immigrants would obey the dictates of Pope Gregory XVI (1831–1846), who in an official 1832 papal declaration (encyclical) had condemned liberty of conscience, freedom of publication, and the separation of church and state. Gregory instructed Catholics to repudiate republicanism and acknowledge the "submission due to princes" and to the papacy itself. Republican-minded Protestants of many denominations shared Morse's fears of papal interference in American life and politics, and *Foreign Conspiracy* became their handbook.

The social tensions stemming from industrialization intensified anti-Catholic sentiment. During busi-

The Drunkard's Progress: From the First Glass to the Grave

This 1846 lithograph, published by N. Currier, suggests the inevitable fate of those who drink. The drunkard's descent into "Poverty and Disease" ends with "Death by suicide," leaving a grieving and destitute wife and child. Temperance reformers urged Americans to take "The Cold Water Cure" by drinking water instead of alcoholic beverages. To promote abstinence among the young, in 1836 revivalist preacher and temperance lecturer Reverend Thomas Poage Hunt founded the Cold Water Army, an organization that grew to embrace several hundred thousand children, all of whom pledged "perpetual hate to all that can Intoxicate."   Library of Congress.

ness recessions, unemployed Protestant mechanics and factory workers joined mobs that attacked Catholics, accusing them of taking jobs and driving down wages. These cultural conflicts undercut trade unionism, because many Protestant wage earners felt that they had more in common with their Protestant employers than with their Catholic coworkers. Other native-born Protestants formed clubs that called for a halt to immigration. Benevolent-minded Protestants supported the anti-Catholic movement for reasons of public policy. As crusaders for public education, they opposed the diversion of tax resources to Catholic schools; as advocates of temperance and civilized manners, they condemned the rowdyism of drunken Irish men.

In many northeastern cities, religious and cultural tensions led to violence. In 1834, in Charlestown, Massachusetts, a quarrel between Catholic laborers repairing a convent owned by the Ursuline order of nuns and Protestant workers in a neighboring brickyard led to a full-scale riot and the convent's destruction. In 1844, in Philadelphia, riots erupted when the Catholic bishop persuaded public-school officials to use both Catholic and Protestant versions of the Bible. Anti-Irish violence incited by the city's nativist clubs lasted for two months and escalated into open warfare between Protestants and the Pennsylvania militia. Even as the economic revolution brought prosperity to many Americans and attracted millions of immigrants, it divided society along lines of class, ethnicity, and religion.

- What social classes were created by the economic revolution? Describe their defining characteristics.

- What were the main goals of the Benevolent Empire? To what extent were they achieved?

- Weigh the relative importance of the Industrial Revolution and the Market Revolution in changing the American economy.

A Debate over Catholic Immigration

Between 1776 and 1830, relatively few Europeans immigrated to the United States. Then, as the text explains, an increase in population and in poverty sparked the migration of increasing numbers of Germans (both Catholics and Protestants) and Irish Catholics. The arrival of hundreds of thousands of foreign Catholics in the midst of the intense Protestantism of the Second Great Awakening led to religious riots, the formation of the nativist American Party, and sharp debates in the public press. By using contemporary newspapers and other writings as a source, historians can gain insight into the public rhetoric (and often the private passions) of the time.

Lyman Beecher

Catholicism Is Incompatible with Republicanism

Lyman Beecher (1775–1863) was one of the leading Protestant ministers of his generation and the father of a family of Christian social reformers and well-known authors: minister Henry Ward Beecher, Harriet Beecher Stowe (*Uncle Tom's Cabin*), and Catharine Beecher (*A Treatise on Domestic Economy*). In *A Plea for the West* (1835), Lyman Beecher alerted his fellow Protestants to the centralized power of the Roman Catholic Church and its opposition to republican institutions. That opposition was formalized in papal encyclicals issued by Pope Gregory XVI (*Mirari Vos*, 1832) and Pope Pius IX (*Quanta Cura*, 1864), both of which condemned republicanism and freedom of conscience as false political ideologies.

Since the irruption of the northern barbarians, the world has never witnessed such a rush of dark-minded population from one country to another, as is now leaving Europe, and dashing upon our shores. . . .

They come, also, not undirected. There is evidently a supervision abroad—and one here—by which they come, and set down together, in city or country, as a Catholic body, and are led or followed quickly by a Catholic priesthood, who maintain over them in the land of strangers and unknown tongues an [absolute] ascendancy. . . .

The ministers of no Protestant sect could or would dare to attempt to regulate the votes of their people as the Catholic priests can do, who at the confessional learn all the private concerns of their people, and have almost unlimited power over the conscience as it respects the performance of every civil or social duty.

There is another point of dissimilarity of still greater importance. The opinions of the Protestant clergy are congenial with liberty—they are chosen by the people who have been educated as freemen, and they are dependent on them for patronage and support. The Catholic system is adverse to liberty, and the clergy to a great extent are dependent on foreigners [the Pope and church authorities in Rome] opposed to the principles of our government.

Nor is this all—the secular patronage at the disposal of an associated body of men, who under the influence of their priesthood may be induced to act as one . . . would enable them to touch far and wide the spring of action through our cities and through the nation. . . . How many mechanics, merchants, lawyers, physicians, in any political crisis, might they reach and render timid . . . ? How will [the priesthood's] power extend and become omnipresent and resistless as emigration shall quadruple their numbers and action on the political and business men of the nation?

A tenth part of the suffrage of the nation, thus condensed and wielded by the Catholic powers of Europe, might decide our elections, perplex our policy, inflame and divide the nation, break the bond of our union, and throw down our free institutions. . . .

[Catholicism is] a religion which never prospered but in alliance with despotic governments, has always been and still is the inflexible enemy of Liberty of conscience and free inquiry, and at this moment is the main stay of the battle against republican institutions.

Source: Lyman Beecher, *A Plea for the West* (Cincinnati: Truman & Smith, 1835), 72–73, 126, 59–63, 85–86, 59.

Orestes Brownson

Catholicism as a Necessity for Popular Government

Like Lyman Beecher, Orestes Brownson was born into the Presbyterian Church, but he quickly grew dissatisfied with its doctrines. After experimenting with Unitarianism, communalism, socialism, and transcendentalism, Brownson converted to Catholicism in 1844. A zealous convert, Brownson defended Catholicism with rigorous, logical, and provocative arguments in this article, "Catholicity Necessary to Sustain Popular Liberty" (1845).

Without the Roman Catholic religion it is impossible to pre-serve a democratic government, and secure its free, orderly, and wholesome action.... The theory of democracy is, Construct your government and commit it to the people to be taken care of ... as they shall think proper.

It is a beautiful theory, and would work admirably, if it were not for one little difficulty, namely, the people are fallible, both individually and collectively, and governed by their passions and interests, which not unfrequently lead them far astray, and produce much mischief.

We know of but one solution of the difficulty, and that is in RELIGION. There is no foundation for virtue but in religion, and it is only religion that can command the degree of popular virtue and intelligence requisite to insure to popular government the right direction.... But what religion? It must be a religion which is above the people and controls them, or it will not answer the purpose. It cannot be Protestantism, ... for Protestantism assumes as its point of departure that Almighty God has indeed given us a religion, but has given it to us not to take care of us, but to be taken care of by us.

[Moreover,] Protestant faith and worship tremble as readily before the slightest breath of public sentiment, as the aspen leaf before the zephyr. The faith and discipline of a sect take any and every direction the public opinion of that sect demands. All is loose, floating,—is here to-day, is there tomorrow, and, next day, may be nowhere. The holding of slaves is compatible with Christian character south of the geographical line, and incompatible north; and Christian morals change according to the prejudices, interests, or habits of the people....

Here, then, is the reason why Protestantism, though it may institute, cannot sustain popular liberty. It is itself subject to popular control, and must follow in all things the popular will, passion, interest, ignorance, prejudice, or caprice.

If Protestantism will not answer the purpose, what religion will? The Roman Catholic, or none. The Roman Catholic religion assumes, as its point of departure, that it is instituted not to be taken care of by the people, but to take care of the people; not to be governed by them, but to govern them. The word is harsh in democratic ears, we admit; but it is not the office of religion to say soft or pleas-ing words.... The people need governing, and must be governed, or nothing but anarchy and destruction await them. They must have a master....

Quote our expression, THE PEOPLE MUST HAVE A MASTER, as you doubtless will; hold it up in glaring capitals, to excite the unthinking and unreasoning multitude, and to doubly fortify their prejudices against Catholicity; be mortally scandalized at the assertion that religion ought to govern the people, and then go to work and seek to

bring the people into subjection to your banks or moneyed corporations....

The Roman Catholic religion, then, is necessary to sustain popular liberty, because popular liberty can be sus-tained only by a religion free from popular control, above the people, speaking from above and able to command them, and such a religion is the Roman Catholic.

Source: Orestes A. Brownson, *Essays and Reviews, Chiefly on Theology, Politics, and Socialism* (New York: D. & J. Sadlier, 1852), 368–370, 372–373, 376, 379–381.

ANALYZING THE EVIDENCE

- According to Beecher, what specific dangers does Catholicism pose to American republican institutions? Why would he argue that Protestant churches do not pose the same dangers?

- Does Brownson disagree with Beecher's criticism of the social and political impact of Catholicism? If so, why does he disagree? If not, on what basis does he defend the values and practices of the Catholic Church? Explain your answer.

- Given Brownson's statement that "the people must have a master," what would be his view of democracy and popular government?

- Would the leaders of the Protestant Benevolent Empire agree with any aspects of Brownson's social and political philosophy? Why or why not?

The Philadelphia Riots of 1844

When riots between nativists and Irish Catholic immigrants broke out in Philadelphia in May 1844, the governor of Pennsylvania called out the militia to restore order. But violence continued. On July 7, battles among Protestants (the well-dressed men in the illustration), Catholics, and state militia left fifteen dead and more than fifty injured. Although the riots were set off by a decision to use both Protestant and Catholic versions of the Bible in the public schools, the causes were more deep-seated. Religious animosities, ethnic differences, and cultural conflicts created an explosive mix that resulted in open warfare.   Library of Congress.

SUMMARY

In this chapter, we examined the causes of the economic transformation of the first half of the nineteenth century. That transformation had two facets: a major increase in production—the Industrial Revolution—and the expansion of commerce—the Market Revolution. Water, steam, and minerals such as coal and iron were crucial ingredients in both revolutions—driving factory machinery, carrying goods to market on canals and rivers, and propelling steamboats and railroad engines.

We also explored the consequences of that transformation: the rise of an urban society, the increasing similarity between the Northeast and Midwest and their growing difference from the South, and the creation of a class-divided society. Seeking to shape the emerging society, benevolent reformers and evangelical revivalists worked to instill moral discipline and Christian values. But artisan republicans, unionized workers, and Irish and German immigrants had their own economic and cultural goals. The result was a fragmented society. Differences of class and culture now split the North just as race and class had long divided the South. As the next chapter suggests, Americans looked to their political system, which was becoming increasingly democratic, to address these divisions. In fact, the tensions among economic inequality, cultural diversity, and political democracy became a troubling—and enduring—part of American life.

CHAPTER REVIEW QUESTIONS

- In what ways was the economy different in 1860 from what it had been in 1800? How would you explain those differences?

- What was the impact of the economic revolution on the lives of women in various social groups and classes?

- Did the Industrial and Market revolutions make America a more or less republican society? How so?

FOR FURTHER EXPLORATION

Charles G. Sellers, *The Market Revolution: Jacksonian America, 1815–1846* (1991), and Richard R. John, *Spreading the News: The American Postal System* (1996), explore the social impact of economic change. Laurel Thatcher Ulrich examines the artifacts and myths of *The Age of Homespun* (2001), while David Freeman Hawke surveys technology in the *Nuts and Bolts of the Past* (1988). Also see the Eli Whitney Museum site (**www.eliwhitney.org**). Scott A. Sandage, *Born Losers: A History of Failure in America* (2005), focuses on failed entrepreneurs.

Stephen Aron, *How the West Was Lost* (1996), analyzes economic conflict in Kentucky, and Peter Way, *Common Labor* (1993), describes the hard lives of the men who dug the canals in the trans-Appalachian west. For the Erie Canal, go to **www.nyscanals.gov/cculture/history**. Documents on white pioneers in Michigan, Minnesota, and Wisconsin (1820–1910) are available at **memory.loc.gov/ammem/umhtml/umhome.html**.

Stuart M. Blumin's *The Emergence of the Middle Class* (1989) discusses the formation of urban classes, while Stephen P. Rice, *Minding the Machine* (2004), probes class, languages, and cultures. David Grimsted, *American Mobbing* (1998), explores urban disorder. In *Home and Work* (1990), Jeanne Boydston exposes the impact of the urban market economy on women's lives. For a textile operative's account of mill life, see **www.fordham.edu/halsall/mod/robinson-lowell.html**. For religion and benevolent societies, consult **www.loc.gov/exhibits/religion/rel07.html**, and William R. Hutchison, *Religious Pluralism in America: The Contentious History of a Founding Ideal* (2003).

TEST YOUR KNOWLEDGE

To assess your command of the material in this chapter, see the Online Study Guide at **bedfordstmartins.com/henretta**.

For Web sites, images, and documents related to topics and places in this chapter, visit **bedfordstmartins.com/makehistory**.

TIMELINE

1782	Oliver Evans builds automated flour mill
1790	Samuel Slater opens spinning mill in Providence, Rhode Island
1792	Congress passes Post Office Act
1793	Eli Whitney devises cotton gin
1800–1830	Shoe entrepreneurs adopt division of labor
1807	Robert Fulton launches the *Clermont*
1814	Boston Manufacturing Company opens cotton mill in Waltham, Massachusetts
1816–1828	Congress levies protective tariffs
1817	Erie Canal begun (completed in 1825)
1820	Minimum price for federal land reduced to $1.25 per acre
1820–1840	Fourfold increase in urban population in Northeast and Midwest
1820s	New England women take textile jobs Rise of Benevolent Empire leads to conservative social reforms
1824	*Gibbons v. Ogden* promotes interstate trade
1830s	Emergence of western commercial cities Labor movement gains strength Urban residence reflects economic class Middle-class culture emerges Growth of temperance movement
1830	Charles G. Finney begins Rochester revivals
1834	Local unions form National Trades' Union John Deere invents steel plow
1840s	Irish and German immigration spark ethnic riots Rise of machine-tool industry
1842	*Commonwealth v. Hunt* legitimizes trade unions
1848	Michigan and Illinois Canal completes water route from New York City to New Orleans
1850s	Expansion of railroads in Northeast and Midwest
1857	Overproduction and speculation trigger a financial panic

A Democratic Revolution, 1820–1844

Europeans who visited the United States in the 1830s generally praised its republican society but not its political parties and politicians. "The gentlemen spit, talk of elections and the price of produce, and spit again," Frances Trollope reported in *Domestic Manners of the Americans* (1832). In her view, American politics was the sport of self-serving party politicians who reeked of "whiskey and onions." Other Europeans lamented the low intellectual level of American political debate. The "clap-trap of praise and pathos" from a Massachusetts politician "deeply disgusted" Harriet Martineau, while Basil Hall was astonished by the shallow arguments advanced by the inept "farmers, shopkeepers, and country lawyers" who sat in the New York assembly.

The negative verdict was unanimous. "The most able men in the United States are very rarely placed at the head of affairs," French aristocrat Alexis de Tocqueville concluded in *Democracy in America* (1835). The reason, Tocqueville suggested, lay in the character of democracy itself. Most citizens ignored important policy issues, jealously refused to elect their intellectual superiors, and listened in awe to "the clamor of a mountebank [a charismatic fraud] who knows the secret of stimulating their tastes."

These Europeans were witnessing the American Democratic Revolution. Before 1815, men of great ability had sat in the seats of government, and the prevailing ideology had been republicanism, or rule by "men of TALENTS and VIRTUE," as a newspaper put it. Such republican leaders feared popular rule. So they wrote constitutions with Bills of Rights, bicameral legislatures, and independent judiciaries, and censured men who campaigned for public office as overambitious politicians. Nonetheless, by the 1820s and 1830s, the watchword was *democracy*, which in practice meant rule by party politicians who avidly sought office by rallying supporters through newspapers, broadsides, and great public processions and meetings. Politics increasingly became a sport — a competitive contest for the votes of ordinary men. "That the majority should govern was a fundamental maxim in all free governments," declared Martin Van Buren, the most talented of the middle-class professional politicians. Criticized by one republican-minded Virginian as "too great an intriguer . . . an adroit, dapper, little managing man," Van Buren often pursued selfish goals; but by encouraging ordinary Americans to burn with "election fever" and support party principles, he and other party politicians provided a sense of identity and purpose amid a fragmented social order.

The Inauguration of President William Henry Harrison, March 4, 1841

After being sworn into office, President Harrison stands on the steps of the U.S. Capitol (in the red box) reviewing a parade of military units. The short balding man to the right of Harrison is Martin Van Buren, the departing president. Although they could not vote, many women attended the ceremony, both to enjoy the festivities and to show their support for the Whig Party's policies of social and moral reform. Anne S. K. Brown Military Collection, Brown University.

The Rise of Popular Politics, 1820–1828

Expansion of the **franchise** (the right to vote) dramatically symbolized the Democratic Revolution. By the 1830s, most states allowed most white men to vote. Nowhere else in the world did ordinary farmers and wage earners exercise such political influence. In England, for example, the Reform Bill of 1832 extended the vote to only 600,000 out of 6 million English men — a mere 10 percent.

The Decline of the Notables and the Rise of Parties

The American Revolution weakened the deferential society of the colonial era, but did not overthrow it. Only two states — Pennsylvania and Vermont — allowed all male taxpayers to vote; even in those states, families of low rank continued to accept the leadership of their social "betters." Consequently, wealthy notables — northern landlords, slave-owning planters, and seaport merchants — dominated the political system in the new republic. And rightly so, thought John Jay, the first chief justice of the Supreme Court. "Those who own the country are the most fit persons to participate in the government of it," Jay declared. Jay and other notables managed local elections by building up an "interest": lending money to small farmers, giving business to storekeepers, and treating their tenants to rum. An outlay of $20 for refreshments, remarked one poll watcher, "may produce about 100 votes." This gentry-dominated system kept men who lacked wealth and powerful family connections from running for office.

The Rise of Democracy The struggle to expand the suffrage began in the 1810s with Maryland reformers invoking the egalitarian language of republicanism: Property qualifications were a "tyranny" because they endowed "one class of men with privileges which are denied to another." To defuse this criticism and deter migration to the West, legislators in Maryland and other seaboard states grudgingly accepted a broader franchise. The new voters quickly changed the tone of politics, rejecting candidates who wore "top boots, breeches, and shoe buckles," their hair in "powder and queues." Instead, they elected men who dressed simply and endorsed democracy.

Smallholding farmers and ambitious laborers in the Midwest and Southwest likewise challenged the old hierarchical order. In Ohio, a traveler reported, "no white man or woman will bear being called a servant." The constitutions of the new states of Indiana (1816), Illinois (1818), and Alabama (1819) prescribed a broad male franchise, and voters usually elected middling men to local and state offices. A well-to-do migrant in Illinois was surprised to learn that the man who plowed his fields "was a colonel of militia, and a member of the legislature." Once in public office, men from modest backgrounds enacted laws that restricted imprisonment for debt, kept taxes low, and allowed farmers to claim squatters' rights to unoccupied land.

By the mid-1820s, many states had given the vote to all white men or to all those who paid taxes or served in the militia. Only a few — North Carolina, Virginia, and Rhode Island — still required the ownership of freehold property for voting. Moreover, between 1818 and 1821, Connecticut, Massachusetts, and New York wrote more democratic constitutions that reapportioned legislative districts on the basis of population and mandated the popular election (rather than the appointment) of judges and justices of the peace.

Democratic politics was contentious and, because it attracted men on the make, often corrupt. Powerful entrepreneurs and speculators — both notables and self-made men — demanded government assistance for their business enterprises and paid bribes to get it. Speculators won land grants by paying off the members of important committees, and bankers distributed shares of stock to key legislators. When the Seventh Ward Bank of New York City received a legislative charter in 1833, the bank's officials set aside one-third of the 3,700 shares of stock for themselves and their friends and almost two-thirds for state legislators and bureaucrats, leaving just 40 shares for public sale.

More political disputes broke out when religious reformers sought laws to enforce the cultural agenda of the Benevolent Empire. In Utica, New York, evangelical Presbyterians called for a town ordinance restricting Sunday entertainment. In response, a member of the local Universalist church — a freethinking Protestant denomination — denounced the measure as coercive and called for "Religious Liberty."

Parties Take Command The appearance of political parties encouraged such debates over government policy. Revolutionary-era Americans had condemned political "factions" as antirepublican and made no mention of political parties in the national and state constitutions. But as the power of notables waned in the 1820s, disciplined political parties appeared in a number of states; usually they were run by professional politicians, often middle-class lawyers and journalists. One observer compared the new organizations to a well-designed textile loom, calling them "machines" that wove the interests of diverse social and economic groups into a coherent legislative program.

Martin Van Buren of New York was the chief architect of the emerging system of party government, at both the state and national levels. The son of a Jeffersonian tavern keeper, Van Buren grew up in the landlord-dominated society of the Hudson River Valley. To get training as a lawyer, he relied on the powerful Van Ness clan; then, determined not to become a dependent "tool" of a notable family, Van Buren repudiated their tutelage. His goal was to create a new political order based on party identity, not family connections. In justifying governments run by party politicians, Van Buren rejected the traditional republican belief that political factions were dangerous. Instead, he claimed that the opposite was true: "All men of sense know that political parties are inseparable from free government," he stated, because they check an elected official's inherent "disposition to abuse power."

Between 1817 and 1821, Van Buren turned his "Bucktail" supporters (so called because they wore a deer's tail on their hats) into the first statewide **political machine**. He purchased a newspaper, the *Albany Argus*, and used it to promote his policies and get out the vote. **Patronage** was an even more important tool. When Van Buren's Bucktails won control of the New York legislature in 1821, they acquired a political interest much greater than that of the notables: the power to appoint some six thousand of their friends to positions in New York's legal bureaucracy of judges, justices of the peace, sheriffs, deed commissioners, and coroners. This **spoils system** was fair, Van Buren suggested, because it "would operate sometimes in favour of one party, and sometimes of another." Party government was thoroughly republican, he added, as it reflected the preferences of a majority of the voters (see Voices from Abroad, "Alexis de Tocqueville: Probing American Politics," p. 306). To ensure the passage of the party's legislative program, Van Buren insisted on disciplined voting as determined by a **caucus**, a meeting of party leaders. On one crucial occasion, the "Little Magician"—a nickname reflecting Van Buren's short stature and political dexterity—gave an elaborate banquet in honor of seventeen New York legislators who sacrificed "individual preferences for the general good" of the party.

The Election of 1824

The advance of political democracy and party government in the states undermined the traditional notable-dominated system of national politics. After the War of 1812, the aristocratic Federalist Party virtually disappeared, and the Republican Party splintered into competing factions (see Chapter 7). As the election of 1824 approached, five Republican candidates campaigned for the presidency. Three were veterans of President James Monroe's cabinet: Secretary of State John Quincy Adams, the son of former president John Adams; Secretary of War John C. Calhoun; and Secretary of the Treasury William H. Crawford. The other candidates were Henry Clay of Kentucky, the hard-drinking, dynamic Speaker of the House of Representatives; and General Andrew Jackson, now a senator from Tennessee. When the Republican caucus in Congress selected Crawford as the party's official nominee, the other candidates refused to withdraw and took their case to the voters. Thanks to democratic reforms, eighteen of the twenty-four states required popular elections (rather than a vote of the state legislature) to choose their representatives to the electoral college.

Each candidate had strengths. Thanks to his diplomatic successes as secretary of state, John Quincy Adams enjoyed national recognition; and his Massachusetts connection ensured him the electoral votes of New England. Henry Clay based his candidacy on his **American System**, an integrated program of national economic development similar to the Commonwealth System of the state governments. Clay wanted to strengthen the Second Bank of the United States and to use tariff revenues to build roads and canals. His nationalistic program won praise in the West, which needed transportation improvements, but elicited sharp criticism in the South, which relied on rivers to market its cotton and had few manufacturing industries to protect. William Crawford of Georgia, an ideological heir of Thomas Jefferson, denounced Clay's American System as a scheme to "consolidate" political power in Washington. Recognizing Crawford's appeal in the South, John C. Calhoun of South Carolina withdrew from the race and endorsed Andrew Jackson.

As the hero of the Battle of New Orleans, Jackson benefited from the surge of patriotism after the War of 1812. Born in the Carolina backcountry, Jackson had settled in Nashville, Tennessee, where he formed ties to influential families through marriage and a career as an attorney and a slave-owning cotton planter. His rise from common origins symbolized the new democratic

All the nations and people I had hitherto passed through resembled
own in their manners, customs and langu

Alexis de Tocqueville
Probing American Politics

In 1831, the French aristocrat Alexis de Tocqueville (1805–1859) came to the United States to report on its innovative penal system. But the major product of Tocqueville's nine-month sojourn was *Democracy in America* (1835, 1840), a brilliant analysis of the new republican society. Tocqueville had collected the raw materials for his great study into fourteen notebooks, where he recorded conversations with hundreds of citizens and pondered their significance.

From a Conversation with Boston intellectual Jared Sparks:
[Sparks:] The political dogma of this country is that the majority is always right. By and large we are very well satisfied to have adopted it, but . . . sometimes the majority has wished to oppress the minority. . . .

From a Conversation with Étienne Mazureau, a French-born lawyer in New Orleans:
[Tocqueville] Q. Before you came under American rule, did you have any of the forms of free government?

[Mazureau] A. No.

Q. Was the change from complete subjection to complete freedom difficult?

A. No. Congress has been careful to give us independence by degrees. At first its rule was almost as absolute as that of our old Governors. Then it gave us the status of a territory. Finally it incorporated us in the Union as an independent State . . . [which promoted our prosperity.]

From a Conversation with Mr. Guillemain, the French Consul at New Orleans:
[Tocqueville] Q. Do you think that part of this prosperity is due to the free institutions given to Louisiana?

[Guillemain] A. One must have seen close up as I have for fifteen years the way business is conducted in a little, completely democratic republic, to be convinced that prosperity is not due to political institutions, but is independent of them. You have no idea of such a Bedlam. The people appoint intriguers without talent to office, while outstanding men seldom achieve it. The legislature ceaselessly makes, alters and repeals the laws. . . . The government is a prey to factions. You see what a state of neglect and dirt the town is in; it has a revenue of a million francs. But much squandering of public money prevails. People say that by widening the franchise one increases the independence of the vote. I think the opposite. In all countries the working classes are at the disposition of those who employ them; . . . However . . . prosperity of Louisiana is very great and is perpetually increasing. This government here has the merit of being very weak, and of not hampering any freedom.

From a Conversation with an Alabama Lawyer:
[Tocqueville] Q. Do the people choose good representatives?

A. No, in general they choose people on their own level who flatter them. . . .

Q. But from these bad choices there must result bad laws and bad government?

A. Not nearly so much as one might expect at first glance. There are always some men of talent in our assemblies; from the first days these overwhelm the others and absolutely dominate business. It is really they who make and discuss the laws. The rest vote as they do.

Tocqueville's Reflections:
The two great social principles which seem to me to rule American society . . . are as follows:

1st. The majority may be mistaken on some points, but finally it is always right. . . .

2nd. Every individual, private person, society, community or nation, is the only lawful judge of its own interest, and provided it does not harm the interests of others, nobody has the right to interfere.

A completely democratic government is so dangerous an instrument that, *even in America*, men have been obliged to take a host of precautions against the errors and passions of Democracy. The establishment of two chambers [in the legislatures], the governor's veto, and above all the establishment of the judges.

Source: Alexis de Tocqueville, *Journey to America*, ed. J. P. Mayer, trans. George Lawrence (Garden City, NY: Anchor Books, 1971), 47, 95, 98–99, 103–104, 148.

ANALYZING THE EVIDENCE

- Who are Tocqueville's informants? How might their social identity affect their perspective on events?
- According to Tocqueville's sources, what are the strengths and weaknesses of the American political system? What is his view?

age, and his reputation as a "plain solid republican" attracted voters in all regions. Still, Jackson's strong showing surprised most political leaders. The Tennessee senator received 99 of the 261 votes cast by members of the electoral college; Adams garnered 84 votes; Crawford, struck down by a stroke during the campaign, won 41; and Clay finished with 37 (Map 10.1).

Because no candidate received an absolute majority, the Twelfth Amendment to the Constitution (ratified in 1804) specified that the House of Representatives would choose the president from among the three highest vote-getters. This procedure hurt Jackson because many congressmen feared that the rough-hewn "military chieftain" might become a tyrant. Out of the race himself, Henry Clay used his influence as Speaker to thwart Jackson's election. Clay assembled a coalition of congressmen from New England and the Ohio River Valley that voted Adams into the presidency. Adams

showed his gratitude by appointing Clay his secretary of state, which was the traditional stepping-stone to the presidency. Clay's appointment was politically fatal for both men: Jackson's supporters accused Clay and Adams of making a secret deal. Condemning what Calhoun labeled a "corrupt bargain" that thwarted the popular mandate for Jackson's election, they vowed to oppose Adams's policies and to prevent Clay's rise to the presidency.

The Last Notable President: John Quincy Adams

As president, Adams called for bold national leadership. "The moral purpose of the Creator," he told Congress, was to use the president and other public officials to "improve the conditions of himself and his fellow men." Adams called for the establishment of a national university in Washington, extensive scientific explorations in the Far West, and a uniform standard of weights and measures. Most important, he endorsed Henry Clay's American System and its three key elements: protective tariffs to stimulate manufacturing, federally subsidized roads and canals to facilitate commerce, and a national bank to control credit and provide a uniform currency.

The Fate of Adams's Policies   Manufacturers, entrepreneurs, and farmers in the Northeast and Midwest welcomed Adams's proposals. But his policies won little support in the South, where planters opposed protective tariffs because they raised the price of manufactures. Southern smallholders also feared powerful banks that could force them into bankruptcy. From his deathbed, Thomas Jefferson condemned Adams for promoting "a single and splendid government of aristocracy [of money] . . . riding and ruling over the plundered ploughman and beggared yeomanry."

Other politicians objected to the American System on constitutional grounds. In 1817, President Madison had vetoed the Bonus Bill, which proposed using the national government's income from the Second Bank of the United States to fund improvement projects in the states. Such projects, Madison had argued, were the sole responsibility of the states, a sentiment widely shared among Jeffersonian Republicans. After a trip to Monticello to meet the aging Patriot statesman, Martin Van Buren declared his allegiance to the constitutional "doctrines of the Jefferson School." Now a member of the U.S. Senate, Van Buren joined other Jeffersonian Republicans in defeating most of Adams's proposed subsidies for roads and canals.

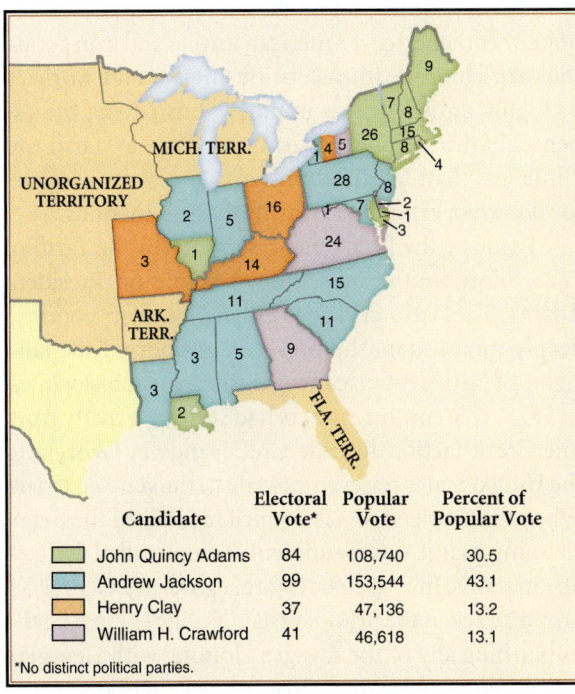

Candidate	Electoral Vote*	Popular Vote	Percent of Popular Vote
John Quincy Adams	84	108,740	30.5
Andrew Jackson	99	153,544	43.1
Henry Clay	37	47,136	13.2
William H. Crawford	41	46,618	13.1

*No distinct political parties.

MAP 10.1

The Presidential Election of 1824

Regional voting was the dominant factor in 1824. John Quincy Adams captured every electoral vote in New England and most of those in New York; Henry Clay carried Ohio and Kentucky, the most populous trans-Appalachian states; and William Crawford took the southern states of Virginia and Georgia. Only Andrew Jackson claimed a national constituency, winning Pennsylvania and New Jersey in the East, Indiana and most of Illinois in the Midwest, and much of the South. Only 356,000 Americans voted, about 27 percent of the eligible electorate.

John Quincy Adams

This famous daguerreotype of the former president, taken about 1843 by Philip Haas, conveys his rigid personality and high moral standards. Although these personal attributes hindered Adams's effectiveness as the nation's chief executive, they contributed to his success as an antislavery congressman from Massachusetts in the 1830s and 1840s. The Metropolitan Museum of Art, Gift of I. N. Phelps Stokes, Edward S. Hawes, Alice Mary Hawes, Marion Augusta Hawes, 1937. Photograph © The Metropolitan Museum of Art.

The Tariff Battle | The farthest-reaching battle of the Adams administration came over tariffs. The Tariff of 1816 had placed relatively high duties on imports of cheap English cotton cloth, allowing New England textile producers to dominate the market for such goods. In 1824, Adams and Clay secured a new tariff that protected manufacturers in New England and Pennsylvania against imports of iron goods and more expensive English woolen and cotton textiles. Without these tariffs, U.S. producers might have shared the fate of India's once world-dominant textile industry, which was destroyed in the early nineteenth century by cheaper British machine-made imports— thanks to the free trade policies imposed by the British imperial regime.

Recognizing the appeal of tariffs, Van Buren and his Jacksonian allies hopped on the bandwagon. By increasing tariffs on wool, hemp, and other imported raw materials, they hoped to win the support of wool- and hemp-producing farmers in New York, Ohio, and Kentucky for Jackson's presidential candidacy in 1828. The tariff had become a prisoner of politics. "I fear this tariff thing," remarked Thomas Cooper, the president of the College of South Carolina and an advocate of free trade. "[B]y some strange mechanical contrivance [it has become] . . . a machine for manufacturing Presidents, instead of broadcloths, and bed blankets." Disregarding southern protests, northern Jacksonians joined with supporters of Adams and Clay to enact the Tariff of 1828, which raised duties significantly on raw materials, textiles, and iron goods.

The new tariff enraged the South. As the producer of the world's cheapest raw cotton, the South did not need a tariff to protect its main industry. Moreover, by raising the price of manufactures, the tariff cost southern planters about $100 million a year. Planters had to buy either higher-cost American textiles and iron goods, thus enriching northeastern businesses and workers, or highly dutied British imports, thus paying the expenses of the national government. The new tariff was "little less than legalized pillage," an Alabama legislator declared, calling it a "Tariff of Abominations."

Ignoring the Jacksonians' support for the Tariff of 1828, most southerners heaped blame on President Adams. They also criticized Adams's Indian policy. A deeply moral man, the president supported the land rights of Native Americans against expansionist whites. In 1825, U.S. commissioners had secured a treaty from one Creek faction to cede Creek lands in Georgia to the United States for eventual sale to the state's citizens. When the Creek National Council repudiated the treaty, claiming that it was fraudulent, Adams called for new negotiations. In response, Georgia governor George M. Troup attacked the president as a "public enemy . . . the unblushing ally of the savages." Joining with Georgia's congressional delegation, Troup persuaded Congress to extinguish the Creeks' land titles, forcing most Creeks to leave the state.

Elsewhere in the nation, Adams's primary weakness was his out-of-date political style. The last notable to serve in the White House, he acted the part: aloof, moralistic, and paternalistic. When Congress rejected his activist economic policies, Adams questioned the wisdom of the voters and advised elected officials not to be "palsied [enfeebled] by the will of our constituents." Ignoring his waning popularity, the president

A CARTOON COMPARING CONDITIONS UNDER FREE TRADE AND
PROTECTIVE TARIFF

From "The United States Weekly Telegram," November 5, 1832.

The "Tariff of Abominations"

Political cartoons enjoyed wide use in eighteenth-century England and became popular in the United States during the political battles of the First Party System (1794–1815). By the 1820s, American newspapers, which were often subsidized by political parties, published cartoons daily. This political cartoon attacks the tariffs of 1828 and 1832 as hostile to the interests and prosperity of the South. The gaunt figure on the left represents a southern planter, starved by exactions of the tariff, while the northern textile manufacturer has grown stout feasting on the bounty of protectionism.   © Bettmann/Corbis.

Jackson's Electoral Strategy, 1828

In 1824, Jackson lost the presidency because of an agreement (a "corrupt bargain," according to the Jacksonians) between the supporters of John Quincy Adams and Henry Clay in the House of Representatives. Four years later, supporters of Old Hickory plastered walls with posters celebrating Jackson as "The Man of the People," who would neither "BARTER NOR BARGAIN" for the presidency, saying it should depend only on the vote of the **"PEOPLE."**
© Collection of the New-York Historical Society.

refused to use patronage to reward his supporters and allowed hostile federal officials to remain in office. Rather than "run" for reelection in 1828, Adams "stood" for it, telling supporters, "If my country wants my services, she must ask for them."

"The Democracy" and the Election of 1828

Martin Van Buren and the politicians handling Andrew Jackson's campaign had no reservations about running for office. The Little Magician wanted to revive the national political coalition created by Thomas Jefferson; he therefore championed policies that appealed both to northern farmers and artisans (the "plain Republicans of the North") and to southern slave owners and smallholding planters. John C. Calhoun, Jackson's running mate, brought his South Carolina allies into Van Buren's party, and Jackson's close friends in Tennessee rallied voters there and throughout the Old Southwest. By forming a national political party, Jackson's friends hoped to reconcile the diverse economic and social

"interests" that, as James Madison had predicted in "Federalist No. 10," would inevitability exist in a large republic.

At Van Buren's direction, the Jacksonians orchestrated a massive publicity campaign. In New York, fifty newspapers declared their support for Jackson on the same day. Elsewhere, Jacksonians used mass meetings, torchlight parades, and barbecues to celebrate the candidate's frontier origin and rise to fame. With the cry of "Jackson for ever!" they praised "Old Hickory" as a "natural" aristocrat, a self-made man.

The Jacksonians called themselves Democrats or "the Democracy," names that conveyed their egalitarian message. As Thomas Morris told the Ohio legislature, he and his fellow Democrats were fighting for equality: The republic had been corrupted by legislative charters that gave "a few individuals rights and privileges not enjoyed by the citizens at large." Morris promised that the Democracy would destroy such "artificial distinction." Jackson himself declared that "equality among the people in the rights conferred by government" was the "great radical principle of freedom."

Jackson's message of equal rights and popular rule appealed to many social groups. His hostility to business corporations and to Clay's American System won support from northeastern artisans and workers who felt threatened by industrialization. Jackson also captured the votes of Pennsylvania ironworkers and New York farmers who had been enriched by the controversial Tariff of Abominations. Yet, by astutely declaring his preference for a "judicious" tariff that would balance regional interests, Jackson remained popular in the South as well. Old Hickory also garnered votes in the Southeast and Midwest, where his well-known hostility toward Native Americans reassured white farmers seeking Indian removal.

The Democrats' celebration of popular rule carried Jackson into office. In 1824, about one-quarter of the eligible electorate had voted; in 1828, more than one-half went to the polls, and 56 percent voted for the senator from Tennessee (Figure 10.1). Jackson received 178 of 261 electoral votes and became the first president from a trans-Appalachian state (Map 10.2). As the president-elect traveled to Washington, he cut a dignified figure. According to an English observer, he "wore his hair carelessly but not ungracefully arranged, and in spite of his harsh, gaunt features looked like a gentleman and a soldier." Still, Jackson's popularity and sharp temper frightened men of wealth. Senator Daniel Webster of Massachusetts, a former Federalist and now a corporate lawyer, warned his clients that the new president would "bring a breeze with him. Which way it will blow, I cannot tell [but] . . . my fear is stronger than my hope." Supreme Court justice Joseph Story shared Webster's apprehensions. Watching an unruly Inauguration Day crowd climb over the elegant White House furniture to congratulate Jackson, Story lamented that "the reign of King 'Mob' seemed triumphant."

- Was there a necessary connection between the growth of democracy and the emergence of political parties? Explain your answer.

- How do you explain John Quincy Adams's great success as secretary of state (see Chapter 7) and his relative lack of success as president?

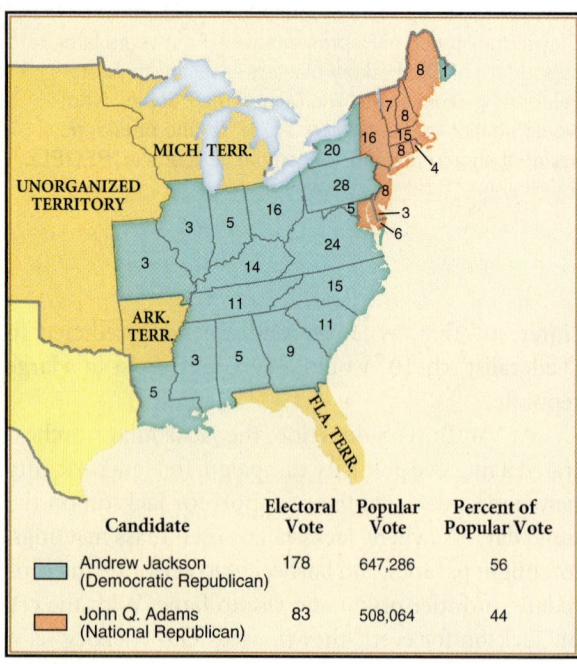

MAP 10.2

The Presidential Election of 1828

As he did in 1824, John Quincy Adams carried all of New England and some of the Mid-Atlantic states. However, Andrew Jackson swept the rest of the nation and won a resounding victory in the electoral college. More than 1.1 million American men cast ballots in 1828, more than three times the number who voted in 1824.

Candidate	Electoral Vote	Popular Vote	Percent of Popular Vote
Andrew Jackson (Democratic Republican)	178	647,286	56
John Q. Adams (National Republican)	83	508,064	44

The Jacksonian Presidency, 1829–1837

American-style political democracy—a broad franchise, a disciplined political party, and policies favoring specific interest groups—ushered Andrew Jackson into office. Jackson used his popular mandate to transform the policies of the national government and the presidency itself. During his two terms in the White House, he enhanced presidential authority, destroyed the nationalistic American System, and established the legitimacy of a new ideology of government. An Ohio supporter summed up Jackson's vision as follows: "the Sovereignty of the People, the Rights of the States, and a Light and Simple Government."

Jackson's Agenda: Rotation and Decentralization

To make policy, Jackson relied primarily on an informal group of advisors: his so-called "Kitchen Cabinet." Its most influential members were Kentuckians Francis

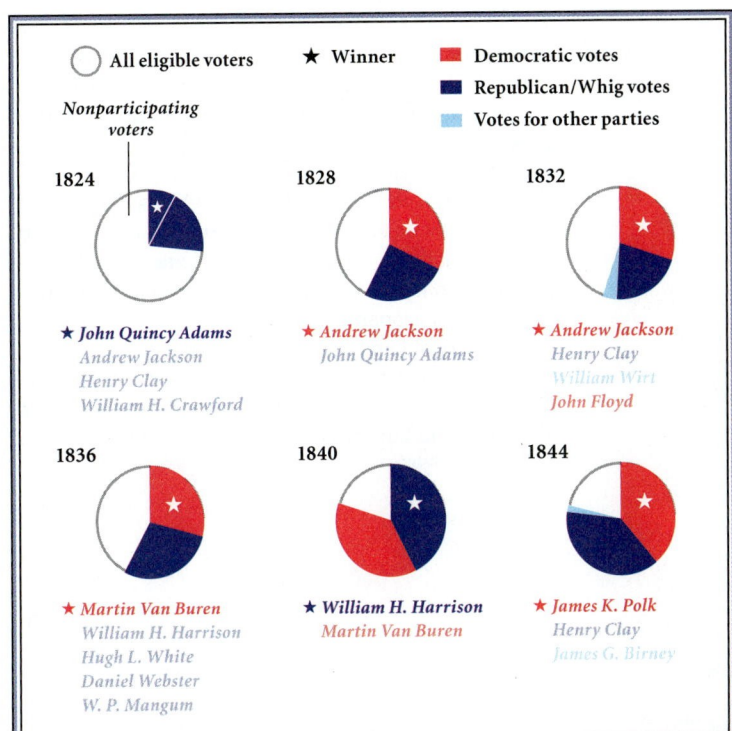

All eligible voters   ★ Winner   ■ Democratic votes
■ Republican/Whig votes
■ Votes for other parties

Nonparticipating voters

1824

★ John Quincy Adams
Andrew Jackson
Henry Clay
William H. Crawford

1828

★ Andrew Jackson
John Quincy Adams

1832

★ Andrew Jackson
Henry Clay
William Wirt
John Floyd

1836

★ Martin Van Buren
William H. Harrison
Hugh L. White
Daniel Webster
W. P. Mangum

1840

★ William H. Harrison
Martin Van Buren

1844

★ James K. Polk
Henry Clay
James G. Birney

FIGURE 10.1

Changes in Voting Patterns, 1824–1840

Between 1824 and 1840, the proportion of eligible voters who cast ballots in presidential elections increased dramatically from 27 percent to 79 percent, and remained thereafter at that level (note the shrinking white sections of these pie graphs). Voter participation soared first in 1828, when Andrew Jackson and John Quincy Adams contested for the White House, and again in 1840, as competition heated up between Democrats and Whigs, who advocated different policies and philosophies of government. Democrats triumphed in most of these contests because their program appealed to more ordinary citizens than did the policies of their Republican-Whig opponents.

Preston Blair, who edited the *Washington Globe*, and Amos Kendall, who wrote Jackson's speeches; Roger B. Taney of Maryland, who became attorney general, treasury secretary, and then chief justice of the Supreme Court; and, most important, Martin Van Buren, whom Jackson named secretary of state.

Following Van Buren's practice in New York, Jackson used patronage to create a disciplined national party. He rejected the idea of "property in office" (that officials held permanent title to an office) and insisted on a rotation of officeholders, so that when an administration was voted out, its bureaucratic appointees would also have to leave government service. Rotation would not lessen expertise, Jackson insisted, because public duties were "so plain and simple that men of intelligence may readily qualify themselves for their performance." William L. Marcy, a New York Jacksonian, put it bluntly: Government jobs were like the spoils of war, and "to the victor belong the spoils of the enemy." Using the spoils system, Jackson dispensed available government jobs to reward his friends and win backing for his policies.

Jackson's priority was to destroy the American System and all national plans for economic development. As Henry Clay noted apprehensively, the new president wanted "to cry down old [expansive] constructions of the Constitution . . . to make all Jefferson's opinions the articles of faith of the new Church." Declaring that the

"voice of the people" called for "economy in the expenditures of the Government," Jackson rejected national subsidies for transportation projects, also on constitutional grounds. In 1830, he vetoed four internal improvement bills, including an extension of the National Road, arguing that they infringed "the reserved powers of states." These vetoes represented an indirect attack on the protective tariffs, another controversial part of the American System, because Clay proposed funding canals and roads with tariff revenues. Jacksonian Senator William Smith of South Carolina agreed, "[D]estroy internal improvements and you leave no motive for the tariff."

The Tariff and Nullification

In fact, The Tariff of 1828 assisted manufacturers and farmers and had helped Jackson win the presidency. But it saddled him with a major political crisis. There was fierce opposition to high tariffs throughout the South, especially in South Carolina. South Carolina was the only state with an African American majority — 56 percent of the population in 1830 — and its slave owners, like the white sugar planters in the West Indies, feared a black rebellion. They also worried about the legal abolition of slavery. The British Parliament had declared that slavery in the West Indies would end in 1833; South Carolina planters, remembering attempts

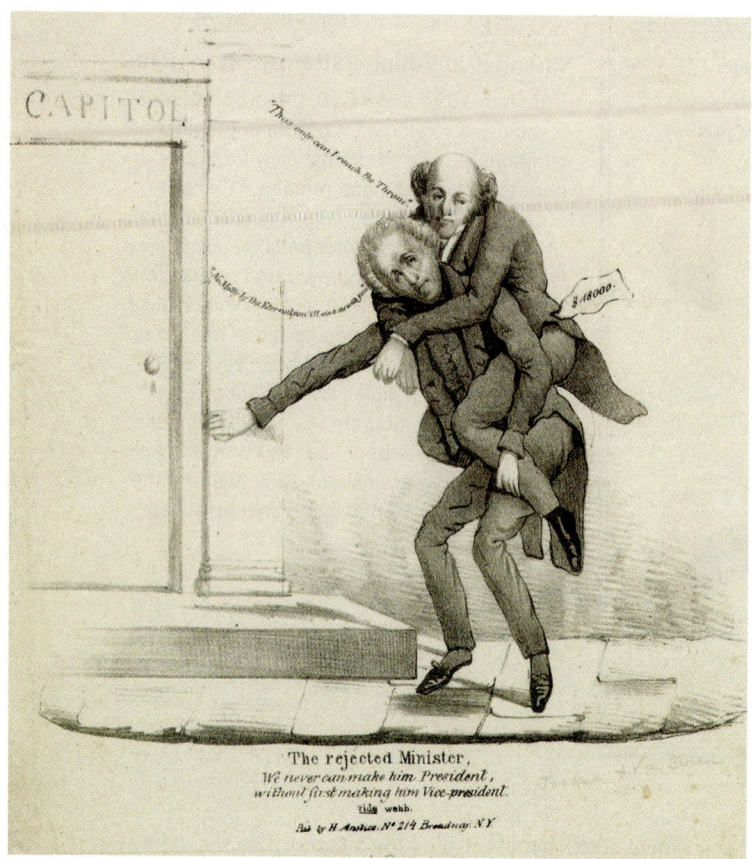

The rejected Minister,
*We never can make him President,
without first making him Vice-president.*
Vide webb.
Pub. by H. Anthra. Nº 214 Broadway. N.Y

Who Will Be Jackson's Heir?

Elected vice president in 1828, John C. Calhoun hoped to succeed Jackson in the White House. But he failed to account for Martin Van Buren, who managed Jackson's campaign and claimed the prized office of secretary of state. When Van Buren resigned as secretary in 1831 and Jackson nominated him as minister to Britain, Calhoun sought to destroy his rival by blocking his confirmation in the Senate. The "Little Magician" pounced on this miscalculation, persuading Jackson, already disillusioned by Calhoun's support for nullification, to oust him from the ticket. Van Buren took his place as vice president in 1832, carried into the office — as the cartoonist tells the tale — on Jackson's back, and succeeded to the presidency in 1836.   © Collection of the New-York Historical Society.

to limit slavery in Missouri (see Chapter 8), worried that the U.S. Congress would follow the British lead. So they attacked the tariff, both to lower rates and to discourage attempts to use federal power to attack slavery.

The crisis began in 1832, when high-tariff congressmen ignored southern warnings that they were "endangering the Union" and reenacted the Tariff of Abominations. In response, leading South Carolinians called a state convention, which in November boldly adopted an Ordinance of Nullification declaring the tariffs of 1828 and 1832 to be null and void; prohibiting the collection of those tariffs in South Carolina after February 1, 1833; and threatening secession if federal officials tried to collect them.

South Carolina's act of **nullification** rested on the constitutional arguments developed in *The South Carolina Exposition and Protest* (1828). Written anonymously by Vice President John C. Calhoun, the *Exposition* gave a localist (or sectional) interpretation to the federal union. Because each state or geographic region had distinct interests, localists argued, protective tariffs and other national legislation that operated unequally on the various states lacked fairness and legitimacy — in fact, they were unconstitutional. An obsessive defender of the interests of southern planters, Calhoun

exaggerated the frequency of such legislation, declaring, "Constitutional government and the government of a majority are utterly incompatible."

In developing his interpretation of the Constitution, Calhoun used the arguments first advanced by Jefferson and Madison in the Kentucky and Virginia resolutions of 1798. Because the Constitution had been ratified by conventions in the various states, the resolutions had suggested, sovereignty lay in the states, not in the people. Beginning from this premise, Calhoun developed a states' rights interpretation, arguing that a state convention could declare a congressional law to be unconstitutional and therefore void within the state's borders. Replying to this argument, which had no support in the text of the Constitution, Senator Daniel Webster of Massachusetts presented a nationalist interpretation that celebrated popular sovereignty and Congress's responsibility to secure the "general welfare."

Jackson hoped to find a middle path between Webster's strident nationalism and Calhoun's radical doctrine of localist federalism. The Constitution clearly gave the federal government the authority to establish tariffs, and Jackson vowed to enforce that power, whatever the cost. He declared that South Carolina's Ordi-

The Great Webster-Hayne Debate, 1830

The "Tariff of Abominations" sparked one of the great debates in American history. When Senator Robert Y. Hayne of South Carolina (seated in the middle of the picture, with his legs crossed) opposed the federal tariffs by invoking the doctrines of states' rights and nullification, Daniel Webster rose to the defense of the Union. Speaking for two days to a spellbound Senate, Webster delivered an impassioned oration that celebrated the unity of the American people as the key to their freedom. His parting words — "Liberty *and* Union, now and forever, one and inseparable!" – quickly became part of the national memory.   *Webster's Reply to Hayne*, by G. P. A. Healy, City of Boston Art Commission.

nance of Nullification not only violated the letter of the Constitution but also was "unauthorized by its spirit . . . and destructive of the great object for which it was formed." More pointedly, he warned, "Disunion by armed force is treason." At Jackson's request, Congress in early 1833 passed the Force Bill, authorizing the president to use military means to compel South Carolina's obedience to national laws. Simultaneously, Jackson addressed the South's objections to high import duties by winning passage of a new tariff act that, by 1842, reduced rates to the modest levels of 1816. Subsequently, duties remained low because western wheat farmers joined southern planters in advocating cheap imports and warning against retaliatory tariffs by foreign nations. "Illinois wants a market for her agricultural products," declared Senator Sidney Breese in 1846. "[S]he wants the market of the world."

Having won the *political* battle by securing a reduction in duties, the South Carolina convention gave up its *constitutional* demand for the right of nullification. Jackson was satisfied. He had addressed the economic demands of the South while upholding the constitutional principle that no state could nullify a law of the United States — a principle that Abraham Lincoln would embrace to defend the Union during the secession crisis of 1861.

The Bank War

As the tariff crisis intensified, Jackson faced a major challenge from politicians who supported the Second Bank of the United States. Founded in Philadelphia in 1816 (see Chapter 7), the bank was privately managed and operated under a twenty-year charter from the federal government, which owned 20 percent of its stock. The bank's most important role was to stabilize the nation's money supply, which consisted primarily of notes and bills of credit — in effect, paper money —

issued by state-chartered banks. Those banks promised to redeem the notes on demand with "hard" money—that is, gold or silver coins (also known as specie). By collecting those notes and regularly demanding specie, the Second Bank kept the state banks from issuing too much paper money and depreciating its value.

This cautious monetary policy pleased creditors—the bankers and entrepreneurs in Boston, New York, and Philadelphia, whose capital investments were underwriting economic development. However, ordinary Americans worried that the Second Bank would force the closure of state banks, leaving people holding worthless paper notes. Some politicians opposed the Second Bank because of the arrogance of its president, Nicholas Biddle. "As to mere power," Biddle boasted, "I have been for years in the daily exercise of more personal authority than any President habitually enjoys." Fearing Biddle's influence, bankers in New York and other states wanted the specie owned by the federal government deposited in their own institutions rather than in the Second Bank. Expansion-minded bankers, including friends of Jackson's in Nashville, wanted to escape supervision by any central bank.

Jackson's Bank Veto | Although the Second Bank had many enemies, a political miscalculation by its friends brought its downfall. In 1832, Henry Clay and Daniel Webster persuaded Biddle to seek an early extension of the bank's charter (which still had four years to run). They had the votes in Congress to enact the required legislation and hoped to lure Jackson into a veto that would split the Democrats just before the 1832 elections.

Jackson turned the tables on Clay and Webster. He vetoed the rechartering bill and issued a masterful veto message that blended constitutional arguments with class rhetoric and patriotic fervor. Adopting Thomas Jefferson's position, Jackson declared that Congress had no constitutional authority to charter a national bank. Then he condemned the bank as "subversive of the rights of the States," "dangerous to the liberties of the people," and a nest of special privilege and monopoly power that promoted "the advancement of the few at the expense of . . . farmers, mechanics, and laborers." Finally, the president noted that British aristocrats owned much of the bank's stock. Such a powerful institution should be "purely American," Jackson declared with patriotic fervor.

Jackson's attack on the bank carried him to victory in 1832. Old Hickory and Martin Van Buren, his longtime ally and new running mate, overwhelmed Henry Clay, who headed the National Republican ticket, by 219 to 49 electoral votes. Jackson's most fervent supporters were eastern workers and western farmers, who blamed the Second Bank for high urban prices and stagnant farm income. "All the flourishing cities of the West are mortgaged to this money power," charged Senator Thomas Hart Benton, a Jacksonian from Missouri. "They may be devoured by it at any moment." But many of Jackson's other supporters had prospered during a decade of strong economic growth. Along with thousands of middle-class Americans—lawyers, clerks, shopkeepers, and artisans—they wanted an equal opportunity to rise in the world and cheered Jackson's attack on privileged corporations.

The Bank Destroyed | Early in 1833, Jackson met their wishes by appointing Roger B. Taney, a strong opponent of corporate privilege, as head of the Treasury Department. Taney promptly withdrew the government's gold and silver from the Second Bank. He deposited the specie in various state banks, which critics called Jackson's "pet banks." To justify this abrupt (and probably illegal) transfer, Jackson declared that his reelection represented "the decision of the people against the bank" and gave him a mandate to destroy it. This sweeping claim of presidential power was new and radical. Never before had a president claimed that victory at the polls allowed him to pursue a controversial policy or to act independently of Congress (see Comparing American Voices, "The Character and Goals of Andrew Jackson," pp. 316–317).

The "bank war" escalated into an all-out political battle. In March 1834, Jackson's opponents in the Senate passed a resolution by Henry Clay censuring the president and warning of executive tyranny: "We are in the midst of a revolution, hitherto bloodless, but rapidly descending towards a total change of the pure republican character of the Government, and the concentration of all power in the hands of one man." Jackson remained undeterred by Clay's charges and Congress's censure. "The Bank is trying to kill me but I will kill it," he vowed to Van Buren. And so he did. When the Second Bank's national charter expired in 1836, Jackson prevented its renewal.

Jackson had destroyed both national banking—the handiwork of Alexander Hamilton—and the American System of protective tariffs and internal improvements created by Henry Clay and John Quincy Adams. The result was a profound check on economic activism and innovative policymaking by the national government. "All is gone," observed a Washington newspaper correspondent. "All is gone, which the General Government was instituted to create and preserve."

Indian Removal

The status of Native American peoples posed an equally complex political problem. By the late 1820s, white voices throughout the South and Midwest were calling for Indian peoples to be resettled west of the Mississippi River. Many eastern supporters of Native Americans also favored resettlement. Removal to the West seemed the only way to protect Indians from alcoholism, financial chicanery, and cultural decline.

However, most Indians did not want to leave their ancestral lands. For centuries Cherokees and Creeks had lived in Georgia, Tennessee, and Alabama; Chickasaws and Choctaws in Mississippi and Alabama; and Seminoles in Florida. During the War of 1812, Andrew Jackson had forced the Creeks to relinquish millions of acres, but Indian tribes still controlled vast tracts and wanted to keep them.

Cherokee Resistance But on what terms? Some Indian peoples had adopted white ways. An 1825 census of the Cherokees revealed that they owned 33 gristmills, 13 sawmills, nearly 2,500 spinning wheels, 760 looms, and 2,900 plows. Many owners were mixed-bloods, the offspring of white traders and Indian women. They had grown up in a bicultural world, knew the political and economic ways of whites, and often favored assimilation into white society. Indeed, some mixed-bloods were indistinguishable from southern planters. James Vann, a Georgia Cherokee, owned more than twenty black slaves, two trading posts, and a gristmill. Forty other mixed-blood Cherokee families each owned twenty or more African American slaves.

To protect their property and the lands of their people, the mixed-bloods sought full integration into American life. In 1821, Sequoyah perfected a system of writing for the Cherokee language; six years later, mixed-bloods devised a new charter of Cherokee government modeled directly on the U.S. Constitution. "You asked us to throw off the hunter and warrior state," Cherokee John Ridge told a Philadelphia audience in 1832. "We did so. You asked us to form a republican government: We did so. . . . You asked us to learn to read: We did so. You asked us to cast away our idols, and worship your God: We did so." Full-blood Cherokees, who made up 90 percent of the population, resisted many of these cultural and political innovations but were equally determined to retain their ancestral lands. "We would not receive money for land in which our fathers and friends are buried," one full-blood chief declared. "We love our land; it is our mother."

What the Cherokees did or wanted carried no weight with the Georgia legislature. In 1802, Georgia had given up its western land claims in return for a federal promise to extinguish Indian landholdings in the state. Now it demanded fulfillment of that pledge. Having spent his military career fighting Indians and seizing their lands, Andrew Jackson gave full support to Georgia. On assuming the presidency, he withdrew the federal troops that had protected Indian enclaves there and in Alabama and Mississippi. The states, he declared, were sovereign within their borders.

The Removal Act and Its Aftermath Jackson then pushed the Indian Removal Act of 1830 through Congress over the determined opposition of evangelical Protestant men—and women. To block removal, Catharine Beecher and Lydia Sigourney

Black Hawk

This portrait of Black Hawk (1767–1838), by Charles Bird King, shows the Indian leader as a young warrior, wearing a medal commemorating an early nineteenth-century agreement with the U.S. government. Later, in 1830, when Congress approved Andrew Jackson's Indian Removal Act, Black Hawk mobilized Sauk and Fox warriors to protect their ancestral lands in Illinois. "It was here, that I was born— and here lie the bones of many friends and relatives," the aging chief declared. "I . . . never could consent to leave it." Courtesy Warner Collection of Gulf States Paper Corporation, Tuscaloosa, AL.

The Character and Goals of Andrew Jackson

From the start of his career, Andrew Jackson was a controversial figure. "Hot-tempered," "Indian-hater," "military despot" — critics hurled many such charges at Jackson, while his friends praised him as an honorable and forthright statesman. His contemporary biographer, the journalist James Parton, found him a man of many faces, an enigma. Others thought they understood his personality and policies: James Hamilton, a loyal Jacksonian and a congressman, recalled Jackson's volatile temper. Henry Clay, his archrival, warned that Jackson's high-handed actions threatened American republican institutions. Even worse, said Philip Hone — a wealthy New York Whig merchant — Jackson and his allies were instigating class warfare. But based on conversations with dozens of Americans, Frenchman Alexis de Tocqueville offered a more moderate interpretation of the man and his goals.

James Parton

From Parton's Preface to *The Life of Andrew Jackson* (1860)

If any one, at the end of a year even, had asked what I had yet discovered respecting General Jackson, I might have answered thus: "Andrew Jackson, I am given to understand, was a patriot and a traitor. He was one of the greatest of generals, and wholly ignorant of the art of war. A writer brilliant, elegant, eloquent, without being able to compose a correct sentence. . . . The first of statesmen, he never devised, he never framed a measure. He was the most candid of men, and was capable of the profoundest dissimulation. A most law-defying, law-obeying citizen. A stickler for discipline, he never hesitated to disobey his superior. A democratic autocrat. An urbane savage. An atrocious saint."

James Hamilton Jr.

Hamilton Recalls an Event of 1827, as Jackson Began His Second Campaign for the Presidency

The steamer Pocahontas was chartered by citizens of New Orleans to convey the General and his party from Nashville to that city. She was fitted out in the most sumptuous manner. The party was General and Mrs. Jackson, . . . Governor Samuel Houston, Wm. B. Lewis, Robert Armstrong, and others. . . . The only freight was the General's cotton-crop.

During the voyage we stopped at the different towns on the river . . . and at the principal ones, committees addressed the General, to whom he made appropriate replies. In the course of the voyage an event occurred, which I repeat, as it is suggestive of [his] character. A steamer of greater speed than ours, going in the same direction, passed us, crossed our bow; then stopped and let us pass her and then passed us again in triumph. This was repeated again and again, until the General, being excited by the offensive course, ordered a rifle to be brought to him; hailed the pilot of the other steamer, and swore that if he did the same thing again he would shoot him.

Philip Hone

A New York Conservative Ruminates in His Diary on the Jacksonians' Victory in the New York Elections of 1834

I apprehend that Mr. Van Buren [Jackson's vice president and successor] and his friends have no permanent cause of triumph in their victory. They . . . have mounted a vicious horse, who, taking the bit in his mouth, will run away with [them]. . . . This battle had been fought upon the ground of the poor against the rich, and this unworthy prejudice, this dangerous delusion, has been encouraged by the leaders of the triumphant party, and fanned into a flame by the polluted breath of the hireling press in their employ. . . .

The cry of "Down with the aristocracy!" mingled with the shouts of victory, and must have grated on the ears of some of their own leaders like the croaking of the evil-boding raven. They have succeeded in raising this dangerous spirit [of the mob], and have gladly availed themselves of its support to accomplish a temporary object; but can they allay it at pleasure? . . . Eighteen thousand men in New York have voted for the high-priest of the party whose professed design is to bring down the property, the talents, the industry, the steady habits of that class which constituted the real strength of the Commonwealth, to the common level of the idle, the worthless, and the unenlightened. Look to it, ye men of respectability in the Jackson party, are ye not afraid of the weapons ye have used in this warfare?

Henry Clay

Clay Introduces a Senate Resolution Censuring Jackson's Actions, December 26, 1833

We are in the midst of a revolution, hitherto bloodless, but rapidly tending toward a total change of the pure republican character of the government, and to the concentration of all power in the hands of one man. The powers of Congress are paralyzed, except when exerted in conformity with his will, by frequent and an extraordinary exercise of the executive veto, not anticipated by the founders of our Constitution, and not practiced by any of the predecessors of the present chief magistrate. . . .

The judiciary has not been exempt from the prevailing rage for innovation. Decisions of the tribunals, deliberately pronounced, have been contemptuously disregarded. And the sanctity of numerous treaties openly violated. Our Indian relations, coeval with the existence of the government, and recognized and established by numerous laws and treaties, have been subverted. . . . The system of protection of improvement lies crushed beneath the veto. The system of protection of American industry [will soon meet a similar fate]. . . . In a term of eight years, a little more than equal to that which was required to establish our liberties [as an independent republican nation between 1776 and 1783], the government will have been transformed into an elective monarchy — the worst of all forms of government.

Alexis de Tocqueville

The French Political Philosopher Analyzes Jackson in *Democracy in America* (1835)

Some persons in Europe have formed an opinion of the influence of General Jackson upon the affairs of his country which appears highly extravagant to those who have seen the subject nearer at hand. We have been told that General Jackson has won battles; that he is an energetic man, prone by nature and habit to the use of force, covetous of power and a despot by inclination.

All this may be true; but the inferences which have been drawn from these truths are very erroneous. It has been imagined that General Jackson is bent on establishing a dictatorship in America, introducing a military spirit, and giving a degree of influence to the central authority that cannot but be dangerous to provincial [state] liberties. But in America the time for similar undertakings, and the age for men of this kind, has not yet come; if General Jackson had thought of exercising his authority in this manner, he would infallibly have forfeited his political station and compromised his life; he has not been so imprudent as to attempt anything of the kind.

Far from wishing to extend the Federal power, the President belongs to the party which is desirous of limiting that power to the clear and precise letter of the Constitution and which never puts a construction upon that act favorable to the government of the Union; far from standing forth as the champion of centralization, General Jackson is the agent of the state jealousies; and he was placed in his lofty station by the passions that are most opposed to the central government. It is by perpetually flattering these passions that he maintains his station and his popularity. General Jackson is the slave of the majority: he yields to its wishes, its propensities, and its demands. . . .

General Jackson stoops to gain the favor of the majority. . . . Supported by a power that his predecessors never had, he tramples on his personal enemies, whenever they cross his path. . . . He even treats the national representatives with a disdain approaching to insult; he puts his veto on the laws of Congress and frequently neglects even to reply to that powerful body. . . . The power of General Jackson perpetually increases, but that of the President declines; in his hands the Federal government is strong, but it will pass enfeebled into the hands of his successor.

Sources: James Parton, *The Life of Andrew Jackson. In Three Volumes* (New York: Mason Brothers, 1860), vol. 1, pp. vii–viii; Sean Wilentz, ed., *Major Problems in the Early Republic, 1787–1848* (Lexington, MA: D. C. Heath, 1991), 374 (Hamilton) and 392–393 (Hone); Calvin Colton, ed., *The Life . . . of Henry Clay*, 6 vols. (New York: A. Barnes, 1857), 576–580; Alexis de Tocqueville, *Democracy in America*, abr. by Thomas Bender (New York: Modern Library, 1981), 271–273.

ANALYZING THE EVIDENCE

- Was Jackson a "democratic autocrat," as Parton puts it? What does he mean by this term? Would the authors of the other excerpts agree with this characterization? Did Jackson instigate class warfare, as Hone suggests?

- In what respects do Clay and Tocqueville agree in their assessment of Jackson and his policies? How do they disagree?

- What did Tocqueville mean by saying that Jackson's power "perpetually increases, but that of the President declines"? Was he correct?

dispatched the Ladies Circular, which urged "benevolent ladies" to use "prayers and exertions to avert the calamity of removal." In response, women from across the nation flooded Congress with petitions. Despite their efforts, Jackson's bill squeaked through the House of Representatives by a vote of 102 to 97.

The Removal Act created the Indian Territory, outside the bounds of any state (on lands in present-day Oklahoma and Kansas). It also promised money and reserved land to Native American peoples who would agree to give up their ancestral holdings east of the Mississippi River. Government officials promised the Indians that they could live on their new land, "they and all their children, as long as grass grows and water runs." But, as one Indian leader noted, in "the wilderness of the West . . . water and timber are scarcely to be

seen." When Chief Black Hawk and his Sauk and Fox followers refused to leave rich, well-watered farmland in western Illinois in 1832, Jackson quickly sent troops to expel them. Following a series of confrontations, the U.S. Army pursued Black Hawk into the Wisconsin Territory and, in the brutal eight-hour Bad Axe Massacre, killed 850 of his 1,000 warriors. Over the next five years, American diplomatic pressure and military power forced seventy Indian peoples to sign treaties and move west of the Mississippi (Map 10.3).

In the meantime, the Cherokees had carried the defense of their lands to the Supreme Court, where they claimed the status of a "foreign nation." In *Cherokee Nation v. Georgia* (1831), Chief Justice John Marshall denied the Cherokees' claim of independence and declared that Indian peoples were "domestic depen-

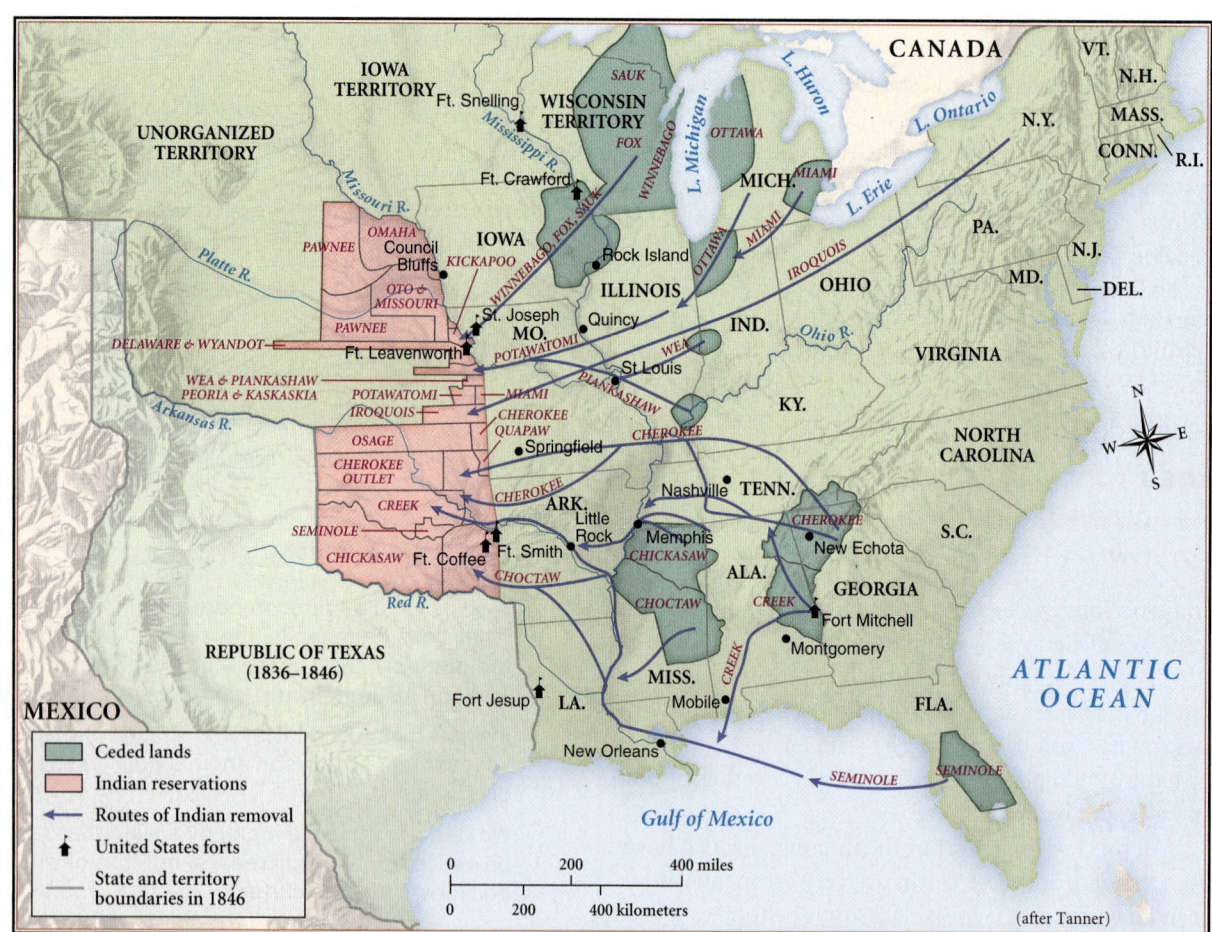

MAP 10.3

The Removal of Native Americans, 1820–1846

Beginning in the 1820s, the U.S. government forced scores of Native American peoples to sign treaties that exchanged Indian lands in the East for money and designated reservations west of the Mississippi River. Then, in the 1830s, the government used military force to expel the Cherokees, Chickasaws, Choctaws, Creeks, and many Seminoles from their ancestral homes in the Old Southeast and to resettle them in the Indian Territory, in the present-day states of Oklahoma and Kansas.

Raising Public Opinion Against the Seminoles

During the eighteenth century, hundreds of black slaves fled South Carolina and Georgia and found refuge in Spanish Florida, where they lived among and intermarried with the Seminole people. This color engraving from the 1830s—showing red and black Seminoles butchering respectable white families—sought to bolster political support for the forced removal of the Seminoles to the Indian Territory. By the mid-1840s, after a decade of warfare, the U.S. Army had forced 2,500 Seminoles to migrate to Oklahoma. However, another 2,500 Seminoles continued their armed resistance and eventually won a new treaty allowing them to live in Florida.   Granger Collection.

dent nations." However, in *Worcester v. Georgia* (1832), Marshall and the court sided with the Cherokees against Georgia. Voiding Georgia's extension of state law over the Cherokees, the court held that Indian nations were "distinct political communities, having territorial boundaries, within which their authority is exclusive [and is] guaranteed by the United States."

Instead of guaranteeing the Cherokees' territory, the U.S. government took it from them. In 1835, American officials negotiated the Treaty of New Echota with a minority Cherokee faction and insisted that all Cherokees move to the new Indian Territory. When only 2,000 of 17,000 Cherokees had moved by the May 1838 deadline, President Martin Van Buren ordered General Winfield Scott to enforce the treaty. Scott's army rounded up some 14,000 Cherokees and marched them 1,200 miles to the Indian Territory, an arduous journey that became known as the Trail of Tears. Along the way, 3,000 Indians died of starvation and exposure. Once in Oklahoma, the Cherokees excluded anyone of "negro or mullato parentage" from governmental office and thus reaffirmed that full citizenship in their nation was racially defined. Just as the United States was a "white man's country," so Indian Territory would be defined as a "red man's country."

After the Creeks, Chickasaws, and Choctaws moved west of the Mississippi, encouraged by generous gifts of land, the Seminoles were the only numerically significant Indian people remaining in the Old South-

west. After years of warfare, about half the Seminole people moved to Indian Territory. But Seminoles who had intermarried with runaway slaves feared the emphasis on "blood purity" there. During the 1840s, they fought a successful guerrilla war against the U.S. Army and retained their lands in Florida, which was still a sparsely settled frontier region. These Seminoles were the exception, however. The Jacksonians had forced the removal of most eastern Indian peoples.

The Jacksonian Impact

Jackson's legacy, like that of every other great president, is complex and rich. On the institutional level, he expanded the authority of the nation's chief executive by identifying it with the voice of the people. As Jackson put it, "The President is the direct representative of the American people." Assuming that role during the nullification crisis, he upheld national authority by threatening the use of military force, laying the foundation for Lincoln's defense of the Union a generation later. At the same time (and somewhat contradictorily), Jackson curbed the reach of the national government. By undermining Henry Clay's American System of national banking, protective tariffs, and internal improvements, Jackson reinvigorated the Jeffersonian tradition of a limited and frugal central government (see Reading American Pictures, "Thomas Cole's Political Allegory of Jacksonian America," p. 320).

Thomas Cole's Political Allegory of Jacksonian America

Andrew Jackson was a polarizing figure whose policies and personality divided Americans. One Jacksonian critic was Thomas Cole (1801–1848). Born in England, Cole came to the United States in 1817 and soon acquired a reputation as a fine landscape painter—a leading member of the so-called Hudson River School. Between 1833 and 1836, Cole executed a series of five large canvases collectively known as *The Course of Empire*, a veiled attack on Jacksonian democracy. (See en.wikipedia.org/wiki/The_Course_of_Empire.)

Thomas Cole, *The Course of Empire: The Consummation of Empire*. © Collection of the New-York Historical Society.

ANALYZING THE EVIDENCE

- Do you recognize the architecture of the buildings? Why would Cole set his allegory in classical Greece or Rome? What political ideologies of the classical world served as models during the Revolutionary era (see Chapter 5)?

- At the lower left of *Consummation*, a red-robed, crowned emperor is borne in triumph on an elephant,

followed by his retainers, officials, and war captives. Cole had read Edward Gibbon's epic history, *The Decline and Fall of the Roman Empire* (1776–1788), which linked Rome's decline to the overthrow of the Roman Republic by Julius Caesar (who was feted in such processions). How might a similar fate befall the American Republic?

- Cole wrote that *The Course of Empire* "anticipated the downfall of pure republican government." *Consummation* offers clues as to the cause of its demise. What is the ideology of "pure republicanism" and how does Cole's imagery suggest its downfall?

The Taney Court Jackson also undermined the constitutional jurisprudence of John Marshall by appointing Roger B. Taney as Marshall's successor. During his long tenure as chief justice (1835–1864), Taney partially reversed the nationalist and vested-property-rights decisions of the Marshall Court and gave constitutional legitimacy to Jackson's policies of states' rights and free enterprise. In the landmark case *Charles River Bridge Co. v. Warren Bridge Co.* (1837), Taney declared that a legislative charter — in this case, to build and operate a toll bridge — did not necessarily bestow a monopoly, and that a legislature could charter a competing bridge to promote the general welfare: "While the rights of private property are sacredly guarded, we must not forget that the community also has rights." This decision directly challenged Marshall's interpretation of the contract clause of the Constitution in *Dartmouth College v. Woodward* (1819), which had stressed the binding nature of public charters (see Chapter 7). By limiting the property claims of existing canal and turnpike companies, Taney's decision allowed legislatures to charter competing railroads that would provide cheaper and more efficient transportation.

The Taney Court also limited Marshall's nationalistic interpretation of the commerce clause by enhancing the regulatory role of state governments. For example, in *Mayor of New York v. Miln* (1837), the Taney Court ruled that New York State could use its "police power" to inspect the health of arriving immigrants. The Court also restored to the states some of the economic powers they had exercised before 1787. In *Briscoe v. Bank of Kentucky* (1837), the justices allowed a bank owned by the state of Kentucky to issue currency, despite the wording of the U.S. Constitution (Article 1, Section 10) that prohibits states from issuing "bills of credit."

States Revise Their Constitutions Inspired by Jackson and Taney's example, Democrats in the various states mounted their own constitutional revolutions. Between 1830 and 1860, twenty states called conventions that wrote new, more democratic constitutions. Most of these constitutions gave the vote to all white men and reapportioned state legislatures on the basis of population. They also brought government "near to the people" by mandating the election, rather than the appointment, of most public officials, including sheriffs, justices of the peace, and judges.

The new constitutions also embodied the principles of **classical liberalism**, or **laissez-faire**, by limiting the government's role in the economy. (Twentieth-century social-welfare liberalism endorses the opposite principle: that government should intervene in economic and social life.) As president, Jackson had destroyed the American System, and his disciples now attacked the state-based Commonwealth System: the use of chartered corporations and state funds to promote economic development. Most Jackson-era constitutions prohibited states from granting special charters to corporations and extending loans and credit guarantees to private businesses. "If there is any danger to be feared in . . . government," declared a New Jersey Democrat, "it is the danger of associated wealth, with special privileges." The revised constitutions also protected taxpayers by setting strict limits on state debt and encouraging judges to enforce them. Said one New York reformer, "We will not trust the legislature with the power of creating indefinite mortgages on the people's property."

"The world is governed too much," the Jacksonians proclaimed as they embraced a small-government, laissez-faire outlook. The first American populists, they celebrated the power of ordinary people to make decisions in the voting booth and the marketplace.

- What were Andrew Jackson's policies on banking and tariffs? Did they help or hurt the American economy? Why?

- Compare and contrast the views of Jackson and John Marshall with respect to the status and rights of Indian peoples.

- How did the constitutional interpretations of the Taney Court and the new Jacksonian state constitutions alter the American legal and constitutional system?

Class, Culture, and the Second Party System

The rise of the Democracy and Jackson's tumultuous presidency sparked the creation in the mid-1830s of a second national party: the **Whigs**. For the next two decades, Whigs and Democrats competed fiercely for votes and found supporters in different cultural groups. Many evangelical Protestants became Whigs, while most Catholic immigrants and traditional Protestants joined the Democrats. By debating issues of economic policy, class power, and moral reform, party politicians offered Americans a choice between competing programs and political leaders. "Of the two great parties," remarked philosopher and essayist Ralph Waldo Emerson, "[the

Democracy] has the best cause . . . for free trade, for wide suffrage, [but the Whig party] has the best men."

The Whig Worldview

The Whig Party arose in 1834, when a group of congressmen banded together to oppose Andrew Jackson's policies and his high-handed, "kinglike" conduct. They took the name *Whigs* to identify themselves with the pre-Revolutionary American and British parties — also called Whigs — that had opposed the arbitrary actions of British monarchs. The Whigs accused "King Andrew I" of violating the Constitution by creating a spoils system and undermining elected legislators, who were the true representatives of the sovereign people. One Whig accused Jackson of ruling in a manner "more absolute than that of any absolute monarchy of Europe."

Initially, the Whigs were a diverse group drawn from various political factions. However, under the leadership of Senators Webster of Massachusetts, Clay of Kentucky, and Calhoun of South Carolina, the new party gradually assumed a distinctive stance. Like the Federalists of the 1790s, the Whigs wanted a political world dominated by men of ability and wealth; unlike the Federalists, though, they advocated an elite based on talent, not birth.

The Whigs celebrated the entrepreneur and the enterprising individual: "This is a country of self-made men," they boasted, pointing to the relative absence of permanent distinctions of class and status among white citizens. Embracing the Industrial Revolution, northern Whigs welcomed the investments of "moneyed capitalists," which provided workers with jobs and so "bread, clothing and homes." As Whig congressman Edward Everett told a Fourth of July crowd in Lowell, Massachusetts, there should be a "holy alliance" among laborers, owners, and governments. Many workers agreed, especially those who labored in the New England textile factories and Pennsylvania iron mills that benefited from protective tariffs. To ensure prosperity, Everett and other northern Whigs called for a return to the American System.

Calhoun's Dissent | Support for the Whigs in the South — less widespread than that in the North — rested on the appeal of specific policies and politicians. Some southern Whigs were wealthy planters who invested in railroads and banks or sold their cotton to New York merchants. But the majority were yeomen whites who resented the power and policies of low-country planters, most of whom

were Democrats. In addition, some Virginia and South Carolina Democrats became Whigs because, like John C. Calhoun, they favored states' rights and condemned Andrew Jackson's crusade against nullification.

Like Calhoun, most southern Whigs rejected the Whig Party's enthusiasm for high tariffs and social mobility. Calhoun was extremely conscious of class divisions in society. He believed that the northern Whig ideal of equal opportunity was contradicted not only by slavery, which he considered a fundamental American institution, but also by the wage-labor system of industrial capitalism. "There is and always has been in an advanced state of wealth and civilization a conflict between labor and capital," Calhoun declared in 1837. He urged slave owners and factory owners to unite against their common foe: a working class composed of enslaved blacks and propertyless whites.

Most northern Whigs rejected Calhoun's class-conscious social ideology. "A clear and well-defined line between capital and labor" might fit the slave South or class-ridden European societies, Daniel Webster conceded, but in the North "this distinction grows less and less definite as commerce advances." Ignoring the ever-increasing mass of propertyless immigrants and native-born wage workers, Webster focused on the growing size of the northern middle class, whose members generally supported Whig candidates. In the election of 1834, the Whigs won a majority in the House of Representatives by appealing to evangelical Protestants and upwardly mobile families — prosperous farmers, small-town merchants, and skilled industrial workers in New England, New York, and the new communities along the Great Lakes.

Anti-Masons Become Whigs | Many Whig voters in 1834 had previously supported the Anti-Masonic Party, a powerful but short-lived political party that formed in the late 1820s. As the name implies, Anti-Masons opposed the Order of Freemasonry. Freemasonry arose in eighteenth-century Europe among men who opposed their monarchical governments and espoused republicanism; it operated as a secret society with complex rituals to avoid police spies. The order spread rapidly in America and attracted political leaders — including George Washington, Henry Clay, and Andrew Jackson — and ambitious businessmen. In New York State alone by the mid-1820s, there were more than 20,000 Masons, organized into 450 local lodges. But after the kidnapping and murder in 1826 of William Morgan, a New York Mason who had threatened to reveal the order's secrets, the Freemasons fell

Celebrating a Political Triumph, 1836
To commemorate Martin Van Buren's election in 1836 and to reward friends for their support, the Democratic Party distributed thousands of snuff boxes inscribed with the new president's portrait. By using gifts and other innovative measures to enlist the loyalty of voters, Van Buren and his allies transformed American politics from an upper-class avocation to a democratic contest for votes and power.
Collection of Janice L. and David J. Frent.

into disrepute. Thurlow Weed, a newspaper editor in Rochester, New York, spearheaded the Anti-Masonic Party, which condemned the Masons as a secret aristocratic fraternity. To oust Masons from local and state offices, the Anti-Masons nominated their own candidates.

The Whigs recruited Anti-Masons to their party by endorsing the Anti-Masons' support for temperance, equality of opportunity, and evangelical morality. Throughout the Northeast and Midwest, Whig politicians advocated legal curbs on the sale of alcohol and local ordinances that preserved Sunday as a day of worship. The Whigs also won congressional seats in the Ohio and Mississippi valleys, where farmers, bankers, and shopkeepers favored Henry Clay's American System. For these citizens of the growing Midwest, the Whigs' program of government subsidies for roads, canals, and bridges was as important as their moral agenda.

In the election of 1836, the Whig Party faced Martin Van Buren, the architect of the Democratic Party and Jackson's handpicked successor. Van Buren denounced the American System and warned that its revival would promote an oppressive "consolidated government." Po-

sitioning himself as a defender of individual rights, Van Buren condemned the efforts of Whigs and moral reformers to enact state laws imposing temperance and national laws abolishing slavery. "The government is best which governs least" became his motto in economic, cultural, and racial matters.

To oppose Van Buren, the Whigs ran four candidates, each with a strong regional reputation. Their plan was to garner enough electoral votes to throw the contest into the House of Representatives. However, the Whig tally—73 electoral votes collected by William Henry Harrison of Ohio, 26 by Hugh L. White of Tennessee, 14 by Daniel Webster of Massachusetts, and 11 by W. P. Magnum of Georgia—fell far short of Van Buren's 170 votes. Still, the four Whig candidates won 49 percent of the popular vote, showing that the party's message of economic and moral improvement had a broad appeal.

Labor Politics and the Depression of 1837–1843

As the Democrats battled Whigs on the national level, they faced local challenges from urban artisans and workers. In 1827, artisans and workers in Philadelphia organized the Mechanics' Union of Trade Associations, a group of fifty unions with 10,000 members. The following year, they founded a Working Men's Party to secure "a just balance of power . . . between all the various classes." In their view, the growth of industry and commerce brought prosperity to bankers and entrepreneurs but not to urban artisans and workers, who suffered from rising prices and stagnant wages. To restore the balance, the new party called for the abolition of private banks, chartered monopolies, and debtors' prisons. And it demanded a fairer system of taxation and universal public education.

Workers Form a Political Party   By 1833, laborers had established Working Men's Parties in fifteen states. The new parties were locally based but shared a common ideology. They rejected "the glaring inequality of society" that subordinated the interests of workers to those of their employers. "Past experience teaches us that we have nothing to hope from the aristocratic orders of society," declared the New York Working Men's Party. It vowed "to send men of our own description, if we can, to the Legislature at Albany." In Philadelphia, the Working Men's Party elected a number of assemblymen; in 1834, they persuaded the Pennsylvania legislature to authorize tax-supported schools so that workers' children could rise in the world.

Indeed, the workers' ultimate goal was a society without dependent wage earners. In such an artisan republic, said labor intellectual Orestes Brownson, "All men will be independent proprietors, working on their own capitals, on their own farms, or in their own shops." Like the rising middle class, artisan republicans demanded equal rights and equal opportunity. Joseph Weydemeyer, a close friend of Karl Marx, reported from New York in the early 1850s that most American workers "are incipient bourgeois, and feel themselves to be such." Thus William Leggett, a leading member of the New York Loco-Foco (Equal Rights) Party, demanded "a system of legislation which leaves to all the free exercise of their talents and industry." Working Men's candidates won office in many cities, but divisions over policy and the parties' weakness in statewide contests soon took a toll. By the mid-1830s, most politically active workers had joined the Democratic Party and were urging it to eliminate protective tariffs and tax the stocks and bonds of wealthy capitalists.

Financial Panic and Economic Depression | At this juncture, the Panic of 1837 threw the American economy—and the union movement—into disarray. The panic began when the Bank of England decided to boost the faltering British economy by sharply curtailing the flow of money and credit to the United States. Since 1822, British manufacturers had extended credit to southern planters to expand cotton production, and British investors had purchased millions of dollars of the canal bonds issued by northern states. Suddenly deprived of British funds, American planters, merchants, and canal corporations had to withdraw gold from domestic banks to pay their commercial debts and interest on their foreign loans. Moreover, as British textile mills drastically reduced their purchases of raw cotton from the South, cotton prices plummeted from 20 cents a pound to 10 cents or less.

Falling cotton prices and the drain of specie to Britain set off a financial panic. On May 8, the Dry Dock Bank of New York City closed its doors, and worried depositors began to withdraw gold and silver coins from other banks. Within two weeks, every bank in the United States had stopped trading specie and curtailed credit, turning a financial panic into an economic crisis. "This sudden overthrow of the commercial credit" had a "stunning effect," observed Henry Fox, the British minister in Washington. "The conquest of the land by a foreign power could hardly have produced a more general sense of humiliation and grief."

A second, longer-lasting downturn began in 1839. To revive the economy after the Panic of 1837, state governments had increased their investments in canals and railroads. As they issued more and more bonds to finance these ventures, bond prices fell sharply in Europe, sparking a four-year-long financial crisis that engulfed state governments in America. Nine states could not meet the interest payments due on their bonds and defaulted, which prompted foreign lenders to cut the flow of new capital to the United States. Bumper crops drove down cotton prices even further, bringing more bankruptcies.

The American economy fell into a deep depression. By 1843, canal construction had dropped by 90 percent and prices had fallen by nearly 50 percent. Unemployment reached almost 20 percent of the workforce in seaports and industrial centers. Minister Henry Ward Beecher described a land "filled with lamentation . . . its inhabitants wandering like bereaved citizens among the ruins of an earthquake, mourning for children, for houses crushed, and property buried forever."

By creating a surplus of unemployed workers, the depression undermined the labor movement. In 1837, six thousand masons, carpenters, and other building-trades workers lost their jobs in New York City, depleting unions' rosters and destroying their bargaining power. By 1843, most local unions and all the national labor organizations had disappeared, along with their newspapers.

"Tippecanoe and Tyler Too!"

Many Americans blamed the Democrats for the depression of 1837–1843. They criticized Jackson for destroying the Second Bank and directing the Treasury Department to issue a Specie Circular in 1836. The Treasury's document required western settlers to use gold and silver coins to buy farms in the national domain and was believed, albeit mistakenly, to have been primarily responsible for the drain of specie from the economy.

The public turned its anger on Van Buren, who took office just as the panic struck. Ignoring the pleas of influential bankers, the new president refused to revoke the Specie Circular or take actions to stimulate economic activity. Holding to his philosophy of limited government, Van Buren advised Congress that "the less government interferes with private pursuits the better for the general prosperity." As the depression deep-

Hard Times

The Panic of 1837 struck Americans hard. As this anti-Democratic political cartoon suggests, unemployed workers turned to drink; women and children begged in the streets; and fearful depositors tried to withdraw funds before banks collapsed. As the plummeting hot-air balloon in the background symbolized, the rising "Glory" of America was crashing to earth.   © Museum of the City of New York, USA /The Bridgeman Art Library.

ened in 1839, this laissez-faire outlook commanded less and less political support. Worse, Van Buren's major piece of fiscal legislation, the Independent Treasury Act of 1840, actually delayed recovery. The act pulled federal specie out of Jackson's pet banks (which had used it to back loans) and placed it in government vaults, where it had little economic impact.

The Log Cabin Campaign   Determined to exploit Van Buren's weakness, the Whigs organized their first national convention in 1840 and nominated William Henry Harrison of Ohio for president and John Tyler of Virginia for vice president. A military hero of the Battle of Tippecanoe and the War of 1812, Harrison was well advanced in age (sixty-eight) and had little political experience. But the Whig leaders in Congress, Clay and Webster, wanted a president

who would rubber-stamp their program for protective tariffs and a national bank. An unpretentious, amiable man, Harrison told voters that Whig policies were "the only means, under Heaven, by which a poor industrious man may become a rich man without bowing to colossal wealth."

Panic and depression stacked the political cards against Van Buren, but the election turned more on style than on substance. It became the great "log cabin campaign"—the first time two well-organized parties competed for the loyalties of a mass electorate through a new style of campaigning. Whig songfests, parades, and well-orchestrated mass meetings drew new voters into politics. Whig speakers assailed "Martin Van Ruin" as a manipulative politician with aristocratic tastes—a devotee of fancy wines and elegant clothes, as indeed he was. Less truthfully, they portrayed Harrison as a

self-made man who lived contentedly in a log cabin and quaffed hard cider, a drink of the common people. In fact, Harrison's father was a wealthy Virginia planter who had signed the Declaration of Independence, and Harrison himself lived in a series of elegant mansions.

The Whigs boosted their electoral hopes by welcoming women to campaign festivities—a "first" for American politics. Jacksonian Democrats considered politics to be a "manly" affair; they likened politically minded females to "public" women, prostitutes who plied their trade in theaters and other public places. But the Whigs recognized that Christian women from Yankee families, a key Whig constituency, had already entered American public life through the temperance movement and other benevolent activities. In October 1840, Daniel Webster addressed a meeting of twelve hundred Whig women, praised their efforts for moral reform, and urged them to back Whig candidates. "This way of making politicians of their women is something new under the sun," exclaimed one Democrat, who worried that it would bring more Whig men to the polls. And it did: More than 80 percent of the eligible male voters cast ballots in 1840, up from fewer than 60 percent in 1832 and 1836. Heeding the Whigs' campaign

slogan "Tippecanoe and Tyler Too," they voted Harrison into the White House with 53 percent of the popular vote and gave the party a majority in Congress.

Tyler Subverts the Whig Agenda

Led by Clay and Webster, the Whigs in Congress prepared to reverse the Jacksonian revolution. But their hopes were short-lived; barely a month after his inauguration, Harrison died of pneumonia, and the nation got "Tyler Too." But in what capacity: as acting president or as president? The Constitution was vague on the issue. Ignoring his Whig associates in Congress, who wanted a weak chief executive, Tyler took the presidential oath of office and declared his intention to govern as he pleased. As it turned out, that would not be like a Whig.

Tyler had served in the House and the Senate as a Jeffersonian Democrat, firmly committed to slavery and states' rights. He had joined the Whigs only to protest Jackson's stance against nullification. On economic issues, Tyler shared Jackson's hostility to the Second Bank and the American System. He therefore vetoed Whig bills that would have raised tariffs and created a new national bank. Outraged by this betrayal,

President John Tyler (1790–1862)

Both as an "accidental" president and as a man, John Tyler left his mark on the world. His initiative to annex Texas made the election of 1844 into a pivotal contest and led to the war with Mexico in 1846. Tyler's first wife, Letitia, give birth to eight children before dying in the White House in 1842. Two years later, he married twenty-four-year-old Julia Gardiner, who bore him seven more children.   White House Historical Association (White House Collection).

most of Tyler's cabinet resigned in 1842, and the Whigs expelled Tyler from their party. "His Accidency," as he was called by his critics, was now a president without a party.

The split between Tyler and the Whigs allowed the Democrats to regroup. The party vigorously recruited subsistence farmers in the North, smallholding planters in the South, and former members of the Working Men's Parties in the cities. It also won support among Irish and German Catholic immigrants—whose numbers had increased during the 1830s—by backing their demands for religious and cultural liberty, such as the freedom to drink beer and whiskey. A pattern of **ethnocultural politics**, as historians refer to the practice of voting along ethnic and religious lines, now became a prominent feature of American life. Thanks to these urban and rural recruits, the Democrats remained the majority party in most parts of the nation. Their program of equal rights, states' rights, and cultural liberty was more attractive than the Whig platform of economic nationalism, moral reform, temperance laws, and individual mobility.

- How did the ideology of the Whigs differ from that of the Jacksonian Democrats?

- Why did the Working Men's and the Anti-Masonic Parties fail and the Whig Party succeed? What do their respective fates suggest about the nature of the American political system?

SUMMARY

In this chapter, we have examined the causes and the consequences of the democratic political revolution that accompanied the economic transformation of the early nineteenth century. We saw that the expansion of the franchise weakened the political system run by notables of high status and encouraged the transfer of power to professional politicians—men like Martin Van Buren who were mostly of middle-class origin.

We also witnessed a revolution in government policy, as Andrew Jackson and his Democratic Party dismantled the mercantilist economic system of government-supported economic development. On the national level, Jackson destroyed Henry Clay's

American System; on the state level, Democrats wrote new constitutions that ended the Commonwealth System of government charters and subsidies to private businesses.

Finally, we watched the emergence of the Second Party System. Following the split in the Republican Party during the election of 1824, two new parties — the Democrats and the Whigs — developed on the national level and eventually absorbed the members of the Anti-Masonic and Working Men's Parties. The new party system established universal suffrage for white men and a mode of representative government that was responsive to ordinary citizens. In their scope and significance, these political innovations matched the economic advances of both the Industrial Revolution and the Market Revolution.

CHAPTER REVIEW QUESTIONS

- How did the Jackson era fundamentally change the American economy, public policy, and society?

- Explain the rise of the Second Party System. How would you characterize American politics in the early 1840s?

- The chapter argues that a democratic revolution swept America in the decades after 1820. What evidence does the text present to support this argument? How persuasive is the evidence?

FOR FURTHER EXPLORATION

Two new studies of American politics are Sean Wilentz, *The Rise of American Democracy* (2005), and Christian G. Fritz, *American Sovereigns: The People and America's Constitutional Tradition* (2008). See also the classic books by George Dangerfield, *The Era of Good Feelings* (1952), and Alexis de Tocqueville, *Democracy in America* (1835). For concise analyses of the Jackson era, consult Harry L. Watson, *Liberty and Power* (1990); Daniel Feller, *The Jacksonian Promise* (1995); and the essays at **xroads.virginia.edu/~hyper/detoc/home.html**. Richard Hofstadter, *The Idea of a Party System* (1969), lucidly explains the triumph of party politics. See **www.ipl.org/div/potus/jqadams.html** for the election of 1824 and the John Quincy Adams administration. For wonderful political cartoons, go to **loc.harpweek.org**.

Robert V. Remini, *The Life of Andrew Jackson* (1988), highlights Jackson's triumphs and shortcomings. For Jackson's Indian policy, read the novel by Robert J. Conley, *Mountain Windsongs* (1992), and two studies by historians: Sean Michael O'Brien, *In Bitterness and in Tears* (2003), and John Buchanan, *Jackson's Way* (2001). For the Cherokees, see **cherokeehistory.com**. Thomas N. Ingersoll, *To Intermix with Our White Brothers* (2005), discusses Indians of mixed racial heritage.

Major L. Wilson, *The Presidency of Martin Van Buren* (1984), offers a shrewd assessment. For the Whigs, consult Merrill D. Peterson's *The Great Triumvirate: Webster, Clay, and Calhoun* (1987). Sean Wilentz, *Chants Democratic* (1986), covers the ideology of working men.

TEST YOUR KNOWLEDGE

To assess your command of the material in this chapter, see the Online Study Guide at **bedfordstmartins.com/henretta**.

For Web sites, images, and documents related to topics and places in this chapter, visit **bedfordstmartins.com/makehistory**.

TIMELINE

1810s States expand white male voting rights
Martin Van Buren creates focused party in New York

1825 John Quincy Adams chosen president by House of Representatives; endorses Henry Clay's American System

1828 Philadelphia artisans found Working Men's Party
"Tariff of Abominations" raises duties
Andrew Jackson elected president
John C. Calhoun's *South Carolina Exposition and Protest*

1830 Jackson vetoes National Road bill
Congress enacts Jackson's Indian Removal Act

1831 *Cherokee Nation v. Georgia* denies Indians' independence, but *Worcester v. Georgia* (1832) upholds their political autonomy

1832 Massacre of 850 Sauk and Fox warriors at Bad Axe
Jackson vetoes renewal of Second Bank
South Carolina adopts Ordinance of Nullification

1833 Congress enacts compromise tariff

1834 Whig Party formed by Clay, Calhoun, and Daniel Webster

1835 Roger Taney named Supreme Court chief justice

1836 Van Buren elected president

1837 *Charles River Bridge* case weakens chartered monopolies
Panic of 1837 derails union movement

1838 Cherokees die in Trail of Tears march to Indian Territory

1839–1843 Loans to American states spark international financial crisis and depression

1840 Whigs win "log cabin" campaign

1841 John Tyler succeeds William Henry Harrison as president

Hannah Roberts Married march 30 1833 Lewis Abbots 1833

Religion and Reform, 1820–1860

"The spirit of reform is in every place," declared the children of legal reformer David Dudley Field in their handwritten monthly *Gazette* in 1842:

The labourer with a family says "reform the common schools"; the merchant and the planter say, "reform the tariff," the lawyer "reform the laws," the politician "reform the government," the abolitionist "reform the slave laws," the moralist "reform intemperance," . . . the ladies wish their legal privileges extended, and in short, the whole country is wanting reform.

Like many Americans, the young Fields sensed that the political whirlwind of the 1830s had transformed the way people thought about themselves and about society. Suddenly, thousands of men and women, inspired by the economic progress and democratic spirit of the age and by the religious optimism of the Second Great Awakening, believed that they could improve their personal lives and society as a whole. Some dedicated themselves to the cause of reform. William Lloyd Garrison began as an antislavery advocate and foe of Indian removal and then went on to embrace women's rights, pacifism, and the abolition of prisons. Such obsessive individuals, warned Unitarian minister Henry W. Bellows, were pursuing "an object, which in its very nature is unattainable – the perpetual improvement of the outward condition."

Reform was complex and contradictory. Some reformers wanted to improve society by promoting morality and enforcing social discipline. The first wave of American reformers, the benevolent religious improvers of the 1820s, championed regular church attendance, temperance, and a strict moral code. Their zeal offended many upright citizens: "A peaceable man can hardly venture to eat or drink, . . . to correct his child or kiss his wife, without obtaining the permission . . . of some moral or other reform society," said one.

A second wave of reformers, which arose during the 1830s and 1840s, undertook to liberate people from archaic customs and traditional lifestyles. These reformers were mostly middle-class northerners and midwesterners who promoted a bewildering assortment of radical ideals: extreme individualism, common ownership of property, the immediate emancipation of slaves, and sexual equality. Although their numbers were small, second-wave reformers challenged well-established cultural practices and prompted the horrified opposition of the majority of Americans. As one fearful southerner saw it, radical reformers favored a chaotic world with "No-Marriage, No-Religion, No-Private Property, No-Law and No-Government."

Hannah Roberts and Lewis Tebbets

During the 1830s, Joseph H. Davis used bright watercolors to paint scores of family portraits – 150 still survive – that capture the comfortable lives of New England's middle classes. This double portrait commemorates the engagement of a young, well-dressed couple of Berwick, Maine. To emphasize their romantic love, Davis shows them gazing into each other's eyes, their hands linked by a prayer book, a symbol of their education and coming sacred union. Such respectable couples – Lewis Tebbets became a minister of the Methodist Episcopal Church – flocked to hear Ralph Waldo Emerson and other lecturers on the lyceum circuit. Terra Foundation for American Art, Chicago/ Art Resource, NY.

Individualism: The Ethic of the Middle Class

Those fears were not exaggerated. Rapid economic growth and geographical expansion had weakened traditional institutions, forcing individuals to fend for themselves. In 1835, Alexis de Tocqueville coined the word *individualism* to describe the result. Native-born white Americans were "no longer attached to each other by any tie of caste, class, association, or family," the French aristocrat lamented, and so lived in social isolation. Even as Tocqueville mourned the loss of social ties, the New England essayist and philosopher Ralph Waldo Emerson (1803–1882) celebrated the liberation of the individual. Emerson's vision influenced thousands of ordinary Americans and a generation of important artists; the result was the **American Renaissance**, a remarkable outpouring of first-class novels, poetry, and essays.

Ralph Waldo Emerson and Transcendentalism

Emerson was the leading voice of **transcendentalism**, an intellectual movement rooted in the religious soil of New England. Its first advocates were Unitarian ministers from well-to-do New England families who questioned the constraints of their Puritan heritage (see Chapter 8). For inspiration, they turned to European romanticism, a new conception of self and society. Romantic thinkers, such as German philosopher Immanuel Kant and English poet Samuel Taylor Coleridge, rejected the ordered, rational world of the eighteenth-century Enlightenment. They embraced human passion and sought deeper insight into the mysteries of existence. By tapping their intuitive powers, the young Unitarians believed, people could come to know the infinite and the eternal.

As a Unitarian, Emerson already stood outside the mainstream of American Protestantism. Unlike most Christians, Unitarians believed that God was a single being, not a trinity of Father, Son, and Holy Spirit. In 1832, Emerson took a more radical step by resigning his Boston pulpit and rejecting all organized religion. He moved to Concord, Massachusetts, and, in influential essays, explored what he called "the infinitude of the private man," the idea of individuality, the radically free person.

The young philosopher argued that people were trapped by inherited customs and institutions. They wore the ideas of earlier times — New England Calvin-

The Founder of Transcendentalism

As this painting of Ralph Waldo Emerson by an unknown artist indicates, the young philosopher was an attractive man, his face brimming with confidence and optimism. With his radiant personality and incisive intellect, Emerson deeply influenced dozens of influential writers, artists, and scholars, and enjoyed great success as a lecturer to the emerging middle class.   The Metropolitan Museum of Art, Bequest of Chester Dale, 1962 (64.97.4) Photograph© 1991 The Metropolitan Museum of Art.

ism, for example — as a kind of "faded masquerade," and they needed to shed those values. "What is a man born for but to be a Reformer, a Remaker of what man has made?" Emerson asked. In his view, individuals could be remade only by discovering their "original relation with Nature" and entering into a mystical union with the "currents of Universal Being." The ideal setting for this transcendent discovery was under an open sky, in solitary communion with nature. The revivalist Charles Grandison Finney described his religious conversion in Emersonian terms: an individual in the woods, alone, joining with God in a mystical union.

Emerson's genius lay in his ability to translate such abstract ideas into examples that made sense to middle-class Americans. His essays suggested that nature was saturated with the presence of God, a pantheistic outlook at odds with traditional Christian doctrine. Emerson also warned that the new market society — the focus on work, profits, and consumption — was

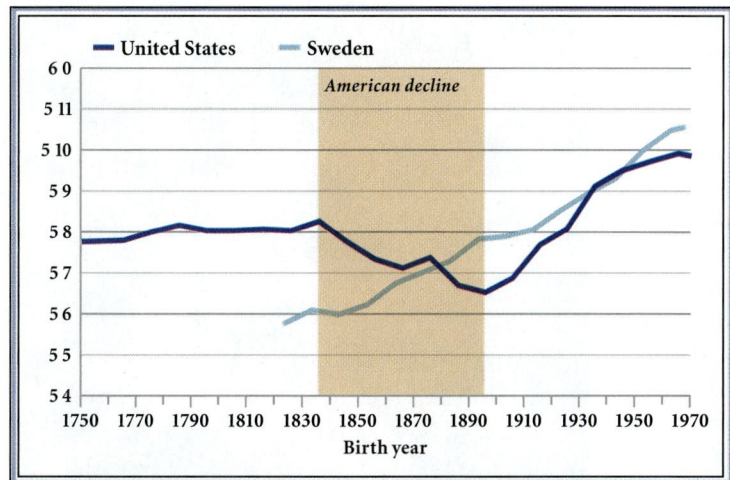

FIGURE 11.1

The Ecology of Health: Average Height of Native-born American and Swedish Men, by Year of Birth, 1750–1970

American transcendentalists sensed that the new urban and industrial society would damage people's health, and modern research suggests they were right. The average height of men born in the United States from the 1830s to the 1930s (as recorded in military records and other sources) was significantly lower than that of men born between 1750 and 1830. Researchers attribute this decline to the men's childhood experience of less adequate nutrition and greater exposure to infectious diseases in urban areas. However, data from Sweden—a predominantly poor, rural society until 1900—suggests that life in the traditional European agricultural world was equally damaging to people's welfare. Source: Richard Steckel, "Health and Nutrition in the Preindustrial Era" (Cambridge, MA: National Bureau of Economic Research, Working Paper 8452, 2001).

debasing Americans' spiritual and material lives (Figure 11.1). "Things are in the saddle," he wrote, "and ride mankind."

The transcendentalist message of individual self-realization reached hundreds of thousands of people through Emerson's writings and lectures. Public lectures had become a spectacularly successful way of spreading information and fostering discussion among the middle classes. Beginning in 1826, the lyceum movement—modeled on the public forum of the ancient Greek philosopher Aristotle—arranged lecture tours by hundreds of poets, preachers, scientists, and reformers. The lyceum became an important cultural institution in the North and Midwest—but not in the South, where the middle class was smaller and popular education had a lower priority. In 1839, nearly 150 lyceums in Massachusetts invited lecturers to address more than 33,000 subscribers. Emerson was the most popular speaker, eventually delivering fifteen hundred lectures in more than three hundred towns in twenty states.

Emerson celebrated those who rejected tradition and practiced self-discipline and civic responsibility. His individualistic ethos spoke directly to the experiences of many middle-class Americans, who had left family farms to make their way in the urban world. His pantheistic view of nature encouraged Unitarians in Boston to create the Mount Auburn Cemetery, a beautiful planned landscape of trees and bushes and burial markers for the dead of all faiths; soon there were similar rural cemeteries in many American cities. And Emerson's optimism inspired preachers such as Finney, who told believers to transcend old doctrines

and constraints. "God has made man a moral free agent," Finney declared.

Emerson's Literary Influence

Emerson sought to remake American literature. In "The American Scholar" (1837), the philosopher issued a literary declaration of independence. He urged American writers to free themselves from the "courtly muse" of Old Europe and instead to find inspiration in the experiences of ordinary Americans: "the ballad in the street; the news of the boat; the glance of the eye; the form and gait of the body."

Thoreau, Fuller, and Whitman One young New England intellectual, Henry David Thoreau (1817–1862), heeded Emerson's call and sought inspiration from the natural world. In 1845, depressed by his beloved brother's death, Thoreau built a cabin near Walden Pond in Concord, Massachusetts, and lived alone there for two years. In 1854, he published *Walden, or Life in the Woods*, an account of his search for meaning beyond the artificiality of civilized society:

> I went to the woods because I wished to live deliberately, to front only the essential facts of life, and see if I could not learn what it had to teach, and not, when I came to die, discover that I had not lived.

Walden's most famous metaphor provides an enduring justification for independent thinking: "If a man does not keep pace with his companions, perhaps it is because he hears a different drummer." Beginning from this premise, Thoreau advocated social nonconformity and civil disobedience against unjust laws — a thoroughgoing individuality.

As Thoreau was seeking self-realization for men, Margaret Fuller (1810–1850) was exploring the possibilities of freedom for women. Born into a wealthy Boston family, Fuller mastered six languages, read broadly in classic literature, and educated her four siblings. Embracing Emerson's ideas, she started a transcendental "conversation," or discussion group, for educated Boston women in 1839. While editing the leading transcendentalist journal, *The Dial*, Fuller published *Woman in the Nineteenth Century* (1844). It proclaimed that a "new era" was changing the relationships between men and women.

Fuller's philosophy began from the transcendental principle that all people — women as well as men — could develop a life-affirming mystical relationship with God. Every woman therefore deserved psychological and social independence: the ability "to grow, as an intellect to discern, as a soul to live freely and unimpeded." She wrote: "We would have every arbitrary barrier thrown down [and] every path laid open to Woman as freely as to Man." Acting on that precept, Fuller became the literary critic of the *New York Tribune* and traveled to Italy to report on the Revolution of 1848. Her adventurous life led to an early death; in 1850, she drowned in a shipwreck en route home to the United States. But Fuller's life and writings inspired a rising generation of women writers and reformers.

Another writer who responded to Emerson's call was the poet Walt Whitman (1819–1892). When Whitman first met Emerson, the poet recalled, he had been "simmering, simmering"; then Emerson "brought me to a boil." Whitman worked as a printer, a teacher, a journalist, an editor of the *Brooklyn Eagle*, and an influential publicist for the Democratic Party. But poetry was the "direction of his dreams." In *Leaves of Grass*, a collection of wild, exuberant poems first published in 1855 and constantly revised and expanded, Whitman recorded in verse his efforts to transcend various "invisible boundaries": between solitude and community, between prose and poetry, even between the living and the dead. At the center of *Leaves of Grass* is the individual — the figure of the poet — "I, Walt." He begins alone: "I celebrate myself, and sing myself." But because he has an Emersonian "original relation" with nature, Whitman claims perfect communion with others: "For every atom belonging to me as good belongs to you." For Emerson, Thoreau, and Fuller, the individual had a divine spark;

***Margaret Fuller*, 1848**

At thirty-eight, American social reformer Margaret Fuller moved to Italy, where she reported on the Revolution of 1848 for a New York newspaper. She fell in love there with Thomas Hicks (1823–1890), a much younger American artist. Hicks rebuffed Fuller's romantic advances but painted this flattering portrait, softening her features and giving her a pensive look. Fuller married a Roman nobleman, Giovanni Angelo, Marchese d'Ossoli, and gave birth to a son in September 1848. Two years later, the entire family died in a shipwreck while en route to the United States.   Constance Fuller Threinen.

for Whitman, the collective democracy assumed a sacred character.

The transcendentalists were optimistic but not naive. Whitman wrote about human suffering with passion, and Emerson laced his accounts of transcendence with twinges of anxiety. "I am glad," he once said, "to the brink of fear." Thoreau was gloomy about everyday life: "The mass of men lead lives of quiet desperation." Still, dark murmurings remain muted in their work, overshadowed by assertions that nothing was impossible for the individual who could break free from tradition.

Darker Visions | Emerson's writings also influenced two great novelists, Nathaniel Hawthorne and Herman Melville, who had more pessimistic worldviews. Both sounded powerful warnings that unfettered egoism could destroy individuals and those around them.

Hawthorne brilliantly explored the theme of excessive individualism in his novel *The Scarlet Letter* (1850). The two main characters, Hester Prynne and Arthur Dimmesdale, blatantly challenged their seventeenth-century New England community by committing adultery and producing a child. Their decision to ignore social restraints results not in liberation but in degradation: a profound sense of guilt and condemnation by the community.

Herman Melville explored the limits of individualism in even more extreme and tragic terms and emerged as a scathing critic of transcendentalism. His most powerful statement was *Moby Dick* (1851), the story of Captain Ahab's obsessive hunt for a mysterious white whale that ends in death for Ahab and all but one member of his crew. Here, the quest for spiritual meaning in nature brings death, not transcendence, because Ahab, the liberated individual, lacks inner discipline and self-restraint.

Moby Dick was a commercial failure. The middle-class audience that devoured sentimental American fiction refused to follow Melville into the dark, dangerous realm of individualism gone mad. What middle-class readers emphatically preferred were the more modest examples of individualism offered by Emerson and Finney: personal improvement through spiritual awareness and self-discipline.

Brook Farm To escape life in America's emerging market society, transcendentalists and other reformers created ideal communities, or utopias. They hoped these planned societies would allow people to realize their spiritual potential. The most important transcendentalist communal experiment was Brook Farm, founded just outside Boston in 1841. Intellectual life at Brook Farm was electric. Emerson, Thoreau, and Fuller were residents or frequent visitors; members recalled that they "inspired the young with a passion for study, and the middle-aged with deference and admiration, while we all breathed the intellectual grace that pervaded the atmosphere."

Whatever its spiritual rewards, Brook Farm was an economic failure. The residents hoped to escape the ups and downs of the market economy by producing their own food and exchanging their surplus milk, vegetables, and hay for manufactures. However, most members were ministers, teachers, writers, and students who had few farming skills; only the cash of affluent residents kept the enterprise afloat. After a devastating fire in 1846, the organizers disbanded the community and sold the farm.

With the failure of Brook Farm, the Emersonians abandoned their quest for a new social system. They accepted the brute reality of the emergent industrial order and tried to reform it, especially through the education of workers and the movement to abolish slavery.

- What were the main beliefs of transcendentalism, and how did American writers incorporate them into their work?

- What is the relationship between transcendentalism and individualism? Between transcendentalism and social reform? Between transcendentalism and the middle class?

Rural Communalism and Urban Popular Culture

Even as Brook Farm collapsed, thousands of Americans were joining communal settlements in rural areas of the Northeast and Midwest (Map 11.1). Many communalists were farmers and artisans seeking refuge during the economic depression that began with the Panic of 1837 and lasted seven years. However, these rural utopias were also symbols of social protest and experimentation. By advocating the common ownership of property and unconventional forms of marriage and family life, the communalists challenged capitalist values and traditional gender roles.

Simultaneously, tens of thousands of rural Americans and European immigrants poured into the larger cities of the United States. There, they created a popular culture that challenged some sexual norms, reinforced traditional racist feelings, and encouraged new styles of dress and behavior.

Mother Ann Lee and the Shakers

The Shakers were the first successful American communal movement. In 1770, Ann Lee Stanley (Mother Ann), a young cook in Manchester, England, had a vision that she was an incarnation of Christ and that sexual lust had caused Adam and Eve to be banished from the Garden of Eden. Four years later, she led a few followers to America, and established a church near Albany, New York. Because of the ecstatic dances that were part of their worship, the sect became known as the Shakers.

After Mother Ann's death in 1784, the Shakers honored her as the Second Coming of Christ, withdrew

MAP 11.1

Major Communal Experiments before 1860

Some experimental communities settled along the frontier, but the vast majority chose rural areas in well-settled regions of the North and Midwest. Because of their opposition to slavery, communalists usually avoided the South. Most secular experiments failed within a few decades, as the founders lost their reformist enthusiasm or died off; religious communities—such as those of the Shakers and the Mormons—were longer-lived.

---

from the profane world, and formed disciplined religious communities. Members embraced the common ownership of property; accepted strict oversight by church leaders; and pledged to abstain from alcohol, tobacco, politics, and war. Shakers also repudiated sexual pleasure and marriage. Their commitment to celibacy followed Mother Ann's testimony against "the lustful gratifications of the flesh as the source and foundation of human corruption." The Shakers' theology was as radical as their social thought. They held that God was "a dual person, male and female." This doctrine prompted Shakers to repudiate male leadership and to place community governance in the hands of both women and men — the Eldresses and the Elders.

Shakers founded twenty communities, mostly in New England, New York, and Ohio. Their agriculture and crafts, especially furniture making, acquired a reputation for quality that made most Shaker communities self-sustaining and even comfortable. Because the Shakers disdained sexual intercourse, they relied on conversions and the adoption of thousands of young orphans to increase their numbers. During the 1830s, three thousand adults, mostly women, joined the Shakers, attracted by their communal intimacy and sexual equality. To Rebecca Cox Jackson, an African American seamstress from Philadelphia, the Shakers seemed to be "loving to live forever." As the supply of orphans dried up during the 1840s and 1850s (with the increase in public and private orphanages), Shaker communities began to decline. By 1900, the Shakers had virtually disappeared, leaving as their material legacy a distinctive plain but elegant style of wood furniture.

Arthur Brisbane and Fourierism

As the Shakers' growth slowed during the 1840s, the American Fourierist movement mushroomed. Charles Fourier (1777–1837) was a French reformer who devised an eight-stage theory of social evolution that predicted the imminent decline of individualism and capitalism. According to Arthur Brisbane, the leading disciple of Fourierism in America, Fourier's utopian socialism—a forerunner of class-based **socialism**—would free workers from the "menial and slavish system of Hired Labor or Labor for Wages," just as republicanism had freed Americans from slavish monarchical government. In a Fourierist society, men and women would work for the community, in cooperative groups called phalanxes. The members of a phalanx would be its shareholders; they would own its property in common, including stores and a bank, a school, and a library.

Fourier and Brisbane saw the phalanx as a humane system that would liberate women as well as men. "In society as it is now constituted," Brisbane wrote, individual freedom was possible only for men, while "woman

Shakers at Prayer

Most Americans viewed the Shakers with a mixture of fascination and suspicion. They feared the sect's radical aspects—such as a commitment to celibacy and communal property—and considered the Shakers' dancing more an invitation to debauchery than a form of prayer. Those apprehensions surfaced in this engraving, "The Shakers of New Lebanon," New York, which expresses both the powerful intensity and the menacing character of the Shaker ritual. The work of the journalist-engraver Joseph Becker, the picture appeared in *Frank Leslie's Illustrated Newspaper* in 1873.   © Bettmann.

is subjected to unremitting and slavish domestic duties." In the "new Social Order . . . based upon Associated households," men would share women's domestic labor and thereby increase sexual equality.

Brisbane skillfully promoted Fourier's ideas in his influential book *The Social Destiny of Man* (1840), a regular column in Horace Greeley's *New York Tribune*, and hundreds of lectures. Fourierist ideas found a receptive audience among educated farmers and craftsmen, who yearned for economic stability and communal solidarity in the wake of the Panic of 1837. During the 1840s, Fourierists started nearly one hundred cooperative communities, mostly in western New York and the Midwest. However, most of these communities collapsed within a decade because of disputes over work

responsibilities and social policies. Fourierism's decline revealed the difficulty of establishing a utopian community in the absence of a charismatic leader or a compelling religious vision.

John Humphrey Noyes and the Oneida Community

John Humphrey Noyes (1811–1886) was both charismatic and religious. He ascribed the Fourierists' failure to their secular outlook and took as his model the pious Shakers, the true "pioneers of modern Socialism." The Shakers' marriageless society also appealed to Noyes and inspired him to create a community that defined sexuality and gender roles in radically new ways.

"Bloomerism – An American Custom"

The hippies of the 1960s weren't the first to draw attention to themselves with their dress (sloppy) and smoking (marijuana). Independent women of the 1850s took to wearing bloomers and puffing on cigars, behaviors that elicited everything from matrons' disapproving stares to verbal and physical assaults from street urchins. Beyond dress and smoking habits, the women's movement questioned existing cultural norms and sought to expand the boundaries of personal freedom. This cartoon appeared in 1851 in *Harper's New Monthly Magazine*, a major periodical of the time. *Harper's New Monthly Magazine* (August 1851)/ Picture Research Consultants & Archives.

Noyes was a well-to-do graduate of Dartmouth College who joined the ministry after hearing a sermon by Charles Grandison Finney. Dismissed as the pastor of a Congregational church for holding unorthodox beliefs, Noyes turned to perfectionism, an evangelical Protestant movement of the 1830s that attracted thousands of New Englanders who had migrated to New York and Ohio. Perfectionists believed that Christ had already returned to earth (the Second Coming); consequently, according to the Bible, people could aspire to sinless perfection in their earthly lives. Unlike most perfectionists, who lived conventional personal lives, Noyes rejected marriage as the major barrier to perfection. "Exclusiveness, jealousy, quarreling have no place at the marriage supper of the Lamb," Noyes wrote. But instead of the Shakers' celibacy, Noyes and his followers embraced "complex marriage," in which all the members of the community were married to one another.

Noyes's teachings highlighted the growing debate over legal and cultural constraints on women. He rejected monogamy partly to free women from their status as the property of their husbands, as they were by custom and by common law. To give women the time and energy to participate fully in the community, Noyes urged them to avoid multiple pregnancies. He asked men to assist in this effort by avoiding orgasm during intercourse. To raise the community's children, Noyes set up nurseries run by both sexes. Symbolizing the quest for equality, Noyes's women followers cut their hair short and wore pantaloons under calf-length skirts.

In 1839, Noyes set up a perfectionist community near his hometown of Putney, Vermont. When, in the mid-1840s, he introduced the practice of complex marriage, local outrage forced Noyes to relocate the community to an isolated area near Oneida, New York. By the mid-1850s, the Oneida settlement had 200 residents; it became financially self-sustaining when the inventor of a highly successful steel animal trap joined the community. With the profits from trap making, the Oneidians diversified into the production of silverware. When Noyes fled to Canada in 1879 to avoid prosecution for adultery, the community abandoned complex marriage but retained its cooperative spirit. Its members founded Oneida Community, Ltd., a jointly owned silverware-manufacturing company that remained a communal venture until the middle of the twentieth century.

The historical significance of the Oneidians, Shakers, and Fourierists does not lie in their numbers, which were small, or in their fine crafts. Rather, their importance stems from their radical questioning of traditional sexual norms and of the capitalist principles and class divisions of the emerging market society. Their utopian communities stood as countercultural blueprints for a more egalitarian social and economic order.

Joseph Smith and the Mormon Experience

The Shakers and the Oneidians were radical utopians, but because their communities remained small, they aroused relatively little hostility. The Mormons, members of the Church of Jesus Christ of Latter-day Saints, were religious utopians with a conservative social agenda: to perpetuate close-knit communities and patriarchal power. Because of their cohesiveness and size, the Mormons provoked more animosity than the radical utopians did.

Joseph Smith | Like many social movements of the era, Mormonism emerged from religious ferment among families of Puritan descent who lived along the Erie Canal. The founder of the Latter-day Church, Joseph Smith Jr. (1805–1844), was born in Vermont to a poor farming and shop-keeping family that migrated to Palmyra in central New York. In religious experiences that began in 1820, Smith came to believe that God had singled him out to receive a special revelation of divine truth. In 1830, he published *The Book of Mormon*, which he claimed to have translated from ancient hieroglyphics on gold plates shown to him by an angel named Moroni. *The Book of Mormon* told the story of ancient civilizations from the Middle East that had migrated to the Western Hemisphere and of the visit of Jesus Christ, soon after his Resurrection, to one of them. Smith's account explained the presence of native peoples in the Americas and integrated them into the Judeo-Christian tradition.

Smith proceeded to organize the Church of Jesus Christ of Latter-day Saints. Seeing himself as a prophet in a sinful, excessively individualistic society, Smith revived traditional social doctrines, including patriarchal authority within the family. Like many Protestant ministers, he encouraged practices that led to individual success in the age of capitalist markets and factories: frugality, hard work, and enterprise. But Smith also stressed communal discipline to safeguard the Mormon "New Jerusalem" from individualism and rival religious doctrines. His goal was a church-directed society that would ensure moral perfection.

Constantly harassed by hostile anti-Mormons, Smith struggled for years to find a secure home for his new religion. At one point, he identified Jackson County in Missouri as the site of the sacred "City of Zion," and his followers began to settle there. Agitation led by Protestant ministers quickly forced them out: "Mormons were the common enemies of mankind and ought to be destroyed," said one cleric. Smith and his growing congregation eventually settled in Nauvoo, Illinois, a

A Mormon Man and His Wives

The practice of polygamy split the Mormon community and, because it deviated from traditional religious principles, enraged other Christian denominations. This Mormon household, pictured in the late 1840s, was unusually prosperous, partly because of the labor of the husband's multiple wives. Although the cabin provides cramped quarters for such a large family, it boasts a brick chimney and — a luxury for any pioneer home — a glass window.   Library of Congress.

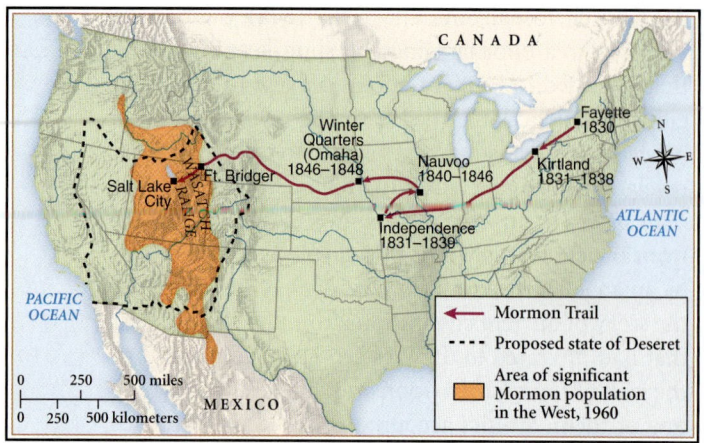

MAP 11.2

The Mormon Trek, 1830–1848

Because of their unorthodox religious views and communal solidarity, Mormons faced hostility first in New York and then in Missouri and Illinois. After founder Joseph Smith Jr. was murdered, Brigham Young led the polygamist faction of Mormons into lands claimed by Mexico and thinly populated by Native Americans. From Omaha, the migrants followed the path of the Oregon Trail to Fort Bridger and then struck off to the southwest. They settled along the Wasatch Range in the basin of the Great Salt Lake in present-day Utah.

town they founded on the Mississippi River (Map 11.2). By the early 1840s, Nauvoo was the largest utopian community in the United States, with 30,000 residents. The rigid discipline and secret rituals of the Mormons — along with their prosperity, hostility toward other sects, and bloc voting in Illinois elections — fueled resentment among their neighbors. That resentment turned to overt hostility when Smith refused to abide by any Illinois law of which he disapproved, asked Congress to turn Nauvoo into a separate federal territory, and declared himself a candidate for president of the United States.

Moreover, Smith claimed to have received a new revelation justifying polygamy, the practice of a man having multiple wives. When leading Mormon men took several wives, they sparked a contentious debate among Mormons and enraged Christians in neighboring towns. In 1844, Illinois officials arrested Smith and charged him with treason for allegedly conspiring to create a Mormon colony in Mexican territory. An anti-Mormon mob stormed the jail in Carthage, Illinois, where Smith and his brother were being held and murdered them.

Brigham Young and Utah   Led by Brigham Young, Smith's leading disciple and an energetic missionary, about 6,500 Mormons fled the United States. Beginning in 1845, they crossed the Great Plains into Mexican territory and settled in the Great Salt Lake Valley in present-day Utah. Using cooperative labor and an irrigation system based on communal water rights, the Mormon pioneers quickly spread planned agricultural communities along the base of the Wasatch Range. Many Mormons who rejected polygamy remained in the United States. Led by Smith's son, Joseph Smith III, they formed the Reorganized Church of Jesus Christ of Latter-day Saints and settled throughout the Midwest.

When the United States acquired title to Mexico's northern territories in 1848, the Salt Lake Mormons petitioned Congress to create a vast new state, Deseret, which would stretch from Utah to the Pacific coast. Instead, Congress set up the much smaller Utah Territory in 1850 and named Brigham Young its governor. Young and his associates ruled in an authoritarian fashion, determined to ensure the ascendancy of the Mormon Church and its practices. By 1856, Young and the Utah territorial legislature were openly vowing to resist federal laws that were "of right not in force in this territory." Pressed by Protestant churches to end polygamy and considering the Mormons' threat of nullification "a declaration of war," the administration of President James Buchanan dispatched a small army to Utah. As the "Nauvoo Legion" resisted the army's advance, aggressive Mormon militia massacred a party of 120 California-bound emigrants and murdered suspicious travelers and Mormons seeking to flee Young's regime. Despite this bloodshed, the "Mormon War" ended quietly in June 1858. President Buchanan, a longtime supporter of the white South, feared that the forced abolition of polygamy would serve as a precedent for ending slavery. So he offered a pardon to Utah citizens who would acknowledge federal authority, an offer accepted by Young and other leaders in order to prolong Mormon rule. (To enable Utah to win admission to the Union in 1896, its citizens ratified a constitution that "forever" banned the practice of polygamy. But the state government has never strictly enforced that ban.)

The Salt Lake Mormons had succeeded even as other social experiments had failed. By endorsing private property and individual enterprise, Mormons became prosperous contributors to the new market society. However, their leaders resolutely used strict religious controls to perpetuate patriarchy and communal discipline, reaffirming traditional values. This blend of

Night Life in Philadelphia

This watercolor by Russian painter Pavel Svinin (1787–1839) captures the diversity and allure of urban America. A respectable gentleman relishes the delicacies sold by a black oysterman. Meanwhile, a young woman—probably a prostitute—engages the attention of two well-dressed young "swells" outside the Chestnut Street Theatre. The Metropolitan Museum of Art, Rogers Fund, 1942 (42.95.18). Photograph © 1989 The Metropolitan Museum of Art.

economic innovation, social conservatism, and hierarchical leadership, in combination with a strong missionary impulse, created a wealthy and expansive church that now claims a worldwide membership of about twelve million people.

Urban Popular Culture

As utopians organized communities in the countryside, rural migrants and foreign immigrants created a new urban culture. In 1800, American cities were overgrown towns with rising death rates: New York had only 60,000 residents, Philadelphia had 41,000, and life expectancy at birth was a mere twenty-five years. Then urban growth accelerated as a huge in-migration outweighed the high death rates. By 1840, New York's population had ballooned to 312,000; Philadelphia and its suburbs had 150,000 residents; and three other cities—

New Orleans, Boston, and Baltimore—each had about 100,000. By 1860, New York had become a metropolis with more than 1 million residents: 813,000 in Manhattan and another 266,000 in the adjacent community of Brooklyn.

Sex in the City These new cities, particularly New York, generated a new urban culture. Thousands of young men and women from rural areas flocked to the city searching for adventure and fortune, but many found only a hard life. Young men labored for meager wages constructing thousands of new buildings each year. Others worked as low-paid clerks or operatives in hundreds of mercantile and manufacturing firms. The young women had an even harder time (see Reading American Pictures, "Looking for Clues in Art about Women's Sphere," p. 342). Thousands toiled as live-in domestic servants, ordered about by the mistress

Looking for Clues in Art about Women's Sphere

This rather somber painting, *The Intelligence Office*, by William Henry Burr (1849), depicts a scene at an urban employment agency. The woman sitting to the right, dressed in formal satins, is deciding whether to hire the two standing women as domestic servants. What does this picture tell us about social relations in nineteenth-century America? Burr's work also incorporates various hallmarks of the new age: contractual labor relations, then-current forms of communication, and the intensification of class identity. Do you see them?

A Nineteenth-Century Job Interview. © Collection of the New-York Historical Society.

ANALYZING THE EVIDENCE

- Study the applicants' clothing. How does their garb differ from that of the employer? Look carefully at their faces and posture. How do you interpret the attitude of the standing girl, facing outward, looking down? How would you interpret the facial expressions of the women seated in the background?

- What events during the antebellum period forced workers to alter their lifestyle and choices for employment?

- Suppose Burr had been painting in 1749, a century earlier. How would a wealthy village squire or a prosperous merchant go about hiring domestic help? What had changed over the decades? Why did an employer in 1849 need the services of a professional agent?

- How did the women applicants come to use the agent's services? What clue has the artist placed in the picture that suggests an answer?

of the household and often sexually exploited by the master. Thousands more scraped out a bare living as needlewomen in New York's booming clothes manufacturing industry. Unwilling to endure domestic service or subsistence wages, many young girls turned to prostitution. In the 1850s, Dr. William Sanger's careful survey found 6,000 women engaged in commercial sex. Three-fifths of them were native-born whites, and the rest were foreign immigrants; most were between fifteen and twenty years old. Half were or had been domestic servants, half had children, and half were infected with syphilis.

Commercialized sex—and sex in general—formed one facet of the new urban culture. "Sporting men" engaged freely in sexual conquests; otherwise respectable married men kept mistresses in handy apartments; and working men frequented bawdy houses. New York City had some two hundred brothels in the 1820s and five hundred by the 1850s. Prostitutes—so-called "public" women—openly advertised their wares on Broadway, the city's most fashionable thoroughfare, and welcomed clients on the infamous "Third Tier" of the theaters. Many men considered access to illicit sex to be a right. "Man is endowed by nature with passions that must be gratified," declared the *Sporting Whip*, a working-class magazine. Reverend William Berrian, pastor of the ultra-respectable Trinity Episcopal Church, did not disagree; he remarked from the pulpit that he had resorted to "a house of ill-fame" a mere ten times.

Prostitution formed only the tip of the urban sexual iceberg. Freed from family oversight, urban men and women pursued wide-ranging romantic adventures. Men formed homoerotic friendships and relationships; as early as 1800, the homosexual "Fop" was an acknowledged character in Philadelphia. Young people discovered their sexual and social identity by moving from partner to partner until they chanced on an ideal mate. To enhance their allure, they strolled along Broadway in the latest fashions: elaborate bonnets and silk dresses for young women; flowing capes, leather boots, and silver-plated walking sticks for young men. Rivaling the elegance on Broadway was the colorful dress on the Bowery, the broad avenue that ran along the east side of lower Manhattan. By day, the "Bowery Boy" worked as an apprentice or journeyman; by night, he prowled the streets as a "consummate dandy," his hair cropped at the back of his head "as close as scissors could cut," with long front locks "matted by a lavish application of *bear's grease*, the ends tucked under so as to form a roll and brushed until they shone like glass bottles." The "B'hoy," as he was called, cut a dashing figure as he walked along with a "Bowery Gal" in a striking dress

and shawl: "a light pink contrasting with a deep blue" or "a bright yellow with a brighter red."

Minstrelsy Popular entertainment was another facet of the new urban culture. In New York, workingmen could partake of traditional rural blood sports—rat and terrier fights—at Sportsmen Hall, or they could crowd into the pit of the Bowery Theatre to see the "Mad Tragedian," Junius Brutus Booth, deliver a stirring performance of Shakespeare's *Richard III*. Middle-class couples enjoyed evenings at the huge Broadway Tabernacle, where they could hear an abolitionist lecture and see the renowned Hutchinson Family Singers of New Hampshire lead the audience in a roof-raising rendition of their antislavery anthem, "Get Off the Track." Or they could visit the museum of oddities (and hoaxes) created by P. T. Barnum, the great cultural entrepreneur and founder of the Barnum & Bailey Circus.

The most popular theatrical entertainments were the minstrel shows, in which white actors in blackface presented comic routines that blended racist caricature and social criticism. Minstrelsy began around 1830, when a few actors put on blackface and performed song-and-dance routines. The most famous was John Dartmouth Rice, whose "Jim Crow" blended a weird shuffle-dance-and-jump with unintelligible lyrics delivered in "Negro dialect." By the 1840s, there were hundreds of minstrel troupes, including a group of black entertainers, Gavitt's Original Ethiopian Serenaders. The actor-singers' rambling improvised lyrics poked racist fun at the African Americans they caricatured, portraying them as lazy, sensual, and irresponsible while simultaneously using them to criticize white society. Minstrels ridiculed the drinking habits of Irish immigrants, parodied the speech of recent German arrivals, denounced women's demands for political rights, and mocked the arrogance of upper-class men.

Immigrant Masses and Nativist Reaction Still, by performing in blackface, the minstrels declared the importance of being white. In particular, their racism encouraged Irish and German immigrants to identify with the dominant culture of native-born whites, which eased their entry into New York society. By 1855, Irish men and women in New York City numbered 200,000, and Germans 110,000 (Figure 11.2). German-language shop signs filled entire neighborhoods, and German foods (sausages, hamburgers, sauerkraut) and food customs (such as drinking beer in family *biergärten*) became part of the city's culture. The mass of impoverished

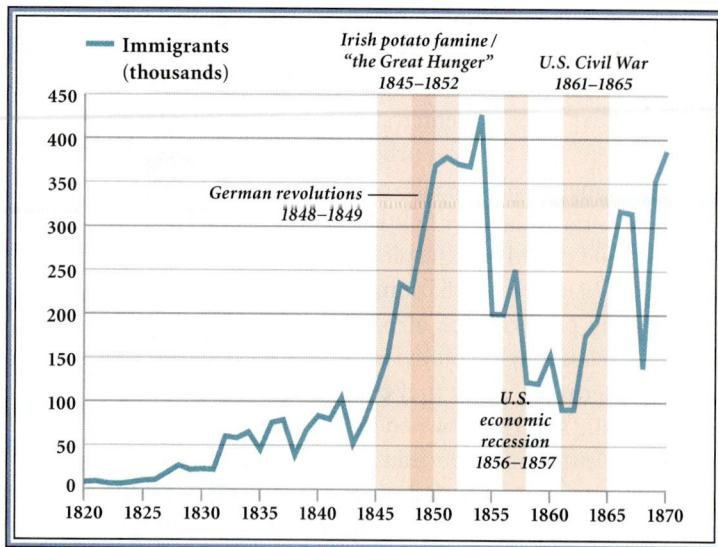

FIGURE 11.2

The Surge in Immigration, 1845–1855

In 1845, the failure of the potato crop in Ireland prompted the wholesale migration to the United States of peasants from the overcrowded farms of its western counties. Population growth and limited economic prospects likewise spurred the migration of tens of thousands of German peasants, while the failure of the liberal republican political revolution of 1848 prompted hundreds of prominent German politicians and intellectuals to follow them. An American economic recession cut the flow of immigrants, but the booming northern economy during the Civil War again persuaded Europeans to set sail for the United States.

Irish migrants found allies in the American Catholic Church, which soon became an Irish-dominated institution, and the Democratic Party, which gave them a foothold in the political process.

Native-born New Yorkers took alarm as hordes of ethnically diverse migrants altered the city's culture. They organized a nativist movement—a final aspect of the new urban world. Beginning in the mid-1830s, nativists called for a halt to immigration and mounted a cultural and political assault on foreign-born residents (see Chapter 9). Gangs of B'hoys assaulted Irish youths in the streets, employers restricted Irish workers to the most menial jobs, and temperance reformers denounced the German fondness for beer. In 1844, the American Republican Party, with the endorsement of the Whigs, swept the city elections by focusing on the culturally emotional issues of temperance, anti-Catholicism, and nativism (see Comparing American Voices, "Saving the Nation from Drink," pp. 346–347).

In the city, as in the countryside, new values were challenging old beliefs. The sexual freedom celebrated by Noyes at Oneida had its counterpart in commercialized sex and male promiscuity in New York City. Similarly, the disciplined rejection of tobacco and alcohol by the Shakers and the Mormons found a parallel in the Washington Temperance Society and other urban reform organizations. American society was in ferment, and the outcome was far from clear.

- **In what respects were the new cultures of the mid-nineteenth century—those of utopian communalists and of urban residents—different from the mainstream culture described in Chapters 8 and 9? How were they alike?**

- **What accounts for the proliferation of rural utopian communities in nineteenth-century America?**

Abolitionism

Like other reform movements, abolitionism drew on the religious enthusiasm of the Second Great Awakening, and the language of protest changed accordingly. Around 1800, antislavery activists had assailed human bondage as contrary to republicanism and liberty. By the 1830s, white abolitionists were condemning slavery as a sin. Their demands for its immediate end led to fierce political debates, urban riots, and sectional conflicts.

Black Social Thought: Uplift, Race Equality, and Rebellion

Beginning in the 1790s, leading African Americans in the North advocated a strategy of social uplift. They encouraged free blacks to "elevate" themselves through education, temperance, and hard work. By securing "respectability," they argued, blacks could become the social equals of whites. To promote that goal, black leaders—men such as James Forten, a Philadelphia sailmaker; Prince Hall, a Boston barber; and ministers Hosea Easton and Richard Allen (see Chapter 8)—founded an array of churches, schools, and self-help associations. Capping this effort in 1827, John Russwurm and Samuel D. Cornish of New York published the first African American newspaper, *Freedom's Journal*.

Rampant Racism

Minstrel shows and music were just one facet of the racist culture of mid-nineteenth-century America. Exploiting the market for almanacs among farmers and city-folk alike, the publishing firm of Fisher and Brother produced the "Black Joke Al-Ma-Nig" for 1852. Like other almanacs, it provided information about holidays, astrological charts, and weather predictions but sought to boost sales by including "new and original nigga' stories, black jokes, puns, parodies" that would "magnetize bofe white an' black." Such racist caricatures influenced white views of African Americans and their culture well into the twentieth century.

The black quest for respectability elicited a violent response from whites in Boston, Pittsburgh, and other northern cities who refused to accept African Americans as their social equals. "I am Mr. _____'s *help*," a white maid informed a British visitor. "I am no *sarvant*; none but *negers* are *sarvants*." Such racial contempt prompted white mobs to terrorize black communities. The attacks in Cincinnati were so violent and destructive that several hundred African Americans fled to Canada for safety.

David Walker's Appeal   Responding to the attacks, David Walker published a stirring pamphlet: *An Appeal . . . to the Colored Citizens of the World* (1829). Its goal was to protest black "wretchedness in this *Republican Land of Liberty!!!!!*" Walker was a free black from North Carolina who had moved to Boston, where he sold secondhand clothes and copies of *Freedom's Journal*. A self-educated man, Walker used history and morality to attack racial slavery. His *Appeal* ridiculed the religious pretensions

Saving the Nation from Drink

The temperance crusade was the first and greatest antebellum reform movement. It mobilized more than a million supporters from all sections of the country and significantly lowered the consumption of alcoholic beverages. Like other reform efforts, however, the crusade divided over questions of strategy and tactics. The following passages, taken from the writings of leading temperance advocates, show that some reformers favored legal regulation while others preferred persuasion and voluntary abstinence.

Lyman Beecher

"Intemperance Is the Sin of Our Land"

A leading Protestant minister and spokesman for the Benevolent Empire, Lyman Beecher conceived of drunkenness as a sin. His *Six Sermons on . . . Intemperance* (1829) condemned the recklessness of working-class drunkards and called on members of the middle class to lead the way to a temperate society.

Intemperance is the sin of our land, and, with our boundless prosperity, is coming in upon us like a flood; and if anything shall defeat the hopes of the world, which hang upon our experiment of civil liberty, it is that river of fire. . . .

In every city and town the poor-tax, created chiefly by intemperance, is augmenting. . . . The frequency of going upon the town [relying on public welfare] has taken away the reluctance of pride, and destroyed the motives to providence which the fear of poverty and suffering once supplied. The prospect of a destitute old age, or of a suffering family, no longer troubles the vicious portion of our community. They drink up their daily earnings, and bless God for the poor-house, and begin to look upon it as, of right, the drunkard's home. . . . Every intemperate and idle man, whom you behold tottering about the streets and steeping himself at the stores, regards your houses and lands as pledged to take care of him, puts his hands deep, annually, into your pockets. . . .

What then is this universal, natural, and national remedy for intemperance? IT IS THE BANISHMENT OF ARDENT SPIRITS FROM THE LIST OF LAWFUL ARTICLES OF COMMERCE, BY A CORRECT AND EFFICIENT PUBLIC SENTIMENT; SUCH AS HAS TURNED SLAVERY OUT OF HALF OUR LAND, AND WILL YET EXPEL IT FROM THE WORLD.

We are not therefore to come down in wrath upon the distillers, and importers, and venders of ardent spirits. None of us are enough without sin to cast the first stone. . . . It is the buyers who have created the demand for ardent spirits, and made distillation and importation a gainful traffic. . . . Let the temperate cease to buy—and the demand for ardent spirits will fall in the market three fourths, and ultimately will fail wholly. . . .

This however cannot be done effectually so long as the traffic in ardent spirits is regarded as lawful, and is patronized by men of reputation and moral worth in every part of the land. Like slavery, it must be regarded as sinful, impolitic, and dishonorable. That no measures will avail short of rendering ardent spirits a contraband of trade, is nearly self-evident.

Abraham Lincoln

"A New Class of Champions"

In Baltimore in 1840, a group of reformed alcoholics formed the Washington Temperance Society, which turned the antidrinking movement in a new direction. By talking publicly about their personal experiences of alcoholic decline and spiritual recovery, they inspired thousands to "sign the pledge" of total abstinence. In 1842, Lincoln, an ambitious lawyer and Illinois legislator who did not drink, praised such "moral suasion" in an address to the Washingtonians of Springfield, Illinois.

Although the temperance cause has been in progress for near twenty years, it is apparent to all that it is just now being crowned with a degree of success hitherto unparalleled. The list of its friends is daily swelled by the additions of fifties, of hundreds, and of thousands.

The warfare heretofore waged against the demon intemperance has somehow or other been erroneous. . . . [Its] champions for the most part have been preachers [such as Beecher], lawyers, and hired agents. Between these and the mass of mankind there is a want of approachability. . . .

But when one who has long been known as a victim of intemperance bursts the fetters that have bound him, and appears before his neighbors "clothed and in his right mind," . . . to tell of the miseries once endured, now to be endured no more . . . there is a logic and an eloquence in it that few with human feelings can resist. . . .

In my judgment, it is to the battles of this new class of champions that our late success is greatly, perhaps chiefly, owing. . . . [Previously,] too much denunciation against dram-sellers and dram-drinkers was indulged in. This I think was both impolitic and unjust. . . . When the dram-seller and drinker were incessantly [condemned] . . . as moral pestilences . . . they were slow [to] . . . join the ranks of their denouncers in a hue and cry against themselves.

By the Washingtonians this system of consigning the habitual drunkard to hopeless ruin is repudiated. . . . They teach hope to all—despair to none. As applying to their cause, they deny the doctrine of unpardonable sin. . . .

If the relative grandeur of revolutions shall be estimated by the great amount of human misery they alleviate, and the small amount they inflict, then indeed will this be the grandest the world shall ever have seen. Of our political revolution of '76 we are all justly proud. It has given us a degree of political freedom far exceeding that of any other nation of the earth. . . . But, with all these glorious results, past, present, and to come, it had its evils too. It breathed forth famine, swam in blood, and rode in fire; and long, long after, the orphan's cry and the widow's wail continued to break the sad silence that ensued. These were the price, the inevitable price, paid for the blessings it brought.

Turn now to the temperance revolution. In it we shall find a stronger bondage broken, a viler slavery manumitted, a greater tyrant deposed; in it, more of want supplied, more disease healed, more sorrow assuaged. By it no orphans starving, no widows weeping.

Glorious consummation! Hail, fall of fury! Reign of reason, all hail!

American Temperance Magazine
"You Shall Not Sell"

In 1851, the Maine legislature enacted a statute prohibiting the sale of alcoholic beverages in the state. The Maine Supreme Court upheld the statute declaring the legislature's "right to regulate by law the sale of any article, the use of which would be detrimental of the morals of the people." As this article from 1852 shows, the American Temperance Magazine became a strong advocate of legal prohibition and, within four years, had won passage of "Maine Laws" in twelve other states (see Chapter 9).

This is a utilitarian age. The speculative has in all things yielded to the practical. Words are mere noise unless they are things [and result in action].

In this sense, moral suasion is moral balderdash. "Words, my lord, words" . . . are a delusion. . . . The drunkard's mental and physical condition pronounces them an absurdity. He is ever in one or other extreme—under the excitement of drink, or in a state of morbid collapse. . . . Reason with a man when all reason has fled, and it is doubtful whether he or you is the greater fool. . . . Moral suasion! Bah!

Place this man we have been describing out of the reach of temptation. He will have time to ponder. His mind and frame recover their native vigor. The public-house does not beset his path. . . . Thus, and thus only, will reformation and temperance be secured. And how is this accomplished? Never except through the instrumentality of the law. If it were possible to reason the drunkard into sobriety, it would not be possible to make the rumseller forego his filthy gains. Try your moral suasion on him. . . . The only logic he will comprehend, is some such ordinance as this, coming to him in the shape and with the voice of law—you shall not sell.

Source: All selections are abridged from David Brion Davis, *Antebellum American Culture: An Interpretive Anthology* (University Park: Pennsylvania State University Press, 1997), 395–398, 403–409.

ANALYZING THE EVIDENCE

- What does Lincoln's address tell us about his general political philosophy?

- Compare Beecher's position to Lincoln's. In what ways are they similar? How are they different? Then compare Beecher's solution to that of the *American Temperance Magazine*. Are they the same? Whose position is closest to that of Orestes Brownson (see Chapter 9, pp. 298–299)?

- Where in these selections do you see the influence of the Second Great Awakening, especially the evangelical message of Charles Grandison Finney? Where do you see the influence of the Market Revolution and the middle-class values of the market economy? Do these selections take the same position as to the role of government in regulating morality?

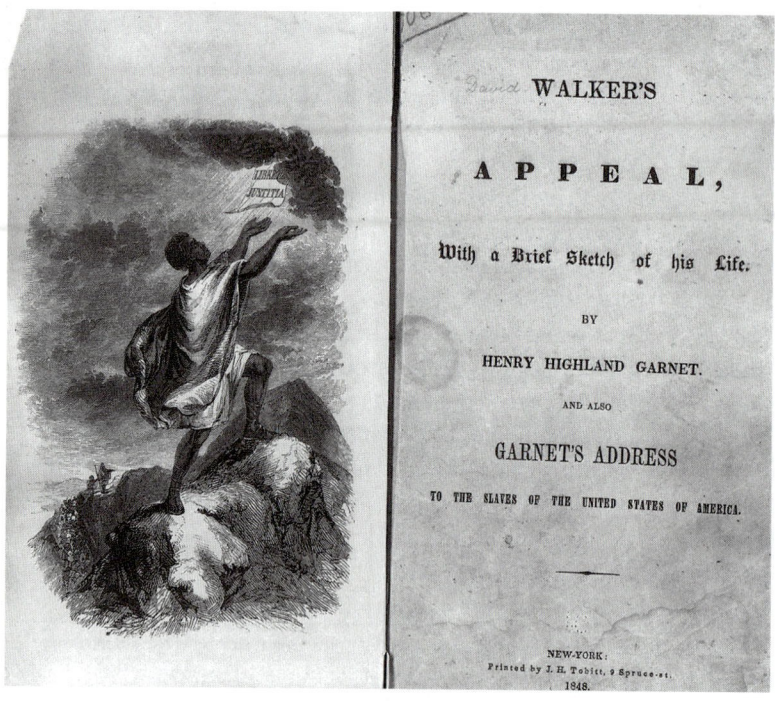

of slaveholders, justified slave rebellion, and in biblical language warned of a slave revolt if justice were delayed. "We must and shall be free," he told white Americans. "And woe, woe, will be it to you if we have to obtain our freedom by fighting. . . . Your DESTRUCTION is at hand, and will be speedily consummated unless you REPENT." Walker's pamphlet quickly went through three printings and, carried by black merchant seamen, reached free African Americans in the South.

In 1830, Walker and other African American activists called a national convention in Philadelphia. The delegates refused to endorse Walker's radical call for a slave revolt or the traditional program of uplift for free blacks. Instead, this new generation of activists demanded freedom and "race-equality" for all those of African descent. They urged free blacks to use every legal means, including petitions and other forms of political protest, to break "the shackles of slavery."

Nat Turner's Revolt As Walker threatened violence in Boston, Nat Turner, a slave in Southampton County, Virginia, staged a bloody revolt—a chronological coincidence that had far-reaching consequences. As a child, Turner had taught himself to read and had hoped for emancipation, but one new master forced him into the fields and another separated him from his wife. Becoming deeply spiritual, Turner had a religious vision in which "the Spirit" explained that "Christ had laid down the yoke he had borne for the sins of men, and that I should take it on

and fight against the Serpent, for the time was fast approaching when the first should be last and the last should be first." Taking an eclipse of the sun in August 1831 as an omen, Turner and a handful of relatives and friends rose in rebellion and killed at least 55 white men, women, and children. Turner hoped that hundreds of slaves would rally to his cause, but he mustered only 60 men. The white militia quickly dispersed his poorly armed force and took their revenge. One company of cavalry killed 40 blacks in two days and put the heads of 15 of them on poles to warn "all those who should undertake a similar plot." Turner died by hanging, still identifying his mission with that of his Savior. "Was not Christ crucified?" he asked.

Deeply shaken by Turner's Rebellion, the Virginia assembly debated a law providing for gradual emancipation and colonization abroad. When the bill failed by a vote of 73 to 58, the possibility that southern planters would voluntarily end slavery was gone forever. Instead, the southern states toughened their slave codes, limited black movement, and prohibited anyone from teaching slaves to read. They would meet Walker's radical *Appeal* with radical measures of their own.

Evangelical Abolitionism

Concurrently with Walker's and Turner's religiously suffused attacks, a cadre of northern evangelical Christians launched a moral crusade to abolish slavery immediately. If planters did not allow blacks their God-given status as

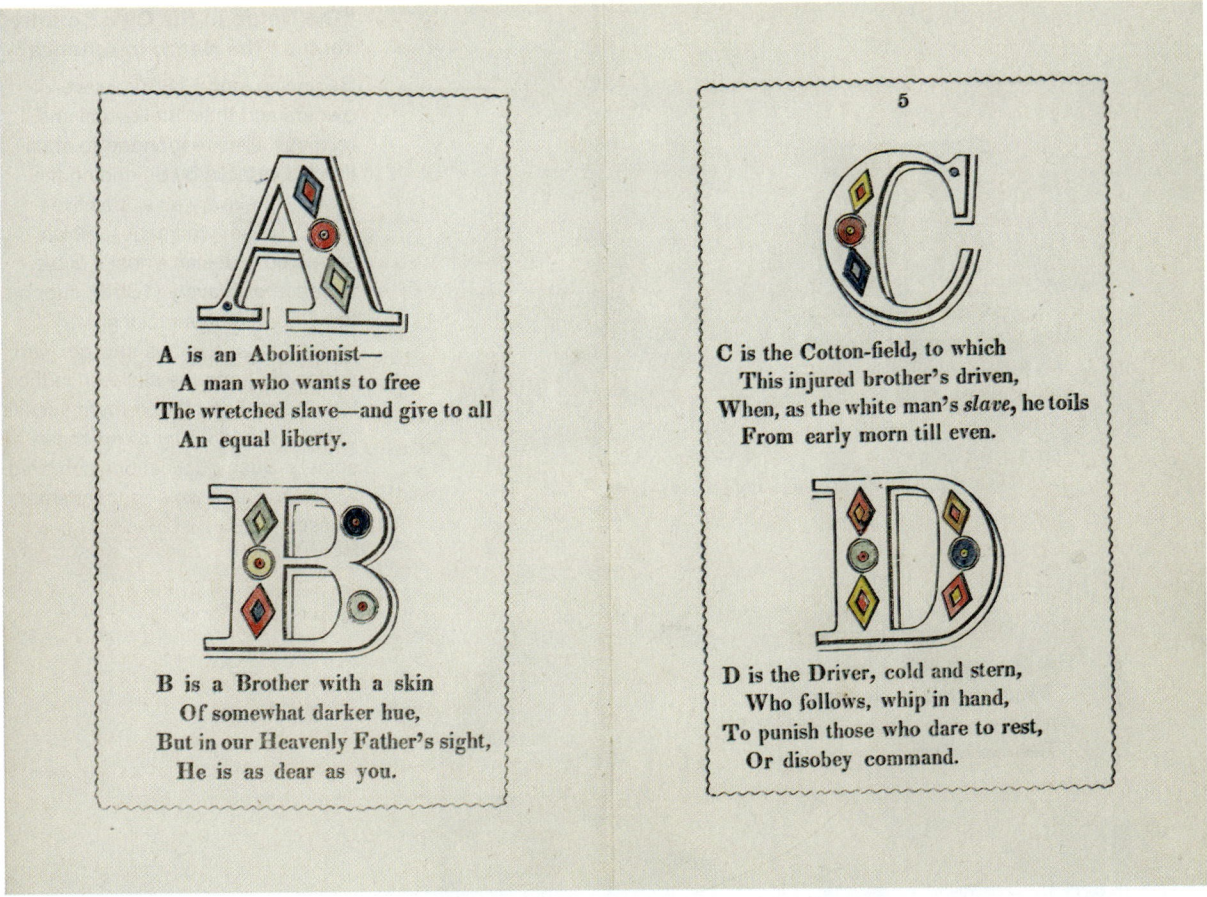

The Anti-Slavery Alphabet

Girding themselves for a long fight, abolitionists took care to convey their beliefs to the next generation. This primer, written by Quakers Hannah and Mary Townsend and published in Philadelphia in 1846, taught young children the alphabet by spreading the antislavery message. "A" was for "Abolitionist," and "B" was for a "Brother," an enslaved black that, though of a "darker hue," was considered by God "as dear as you." The Huntington Library, San Marino, California.

free moral agents, these radical Christians warned, they faced revolution in this world and damnation in the next.

William Lloyd Garrison, Theodore Weld, and Angelina and Sarah Grimké The most determined abolitionist was William Lloyd Garrison (1805–1879). A Massachusetts-born printer, Garrison had worked in Baltimore during the 1820s helping to publish the *Genius of Universal Emancipation*, an antislavery newspaper. In 1830, Garrison went to jail, convicted of libeling a New England merchant engaged in the domestic slave trade. The following year, Garrison moved to Boston, where he started his own weekly, *The Liberator*, and founded the New England Anti-Slavery Society.

From the outset, *The Liberator* demanded the immediate abolition without compensation to slavehold-

ers. "I will not retreat a single inch," Garrison declared, "AND I WILL BE HEARD." Garrison accused the American Colonization Society (see Chapter 8) of perpetuating slavery, and assailed the U.S. Constitution as "a covenant with death and an agreement with Hell" because it implicitly accepted racial bondage.

In 1833, Garrison, Theodore Weld, and sixty other abolitionists, black and white, established the American Anti-Slavery Society. The society received financial support from Arthur and Lewis Tappan, wealthy silk merchants in New York City. Women abolitionists established separate organizations, including the Philadelphia Female Anti-Slavery Society, founded by Lucretia Mott in 1833, and the Anti-Slavery Conventions of American Women, a network of local societies. The women raised money for *The Liberator* and carried the movement to the farm villages of the Midwest, where

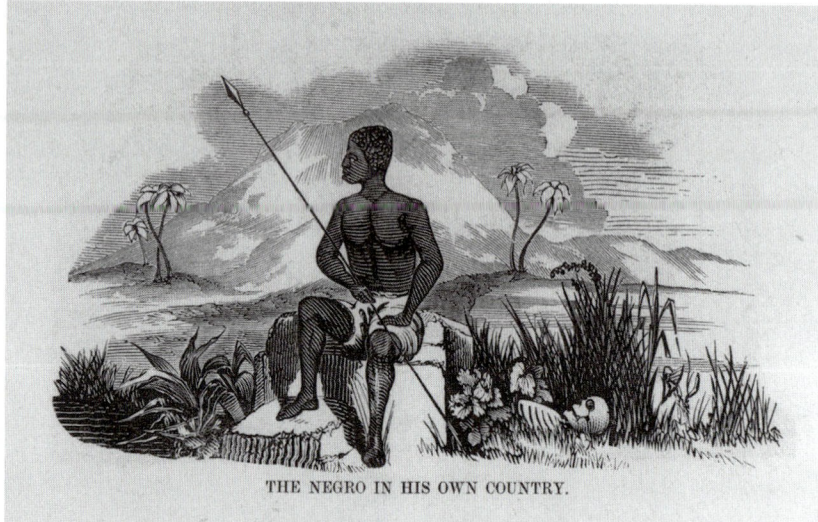

THE NEGRO IN HIS OWN COUNTRY.

THE NEGRO IN AMERICA.

"The Negro in His Own Country" versus "The Negro in America"

Beginning in the 1830s, slave owners and their intellectual and religious allies responded to abolitionists' attacks by defending the system of slavery as a "positive good." These two images, which appeared in Josiah Priest's *Bible Defence of Slavery* (1852), support the argument that racial slavery saved Africans from a savage, war-ridden life (note the skeleton in the top image) and offered them access to the civilized luxury of American society. Such publications achieved wide circulation among the planter classes.   Library of Congress. / Chicago History Museum.

they distributed abolitionist literature and collected thousands of signatures on antislavery petitions.

Abolitionist leaders developed a three-pronged plan of attack. They began by appealing to religious believers. In 1837, Weld published *The Bible Against Slavery*, which used passages from Christianity's holiest book to discredit slavery. Two years later, Weld teamed up with the Grimké sisters — Angelina, whom he married, and Sarah. The Grimkés had left their father's plantation in South Carolina, converted to Quakerism, and taken up the abolitionist cause in Philadelphia. In *American Slavery as It Is: Testimony of a Thousand Witnesses* (1839), Weld and the Grimkés addressed a simple question: "What is the actual condition of the slaves in the United States?" Using reports from southern newspapers and firsthand testimony, they presented a mass of incrimi-

nating evidence. Angelina Grimké told of a treadmill that South Carolina slave owners used for punishment:

> One poor girl, [who was] sent there to be flogged, and who was accordingly stripped naked and whipped, showed me the deep gashes on her back—I might have laid my whole finger in them—large pieces of flesh had actually been cut out by the torturing lash.

Filled with such images of pain and suffering, the book sold more than 100,000 copies in a single year.

The American Anti-Slavery Society   To spread their message, the abolitionists used the latest techniques of mass communication. Using new steam-powered presses, the American Anti-Slavery Society printed thousands of pieces of literature in 1834. In 1835, the society launched a "great postal campaign" to flood the nation, including the South, with a million pamphlets.

The abolitionists' second tactic was to aid fugitive slaves. They provided lodging and jobs for escaped blacks in free states and created the Underground Railroad, an informal network of whites and free blacks in Richmond, Charleston, and other southern towns that assisted fugitives from the Lower South (Map 11.3). In Baltimore, a free African American sailor loaned his identification papers to future abolitionist Frederick Douglass, who used them to escape to New York. Harriet Tubman and other runaways risked reenslavement or death by returning repeatedly to the South to help others escape. "I should fight for . . . liberty as long as my strength lasted," Tubman explained, "and when the time came for me to go, the Lord would let them take me." Thanks to the Railroad, about 1,000 African Americans reached freedom in the North each year.

There, they faced an uncertain future because most whites did not favor civic or social equality for African Americans. Voters in six northern and midwestern states adopted constitutional amendments that denied or limited the franchise for free blacks. "We want no masters," declared a New York artisan, "and least of all no negro masters." Moreover, the Fugitive Slave Law (1793) allowed owners and their hired slave catchers to seize suspected runaways and return them to bondage. To thwart these efforts, white abolitionists and free blacks in northern cities formed mobs that attacked slave catchers, released their captives, and often spirited them off to Canada, which refused to extradite fugitive slaves.

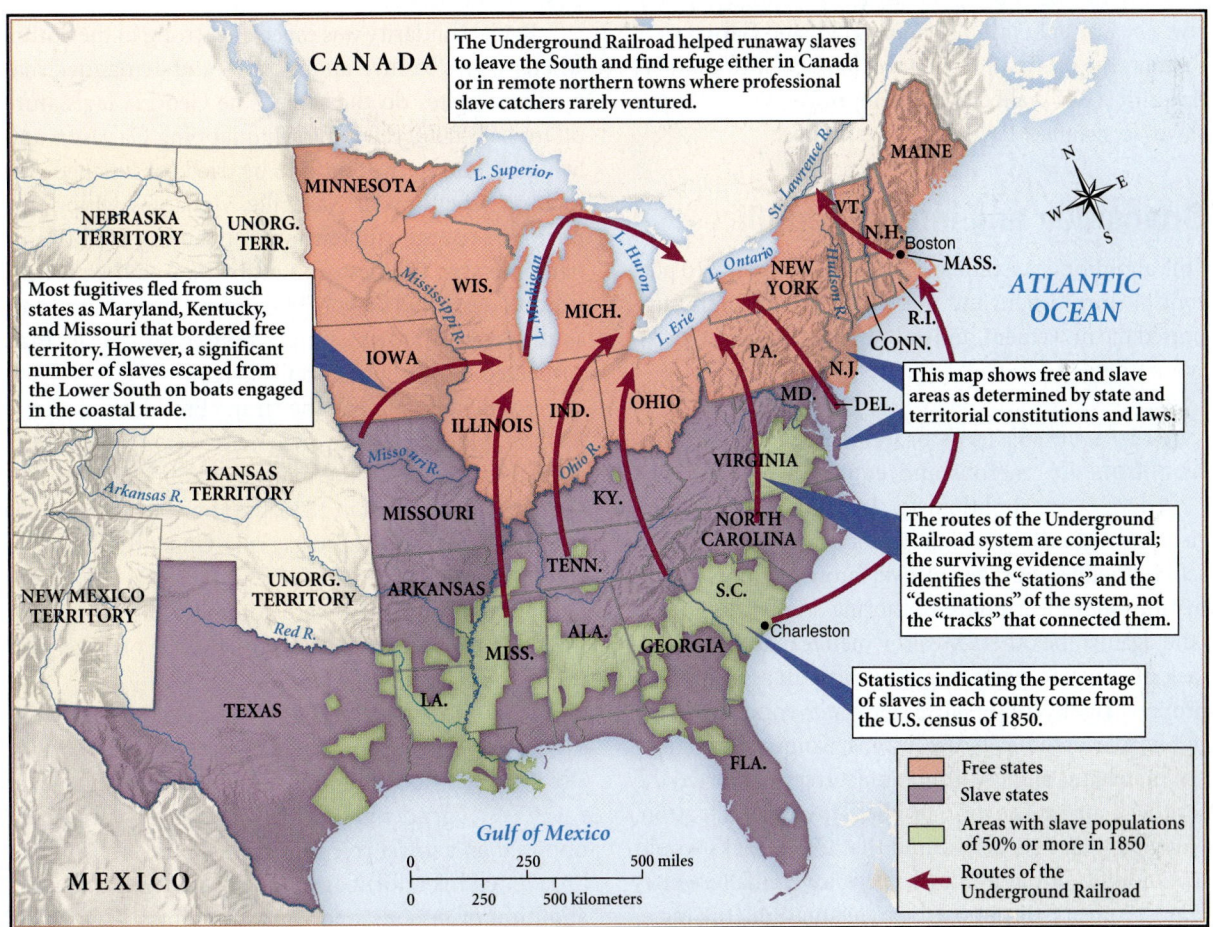

MAP 11.3

The Underground Railroad in the 1850s

Before 1840, most African Americans who fled slavery did so on their own or with the help of family and friends. Thereafter, they could count on support from members of the Underground Railroad. Provided with food, directions, and free black guides in the South, fugitive slaves crossed into free states. There, they received protection and shelter from sympathetic men and women who arranged for their transportation to Canada or to "safe" American cities and towns.

A political campaign was the final element of the abolitionists' program. In 1835, the American Anti-Slavery Society bombarded Congress with petitions demanding the abolition of slavery in the District of Columbia, an end to the interstate slave trade, and a ban on admission of new slave states. By 1838, petitions with nearly 500,000 signatures had arrived in Washington.

Such activities drew support from thousands of deeply religious farmers and small-town proprietors. The number of local abolitionist societies grew from 200 in 1835 to 2,000 by 1840, with nearly 200,000 members, including many transcendentalists. Emerson condemned Americans for supporting slavery, and Thoreau, seeing the Mexican War as an attempt to extend slavery, refused to pay taxes and submitted to arrest. In 1848, he published "Resistance to Civil Government," an essay urging individuals to follow a higher moral law. The black abolitionist Henry Highland Garnet went further; his *Address to the Slaves of the United States of America* (1841) called for "Liberty or Death" and urged slave "Resistance! Resistance! Resistance!"

Opposition and Internal Conflict

Still, abolitionists remained a minority. Perhaps 10 percent of northerners and midwesterners strongly supported the movement, and only another 20 percent were sympathetic to its goals.

Attacks on Abolitionism Slavery's proponents were more numerous and equally aggressive. The abolitionists' agitation, they warned, risked "embroiling neighborhoods and families—setting friend against friend, overthrowing churches and institutions of learning, embittering one portion of the land against the other." Wealthy men feared that the attack on slave property might become an assault on all property rights, conservative clergymen condemned the public roles assumed by abolitionist women, and northern merchants and textile manufacturers supported the southern planters who supplied them with cotton. Northern wage earners feared that freed blacks would work for lower wages and take their jobs. Finally, whites almost universally opposed "amalgamation," the racial mixing and intermarriage that Garrison seemed to support by holding meetings of blacks and whites of both sexes.

Racial fears and hatreds led to violent mob actions. White workers in northern towns laid waste to taverns and brothels where blacks and whites mixed, and van-

dalized "respectable" African American institutions such as churches, temperance halls, and orphanages. In 1833, a mob of 1,500 New Yorkers stormed a church in search of Garrison and Arthur Tappan. Another white mob swept through Philadelphia's African American neighborhoods, clubbing and stoning residents and destroying homes and churches. Fearing change, "gentlemen of property and standing"—lawyers, merchants, and bankers—broke up an abolitionist convention in Utica, New York, in 1835. Two years later, a mob in Alton, Illinois, shot and killed Elijah P. Lovejoy, editor of the abolitionist *Alton Observer*. By pressing for emancipation and equality, the abolitionists had revealed the extent of racial prejudice and the deep white resistance to accepting "respectable" blacks into the middle class. In fact, the abolitionist crusade had heightened race consciousness, as both whites and blacks identified across class lines with members of their own race.

Racial solidarity was especially strong in the South, where whites banned abolitionists and demanded that northern states do the same. The Georgia legislature offered a $5,000 reward for kidnapping Garrison and bringing him to the South to be tried (or lynched) for inciting rebellion. In Nashville, vigilantes whipped a northern college student for distributing abolitionist pamphlets; in Charleston, a mob attacked the post office and destroyed sacks of abolitionist mail. After 1835, southern postmasters simply refused to deliver mail suspected to be of abolitionist origin.

Politicians joined the fray. President Andrew Jackson, a longtime slave owner, asked Congress in 1835 to restrict the use of the mails by abolitionist groups. Congress refused, but in 1836, the House of Representatives adopted the so-called gag rule. Under this informal rule, which remained in force until 1844, antislavery petitions to the House were automatically tabled and not discussed, keeping the explosive issue of slavery off the congressional stage.

Internal Divisions Assailed by racists from the outside, abolitionists fought among themselves over gender issues. Many antislavery clergymen opposed an activist role for women, but Garrison had broadened his reform agenda to include pacifism, the abolition of prisons, and women's rights: "Our object is universal emancipation, to redeem women as well as men from a servile to an equal condition." In 1840, Garrison's demand that the American Anti-Slavery Society support women's rights helped split the abolitionist movement. Abby Kelley, Lucretia Mott, and Elizabeth Cady Stanton, among others, remained with Garrison

AN AFFECTING SCENE IN KENTUCKY.

The Complexities of Race

This cartoon takes aim at Richard Mentor Johnson of Kentucky, the distraught man being comforted by prominent abolitionists Frederick Douglass and William Lloyd Garrison. A congressman (1806–1819, 1829–1837) and senator (1819–1829), Johnson was the Democrats' vice presidential candidate in 1836. Although the party stood for the South and slavery—and condemned mixed-race unions—Johnson lived openly with an enslaved woman, Julia Chinn, whose portrait is held by his mixed-race daughters. Future Supreme Court justice John Catron noted with disgust that Johnson often tried "to force his daughters into society," and that they and their mother "rode in carriages, and claimed equality." Racial prejudice cost Johnson some votes, but he won a plurality in the electoral college and, on a party-line vote, Democrats in the Senate elected him Martin Van Buren's vice president.   Library of Congress.

in the American Anti-Slavery Society and assailed both the institutions that bound blacks and the customs that constrained free women.

Garrison's opponents founded a new organization, the American and Foreign Anti-Slavery Society, which focused its energies on ending slavery through political means. Its members mobilized their churches to oppose racial bondage and organized the Liberty Party, the first antislavery political party. In 1840, the new party nominated James G. Birney, a former Alabama slave owner, for president. Birney and the Liberty Party argued that the Constitution did not recognize slavery and, conse-

quently, that slaves automatically became free when they entered areas of federal authority, including the District of Columbia and the national territories. However, Birney won few votes, and the future of political abolitionism appeared dim.

Popular violence in the North, government-aided suppression in the South, and internal schisms stunned the abolitionist movement. By melding the energies and ideas of evangelical Protestants, moral reformers, and transcendentalists, it had raised the banner of antislavery to new heights, only to face a hostile and widespread backlash. "When we first unfurled the banner of *The Liberator*," Garrison admitted, "it did not occur to us that nearly every religious sect, and every political party would side with the oppressor."

- How did black social thought change over the first half of the nineteenth century? What role did black activists play in the abolitionist movement?

- How did the abolitionists' proposals and methods differ from those of earlier antislavery movements (see Chapter 8)? Why did those proposals and methods arouse such hostility in the South and in the North?

The Women's Rights Movement

The prominence of women among the abolitionists reflected a broad shift in American culture. By joining religious revivals and reform movements such as the temperance crusade and the abolitionist movement, women entered public life. Their activism caused many gender issues—sexual behavior, marriage, family authority—to become subjects of debate. The debate entered a new phase in 1848, when some reformers focused on women's rights and demanded complete equality with men.

Origins of the Women's Movement

"Don't be afraid, not afraid, fight Satan; stand up for Christ; don't be afraid." So spoke Mary Walker Ostram on her deathbed in 1859. Her religious convictions were as firm at the age of fifty-eight as they had been in 1816, when she helped to found the first Sunday school in Utica, New York. Married to a lawyer-politician and childless, Ostram had devoted her life to evangelical Presbyterianism and its program of benevolent social reform. In a eulogy after her death, minister Philemon Fowler celebrated Ostram as a "living fountain" of faith, an exemplar of "Women's Sphere of Influence" in the world.

Even as Reverend Fowler heaped praise on Ostram, he rejected a public presence for women. Like men of the Revolutionary era, Fowler thought women should limit their political role to that of "republican mother," instructing "their sons in the principles of liberty and government." Women inhabited a "separate sphere," he said, and had no place in "the markets of trade, the scenes of politics and popular agitation, the courts of justice and the halls of legislation." He concluded: "Home is her peculiar sphere and members of her family her peculiar care."

But Ostram and many other middle-class women had already rejected the notion of **separate spheres** by joining in the Second Great Awakening. Their spiritual activism bolstered their authority within the household and allowed them to influence many areas of family life, including the timing of pregnancies. Publications such as *Godey's Lady's Book*, a popular monthly periodical, and Catharine Beecher's *Treatise on Domestic Economy* (1841) taught women how to make their homes examples of middle-class efficiency and domesticity. Women in propertied farm families were equally vigilant. To protect their homes and husbands from alcoholic excess, they joined the Independent Order of Good Templars, a family-oriented temperance organization in which they were full members.

Moral Reform | Some religious women sought to assist other women. In 1834, a group of middle-class women in New York City founded the Female Moral Reform Society and elected Lydia Finney, the wife of revivalist Charles Grandison Finney, as its president. The society tried to curb prostitution in New York City and to protect single women from moral corruption. Rejecting the sexual double standard, its members demanded chastity for men as well as for women. By 1840, the Female Moral Reform Society had grown into a national association, with 555 chapters and 40,000 members throughout the North and Midwest. Employing only women as agents, the society provided moral guidance for young women who were living away from their families and working as factory operatives, seamstresses, or servants. Society members visited brothels, where they sang hymns, offered prayers, searched for runaway girls, and noted the names of clients. They also founded homes of refuge for prostitutes and won the passage of laws in Massachusetts and New York that made seduction a crime.

Improving Prisons, Creating Asylums, Expanding Education | Other women set out to improve public institutions, and Dorothea Dix (1801–1887) was their model. Dix's paternal grandparents were prominent Bostonians, but her father, a Methodist minister, ended up an impoverished alcoholic. Emotionally abused as a child, Dix grew into a compassionate young woman with a strong sense of moral purpose. She used money from her grandparents to set up charity schools to "rescue some of

A Well-Ordered Family

This lithograph, "The Good Husband," thousands of which were printed by the firm of Currier and Ives, ascribed the family's upper-middle-class lifestyle to the husband and father's "Temperance and Industry." Through such means, the bourgeois values of achievement and respectability achieved a wide circulation and defined the cultural goals embraced by many aspiring American families. Library of Congress Prints and Photographs Division.

America's miserable children from vice" and became a successful author. By 1832, she had published seven books, including *Conversations on Common Things* (1824), an enormously successful treatise on natural science and moral improvement.

In 1841, Dix took up a new cause. Discovering that insane women were jailed alongside male criminals, she persuaded Massachusetts lawmakers to enlarge the state hospital to accommodate indigent mental patients. Exhilarated by that success, Dix began a national movement to establish state asylums for those with mental illnesses. By 1854, she had traveled more than 30,000 miles and had visited eighteen state penitentiaries, three hundred county jails, and more than five hundred almshouses in addition to innumerable hospitals. Issuing dozens of reports, Dix prompted many states to expand their public hospitals and improve their prisons.

Both as reformers and teachers, other northern women transformed public education. From Maine to Wisconsin, women vigorously supported the movement led by Horace Mann to increase elementary schooling and improve the quality of instruction. As secretary of the Massachusetts Board of Education from 1837 to 1848, Mann lengthened the school year; established teaching standards in reading, writing, and arithmetic; and recruited well-educated women as teachers. The

intellectual leader of the new women educators was Catharine Beecher, who founded academies for young women in Hartford, Connecticut, and Cincinnati, Ohio. In widely read publications, Beecher argued that "energetic and benevolent women" were better qualified than men were to impart moral and intellectual instruction to the young. By the 1850s, most teachers were women, both because local school boards heeded Beecher's arguments and because they could hire women at lower salaries than men. As secular educators as well as moral reformers, women were now part of American public life.

Abolitionist Women

Women were central to the antislavery movement. One of the first abolitionists recruited by William Lloyd Garrison was Maria W. Stewart, an African American, who spoke to mixed audiences of men and women in Boston in the early 1830s. As abolitionism blossomed, scores of white women delivered lectures condemning slavery, and thousands more made home "visitations" to win converts to their cause (Map 11.4).

Women abolitionists were particularly aware of the special horrors of slavery for their sex. In her autobiography, *Incidents in the Life of a Slave Girl*, black abolitionist Harriet Jacobs described being forced to

Sojourner Truth

Few women had as interesting a life as Sojourner Truth. Born "Isabella" in Dutch-speaking rural New York about 1797, she labored as a slave until emancipated in 1827. Following a religious vision, Isabella moved to New York City, perfected her English, and worked for deeply religious — and ultimately fanatical — Christian merchants. In 1843, seeking further spiritual enlightenment, she took the name "Sojourner Truth" and left New York. After briefly joining the Millerites (who believed the world would end in 1844), Truth won fame as a forceful speaker for abolitionism and woman's rights. This illustration, showing Truth addressing a black audience, suggests her powerful personal presence. Picture Research Consultants & Archives.

have sexual relations with her white owner. "I cannot tell how much I suffered in the presence of these wrongs," she wrote. According to Jacobs and other enslaved women, such sexual assaults were compounded by the cruel treatment they suffered at the hands of their owners' wives, who were enraged by their husbands' promiscuity. In her best-selling novel, *Uncle Tom's Cabin* (1852), Harriet Beecher Stowe charged that one of the greatest moral failings of slavery was the degradation of slave women.

When men challenged their public activism, white abolitionist women grew increasingly conscious of the inferiority of their own social and legal status. In 1836, Congregationalist clergymen in New England assailed

Angelina and Sarah Grimké for addressing mixed male and female audiences. For justification, Sarah Grimké turned to the Bible: "The Lord Jesus defines the duties of his followers in his Sermon on the Mount . . . without any reference to sex or condition," she wrote. "Men and women are CREATED EQUAL! They are both moral and accountable beings and whatever is right for man to do is right for woman." In a pamphlet debate with Catharine Beecher (who believed that women should exercise authority primarily as wives, mothers, and schoolteachers), Angelina Grimké pushed the argument beyond religion by invoking Enlightenment principles to claim equal civic rights for women:

> It is a woman's right to have a voice in all the laws and regulations by which she is governed, whether in Church or State. . . . The present arrangements of society on these points are a violation of human rights, a rank usurpation of power, a violent seizure and confiscation of what is sacredly and inalienably hers.

By 1840, female abolitionists were asserting that traditional gender roles amounted to the "domestic slavery" of women. "How can we endure our present marriage relations," asked Elizabeth Cady Stanton, "[which give a woman] no charter of rights, no individuality of her own?" As another female reformer put it: "The radical difficulty . . . is that women are considered as *belonging* to men" (see Voices from Abroad, "Ernestine Rose: Woman's Rights in America," p. 358). Having acquired a public voice and political skills in the crusade for African American freedom, thousands of northern women now advocated greater rights for themselves.

The Program of Seneca Falls and Beyond

During the 1840s, women's rights activists devised a pragmatic program of reform. They did not challenge the institution of marriage or the conventional division of labor within the family. Instead, they tried to strengthen the legal rights of married women, especially to allow them to own property. This initiative won crucial support from affluent men, who feared bankruptcy in the volatile market economy and desired to put some family assets in their wives' names. Fathers also wanted to ensure that married daughters had property rights in order to protect them (and their inheritances) from financially irresponsible sons-in-law. These considerations prompted legislatures in three states — Mississippi, Maine, and Massachusetts — to enact married women's property laws between 1839 and 1845. Three years later, women activists in New York won a

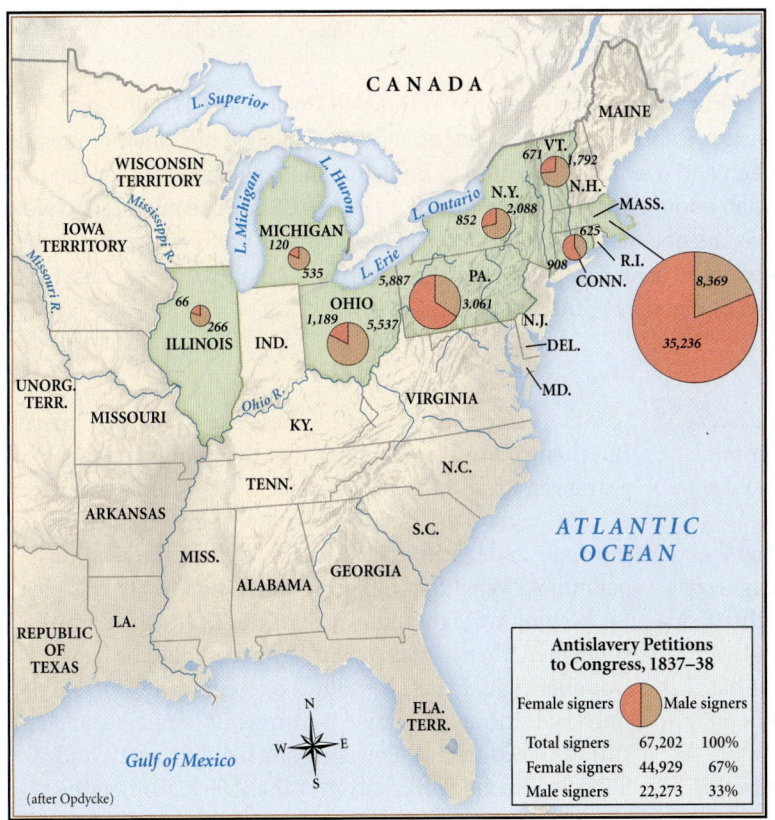

MAP 11.4

Women and Antislavery, 1837–1838

Beginning in the 1830s, abolitionists and antislavery advocates dispatched dozens of petitions to Congress demanding an end to slavery. Women accounted for two-thirds of the 67,000 signatures on the petitions submitted in 1837–1838, a fact that suggests not only the influence of women in the antislavery movement but also the extent of female organizations and social networks. Lawmakers, eager to avoid sectional conflict, devised an informal agreement (the "gag rule") to table the petitions without discussion.

more comprehensive statute that became the model for fourteen other states. The New York statute of 1848 gave women full legal control over the property they brought to a marriage.

That same year, Elizabeth Cady Stanton and Lucretia Mott organized a gathering of women's right activists in the small New York town of Seneca Falls. Seventy women and thirty men attended the meeting, which issued a rousing manifesto that extended the egalitarian republican ideology of the Declaration of Independence to women. "All men and women are created equal," the Declaration of Sentiments declared, "[yet] the history of mankind is a history of repeated injuries and usurpations on the part of man toward woman [and] the establishment of an absolute tyranny over her." To persuade Americans to right this long-standing wrong, the activists resolved to "employ agents, circulate tracts,

petition the State and National legislatures, and endeavor to enlist the pulpit and the press on our behalf." By staking out claims for equality for women in public life, the Seneca Falls reformers repudiated both the natural inferiority of women and the ideology of separate spheres.

Most men dismissed the Seneca Falls declaration as nonsense, and many women also repudiated the activists and their message. Writing in her diary, one small-town mother and housewife lashed out at the female reformer who "aping mannish manners . . . wears absurd and barbarous attire, who talks of her wrongs in harsh tone, who struts and strides, and thinks that she proves herself superior to the rest of her sex."

Still, the women's rights movement grew in strength and purpose. In 1850, delegates to the first national women's rights convention in Worcester, Massachusetts,

All the nations and people I had hitherto passed through resembled [...] own in their manners, customs and langu[...]

VOICES
FROM
ABROAD

Ernestine Rose
Woman's Rights in America

Ernestine Potowsky Rose was born in Russian Poland in 1810, the daughter of a wealthy rabbi. Facing an arranged marriage, she left her family at the age of seventeen and eventually migrated to England. There she associated with radical Christian reformers and married one of them. In 1836, Rose migrated to New York, where she emerged as a major force in the woman's rights movement. In this 1851 speech, she uses European events to inspire her American colleagues. Rose returned to England in 1869 and died there in 1892.

After having heard the letter read from our poor incarcerated sisters of France, well might we exclaim, Alas poor France! Where is thy glory? Where is the glory of the Revolution of 1848[?]

... But need we wonder that France, governed as she is by Russian and Austrian despotism, does not recognize the rights of humanity in the recognition of the Rights of Woman, when even here, in this far-famed land of freedom ... woman, the mockingly so-called "better half" of man, has yet to plead for her rights. ... In the laws of the land, she has no rights; in government she has no voice. And in spite of another principle recognized in this Republic, namely, that "taxation without representation is tyranny," she is taxed without being represented. Her property may be consumed by taxes to defray the expenses of that unholy, unrighteous custom called war, yet she has no power to give her vote against it. From the cradle to the grave she is subject to the power and control of man. Father, guardian, or husband, one conveys her like some piece of merchandise over to the other.

At marriage she loses her entire identity, and her being is said to have become merged in her husband. Has nature thus merged it? Has she ceased to exist and feel pleasure and pain? When she violates the laws of her being, does her husband pay the penalty? When she breaks the moral law does he suffer the punishment? When he satisfies his wants, is it enough to satisfy her nature? ...

But it will be said that the husband provides for the wife, or in other words, he feeds, clothes and shelters her! I wish I had the power to make every one before me fully realize the degradation contained in that idea. Yes! He keeps her, and so he does a favorite horse; by law they are both considered his property. ...

Not long ago, I saw an account of two offenders, brought before a Justice of New York. One was charged with stealing a pair of boots, for which offense he was sentenced to six months' imprisonment; the other crime was assault and battery upon his wife; he was let off with a reprimand by the judge! ... The judge showed us the comparative value which he set on these two kinds of property. But then you must remember that the boots were taken by a stranger, while the wife was insulted by her legal owner! ...

But say some, would you expose woman to the contact of rough, rude, drinking, swearing, fighting men at the ballot box? What a humiliating confession lies in this plea for keeping woman in the background! Is the brutality of some men, then, a reason why woman should be kept from her rights? ... Carry out the republican principle of universal suffrage, or strike it from your banners and substitute "Freedom and Power to one half of society, and Submission and Slavery to the other." Give women the elective franchise. Let married women have the same right to property that their husbands have. ...

There is no reason against woman's elevation, but ... prejudices. The main cause is a pernicious falsehood propagated against her being, namely that she is inferior by her nature. Inferior in what? What has man ever done that woman, under the same advantages could not do? In morals, bad as she is, she is generally considered his superior. In the intellectual sphere ... there is no need of naming the [Madame] de Staels, ... the [Mary] Wollstonecrafts, the [Lydia] Sigourneys, the [Fanny] Wrights, the [Harriet] Martineaus, ... and the [Margaret] Fullers ... to prove her mental powers, her patriotism, her self-sacrificing devotion to the cause of humanity.

Source: *History of Woman Suffrage*, ed. Elizabeth Cady Stanton, Susan B. Anthony, and Matilda Joslyn Gage (New York: Fowler & Wells, 1887), 1: 237–242.

ANALYZING THE EVIDENCE

- Rose makes at least four distinct arguments for woman's equality. What are they? Which one is the most convincing? The least powerful?

- How would most American men of this time have justified their privileged legal and social position over women?

Crusading Women Reformers

Elizabeth Cady Stanton (1815–1902) and Susan B. Anthony (1820–1906) were a dynamic duo of social reformers. Stanton, the well-educated daughter of a prominent New York judge, was an early abolitionist, and the mother of seven children. Anthony was raised as a Quaker and worked as a teacher and a temperance activist. After meeting in 1851, Stanton and Anthony became friends and co-organizers. From 1854 to 1860, they led a successful struggle to expand New York's Married Women's Property Law of 1848. During the Civil War, they set up the Women's Loyal National League, which helped win passage of the Thirteenth Amendment, ending slavery. In 1866, they joined the American Equal Rights Association, which demanded the vote for women and African Americans.
© Corbis/Bettmann.

hammered out a program of action. The women called on churches to revise notions of female inferiority in their theology. Addressing state legislatures, they proposed laws to guarantee the custody rights of mothers in the event of divorce or a husband's death and to allow married women to institute lawsuits and testify in court. Finally, they began a concerted campaign to win the vote for women. Delegates to the 1851 convention declared that suffrage was "the corner-stone of this enterprise, since we do not seek to protect woman, but rather to place her in a position to protect herself."

The activists' legislative campaign required talented organizers and lobbyists. The most prominent political operative was Susan B. Anthony (1820–1906), who came from a Quaker family and, as a young woman, had acquired political skills in the temperance and antislavery movements. Those experiences, Anthony explained, taught her "the great evil of woman's utter dependence on man." Joining the women's right movement, she worked closely with Elizabeth Cady Stanton. Anthony created an activist network of political "captains," all women, who relentlessly lobbied state legislatures. In 1860, her efforts secured a New York law granting women the right to control their own wages (which fathers or husbands had previously managed); to own property acquired by "trade, business, labors, or services"; and, if widowed, to assume sole guardianship of their children. Genuine individualism for women, the dream of transcendentalist Margaret Fuller, had advanced a tiny step closer to reality. In such small and much larger ways, the midcentury reform movements had altered the character of American culture.

- Why did religious women such as Mary Walker Ostram and the Grimké sisters become social reformers?

- How do you explain the appearance of the women's rights movement? What were the movement's goals, and why did they arouse intense opposition?

- What was the relationship between the abolitionist and women's rights movements? Why did women's issues suddenly become so prominent in American culture?

SUMMARY

In this chapter, we examined four major cultural movements of the mid-nineteenth century and analyzed the new popular culture in New York City. Our discussion of the transcendentalists highlighted the influence of Ralph Waldo Emerson on the great literary figures of the era; we also linked transcendentalism to the rise of individualism and the character of middle-class American culture.

Our analysis of communal movements probed the efforts of communalists to devise new rules for sexual behavior, gender relationships, and property ownership. We saw in this chapter that successful communal experiments—Mormonism, for example—began with a charismatic leader and a religious foundation and endured if they developed strong, authoritarian institutions.

We also traced the personal and ideological factors that linked the abolitionist and women's rights movements. Lucretia Mott, Elizabeth Cady Stanton, and the Grimké sisters began as antislavery advocates, but—denied access to lecture platforms by male abolitionists—they became staunch advocates of women's rights. This transition was a logical one: Both enslaved blacks and married women were "owned" by men, either as property or as their legal dependents.

Consequently, the efforts of women's rights activists to abolish the legal prerogatives of husbands were as controversial as the abolitionists' efforts to end the legal property rights of slave owners. As reformers took aim at such deeply rooted institutions and customs, many Americans feared that their activism would not perfect society but destroy it.

CHAPTER REVIEW QUESTIONS

- Did the era of reform increase or decrease the belief in, and practice of, liberty in American society?

- Explain the relationship between individualism and communalism as presented in the chapter. How were these two movements related to the social and economic changes in America in the decades after 1820?

- Explain the relationship between religion and reform in the decades from 1820 to 1860. Why did many religious people feel compelled to remake society? What was their motivation? How successful were they? Do you see any parallels with social movements today?

FOR FURTHER EXPLORATION

Ronald Walters, *American Reformers, 1815–1860* (1978), surveys the major reform movements, and Robert H. Abzug, *Cosmos Crumbling* (1994), shows their religious roots. David S. Reynolds, *Walt Whitman's America* (1995), assesses the poet and his society. Charles Capper, *Margaret Fuller* (1992), illuminates Fuller's intellectual milieu, as does Nathaniel Hawthorne's novel, *The Blithedale Romance* (1852). Peter S. Field, in *Ralph Waldo Emerson* (2003), sketches a convincing profile. A good site on transcendentalism is "The Web of American Transcendentalism," found at **www.vcu.edu/engweb/ transcendentalism**. For religious utopianism gone mad, read Paul E. Johnson and Sean Wilentz, *The Kingdom of Matthias* (1995).

James B. Stewart, *Holy Warriors* (1976), explores Garrison's abolitionist movement. Also see Mark Perry's study of the Grimké family, *Lift Up Thy Voice* (2001). Stephen B. Oates, *The Fires of Jubilee* (1975), explores the life Nat Turner; Turner's testimony is at **docsouth .unc.edu/neh/turner/menu.html**. *The Narrative of the Life of Frederick Douglass* (1845) is a literary masterpiece. Biographies of abolitionists include John Stauffer, *The Black Hearts of Men* (2001), and Catherine Clinton, *Harriet Tubman* (2004). For antiabolitionism, see Leonard L. Richards, *"Gentlemen of Property and Standing"* (1970), and David Roediger, *The Wages of Whiteness* (1995). Additional material is available from the *Africans in America* series Web site at **www.pbs .org/wgbh/aia/part4/**.

Anne M. Boylan, *The Origins of Women's Activism* (1992), and Mary Ryan, *Women in Public* (1990), explore women's civic activities. Also see Eleanor Flexner, *Century of Struggle* (1959), and the Seneca Falls Women's Rights National Historical Park Web site at **www.nps .gov/wori/index.htm**.

TEST YOUR KNOWLEDGE

To assess your command of the material in this chapter, see the Online Study Guide at **bedfordstmartins.com/henretta**.

For Web sites, images, and documents related to topics and places in this chapter, visit **bedfordstmartins.com/makehistory**.

TIMELINE

1826	Lyceum movement begins
1829	David Walker's *Appeal . . . to the Colored Citizens of the World*
1830	Joseph Smith publishes *The Book of Mormon*
1830s	Emergence of minstrelsy shows Nativist citizens question immigration policy
1831	William Lloyd Garrison founds *The Liberator* Nat Turner's uprising in Virginia
1832	Ralph Waldo Emerson turns to transcendentalism
1833	Garrison organizes American Anti-Slavery Society
1834	New York activists create Female Moral Reform Society
1835	Abolitionists launch mail campaign; antiabolitionists riot against them
1836	House of Representatives adopts gag rule Grimké sisters defend public roles for women
1840	Liberty Party runs James G. Birney for president
1840s	Fourierist communities arise in Midwest Commercialized sex flourishes in New York City
1841	Transcendentalists found Brook Farm Dorothea Dix promotes hospitals for mentally ill
1844	Margaret Fuller publishes *Woman in the Nineteenth Century*
1845	Henry David Thoreau goes to Walden Pond
1846	Brigham Young leads Mormons to Salt Lake
1848	John Humphrey Noyes founds Oneida Seneca Falls convention proposes women's equality
1850	Nathaniel Hawthorne's *The Scarlet Letter*
1851	Herman Melville publishes *Moby Dick*
1852	Harriet Beecher Stowe writes *Uncle Tom's Cabin*
1855	Walt Whitman's *Leaves of Grass*
1858	"Mormon War" over polygamy

CHAPTER 12

The South Expands: Slavery and Society, 1800–1860

Life in South Carolina had been good to James Lide. A slave-owning planter who lived near the Pee Dee River, Lide and his wife had raised twelve children. Living in relative comfort, Lide had long resisted the "Alabama Fever" that had prompted thousands of Carolina families to move west. Finally, at age sixty-five, probably seeking land for his many offspring, he moved his slaves and family—including six children and six grandchildren—to a plantation near Montgomery, Alabama. There, the family lived initially in a squalid double log cabin with airholes but no windows. Even as their housing conditions improved, the Lides' family life remained unsettled. "Pa is quite in the notion of moving somewhere," his daughter Maria reported a few years later. Although James Lide lived out his years in Alabama, many of his children did not. In 1854, at the age of fifty-eight, Eli Lide moved to Texas, telling his father, "Something within me whispers onward and onward."

The story of the Lide family was the story of American society. Between 1800 and 1860, white planters from the South as well as yeomen farmers from the North were moving west. The South's "master class was one of the most mobile in history," notes historian James Oakes. The planters' goal was to make the West into a "slave society" similar to those their fathers and grandfathers had built in Virginia and South Carolina. Using the muscles and sweat of a million enslaved African Americans, the planters brought millions of acres into cultivation. By 1840, the South was at the cutting edge of the American Market Revolution. It annually produced and exported 1.5 million bales of raw cotton—over two-thirds of the world's supply—and its economy was larger and richer than that of most nations. "Cotton is King," boasted the *Southern Cultivator*, the leading Georgia farm journal, "and wields an astonishing influence over the world's commerce."

No matter how rich they were, few cotton planters in the southwestern states of Alabama, Mississippi, and Texas lived in elegant houses or led cultured lives. Abandoning the aristocratic gentility of Chesapeake and the Carolinas, these agricultural capitalists wanted to make money. "To sell cotton in order to buy negroes—to make more cotton to buy more negroes, 'ad infinitum,' is the aim ... of the thorough-going cotton planter," a New England traveler reported from Mississippi in 1835. "His whole soul is wrapped up in

Generations in Slavery

In 1862, traveling photographer Timothy O'Sullivan took this picture at the plantation of J. J. Smith in Beaufort, South Carolina. It shows four—perhaps five—generations of a slave family, most of whom were born on the plantation. As you read this chapter, consider whether the experience of this African American family was the exception or the rule. Who might be missing from this family photograph? For example, what happened to the brothers and sisters of the man standing in the back? Library of Congress.

the pursuit." A generation later, Frederick Law Olmsted found that the plantations in Mississippi were large but their owners mostly had "but small and mean residences." Plantation women were especially aware of the loss of genteel surroundings and polite society. Raised in North Carolina, where she was "blest with every comfort, & even luxury," a "discontented" Mary Drake found Mississippi and Alabama "a dreary waste."

Hundreds of thousands of enslaved African Americans in the Lower Mississippi River Valley knew what "dreary waste" really meant: unremitting toil, unrelieved poverty, and profound sadness. Sold south from Maryland, where his family had lived for generations, Charles Ball's father became "gloomy and morose"; when threatened again with sale, he ran off and disappeared. With good reason: On new cotton plantations, slaves labored from "sunup to sundown" and from one end of the year to the other. As one field hand put it, there was "no time off [between] de change of de seasons. . . . Dey was allus clearin' mo' lan' or sump'." Day by day, the forced labor of unwilling black migrants produced the wealth of the Cotton South. Always wanting more, southern planters and politicians plotted to extend their plantation economy across the continent.

Creating the Cotton South

American slavery took root on the tobacco plantations of the Chesapeake and in the rice fields of the Carolina Low Country. It grew to maturity on the sugar fields of Louisiana, the hemp farms of Kentucky and Tennessee, and especially in the cotton states bordering the Gulf of Mexico: Alabama, Mississippi, and Texas (Figure 12.1). This massive transplantation of slavery led planters to believe that it could keep expanding. "We want land, and have a right to it," declared a Georgia planter on the eve of the Civil War.

The Domestic Slave Trade

In 1817, when the American Colonization Society began to return a few freed blacks to Africa (see Chapter 8), the southern plantation system was expanding rapidly. In 1790, its western boundary ran through the middle of Georgia; by 1830, it stretched through western Louisiana; by 1860, the slave frontier extended far into Texas (Map 12.1). That advance of 900 miles more than doubled the geographical area cultivated by slave labor and raised the number of slave states from eight in 1800 to fifteen by 1850. The federal government assisted this expansion by buying Louisiana from the French in 1803, removing Native Americans from the southeastern states in the 1830s, and annexing Texas and Mexican lands in the 1840s.

To cultivate this vast area, white planters looked for enslaved laborers first in Africa and then in the Chesapeake region. Between 1776 and 1809, when Congress outlawed the Atlantic slave trade, planters imported about 115,000 Africans. "The Planter will . . . sacrifice every thing to attain Negroes," declared one slave trader. Despite the influx, the demand for labor far exceeded the supply. Consequently, planters imported new African workers illegally, through the Spanish colony of Florida until 1819 and then through the Mexican province of Texas. Yet these Africans—about 50,000 between 1810 and 1869—did not meet the demand.

The Upper South Exports Slaves So planters looked to the Chesapeake region, home in 1800 to nearly half of the nation's black population. There, the African American population was growing rapidly from natural increase—an average of 27 percent a decade—and creating a surplus of enslaved laborers. By 1815, so-called Georgia traders had created a large and growing domestic trade in slaves. Between 1818 and 1829, planters in just one Maryland county—Frederick—sold at least 952 slaves to traders or cotton planters. Seventy-five thousand slaves left Virginia during the 1810s and again during the 1820s. The number of unwilling Virginia migrants jumped to nearly 120,000 during the 1830s and then averaged 85,000 during the 1840s and 1850s. In Virginia alone, then, 440,000 African Americans were ripped from com-

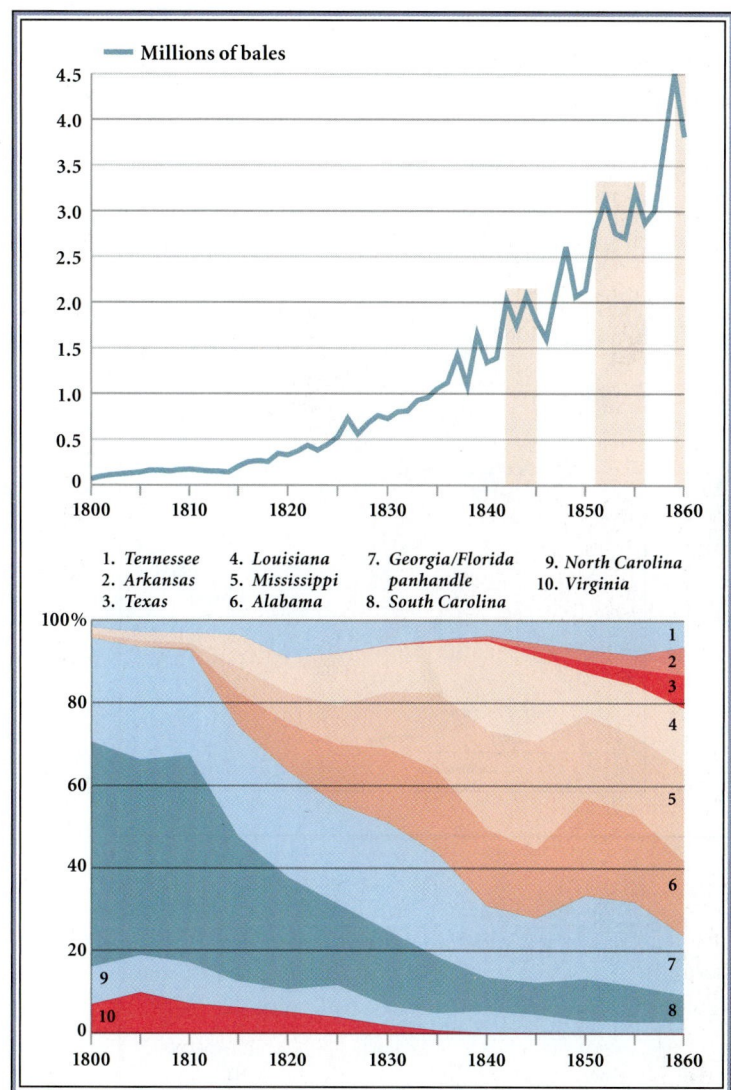

FIGURE 12.1

Cotton Production and Producers, 1800–1860

Until the mid-1830s, most cotton was grown in Georgia and South Carolina (7 and 8 in the lower graph) and production increased at a steady pace. Then came a series of dramatic changes. By the early 1840s, those southeastern states grew only one-third of the cotton because planters had moved hundreds of thousands of slaves to the Mississippi Valley (Louisiana, Mississippi, and Alabama— 4, 5, and 6 in the lower graph). Simultaneously, production burst upward in a series of leaps, reaching 2 million bales a year by the mid-1840s, 3 million by the mid-1850s, and 4 million on the eve of the Civil War.   Source: *Historical Statistics of the United States* (Washington, D.C.: U.S. Government Printing Office, 1957), Sec. K 534; lower graph adapted from Alan L. Olmstead and Paul W. Rhode, "'Wait a Cotton Picking Minute': A New View of Slave Productivity" (unpublished paper, 2005), Fig. 5.

munities where their families had lived for three or four generations. By 1860, the "mania for buying negroes" had resulted in a massive forced migration from the Upper South of more than 1 million slaves (Figure 12.2).

This movement of African Americans took two forms: transfer and sale. Looking for new opportunities, thousands of Chesapeake and Carolina planters—men like James Lide—sold their plantations and moved to the Southwest with their slaves. Many other planters in the Old South gave slaves to sons and daughters who were moving west. This transfer of entire or partial plantations accounted for about 40 percent of the African American migrants. The rest—about 60 percent of the one million migrants—were "sold south" through traders. By 1860 a majority of African Americans lived and worked in the Deep South, the lands that stretched from Georgia to Texas.

Just as the Atlantic slave trade was a major eighteenth-century commercial enterprise that enriched English merchants, so the domestic slave trade became a great business between 1800 and 1860. The domestic trade involved both a coastal system through Atlantic seaports and inland routes using rivers and roads. The coastal system sent thousands of slaves to the sugar plantations in Louisiana, the former French territory which entered the Union in 1812. Slave traders scoured the countryside near the port cities of the Chesapeake and the Carolinas—Baltimore, Alexandria, Richmond, Charleston—searching, as one of them put it, for "likely young men such as I think would suit the New Orleans market." Each year, hundreds of muscular young slaves passed through the auction houses of the port cities bound for the massive trade mart in New Orleans. Because this traffic in laborers was highly

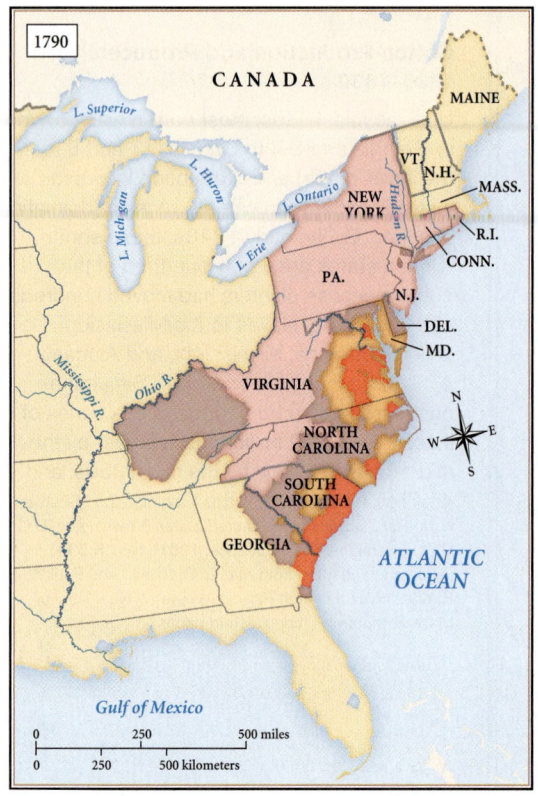

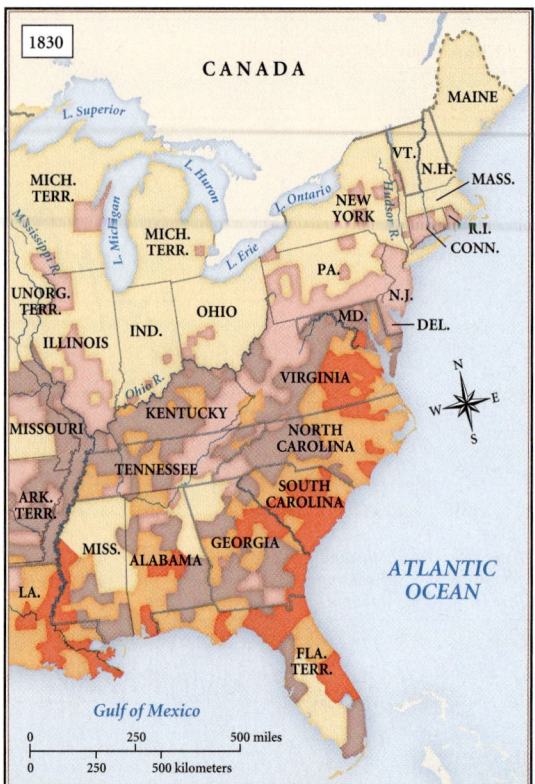

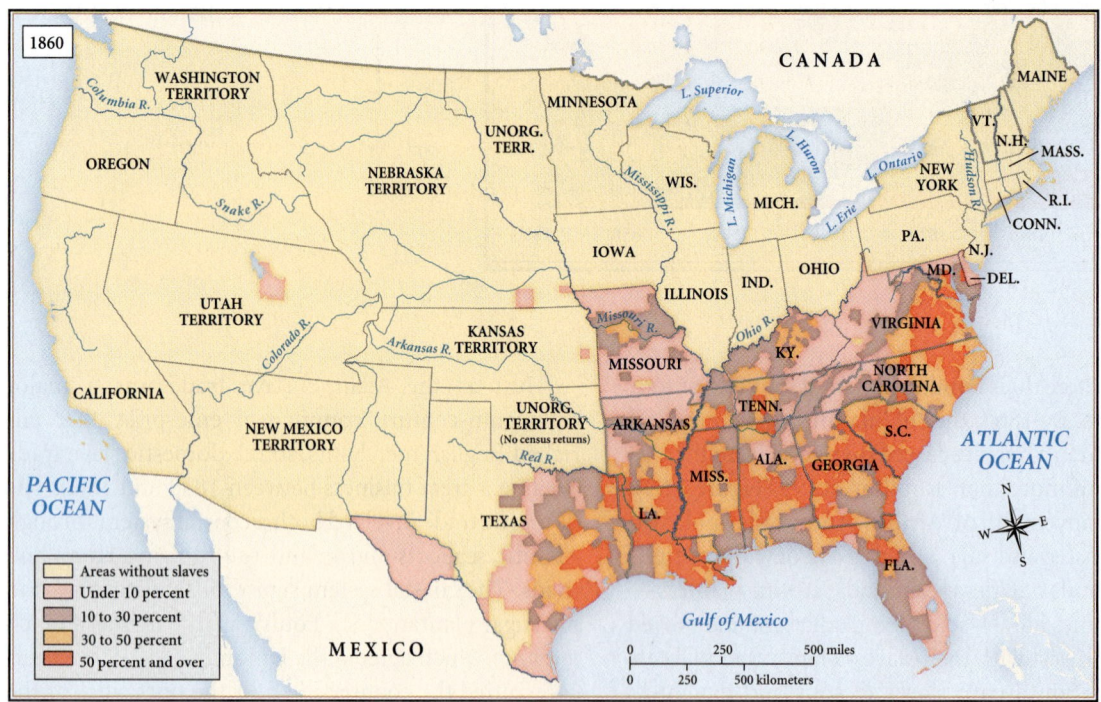

MAP 12.1

Distribution of the Slave Population in 1790, 1830, and 1860

The cotton boom shifted many African Americans to the Old Southwest. In 1790, most slaves lived and worked on Chesapeake tobacco and Carolina rice and indigo plantations. By 1830, hundreds of thousands of enslaved blacks were laboring on the cotton and sugar lands of the Lower Mississippi Valley and on cotton plantations in Georgia and Florida. Three decades later, the centers of slavery lay along the Mississippi River and in an arc of fertile cotton land—the "black belt"—sweeping from Mississippi through Georgia.

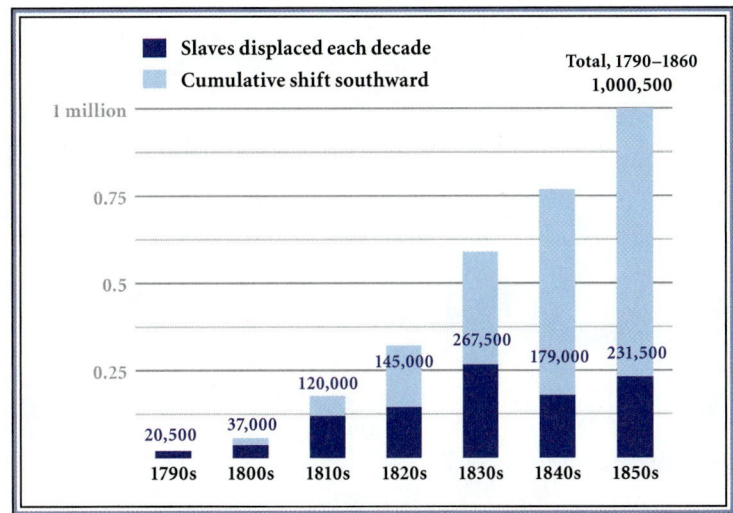

Slaves displaced each decade
Cumulative shift southward

Total, 1790–1860
1,000,500

1 million

0.75

0.5

0.25

| 1790s | 1800s | 1810s | 1820s | 1830s | 1840s | 1850s |
| 20,500 | 37,000 | 120,000 | 145,000 | 267,500 | 179,000 | 231,500 |

FIGURE 12.2

Forced Migration of Slaves from the Upper South to the Lower South, 1790–1860

The cotton boom that began in the 1810s set in motion a vast redistribution of the African American population. Between 1790 and 1860, white planters moved or sold more than a million slaves from the Upper to the Lower South, a process that broke up families and long-established black communities. Source: Based on data in Robert William Fogel and Stanley L. Engerman, *Time on the Cross* (Boston: Little, Brown, 1974), and Michael Tadman, *Speculators and Slaves: Masters, Traders, and Slaves in the Old South* (Madison: University of Wisconsin Press, 1996).

visible, it elicited widespread condemnation by northern abolitionists.

Sugar was a "killer" crop, and Louisiana (like the eighteenth-century West Indies) soon had a well-deserved reputation among African Americans "as a place of slaughter." Hundreds died each year from disease, overwork, and brutal treatment. Maryland farmer John Anthony Munnikhuysen refused to consent to his daughter Priscilla's marriage to a Louisiana sugar planter, remarking: "Mit has never been used to see negroes flayed alive and it would kill her."

The inland system that sent slaves to the Cotton South was less visible than the coastal trade but much more extensive. It also relied on professional slave traders, who went from one rural village to another buying "young and likely Negroes." The traders then marched

their purchases in coffles — columns of slaves bound to one another — to Alabama, Mississippi, and Missouri in the 1830s and to Arkansas and Texas in the 1850s. One slave described the arduous journey: "Dem Speckulators would put the chilluns in a wagon usually pulled by oxens and de older folks was chained or tied together sos dey could not run off." Once a coffle reached its destination, the trader would sell slaves "at every village in the county."

Chesapeake and Carolina planters provided the human cargo. Some planters sold slaves when poor management or their "own extravagances" threw them into debt. "Trouble gathers thicker and thicker around me," Thomas B. Chaplin of South Carolina lamented in his diary. "I will be compelled to send about ten prime Negroes to Town on next Monday, to be sold." Many

The Internal Slave Trade

Mounted whites escort a convoy of slaves from Virginia to Tennessee in Lewis Miller's *Slave Trader, Sold to Tennessee* (1853). For white planters, the interstate trade in slaves was lucrative; it pumped money into the declining Chesapeake economy and provided young workers for the expanding plantations of the cotton belt. For blacks, it was a traumatic journey, a new Middle Passage that broke up their families and communities. "Arise, Arise and weep no more, dry up your tears, we shall part no more," the slaves sing hopefully as they journey to new lives in Tennessee. Abby Aldrich Rockefeller Folk Art Museum, Williamsburg, VA.

The Business of Slavery

In the 1850s, Virginia slaves were still being "sold south." This painting, *Slave Auction in Richmond, Virginia* (1852), captures the pensive and apprehensive emotions of the women and the discontent of the man, none of whom can control their fate. Whites — plantation overseer, slave trader, top-hatted aristocratic planter — lurk in the background, where they are completing the commercial transaction. The illustration on page 369, a public notice for a slave auction to be held in Iberville, Louisiana, advertises "24 Head of Slaves" as if they were cattle — a striking commentary on the business of slavery.   The Granger Collection, New York/Library of Congress.

more planters doubled as slave traders, earning substantial profits by traveling south to sell some of their slaves and those of their neighbors. Prices marched in step with those for cotton; during the boom years of the 1850s, said one planter, a slave "will fetch $1000, cash, quick, this year." Exploiting this demand, Thomas Weatherly of South Carolina drove his surplus slaves to Hayneville, Alabama, where he "sold ten negroes." Colonel E. S. Irvine, a member of the South Carolina legislature and "a highly respected gentleman" in white circles, likewise traveled frequently "to the west to sell a drove of Negroes."

The domestic slave trade was crucial to the prosperity of the South. It provided workers to fell the forests and plant cotton in the Gulf states and bolstered the economy of the Upper South. By selling surplus workers, tobacco, rice, and grain, planters in the Chesapeake and Carolinas added about 20 percent to their income. As a Maryland newspaper remarked in 1858, "[The domestic slave trade serves as] an almost universal resource to raise money. A prime able-bodied slave is worth three times as much to the cotton or sugar planter as to the Maryland agriculturalist."

The Impact on Blacks   For African American families, the domestic slave trade was a personal disaster that accentuated their status — and vulnerability — as property. On this issue, blacks and whites agreed. W. C. Pennington, a former slave, reflected, "The being of slavery, its soul and its body, lives and moves in the chattel principle, the property principle, the bill of sale principle." A South Carolina master put it more crudely: "[The slave's earnings] belong to *me* because I bought him." Indeed, slave property

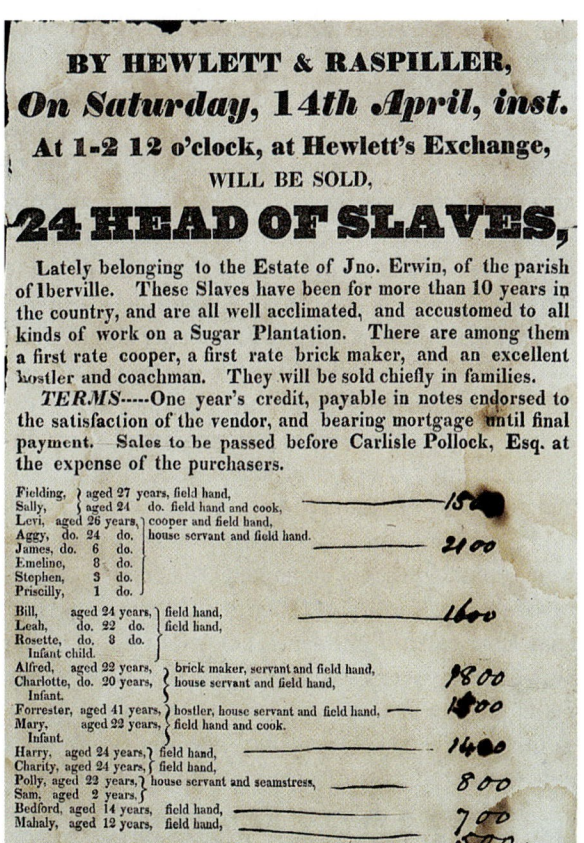

BY HEWLETT & RASPILLER,

On Saturday, 14th April, inst.

At 1-2 12 o'clock, at Hewlett's Exchange,

WILL BE SOLD,

24 HEAD OF SLAVES,

Lately belonging to the Estate of Jno. Erwin, of the parish of Iberville. These Slaves have been for more than 10 years in the country, and are all well acclimated, and accustomed to all kinds of work on a Sugar Plantation. There are among them a first rate cooper, a first rate brick maker, and an excellent hostler and coachman. They will be sold chiefly in families.

TERMS-----One year's credit, payable in notes endorsed to the satisfaction of the vendor, and bearing mortgage until final payment. Sales to be passed before Carlisle Pollock, Esq. at the expense of the purchasers.

Fielding,	aged 27 years, field hand,	15
Sally,	aged 24 do. field hand and cook,	
Levi, aged 26 years, cooper and field hand,		
Aggy, do. 24 do. house servant and field hand.		21 00
James, do. 6 do.		
Emeline, 8 do.		
Stephen, 3 do.		
Priscilly, 1 do.		
Bill, aged 24 years, field hand,		16 00
Leah, do. 22 do. field hand,		
Rosette, do. 3 do.		
Infant child.		
Alfred, aged 22 years, brick maker, servant and field hand,		18 00
Charlotte, do. 20 years, house servant and field hand,		
Infant.		
Forrester, aged 41 years, hostler, house servant and field hand,		12 00
Mary, aged 22 years, field hand and cook.		
Infant.		
Harry, aged 24 years, field hand,		14 00
Charity, aged 24 years, field hand,		
Polly, aged 22 years, house servant and seamstress,		8 00
Sam, aged 2 years.		
Bedford, aged 14 years, field hand,		7 00
Mahaly, aged 12 years, field hand,		5 00 .
		11 00

formed the foundation of the entire southern economic system. As Whig politician Henry Clay observed, the "immense amount of capital which is invested in slave property . . . is owned by widows and orphans, by the aged and infirm, as well as the sound and vigorous. It is the subject of mortgages, deeds of trust, and family settlements." The Whig politician concluded: "I know that there is a visionary dogma, which holds that negro slaves cannot be the subject of property. I shall not dwell long on this speculative abstraction. That is property which the law declares to be property."

As a slave owner, Clay knew that property rights were a key to slave discipline. As one master put it, "I govern them . . . without the whip by stating . . . that I should sell them if they do not conduct themselves as I wish." The threat was effective. "The Negroes here dread nothing on earth so much as this," an observer in Maryland noted. "They regard the south with perfect horror, and to be sent there is considered as the worst punishment that could be inflicted on them."

But thousands of slaves suffered that fate, which destroyed about one in every four slave marriages. "I am Sold to a man by the name of Peterson a trader," lamented a Georgia slave. "My Dear wife for you and my

Children my pen cannot Express the griffe I feel to be parted from you all." The trade encompassed children and youth as well as adults; in northern Maryland, boys and girls were sold away at an average age of 17 years. "Dey sole my sister Kate," Anna Harris remembered decades later, "and I ain't seed or heard of her since." The trade also separated almost a third of all slave children under the age of fourteen from one or both of their parents. Sarah Grant remembered, "Mamma used to cry when she had to go back to work because she was always scared some of us kids would be sold while she was away." Well might she worry, for slave traders worked quietly and quickly. "One night I lay down on de straw mattress wid my mammy," Vinny Baker recalled, "an' de nex' mo'nin I woke up an' she wuz gone." When their owner sold seven-year-old Laura Clark and ten other children from their plantation in North Carolina, Clark sensed that she would see her mother "no mo' in dis life."

Despite these sales, 75 percent of slave marriages remained unbroken, and the majority of children lived with one or both parents until puberty. Consequently, the sense of family among African Americans remained strong. Sold from Virginia to Texas in 1843, Hawkins Wilson carried with him a detailed mental picture of his family. Twenty-five years later and now a freedman, Wilson set out to find his "dearest relatives" in Virginia. "My sister belonged to Peter Coleman in Caroline County and her name was Jane. . . . She had three children, Robert, Charles and Julia, when I left — Sister Martha belonged to Dr. Jefferson. . . . Sister Matilda belonged to Mrs. Botts."

During the decades between sale and freedom, Hawkins Wilson and thousands of other African American migrants constructed new lives for themselves in the Mississippi River Valley. Undoubtedly, many of them did so with a sense of foreboding: From personal experience, they knew that their lives could be shaken to the core at any moment. Like Charles Ball, some "longed to die, and escape from the bonds of my tormentors." Even moments of joy were shadowed by the darkness of slavery. Knowing that sales often ended slave marriages, a white minister blessed one couple "for so long as God keeps them together."

Many white planters "saw" only the African American marriages that endured and ignored those they had broken. Accordingly, many slave owners considered themselves benevolent masters, committed to the welfare of "my family, black and white." Some masters gave substance to this paternalist ideal by treating with kindness various "loyal and worthy" slaves — the drivers, the mammy who raised their children, and trusted house servants. By safeguarding the families of these slaves from sale, planters convinced themselves that they "sold south" only "coarse" troublemakers and uncivilized slaves who had "little sense of family." Other owners were more honest about the human cost of their pursuit of wealth. "Tomorrow the negroes are to get off [to Kentucky]," a slave-owning woman in Virginia wrote to a friend, "and I expect there will be great crying and moaning, with children Leaving there mothers, mothers there children, and women there husbands."

Whether or not they acknowledged the slaves' pain, few southern whites questioned the morality of the domestic slave trade. Responding to criticism by abolitionists, the city council of Charleston, South Carolina, declared that slavery was completely consistent "with moral principle and with the highest order of civilization," as was "the removal of slaves from place to place, and their transfer from master to master, by gift, purchase, or otherwise."

The Dual Cultures of the Planter Elite

A small elite of extraordinarily wealthy planter families stood at the top of southern society. These families — about three thousand in number — each owned more than one hundred slaves and huge tracts of the most fertile lands. Their ranks included many of the richest families in the United States. On the eve of the Civil War, southern planters accounted for nearly two-thirds of all American men with wealth of $100,000 or more.

The Traditional Southern Gentry | The westward movement split the plantation elite into two distinct groups: the traditional aristocrats of the Old South, and the upstart capitalist-inclined planters of the cotton states. The Old South gentry, having gained their wealth from tobacco and rice, dominated the Tidewater region of the Chesapeake and the low country of South Carolina and Georgia. During the eighteenth century, these planters built impressive mansions and adopted the manners and values of the English landed gentry (see Chapter 3). Their aristocratic culture survived the revolution of 1776 and soon took on a republican character. Classical republican theory had its roots in the slave-owning societies of Greece and Rome, and had long identified political tyranny (not slavery) as the major threat to liberty. That variety of republican ideology appealed to southern aristocrats, who feared government interference with their property in slaves. To prevent despotic rule by democratic demagogues or radical legislatures, planters demanded that authority rest in the hands of incorruptible men of "virtue."

Affluent planters cast themselves as the embodiment of this ideal — a republican aristocracy (see Chapter 8). "The planters here are essentially what the nobility are in other countries," declared James Henry Hammond of South Carolina. "They stand at the head of society & politics . . . [and form] an aristocracy of talents, of virtue, of generosity and courage." Wealthy planters criticized the increasingly democratic polity and middle-class society that was developing in the Northeast and Midwest. "Inequality is the fundamental law of the universe," declared one aristocratic-minded planter. Others condemned professional politicians as "a set of demagogues" and questioned the legitimacy of universal suffrage. "Times are sadly different now to what they were when I was a boy," lamented David Gavin, a prosperous South Carolinian. Then, the "Sovereign people, alias mob" had little influence; now they vied for power with the elite. "[How can] I rejoice for a freedom," Gavin demanded to know, "which allows every bankrupt, swindler, thief, and scoundrel, traitor and seller of his vote to be placed on an equality with myself?"

To maintain their privileged identity, aristocratic planters married their sons and daughters to one another and expected them to follow in their footsteps — the men working as planters, merchants, lawyers, newspaper editors, and ministers, and the women hosting plantation balls and church bazaars. To confirm their social preeminence, they lived extravagantly and entertained graciously. James Henry Hammond built a Greek Revival mansion with a center hall 53 feet by 20 feet, its floor embellished with stylish Belgian tiles and expensive Brussels carpets. "Once a year, like a great feudal landlord," a guest recounted, "[Hammond] gave a fete or grand dinner to all the country people."

Rice planters remained at the apex of the plantation aristocracy. In 1860, the fifteen proprietors of the vast plantations in All Saints Parish in the Georgetown district of South Carolina owned 4,383 slaves — nearly 300 apiece — who annually grew and processed 14 million pounds of rice. As inexpensive Asian rice entered the world market in the 1820s and cut their profit margins, Carolina planters sold some slaves and worked the others harder — allowing them to sustain their luxurious lifestyle. The "hospitality and elegance" of Charleston and Savannah impressed savvy English traveler John Silk Buckingham. Buckingham likewise found "polished" families among long-established French Catholic planters in New Orleans and along the Mississippi River: "The sugar and cotton planters live in splendid

A Louisiana Plantation, 1861

This view of the St. John plantation in Louisiana by Marie Adrien Persac, a French-born artist, presents an exquisitely detailed but romanticized vision of the planter lifestyle. Well-dressed slaves stand amid neatly spaced rows of cotton as the women of the household prance by on well-groomed horses. Off to the right, smoke rises from the chimneys of a small mill, probably used to process the sugarcane grown elsewhere on the plantation.   Louisiana State University Museum of Art.

edifices, and enjoy all the luxury that wealth can impart" (see Voices from Abroad, "Bernhard, Duke of Saxe-Weimar-Eisenach: The Racial Complexities of Southern Society," p. 372).

In tobacco-growing regions, the lives of the planter aristocracy followed a different trajectory, in part because slave ownership was widely diffused. In the 1770s, about 60 percent of white families in the Chesapeake region owned at least one African American slave. As many wealthy tobacco planters moved their plantations and slaves to the Cotton South, middling planters (who owned between five and twenty slaves) came to dominate the Chesapeake economy. The descendants of the old tobacco aristocracy remained influential, but increasingly as slave-owning grain farmers, lawyers, merchants, industrialists, and politicians. They either hired out slaves they didn't need for their businesses or sold them south or allowed them to purchase their freedom.

The Ideology and Reality of "Benevolence" Although the genteel planter aristocracy flourished primarily around the periphery of the South—in Virginia, South Carolina, and Louisiana—its members took the lead in defending slavery. Ignoring the old Jeffersonian response to slavery as a

Bernhard, Duke of Saxe-Weimar-Eisenach

The Racial Complexities of Southern Society

In 1825 and 1826, Bernhard, duke of the German principality of Saxe-Weimar-Eisenach, traveled throughout the United States, and published an account of his adventures in 1828. Subsequently, he compiled a distinguished military record serving the king of the Netherlands and then ruled his principality from 1853 until his death in 1862. In this selection from his *Travels*, Bernhard notes the migration to the cotton belt and describes the racial intricacies of New Orleans society.

[On our way to New Orleans] we met several parties of emigrants from the eastern sections of Georgia on their way to Butler County in Alabama. They proposed to settle on lands that they had acquired very cheaply from the federal government. The number of their Negroes, horses, wagons, and cattle showed that these wanderers were well off.

In New Orleans we were invited to a subscription ball. . . . Only good society is invited to these balls. The first to which we came was not very well attended; but most of the ladies were very nice looking and well turned out in the French manner. Their clothing was elegant after the latest Paris fashions. They danced very well and did credit to their French dancing masters. Dancing and some music are the main branches of the education of a Creole [an American-born white] woman. . . .

The native men are far from matching the women in elegance. And they stayed only a short time, preferring to escape to a so-called "Quarterons Ball" which they find more amusing and where they do not have to stand on ceremony. . . .

A "quarteron" (octoroon) is the offspring of a mestizo mother and a white father, just as the mestizo is the child of a mulatto and a white man. The "quarterons" are almost completely white. There would be no way of recognizing them by their complexion, for they are often fairer than the Creoles. Black hair and eyes are generally the signs of their status, although some are quite blond. The ball is attended by the free "quarterons." Yet the deepest prejudice reigns against them on account of their colored origin; the white women particularly feel or affect to feel a strong repugnance to them.

Marriage between colored and white people is forbidden by the laws of the state. Yet the "quarterons," for their part, look upon the Negroes and mulattoes as inferiors and are unwilling to mix with them. The girls therefore have no other recourse than to become the mistresses of white men. The "quarterons" regard such attachment as the equivalent of marriage. They would not think of entering upon it other than with a formal contract in which the man engages to pay a stipulated sum to the mother or father of the girl. The latter even assumes the name of her lover and regards the affair with more faithfulness than many a woman whose marriage was sealed in a church.

Some of these women have inherited from their fathers and lovers, and possess considerable fortunes. Their status is nevertheless always very depressed. They must not ride in the street in coaches, and their lovers can bring them to the balls in their own conveyances only after nightfall. They must never sit opposite a white lady, nor may they enter a room without express permission. . . . But many of these girls are much more carefully educated than the whites, behave with more polish and more politeness, and make their lovers happier than white wives their husbands. And yet the white ladies speak of these unfortunate depressed creatures with great disdain, even bitterness. Because of the depth of these prejudices, many fathers send their daughters, conceived after this manner, to France where good education and wealth are no impediments to the attainment of a respectable place.

Source: C. J. Jeronimus, ed., *Travels by His Highness Duke Bernhard of Saxe-Weimar-Eisenach Through North America in the Years 1825 and 1826*, trans. William Jeronimus (1828; repr., Lanham, Md.: University Press of America, 2001), 296–297, 343, 346–347.

ANALYZING THE EVIDENCE

- What does this passage suggest about the effect of racial slavery on white marriages?
- Why were France and French fashions so important in the lives of the white and "quarteron" population of New Orleans?
- How does Bernhard's account help explain the values and outlook of the free black population in the South?
- In the United States, the kind of racial mixing Bernhard noted in New Orleans society was unique. Why did it not appear in Charleston, Richmond, and other southern cities?

"misfortune" or a "necessary evil" (see Chapter 8), southern apologists began in the 1830s to argue that slavery was a "positive good" that allowed a civilized lifestyle for whites and provided tutelage for genetically inferior Africans. "As a race, the African is inferior to the white man," declared Alexander Stephens, the future vice president of the Confederacy. "Subordination to the white man, is his normal condition." Apologists depicted planters and their wives as aristocratic models of "disinterested benevolence," who paternalistically provided food and housing for their workers and cared for them in old age. One wealthy Georgian declared, "Plantation government should be eminently patriarchal . . . the *pater-familias*, or head of the family, should, in one sense, be the father of the whole concern, negroes and all."

Those planters who embraced Christian stewardship tried to shape the behavior of their slaves. Some built cabins for their workers and insisted slaves whitewash the cabins regularly. Many others built churches on their plantations, welcomed evangelical preachers, and often required their slaves to attend services. A few encouraged African Americans with spiritual "gifts" to serve as exhorters and deacons. The motives of the planters were mixed. Some acted from sincere Christian belief, while others wanted to counter abolitionist criticism or to use religious teachings to control their workers.

Indeed, religion served increasingly as a justification for human bondage. Protestant ministers in the South pointed out that the Hebrews, God's chosen people, had owned slaves and that Jesus Christ had never condemned slavery. As Hammond told a British abolitionist in 1845: "What God ordains and Christ sanctifies should surely command the respect and toleration of man." But many aristocratic apologists were absentee owners or delegated authority to overseers, and rarely glimpsed the day-to-day brutality of the slave regime. "I was at the plantation last Saturday and the crop was in fine order," an absentee's son wrote to his father, "but the negroes are most brutally scarred & several have run off."

Cotton Entrepreneurs There was much less hypocrisy and far less elegance among the second group of elite planters: the market-driven entrepreneurs of the Cotton South. "The glare of expensive luxury vanishes" in the black soil regions of Alabama and Mississippi, John Silk Buckingham remarked as he traveled through the Cotton South, and aristocratic paternalism vanished as well. A Mississippi planter put it plainly: "Everything has to give way

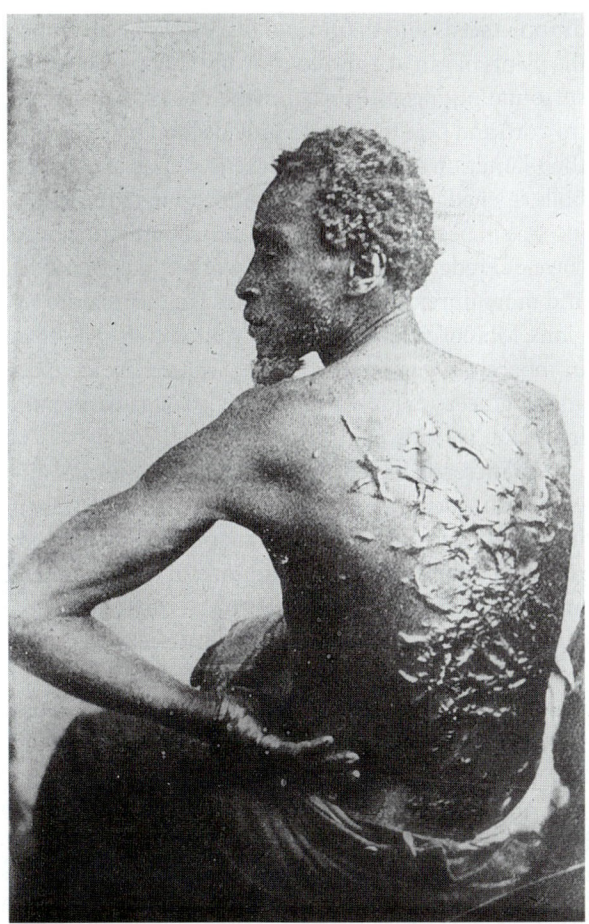

The Inherent Brutality of Slavery

Like all systems of forced labor, American racial slavery relied on physical coercion. Slave owners and overseers routinely whipped slaves who worked slowly or defied their orders. On occasion, they applied the whip with such ferocity that the slave was permanently injured or killed. This photograph of a Mississippi slave named Gordon, taken after he fled to the Union Army in Louisiana in 1863 and published in *Harper's Weekly*, stands as graphic testimony to the inherent brutality of the system.   National Archives.

to large crops of cotton, land has to be cultivated wet or dry, negroes [must] work, hot or cold." Angry at being sold south and pressed to hard labor, many slaves grew "mean" and stubborn. Those who would not labor were subject to the lash. "Whiped all the hoe hands," Alabama planter James Torbert wrote matter-of-factly in his journal. Overseers pushed their workers hard because their salaries often depended on the quantity of cotton they were able "to make for the market." A Mississippi slave recalled, "When I wuz so tired I cu'dnt hardly stan', I had to spin my cut of cotton befor' I cu'd go to sleep. We had to card, spin, an' reel at nite."

Cotton was a demanding crop because of its long growing season. Slaves plowed the land in March;

dropped seeds into the ground in early April; and, once the plants began to grow, continually chopped away the surrounding grasses. In between these tasks, they planted the corn and peas that would provide food for them and the plantation's hogs and chickens. When the cotton bolls ripened in late August, the long four-month picking season began. Slaves in the Cotton South, concluded traveler Frederick Law Olmsted, worked "much harder and more unremittingly" than those in the tobacco regions. Moreover, fewer of them acquired craft skills than in tobacco, sugar, and rice areas, where slave coopers and engineers made casks, processed sugar, and built irrigation systems.

To increase output, profit-conscious cotton planters began during the 1820s to use a rigorous **gang-labor system**. Previously, many planters had either supervised their workers sporadically or assigned them jobs and let them work at their own pace. Now masters with twenty or more slaves organized disciplined teams, or "gangs," supervised by black drivers and white overseers. They instructed the supervisors to work the gangs at a steady pace, clearing and plowing land or hoeing and picking cotton. A traveler in Mississippi described two gangs returning from work:

> First came, led by an old driver carrying a whip, forty of the largest and strongest women I ever saw together; they were all in a simple uniform dress of a bluish check stuff, the skirts reaching little below the knee; . . . they carried themselves loftily, each having a hoe over the shoulder, and walking with a free, powerful swing.

Next marched the plow hands with their mules, "the cavalry, thirty strong, mostly men, but a few of them women." Finally, "a lean and vigilant white overseer, on a brisk pony, brought up the rear."

The cotton planters' quest for profits was ecologically costly. Cotton monoculture and little crop rotation depleted the nutrients in the soil and gradually reduced the output per acre. Still, the crop was a financial bonanza. Because a slave working in a gang finished as much work in thirty-five minutes as a white yeoman planter did in an hour, gang labor became ever more prevalent. In one Georgia county, the percentage of slaves working in gangs doubled between 1830 and 1850 and increased further during the 1850s. As the price of raw cotton surged after 1846, the wealth of the planter class skyrocketed. And no wonder: Nearly 2 million enslaved African Americans now labored on the plantations of the Cotton South and annually produced 4 million bales of the valuable fiber.

Planters, Smallholding Yeomen, and Tenants

Although the South was a "slave society"—that is, the institution of slavery affected all aspects of life there— most white southerners did not own slaves. The percentage of white families who held blacks in bondage steadily decreased—from 36 percent in 1830, to 31 percent in 1850, to about 25 percent a decade later. However, slave ownership varied by region. In some cotton-rich counties, 40 percent or more of the white families owned slaves; in the hill country near the Appalachian Mountains, the proportion dropped to 10 percent.

Planter Elites   Among the privileged minority of 395,000 families who owned slaves in 1860, there was a strict hierarchy. The top one-fifth of these families owned twenty or more slaves. This elite—just 5 percent of the South's white population— dominated the economy, owning over 50 percent of the entire slave population of 4 million, and growing 50 percent of the South's cotton crop. The average wealth of these planters was $56,000 (about $1.5 million today); by contrast, the average southern yeoman or northern farmer owned property worth a mere $3,200.

Substantial proprietors, another fifth of the slave-owning population, held title to six to twenty bondsmen and -women. These middling planters owned almost 40 percent of the slave population and produced more than 30 percent of the cotton. Often they pursued dual careers as skilled artisans or professional men. For example, many of the fifteen slaves owned by Samuel L. Moore worked in his brick factory; the others labored on his Georgia farm. In Macon County, Alabama, James Tolbert owned a plantation that yielded 50 bales of cotton a year; but Tolbert also ran a sawmill, "which pays as well as making Cotton." Dr. Thomas Gale used the income from his medical practice to buy a Mississippi plantation that annually produced 150 bales of cotton. In Alabama, lawyer Benjamin Fitzpatrick used his legal fees to buy ten slaves.

Like Fitzpatrick, many lawyers either owned slaves or managed the affairs of the slave-owning elite. They became well known in their communities by representing merchants and storekeepers in suits for debt, settling disputes over property, and helping smallholders and tenants register their deeds and contracts. Standing at the legal crossroads of their small towns and personally known by many residents, lawyers regularly won election to public office. Less than 1 percent of the male population, in 1828 lawyers made up 16 percent of the Alabama legislature, and an astounding 26 percent in 1849.

Smallholding Planters and Yeomen

The smallholders who made up the majority of slave owners were much less visible than the wealthy grandees and the middling lawyer-planters. These slave owners held from one to five black laborers in bondage and claimed title to a few hundred acres of land. Some smallholders were well-connected young men who would rise to wealth when their father's death blessed them with more land and slaves. Others were poor but ambitious men trying to pull themselves up by their bootstraps, with the encouragement of elite planters and proslavery advocates. "Ours is a pro-slavery form of Government, and the pro-slavery element should be increased," declared a Georgia newspaper. "We would like to see every white man at the South the owner of a family of negroes."

Taking this advice to heart, aspiring planters saved or borrowed enough to acquire more land and more laborers. Some achieved modest prosperity. One German settler in Alabama reported in 1855 that "nearly all his countrymen" who emigrated with him were now slaveholders. "They were poor on their arrival in the country; but no sooner did they realize a little money than they invested it in slaves," whose labor made them well-to-do.

Bolstered by the patriarchal ideology of the planter class, yeomen farmers ruled their smallholdings with a firm hand. The male head of the household had authority over all the dependents—wives, children, and slaves—and, according to one South Carolina judge, the legal right on his property "to be as churlish as he pleases." The wives of southern yeomen had little power; like women in the North, they lost their legal identity when they married. To express their concerns and interests, many southern women joined churches, where they usually outnumbered men by a margin of two to one. Women especially welcomed the message of spiritual equality preached in evangelical Baptist and Methodist churches, and hoped that the church community would hold their husbands to the same standards of Christian behavior to which they were held. But most churches supported patriarchal rule and told female members to remain in "wifely obedience," whatever the actions of their husbands.

Whatever their authority within the household, most southern yeomen lived and died as hardscrabble farmers. They worked alongside their slaves in the fields, struggled to make ends meet as their families grew, and moved regularly in search of opportunity. Thus, in 1847, James Buckner Barry left North Carolina with his new wife and two slaves to settle in Bosque County, Texas. There he worked part-time as an Indian fighter while his slaves toiled on a drought-ridden farm that barely kept the family in food. In South Carolina, W. J. Simpson struggled for years as a smallholding cotton planter and then gave up. He hired out one of his two slaves and went to work as an overseer on his father's farm.

Other smallholders fell from the privileged ranks of the slave-owning classes. Selling their land and slaves to pay off debts, they joined the large group of propertyless tenants who farmed the estates of wealthy landlords. In 1860, in Hancock County, Georgia, there were 56 slave-owning planters and 300 propertyless white farm laborers and factory workers; in nearby Hart County, 25 percent of the white farmers were tenants. Across the South, about 40 percent of the white population worked as tenants or farm laborers; as the *Southern Cultivator* observed, they had "no legal right nor interest in the soil [and] no homes of their own."

Poor Freemen

Propertyless whites enjoyed few of the benefits of slavery and suffered many of its ill consequences. Because hard labor was deemed fit only for enslaved blacks, white workers received little respect. Nor could they hope for a better life for their children, because slave owners refused to pay taxes to fund public schools. Moreover, wealthy planters bid up the price of African Americans, depriving white laborers and tenants of easy access to the slave labor required to accumulate wealth. Finally, planter-dominated legislatures forced all white men—whether they owned slaves or not—to serve in the patrols and militias that deterred black uprisings. For their sacrifices, poor whites gained only the psychological satisfaction that they ranked above blacks. As Alfred Iverson, a U.S. senator from Georgia (1855–1861), explained: A white man "walks erect in the dignity of his color and race, and feels that he is a superior being, with the more exalted powers and privileges than others." To reinforce this sense of racial superiority, planter James Henry Hammond told his poor white neighbors, "In a slave country every freeman is an aristocrat."

Rejecting that half-truth, many southern whites fled planter-dominated counties and sought farms in the Appalachian hill country and beyond—in western Virginia, Kentucky, Tennessee, the southern regions of Illinois and Indiana, and Missouri. Living as yeomen farmers, they used family labor to grow foodstuffs for sustenance. To obtain cash or store credit to buy agricultural implements, cloth, shoes, salt, and other necessities, yeomen families sold their surplus crops, raised hogs for market sale, and—when the price of cotton rose sharply—grew a few bales. Their goals were modest: On the family level, they wanted to preserve their holdings and buy enough land to set up their children as small-scale farmers. As citizens, smallholders wanted to control their local government and elect men of their own kind to public office. However, thoughtful yeomen realized that the cotton revolution had sentenced family farmers to a subordinate place in the southern social order. They could hope for a life of independence and dignity only by moving north or farther west, where labor was "free" and hard work was respectable.

The Settlement of Texas

By the 1830s, settlers from the South had carried both yeoman farming and plantation slavery into Arkansas and Missouri. Between those states and the Rocky Mountains stretched great grasslands. An army explorer, Major Stephen H. Long, thought the plains region "almost wholly unfit for cultivation" and in 1820 labeled it the Great American Desert. Americans looking for land therefore turned south, to the Mexican province of Texas.

After winning independence from Spain in 1821, the Mexican government encouraged this migration by offering large land grants (and citizenship) to Americans. One early grantee was Moses Austin, an American land speculator who settled smallholding farmers on his vast grant. His son, Stephen F. Austin, acquired even more land from the Mexican government—some 180,000 acres—which he sold to newcomers. By 1835, about 27,000 white Americans and 3,000 African American slaves were raising cotton and cattle in eastern and central Texas. They far outnumbered the 3,000 Mexican residents, who lived primarily near the southwestern Texas towns of Goliad and San Antonio.

When Mexico's central government asserted greater political control over Texas and other provinces in the 1830s, the Americans split into two groups. Members of the "peace party," led by Stephen Austin, accepted Mexican rule but campaigned for greater political autonomy. They wanted Texas to flourish within a decentralized Mexican republic, the sort of "federalism" demanded by the Liberal Party in Mexico and Jacksonian Democrats in the United States. But the "war party," headed mostly by recent migrants from Georgia, demanded independence for Texas. Austin won significant concessions from Mexican authorities, including an exemption from a law ending slavery, but in 1835 Mexico's president, General Antonio López de Santa Anna, nullified them. Santa Anna wanted to impose national authority throughout Mexico. Fearing that outcome, the Texas war party provoked a rebellion that most of the American settlers ultimately supported. On

Assault on the Alamo

After a thirteen-day siege, on March 6, 1836, a Mexican army of 4,000 stormed the walls of the small San Antonio fort known as the Alamo (originally a Spanish mission). "The first to climb were thrown down by bayonets . . . or by pistol fire," reported a Mexican officer. After a half-hour of continuous and costly assaults, the attackers won control of a wall. This contemporary woodcut suggests the fierceness of the battle, which took the lives of all 250 Texas defenders; 1,500 Mexicans were killed or wounded in the fighting.   Archives Division, Texas State Library.

Starting Out in Texas

Thousands of white farmers, some owning a few slaves, moved onto small farms in Texas and Arkansas during the 1840s and 1850. They lived in crudely built log huts; owned a few cows, horses, and oxen; and eked out a meager living by planting a few acres of cotton in addition to their crops of corn. Their aspirations were simple: to achieve modest prosperity during their lives and to leave their property to their children.   Daughters of the Republic of Texas Library.

March 2, 1836, the American rebels proclaimed the independence of Texas and adopted a constitution legalizing slavery.

President Santa Anna vowed to put down the rebellion. On March 6, he led an army that wiped out the Texan garrison defending the Alamo in San Antonio; then his forces captured Goliad and executed 371 rebel prisoners. Santa Anna thought that he had crushed the rebellion, but New Orleans and New York newspapers romanticized the heroism of the Texans and the deaths at the Alamo of folk heroes Davy Crockett and Jim Bowie. Drawing on anti-Catholic sentiment aroused by Irish immigration, journalists urged Americans to "Remember the Alamo" and depicted the Mexicans as tyrannical butchers in the service of the pope. Scores

of American adventurers, lured by offers of land grants, flocked to Texas to join the rebel forces. Commanded by General Sam Houston, the Texans routed Santa Anna's overconfident army in the Battle of San Jacinto in April 1836, winning de facto independence. The Mexican government refused to recognize the Texas Republic but abandoned efforts to reconquer it.

The Texans voted for annexation by the United States, but President Martin Van Buren refused to bring the issue before Congress. As a Texas diplomat reported, Van Buren and other American politicians feared that annexation would spark a war with Mexico and, beyond that, a "desperate death-struggle . . . between the North and the South [over the extension of slavery]; a struggle involving the probability of a dissolution of the Union."

The Politics of Democracy

As American men asserted their claim to a voice in government affairs, politicians catered to their prejudices and preferences. And they took their message to voters, wherever they found them. This detail from George Caleb Bingham's *Stump Speaking* (1855) shows a well-dressed politician on an improvised stage seeking the votes of an audience of farmers—identified by their broad-brimmed hats and casual clothes.   · Private Collection/The Bridgeman Art Library Ltd.

The Politics of Democracy

As national politicians refused admission to Texas, elite planters struggled to control state governments in the Cotton South. Unlike the planter-aristocrats of the eighteenth century, they lived in a republican society with democratic institutions. The Alabama Constitution of 1819 granted suffrage to all white men; it also provided for a **secret ballot**; apportionment based on population; and the election of county supervisors, sheriffs, and clerks of court. Given these democratic provisions, political factions in Alabama had to compete with one another for popular favor. When a Whig newspaper sarcastically asked whether the state's policies should "be governed and controlled by the whim and caprice of the majority of the people," Democrats stood forth as champions of the common folk. They called on "Farmers, Mechanics, laboring men" to repudiate

Whig "aristocrats . . . the soft handed and soft headed gentry."

The Politics of Taxation Whatever the rhetoric, most candidates from both parties were men of substance. In the early 1840s, nearly 90 percent of Alabama's legislators owned slaves, testimony to the power of the slave-owning minority. But relatively few lawmakers—only about 10 percent—were rich planters, a group voters by and large distrusted. "A rich man cannot sympathize with the poor," declared one candidate. Consequently, the majority of elected state officials, and most county officials in the Cotton South, came from the ranks of middle-class planters and planter-lawyers. To curry favor among voters, Alabama Democrats advanced policies that would command popular support, such as low taxes. Their

Whig opponents favored higher taxes, in order to provide government subsidies for banks, canals, roads, and other internal improvements; but they also ran candidates who appealed to the common people.

Regardless of party, Alabama's legislators usually enacted policies supported by slave owners. However, they took care not to anger the mass of yeomen farmers and propertyless whites by favoring too many expensive measures, such as the public works projects favored by the Whigs. "Voting against appropriations is the safe and popular side," one senator declared, and his colleagues agreed; until the 1850s, they rejected most of the bills that would have granted subsidies to railroads, canals, and banks. They also refrained from laying "oppressive" taxes on the people, particularly the poor white majority who owned no slaves. Between 1830 and 1860, the Alabama legislature obtained about 70 percent of the state's revenue from taxes on slaves and land. Another 10 to 15 percent came from levies on carriages, gold watches, and other luxury goods, and on the capital invested in banks, transportation companies, and manufacturing enterprises.

If taxes in Alabama had a democratic thrust, those elsewhere in the South did not. In some states, wealthy planters used their political influence to exempt slave property from taxation. And they shifted the burden of land taxes to backcountry yeomen by taxing farms according to acreage rather than value. Planter-legislators also spared themselves the cost of building fences around their large fields by enacting laws that required yeomen to fence in their livestock. And, during the 1850s, wealthy legislators throughout the South used public funds to subsidize the canals and railroads in which they had invested.

The Paradox of Southern Prosperity

Seen from one perspective, the southern states' subsidies for transportation were unnecessary. If the South had been a separate nation in 1860, its economy would have been the fourth most prosperous in the world, with a per capita income higher than that of France and Germany. As a contributor to a Georgia newspaper argued in the 1850s, it was beside the point to complain about "tariffs, and merchants, and manufacturers" because "the most highly prosperous people now on earth, are to be found in these very [slave] States."

Yet such arguments tell only part of the story. Many white southerners—especially those who were slave owners—did enjoy higher living standards than other peoples of the world, but most African Americans—30 percent of the population—lived in dire and permanent poverty. And the South's standard of living fell behind that of the North. Both in 1840 and in 1860, the per capita wealth of the South was only 80 percent of the national average, while that in the industrializing Northeast was 139 percent of the average.

Influential southerners blamed the shortcomings of their plantation-based economy on outsiders: "Purely agricultural people," intoned planter-politician James Henry Hammond, "have been in all ages the victims of rapacious tyrants grinding them down." And they steadfastly defended their way of life. "We have no cities—we don't want them," boasted former U.S. senator Louis Wigfall of Texas in 1861. "We want no manufactures: we desire no trading, no mechanical or manufacturing classes. . . . As long as we have our rice, our sugar, our tobacco, and our cotton, we can command wealth to purchase all we want." And so wealthy southerners continued to buy land and slaves, a strategy that brought substantial short-run profits but neglected investments in the great technological innovations of the nineteenth century—water- and steam-powered factories, machine tools, steel plows, and crushed-gravel roads, for example—that would have raised the South's productivity and wealth.

Urban growth—the key to prosperity in Europe and the North—occurred mostly in the commercial cities around the periphery of the South: New Orleans, St. Louis, and Baltimore. Factories—often staffed by slave labor—likewise appeared primarily in the Chesapeake, which had a more diverse economy and a surplus of bound workers. Within the Cotton South, wealthy planters invested in railroads but only to open up new lands for commercial farming; when the Western & Atlantic Railroad reached the Georgia upcountry, the cotton crop quickly doubled. Cotton—and agriculture—remained King.

Slavery also deterred European migrants from settling in the South, because they feared competition from bound labor. Their absence deprived the region of hardworking families and of laborers to drain swamps, dig canals, smelt iron, and work on railroads. When entrepreneurs tried to hire slaves for such tasks, planters replied that "a negro's life is too valuable to be risked" at the dangerous work. Other slave owners feared that hiring out would make their slaves too independent. As a planter explained to Frederick Law Olmsted, such workers "had too much liberty . . . and got a habit of roaming about and taking care of themselves."

Thus, despite its increasing size and booming exports, the South remained an economic colony: Great Britain and the North bought its staple crops and provided its manufactures, financial services, and shipping facilities. In 1860, most southerners—some 84 percent, more than double the percentage in the northern states—still worked in agriculture and southern factories turned out only 10 percent of the nation's manufactured goods. The South's fixation on an "exclusive and exhausting" system of agriculture filled South Carolina textile entrepreneur William Gregg with "dark forebodings." Gregg feared that the combination of cotton and slavery had been to the South

> what the [gold and silver] mines of Mexico were to Spain. It has produced us such an abundant supply of all the luxuries and elegances of life, with so little exertion on our part, that we have become enervated, unfitted for other and more laborious pursuits.

- How would you explain the large and expanding domestic trade in slaves between 1800 and 1860? What combination of factors produced this result?

- By 1860, what different groups made up the South's increasingly complex society? How did these groups interact in the political arena?

The African American World

By the 1820s, the cultural life of most slaves reflected both the values and customs of their West African ancestors and the language, laws, and religious beliefs of the South's white population. This mix of African and American cultural values persisted for decades because whites discouraged blacks from assimilating and because slaves prized their African heritage.

Evangelical Black Protestantism

The appearance of black Christianity exemplified the synthesis of African and European cultures. Evangelical Protestantism swept over the white South during the Second Great Awakening, from the 1790s to the 1840s. Baptist and Methodist preachers converted thousands of white families and hundreds of enslaved blacks (see Chapter 8). Until that time, African-born blacks, often identifiable by their ritual scars, had maintained the religious practices of their homelands: Some practiced Islam, but the majority relied on African gods and spirits. As late as 1842, Charles C. Jones, a Presbyterian minister, noted that the blacks on his family's plantation in Georgia believed "in second-sight, in apparitions, charms, witchcraft . . . [and other] superstitions brought from Africa." Fearing "the consequences" for their own

souls if they withheld "the means of salvation" from African Americans, Jones and other zealous white Protestant preachers and planters set out to convert slaves to Christianity.

Other Protestant crusaders came from the ranks of pious black men and women who were swept from the Chesapeake to the Cotton South by the domestic slave trade and carried the evangelical message of emotional conversion, ritual baptism, and communal spirituality with them. Equally important, these crusaders adapted Protestant doctrines to black needs. Enslaved Christians pointed out that blacks as well as whites were "children of God" and should be dealt with according to the Golden Rule—treat others as you would be treated by them. Moreover, black preachers generally ignored the doctrines of original sin and predestination as well as biblical passages that encouraged unthinking obedience to authority. A white minister in Liberty County, Georgia, reported that when he urged slaves to obey their masters, "one half of my audience deliberately rose up and walked off" (see Reading American Pictures, "Slave Life on a Cotton Plantation," p. 381).

Black Protestantism Indeed, some African American converts envisioned the deity as the Old Testament warrior who had liberated the Jews and so would also liberate them. Inspired by a vision of Christ, Nat Turner led his bloody rebellion against slavery in Virginia (see Chapter 11). Other black Christians saw themselves as Chosen People: "de people dat is born of God." Charles Davenport, a Mississippi slave, recalled black preachers' "exhort[ing] us dat us was de chillun o' Israel in de wilderness an' de Lawd done sont us to take dis lan' o' milk an' honey."

As successive generations of slaves worshipped a European god, they expressed their Christianity in distinctively African ways. The thousands of African Americans who joined the Methodist Church respected its ban on profane dancing but praised the Lord in the African-derived "ring shout." Minister Henry George Spaulding explained the "religious dance of the Negroes" this way:

> Three or four, standing still, clapping their hands and beating time with their feet, commence singing in unison one of the peculiar shout melodies, while the others walk around in a ring, in single file, joining also in the song.

The songs themselves were usually collective creations, devised spontaneously from bits of old hymns and tunes. Recalled an ex-slave:

Slave Life on a Cotton Plantation

By the middle decades of the nineteenth century, a majority of enslaved African Americans labored on the cotton plantations that stretched from South Carolina to Texas. What was it like to work and live on a cotton plantation? Historians can consult a mass of evidence to answer this question—the testimonials of escaped slaves, the recollections of former slaves, travelers' accounts, and contemporaneous engravings and photographs. These two images tell a very small part of that story and, like all historical sources, have to be carefully interrogated.

ANALYZING THE EVIDENCE

- Picking the cotton—thousands of small bolls attached to 3-foot-high woody stalks—was a tedious and time-consuming task. The photograph here was taken on a cotton plantation near Savannah, Georgia. Who is harvesting the cotton? (Note the collection bags draped over some of the pickers' shoulders.) Why could this work be done by both sexes and all ages? Why might children have been adept as pickers? Without directly supervising the family's labor, how might the owner have ensured that the work was getting done?

- What does the photo of cotton pickers suggest about women's lives, family relations, and living conditions?

- Why would the planter pictured in *Family Worship in a Plantation in South Carolina*, an engraving printed in a British magazine, have encouraged Christian services? Why might the planter and his wife and children have been attending the service?

- Is it significant that the minister is black? How do we know that he is literate? How is the African American audience reacting to his message?

A Slave Family Picking Cotton. © Collection of the New-York Historical Society.

Family Worship in a Plantation in South Carolina. *The Illustrated London News*/Picture Research Consultants and Archives.

- Would either of these images be used by abolitionists to further their demands for immediate emancipation? Would either be used by authors who defended slavery? Specifically, how might either one be used to attack or defend the slave regime?

We'd all be at the "prayer house" de Lord's day, and de white preacher he'd splain de word and read whar Esekial done say — *Dry bones gwine ter lib ergin.* And, honey, de Lord would come a-shinin' thoo dem pages and revive dis ole nigger's heart, and I'd jump up dar and den and holler and shout and sing and pat, and dey would all cotch de words and I'd ring it to some ole shout song I'd heard 'em sing from Africa, and dey'd all take it up and keep at it, and keep a-addin' to it, and den it would be a spiritual.

By such African-influenced means, black congregations devised a distinctive and joyous brand of Protestant worship to sustain them on the long journey to emancipation and the Promised Land. "O my Lord delivered Daniel," the slaves sang, "O why not deliver me too?"

Forging Families and Creating Culture

Black Protestantism was one facet of an increasingly homogeneous African American culture in the rural South. Even in South Carolina — a major point of entry for imported slaves — only 20 percent of the black residents in 1820 had been born in Africa. The domestic slave trade mingled blacks from many states, erased regional differences, and prompted the emergence of a core culture in the Lower Mississippi Valley. A prime example was the fate of the Gullah dialect (see Chapter 3). Spoken by blacks in the Carolina low country well into the twentieth century, Gullah did not take root on the cotton plantations of Alabama and Mississippi. There, slaves from Carolina were far outnumbered by migrants

Black Kitchen Ball

From time to time, the hardships and demanding work routine of slaves' lives were punctuated by festive celebrations. In this 1838 painting, *Kitchen Ball at White Sulphur Springs*, in Virginia, African Americans dance to the music of a fiddle and a fife (on the right). Note the light complexions and Europeanized features of the most prominent figures, the result of either racial mixing or the cultural perspective of the artist. The painter, Christian Mayr, was born in Germany in 1805 and migrated to the United States in 1833. After working for years as a traveling portrait painter, Mayr settled in New York City in 1845 and died there in 1850.   The North Carolina Museum of Art. Purchased with funds from the State of North Carolina, 52.9.23.

Antebellum Slave Quarters

During the colonial period, owners often housed their slaves by gender in communal barracks. In the nineteenth century, slaves usually lived in family units in separate cabins. The slave huts on this South Carolina plantation were sturdily built but had few windows. Inside, they were sparsely furnished.   William Gladstone.

from the Chesapeake, who spoke black English. Like Gullah, black English used double negatives and other African grammatical forms, but consisted primarily of English words rendered with West African pronunciation (for example, with *th* pronounced as *d*—"de preacher").

African Influences As the black population of the Mississippi Valley increased, African influences remained important. At least one-third of the slaves who entered the United States between 1776 and 1809 came from the Congo region of West-Central Africa, and they brought their regional cultures with them. As traveler Isaac Holmes reported in 1821: "In Louisiana, and the state of Mississippi, the slaves . . . dance for several hours during Sunday afternoon. The general movement is in what they call the Congo dance." Similar descriptions of blacks who "danced the Congo and sang a purely African song to the accompaniment of . . . a drum" appeared as late as 1890.

African Americans also continued to respect African incest taboos by shunning marriages between cousins. On the Good Hope Plantation on the Santee River in South Carolina, nearly half of the slave children born between 1800 and 1857 were related by blood to one another; yet when they married, only one of every forty-one unions took place between cousins. This taboo was not copied from white planters: Cousin marriages were frequent among the 440 South Carolina men and women who owned at least 100 slaves in 1860, in part because such unions kept wealth within an extended family.

Unlike white marriages, slave unions were not recognized in law. Southern legislatures and courts prohibited legal marriages among slaves so that their sale would not break a legal bond. Still, many African Americans took marriage vows before Christian ministers. Others publicly marked their married state in ceremonies that included the West African custom of jumping over a broomstick together. Once married, newly arrived young people in the Cotton South whose parents remained in the Chesapeake region often chose older people in their new communities as fictive "aunts" and "uncles." The slave trade had destroyed their family, but not their family values.

The creation of fictive kinship ties was part of a community-building process. Naming children was another. Recently imported slaves frequently gave their children African names. Males born on Friday, for example, were often called Cuffee — the name of that day in several West African languages. Many American-born parents chose names of British origin, but they usually named sons after fathers, uncles, or grandfathers, and daughters after grandmothers. Those transported to the Cotton South often named their children for relatives left behind. Like incest rules and marriage rituals, this intergenerational sharing of names evoked memories of a lost world and bolstered kin ties in the present one.

Negotiating Rights

By forming stable families and communities, African Americans gradually created a sense of order in the harsh and arbitrary world of slavery. In a few regions, slaves won substantial control over their lives. Blacks in the rice-growing lowlands of South Carolina successfully asserted the right to labor by the "task" rather than to work under constant supervision. Each day, task workers had to complete a precisely defined job — for example, digging up a quarter-acre of land, hoeing half an acre, or pounding seven mortars of rice. By working hard, many finished their tasks by early afternoon, a Methodist preacher reported, and had "the rest of the day for themselves, which they spend in working their own private fields . . . planting rice, corn, potatoes, tobacco &c. for their own use and profit." Slaves on sugar and cotton plantations were less fortunate. There, the gang-labor system imposed a regimented work schedule, and owners prohibited slaves from growing crops on their own. "It gives an excuse for trading," explained one slave owner, and that encouraged roaming and independence.

Planters worried constantly that enslaved African Americans — a majority of the population in most counties of the Cotton South — would rise in rebellion. Slave owners knew that, legally speaking, they had virtually unlimited power over their slaves. As Justice Thomas Ruffin of the North Carolina Supreme Court wrote in a decision in 1829: "The power of the master must be absolute to render the submission of the slave perfect." But absolute power required brutal coercion, and only the most hardened or most sadistic masters had the stomach for that. Some southern whites wanted no part of such violence. "These poor negroes, receiving none of the fruits of their labor, do not love work," explained one farm woman, "if we had slaves, we should have to . . . beat them to make use of them."

Moreover, passive resistance by African Americans seriously limited the power of their owners. Slaves slowed the pace of work by feigning illness and "losing" or breaking tools. Some blacks insisted that people be sold "in families." One Maryland slave faced with transport to Mississippi and separation from his wife "neither yields consent to accompany my people, or to be exchanged or sold," his owner reported. Masters ignored such feelings at their peril. A slave (or a relative) might retaliate by setting fire to the master's house and barns, poisoning his food, or destroying crops or equipment. Fear of resistance, as well as the increasingly critical scrutiny of abolitionists, prompted many masters to reduce their reliance on the lash. Instead, they tried to devise "a wholesome and well regulated system" for managing their laborers by using positive incentives like food and special privileges. Noted Frederick Law Olmsted: "Men of sense have discovered that it was better to offer them rewards than to whip them." Nonetheless, owners always had the option of resorting to violence, and many masters continued to assert their power by raping their female slaves.

Slavery remained an exploitative system grounded in fear and coercion. Over the decades, hundreds of individual slaves responded to this violence by attacking their masters and overseers. But only a few blacks — among them Gabriel and Martin Prosser (1800) and Nat Turner (1832) — plotted or mounted mass uprisings that involved taking revenge on their white captors. Most slaves recognized that uprisings would be futile; they lacked the autonomous institutions — such as the communes of peasants or serfs in Europe, for example — needed to organize a successful rebellion. Moreover, whites were numerous, well armed, and determined to maintain their position of racial superiority (see Comparing American Voices, "Slaves and Masters," pp. 386–387).

Escape was equally problematic. Blacks in the Upper South could flee to the North, but only by leaving their family and kin. Slaves in the Lower South could seek freedom in Spanish Florida until 1819, when the United States annexed that territory. Even then, hundreds of blacks continued to flee to Florida, where some intermarried with the Seminole Indians. Elsewhere in the South, small groups of escaped slaves eked out a meager existence in deserted marshy areas or mountain

CLASS No. 1.

Comprises those prisoners who were found guilty and executed.

Prisoners Names.	Owners' Names.	Time of Commit.	How Disposed of.
Peter	James Poyas	June 18	
Ned	Gov. T. Bennett,	do.	Hanged on Tuesday
Rolla	do.	do	the 2d July, 1822,
Batteau	do.	do.	on Blake's lands,
Denmark Vesey	A free black man	22	near Charleston.
Jessy	Thos. Blackwood	23	
John	Elias Horry	July 5	Do. on the Lines near
Gullah Jack	Paul Pritchard	do.	Ch.; Friday July 12.
Mingo	Wm. Harth	June 21	
Lot	Forrester	27	
Joe	P. L. Jore	July 6	
Julius	Thos. Forrest	8	
Tom	Mrs. Russell	10	
Smart	Robt. Anderson	do.	
John	John Robertson	11	
Robert	do.	do.	
Adam	do.	do.	
Polydore	Mrs. Faber	do.	Hanged on the Lines
Bacchus	Benj. Hammet	do.	near Charleston,
Dick	Wm. Sims	13	on Friday, 26th
Pharaoh	— Thompson	do.	July.
Jemmy	Mrs. Clement	18	
Mauidore	Mordecai Cohen	19	
Dean	— Mitchell	do.	
Jack	Mrs. Purcell	12	
Bellisle	Est. of Jos. Yates	18	
Naphur	do.	do.	
Adam	do.	do.	
Jacob	John S. Glen	16	
Charles	John Billings	18	
Jack	N. McNeill	22	
Cæsar	Miss Smith	do.	Do. Tues. July 30.
Jacob Stagg	Jacob Lankester	23	
Tom	Wm. M. Scott	24	
William	Mrs. Garner	Aug. 2	Do. Friday, Aug. 9.

"An Account of the Late Intended Insurrection, Charleston, South Carolina"

In 1820, Charleston had a free black population of 1,500 and an array of African American institutions, including the Brown Fellowship Society (for those of mixed racial ancestry) and an African Methodist Episcopal (AME) church. In 1822, Charleston authorities accused a free black, Denmark Vesey, of organizing a revolt to free the city's slaves. Although historians long accepted the validity of that charge, recent scholarship suggests that Vesey's only offense was antagonizing some whites by claiming his rights as a free man and that the alleged insurrection was a figment of the imagination of fearful slave owners. Regardless, South Carolina officials hanged Vesey and thirty-four alleged co-conspirators and tore down the AME church where they were said to have plotted the uprising. Rare Book, Manuscript & Special Collections, Duke University Library.

valleys. However, as Frederick Douglass observed, most slaves were "pegged down to one single spot, and must take root there or die."

Given these limited options, most slaves struggled to build the best possible lives for themselves on the plantations where they lived. Over time, they pressed their owners for a greater share of the product of their labor—much like unionized workers in the North were

trying to do. Thus, slaves insisted on getting paid for "overwork" and on their right to cultivate a garden and sell its produce. "De menfolks tend to de gardens round dey own house," recalled a Louisiana slave. "Dey raise some cotton and sell it to massa and git li'l money dat way." That money was theirs to do with as they wished. An Alabama slave remembered buying "Sunday clothes with dat money, sech as hats and pants and shoes and dresses." By the 1850s, thousands of African Americans were reaping the small rewards of this underground economy.

Even if their material circumstances improved, however, few slaves accepted the legitimacy of their status. Although he was well fed and never whipped, a former slave explained to an English traveler that he knew he had been oppressed: "I was cruelly treated because I was kept in slavery."

The Free Black Population

Some African Americans escaped slavery through flight, manumission, or gradual emancipation laws. The proportion of free blacks rose from 8 percent of the African American population in 1790 to about 13 percent between 1820 and 1840, and then fell to 11 percent. Still, in Maryland in 1860, half of all blacks were free and many more were "term" slaves, guaranteed their freedom in exchange for a few more years of work. Nearly half of free blacks in the United States in 1840 (some 170,000) and again in 1860 (250,000) lived in the free states of the North.

Northern Free Blacks In the North, few free blacks enjoyed unfettered freedom. Most whites regarded African Americans as their social inferiors and confined them to low-paying jobs. In rural areas, free blacks worked as farm laborers or tenant farmers; in towns and cities, they toiled as domestic servants, laundresses, or day laborers. Only a small number of free African Americans owned land. "You do not see one out of a hundred . . . that can make a comfortable living, own a cow, or a horse," a traveler in New Jersey noted. In addition, northern blacks were usually forbidden to vote, attend public schools, or sit next to whites in churches. Only a few states extended the vote to free blacks, and blacks could testify in court against whites only in Massachusetts. The federal government did not allow free African Americans to work for the postal service, claim public lands, or hold a U.S. passport. As black activist Martin Delaney remarked in 1852: "We are slaves in the midst of freedom."

Thus I have given you, I think, the Substance of the Arguments o
both sides of that great and important Questic

Slaves and Masters

Slavery consisted of a multitude of individual relationships between African Americans and their white owners. But it was also a system of chattel property, forced labor, and sexual abuse. These selections—interviews with former slaves and a diary entry written by a cotton planter—suggest how people's lives were shaped by the slave-master relationship. The Works Project Administration (WPA), a government relief program in the 1930s, conducted hundreds of these interviews, creating a valuable documentary record. However, most of the interviewers were white and the former slaves were very old, so that the resulting stories were less graphic than the actual slave experience.

Mollie Dawson

Memories of a Slave Childhood

Mollie Dawson was born into slavery in Texas, where her owner had migrated from Tennessee. When Dawson told her story to a WPA interviewer, she was eighty-five years old.

Dat makes me bo'n in january sometime, of 1852. . . . Mah maw was de slave of Nath Newman and dat made me his slave. Mah maw's name was Sarah Benjamin. Mah father's name was Carrol Benjamin, and he belonged ter different white folks. . . .

De plantation dat he worked on was j'inin' our'n. I would go ovah ter see him once in a while when I was little, and de last time I goes ovah dar dey whips a man. . . . Dat was the only slave I ever seed gits a whippin', and I never did wants ter see dis white man anymo'. . . .

Mah mother and father was slavery time married darkies. Dat didn't mean nuthin' dem days, but jest raisin' mo' darkies, and every slave darkie woman had ter do dat whether she wanted to or not. Dey would let her pick out a man, or a man pick him out a woman, and dey was married, and if de woman wouldn't have de man dat picks her, dey would take her ter a big stout high husky nigger somewhere and leave her a few days, jest lak dey do stock now'days, and she bettah begin raisin' chilluns, too. . . .

Mah mother and father never did love each other lak dey ought to, so dey separated as soon as dey was free. Mah father married another woman by law. Mah mother married George Baldwin, and dey lives together fer about twelve years. Dey separated den, and she married Alfred Alliridge and dey lives together till she dies. . . .

I was too young ter do much work durin' slavery time, but I picks lots of cotton, and all de pay we got fer it was a place ter stay, water ter drink, wood ter burn, food ter eat, and clothes ter wear, and we made de food and clothes ourselves. We eats corn pones three times a day, 'ceptin' Sunday and Christmas mornings; Maser Newman lets us

have flour fer biscuits, den. In de summah we wore cotton clothes. All of dem was made on de plantation. Some of de women would spin and some would weave and some would make clothes. . . .

Maser Newman was a tall, slender man nearly six foot tall and was blue-eyed. He sho' was good ter all us slaves, but we all knew he means fer us ter work. He never whipped any of us slaves, but he hit one of de men wid a leather line 'bout two times once, 'cause dis slave kinda talked back ter him. . . .

Maser Newman was a slow easy-goin' sort of a man who took everything as it comes, takin' bad and good luck jest alak. . . . Maser Newman was lots older dan his wife. She was a real young woman, and they 'peared ter think quite a bit of each other. . . . Maser and Missus Newman jest had two chilluns and both of dem was little girls. . . . Dey sho' was pretty little gals and dey was smart, too. Dey played wid de little slave chilluns all de time, and course dey was de boss, same as deir mother and father.

Maser Newman was a poor man, compared wid some of de other slave owners. He only had about seven slaves big enough ter work all de year round in de fields. . . . He didn't have no drivah; he would jest start dem all out ter work, and dey kept at it all day. But he generally worked around pretty close ter dem.

Source: James Mellon, ed., *Bullwhip Days* (New York: Weidenfeld & Nicolson, 1988), 421–428.

Louisa Picquet

Sexual Exploitation Under Slavery

Louisa Picquet was born into slavery in Georgia in 1827; around 1840, she became the property of a John Williams of New Orleans. On his death in 1848, she was freed and moved to Ohio with her four children. In 1860, she related the story of her life to Hiram Mattison, a white abolitionist minister, who published it.

Q: How did you say you come to be sold?

A: Well, you see, Mr. Cook [my master] made great parties, and go off to watering-places, and get in debt, and had to break up, and then he took us to Mobile. . . . Then, after a while, the sheriff came from Georgia after Mr. Cook's debts, and found us all, and took us to auction, and sold us. My mother and brother was sold to Texas, and I was sold to New Orleans.

Q: How old were you, then?

A: Well, I don't know exactly, but the auctioneer said I wasn't quite fourteen. . . .

Q: Were there others there white like you?

A: Oh yes, plenty of them. . . . Then I was sold. . . . Mr. Williams allowed that he did not care what they bid, he was going to have me anyhow. Then he bid fifteen hundred. Mr. Horton said 'twas no use to bid anymore, and I was sold to Mr. Williams. I went right to New Orleans then.

Q: Who was Mr. Williams?

A: I didn't know then, only he lived in New Orleans. Him and his wife had parted, some way he had three children, boys. When I was going away I heard someone cryin' and prayin' the Lord to go with her only daughter, and protect me.

Q: Have you never seen her [Picquet's mother] since?

A: No, never since that time. I went to New Orleans, and she went to Texas. So I understood.

A: Mr. Williams told me what he bought me for, soon as we started for New Orleans. He said he was getting old, and when he saw me he thought he'd buy me, and end his days with me. He said if I behave myself he'd treat me well; but, if not, he'd whip me almost to death.

Q: How old was he?

A: He was over forty; I guess pretty near fifty. He was gray-headed. That's the reason he was always so jealous. He never let me go out anywhere. . . .

Q: Had you any children while in New Orleans?

A: Yes, I had four.

Q: Who was their father?

A: Mr. Williams. . . .

Q: Were your children mulattoes?

A: No, sir! They were all white. They look just like him. The neighbors all see that.

Source: H. Mattison, Louisa Picquet, *The Octoroon: Or Inside Views of Southern Life* (New York: Published by the Author, 1861), 17–19.

Bennet Barrow
Enforcing Labor Discipline

Bennet Barrow (1811–1854) inherited a substantial cotton plantation in Louisiana. From 1837 to 1845, he kept a diary that consisted of brief remarks on the day's events.

January 1838

14 Appearance of rain—pressed 7 B. [bales of cotton] last Sunday—pressing to day at Gibsons—will ship on Tuesday next 66 B . . . to Gin—On selling from 5 to 11-1/2 cts.— The times are seriously hard all most impossible to raise one dollar . . . great Excitement in Congress, Northern States medling with slavery—first they com'ced by petition— now by openly speaking of the sin of Slavery in the southern states . . . must eventually cause a separation of the Union.

October 1838

12 Clear verry cold morning—hands picked worse yesterday than they have done this year. . . . Whiped near half the hands to day for picking badly & trashy. . . .

26 Clear pleasant weather—Cotton picks very trashy— Whiped 8 or 10 for weight today. . . .

May 1839

21 Clear verry warm—Finished hilling Cotton—Darcas & Fanny are the greatest shirks of any negroes I have— laid up twicet a month—Went to Town—man tried for whipping a negro to Death. trial will continue till to morrow—deserves death—Cleared!

July 1841

18 . . . Received a note from Ruffin stating that several of my negroes were implicated in an intended insurrection on the 1st of August next. . . .

27 Cloudy. Verry warm, Negros all Cleared. But will be tried by the Planters themselves &c.

Source: Edwin Davis Adams, *Plantation Life in the Florida Parishes of Louisiana, 1836–1845 as Reflected in the Diary of Bennet H. Barrow* (New York: AMS Press, 1967 [c. 1943]), 105–106, 133, 135, 148, 236, 237.

ANALYZING THE EVIDENCE

- **How strong is the evidence in these selections? Is there any reason to question its accuracy? Mollie Dawson was eighty-five when she was interviewed. How reliable was her memory? An abolitionist published Louisa Picquet's account as an indictment of slavery. Is his account trustworthy? Is Bennet Barrow's diary a more reliable source than the other two? Explain your answer.**

- **Were you surprised by any of these accounts? If so, why? What did they tell you about day-to-day life under slavery that you did not know?**

- **Why do you suppose Picquet was freed in 1848?**

A Master Bridge Builder

Horace King (1807–1885) was a self-made man of color, a rarity in the nineteenth-century South. Born a slave of mixed European, African, and Native American (Catawba) ancestry, King built major bridges in Georgia, Alabama, and Mississippi during the early 1840s. After winning his freedom in 1846, he built and ran a toll bridge across the Chattahoochee River in Alabama. During the Civil War, King worked as a contractor for the Confederacy; during Reconstruction, he served two terms as a Republican in the Alabama House of Representatives. Collection of the Columbus Museum, Columbus, Georgia; Museum Purchase.

Of the few African Americans who were able to make full use of their talents, several achieved great distinction. Mathematician and surveyor Benjamin Banneker (1731–1806) published an almanac and helped lay out the new capital in the District of Columbia; Joshua Johnston (1765–1832) won praise for his portraiture; and merchant Paul Cuffee (1759–1817) acquired a small fortune from his business enterprises. More impressive and enduring were the community institutions created by free African Americans. Throughout the North, these largely unknown men and women founded schools, mutual-benefit organizations, and fellowship groups, often called Free African Societies. Discriminated against by white Protestants, they formed their own congregations and a new religious denomination—the African Methodist Episcopal Church, headed by Bishop Richard Allen (see Chapter 8).

These institutions gave free African Americans a measure of cultural autonomy, even as they institutionalized sharp social divisions among blacks. "Respectable" blacks tried through their dress, conduct, and attitude to win the "esteem and patronage" of prominent whites—first Federalists and then Whigs and abolitionists—who were sympathetic to their cause. Those efforts separated them from impoverished blacks, who distrusted not only whites but also blacks who "acted white."

Standing for Freedom in the South The free black population in the slave states numbered approximately 94,000 in 1810 and 225,000 in 1860. Most of these men and women lived in coastal cities—Mobile, Memphis, New Orleans—and in the Upper South. Partly because skilled Europeans avoided the South, free blacks formed the backbone of the region's urban artisan workforce. African American carpenters, blacksmiths, barbers, butchers, and shopkeepers played prominent roles in the economies of Baltimore, Richmond, Charleston, and New Orleans. But free blacks faced many dangers. Those accused of crimes were often denied a jury trial, and those charged with vagrancy were sometimes forced back into slavery. Other free blacks were simply kidnapped and taken elsewhere by their captors to be sold.

As a privileged group among African Americans, free blacks in the South had divided loyalties. To advance the welfare of their families, they were tempted to distance themselves from plantation slaves and assimilate white culture and values. Indeed, some privileged blacks became adjunct members of the planter class. David Barland, one of twelve children born to a white Mississippi planter and his black slave Elizabeth, himself owned no fewer than eighteen slaves. In neighboring Louisiana, some free blacks supported secession because they owned slaves and were "dearly attached to their native land."

Such men were exceptions. Most free African Americans acknowledged their ties to the great mass of slaves, some of whom were their relatives. "We's different [from whites] in color, in talk and in 'ligion and beliefs," said one. White planters reinforced black unity in the 1840s and 1850s by calling for the reenslavement of free African Americans. Knowing their own liberty was not secure so long as slavery existed, free

An African American Clergyman

This flattering portrait is one of two paintings of African Americans by black artist Joshua Johnston (who also went by the surname Johnson). Born into slavery in 1765, Johnston somehow became a free man and a successful artist. In an advertisement in the *Baltimore Intelligence* in 1798, he described himself as a "Portrait Painter . . . a self-taught genius deriving from nature and industry his knowledge of the Art." White merchant families in Maryland and Virginia held Johnston's work in high regard and commissioned most of his thirty or so extant works. Bowdoin College Museum of Art, Brunswick, Maine. Museum Purchase, George Otis Hamlin Fund.

blacks celebrated West Indian Emancipation Day (August 1) and sought freedom for all Americans of African ancestry. As a delegate to the National Convention of Colored People in 1848 put it, "Our souls are yet dark under the pall of slavery." In the rigid American caste system, free blacks stood as symbols of hope to enslaved African Americans and as symbols of danger to most whites.

- Why did certain African cultural practices (the ring shout and incest taboos, for example) persist in the United States while others (ritual scarring, for example) disappeared?

- What were some of the successes of African Americans in the period 1800–1860? In what endeavors did they not succeed?

SUMMARY

In this chapter, we focused on the theme of an expanding South. Beginning about 1800, planters carried the plantation system from its traditional home in the Upper South to the Mississippi Valley and beyond. Powered by cotton, this movement westward divided the planter elite into aristocratic paternalists and entrepreneurial capitalists, and involved the forced migration of more than 1 million enslaved African Americans.

We also examined the character of white and black societies in the Cotton South. After 1820, less than a third of white families owned slaves and another third were yeoman farmers; propertyless tenant farmers and laborers made up the rest. Many whites joined evangelical Protestant churches, as did blacks, who infused their churches with African modes of expression. Indeed, church and family became core institutions of African American society, providing strength and solace amid the tribulations of slavery. Finally, we explored the initiatives taken by the free black population, in both the northern and southern states, to achieve individual mobility and to build community institutions. These efforts produced a church-based leadership class and a black abolitionist movement.

CHAPTER REVIEW QUESTIONS

- How did plantation crops and the system of slavery change between 1800 and 1860? Why did these changes occur?

- Why in 1860 did white southerners remain committed to the institution of slavery and its expansion? Based on what you've learned so far in Part 3, compare and contrast society in the American South with that of the North. Is it fair to say that America was, in fact, two distinct societies by 1860?

FOR FURTHER EXPLORATION

Charlene M. Boyer Lewis explores the lives of the planter class in *Ladies and Gentlemen on Display* (2001). Other studies of slave owners are William Kauffman Scarborough, *Masters of the Big House* (2003), and Jeffrey Robert Young, *Domesticating Slavery* (1999). For the planters' intellectual pursuits, read Michael O'Brien, *Conjectures of Order* (2004). Edward Ball's *Slaves in the Family* (1998) recounts his ancestors' ownership of slaves, their illicit sexual unions, and the family's diverse racial identity. Stephanie McCurry's *Masters of Small Worlds* (1995) evokes the patriarchal lives of yeomen families. For plantation discipline, see Sally E. Hadden, *Slave Patrols* (2001), and John Hope Franklin and Loren Sweninger, *Runaway Slaves* (1999). On slavery's decline in the North, read Joanne Pope Melish, *Disowning Slavery* (1998).

Ira Berlin, *Generations of Captivity* (2003), Adam Rothman, *Slave Country: American Expansion and the Origins of the Deep South* (2005), and Michael Tadman, *Speculators and Slaves* (1996), analyze the changing character of slavery and African American society. See also Charles Joyner, *Down by the Riverside* (1984), and the material at **www.pbs.org/wnet/slavery/about/index.html**. For primary documents on the black Christian church, consult **docsouth.unc.edu/church/index.html**. Marcus Wood, *Blind Memory* (2000), offers many images of slave life, while Walter Johnson, *Soul by Soul* (1999), closely examines the New Orleans slave mart. Two document-rich Web sites are "The African-American Mosaic" at **www.loc.gov/exhibits/african/intro.html** and "Slaves and the Courts, 1740–1860" at **lcweb2.loc.gov/ammem/aaohtml**.

TEST YOUR KNOWLEDGE

To assess your command of the material in this chapter, see the Online Study Guide at **bedfordstmartins.com/henretta**.

For Web sites, images, and documents related to topics and places in this chapter, visit **bedfordstmartins.com/makehistory**.

TIMELINE

1810s	Africans from Congo region influence black culture
	Natural increase produces surplus of slaves in Old South
	Domestic slave trade expands, disrupting black family life
1812	Louisiana becomes a state, and its sugar output increases
1817	Mississippi becomes a state; Alabama follows (1819)
1820s	Growth in free black population in North and South
	Slave-owning gentry in Old South adopt paternalistic ideology
	Entrepreneurial planters in Cotton South turn to gang labor
	Southern Methodists and Baptists become socially conservative
	African Americans adopt Christian beliefs
1830s	Advocates of slavery argue it is a "positive good"
	Boom in cotton production
	Percentage of slave-owning white families falls
	Yeomen farm families retreat to hill country
	Lawyers become influential in southern politics
1840s	Southern Whigs advocate economic diversification
	Gradual emancipation completed in North
1850s	Cotton prices and production increase; slave prices rise
	Southern states subsidize railroads, but industrialization remains limited

PART 4

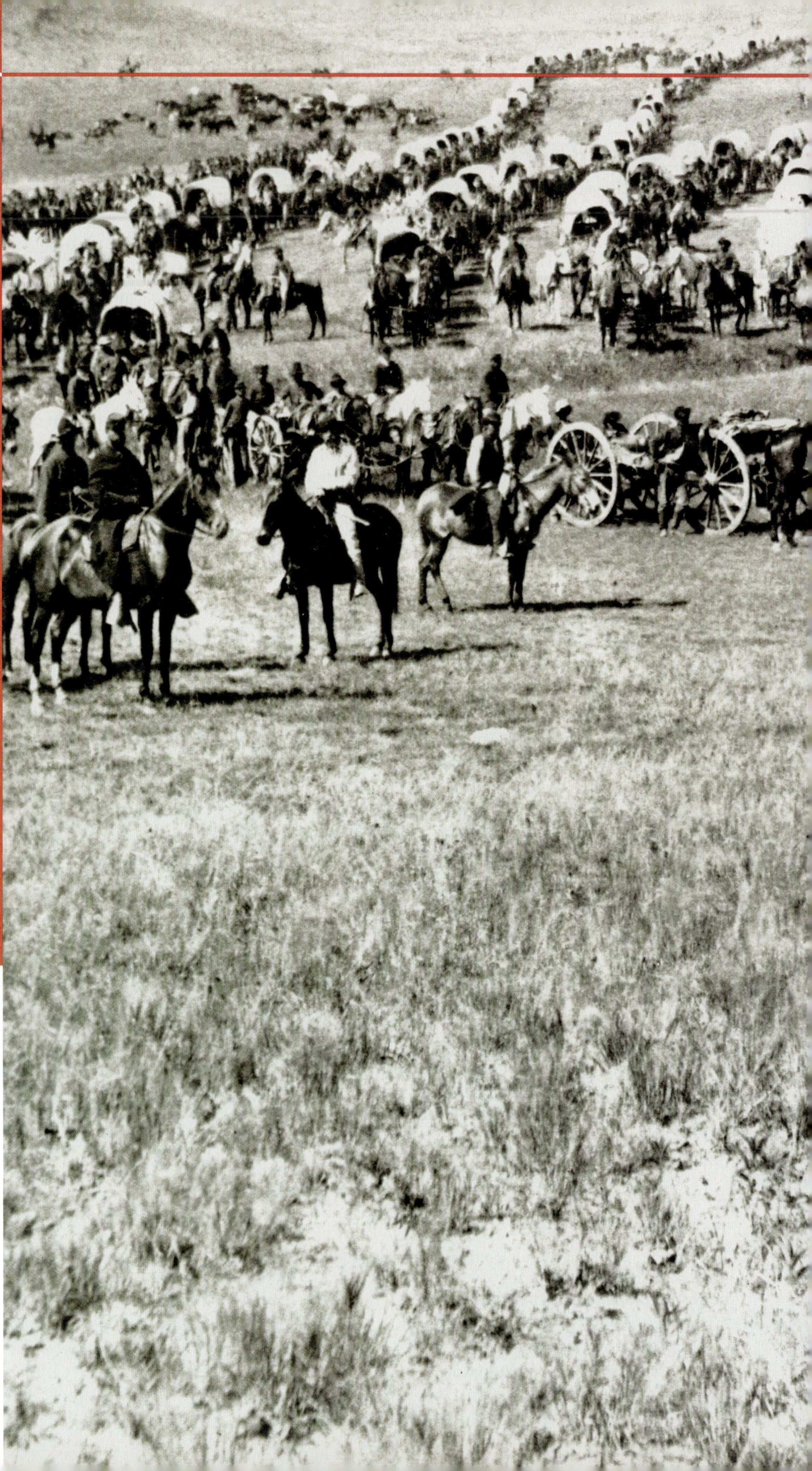

CHAPTERS

CREATING AND PRESERVING A CONTINENTAL NATION, 1844-1877

Between 1844 and 1877, the United States became a continental nation by fighting—and winning—three wars and creating a stronger central government. In the 1840s, it took over much of western North America through diplomatic negotiations with Great Britain and a war of conquest with Mexico. Geographic expansion sharpened political conflicts between the free and slave states and led to the South's secession in 1861. The Union government consolidated national authority by defeating the secessionists in a long Civil War, freeing millions of slaves, and reconstructing the Union under the ideals of the Republican Party.

Reconstruction included far more than reincorporating the South. After the war, the national government opened up newly acquired western lands for Euro-Americans by conquering Indian peoples and confining them to reservations. These events created new conflicts and systems of race relations. Native Americans found themselves negotiating between policies of "race uplift" and potential citizenship, and their desire to retain their traditional cultural and tribal ties. Meanwhile, Reconstruction offered hope for millions of workers of African ancestry, who fought for a fairer labor system and equal citizenship rights as African *Americans*. The story of these transforming events falls into five interconnected parts.

CONTINENTAL EMPIRE

The quest for western lands sparked wars against Mexico and . . . Indian peoples

Diplomatic and Military Expansion

The romantic spirit of Manifest Destiny pervaded American culture during the 1840s, prompting southerners to push for the annexation of Texas and Midwesterners to demand control over Oregon. Railroad entrepreneurs championed expansionism, as did northeastern merchants eager to expand trade across the Pacific. The quest for western lands sparked wars against Mexico and the Cheyennes, Sioux, and Comanches, among other Indian peoples. The purchase of Russian claims to Alaska, and efforts to acquire overseas coaling stations, marked policymakers' rising interest in foreign markets. On the continent, Anglo-American settlement of California and the Southwest overturned Spanish and Mexican customs and land claims and rapidly opened up the region to white miners, farmers, and ranchers.

SECTIONALISM

. . . a downward spiral of conflict . . . ended in the Civil War

Secession and Reunion

The Mexican War prompted a decade-long debate over the constitutional status of newly acquired lands. This increasingly bitter political struggle led to the Compromise of 1850, a multifaceted legislative agreement that won little support either in the North or the South. The Kansas-Nebraska Act of 1854 and the 1857 *Dred Scott* decision began a downward spiral of conflict that ended in the Civil War. Though sectional conflict would continue, the Union emerged stronger from the Civil War, as Republican policies bound the nation together. Never again would a region seek to leave the nation and establish its independence.

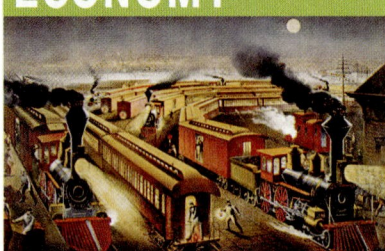

The Civil War greatly enhanced [federal] military power and constitutional authority

[Republicans] enacted aggressive policies to promote economic development

Irish, German, and British immigrants prompted a sharp nativist reaction

Democracy Challenged

Continental expansion and sectional conflict triggered the disintegration of the Second Party system. As Southern Whigs became Democrats and Northern Whigs turned into Republicans, party allegiances split along sectional lines and created political divisions that persisted well into the twentieth century. Political developments brought about by the Civil War greatly enhanced the military power and the constitutional authority of the national government. Three wartime constitutional amendments changed the nature of federalism by altering the nature of American citizenship— prohibiting slavery, mandating suffrage for black men, and forbidding state action that denied people equal protection under the law. After the war, the U.S. Army remained a significant force, enforcing Reconstruction in the South, suppressing Indian peoples, and upholding legal authority in the West.

Public Support for Private Enterprise

The Civil War created a powerful American state. To fight the war, the Union government mobilized millions of men and billions of dollars. In the process, it created a modern fiscal system, an elaborate network of national banks, and—for the first time in American history—a significant national bureaucracy. Inspired by Whig ideology, Republican-run Congresses enacted aggressive policies to promote economic development. They granted huge subsidies to railroad companies, protected industries and workers through high protective tariffs, promoted education and economic research, gave western land to farmers and cattlemen, and mapped and distributed western resources, including timber and mineral rights. A great postwar boom in railway construction, land speculation, and agricultural production collapsed in 1873, as a worldwide decline in prices led to a lengthy depression.

New Peoples, New Statuses

The ethnic composition and racial distinctions of the United States changed dramatically during the decades before, during, and just after the Civil War. Millions of Irish, German, and British immigrants prompted a sharp nativist reaction. Increasingly, the elite classes of the North doubted the wisdom of universal male suffrage. The freedom granted to 4 million African Americans raised a similar issue for southern whites, who maintained their privileged racial status by denying full political and civil rights for freedmen. In the trans-Mississippi West, whites jostled uneasily with conquered Hispanic residents, subject Indian peoples, and despised Chinese immigrants. These decades, which began with the romantic quest for continental empire, ended on the bitter notes of racial struggles and half-won freedoms.

Nonetheless, many European Americans looked back on the era as one of unprecedented progress. The United States had claimed a vast, resource-rich empire in the West. Railroads and industrial cities were growing from Chicago to San Francisco, and merchants and traders looked eagerly across the Pacific. The nation had fought a great war that preserved the Union and vanquished slavery. And America's dynamic postwar economy began to draw immigrants from many continents. These achievements, by no means predictable in 1840, had set the nation on a course toward global power.

CREATING AND PRESERVING A CONTINENTAL NATION, 1844–1877

	CONTINENTAL EMPIRE	SECTIONALISM	GOVERNMENT	ECONOMY	SOCIETY
1840	• Texas annexation (1845), acquisition of Oregon (1846), and Mexican War (1846–1848) extend U.S. borders to Pacific • Wars against Seminoles in Florida (1835–1842, 1855–1858)	• Mexican War and Wilmot Proviso (1846) increase sectional conflict • Gold Rush makes California eligible for statehood—free or slave?	• Free-Soil Party (1848) • Seneca Falls convention seeks votes for women (1848)	• Recession causes some states to default on bonds issued to build canals • Walker Tariff (1846) lowers rates, increases trade	• Whites migrate to Oregon and California • Hispanics incorporated as citizens in Southwest
1850	• President Pierce opens Japan to trade; seeks expansion of American territory and slavery into Caribbean • Comanches and Sioux dominate Great Plains trade in horses and buffalo hides	• Compromise of 1850 • Harriet Beecher Stowe's *Uncle Tom's Cabin* (1852) • Kansas-Nebraska Act (1854) and "Bleeding Kansas"	• Whig Party disintegrates; Know-Nothing Party emerges • Republican Party founded (1854) • Rise of southern secessionists	• Surge of cotton output in South • Expansion of farm society into trans-Mississippi west • Railroads and manufacturing intensify in North and Midwest	• Indians resettled throughout West • Arrival of millions of German and Irish immigrants • *Dred Scott* decision (1857) implies slavery throughout United States
1860	• Union triumphs in Civil War, preserving a continental nation • Secretary of State Seward buys Alaska from Russia (1867) • Homesteaders, cattlemen, and miners settle Plains and West	• South Carolina leads secession movement (1860) • Confederate States of America (1861–1865) • Radical Republicans seek to reconstruct postwar South	• Freedman's Bureau assists ex-slaves • Fourteenth Amendment (1868) extends legal and political rights	• Republicans enact Whigs' policy agenda: Homestead Act (1862), railroad aid, high tariffs, and national banking	• Emancipation Proclamation (1863) and Thirteenth Amendment (1865) end slavery • Blacks in the South struggle for freedom, land, and education
1870	• Wars against Plains Indians: Cheyennes, Sioux, Apaches, and Nez Perce	• Ku Klux Klan and white vigilantes attack Reconstruction governments • Compromise of 1877 ends Reconstruction	• Fifteenth Amendment (1870) extends vote to black men • Rollback of Republican control of Congress (1874)	• Rise of sharecropping in the South • Depression of 1873 halts railway expansion	• White elites challenge ideal of universal suffrage • Dawes Act (1887) seeks Indian assimilation

Expansion, War, and Sectional Crisis, 1844-1860

The American expansionist surge of the 1840s had deep roots. Visionaries had long predicted a glorious expansion across the continent. "It belongs of right to the United States to regulate the future destiny of North America," declared a writer in the *New-York Evening Post* in 1803. Two decades later, politicians had taken up the refrain. "Our natural boundary is the Pacific Ocean," asserted Massachusetts congressman Francis Baylies in 1823. "The swelling tide of our population must and will roll on until that mighty ocean interposes its waters." Yet the creation of a continental republic was far from inevitable; it required a transportation revolution – canals and railways – that would connect far-flung regions, a growing land-hungry population, and a dynamic economy. By the 1840s, all of those factors were in place.

Other obstacles remained. Strong, well-armed Indian peoples controlled the Great Plains, Mexico held sovereignty over Texas and the lands west of the Rocky Mountains, and Great Britain laid claim to the Oregon Country. To extend the American republic would likely involve new Indian wars and armed conflict with Mexico (perhaps aided by France, its creditor) and Great Britain. An ardent imperialist, President James Polk willingly assumed those risks. "I would meet the war which either England or France or all the powers of Christendom might wage," he told Secretary of State James Buchanan in 1846, "and fight until the last man."

Polk's aggressive expansionism sparked fighting abroad and conflict at home. A war with Mexico intended to be "brief, cheap, and bloodless" became, as Senator Thomas Hart Benton of Missouri complained, "long, costly, and sanguinary." Even Polk's great territorial acquisitions – New Mexico, California, the Oregon Country – proved double-edged, because they reignited a bitter debate over the extension of slavery. Southerners threatened to secede from the Union in 1850, Northerners responded with anger, and rhetoric spiraled downward into violence. When Massachusetts Senator Charles Sumner accused Senator Andrew P. Butler of South Carolina in 1856 of taking "the harlot slavery" as his mistress, South Carolina representative Preston Brooks beat Sumner unconscious with a walking cane. As Brooks struck down Sumner in Washington, Axalla Hoole of South Carolina and other proslavery migrants in the Kansas Territory fought armed New England abolitionists. Passion had replaced political compromise as the hallmark of American public life.

War News from Mexico, 1848

In this painting of men at the "American Hotel," artist Richard Caton Woodville (1825–1855) captures the public's hunger for news of the Mexican War, the first foreign conflict since the War of 1812. As a journalist in Baltimore, Woodville's hometown, noted, "People begin to collect every evening, about 5 o'clock at the telegraph and newspaper offices, waiting for extras and despatches." Note the subordinate placement of African Americans and a woman (in the window at the right edge of the painting). Private Collection, on loan to the National Gallery of Art, Washington, Photograph © 2002 Board of Trustees, National Gallery of Art.

Manifest Destiny: South and North

The upsurge in violence reflected a generational shift in culture and politics. The Missouri crisis of 1819–1822 (see Chapter 8) had thrown a fright into the nation's leaders. For the next two decades, the professional politicians who managed the Second Party System avoided policies, such as the annexation of the slave-holding Republic of Texas, that would prompt regional strife. Then, during the 1840s, many citizens embraced an ideology of conquest that proclaimed their God-given duty to extend American republicanism and capitalism to the Pacific Ocean. But whose republican institutions and economic system: the hierarchical racial order of the slaveholding South, or the more democratic, reform-minded society of the North and Midwest? Or both? Ultimately, the failure to find a politically acceptable answer to this question would rip the nation apart.

The Push to the Pacific

As expansionists developed continental ambitions, the term **Manifest Destiny** captured those dreams. John L. O'Sullivan, editor of the *Democratic Review*, coined the phrase in 1845: "Our manifest destiny is to overspread the continent allotted by Providence for the free development of our yearly multiplying millions." Underlying the rhetoric of Manifest Destiny was a sense of Anglo-American cultural and racial superiority: The "inferior"

peoples who lived in the Far West — Native Americans and Mexicans — were to be brought under American dominion, taught republicanism, and converted to Protestantism (see Reading American Pictures, "Visualizing 'Manifest Destiny,'" p. 401).

Oregon | Land-hungry farmers of the Ohio River Valley had already cast their eyes toward the fertile valleys of the Oregon Country. This region stretched along the Pacific coast between the Mexican province of California and Russian settlements in Alaska and was claimed by both Britain and the United States. Since 1818, a British-American agreement had allowed people from both nations to live there. The British-run Hudson's Bay Company developed a lucrative fur trade north of the Columbia River, while Methodist missionaries and a few hundred Americans settled to the south, in the Willamette Valley (Map 13.1).

In 1842, American interest in Oregon increased dramatically. The U.S. Navy published a glowing report of fine harbors in the Puget Sound, which were already being used by New England merchants trading with China. In the same year, a party of one hundred farmers journeyed along the Oregon Trail, which fur traders and explorers had blazed from Independence, Missouri, across the Great Plains and the Rocky Mountains (Map 13.2). Their letters from Oregon told of a mild climate and rich soil.

"Oregon fever" suddenly raged. A thousand men, women, and children — with a hundred wagons and 5,000 oxen and cattle — had gathered in Independence

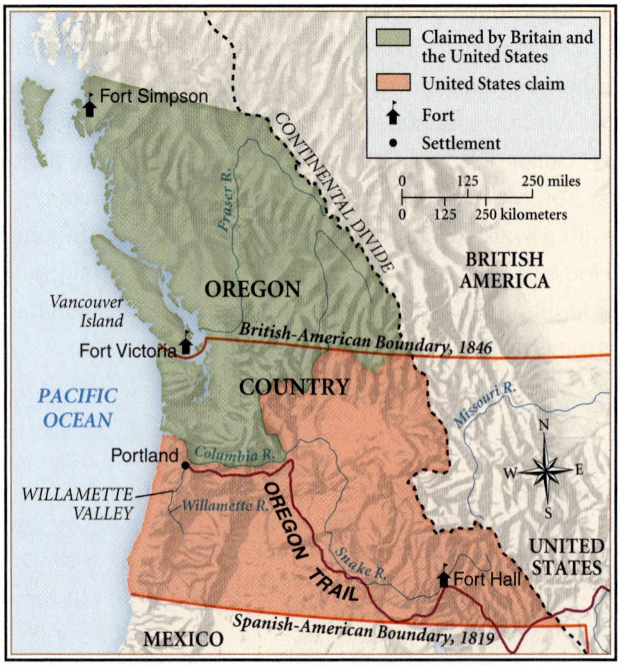

MAP 13.1

Territorial Conflict in Oregon, 1819–1846

As thousands of American settlers poured into the Oregon Country in the early 1840s, British authorities tried to keep them south of the Columbia River. However, the migrants — and fervent midwestern expansionists — asserted that Americans could settle anywhere in the territory, raising the prospect of armed conflict. In 1846, British and American diplomats resolved the dispute by dividing the region at the 49th parallel.

Settling Oregon

It did not take long for Americans to populate the Far West and re-create there the small-town life of the eastern states. As early as 1845, as this drawing by a British military officer shows, Oregon City boasted a steepled church, several large merchandise warehouses, and several dozen houses. On the riverbank opposite the town stand several Indians, who had a very different way of life and would be steadily pushed off the lands of their ancestors.   Library of Congress from Henry James Warre, *Sketches from North America and the Oregon Territory* (London: Dickson & Co., 1848).

by late April 1843. As the spring mud dried, they began their six-month trek, hoping to miss the winter snows. Another 5,000 settlers, mostly yeomen farm families from the southern border states (Missouri, Kentucky, and Tennessee), set out over the next two years. These pioneers overcame floods, dust storms, livestock deaths, and a few armed encounters with Indians before reaching the Willamette Valley, a journey of 2,000 miles.

By 1860, about 250,000 Americans had braved the Oregon Trail, with 65,000 heading for Oregon and 185,000 to California. More than 34,000 migrants died in the effort, mostly from disease and exposure; fewer than 500 deaths resulted from Indian attacks. The walking migrants wore paths 3 feet deep, and their wagons carved 5-foot ruts across sandstone formations in southern Wyoming—tracks that are visible today. Women found the trail especially difficult; in addition to their usual chores and the new work of driving wagons and animals, they lacked the support of female kin and the security of their domestic space. About 2,500 women endured pregnancy or gave birth during the long journey, and some did not survive. "There was a woman died in this train yesterday," Jane Gould Tortillott noted in her diary. "She left six children, one of them only two days old."

The 10,000 migrants who made it to Oregon in the 1840s mostly settled in the Willamette Valley. Many families squatted on 640 acres and hoped Congress would legalize their claims so that they could profit from the sale of their surplus acreage to new settlers. They quickly created a race- and gender-defined polity by restricting voting to a "free male descendant of a white man."

California | About 3,000 other early pioneers ended up in the Mexican province of California. They left the Oregon Trail along the Snake River, trudged down the California Trail, and settled in the interior along the Sacramento River, where there were few Mexicans. A remote outpost of Spain's American empire, California had been settled only in the 1770s, when Spanish authorities built a chain of presidios—religious missions and forts—along the Pacific coast.

MAP 13.2

The Great Plains: Indian Peoples and Settler Trails

By the 1850s, the Mormon, Oregon, and Santa Fe trails ran through "Indian Country," the semi-arid, buffalo-filled area of the Great Plains west of the 95th meridian, through the Rocky Mountains. Tens of thousands of Americans set out on these trails to found new communities in Utah, Oregon, New Mexico, and California. This mass migration increasingly exposed Indian peoples to American diseases, guns, and manufactures. But their lives were even more significantly affected by U.S. soldiers, and the traders who provided a ready market for Indian horses and mules, dried meat, and buffalo skins.

After Mexican independence in 1821, the government took over the Franciscan-run missions and freed the 20,000 Indians who had been coerced into working on them. Some mission Indians rejoined their tribes, but many intermarried with mestizos (Mexicans of mixed Spanish and Indian ancestry) and worked on large ranches. To promote California's development, Mexican authorities bestowed large land grants on entrepreneurs, who raised Spanish cattle, prized for their hides and tallow.

Visualizing "Manifest Destiny"

In 1845, newspaper editor John O'Sullivan coined the term *Manifest Destiny* to describe Americans' suddenly urgent longing to extend the nation to the Pacific Ocean. John Gast's painting, *American Progress* (1872), gave visual form to that aspiration and was widely distributed through color lithographs. What do the details of the painting tell us about the meaning of Manifest Destiny?

John Gast, *American Progress.* Library of Congress.

ANALYZING THE EVIDENCE

- The painting is an allegory: The artist uses symbols to depict America's expansion to the Pacific. The central symbol of the goddess Liberty floats westward, her forehead emblazoned with the "Star of Empire." Why did Gast choose Liberty to lead the republic west? Why is she wearing the Star of Empire? What is the meaning of the "School Book" in her right hand? Of the telegraph lines?

- The painting has three horizontal planes—foreground, middle ground, and background—and each tells a story. What stages of social evolution are pictured in each plane? What symbols of progress does Gast employ? What role does technology play in the artist's rendition of progress?

- Gast also divided the painting into two vertical planes by altering the brightness of the image. What might a transition from light to dark symbolize?

- In the background on the far right stands New York City, with the magnificent Brooklyn Bridge (still under construction in 1872) spanning the East River. Far to the left is the Pacific Ocean. Why did Gast include these elements?

- Aside from the goddess, there are no clearly visible white women in the picture (though two Native American women can be seen in the foreground at left)—nor are there any black men or women. Why might Gast have excluded Euro-American women and African Americans?

William Henry Jackson, *California Crossing, South Platte River*, detail, 1867
The South Platte River was wide (stretching from the foreground to the low bluff in the middle of the picture) but shallow, allowing relatively easy passage for the migrants' cattle and covered wagons. During the late spring and early summer, wagon trains often stretched across the Great Plains as far as the eye could see.   National Park Service/ Picture Research Consultants & Archives.

The ranches soon linked California to the American economy. New England merchants dispatched dozens of agents to buy leather for the booming Massachusetts boot and shoe industry and tallow to make soap and candles. Many agents married the daughters of the elite Mexican landowners and ranchers—the Californios— and adopted their manners, attitudes, and Catholic religion. A crucial exception was Thomas Oliver Larkin, a successful merchant in the coastal town of Monterey. Larkin worked closely with Mexican ranchers, but he remained an American in outlook and eventually fostered California's annexation to the United States.

Like Larkin, the American migrants in the Sacramento River Valley did not want to assimilate into Mexican society. Some hoped to emulate the Americans in Texas by colonizing the country and then seeking annexation to the United States. However, in the early 1840s, these settlers numbered only about 1,000; by contrast, 7,000 Mexicans and 300 American traders lived along the coast.

The Plains Indians

As the Pacific-bound wagon trains rumbled across Nebraska along the broad Platte River, the migrants encountered the unique ecology of the Great Plains. A vast sea of grass stretched north from Texas to Saskatchewan in Canada, and west from the Missouri River to the Rocky Mountains. Tall grasses flourished in the eastern regions of the future states of Kansas, Nebraska, and the Dakotas, where there was ample rainfall. To the west—in the semiarid region beyond the 100th meridian—the migrants found short grasses that sustained a rich wildlife dominated by buffaloes and grazing antelopes. Nomadic buffalo-hunting Indian peoples roamed the western plains, while the tall grass-

lands and river valleys to the east were home to semi-sedentary tribes and, since the 1830s, the Indian peoples whom Andrew Jackson had "removed" to the west. A line of military forts—stretching from Fort Jesup in Louisiana to Fort Snelling in Minnesota—policed the boundary between white America and what Congress in 1834 designated as Permanent Indian Territory.

For centuries, the Indians who lived on the eastern edge of the plains, such as the Pawnees and the Mandan on the Upper Missouri River, subsisted primarily on food crops—corn and beans—supplemented by buffalo meat. They hunted the buffalo on foot, driving them over cliffs or into canyons for the kill. To the south, the nomadic Apaches acquired horses from Spanish settlers in New Mexico. No longer dependent on dogs to move their goods, the Apaches ranged widely across the southern plains. But it was the Comanches, who migrated down the Arkansas River from the Rocky Mountains around 1750, who first developed a specialized horse culture. Fierce warriors and skilled buffalo hunters, the Comanches pushed the Apaches to the southern edge of the plains. Then the Comanches evolved into pastoralists; each Comanche family owned thirty to thirty-five horses or mules, far more than the five or six required for buffalo hunting. They sold both horses and mules to northern Indian peoples and Euro-American farmers in Missouri and Arkansas. They also exchanged goods with traders and travelers along the Sante Fe Trail, which cut through Comanche and Kiowa territory as it connected Missouri and New Mexico. By the early 1840s, goods worth nearly $1 million moved along the trail each year.

By the 1830s, the Kiowas, Cheyennes, and Arapahos had also adopted this horse culture and, allied with the Comanches, dominated the plains between the Arkansas and Red rivers. With the new culture came sharper social divisions. Some Kiowa men owned hundreds of horses and had several "chore wives" and captive children who worked for them. Poor men, who owned only a few horses, could not find marriage partners and often had to work for their wealthy kinsmen.

However, even as European horses enhanced the mobility and wealth of the Plains Indians, European diseases and guns thinned their ranks. A devastating smallpox epidemic spread northward from New Spain in 1779–1781, taking the lives of half of the Plains Indians. Twenty years later, another smallpox outbreak left dozens of deserted villages along the Missouri River. Smallpox struck the northern plains again from 1837 to 1840, killing half of the Assiniboines and Blackfeet and nearly a third of the Crows and Pawnees. "If I could see this thing, if I knew where it came from, I would go there and fight it," exclaimed a distressed Cheyenne warrior as an epidemic ran through his tribe.

European weapons also altered the geography of native peoples. Around 1750, the Crees and Assiniboines, who lived on the far northern plains, acquired guns by trading wolf pelts and beaver skins to the British-run Hudson's Bay Company. Once armed, they drove the Blackfeet peoples westward into the Rocky Mountains and took control of the Saskatchewan and Upper Missouri River basins. When the Blackfeet obtained guns and horses around 1800, they emerged from the mountains and pushed the Shoshones and Crows to the south. Because horses could not easily find winter forage in the cold, snow-filled plains north of the Platte River, the Blackfeet could not maintain large herds; most families kept five to ten horses and remained hunters, not pastoralists.

The powerful Sioux, who acquired guns and ammunition from French, Spanish, and American traders along the Missouri River, also remained buffalo hunters. As nomadic people who traveled in small groups, the Sioux largely avoided major epidemics and increased their numbers. They kept some sedentary peoples, such as the Arikaras, in subjection and raided others for their crops and horses. By the 1830s, the Sioux were the dominant tribe on the central as well as the northern plains. "Those lands once belonged to the Kiowas and the Crows," boasted the Oglala Sioux chief Black Hawk, "but we whipped those nations out of them, and in this we did what the white men do when they want the lands of the Indians."

The Sioux's prosperity came at the expense not only of other Indian peoples but also of the buffalo, which provided them with a diet rich in protein and with hides and robes to sell. The number of hides and robes shipped down the Missouri River each year by the American Fur Company and the Missouri Fur Company increased from 3,000 in the 1820s, to 45,000 in the 1830s, and to 90,000 annually after 1840. North of the Missouri, the story was much the same. The 24,000 nomadic Indians of that region—Blackfeet, Crees, and Assiniboines—annually killed about 160,000 buffalo. The women dried the meat to feed their people and to sell to white traders and soldiers. They also undertook the arduous work of skinning and tanning the hides, which were used primarily for their own needs—for tepees, buffalo robes, and sleeping covers. But they traded surplus hides and robes, about 40,000 annually, for pots, knives, guns, and other manufactures. As among the Kiowas, trade with Euro-Americans increased social divisions. "It is a fine sight," a traveler noted around 1850, "to see one of those big men among the Blackfeet, who has two or three lodges, five or six wives, twenty or thirty children, fifty to a hundred head of horses; for his trade amounts to upward of $2,000 per year."

Although the Blackfeet, Kiowas, and Sioux contributed to the market economy, its workings remained largely unknown to them. Not understanding the value of their buffalo hides in world markets—as winter clothes, leather accessories, and industrial drive belts—they could not demand the best price. Nor was the future bright, because the Indians' subsistence needs and the overkill for the export trade was cutting the size of the buffalo herds. In the 1820s, the northern herd had numbered more than 5 million; by the late 1860s, it had shrunk to less than 2 million. According to Assiniboines' beliefs, when their cultural hero Inkton'mi taught the people how to kill the buffalo, he said: "The buffalo will live as long as your people. There will be no end of them until the end of time." Rather than a perpetual guarantee, by the 1860s Inkton'mi's words prefigured the end of time—the end of traditional buffalo-hunting and, perhaps, of the Assiniboines as well.

The Fateful Election of 1844

The election of 1844 changed the American government's policy toward the Great Plains, the Far West, and Texas. Since 1836, when Texas sought annexation, southern leaders had advocated American expansion to extend slavery, only to be rebuffed by cautious party politicians and northern abolitionists. Now rumors swirled that Great Britain wanted California as payment for the large debts owed to British investors; that it was encouraging Texas to remain independent; and that it had designs on Spanish Cuba, which some slave owners wanted to annex to the United States. To thwart such imagined schemes, southern expansionists demanded the immediate annexation of Texas.

At this crucial juncture, Oregon fever and Manifest Destiny altered the political landscape in the North. In 1843, Americans in the Ohio River Valley and the Great Lakes states organized "Oregon conventions," and Democratic and Whig politicians alike called for American control of the entire Oregon Country, from Spanish California to Russian Alaska (which began at 54°40' north latitude). With northerners demanding Oregon, southern Democrats again called for the annexation of Texas. The southerners had the support of President John Tyler, a proslavery zealot. Disowned by the Whigs because of his opposition to Henry Clay's nationalist economic program, Tyler hoped to win reelection in

1844 as a Democrat. To curry favor among northern expansionists of both parties, Tyler proposed to seize all of Oregon.

In April 1844, Tyler and John C. Calhoun, his expansionist-minded secretary of state, sent the Senate a treaty to bring Texas into the Union. But the two major presidential hopefuls, Democrat Martin Van Buren and Whig Henry Clay, opposed Tyler's initiative. Fearful of raising the issue of slavery, they persuaded the Senate to reject the treaty.

Expansion into Texas and Oregon became the central issue in the election of 1844. Most southern Democrats favored expansion and refused to support Van Buren, because of his opposition to annexing Texas. The party also passed over Tyler, whom they did not trust. Instead, the Democrats selected Governor James K. Polk of Tennessee, an avowed expansionist and a slave owner. Known as "Young Hickory" because he was a protégé of Andrew Jackson, Polk shared his mentor's iron will, boundless ambition, and determination to open up lands for white settlement. Accepting the false claim in the Democratic Party platform that both areas already belonged to the United States, Polk campaigned for the "Re-occupation of Oregon and the Re-annexation of Texas." He insisted that the United States claim "the whole of the territory of Oregon" to the Alaskan border. "Fifty-four forty or fight!" became his jingoistic cry.

The Whigs nominated Henry Clay, who again advocated his American System of high tariffs, internal improvements, and national banking. Clay initially dodged the issue of Texas but, seeking southern votes, ultimately supported annexation. Northern Whigs who opposed the admission of a new slave state expressed their disappointment in Clay by casting their ballots for James G. Birney of the Liberty Party (see Chapter 11). Birney garnered less than 3 percent of the national vote but took enough Whig votes in New York to cost Clay that state—and the presidency.

Following Polk's narrow victory, congressional Democrats called immediately for Texas statehood. However, they lacked the two-thirds majority in the Senate needed to ratify a treaty of annexation. So the Democrats admitted Texas using a joint resolution of Congress, which required just a majority vote in each house, and Texas became the twenty-eighth state in December 1845. Polk's strategy of linking Texas and Oregon had put him in the White House and Texas in the Union. Shortly, it would make the expansion of the South—and its system of slavery—the central topic of American politics.

- What ideas did the term *Manifest Destiny* reflect? Did it cause historical events, such as the new political support for territorial expansion, or was it merely a description of events?

- Which of the peoples native to the Great Plains increased in numbers and in wealth between 1750 and 1860? Why did they flourish while other peoples did not?

War, Expansion, and Slavery, 1846–1850

The acquisition of Texas whetted Polk's appetite for all the Mexican lands between Texas and the Pacific Ocean. If necessary, he was ready to go to war to get them. What he and many Democrats consciously ignored was the crisis over slavery that this expansion would unleash. Like other American presidents, Polk would learn that war can be a costly military and political option.

The War with Mexico, 1846–1848

Since gaining independence in 1821, Mexico had not prospered. Its civil wars and political instability resulted in a stagnant economy, a weak government, and modest tax revenues, which were quickly devoured by a bloated bureaucracy and debt payments to European bankers. Although the distant northern provinces of California and New Mexico contributed little to the national economy and remained sparsely settled, with a Spanish-speaking population of only 75,000 in 1840, Mexican officials vowed to preserve their nation's historic boundaries. When its former province of Texas voted to join the American union in July 1845, Mexico broke off diplomatic relations with the United States.

Polk's Expansionist Program | President Polk quickly set in motion his plans to acquire Mexico's other northern provinces. He hoped to foment a revolution in California that, like the 1836 rebellion in Texas, would lead to annexation. In October 1845, Secretary of State James Buchanan told merchant Thomas Oliver Larkin, now the U.S. consul in the port of Monterey, to encourage influential Californios to seek independence and union with the United States. To add military muscle to this scheme, Polk ordered American naval commanders to seize San Francisco Bay and California's coastal towns in case of war with Mexico. The president also instructed the War Department to dispatch Captain John C. Frémont and an "exploring" party of heavily armed soldiers into Mexican territory. By December 1845, Frémont's force had reached California's Sacramento River Valley.

With these preparations in place, Polk launched a secret diplomatic initiative: He sent Louisiana congressman John Slidell to Mexico, telling him to secure the Rio Grande boundary and to buy the provinces of California and New Mexico for $30 million. However, Mexican officials declared that the annexation of Texas violated Mexican sovereignty and refused to see Slidell.

Events now moved quickly toward war. Polk ordered General Zachary Taylor and an American army of 2,000 soldiers to occupy disputed lands between the Nueces River (the historic southern boundary of Spanish Texas) and the Rio Grande, which the Republic of Texas had claimed as its border with Mexico. "We were sent to provoke a fight," recalled Ulysses S. Grant, then a young officer serving with Taylor, "but it was essential that Mexico should commence it." When the armies clashed near the Rio Grande in May 1846, Polk delivered the war message he had drafted long before. Taking liberties with the truth, the president declared that Mexico "has passed the boundary of the United States, has invaded our territory, and shed American blood upon the American soil." Ignoring pleas by some Whigs for a negotiated settlement, an overwhelming majority in Congress voted for war—a decision greeted with great popular acclaim. To avoid a simultaneous war with Britain, Polk retreated from his demand for "fifty-four forty or fight" and accepted a British proposal to divide the Oregon Country at the forty-ninth parallel.

American Military Successes Meanwhile, American forces in Texas established their military superiority. Zachary Taylor's army crossed the Rio Grande; occupied the Mexican city of Matamoros; and, after a fierce six-day battle in September 1846, took the interior Mexican town of Monterrey. Two months later, a U.S. naval squadron in the Gulf of Mexico seized Tampico, Mexico's second most important port. By the end of 1846, the United States controlled much of northeastern Mexico (Map 13.3).

MAP 13.3

The Mexican War, 1846–1848

After moving west from Fort Leavenworth in present-day Kansas, American forces commanded by Captain John C. Frémont and General Stephen Kearney defeated Mexican armies in California in 1846 and early 1847. Simultaneously, U.S. troops under General Zachary Taylor and Colonel Alfred A. Doniphan won victories over General Santa Anna's forces south of the Rio Grande. In mid-1847, General Winfield Scott mounted a successful seaborne attack on Veracruz and Mexico City, ending the war.

Street Fighting in the Calle de Iturbide, 1846

Monterrey, which had resisted Spanish troops during Mexico's war for independence (1820–1821), was captured by the Americans only after bloody house-to-house fighting in the Mexican War (1846–1848). Protected by thick walls and shuttered windows, Mexican defenders pour a withering fire on the dark-uniformed American troops and buckskin-clad frontier fighters. A large Catholic cathedral looms in the background, its foundations obscured by the smoke from the Mexicans' cannons.   West Point Museum, United States Military Academy, West Point, N.Y.

Fighting had also broken out in California. In June 1846, naval commander John Sloat landed 250 marines in Monterey and declared that California "henceforward will be a portion of the United States." Almost simultaneously, American settlers in the Sacramento River Valley staged a revolt and, supported by Frémont's force, captured the town of Sonoma, where they proclaimed the independence of the "Bear Flag Republic." To cement these victories, Polk ordered army units to capture Santa Fe in New Mexico and then march to southern California. Despite stiff Mexican resistance,

American forces secured control of California early in 1847.

Polk expected these American victories to end the war, but he had underestimated the Mexicans' national pride and the determination of President Santa Anna. In February 1847 in the Battle of Buena Vista, Santa Anna nearly defeated Taylor's army in northeastern Mexico. To bring Santa Anna to terms, Polk approved General Winfield Scott's plan to attack the Mexican capital. In March 1847, Scott captured the port of Veracruz and, with a force of 14,000 soldiers, began the

260-mile march to Mexico City. Scott's troops crushed Santa Anna's forces and seized the Mexican capital in September 1847. Those defeats cost Santa Anna his presidency, and a new Mexican government made peace with the United States.

A Divisive Victory

Initially, the war with Mexico sparked an explosion of patriotic support. The *Nashville Union* hailed it as a noble struggle to extend "the principles of free government." However, the war soon divided the nation (see Comparing American Voices, "The Mexican War: Expansion and Slavery," pp. 410–411). Some northern Whigs—among them Charles Francis Adams of Massachusetts (the son of John Quincy Adams) and Chancellor James Kent of New York—opposed the war on moral grounds. It was "causeless & wicked & unjust," declared Kent. Adams, Kent, and other so-called **conscience Whigs** accused Polk of waging a war of conquest to add new slave states and give slave-owning Democrats permanent control of the federal government. The Whig party grew bolder when voters repudiated Polk's war policy in the elections of 1846 and gave them control of Congress. Whig leaders now called for "No Territory"—a Congressional pledge that the United States would not seek any land from the Mexican republic. "Away with this wretched cant about a 'manifest destiny,' a 'divine mission'... to civilize, and Christianize, and democratize our sister republics at the mouth of a cannon," declared New York Senator William Duer.

The Wilmot Proviso | Moreover, Polk's expansionist policies split the Democrats along sectional lines. As early as 1839, Ohio Democrat Thomas Morris had warned that "the power of slavery is aiming to govern the country, its Constitutions and laws." In 1846, David Wilmot, an antislavery Democratic congressman from Pennsylvania, took up that refrain. Wilmot proposed that slavery be prohibited in any territories gained from the war. His plan rallied Whigs and antislavery Democrats in the House of Representatives, which passed the Wilmot Proviso. Congress had begun to divide along sectional lines. "The madmen of the North...," grumbled the *Richmond Enquirer*, "have, we fear, cast the die and numbered the days of this glorious Union." Fearing that outcome, a few proslavery northern senators joined their southern colleagues to kill the proviso.

Fervent Democratic expansionists now became even more aggressive. President Polk, Secretary of State Buchanan, and Senators Stephen A. Douglas of Illinois and Jefferson Davis of Mississippi called for the annexation of a huge swath of Mexican territory south of the Rio Grande. However, John C. Calhoun and other politicians feared this demand would extend the costly war and require the assimilation of a huge number of Mexicans of mixed Indian and Spanish ancestry. So they favored only the annexation of sparsely settled New Mexico and California. "Ours is a government of the white man," proclaimed Calhoun, and should never welcome "into the Union any but the Caucasian race."

To unify the Democratic Party, Polk and Buchanan abandoned their hyperexpansionist dreams and accepted Calhoun's policy. In February 1848, Polk signed the Treaty of Guadalupe Hidalgo, in which the United States agreed to pay Mexico $15 million in return for more than one-third of its territory. The Senate ratified the treaty in March 1848 (Map 13.4). The same year, Congress created the Oregon Territory, and in 1850 it enacted the Oregon Donation Land Claim Act, which granted farm-sized plots of "free land" to settlers who took up residence before 1854. Soon, treaties with Indian peoples extinguished their titles to much of the new territory. With the settlement of Oregon and the acquisition of New Mexico and California, the first stage of the American conquest of the Far West was complete.

Free Soil | But the political debate was far from over and dominated the election of 1848. The Senate's rejection of the Wilmot Proviso revived Thomas Morris's charge that white southerners were engaged in a "Slave Power" conspiracy to dominate national life. To thwart any such plan, thousands of ordinary northerners, including farmer Abijah Beckwith of Herkimer County, New York, joined the **free-soil movement**. To Beckwith, slavery was an institution of "aristocratic men" and a danger to "the great mass of the people [because it]... threatens the general and equal distribution of our lands into convenient family farms."

The free-soilers quickly organized the Free-Soil Party. The new party abandoned the Liberty Party's emphasis on the sinfulness of slavery and the natural rights of African Americans. Instead, like Beckwith, it depicted slavery as a threat to republicanism and the Jeffersonian ideal of a freeholder society. Their call for free soil, which extended the principle of the Wilmot Proviso, was the first antislavery proposal to attract broad support. Hundreds of men and women in the Great Lakes states joined the free-soil organizations formed by the American and Foreign Anti-Slavery Society. So, too, did Frederick Douglass, the foremost black abolitionist, who attended the convention that estab-

As part of the Compromise of 1850, Texas ceded to the United States some of the disputed lands. These lands and other parts of the Mexican cession were then organized into the territories of New Mexico and Utah.

Dotted lines show the eventual state boundaries for Mexican cession territories.

After winning independence from Mexico in 1836, the Republic of Texas remained an independent nation until admitted to the U.S. as the twenty-eighth state in December 1845.

Under terms of the Compromise of 1850, California became a free state.

In the Gadsden Purchase of 1853, the United States acquired additional land from Mexico to facilitate the construction of a railroad from Texas to California.

Territory ceded by Mexico to U.S., 1848

Claim waived by Texas, 1850

Gadsden Purchase, 1853

REPUBLIC OF TEXAS (1836–1845)

UNITED STATES

PACIFIC OCEAN

MEXICO

Galveston Bay

Corpus Christi Bay

Gulf of Mexico

Mississippi R.

Missouri R.

Arkansas R.

Red R.

Colorado R.

Gila R.

Pecos R.

Nueces R.

Rio Grande

Brazos R.

Trinity R.

Sabine R.

0   100   200 miles

0   100   200 kilometers

MAP 13.4

The Mexican Cession, 1848

In the Treaty of Guadalupe Hidalgo (1848), Mexico ceded to the United States its vast northern territories—the present-day states of California, Nevada, Utah, Arizona, New Mexico, and half of Colorado. These new territories, President Polk boasted to Congress, "constitute of themselves a country large enough for a great empire, and the acquisition is second in importance only to that of Louisiana in 1803."

lished the Free-Soil Party in 1848 and endorsed its strategy for broadening the appeal of antislavery. However, William Lloyd Garrison and other radical abolitionists condemned the Free-Soilers' stress on white freehold farming as racist "whitemanism."

The Election of 1848 The conflict over slavery took a toll on Polk and the Democratic Party. Scorned by Whigs and Free-Soilers and exhausted by his rigorous dawn-to-midnight work regime, Polk declined to run for a second term; he would die just three months after leaving office. In his place, the Democrats nominated Senator Lewis Cass of Michigan, an avid expansionist who had advocated buying Cuba, annexing Mexico's Yucatán Peninsula, and taking all of Oregon. To maintain party unity on the slavery issue, Cass promoted a new idea—squatter sovereignty—Congressional legislation that would al-

low settlers in each territory to determine its status as free or slave.

Cass's doctrine of squatter sovereignty failed to persuade some northern Democrats, who opposed the expansion of slavery into any territories. They joined the Free-Soil Party, as did Martin Van Buren, who became its candidate for president. To attract Whig votes, the Free-Soilers chose conscience Whig Charles Francis Adams for vice president.

The Whigs nominated General Zachary Taylor for president. Taylor was a Louisiana slave owner firmly committed to the defense of slavery in the South but not in the territories, a position that won him support in the north. Moreover, the general's military exploits had made him a popular hero, known affectionately among his troops as "Old Rough and Ready." In 1848, as in 1840, running a military hero worked for the Whigs. Taylor took 47 percent of the popular vote to

The Mexican War: Expansion and Slavery

Conflict with Mexico prompted debates over the Polk administration's aggressive efforts to acquire territory and spread slavery. The expansionists are represented here by John L. O'Sullivan, the editor of the *United States Magazine and Democratic Review*, and Secretary of State James Buchanan. Polk's critics are the poet Walt Whitman, the editor of the *Brooklyn Eagle*, and Charles Sumner, a future Republican senator from Massachusetts.

John L. O'Sullivan
"Manifest Destiny," July 1845

Texas is now ours . . . her star and her stripe may already be said to have taken their place in the glorious blazon of our common nationality. . . .

Other nations [Britain and France] have undertaken to intrude themselves [into Texas affairs] . . . for the avowed object of thwarting our policy and hampering our power, limiting our greatness and checking the fulfillment of our manifest destiny to overspread the continent allotted by Providence for the free development of our yearly multiplying millions. . . .

The independence of Texas was complete and absolute. It was an independence, not only in fact, but of right. No obligation of duty towards Mexico tended in the least degree to restrain our right to [annex it]. . . . What then can be more preposterous than all this clamor by Mexico and the Mexican interest, against Annexation, as a violation of any rights of hers . . . ?

Nor is there any just foundation for the charge that Annexation is a great pro-slavery measure—calculated to increase and perpetuate that institution. Slavery had nothing to do with it. . . . That it will tend to facilitate and hasten the disappearance of Slavery from all the northern tier of the present Slave States, cannot surely admit of serious question. The greater value in Texas of the slave labor now employed in those States, must soon produce the effect of draining off that labor southwardly. . . .

California will, probably, next fall away from the loose adhesion which, in such a country as Mexico, holds a remote province in a slight equivocal kind of dependence on the metropolis. . . . Already the advance guard of the irresistible army of Anglo-Saxon emigration has begun to pour down upon it, armed with the plough and the rifle, and marking its trail with schools and colleges, courts and representative halls, mills and meeting-houses. A population will soon be in actual occupation of California, over which it will be idle for Mexico to dream of dominion. . . . And they will have a right to independence—to self-government . . . a better and a truer right than the artificial title of sovereignty in Mexico, a thousand miles distant, inheriting from Spain a title good only against those who have none better.

Source: Sean Wilentz, ed., *Major Problems in the Early Republic, 1787–1848* (D. C. Heath: Lexington, MA, 1991), 525–528.

James Buchanan
Letter to John Slidell, November 1845

In your negotiations with Mexico, the independence of Texas must be considered a settled fact, and is not to be called in question. . . .

It may, however, be contended on the part of Mexico, that the Nueces and not the Rio del Norte [Rio Grande], is the true western boundary of Texas. I need not furnish you arguments to controvert this position. . . . The jurisdiction of Texas has been extended beyond that river [the Nueces] and . . . representatives from the country between it and the Del Norte have participated in the deliberations both of her Congress and her Convention. . . .

The case is different in regard to New Mexico. Santa Fe, its capital, was settled by the Spaniards more than two centuries ago; and that province has been ever since in their possession and that of the Republic of Mexico. The Texans never have conquered or taken possession of it. . . . [However,] . . . a great portion of New Mexico being on this side of the Rio Grande and included within the limits already claimed by Texas, it may hereafter, should it remain a Mexican province, become a subject of dispute. . . .

If in adjusting the boundary, the province of New Mexico should be included within the limits of the United States, this would obviate the danger of future collisions. Mexico would part with a remote and disturbed province, the possession of which can never be advantageous to her. . . . It would seem to be equally the interest of both Powers, that New Mexico should belong to the United States. . . .

It is to be seriously apprehended that both Great Britain and France have designs upon California. . . . This Government . . . would vigorously interpose to prevent the latter from becoming either a British or a French Colony. . . .

The possession of the Bay and harbor of San Francisco, is all important to the United States.

The Government of California is now but nominally dependent on Mexico. . . . It is the desire of the President that you shall use your best efforts to obtain a cession of that Province. . . . Money would be no object.

Source: Victoria Bissell Brown and Timothy J. Shannon, eds., *Going to the Source: The Bedford Reader in American History* (Bedford/St Martin's: Boston, 2004), I, 260–262.

Charles Sumner
Letter to Robert Winthrop, October 25, 1846

By virtue of an unconstitutional Act of Congress, in conjunction with the de facto government of Texas, the latter was annexed to the United States some time in the month of December, 1845. If we regard Texas as a province of Mexico, its boundaries must be sought in the geography of that republic. If we regard it as an independent State, they must be determined by the extent of jurisdiction which the State was able to maintain. Now it seems clear that the river Nueces was always recognized by Mexico as the western boundary; and it is undisputed that the State of Texas, since its Declaration of Independence, never exercised any jurisdiction beyond the Nueces. . . .

In the month of January, 1846, the President of the United States directed the troops under General Taylor, called the Army of Occupation, to take possession of this region [west of the Nueces river]. Here was an act of aggression. As might have been expected, it produced collision. The Mexicans, aroused in self-defence, sought to repel the invaders. . . .

Here the question occurs, What was the duty of Congress in this emergency? Clearly to withhold all sanction to unjust war,—to aggression upon a neighboring Republic,—to spoliation of fellow-men. Our troops were in danger only because upon foreign soil, forcibly displacing the jurisdiction and laws of the rightful government. . . . The American forces should have been directed to *retreat*, not from any human force, but from *wrongdoing*; and this would have been a true victory.

Alas! This was not the mood of Congress. With wicked speed a bill was introduced, furnishing large and unusual supplies of men and money. . . . This was adopted by a vote of 123 to 67; and the bill then leaped forth, fully armed, as a measure of open and active hostility against Mexico.

Source: Sean Wilentz, ed., *Major Problems in the Early Republic, 1787–1848* (D. C. Heath: Lexington, MA, 1991), 541.

Walt Whitman
Editorial in the *Brooklyn Eagle*, September 1, 1847

The question whether or no there shall be slavery in the new territories which . . . we are largely to get through this Mexican war, is a question between *the grand body of white workingmen, the millions of mechanics, farmers, and operatives of our country*, with their interests on the one side—and the interests of the few thousand rich, "polished," and aristocratic owners of slaves at the South, on the other side.

Experience has proved . . . that a stalwart mass of respectable workingmen, cannot exist, much less flourish, in a thorough slave State. Let any one think for a moment what a different appearance New York, Pennsylvania, or Ohio, would present—how much less sturdy independence and family happiness there would be—were slaves the workmen there, instead of each man as a general thing being his own workman. . . .

Slavery is a good thing enough . . . to the rich—the one out of thousands; but it is destructive to the dignity and independence of all who work, and to labor itself. . . . All practice and theory . . . are strongly arrayed in favor of limiting slavery to where it already exists.

Source: Sean Wilentz, ed., *Major Problems in the Early Republic, 1787–1848* (D. C. Heath: Lexington, MA, 1991), 525–528, 541, 543.

ANALYZING THE EVIDENCE

- **What arguments do Buchanan and Sumner make about the boundaries of Texas, the issue that sparked the fighting? Whose argument is more persuasive?**

- **What are O'Sullivan's and Buchanan's views with respect to California? Do they support or undercut the proposition that the Polk administration undertook an imperialist war of aggression?**

- **O'Sullivan raises the issue of who has a "right" to California. What is your view?**

- **Why does Whitman oppose the expansion of slavery? Given Whitman's views, who might have gotten his vote in the election of 1848? Why?**

"This Is the House That Polk Built"

President James Polk's administration started off with a bang—a long-sought Democratic free-trade tariff, a compromise settlement of the Oregon boundary dispute with Great Britain, and a war to seize California and other Mexican provinces. This ambitious agenda promised fame for the president, but the cartoonist pictures Polk as a worried man, afraid that he has built a house of cards that might collapse at any time.   Bettmann/Corbis.

Cass's 42 percent. However, Taylor won a majority in the electoral college (163 to 127) only because Van Buren and the Free-Soil ticket took enough votes in New York to deny Cass a victory there. The bitter debate over the expansion of slavery had changed the dynamics of national politics, as antislavery voters denied the presidency to Clay in 1844 and to Cass in 1848.

California Gold and Racial Warfare

Even before Taylor took office, events in California took center stage. In January 1848, workers building a mill for John A. Sutter in the Sierra Nevada foothills discovered flakes of gold. Sutter was a Swiss immigrant who had arrived in California in 1839, became a Mexican

citizen, and accumulated an estate in the Sacramento River Valley. He tried to hide the discovery, but by mid-1848 Americans from Monterey and San Francisco were pouring into the foothills, along with hundreds of Indians and Californios and scores of Australians, Mexicans, and Chileans. The gold rush was on. By January 1849, sixty-one crowded ships had left northeastern ports to sail around Cape Horn to San Francisco; by May, twelve thousand wagons had crossed the Missouri River bound for the goldfields (Map 13.5). For Bernard Reid, the overland trip on the Pioneer Line was "a long dreadful dream," beset by cholera, scurvy, and near starvation. Still, by the end of 1849, more than 80,000 people, mostly men, had arrived in California.

The Forty-Niners   The "forty-niners" lived in crowded, chaotic towns and mining camps amid gamblers, saloon keepers, and prostitutes. They fashioned a rudimentary legal system based on practice in the East and set up "claims clubs" that settled mining disputes. The American miners usually treated fellow whites fairly but ruthlessly expelled Indians, Mexicans, and Chileans from the gold fields or confined them to marginal diggings. When substantial numbers of Chinese migrants arrived in 1850, they were often forced off independent claims and so had to work for wages (see Voices from Abroad, "Norman Assing (Yuan Sheng): Equality for Chinese Immigrants," p. 414).

The first miners to exploit a site often struck it rich. They scooped up the easily reached deposits and left small pickings for later arrivals. His "high hopes" wrecked, one latecomer saw himself and most other California miners as little better than "convicts condemned to exile and hard labor." They were often condemned to disease as well: "Diarrhea was so general during the fall and winter months" and so often fatal, a Sacramento doctor remarked, that it was called "the disease of California." Like many other migrants, William Swain gave up the search for gold; at the end of 1850, he borrowed funds and returned to his wife, infant daughter, and aged mother on a New York farm. "O William," his wife Sabrina had written, "I wish you had been content to stay at home, for there is no real home for me without you."

Thousands of other disillusioned forty-niners were either too ashamed or too tired or too adventurous to go home. Some became wage workers for companies that engaged in hydraulic or underground mining; many others turned to farming. "Instead of going to the mines where fortune hangs upon the merest chance," a frustrated miner advised emigrants, "[you] should at once commence the cultivation of the soil." Farming required

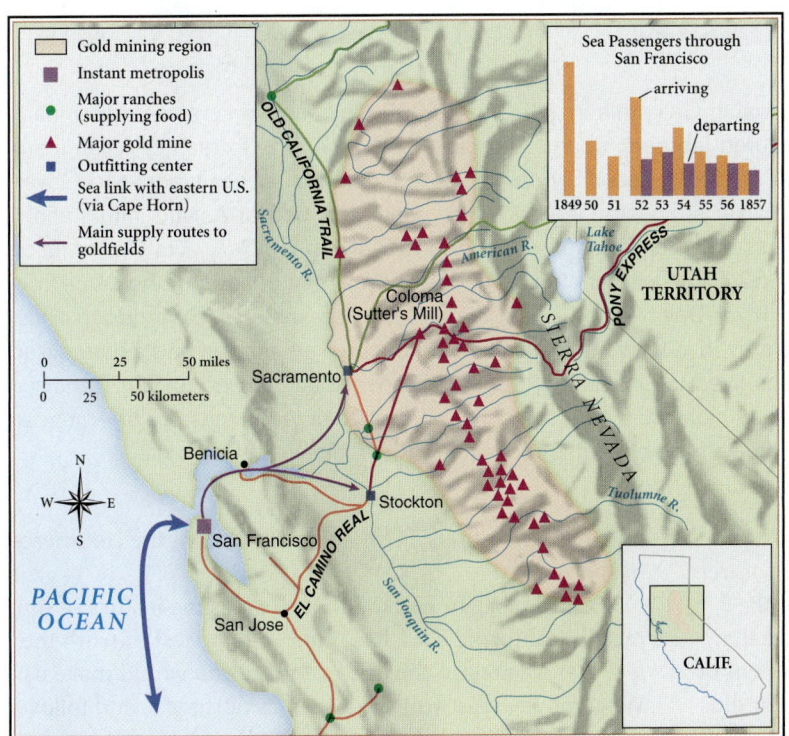

Gold mining region
Instant metropolis
Major ranches (supplying food)
Major gold mine
Outfitting center
Sea link with eastern U.S. (via Cape Horn)
Main supply routes to goldfields

Sea Passengers through San Francisco
arriving
departing
1849 50 51 52 53 54 55 56 1857

MAP 13.5

The California Gold Rush, 1849–1857

Traveling from all parts of the world—South America, Europe, China, and Australia, as well as the eastern United States—hundreds of thousands of bonanza-seekers converged on the California goldfields. Miners traveling by sea landed at San Francisco, which mushroomed into a substantial city; many other prospectors trekked overland to the goldfields on the Old California Trail. By the mid-1850s, the gold rush was over: Almost as many people were sailing from San Francisco each year as were arriving to seek their fortune.

California Drinking, 1855

Men—and women—from around the globe joined the California gold rush in search of easy money. This lithograph by Frank Marryat, *The Bar of a Gambling Saloon*, suggests this geographic diversity by picturing Mexicans, Chinese, and Americans in their national dress. Some patrons drink to their success in the fields or at the gambling tables, while a crowd of men in the adjacent room ogles scantily clad "public women" dancing on a platform.   © Collection of the New-York Historical Society, USA /The Bridgeman Art Library.

All the nations and people I had hitherto passed through resembled own in their manners, customs and langua

Norman Assing (Yuan Sheng)
Equality for Chinese Immigrants

The arrival in California in 1852 of 20,000 Chinese workers, including many indentured laborers, sparked Anglo-American efforts to restrict Asian immigration. A California assembly committee condemned "coolie labor" and Governor John Bigler suggested legislation to "check this tide of Asiatic immigration." Norman Assing (Yuan Sheng) responded to Bigler in the *Daily Alta California* on May 5, 1852. Like most nineteenth-century Chinese migrants, Assing came from the Pearl River Delta region of southern China (present-day Guangdong Province). He arrived in New York City in 1820, became a Christian and a naturalized citizen, and lived in Charleston, South Carolina. Assing moved to San Francisco and emerged as a prominent merchant and—thanks to his mastery of American culture—the self-appointed spokesman for the Chinese in California.

To His Excellency Gov. Bigler

Sir: I am a Chinaman, a republican, and a lover of free institutions; am much attached to the principles of the Government of the United States, and therefore take the liberty of addressing you as the chief of the government of this state.... The effect of your late message has been thus far to prejudice the public mind against my people, to enable those who wait the opportunity to hunt them down, and rob them of the rewards of their toil....

You are deeply convinced you say "that to enhance the prosperity and to preserve the tranquility of this state, Asiatic immigration must be checked." This, your Excellency, is but one step towards a retrograde movement of the government ... which the citizens of this country ought never to tolerate. It was one of the principal causes of quarrel between you (when colonies) and England; when the latter pressed laws against emigration, you looked for immigration; it came, and immigration made *you what you are*, your nation what it is....

You argue that this is a republic of a particular race that the constitution of the United States admits of no asylum to any other than the pale face. This proposition is false in the extreme; and you know it. The declaration of your independence, and all the acts of your government, your people, and your history, are against you.

It is true, you have degraded the negro because of your holding him in involuntary servitude, and because for the sake of union in some of your states such was tolerated. And amongst this class you would endeavor to place us; and no doubt it would be pleasing to some would-be free-men to mark the brand of servitude upon us. But we would beg to remind you that when your nation was a wilderness, and the nation from whom you sprung *barbarous*, we [Chinese] exercised most of the arts and virtues of civilized life; that we are possessed of a language and literature, and that men skilled in science and the arts are numerous amongst us; that the productions of our manufactories, our

sail and work-shops, form no small share of the commerce of the world....

And we beg to remark, that so far as the history of our race in California goes, it stamps with the test of truth the fact that we are not the degraded race you would make us. We came amongst you as mechanics or traders, and following every honorable business of life. You do not find us pursuing occupations of a degrading character, except you consider labor degrading, which I am sure you do not....

You say "you desire to see no change in the generous policy of this Government as far as regards Europeans." It is out of your power to say, however, in what way or to whom the doctrines of the Constitution shall apply. You have no more right to propose a measure for checking immigration, than you have to assume the right of sending a message to the Legislature on the subject.

As far as regards the color and complexion of our race, we are perfectly aware that our population have been a little more tanned than yours. Your Excellency will discover, however, ... that as far as the aristocracy of *skin* is concerned, ours might compare with many of the European races; nor do we consider that your Excellency, as a Democrat, will make us believe that the framers of your declaration of rights ever suggested the propriety of establishing an aristocracy of *skin*.

Source: *Daily Alta California*, May 5, 1852.

ANALYZING THE EVIDENCE

- What are the major arguments Assing uses to defend the rights of Chinese immigrants in California?
- Why does Assing claim that Bigler (and California) cannot limit immigration?
- The Naturalization Act of 1790 limits naturalization to aliens who are "free white persons." How does that law affect Assing's arguments?

arable land, which was owned by Mexican grantees or occupied by Indian peoples. The American arrivals brushed aside both groups, brutally eliminating the Indians and wearing down Mexican claimants with legal tactics and political pressure.

Racial Warfare and Land Rights The subjugation of the Indians came first. When the gold rush began in 1848, there were about 150,000 Indians in California; by 1861, there were only 30,000. As elsewhere in the Americas, European diseases took the lives of thousands of natives. But in California, white settlers also undertook systematic campaigns of extermination and local political leaders did little to stop them: "A war of extermination will continue to be waged . . . until the Indian race becomes extinct," predicted Governor Peter Burnett in 1851. Congress abetted these assaults. At the bidding of white Californians, it repudiated treaties that federal agents had negotiated with 119 tribes, and that provided the Indians with 7 million acres of land. Instead, in 1853, Congress authorized five reservations of only 25,000 acres each and refused to provide the Indians with military protection.

Consequently, some settlers simply murdered Indians to push them off non-reservation lands. The Yuki people, who lived in the Round Valley in northern California, were one target. As the *Petaluma Journal* reported in April 1857: "Within the past three weeks, from 300 to 400 bucks, squaws and children have been killed by whites." Other white Californians turned to slave trading: "Hundreds of Indians have been stolen and carried into the settlements and sold," the state's Indian Affairs superintendent reported in 1856. Labor-hungry farmers quickly put them to work. Indians were "all among us, around us, with no house and kitchen without them," recalled one farmer. Expelled from their lands and widely dispersed, many Indian peoples simply vanished as distinct communities. Those tribes that survived were a shadow of their former selves. In 1854, Round Valley was home to at least 5,000 Yukis; a decade later, only 85 men and 215 women remained.

The Mexicans and Californios who held grants to thousands of acres were harder to dislodge. The Treaty of Guadalupe Hidalgo guaranteed that the land grants made by Spanish and Mexican authorities would be "inviolably respected." Despite the fact that many of the 800 grants in California were either fraudulent or questionable, the Land Claims Commission created by Congress upheld the validity of 75 percent of them. In the meantime, hundreds of Americans had set up farms on the grants, many of which had never been settled. Having come of age in the anti-monopoly Jacksonian era, these American squatters rejected the notion that so much unoccupied and unimproved land could be held by a few families. They pressured local land commissioners and judges to void suspect grants, with considerable success. Although the squatters failed to secure legislation transferring unoccupied grants to the public domain, the Americans' clamor for land was so intense and their numbers so large that even successful Mexican and Californio claimants decided to sell off their properties at bargain prices.

In northern California, farmers found that they could grow most eastern crops: corn and oats to feed work horses, pigs, and chickens; potatoes, beans, and peas for the farm table; and refreshing grapes, apples, and peaches. Ranchers gradually replaced Spanish cattle with American breeds that yielded more milk and meat, which found a ready market as California's population shot up to 380,000 by 1860 and 560,000 by 1870. Most important, wheat and barley farmers cultivated hundreds of acres, using the latest technology and scores of hired workers to produce huge crops, which San Francisco merchants exported to Europe at high prices. The gold rush gradually turned into a wheat boom.

1850: Crisis and Compromise

The rapid settlement of California qualified it for admission to the Union. Hoping to avoid an extended debate over slavery, President Taylor advised the settlers to skip the territorial phase and immediately apply for statehood. When Californians ratified a state constitution prohibiting slavery in November 1849, the president urged Congress to admit California as a free state.

Constitutional Conflict Taylor's effort to avoid sectional conflict failed. California's bid for admission produced passionate debates in Congress and four distinct positions with respect to the expansion of slavery. On the verge of death, John C. Calhoun took his usual extreme stance. Calhoun deeply resented the North's "long-continued agitation of the slavery question." To uphold southern honor (and political power), he proposed a constitutional amendment to create a dual presidency, thus permanently dividing executive power within the national government between the North and the South. Calhoun also advanced the radical argument that Congress had no constitutional authority to regulate slavery in the territories. Slaves were property, Calhoun pointed out, and the Constitution restricted Congress's power to abrogate or limit property rights. That argument ran counter to a half century of practice. Congress had prohibited slavery

Resolving the Crisis of 1850
By 1850, Whig Henry Clay had been in Congress for nearly four decades. Now in partnership with fellow Whig Daniel Webster and Democrat Stephen Douglas, Clay fashioned a complex—and controversial—compromise that preserved the Union. In this engraving, he addresses a crowded Senate chamber, with Webster sitting immediately to his left. Clay addresses his remarks to his prime antagonist, Southern nationalist John C. Calhoun, the man with the long white hair at the far right of the picture. Library of Congress Prints and Photographs Division, LC-DIG-ppmsca-09398.

in the Northwest Territory in 1787, and it had extended that ban to most of the Louisiana Purchase in the Missouri Compromise of 1820.

Calhoun's assertion that "slavery follows the flag" won support in the Deep South, but many southerners favored a more moderate proposal to extend the Missouri Compromise line to the Pacific Ocean. This plan won the backing of Pennsylvanian James Buchanan and other influential northern Democrats. It would guarantee slave owners access to some western territory, including a separate state in southern California.

A third alternative was squatter sovereignty. Lewis Cass had advanced this idea in 1848, and Democratic senator Stephen Douglas of Illinois now became its champion. Douglas called his plan popular sovereignty to link it to the ideology of republicanism, which placed ultimate power in the hands of the people (see Chapter 5), and it had considerable appeal. Politicians hoped it would remove the explosive issue of slavery from the national agenda, and local settlers welcomed the power it would give them. However, popular sovereignty was a slippery concept. Could residents accept or ban slavery when a territory was first organized? Or must they delay that decision until a territory had enough people to frame a constitution and apply for statehood? To promote their plan, advocates of popular sovereignty evaded answering such questions.

For their part, antislavery advocates refused to accept any plan for California that might allow slavery there or elsewhere. Senator Salmon P. Chase of Ohio, elected by a Democratic–Free-Soil coalition, and Senator William H. Seward, a New York Whig, urged a fourth position: that federal authorities restrict slavery within its existing boundaries and eventually extinguish it completely. Condemning slavery as "morally unjust, politically unwise, and socially pernicious" and invoking "a higher law than the Constitution," Seward demanded bold action to protect freedom, "the common heritage of mankind."

A Complex Compromise Standing on the brink of disaster, senior Whig and Democratic politicians worked desperately to preserve the Union. Aided by Millard Fillmore, who became president in 1850 after Zachary Taylor's sudden death, Whig leaders Henry Clay and Daniel Webster and Democrat Stephen A. Douglas won the passage of five separate laws known collectively as the Compromise of 1850. To mollify the South, the compromise included a new Fugitive Slave Act that gave federal support to slave catchers. To satisfy the North, the legislation admitted California as a free state, resolved a boundary dispute between New Mexico and Texas in favor of New Mexico, and abolished the slave trade (but not slavery) in

Compromise of 1850
- Voters allowed to decide whether to permit slavery
- Territory left unorganized

Kansas-Nebraska Act, 1854
- Voters allowed to decide whether to permit slavery
- New boundaries
- Free states and territories
- Slave states

MAP 13.6

The Compromise of 1850 and the Kansas-Nebraska Act of 1854

The contest over the expansion of slavery involved vast territories. The Compromise of 1850 peacefully resolved the status of the Far West: California would be a free state, and settlers in the Utah and New Mexico territories would vote for or against slavery (the doctrine of popular sovereignty). However, the Kansas-Nebraska Act of 1854 voided the Missouri Compromise (1820) and instituted popular sovereignty in those territories. That decision sparked a bitter local war and revealed a fatal flaw in the doctrine.

the District of Columbia. Finally, the compromise organized the rest of the lands acquired from Mexico into the territories of New Mexico and Utah and, invoking popular sovereignty, left the issue of slavery in their hands (Map 13.6).

The Compromise of 1850 preserved the Union, but only barely. During the debate, South Carolina's governor warned that his state might well secede. He and other militant secessionists (or "fire-eaters") in Georgia, Mississippi, and Alabama organized special conventions to promote the goal of safeguarding "southern rights" by leaving the Union. Georgia congressman Alexander H. Stephens called on the delegates of one such convention to make "the necessary preparations of men and

money, arms and munitions, etc. to meet the emergency." However, a majority of convention delegates remained committed to the Union—though now only conditionally. They agreed to leave the Union if Congress abolished slavery anywhere or refused to grant statehood to a territory with a proslavery constitution. Political wizardry had solved the immediate crisis, but the underlying issues remained unresolved.

- Why did President Polk go to war with Mexico? Why did the war become so divisive in Congress and the country?

- What issues did the Compromise of 1850 resolve? Who benefited more from its terms: the North or the South? Why?

The End of the Second Party System, 1850–1858

The architects of the Compromise of 1850 expected it to last for a generation, as the Missouri Compromise had. Their hopes were quickly dashed. Demanding freedom for fugitive slaves and free soil in the West, antislavery northerners refused to accept the compromise. For their part, proslavery southerners plotted to extend slavery into the West, the Caribbean, and Central America. The resulting disputes destroyed the Second Party System and deepened the crisis of the Union.

Resistance to the Fugitive Slave Act

The Fugitive Slave Act proved the most controversial element of the Compromise. Under its terms, federal magistrates in the northern states determined the status of alleged runaway slaves. The law denied a jury trial to the accused blacks and even the right to testify. Using its provisions, southern owners reenslaved about 200 fugitives (as well as some free northern blacks).

The plight of the runaways and the appearance of slave catchers in the North and Midwest aroused popular hostility. Ignoring the threat of substantial fines and prison sentences, free blacks and white abolitionists prevented the return of fugitive slaves. In October 1850, Boston abolitionists helped two slaves escape and drove a Georgia slave catcher out of town. Rioters in Syracuse, New York, broke into a courthouse, freed a fugitive slave, and accused the U.S. marshal of kidnapping. Abandoning nonviolence, Frederick Douglass declared, "The only way to make a Fugitive Slave Law a dead letter is to make half a dozen or more dead kidnappers." Precisely such a deadly result occurred in Christiana, Pennsylvania, in September 1851. About twenty African Americans exchanged gunfire with Maryland slave catchers, killing two of them. Federal authorities indicted thirty-six blacks and four whites for treason and other crimes. But a Pennsylvania jury acquitted one defendant, and northern public opinion forced the government to drop the charges against the rest.

Harriet Beecher Stowe's novel, *Uncle Tom's Cabin* (1852), boosted opposition to the Fugitive Slave Act and to slavery. Conveying the moral principles of abolitionism in heartrending personal situations, Stowe's melodramatic book evoked empathy for enslaved women and men and outrage toward the internal slave trade. In Britain, the novel sold 1 million copies in eight months and resulted in the Stafford House Address, an antislavery petition signed by 560,000 English women. Northern states' legislators declared that the Fugitive Slave Act violated state sovereignty and passed **personal-liberty laws** that enhanced the legal rights of their residents, including accused fugitives. In 1857, the Wisconsin Supreme Court went even further, ruling in *Ahleman v. Booth* that the act violated the constitutional rights of Wisconsin's citizens. Taking a states' rights stance—traditionally a southern position—the Wisconsin court denied the authority of federal courts to review its decision. In 1859, Chief Justice Roger B. Taney led a unanimous Supreme Court in affirming the supremacy of federal courts—a position that has withstood the test of time—and upheld the constitutionality of the act. But by then, as Frederick Douglass had hoped, popular opposition had made the law a "dead letter."

The Political System in Decline

The conflict over slavery split both major political parties along sectional lines. Hoping to unify their party, the Whigs ran another war hero, General Winfield Scott, as their presidential candidate in 1852. Among the Democrats, southerners demanded a candidate who accepted Calhoun's constitutional argument that all territories were open to slavery. However, northern and midwestern Democrats advocated popular sovereignty, as did the three leading candidates—Lewis Cass of Michigan, Stephen Douglas of Illinois, and James Buchanan of Pennsylvania. Ultimately, the party settled on a compromise candidate, Franklin Pierce of New Hampshire, a congenial man who was sympathetic to the South, and swept to victory. Many Free-Soilers voted for Pierce, reuniting the Democratic Party. The Whig Party fragmented along sectional wings over slavery and would never again wage a national campaign.

As president, Pierce pursued an expansionist foreign policy. To assist northern merchants, who wanted a commercial empire, he negotiated a treaty with Japan. To mollify southern expansionists, who desired a landed empire, he tried to purchase extensive Mexican lands south of the Rio Grande. Ultimately, Pierce settled for a narrow slice of land—the Gadsden Purchase of 1853—that enabled his negotiator, James Gadsden, to build a transcontinental rail line from New Orleans to California.

Pierce's most controversial initiatives came in the Caribbean and Central America. Southern expansionists had long urged Cuban slave owners to declare independence and join the United States; to assist them, and the American traders who carried thousands of African slaves to Spanish-owned Cuba each year, Pierce covertly supported military expeditions to Cuba and Nicaragua and threatened war with Spain. Northern Democrats in Congress denounced this aggressive diplomacy and reacted strongly when Secretary of State William L. Marcy arranged for American diplomats in Europe to compose the Ostend Manifesto, which urged Pierce to seize Cuba. They denounced the manifesto and scuttled the planters' dreams of American expansion into the Caribbean.

The Kansas-Nebraska Act and the Rise of New Parties

The Caribbean was a sideshow. The main stage was the trans-Mississippi west, where a major controversy in 1854 destroyed the Second Party System and sent the Union spinning toward disaster. The Missouri Compromise prohibited new slave states in the Louisiana Purchase north of 36°30'. Consequently, southern senators had long prevented the creation of new territories there; it remained Permanent Indian Territory. Now Senator Stephen A. Douglas of Illinois hoped to open it up, so that a transcontinental railroad could link Chicago to California. Without a railroad, Douglas asked, "How are we to develop our immense interests and possessions on the Pacific? . . . The Indian barrier must be removed." Douglas introduced a bill extinguishing Native American rights on the Great Plains, organiz-

ing the large free territory of Nebraska, and opening it up to white settlers.

Southern politicians opposed Douglas's initiative. They hoped to extend slavery throughout the Louisiana Purchase and to have a southern city — New Orleans, Memphis, or St. Louis — as the eastern terminus of a transcontinental railroad. To win their support, Douglas amended his bill so that it explicitly repealed the Missouri Compromise and organized the region on the basis of popular sovereignty. He also agreed to the formation of two territories, Nebraska and Kansas, allowing southerners to hope that Kansas would become a slave state. Knowing that the revised bill would "raise a hell of a storm" in the North, Douglas argued that Kansas was not suited to plantation agriculture and would become a free state. After weeks of bitter debate, the Senate enacted the Kansas-Nebraska Act. In the House of Representatives, sixty-six northern Democrats refused to follow the party line and opposed the act. But Pierce used pressure and patronage to persuade twenty-two of them to change their votes, and the measure squeaked through.

The American and Republican Parties | The Kansas-Nebraska Act of 1854 was a disaster for the American political system. It finished off the Whig Party and nearly destroyed the Democrats as a national party. Denouncing the act as "part of a great scheme for extending and

An Excursion of the New York Turners, 1854

Friedrich Ludwig Jahn, a Prussian educator and nationalist, founded the Turner (or gymnastics) movement in 1811. Intended to develop moral character and patriotic élan as well as physical strength among German men, Turner societies advocated public schooling, free speech, and political democracy. Brought to the United States by German refugees from the failed democratic Revolution of 1848, the Turner movement preserved German culture and served as a home for German abolitionists and reformers. Here, some Turners display their physical fitness while others discuss politics, sing German songs, and drink beer. Museum of the City of New York, The J. Clarence Davies Collection.

perpetuating supremacy of the slave power," northern Whigs and "anti-Nebraska" Democrats abandoned their old parties. They joined with Free-Soilers and abolitionists in a new Republican Party.

The new party was a coalition of "strange, discordant and even hostile elements," one Republican observed, but its leaders were united in opposing slavery. Republicans repudiated slavery because it degraded the dignity of manual labor and drove down the wages and working conditions of free white workers. Like Thomas Jefferson, they praised a society based on "the middling classes who own the soil and work it with their own hands." Abraham Lincoln, an Illinois Whig who became a Republican, conveyed the party's vision of social mobility. "There is no permanent class of hired laborers among us," he declared; every free man had a chance to become a property owner. Ignoring the increasing class divisions in the industrializing North and Midwest, Lincoln and his fellow Republicans celebrated republican liberty and individual enterprise.

The Republicans faced strong competition from the American, or Know-Nothing, Party. The party had its origins in the anti-immigrant and anti-Catholic movements of the 1840s (see Chapter 9). In 1850, these secret nativist societies banded together as the Order of the Star-Spangled Banner; the following year, they formed the American Party. When faced with outsiders' questions, the party's secrecy-conscious members often replied, "I know nothing," hence the nickname. The Know-Nothing Party's program was far from secret, however: It wanted to unite native-born Protestants against the "alien menace" of Irish and German Catholics, prohibit further immigration, and institute literacy tests for voting. In 1854, voters elected dozens of Know-Nothing candidates to the House of Repre-

sentatives and gave the American Party control of the state governments of Massachusetts and Pennsylvania. The emergence of a major nativist party became a real possibility.

Bleeding Kansas | Meanwhile, thousands of settlers rushed into the Kansas Territory, putting Douglas's concept of popular sovereignty to the test. On the side of slavery, Missouri senator David R. Atchison encouraged residents of his state to cross temporarily into Kansas to vote in crucial elections there. Opposing Atchison was the abolitionist New England Emigrant Aid Society, which dispatched freesoilers to Kansas. In 1855, the Pierce administration accepted the legitimacy of a proslavery legislature in Lecompton, Kansas, which had been elected by border-crossing Missourians. However, the majority of Kansas residents favored free soil and refused allegiance to the Lecompton government.

In 1856, both sides turned to violence, prompting Horace Greeley of the *New York Tribune* to label the territory "Bleeding Kansas." A proslavery force, seven hundred strong, looted and burned the free-soil town of Lawrence. The attack enraged John Brown, a fifty-six-year-old abolitionist from New York and Ohio, who commanded a free-state militia. Brown was a complex man with a long record of failed businesses, but he had an intellectual and moral intensity that won the trust of influential people. Taking vengeance for the sack of Lawrence, Brown and his followers murdered five proslavery settlers at Pottawatomie. Abolitionists must "fight fire with fire" and "strike terror in the hearts of the proslavery people," Brown declared. The attack on Lawrence and the Pottawatomie killings started a guerrilla war in Kansas that took nearly two hundred lives.

Armed Abolitionists in Kansas, 1859
The confrontation between North and South in Kansas took many forms. In the spring of 1859, Dr. John Doy (seated) slipped across the border into Missouri and tried to lead thirteen escaped slaves to freedom in Kansas, only to be captured and jailed in St. Joseph, Missouri. The serious-looking men standing behind Doy, well armed with guns and Bowie knives, attacked the jail and carried Doy back to Kansas. The photograph celebrated—and memorialized—their successful exploit.
Kansas State Historical Society.

Buchanan's Failed Presidency

The violence in Kansas dominated the presidential election of 1856. The new Republican Party counted on anger over Bleeding Kansas to boost the party's fortunes. Its platform denounced the Kansas-Nebraska Act and demanded that the federal government prohibit slavery in all the territories. Republicans also called for federal subsidies for transcontinental railroads, reviving a Whig economic proposal popular among midwestern Democrats. For president, the Republicans nominated Colonel John C. Frémont, a free-soiler who had won fame in the conquest of Mexican California.

The Election of 1856   The American Party entered the election with equally high hopes, but like the Whigs and Democrats, it split along sectional lines over slavery. The southern faction of the American party nominated former Whig president Millard Fillmore, while the northern contingent endorsed Frémont—thanks to clever maneuvering by Republican politicians. During the campaign, the Republicans won the votes of many Know-Nothing workingmen in the North by demanding a ban on foreign immigrants and high tariffs on foreign manufactures. As a Pennsylvania Republican put it, "Let our motto be, protection to everything American, against everything foreign." In New York, Republicans campaigned on a reform platform designed "to cement into a harmonious mass . . . all of the Anti-Slavery, Anti-Popery and Anti-Whiskey" voters.

The Democrats reaffirmed their support for popular sovereignty and the Kansas-Nebraska Act, and nominated James Buchanan of Pennsylvania. A tall, dignified man and an experienced but unimaginative politician, Buchanan was staunchly prosouthern. He won the three-way race with 1.8 million popular votes (45.3 percent) and 174 electoral votes. Frémont polled 1.3 million popular votes (33.2 percent) and 114 electoral votes; Fillmore won 873,000 popular votes (21.5 percent) but captured only 8 electoral votes.

The dramatic restructuring of parties was now apparent (Map 13.7). With the splintering of the American Party, the Republicans had replaced the Whigs as the second major party. However, Republicans were a sectional party. Frémont had not won a single vote in the South; had he triumphed, a North Carolina newspaper warned, the result would have been "a separation

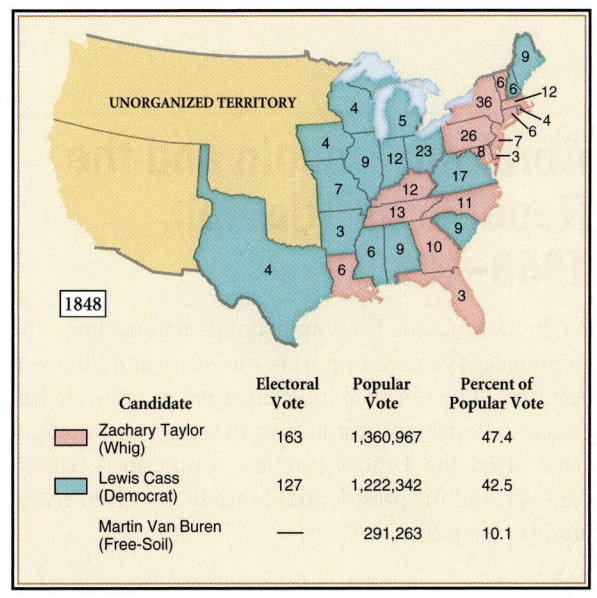

Candidate	Electoral Vote	Popular Vote	Percent of Popular Vote
Zachary Taylor (Whig)	163	1,360,967	47.4
Lewis Cass (Democrat)	127	1,222,342	42.5
Martin Van Buren (Free-Soil)	—	291,263	10.1

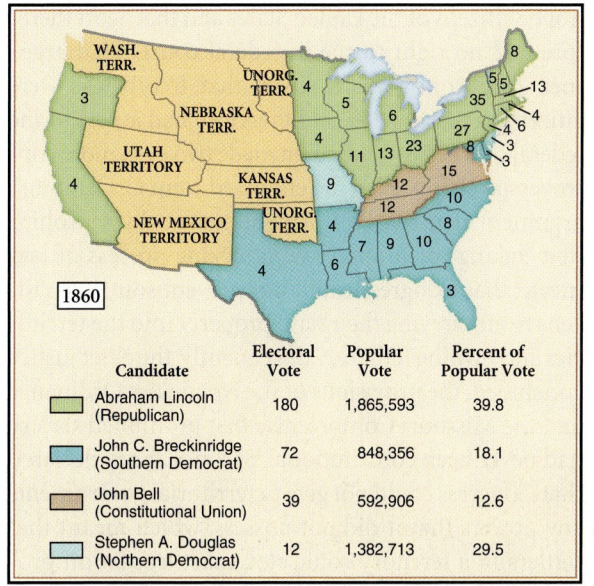

Candidate	Electoral Vote	Popular Vote	Percent of Popular Vote
Abraham Lincoln (Republican)	180	1,865,593	39.8
John C. Breckinridge (Southern Democrat)	72	848,356	18.1
John Bell (Constitutional Union)	39	592,906	12.6
Stephen A. Douglas (Northern Democrat)	12	1,382,713	29.5

MAP 13.7

Political Realignment, 1848 and 1860

In the presidential election of 1848, both the Whig and the Democratic candidates won electoral votes throughout the nation. Subsequently, the political conflict over slavery and the Compromise of 1850 destroyed the Whig Party in the South. As the only nationwide party, the Democrats won easily over the Whigs in 1852 and, because of the split between Republicans and Know-Nothings, triumphed in 1856 as well. However, a new regional-based party system had taken shape by 1860 and would persist for the next seventy years—with Democrats dominant in the South and Republicans usually controlling the Northeast, Midwest, and Far West.

of the states." The fate of the republic hinged on President Buchanan's ability to quiet the passions of the past decade and to hold the Democratic Party—the only national party—together.

Dred Scott: Petitioner for Freedom

Events—and his own values and weaknesses—conspired against Buchanan. In 1856, the Supreme Court decided the case of *Dred Scott v. Sandford*, which raised the controversial issue of Congress's constitutional authority over slavery in the territories. Dred Scott was an enslaved African American who had lived for a time with his owner, an army surgeon, in the free state of Illinois and in the Wisconsin Territory, where the Northwest Ordinance (1787) prohibited slavery. Scott claimed that residence in a free state and a free territory had made him free. Buchanan wanted the Court to reject Scott's appeal and pressured the two justices from Pennsylvania to side with their southern colleagues. Seven of the nine justices issued opinions declaring that Scott was still a slave. But they disagreed on the legal rationale, so the case did not create a binding principle of constitutional law.

Chief Justice Roger B. Taney of Maryland, a slave owner himself, wrote the most influential opinion. He declared that Negroes, whether enslaved or free, could not be citizens of the United States and that Scott therefore had no right to sue in federal court. That argument was controversial, given that free blacks were citizens in many states and therefore had access to the federal courts. But Taney then made two even more controversial claims. First, he endorsed John C. Calhoun's argument that the Fifth Amendment, which prohibited "taking" of property without due process of law, meant that Congress could not prevent southern citizens from carrying their slave property into the territories and owning it there. Consequently, the chief justice concluded, the provisions of the Northwest Ordinance and the Missouri Compromise that prohibited slavery had never been constitutional. Second, Taney declared that Congress could not give to territorial governments any powers that it did not possess, which meant that settlers in a territory could not enact legislation prohibiting slavery. Taney thereby endorsed Calhoun's interpretation of popular sovereignty: Only when settlers wrote a constitution and requested statehood could they prohibit slavery.

In a single stroke, Taney had declared the Republicans' stance against the expansion of slavery to be unconstitutional. The Republicans could never accept the legitimacy of Taney's arguments. Led by Senator Seward of New York, they accused the chief justice and President Buchanan of participating in the Slave Power conspiracy.

Buchanan then added fuel to the raging constitutional fire. Ignoring reports that antislavery residents held a clear majority in Kansas, he refused to allow a popular vote on the proslavery Lecompton constitution and recommended the admission of Kansas as a slave state. Angered by Buchanan's machinations, Stephen Douglas, the most influential Democratic senator and architect of the Kansas-Nebraska Act, broke with the president and persuaded Congress to deny statehood to Kansas. (Kansas would enter the Union as a free state in 1861.) Still determined to aid the South, Buchanan informed Congress in December 1858 that he was resuming negotiations to buy Cuba. By pursuing a proslavery agenda—first in *Dred Scott* and then in Kansas and Cuba—Buchanan widened the split in his party and the nation.

- Why did the Compromise of 1850 fail? Would it have succeeded if the Kansas-Nebraska Act of 1854 either had not been enacted or had contained different provisions?

- What were the main constitutional arguments advanced during the debate over slavery in the territories? Which of those arguments influenced Chief Justice Taney's opinion in *Dred Scott*?

Abraham Lincoln and the Republican Triumph, 1858–1860

As the Democratic Party split along sectional lines, the Republicans gained support in the North and Midwest. Abraham Lincoln of Illinois emerged as the only Republican leader whose policies and temperament might have saved the Union. But few southerners trusted Lincoln, and his presidential candidacy revived secessionist agitation.

Lincoln's Political Career

The middle-class world of storekeepers, lawyers, and entrepreneurs in the small towns of the Ohio River Valley shaped Lincoln's early career. He came from a hardscrabble yeoman farm family that was continually on the move—from Kentucky, where Lincoln was born in 1809, to Indiana, and then to Illinois. In 1831, Lincoln rejected his father's life as a subsistence farmer and be-

Abraham Lincoln, 1859

Lincoln was not a handsome man, and he photographed poorly. His campaign photographs were often retouched to hide his prominent cheekbones and nose. More important, no photograph ever captured Lincoln's complex personality and wit or the intensity of his spirit and intellect. To grasp Lincoln, it is necessary to read his words. Chicago Historical Society.

came a store clerk in New Salem, Illinois. Socially ambitious, Lincoln sought entry into the middle class by mastering its culture; he joined the New Salem Debating Society, read Shakespeare, and studied law.

Admitted to the bar in 1837, Lincoln moved to Springfield, the new state capital. There, he met Mary Todd, the cultured daughter of a Kentucky banker; they married in 1842. Her tastes were aristocratic; his were humble. She was volatile; he was easygoing, but suffered bouts of depression that tried her patience and tested his character.

An Ambitious Politician | Lincoln's ambition was "a little engine that knew no rest," his closest associate remarked, and it propelled him into politics. An admirer of Henry Clay, Lincoln joined the Whig Party and won election to four terms in the Illinois legislature, where he promoted education, banks, canals, and railroads. He became a dexterous party politician, adept in the distribution of patronage and the passage of legislation.

In 1846, the rising lawyer-politician won election to a Congress that was bitterly divided over the Wilmot Proviso. Lincoln believed that human bondage was unjust but doubted that the federal government had the constitutional authority to tamper with slavery in the South. With respect to the Mexican War, he took a middle ground. Lincoln voted for military appropriations, but he also supported Wilmot's proposal to prohibit slavery in any acquired territories. And he introduced legislation that would require the gradual (and thus compensated) emancipation of slaves in the District of Columbia. Lincoln advocated firm opposition to the expansion of slavery, gradual emancipation, and, to resolve the issue of racial diversity, the colonization of freed blacks in Africa. Both abolitionists and proslavery activists heaped scorn on Lincoln's middle-of-the-road policies, and he lost his bid for reelection. Dismayed by the rancor of ideological debate, he withdrew from politics and prospered as a lawyer representing railroads and manufacturers.

Lincoln returned to the political fray because of the Kansas-Nebraska Act. Shocked by the act's repeal of the Missouri Compromise and Douglas's advocacy of popular sovereignty, Lincoln reaffirmed his position that slavery should be excluded from the territories. Beyond that, he likened slavery to a cancer that had to be cut out if the nation's republican ideals and moral principles were to endure.

The Lincoln-Douglas Debates | Abandoning the Whigs, Lincoln quickly emerged as the Republican leader in Illinois. Campaigning for the U.S. Senate against Douglas in 1858, Lincoln explained that the proslavery Supreme Court might soon declare that the Constitution "does not permit a state to exclude slavery from its limits," just as it had decided in *Dred Scott* that "neither Congress nor the territorial legislature" could ban slavery in a territory. In that event, he warned, "we shall awake to the reality . . . that the Supreme Court has made Illinois a slave state." The prospect of slavery spreading into the North informed Lincoln's famous "House Divided" speech. Quoting from the Bible, "A house divided against itself cannot stand," he predicted that American society "cannot endure permanently half slave and half free. . . . It will become all one thing, or all the other."

The Senate race in Illinois attracted national interest because of Douglas's prominence and Lincoln's reputation as a formidable speaker. During a series of seven debates, Douglas declared his support for white supremacy: "This government was made by our fathers, by white men for the benefit of white men," he said, and attacked Lincoln for supporting "negro equality." Lincoln parried Douglas's racist attacks by advocating economic opportunity for free blacks but not equal political rights. Taking the offensive, he asked how Douglas could accept the *Dred Scott* decision (which protected slave owners' property in the territories) yet advocate popular sovereignty (which asserted the settlers' power to exclude slavery). Douglas responded with the so-called Freeport Doctrine: that a territory's residents could exclude slavery by not adopting laws to protect it. That position pleased neither proslavery nor antislavery advocates. Nonetheless, the Democrats won a narrow majority in the state legislature, which reelected Douglas to the U.S. Senate.

The Union under Siege

The debates with Douglas gave Lincoln a national reputation, and in the election of 1858 the Republican Party won control of the U.S. House of Representatives.

The Rise of Radicalism   Shaken by the Republicans' advance, southern Democrats divided again into moderates and fire-eaters. The moderates, who included Senator Jefferson Davis of Mississippi, strongly defended "southern rights"; they demanded ironclad political or constitutional protections for slavery. The fire-eaters — men such as Robert Barnwell Rhett of South Carolina and William Lowndes Yancey of Alabama — repudiated the Union and actively promoted secession. Radical antislavery northerners likewise took a strong stance. Senator Seward of New York declared that freedom and slavery were locked in "an irrepressible conflict," and militant abolitionist John Brown, who had perpetrated the Pottawatomie massacre, showed what that might mean. In October 1859, Brown led eighteen heavily armed black and white men in a raid on the federal arsenal at Harpers Ferry, Virginia. Brown hoped to arm slaves with the arsenal's weapons and mount a major rebellion that would end slavery.

Republican leaders condemned Brown's unsuccessful raid, but Democrats called his plot "a natural, logical, inevitable result of the doctrines and teachings of the Republican party." When the state of Virginia charged Brown with treason and sentenced him to be hanged, transcendentalist reformers Henry David Thoreau and Ralph Waldo Emerson defended him as "an angel of light" and a "saint awaiting his martyrdom." The slaveholding states looked to the future with terror. "The aim of the present black republican organization is the destruction of the social system of the Southern States, without regard to consequences," warned one newspaper. Once Republicans came to power, another cau-

tioned, they "would create insurrection and servile war in the South — they would put the torch to our dwellings and the knife to our throats."

Nor could the South count on the Democratic Party to protect its interests. At the party's convention in April 1860, northern Democrats rejected Jefferson Davis's proposal to protect slavery in the territories, prompting the delegates from eight southern states to quit the meeting. At a second Democratic convention in Baltimore, northern and midwestern delegates nominated Stephen Douglas for president; meeting separately, southern Democrats nominated the sitting vice president, John C. Breckinridge of Kentucky.

The Election of 1860   With the Democrats divided, the Republicans sensed victory. They courted white voters with a free-soil platform that opposed both slavery and racial equality: "Missouri for white men and white men for Missouri," declared that state's Republican platform. The national Republican convention chose Lincoln as its presidential candidate because his position on slavery was more moderate than the abolitionist stance taken by the best-known Republicans, Senators William Seward of New York and Salmon Chase of Ohio. Lincoln also conveyed a compelling egalitarian image that appealed to small-holding farmers, wage earners, and Midwestern voters.

The Republican strategy worked. Although Lincoln received only 40 percent of the popular vote, he won every northern and western state except New Jersey, giving him 180 (of 303) electoral votes and an absolute majority in the electoral college. Breckinridge took 72 electoral votes by sweeping the Deep South and picking up Delaware, Maryland, and North Carolina. Douglas won 30 percent of the popular ballot but secured electoral votes only in Missouri and New Jersey. The Republicans had united voters in the Northeast, Midwest, and Pacific Coast behind free soil.

A revolution was in the making. Slavery had permeated the American federal republic so thoroughly that southerners saw it as a natural part of the constitutional order — an order that was now under siege. Fearful of a massive black uprising, Chief Justice Taney recalled "the horrors of St. Domingo [Haiti]." At the very least, warned John Townsend of South Carolina, a Republican administration in Washington would suppress "the inter-State slave trade" and thereby "*cripple this vital Southern institution* of slavery." To many southerners, it seemed time to think carefully about Lincoln's 1858 statement that the Union must "become all one thing, or all the other."

THE NATIONAL GAME. THREE "OUTS" AND ONE "RUN".
ABRAHAM WINNING THE BALL.

Lincoln on Home Base

As early as 1860, the language and imagery of sports had penetrated politics. Sporting a long, rail-like bat labeled "EQUAL RIGHTS AND FREE TERRITORY," Abraham Lincoln appears ready to score a victory in the election. His three opponents—from left to right, John Bell (the candidate of a new Constitutional Union party), Stephen A. Douglas, and John C. Breckinridge—will soon be "out." Indeed, according to the pro-Lincoln cartoonist, they were about to be "skunk'd." As Douglas laments, their attempt to put a "short stop" to Lincoln's presidential ambitions had failed.   Museum of American Political Life.

- What was Lincoln's position on slavery during the 1850s? Did it differ from that of Stephen Douglas? Explain your answer.

- What was the relationship between the collapse of the Second Party System of Whigs and Democrats and the Republican victory in the election of 1860?

SUMMARY

In this chapter, we examined four related themes: the ideology of Manifest Destiny and the westward movement of Americans in the 1840s, the impact of American traders and settlers on the Great Plains and California Indians, the causes and consequences of the Mexican War (1846–1848), and the disintegration of the Second Party System during the 1850s.

We saw that the determination of Presidents John Tyler and James Polk to add territory and slave states to the Union pushed the United States into the Mexican War and into a new debate over the expansion of slavery. To resolve the resulting crisis, Henry Clay, Daniel Webster, and Stephen Douglas devised the Compromise of 1850. Their efforts were in vain: Antislavery northerners defied the Fugitive Slave Act, and expansionist-minded southerners sought new slave states in the Caribbean. *Ideology* (the pursuit of absolutes) replaced *politics* (the art of compromise) as the ruling principle of American political life.

The Second Party System rapidly disintegrated. The Whig Party vanished, and two issue-oriented parties, the nativist American Party and the antislavery Republican Party, competed for its members. As the Republicans gained strength, the Democratic Party splintered into sectional factions over Bleeding Kansas and other slavery-related issues. The stage was set for Lincoln's victory in the climactic election of 1860.

CHAPTER REVIEW QUESTIONS

- What were the links between the Mexican War of 1846–1848 and Abraham Lincoln's election as president in 1860?

- When and why did the Second Party System of Whigs and Democrats collapse?

- Some historians claim that the mistakes of a "blundering generation" of political leaders led, by 1860, to the imminent breakup of the Union. Do you agree with their assessment? Why or why not?

FOR FURTHER EXPLORATION

Patricia Nelson Limerick, *The Legacy of Conquest* (1989), highlights social conflicts in the West. See also the PBS documentary *The West* (6 hours) and its Web site (**www.pbs.org/weta/thewest**). For "California as I Saw It," a resource of first-person narratives of California settlers, go to **memory.loc.gov/ammem/ cbhtml/cbhome.html**. On early Texas history, see **www.tsl.state.tx.us/treasures**. The PBS documentary *U.S.-Mexican War: 1846–1848* (4 hours) and its Web site (**www.pbs.org/usmexicanwar**) cover both American and Mexican perspectives.

David Potter, *The Impending Crisis, 1848–1861* (1976), covers the political history of the 1850s. John Patrick Daly, *When Slavery Was Called Freedom: Evangelicalism, Proslavery, and the Causes of the Civil War* (2002), and Leonard L. Richards, *The Slave Power: The Free North and Southern Domination, 1780–1860* (2000), offer broad cultural analyses. For good state-focused studies of Virginia and South Carolina, read William A. Link, *Roots of Secession* (2003), and Manisha Sinha, *The Counterrevolution of Slavery* (200 0).

Eric Foner, *Free Soil, Free Labor, Free Men* (1970), covers the ideology of the Republican Party, while Michael Holt's *The Political Crisis of the 1850s* (1978) traces the collapse of the Second Party System. For Lincoln, read Stephen Oates, *With Malice Toward None* (1977). The court's decision in the *Dred Scott* case, as well as links to the justices' concurring and dissenting opinions, can be found at **www.tourolaw.edu/patch/ scott**. "*Uncle Tom's Cabin* and American Culture" (**utc.iath.virginia.edu**) places the novel in its literary and cultural context.

TEST YOUR KNOWLEDGE

To assess your command of the material in this chapter, see the Online Study Guide at **bedfordstmartins.com/henretta**.

For Web sites, images, and documents related to topics and places in this chapter, visit **bedfordstmartins.com/makehistory**.

TIMELINE

1844	James Polk elected president
1845	Texas admitted into Union
1846	United States declares war on Mexico
	Treaty with Britain divides Oregon Country
	Wilmot Proviso approved by House but not by Senate
1847	American troops capture Mexico City
1848	Gold found in California
	Treaty of Guadalupe Hidalgo gives Mexican provinces of California, New Mexico, and Texas to United States
	Free-Soil Party forms
	Zachary Taylor elected president
1850	President Taylor dies; Millard Fillmore assumes presidency
	Compromise of 1850 preserves Union
	Northern abolitionists reject Fugitive Slave Act
	South seeks to acquire Spanish Cuba to expand slavery
1851	American (Know-Nothing) Party forms
1852	Harriet Beecher Stowe publishes *Uncle Tom's Cabin*
1854	Ostend Manifesto urges seizure of Cuba
	Kansas-Nebraska Act tests policy of popular sovereignty
	Republican Party forms
1856	Turmoil in Kansas undermines popular sovereignty
	James Buchanan elected president
1857	*Dred Scott v. Sandford* allows slavery in U.S. territories
1858	President Buchanan backs Lecompton constitution
	Abraham Lincoln and Stephen Douglas debate in U.S. Senate race
1859	John Brown raids federal arsenal at Harpers Ferry
1860	Abraham Lincoln elected president in four-way contest

Two Societies at War, 1861–1865

"What a scene it was," Union soldier Elisha Hunt Rhodes wrote in his diary at Gettysburg in July 1863. "Oh the dead and the dying on this bloody field." Thousands of men had already died and the slaughter would continue for almost two more years. "What is this all about?" asked Confederate lieutenant R. M. Collins as another gruesome battle ended. "Why is it that 200,000 men of one blood and tongue . . . [are] seeking one another's lives? We could settle our differences by compromising and all be at home in ten days." But, almost inexplicably, there was no compromise. "God wills this contest, and wills that it shall not yet end," President Abraham Lincoln reflected in 1862. Even on the eve of victory in 1865, Lincoln felt the nation in the grip forces beyond human control: "The Almighty has His own purposes."

To explain why southerners seceded and fought to the bitter end is not simple, but racial slavery is an important part of the answer. To southern whites, the Republican victory in 1860 presented an immediate danger to the slave-owning republic that had existed since 1776. Lincoln won not a single electoral vote in the South, and many Republicans vowed to limit (and perhaps even end) the slave system. "We are resisting revolution," leading southerners protested. "[O]ur struggle is for inherited rights." Southerners did not believe Lincoln when he promised not "directly or indirectly, to interfere with the institution of slavery in the States where it exists." To the contrary, a southern newspaper declared: "The mission of the Republican party was to meddle with everything – to meddle with the domestic institutions of other States, and to meddle with family arrangements in their own states – to overthrow Democracy, Catholicism and Slavery." Soon, a southern senator warned, "cohorts of Federal office-holders, Abolitionists, may be sent into [our] midst" to mobilize enslaved blacks. Remembering John Brown's raid, southerners were terrified that federal officials would encourage bloody slave revolts and racial mixture. By *racial mixture*, white southerners meant sexual relations between black men and white women, given that white owners had already fathered untold thousands of children by their enslaved black women. "Better, far better! [to] endure all horrors of civil war," insisted a Confederate recruit from Virginia, "than to see the dusky sons of Ham leading the fair daughters of the South to the altar." To preserve the subordination of blacks and the supremacy of white men, radical southerners chose the dangerous enterprise of secession.

Lincoln and the North would not let them go in peace. Living in a world still ruled by kings and princes, northern leaders believed that the collapse of

Fields of Death

Fought with mass armies and new weapons, the Civil War took a huge toll in human lives, as evidenced by this grisly photograph of a small section of the battlefield at Antietam, Maryland. At Shiloh, Tennessee, General Ulysses Grant surveyed a field "so covered with dead that it would have been possible to walk . . . in any direction, stepping on dead bodies, without a foot touching the ground." Library of Congress.

the American Union might destroy for all time the possibility of a democratic republican government. "We cannot escape history," the new president eloquently declared. "We shall nobly save, or meanly lose, the last best hope of earth." A young Union army recruit from Ohio put the issue simply: "If our institutions prove a failure . . . of what value will be house, family, or friends?"

And so came the Civil War. Called the War Between the States by southerners and the War of the Rebellion by northerners, the struggle continued until the great issues of the Union and slavery had finally been resolved. The cost was incredibly high: more American lives lost than the combined total for all the nation's other wars, and a century-long legacy of bitterness between the triumphant North and the vanquished white South.

Secession and Military Stalemate, 1861–1862

Following Lincoln's election in November 1860, secessionist fervor swept through the Deep South. But veteran party leaders in Washington still hoped to save the Union. In the four months between Lincoln's election and his inauguration on March 4, 1861, they sought a new compromise.

The Secession Crisis

The Union collapsed first in South Carolina, the home of John C. Calhoun, nullification, and southern rights. Robert Barnwell Rhett and other fire-eaters had demanded secession since the Compromise of 1850, and their goal was now within reach. "Our enemies are about to take possession of the Government," warned one South Carolinian, predicting that those "enemies" would act like a "conqueror." Frightened by that prospect, a special state convention voted unanimously on December 20, 1860, to dissolve "the union now subsisting between South Carolina and other States."

The Lower South Secedes Fire-eaters elsewhere in the Deep South quickly called similar conventions and organized mobs to attack local Union supporters. In early January, white Mississippians joyously enacted a secession ordinance. Within a month, Florida, Alabama, Georgia, Louisiana, and Texas had also left the Union (Map 14.1). In February, the jubilant secessionists met in Montgomery, Alabama, to proclaim a new nation: the Confederate States of America. Adopting a provisional constitution, the delegates named Mississippian Jefferson Davis, a former

U.S. senator and secretary of war, as the Confederacy's president and Georgia congressman Alexander Stephens as vice president.

Secessionist fervor was less intense in the four states of the Middle South (Virginia, North Carolina, Tennessee, and Arkansas), where there were fewer slaves. White opinion was especially divided in the four border slave states (Maryland, Delaware, Kentucky, and Missouri), where yeomen farmers held greater political power. During the 1850s, journalist Hinton Helper of North Carolina had warned yeomen that "the slaveholders . . . have hoodwinked you." Influenced partly by such sentiments, the legislatures of Virginia and Tennessee refused to join the secessionist movement and urged a compromise.

Meanwhile, the Union government floundered. The president declared secession illegal but — in line with his pro-South, states' rights outlook — claimed that the federal government lacked authority to restore the Union by force. Buchanan's timidity prompted South Carolina's new government to demand the surrender of Fort Sumter (a federal garrison in Charleston Harbor) and to cut off its supplies. The president again backed down, refusing to order the navy to escort a supply ship into the harbor.

The Crittenden Compromise Instead, the outgoing president urged Congress to find a compromise. The plan proposed by Senator John J. Crittenden of Kentucky received the most support. Crittenden's plan had two parts. The first, which Congress approved, called for a constitutional amendment to protect slavery from federal interference in any state where it already existed. Crittenden's second provision called for the westward extension of the Missouri Compromise line (36°30' north latitude) to the Califor-

Agitating for Secession

Lincoln's election triggered a vigorous response from South Carolina's fire-eaters, who called a secession rally in Charleston. On December 1, 1860, hundreds of well-dressed planters and merchants met at the Mills Hotel to hear prominent secessionists demand withdrawal from the Union. Three weeks later, in a unanimous vote, a special state convention did just that.   Library of Congress.

nia border. Slavery would be barred north of the line and protected to the south, including any territories "hereafter acquired," thus raising the prospect of expansion into Cuba or Central America. Congressional Republicans rejected Crittenden's second proposal on strict instructions from Lincoln, the president-elect. With good reason, Lincoln feared that it would prompt new imperialist adventures. "I want Cuba," Senator Albert G. Brown of Mississippi had candidly stated in 1858. "I want Tamaulipas, Potosi, and one or two other Mexican States . . . for the planting or spreading of slav-

ery." In 1787, 1821, and 1850, the North and South had resolved their differences over slavery. In 1861, there would be no compromise.

In his March 1861 inaugural address, Lincoln carefully outlined his views on slavery and the Union. He promised to safeguard slavery where it existed but vowed to prevent its expansion. Beyond that, Lincoln declared that the Union was "perpetual"; consequently, the secession of the Confederate states was illegal. The Republican president declared his intention to "hold, occupy, and possess" federal property in the seceded states and

The states colored orange practiced slavery before and during the Civil War but did not secede from the Union. Why? Was it the presence of federal troops? Or was it because, as Figure 14.1 shows, there were relatively few slaves (and slaveholders) in those states?

This map records the votes for and against secession in each county or parish.

The numbers show the chronological sequence of secession of the Confederate states. Did a state's place in the sequence reflect the unanimity of its vote?

For secession	
Against secession	
Delegation divided	
No returns	
Border states that did not secede	

1 Numbers indicate order of secession

——— Northern limit of secession before Ft. Sumter

---- Northern limit of secession after Ft. Sumter

0   200   400 miles
0   200   400 kilometers

MAP 14.1

The Process of Secession, 1860–1861

The states of the Lower South had the highest concentration of slaves, and they led the secessionist movement. After the attack on Fort Sumter in April 1861, the states of the Upper South joined the Confederacy. Yeomen farmers in Tennessee and the backcountry of Alabama, Georgia, and Virginia opposed secession but, except in the future state of West Virginia, initially rallied to the Confederate cause. Consequently, the South entered the Civil War with its white population relatively united.

"to collect duties and imposts" there. If military force was necessary to preserve the Union, Lincoln—like Andrew Jackson during the nullification crisis—would use it. The choice was the South's: Return to the Union, or face war.

The Upper South Chooses Sides

The South's decision came quickly. When Lincoln dispatched an unarmed ship to resupply Fort Sumter, Jefferson Davis and his associates in the Provisional Government of the Confederate States decided to seize the fort. The Confederate forces opened fire on April 12, with ardent fire-eater Edmund Ruffin supposedly firing the first cannon. Two days later, the Union defenders capitulated. On April 15, Lincoln called 75,000 state militiamen into federal service for ninety days to put down an insurrection "too powerful to be suppressed by the ordinary course of judicial proceedings."

Northerners responded to Lincoln's call to arms with wild enthusiasm. Asked to provide thirteen regiments of volunteers, Republican governor William Dennison of Ohio sent twenty. Many northern Democrats also lent their support. "Every man must be for the United States or against it," Democratic leader Stephen Douglas declared. "There can be no neutrals in this war, only patriots—or traitors." How then might the Democratic Party function as a "loyal opposition," supporting the Union while challenging certain Republican policies? It would not be an easy task.

Whites in the Middle and Border South now had to choose between the Union and the Confederacy, and their decision was crucial. Those eight states accounted for two-thirds of the whites in the slaveholding states, three-fourths of their industrial production, and well over half of their food. They were home to many of the nation's best military leaders, including Colonel Robert E. Lee of Virginia, a career officer whom veteran General Winfield Scott recommended to Lincoln to lead the new Union army. Those states were also geographically strategic. Kentucky, with its 500-mile border on the Ohio River, was essential to the movement of troops and supplies. Maryland was vital to the Union's security because it bordered the nation's capital on three sides.

The weight of its history as a slave-owning colony and state decided the outcome in Virginia. A convention approved secession by a vote of 88 to 55, with dissenters coming mainly from the state's yeomen-dominated northwestern counties. Elsewhere, Virginia whites embraced the Confederate cause. "The North was the aggressor," declared Richmond lawyer William Poague as he enlisted. "The South resisted her invaders." Refusing Scott's offer of the Union command, Robert E. Lee resigned from the U.S. Army. "Save in defense of my native state," Lee told Scott, "I never desire again to draw my sword." Arkansas, Tennessee, and North Carolina quickly joined Virginia in the Confederacy.

Lincoln moved aggressively to hold strategic areas where relatively few whites owned slaves (see Figure 14.1). To secure the railway line connecting Washington to the Ohio River Valley, the president ordered General George B. McClellan to take control of northwestern Virginia. "I am armed like a desperado," wrote a Unionist there. "Friends have become enemies to one another." In October 1861, the yeoman-dominated electorate voted overwhelmingly to set up a separate breakaway territory, West Virginia, which was admitted to the Union in 1863. Unionists also carried the day in Delaware. In Maryland, where slavery was still entrenched, a pro-Confederate mob attacked Massachusetts troops traveling through Baltimore, causing the war's first combat deaths: four soldiers and twelve civilians. When Maryland secessionists destroyed railroad bridges and telegraph lines, Lincoln ordered Union troops to occupy the state and arrest Confederate sympathizers, including legislators. He released them only in November 1861, after Unionists had secured control of Maryland's government.

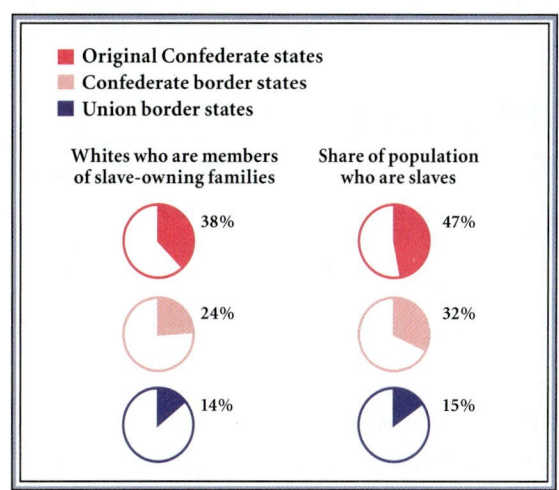

FIGURE 14.1

Slavery and Secession

As these graphs indicate, the Confederate states that initially seceded from the Union were heavily invested in slavery. Nearly 40 percent of whites in those Deep South states were members of families that owned slaves, who numbered nearly half that region's population. By contrast, only 14 percent of the whites owned slaves in the pro-Union border states, such as Missouri and Maryland, where enslaved people formed only 15 percent of the population.

Lincoln was equally energetic in the Mississippi River Valley. To win control of Missouri (along with the Missouri River and the Upper Mississippi River), Lincoln mobilized the state's German American militia, which strongly opposed slavery; in July, the German Americans defeated a force of Confederate sympathizers commanded by the state's governor. Despite continuing raids by Confederate guerrilla bands, which included the notorious outlaws Jesse and Frank James, the Union retained control of Missouri (see Voices from Abroad, "Ernest Duvergier de Hauranne: Germans and the War in Missouri," p. 434). In Kentucky, secessionist and Unionist sentiment was evenly balanced, so Lincoln moved cautiously. He allowed Kentucky's thriving trade with the Confederacy to continue until Unionists took over the state government in August 1861. When the Confederacy responded to the cutoff of trade by invading Kentucky in September, Illinois volunteers commanded by Ulysses S. Grant drove them out. Mixing military force with political persuasion, Lincoln had kept four border states (Delaware, Maryland, Missouri, and Kentucky) and the northwestern portion of Virginia in the Union.

All the nations and people I had hitherto passed through resembled [my] own in their manners, customs and langu[age]

Ernest Duvergier de Hauranne
Germans and the War in Missouri

Tens of thousands of German immigrants settled in Missouri and other mid-western states in the two decades before the Civil War. As this letter written by Ernest Duvergier de Hauranne indicates, most of them supported the Union cause. A French citizen, Duvergier de Hauranne (1843–1877) traveled widely, and his letters home offer intelligent commentary on American politics and society during the Civil War.

St. Louis, September 12, 1864

Missouri is to all intents and purposes a rebel state, an occupied territory where the Federal forces are really nothing but a garrison under siege; even today it is not certain what would happen if the troops were withdrawn. Party quarrels here are poisoned by class hatreds. Not only are questions of peace and war, of national honor and humiliation, hotly debated, but so is the much more explosive question of slavery versus abolition. . . . It is a war over private interests between two irreconcilable classes. The old Anglo-French families, attached to Southern institutions, harbor a primitive, superstitious prejudice in favor of slavery. Conquered now, but full of repressed rage, they exhibit the implacable anger peculiar to the defenders of lost causes. They no longer have any hope of reviving slavery or their own past fortunes; . . . they seem to be lying low while hoping for an opportunity to take their revenge.

The more recent German population is strongly abolitionist. They have brought to the New World the instincts of European democracy, together with its radical attitudes and all-or-nothing doctrines. Ancient precedents and worn-out laws matter little to them. They have not studied history and have no respect for hallowed injustices; but they do have, to the highest degree, that sense of moral principle which is more or less lacking in American democracy. They aren't afraid of revolution: to destroy a barbarous institution they would, if necessary, take an axe to the foundations of society. Furthermore, their interests coincide with their principles. . . . Even if their democratic beliefs and innate sense of justice did not cause them to rise up against slavery, they would still detest it as an obstacle to their prosperity and as a source of unfair competition with their labor.

The immigrant arrives poor and lives by his work. A newcomer, having nothing to lose and caring little for the interests of established property owners, sees that the subjection of free labor to the ruinous competition of slave labor must be ended. At the same time, his pride rebels against the prejudice attached to work in a land of slavery; he wants to reestablish its value. . . .

There is no mistaking the hatred the two parties, not to say the two peoples, have for each other. . . .

As passions were coming to a boil, the Federal government sent General [John C.] Frémont here as army commander and dictator. . . . An abolitionist and a self-made man, he put himself firmly at the head of the German party, determined to crush the friends of slavery. He formed an army of Germans. . . . He left the abolitionist party in the West organized, disciplined, stronger and more resolute, but he also left the pro-Southern party more exasperated than ever, and society divided, without intermediaries, into two hostile camps. . . .

Everyone is an extremist; between the radical abolitionists and the friends of the South there is no moderate Unionist middle ground. Bands of guerrillas hold the countryside, where they raid as much as they please; politics serves as a fine pretext for looting. Their leaders are officers from the army of the South who receive their orders from the Confederate government. . . . These "bushwackers," who ordinarily rob indiscriminately, maintain their standing as political raiders by occasionally killing some poor, inoffensive person. Finally, people bent on personal vengeance take advantage of the state of civil war: sometimes one hears of villages divided against themselves so bitterly that massacres are carried on from door to door with incredible ferocity. . . . You can see what emotions are still boiling in this region that is supposed to be pacified.

Source: Ernest Duvergier de Hauranne, *A Frenchman in Lincoln's America* (Chicago: Lakeside Press, 1974), 1: 305–309.

ANALYZING THE EVIDENCE

- According to Duvergier de Hauranne, why did German immigrants oppose slavery? How does his explanation provide insight into the free-soil movement?

- Why, even in 1864, did the federal government lack control over Missouri, a border state that remained in the Union? What clues does Duvergier de Hauranne provide?

- Ethnic rivalries loomed large in the civil warfare in Missouri. As you read the chapter, look for other ethnic conflicts that exploded during the war. Why did they do so?

Setting War Objectives and Devising Strategies

Speaking as provisional president of the Confederacy in April 1861, Jefferson Davis identified the Confederates' cause with that of the Patriots of 1776: Like their grandfathers, he said, white southerners were fighting for the "sacred right of self-government." The Confederacy sought "no conquest, no aggrandizement . . . ; all we ask is to be let alone." Davis's renunciation of expansion was probably a calculated short-run policy; after all, the slave owners' quest to extend slavery had sparked Lincoln's election and southern secession. Still, this decision simplified the Confederacy's military strategy; it needed only to defend its boundaries to achieve independence. Ignoring strong antislavery sentiment among potential European allies, the Confederate constitution explicitly ruled out gradual emancipation or any other law "denying or impairing the right of property in negro slaves." Indeed, Confederate vice president Alexander Stephens insisted that his nation's "cornerstone rests upon the great truth that the Negro is not equal to the white man, that slavery—subordination to the superior race—is his natural or normal condition."

Lincoln responded to Davis in a speech to Congress on July 4, 1861. He portrayed secession as an attack on popular government, America's great contribution to world history. The issue, Lincoln declared, was "whether a constitutional republic" had the will and the means to "maintain its territorial integrity against a domestic foe." Determined to crush the rebellion, Lincoln rejected General Winfield Scott's strategy of peaceful persuasion through economic sanctions and a naval blockade. Instead, the president insisted on an aggressive military campaign to restore the Union.

Union Thrusts Toward Richmond Lincoln hoped that a quick strike against the Confederate capital of Richmond, Virginia, would end the rebellion. Many northerners were equally optimistic. "What a picnic," thought one New York volunteer, "to go down South for three months and clean up the whole business." So in July 1861, Lincoln ordered General Irvin McDowell and an army of 30,000 men to attack General P. G. T. Beauregard's force of 20,000 troops at Manassas, a Virginia rail junction 30 miles southwest of Washington. McDowell launched a strong assault near Manassas Creek (also called Bull Run), but panic swept his troops when the Confederate soldiers counterattacked, shouting the hair-raising "rebel yell." "The peculiar corkscrew sensation that it sends down your backbone under these circumstances

can never be told," one Union veteran wrote. "You have to feel it." McDowell's troops—along with the many civilians who had come to observe the battle—retreated in disarray to Washington.

The rout at Bull Run made it clear that the rebellion would not be easily crushed. Lincoln replaced McDowell with General George McClellan and enlisted an additional million men to serve for three years in the newly created Army of the Potomac. A cautious military engineer, McClellan spent the winter of 1861 training the recruits; then, early in 1862, he launched a major offensive. With great logistical skill, the Union general transported 100,000 troops by boat down the Potomac River to the Chesapeake Bay and landed them on the peninsula between the York and James rivers (Map 14.2). Ignoring Lincoln's advice to "strike a blow," McClellan advanced slowly toward the South's capital, allowing the Confederates to mount a counterstrike. To relieve the pressure on Richmond, a Confederate army under Thomas J. "Stonewall" Jackson marched rapidly northward through the Shenandoah Valley in western Virginia and threatened Washington. Lincoln recalled 30,000 troops from McClellan's army to protect the Union capital, and Jackson returned quickly to Richmond to bolster the main Confederate army commanded by General Robert E. Lee. Lee launched a ferocious attack that lasted from June 25 to July 1 and cost the Confederates 20,000 casualties to the Union's 10,000. When McClellan failed to exploit the Confederates' losses, Lincoln ordered a withdrawal and Richmond remained secure.

Lee Moves North: Antietam Hoping for victories that would humiliate Lincoln's government, Lee went on the offensive. Joining with Jackson in northern Virginia, he routed Union troops in the Second Battle of Bull Run (August 1862) and then struck north through western Maryland. There, he nearly met with disaster. When Lee divided his force, sending Jackson to capture Harpers Ferry in West Virginia, a copy of Lee's orders fell into McClellan's hands. But the Union general again failed to exploit his advantage, delaying his attack, and allowing Lee's depleted army to occupy a strong defensive position on the high ground west of Antietam Creek, near Sharpsburg, Maryland. Outnumbered 87,000 to 50,000, Lee desperately fought off McClellan's attacks until Jackson's troops arrived and saved the Confederates from a major defeat. Appalled by the Union casualties, McClellan allowed Lee to retreat to Virginia.

The fighting at Antietam was savage. A Wisconsin officer described his men "loading and firing with demoniacal fury and shouting and laughing hysterically."

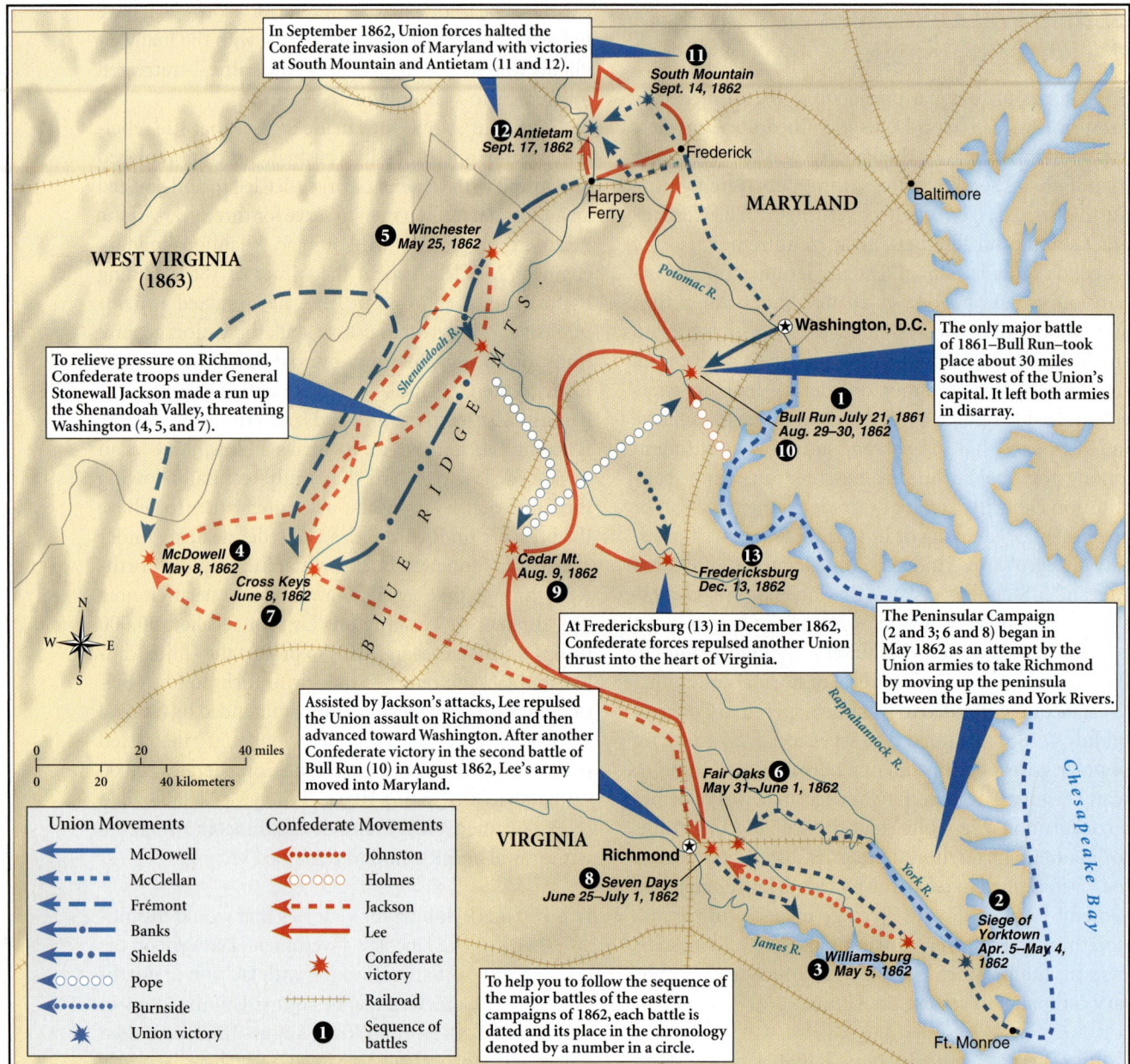

In September 1862, Union forces halted the Confederate invasion of Maryland with victories at South Mountain and Antietam (11 and 12).

South Mountain Sept. 14, 1862

Antietam Sept. 17, 1862

Winchester May 25, 1862

WEST VIRGINIA (1863)

To relieve pressure on Richmond, Confederate troops under General Stonewall Jackson made a run up the Shenandoah Valley, threatening Washington (4, 5, and 7).

McDowell May 8, 1862

Cross Keys June 8, 1862

Harpers Ferry

Frederick

MARYLAND

Baltimore

Potomac R.

Washington, D.C.

The only major battle of 1861–Bull Run–took place about 30 miles southwest of the Union's capital. It left both armies in disarray.

Bull Run July 21, 1861 Aug. 29–30, 1862

Cedar Mt. Aug. 9, 1862

Fredericksburg Dec. 13, 1862

At Fredericksburg (13) in December 1862, Confederate forces repulsed another Union thrust into the heart of Virginia.

The Peninsular Campaign (2 and 3; 6 and 8) began in May 1862 as an attempt by the Union armies to take Richmond by moving up the peninsula between the James and York Rivers.

Assisted by Jackson's attacks, Lee repulsed the Union assault on Richmond and then advanced toward Washington. After another Confederate victory in the second battle of Bull Run (10) in August 1862, Lee's army moved into Maryland.

VIRGINIA

Richmond

Fair Oaks May 31–June 1, 1862

Seven Days June 25–July 1, 1862

Williamsburg May 5, 1862

Siege of Yorktown Apr. 5–May 4, 1862

Ft. Monroe

Rappahannock R.

Chesapeake Bay

York R.

James R.

Shenandoah R.

BLUE RIDGE MTS.

N W E S

0   20   40 miles
0   20   40 kilometers

Union Movements	Confederate Movements
McDowell	Johnston
McClellan	Holmes
Frémont	Jackson
Banks	Lee
Shields	Confederate victory
Pope	Railroad
Burnside	Sequence of battles
Union victory	

To help you to follow the sequence of the major battles of the eastern campaigns of 1862, each battle is dated and its place in the chronology denoted by a number in a circle.

MAP 14.2

The Eastern Campaigns of 1862

Many of the great battles of the Civil War took place in the 125 miles separating the Union capital, Washington, D.C., and the Confederate capital, Richmond, Virginia. During 1862, Confederate generals Thomas Jonathan "Stonewall" Jackson and Robert E. Lee won battles that defended the Confederate capital (3, 6, 8, and 13) and launched offensive strikes against Union forces guarding Washington (1, 4, 5, 7, 9, and 10). They also suffered a defeat—at Antietam (12), in Maryland—that was almost fatal. As was often the case in the Civil War, the victors in these battles were either too bloodied or too timid to exploit their advantage.

The Battle of Pea Ridge, Arkansas, March 1862

Pea Ridge was the biggest battle of the Civil War fought west of the Mississippi and was of considerable strategic significance. By routing one Confederate army and holding another to a draw, outnumbered Union forces maintained their control of Missouri — just to the north of the battleground — for the duration of the war. The painting shows the main Confederate advance to the Elkhorn Tavern, a position its troops were not able to hold on the second day of the battle. Each side had about 1,000 men killed or wounded, with another 200 taken prisoner. Museum of the Confederacy, Richmond, Virginia.

A sunken road — nicknamed Bloody Lane — was filled with Confederate bodies two and three deep, and the advancing Union troops knelt on this "ghastly flooring" to shoot at the retreating Confederates. The battle at Antietam on September 17, 1862, remains the bloodiest single day in U.S. military history. Together, the Confederate and Union dead numbered 4,800 and the wounded 18,500, of whom 3,000 soon died. (By comparison, there were 6,000 American casualties on D-Day, which began the invasion of Nazi-occupied France in World War II.)

In public, Lincoln claimed Antietam as a Union victory; privately, he criticized McClellan for not fighting Lee to the bitter end. A masterful organizer of men and supplies, McClellan refused to risk his troops, fearing that heavy casualties would undermine public support for the war. Lincoln was more worried by the prospect of a lengthy war. He dismissed McClellan and began a long search for a more aggressive commanding general. His first choice, Ambrose E. Burnside, proved to be more daring but less competent than McClellan. In December, after heavy losses in futile attacks against well-entrenched Confederate forces at Fredericksburg, Virginia, Burnside resigned his command, and Lincoln replaced him with Joseph "Fighting Joe" Hooker. As 1862 ended, Confederates were optimistic: They had won a stalemate in the East.

The War in the Mississippi Valley During the same months of 1862, Union commanders in the Midwest had been more successful (Map 14.3). Their goal was to control the Ohio, Mississippi, and Missouri rivers, dividing the Confederacy and reducing the mobility of its armies. Because Kentucky did not join the rebellion, the Union already dominated the Ohio River Valley. In February 1862, the

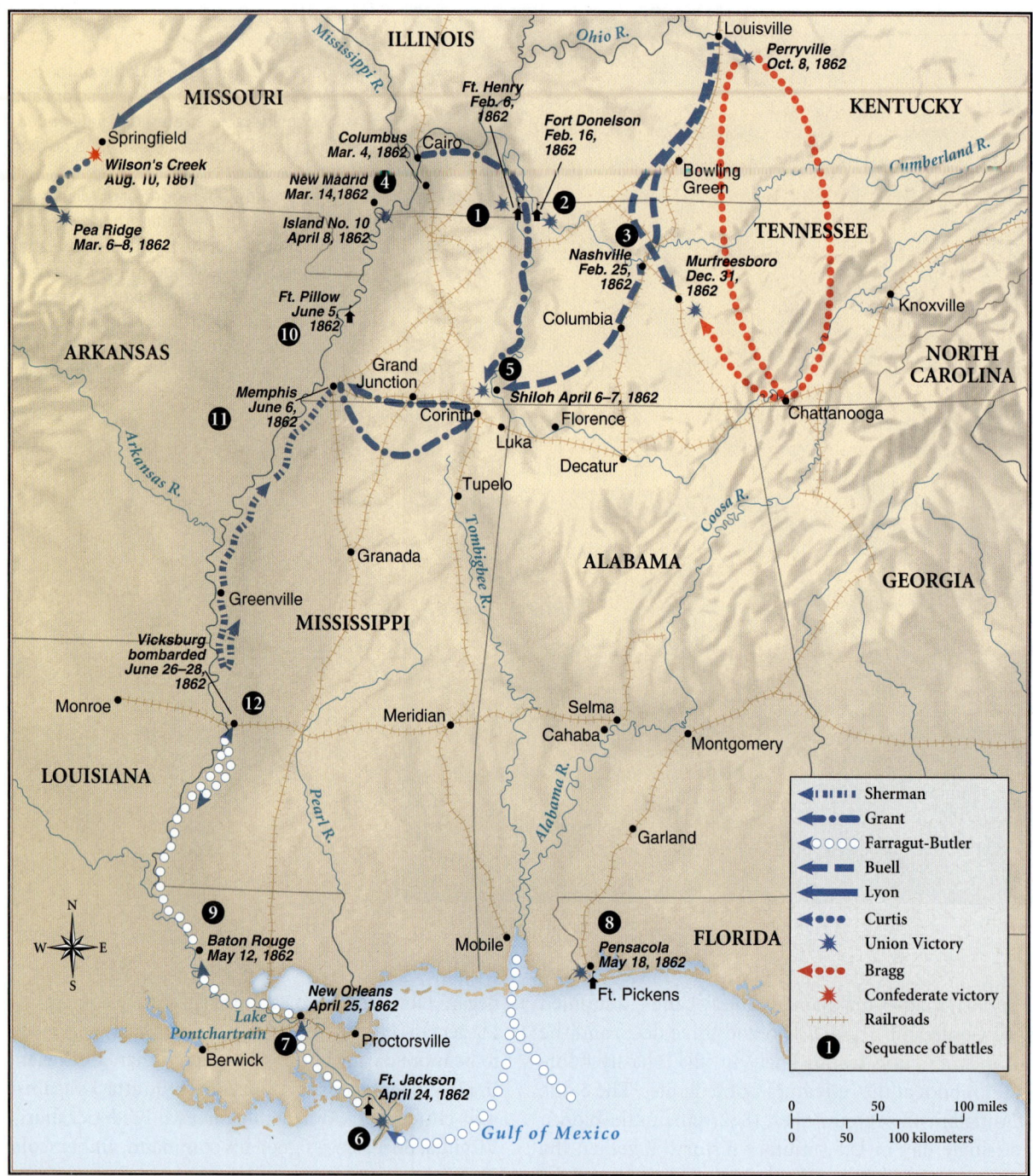

MAP 14.3

The Western Campaigns, 1861–1862

As the Civil War intensified in 1862, Union and Confederate military and naval forces sought control of the great valleys of the Ohio, Tennessee, and Mississippi rivers. From February through April 1862, Union armies moved south through western Tennessee (1–3 and 5). By the end of June, Union naval forces controlled the Mississippi River north of Memphis (4, 10, and 11) and from the Gulf of Mexico to Vicksburg (6, 7, 9, and 12). These military and naval victories gave the Union control of crucial transportation routes, kept Missouri in the Union, and carried the war to the borders of the states of the Lower South.

Union army used an innovative tactic to take charge of the Tennessee and Mississippi rivers as well. General Ulysses S. Grant used riverboats clad with iron plates to capture Fort Henry on the Tennessee River and Fort Donelson on the Cumberland River. When Grant moved south to seize critical railroad lines, Confederate troops led by Albert Sidney Johnston and P. G. T. Beauregard caught his army by surprise near a small log church named Shiloh. But Grant relentlessly committed troops until he forced a Confederate withdrawal. As the fighting at Shiloh ended on April 7, Grant surveyed a large field "so covered with dead that it would have been possible to walk over the clearing in any direction, stepping on dead bodies, without a foot touching the ground." The cost in lives was horrific, but Lincoln was resolute: "What I want . . . is generals who will fight battles and win victories."

Three weeks later, Union naval forces commanded by David G. Farragut struck the Confederacy from the Gulf of Mexico. They captured New Orleans and took control of fifteen hundred plantations and 50,000 slaves in the surrounding region. The Union now held the South's financial center and largest city and had struck a strong blow against slavery. Workers on many plantations looted their owners' mansions and refused to labor unless they were paid wages. "[Slavery there] is forever destroyed and worthless," declared one Northern reporter. Union victories had significantly undermined Confederate strength in the Mississippi River Valley.

- Why was there no new compromise over slavery in 1861? How important was the conflict at Fort Sumter? Would the Confederacy — and the Union — have decided to go to war in any event?

- In the first years of the war, what were the political and military strategies of each side? Which side was the more successful? Why?

Toward Total War

The military carnage in 1862 revealed that the war would be long and costly. Grant later remarked that, after Shiloh, he "gave up all idea of saving the Union except by complete conquest." Increasingly, the Civil War resembled the **total wars** that would come in the twentieth century. In such wars, governments mobilized the entire resources of their societies and decreed that the lives and property of enemy civilians were legitimate objects of attack. Aided by the Republican Party and a talented cabinet, Lincoln gradually organized an effective

central government able to wage all-out war. Jefferson Davis had less success at harnessing southern resources, because the eleven states of the Confederacy remained suspicious of centralized rule and southern yeomen grew increasingly skeptical of the war effort.

Mobilizing Armies and Civilians

Initially, patriotic fervor filled both armies with eager young volunteers. One Union recruit recalled that all he heard was "War! War! War!" Even those of sober minds joined up. "I don't think a young man ever went over all the considerations more carefully than I did," reflected William Saxton of Cincinnatus, New York. "It might mean sickness, wounds, loss of limb, and even life itself. . . . But my country was in danger." The southern call for volunteers was even more successful, thanks to its strong military tradition, supply of trained officers, and a culture that stressed duty and honor. "Would you, My Darling, . . . be willing to leave your Children under such a [despotic Union] government?" James B. Griffin of Edgefield, South Carolina, asked his wife. "No — I know you would sacrifice every comfort on earth, rather than submit to it." Enlistments declined, however, as potential recruits learned the realities of mass warfare: epidemic diseases in the camps and wholesale death on the battlefields. Both governments soon faced the need for conscription.

The Military Draft The Confederacy acted first. In April 1862, following the bloodshed at Shiloh, the Confederate Congress imposed the first legally binding draft in American history. New laws required existing soldiers to serve for the duration of the war and demanded three years of military service from all men between the ages of eighteen and thirty-five. In September 1862, after the heavy casualties at Antietam, the age limit jumped to forty-five. The South's draft had two loopholes, both controversial. First, it exempted one white man — the planter, a son, or an overseer — for each twenty slaves, allowing some whites on large plantations to avoid military service. This provision, a legislator from Mississippi warned Jefferson Davis, "has aroused a spirit of rebellion in some places." Second, draftees could hire substitutes. By the time this loophole was closed in 1864, the price of a substitute had risen to $300 in gold, three times the annual wage of a skilled worker. Laborers and yeomen farmers angrily complained that it was "a rich man's war and a poor man's fight."

Consequently, some southerners refused to serve. Because the Confederate constitution vested sovereignty

Kansas Volunteers, 1862

When they posed for this tintype photograph in 1862, these men from Company E, 8th Kansas Volunteer Infantry, had marched hundreds of miles through Kentucky and Tennessee in a largely fruitless pursuit of the Confederate Army and wore the look of battle-hardened troops. Some of these volunteers appear to be in their thirties or forties, and perhaps were abolitionist veterans of the civil strife in Bloody Kansas during the 1850s.   Kansas State Historical Society.

in the individual states, the government in Richmond could not compel military service. Independent-minded governors such as Joseph Brown of Georgia and Zebulon Vance of North Carolina simply ignored President Davis's first draft call in early 1862. Elsewhere, state judges issued writs of **habeas corpus**—legal instruments used to protect people from arbitrary arrest—and ordered the Confederate army to release reluctant draftees. However, the Confederate Congress overrode the judges' authority to free conscripted men, so the government was able to keep substantial armies in the field well into 1864.

The Union government acted more ruthlessly toward Confederate sympathizers and those who opposed the draft. In Missouri and other border states, Union commanders levied special taxes on southern supporters. Lincoln went further, suspending habeas corpus and, over the course of the war, temporarily imprisoning about 15,000 people without trial. The president placed civilians who discouraged enlistments or resisted the draft under the jurisdiction of military courts, preventing acquittals by sympathetic local juries. But Union governments primarily used incentives

to lure recruits. When the Militia Act of 1862 set local quotas, states, counties, and towns avoided conscription by using cash bounties of as much as $600 (about $11,000 today) and signed up nearly 1 million men. The Union also allowed men to avoid military service by providing a substitute or paying a $300 fee.

When the Enrollment Act of 1863 finally initiated conscription in the North, recent German and Irish immigrants often refused to serve. It was not their war, they said. Northern Democrats used the furor over conscription to bolster support for their party, which increasingly criticized Lincoln's policies. They accused Lincoln of drafting poor whites to liberate blacks, who would then flood the cities and take their jobs. Slavery was nearly "dead," declared a Democratic newspaper in Cincinnati, "[but] the negro is not, there is the misfortune." In July 1863, the immigrants' hostility to conscription and blacks led to riots in New York City. For five days, Irish and German workers ran rampant, burning draft offices, sacking the homes of influential Republicans, and attacking the police. The rioters lynched and mutilated a dozen African Americans, drove hundreds of black families from their homes, and burned

The Business of Recruiting an Army

Following the New York City draft riots in July 1863, Union governments used monetary bonuses to induce men to join the army. This painting by George Law shows a recruiting post in 1864. To meet New York's draft quota of 30,000 men, the county and state governments offered volunteers bounties of $300 and $75 – on top of a U.S. government bounty of $302. The total – some $677 – was serious money at a time when the average worker earned $1.70 for a ten-hour day.   Anne S. K. Brown Military Collection, Brown University Library.

down the Colored Orphan Asylum. Lincoln rushed in Union troops who had just fought at Gettysburg; they killed more than a hundred rioters and suppressed the immigrant mobs.

The Union government won greater support among native-born middle-class citizens. In 1861, prominent New Yorkers established the U.S. Sanitary Commission to provide medical services and prevent the spread of epidemic diseases among the troops. Through its network of seven thousand local auxiliaries, the commission collected clothing and food. "I almost weep," reported a local agent, "when these plain rural people come to send their simple offerings to absent sons and brothers." The commission also recruited battlefield nurses and doctors for the Union Army Medical Bureau. Despite these efforts, dysentery, typhoid, and malaria spread through the camps, as did mumps and measles, viruses that were often deadly to rural recruits. Diseases and

infections killed about 250,000 Union soldiers, nearly twice the 135,000 who died in combat. Still, thanks to the Sanitary Commission, Union troops had a far lower mortality rate than soldiers fighting in nineteenth-century European wars. Confederate troops were less fortunate. Thousands of women volunteered as nurses, but the Confederate army's health system was poorly organized. Scurvy was a special problem for southern soldiers, who lacked vitamin C in their diets, and they died from camp diseases at a high rate.

So much death created new industries and cultural rituals. Embalmers devised a zinc chloride fluid to preserve soldiers' bodies, allowing them to be shipped home for burial; this innovation marked the beginning of modern funeral practices. Military cemeteries with hundreds of crosses in neat rows replaced the landscaped "rural cemeteries" in vogue in American cities before the Civil War. And thousands of mothers, wives, and sisters mourned the deaths of fallen soldiers. Facing utter deprivation, working-class women grieved for the loss of a breadwinner; meanwhile, middle-class wives, bound by the affectionate tenets of domesticity, lamented the death of their partner in life. Clothing stores set aside space for black crape "mourning" dresses and other personal accessories of death. The destructive war, in concert with the emerging consumer culture and ethic of domesticity, had produced a new "cult of mourning" among the middle and upper classes.

Women in Wartime | As tens of thousands of wounded husbands and sons limped home from the war, their wives and sisters helped them rebuild their lives. Another 200,000 women worked as volunteers in the Sanitary Commission and the Freedman's Aid Society, which collected supplies for liberated slaves.

The war drew more women into the wage-earning work force as nurses, clerks, and factory operatives. Dorothea Dix (see Chapter 11) served as superintendent of female nurses and, by successfully combating the prejudice against women providing medical treatment to men, opened a new occupation to women. Thousands of educated Union women became government clerks, while southern women staffed the efficient Confederate postal service. In both societies, millions of women took over farm tasks; filled jobs in schools and offices; and worked in textile, shoe, and food-processing factories. A few even became spies, scouts, and (disguising themselves as men) soldiers. As Union nurse Clara Barton, who later founded the American Red Cross, recalled, "At the war's end, woman was at least fifty years in advance of the normal position which continued peace would have assigned her."

Mobilizing Resources

Wars are usually won by the side that possesses greater resources. In that regard, the Union had a distinct advantage. With nearly two-thirds of the nation's popu-

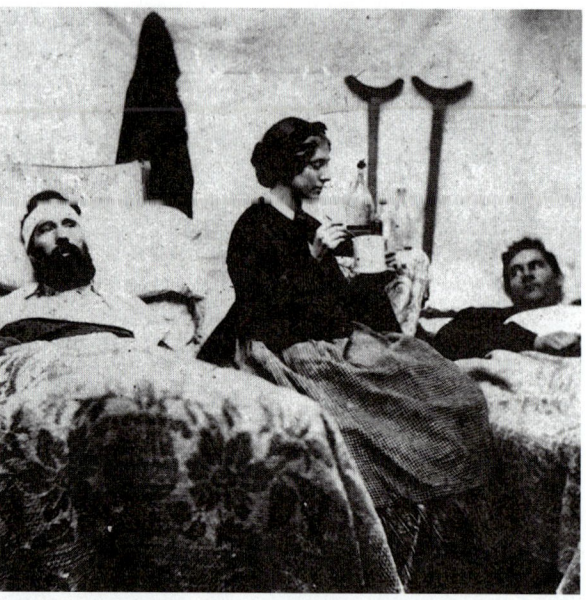

Hospital Nursing

Working as nurses in battlefront hospitals, thousands of Union and Confederate women gained firsthand experience of the horrors of war. A sense of calm prevails in this behind-the-lines Union hospital in Nashville, Tennessee, as nurse Anne Belle tends to the needs of soldiers recovering from their wounds. Most Civil War nurses were volunteers; they spent time cooking and cleaning for their patients as well as tending their injuries.   U.S. Army Military History Institute.

lation, two-thirds of the railroad mileage, and accounting for almost 90 percent of the industrial output, the North's economy was far superior to that of the South (Figure 14.2). The North had a further great advantage in the manufacture of cannon and rifles because many of its arms factories were equipped for mass production.

But the Confederate position was far from weak. Virginia, North Carolina, and Tennessee had substantial industrial capacity. Richmond, with its Tredegar Iron Works, was an important manufacturing center, and in 1861 its armory acquired the gun-making machinery from the U.S. armory at Harpers Ferry. The produc-

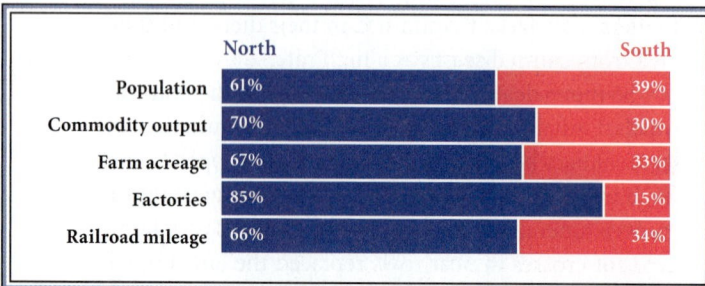

	North	South
Population	61%	39%
Commodity output	70%	30%
Farm acreage	67%	33%
Factories	85%	15%
Railroad mileage	66%	34%

FIGURE 14.2

Economies, North and South, 1860

The military advantages of the North were even greater than this chart suggests. The population figures for the South include slaves, whom the Confederacy feared to arm. Also, the South's commodity output was primarily in farm goods rather than manufactures. Finally, southern factories were much smaller on average than those in the North.   Sources: Stanley Engerman, "The Economic Impact of the Civil War," in *The Reinterpretation of American Economic History*, ed. Robert W. Fogel and Stanley L. Engerman (New York: Harper & Row, 1971); and U. S. census data.

Richmond: Capital City and Industrial Center

The Confederacy chose Richmond as its capital because of the historic importance of Virginia as the home of Washington, Jefferson, Madison, and Monroe. However, Richmond was also a major industrial center. Exploiting the city's location at the falls of the James River, the city's entrepreneurs had developed a wide range of industries: flour mills, tobacco factories, railroad and port facilities, and, most important, a substantial iron industry. In 1861, the Tredegar Iron Works employed nearly a thousand workers and, as the only facility in the South that could manufacture large machinery and heavy weapons, made a major contribution to the Confederate war effort.   The Library of Virginia.

tion at the Richmond armory, the purchase of Enfield rifles from Britain, and the capture of 100,000 Union guns enabled the Confederacy to provide every infantryman with a modern rifle-musket by 1863.

Moreover, with 9 million people, the Confederacy could mobilize enormous armies. Enslaved blacks, one-third of the population, assisted the war effort by producing food for the army and cotton for export. Confederate leaders counted on **King Cotton** to purchase clothes, boots, blankets, and weapons from abroad. They also saw it as a diplomatic weapon that would persuade Britain and France, whose textile factories needed raw cotton, to assist the Confederacy. British manufacturers had stockpiled cotton, however, and exploited new sources in Egypt and India. Still, the South's hope was partially fulfilled. Although Britain never recognized the Confederacy as an independent nation, it treated the rebel government as a belligerent power — with the right under international law to borrow money and purchase weapons. The odds, then, did not necessarily favor the Union, despite its superior resources.

Republican Economic and Fiscal Policies   To mobilize northern resources, the Republican-dominated Congress enacted a neomercantilist program of government-assisted economic development that far surpassed Henry Clay's American System. The Republicans imposed high tariffs (averaging nearly 40 percent) on various foreign goods, thereby encouraging domestic industries. To boost agricultural output, they offered "free land" to farmers. The Homestead Act of 1862 gave settlers the title to 160 acres of public land after five years of residence. To create an integrated national banking system (far more powerful than the First and Second Banks of the United States), Secretary of the Treasury Salmon P. Chase forced thousands of local banks to accept federal charters and regulations.

Finally, the Republican Congress implemented Clay's program for a nationally financed transportation system. Expansion to the Pacific, the California gold rush, and subsequent discoveries of gold, silver, copper, and other metals in Nevada, Montana, and other western lands had revived demands for such a network. So, in 1862, Congress chartered the Union Pacific and Central Pacific companies to build a transcontinental railroad line and granted them lavish subsidies. This comprehensive economic program won the Republican Party the allegiance of farmers, workers, and entrepreneurs and bolstered the Union's ability to fight a long war.

New industries sprang up to provide the Union army—and its 1.5 million men—with guns, clothes, and food. Over the course of the war, soldiers consumed more than half a billion pounds of pork and other packed meats. To meet this demand, Chicago railroads built new lines to carry thousands of hogs and cattle to the city's ever-larger stockyards and slaughterhouses. By 1862, Chicago had passed Cincinnati as the meatpacking capital of the nation, bringing prosperity to thousands of midwestern farmers and great wealth to Philip D. Armour and other meatpacking entrepreneurs.

Bankers and financiers likewise found themselves pulled into the war effort. The annual spending of the Union government shot up from $63 million in 1860 to more than $865 million in 1864 (Figure 14.3). To raise that enormous sum, the Republicans created a modern system of public finance that secured funds in three ways. First, the government increased tariffs; placed high duties on alcohol and tobacco; and imposed direct taxes on business corporations, large inheritances, and the incomes of wealthy citizens. These levies paid about 20 percent of the cost. Interest-paying bonds issued by the U.S. Treasury financed another 65 percent. The National Banking Acts of 1863 and 1864 forced most banks to buy those bonds; and Jay Cooke, a Philadelphia banker working for the Treasury Department, used newspaper ads and 2,500 subagents to persuade nearly a million northern families to buy them.

The Union paid the remaining 15 percent by printing paper money. The Legal Tender Act of 1862 authorized $150 million in paper currency—soon known as **greenbacks**—and required the public to accept them as legal tender. Like the Continental currency of the Revolutionary era, greenbacks could not be exchanged for specie; however, because they were issued in relatively limited amounts, they only lost a small part of their face value.

If a modern fiscal system was one result of the war, immense concentrations of capital in many industries was another. The task of supplying the huge war machine, an observer noted, gave a few men "the command of millions of money." Such massed financial power threatened not only the prewar society of small producers but also the future of democratic self-government. Americans "are never again to see the republic in which we were born," lamented abolitionist and social reformer Wendell Phillips.

The South Resorts to Coercion and Inflation

The economic demands on the South were equally great but, true to its states' rights philosophy, the Confederacy initially left most matters to the state governments. However, as the realities of total war became clear, Jefferson Davis's administration took extraordinary measures: It built and

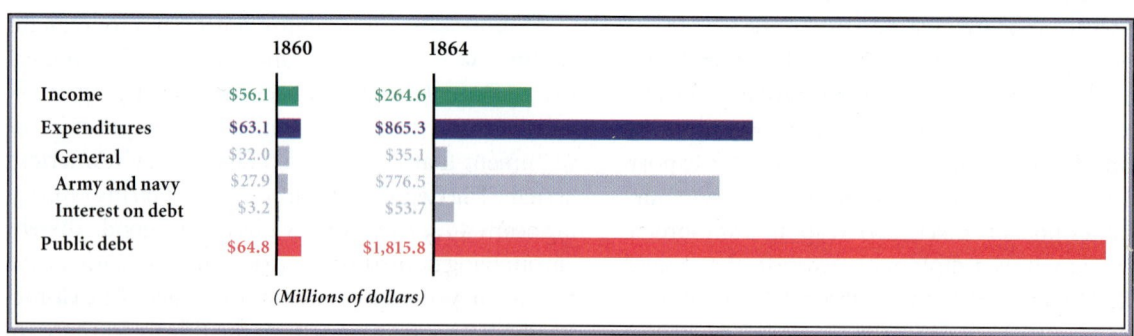

FIGURE 14.3

The High Cost of War: Union Finances, 1860 and 1864

In 1864, the Union government received almost 5 times as much in tax revenues as it had in 1860, but it spent nearly 14 times as much, mostly to pay soldiers and buy military supplies. In four years, the public debt had risen by a factor of 28, so that in 1864 the interest payment on the debt alone nearly equaled the level of *all* federal government spending in 1860.

A Southern Refugee Family

As Union and Confederate armies swept back and forth across northern Virginia and other war zones, the civilian population feared for its property and personal security. Here, two southern women – their husbands presumably away at war – have hitched up their mules and piled their goods and children on a farm wagon in order to flee the fighting. Lucky refugees had relatives in safe areas; others had to rely on the goodwill of strangers.   National Archives.

operated shipyards, armories, foundries, and textile mills; commandeered food and scarce raw materials such as coal, iron, copper, and lead; requisitioned slaves to work on fortifications; and directly controlled foreign trade.

The Confederate Congress and ordinary southern citizens opposed many of Davis's initiatives, particularly those involving taxes. The Congress refused to tax cotton exports and slaves, the most valuable property held by wealthy planters, and the urban middle classes and yeomen farm families refused to pay more than their fair share. Consequently, the Confederacy covered less than 10 percent of its expenditures through taxation. The government paid another 30 percent by borrowing, but wealthy planters and foreign bankers grew increasingly wary of investing in Confederate bonds that might never be redeemed.

So the Confederacy had to pay 60 percent of the war costs by printing paper money. The flood of currency created a spectacular inflation: By 1865, prices had risen to ninety-two times their 1861 level. As food prices soared, riots erupted in more than a dozen southern cities and towns. In Richmond, several hundred women broke into bakeries, crying, "Our children are starving while the rich roll in wealth." In Randolph County, Alabama, women confiscated grain from a government warehouse "to prevent starvation of themselves and their families." As inflation continued, southerners refused to accept paper money, whatever the consequences. When South Carolina storekeeper Jim Harris rejected the currency presented by Confederate soldiers, they raided his storehouse and, he claimed, "robbed it of about five thousand dollars worth of goods." Army supply officers likewise seized goods from merchants and offered payment in worthless IOUs. Facing a public that feared strong government and high taxation, the Confederacy could sustain the war effort only by seizing its citizens' property and by championing white supremacy: President Davis warned that a

Union victory would destroy slavery "and reduce the whites to the degraded position of the African race."

- **How did the governments — the Union or the Confederacy — go about mobilizing soldiers, citizens, and resources to wage a total war? How successful were their respective strategies?**

- **What were the main economic policies enacted by the Republican-controlled Congress?**

The Turning Point: 1863

By 1863, the Lincoln administration had finally created an efficient war machine and a set of strategic priorities. Henry Adams, the grandson of John Quincy Adams and a future novelist and historian, noted the change from his diplomatic post in London: "Little by little, one began to feel that, behind the chaos in Washington power was taking shape; that it was massed and guided as it had not been before." Slowly but surely, the tide of the struggle had turned against the Confederacy.

Emancipation

When the war began, antislavery Republicans demanded that abolition — as well as restoration of the Union — be a goal of the war. The fighting should continue, said a Massachusetts abolitionist, "until the Slave power is completely subjugated, and *emancipation made certain*." Because slave-grown crops sustained the Confederacy, activists justified black emancipation on military grounds. As Frederick Douglass put it, "Arrest that hoe in the hands of the Negro, and you smite the rebellion in the very seat of its life."

"Contrabands" As abolitionists pressed their case, African Americans exploited wartime chaos to seize freedom for themselves. When three slaves reached the camp of Union general Benjamin Butler in Virginia in May 1861, he labeled them "contraband of war" (a term for enemy property that can be legitimately seized, according to international law) and refused to return them. Butler's term stuck, and soon thousands of "contrabands" were camping with Union armies. Near Fredericksburg, Virginia, an average of 200 blacks appeared every day, "with their packs on their backs and handkerchiefs tied over their heads — men, women, little children, and babies." To provide legal status to these fugitives, Congress passed the Confiscation Act in August 1861; it authorized the seizure of property, including slave property, used to support the rebellion.

Radical Republicans — Treasury Secretary Salmon Chase, Senator Charles Sumner of Massachusetts, and Representative Thaddeus Stevens of Pennsylvania — now began to use wartime legislation to destroy slavery. A longtime member of Congress, Stevens was a masterful politician, skilled at fashioning legislation that could win majority support. In April 1862, Stevens and the Radicals persuaded Congress to end slavery in the District of Columbia by providing compensation for owners; in June, Congress outlawed slavery in the federal territories (finally enacting the Wilmot Proviso of 1846); and in July, it passed a second Confiscation Act. This act overrode the property rights of Confederate planters by declaring "forever free" the thousands of fugitive slaves and all slaves captured by the Union army. Emancipation had become an instrument of war.

The Emancipation Proclamation Initially, Lincoln had rejected emancipation as a war aim, but faced with thousands of contrabands and Radical Republican pressure, he moved cautiously toward that goal. The president drafted a general proclamation of emancipation in July 1862, and he publicly linked black freedom with the preservation of the Union in August. "If I could save the Union without freeing any slave, I would do it," Lincoln told Horace Greeley of the *New York Tribune*, "and if I could save it by freeing all the slaves, I would do it."

Now he waited for a Union victory. Considering the Battle of Antietam "an indication of the Divine Will," Lincoln issued a preliminary proclamation of emancipation five days later, on September 22, 1862, and based its legal authority on his duty as commander in chief to suppress the rebellion. The proclamation stated that slavery would be legally abolished in all states that remained out of the Union on January 1, 1863. The rebel states could preserve slavery by renouncing secession. None chose to do so.

The proclamation was politically astute. Lincoln conciliated slave owners in the Union-controlled border states, such as Maryland and Missouri, by leaving slavery intact in those states. It also permitted slavery to continue in areas occupied by Union armies: western and central Tennessee, western Virginia, and southern Louisiana. In Indian Territory, also under Union control, most mixed-blood Cherokee slave owners remained committed to the Confederacy. They did not formally free their 4,000 slaves until July 1866, when a new treaty with the U.S. government specified that their ex-slaves "shall have all the rights of native Cherokee."

Consequently, the Emancipation Proclamation did not immediately free a single slave. Yet, as abolitionist Wendell Phillips understood, Lincoln's proclamation had moved slavery to "the edge of Niagara," and it would soon be swept over the brink. Advancing Union troops became the agents of slavery's destruction. "I became free in 1863, in the summer, when the yankees come by and said I could go work for myself," recalled Jackson Daniel of Maysville, Alabama. As Lincoln now saw it, "the old South is to be destroyed and replaced by new propositions and ideas"—a system of free labor.

Emancipation was extraordinarily controversial. In the Confederacy, Jefferson Davis labeled it the "most execrable measure recorded in the history of guilty man"; in the North, it unleashed a racist backlash among white voters. During the elections of 1862, the Democrats denounced emancipation as unconstitutional, warned of slave uprisings, and predicted that freed blacks would take white jobs. Every freed slave, suggested a nativist-minded New Yorker, should "shoulder an Irishman and leave the Continent." Such sentiments propelled Democrat Horatio Seymour into the governor's office in New York; if abolition was a war goal, Seymour argued, the South should not be conquered. According to one observer, many Democrats viewed "every success of the rebels . . . [as] a party victory & hail it with triumph." Their party swept to victory in Pennsylvania, Ohio, and Illinois, and gained thirty-four seats in Congress. But Republicans still held a twenty-five-seat majority in the House and gained five seats in the Senate. Lincoln refused to retreat. Calling emancipation an "act of justice," he signed the final proclamation on New Year's Day 1863. "If my name ever goes into history," he said, "it was for this act."

Vicksburg and Gettysburg

The Emancipation Proclamation's fate would depend on Republican political success and Union military victories. The outlook was not encouraging on either front. Democrats had made significant gains in 1862, and popular support was growing for a negotiated peace. Two brilliant victories in Virginia by General Robert E. Lee, whose army defeated Union forces at Fredericksburg (December 1862) and Chancellorsville (May 1863), further eroded northern support for the war.

The Battle for the Mississippi | At this critical juncture, General Grant mounted a major offensive to split the Confederacy in two. Grant drove south along the west bank of the Mississippi in Arkansas and then crossed the river near Vicksburg, Mississippi. There, he defeated two Confederate armies and laid siege to the city. After repelling Union assaults for six weeks, the exhausted and starving Vicksburg garrison surrendered on July 4, 1863. Five days later, Union forces took Port Hudson, Louisiana (near Baton Rouge), and seized control of the Mississippi River. Grant had taken 31,000 prisoners; cut off Louisiana, Arkansas, and Texas from the rest of the Confederacy; and prompted thousands of slaves to desert their plantations or demand wages.

As Grant had advanced toward Vicksburg in May, Confederate leaders had argued over the best strategic response. President Davis and other politicians wanted to send an army to Tennessee to relieve the Union pressure along the Mississippi River. But General Lee, buoyed by his recent victories, favored a new invasion of the North. That strategy, Lee suggested, would either draw Grant's forces to the east or give the Confederacy a major victory that would destroy the North's will to fight.

Lee's Advance and Defeat | Lee won out. In June 1863, he maneuvered his army north through Maryland into Pennsylvania. The Army of the Potomac moved along with him, positioning itself between Lee and Washington, D.C. On July 1, the two great armies met by accident at Gettysburg, Pennsylvania, in what became a decisive confrontation (Map 14.4). On the first day of battle, Lee drove the Union's advance guard to the south of town. But Union commander George G. Meade placed his troops in well-defended hilltop positions and called up reinforcements. By the morning of July 2, Meade had 90,000 troops to Lee's 75,000. Aware that he was outnumbered but intent on victory, Lee ordered assaults on Meade's flanks but failed to turn them.

On July 3, Lee decided on a dangerous frontal assault against the center of the Union line. After the heaviest artillery barrage of the war, Lee sent General George E. Pickett and his 14,000 men to take Cemetery Ridge. When Pickett's men charged across a mile of open terrain, they were met by deadly fire from artillery and massed riflemen; thousands were killed, wounded, or captured. As the three-day battle ended, the Confederates had suffered 28,000 casualties, one-third of the Army of Northern Virginia, while 23,000 of Meade's soldiers lay killed or wounded. Shocked by the bloodletting, Meade allowed the Confederate units to escape. Lincoln was furious. "As it is," the president brooded, "the war will be prolonged indefinitely."

Still, Gettysburg was a great Union victory and, together with the simultaneous triumph at Vicksburg, was the major turning point in the war. Southern armies

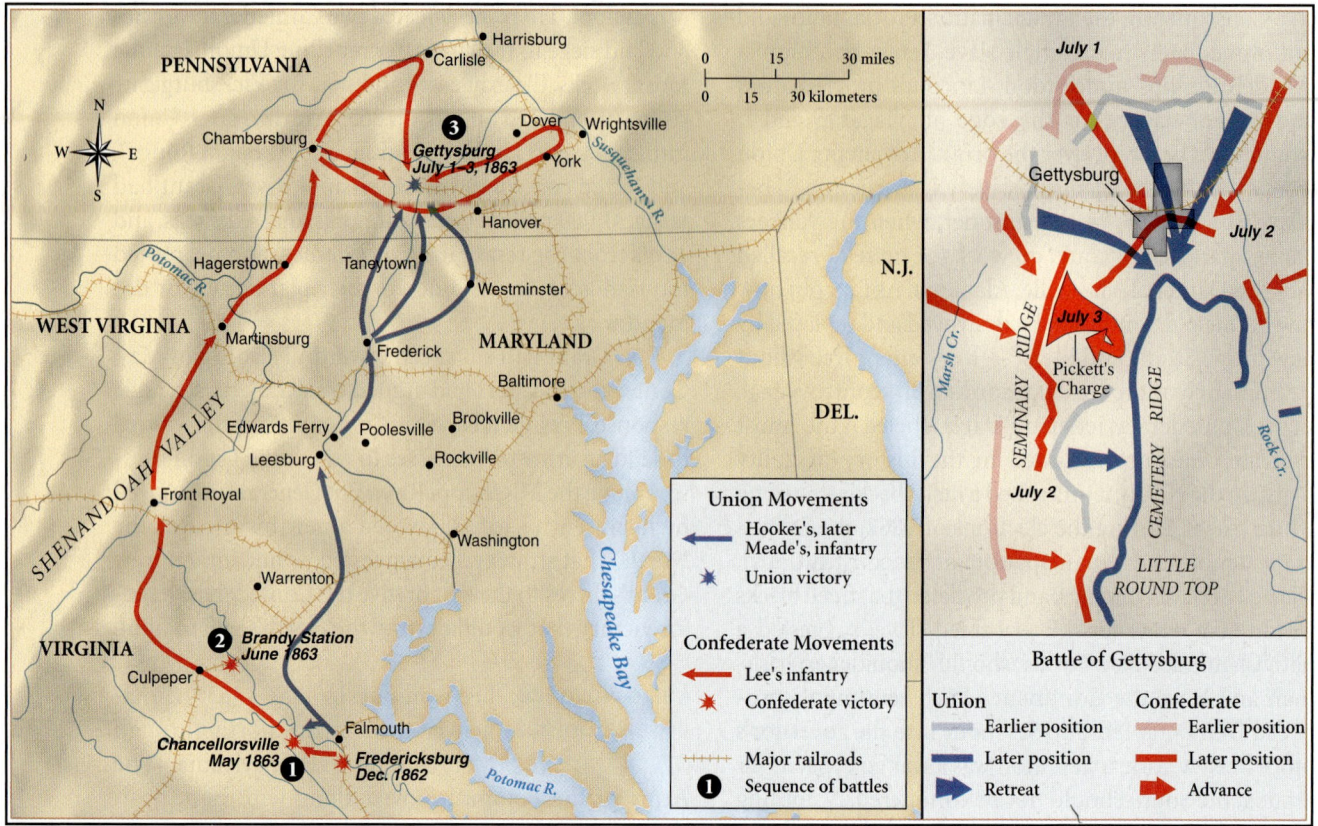

MAP 14.4

Lee Invades the North, 1863

After Lee's victories at Chancellorsville (1) in May and Brandy Station (2) in June, the Confederate forces moved northward, constantly shadowed by the Union army. On July 1, the two armies met accidentally near Gettysburg, Pennsylvania. In the ensuing battle (3), the Union army, commanded by General George Meade, emerged victorious, primarily because it was much larger than the Confederate force and held well-fortified positions along Cemetery Ridge, which gave its units a major tactical advantage.

would never again invade the North, and Southern citizens grew increasingly critical and worried. The Confederate elections of 1863 went sharply against the politicians who supported Jefferson Davis.

Vicksburg and Gettysburg transformed the political and diplomatic situation. In the fall of 1863, Republicans swept state elections in Pennsylvania, Ohio, and New York. In Europe, the victories boosted the leverage of American diplomats. Since 1862, the British-built ironclad cruiser the *Alabama* had sunk or captured more than a hundred Union merchant ships, and the Confederacy was about to accept delivery of two more cruisers. But with a Union victory increasingly likely, the British government decided to stop the flow of advanced weapons to the Confederacy and impound the

warships. British workers and reformers had long condemned slavery; now, because of poor grain harvests, Britain depended on imports of wheat and flour from the American Midwest. King Cotton diplomacy had failed; King Wheat stood triumphant. "Rest not your hopes in foreign nations," President Jefferson Davis advised his people. "This war is ours; we must fight it ourselves."

- Some historians argue that emancipation happened because thousands of slaves "freed themselves" by fleeing to Union armies. How persuasive is their argument?

- Why were the battles at Gettysburg and Vicksburg significant? How did they change the tide of war strategically, diplomatically, and psychologically?

Black Soldiers in the Union Army

Determined to end racial slavery, tens of thousands of African Americans volunteered for service in the Union army in 1864 and 1865, boosting the northern war effort at a critical moment. These proud soldiers were members of the 107th Colored Infantry, stationed at Fort Corcoran near Washington, D.C. In January 1865, their regiment saw action in the daring capture of Fort Fisher, which protected Wilmington, North Carolina, the last Confederate port open to blockade runners.   Library of Congress.

The Union Victorious, 1864–1865

The Union victories of 1863 meant that the South could not win independence through a decisive military triumph. However, the Confederacy could still hope for a battlefield stalemate and a negotiated peace. To keep the Union in Republican hands, Lincoln faced the daunting task of conquering the South.

Soldiers and Strategy

Two developments allowed the Union to prosecute the war vigorously: the promotion of aggressive generals and the enlistment of African American soldiers. As early as 1861, free African Americans and fugitive slaves had volunteered for the Union army, both to fight against slavery and, as Frederick Douglass put it, to win "the right to citizenship." But military service for blacks offended many northern whites. "I am as much

opposed to slavery as any of them," a New York soldier wrote to his local newspaper, "but I am not willing to be put on a level with the negro and fight with them." Although Union generals opposed the enlistment of African Americans, doubting that former slaves would make good soldiers, free and contraband blacks formed volunteer regiments in New England, South Carolina, Louisiana, and Kansas.

The Impact of Black Troops   The Emancipation Proclamation changed military policy and popular sentiment. The proclamation invited former slaves to serve in the Union army, and northern whites, having suffered thousands of casualties, now accepted that blacks should share in the fighting and dying. The valor of the first African American regiments to go into combat also influenced northern opinion. In 1863, a heroic and costly attack on Fort Wagner, South Carolina, by the Fifty-fourth Massachusetts Infantry convinced Union officers of the value of black soldiers. The Lincoln administration now recruited as many

Grant Planning a Strategic Maneuver

On May 21, 1864, the day this photograph was taken, Grant pulled his forces from the Spotsylvania Court House, where a bitter two-week battle (May 8–21) resulted in 18,000 Union and 10,000 Confederate casualties. He moved his army to the southeast, seeking to outflank Lee's forces. Photographer Timothy H. O'Sullivan caught up to the Union high command at Massaponax Church, Virginia, and captured this image of Grant (to the left) leaning over a pew and reading a map held by General George H. Meade. As Grant plots the army's movement, his officers smoke their pipes and read reports of the war in newspapers that had just arrived from New York City. Intercepting Grant's forces, Lee took up fortified positions first at the North Anna River and then at Cold Harbor, where the Confederates scored their last major victory of the war (May 31–June 3).   Library of Congress.

African Americans as it could. By the spring of 1865, nearly 200,000 African Americans were serving the Union. Without black soldiers, the president suggested, "we would be compelled to abandon the war in three weeks."

Military service did not end racial discrimination. Black soldiers were initially paid less than white soldiers

($10 a month versus $13) and won equal pay only by threatening to quit. Moreover, blacks served under white officers in segregated regiments and were used primarily to build fortifications, garrison forts, and guard supply lines. Nonetheless, African Americans continued to volunteer, knowing they were fighting for freedom and a new social order. "Hello, Massa," said one black soldier to his former master, who had been taken prisoner. "Bottom rail on top dis time." The worst fears of the secessionists had come true: Through the agency of the Union army, blacks had risen in a great rebellion against slavery.

Capable Generals Take Command As African Americans bolstered the army's ranks, Lincoln finally found an efficient and ruthless commanding general. In March 1864, Lincoln placed General Ulysses S. Grant in charge of all Union armies; from then on, the president determined overall strategy and Grant implemented it. Lincoln favored a simultaneous advance against the major Confederate armies, a strategy Grant had long favored, in order to achieve a decisive victory before the election of 1864.

Grant knew how to fight a war that relied on industrial technology and targeted an entire society. At Vicksburg, he had besieged the whole city and forced its surrender. Then, in November 1863, he had used railroads to charge to the rescue of an endangered Union army near Chattanooga, Tennessee. Grant believed that the efforts of earlier Union commanders "to conserve life" through cautious tactics had merely prolonged the war. He was willing to accept heavy casualties, a stance that earned him a reputation as a butcher of enemy armies and his own men.

In May 1864, Grant ordered two major offensives. Personally taking charge of the 115,000-man Army of the Potomac, he set out to destroy Lee's force of 75,000 troops in Virginia. And Grant instructed General William Tecumseh Sherman, who shared his harsh outlook, to invade Georgia and take Atlanta. "All that has gone before is mere skirmish," Sherman wrote as he prepared for battle. "The war now begins."

Grant advanced toward Richmond, hoping to force Lee to fight in open fields, where the Union's superior manpower and artillery would prevail. Remembering his tactical errors at Gettysburg, Lee remained in strong defensive positions and attacked only when he held an advantage. The Confederate general seized that opportunity twice, winning costly victories in early May 1864 at the bloody battles of the Wilderness and Spotsylvania Court House. At Spotsylvania, the troops fought at point-blank range; an Iowa recruit recalled "lines of blue and grey [soldiers firing] into each other's faces; for an hour and a half." Despite heavy losses in these battles and then at Cold Harbor, Grant drove on (Map 14.5). His attacks severely eroded Lee's forces, which suffered 31,000 casualties, but Union losses were even higher: 55,000 men.

Stalemate The fighting took a heavy psychological toll. "Many a man has gone crazy since this campaign began from the terrible pressure on mind and body," observed a Union captain. As morale declined, soldiers deserted. In June 1864, Grant laid siege to Petersburg, an important railroad center near

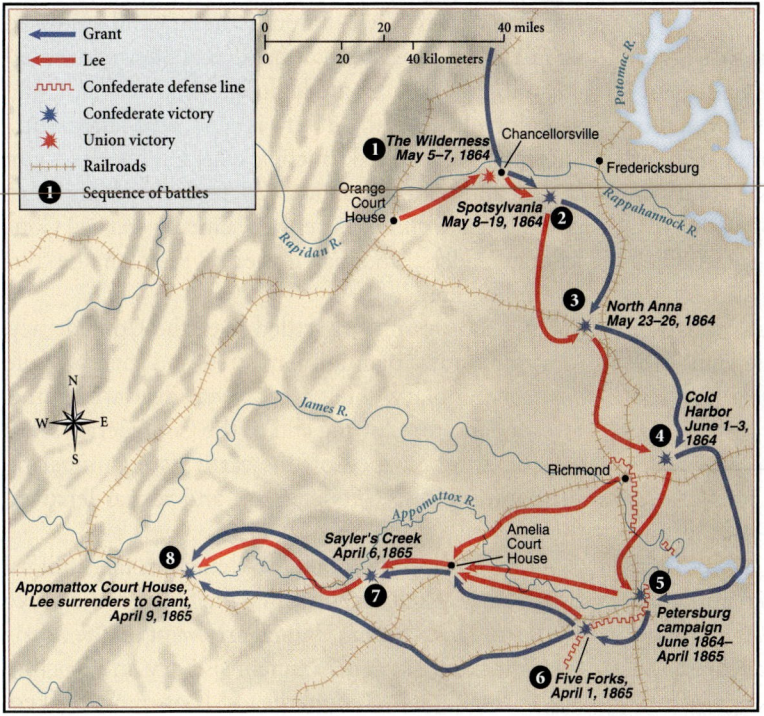

MAP 14.5

The Closing Virginia Campaign, 1864–1865

Beginning in May 1864, General Ulysses S. Grant launched an all-out campaign against Richmond. By threatening to cut General Robert E. Lee's lines of supply, Grant tried to lure him into open battle. Lee avoided a major test of strength. Instead, he retreated to defensive positions and inflicted heavy casualties on Union attackers at the Wilderness, Spotsylvania Court House, North Anna, and Cold Harbor (1–4). From June 1864 to April 1865, the two armies faced each other across defensive fortifications outside Richmond and Petersburg (5). Grant finally broke this ten-month siege by a flanking maneuver at Five Forks (6). Lee's surrender followed shortly.

Richmond. Protracted trench warfare—foreshadowing that in France in World War I—was devastating. Union and Confederate soldiers built complex networks of trenches, tunnels, and artillery emplacements stretching for 40 miles along the eastern edge of Richmond and Petersburg. Invoking the intense imagery of the Bible, an officer described the continuous artillery barrages and sniping as "living night and day within the 'valley of the shadow of death.'" The stress was especially great for the outnumbered Confederate troops, who spent months in the muddy, hellish trenches without rotation to the rear.

As time passed, Lincoln and Grant felt pressures of their own. The enormous casualties and military stalemate threatened Lincoln with defeat in the November election. The Republican outlook worsened in July, when Jubal Early's cavalry burned the Pennsylvania town of Chambersburg and threatened Washington, forcing Grant to divert troops from the Petersburg campaign. To punish farmers in the Shenandoah Valley who had aided the Confederate raiders, Grant ordered General Philip H. Sheridan to turn the region into "a barren waste." Sheridan's troops conducted a scorched-earth campaign, destroying grain, barns, and gristmills. These tactics, like Early's raid, violated the military norms of the day, which treated civilians as noncombatants. On both sides, rising desperation and anger were changing the definition of conventional warfare.

The Election of 1864 and Sherman's March

As the siege at Petersburg dragged on, Lincoln's hopes for reelection depended on General Sherman in Georgia. Sherman's army of 90,000 men had advanced methodically toward Atlanta, a railway hub at the heart of the Confederacy. Then, in June 1864, Sherman engaged General Joseph E. Johnson's army of 60,000 in a set battle at Kennesaw Mountain, only to suffer 3,000 casualties—five times the Confederates' losses. By late July, the Union army reached the northern outskirts of Atlanta, but the next month brought little gain. Like Grant, Sherman seemed bogged down in a hopeless campaign.

The National Union Party versus the Peace Democrats Meanwhile, the presidential campaign of 1864 was heating up. In June, the Republican Party's convention rebuffed attempts to prevent Lincoln's renomination. It endorsed the president's war strategy, demanded the Confederacy's unconditional surrender, and called for a consti-

tutional amendment to abolish slavery. The delegates likewise embraced Lincoln's political strategy. To attract border-state and Democratic voters, the Republicans took a new name, the National Union Party, and chose Andrew Johnson, a Tennessee slave owner and Unionist Democrat, as Lincoln's running mate.

The Democratic Party met in August and nominated General George B. McClellan for president. Lincoln had twice removed McClellan from military commands: first for an excess of caution and then for his opposition to emancipation. Like McClellan, the Democratic delegates rejected emancipation and condemned Lincoln's repression of domestic dissent. However, they split into two camps over the issue of continuing the war. War Democrats vowed to continue fighting until the Union was restored, while Peace Democrats called for a "cessation of hostilities" and a constitutional convention to negotiate a peace settlement. Although personally a War Democrat, McClellan promised if elected to recommend to Congress an immediate armistice and a peace convention. Hearing this news, Confederate vice president Alexander Stephens celebrated "the first ray of real light I have seen since the war began." He predicted that if Atlanta and Richmond held out, Lincoln would be defeated and McClellan could be persuaded to accept an independent Confederacy.

The Fall of Atlanta and Lincoln's Victory Stephens's hopes collapsed on September 2, 1864, as Atlanta fell to Sherman's army. In a stunning move, the Union general pulled his troops from the trenches, swept around the city, and destroyed its rail links to the south. Fearing that Sherman would encircle his army, Confederate general John B. Hood abandoned the city. "Atlanta is ours, and fairly won," Sherman telegraphed Lincoln, sparking hundred-gun salutes and wild Republican celebrations in northern cities. "We are *gaining* strength," Lincoln warned Confederate leaders, "and may, if need be, maintain the contest indefinitely."

A deep pessimism settled over the Confederacy. Mary Chesnut, a plantation mistress and general's wife wrote in her diary, "I felt as if all were dead within me, forever," and foresaw the end of the Confederacy: "We are going to be wiped off the earth" (see Comparing American Voices, "Gender, Class, and Sexual Terror in the Invaded South," pp. 454–455).

Recognizing the dramatic change in the military situation, McClellan repudiated the Democratic peace platform. The National Union Party went on the offensive, attacking McClellan's inconsistency and labeling Peace Democrats as "copperheads" (poisonous snakes) who were hatching treasonous plots. "A man must go for the Union at all hazards," declared a Republican legislator in Pennsylvania, "if he would entitle himself to be considered a loyal man."

Lincoln won a clear-cut victory in November. The president received 55 percent of the popular vote and won 212 of 233 electoral votes. Republicans and National Unionists captured 145 of the 185 seats in the House of Representatives and increased their Senate majority to 42 of 52 seats. Many Republicans owed their victory to the votes of Union troops, who wanted to crush the rebellion and end slavery.

Legal emancipation was already under way at the edges of the South. In 1864, Maryland and Missouri amended their constitutions to end slavery, and the three Confederate states occupied by the Union army — Tennessee, Arkansas, and Louisiana — followed suit. Still, abolitionists worried that the Emancipation Proclamation, which was based on the president's wartime powers, would lose its force at the end of the war. Urged on by Lincoln and National Equal Rights League, the Republican Congress approved the Thirteenth Amendment, ending slavery, in January 1865 and sent it to the states for ratification. Slavery was nearly dead.

William Tecumseh Sherman: "Hard War" Warrior

Thanks to William Tecumseh Sherman, the Confederacy was nearly dead as well. As a young military officer stationed in the South, Sherman sympathized with the planter class and felt that slavery upheld social stability. But Sherman believed in the Union. Secession meant "anarchy," he told his southern friends in early 1861: "If war comes . . . I must fight your people whom I best love." Serving under Grant, Sherman distinguished himself at Shiloh and Vicksburg. Taking command of the Army of the Tennessee, he developed the philosophy and tactics of "hard war." "When one nation is at war with another, all the people of one are enemies of the other," Sherman declared, turning his troops loose against civilians suspected of helping Confederate guerrillas. When guerrillas fired on a boat carrying Unionist civilians near Randolph, Tennessee, Sherman sent a regiment to destroy the town, asserting, "We are justified in treating all inhabitants as combatants."

After capturing Atlanta, Sherman decided on a bold strategy. Instead of pursuing the retreating Confederate army northward into Tennessee, he proposed to move south, live off the land, and "cut a swath through to the sea." To persuade Lincoln and Grant to approve his unconventional plan, Sherman argued that his march would be "a demonstration to the world, foreign and

William Tecumseh Sherman

A man of nervous energy, Sherman smoked cigars and talked continuously. When seated, he crossed and uncrossed his legs incessantly, and a journalist described his fingers as constantly "twitching his red whiskers – his coat buttons – playing a tattoo on the table – or running through his hair." But on the battlefield Sherman was a decisive general who commanded the loyalty of his troops. This 1865 photograph was taken after Sherman's devastating march through Georgia and the Carolinas.   Library of Congress.

domestic, that we have a power [Jefferson] Davis cannot resist." The Union general lived up to his pledge. "We are not only fighting hostile armies," Sherman wrote, "but a hostile people, and must make old and young, rich and poor, feel the hard hand of war." He left Atlanta in flames, and during his 300-mile march to the sea (Map 14.6) his army consumed or demolished everything in its path. A Union veteran wrote, "[We] destroyed all we could not eat, stole their niggers, burned their cotton & gins, spilled their sorghum, burned & twisted their R.Roads and raised Hell generally." Although Sherman's army usually did not harm noncombatants who kept to their peaceful business, the havoc so demoralized Confederate soldiers that many deserted their units and returned home. When Sherman reached Savannah in mid-December, the city's 10,000 defenders left without a fight.

Gender, Class, and Sexual Terror in the Invaded South

When the white men of the South marched off to war, they left behind their wives and children. Soon, Confederate women in the border states confronted an enemy army of occupation. Southern women feared sexual abuse by occupying troops, especially as Union armies invaded the Confederacy and exposed women to a dangerous army of destruction. As the following selections show, rules of culture and class (for example, how "gentlemen" should act) and assumptions of male sexual privilege meant these interactions had varied outcomes.

Cornelia Peake McDonald

Journal

Cornelia Peake McDonald was the wife of an affluent lawyer in Winchester, Virginia, which was occupied during the Civil War; her nine children were born between 1848 and 1861.

[May 1863] 22nd . . . To day I received another intimation that my house would be wanted for a [Union] regimental hospital. I feel a sickening despair when I think of what will be my condition if they do take it. . . .

Major Butterworth . . . told me that he was a quarter master, and that he had been sent to inform me that I must give up the house, as they must have it for a hospital. . . . I lost no time in seeking [General] Milroy's presence. . . . "Gen. Milroy," said I. He looked around impatiently. "They have come to take my house from me." . . . [He replied,] "Why should you expect me to shelter you and your family, you who are a rebel, and whose husband and family are in arms against the best government the world ever saw?" . . . "But Gen. Milroy, you are commandant here . . . and you can suffer me to remain in mine, where at least I can have a shelter for my sick children. . . . At last he raised his head and looked in my face. "You can stay but I allow it at the risk of my commission."

Source: *A Woman's Civil War*, ed. Minrose C. Gwin (Madison: University of Wisconsin, 1992), 101, 150–153.

Judith White Brockenbrough McGuire

Diary

Judith White Brockenbrough McGuire, of Alexandria, Virginia, spent most of the war as a refugee in Richmond.

June 11, 1865
These particulars . . . I have [heard] from our nephew, J. P. [in occupied central Virginia. He reports that] . . . the

Northern officers seemed disposed to be courteous to the ladies, in the little intercourse which they had with them. General Ferrera, who commanded the negro troops, was humane, in having a coffin made for a young Confederate officer. . . . The surgeons, too, assisted in attending to the Confederate wounded. An officer one morning sent for Mrs. N. [to return an item stolen by Union soldiers]. . . . She thanked him for his kindness. He seemed moved and said, "Mrs. N., I will do what I can for you, for I cannot be too thankful that my wife is not in an invaded country."

Source: Rod Gragg, *The Illustrated Confederate Reader* (Harper & Row: New York, 1989), 88–89.

Henrietta E. Lee

Letter to Union General David Hunter

Henrietta E. Lee was the wife of Edmund J. Lee, a wealthy relative of Robert E. Lee. David Hunter was fighting Confederate forces in the Shenandoah Valley.

Shepherdstown, Va., July 20, 1864
General Hunter:
Yesterday your underling, Captain Martindale, of the First New York Calvary, executed your infamous order and burned my house. . . . I, therefore, a helpless woman whom you have cruelly wronged, address you, a Major-General of the United States Army, and demand why this was done? . . .

A colonel of the Federal Army has stated that you deprived forty of your officers of their commands because they refused to carry out your malignant mischief [of burning]. All honor to their names for this, at least! They are men, and have human hearts and blush for such a commander! . . . Your name will stand on history's pages as the Hunter of weak women, and innocent children.

Source: *The Women of the South in War Times*, comp. Matthew Pace Andrews (Baltimore: Norman, Remington, 1924), 382–383.

Anna Maria Green

Diary

Twenty-year-old Anna Maria Green kept a diary as General William Tecumseh Sherman's army of 60,000 men approached Milledgeville, Georgia.

Saturday evening November 19th [1864]—Again we are in a state of excitement caused by the near approach to our town of the enemy. Last night they were two thousand strong at Monticello. . . . Minnie came in to call me to look at a fire in the west. My heart sank, and almost burst with grief as I beheld the horizon crimson and the desolation our hated foe was spreading. Great God! Deliver us, oh! Spare our city. . . .

Nov. 25th Friday evening . . . This morning the last of the vandals left our city and burned the bridge after them—leaving suffering and desolation behind them, and embittering every heart. The worst of their acts was committed to poor Mrs. Nichols—violence done, and atrocity committed that ought to make her husband an enemy unto death. Poor woman. I fear she has been driven crazy.

Source: Rod Gragg, *The Illustrated Confederate Reader* (Harper & Row: New York, 1989), 175–176.

Unknown Woman

Letter to Her Daughter

This letter was written by a woman in Columbia, South Carolina.

Columbia March 3, 1865
My dear Gracia
Doubtless your anxiety is very great to hear something about us after the great calamity that has befallen our town. We have lost everything, but thank God, our lives have been spared. Oh Gracia, what we have passed through no tongue can tell, it defies description! . . .

The first regiment sent into the city was what Sherman calls his "Tigers." Whenever he sends these men ahead, he intends to do his worst. . . . The first thing they did was break open the stores and distribute the goods right and left. They found liquor and all became heartily drunk. . . . When night came on, the soldiers . . . fired the houses. It was a fearful sight. . . .

We stayed all night in the street, protected by a Yankee Captain from Iowa who was very kind to us.

Source: Rod Gragg, *The Illustrated Confederate Reader* (Harper & Row: New York, 1989), 189–190.

Daniel Heyward Trezevant

Report

Daniel Heyward Trezevant, a doctor in Columbia, South Carolina, wrote a brief report after Sherman's departure.

The Yankees' gallantry, brutality and debauchery were afflicted on the negroes. . . . The case of Mr. Shane's old negro woman, who, after being subjected to the most brutal indecency from seven of the Yankees, was, at the proposition of one of them to "finish the old Bitch," put into a ditch and held under water until life was extinct. . . .

Mrs. T.B.C. was seized by one of the soldiers, an officer, and dragged by the hair and forced to the floor for the purpose of sensual enjoyment. She resisted as far as practical—held up her young infant as a plea for sparing her and succeeded, but they took her maid, and in her presence, threw her on the floor and had connection with her. . . . They pinioned Mrs. McCord and robbed her. They dragged Mrs. Gynn by the hair of her head about the house. Mrs. G. told me of a young lady about 16, Miss Kinsler, who . . . three officers brutally ravished and who became crazy. . . .

Source: Rod Gragg, *The Illustrated Confederate Reader* (Harper & Row: New York, 1989), 192.

ANALYZING THE EVIDENCE

- Why does General Milroy allow Cornelia McDonald to stay in her home? Was it because they were both members of the American upper classes? Or because the general held cultural values that protected women and children? How do the actions of the "Yankee Captain from Iowa" compare with Milroy's decision? What does the report about Mrs. N. and the kindness of the unnamed officer in the diary of Judith McGuire suggest about that officer's motivation?

- Why did Henrietta E. Lee call herself "helpless"? What did she mean—and what was her aim—in praising the officers allegedly dismissed by General Hunter?

- Although none of these writers used the word *rape* (why not?), we can assume that Mrs. Nichols was raped, as were Miss Kinsler and the enslaved African American maid in Columbia. What about Mrs. T.B.C., Mrs. McCord, and Mrs. Gynn? Should we believe these sources (and other, similar accounts written by whites) when they assert or imply that Union troops raped enslaved women and spared white women?

- What impact might accounts of the Union soldiers' brutality toward women have had on the Confederate army? Were such acts of brutality an inevitable result of the practice of "hard war"?

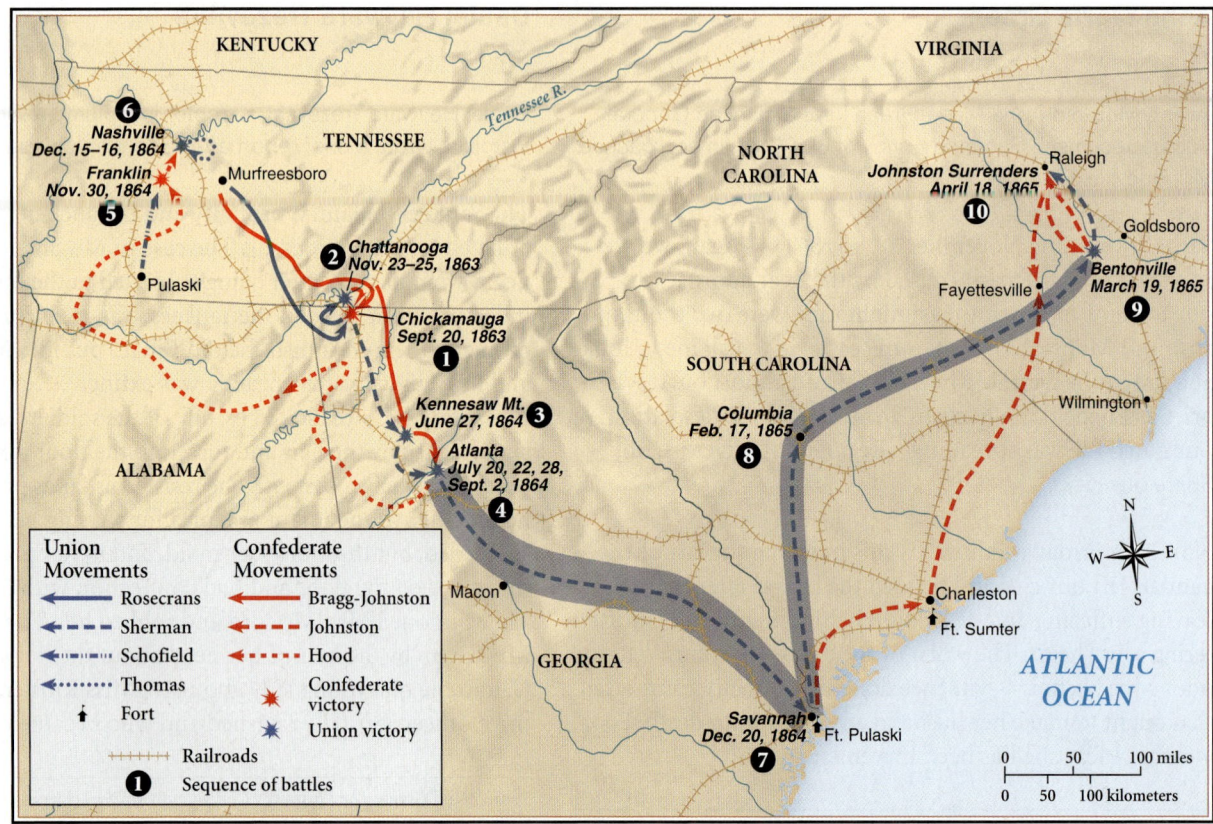

MAP 14.6

Sherman's March through the Confederacy, 1864–1865

The Union victory in November 1863 at Chattanooga, Tennessee (2), was almost as critical as the victories in July at Gettysburg and Vicksburg, because it opened up a route of attack into the heart of the Confederacy. In mid-1864, General William Tecumseh Sherman advanced on the railway hub of Atlanta (3 and 4). After finally taking the city in September 1864, Sherman relied on other Union armies to stem General Hood's invasion of Tennessee (5 and 6) while he began his devastating "March to the Sea." By December, he had reached Savannah (7); from there, he cut a swath through the Carolinas (8–10).

Georgia's African Americans treated Sherman as a savior. "They flock to me, old and young," he wrote. "[T]hey pray and shout and mix up my name with Moses . . . as well as 'Abram Linkom,' the Great Messiah of 'Dis Jubilee.'" To provide for the hundreds of blacks now following his army, Sherman issued Special Field Order No. 15, which set aside 400,000 acres of prime rice-growing land for the exclusive use of freedmen. By June 1865, about 40,000 blacks were cultivating "Sherman lands." Many freedmen believed that the lands were to be theirs forever, belated payment for generations of unpaid labor: "All the land belongs to the Yankees now and they gwine divide it out among de coloured people."

In February 1865, Sherman invaded South Carolina to link up with Grant at Petersburg and to punish the instigators of nullification and secession. His troops ravaged the countryside as they cut a narrow swath across the state. After capturing South Carolina's capital, Columbia, they burned the business district, most churches, and the wealthiest residential neighborhoods. "This disappointment to me is extremely bitter," lamented Jefferson Davis. By March, Sherman had reached North Carolina, ready to link up with Grant and crush Lee's army.

The Confederate Collapse Grant's war of attrition in Virginia had already exposed a weakness in the Confederacy: rising class resentment among poor whites. Angered by slave owners' exemptions from military service and fearing that the Confederacy was doomed, ordinary southern farmers now repudiated the draft. "All they want is to git you . . . to fight for their infurnal negroes," grumbled an Alabama hill farmer. More and more soldiers fled their units. "I am now going to work instead of to the war," vowed David Harris, another backcountry yeoman. By 1865, at least 100,000 men had deserted from Confederate armies, prompting reluctant Confederate leaders to allow the enlistment of black soldiers and promising freedom to those who served. But the fighting ended too soon to reveal whether any slaves would have fought for the Confederacy.

The symbolic end of the war took place in Virginia. In April 1865, Grant finally gained control of the crucial railroad junction at Petersburg and forced Lee to abandon Richmond. As Lincoln visited the ruins of the Confederate capital and was mobbed by joyful ex-slaves, Grant cut off Lee's escape route to North Carolina. On April 9, almost four years to the day after the attack on Fort Sumter, Lee surrendered at Appomattox Court House, Virginia. By late May, all the

Confederate generals had stopped fighting, and the Confederate army and government simply melted away (Map 14.7).

The hard and bitter conflict was finally over. Union armies had destroyed slavery and the Confederacy; many of the South's factories, railroads, and cities were in ruins, and its farms and plantations had suffered years of neglect. Almost 260,000 Confederate soldiers had paid for secession with their lives. On the other side, more than 360,000 northerners had died for the Union, and thousands more had been maimed (see Reading American Pictures, "What Do Photographs Tell Us about the Civil War?" p. 458). Was it all worth the price? Delivering his second inaugural address in March 1865, Abraham Lincoln could justify the hideous carnage only by alluding to divine providence: "[S]o still it must be said 'the judgments of the Lord are true and righteous altogether.'"

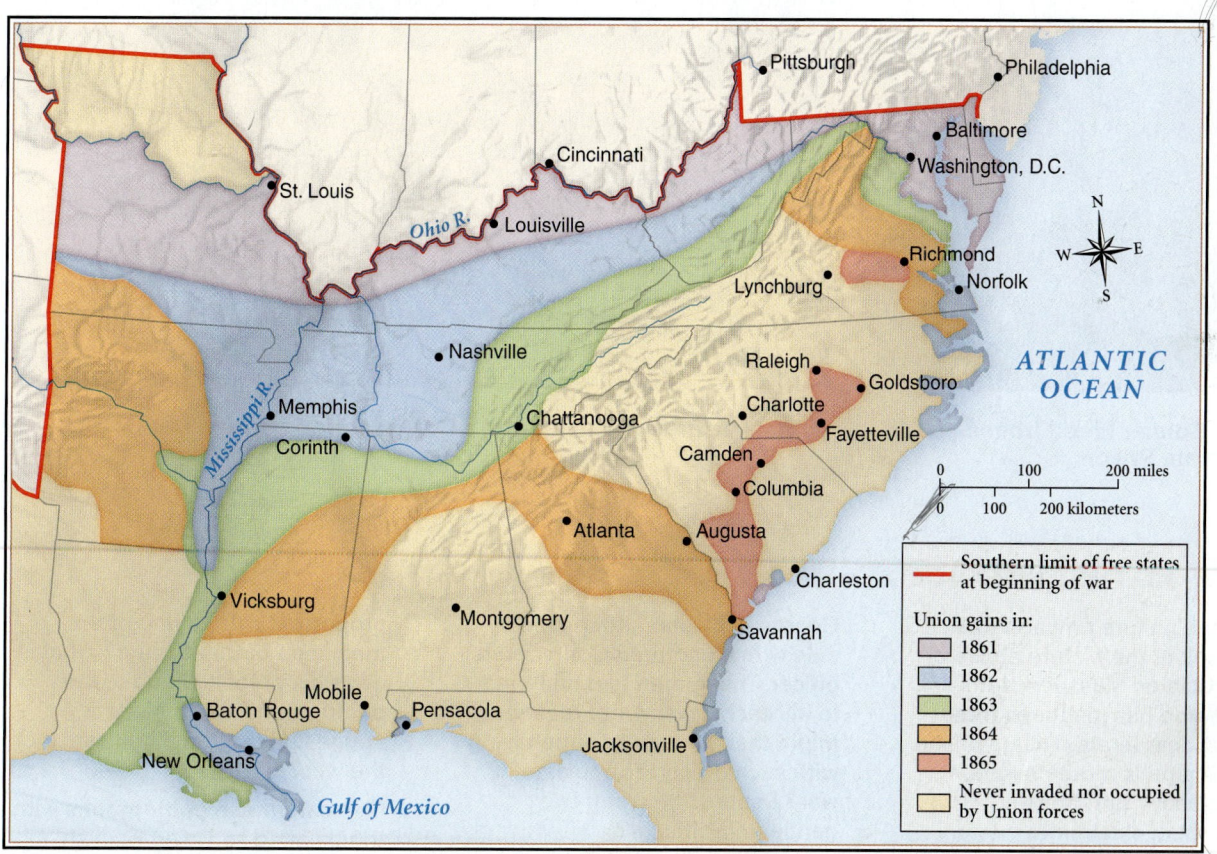

MAP 14.7

The Conquest of the South, 1861–1865

It took four years for the Union armies to defeat the Confederate forces. Until 1864, most of the South remained in Confederate hands; even at the end of the war, Union armies had never entered many parts of the rebellious states. Most of the Union's territorial gains came on the vast western front, where its control of strategic lines of communication (the Ohio and Mississippi rivers and major railroads) gave its forces a decisive advantage.

What Do Photographs Tell Us about the Civil War?

The Civil War was the first military conflict recorded extensively by photographers. As the full-page photograph at the beginning of this chapter attests, the results were not pretty. Many Civil War photos portray military encampments and hundreds show the bodies of dead men scattered across fields of battle—grim scenes, indeed. But what was the impact of these photographs of death, given that few of them achieved wide distribution at the time? What insight can other photographs give us into the nature of the conflict?

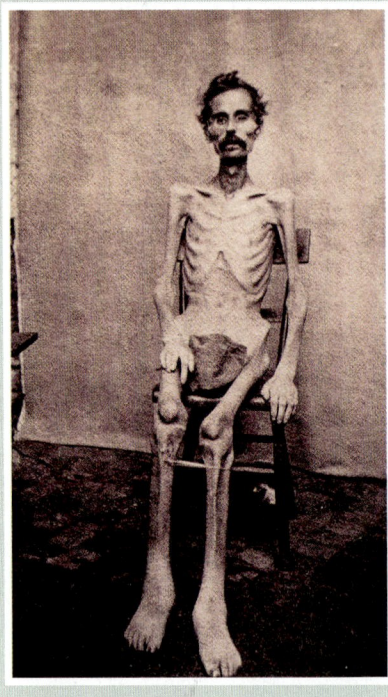

A Union Soldier Freed from a Confederate Prison. © Corbis.

Captain George A. Custer and a Confederate Prisoner. Library of Congress.

ANALYZING THE EVIDENCE

- Study the picture on page 428. Then look at the picture above of the emaciated Massachusetts soldier who has just been freed from a Confederate military prison. Which image is more powerful intellectually? Emotionally? How do you think nineteenth-century Americans would have responded to the two photographs? And how would you explain the Confederates' treatment of that prisoner (who was only one among many)?

- The other photograph above shows Captain (later General) George A. Custer sitting side by side with a captured Confederate officer. These men had just tried to kill each other. What reasons might they have had for behaving with such civility: The rules of war? Respect between two gentlemen-officers?

- Why did the photographer, the famous Mathew Brady, take this picture of Custer and the prisoner? Brady chose his images carefully so that they conveyed a message or a perspective on events. Is the African American boy, the southerner's slave property, a clue to one of the meanings of this picture? What does his presence add to the photograph? What might it suggest about the significance of the war?

- Compare these photographs with the painting by David English Henderson, *The Return to Fredericksburg after the Battle* (p. 459). What are the advantages (and drawbacks) of the two mediums—photography and art—in conveying the experience of war?

The Harsh Aftermath

The end of the war was not the end of the suffering, as David English Henderson's *The Return to Fredericksburg after the Battle* (1865) shows. Many southern soldiers and families returned to devastated homes and cities. Shocked by the destruction, the members of this well-to-do family stare blankly into space, unable yet to comprehend how they will rebuild their shattered lives.   Gettysburg National Military Park.

But what of the war's effects on society? A New York census taker suggested that the conflict had undermined "autocracy" and had an "equalizing effect." Slavery was gone from the South, he reflected, and in the North, "military men from the so called 'lower classes' now lead society, having been elevated by real merit and valor." However perceptive these remarks, they ignored the wartime emergence of a new financial aristocracy that would soon preside over what Mark Twain would label the Gilded Age. Nor was the sectional struggle yet concluded. As the North began to reconstruct the South and the Union, it found those tasks to be almost as hard and bitter as the war itself.

- How did the Emancipation Proclamation affect the politics and military affairs of the North?

- What were the strengths and weaknesses of Grant's and Sherman's military strategy and tactics? How were their ways of warfare different from traditional military practice?

SUMMARY

In this chapter, we surveyed the dramatic events of the Civil War. Looking at the South, we watched the fire-eaters declare secession, form a new Confederacy, and attack Fort Sumter. Subsequently, we saw its generals repulse Union attacks against Richmond and go on the offensive. However, as the war continued, the inherent weaknesses of the Confederacy came to the fore. Enslaved workers fled or refused to work, and yeomen farmers refused to fight for an institution that primarily benefited wealthy planters.

Examining the North, we witnessed its military shortcomings. Its generals—McClellan and Meade—moved slowly to attack and refused to pursue their weakened foes. However, the Union's significant advantages in industrial output, financial resources, and military manpower became manifest over time. Congress created efficient systems of banking and war finance, Lincoln found efficient and ruthless generals, and the emancipation and recruitment of African Americans provided an abundant supply of soldiers determined to end slavery.

We explored the impact of the war on civilians in both regions: the imposition of conscription and high taxes, the increased workload of farm women, and the constant food shortages and soaring prices. Above all else, there was the omnipresent fact of death—a tragedy that touched nearly every family, North and South.

CHAPTER REVIEW QUESTIONS

- As the Civil War began, politicians and ordinary citizens in both the North and the South were supremely confident of victory. Why did southerners believe they would triumph? Why did the North ultimately win the war?

- In 1860, the institution of slavery was firmly entrenched in the United States; by 1865, it was dead. How did this happen? How did Union policy toward slavery and enslaved people change over the course of the war? Why did it change?

FOR FURTHER EXPLORATION

Charles P. Roland, *An American Iliad* (1991), and James M. McPherson, *The Battle Cry of Freedom* (1988), are fine histories of the Civil War. Recent important studies include Nicholas Onuf and Peter Onuf, *Nations, Markets, and War* (2006); Drew Gilpin Faust, *This Republic of Suffering: Death and the American Civil War* (2008); and Dora L. Costa and Matthew E. Kahn, *Heroes and Cowards: The Social Face of War* (2008).

For military matters, consult Nancy Scott Anderson and Dwight Anderson, *The Generals: Ulysses S. Grant and Robert E. Lee* (1988); Mark Grimsley, *The Hard Hand of War* (1995); and Gary W. Gallagher, *The Confederate War* (1997). William W. Freehling's *The South vs. the South* (2001) explores anti-Confederate sentiment.

James M. McPherson, *For Cause and Comrades* (1997), presents accounts of ordinary soldiers, as does Ira Berlin et al., eds., *Freedom's Soldiers: The Black Military Experience in the Civil War* (1998). Earl J. Hess, *The Union Soldier in Battle* (1997), vividly describes the smell, sound, and feel of combat, as does Michael Shaara's novel, *Killer Angels* (1974).

For southern women, read Drew Gilpin Faust, *Mothers of Invention* (1996); Laura F. Edwards, *Scarlett Doesn't Live Here Anymore* (2000); and *Mary Chesnut's Civil War*, edited by C. Vann Woodward (1981). See also Jane E. Schultz, *Women at the Front* (2004).

For Civil War photographs from the Library of Congress collection, visit **memory.loc.gov/ammem/cwphtml/cwphome.html**. A fine Web site is "The Valley of the Shadow" (**valley.lib.virginia.edu**), and the companion book by Edward L. Ayers, *In the Presence of Mine Enemies* (2003). For firsthand documents relating to emancipation, see **www.history.umd.edu/Freedmen/home.html**.

TEST YOUR KNOWLEDGE

To assess your command of the material in this chapter, see the Online Study Guide at **bedfordstmartins.com/henretta**.

For Web sites, images, and documents related to topics and places in this chapter, visit **bedfordstmartins.com/makehistory**.

TIMELINE

1860
- Abraham Lincoln elected president (November 6)
- South Carolina secedes (December 20)

1861
- Lincoln inaugurated (March 4)
- Confederates fire on Fort Sumter (April 12)
- Virginia leaves Union (April 17)
- General Butler declares runaway slaves "contraband of war" (May)
- Confederates win Battle of Bull Run (July 21)
- First Confiscation Act (August)

1862
- Legal Tender Act authorizes greenbacks (February)
- Union triumphs at Shiloh (April 6–7)
- Confederacy introduces draft (April)
- Congress passes Homestead Act (May)
- Congress subsidizes transcontinental railroads (July)
- Second Confiscation Act (July)
- Union halts Confederates at Antietam (September 17)
- Preliminary emancipation proclamation (September 22)

1863
- Lincoln signs Emancipation Proclamation (January 1)
- Union wins battles at Gettysburg (July 1–3) and Vicksburg (July 4)
- Union initiates draft (March), sparking riots in New York City (July)

1864
- Ulysses S. Grant named Union commander (March)
- Grant advances on Richmond (May)
- William Tecumseh Sherman takes Atlanta (September 2)
- Lincoln reelected (November 8)
- Sherman marches through Georgia (November and December)

1865
- Congress approves Thirteenth Amendment (January 31)
- Robert E. Lee surrenders (April 9)
- Lincoln assassinated (April 14)
- Thirteenth Amendment ratified (December 6)

Reconstruction, 1865–1877

In 1869, Wyoming Territory did something few Americans could have imagined before the Civil War: It gave women full voting rights. A few local women's rights advocates supported the measure, but one legislator endorsed it in a spirit of revenge. "Damn it," he said, "if you are going to let the niggers and pigtails [Chinese] vote, we will ring in the women, too." A decade later, similar arguments surfaced in California. "We give negroes, and Chinamen, and everything else, a right to vote," pointed out one delegate to a state constitutional convention. Another challenged him: "Are you going over to that doctrine of the universal brotherhood of man?" He answered, "In regard to women, I am."

In other spheres, as well, "universal brotherhood" was a subject of intense debate. Congress overhauled the Naturalization Act of 1790, which had limited citizenship to immigrants who were "free white persons." The most radical congressmen argued that racial barriers to citizenship should be dropped entirely. But their proposal foundered, largely because of opposition to Chinese immigration. One U.S. senator warned that Chinese American citizenship would put "an end to republican government" on the Pacific coast. In the end, Congress offered citizenship rights to people of African descent, but not to those from Asia.

As these debates suggest, the Civil War opened enormous questions about citizenship and nationhood. Americans engaged in intense, often violent struggles over the postwar order. Slavery was finished—that much was certain—and the South had been forcibly reattached to the Union. But how should the United States reincorporate former rebels into the political system? Could it also define a secure place for four million former slaves? What about immigrants from many parts of the world? And if the United States was no longer a "white man's country," might citizenship extend to women as well as to black men?

Reconstruction is often thought of as something that happened in the South. But events there were part of a much broader transformation. Far beyond the ex-Confederacy, the United States embarked on an ambitious process of nation building. Chapter 16 will explore events in the West. There, the United States knit together a continental empire; military conflict with Native Americans entered its final phase, and the arrival of Asian immigrants raised new issues of citizenship and trade. In Chapter 15, we will focus on events in Washington, D.C., and in the former Confederacy, where freed slaves, former slave owners, and other southerners found their worlds turned upside down.

Chloe and Sam, **1882**

After the Civil War, the country went through the wrenching peacemaking process known as Reconstruction. The struggle between the victorious North and the vanquished Confederacy was fought out on a political landscape, but Thomas Hovenden's painting reminds us of the deeper meaning of Reconstruction: that Chloe and Sam, after lives spent in slavery, might end their days in the dignity of freedom. Amon Carter Museum of Western Art.

The Struggle for National Reconstruction

The U.S. Constitution does not address the question of how to restore rebellious states. After the Civil War, the nation had to determine whether the Confederate states, upon seceding, had legally left the Union. If so, then their reentry required action by Congress. If not—if even during secession they had retained their constitutional status—then restoring these states might be an administrative matter, best left to the president. Lack of clarity on this fundamental question made for explosive politics. In the early years of Reconstruction, the president and Congress struggled over who was in charge. Only by winning this fight did Republicans in Congress open the way for the sweeping achievements of radical Reconstruction.

Presidential Approaches: From Lincoln to Johnson

As wartime president, Lincoln had offered amnesty to all but high-ranking Confederates. When 10 percent of a rebellious state's voters had taken an oath of loyalty, he proposed, the state would be restored to the Union, provided that it approved the Thirteenth Amendment abolishing slavery (see Chapter 14). But Confederate states rejected Lincoln's Ten Percent Plan, and Congress proposed a tougher substitute. The Wade-Davis Bill, passed on July 2, 1864, required an oath of allegiance to the Union by a majority of each state's adult white men, new governments formed only by those who had never taken up arms against the North, and permanent disenfranchisement of Confederate leaders. Lincoln used a **pocket veto** to kill the Wade-Davis Bill; that is, he left it unsigned when Congress adjourned, while initiating talks with congressional leaders aimed at a compromise.

We will never know what would have happened had Lincoln lived. His assassination in April 1865 plunged the nation into political uncertainty and fueled Unionist fury against the South. As a special train bore Lincoln's flag-draped coffin slowly home to Illinois, tens of thousands of Americans lined the railroad tracks to pay respects. Grieving northerners blamed all Confederates for the acts of southern sympathizer John Wilkes Booth and his accomplices in the assassination. At the same time, Lincoln's death left the presidency in the hands of a man utterly lacking in Lincoln's moral sense and political judgment, Vice President Andrew Johnson.

Johnson was a self-styled "common man" from the hills of eastern Tennessee. Trained as a tailor, he built a career on the support of farmers and laborers. Loyal to the Union, Johnson refused to leave the U.S. Senate when Tennessee seceded. After federal forces captured Nashville in 1862, Lincoln appointed Johnson as Tennessee's military governor. In the election of 1864, placing this War Democrat on the Republican ticket had seemed a smart move, designed to promote unity and court southern Unionists. But after Lincoln's death, Johnson's presidency wreaked political havoc. Johnson, who was not even a Republican, often seemed to view ex-Confederates as his friends and abolitionists as his enemies.

In May 1865, with Congress out of session for months to come, Johnson advanced his own version of Reconstruction. He offered amnesty to all southerners who swore allegiance to the United States, except for the highest-ranking Confederates. Johnson appointed provisional governors for the southern states and required only that they revoke secession, repudiate Confederate debts, and ratify the Thirteenth Amendment. Within months, all the former Confederate states had met Johnson's terms and created functioning elected governments.

Many northerners were disgusted with Johnson. "The rebels have gotten back all their rights and have all been pardoned," wrote one angry Union army veteran in Missouri. He called Johnson "a traitor to the loyal people of the Union." Meanwhile, despite military defeat (see Voices from Abroad, "David Macrae: The Devastated South," p. 465), southerners' new legislatures moved to restore slavery in all but name. They enacted laws, known as **Black Codes**, designed to force former slaves back to plantation labor. The codes, for example, imposed severe penalties on blacks who did not hold full-year labor contracts and set up procedures for taking black children away from their parents and apprenticing them to former slave owners. Johnson, moreover, talked tough but then forgave ex-Confederate leaders easily when they appealed for pardons. Emboldened by Johnson's indulgence, ex-Confederates began to filter back into the halls of power. When Georgians elected Alexander Stephens, former vice president of the Confederacy, to represent them in Congress, many outraged Republicans saw this as the last straw.

Congress versus the President

Under the Constitution, Congress is "the judge of the Elections, Returns and Qualifications of its own Members" (Article 1, Section 5). Using this power, Republican

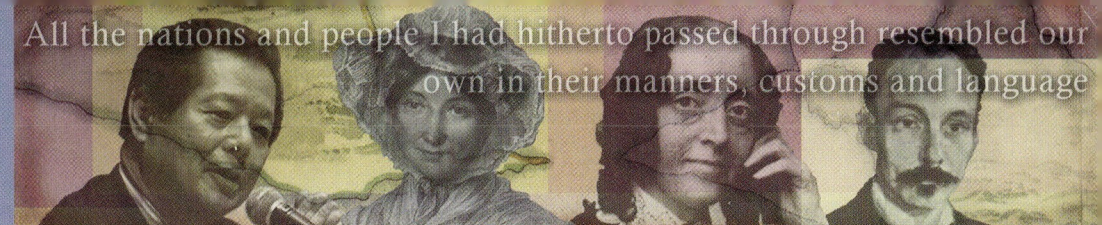

All the nations and people I had hitherto passed through resembled our own in their manners, customs and language

David Macrae
The Devastated South

In this excerpt from *The Americans at Home* (1870), an account of his tour of the United States, Scottish clergyman David Macrae describes the war-stricken South as he found it in 1867–1868, at a time when the crisis over Reconstruction was boiling over.

I was struck with a remark made by a Southern gentleman in answer to the assertion that Jefferson Davis [the president of the Confederacy] had culpably continued the war for six months after all hope had been abandoned.

"Sir," he said, "Mr. Davis knew the temper of the South as well as any man in it. He knew if there was to be anything worth calling peace, the South must win; or, if she couldn't win, she wanted to be whipped—well whipped—thoroughly whipped."

The further south I went, the oftener these remarks came back upon me. Evidence was everywhere that the South had maintained the desperate conflict until she was utterly exhausted. . . . Almost every man I met at the South, especially in North Carolina, Georgia, and Virginia, seemed to have been in the army; and it was painful to find many who had returned were mutilated, maimed, or broken in health by exposure. When I remarked this to a young Confederate officer in North Carolina, and said I was glad to see that he had escaped unhurt, he said, "Wait till we get to the office, sir, and I will tell you more about that." When we got there, he pulled up one leg of his trousers, and showed me that he had an iron rod there to strengthen his limb, and enable him to walk without limping, half of his foot being off. He showed me on the other leg a deep scar made by a fragment of a shell; and these were but two of seven wounds which had left their marks upon his body. When he heard me speak of relics, he said, "Try to find a North Carolina gentleman without a Yankee mark on him."

Nearly three years had passed when I traveled through the country, and yet we have seen what traces the war had left in such cities as Richmond, Petersburg, and Columbia. The same spectacle met me at Charleston. Churches and houses had been battered down by heavy shot and shell hurled into the city from Federal batteries at a distance of five miles. Even the valley of desolation made by a great fire in 1861, through the very heart of the city, remained unbuilt. There, after the lapse of seven years, stood the blackened ruins of streets and houses waiting for the coming of a better day. . . . Over the country districts the prostration was equally marked. Along the track of Sherman's army, especially, the devastation was fearful—farms laid waste,

fences burned, bridges destroyed, houses left in ruins, plantations in many cases turned into wilderness again.

The people had shared in the general wreck, and looked poverty-stricken, careworn, and dejected. Ladies who before the war had lived in affluence, with black servants round them to attend to their every wish, were boarding together in half-furnished houses, cooking their own food and washing their own linen, some of them, I was told, so utterly destitute that they did not know when they finished one meal where they were to find the next. . . . Men who had held commanding positions during the war had fallen out of sight and were filling humble situations—struggling, many of them, to earn a bare subsistence. . . . I remember dining with three cultured Southern gentlemen, one a general, the other, I think, a captain, and the third a lieutenant. They were all living together in a plain little wooden house, such as they would formerly have provided for their servants. Two of them were engaged in a railway office, the third was seeking a situation, frequently, in his vain search, passing the large blinded house where he had lived in luxurious ease before the war.

Source: Allan Nevins, ed., *America through British Eyes* (Gloucester, MA: Peter Smith, 1968), 345–347.

ANALYZING THE EVIDENCE

- In general, we value accounts by foreigners for insights they provide into America that might not be visible to its own citizens. Do you find any such insights in the Reverend Macrae's account of the postwar South?

- The South proved remarkably resistant to northern efforts at reconstruction. Can we find explanations for that resistance in Macrae's account?

- The North quickly became disillusioned with radical Reconstruction (see p. 483). Is there anything in Macrae's sympathetic interviews with wounded southern gentlemen and destitute ladies that sheds light on the susceptibility of many northerners to propaganda depicting a South in the grip of "a mass of black barbarism"?

Memphis Riot, 1866

Whites in postwar Memphis, as in much of the South, bitterly resented the presence in their city of former black soldiers mustered out of service with the U.S. Army. On April 30, 1866, when some black veterans—no longer protected by their uniforms—celebrated the end of their Army service by drinking, violence broke out. For three days, whites burned black neighborhoods, churches, and schools, raped several African American women, and killed dozens of black residents. Two whites also died in the rioting, which hardened Northern public opinion and prompted calls for stronger measures to put down ex-Confederate resistance. This tinted illustration is based on a lithograph that appeared in *Harper's Weekly*.
Harper's Weekly/Picture Research Consultants & Archives.

majorities in both houses refused to admit southern delegations when Congress convened in December 1865, effectively blocking Johnson's program. Hoping to mollify Congress, some southern states dropped the most objectionable provisions from the Black Codes. But at the same time, antiblack violence erupted in various parts of the South. A Nashville newspaper reported that white gangs were "riding about whipping, maiming and killing all negroes who do not obey the orders of their former masters."

Congressional Republicans concluded that the South planned to circumvent the Thirteenth Amendment. The federal government had to intervene. Back in March 1865, Congress had established the Freedmen's Bureau to aid former slaves. Now, in early 1866, Congress voted to extend the bureau, gave it direct funding for the first time, and authorized its agents to investigate mistreatment of blacks. Even more extraordinary was a civil rights bill that declared formerly enslaved people to be citizens and granted them equal protection and rights of contract, with full access to the courts.

These bills provoked bitter conflict with Johnson, who vetoed them both. Johnson's racism, hitherto publicly muted, now blazed forth: "This is a country for white men, and by God, as long as I am president, it shall be a government for white men." Galvanized, Re-

publicans in Congress gathered two-thirds majorities and overrode both vetoes, passing the Civil Rights Act in April 1866 and the Freedmen's Bureau law four months later. Their resolve was reinforced by continued violence in the South, which culminated in three days of rioting in Memphis, Tennessee, that left forty-six blacks dead and hundreds of African American homes, churches, and schools burned.

Radical Republicans and the Fourteenth Amendment   Anxious to protect freedpeople and reassert Republican power in the South, Congress moved to ensure black civil rights. In what became the Fourteenth Amendment to the Constitution, they declared that "all persons born or naturalized in the United States" were citizens. No state could abridge "the privileges or immunities of citizens of the United States"; deprive "any person of life, liberty, or property, without due process of law"; or deny anyone "equal protection of the laws." Johnson was right on one thing: Republicans were tending toward "centralization." In a stunning increase in federal power, the Fourteenth Amendment declared that when people's essential rights were at stake, national citizenship henceforth took precedence over citizenship in a state.

Johnson urged the states not to ratify the amendment, but public opinion had swung against him. In August 1866, Johnson embarked on a disastrous speaking tour, during which he made matters worse by shouting at hecklers and insulting hostile crowds. In the 1866 congressional elections, voters inflicted humiliation on Johnson by giving Republicans a three-to-one majority in Congress.

Power had shifted to the so-called Radical Republicans, who sought sweeping transformations in the defeated South. The Radicals' leader in the Senate was Charles Sumner of Massachusetts, the fiery abolitionist who in 1856 had been nearly beaten to death by South Carolina congressman Preston Brooks. Radicals in the House followed Thaddeus Stevens of Pennsylvania, a passionate advocate of freedpeople's political and eco-

nomic rights. With such men at the fore, and with congressional Republicans now numerous and united enough to override Johnson's vetoes on many questions, Republicans proceeded to remake Reconstruction.

Radical Reconstruction

The Reconstruction Act of 1867, enacted in March, divided the conquered South into five military districts, each under the command of a U.S. general (Map 15.1). To reenter the Union, each former Confederate state had to grant the vote to freedmen and deny it to leading ex-Confederates. Each military commander was required to register all eligible adult males, black as well as white; supervise new state constitutional conventions; and ensure that new constitutions guaranteed black

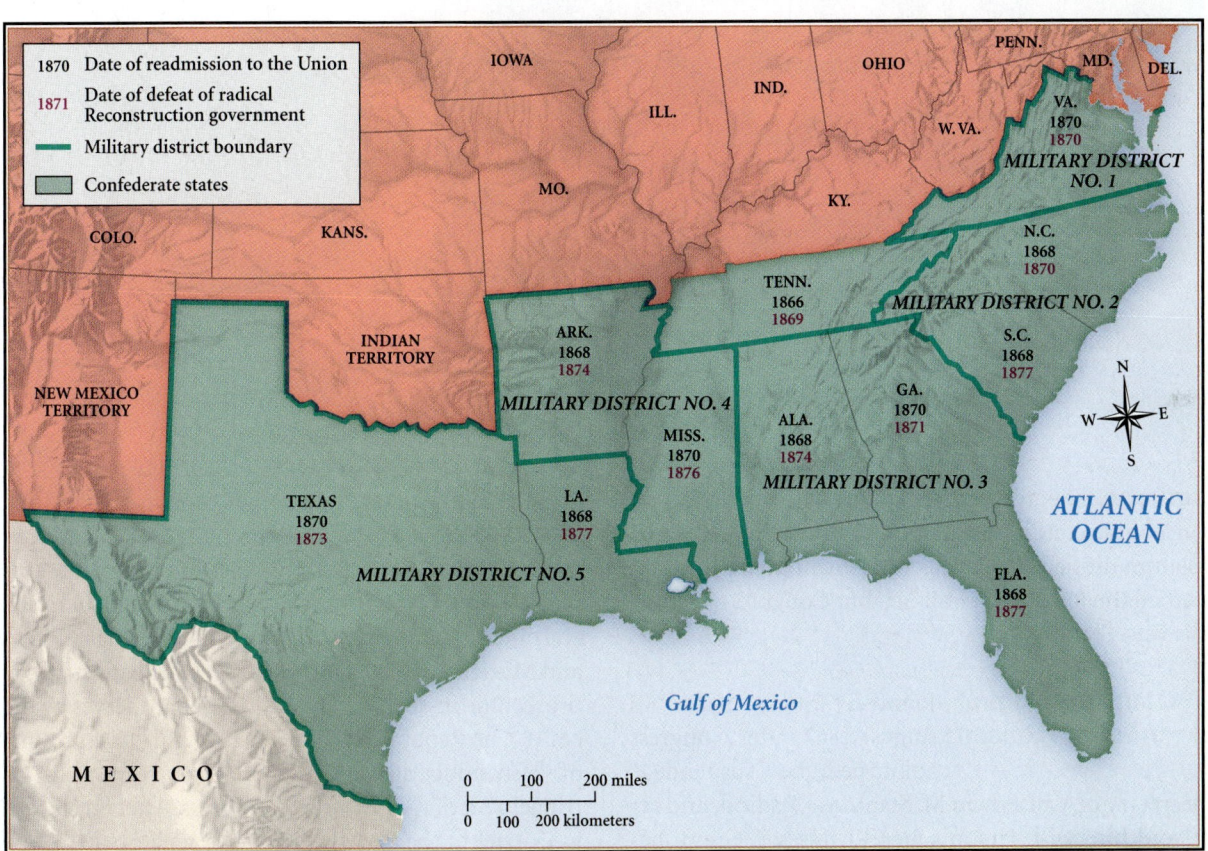

MAP 15.1

Reconstruction

The federal government organized the Confederate states into five military districts during radical Reconstruction. For the states shown in this map, the first date indicates when that state was readmitted to the Union; the second date shows when Radical Republicans lost control of the state government. All the ex-Confederate states rejoined the Union between 1868 and 1870, but the periods of radical rule varied widely. Republicans lasted only a few months in Virginia; they held on until the end of Reconstruction in Louisiana, Florida, and South Carolina.

"The First Vote"

In this pastel drawing, based on an engraving by Alfred Waud that appeared in *Harper's Weekly* in November 1867, the voters shown represent elements of African American political leadership: an artisan with tools, a well-dressed member of the middle class, and a Union soldier. After ratification of the Fifteenth Amendment in 1870, African American men voted in every state of the Union. © Bettmann/Corbis.

suffrage. Congress would readmit a state to the Union once these conditions were met and the new state legislature ratified the Fourteenth Amendment. Johnson vetoed the Reconstruction Act, but Congress overrode his veto (Table 15.1).

The Impeachment of Andrew Johnson

Johnson fought back. In August 1867, after Congress adjourned, he "suspended" Secretary of War Edwin M. Stanton, a Radical, and replaced him with Union general Ulysses S. Grant, believing Grant would be a good soldier and follow orders. Johnson, however, had misjudged Grant, who publicly objected to the president's machinations. When the Senate reconvened in the fall, it overruled Stanton's suspension. Grant, now an open enemy of Johnson, resigned so that Stanton could resume his place as secretary of war. On February 21, 1868, Johnson formally dismissed Stanton. The feisty secretary of war responded by barricading himself in his office, precipitating a crisis.

Three days later, for the first time in U.S. history, legislators in the House of Representatives introduced articles of **impeachment** against the president, employing their constitutional power to charge high federal officials with "Treason, Bribery, or other high Crimes and Misdemeanors." The House serves, in effect, as the prosecutor in such cases, and the Senate serves as the court. The Republican majority brought eleven counts of misconduct against Johnson, most relating to infringement of the powers of Congress. After an eleven-week trial in the Senate, thirty-five senators voted for conviction—one vote short of the two-thirds majority required. Seven Republicans voted for acquittal along with twelve Democrats. The dissenting Republicans felt that removing a president for defying Congress was too damaging to the constitutional system of checks and balances. But despite the president's acquittal, Congress had shown its power. For the brief months remaining in his term, Johnson was largely irrelevant to Reconstruction policy.

TABLE 15.1

Primary Reconstruction Laws and Constitutional Amendments

Law (Date of Congressional Passage)	Key Provisions
Thirteenth Amendment (December 1865*)	Prohibited slavery
Civil Rights Act of 1866 (April 1866)	Defined citizenship rights of freedmen
	Authorized federal authorities to bring suit against those who violated those rights
Fourteenth Amendment (June 1866†)	Established national citizenship for persons born or naturalized in the United States
	Prohibited the states from depriving citizens of their civil rights or equal protection under the law
	Reduced state representation in House of Representatives by the percentage of adult male citizens denied the vote
Reconstruction Act of 1867 (March 1867)	Divided the South into five military districts, each under the command of a Union general
	Established requirements for readmission of ex-Confederate states to the Union
Tenure of Office Act (March 1867)	Required Senate consent for removal of any federal official whose appointment had required Senate confirmation
Fifteenth Amendment (February 1869‡)	Forbade states to deny citizens the right to vote on the grounds of race, color, or "previous condition of servitude"
Ku Klux Klan Act (April 1871)	Authorized the president to use federal prosecutions and military force to suppress conspiracies to deprive citizens of the right to vote and enjoy the equal protection of the law

*Ratified by three-fourths of all states in December 1865.
†Ratified by three-fourths of all states in July 1868.
‡Ratified by three-fourths of all states in March 1870.

The Election of 1868 and the Fifteenth Amendment The impeachment controversy made Grant, already the Union's greatest war hero, a Republican idol as well, and he easily won the party's presidential nomination in 1868. Although he supported radical Reconstruction, Grant also urged reconciliation between the sections. His Democratic opponent, Horatio Seymour, a former governor of New York, almost declined the nomination because he understood that Democrats could not yet overcome the stain of disloyalty. Grant won by an overwhelming margin, receiving 214 out of 294 electoral votes. Republicans retained two-thirds majorities in both houses of Congress.

In February 1869, in the wake of this smashing victory, Republicans produced the last Reconstruction amendment, the Fifteenth. It protected male citizens' right to vote irrespective of race, color, or "previous condition of servitude." Despite Radical Republicans' protests, the amendment left room for a **poll tax** (a tax paid for the privilege of voting) and literacy requirements, both necessary concessions to northern and western states that already relied on such provisions to keep immigrants and the "unworthy" poor from the polls. Congress required the four states remaining under federal control to ratify it as a condition for being readmitted to the Union. A year later, the Fifteenth Amendment became part of the Constitution.

Passage of the Fifteenth Amendment, despite its limitations, was an astonishing feat. Elsewhere in the Western Hemisphere, lawmakers had left emancipated slaves in a condition of semicitizenship, with no voting rights. But, like almost all Americans, congressional Republicans had extraordinary faith in the power of the ballot. African American leaders agreed. "The colored people of these Southern states have cast their lot with the Government," declared a delegate to Arkansas's constitutional convention, "and with the great Republican Party. . . . The ballot is our only means of protection." After the amendment was ratified, hundreds of

Women's Rights, 1870s

This engraving of a National Woman's Suffrage Association (NWSA) meeting in the 1870s shows that it was an all women's organization, and female led. The NWSA investigated the "labor question" and called for equal pay for wage-earning women.   The Granger Collection, New York.

thousands of African Americans flocked to the polls across the South, in an atmosphere of collective pride and celebration.

Woman Suffrage Denied

Northern women had played key roles in the antislavery movement and Union victory. Women's rights leaders, who had campaigned for women's voting rights since the Seneca Falls convention of 1848, fervently hoped that Reconstruction would bring votes for women as well as for black men. As Elizabeth Cady Stanton put it, women could "avail ourselves of the strong arm and the blue uniform of the black soldier to walk in by his side." The addition of a single word in the Fifteenth Amendment would have done it: The protected categories for voting could have read "race, color, *sex*, or

previous condition of servitude." But that word proved impossible to obtain. For the authors of Reconstruction, enfranchising black men had clear benefits. It punished ex-Confederates and ensured Republican support in the South. But a substantial majority of northern voters—all men, of course—opposed women's enfranchisement. Even Radicals feared that this "side issue" would defeat the Fourteenth Amendment and overburden the party's program.

At the May 1869 convention of the Equal Rights Association, black abolitionist and women's rights advocate Frederick Douglass pleaded for white women to understand the plight in which former slaves found themselves, and to allow black male suffrage to take priority. "When women, because they are women, are hunted down, . . . dragged from their homes and hung upon lamp posts, . . . then they will have an urgency to

OUT IN THE COLD.

"Out in the Cold"

Though many women, including African American activists in the South, went to the polls in the early 1870s to test whether the new Fourteenth Amendment had given them the vote, federal courts subsequently rejected women's voting rights. Only the Wyoming and Utah territories fully enfranchised women. At the same time, revised naturalization laws allowed immigrant men of African descent—though not of Asian descent—to become citizens. With its crude Irish, African, and Chinese racial caricatures, this 1884 cartoon from the humor magazine *The Judge* echoes the arguments of some white suffragists that though men of races stereotyped as inferior had been enfranchised, white women were not. The woman knocking on the door is also a caricature, with her harsh appearance and masculine style of dress.   Library of Congress.

obtain the ballot equal to our own." Some women's rights leaders joined Douglass in backing the Fifteenth Amendment, even without the word *sex*. But most white women in the audience rebelled. One African American woman remarked that they "all go for sex, letting race occupy a minor position." In her despair, Elizabeth Cady Stanton lashed out against "Patrick and Sambo and Hans and Ung Tung," maligning uneducated freedmen and immigrants who could vote while educated white women could not. Douglass's resolution in support of the Fifteenth Amendment failed, and the convention broke up in bitterness.

At this searing moment, a rift opened in the women's movement. The majority, led by Lucy Stone and Julia Ward Howe, reconciled themselves to disappointment. Organized into the American Woman Suffrage Association, they remained loyal to the Republican Party in hopes that once Reconstruction had been settled, it would be women's turn. A group led by Elizabeth Cady Stanton and Susan B. Anthony struck out in a new direction. They saw that the moment of radical innovation had passed and woman suffrage was unlikely in the near future. Stanton declared that woman "must not put her trust in man." The new organization that she headed, the National Woman Suffrage Association (NWSA) focused exclusively on women's rights and took up the battle for a federal suffrage amendment.

In 1873, NWSA members decided to test the limits of the new constitutional amendments. Suffragists all over the United States, including some African American women in the South, tried to register and vote. Most were turned away. In Rochester, New York, Susan B. Anthony cast a straight Republican ballot and was arrested afterward in her home, by a polite and rather embarrassed U.S. marshal. In one of a series of ensuing lawsuits, suffrage advocate Virginia Minor of Missouri argued that the registrar who rejected her had violated her rights under the Fourteenth Amendment. In *Minor v. Happersett* (1875), the Supreme Court dashed suffragists' hopes. It ruled that suffrage rights were not inherent in citizenship; women were citizens, but state legislatures could deny women the ballot if they wished.

Despite these defeats, radical Reconstruction created the conditions for a high-profile, nationwide movement for women's voting rights. Amid debates over the Fourteenth and Fifteenth Amendments, some Americans argued for the measure as part of a bold expansion of democracy. Others saw white women's votes as a possible counterweight to the votes of African American or Chinese men (while opponents pointed out that black and immigrant women would likely be enfranchised, too). When Wyoming Territory gave women the vote in 1869, its governor received telegrams of congratulation from as far away as Europe. Afterward, contrary to antisuffragist warnings, female voters in Wyoming did not appear to neglect their homes, abandon their children, or otherwise "unsex" themselves. In fact, suffragists argued that women's presence helped make

Wyoming politics less corrupt and more respectable. The goal of votes for women could no longer be dismissed as the absurd notion of a tiny minority. It became a serious issue for national debate.

- **How did Lincoln and Johnson each approach Reconstruction?**

- **Over what issues did Johnson and Congress clash? What measures and policies emerged from that conflict?**

- **What did the supporters of radical Reconstruction do to advance their vision for the postwar South?**

- **How did Reconstruction affect the movement for women's voting rights?**

The Meaning of Freedom

While political leaders in Washington struggled over Reconstruction, emancipated slaves acted on their own ideas about freedom (see Comparing American Voices, "Freedom," pp. 474–475). Freedom meant many things—the end of punishment by the lash; the ability to move around; the reunion of families; and the opportunity to build schools and churches, and publish and read newspapers. Topmost among freedmen's demands was the right to vote. To achieve a true measure of freedom, former slaves had to overcome both the hostility of former Confederates and the ambivalence of many Unionist allies.

The Quest for Land

One of freedmen's most pressing goals was landownership. In the chaotic final months of war, freedmen had seized control of plantations where they could. In Georgia and South Carolina, General William Tecumseh Sherman had reserved large coastal tracts for liberated slaves and settled them on forty-acre plots. Sherman simply did not want to be bothered with refugees as his army crossed the region, but the freedmen assumed that Sherman's order meant that the land was theirs. After the war, resettlement became the responsibility of the Freedmen's Bureau. Thousands of rural blacks hoped for land distributions. "I have gone through the country," reported a black spokesman in South Carolina, "and on every side I was besieged with questions: How are we to get homesteads, to get lands?"

Johnson's amnesty plan, enabling pardoned Confederates to recover property seized during the war, blasted freedmen's hopes. In October 1865, Johnson ordered General Oliver O. Howard, head of the Freedmen's Bureau, to restore plantations on the Sea Islands off the South Carolina coast to their white owners. Dispossessed blacks protested: "Why do you take away our lands? You take them from us who have always been true, always true to the Government! You give them to our all-time enemies! That is not right!" Former slaves resisted efforts to evict them. Led by black Union veterans, they fought pitched battles with plantation owners and bands of ex-Confederate soldiers. But white landowners, sometimes aided by federal troops, generally prevailed.

Freed Slaves and Northerners: Conflicting Goals | The problem of land was broader than Johnson's policies or even ex-Confederate resistance. A profound gap lay between the goals of freed slaves and those of Republicans in Washington. The economic revolution of the antebellum period had transformed New England and the Mid-Atlantic states. Most congressional leaders believed, following in the tradition of antebellum Whigs, that once slavery was dead, the same kind of economic development would revolutionize the South. Republicans sought to restore cotton as the country's leading export. They envisioned former slaves as wageworkers on cash-crop plantations, not as independent farmers. Only a handful of radicals, like Thaddeus Stevens, argued that freed slaves had already *earned* a right to the land, through what Lincoln once referred to as "four hundred years of unrequited toil." Stevens proposed that large southern plantations be treated as "forfeited estates of the enemy" and broken up into small farms for the former slaves.

Today, most historians of Reconstruction agree with Stevens: Policymakers did not go far enough to ensure freedpeople's economic welfare. Left without land, former slaves were rendered poor and vulnerable. At the time, however, men like Stevens had few allies. Though often accused of harshness toward the defeated Confederacy, most Republicans—even Radicals—recoiled at the idea of confiscating private land. They could not imagine "giving" land to former slaves. The same congressmen, of course, had no difficulty giving homesteaders land on the frontier that had been taken from Indians. But Republicans were deeply reluctant to confiscate white-owned plantations. Some southern Republican state governments did try, without much success, to use tax policy to break up large landholdings and get them into the hands of poorer whites and blacks. In 1869, South Carolina established a land commission to buy property and resell it on easy terms to the landless; about 14,000 black families acquired farms through

Wage Labor of Former Slaves

This photograph, taken in South Carolina shortly after the Civil War, shows former slaves leaving the cotton fields. Many freedpeople were organized into work crews probably not that different from earlier slave gangs, although they now labored for wages. Freedmen resisted such working conditions and sought greater freedom from constant threats and oversight.   © Collection of the New-York Historical Society.

the program. But such initiatives were the exception, not the rule.

Wage Labor and Sharecropping Freedmen and freedwomen wanted as much independence of work and life as they could achieve. Obtaining no land, however, most began with few options but to work for former slave owners. Serious conflict ensued. Landowners wanted to retain the old **gang-labor system**, with wages replacing the food, clothing, and shelter that slaves had once received. Southern planters—who had recently scorned the North for the cruelties of the wage-labor system—now embraced waged work with apparent satisfaction. Maliciously comparing freedpeople to free-roaming pigs, landowners told them to "root, hog, or die." Former slaves found themselves with rock-bottom wages, especially in agriculture; it was a shock to find that Emancipation and a "free labor" system did not prevent a hardworking family from nearly starving. African American workers used a variety of tactics to fight back. Some left the fields and traveled long distances to seek work on the railroads or in turpentine and lumber camps. Others organized to bargain for fairer wages. Not only black farmworkers but also factory workers and laundrywomen went on strike.

At the same time, a major conflict raged between employers and freedpeople over the labor of women. In slavery, African American women's bodies had been the sexual property of white men. Protecting black women from such abuse, as much as possible, was a crucial priority for freedpeople. When planters demanded that black women go back into the fields, African Americans resisted resolutely. "I seen on some plantations," one freedman recounted, "where the white men would . . . tell colored men that their wives and children could not live on their places unless they work in the fields. The colored men [answered that] whenever they wanted their wives to work they would tell them themselves."

There was a profound irony in this man's definition of freedom: It designated a wife's labor as her husband's property. In that, of course, freedpeople were adapting to white norms. Some black women asserted their independence and headed their own households—though in a society utterly disrupted by war, this was often a matter of necessity rather than choice. For many freedwomen and freedmen, the opportunity for a stable family life was one of the greatest achievements of emancipation. Many enthusiastically accepted the northern ideal of **domesticity**. Missionaries, teachers, and editors of black newspapers urged men to work diligently and support their families, and women (though many worked for wages) to devote themselves to motherhood and the home. Like their northern allies, many southern African Americans believed domesticity was the key to civilization and progress.

Thus I have given you, I think, the Substance of the Arguments o both sides of that great and important Questic

Freedom

Slavery meant one thing to slave owners, something altogether different to slaves. When freedom came, there was no bridging this bottomless gulf. The following documents offer vivid testimony to the bitter legacy of slavery.

Henry William Ravenel
Diary Entry, March 8, 1865

Henry William Ravenel was from a (formerly) wealthy plantation family; his diary was written amid the Confederacy's collapse and the aftermath of defeat in South Carolina.

The breath of Emancipation has passed over the country, & we are now in that transition state between the new & the old systems—a state of chaos & disorder. Will the negro be materially benefitted by the change? Will the condition of the country in its productive resources, in material prosperity be improved? Will it be a benefit to the landed proprietors? These are questions which will have their solution in the future. They are in the hands of that Providence which over-ruleth all things for good. It was a strong conviction of my best judgment that the old relation of master & slave, had received the divine sanction & was the best condition in which the two races could live together for mutual benefit. There were many defects to be corrected & many abuses to be remedied. Among these defects I will enumerate the want of legislation to make the marriage contract binding—to prevent the separation of families, & to restrain the cupidity of cruel masters. Perhaps it is for neglecting these obligations that God has seen fit to dissolve that relation. I believe the negro must remain in this country & that his condition although a freed-man, must be to labour on the soil. Nothing but necessity will compel him to labour. Now the question is, will that necessity be so strong as to compel him to labour, which will be profitable to the landed proprietors? Will he make as much cotton, sugar, rice & tobacco for the world as he did previously? They will now have a choice *where* to labour. This will ensure good treatment & the best terms. The most humane, the most energetic & the most judicious managers have the best chances in the race for success. I expect to see a revolution in the ownership of landed estates. Those only can succeed who bring the best capacity for the business. Time will show.

Source: *The Civil War and Reconstruction: A Documentary Collection*, ed. William E. Gienapp (New York: W. W. Norton, 2001), 304–05.

Edward Barnell Heyward
Letter, January 22, 1866

This letter is from the son of a South Carolina plantation owner to a friend in the North. Perhaps most telling, in this letter, is Heyward's despair over the future of his former slaves. He believes that, after emancipation, "their best days are over."

My dear Jim

Your letter of date July 1865, has just reached me and you will be relieved by my answers, to find that I am still alive, and extremely glad to hear from you. . . . I have served in the Army, my brother died in the Army, and every family has lost members. No one can know how reduced we are, particularly the refined & educated. . . .

My father had five plantations on the coast, and all the buildings were burnt, and the negroes, now left to themselves, are roaming in a starvation condition . . . like lost sheep, with no one to care for them.

They find the Yankee only a speculator, and they have no confidence in anyone. They very naturally, poor things, think that freedom means doing nothing, and this they are determined to do. They look to the government, to take care of them, and it will be many years, before this once productive country will be able to support itself. The former kind and just treatment of the slaves, and their docile and generous temper, make them now disposed to be [quiet] and obedient: but the determination of your Northern people to give them a place in the councils of the Country and make them the equal of the white man, will at last, bear its fruit, and we may *then* expect them, to rise against the whites, and in the end, be exterminated themselves.

I am now interested in a school for the negroes, who are around me, and will endeavor to do my duty, to them, as ever before, but I am afraid their best days are past. . . .

I feel now that I have *no country*, I *obey* like a subject, but I cannot love such a government. Perhaps the next letter, you get from me, will be from England. . . .

Source: Stanley I. Kutler, ed., *Looking for America: The People's History*, 2nd ed., 2 vols. (New York: W. W. Norton, 1979), 2: 4–6.

Isabella Soustan
Letter, July 10, 1865

Isabella Soustan, a freedwoman in Virginia, wrote this letter to her former master not long after the Civil War's end.

I have the honor to appeal to you one more for assistance, Master. I am cramped hear nearly to death and no one ceares for me heare, and I want you if you please Sir, to Send for me. I dont care if I am free. I had rather live with you. I was as free while with you, as I wanted to be. Mas Man you know I was as well Satisfied with you as I wanted to be. Now Affectionate Master pleas, oh, please come or Sind for me. John is still hired out at the same and doing Well and well Satisfied only greaveing about home, he want to go home as bad as I do, if you ever Send for me I will Send for him immediately, and take him home to his kind Master. Mas Man. Pleas to give my love to all of my friends, and especially to my young mistress don't forget to reserve a double portion for yourself. I Will close at present, hoping to bee at your Service Soon yes before yonder Sun Shal rise and set any more.

May I subscribe myself your Most affectionate humble friend and Servt.
Isabella A. Soustan

Source: Leon F. Litwack, *Been in the Storm So Long: The Aftermath of Slavery* (New York: Knopf, 1979), 332.

Jourdon Anderson
Letter, August 7, 1865

Anderson had escaped with his family from Tennessee and settled in Dayton, Ohio. He dictated this letter, which then was printed in the *New York Daily Tribune*. Folklorists have recorded the ways that slaves found, even in bondage, for "puttin' down" their masters. But only in freedom — and in a northern state — could Anderson's sarcasm be expressed so openly.

To My Old Master, Colonel P. H. Anderson, Big Spring, Tennessee.

Sir:
I got your letter, and was glad to find that you had not forgotten Jourdon.... I thought the Yankees would have hung you long before this, for harboring Rebs....

I want to know particularly what the good chance is you propose to give me. I am doing tolerably well here. I get twenty-five dollars a month, with victuals and clothing; have a comfortable home for Mandy, — the folks here call her Mrs. Anderson, — and the children — Milly, Jane, and Grundy — go to school and are learning well....

Mandy says she would be afraid to go back without some proof that you were disposed to treat us justly and kindly; and we have concluded to test your sincerity by asking you to send us our wages for the time we served you. This will make us forget and forgive old scores, and rely on your justice and friendship in the future. I served you faithfully for thirty-two years, and Mandy twenty years. At twenty-five dollars a month for me and two dollars a week for Mandy, our earnings would amount to eleven thousand six hundred and eighty dollars. Add to this the interest for the time our wages have been kept back, and deduct what you paid for our clothing, and three doctor's visits to me, and pulling a tooth for Mandy, and the balance will show what we are in justice entitled to. Please send the balance by Adams Express, in care of V. Winters, esq., Dayton, Ohio. If you do not pay us for faithful labors in the past we can have little faith in your promises in the future....

In answering this letter, please state if there would be any safety for my Milly and Jane, who are now grown up, and both good-looking girls.... I would rather stay here and starve — and die, if it come to that — than have my girls brought to shame by the violence and wickedness of their young masters. You will also please state if there has been any schools opened for the colored children in your neighborhood. The great desire of my life now is to give my children an education, and have them form virtuous habits.

From your old servant,
Jourdon Anderson

P.S. Say howdy to George Carter, and thank him for taking the pistol from you when you were shooting at me.

Source: Leon F. Litwack, *Been in the Storm So Long: The Aftermath of Slavery* (New York: Knopf, 1979), 333–335.

ANALYZING THE EVIDENCE

- What were Ravenel's and Heyward's attitudes toward freedmen and freedwomen? How did their views differ, and on what points did they agree?

- What predictions do Ravenel and Heyward make about the South's postwar future? How might their expectations have shaped their own actions?

- Soustan and Anderson are both writing to men who formerly claimed them as property. How do you account for the differences in their approach and tone? What conditions of life does each writer mention? What conclusions might be drawn from this about the varied postwar experiences of freedpeople?

Even in rural areas, former slaves refused to work under the conditions of slavery. There would be no gang work, they vowed: no overseers, no whippings, no regulation of their private lives. All across the South, planters who needed labor were forced to yield to what one planter termed "the inveterate prejudices of the freedmen, who desire to be masters of their own time." In a few areas, waged work became the norm—for example, on the giant sugar plantations of Louisiana financed by northern capital. But cotton planters lacked the money to pay wages, and sometimes, in lieu of a straight wage, they offered a share of the crop. Freedmen, in turn, paid their rent in shares of the harvest.

Thus sprang up the distinctive laboring system of cotton agriculture known as **sharecropping**, in which freedmen worked as renters, exchanging their labor for the use of land, house, implements, and sometimes seed and fertilizer. Sharecroppers typically turned over half of their crops to the landlord (Map 15.2). In a credit-starved agricultural region that grew crops for a world economy, sharecropping was an effective strategy, through which laborers and landowners shared risks and returns. But it was a very unequal relationship, given sharecroppers' dire economic circumstances. Starting out penniless, they had no way of making it through the first growing season without borrowing for food and supplies.

Country storekeepers stepped in. Bankrolled by northern suppliers, they furnished the sharecropper with provisions and took as collateral a **lien** on the crop, effectively assuming ownership of the cropper's share and leaving him only the proceeds that remained after

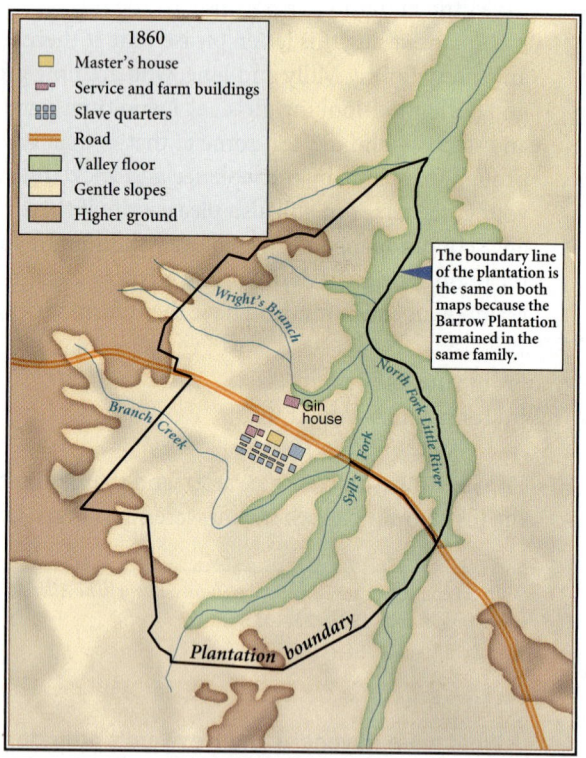
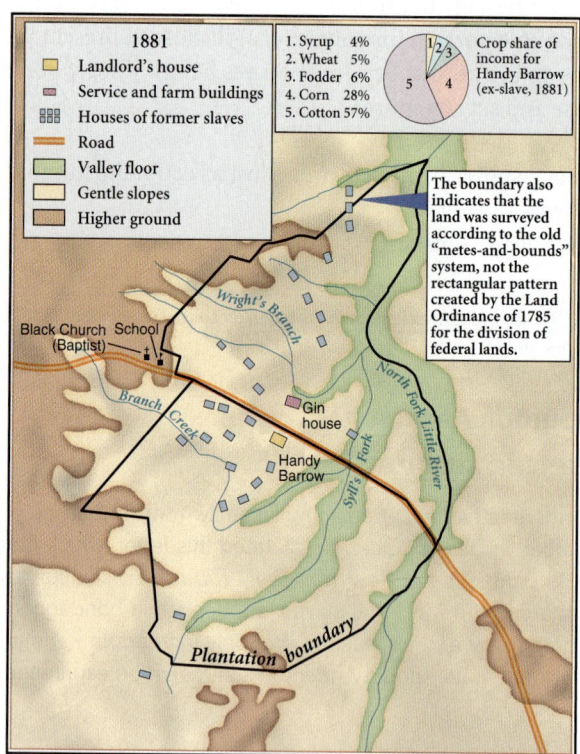

MAP 15.2

The Barrow Plantation, 1860 and 1881

This map is a modern redrawing of one that first appeared in the popular magazine *Scribner's Monthly* in April 1881, accompanying an article about the Barrow plantation. The boundary line is the same on both maps because the plantation remained in the same family. Comparing the 1860 map of this central Georgia plantation with the 1881 map reveals the impact of sharecropping on patterns of black residence. In 1860, the slave quarters were clustered near the planter's house. In contrast, by 1881 the sharecroppers were scattered across the plantation's 2,000 acres, having built cabins on the ridges between the low-lying streams. The surname Barrow was common among the sharecropping families, which means almost certainly that they had been slaves who, years after emancipation, still had not moved on. For sharecroppers, freedom meant not only their individual lots and cabins but also the school and church shown on the map.

Cotton Farmers, Marietta, Georgia, c. 1880

Before the Civil War, the South had proudly called itself the "Cotton Kingdom": After the war, cotton was still king, but few southerners got rich on cotton profits. Instead, thousands of small-scale farmers, white and black, struggled with plunging crop prices, debt, and taxes on land to support an array of ambitious Reconstruction programs. The farmers here have baled their cotton for market and pose with their wagons in Marietta's courthouse square. Courtesy Georgia Department of Archives, Vanishing Georgia Collection, cob262.

his debts had been paid. Once indebted at one store, sharecroppers could no longer shop around. They became easy targets for exorbitant prices, unfair interest rates, and crooked bookkeeping. As cotton prices declined during the 1870s, more and more sharecroppers failed to settle accounts and fell into permanent debt. If the merchant was also the landowner or conspired with the landowner, the debt became a pretext for forced labor, or **peonage**, though when things became hopeless, sharecroppers sometimes managed to pull up stakes and move on.

Sharecropping—a product of the struggles of Reconstruction—endured in part because it was a good fit for cotton agriculture. Cotton, unlike sugarcane, could be raised efficiently by small farmers (provided they had the lash of indebtedness always on their backs). We can see this in the experience of other countries that became major producers in response to the global cotton famine set off by the Civil War. In India, Egypt, Brazil, and West Africa, variants of the sharecropping system emerged. Most striking was the adoption everywhere of crop-lien laws, at the behest of international merchants and bankers who put up the capital. Indian and Egyptian villagers got the advances they needed to shift from subsistence agriculture to cotton but at the price of being placed, as in America, perma-

nently under the thumb of furnishing merchants. American planters resisted sharecropping at first because they started at a different place: not traditional, subsistence economies that had to be converted to cotton but a proven plantation system over which they had been absolute masters.

For freedmen, sharecropping was not the worst choice, in a world where former masters threatened to impose labor conditions that were close to slavery (see Reading American Pictures, "Why Sharecropping?" p. 478). But for southern agriculture, the costs were devastating. With farms leased on a year-to-year basis, neither tenant nor owner had much incentive to improve the property. The crop-lien system rested on expensive interest payments—money that might otherwise have gone into agricultural improvements. And sharecropping committed the South inflexibly to cotton, which as a market crop generated the cash required by landlords and furnishing merchants. The result was a stagnant farm economy that blighted the South's future. As Republican governments tried to remake the South, they faced not only the challenges of wartime destruction and widespread poverty but also the failure of their hopes that free labor would create a modern, prosperous South, built in the image of the industrializing North. Instead, a rural economy emerged that remained

Why Sharecropping?

The account of sharecropping on the neighboring pages describes the experience of hundreds of thousands of ex-slaves and plantation owners. How do we know that our generalizations are true? Or, more concretely, that a sharecropper reading our account might nod and say, "Yes, that's the way it was"? One sliver of evidence is this photograph of a family of freedpeople standing proudly by their new cabin and young cotton crop. In what ways does this contemporary photograph confirm or amplify our account of sharecropping?

Sharecroppers in Georgia. Brown Brothers.

ANALYZING THE EVIDENCE

- The cotton rows go right up to the house. Why might this family not have land set aside for a garden and livestock? What does this suggest about the historians' claim that sharecropping doomed the South to a cash-crop monoculture?

- Note the gent in the background—most likely the landowner—with his handsome horse and carriage. The tenant farmers and children in the foreground look directly at the photographer, yet this man chooses to remain in the background and look straight ahead. Presuming that this man is the landowner, which seems likely, he has probably rented out the cabins and farmland to these tenants but still has the run of the place. What does his presence suggest about the limits of sharecropping as a means of freedpeople achieving independence?

- In the struggle for economic independence, everything was relative. What elements in the photograph suggest that, compared to the lives they knew as slaves or, after emancipation would have faced as day laborers, these farmers might have thought they were not faring so badly? Consult Map 15.2 on page 476 while considering your answer (bearing in mind of course that the family in this photograph did not live on the Barrow plantation).

mired in widespread poverty and based on an uneasy compromise between landowners and laborers.

Republican Governments in the South

Between 1868 and 1871, all the former Confederate states met congressional stipulations and rejoined the Union. Protected by federal troops, Republican administrations in these states retained power for periods ranging from a few months in Virginia to nine years in South Carolina, Louisiana, and Florida. These governments remain some of the most misunderstood institutions in all U.S. history. Ex-Confederates never accepted their legitimacy. Many contemporaries agreed, focusing particularly on the role of African American Republicans who began to serve in public office. "It is strange, abnormal, and unfit," declared one British visitor to Louisiana, "that a *negro* Legislature should deal . . . with the gravest commercial and financial interests."

During much of the twentieth century, historians echoed such critics, condemning Reconstruction leaders as ignorant and corrupt. These historians shared, at root, the racist assumptions of the British observer: Blacks were simply unfit to legislate. (In the early twentieth century, U.S. historians lived in a country that once again elected, year after year, an all-white Congress; the prospect of a nonwhite president was completely unthinkable.) In fact, Reconstruction governments were ambitious. They were hated, in part, because they undertook impressive reforms in public education, family law, social services, commerce, and transportation. Like their northern allies, southern Republicans admired the economic and social transformations that had occurred in the North before the Civil War, and during Reconstruction they worked energetically to import them.

The southern Republican Party included former Whigs, a few former Democrats, black and white newcomers from the North, and southern African Americans. From the start its leaders faced the dilemma of racial prejudice. In the upcountry, white Unionists were eager to join the party. But in most areas the Republicans also needed African American voters, who constituted a majority of registered voters in Alabama, Florida, South Carolina, and Mississippi.

For a brief moment in the late 1860s, black and white Republicans joined forces through the Union League, a secret fraternal order. Formed in border states and northern cities during the Civil War, the Union League became a powerful political club that spread through the former Confederacy. Functioning as a grassroots wing of Radical Republicanism, league members pressured Congress to uphold justice to freedmen. After blacks won voting rights, the Union League organized meetings at churches and schoolhouses to instruct freedmen on political issues and voting procedures. League clubs also held parades and military drills, giving a public face to the new political order.

The Freedmen's Bureau also supported grassroots Reconstruction efforts. Though some bureau officials were hostile to freedmen and sympathized with planters' interests, most were dedicated, often idealistic men who tried valiantly to reconcile opposing interests. Bureau men kept a sharp eye out for unfair labor contracts and often forced landowners to bargain with workers and tenants. Bureau leaders advised freedmen

Hiram R. Revels

In 1870, Hiram R. Revels (1827–1901) was elected to the U.S. Senate from Mississippi to fill Jefferson Davis's former seat. Revels was a free black from North Carolina who had moved to the North and attended Knox College in Illinois. During the Civil War he had recruited African Americans for the Union army and, as an ordained Methodist minister, served as chaplain of a black regiment in Mississippi, where he settled after the war.   The Granger Collection, New York.

Fisk Jubilee Singers, 1873

Fisk University in Nashville, Tennessee, was established in 1865 to provide higher education for African Americans from all across the South. When university funds ran short in 1871, the Jubilee Singers choral group was formed and began touring to raise money for the school. They performed African American spirituals and folksongs, such as "Swing Low, Sweet Chariot," arranged in ways that appealed to white audiences, making this music nationally popular for the first time. In 1872 the group performed for President Grant at the White House. Money raised by this acclaimed chorale saved Fisk from bankruptcy. Edmund Havel's portrait of the group was painted during their first European tour.   Fisk University Art Galleries.

on economic matters; provided direct payments to desperate families, especially women and children; and helped establish freedpeople's schools. In cooperation with northern aid societies, the bureau played a key role in founding African American colleges and universities such as Fisk, Tougaloo, and the Hampton Institute. These institutions, in turn, focused first on training teachers. By 1869 there were more than three thousand teachers instructing freedpeople in the South. More than half were themselves black.

Ex-Confederates viewed the Union League, Freedmen's Bureau, and Republican Party as illegitimate forces in southern affairs, and they bitterly resented the political education of freedpeople. They referred to southern whites who supported Reconstruction as **scalawags**—an ancient Scots-Irish term for worthless animals—and they denounced northern whites as **carpetbaggers**, self-seeking interlopers who carried

all their property in cheap suitcases called carpetbags. Such labels glossed over the actual diversity of white Republicans. Many new arrivals from the North, while motivated by personal profit, also brought capital and skills. Interspersed with ambitious schemers were idealists hoping to advance the cause of freedmen's rights. The so-called scalawags were even more varied. Some were former slave owners; others were ex-Whigs or even ex-Democrats drawn to Republicanism as the best way to attract northern capital. But most hailed from the backcountry and wanted to rid the South of its slaveholding aristocracy. They had generally fought against, or at least refused to support, the Confederacy, believing that slavery had victimized whites as well as blacks.

Southern Democrats' contempt for black leaders, whom they regarded as ignorant field hands, was just as misguided as their stereotypes about white Republicans. The first African American leaders in the South

Outside the Freedmen's Bureau Office, Beaufort, South Carolina

This photograph, taken in the 1870s, shows how offices of the Freedmen's Bureau became hubs of activity in southern cities and towns. Southerners, both black and white, gathered at the offices to sign contracts, resolve labor disputes, obtain official advice — even get married and mediate family conflicts. Bureau officials, whose numbers were pitifully small in comparison with the scope and number of their duties, had limited resources to address postwar devastation and the arrival of "free labor." Nonetheless, in the power vacuum of the ex-Confederacy, many bureau officials played a central role in restoring order and upholding justice.   Miriam and Ira D. Wallach Division of Art, Prints and Photographs, The New York Public Library. Astor, Lenox and Tilden Foundations.

came from the ranks of antebellum free blacks. They were joined by northern blacks who moved south to support Reconstruction. Many were Union veterans; some were employees of the Freedmen's Bureau and northern missionary societies. Others had escaped from slavery and were returning home. One of these ex-slaves was Blanche K. Bruce, who had been tutored on a Virginia plantation by his white father. During the war, Bruce escaped and established a school for freedmen in Missouri. In 1869, he moved to Mississippi and became active in politics; in 1874, he became Mississippi's second black U.S. senator.

During radical Reconstruction, African American speakers, some financed by the Republican Party, fanned out into the old plantation districts and recruited former slaves to participate in politics. Still, few of the new leaders were field hands; most had been preachers or artisans. Literacy helped freedman Thomas Allen, a Baptist minister and shoemaker, win election to the Georgia legislature. "In my county," Allen recalled, "the colored people came to me for instructions, and I gave them the best instructions I could. I took the *New York Tribune* and other papers, and in that way I found out a great deal, and I told them whatever I thought was right." Though never proportionate to their numbers in the population, blacks became officeholders across the South. In South Carolina, African Americans constituted a majority in the lower house of the legislature

Freedmen's School, Petersburg, Virginia, 1870s

A Union veteran, returning to Virginia in the 1870s to photograph battlefields, captured this image of an African American teacher and her students at a freedmen's school. Note the difficult conditions in which they study: Many are barefoot, and there are gaps in the walls and floor of the school building. Nonetheless, the students have a few books. Despite poverty and relentless hostility from many whites, freedpeople across the South were determined to get a basic education for themselves and their children. William L. Clements Library, University of Michigan.

in 1868. Over the course of Reconstruction, twenty African Americans served in state administrations as governor, lieutenant governor, secretary of state, or lesser offices. More than six hundred served as state legislators and sixteen as congressmen.

Southern Republicans had big plans. Their Reconstruction governments eliminated property qualifications for the vote and abolished the Black Codes that hemmed in freedpeople. Their new state constitutions expanded the rights of married women, enabling them to hold property and wages independent of their husbands'—"a wonderful reform," one white woman in Georgia wrote, for "the cause of Women's Rights." Like their counterparts in the North, southern Republicans also believed in using government to foster economic growth. They sought to diversify the economy beyond cotton agriculture, and they poured money into railroads and other building projects to expand the region's shattered economy.

In myriad ways, Republicans brought southern state and city governments up to date. They outlawed corporal punishments such as whipping and branding. They established more humane penitentiaries as well as hospitals and asylums for orphans and the disabled. South Carolina offered free public health services, while Alabama provided free legal representation for defendants who could not pay. Some municipal governments paved the streets and installed streetlights. Petersburg, Virginia, established a board of health that offered free medical care during the smallpox epidemic of 1873. Nashville, Tennessee, created soup kitchens for the poor.

Most impressive of all were achievements in public education, where the South had lagged woefully. Republicans viewed education as the foundation of a true democratic order. By 1875, over half of black children were attending school in Mississippi, Florida, and South Carolina. African Americans of all ages rushed to the newly established schools, even when they had to pay tuition. They understood why slaveholders had criminalized slave literacy: The practice of freedom rested on the ability to read newspapers, labor contracts, history books, and the Bible. A school official in Virginia reported that freedpeople were "*crazy to learn.*" One Louisiana man explained why he was sending his children to school, even though he needed their help in the field. It was "better than leaving them a fortune; because if you left them even five hundred dollars, some man having more education than they had would come along and cheat them out of it all." Meanwhile, thousands of white children, particularly girls and the sons of poor farmers and laborers, also benefited from the new public education system. Young white women's graduation from high school, an unheard of occurrence before the Civil War, became accepted and even celebrated in southern cities and towns.

Building Black Communities

In slavery days, African Americans had built networks of religious worship and mutual aid to sustain one another, but these operated largely underground. After emancipation, southern blacks could engage in open community building. In doing so, they cooperated with northern missionaries and teachers who came to help in the great work of freedom. "Ignorant though they may be, on account of long years of oppression, they exhibit a desire to hear and to learn, that I never imagined," reported African American minister Reverend James Lynch, who had traveled from Maryland to the Deep South. "Every word you say while preaching, they drink down and respond to, with an earnestness that sets your heart all on fire."

Independent churches quickly became central institutions of black life, as blacks across the South left white-dominated congregations, where they had sat in segregated balconies, and built churches of their own. These churches joined their counterparts in the North to become national denominations, including, most prominently, the National Baptist Convention and the African Methodist Episcopal Church. Everywhere, black churches served not only as sites of worship but also as schools, social centers, and meeting halls. Black ministers were community leaders and often political spokesmen as well. As Charles H. Pearce, a Methodist minister in Florida, declared, "A man in this State cannot do his whole duty as a minister except he looks out for the political interests of his people." Calling forth the special destiny of formerly enslaved southerners as the new "Children of Israel," black ministers provided a powerful religious underpinning for the politics of their congregations.

The flowering of southern black churches, schools, newspapers, and civic groups was one of the most enduring initiatives of the Reconstruction era. Dedicated teachers and charity leaders embarked on a project of "race uplift" that never ceased thereafter, while black entrepreneurs were proud to build businesses that served their own communities. The issue of **desegregation**—sharing public facilities with whites—was a trickier one. Some black leaders pressed for desegregated public facilities, but they were keenly aware of the backlash this was likely to provoke. Many freedpeople made it clear that they preferred their children to attend all-black schools, especially if they had encountered hostile or condescending white teachers. Others had pragmatic concerns. Asked whether she wanted her boys to attend an integrated school, one woman in New Orleans said no: "I don't want my children to be pounded by dem white boys. I don't send them to school to fight, I send them to learn."

At the national level, congressmen wrestled with similar issues as they debated an ambitious civil rights bill championed by Radical Republican senator Charles Sumner. Sumner first introduced his bill in 1870, seeking to enforce, among other things, equal access to schools, public transportation, hotels, and churches. Through a series of defeats and delays, the bill remained on Capitol Hill for five years. Opponents charged that shared use of public spaces would lead to race mixing and intermarriage. Some sympathetic Republicans feared a backlash, while others questioned whether, because of the First Amendment, the federal government had the right to regulate churches. On his deathbed in 1874, Sumner exhorted a visitor to remember the civil rights bill: "Don't let it fail." In the end, the Senate removed Sumner's provision for integrated churches, and the House removed the clause requiring integrated schools. But to honor the great Massachusetts abolitionist, Congress passed the Civil Rights Act of 1875. The law required "full and equal" access to jury service and to transportation and public accommodations, irrespective of race. It was the last such act for almost a hundred years—until the Civil Rights Act of 1964.

- In what ways did the freedmen's goal of landownership clash with the goals of northern Republicans and of southerners? What were the results of that clash?

- What were the goals of southern Republican governments? In what ways did they succeed in realizing these aims?

- How did black communities develop during Reconstruction? Based on their collective activities, what priorities did they appear to have had in the wake of emancipation?

The Undoing of Reconstruction

Sumner's death marked the waning of radical Reconstruction. Leaders of that movement had accomplished more than anyone dreamed a few years earlier. But a chasm had opened between the goals of freedmen, who wanted autonomy, and policymakers, whose first priorities were to reincorporate ex-Confederates into the nation and build a powerful national economy. Meanwhile, the North was flooded with one-sided, often racist reports such as James M. Pike's *The Prostrate State* (1873), which described South Carolina in the grip of "black barbarism." Events of the 1870s deepened the northern public's disillusionment. Scandals rocked the Grant administration, and a sudden economic depression placed severe restraints on both private investment and public spending. At the same time, northern resolve was worn down by ex-Confederates' continued refusal to accept Reconstruction. Only full-scale military intervention could reverse the situation in the South, and by the mid-1870s the North had no political willpower to renew the occupation. Besieged by economic hardship and ex-Confederate resistance, Reconstruction faltered.

The Republican Unraveling

Republicans who banked on economic growth to underpin their ambitious programs found their hopes dashed by a severe depression that began in 1873. This global downturn affected much of Europe and even touched other parts of the world. In the United States, the initial panic was triggered by the bankruptcy of the Northern Pacific Railroad, backed by leading financier Jay Cooke. Cooke's supervision of Union finances during the Civil War had made him a national hero; his downfall was a shock, and since Cooke was so well connected in Washington, it raised suspicions that Republican financial manipulation had caused the depression. Grant's officials deepened public resentment toward their party when they rejected pleas to increase the money supply and provide relief from debt and unemployment.

The impact of the depression varied in different parts of the United States. But many farmers found themselves in a terrible plight as crop prices plunged, while industrial workers faced layoffs and sharp reductions in pay. Within a year, 50 percent of American iron manufacturing had stopped. By 1877, half the nation's railroad companies had filed for bankruptcy. Rail construction halted. With hundreds of thousands thrown out of work, people took to the road. Wandering "tramps," who camped beside railroad tracks and knocked on doors to beg for work and food, became a source of fear and anxiety for prosperous Americans.

In addition to discrediting Republicans, the depression directly undercut their policies, most dramatically in the South. The ex-Confederacy was still recovering from the ravages of war, and the region's new economic and social order, negotiated in the wake of emancipation, remained fragile. The ambitious policies of southern Republicans—for education, public health, and grants to railroad builders—cost a great deal of money. Federal support, offered through programs like the Freedmen's Bureau, had begun to fade even before 1873. Republicans had banked on major infusions of northern and foreign investment capital into the South; for the most part, these failed to materialize. Investors who had sunk money into Confederate bonds, only to have those repudiated, were especially wary. The South's economy grew more slowly than Republicans had hoped, and when the depression hit, growth screeched to a halt. State debts mounted rapidly, and as crushing interest on bonds fell due, public credit collapsed.

Not only had Republican officials failed to anticipate a severe depression; during the era of generous spending, considerable funds had been wasted or ended up in the pockets of public officials. Corruption was common in an era of railroad building and ambitious public contracts, and some notorious cases in the South rivaled the scandals that would soon be uncovered in Washington, D.C. Two swindlers in North Carolina, one of them a former Union general, were found to have distributed more than $200,000 in bribes and loans to legislators to gain millions in state funds for rail construction. Instead of building railroads, they used the money to travel to Europe and speculate in stocks and bonds. Not only Republicans were on the take. "You are mistaken," wrote one Democrat to a northern friend, "if you suppose that all the evils . . . result from the carpetbaggers and negroes. The Democrats are leagued with them when anything is proposed that promises to pay." Bipartisan or not, such corruption severely damaged the cause of Reconstruction.

One of the depression's most tragic results was the failure of the Freedman's Savings and Trust Company. This private bank, founded in 1865, had worked closely with the Freedmen's Bureau and Union army across the South. Former slaves associated it with the party of Lincoln, and thousands responded to northerners' call for thrift and savings by bringing their small deposits to the nearest branch. Not only African American farmers and entrepreneurs but also churches and charitable groups opened accounts at the bank. But in the early 1870s, the bank's directors sank their money into risky loans and speculative investments. In June 1874, the bank failed.

Some Republicans believed that, because the bank had been so closely associated with the U.S. Army and other federal agencies, Congress had a duty to step in. Even a southern Democratic representative argued that the government was "morally bound to see to it that not a dollar is lost." But in the end, Congress refused to compensate the sixty-one thousand depositors; about half recovered small amounts—averaging $18.51—but the other half received nothing. Abandonment of the bank signaled that the party of Reconstruction was losing its moral leadership.

The Disillusioned Liberals   As a result of both the depression and a backlash against the activist government of the postwar years, a revolt took shape inside the Republican Party. It was led by influential intellectuals, journalists, and businessmen who were **classical liberals**—believers in free trade, smaller government, and limited voting rights. Unable to block Grant's renomination in 1872, these dissidents broke away and formed a new party under the name Liberal Republican. Their candidate was Horace Greeley, longtime publisher of the *New York Tribune* and veteran reformer and abolitionist. The Democrats, still in disarray, also nominated Greeley, notwithstanding his editorial diatribes against them. A poor campaigner, Greeley was assailed so bitterly that, as he said, "I hardly knew whether I was running for the Presidency or the penitentiary."

Grant won re-election overwhelmingly, capturing 56 percent of the popular vote and every electoral vote. Yet the Liberal Republicans had managed to shift the terms of political debate. The agenda they had advanced—civil service reform, smaller government, restricted voting rights, and reconciliation with the South—resonated with Democrats, who were working to reclaim their status as a legitimate national party. Democrats had long been the party of limited government, and the rise of Liberal Republicanism provided an opportunity to revive that message. Liberalism thus crossed party lines, uniting disillusioned Republicans with Democrats who denounced government activism, especially social welfare programs. E. L. Godkin of *The Nation* and other classical liberal editors played key roles in turning northern public opinion against Reconstruction. With unabashed elitism, liberals claimed freedmen were unfit to vote. They denounced universal suffrage, which "can only mean in plain English the government of ignorance and vice."

The second Grant administration gave the liberals plenty of ammunition for their anticorruption guns. The most notorious scandal involved Crédit Mobilier, a sham corporation set up by shareholders in the Union Pacific Railroad to secure government grants at an enormous profit. Organizers of the scheme protected it from federal investigation by providing gifts of Crédit Mobilier stock to powerful members of Congress. Another major scandal involved the Whiskey Ring, a network of liquor distillers and treasury agents who defrauded the government of millions of dollars of excise taxes on whiskey. The ringleader was a Grant appointee, and Grant's private secretary, Orville Babcock, had a hand in the thievery. The others went to prison, but Grant stood by Babcock, possibly perjuring himself to save his secretary from jail. The stench of scandal permeated the White House.

Counterrevolution in the South

While northerners became preoccupied with scandals and the shock of economic depression, ex-Confederates seized the initiative in the South. Most believed (as northern liberals had also begun to argue) that southern Reconstruction governments were illegitimate "regimes." Led by the planters, ex-Confederates staged a massive counterrevolution designed to take back the South.

Insofar as they could win at the ballot box, southern Democrats took that route. They got ex-Confederate voting rights restored and campaigned against "negro rule." But when violence was necessary, southern Democrats used it. Present-day Americans, witnessing violence and political instability in other countries, seldom remember that our own history includes the overthrow of elected governments by paramilitary groups. But this is exactly how Reconstruction ended in many parts of the South. Ex-Confederates organized to terrorize Republicans, especially in districts with large proportions of black voters. Black political leaders were shot, hanged, beaten to death, and in one case even beheaded. Many Republicans, both black and white, went into hiding or fled for their lives. Southern Democrats called this violent process "Redemption."

No one looms larger in this bloody story than Nathan Bedford Forrest, a decorated Confederate general. Born in poverty in 1821, Forrest had scrambled in the booming cotton economy to become a big-time slave trader and Mississippi plantation owner. A fiery champion of secession, Forrest had formed a Tennessee Confederate cavalry regiment, fought bravely at the battle of Shiloh, and won fame as a daring raider. On April 12, 1864, his troopers perpetrated one of the war's worst atrocities, the slaughter of black Union troops at Fort Pillow, Tennessee. Forrest's troops refused to take prisoners, instead shooting down black soldiers as they tried to surrender.

Forrest's determination to uphold white supremacy emerged again after the war's end, altering the course of Reconstruction. William G. Brownlow, elected

Nathan Bedford Forrest in Uniform, c. 1865
Before he became Grand Wizard of the Ku Klux Klan, Forrest had been a celebrated cavalry general in the Confederate army. This photograph shows him in uniform before he was mustered out.   Library of Congress.

as Tennessee's Republican governor in 1865, was a tough man, a former prisoner of the Confederates who was not shy about calling his enemies to account. Ex-Confederates struck back with a campaign of terror, targeting especially Brownlow's black supporters. Amid the mayhem, some ex-Confederates formed the first Ku Klux Klan group in late 1865 or early 1866. As it proliferated across the state, the Klan turned to Forrest, who had been trying, unsuccessfully, to rebuild his prewar fortunes. Late in 1866, at a secret meeting in Nashville, Forrest donned the robes of Grand Wizard. His activities are mostly cloaked in mystery, but there is no mistake about his goals: The Klan would strike blows against the despised Republican government of Tennessee.

In many towns, the Klan became virtually identical to the Democratic Party. In fact, Klan members—including Forrest—dominated Tennessee's delegation to the Democratic national convention of 1868. At home, the Klan unleashed a murderous campaign of terror, and though Governor Brownlow responded resolutely, in the end the Republicans cracked. By March 1869, Brownlow retreated to the U.S. Senate. The Klan spread in the meantime to other states, where its members burned freedmen's schools, beat teachers, murdered

and threatened Republican politicians, and attacked Republican gatherings. By 1870, Democrats had seized power in Georgia and North Carolina and were making headway across the South.

In responding to the Klan between 1869 and 1871, the federal government showed it could still exert power effectively in the South. Determined to end Klan violence, Congress held extensive hearings and passed laws designed to put down the Klan and enforce freedmen's rights under the Fourteenth and Fifteenth Amendments. These so-called Enforcement Laws authorized federal prosecutions, military intervention, and martial law to suppress terrorist activities. The Grant administration made full use of these new powers. In South Carolina, where the Klan became deeply entrenched, U.S. troops occupied nine counties, made hundreds of arrests, and drove as many as 2,000 Klansmen from the state.

This assault on the Klan, while raising the spirits of southern Republicans, also revealed how dependent they were on Washington. The potency of the anti-Klan legislation, a Mississippi Republican wrote, "derived alone from its source" in the federal government. "No such law could be enforced by state authority, the local power being too weak." But northern Republicans were growing disillusioned with Reconstruction, and in the South, prosecuting Klansmen was an uphill battle against all-white juries and unsympathetic federal judges. After 1872, prosecutions began to drop off. In the meantime, Texas fell to the Democrats in 1873 and Alabama and Arkansas in 1874.

As the increasingly divided Republicans debated how to respond, voters in the congressional election of 1874 handed the ruling party one of the most stunning defeats of the entire nineteenth century. Responding particularly to the severe depression that gripped the nation, they defeated almost half of the party's 199 representatives in the House. Democrats, who had held 88 seats, now commanded an overwhelming majority of 182. "The election is not merely a victory but a revolution," exulted one Democratic newspaper in New York.

After 1874, with Democrats in firm control of the House, Republicans who tried to shore up their southern wing had limited options. Bowing to election results, the Grant administration began to reject southern Republicans' appeals for aid. Events in Mississippi showed the results. As state elections neared in 1875, paramilitary groups such as the Red Shirts operated openly. Mississippi's Republican governor, Adelbert Ames, a Union veteran from Maine, appealed to the president for federal troops, but Grant refused. "The whole public are tired out with these annual autumnal outbreaks in the South," complained one Grant official, who went on to tell southern Republicans that they were responsible for their own fate. As Mississippi Republicans faced a rising tide of brutal murders, Governor Ames — realizing that nothing could result but further bloodshed — urged his allies to give up the fight. Brandishing guns and stuffing ballot boxes, Democratic "Redeemers" swept the 1875 elections and took control of Mississippi. Thus, by 1876, Reconstruction was largely over. Republican governments, backed by token U.S. military units, remained in only three southern states: Louisiana, South Carolina, and Florida. Elsewhere, former Confederates and their allies were back in power.

The Supreme Court Rejection of Equal Rights Northern Democrats and so-called Redeemers in the South played decisive roles in ending Reconstruction. But even though, for the moment, Democrats had won control of the House and ex-Confederates had seized power in southern states, new landmark constitutional amendments and federal laws remained in force. If the Supreme Court had left these intact, subsequent generations of civil rights advocates could have used the federal courts to combat discrimination and violence. Instead, the court closed off this avenue for the pursuit of justice and equal rights, just as it had dashed the hopes of women's rights advocates.

As early as 1873, in a group of decisions known collectively as the *Slaughterhouse Cases*, the Court began to undercut the power of the Fourteenth Amendment. In these cases and a related ruling, *U.S. v. Cruikshank* (1876), the justices argued that the Fourteenth Amendment offered only a few, rather trivial federal protections to citizens (such as access to navigable waterways). In *Cruikshank* — a case that emerged from the massacre of African American farmers by ex-Confederates in Colfax, Louisiana, which was followed by a Democratic political coup — the Court ruled that voting rights remained a state prerogative unless the state *itself* violated those rights. So long as the civil rights of former slaves were being violated by individuals or private groups (including the Klan), that was a state responsibility and beyond federal jurisdiction. Therefore, the Fourteenth Amendment did not protect citizens from armed vigilantes, even if those vigilantes seized political power. The Court thus gutted the Fourteenth Amendment. In the *Civil Rights Cases* (1883), the justices also struck down the Civil Rights Act of 1875. The impact of these decisions endured for decades.

The Political Crisis of 1877

After the grim election results of 1874, Republicans faced an uphill battle in the presidential election of 1876. Abandoning Grant, they nominated Rutherford B. Hayes, a former Union general who was untainted by corruption and — even more important — was governor of the key swing state of Ohio. Hayes's Democratic opponent was New York governor Samuel J. Tilden, a Wall Street lawyer with a reform reputation. Tilden favored **home rule** for the South, but so, more discreetly, did Hayes. With enforcement on the wane, Reconstruction did not figure prominently in the campaign, and little was said about the states still ruled by Reconstruction governments: Florida, South Carolina, and Louisiana.

Once returns started coming in on election night, however, those three states began to loom very large. Tilden led in the popular vote and seemed headed for victory until sleepless politicians at Republican headquarters realized that the electoral vote stood at 184 to 165, with the 20 votes from Florida, South Carolina, and Louisiana still uncertain. If Hayes took those votes, he would win by a margin of 1. Republicans still controlled the election process in the three states; citing Democratic fraud and intimidation, they certified Republican victories. The "Redeemer" Democrats who had seized the states sent in their own electoral votes, for Tilden. When Congress met in early 1877, it confronted two sets of electoral votes from those states.

The Constitution does not provide for such a contingency. All it says is that the president of the Senate (in 1877, a Republican) opens the electoral certificates before the House (Democratic) and the Senate (Republican) and that "the Votes shall then be counted" (Article 2, Section 1). Suspense gripped the country. There was talk of inside deals, of a new election, even of a violent coup. Finally, Congress appointed an electoral commission to settle the question. The commission included seven Republicans, seven Democrats, and, as the deciding member, David Davis, a Supreme Court justice not known to have fixed party loyalties. Davis, however, disqualified himself by accepting an Illinois seat in the Senate. He was replaced by Republican justice Joseph P. Bradley, and by a vote of 8 to 7, on party lines, the commission awarded the disputed votes to Hayes.

In the House of Representatives, outraged Democrats vowed to stall the final count of electoral votes so as to prevent Hayes's inauguration on March 4. But in the end, they went along — partly because Tilden himself urged that they do so. Hayes had publicly indicated his desire to offer substantial patronage to the South,

"Grantism"

President Grant was lampooned on both sides of the Atlantic for the problems of his scandal-ridden administration. The British magazine *Puck* shows Grant barely defying gravity to keep himself and his corrupt subordinates aloft and out of jail. To a great extent, however, the hero of the Union Army remained personally popular at home and abroad. The British public welcomed Grant with admiration on his triumphant foreign tour in 1877. Library of Congress.

including federal funds for education, internal improvements, and economic growth. He promised "a complete change of men and policy"—naively hoping, at the same time, that he could count on support from old-line southern Whigs and protect black voting rights. Hayes was inaugurated on schedule. He expressed hope in his inaugural address that the federal government could protect "the interests of both races carefully and equally." But, setting aside the U.S. troops who were serving on border duty in Texas, only 3,000 Union soldiers remained in the South. As soon as the new president ordered them back to their barracks, the last Republican administrations in the South fell. Reconstruction had ended.

Lasting Legacies

In the short run, the fall of the last state Republican governments had little impact on the lives of most southerners. Much of the violent work of "Redemption" had already been done. What mattered was the broad political trend: the long, slow decline of Radical Republican power from the early 1870s through the mid-1880s, and the corresponding rise of ex-Confederate power in the South and Democrats on the national stage. It was obvious to most Americans that so-called Redeemers in the South had assumed power through violence. But many—including prominent classical liberals who shaped public opinion—believed that ex-Confederates had overthrown corrupt, illegitimate governments and that the end justified the means. Those who deplored the results had little political traction. The only remaining question was how far the revolution would be rolled back. In 1884, when Democrats elected their first post–Civil War president, Grover Cleveland, many freedpeople feared that he would seek to repeal the Thirteenth Amendment and reinstate slavery.

But the South never went back to the antebellum status quo. Sharecropping, for all its flaws and injustices, was not slavery. Freedmen and freedwomen managed to resist gang labor and work on their own terms. They had established their right to marry, read and write, worship as they pleased, and travel in search of a better life—rights that were not easily revoked. Across the South, black farmers overcame great odds to buy and work their own land. African American businessmen built thriving enterprises. Parents sacrificed to send their children to school, and a few proudly watched their sons and daughters graduate from college. Black religious and charitable leaders sustained networks of mutual aid. At the grassroots level, Reconstruction never entirely ended.

Reconstruction had also shaken, if not entirely overturned, the legal and political framework that had, since the founding of the United States, made it a white man's country. This was a stunning achievement, and though hostile courts and violent resistance undercut it, no one ever repealed the Thirteenth, Fourteenth, and Fifteenth Amendments. They remained in the Constitution, an enduring statement of belief in equality, even if equality in practice was as yet unfulfilled. It was on this constitutional framework that the civil rights movement of the twentieth century would be built (Chapter 26). Meanwhile, legal cases brought by Asian immigrants, Mexicans in the Southwest, and American-born women would show that the Fourteenth and Fifteenth Amendments had transformed the nature of American citizenship.

In fact, the new federal powers asserted in Reconstruction—what Andrew Johnson disparaged as "centralization"—were in some ways more potent in the West than in the South. Republicans boldly carried their nation-building project into the West, to consolidate a continental empire. U.S. policymakers and

businessmen also developed networks of trade and finance that stretched overseas. Before 1865, Americans had often worried about European interference in their domestic affairs. After the Civil War, Americans seldom brooded over such matters. Instead, the United States proudly began to describe itself as Britain's leading rival, not only in championing Emancipation and other marks of "advancing civilization" but also as a naval and commercial power around the world. Though the cause of freedom did not always advance, the federal powers that had secured emancipation would find new outlets in the postwar era.

- **What factors undermined Republican control of the federal government during the 1870s? What were the consequences of this development for Reconstruction?**

- **How did ex-Confederates achieve their counterrevolution against Reconstruction? What role did northern Democrats and the Supreme Court play in that counterrevolution?**

- **What was the political crisis of 1877, and what were its consequences for Reconstruction?**

- **What economic, social, and political legacies persisted after the end of Reconstruction?**

SUMMARY

Postwar Republicans confronted two great tasks: restoring the rebellious states to the Union and defining the role of emancipated slaves. After Lincoln's assassination, his successor, Andrew Johnson, hostile to Congress, unilaterally offered the South easy terms for reentering the Union. Exploiting this opportunity, southerners adopted oppressive Black Codes and welcomed ex-Confederates back into power. Congress impeached Johnson, and though failing to convict him, seized the initiative. They placed the South under military rule. In this second, or radical, phase of Reconstruction, Republican state governments tried to transform the South's economic and social institutions. Congress passed innovative civil rights acts and funded new agencies like the Freedmen's Bureau. The Fourteenth Amendment defined U.S. citizenship and asserted that states could no longer limit or supersede it. The Fifteenth Amendment gave full voting rights to formerly enslaved men. Debate over this amendment precipitated a split among women's rights advocates, since women did not win inclusion.

Freedmen found that their goals conflicted with those of Republican leaders, who counted on cotton to fuel economic growth. Like Southern landowners, they envisioned former slaves as wage workers, while freedmen wanted their own land. Sharecropping, which satisfied no one completely, emerged as a compromise suited to the needs of the cotton market and an impoverished, credit-starved region.

Nothing could reconcile ex-Confederates to Republican government, and they staged a violent counterrevolution in the name of white supremacy and "Redemption." Meanwhile, struck by a massive economic depression, Northern voters handed Republicans a crushing defeat in the election of 1874. By 1876, Reconstruction was dead. Rutherford B. Hayes's extremely narrow victory in the presidential election of that year, decided by a federal commission, resulted in the withdrawal of the last Union troops from the South. A series of Supreme Court decisions also undermined the Fourteenth Amendment and civil rights

laws, setting up legal parameters through which, over the long term, disenfranchisement and segregation would flourish. Nonetheless, grassroots community-building among African Americans continued in the South, even after national Reconstruction faded.

CHAPTER REVIEW QUESTIONS

- How might the outcome of Reconstruction have been different had Lincoln lived, or chosen a different vice presidential running mate in 1864?

- What were the goals of Radical Republicans and of freedpeople during Reconstruction? How did these differ, and what were the results?

- Why did Reconstruction falter? To what extent was its failure the result of events in the South, in the North, and in Washington, D.C.?

FOR FURTHER EXPLORATION

The best modern book on Reconstruction is Eric Foner's major synthesis, *Reconstruction: America's Unfinished Revolution, 1863–1877* (1988). Foner's *Nothing But Freedom* (1983) helpfully places Reconstruction in a comparative context. See also Michael Perman, *Emancipation and Reconstruction*, 2nd ed. (2003). *Black Reconstruction in America* (1935), by African American activist and scholar W. E. B. Du Bois, deserves attention as the first book on Reconstruction that stressed the role of blacks in their own emancipation. On freedmen's experiences, see Leon F. Litwack, *Been in the Storm So Long: The Aftermath of Slavery* (1979). More recent studies include Julie Saville, *The Work of Reconstruction: From Slave to Wage Laborer in South Carolina, 1860–1870* (1994). In *Gendered Strife and Confusion* (1997), Laura F. Edwards explores the impact of ordinary women and men on Reconstruction. For recent views of the Freedmen's Bureau, see Paul A. Cimbala and Randall M. Miller, eds., *The Freedmen's Bureau and Reconstruction* (1999). For national politics, see (in addition to Foner) *The Reconstruction Presidents* (1998), by Brooks D. Simpson. On Americans' fading support for Reconstruction at the national level, see Heather Cox Richardson, *The Death of Reconstruction* (1991), and David W. Blight's sweeping *Race and Reunion* (1991). The site for the PBS documentary *Reconstruction: The Second Civil War* (**www.pbs.org/wgbh/amex/reconstruction/index.html**) features many helpful primary documents and images.

TEST YOUR KNOWLEDGE

To assess your command of the material in this chapter, see the Online Study Guide at **bedfordstmartins.com/henretta**.

For Web sites, images, and documents related to topics and places in this chapter, visit **bedfordstmartins.com/makehistory**.

TIMELINE

1864	Wade-Davis Bill passed by Congress but killed by Lincoln's pocket veto
1865	Freedmen's Bureau established
	Lincoln assassinated; Andrew Johnson succeeds him as president
	Johnson implements Lincoln's restoration plan
1866	Civil Rights Act passes over Johnson's veto
	Republican gains in congressional elections
1867	Reconstruction Act
1868	Impeachment crisis
	Fourteenth Amendment ratified
	Ulysses S. Grant elected president
1870	Ku Klux Klan at peak of power
	Fifteenth Amendment ratified
1872	Grant reelected
1873	Panic of 1873 ushers in severe economic depression of 1873–1877
1874	Sweeping Democratic gains in congressional election
1875	Whiskey Ring scandal undermines Grant administration
	Minor v. Happersett Supreme Court rules that Fourteenth Amendment does not extend voting rights to women
1877	Rutherford B. Hayes becomes president
	Reconstruction ends

THE GREAT WEST

Conquering a Continent

On May 10, 1869, people across the United States poured into the streets for a giant party. In Chicago and other large cities, the racket was incredible. Cannons boomed, church bells rang, train whistles shrilled. New York fired a hundred-gun salute at City Hall. Congregations sang anthems, while the less religious gathered in saloons to celebrate with whiskey. In Philadelphia, joyful throngs at the statehouse reminded one observer of the day, four years earlier, when news had arrived of Lee's surrender. The festivities were triggered by a long-awaited telegraph message: Executives of the Union Pacific and Central Pacific Railroads had driven a golden spike at Promontory Point, Utah, linking up their lines. An unbroken track now stretched from the Atlantic to the Pacific. A journey across the United States, which until recently had taken several months, could now be made in less than a week.

The transcontinental railroad meant economic growth. When they heard the news, San Francisco residents got right to business: After firing a cannon salute, they loaded a shipment of Japanese tea onto a train bound for St. Louis, marking California's first overland delivery to the East. In the coming decades, trade and tourism in areas west of the Mississippi River fueled tremendous economic development. San Francisco, which in 1860 had handled $7.4 million in imports, increased that figure to $49 million by 1890. The new railroad would, as one speaker predicted in 1869, "populate our vast territory" and make America "the highway of nations."

The railroad was a political as well as an economic triumph for the Union. The Republicans who emerged victorious from the Civil War saw themselves as heirs to the American System envisioned by Henry Clay and other antebellum Whigs. They believed that government intervention in the economy was the key to nation building. Unlike the Whigs, whose plans had been stalled by Democratic opposition, Republicans enjoyed a decade of unparalleled power in Washington. They used that power vigorously: Federal spending per person, which skyrocketed during the Civil War, afterward remained well above earlier levels. Republicans argued that industrialization and economic integration were the best guarantors of lasting peace. As a New York minister declared, the transcontinental railroad would "preserve the Union of these states."

The minister was wrong on one point, however. He claimed the railroad was a peaceful achievement, in contrast to battlefield victories that had brought "desolation, devastation, misery, and woe." In fact, creating a conti-

The Great West

In the wake of the Civil War, Americans looked westward. Republicans implemented an array of policies to foster economic development and the making of continental fortunes in the "Great West." Ranchers, farmers, and lumbermen cast hungry eyes on the remaining lands held by Native Americans. Steamboats and railroads, both visible in the background of this image, became celebrated as symbols of the expanding reach of U.S. economic might. This 1881 promotional poster illustrates the bountiful natural resources to be found out west, as well as the land available for ranching, farming, and commerce. The men in the lower left corner are surveying land for sale. Library of Congress.

nental empire caused plenty of woe. Incorporating the areas west of the Mississippi into the national economy required the conquest of native peoples and the establishment of friendly conditions for international investors — often at great domestic cost. Conquering the West helped make the United States into a major industrial power, yet it also deepened America's rivalry with the imperial powers of Europe and created new patterns of investment and exploitation in Latin America and Asia.

The Republican Vision

Reshaping the former Confederacy was only one part of Republicans' plan for a reconstructed nation. They remembered the era after Andrew Jackson's destruction of the Second National Bank as a period of economic chaos, when the United States had become vulnerable to international creditors and market fluctuations. Land speculation on the frontier had provoked dizzying cycles of boom and bust. Failure to fund a transcontinental railroad had left different regions of the country disconnected. This, Republicans believed, had helped trigger the Civil War, and they were determined to take economic policy in a new direction.

Even as the war still raged, the Republican-dominated Congress made vigorous use of federal power, launching the transcontinental rail project, developing a new national banking system, and passing the Homestead Act. Congress also raised the **protective tariff** on a range of manufactured goods, from textiles to steel, and on some agricultural products, like wool and sugar. At federal customhouses in each port, foreign manufacturers who brought merchandise into the United States had to pay import fees. These tariff revenues gave U.S. manufacturers, who did not pay the fees, a competitive advantage in America's giant domestic market.

The massive economic depression that began in 1873 set limits on Republicans' ambitious economic program, just as it hindered their Reconstruction policies in the South. But key policies endured. Tariffs, the national banking system, and public subsidies to railroads, in particular, continued to shape the economy. Though some historians argue that the late nineteenth century was an era of unrestrained capitalism, in which government sat passively by, the industrial United States was actually the product of a massive public-private partnership, in which government played a critical role. Secretary of State William Seward, already looking abroad for markets and raw materials, provided a blueprint for international trade, resource exploitation, and investment for a century to come.

Integrating the National Economy

Railroad development in the United States began well before the Civil War, with the first locomotives arriving from Britain in the early 1830s. Unlike canals or roads, railroads offered the promise of year-round, all-weather service. Locomotives could run in the dark and never needed to rest, except to take on coal and water. Steam engines carried them over steep mountains and rocky gorges, where pack animals could find no fodder and canals could never reach. West of the Mississippi, railroads opened vast regions for conquest, farming, trade, and tourism. Railroads "do wonders — they work miracles," declared one booster. Looking back later, a transcontinental railroad executive was only half joking when he said, "[T]he West is purely a railroad enterprise."

Railroads could be run by the government or financed by private investors. Unlike most European countries, the United States chose the private approach, but the federal government provided essential incentives in the form of loans, subsidies, and land grants. States and localities also lured railroads with offers of financial aid, mainly by buying railroad bonds. Without this aid, the rail network would have grown much more slowly and would most likely have concentrated in urban regions. With it, railroads enjoyed an enormous boom. By 1900, virtually no corner of the country lacked rail service (Map 16.1).

Railroad companies transformed American capitalism. They adopted a legal form of organization, the corporation, that enabled them to raise private capital in prodigious amounts. In earlier decades, state legislatures had chartered corporations for specific public purposes, binding these creations to government goals

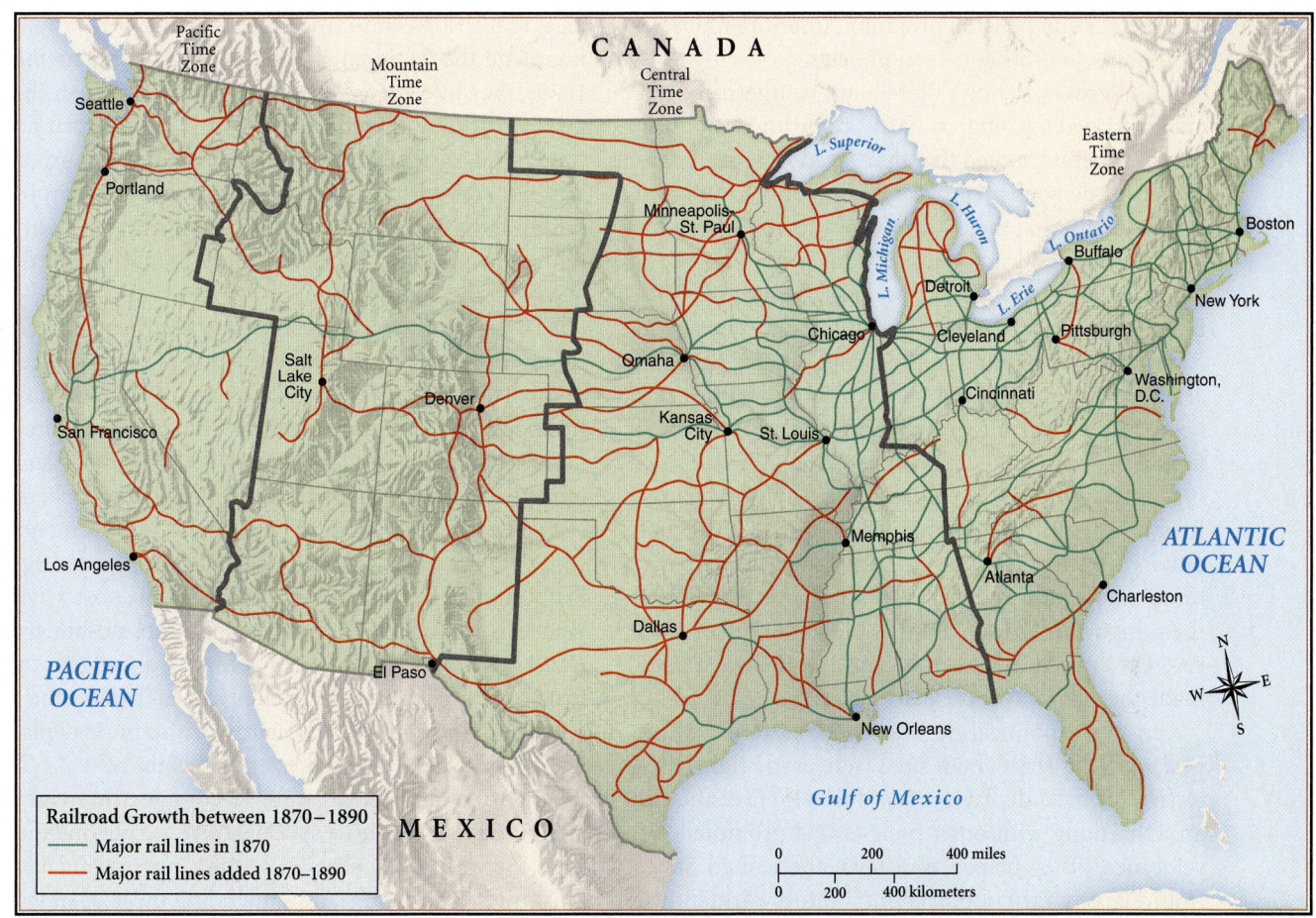

MAP 16.1

The Expansion of the Railroad System, 1870–1890

In 1860, the nation had 30,000 miles of rail track; by 1890, it had 167,000 miles. The tremendous burst of construction during the last twenty years of that period essentially completed the nation's rail network, although there would be additional expansion for the next two decades. The main areas of growth were in the South and in the lands west of the Mississippi. Time zones—introduced by the railroad companies in 1883—are marked by the gray lines.

and oversight. But over the course of the nineteenth century, legislatures gradually began to allow any business to become a corporation by simply applying for a state charter. Among the first corporations to become large interstate enterprises, private railroads were much freer than earlier corporations to do as they pleased, and after the Civil War they received lavish grants of public resources with few strings attached. In this, their position was not unlike that of American banks in late 2008, after the big federal bailout: Even critics acknowledged that public aid to these giant companies was good for the economy, but they observed that it also lent government support to fabulous accumulations of private wealth.

Protective Tariffs and Economic Growth Along with the transformative power of railroads, the Republicans' protective tariffs helped build other U.S. industries, including textile and steel manufacturing in the Northeast and Midwest and (through a tariff on imported wool) sheep ranching in the West. Tariffs also funded government itself. In an era when the United States did not levy income taxes on corporations or individuals, tariffs provided the largest share of revenue for the treasury. The Civil War had left the Union with a staggering debt of $2.8 billion. Tariff income—which totaled $2.1 billion during the 1880s alone—erased that debt in two decades and then generated huge surpluses. These paid for a generous

Union veterans' pension program, America's first steel battleships, and other federal projects.

As Reconstruction faltered and southern Democrats returned to Congress, tariffs came under political fire. Democrats argued that they taxed American consumers by denying them access to low-priced imported goods and forcing them to pay subsidies to U.S. manufacturers. Republicans claimed, conversely, that tariffs benefited ordinary workers because they created jobs, blocked low-wage foreign competition, and safeguarded America from the kind of industrial poverty that had arisen in Europe. According to this argument, tariffs helped American men earn enough to support their families; wives could devote themselves to homemaking, and children could go to school, not the factory. Republican campaign pamphlets described lurid conditions in "free trade" England, where women labored in mines and iron forges. For protectionist Republicans, then, high tariffs were akin to the abolition of slavery: They protected the most vulnerable workers and made the economy more just.

In fierce political debates over the tariff, which peaked in the 1880s, both sides were partly right. Protective tariffs did play a powerful role in economic growth. Along with other policies that promoted development, they helped transform the United States from a largely agricultural country into a world industrial power. Eventually, though, even protectionist Republicans had to admit that Democrats had a point: Tariffs had not prevented poverty in the United States. U.S. companies accumulated many benefits from tariffs but failed to pass most of these along to workers, who often toiled long hours for low wages. Furthermore, protective tariffs helped foster **trusts**, corporations that dominated whole sectors of the economy and wielded monopoly or near-monopoly power.

The Role of Courts

The rise of railroads and other giant corporations prompted many proposals for government regulation of these monster enterprises. But in this aspect of their economic policies, most historians agree, Republicans did not make government powerful enough. State legislatures did pass hundreds of regulatory laws after the Civil War, but with the federal government asserting new powers, interstate companies challenged such laws in federal courts. In *Munn v. Illinois* (1877), the U.S. Supreme Court acknowledged that states did have the right to regulate those businesses that served important public purposes, such as railroads and grain elevators. However, the justices feared that too many state and local regulations and impediments to business would fragment the national marketplace. Starting in the 1870s, they interpreted the "due process" clause of the new Fourteenth Amendment—which dictated that no state could "deprive any person of life, liberty, or property, without due process of law"—as shielding corporations from excessive regulation. Ironically, the Court refused to use that same amendment to protect freedpeople in the South.

In the Southwest, as well, federal courts promoted economic development at the expense of racial justice. Though the United States had taken control of New Mexico and Arizona after the Mexican War (1846–1848), economic change occurred slowly. In the 1870s, much land remained in the hands of Mexican farmers and ranchers. Many lived as *peónes*, under long-standing agreements with *patrónes*, or landowners, who held large tracts originally granted by the Spanish crown. But the post–Civil War years brought railroads and an influx of land-hungry Anglos. New Mexico's governor reported indignantly that Mexican shepherds were often "asked" to leave their ranges "by a cowboy or cattle herder with a brace of pistols at his belt and a Winchester in his hands."

Existing land claims were so complex that Congress eventually set up a special court to rule on land titles. Between 1891 and 1904, the court invalidated most traditional land claims, including those of *ejidos*, or village commons, in New Mexico. Mexican Americans lost about 64 percent of the contested lands on which the court ruled. In addition, much land was sold or appropriated through legal machinations like those of a notorious group of politicians and lawyers known as the Santa Fe Ring. The result was the displacement of thousands of Mexican American villagers and farmers.

Silver and Gold

In an era of nation building, U.S. and European policymakers sought new ways to rationalize economic markets. At a series of conferences, for example, industrializing nations tried to develop an international system of standard measurements and even a unified currency. Though this vision failed as each nation succumbed to self-interest, governments did increasingly agree that, for "scientific" reasons, money should be based on gold, which was thought to have an intrinsic worth above other metals. Great Britain had long been on the **gold standard**, meaning that paper notes from the Bank of England could be backed by gold held in the bank's vaults. During the 1870s and 1880s, the United States, Germany, France, Norway, and other countries also converted to gold.

Before they made the shift, these nations had been on a bimetallic standard: They issued both gold and silver coins, with the respective weights fixed at a relative value. The United States switched to the gold standard in part because treasury officials and financiers were watching developments out west. Geologists accurately predicted the discovery of immense lodes of silver, such as the Comstock Lode found at Virginia City, Nevada, without comparable new gold strikes. A massive influx of silver would clearly upset the long-standing ratio. Thus, with a law that became infamous to later critics as "the Crime of 1873," Congress chose gold. It directed the U.S. Treasury to cease minting silver dollars, and over a six-year period, to retire the **greenbacks** (paper dollars) that had been issued during the Civil War and replace them with notes from an expanded system of national banks. After this process was complete, in 1879, the treasury exchanged such notes for gold on request. (Advocates of bimetallism did achieve one small victory: The Bland-Allison Act of 1878 required the U.S. Mint to coin a modest amount of silver.)

By putting the United States on the gold standard, Republican policymakers sharply limited the nation's money supply, to the level of available gold. The amount of money circulating in the United States had been $30.35 per person in 1865; by 1880, it fell to only $19.36 per person. Today, few economists would sanction such a plan, especially for an economy growing at breakneck speed. They would recommend, instead, increasing money supplies to keep pace with development. But at the time, policymakers were reacting to the antebellum years of rampant speculation and the keenly felt hardships of inflation during the Civil War. The United States, as a developing country, also needed to attract investment capital from Britain, Belgium, and other European nations that were on the gold standard. Making it easy to exchange U.S. bonds and currency for gold encouraged European investors to bring their capital to the United States.

Republican policies fostered exuberant growth and a breathtakingly rapid integration of the economy. Railroads and telegraphs tied the nation together. U.S. manufacturers amassed staggering amounts of capital and built corporations of national and even global scope. To a large extent, the courts rejected federal regulation of these new enterprises. In 1900, census officials reported that "the mainland of the United States is the largest area in the civilized world . . . unrestricted by customs, excises, or national prejudice." With its immense, integrated marketplace of workers, consumers, raw mate-

rials, and finished products, the United States was poised to become a mighty industrial power.

The New Union and the World

The United States emerged from the Civil War with new leverage in its negotiation with European countries, especially Great Britain, whose navy dominated the high seas. Britain, which had permitted Confederate raiding vessels such as the CSS *Alabama* to be built in its shipyards, agreed afterward to submit to arbitration and pay the United States $15.5 million in damages. In the flush of victory, many Americans expected more British or Spanish territories to fall easily into the Union's lap. Senator Charles Sumner initially proposed, in fact, that Britain settle the *Alabama* claims by handing over Canada.

Such grand dreams were a logical extension of pre–Civil War conquests, especially in the Mexican War. With the East now linked to San Francisco by rail, merchants and manufacturers cast their eyes across the Pacific, hungry for trade with Asia. Americans had already established a dominant presence in the Hawaiian Islands, where U.S. whalers and merchant ships stopped for food and repairs. With the advent of steam-powered vessels, both the U.S. Navy and private shippers wanted more refueling points in the Caribbean and Pacific.

Even before the Civil War, these commercial aims had prompted the U.S. government to force Japan to open trade. For two centuries, after unpleasant encounters with Portuguese traders in the 1600s, Japanese leaders had adhered to a policy of strict isolation. Americans, who wanted refueling stations in Japan, argued that international trade would extend what one missionary called "commerce, knowledge, and Christianity, with their multiplied blessings." Whether or not Japan wanted these blessings was irrelevant. In 1854, Commodore Matthew Perry succeeded in getting Japanese officials to sign a treaty at Kanagawa, allowing U.S. ships to refuel at two ports. By 1858, America and Japan had commenced trade, and a U.S. consul took up residence in the Japanese capital, Edo (now known as Tokyo).

Union victory paved the way not only for increased trade with Japan and other parts of Asia but also for economic expansion in Latin America. While the United States was preoccupied with its internal war, France had deposed Mexico's government and installed an emperor. On May 5, 1867, Mexico overthrew the French invaders and executed Emperor Maximilian, events that have been celebrated ever since on Cinco de Mayo. Mexico—the part, that is, that the United States had

An American Merchant Ship in Yokohama Harbor, 1861

After the United States forcibly "opened" Japan to foreign trade in 1854, American and European ships and visitors became a familiar sight in the port of Yokohama. In these 1861 prints (which are two panels of a five-panel series), artist Hashimoto Sadahide meticulously details the activity on and around a merchant ship in Yokohama Harbor. On the left goods are carried onto the ship; on the right, two women dressed in Western style watch the arrival of another boat. In the background a steamship flies the French flag. Library of Congress.

not annexed in 1848—regained independence. But without European backing, Mexico lay open to the economic designs of its increasingly powerful northern neighbor.

U.S. policymakers developed a new model for asserting power in Latin America and Asia, not by direct conquest of land and people but through international trade. The architect of this vision was William Seward, secretary of state from 1861 to 1869, under Lincoln and Johnson. A New Yorker of grandiose ambition and ego, Seward had been Lincoln's main rival for the presidential nomination in 1860. He believed, like many contemporaries, that Asia would soon become "the chief theatre of [world] events" and that trade there was key to America's prosperity. Seward urged the Senate to purchase sites in both the Pacific and the Caribbean for naval bases and refueling stations. When Japan changed policy and tried to close its ports to foreign trade, Seward dispatched U.S. Navy vessels to join those

of Britain, France, and the Netherlands. They reopened trade by force. At the same time, Seward urged annexation of Hawaii. He predicted that the United States would one day claim the Philippines and build a canal across the isthmus of Panama.

Seward's short-term achievements were modest. During his term of office, Congress was preoccupied with the Civil War and Reconstruction. After Lee's surrender, Americans had little enthusiasm for further military exploits. Seward achieved only two significant victories. In 1868, he secured congressional approval for the Burlingame Treaty with China, which guaranteed the rights of U.S. missionaries in China and set official terms for the emigration of Chinese laborers, some of whom were already clearing farmland and building railroads across the West. In the same year, Seward negotiated the purchase of Alaska from Russia. After the Senate approved the deal, Seward waxed poetic about his long-term dream:

Building the Central Pacific Railroad
In 1865, Chinese workers had labored to build the 1,100-foot-long, 90-foot-high trestle over the divide between the American and Bear rivers at Secret Town in the Sierra Nevada mountains. In 1877, the Chinese workers shown in this photograph by Carleton Watkins were again at work on the site, burying the trestle to avoid replacement of the aging timbers, which had become a fire hazard. University of California at Berkeley, Bancroft Library.

> Our nation with united interests blest
> Not now content to poise, shall sway the rest;
> Abroad our empire shall no limits know,
> But like the sea in endless circles flow.

Many Americans scoffed at the purchase of Alaska, a frigid arctic tract that the secretary of state's critics nicknamed "Seward's Icebox." But Seward mapped out a path that his Republican successors would follow thirty years later in an aggressive bid for global power. In the meantime, the United States laid foundations for its military and economic ascendance closer to home, through final conquest of the American West.

- **What factors helped advance the integration of the national economy after the Civil War?**

- **How did the post–Civil War nation's economic goals shape its foreign policy? What role did William Seward play in advancing that policy?**

Incorporating the West

In the national economy they hoped to build, Republicans made a place for farms as well as factories. They sought to attract families to the West through the Homestead Act, which gave free public plots of 160 acres each to applicants who occupied and improved them. Lincoln administration officials not only promoted the Homestead Act in America but also advertised it in Europe, hoping to attract immigrants to serve in the Union Army and then settle the Great Plains. As early as 1860, Republicans hailed the future of "Uncle Sam's Farm" in popular lyrics written by the abolitionist Hutchinson Family Singers:

> A welcome, warm and hearty, do we give the sons
> of toil,
> To come west and settle and labor on Free Soil;

We've room enough and land enough, they needn't feel alarmed—
Oh! Come to the land of Freedom and vote yourself a farm.

Republicans hoped that hardworking families would cross the Mississippi River, claim homesteads, and help build up a continental empire—especially in the interior West, which was inhabited by Indian peoples but remained "empty" on U.S. government survey maps. They were eager to send miners and ranchers on the same mission.

Implementing this plan required innovative federal policies. In 1862, Congress created the federal Department of Agriculture to conduct research and distribute experimental seeds and advice to farmers. That same year, through the Morrill Act, Congress set aside 140 million acres of federal land to be sold by the states, to raise money for public universities; the goal, in part, was to foster technical expertise and scientific research. After the Civil War, Congress funded several geological surveys, dispatching U.S. Army officers, scientists, artists, and photographers west to map unknown terrain and catalog natural resources. In 1879, Congress consolidated these efforts into an influential new bureau in the Department of the Interior, the U.S. Geological Survey (USGS).

To a large extent, these policies succeeded in incorporating lands west of the Mississippi. European investors sank millions into mines and cattle operations. Railroads soon crisscrossed the West, and homesteaders and their families filed land claims by the thousands. The United States began to fully exploit its continental empire for minerals, lumber, and other raw materials that European nations obtained through overseas conquest. But in many parts of the West, dreams of unlimited growth outran reality. The Great Plains, in particular, proved resistant to conquest. After prospering in the 1870s, ranchers and farmers faced devastating blizzards and drought in the following decade. Republicans' bold initiatives proved insufficient to meet the challenges of life on the plains.

Cattlemen and Miners

As late as the Civil War years, great bison herds roamed the western grasslands. But overhunting and the introduction of European animal afflictions, like the bacterial disease brucellosis, were already decimating

Cowboys on the Open Range

Cowboys were really farmhands on horseback, with the skills to work on the range. An ethnically diverse group, including blacks and Hispanics, they earned $25 a month, plus meals and a bed in the bunkhouse, in return for long hours of grueling, lonesome work. Cowboys were part of the system of open-range ranching, in which cattle (branded with their owners' mark) from different ranches grazed together. At roundups, cowboys separated the cattle by owner and branded the calves.   Library of Congress.

the herds. In the 1870s, hide hunters finished them off so thoroughly that, at one point, fewer than a hundred of the animals remained in U.S. territory. Hunters hidden downwind of a herd, under the right conditions, could kill four or five dozen bison at a time without moving from the spot. One Montana hunter told a visitor that he had killed sixty-three of the animals in less than an hour. Hunters took the hides but left the meat to rot, an act of vast wastefulness that shocked native peoples. An early conservationist called it "butchery [of the] most cruel kind."

Where bison had grazed, ranchers envisioned cow country. South Texas provided an early model for their ambitious plans. By the end of the Civil War, about five million head of longhorn cattle grazed on Anglo ranches there. In 1865, the Missouri Pacific Railroad reached Sedalia, Missouri, far enough west to be accessible as the Confederacy surrendered and Texas re-entered the Union. A longhorn worth $3 in Texas might command $40 at Sedalia. With this incentive, Texas ranchers inaugurated the Long Drive, hiring cowboys to herd cattle hundreds of miles north to the new rail lines, which soon extended into Kansas. At Abilene and Dodge City, Kansas, ranchers sold their longhorns, and trail-weary cowboys crowded into saloons. These cattle towns captured the nation's imagination as symbols of the "Wild West." The reality was much less exciting. Cowboys, many of them African American and Hispanic, were actually farmhands on horseback who worked long, harsh hours for low pay.

News of easy money traveled fast. North of Texas, where land remained in the public domain, the grass was free and the rush was on. Open lands drew investors and adventurers eager for a taste of the West. By the early 1880s, as many as 7.5 million cattle were destroying the native grasses and trampling water holes on the plains, creating the conditions for a long-term ecological catastrophe. A cycle of good weather only postponed disaster, which arrived in 1886: record blizzards and bitter cold. An awful scene of rotting carcasses greeted cowhands as they rode onto the range in the spring. Further damaged by a severe drought the following summer, the cattle boom collapsed.

Thanks to new strategies, however, cattle ranching survived and became part of the integrated national economy. Ranchers had abandoned the Long Drive as railroads reached Texas in the 1870s. Meanwhile, northern cattlemen began to fence small areas of land and plant hay. Stockyards appeared beside the rapidly extending railroad tracks. Ranchers brought cattle there for sale, and trains took the gathered animals to giant slaughterhouses in Chicago and other midwestern cen-

MAP 16.2

The Mining Frontier, 1848–1890

The Far West was America's gold country because of its geological history. Veins of gold and silver form when molten material from the earth's core is forced up into fissures caused by the tectonic movements that create mountain ranges, such as the ones that dominate the far western landscape. It was these veins, the product of mountain-forming activity many thousands of years earlier, that prospectors began to discover after 1848 and furiously exploit. Although widely dispersed across the Far West, the lodes that they found followed the mountain ranges bisecting the region and bypassing the great plateaus not shaped by the ancient tectonic activity.

ters, which turned them into cheap beef for customers back east. Hispanic shepherds from New Mexico also brought sheep to feed on the mesquite and prickly pear that supplanted native grasses. Sheep raising, previously scorned by ranchers as unmanly and threatening to cattle, became a major enterprise in the sparser high country of the Sierras and Rockies.

In these same years, extraction of mineral wealth became the basis for development in the Far West (Map 16.2). In the late 1850s, as easy pickings in the

Hydraulic Mining

When surface veins of gold played out, miners turned to hydraulic mining, the modern form of which was invented in California in 1853. The technology was simple, using high-pressure streams of water to wash away hillsides of gold-bearing soil. Although building the reservoirs, piping systems, and sluices cost money, the profits from hydraulic mining helped transform western mining into big business. But, as this daguerreotype suggests, the large scale on which hydraulic mining was done wreaked large-scale havoc on the environment.   Collection of Matthew Isenberg.

California gold rush diminished, prospectors had spread across the West in hopes of striking it rich elsewhere. They had found gold at many sites, including Nevada, the Colorado Rockies, and in South Dakota's Black Hills. As news of each gold strike spread, a wild remote area turned almost overnight into a mob scene of prospectors, traders, prostitutes, and saloon keepers (see Voices from Abroad, "Baron Joseph Alexander von Hübner: A Western Boom Town," p. 503). At community meetings, prospectors would make their own laws, often using them as an instrument for excluding or discriminating against Mexicans, Chinese, and blacks.

At some sites, miners found other metals, including the copper, lead, and zinc that eastern industries demanded. The silver from Nevada's immense Comstock Lode, discovered in 1859, built the boom-town of Virginia City, which soon acquired fancy hotels, a Shakespearean theater, and even its own stock exchange. In 1870, a hundred saloons operated in Virginia City, brothels lined D Street, and men outnumbered women two to one. In the 1880s, however, as the Comstock Lode played out, Virginia City suffered the fate of many mining camps: It became a ghost town. What remained was a ravaged landscape with mountains of debris, poisoned water sources, and surrounding lands stripped of timber. The insatiable demands of mining triggered the growth of smelting, lumbering, and other industries at many far-flung sites. Comstock, one critic remarked, was "the tomb of the forests of the Sierra." At the same time, booming California created a market for timber and produce from the Pacific Northwest. By the 1880s, Portland

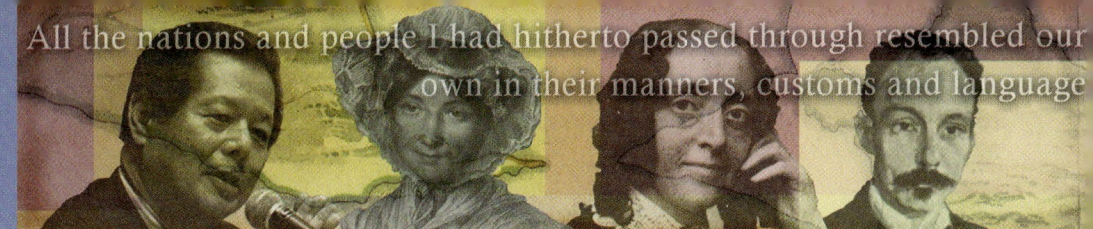
Baron Joseph Alexander von Hübner

A Western Boom Town

During a leisurely trip around the world in 1871, Baron Joseph Alexander von Hübner, a distinguished Austrian diplomat, traveled across the United States, taking advantage of the newly completed transcontinental railroad to see the Wild West. After observing Mormon life in Salt Lake City, he went northward to Corinne, Utah, near the juncture where the Central Pacific and Union Pacific railroads met. The baron might have arrived with romantic notions of the Wild West popular among Europeans of his class. That was not, however, how he departed.

Corinne has only existed for four years. Sprung out of the earth as if by enchantment, this town now contains upwards of 2,000 inhabitants, and every day increases in importance. It is a victualing center for the advanced posts of the [miners] in Idaho and Montana. A coach runs twice a week to Virginia City and to Helena, 350 and 500 miles to the north. Despite the serious dangers and the terrible fatigue of the journeys, these diligences are always full of passengers. Various articles of consumption and dry goods of all sorts are sent in wagons. The "high road" is but a rough track in the soil left by the wheels of the previous vehicles.

The streets of Corinne are full of white men armed to the teeth, miserable looking Indians dressed in the ragged shirts and trousers furnished by the federal government, and yellow Chinese with a business-like air and hard, intelligent faces. No town in the Far West gave me so good an idea as this little place of what is meant by "border life," the struggle between civilization and savage men and things. . . .

All commercial business centers in Main Street. The houses on both sides are nothing but boarded huts. I have seen some with only canvas partitions. . . . The lanes alongside of the huts, which are generally the resort of Chinese women of bad character, lead into the desert, which begins at the doors of the last houses. . . .

To have on your conscience a number of man-slaughters committed in full day, under the eyes of your fellow citizens; to have escaped the reach of justice by craft, audacity, or bribery; to have earned a reputation for being "sharp," that is, for knowing how to cheat all the world without being caught—those are the attributes of the true rowdy in the Far West. . . . Endowed as they often are with really fine qualities—courage, energy, and intellectual and physical strength—they might in another sphere and with the moral sense which they now lack, have become valuable members of society. But such as they are, these adventurers have a reason for being, a providential mission to fulfill. The qualities needed to struggle with and conquer savage nature have naturally their corresponding defects.

Look back, and you will see the cradles of all civilization surrounded with giants of Herculean strength ready to run every risk and to shrink from neither danger nor crime to attain their ends. It is only by the peculiar temper of the time and place that we can distinguish them from the backwoodsman and rowdy of the United States.

Source: Oscar Handlin, ed., *This Was America* (Cambridge, MA: Harvard University Press, 1949), 313–315.

ANALYZING THE EVIDENCE

- We read foreign impressions of America to find in them insights that Americans themselves might not have had. In what ways, if any, do you find such insights in Baron von Hübner's account of Corinne?

- The baron describes Corinne as a booming supply center for the hard-rock mining industry of Montana and Idaho. Yet his explanation of Corinne is more romantic. He sees in its activities a "struggle between civilization and savage men and things." Is that a helpful insight for us? Would it have been shared or seen as helpful, say, by a Boston businessman looking to invest in real estate in Corinne?

- The baron is unsparing in his description of the "Chinese women of bad character," "miserable looking" Indians, and other unsavory inhabitants of Corinne. But he makes an exception for the gunmen roaming the streets. Despite their "defects," they have "a providential mission to fulfill." What does he mean by that? Would his view have made sense to the hypothetical Boston businessman mentioned above? Or to other Americans who saw in the West the economic opportunity of a lifetime?

and Seattle blossomed into populous and important commercial centers (Map 16.3).

Homesteaders

Before farmers would settle the western plains, they had to be persuaded that crops would grow there. Powerful interests worked hard to overcome the popular idea that the grassland was the **Great American Desert** (Map 16.4). Railroads, eager to sell land the government had granted them, advertised aggressively. Land speculators, transatlantic steamship lines, and western states and territories joined the campaign. "Why emigrate to Kansas?" asked a testimonial in *Western Trail*, the Rock Island Railroad's gazette. "Because it is the garden spot of the world. Because it will grow anything that any other country will grow, and with less work."

Newcomers found the soil beneath the native prairie grasses deep and fertile. Steel plows enabled them to break through the tough roots, while barbed wire provided cheap, effective fencing against roaming cattle. European immigrants brought strains of hard-kernel wheat that tolerated the extreme temperatures of the plains. As if to confirm the promoters' optimism, a wet cycle occurred between 1878 and 1886, shifting the zone of greater rainfall toward the Rockies. Ameri-

cans decided that "rain follows the plow." Some attributed the increased rain to soil cultivation and tree planting. Others credited God. As one settler on the southern plains remarked, "The Lord just knowed we needed more land an' He's gone and changed the climate."

The motivation for most settlers, American or European, was to better themselves economically. Union veterans, who received favorable terms in staking homestead claims, played a major role in settling Kansas and other plains states. When a severe depression hit northern Europe in the 1870s, Norwegians and Swedes joined German emigrants in large numbers. At the peak of "American fever" in 1882, more than 105,000 Scandinavians left for the United States. Swedish and Norwegian became the primary languages in parts of Minnesota and the Dakotas.

For African Americans, the plains could represent a promised land of freedom. In 1879, some black communities chose to leave the South in a quest to escape poverty and white vengeance. Some six thousand blacks walked out of Mississippi and Louisiana, most carrying little but the clothes on their backs and faith in God. They called themselves **Exodusters**, participants in a great exodus to the prairie. The 1880 census reported 40,000 blacks in Kansas, by far the largest African American concentration in the West aside from Texas, where

MAP 16.3

The Settlement of the Pacific Slope, 1860–1890

In 1860, the economic development of the Pacific slope was remarkably uneven—fully under way in northern California and scarcely begun anywhere else. By 1890, a new pattern had begun to emerge, with the swift growth of southern California foreshadowed and the Pacific Northwest incorporated into the regional and national economy.

MAP 16.4

The Natural Environment of the West, 1860s

As cattle ranchers and homesteaders pushed into the Great Plains and beyond the line of semiaridity, they sensed the overwhelming power of the natural environment. In a landscape without trees for fences and barns, and without adequate rainfall, ranchers and farmers had to relearn their business. The Native Americans peopling the plains and mountains had learned to live in this environment, but their knowledge counted for little against the ruthless pressure of the settlers to domesticate the West.

the expanding cotton frontier attracted hundreds of thousands of black migrants.

For all newcomers, taming the plains differed from "pioneering" in antebellum Iowa or Oregon. Dealers sold big new machines to help with plowing and harvesting. Western wheat traveled by rail to giant grain elevators, and it traded immediately on world markets. Hoping that frontier land values would appreciate rap-

idly, many farmers planned to profit from selling acreage as much as (or more than) from selling their crops. In boom times, many rushed into debt to acquire more land and better equipment. All these enthusiasms — for cash crops, land speculation, borrowed money, and new technology — bore witness to the conviction that farming was, as one agricultural journal remarked, a business "like all other business."

The Shores Family, Custer County, Nebraska, 1887

Whether the Shores family came west as Exodusters, we do not know. But in 1887, when this photograph was taken, they were well settled on their Nebraska farm, although still living in sod houses. The matriarch and patriarch of the family, Rachel and Jerry Shores (an ex-slave), are third and second from the right. Nebraska State Historical Society.

Women in the West Those who came west to mine ore, to harvest lumber, or to tend cattle were overwhelmingly male, but homesteaders most often arrived as families. Women and children played critical roles in running farms. For this reason, farmers held a special place in Republicans' vision of a transformed nation. According to the ideal of domesticity, which had spread widely in the North before the Civil War, it was a man's devotion to his wife and children that caused him to work hard, be thrifty, and contribute to national progress. Meanwhile, women's commitment to the home, motherhood, and female Christian charity were considered crucial to the improvement of American civilization. Respectable settlers did not, of course, include in this vision of domesticity the thousands of prostitutes who worked in western mining camps and cattle towns.

Domesticity precipitated a political clash with a distinctive religious group that had already conquered part of the West: Mormons, or members of the Church of Jesus Christ of Latter-Day Saints (LDS). Most Americans at the time were deeply hostile to Mormonism, especially the LDS practice of plural marriage—sanctioned by church founder Joseph Smith—through which some Mormon husbands married more than one wife. Mormons had their own view of women's role. In 1870, the Utah legislature granted full voting rights to women. This measure increased LDS power—since most Utah women were Mormons, and many men in mining camps were not—and recognized the central role of women in Mormon life. Amid the upheaval of Reconstruction, **polygamy** and women's voting rights became intertwined political controversies (see Comparing American Voices, "Women's Rights in the West," pp. 508–509).

Utah was not the only place in the West where women found new rights and opportunities. As noted in Chapter 15, legislators in Wyoming Territory were the first to grant women full voting rights, in 1869. Western women also ran for public office and held government posts more often than in other regions of the country. Kansas women took the lead: Starting with Argonia in 1887, six towns elected women as mayors, and Oskaloosa boasted the nation's first all-female city council. Such work was part of a broader pattern of women's employment outside the home. Female lawyers, doctors, and entrepreneurs—even single female ranchers and homesteaders—were not uncommon in the West. A shortage of skilled labor and women's frontier self-reliance may have contributed to this marked trend.

Yet the vast majority of rural women endured considerable frontier hardship. This was especially true of those who bore and raised children on homesteads. For many, life on the plains was monotonous and isolated, especially when prosperity proved elusive. "Such an air of desolation," wrote a woman when she moved to the grasslands of Nebraska. Another, in Texas, spoke of "such a lonely country." In his novel *Giants in the Earth*, O. E. Rolvaag dramatically portrayed the fear and iso-

Promoting the Prairie, 1870s

This sketch by Henry Worrall is a classic "booster" image, promoting the plains farming life. After ten years' labor, the woodland farmer will still be poor, as he's spent the time cutting down trees. But after only six years on the prairie, a farmer would see far greater results from his labor: a larger home, vines, orchards, flourishing grain crops, as well as a church and neighbors nearby. And if trees are a necessity, they can be grown quickly: Worrell also claims that one Topeka cottonwood grew 26 feet tall in four years. Such images—accompanied by glowing testimonials from scientists, government experts, and newspaper editors—helped lure farmers to the plains. This image soon found its way onto posters advertising the Atchison, Topeka, and Santa Fe Railway.   Kansas State Historical Society.

lation of late-nineteenth-century Norwegian immigrant women on the Dakota prairie, far from the coastal fishing villages of their childhoods. Farmers' advocates soon warned that many farmwives on the plains were ending up in insane asylums. Though the claim was exaggerated, it circulated widely, suggesting that it resonated with homesteaders' personal experiences.

Debt and Aridity

Homesteading men suffered alongside women and children. In the late nineteenth century, due to technological innovation and the global expansion of export agriculture, farm products glutted world markets. The result was a long, precipitous drop in crop prices. Wheat, cotton, and corn farmers were especially vulnerable. In some years during the 1880s, the price of

corn fell so low that Iowa farmers found it more cost-effective to keep their harvest and burn it in their stoves for winter heat than to sell it.

Farmers faced another problem: They were individual businessmen in a marketplace that rewarded **economies of scale**. Thus, they faced serious disadvantages in negotiating with the railroads and merchant companies that transported and sold their products, as well as bankers and equipment dealers who supplied them with machinery and loans. Many understood their dilemma all too keenly, and in the 1880s farmers in the West and South would build one of the most powerful protest movements in the history of American politics.

In the meantime, farmers on the Great Plains faced the additional challenge of a hostile environment. In the grasslands, a cloud of grasshoppers could descend and

Women's Rights in the West

In 1870, Utah's territorial legislature granted voting rights to women. The decision was a shock to advocates of women's suffrage in the East: They expected their first big victories would come in New England, not in the West. Furthermore, Utah was overwhelmingly peopled by Mormons—members of the Church of Jesus Christ of Latter Day Saints (LDS). Critics saw Mormonism as a harshly patriarchal religion. They especially loathed the Mormon practice of "plural marriage," in which some Mormon men took more than one wife. Most Easterners thought this practice was barbaric and demeaning to women. Over the next two decades, Republicans pressured Mormons to abolish plural marriage. They also disenfranchised Mormon women and, a few years later, all Mormons; Congress refused to admit Utah as a state. Only after 1890, when the LDS church officially abolished plural marriage, was Utah statehood possible. In 1896, when Utah became a state, women's voting rights were finally reinstated.

Fanny Stenhouse

Exposé of Polygamy: A Lady's Life among the Mormons (1872)

An Englishwoman who converted to the faith and moved to Utah, Stenhouse became disillusioned and published her book to criticize the practice of Mormon polygamy.

How little do the Mormon men of Utah know what it is, in the truest sense, to have a wife, though they have so many "wives," after their own fashion. Almost imperceptibly to the husband, and even the wife herself, a barrier rises between them the very day that he marries another woman. It matters not how much she believes in the doctrine of plural marriages, or how willing she may be to submit to it; the fact remains the same. The estrangement begins by her trying to hide from him all secret sorrow; for she feels that what has been can not be undone now, and she says, "I cannot change it; neither would I if I could, because it is the will of God, and I must bear it; besides, what good will it do to worry my husband with all my feelings?"

. . . A man may have a dozen wives; but from the whole of them combined he will not receive as much real love and devotion as he might from one alone, if he had made her feel that she had his undivided affection and confidence. How terribly these men deceive themselves! When peace, or rather quiet, reigns in their homes, they think that the spirit of God is there. But it is not so! It is a calm, not like the gentle silence of sleep, but as the horrible stillness of death—the death of the heart's best affections, and all that is worth calling love. All true love has fled, and indifference has taken its place. The very children feel it. What do they—what can they care about their fathers? They seldom see them.

Whatever, in the providence of God, may be the action of Congress toward Utah, if the word of a feeble woman can be listened to, let me respectfully ask the Honorable Senators and Representatives of the United States that, in the abolition of Polygamy, if such should be the decree of the nation, let no compromise be made where subtlety can bind the woman now living in Polygamy to remain in that condition.

Source: *Exposé of Polygamy: A Lady's Life among the Mormons*, ed. Linda Wilcox DeSimone (Logan: Utah State University Press, 2008), 72–73, 155.

Eliza Snow, Harriet Cook Young, Phoebe Woodruff

A Defense of Plural Marriage

The vast majority of Mormon women defended their faith and the practice of plural marriage. The statements by Eliza Snow, Harriet Cook Young, and Phoebe Woodruff, below, were made at a public protest meeting in Salt Lake City in 1870. LDS women pointed proudly to their new suffrage rights as proof of their religion's just treatment of women. Why did Mormons, who dominated the Utah legislature, give women full voting rights? In part, they sought to protect their church by increasing Mormon voting power: Most of the non-Mormons were single men who worked on ranches or in mining camps. But the LDS Church also celebrated women's central role in the family and community. Some women achieved prominence as midwives, teachers, and professionals.

Eliza Snow: Our enemies pretend that, in Utah, woman is held in a state of vassalage—that she does not act from choice, but by coercion—that we would even prefer life elsewhere, were it possible for us to make our escape. What nonsense! We all know that if we wished we could leave at any time—either go singly, or to rise en masse, and there is no power here that could, or would wish to, prevent us. I will now ask this assemblage of intelligent ladies, do you know of anyplace on the face of the earth, where woman has more liberty, and where she enjoys such high and glorious privileges as she does here, as a latter-day saint? No! The very idea of woman here in a state of slavery is a burlesque on good common sense.

Harriet Cook Young: Wherever monogamy reigns, adultery, prostitution and foeticide, directly or indirectly, are its concomitants. . . . The women of Utah comprehend this; and they see, in the principle of plurality of wives, the only safeguard against adultery, prostitution, and the reckless waste of pre-natal life, practiced throughout the land.

Phoebe Woodruff: God has revealed unto us the law of the patriarchal order of marriage, and commanded us to obey it. We are sealed to our husbands for time and eternity, that we may dwell with them and our children in the world to come; which guarantees unto us the greatest blessing for which we are created. If the rulers of the nation will so far depart from the spirit and letter of our glorious constitution as to deprive our prophets, apostles and elders of citizenship, and imprison them for obeying this law, let them grant this, our last request, to make their prisons large enough to hold their wives, for where they go we will go also.

Source: Edward W. Tullidge, *Women of Mormondom* (New York: Tullidge & Crandall, 1877), 390–391, 396, 400.

Susan B. Anthony
Letter to *The Revolution*, July 5, 1871

National women's suffrage leaders responded awkwardly to the Utah suffrage victory. Being associated with Mormons, they understood, damaged their fragile new movement in the eyes of most Americans. But they tried tentatively to forge alliances with Mormon women they viewed as progressive, as well as dissidents in the church. Suffrage leader Susan B. Anthony traveled to Salt Lake City in 1871 to try to forge alliances with Mormon women, especially dissidents such as Fanny Stenhouse. Anthony expressed strong disapproval of polygamy, but she also tried to change the debate to focus on the vulnerability of all married women to exploitation by their husbands. Her report from Utah, published in her journal *The Revolution*, is below.

Woman's work in monogamy and polygamy is essentially one and the same—that of planting her feet on the solid ground of self-support; . . . there is and can be no salvation for womanhood but in the possession of power over her own subsistence.

The saddest feature here is that there really is nothing by which these women can earn an independent livelihood for themselves and children. No manufacturing establishments; no free schools to teach. Women here, as everywhere, must be able to live honestly and honorably without men, before it can be possible to save the masses of them from entering into polygamy or prostitution, legal or illegal. Whichever way I turn, whatever phase of social life presents itself, the same conclusion comes—independent bread alone can redeem woman from her sure subjection to man. . . .

Here is missionary ground. Not for and "thus saith the Lord," divine rights, canting priests, or echoing priestesses of any sect whatsoever; but for great, god-like, humanitarian men and women, who "feel for them in bonds as bound with them," . . . a simple, loving, sisterly clasp of hands with these struggling women, and an earnest work with them. Not to modify nor ameliorate, but to ABOLISH the whole system of woman's subjection to man in both polygamy and monogamy.

Source: *The Revolution*, 20 July 1871.

ANALYZING THE EVIDENCE

- What arguments did the Mormon women make in defense of plural marriage? On what grounds did Stenhouse argue for its abolition?

- Susan B. Anthony's letter was published in Boston. How might Mormon women have reacted to it? Would they have been persuaded? How might non-Mormon women have reacted to the statements by Snow, Young, and Woodruff?

- How do you account for the very different experiences of plural marriage described by Stenhouse, on the one hand, and Snow, Young, and Woodruff, on the other?

destroy a crop in a day; a prairie fire or hailstorm could do the job in an hour. In spring, homesteaders could face sudden, terrifying tornados; their winter experiences added the word *blizzard* to the American vocabulary in the 1870s. On the plains, also, farmers did not find what forested land had always provided—ample water and lumber for both fuel and construction. Newly arrived families often cut dugouts into hillsides and then, after a season or two, erected houses made of turf cut from the ground.

Over the long term, homesteaders discovered that the western grasslands did not receive enough rain to grow wheat and other grains. Despite the belief that "rain followed the plow," the cycle of rainfall shifted from wet to dry. "A wind hot as an oven's fury," reported the budding novelist Stephen Crane from Nebraska, "[f]rom day to day . . . raged like a pestilence," destroying the crops and leaving "farmers helpless, with no weapon against this terrible and inscrutable wrath of nature." By the late 1880s, some recently settled lands emptied as homesteaders fled in defeat—50,000 of them from the Dakotas alone. It had become obvious that farming in the arid West required methods other than those used east of the Mississippi.

Clearly, 160-acre homesteads were the wrong size: Farmers needed either small, intensively irrigated plots or immense tracts that could support capital-intensive farming. The latter approach included dry farming, which involved deep planting to bring subsoil moisture to the roots and quick harrowing after rainfalls to turn over a dry mulch that slowed evaporation. Dry farming developed most fully on huge corporate farms in the Red River Valley of North Dakota. But even family farms, the norm elsewhere, could not survive on less than 300 acres of grain crops plus machinery for plowing, planting, and harvesting. Crop prices were too low, and the climate too unpredictable, to allow farmers to get by on less.

In this struggle, settlers regarded themselves as nature's potential conquerors, striving, as one pioneer remarked, "to get the land subdued and the wilde nature out of it." Much about its "wilde nature" was, of course, hidden to these strangers to the plains. They did not know that destroying biodiversity, which was what farming the plains really meant, opened pathways for exotic, destructive pests and weeds, and that plowing under the native bunch grasses rendered the soil vulnerable to erosion. By the turn of the twentieth century, about half the nation's cattle and sheep, one-third of its cereal crops, and nearly three-fifths of its wheat came from the Great Plains. But it was not a sustainable achievement. In the twentieth century, this renowned breadbasket was revealed to be, in the words of one historian, "the largest, longest-run agricultural and environmental miscalculation in American history."

John Wesley Powell, a one-armed veteran of the Battle of Shiloh, predicted this catastrophe from an early date. Powell, employed by the new U.S. Geological Survey, led celebrated expeditions in the West. During one of these, he and his survey team navigated the rapids of the Colorado River in wooden boats through the Grand Canyon. In his *Report on the Lands of the Arid Regions of the United States* (1878), Powell told Congress bluntly that individual 160-acre homesteads would not work in dry regions. Impressed with the success of Mormon irrigation projects in Utah, Powell urged the United States to follow that model. He proposed that the government develop the West's water resources, building dams and canals and organizing landowners into local districts that would operate these democratically. Doubting that rugged individualism would succeed in the West, Powell proposed massive cooperation under government control.

Unfortunately, after heated debate, Congress rejected Powell's plan. His critics accused him of playing into the hands of large ranching corporations; boosters and would-be farmers were not yet willing to give up the dream of small homesteads dotted across the plains. But Powell turned out to be right. Though environmental historians do not always agree with Powell's proposed solution, they point to his *Report on Arid Lands* as a cogent critique of what went wrong on the Great Plains. By 1900, Americans would begin to agree with Powell that the federal government should not sell off this public land but instead hold and manage much of it in trust for the American people. At the same time, federal funding eventually paid for the dams and canal systems that supported intensive agriculture in many parts of the West.

Yellowstone | Though it took decades for Americans to accept irrigation and cooperative farming, the conquest of the West precipitated other innovations. So rapid and thorough was the West's incorporation into the national marketplace that some officials began to fear rampant overdevelopment. Amid the heady initiatives of Reconstruction, Congress therefore began to preserve sites of unusual natural splendor. As early as 1864, Congress gave 10 square miles of the Yosemite Valley to California for "public use, resort, and recreation." (In 1890, Yosemite reverted to federal control.) Praising the austere beauty of western landscapes, leading writers urged the United States to create

The Yo-Hamite Falls, 1855
This is one of the earliest artistic renderings of the Yosemite Valley, drawn, in fact, before the place came to be called Yosemite. The scale of the waterfall, which drops 2,300 feet to the valley below, is dramatized by artist Thomas A. Ayres's companions in the foreground. In this romantic lithograph, one can already see the grandeur of the West that Yosemite came to represent for Americans. University of California at Berkeley, Bancroft Library, Honeyman Collection.

more preserves. Congress responded in 1872 by setting aside 2 million acres of Wyoming's Yellowstone Valley "as a public park or pleasuring ground for the benefit and enjoyment of the people."

Tourism was at least as important a motive for Yellowstone's creation as dawning environmental consciousness. Here, again, railroads played a central role. Jay Cooke, owner of the Northern Pacific Railroad, lobbied Congress vigorously to get Yellowstone established. Luxury Pullman cars soon ushered visitors to Yellowstone's grand hotel, operated by the railroad itself. Thus, tourism became a booming enterprise in parts of the West at the same moment that farming, ranching, and mining did. Yellowstone and Yosemite became symbols of national pride, grander than Europe's castles. Busy urban Americans — especially members of the elite — began to find a refuge in the solitude of the natural parks. The national preserves of the West, as one senator put it, became a "great breathing-place for the national lungs."

The creation of Yellowstone National Park was fraught with complications. No one knew exactly what a "national park" was or how to operate it. The U.S. Army was dispatched to take charge of Yellowstone; only in the 1890s and early 1900s, when Congress established many more parks in the West, did consistent management policies emerge. In the meantime, soldiers spent much of their time evicting native peoples who hunted in the Yellowstone Valley. Congress's stipulation that the government keep the park in a "natural condition" required removing any Indians who might spoil its "natural" qualities. Yet, though native hunting was prohibited, wealthy eastern sportsmen quickly came out to hunt the big-game animals that had sustained Indian peoples like the Crows.

The creation of Yellowstone was an early, important step toward a public ethic of preservation and respect for land and wildlife. At the same time, the eviction of Indians from the park showed how creating small preserves of "uninhabited wilderness" was

Killing the Bison
This woodcut shows passengers shooting bison from a Kansas Pacific Railroad train—a small thrill added to the modern convenience of traveling west by rail. By the end of the 1870s, the plains bison shown here, which once numbered in the tens of millions and had been a large part of the Plains Indians' way of life, had been hunted almost to extinction. North Wind Picture Archives.

part of the process of conquest itself. Nothing demonstrated this more dramatically than what took place in Yellowstone in 1877. That year, the federal government forcibly removed the Nez Perce tribe from their ancestral lands in Idaho. Under the leadership of young Chief Joseph, the Nez Perce tried to flee to Canada. After a journey of 1,100 miles, they were forced to surrender just short of the border. On the way, five bands fled across Yellowstone; as Nez Perce warrior Yellow Wolf remembered, they "knew that country well." For thirteen days, Nez Perce men raided the valley for supplies, waylaying several groups of tourists. The following summer, just east of the park border, U.S. troops defeated a desperate group of Bannock Indians who, facing starvation on an assigned reservation, had fled to Yellowstone.

Both conflicts made headlines across the country. Americans, proud of their nation's new "pleasuring ground" at Yellowstone, were startled to find that the park was still a site of native resistance. Throughout the postwar decades, such conflicts reminded Americans that they were not, in fact, "settling" empty territory in the West. They were *un*settling it from native peoples who already lived there. The drive toward settlement often trumped environmentalism. In 1874, for example, Congress tried to enact America's first wildlife protection bill, seeking to prohibit the killing of female bison by non-Indians. President Grant vetoed the bill. Treaties the United States had signed in 1867 and 1868 promised various Plains Indian tribes that they could live free

and hunt as long as bison ranged "in such numbers as to justify the chase." Grant and the army knew that killing bison would cripple Indian resistance. To complete the work of conquest, the great herds of bison had to vanish from the plains.

- How did cattle ranching develop on the western grasslands and become part of the integrated national economy?

- What factors drew homesteaders to the Great Plains, and what role did they play in the Republicans' vision for the post–Civil War nation?

- What environmental conditions did the homesteaders confront on the Great Plains? How did they respond to those conditions, and what were the consequences of that response?

- What prompted the U.S. government to set aside natural reserves such as Yellowstone? What were the results of that policy?

A Harvest of Blood: Native Peoples Dispossessed

Before the Civil War, Congress reserved the Great Plains for nomadic peoples. After all, they did not believe the western prairie could be farmed. But in the era of railroads, steel plows, and Union victory, Americans suddenly had the power and desire to incorporate the whole plains. The U.S. Army fought against not only the loosely federated Sioux—who had become the major power on the grasslands—but also many other peoples who had agreed to live on reservations but found conditions so desperate that they fled in protest (Map 16.5). These "reservation wars," caused largely by inconsistencies in federal policy, were messy and bitter. Faced with inconsistent policies, failed military campaigns, a series of army atrocities, and egregious corruption in the Indian Bureau, Americans began to heed reformers who called for a new, more humane policy—one that would destroy native ways of life but "save" Indians themselves.

The Civil War and Indians on the Plains

In August 1862, the attention of most Unionists and Confederates was riveted on General George McClellan's failed campaign on the Chesapeake Bay peninsula. But in Minnesota, the Dakota Sioux were increasingly restive. In 1858, they had agreed to settle on a strip of land reserved for them by the government, in exchange for receiving regular payments and supplies. But Indian agents, contractors, and even Minnesota's territorial governor pocketed most of the funds meant for the Dakotas. When

MAP 16.5

Indian Country in the West, to 1890

As settlement pushed onto the Great Plains after the Civil War, native peoples put up bitter resistance but ultimately to no avail. Over a period of decades, they ceded most of their lands to the federal government, and by 1890 they were confined to scattered reservations.

Enclosed Dakota Camp at Fort Snelling, Minnesota, 1862

During the trial of Dakota warriors involved in the 1862 rebellion, and through the harsh Minnesota winter that followed, more than a thousand members of the tribe were imprisoned inside an enormous enclosure on Pike Island, across from Fort Snelling, near St. Paul. A measles epidemic broke out in the crowded Dakota camp and dozens died, especially children. Though U.S. soldiers were often unfriendly toward their captives, local sentiment was even more hostile, and troops regularly marched through the camp, in part to protect the Dakota from vigilante violence. In 1863 all members of the tribe were forcibly removed from the state. In November 1862, photographer Benjamin Franklin Upton captured this image of Dakota tents within the Pike Island enclosure.   Minnesota Historical Society.

the Dakotas protested that their children were starving, state officials dismissed their appeals. Corruption was so egregious that one leading Minnesota clergyman, Episcopal bishop Henry Whipple, wrote an urgent appeal to President James Buchanan. "A nation which sows robbery," he warned, "will reap a harvest of blood."

Whipple's prediction proved correct: In the summer of 1862, a decade of anger boiled over. In a surprise attack, Dakota warriors fanned out through the Minnesota countryside, killing settlers and burning farms. They planned to sweep eastward to St. Paul but were repulsed at Fort Ridgely and the town of New Ulm. In the end, more than four hundred whites lay dead and thousands had fled. Panicked officials telegraphed for aid, spreading hysteria from Wisconsin to Colorado.

Minnesotans' fierce response to the Dakota uprising set the stage for further conflict. A hastily appointed military court, bent on revenge, sentenced 307 Dakotas to death, making it clear that Indians who rebelled would be treated as criminals rather than captured warriors. Abraham Lincoln, who insisted on reviewing the trial records, commuted most of the sentences but authorized the deaths of 38 Dakota men. They were

hanged just after Christmas 1862 in the largest mass execution in U.S. history. Two months later, Congress canceled all treaties with the Dakotas, revoked their annuities, and expelled them from Minnesota. Faced with these cruel conditions, scattered bands fled farther west to join nonreservation allies.

As this rebellion showed, the Civil War had created two dangerous conditions in the West. First, with the Union Army fighting the Confederacy, western whites felt especially vulnerable to Indian attacks. Second, fearful westerners found that when they chose to, they could fight Indians with minimal federal oversight. In the wake of the Dakota uprising, worried Coloradans favored a military campaign against the Cheyennes—allies of the Sioux—even though the Cheyennes had shown little evidence of hostility. Colorado militia leader John M. Chivington, an aspiring politician, determined to quell public anxiety and make his own career.

In May 1864, Chivington's militia attacked a Cheyenne encampment, shooting down a chief who had made peace terms with the United States. After witnessing this murder, Cheyenne chief Black Kettle surrendered his own band to federal agents, who instructed them to camp in the area of Sand Creek, in eastern Colorado, until a treaty could be signed. On November 29, 1864, Chivington's Colorado militia attacked this camp while most of the warriors were out hunting. They killed Black Kettle and hunted down more than a hundred women, children, and even infants, following an officer's orders to leave none alive. The militia rode back for a celebration in Denver, where they hung Cheyenne scalps (and women's genitals) from the rafters of the Apollo Theater.

The northern plains exploded in conflict. Infuriated by the Sand Creek massacre, Cheyennes carried war pipes to the Arapahos and Sioux, who attacked and burned settlements along the South Platte River. Ordered to subdue these peoples, the U.S. Army failed miserably: Officers were not even able to locate the enemy, who traveled rapidly in small bands and knew the country well. This humiliation was compounded in December 1866 when 1,500 Sioux warriors executed a perfect ambush, luring Captain William Fetterman and 80 soldiers from a Wyoming fort and wiping them out. With this victory the Sioux succeeded in closing the Bozeman Trail, a private road under army protection that had served as the main route into Montana.

General William Tecumseh Sherman, who had taken command of the army in the West, swore to defeat the Plains Indians, "even to their extermination." But the Union hero who had helped defeat the Confederacy met his match on the plains. Another year of fighting proved expensive, exhausting, and inconclusive. In 1868, the Sioux, led by the Oglala band under Chief Red Cloud, told a peace commission they would not sign any treaty unless the United States pledged to abandon all its forts along the Bozeman Trail. The commission agreed. Red Cloud had won.

In the wake of these events, eastern public opinion turned against the Indian wars, which seemed at best ineffective and costly, and at worst brutal. Congress held hearings on the slaughter at Sand Creek. Though Chivington, now a civilian, was never prosecuted, the massacre became an infamous example of western vigilantism. By the time Ulysses Grant entered the White House in 1869, the congressional leaders orchestrating radical Reconstruction in the South also began to seek solutions to the "Indian problem" out West.

Grant's Peace Policy

When he entered the White House, Ulysses S. Grant inherited an Indian policy in disarray. Federal incompetence was highlighted by yet another mass killing of friendly Indians in January 1870, this time on the Marias River in Montana, by an army detachment that shot and burned to death 173 Piegan (Blackfoot) women and children. Having run out of other promising options, Grant developed a peace policy for the West, based on recommendations from Christian reformers. He put reformers themselves in charge. These men and women, including many former abolitionists, had created such organizations as the Indian Rights Association and the Women's National Indian Association. They rejected the racism of many westerners and soldiers like General Philip Sheridan, who once declared, "The only good Indians I ever saw were dead."

Reformers argued that native peoples had the innate capacity to become equal with whites. They believed, however, that Indians could achieve that goal only if they were Christianized and educated in white ways. Reformers thus aimed to destroy native languages, cultures, and religions. As one put it, they would "kill the Indian and save the man." Despite their humane intentions, peace advocates' condescension was obvious. They ignored dissenters like Dr. Thomas Bland of the National Indian Defense Association, who suggested that instead of an "Indian problem" there might be a "white problem"—the refusal to permit Indians to live according to their own traditional ways. To most nineteenth-century Americans, such a notion was shocking and uncivilized.

Indian Boarding Schools | Reformers focused their greatest energy on educating the next generation. Realizing that **assimilation**, or adoption of white ways, was difficult when children lived at home, agents and missionaries worked hard to enroll children in off-reservation schools. The most famous of these, Pennsylvania's Carlisle School, was founded in 1879. Native families were exhorted, bullied, and bribed into sending their children to such schools, where Indian children were required to speak only English and missionaries forced them to take up white ways. The Lakota boy Plenty Kill, who became one of Carlisle's first students at age eleven and received the new name Luther, remembered his loneliness and terror upon arrival: "The big boys would sing brave songs, and that would start the girls to crying. . . . The girls' quarters were about a hundred and fifty yards from ours, so we could hear them." After having his hair cut short, Plenty Kill felt a profound change in his identity. "None of us slept well that night," he recalled. "I felt that I was no more Indian, but would be an imitation of a white man."

Indian School

This photograph was taken at the Riverside Indian School in Anadarko, Oklahoma Territory. The pupils have been shorn of their braids and clothed in Mother Hubbard dresses and shirts and trousers — one step on the journey into the mainstream of white American society. Children as young as five were separated from their families and sent to Indian schools that taught them new skills while pressuring them to abandon traditional Indian ways.   University of Oklahoma, Western History Collections.

Even in the first flush of reform zeal, Grant's peace policy faced daunting hurdles. Most Indian peoples had been yanked off their traditional lands and assigned to barren ground that would have defeated the most enterprising farmer. Poverty and dislocation made Indians especially vulnerable to the ravages of infectious diseases like measles and scarlet fever. In the meantime, Quaker, Presbyterian, and Methodist reformers fought nasty turf battles among themselves and with Catholic missionaries. Also, despite the efforts of reformers, agents and traders continued to skim off money and supplies from the people they were supposed to protect. Rutherford B. Hayes's administration (1877–1881) undertook housecleaning at the Bureau of Indian Affairs, but corruption lingered.

From the Indian point of view, reformers often became just another interest group in a crowded field of whites who sent hopelessly mixed messages. Individual army officers, agents, and missionaries ranged from sympathetic to utterly ruthless. Many times, after chiefs thought they had reached a face-to-face agreement, they found it denied or drastically altered by Congress or the Bureau of Indian Affairs. The Nez Perce chief Joseph observed, "[T]he white people have too many chiefs. They do not understand each other. They do not all talk alike. . . . I cannot understand why so many chiefs are allowed to talk so many different ways, and promise so many different things." A Kiowa chief agreed: "We make but few contracts, and them we remember well. The whites make so many they are liable to forget them. The white chief seems not to be able to govern his braves."

Native peoples were nonetheless forced to accommodate, as independent tribal governance and treaty making came to an end. Back in the 1830s, the U.S. Supreme Court had declared Indians no longer sovereign but rather "domestic dependent nations." On a practical basis, however, officers in the field and the Senate in Washington had continued to negotiate treaties as late as 1869. In 1871, the House of Representatives, long jealous of Senate privileges, passed a bill to abolish all treaty making with Indians. The Senate agreed, provided that existing treaties remained in force. It was one more step in a long, torturous erosion of native rights. Eventually, the U.S. Supreme Court ruled in *Lone Wolf v. Hitchcock* (1903) that Congress could make whatever Indian policies it chose, ignoring all existing treaties. That same year, in *Ex Parte Crow Dog*, the Court ruled that no Indian was a citizen unless Congress designated him so. Indians were henceforth wards of the government. These rulings remained in force until the New Deal of the 1930s.

Breaking Up Tribal Lands   While the United States exerted increasing legal power over native peoples, reformers made another effort to assimilate them through the Dawes Severalty Act, passed in 1887. This law had long been the dream of Senator Henry L. Dawes of Massachusetts, a leader of the Indian Rights' Association. Dawes saw the reservation system as an ugly relic of the past. He hoped to break up tribal landholding and give Indians **severalty** (individual ownership of land) by dividing reservations into homesteads, just like those of white farmers in the West. Supporters of the plan believed that ownership of private property would encourage Indians to adopt white ways. It would lead, Dawes wrote, to "a personal sense of independence." Property ownership, echoed another reformer, would make the Indian man "intelligently selfish, . . . with a *pocket that aches to be filled with dollars!*"

The Dawes Act was a disaster. It played into the hands of whites who coveted Indian land: They quickly urged that all reservation lands not needed for allotments be sold to non-Indians. Further, the Bureau of Indian Affairs (BIA) implemented the law carelessly, to the shock of Dawes and other sponsors. In Indian Territory, a government commission seized more than 15 million "surplus" acres from native tribes by 1894. This opened the way for whites to convert the last federal territory set aside for native peoples into the state of Oklahoma. Before the Dawes Act, American Indians had held more than 155 million acres of land across the United States; by 1900, this had dropped to 77 million acres. By the time of the Indian Reorganization Act of 1934, native peoples had also lost 66 percent of their individually allotted lands through fraud, BIA mismanagement, and pressure to sell to whites.

The End of Armed Resistance

Despite the glaring flaws that soon became apparent, Americans by the mid-1870s believed they had solved the "Indian problem" in the lands west of the Mississippi. In the Southwest, such formidable peoples as the Kiowas and Comanches had been forced onto designated reservations. The Navajo (or Diné) people, exiled under horrific conditions during the Civil War, were permitted to reoccupy their traditional homeland and abandoned further military resistance. An outbreak among California's Modoc people in 1873 — again, humiliating to the army — had at last been subdued. Only

Little Plume and Yellow Kidney

Photographer Edward S. Curtis took this photograph of Piegan (Blackfeet) warrior Little Plume and his son Yellow Kidney. Curtis's extensive collection of photographs of Native Americans remains a valuable resource for historians. Curtis, however, altered his images for publication to make his native subjects seem more "authentic": Even though Indians made widespread use of non-native furniture, clothes, and other consumer goods (even Singer sewing machines), Curtis removed those from the frame. He also retouched photographs to remove items such as belts and watches. Note the circular "shadow" here, against the lodge wall, near Little Plume's right arm: The original photograph included a clock.   Library of Congress.

Sitting Bull, a leader of the powerful Lakota Sioux on the northern plains, openly refused to go to a reservation. He often crossed into Canada, where he told reporters that "the life of white men is slavery. . . . I have seen nothing that a white man has, houses or railways or clothing or food, that is as good as the right to move in open country and live in our own fashion."

Sitting Bull and Custer   In 1874, the Lakotas faced a direct provocation. General George Armstrong Custer, a brash self-promoter who had graduated last in his class at West Point, led an expedition into South Dakota's Black Hills and loudly proclaimed the discovery of gold. Amid the severe depression that began in 1873, prospectors rushed in. The United States, reneging on its 1868 treaty, pressured Sioux leaders to sell the Black Hills, but the chiefs said no. Ignoring this answer, the government demanded in 1876 that all Sioux gather at the federal agencies. The policy backfired: Not only did Sitting Bull and others refuse to report, but other Sioux, Cheyennes, and Arapahos slipped away from reservations to join Sitting Bull.

Amid the nation's centennial celebration in July 1876, Americans received awful news. On June 25–26, General Custer had led 210 men of the Seventh Cavalry in an ill-considered assault on Sitting Bull's camp beside the Little Big Horn River in Montana. In defense, the Sioux and their allies had killed the attackers to the last man. The story of Custer's "last stand" quickly served to justify American conquest. Long after Americans forgot the massacres of Cheyenne women and children at Sand Creek and Piegan people on the Marias River, prints of the Battle of Little Big Horn hung in barrooms across the country. William F. "Buffalo Bill" Cody, in his traveling Wild West performances, enacted a revenge killing of the Cheyenne warrior Yellow Hand, in a tableau that Cody called "first scalp for Custer." Notwithstanding that the tableau featured a white man scalping a Cheyenne, Cody depicted this as a triumph for civilization in the West.

Little Big Horn was the last major military victory of Plains Indians against the U.S. Army. Pursued relentlessly after Custer's defeat, Sioux warriors watched their children starve through a bitter winter. Slowly, families trickled into the agencies, accommodating themselves to life on reservations that the U.S. government fragmented and drastically reduced in size (Map. 16.6). The next year the Nez Perce, fleeing desperately for the Canadian border, also surrendered. The last holdout was in the Southwest: Chiricahua Apache leader Geronimo. Like many others, Geronimo had accepted reservation

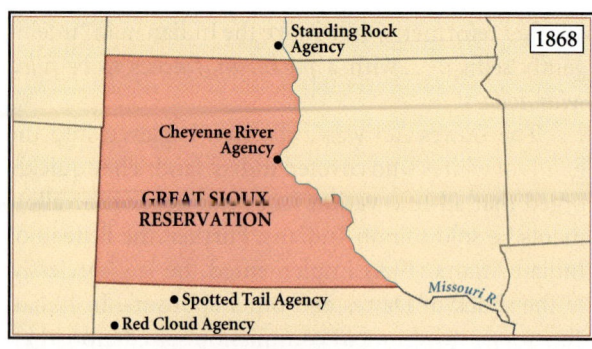

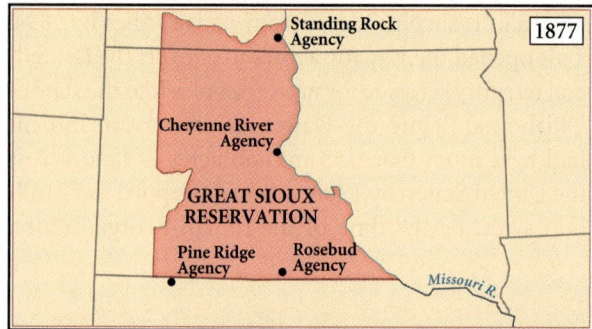

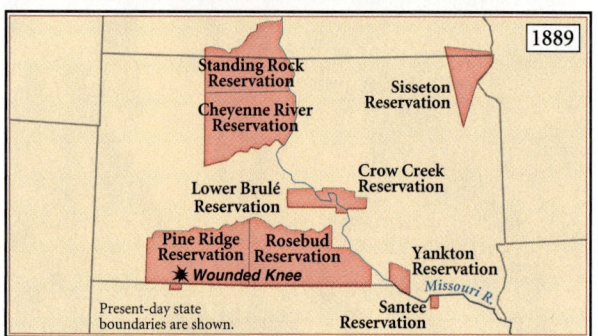

MAP 16.6

The Sioux Reservations in South Dakota, 1868–1889

In 1868, when they bent to the demand that they move onto the reservation, the Sioux thought they had gained secure rights to a substantial part of their ancestral hunting grounds. But harsh conditions on reservations led to continuing military conflicts. Land-hungry whites exerted continuous local pressure, and officials in Washington repeatedly changed the terms of Sioux land holdings—always eroding native claims.

life but then took up arms out of sheer desperation. Recalling the desolate land the tribe had been allotted, one Apache said, "[T]here was nothing but cactus, rattlesnakes, heat, rocks, and insects. . . . Many, many of our people died of starvation." The army recruited other Apaches to track Geronimo into the hills; in September 1886, he surrendered for the last time. The Chiracahua Apaches never returned to their homeland. The United States had completed its military conquest of the West.

Dime Novel Cover, 1872

During and after the Civil War, publishers found an immense market for two types of cheap, sensational novels: urban detective stories and tales of the frontier. The cover of this 1872 novel is typical of the latter. Dime novel Westerns featured such fictional heroes as Deadwood Dick and alleged "real-life" stories about Jesse James or Buffalo Bill. Such novels did not reflect real life in the West, but they were very popular nationwide, particularly among young people and working-class readers. The "Western," as a later film genre, relied heavily on the stories and stereotypes that dime novels popularized.   Library of Congress.

Strategies of Survival

Even though the warpath closed, many native peoples continued secretly to practice traditional customs. Away from the disapproving eyes of agents, missionaries, and teachers, they passed on their languages, oral histories, and traditional arts and medicine from each generation to the next. Frustrated missionaries often concluded that little could be accomplished on the reservations because bonds of kinship and custom were so strong. Yet they

had difficulty enrolling students in off-reservation boarding schools because so many parents hated to relinquish their children. Thus, most Indian schools ended up on or near reservations, and white teachers were forced to accept their pupils' continued participation in the rhythms of reservation life.

Selectively, at least, most native peoples accepted some white ways. Many parents urged their sons and daughters to study hard at white-run schools, learn English, and develop skills to help them succeed in the new world that confronted them. Some of these children grew up to be writers and artists who interpreted native experiences for national audiences. Others took up law and medicine. While enrolled at the Carlisle School in Pennsylvania, the son of a Quechan chief from Arizona wrote to the agent on his family's reservation. He warned, in fluent English, that he knew about the agent's thievery and would write to Washington to expose him if he did not stop.

In practice, most native people relied upon both tradition and innovation as they sought the best path forward (see Reading American Pictures, "A Sioux Chief Blends Old and New Ways," p. 521). One of the most famous examples was a Dakota boy named Ohiyesa, who grew up to become Dr. Charles Eastman. Posted to the Pine Ridge Reservation in South Dakota, Eastman practiced medicine side by side with traditional healers, whom he respected. While assimilating to European American culture, Eastman wrote many popular books under his Dakota name, Ohiyesa. He remembered that when he left for boarding school, his father said, "We have now entered upon this life, and there is no going back. . . . Remember, my boy, it is the same as if I sent you on your first war-path. I shall expect you to conquer."

Nothing exemplified this syncretism better than the Ghost Dance movement of the late 1880s, which fostered the hope that native peoples could, through sacred dances, resurrect the bison and create a great storm that would drive whites back across the Atlantic. The Ghost Dance drew on significant Christian elements as well as native ones. As it spread from reservation to reservation—from Paiutes to Arapahos to Sioux—native peoples across the West began to develop new forms of pan-Indian identity and cooperation.

Unfortunately, the outcome of the Ghost Dance movement bore witness to the lethal exertion of authority by misunderstanding whites. When a group of Lakota Sioux Ghost Dancers left their South Dakota reservation after police there killed Sitting Bull in December 1890, they were pursued by the U.S. Seventh Cavalry, in the fear that further spread of the Ghost Dance would provoke war. On December 29, at Wounded Knee Creek,

BUFFALO BILL'S WILD WEST AND CONGRESS OF **ROUGH RIDERS OF THE WORLD.**

COL. W. F. CODY (BUFFALO BILL) A CLOSE CALL.

"A Close Call"

Part of the appeal of Buffalo Bill's Wild West, for contemporary audiences, was that it reenacted exploits of his that actually happened or, at any rate, that Buffalo Bill claimed to have happened. In fact, Bill never called the Wild West a "show"; he placed tremendous emphasis on its allegedly authentic re-enactments. In this poster advertising the 1894 season, U.S. troopers are rescuing him in the nick of time from a scalping. Such advertisements contributed to the glorification of wars of conquest against "savages." Granger Collection, New York.

the army caught up with the fleeing Indians and killed more than 150 Lakota men, women, and children. Like so many others—such as Sand Creek and the killing of Piegan on the Marias River—this massacre could have been avoided if U.S. officials had had a clearer understanding of native viewpoints, and had pursued a fairer and more consistent course of action. The deaths at Wounded Knee stand as a final indictment against decades of relentless U.S. expansion, chaotic and conflicting policies, and bloody mistakes.

Less than two months after the Wounded Knee massacre, General William T. Sherman died in New York. As the nation marked his passing with pomp and speech-making, commentators noted that Sherman's career had paralleled the rise of the United States. Sherman's first military exploits had been against Seminoles in

Florida; later, during the Mexican War (1846–1848), the army sent him west to help claim California. After a stint in civilian life, Sherman returned to the military when the Civil War broke out, warning a friend in Virginia that northerners were "not going to let this country be destroyed." Before war's end, Sherman's name was infamous throughout the South. It was appropriate that this general who helped subdue the South was then sent west to defeat the Sioux and Cheyennes, until he declared that "the Indian question has become one of sentiment and charity, but not of war."

When Sherman had graduated from West Point in 1840, the United States counted twenty-six states, none of them west of Missouri. At his death in 1891, the nation boasted forty-four states, in settled territory stretching to the Pacific coast. The United States now rivaled

A Sioux Chief Blends Old and New Ways

Late-nineteenth-century Americans developed a keen anthropological interest in Native American cultures, but most also believed that Indians were a "vanishing race," too primitive to survive modern life in an industrial society. Photographers, notably Edward S. Curtis, created individual portraits of people from many different tribes. Wherever possible, Curtis removed from his photographs any objects of modern manufacture (see "Little Plume and Yellow Kidney," p. 517).

The photograph shown here offers a different perspective. Taken by photographer C. G. Morledge in 1891, on the Pine Ridge reservation in South Dakota, it shows the bedroom of Red Cloud, a distinguished chief of the Oglala Lakota (Sioux) tribe. Red Cloud had won a war against the U.S. Army just after the Civil War, and he remained a trusted and powerful leader. He confronted what he saw as meddlesome agents with such tenacity and shrewdness that the Sioux nicknamed Pine Ridge "The Place Where Everything Is Disputed."

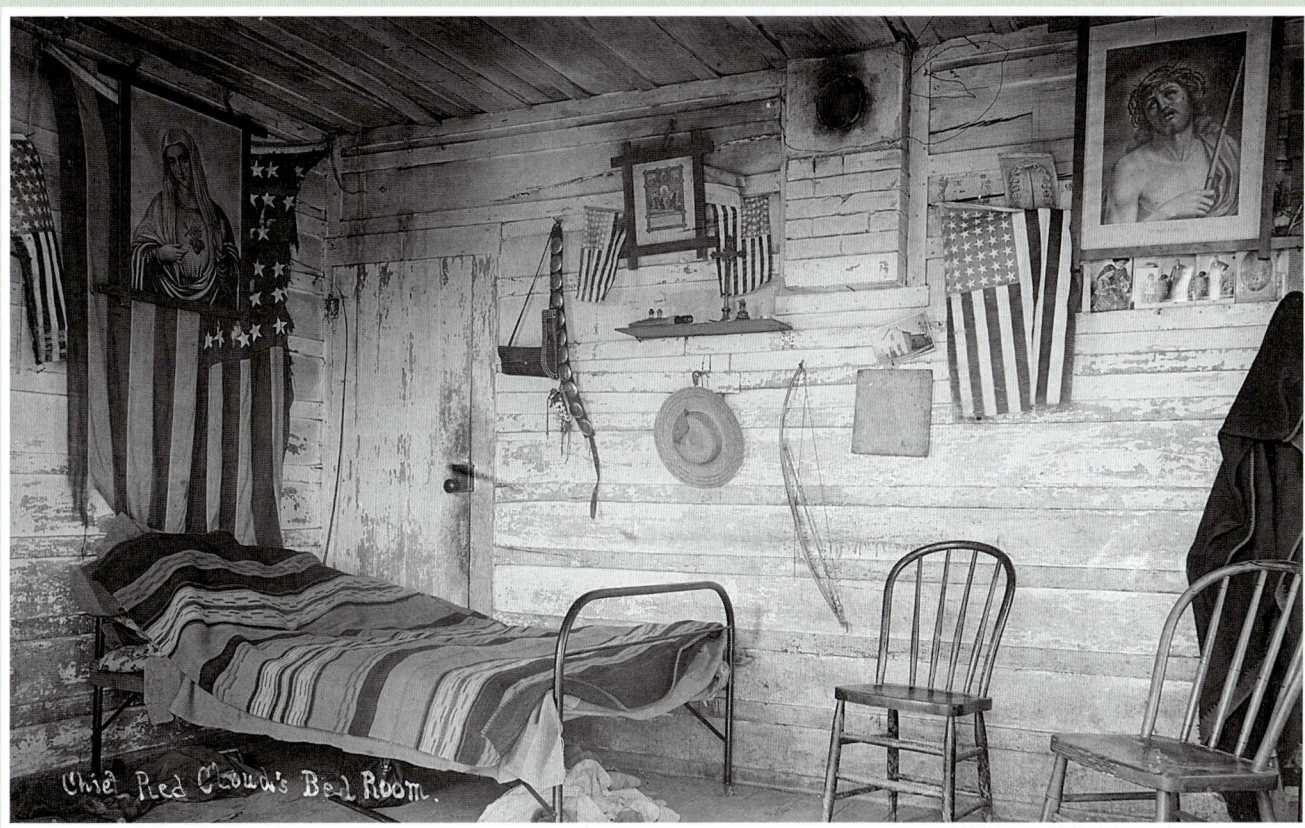

Red Cloud's Bedroom. Denver Public Library, Western History Division.

ANALYZING THE EVIDENCE

- As shown in this photograph, Red Cloud's bedroom brings together objects from different traditions. What objects do you see? From what sources did Red Cloud likely obtain them?

- How do you interpret the presence of five American flags? The portrait of Abraham Lincoln (located between the two small flags in the middle)?

- What continuities in Red Cloud's daily life — traditions and practices passed down by his Oglala Lakota elders — might not be reflected in the photo?

Britain and Germany as an industrial giant, and its dynamic economy was drawing immigrants from Asia, Latin America, and Eastern and Southern Europe to join those from Africa and Western Europe. Over the span of Sherman's career, the United States had become a major player on the world stage. It had done so, in part, through the kind of fierce military conquest that Sherman himself made famous, as well as through bold expansions of federal power. Because of the conflicts and decisions made in Sherman's lifetime, the children and grandchildren of Civil War heroes inherited a vast empire. In the coming decades, it would be up to them to determine how to use the nation's new power at home and abroad.

- How did the Civil War affect relations between the Sioux and their allies, white settlers, and the U.S. government?

- What effect did Grant's peace policy and subsequent U.S. Indian policy have on native peoples? What role did white reformers play in those policies?

- What were the last acts of native peoples' armed resistance? What were the consequences of that resistance?

- What survival strategies did conquered native peoples develop?

SUMMARY

Between 1861 and 1877, the United States completed its conquest of the continent. After the Civil War, the expansion of railroads fostered the integration of the national economy. Republicans in the federal government promoted this integration by erecting protective tariffs, while federal courts made rulings that facilitated economic growth and strengthened corporations. To attract foreign investment, Republican policymakers placed the nation on the gold standard. These policymakers also pursued a vigorous foreign policy, acquiring Alaska and asserting U.S. power indirectly through control of international trade in Latin America and Asia.

An important result of economic integration was the incorporation of the Great Plains. Cattlemen built an industry linked to the integrated economy, though in the process nearly driving the native bison to extinction. Homesteaders confronted harsh environmental conditions as they converted the grasslands for agriculture. Republicans championed homesteader families as representatives of domesticity, an ideal opposed to Mormon plural marriage in Utah. Homesteading accelerated the rapid, often violent, transformation of the western environment. Perceiving this transformation, the federal government began setting aside natural preserves such as Yellowstone, often clashing with Native Americans who wished to hunt on the land.

Such conflict over land ultimately led to the conquest of Native Americans. During the Civil War, white settlers clashed with the Sioux and their allies. Grant's peace policy sought to end this conflict by forcing Native Americans to assimilate western practices. Native American armed resistance continued through the 1870s and 1880s, ending with Geronimo's surrender in 1886. Thereafter, Native Americans survived, though not without further conflict, by either secretly continuing their traditions or selectively adopting white ways. Due in part to the determined military conquest of this period, the United States claimed for itself a major role on the world stage.

CHAPTER REVIEW QUESTIONS

- What national economic development policies did Republicans pursue during the Civil War and Reconstruction? What were the resulting achievements and costs?

- What were some of the impacts of the settlement of the Great Plains and Far West on the natural environment?

- Why did U.S. policies toward Native Americans in this era result in so much continued violence? In what ways did American Indians in the West respond to U.S. encroachment on their traditional lands, and to assimilation efforts?

FOR FURTHER EXPLORATION

On the subject of the economic consolidation of the West, see William Cronon's *Nature's Metropolis* (1991). John Stover's *American Railroads*, 2nd ed. (1997), is a good overview. On Republican policies, see Richard Bensel, *The Political Economy of American Industrialization, 1877–1900* (2000); on tariff debates, Joanne Reitano, *The Tariff Question in the Gilded Age* (1994); on monetary policy, Walter T. K. Nugent, *The Money Question During Reconstruction* (1967). On foreign policy after the Civil War, see the relevant sections of Walter LaFeber, *The American Search for Opportunity* (1993). Thomas Bender explores U.S. nation building in *A Nation Among Nations* (2006).

On the West see Patricia Nelson Limerick's *The Legacy of Conquest* (1987), Richard White's *"It's Your Misfortune and None of My Own"* (1991), and Andrew Isenberg, *The Destruction of the Bison* (2000). On farming see Frieda Knobloch, *The Culture of Wilderness* (1996); on women, Susan Armitage and Elizabeth Jameson, eds., *The Women's West* (1987), and Sarah Barringer Gordon, *The Mormon Question* (2002). María Montoya explores Mexican displacement in *Translating Property* (2002). On the Indian wars see Robert Utley, *The Indian Frontier of the American West* (1984), and Mark David Spence, *Dispossessing the Wilderness* (1999). Assimilation policies are covered in Frederick Hoxie, *A Final Promise* (1984), and David Wallace Adams, *Education for Extinction* (1995). Good sites are **www.americanwest.com** and **www.pbs.org/nationalparks**.

TEST YOUR KNOWLEDGE

To assess your command of the material in this chapter, see the Online Study Guide at **bedfordstmartins.com/henretta**.

For Web sites, images, and documents related to topics and places in this chapter, visit **bedfordstmartins.com/makehistory**.

TIMELINE

1854	United States "opens" Japan to trade
1859	Comstock silver lode discovered in Nevada
1862	Homestead Act Dakota Sioux uprising in Minnesota
1864	Sand Creek massacre of Cheyenne in Colorado Yosemite Valley reserved as public park
1865	Long Drive of Texas longhorns begins
1866	Sioux under Red Cloud succeed in closing Bozeman Trail in Montana
1868	Treaty confirms Sioux rights to Powder River hunting grounds Burlingame Treaty with China
1869	Transcontinental railroad completed
1870	Utah gives full voting rights to women Wyoming gives full voting rights to women
1875	John Wesley Powell publishes *Report on Arid Lands* Sioux ordered to vacate Powder River hunting grounds; war breaks out
1876	Battle of the Little Big Horn
1877	San Francisco anti-Chinese riots *Munn v. Illinois* Supreme Court decision
1879	Exoduster migration to Kansas United States placed fully on gold standard
1886	Dry cycle begins on the Great Plains
1887	Dawes Severalty Act
1890	Massacre of Indians at Wounded Knee, South Dakota

PART

5

BOLD EXPERIMENTS IN AN ERA OF INDUSTRIALIZATION, 1877–1929

Visiting the United States in 1905, British visitor James Bryce remarked on its "prodigious material development." He wrote that "rural districts are being studded with villages, the villages are growing into cities, the cities are stretching out long arms of suburbs." Bryce was witnessing America's birth as a global industrial power. In 1866 the nation was overwhelmingly rural and dependent on foreign capital as it recovered from a crippling civil war. By 1929, industrialization had introduced new ways of working and living. The United States also began to assert itself on the world stage, claiming overseas territories and playing a decisive role in World War I.

Industrialization required political innovation. As former president Theodore Roosevelt declared in 1910, American citizens needed to "effectively control the mighty commercial forces which they have called into being." Workers, farmers, and urban progressives worked to clean up politics, regulate corporations, and fight poverty. In their creative responses to the problems of a new industrial age, such reformers gave their name to the Progressive Era.

ECONOMY

The post–Civil War economy grew rapidly . . . millions of immigrants arrived

POLITICS AND LAW

Politics centered on the scope of government power

Industrialization and the Rise of Corporations

The post–Civil War economy grew rapidly, a trend intensified by industrial production during World War I. Millions of immigrants arrived from around the globe; though millions found places in the economy, Asians faced legal exclusion, and restrictions on overall numbers of immigrants were enacted in the 1920s. Giant corporations developed national and even global networks of production, marketing, and finance. Their complex structures opened new career opportunities for middle-class managers, salesmen, and women office workers. Traditional craftsmen, however, found themselves displaced, while factory workers and miners endured harsh conditions, low pay, and cycles of unemployment. Farmers also suffered from falling crop prices, caused by expanding world production.

State-building and Economic Regulation

The fierce struggles of post-Reconstruction politics centered on the scope of government power. In the 1880s, Republicans increasingly became champions of business. Though Republican Theodore Roosevelt championed key reforms during his presidency (1901–1909), much reform energy passed to other parties. The Greenback-Labor, People's (or Populist), and Progressive parties all proposed expanding government powers in response to industrialization and concentrated wealth. While none won national power, these parties shaped the course of reform. Democrats, who had long called for limited government, began in the 1890s to advocate stronger government intervention to fight poverty and restrain big business. The party had little opportunity to enact national programs during the Republican-dominated years of 1894–1910 and the prosperous, complacent decade of the 1920s. But in between, during the presidency of Democrat Woodrow Wilson ▶

(1913–1921), the party enacted an impressive slate of reforms. By 1929, when the Great Depression hit, Democrats were poised to enact the New Deal.

REFORM

An array of reformers . . . responded to the problems caused by industrialization

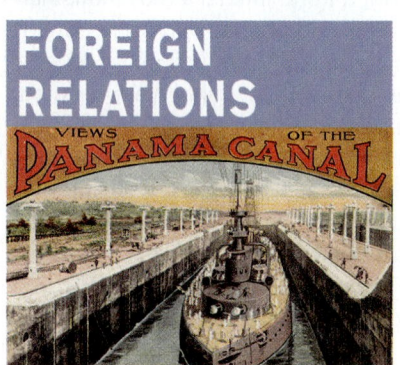

CULTURE

Consumer culture encouraged Americans to spend money and have fun

FOREIGN RELATIONS

The United States claimed overseas colonies and asserted . . . tremendous clout in global affairs

Labor, Reform, and Protest Movements

An array of reformers, loosely known as progressives, responded to the problems caused by industrialization. More radical proposals tended to come from mass-based coalitions of workers and farmers; pressure from such groups combined with the efforts of middle-class and urban reformers to generate new policies. Reformers sought to enhance democracy, rein in the power of corporations, uphold labor rights, and promote public health and safety. Progressives ran up against formidable political obstacles, especially from the Supreme Court. Nonetheless, by 1920, national, state, and local governments enacted a range of landmark laws, representing the early emergence of the modern state.

Immigration and Urbanization: The Origins of Modern Mass Culture

While the nineteenth-century values of thrift, piety, and domesticity never entirely faded, they faced serious challenges in the era of industrialization. Women asserted more independent roles within the family and in public life. The secular pleasures of consumer culture encouraged Americans to spend money and have fun. Americans cheered for professional sports teams, and by the 1920s flocked to the movies and purchased millions of automobiles. As early as the 1880s, literary realism marked a break with Victorian culture as one element of the modernism that led to such innovations as jazz music and abstract art.

An Emerging World Power

Policymakers of the post–Civil War era focused on overseas trade. Victorious against Spain in the War of 1898, the United States claimed overseas colonies and asserted control over the Caribbean basin. Though President Woodrow Wilson attempted to maintain neutrality at the start of World War I, trade ties helped draw America into the conflict on the Allied side. Wilson sought to influence the peace, but Allied leaders ignored his proposals and the U.S. Senate rejected the treaty altogether. At war's end, though America exerted tremendous clout in global affairs, its role on the world stage remained uncertain.

BOLD EXPERIMENTS IN AN ERA OF INDUSTRIALIZATION, 1877–1929

	ECONOMY	POLITICS AND LAW	REFORM	CULTURE	FOREIGN RELATIONS
1870	• Economic depression of 1870s	• Reconstruction ends (1877)	• Great Railroad Strike of 1877	• National League launches professional baseball (1876)	• Treaty brings Hawaii within U.S. orbit
1880	• First vertically integrated firms • Rockefeller establishes Standard Oil Trust • Emergence of white-collar managerial work • Women enter paid labor as office workers	• Era of close party competition, 1876–1894 • Chinese Exclusion (1882–1943) • Pendleton Act (1883) • Interstate Commerce Act (1887)	• Woman's Christian Temperance Union (WCTU) becomes largest women's reform movement • Knights of Labor at peak (mid-1880s) • Hull House (1889)	• William Dean Howells calls for realism in literature (1881)	
1890	• Economic depression (1893–1897)	• Sherman Antitrust Act (1890) • Republican victories (1894–1896) • Rise of Democratic "Solid South" • Supreme Court upholds segregation in *Plessy v. Ferguson* (1896)	• People's Party (1890) • Sierra Club (1892) • Coxey's Army (1894) • Consumers' League (1899)	• William Randolph Hearst pioneers "yellow journalism" • Disenfranchisement and Jim Crow in the South • Rise of Social Gospel	• War of 1898 • Hawaii annexed (1898) • Philippine-American War (1899–1902)
1900	• U.S. Steel becomes first corporation with billion-dollar valuation (1901)	• William McKinley assassinated; Theodore Roosevelt becomes president (1901) • Hepburn Act (1906)	• Growth of American Federation of Labor (AFL) • American Socialist Party (1901) • NAACP (1909)	• Popularity of ragtime music • First World Series in baseball (1903)	• Platt Amendment (1902) • Roosevelt corollary to Monroe Doctrine (1904) • Panama Canal begun (1904)
1910	• Triangle Shirtwaist fire (1911) • United States becomes a creditor nation • Great Migration of African Americans	• Woodrow Wilson elected president (1913) • Eighteenth Amendment: federal income tax (1913)	• Women's suffrage movement grows	• Armory Show (1913) • Anti-German nativism during World War I • "Red Scare" (1919)	• Wilson intervenes in Mexico (1914) • United States enters World War I (1917) • Wilson's Fourteen Points (1918)
1920	• Economic prosperity (1922–1929)	• Republican ascendancy (1920–1932) • Nineteenth Amendment: national women's suffrage (1921) • Heyday of second Ku Klux Klan	• Prohibition (1921–1933)	• Rise of Hollywood • Harlem Renaissance • Emergence of jazz	• Treaty of Versailles rejected by U.S. Senate (1920)

CHAPTER 17

The Busy Hive: Industrial America at Work, 1877–1911

For millions of his contemporaries, the life of Andrew Carnegie exemplified American success. Arriving from Scotland as a poor twelve-year-old in 1848, Carnegie found work as an errand boy for the Pennsylvania Railroad and rapidly scaled the managerial ladder. In 1865, he struck out on his own as an iron manufacturer, selling to his network of friends in the railroad business, and he soon built a massive steel mill outside Pittsburgh. Its centerpiece was a state-of-the-art Bessemer converter, which broke a bottleneck in the process of the refining of iron into steel. With Carnegie showing the way, steel soon became a major U.S. industry, reaching an annual production of 10 million metric tons by 1900 — almost as much as the *combined* output of the world's other top producers, Germany (6.6 million tons) and Great Britain (4.8 million tons).

Americans hailed Carnegie as a genius, eagerly absorbing his ideas about the economic upheavals he was helping to cause. In his popular 1887 essay, "Wealth," Carnegie acknowledged that industrialization increased the gap between rich and poor. But that, he said, was progress. Industrialization brought cheap products to the masses; even if the benefits were unequal, everyone's standard of living rose. "The poor enjoy what the rich could not before afford," Carnegie wrote. "What were the luxuries have become the necessaries of life."

At the time Carnegie was writing that essay, skilled workers at his mill in Homestead, Pennsylvania, might have agreed with many of his views. Most earned good wages and lived comfortably. They had a strong union, and Carnegie had affirmed workers' right to organize. But by 1892, Carnegie — confident that new machinery gave him the upper hand — decided that collective bargaining was too expensive. The steel magnate withdrew to his estate in Scotland, leaving his partner, Henry Clay Frick, in command. A former coal magnate and veteran of labor wars in the coal fields, Frick was well qualified to do the dirty work. He announced that after July 1, 1892, members of the Amalgamated Association of Iron and Steel Workers would be locked out of the Homestead mill. If they wanted to return to work, they would have to abandon the union and sign new individual contracts. Frick had fortified the mill and prepared to bring in replacement workers if needed. The battle was on.

Industrial Landscape

Artist Aaron Henry Gorson painted this landscape along the Monongahela River near Pittsburgh, depicting one of the steel mills that became symbols of America's industrial prowess but also, as the clouds of smoke suggest, a major source of the Pittsburgh area's polluted air. Gorson, born a Lithuanian Jew, followed his brother to Philadelphia in 1888 and studied art in night school. He found a patron in Rabbi Leonard Levy, and Gorson followed Levy to Pittsburgh when he moved there to lead a Reform synagogue. Fascinated by the mills of Pittsburgh's industrial districts, Gorson made them his chief subject. He painted commissioned works for Andrew Carnegie and other leading manufacturers and financiers. Courtesy of Arader Galleries.

At dawn on July 6, barges chugged up the Monongahela River, bringing dozens of armed guards from the Pinkerton Detective Agency, hired to take possession of the steelworks. Some of the locked-out workers opened fire, beginning a gunfight that left seven workers and three Pinkertons dead. Frick appealed to Pennsylvania's governor, who called out the state militia. Labor leaders and town officials were arrested on charges of riot and murder. Most of the locked-out workers lost their jobs. The union was dead.

By the time of the bloody clash at Homestead, industrialization had transformed the United States. More and more Americans worked not as self-employed farmers or artisans, but as employees of large corporations whose operations spanned national and even global markets. Conditions of work had changed for people of all economic classes and backgrounds. The stream of immigration into the United States had become a torrent, creating a new American working class that was strikingly diverse. In many places, as at Homestead, these dramatic changes provoked working people to protest—not only through strikes, but also through new movements for political reform.

Business Gets Bigger

In the late 1800s, the industrialization of Europe and the United States revolutionized the world economy. It brought large-scale commercial agriculture to many parts of the globe, consolidating land in fewer hands and uprooting traditional farmers. It prompted millions of migrants—including both skilled workers and displaced peasants—to travel across continents and oceans in search of jobs. Industrialization also created a production glut. Because of the immense scale of production, prices fell worldwide, not only for crops and raw materials but also for manufactured goods.

Falling prices normally signal low demand for goods and services, and thus stagnation. In England, a mature industrial power, the late nineteenth century did bring economic decline. But in the United States, industrial production expanded. Between 1877 and 1900, Americans' average real income increased from $388 to $573 per capita. In this sense, Andrew Carnegie was right: Industrialization raised the average standard of living. Technological and business efficiencies allowed American firms to grow, invest in new equipment, and earn profits even as prices for their products fell. Growth depended, in turn, on America's large and rapidly growing population, its expansion into the West, and its integrated national marketplace.

Republican economic policies, such as high protective tariffs and subsidies for transcontinental railroads, played a key role in promoting growth. But while they created jobs, such policies also fostered the rise of giant corporations, which in many industries crowded out or swallowed up small competitors. Though small-scale manufacturers and merchants survived in many fields, large corporations became the dominant form of business. These big companies quickly expanded overseas. As early as 1868, the Singer Manufacturing Company established a factory in Scotland to produce sewing machines. Rockefeller's Standard Oil became a multinational player. By World War I, such brands as Ford and General Electric had become familiar around the world.

The Rise of the Corporation

The United States became an industrial power by tapping North America's vast natural resources, including minerals, lumber, and coal, particularly in the newly developed West. Industries that had once depended on waterpower began to use prodigious amounts of coal. Steam engines replaced human and animal labor, and kerosene replaced whale oil and wood. By 1900, America's factories and urban homes were converting to electric power. Dependence on fossil fuels (oil, coal, natural gas), which powered machines of unprecedented speed and strength, transformed both the economy and the country's natural and built environments.

Vertical Integration The use of fossil fuels was a starting point for a broader array of innovations. After Chicago's Union Stock Yards opened in 1865, middlemen shipped cows by rail from the Great Plains to Chicago and from there to eastern cities, where slaughter took place in local butchertowns. Such a system—a national livestock market with local processing—could have lasted, as it did in Europe. But Gustavus Swift, a shrewd Chicago cattle dealer, saw that local slaughterhouses lacked the scale to utilize waste by-products and cut labor costs. He realized that, through new slaughtering practices, he could reduce production expenses (see Reading American Pictures, "The Killing Floor," p. 532). Further, he understood that if he could keep beef fresh in transit, he could centralize processing in Chicago and cut beef prices below what local butchers could offer.

Building on his insights, Swift pioneered **vertical integration**, a business model in which one company controlled all aspects of production from raw materials to finished goods. Once his engineers designed a cooling system, Swift invested in a fleet of refrigerator cars and constructed a packing plant near Chicago's stockyards. In cities that received his chilled meat, Swift built branch houses and fleets of delivery wagons. He constructed factories to make fertilizer and chemicals from the by-products of slaughter, and he developed marketing strategies for those products as well. Several other Chicago pork packers followed Swift's lead. By 1900, five firms, all vertically integrated, produced nearly 90 percent of the meat shipped in interstate commerce (Map 17.1).

Big packers also invented new sales tactics. For example, Swift & Company periodically slashed prices in certain markets to below production costs, driving

Rank of largest slaughtering and meatpacking centers, with percentage of national total:

1 Chicago (36%) 4 New York (5%)
2 Kansas City (9%) 5 St. Louis (4%)
3 Omaha (9%)

▲ Packing centers
— Major railroads
▉ Important livestock raising area

0   150   300 miles
0   150   300 kilometers

MAP 17.1

The Dressed Meat Industry, 1900

A map of the meatpacking industry clearly shows how transportation, supply, and demand combined to foster the growth of the American industrial economy. The main centers of beef production in 1900— Chicago, Omaha, Kansas City, and St. Louis—were rail hubs with connections westward to the cattle regions and eastward to cities hungry for cheap supplies of meat. Vertically integrated enterprises sprang from these elements, linked by an efficient and comprehensive railroad network.

The Killing Floor: Site of America's Mass-Production Revolution?

The invention of the refrigerator car (p. 531) enabled Gustavus Swift to concentrate his meat-processing operations at a giant packing plant next to the Chicago stockyards. But what did Swift have to gain by processing cattle in bulk? In this 1882 engraving of a Chicago packing plant, we have visual evidence of the system of high-volume meat processing that Swift introduced. It was, in fact, a variant of the mass-production manufacturing system and, like other examples of that system, yielded far higher output per worker and lower labor costs than had been possible under traditional methods. Swift's competitive advantage helped drive his locally based competitors out of business and make him a multimillionaire.

Chicago Meatpacking Plant, 1882. Library of Congress.

ANALYZING THE EVIDENCE

- As you inspect this engraving, you will see many workers but no machinery. All the work is done by hand. Can you explain, by looking at the tasks the workers are doing, why, even without machinery, they would be more efficient collectively than the same number of butchers working in the traditional way, each one handling his own cow? Can you think of a term that describes the system of labor depicted in the engraving?

- Although lacking any mechanized tools, Swift's mass-production system did benefit from one key technological advance: an overhead pulley system. (This one appears to be manual; eventually such systems would be power-driven.) Can you explain, by inspecting the engraving, what this pulley system did and why it was important, crucially important in fact, for Swift's new system of production?

- Can you explain why Henry Ford, whose great innovation in car manufacture was the moving assembly line, claimed he got the idea after visiting a meatpacking plant like the one in this engraving?

- In the text, we say that mass production relied on the de-skilling of labor. Is there any evidence of that process in this engraving?

independent distributors to the wall. With profits from sales elsewhere, a large firm like Swift could survive temporary losses in one locality until competitors went under. Afterward, Swift could raise prices again. This technique, known as **predatory pricing**, helped give a few firms unprecedented market control.

Standard Oil and the Rise of the Trusts | No one used ruthless business tactics more skillfully than the king of petroleum products, John D. Rockefeller of Standard Oil. Inventors in the 1850s had figured out how to extract kerosene, a clean-burning fuel that was excellent for domestic heating and lighting, from crude oil. Then an enormous supply of oil was located at Titusville, Pennsylvania, just as the Civil War severely disrupted the whaling industry and forced whale-oil customers to look for an alternative lighting source. Overnight, a forest of oil wells sprang up around Titusville. Connected to the Pennsylvania oil fields by rail in 1863, Cleveland, Ohio, became a great refining center. At that time, John D. Rockefeller was an up-and-coming Cleveland grain dealer, prospering due to the Civil War (during which he, like Carnegie and most other budding tycoons of that generation, hired a substitute to fight on his behalf). Rockefeller had strong nerves, a sharp eye for able partners, and a genius for finance. He went into the kerosene business and borrowed heavily to expand capacity. Within a few years, his firm—Standard Oil of Ohio—was Cleveland's leading refiner.

Like Carnegie and Swift, Rockefeller succeeded through vertical integration: to control production and sales all the way from the oil well to the kerosene lamp, he took a big stake in the oil fields, added pipelines, and developed a vast distribution network. Rockefeller allied with railroad executives who, like him, hated the boom-and-bust cycles in the oil market. What they wanted was predictable, high-volume traffic. The railroads offered Rockefeller secret rebates that gave him a leg up on competitors.

Rockefeller also pioneered a strategy that became known as **horizontal integration**. Like Swift, he pressured competitors through predatory pricing, but when he had driven them to failure, he invited rivals to merge their companies into his conglomerate. Most accepted the offer, often because they had no choice. Through such mergers, Standard Oil had wrested control of 95 percent of the nation's oil refining capacity by the 1880s. In 1882, Rockefeller's lawyers created a new legal form, the trust. In a trust, business owners assigned a small group of associates—the board of trustees—to hold stock from all the combined firms, managing them

as a single entity. Rockefeller was soon investing in Mexican oil fields and competing in world markets against Russian and Middle Eastern oil producers. Other companies followed his lead, creating trusts to sell such products as linseed oil, sugar, and salt.

Distressed by the development of near monopolies, reformers began to denounce "the trusts," a term that in popular usage referred to any large corporation that seemed to wield excessive power. Some states outlawed trusts as a legal form. But in an effort to attract corporate headquarters to its state, New Jersey broke ranks in 1889, passing a law that permitted the creation of holding companies and other corporate combinations. Despite reformers' efforts, a huge wave of mergers in the 1890s further concentrated corporate power. By 1900, America's largest one hundred companies controlled a third of the nation's productive capacity. Such familiar firms as DuPont, Eastman Kodak, and Singer had assumed dominant places in their respective industries. The immense power of these corporations would henceforth be a recurring political concern.

A National Consumer Culture

In addition to vertical and horizontal integration, corporations innovated in other ways. Companies such as Bell Telephone and Westinghouse set up research laboratories. Steelmakers invested in chemistry and materials science to make their products cheaper, better, and stronger. Americans, introduced to awe-inspiring technological wonders, celebrated inventors as heroes. The most famous, Thomas Edison, operated an independent laboratory rather than working for a corporation. Edison, like many of the era's businessmen, was a shrewd entrepreneur who focused on commercial success. He and his colleagues helped introduce such lucrative products as the incandescent lightbulb, the phonograph, and moving pictures.

In retailing, the lure of a mass market brought comparable advances. New rail lines whisked Florida oranges and other fresh produce to the shelves of grocery stores. Retailers such as the F. W. Woolworth Company and the Great Atlantic and Pacific Tea Company (A&P) opened chains of stores that soon stretched nationwide. The department store, which sold many different products in separate "departments," was pioneered by John Wanamaker in Philadelphia and soon became an urban fixture, displacing many small retail shops. Department stores introduced large display windows, elaborate Christmas decorations, lavish newspaper advertisements, and other methods of dangling temptation in front of shoppers' eyes.

While department stores became fixtures in the city, retailers did not neglect the vast market of rural customers. At county fairs and agricultural expositions, farm families could examine the latest washing machines and kerosene lamps, or meet a promoter dressed as Quaker Oats' symbolic Quaker. Even more influential were huge mail-order enterprises built by such retailers as Montgomery Ward and Sears. Rural families from Vermont to California pored over these companies' annual catalogs, making wish lists of tools, clothes, furniture, and toys. At first, mail-order companies had to coax wary customers to buy products they could not see or touch. Sears and its competitors offered money-back guarantees and simple instructions. "Don't be afraid to make a mistake," the Sears catalog counseled. "Tell us what you want, in your own way." By 1900, America counted more than twelve hundred mail-order companies, some of which produced specialized catalogs of bicycles, baby gear, or women's fashions.

The active attempt to shape consumer demand became, in itself, a new field of enterprise. The 1880s and 1890s brought a boom in colorful trade cards, small business cards that companies circulated to potential customers. By the turn of the century, magazine ads made use of vivid color images and lavish artwork. "It is hard to get mental activity with cold type; *you feel a picture*," wrote one advertiser. Outdoors, advertisements appeared everywhere. In New York's Madison Square, the Heinz Company installed a 45-foot pickle made of green electric lights. Tourists had difficulty admiring Niagara Falls because billboards obscured the view.

Thus modern advertising was born. By 1900, companies were spending more than $90 million a year ($2.3 billion in today's money) to promote their wares in newspapers and magazines, as the press itself became a mass-market industry. Rather than charging subscribers the cost of production, newspapers and magazines began to cover their costs by selling ads. This

Kellogg's Toasted Corn Flakes

Like crackers, sugar, and other nonperishable foods, cereal was traditionally sold in bulk from barrels. In the 1880s, the Quaker Oats Company hit on the idea of selling oatmeal in boxes of standard size and weight. A further innovation by manufacturers was to process cereal so that it could be consumed right from the box (with milk) for breakfast. Lo and behold: Kellogg's Corn Flakes! This is one of Kellogg's earliest advertisements.   Picture Research Consultants & Archives.

allowed them to offer cheap subscriptions, which built a mass readership, which in turn attracted more advertisers. In 1903, the *Ladies' Home Journal* became the first magazine with a million subscribers. Along with articles on home decoration and family life, its pages encouraged Americans to bathe with Pears soap and use Western Electric vacuum cleaners.

Many Americans could not afford such luxuries. But the late nineteenth century was an era of price deflation (Figure 17.1) and, while wages suffered during periods of economic depression, consumer goods did become more affordable. By the early twentieth century, the proliferation of consumer goods had begun to reshape Americans' expectations and goals. For some, long hours on the job were worth it if payday brought the possibility of shopping for new clothes or putting favorite treats on the table. When asked to reflect on the difference between the Old Country and America, a railroadman who had emigrated from the Netherlands spoke of food: "In the good old USA we have two or three kinds of meat every day." A visiting German sociologist suggested that material abundance—or at least the *promise* of it—blunted the attractiveness of socialism and other radical political doctrines. In America, he suggested, protests against the new capitalist order would, like little storm-tossed boats, wreck on the "reefs of roast beef and apple pie."

The Corporate Workplace

Before the Civil War, most American boys had hoped to become farmers, small-business owners, or independent craft workers. Afterward, more and more Americans (both male and female) became accustomed to working for someone else. This change affected not only wage earners but also managers, salespeople, and engineers.

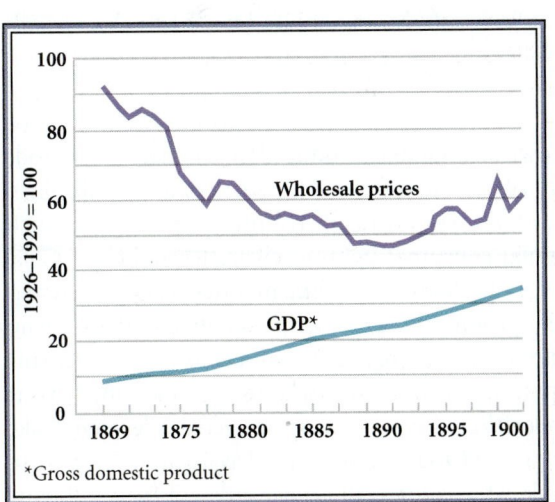

FIGURE 17.1

Business Activity and Wholesale Prices, 1869–1900

This graph shows the key feature of the performance of the late-nineteenth-century economy: While output was booming, wholesale prices were, on the whole, falling. Thus, while workers often struggled with falling wages—especially during decades of severe economic crisis—consumer products also became cheaper to buy.

Because they wore white shirts with starched collars, those who held professional positions within a corporation became known as **white-collar workers,** a term that differentiated them from **blue-collar workers** on the shop floor. For both managers and laborers, however, the shift from independent to corporate work had wide-ranging consequences. Blue-collar workers, for example, were more likely to join a labor union if they did not view the company that hired them as a temporary way station on the path to self-employment.

The Managerial Revolution

As their trunk lines stretched westward, railroad companies faced a management crisis. As Erie Railroad executive Daniel C. McCallum observed, a railroad superintendent on a 50-mile line could personally attend to every detail. But supervising a 500-mile line was an impossible task; trains ran late, communications failed, and crashes were frequent. Between the 1850s and the 1880s, railroad executives gradually invented the systems they needed to solve these problems. They distinguished top corporate managers from those responsible for day-to-day operations. They departmentalized operations by function (purchasing, machinery, freight traffic, passenger traffic) and established clear lines of communication. They perfected cost accounting, which allowed managers to assess performance in various operating units. Cost accounting allowed an industrialist like Andrew Carnegie to keep careful track of expenses and revenues, and thus to follow, on a sweeping scale, his Scottish mother's advice: "Take care of the pennies, and the pounds will take care of themselves."

With few exceptions, the vertically integrated corporations of the post–Civil War years drew on the railroad model. The headquarters of major corporations began to house executives and an array of departments handling specific activities such as purchasing, accounting, and auditing. These departments were supervised by "middle managers," something not seen before in American industry. Though managers of operating units functioned much like earlier factory owners, middle managers took on entirely new tasks, directing the flow of goods, labor, and information throughout the enterprise. Middle managers were key innovators, counterparts to the engineers in research laboratories who, in the same decades, worked to reduce costs and improve efficiency.

Company Salesmen

As early as the 1870s, the "drummer," or traveling salesman, became a familiar site on city streets and in remote country stores. Riding the rail networks from town

The Salesman as Professional, 1906

Salesmanship magazine featured this image in its June 1906 issue – depicting the traveling salesman as an energetic, well-dressed professional. The advertisement urges salesmen to join the United Commercial Travelers of America, a fraternal organization founded by salesmen in 1888 (and still in existence today). UCTA offered its members the opportunity to purchase insurance and build business networks with fellow salesmen. Through such organizations, white-collar workers and managers (who were almost never unionized) banded together to pursue their common interests and express professional pride.   Library of Congress.

to town, drummers introduced merchants to new products, offered incentives, and suggested sales displays. They built nationwide distribution networks for such popular consumer items as cigarettes and Coca-Cola. By the late 1880s, the leading manufacturer of cash registers produced a sales script for its employees, who presented their product as an aid to local merchants hoping to increase profits. "After you have made your proposition clear," the script directed salesmen, "take for granted that he will buy. Say to him, 'Now, Mr. Blank, what color shall I make it?' . . . Take out the order blank, fill it out, and handing him your pen say, 'Just sign here where I have made the cross.'"

With such companies in the vanguard, sales became systematized. Managers set individual sales quotas—one company awarded silver and gold crosses to its top salesmen, while those who sold too little were singled out for remedial training or dismissal. Business leaders eagerly embraced the ideas of business psychologist Walter Dill Scott, who published *The Psychology of Advertising* in 1908. Scott's principles—which included selling to customers based on their presumed "instinct of escape" and "instinct of combat"—were soon taught at Harvard Business School.

Women in the Corporate Workplace

Beneath the ranks of managers, another class of employees emerged: female office workers. Before the Civil War, most clerks at small firms had been young men who expected to rise through the ranks. In a large corporation, secretarial work became a dead-end job, and employers began to assign it to women. By the turn of the twentieth century, 77 percent of all stenographers and typists were female; by 1920, women held half of all low-level office jobs.

In the retail field, department stores hired increasing numbers of saleswomen to interact directly with customers. Though many women viewed sales jobs as far better than factory labor or domestic service, the work was poorly paid and grueling. "Our business was first to dust and condense the stock, and then to stand ready for customers," wrote an investigator who worked undercover at Chicago department stores. "We all served in the double capacity of floorwalkers and clerks, and our business was to see that no one escaped without making a purchase." When customers arrived, she continued, "there was one mad rush of clerks with a quickly spoken, 'What would you like, madam?'" Employees had to use aggressive sales tactics to earn the small commissions that made up their weekly pay.

For white working-class women, clerking and office work represented new opportunities. In an era before day care, married women most often worked at

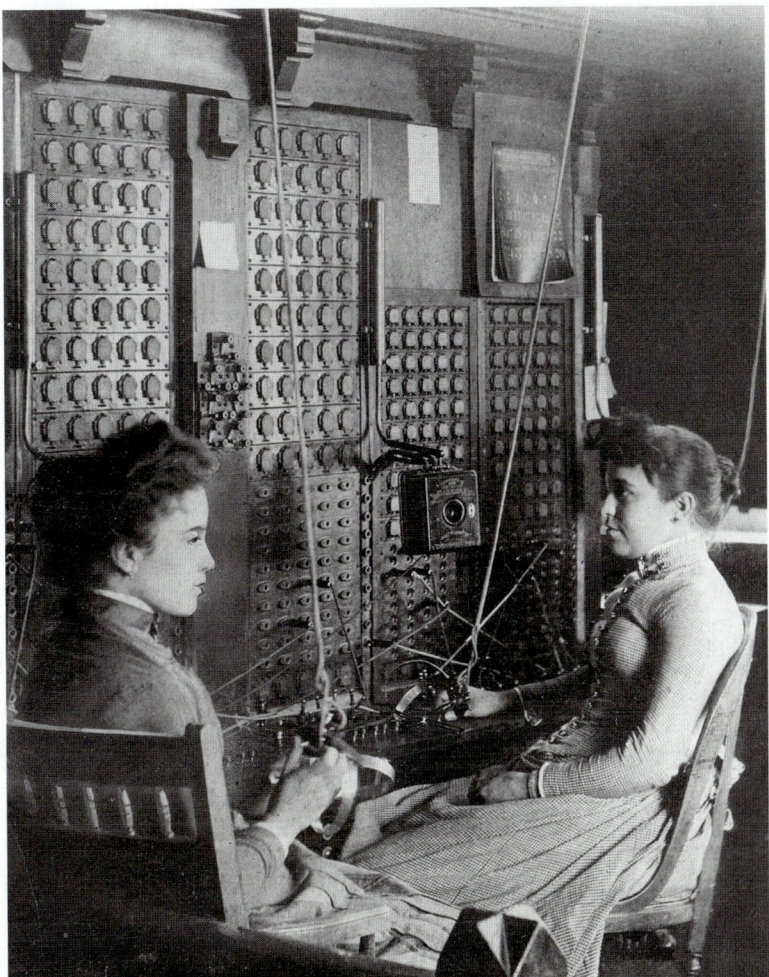

Telephone Operators, 1888

Like other women office workers, these switchboard operators enjoyed relatively high pay and comfortable working conditions—especially in the early years of the telephone industry, before operators' work routines speeded up. These young women worked for the Central Union Telephone Company in Canton, Ohio. Ohio Historical Society.

Working Women

Shoe manufacturing was a pioneering American industry, one of the first to use a division of labor and move into factories. It was also, like textiles, an industry that relied heavily on female workers, who were generally girls or young married women without children. Mostly women worked as stitchers, using sewing machines to finish the shoe uppers. The lasting of the shoes — shaping the shoe by hand on a last (a wooden mold) — was the province of male shoe workers, who belonged to a strong trade union, the Knights of St. Crispin (St. Crispin was the saint of shoemakers). The union's sister organization was the Daughters of St. Crispin. During the 1870s, when wages fell and work was harder to come by, more married women entered the mills, and tensions rose between them and the women already in the labor force.

Wives in the Mills: A Debate

The documents that follow take the form of letters to the editor in the *Lynn Record*, a weekly paper catering to local factory workers in Lynn, Massachusetts. As was customary at the time, the authors adopted assumed names — in this case, A Stitcher, Americus, and Married Stitcher. Modern readers might be skeptical of the ladylike tone of the letters, but New England factory women, thanks to the region's excellent common schools, actually talked and wrote that way. These letters should be read on two levels. At first sight, they reveal sharp differences among working women over the employment of wives. But what of the larger employment system in which all of them are enmeshed? Do they question the role of gender in defining their place in the labor force?

[February 1, 1879]

Mr. Editor, — In last week's *Record* . . . I notice this: "Working women, why don't you organize?" . . . I grew more and more indignant and resolved to write the *Record* a letter giving some of the reasons why the Daughters of St. Crispin's membership fails to increase. . . . Why my blood fairly boils and I get righteously angry when I think of some of the causes which have brought down the price of our labor! But let me tell you: In the first place, the shops are thronged with married women, the greater part of whom (and these are the ones I censure) have good, comfortable homes, and girls whose fathers are amply able to provide them with all the comforts and necessaries of life, but their inordinate love of dress, and a desire to vie in personal adornments with their more wealthy sisters, takes them into the workshops. . . . Ask *them* to join the order, and they are horrified at the thought! They don't want any better wages: they have a home, no board to pay, and so long as they can get enough for pin money, they are content. . . .

Our brother workmen can organize, and redress their wrongs; but for us there is no hope, and the bosses know it just as well as we; so they snap their fingers at us, and as

each returning season comes round, they give us an extra cut in lieu of cutting down the men, knowing full well there are plenty of married women, with well-to-do husbands, and half-supported girls who stand ready to work the few short weeks in which work is given out, at any price they can get. . . .

A Stitcher

[February 8, 1879]

Mr. Editor, — . . . I cannot quite agree with "A Stitcher" in thinking that "married women" and "half-supported girls" are stumbling blocks in the way of organization. The great majority are not "half supported," neither are the majority of married women employed in our shops blessed with "comfortable homes" and "well-to-do husbands": if there are a few of this class, they are *very* few compared with the many who are obliged to work for their daily bread. . . . Married women have been well represented in the D.O.S.C. organization, and . . . they have always proved zealous and ardent supporters of that order. . . .

Americus

[February 15, 1879]

Mr. Editor, — . . . I am a married woman. I have worked in the shops some years, and never but one married woman have I met but what claimed to work from necessity, not from choice. What sent many of the married women into the shops are the girls who [would] rather work with a crowd of men [as lasters] than in the stitching room with their own sex. They have been the cause of many men being cut down [assigned to fewer work hours]; many men with families to maintain. I for one, and I know many more situated in the same way, work to get bread for my children; my husband has been cut down so that in the short time he has work he cannot support us. . . . I consider myself a Crispin in principle. But I will never join an order that takes in girl-lasters! Stitcher is altogether too hard on married women. I think some married woman of her acquaintance must have come out with a smarter silk [dress] or longer train than hers.

Married Stitcher

[February 15, 1879]

Mr. Editor,—I do not believe any woman, married or single, works for the fun of it in these times; neither do I believe most married women work in the shop because they are obliged to—that is, to provide themselves with the actual necessaries of life. To be sure, some of them may have shiftless husbands, but I think the men would make greater exertions if the women were not so eager and willing to take a man's place. If married women had to pay board bills, washing bills, and then had to be denied all the comforts of home, with no one to look to for aid or support, they would be less content to sit quietly down and submit to reduction after reduction, but would be ready to join any honorable scheme which would bring relief.

Were times good, work and money plenty, why, then, if married [women] wanted to work out and neglect their homes, they could do so for all [I care]. But so long as there are a surplus of laborers, with scarcity of work, I shall protest against the married woman question, even though I stand alone. . . .

A Stitcher

[February 22, 1879]

Mr. Editor,—Ah! my dear Stitcher . . . when the husband and father cannot provide for his wife and children, it is perfectly natural that the wife and mother should desire to work for her husband and her little ones, and we have no right to deny her that privilege.

My dear child, don't blame married women if the land of the free has become a land of slavery and oppression. Women are not to blame. . . .

Americus

[March 1, 1879]

Mr. Editor,—For years I have been homeless, thrown here and there by circumstances, but have kept my eyes and ears open to all that has been going on around me; and many times I have been deeply pained at the utter selfishness manifested by a certain class of married women in the shops, till I have been thoroughly disgusted with them all. . . .

From statistical reports there is found to be sixty odd thousand more females than males in the state of Massachusetts, and it is safe to say three-fourths of them have to earn their own support. Now these can never have homes of their own unless they make them. No strong arm on which to lean can ever rightfully be theirs. In the face and eyes of this, can it be fair for them to have to compete with married women who have protectors, in the struggle for bread, besides all the other obstacles in their way?

It is no use, "Americus," since the days of Mother Eve women have been at the bottom of nearly every trouble: and . . . I think a foolish extravagance in dress and love of display on the part of women, has caused many a once honest man to turn thief, and has helped, if did not wholly, bring about this fearful crisis of distress and want. . . .

A Stitcher

Source: Mary H. Blewett, ed., *We Will Rise in Our Might: Workingwomen's Voices from Nineteenth-Century New England* (Ithaca, NY: Cornell University Press, 1991), 140–144.

ANALYZING THE EVIDENCE

- How do you explain A Stitcher's objection to married women working in the shoe factories?

- Married Stitcher, like Americus, defends the employment of married women, but she also has a complaint, which in her case is against single women. Why does she claim they wrong married women? And what does this suggest about her attitude to the sex-typing that confined women in inferior gender-defined jobs?

- Is there any evidence in these documents that the other letter writers share Married Stitcher's conservative views about the segregation of women? Consider what they say about the trade unions in their industry.

- In our time—at the beginning of the twenty-first century—it is taken for granted that if a woman wants to work, that's her personal choice and her right. How might the three letter writers each respond to the idea that women have the right to work for no other reason than personal choice?

Ironworkers – Noontime, 1880
The ideal qualities of the nineteenth-century craft worker — dignity, brotherhood, manliness — shine through in this painting by Thomas P. Anschutz. *Ironworkers – Noontime* became a popular painting after it was reproduced as an engraving in *Harper's Weekly* in 1884.   Fine Arts Museum of San Francisco.

home, where they could tend children while also taking in laundry, boarders, or **piecework** (sewing or other assembly projects that were paid on a per-item basis). Unmarried daughters could leave the home for domestic service or factory work, but clerking and secretarial work were cleaner and better paid. Telegraph operators told one reporter that they felt they held "a social position not inferior to that of a teacher or governess." In 1900, more than 4 million women worked for wages. About a third worked in domestic service; another third in industry; and the rest in office work, teaching, nursing, or sales. As new opportunities arose, the percentage of wage-earning women in domestic service dropped dramatically, a trend that continued in the twentieth century.

On the Shop Floor

Despite the managerial revolution at the top, skilled craft workers — almost all of them men — retained considerable autonomy in many industries. A coal miner, for example, was not an hourly wageworker but essentially an independent contractor, paid by the amount of coal he produced. He provided his own tools, worked at his own pace, and knocked off early when he chose. The same was true for puddlers and rollers in iron works; molders in stove making; and machinists, glass blowers, and skilled workers in many other industries. Such workers abided by the stint, a self-imposed limit on how much they would produce each day. This informal system of restricting output infuriated efficiency-minded engineers, but to the workers it signified personal dignity, manly pride, and brotherhood with fellow employees. One shop in Lowell, Massachusetts, posted regulations requiring all employees to be at their posts by the time of the opening bell and to remain, with the shop door locked, until the closing bell. A machinist promptly packed his tools, declaring that he had not "been brought up under such a system of slavery."

Skilled workers — craftsmen, inside contractors, and foremen — enjoyed a high degree of autonomy. But those who paid helpers from their own pocket could also exploit them. Subcontracting arose, in part,

The Singer Sewing Machine

The sewing machine was an American invention that swiftly found markets abroad. The Singer Manufacturing Company, the dominant firm by the time the Civil War began, exported sewing machines to markets as far-flung as Ireland, Russia, China, and India. The company also moved some manufacturing operations abroad, producing 200,000 machines annually at a Scottish plant that employed 6,000 workers. Singer's advertising rightly boasted of the international appeal of a product that the company dubbed "The Universal Sewing Machine."   © Collection of the New-York Historical Society.

to enable manufacturers to distance themselves from the consequences of shady labor practices. In Pittsburgh steel mills, foremen were known as "pushers," notorious for driving their gangs mercilessly. On the other hand, industrial labor operated on a human scale, through personal relationships that could be close and enduring. Striking craft workers would commonly receive the support of helpers and laborers, and labor gangs would sometimes walk out on behalf of a popular foreman.

As technology advanced, however, workers increasingly lost the proud independence characteristic of craft work. The most important cause of this was the de-skilling of labor under a new system of mechanized manufacturing that industrialist Henry Ford would soon call **mass production**. Over the course of the nineteenth and early twentieth centuries, everything from typewriters to automobiles came to be assembled from standardized parts. The machine tools that cut, drilled, and ground the metal parts were originally operated by skilled workers, but the machines soon could operate without human oversight. A machinist protested in 1883 that the sewing machine industry was so "subdivided" that "one man may make just a particular part of a machine and may not know anything

whatever about another part of the same machine." Such a worker, noted an observer, "cannot be master of a craft, but only master of a fragment."

Employers, who originally favored automatic machinery because it increased output, quickly found that it also helped them control workers and cut labor costs. With mass production, corporations needed fewer skilled workers. They could pay unskilled workers less and replace them easily. Blue-collar workers—those who labored with their hands—therefore had little freedom to negotiate with their employers, and their working conditions deteriorated markedly as mass production took hold.

By the early twentieth century, managers had come to believe that they could further reduce costs by getting employees to work harder and more efficiently. The pioneer in industrial efficiency was Frederick W. Taylor, an expert on metal-cutting methods who dubbed his strategy **scientific management**. To get maximum output from the individual worker, Taylor suggested two basic reforms. First, eliminate the brain work from manual labor: Hire experts to develop "rules, laws, and formulae" for the shop floor. Second, withdraw workers' authority and require that they "do what they are told promptly and without asking questions or making

Child Labor

For many working-class families, children's wages — even though they were low — made up an essential part of the household income. These boys worked the night shift in a glass factory in Indiana. Lewis Hine, an investigative photographer for the National Child Labor Committee, took their picture at midnight, as part of a campaign to educate more prosperous Americans about the widespread employment of child labor, as well as the harsh conditions in which many children worked.   Library of Congress.

suggestions." Decision making would lie in the hands of "management alone." In its most extreme form, scientific management called for engineers to time each task with a stopwatch; companies would then pay workers more if they met the stopwatch standard. Taylor assumed that workers cared only about money and that they would respond automatically to the lure of higher earnings.

Scientific management was not, in practice, a great success. Implementing it proved to be expensive, and workers stubbornly resisted the stopwatch method. One union leader declared, "This system is wrong, because we want our heads left on us." Far from solving the labor problem, scientific management created new conflicts. Corporate managers, however, adopted many bits and pieces of Taylor's system, and they enthusiastically adopted his idea that brain work should be the job of "management alone." Taylor's disciples went on to create the fields of personnel work and industrial psychol-

ogy, whose practitioners purported to know how to extract more and better labor from workers. Over time, in comparison with their counterparts in other countries, American corporations created a particularly wide gap between the perspectives and experiences of white-collar managers and those of the blue-collar workforce.

As production was de-skilled, the ranks of factory workers came to include more and more women and children, who were almost always unskilled and lower paid (see Comparing American Voices, "Working Women," pp. 538–539). Men often resented women's presence in factories. By the early twentieth century, male labor unions also became outspoken leaders in the fight against child labor. In 1900, one of every five children under the age of sixteen worked outside the home. Child labor was most widespread in the South, where a low-wage industrial sector emerged after Reconstruction (Map 17.2). Textile mills sprouted in the Carolinas and Georgia, recruiting workers from surrounding farms.

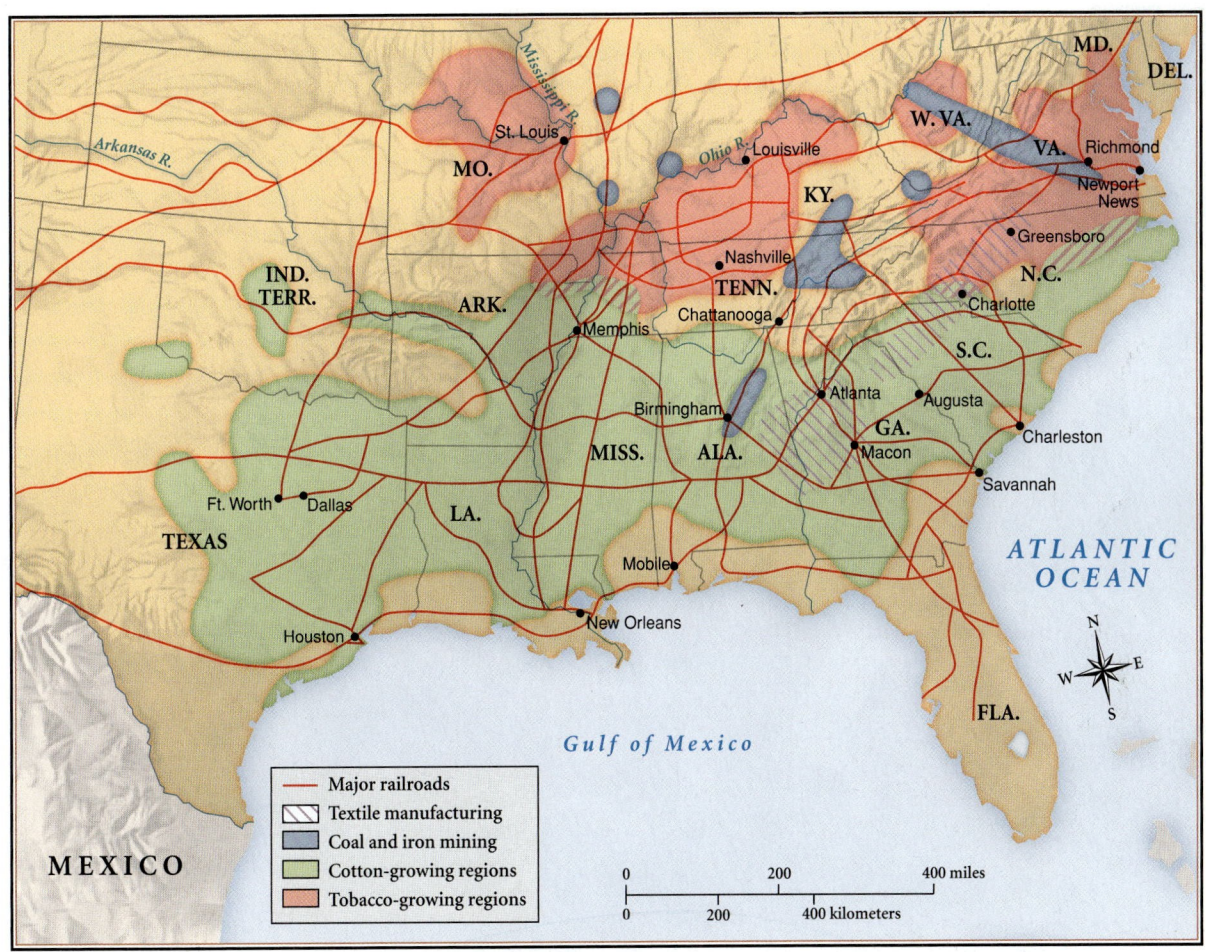

MAP 17.2

The New South, 1900

The economy of the Old South focused on raising staple crops, especially cotton and tobacco. In the New South, staple agriculture continued to dominate, but there was marked industrial development as well. Industrial regions evolved, producing textiles, coal, and iron. By 1900 the South's industrial pattern was well defined, though the region still served—like the West—as a major producer of raw materials for the industrial core region that stretched from New England to Chicago.

Also at the bottom of the pay scale were most African American workers. Corporations and industrial manufacturers widely discriminated on the basis of race, and such racial prejudice was hardly limited to the South. In the decades after the Civil War, African American women who moved to northern cities found that they were largely excluded from office work and other new employment options; instead, they remained heavily concentrated in domestic service, with more than half employed as cooks or servants. African American men confronted the same exclusion. America's booming vertically integrated corporations turned away black men from all but the most menial jobs. In 1890, almost a third of African American men worked in personal service. Employers in the North and West recruited, instead, a different kind of low-wage labor: newly arrived immigrants.

- **What factors led to the rise of the corporation after 1865? What means did corporate leaders use to expand their control of markets?**

- **What new patterns of work developed in the corporate and industrial workplaces? What were the consequences of these patterns for men and women?**

- **Did the benefits of industrialization, as Andrew Carnegie suggested, outweigh its costs? How might a corporate manager, a factory worker, and a shopper at a department store have answered that question?**

German Beer, Mexican Workers, c. 1900
Immigrants from Germany owned and managed most of the breweries in the United States. But workers at the Maier and Zoblein Brewery in Los Angeles came from many nations, including Mexico. At that time, about 4,000 Mexicans lived in Los Angeles County (about 4 percent of the population); by 1930, 150,000 Mexican-born immigrants lived in Los Angeles, making up about 7 percent of the city's rapidly growing population.   Los Angeles Public Library.

Immigrants, East and West

Across the globe, industrialization set people in motion. Farmers' children migrated to cities. Craftsmen entered factories. The lure of jobs, along with cheap steam transportation, pulled opportunity seekers to the United States from across the Atlantic and Pacific and over the Canadian and Mexican borders. Between the Civil War and World War I, 25 million immigrants entered the United States. They began to make the American working class truly global: Joining it were not only people of African and Western European descent but also Southern and Eastern Europeans, Mexicans, and Asians. In 1900, census takers found that more than 75 percent of all residents of San Francisco and New York City had at least one parent who was foreign-born.

For the new industrial order, immigrants made an ideal labor supply. They took the worst jobs at low pay; during economic downturns, many left the labor market and returned to their home countries, reducing the shock of unemployment within the United States. But many native-born Americans viewed immigrants with hostility, through the lens of racial, ethnic, and religious prejudices. They also feared that immigrants would

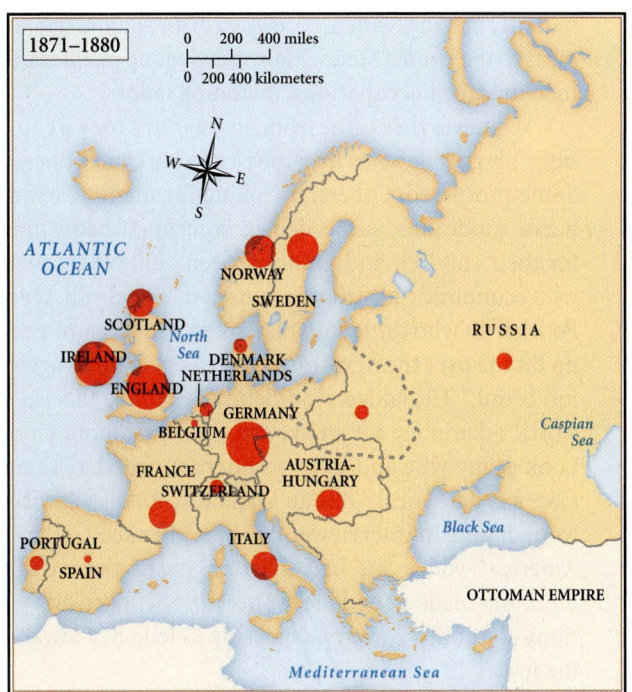

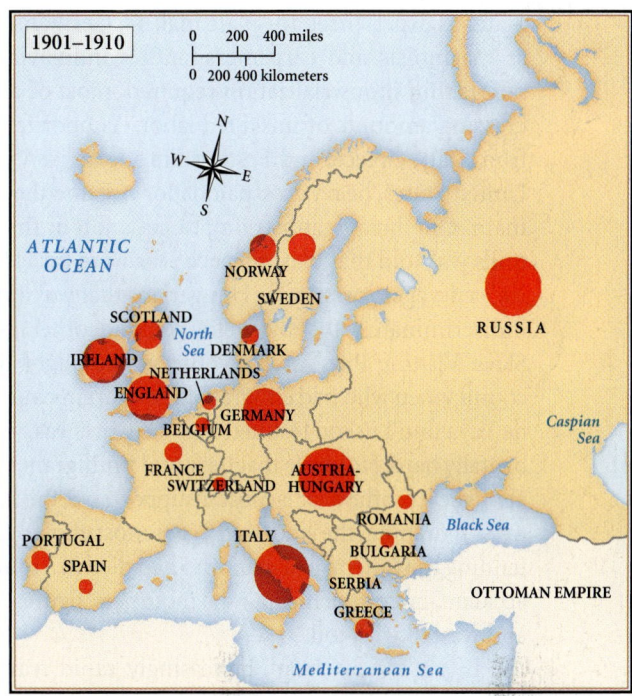

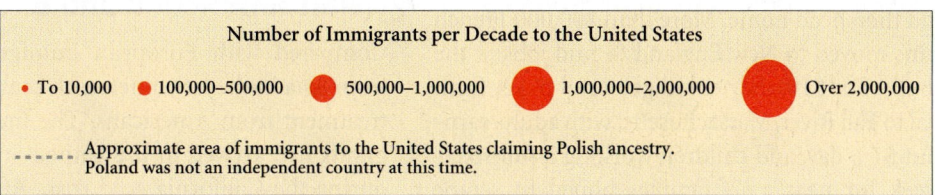

MAP 17.3

Sources of European Immigration to the United States, 1871–1910

Around 1900, Americans began to speak of the "new" immigration. They meant the large numbers of immigrants arriving from Eastern and Southern Europe—Poles, Slovaks and other Slavic peoples, Yiddish-speaking Jews, Italians—and overwhelming the still substantial number of immigrants from the British Isles and Northern Europe.

compete for jobs and erode wages. For immigrants themselves, America was a new world—by turns disorienting, liberating, and disappointing.

Newcomers from Europe

Mass migration from Western Europe had started in the 1840s, when more than 1 million Irish fled a terrible famine. In the following decades, as European populations grew rapidly and agriculture became commercialized, peasant economies suffered, first in Germany and Scandinavia, and then across Austria-Hungary, Russia, Italy, and the Balkans. This upheaval displaced millions of rural people. Some went to Europe's mines and factories; others headed for South America. Millions more sailed for the United States (Map 17.3).

"America was known to foreigners," remembered one Jewish woman from Lithuania, "as the land where you'd get rich. . . . There's gold on the sidewalk! All you have to do is pick it up." But the reality was much harsher. Even in the age of steam, the voyage to America was grueling. For ten to twenty days, passengers in steerage class crowded below-decks, eating terrible food and struggling with seasickness. An investigative reformer who traveled with immigrants from Naples asked, "How can a steerage passenger remember that he is a human being when he must first pick the worms from his food . . . and eat in his stuffy, stinking bunk?" After 1892, European immigrants were routed through the enormous receiving station at New York's Ellis Island.

Some immigrants were skilled, seasoned workers. Many Welshmen, for example, arrived in the United

States as experienced tin-plate makers; Germans came as machinists and carpenters, and Scandinavians as sailors. But industrialization required, most of all, increasing amounts of unskilled labor. As poor farmers from Italy, Greece, and Eastern Europe arrived in the United States, heavy, low-paid labor became their domain. One investigator trying to get a job in the steel mills was told that blast furnace jobs were for "Hunkies," a derogatory term for Hungarians that was applied indiscriminately to Poles, Slovaks, and other ethnic Slavs. Visiting Pittsburgh to observe the plight of his countrymen who had emigrated, Hungarian count Vay de Vaya und Luskod testified that the work was, in fact, brutally hard. He wrote that he found immigrant workers "wherever the heat is most insupportable, the flames most scorching, the smoke and soot most choking." Attending the funeral of a man who had died in a foundry accident, he commented on the mourners' figures "bent and wasted with toil."

In an era of cheap, increasingly rapid travel by railroad and steamship, many immigrants came as "sojourners": They expected to work and save for a few years and then head home. More than 800,000 French Canadians moved to New England to find jobs in the textile mills. For $10, they could get a rail ticket from Montreal to Fall River, Massachusetts; with adults earning about $1 a day, and children working a full sixty-hour week for nearly $2, families hoped to scrape together enough savings to return to Quebec and buy a farm. Thousands of men came alone, especially from Ireland, Italy, and Greece. Many single Irishwomen also immigrated. Circumstances often changed their plans. Some would-be sojourners ended up staying a lifetime, while many immigrants who had expected to settle permanently found themselves forced out of the country by a workplace accident or a sudden economic depression. One historian has estimated that one-third of immigrants to the United States in this era returned home.

Along with Italians and Greeks, Eastern European Jews were among the most numerous arrivals. The first American Jews, who numbered around 50,000 in 1880, were mostly of German-Jewish descent. In the next four decades, more than 3 million poverty-stricken Jews arrived from Russia, Ukraine, Poland, and other parts of Eastern Europe, transforming the Jewish presence in the United States. Like other immigrants, Eastern European Jews sought economic opportunity, but they also came to escape religious repression. These problems were especially acute after Russian officials made Jews scapegoats following the assassination of Czar Alexander II

in 1881. Fleeing violence, Jews fled through German ports to the United States. Many were young people and men in skilled occupations, including tailors.

Wherever they came from, immigrants took a considerable gamble when they traveled to the United States. Some prospered. Others, by toiling for many years in harsh conditions, succeeded in securing a better life for their children and grandchildren. Still others met with economic catastrophe, injury, or early death. One Polish man who came with his parents in 1908 summed up his life over the next thirty years as "a mere struggle for bread." He added: "Sometimes I think life isn't worth a damn for a man like me. I get little money. . . . Look at my wife and kids — undernourished, seldom have a square meal." But an Orthodox Russian Jewish woman told an interviewer that she "thanked God for America," where she had married, raised three children, and made a good life for herself. She "liked everything about this country, especially its leniency toward the Jews."

Asian Americans and Exclusion

Compared with European immigrants, newcomers from Asia in the late nineteenth century faced harsher treatment from Americans. The first Chinese immigrants had arrived in the United States in the 1840s, during the California gold rush. After the Civil War, the Burlingame Treaty between the United States and China opened the way for increasing numbers to emigrate. Fleeing poverty and upheaval in southern China, they, like European immigrants, filled low-wage jobs in the American labor market. But the Chinese confronted far more intense hostility in the form of abysmal pay and threats from coworkers, leading many men to withdraw to the only niches open to them: running restaurants and laundries. Nonetheless, some managed to build profitable businesses and farms. During the depression of the 1870s, hostility in the form of a rising tide of outrage against "Asiatics" was especially extreme in the Pacific coast states, where the majority of Chinese immigrants lived. "The Chinese must go!" railed Dennis Kearney, leader of the California Working Men's Party, who referred to Asians as "almond-eyed lepers." Incited by Kearney, a mob burned San Francisco's Chinatown and beat up residents in July 1877.

Facing intense political pressure, lawmakers shut out Chinese immigrants. In 1882, Congress passed the Chinese Exclusion Act, which specifically barred Chi-

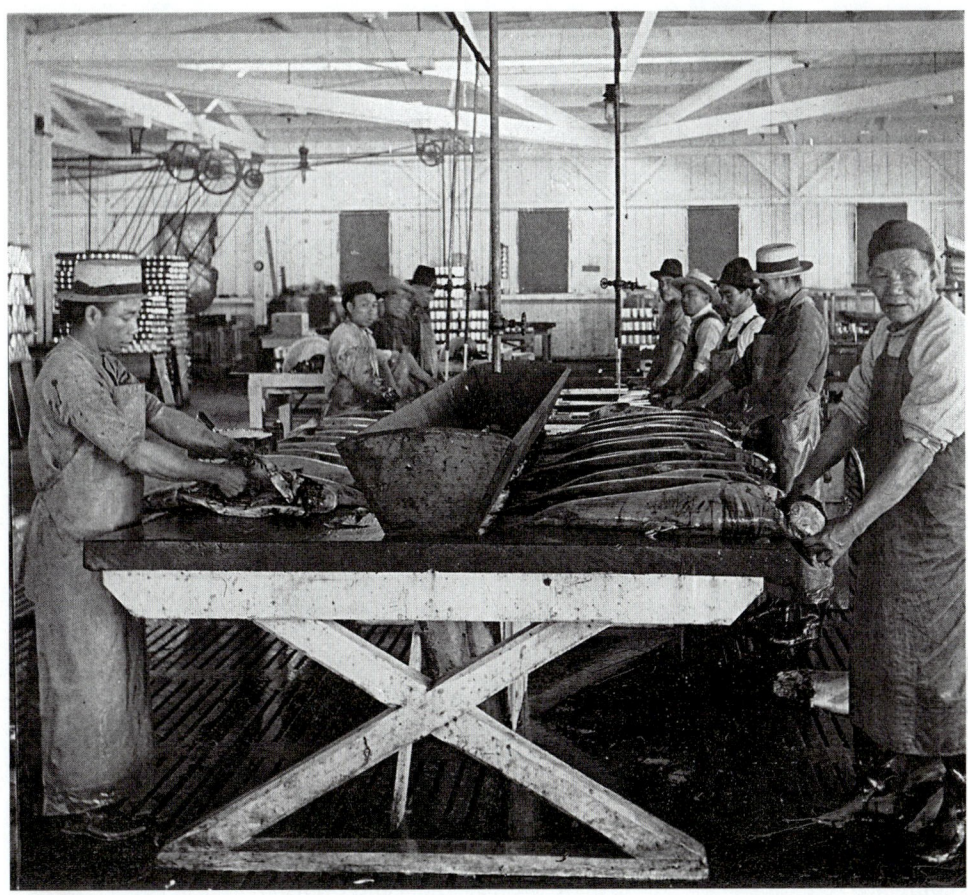

Chinese Workers in a Salmon Cannery, c. 1900

Shut out of many fields of employment by racial discrimination, many Chinese immigrants founded their own restaurants, laundries, and other small businesses. Others, like these cannery workers in Astoria, Oregon, took on some of the most grueling and lowest-paid work in the American economy. Job segregation reinforced, in turn, racial prejudice. Visiting British author Rudyard Kipling, touring canneries along the Columbia River, described Chinese workers in the plants as "blood-besmeared yellow devils." These workers, refuting Kipling's slur, appear clean and respectable. Notice the man in an apron, on the left, who wears his traditional queue, or braided pigtail, tucked into his straw hat.   Oregon Historical Society.

nese laborers from entering the United States (see Voices from Abroad, "Huang Zunxian: Expulsion of the Immigrants," p. 548). Each decade thereafter, Congress renewed the law and tightened its provisions; it was not repealed until 1943. Exclusion laws barred entry of almost all Chinese women, forcing husbands and wives to spend many years apart when men took jobs in the United States. Some immigrants made vigorous use of the courts to protect their rights. In a series of cases brought by Chinese and later Japanese immigrants, the U.S. Supreme Court ruled that all persons born in the United States had citizenship rights that could not be revoked, even if their parents had been born abroad.

Nonetheless, well into the twentieth century, Chinese immigrants (as opposed to native-born Chinese Americans) could not apply for citizenship. By the turn of the twentieth century, Japanese and Korean immi-

grants had also begun to arrive; by 1909, there were 40,000 Japanese immigrants working in agriculture, 10,000 on railroads, and 4,000 in canneries. A few Japanese managed to become U.S. citizens, but in 1906 the U.S. attorney general ruled that they, like other Asians, were barred. In the meantime, Chinese exclusion did not halt violence and discrimination against those who had found a place in the United States. Most labor unions steadfastly refused to allow Chinese workers to join. During the depression of the 1890s, angry unemployed whites attacked Chinese farmworkers in California. In what many Chinese later remembered as "the driving out," they were rounded up, forced onto rail cars, and sent out of the state.

The Chinese Exclusion Act created the legal foundations on which exclusionary immigration policies would be built after the 1920s. To enforce the law, Congress and the courts gave sweeping new powers to

VOICES FROM ABROAD

Huang Zunxian
Expulsion of the Immigrants

From 1882 to 1885, Huang Zunxian was the Chinese consul general in San Francisco, working to protect the rights of Chinese residents. Huang hoped the United States would offer opportunity to growing numbers of his desperately poor countrymen. But violence and discrimination, especially passage of the Chinese Exclusion Act in 1882, left him disillusioned. In his poem "Expulsion of the Immigrants," excerpted below, Huang reflects on Chinese immigration to the United States.

When the Chinese first crossed the ocean,
They were the same as pioneers.
They lived in straw hovels, cramped as snail shells;
For protection gradually built bamboo fences.
Dressed in tatters, they cleared mountain forests;
Wilderness and waste turned into towns and villages.
Mountains of gold towered on high,
Which men could grab with their hands left and right.
Eureka! They return with a load full of gold,
All bragging this land is paradise. . . .
Bartenders lead along cooks;
Some hold tailors' needles, others workmen's axes.
They clap with excitement, traveling overseas;
Everyone surnamed Wong creates confusion. . . .
Gradually the natives turned jealous.
Time to time spreading false rumors,
They say these Chinese paupers
Only wish to fill their money bags.
Soon as their feet touch the ground,
All the gold leaps out of the Earth
They hang ten thousand cash on their waists,
And catch the next boat back to China.
Which of them is willing to loosen his queue,
And do some hard labor for us?
Some say the Chinese are shiftless; . . .
Others say the Chinese are a bunch of hoodlums,
By nature all filthy and unclean.
Their houses are as dirty as dogs';
Their food even worse than pigs'.
All they need is a dollar a day;
Who is as scrawny as they are?
If we allow this cheap labor of theirs,
Then all of us are finished. . . .
From now on they set up a strict ban,
Establishing customs posts everywhere.
They have sealed all the gates tightly,
Door after door with guards beating alarms. . . .
Those who do not carry passports
Are arrested as soon as they arrive.
Anyone with a yellow-colored face

Is beaten even if guiltless.
I sadly recollect George Washington,
Who had the makings of a great ruler.
He proclaimed that in America,
There is a broad land to the west of the desert.
All kinds of foreigners and immigrants,
Are allowed to settle in these new lands,
The yellow, white, red, and black races
Are all equal with our native people.
Not even a hundred years till today,
But they are not ashamed to eat his words.
Alas! In the five great continents,
Each race is distinct and different.
We drive off foreigners and punish barbarians,
Hate one another, call each other names.
Today is not yet the Age of Great Unity;
We only compete in cleverness and power.
The land of the red man is vast and remote;
I know you are eager to settle and open it.
The American eagle strides the heavens soaring,
With half of the globe clutched in his claw.
Although the Chinese arrived later,
Couldn't you leave them a little space?

Source: *Land Without Ghosts: Chinese Impressions of America from the Mid-Nineteenth Century to the Present*, trans. and ed. R. David Arkush and Leo O. Lee (Berkeley: University of California Press, 1989), 61–65.

ANALYZING THE EVIDENCE

- **How does Huang represent the initial experience of Chinese immigrants? In what ways does their experience resemble that of other immigrant groups, according to this account?**

- **Drawing on the poem's images and descriptions, can you imagine what experiences Huang had as a diplomat that caused his disillusionment toward Americans and the United States?**

Anti-Chinese Racism

This cartoon from the magazine *Puck*, drawn by James A. Wales during the 1880 presidential campaign, offers vivid evidence of the widespread and virulent American prejudice against Chinese immigrants. Republican candidate James Garfield, on the left, and Democratic candidate Winfield Scott Hancock, on the right, both nail up their party's "planks" in favor of restricting Chinese immigration. Asian immigrants were not permitted to apply for naturalization as U.S. citizens; they thus had "no vote" and no power in politics. Congress passed the Chinese Exclusion Act, with bipartisan support, soon after Garfield's victory. Library of Congress.

immigration officials, transforming the Chinese into America's first illegal immigrants. Drawn, like others, by the promise of jobs in America's expanding economy, Chinese men stowed away on ships and walked across the borders. Disguising themselves as Mexicans—who at that time could freely enter the United States—some perished in the desert as they tried to reach California.

Other would-be immigrants, known as "paper sons," relied on Chinese residents in the United States, who generated documents falsely claiming the newcomers as American-born children. (One federal judge commented in 1901: "If the story told in the courts were true, every Chinese woman who was in the United States twenty-five years ago must have had at least 500 children.") "Paper sons" memorized pages of information about their supposed relatives and hometowns. The San Francisco earthquake of 1906 helped their cause by destroying all of the port's records. "That was a big chance for a lot of Chinese," remembered one Chinese American. "They forged themselves certificates saying they could go back to China and bring back four or five sons, just like that!" Such ingenuity and persistence ensured that, despite the harsh policies of Chinese exclusion, the flow of Asian immigrants never entirely ceased.

- **How did patterns of immigration to the United States change between 1840 and 1900?**

- **What factors typically shaped the experience of immigrants in the United States? How did these differ among different ethnic and racial groups?**

- **What impact did Americans' response to Asian newcomers have on immigration policies?**

Labor Gets Organized

In the American political system, labor has always been weak. Industrial workers have tended to cluster in cities, near factories and jobs. But in comparison with voters in small towns and rural areas, those in urban areas have been underrepresented in state legislatures, the U.S. Senate, and the electoral college. This problem became acute in the era of industrialization, and it has lingered. Today, for example, the twenty-two U.S. senators elected from Alaska, Idaho, Iowa, Maine, Mississippi, Montana, New Mexico, North Dakota, Vermont, West Virginia, and Wyoming represent a smaller number of people, *combined*, than the two U.S. senators who represent California.

Faced with this obstacle, labor advocates could adopt one of two strategies. First, they could try to make political alliances with sympathetic rural voters who shared their problems. Second, they could reject politics and create narrowly focused **trade unions** to negotiate directly with employers. In general, labor advocates emphasized the first strategy between the 1870s and the early 1890s, and the latter in the early twentieth century. Across this era, while industrialization made America increasingly rich and powerful, it also brought large-scale conflict between labor and capital.

The Emergence of a Labor Movement

The problem of industrial labor entered Americans' consciousness dramatically with the Great Railroad Strike of 1877. Protesting steep wage cuts during the

Houston's Cotton Depot, c. 1909

After the Civil War, cotton agriculture blossomed on the rich lands of east Texas, and Houston simultaneously blossomed as the region's commercial center. This tinted photograph from the 1890s reveals the tremendous volume of traffic that came through Houston, where Texas cotton was compacted in steam-powered cotton presses, loaded onto railcars, and shipped to cotton mills in the Southeast and Britain to be made into cloth.   Houston Public Library, Houston Metropolitan Research Center.

depression that had begun in 1873, thousands of railroad workers walked off the job. Their strike paralyzed the U.S. transportation network, bringing rail travel and commerce to a halt. Thousands of people poured into the streets of Buffalo, Pittsburgh, and Chicago to join the rail workers and protest the economic injustice wreaked by the railroads—as well as the fires caused by stray sparks from locomotives, and the injuries and deaths on train tracks in urban neighborhoods. When Pennsylvania's governor sent in the state militia to break the railroad workers' strike, Pittsburgh crowds reacted by burning railroad property and overturning locomotives. Similar clashes between police and protesters occurred in other cities across the country, from Galveston, Texas, to San Francisco, California.

The 1877 strike left more than fifty people dead and caused $40 million worth of damage, primarily to property owned by the railroads. "It seemed as if the whole social and political structure was on the very brink of ruin," wrote one journalist. For their role in the strike, many railroad workers were fired and **blacklisted**: Rail-

road companies circulated their names on a "do not hire" list to prevent them from getting any work in the industry. In the wake of the strike, the U.S. government also created the National Guard, not to protect Americans against foreign invasion, but to enforce order at home. National Guard armories—fortresses designed to withstand assault by future strikers and rioters—became part of the urban landscape.

In the post–Civil War decades, many rural people believed they faced the same enemies as industrial workers. In the new economy, they found themselves at the mercy of large corporations, from equipment dealers that sold them harvesters and plows, to railroads and grain elevators that shipped and stored their products. Though farmers appeared to have more independence than corporate employees, many felt increasingly caught up in a web of middlemen who chipped away at their profits, with international forces robbing them of decision-making power.

Farmers denounced not only corporations, but also the previous two decades of government policy.

During the Civil War and Reconstruction, Republicans had passed an array of laws to foster economic development in the West. But those policies seemed wrongheaded to many farmers, especially those in the South and West. Farmers' advocates argued that high tariffs forced rural families to pay too much for basic necessities while failing to protect America's great export crops, cotton and wheat. At the same time, they charged, Republican financial policies benefited banks, not ordinary borrowers. The effect on interest rates was sharply regional. Despite expansion of the national bank system, most national banks lay in the Northeast, where loans were relatively easy to get. Farmers also blamed railroad companies, which had built their lines with the support of government land grants and subsidies but charged unequal rates that privileged big eastern manufacturers. From the farmers' point of view, public money had been used to build giant railroad companies that turned around and exploited ordinary people.

The most prominent rural protest group of the early postwar decades was the National Grange of the Patrons of Husbandry, founded in 1867. Like workingmen, Grange farmers sought to counter the new power of corporate middlemen through cooperation and mutual aid. Local Grange halls brought farm families together for recreation and conversation. The Grange set up its own banks, insurance companies, and grain elevators, and, in Iowa, even a manufacturing plant for farm implements. Many Grange members also advocated political action, building independent local parties that ran on anticorporate platforms.

In the wake of the 1870s depression, Grangers, labor advocates, and local workingmen's parties forged a national political movement: the Greenback-Labor Party. In the South, Greenbackers protested the fading of Reconstruction, opposed convict labor, and urged that every man's vote be protected. Across the country, Greenbackers advocated laws to regulate corporations and enforce an eight-hour limit on the workday. They called for the federal government to print more greenback dollars and increase the amount of money in circulation; this, they argued, would stimulate the economy, create jobs, and help borrowers by allowing them to pay off debts in dollars that, over time, slowly decreased in value. Overall, Greenbackers subscribed to the ideal of **producerism**. They dismissed middlemen, bankers, lawyers, and investors as idlers who lived off the sweat of those who labored with their hands.

The Greenback movement radicalized thousands of farmers, miners, and industrial workers. In Alabama's coal-mining regions, black and white miners worked together in the party. Texas boasted seventy African American Greenback clubs. In 1878, Greenback-Labor candidates won more than a million votes and the party elected fifteen congressmen: seven from the Northeast, five from the Midwest, and three from the South. Greenback pressure helped trigger a wave of economic regulatory actions, known in the Midwest, especially, as Granger laws. By the early 1880s, twenty-nine states had created railroad commissions to supervise railroad rates and policies; others formed commissions to regulate insurance and utility companies. Such early regulatory efforts were not always effective, but they were important starting points for reform. While short-lived, the Greenback movement created the foundation for subsequent farmer-labor movements and more sustained, vigorous efforts to regulate big business.

The Knights of Labor

The most important union of the late nineteenth century, the Knights of Labor, was founded in 1869 as a secret society of garment workers in Philadelphia. In 1878, when the Greenback movement was reaching its height, Knights from Ohio, Pennsylvania, Michigan, and other states served as delegates to Greenback-Labor conventions. Like the Grangers, the Knights believed that ordinary people needed control over the enterprises in which they worked. They proposed to set up factories and shops owned by employees, transforming America into what they called "the cooperative commonwealth." In keeping with this broad-based vision, the order practiced open membership, irrespective of race, gender, or field of employment (though, like other labor groups, the Knights excluded Chinese workers). The Knights had a strong political bent. They believed that only political action could bring about many of their goals, such as government regulation of corporations and mandatory arbitration of strikes. The Knights also advocated personal responsibility and self-discipline, including temperance. Their leader, Terence Powderly, warned that the abuse of liquor robbed as many workers of their wages as did greedy employers.

Growing rapidly in the 1880s, the Knights became a sprawling, decentralized organization. The union included not only skilled craftsmen such as carpenters and ironworkers but also German beer brewers in Omaha, textile workers in Rhode Island, domestic workers in Georgia, and tenant farmers in Arkansas. Urban Knights organized workingmen's parties to advocate a host of reforms, ranging from an eight-hour workday to cheaper streetcar fares and better garbage collection. One of the Knights' key innovations was hiring a full-time women's

"BY INDUSTRY WE THRIVE."

The Knights of Labor

The caption on this union card – "By Industry we Thrive" – expresses the core principle of the Knights of Labor that everything of value is the product of honest labor. The two figures are ideal representations of that "producerist" belief – handsome workers, respectably attired, doing productive labor. A picture of the Grand Master Workman, Terence V. Powderly, hangs on the wall, benignly watching them. Picture Research Consultants & Archives.

organizer, Leonora Barry. An Irish American widow who was forced into factory work after her husband's death, Barry became a labor advocate out of horror at the conditions she found on the job.

The pattern of the Knights' growth showed the grassroots nature of labor activism in the 1880s. Increases in membership were often prompted by "wildcat strikes"—those that workers started spontaneously, without consulting union leaders. Powderly urged local Knights to avoid strikes, which he saw as costly and risky. But the organization's greatest successes resulted from grassroots strikes. In 1885, thousands of workers on the Southwest Railroad walked off the job to protest wage cuts; afterward, they telegraphed the Knights and asked to be admitted as members. The strike enhanced

the Knights' reputation among workers and built membership to 750,000. By the following year, local assemblies had sprung up in every state and almost every county in the United States.

Just as the Knights reached a pinnacle of influence, an episode of violence brought them down. In May 1886, a protest at the McCormick reaper works in Chicago led to a clash with police that left four strikers dead. (Three unions, including a Knights of Labor assembly, had struck against the plant, but the Knights had reached an agreement and returned to work. Only the machinists' union remained on strike when the incident occurred.) Chicago was a hotbed of **anarchism**—the revolutionary advocacy of a stateless society. Local anarchists, many of them German immigrants, called a protest meeting the next day, May 4, 1886, at Haymarket Square. When police tried to disperse the crowd, someone threw a bomb that killed several policemen. The officers responded with gunfire. In the trial that followed, eight anarchists were found guilty of murder and criminal conspiracy. All were convicted, not on any definitive evidence that they threw the bomb (the bomber's or bombers' identity still remains unknown) but because they had given antigovernment speeches. Four of the eight anarchists were executed by hanging, one committed suicide, and the others received long prison sentences.

The Haymarket violence caused profound damage to the American labor movement. Seizing on anti-union hysteria set off by the incident, employers went on the offensive against the Knights. They broke strikes violently and forced workers to sign contracts in which they pledged not to join labor organizations. The Knights of Labor never recovered. In the view of the press and many prosperous Americans, the Knights were tainted by their supposed links with anarchism. Novelist and literary critic William Dean Howells, one of a handful of famous Americans who publicly opposed the hanging of the Haymarket anarchists, found that when he spoke out in defense of labor, former friends in Boston shunned him, even refusing to speak when he met them on the street.

Farmers and Workers: The Cooperative Alliance

Despite the aftermath of the Haymarket incident, the Knights' cooperative vision did not entirely fade. A new rural movement, the Farmers' Alliance, arose to take up many of the issues that Grangers and Greenbackers had earlier sought to address. Founded in Texas during the depression of the 1870s, the Farmers' Alliance spread across the Plains states and the South, becoming

Industrial Violence: A Dynamited Mine, 1894

Strikes in the western mining regions pitted ruthless owners, bent on control of their property and workforce, against fiercely independent miners who knew how to use dynamite. Some of the bloodiest conflicts occurred in Colorado mining towns, where the Western Federation of Miners (WFM) had strong support and a series of Republican governors sent state militia to back the mine owners. Violence broke out repeatedly between the early 1890s and the 1910s. At Victor, Colorado, in May 1894, as dozens of armed sheriffs' deputies closed in on angry WFM members occupying the Strong Mine in protest, the miners blew up the mine's shaft house and boiler. Showered with debris, the deputies boarded the next train out of town. Because Colorado then had a Populist governor, Davis Waite, who sympathized with the miners and ordered the deputies to disband, this strike was one of the few in which owners and miners reached a peaceful settlement—a temporary victory for the union.   Library of Congress.

by the late 1880s the largest farmer-based movement in American history. The harsh conditions farmers were enduring—including drought in the West and plunging global prices for corn, cotton, and wheat—intensified the movement's appeal. Traveling Farmers' Alliance lecturers exhorted farmers to "stand as a great conservative body against the encroachments of monopolies and . . . the growing corruption of wealth and power."

Alliance leaders pinned their initial hopes on cooperative stores and exchanges that would circumvent middlemen. **Cooperatives (co-ops)** gathered farmers' orders and bought in bulk at wholesale prices, passing the savings on to farmers. Alliance cooperatives suffered from chronic underfunding and lack of credit. They also faced hostility from the merchants and lenders they tried to circumvent. But they achieved notable victories in the late 1880s. The Dakota Farmers' Alli-

ance, for example, offered members cheap hail insurance and low prices on machinery and farm supplies. The Texas Farmers' Alliance established a huge cooperative enterprise to market cotton and provide farmers with cheap loans.

When cotton prices fell further in 1891, however, the Texas exchange failed. The Texas Farmers' Alliance then proposed a federal price-support system for farm products, modeled on the national banking system. Under this plan, the federal government would hold crops in public warehouses and issue loans on their value until they could be profitably sold. When the Democratic Party—still wary of big-government schemes—declared the idea too radical, the Texas Farmers' Alliance joined the alliances of Kansas, Nebraska, South Dakota, and elsewhere to create a new political party.

Expanding on the earlier work of the Grange, and carrying it into the South and West, the Farmers' Alliance cooperated with the Knights of Labor, using rural reformers' substantial political clout on behalf of urban workers who shared their political vision. By this time, the farmer-labor coalition had made a considerable impact on state politics. But state laws and commissions were proving ineffective against corporations of national and even global scope. It was difficult for a state like Minnesota, for example, to enforce new laws against a railroad company whose lines might stretch from Chicago to Seattle and whose corporate headquarters might be in New York. Militant farmers and labor advocates began to demand federal action.

In 1887, Congress sent President Grover Cleveland two groundbreaking bills that he signed into law. The Hatch Act provided federal funding for agricultural research and education, directly meeting farmers' demands for government aid to agriculture. The landmark Interstate Commerce Act counteracted a Supreme Court decision of the previous year, *Wabash v. Illinois*, that had struck down states' authority to regulate railroads. The act created the Interstate Commerce Commission (ICC), charged with investigating interstate shipping; forcing railroads to make their rates public; and, when necessary, suing in court to force companies to reduce "unjust or unreasonable" rates.

Though creation of the ICC was a direct response to pressure from farmer-labor constituents, its final form represented a compromise. The most radical rural representatives, like Texas congressman John Reagan, wanted Congress to establish a direct set of regulations under which railroads must operate. If a railroad did not comply, any citizen could take the company to court; and if the new rules triggered bankruptcy, the railroad could convert to public ownership. But getting such a plan through Congress proved impossible. Lawmakers more sympathetic to business called instead for an expert commission to oversee the railroad industry. In a pattern that was repeated frequently over the next few decades, the "commission" model proved more acceptable to the majority of congressmen, but probably less effective in practice than the original plan would have been.

The ICC faced formidable challenges. Though the new law forbade railroads from reaching secret rate-setting agreements, evidence was very difficult to gather; secret "pooling" continued. At the same time, a hostile Supreme Court eroded the commission's powers. In a series of sixteen decisions over the two decades after the ICC was created, the Court sided with railroads fifteen times. The justices delivered a particularly hard blow in 1897, when they ruled that the ICC had no power to interfere with shipping rates. Nonetheless, creation of the ICC was a major achievement. In the early twentieth century, Congress would strengthen the commission's powers and the ICC would become one of the most powerful federal agencies charged with overseeing private business.

Another Path: The American Federation of Labor

While the Knights of Labor exerted political pressure, some workers pursued a different strategy. In the 1870s, printers, molders, ironworkers, bricklayers, and about thirty other groups of skilled workers organized nationwide trade unions. These "brotherhoods" focused in narrow, specific ways on the everyday needs of workers in skilled occupations. Trade unions sought a **closed shop**—with all jobs reserved for union members—that kept out lower-wage workers. Union rules specified the terms of work, sometimes in minute detail. Some unions emphasized mutual aid. Because operating trains was a high-risk occupation, for example, railroad brotherhoods pooled their contributions in funds that provided accident and death benefits. Above all, trade unionism defended craft workers' traditional rights and asserted their role as active decision-makers in the workplace, not just cogs in a management-run machine.

For a while, in the 1880s, many trade unionists joined the Knights of Labor coalition. But the catastrophe of Haymarket persuaded them to leave the order and create the separate American Federation of Labor (AFL). The man who led them out of the Knights was Samuel Gompers, a Dutch-Jewish cigar maker whose family had emigrated to New York in 1863. Gompers headed the new AFL until 1924. He believed that the Knights relied too much on electoral politics, where victories were likely to be limited and fleeting, and he did not share their sweeping critique of **capitalism**. The AFL, made up of relatively skilled and well-paid workers, was less interested in challenging the corporate order than in winning a larger profit share for skilled workers.

Having gone to work at age ten, Gompers always contended that what he missed at school he more than made up for in the shop, where cigar makers paid one of their members to read to them while they worked. As a young worker-intellectual, Gompers gravitated to New York's radical circles, where he participated in lively debates about the best strategy for workingmen to pursue. Partly out of these debates, and partly from his own experience in the Cigar Makers Union, Gompers hammered out a doctrine that he called "pure-and-simple unionism." *Pure* referred to membership: strictly

Samuel Gompers, c. 1890s

Samuel Gompers (1850–1924) was one of the founders of the American Federation of Labor, and its president for nearly forty years. A company detective took this photograph when the labor leader was visiting striking miners in West Virginia, an area where mine operators resisted unions with special fierceness.   George Meany Memorial Archives.

limited to workers, organized by craft and occupation, with no reliance on outside advisers or allies. *Simple* referred to goals: only those that immediately benefited workers—better wages, hours, and working conditions. Pure-and-simple unionists distrusted politics. Their aim was collective bargaining with employers.

On one level, pure-and-simple unionism worked. The AFL was small at first, but between 1897 and 1904, its membership rose from 447,000 to more than 2 million. In the early twentieth century, it became the nation's leading voice for workers, lasting far longer than movements like the Knights of Labor. The AFL's strategy—personified by Gompers, who became the union's towering leader—was especially well suited to an era when Congress and the courts were hostile to labor. By the 1910s the political climate would become more re-

sponsive; at that later moment, Gompers would soften his antipolitical stance and AFL leaders joined the battle for new laws to protect workers.

What Gompers gave up most crucially, in the meantime, was the inclusiveness of the Knights of Labor. Compared with the Knights, the AFL was far less welcoming to women and blacks, and it was limited mostly to skilled craftsmen. There was little room in the AFL for department-store clerks and other service workers, much less the farmworkers and domestic servants whom the Knights of Labor had organized. Despite the AFL's great success among skilled craftsmen, the narrowness of its base was a flaw that would come back to haunt the labor movement later on. Gompers made a crucial choice when he limited the AFL's scope because the impact of industrialization reached far beyond skilled workers—and even beyond the workplace, immigrants, and the political sphere. Industrialization was, in these decades, transforming the whole of American society and culture.

- **What factors prompted the emergence of the labor movement? In what ways did farmers and industrial workers cooperate?**
- **How did the goals and practices of the AFL resemble and differ from those of the Knights of Labor?**
- **Which of the national labor organizations that formed after 1865 do you think was most successful? In what ways, and why?**

SUMMARY

The end of the Civil War ushered in the era of American big business. Exploiting the continent's vast resources, vertically integrated corporations emerged as the dominant business form and giant companies built near monopolies in some sectors of the economy. Corporations devised new modes of production, distribution, and marketing, extending their reach through the department store, the mail-order catalog, and the new advertising industry. These developments laid the groundwork for mass consumer culture.

Rapid industrialization drew immigrants from around the world. Until the 1920s, most European and Latin American immigrants were welcome to enter the United States, though they often endured harsh conditions after they arrived. Asian immigrants, by contrast, met with severe discrimination. The Chinese Exclusion Act blocked all Chinese laborers from coming to the United States; it was later extended to other Asians, and it built the legal framework for broader forms of exclusion later on.

Nationwide movements for workers' rights arose in response to industrialization. During the 1870s and 1880s, coalitions of workers and farmers, notably the Knights of Labor and the Farmers' Alliance, organized to seek political solutions to what they saw as large corporations' exploitation of working people. Pressure from such movements led to the first major attempts to regulate corporations, such as the federal Interstate Commerce Act. Radical protest movements were weakened, however, after public condemnation of anarchist violence in 1886 at Chicago's Haymarket Square—even though the Knights and Farmers' Alliance were obviously not responsible. Meanwhile, trade unions pursued a pure-and-simple approach to organization and negotiation, organizing skilled workers to negotiate directly with employers. Such unions became the most popular form of labor organizing in the early twentieth century.

CHAPTER REVIEW QUESTIONS

- What factors led to the rise of big business in the United States? For working people, what were the results of that economic transformation?

- What roles did newly arrived immigrants play in the economy during the late nineteenth and early twentieth centuries?

- What were the long-term consequences of the Chinese Exclusion Act for U.S. immigration policy?

- Compare the accomplishments and limitations of American farmer-labor movements of the 1870s and 1880s, such as the Greenback-Labor Party and the Knights of Labor, with those of the American Federation of Labor. Why did the latter choose a different strategy?

FOR FURTHER EXPLORATION

Important works on industrialization include Walter Licht, *Industrializing America* (1995); Mira Wilkins, *The Emergence of Multinational Enterprise* (1970); and Alfred Chandler, *The Visible Hand* (1977). On managers and salesmen see Olivier Zunz, *Making America Corporate* (1990), and Walter Friedman, *Birth of a Salesman* (2004). On changing views of wage work see Lawrence Glickman, *A Living Wage* (1997); on women, Susan Porter Benson, *Counter Cultures* (1986), and Angel Kwolek-Folland, *Engendering Business* (1994). Biographies include Joseph Frazier Wall, *Andrew Carnegie* (1970), and, on John D. Rockefeller, Ron Chernow, *Titan* (1998).

On immigration see Roger Daniels, *Coming to America* (1990); Walter T. K. Nugent, *Crossings* (1992); Mark Wyman, *Round-Trip to America* (1993); Ronald Takaki, *Strangers from a Different Shore* (1989); and Erika Lee, *At America's Gates* (2003). On 1877 see David Stowell, ed., *The Great Strikes of 1877* (2008). Studies of labor include David Montgomery, *The Fall of the House of Labor* (1987) and *Citizen Worker* (1993); Leon Fink, *Workingmen's Democracy* (1983); David Brody, *Steelworkers in America* (1960); and Paul Krause, *The Battle for Homestead* (1992). On the role of farmers and labor in state-building see Elizabeth Sanders, *Roots of Reform* (1999). On Gompers see Harold Livesay, *Samuel Gompers and Organized Labor in America* (1978), and the treasure trove at the Gompers Papers site, **www.history.umd.edu/Gompers**. Also see *Who Built America?* (second edition; 2008) by the American Social History Project.

TEST YOUR KNOWLEDGE

To assess your command of the material in this chapter, see the Online Study Guide at **bedfordstmartins.com/henretta**.

For Web sites, images, and documents related to topics and places in this chapter, visit **bedfordstmartins.com/makehistory**.

TIMELINE

1863	Cleveland, Ohio, becomes nation's petroleum refining center
1865	Chicago's Union Stock Yard opens
1867	National Grange of the Patrons of Husbandry founded
1869	Knights of Labor founded
1875	John Wanamaker opens nation's first department store in Philadelphia
1877	San Francisco mob attacks Chinatown; Great Railroad Strike
1882	Congress passes Chinese Exclusion Act
1886	McCormick reaper works strike Haymarket Square violence American Federation of Labor (AFL) founded
1887	Interstate Commerce Act
1900	America's one hundred largest companies control one-third of national productive capacity

Tip Top Weekly

An ideal publication for the American Youth

Issued Weekly. By Subscription $2.50 per year. Entered as Second Class Matter at New York Post Office by STREET & SMITH, 238 William St., N. Y.

No. 276.

Price, Five Cents.

FRANK MERRIWELL'S CHUMS

or OUT AGAIN FOR SPORT

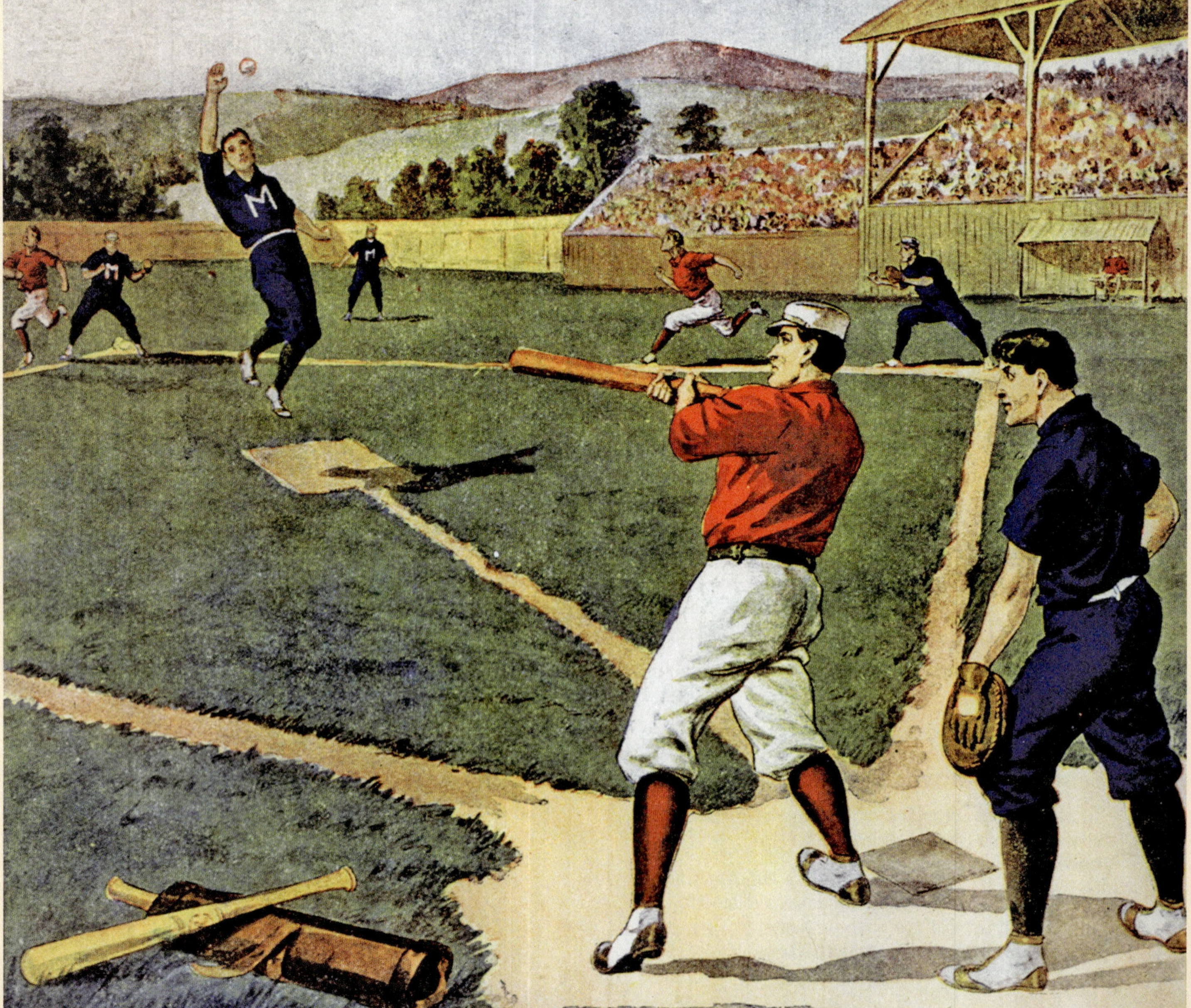

BY BURT L. STANDISH

LIKE A FLASH, MERRY SHOT INTO THE AIR AND PULLED THE BALL DOWN WITH ONE HAND.

The Victorians Meet the Modern, 1880–1917

In 1876, a popular biography of presidential candidate Rutherford B. Hayes told American boys and girls why he had achieved success. As a child, Hayes had always obeyed his loving mother. He "shunned the coarse and rude boys upon the street." At school, he "did not splinter his desk with his penknife, nor throw paper balls or apple-cores. . . . He was a model boy." Hayes grew up to marry a refined and educated woman, Lucy Ware Webb. She devoted herself to her children, while Rutherford, in turn, appreciated his wife's moral guidance. The two were faithful churchgoers; one of their favorite pastimes was gathering the family to sing hymns.

Hayes's biography summed up the ideal of domesticity that prevailed during the Victorian era (that is, the time of Queen Victoria's rule in Great Britain, 1837–1901, when English mores and culture profoundly influenced the United States). Domesticity called for masculine restraint and female moral influence. But industrialization was transforming domesticity, as Americans confronted modern conditions of life. While Hayes served as president, authors of children's books were already undermining older views. Boys and girls were snapping up flamboyant dime novels with titles like *Buffalo Bill's Death-Deal*. From playgrounds to summer camps, children's vigorous physical exercise became a national priority. By 1905, one of the most popular children's books was Ralph Henry Barbour's *The Crimson Sweater*, the story of a schoolboy who proves himself through rugged feats in football and hockey. The story's sassy heroine, Harriet, insists on the nickname "Harry" and sneaks out at night for adventures with the boys.

The shift in children's literature was a marker of America's changing culture. More and more, women sought to exert their influence outside the home, through involvement in politics, reform movements, and civic life. Women also expanded their place in the public sphere through their increasing presence as wage-earners. At the same time, the ideal of restrained Christian manhood gave way to aggressive calls for masculine fitness and self-assertion, exemplified in the rising popularity of athletics. An ethos of duty, self-restraint, and moral uplift gave way to new expectations of leisure and fun.

Manhood: The New Athletic Ideal

By the turn of the century, American boys became avid readers of sports stories in five-cent tabloids like this one, *Tip Top Weekly*. Frank Merriwell, the fictional creation of writer Gilbert Patten (who wrote under the name Burt L. Standish), excelled not only at baseball but in football, basketball, crew, and track. While showing toughness and strength in sports, Frank also solved exciting mysteries and simultaneously educated his Yale classmates on the need to stay physically fit and avoid smoking and strong drink. Frank's adventures, featured in *Tip Top* from 1896 through 1912, became the basis for a later comic strip and a 1930s radio show. Frank Merriwell and his fictional son, Frank Jr., served as models for later boy heroes such as the Hardy Boys. Picture Research Consultants & Archives.

In the same decades, stunning scientific discoveries — from dinosaur fossils to distant galaxies — challenged nineteenth-century beliefs about humans' place in the universe. Faced with such wonders as electricity and medical vaccines, Americans celebrated technological solutions to human problems. But while scientific ways of thinking gained tremendous popularity, religion hardly faded. In fact, the diversity of religious practice grew — not only because immigrants brought new faiths from abroad, but also because religious innovators, confronted with the problems caused by industrialization, developed such creative ideas and institutions as the Social Gospel and the Salvation Army.

In these decades, Americans found themselves living in a **modern** society — one in which their grandparents' beliefs, assumptions, and ways of life no longer seemed to apply. Living in an increasingly market-driven economic order, many Americans championed the freedom of each individual to choose his or her path. At the same time, they expressed anxiety and distress over the attendant risks and upheavals. In the decades between the end of the Civil War and the start of World War I, industrialization transformed family life, education, leisure, religion, and the arts. During this era of dynamic change, Americans reshaped — without necessarily discarding — older attachments and beliefs.

Women, Men, and the Solitude of Self

Appearing before Congress in 1892, women's rights advocate Elizabeth Cady Stanton described what she called the "solitude of self." Stanton rejected the claim that women had no need for equal rights because they enjoyed the protection of male kin. "The talk of sheltering woman from the fierce storms of life is the sheerest mockery," she declared. "They beat on her from every point of the compass, just as they do on man, and with more fatal results, for he has been trained to protect himself." Stanton's arguments suited an era when women were taking up reform work and paid employment outside the home. Meanwhile, in a market-driven economy men faced increasing pressure to strive for success in "the battle of life."

Changes in Family Life

The average American family — especially among the middle class — decreased in size in the post–Civil War decades. A long decline in the birthrate, which began in the late eighteenth century, continued in this era. In 1800, white women who survived to menopause had borne an average of 7.0 children; by 1900, the average was 3.6. On the farm and in many working-class families, children were assets on the family balance sheet: at a young age, they went to work in the fields or factory. But in an industrial society, parents who had fewer sons and daughters could concentrate their resources, educating and preparing each child for success in the new economy. Family limitation was one of the keys to upward mobility.

Several factors limited childbearing. Americans married at older ages, and many mothers tried — as they had for decades — to space pregnancies more widely by nursing young children for several years, which suppressed fertility. By the late nineteenth century, couples also used a range of other contraceptive methods, such as condoms and diaphragms, though they rarely wrote about them. Their reluctance to do so was understandable, since contraceptives were deeply stigmatized. In 1873, Anthony Comstock, the crusading secretary of the New York Society for the Suppression of Vice, secured a federal law that banned obscene materials from the U.S. mail. The Comstock Act prohibited circulation of almost any information about sex and birth control. It appears, however, that Comstock had limited success in preventing the spread of contraceptives.

As they grew to adulthood, rural young people faced new dilemmas and choices. Traditionally, daughters had provided essential labor for spinning and weaving cloth, but industrialization had relocated those tasks from the household to the factory. "Fewer women than men

are needed on the farm," reported one investigator. "One woman, ordinarily, does the work of the family." Finding themselves without a useful role in the household, many farm daughters sought paid employment. In an age of declining rural prosperity, many sons also left the farm and—like immigrants arriving from other countries—set aside part of their pay to help the folks at home. Explaining why she moved to Chicago, an African American woman from Louisiana declared, "A child with any respect about herself or hisself wouldn't like to see their mother and father work so hard and earn nothing. I feel it my duty to help."

The Rise of High School

For young people who hoped to secure respectable and lucrative jobs, the watchword was *education*. A high school education was particularly valuable for boys from affluent families who hoped to enter professional or managerial work. Daughters attended in even larger numbers than their brothers (Table 18.1). Parents of the Civil War generation, who had witnessed the plight of thousands of war widows and orphans, encouraged daughters to educate themselves for teaching or office work, so they could find employment before marriage and would have skills to fall back on, "just in case." Both urban reformers and rural groups such as the Farmers' Alliance pushed for better public schools and for technical and business education. By 1900, 71 percent of Americans between the ages of five and eighteen attended school. That figure rose even further in the early twentieth century, as public officials adopted and enforced laws requiring school attendance.

Most high schools were coeducational. The curriculum included literature and composition, history and geography, biology and mathematics, and a mix of

TABLE 18.1

High School Graduates, 1870–1910

Year	Number	Percent 17-Year-Olds	Male	Female
1870	16,000	2.0	7,000	9,000
1800	44,000	3.0	19,000	25,000
1910	156,000	8.6	64,000	93,000

SOURCE: *Historical Statistics of the United States*, 2 vols. (Washington, DC: U.S. Bureau of the Census, 1975), 1: 386.

ancient and modern languages. Boys and girls engaged in friendly — and sometimes not-so-friendly — rivalry when girls captured an outsize share of academic prizes. In 1884, a high school newspaper in Concord, New Hampshire, published this poem from a disgruntled boy who caricatured his female classmates:

> We know many tongues of living and dead,
> In science and fiction we're very well read,
> But we cannot cook meat and cannot make bread
> And we've wished many times that we were all dead.

A female student promptly shot back a poem of her own, denouncing male students' smoking habit:

> But if boys will smoke cigarettes
> Although the smoke may choke them,
> One consolation still remains —
> *They kill the boys that smoke them.*

Almost every high school featured athletics, and girls found a place there, too. Recruited first as cheerleaders for high school boys' teams, they soon established field hockey and other teams of their own.

College Men and Women

Through most of the nineteenth century, the rate of Americans who attended college had hovered around 2 percent. Driven partly by the expansion of public universities, the rate began to rise steadily in the 1880s, reaching 8 percent by 1920. Much larger numbers attended the rapidly growing network of business and technical schools. "GET A PLACE IN THE WORLD," advertised one Minneapolis business college in 1907, "where your talents can be used to the best advantage." Typically, the school offered both day and night classes in subjects such as bookkeeping, typewriting, and shorthand.

The needs of the changing economy also influenced the curriculum at more traditional institutions. State universities emphasized agricultural and technical training. They fed the growing professional workforce with graduates trained in fields such as engineering. Many private colleges distanced themselves from such practical pursuits; their administrators argued that students who aimed to be leaders in business, politics, and society needed a broad-based knowledge of history and culture. They modernized their course offerings, emphasizing languages such as French and German, for example, rather than Latin and Greek. Harvard College, under dynamic president Charles W. Eliot from 1869 to 1909, pioneered the liberal arts. Students at the all-male college chose from a range of electives, as Eliot called for classes that developed each young man's "individual reality and creative power."

African American Education In the South, one of the most famous educational projects was Booker T. Washington's Tuskegee Institute, founded in 1881. Washington, born in slavery, not only taught but exemplified the goal of self-help, and his autobiography, *Up from Slavery*, became an immediate bestseller in 1901. Because of the deep poverty in which most southern African Americans lived, Washington concluded that "book education" for most "would be almost a waste of time." He focused instead on industrial education. Students, he argued, would "be sure of knowing how to make a living after they had left us." Tuskegee sent many female graduates into teaching and nursing; men more often entered the industrial trades or farmed by the latest scientific methods.

Washington became the most prominent black leader of his generation. His style of leadership, based on avoiding confrontation with whites and cultivating patronage and private influence, was well suited to the difficult era after Reconstruction. Washington believed that money was color-blind: Whites, he argued, would respect economic success. Washington represented the hopes of millions of African Americans who expected that education, hard work, and respectability would erase white prejudice. That optimism proved ill-founded. As a tide of disfranchisement, segregation, and lynch-

Booker T. Washington

In an age of severe racial oppression, Booker T. Washington emerged as the leading public voice of African Americans. He was remarkable both for his effectiveness in speaking to white Americans and for his deep understanding of the aspirations of blacks. Born a slave, Washington had plenty of firsthand experience with racism. But having befriended several whites in his youth, he also believed that African Americans could appeal to whites of good will—and maneuver around those who were hostile—in the struggle for equality. He hoped, most of all, that economic achievement would erase white prejudice. Brown Brothers.

ing rolled in during the 1890s, educated and prosperous blacks became targets of white anger. Washington soon came under fire from a younger generation of race leaders, who argued that he accommodated too much to white racism. Nonetheless, Tuskegee endured as an educational beacon.

Higher Education for Women | In the Northeast and South, women most often attended single-sex institutions or teacher-training colleges where the student body was overwhelmingly female. For students from affluent families, private colleges offered an education equivalent to men's. Vassar College started the trend when it opened in 1861; Smith,

Wellesley, and others soon followed. Some doctors warned that these institutions were dangerous: Intensive brain work, they said, would unsex young women and drain energy from their ovaries, leading them to bear weak children later in life. In response to such critics, Vassar implemented a strict regimen of regular exercise, nutritious meals, naps, and curfews to ensure that students stayed healthy. But as thousands of women earned degrees and suffered no apparent harm, fears faded. Single-sex higher education for women spread from private to public institutions, especially in the South, where the Mississippi State College for Women (1885) led the way.

Coeducation was more prevalent in the Midwest and West, where state universities opened their doors to female students after the Civil War. Women were also admitted to most of the southern African American colleges founded during Reconstruction. By 1910, 58 percent of America's 1,083 colleges and universities were coeducational. While women at single-sex institutions forged strong bonds with one another, women also gained many benefits from learning with men. When male students were friendly, they forged comfortable working relationships; when men were hostile, women learned coping skills that served them well when they later took up reform work or paid employment. One doctor who studied at the University of Iowa remembered later that he and his friends mercilessly harassed the first women who entered the medical school. But when the women showed they were good students, the men's attitudes changed to "wholesome respect."

Whether or not they got a college education, more and more women recognized, in the words of Elizabeth Cady Stanton, their "solitude of self." The rapidly changing economy offered both opportunities and dangers; it rewarded mobility and individual risk-taking. In such a world, women could not always count on the protection or support of fathers, husbands, and sons. Women who needed to support themselves could choose from dozens of guidebooks such as *What Girls Can Do* (1880) and *How to Make Money Although a Woman* (1895). Members of the Association for the Advancement of Women, founded in 1873, argued that women's paid employment was a positive good.

Today, many economists argue that education and high-quality jobs for women are keys to poverty reduction in the developing world. In the United States, that process also led to broader gains in women's political rights. As women began to earn advanced degrees, gain footholds in respectable and professional employments, and live independently, it became harder to argue that women were "dependents" who did not need to vote.

Class of 1896, Radcliffe College

When Harvard University, long a bastion of male education, created an "Annex" for women's instruction in 1879, it was a sure sign of growing support for women's higher education. The Annex became Radcliffe College in 1894. Two years later, this graduating class of thirty posed for their portrait. Among them was Alice Sterling of Bridgeport, Connecticut, who went on to marry Harvard graduate Frank Cook and devote herself to Protestant foreign missions. On two trips around the world, Alice Sterling Cook visited all the women's colleges that missionaries had founded in India, China, and Japan. Cook's energetic public activities were typical of those of many alumnae of women's colleges.   Schlesinger Library, Radcliffe Institute for Advanced Study, Harvard University.

Masculinity and the Rise of Sports

In the decades after the Civil War, gender expectations also changed for middle-class men. Traditionally, the mark of a successful American man was his economic independence: He was his own boss. But by the late nineteenth century, more and more men worked in salaried positions or for wages. Increasing numbers also did brain work in an office, rather than using their muscles outdoors. Anxieties arose that the American male was becoming, as one magazine editor warned, "weak, effeminate, decaying." How could men assert their independence in the modern world? How could

they develop toughness and physical strength? One answer was athletics. Before the Civil War, there were no distinctively American games except for Native American lacrosse. The most popular team sport was cricket. Over the next six decades sports became a fundamental part of American manhood.

The YMCA and "Muscular Christianity" One of the first promoters of physical fitness was the Young Men's Christian Association (YMCA). Adapted from Britain and introduced to Boston in 1851, the YMCA combined vigorous activities for young men with an evangelizing appeal. In cities and towns across America, the YMCA built gymnasiums and athletic facilities where men could exercise their bodies and make themselves "clean and strong."

Begun as a Protestant effort to promote "muscular Christianity" for white-collar workers, the YMCA also developed a substantial industrial program between 1900 and 1917. Railroad managers and other corporate titans hoped that YMCAs would head off labor unrest, fostering a loyal and contented workforce. Business leaders also relied on sports to foster physical and mental discipline, and to help men adjust their bodies to the demands of the clock and stopwatch, enhancing performance on the job. Sports fostered men's competitive spirit, they believed; serving on employer-sponsored teams could instill a sense of teamwork and company pride.

But working-class men and boys had their own ideas about sports and leisure. YMCAs quickly became a site of negotiation. Could workingmen come to the "Y" to play billiards or cards? Could they smoke? At first YMCA leaders said no, but to attract working-class men, they had to make concessions. At the same time, the institution became a site for athletic innovation. YMCA instructors, searching for wintertime fitness activities in the 1890s, invented the new games of basketball and volleyball.

The YMCA sought to provide some of the amenities of elite athletic clubs that also flourished after the Civil War. Exclusive country clubs, which appeared in many affluent neighborhoods, combined facilities for tennis, golf, and swimming with a dining room and calendar of social events. By the turn of the century — perhaps because women were rapidly encroaching on their athletic turf — elite men took up even more aggressive physical sports, including boxing, weightlifting, and martial arts. Theodore Roosevelt became one of the first American devotees of jujitsu; during his presidency, from 1901 to 1909, he designated a judo room in the White House and hired an expert Japanese instructor. Roosevelt also famously wrestled and boxed, urging other American men to join him in pursuing the "strenuous life."

America's Game | In the summer of 1907, famous lawyer Clarence Darrow sweated in a Boise courtroom, defending three leaders of the Western Federation of Miners against charges that they had assassinated Idaho's ex-governor. The atmosphere was tense; when Darrow won acquittals on all counts, the outcome was a sensation. But the seriousness of the trial did not prevent the judge, jury, and lawyers on both sides from adjourning to the local baseball diamond. "Never has life held for me," Darrow once remarked, "anything quite so entrancing as baseball." He and other lawyers cheered as they watched a local telephone company employee, Walter Johnson, pitch a series of spectacular shut-outs in the Idaho State League. Johnson, promptly signed by the Washington Senators, went on to become one of the game's legendary pitchers.

In the post–Civil War years, no other sport in America was as successful as baseball. As early as the late 1700s, Americans had begun to play various stick and ball games, some of which came to be called "base ball." More formal rules developed in the 1840s and 1850s, and baseball's popularity spread in military camps during the Civil War. Afterward, the idea that baseball "received its baptism in the bloody days of our Nation's direst danger," as one promoter put it, became part of the game's mythology.

Big-time professional baseball arose after the war, with the launching of the National League in 1876. The league quickly built more than a dozen teams in the large cities of the Northeast and Midwest, from the Brooklyn Trolley Dodgers to the Cleveland Spiders. Team owners were profit-minded businessmen who shaped the sport to please fans. Wooden grandstands gave way to the concrete and steel stadiums of the early twentieth century, such as Fenway Park in Boston and Forbes Field in Pittsburgh. By 1900, boys collected lithographed cards of their favorite players, and the baseball cap came into fashion. In 1903, two years after the creation of the American League, the Boston Americans defeated the Pittsburgh Pirates in the first World Series.

American men not only rooted for professional baseball teams; they got out on the diamond to play. Until the 1870s, most amateur players were clerks and white-collar workers who had the leisure time to play and the income to buy their own uniforms. Business frowned on baseball and other sports as a waste of time, especially for working-class men. But after the Civil War, employers came to see baseball, like other athletic pursuits, as healthy and uplifting. It provided fresh air and exercise, kept workers out of saloons, and promoted discipline and teamwork. Company teams became a widespread institution. The best players, wearing uniforms emblazoned with their companies' names, competed on paid work time during the ball season. Baseball thus set a pattern for how other American sports developed. Begun among independent craftsmen, it was taken up by elite men anxious to prove their strength and fitness. Well-to-do Americans then decided such sports could benefit wage-earning men.

Football Practice, Chilocco Indian School, 1911

Football became widely popular, spreading from Ivy League schools and state universities to schools like this one, built on Cherokee land in Oklahoma. The uniforms of this team, typical of the day, show very limited padding and protection—a factor that contributed to high rates of injury and even death on the field. As they practiced in 1911, these Chilocco students had an inspiring model to look up to: In the same year Jim Thorpe, a fellow Oklahoman and a member of the Sac and Fox tribes, was winning national fame by leading the all-Indian team at Pennsylvania's Carlisle School to victory against Harvard. Thorpe, one of the finest athletes of his generation, went on to win gold medals in the pentathlon and decathlon at the 1912 Olympics in Stockholm, Sweden.   National Archives.

Rise of the Negro Leagues

Baseball was a site of negotiations over race as well as class. In the 1880s and 1890s, managers hired a few African American players into the major leagues. As late as 1901, the manager of the Baltimore Orioles succeeded in hiring Charlie Grant, a light-skinned black player from Cincinnati, by renaming him Charlie Tokohoma and claiming he was Cherokee. But as the manager's subterfuge suggested, black players were increasingly barred. A Toledo team with a black player received a threatening note before one game in Richmond, Virginia: If the "negro catcher" played, the writer warned, he would be lynched. Toledo put a substitute on the field, and at the end of the season the club terminated the black player's contract.

Shut out of white leagues, black players and fans turned instead to segregated professional teams. These emerged as early as Reconstruction, showcasing both athletic talent and race pride. Louisiana's top team, the New Orleans Pinchbacks, pointedly named themselves after the state's black Reconstruction governor. By the early 1900s, such teams organized into separate Negro Leagues. Though their players endured erratic pay and rundown ball fields, the popular leagues thrived until the desegregation of baseball after World War II. In an era of stark discrimination, they showcased the manhood and talent of black men. "I liked the way their uniform fit, the way they wore their cap," wrote an admiring fan of the Newark Eagles. "They showed a style in almost everything they did." Looking back on his career for Chicago's American Giants and other clubs, player-manager John Henry "Pop" Lloyd remarked, "I had a chance to prove the ability of our race in this sport. . . . We have given the Negro a greater opportunity now to be accepted into the major leagues with other Americans."

American Football The most controversial sport was football, which began at elite Ivy League colleges during the 1880s. The great powerhouse was the Yale team, whose legendary coach Walter Camp went on to become a watch manufacturer. Between 1883 and 1891, under Camp's direction, Yale scored 4,660 points while its opponents scored 92. Camp emphasized drill and precision, drawing on the emerging ideals of scientific management, which taught humans to move with machinelike efficiency. Coaches like Camp argued that football offered perfect training for the competitive world of business. The game was violent: The deaths of six players in the 1908 college season provoked a public outcry. Eventually, new rules protected quarterbacks and required coaches to remove injured players from the game. But such measures were adopted grudgingly, with supporters arguing that they ruined football as a site of manly combat.

Like baseball and the YMCA, football soon attracted business sponsorship. The first professional teams emerged around the turn of the twentieth century in western Pennsylvania's steel towns. Executives of Carnegie Steel organized teams in Homestead and Braddock, and the first league appeared during the anthracite coal strike of 1902. Most early professional teams arose in the industrial heartland. The Green Bay Packers were sponsored by the Indian-Acme Packing Company; the future Chicago Bears, first known as the Decatur Staleys, were funded by a maker of laundry starch. Like baseball, football initially encouraged men to develop their own strength and skills, but its professional form encouraged most men to buy in as spectators and fans.

The Great Outdoors

As the rise of sports suggests, Americans began to look back on Victorian life as stuffy and claustrophobic, and they revolted by heading outdoors. A craze for bicycling swept the country; in 1890, at the height of the mania, U.S. manufacturers sold an astonishing ten million bikes. Women were not far behind men in taking up athletics. By the 1890s even elite women—long confined to corsets and heavy, elaborate clothes that restricted their movement—donned lighter clothes and took up sports like archery and golf. Artist Charles

Frances Benjamin Johnston, Self Portrait, 1903

Like other artists and writers of her day, Frances Benjamin Johnston (1864–1953) found inspiration in the landscapes of the West. She worked extensively at Yellowstone National Park, where she took this photograph of herself, seated in the rugged landscape. Johnston played a major role in bringing public attention to the beauty of Yellowstone. A proudly independent woman who never married, Johnston also served as a model for women's entry into professional work. In 1897, she gave advice to readers of *Ladies' Home Journal* on "What a Woman Can Do with a Camera," promoting professional photography as a career.   Library of Congress.

Gibson became famous for his portraits of the "Gibson Girl," an elite beauty whom he often depicted playing on the tennis court or swimming at the beach. Commentators hailed the "New Woman" for her athleticism and public spirit (see Reading American Pictures, "Challenging Female Delicacy: The New Woman," p. 568).

Those with leisure time used the rail networks to get outdoors and closer to nature. For people of modest means, this most often meant Sunday afternoon by the lake. By the turn of the century, camping had become a recognized form of fun. As early as 1904, Coronado Beach in California was offering tent rentals for $3 a week. By the 1910s, campgrounds and cottages in many parts of the country catered to a working-class clientele. In an industrial and increasingly urban society, the

Challenging Female Delicacy: The New Woman

John Singer Sargent, *Mr. and Mrs. I. N. Phelps Stokes*, 1897.
Image copyright © The Metropolitan Museum of Art/Art Resource, NY.

Recalling her Baltimore girlhood in the 1860s, M. Carey Thomas, the second president of Bryn Mawr College, remembered "the awful doubt, felt by women themselves as well as by men, as to whether women as a sex were physically and mentally fit for" higher education. Those words might sound silly if someone were to say them today, but they were not ridiculous at the time. To document changing assumptions about women in the late nineteenth century, we turn to an unexpected historical source—fine art. This painting by John Singer Sargent, the greatest portraitist of the age, depicts a pair of wealthy newlyweds. Heir to his father's fortune in trading and mining, Isaac Newton Phelps Stokes graduated from Harvard in 1891 and became an architect and New York housing reformer. In 1895 he married Edith Minturn, an heiress "widely known for her beauty" (as the *New York Times* reported in its account of their wedding) and active in charitable organizations. This portrait was a wedding gift to the couple from a wealthy friend.

ANALYZING THE EVIDENCE

- Sargent presents Edith Minturn Stokes in a shirtwaist and long skirt, an outfit more practical than traditional heavy dresses with bustles, which by the 1890s was widely adopted by "New Women." Does anything else about this young wife's appearance convey independence and strength?

- Implicit in the concept of the New Woman was a repudiation of the idea of wives as "the companion or ornamental appendage of man." Is there anything about the portrait that suggests this marital revolution? How might we reconcile that with the painting's title, which identifies the central figure as "Mrs. I. N. Phelps Stokes," not as "Edith"?

- Sargent was a high-society painter. His subjects were almost exclusively elite women, decked out in their finest. Wealthy patrons prized his portraits partly because they enjoyed seeing their women adorned with the objects of conspicuous consumption. But in this portrait, Sargent simply shows Edith Minturn Phelps Stokes in everyday dress. Does this fact throw any light on the changing relations between men and women in this period—especially among the elite?

outdoors became a site of leisure and renewal rather than danger and hard work. One journalist, looking at urban life from the vantage point of a vacation in the West, wrote, "How stupid it all seems: the mad eagerness of money-making men, the sham pleasures of conventional society." In the wilderness, he went on, "your blood clarifies; your brain becomes active. You get a new view of life."

Preservation As Americans went searching for such renewal, national and state governments set aside more public lands for preservation and recreation. The United States substantially expanded its park system and, during Theodore Roosevelt's presidency, extended the reach of national forests, now overseen by the U.S. Forest Service. By 1916, President Woodrow Wilson provided consistent administrative oversight of the national parks, signing an act creating the National Park Service (Map 18.1). A year later the system numbered thirteen parks—including Maine's Acadia, the first that lay east of the Mississippi River.

National parks became increasingly popular places to hike, camp, and contemplate natural beauty.

Further preservation was carried out after 1906 through the Lacey Act, which allowed the U.S. president, without congressional approval, to set aside "objects of historic and scientific interest" as national monuments. Two years later, Theodore Roosevelt used these powers to preserve 800,000 acres at Arizona's Grand Canyon. The Lacey Act proved to be a mixed blessing for conservation. Monuments received weaker protection than did national parks, and many fell under the authority of the U.S. Forest Service, which permitted logging and grazing. Thus, while many areas were preserved under the Lacey Act, business interests lobbied after 1906 to have coveted lands designated as "monuments" rather than "parks" so that businesses could more easily exploit resources. Nonetheless, more and more Americans called for preservation of the last remnants of unexploited land.

John Muir, who fell in love with the Yosemite Valley in 1869, was one of the first famous voices of this

MAP 18.1

National Parks and Forests, 1872–1980

Yellowstone, the first national park in the United States, dates from 1872. In 1893, the federal government began to intervene to protect national forests. Without Theodore Roosevelt, however, the national forest program might have languished; during his presidency he added 125 million acres to the forest system, plus six national parks in addition to several that had already been created during the 1890s. America's national forest and park systems remain one of the most visible and beloved legacies of federal policy innovation in the decades between the Civil War and World War I.

environmental movement. Muir, an imaginative inventor who grew up on a Wisconsin farm, was a keen observer of nature. Raised in a stern Scots Presbyterian family, he knew much of the Bible by heart and developed a deeply spiritual relationship with the natural world. His contemporary Mary Austin, whose book *Land of Little Rain* (1905) celebrated the austere beauty of the California desert, called him "a devout man." In cooperation with his editor at *Century* magazine, Muir founded the Sierra Club in 1892. Similar to the Appalachian Mountain Club, founded in Boston in 1876, the Sierra Club dedicated itself to preserving and enjoying mountain regions.

Environmentalists worked not only to preserve land but also to protect wildlife. Soon after the Civil War, Congress created preserves on the Alaskan coast to protect sea lions and fur seals. By the turn of the twentieth century, local Audubon Societies began to advocate broader protections for wild birds, especially herons and egrets that were being slaughtered by the thousands for their plumes. Women played prominent roles in the movement, lobbying to protect wild birds and organizing campaigns to persuade women to avoid hats with plume decorations. In 1903, President Theodore Roosevelt created the first National Wildlife Refuge at Pelican Island, Florida. By the end of his term as president, Roosevelt had signed fifty-one executive orders creating wildlife refuges in twenty territories and states.

Many states also passed game laws to protect wildlife and regulate hunting and fishing, redefining these as recreational rather than subsistence activities. Such laws were often selectively enforced in ways that reflected prevailing racial biases. In New Mexico, for example, where Anglos and Hispanics were terrified by the prospect of Indians armed with guns, the territory's first fish and game warden argued that his job was to "protect the game and fish and see that Indians in particular are kept off the range."

In all parts of the country, new game laws triggered controversy over the uses of wildlife. In the South, conservationists got many game laws passed in the early twentieth century, but not until the late 1910s and 1920s did judges and juries begin taking them seriously. Results were mixed. Shifting from year-round subsistence hunting to a recreational hunting season brought hardship to many poor rural families who depended on game meat for food. At the same time, most Americans came to agree that regulation was beneficial: It suppressed such popular practices as the hunting of songbirds and the use of dynamite to kill fish in lakes and ponds. Looking back on the era before game laws,

one Alabama hunter remembered that "the slaughter was terrific." While making it more difficult for rural people to support themselves by the bounty of the land, regulation prevented further extinctions like that of the passenger pigeon, which vanished around 1900.

- What new educational opportunities arose for young Americans in the late nineteenth century? How did those change the experiences and expectations of young men and women? Of African Americans, in particular?

- What role did sports play in the redefinition of masculine identities? How did sports reflect the racial and economic divisions of the era?

- What policy changes resulted, in part, from Americans' new zest for outdoor recreation? Do you think those policies were beneficial? Why or why not?

Women in the Public Sphere

In the early nineteenth century, many public spaces—from city streets and election polls to saloons and circus shows—remained the domains of men. A woman who ventured into such places without a chaperone risked damaging her reputation. But industrialization transformed public space. To attract an eager public, purveyors of consumer culture invited women and families to linger in department stores and enjoy new public amusements. Gradually, women of all classes and backgrounds began to claim their right to public space. At the same time, middle-class women sought in other ways to expand their place beyond the household, by building reform movements and taking political action. "Women's place is Home," journalist Rheta Childe Dorr wrote, but then added, "Home is the community. The city full of people is the Family. . . . Badly do the Home and Family need their mother."

Negotiating Public Space

No one promoted commercial domesticity more successfully than showman P. T. Barnum (1810–1891), who used the country's expanding rail network to develop his famous traveling circus. Barnum condemned earlier circus managers who had opened their tents to "the rowdy element." Proclaiming that his most important audience was children, Barnum set out to make his show a family entertainment for audiences of all classes and races (though in the South, black audiences

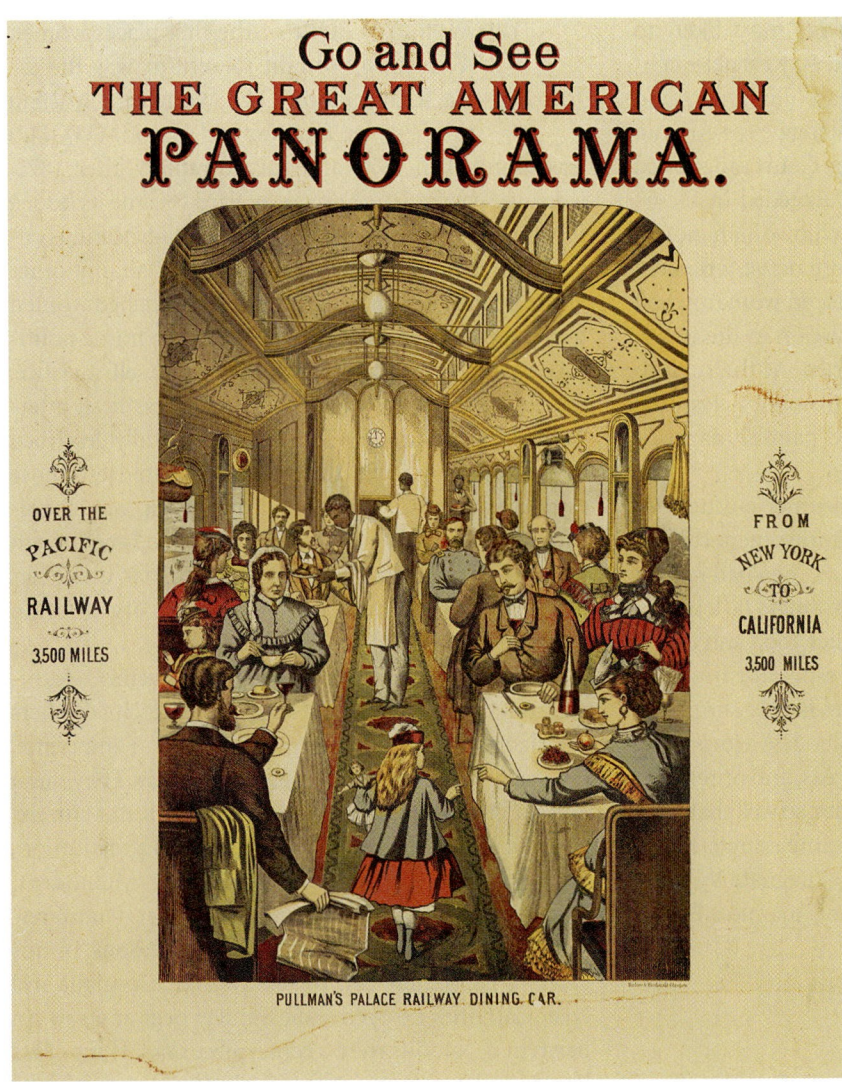

Go and See THE GREAT AMERICAN PANORAMA.

OVER THE PACIFIC RAILWAY 3,500 MILES

FROM NEW YORK TO CALIFORNIA 3,500 MILES

PULLMAN'S PALACE RAILWAY DINING CAR.

Pacific Railway Poster, c. 1900

This color lithograph advertised the Pacific Railway's continental route from New York to California. It emphasizes the excellent service and family atmosphere available in the railroad's Pullman Palace Dining Cars. Pullman, a Chicago-based manufacturer, became a household name by providing high-class sleeping and dining cars to the nation's railroads. Note the African American waiter: In railroad work, as in other industries, blacks were largely barred from higher-paid jobs (often at white workers' insistence) and segregated into service positions. Nonetheless, by the 1920s African American labor activist A. Philip Randolph developed the Brotherhood of Sleeping Car Porters into the nation's first prominent African American labor union. Wisconsin Historical Society.

sat in segregated seats or attended separate shows). He promised parents that his show would teach children about courage and promote the benefits of exercise. To make the show comfortable for women, Barnum's circus featured female performers and emphasized their respectability and refinement. Barnum's managers claimed, for example, that Isabella Butler, who in the early 1900s drove her miniature car in an act called the "Dip of Death," was a student at Vassar.

Finding Americans eager for excursions, railroad companies made their cars comfortable for families. Boston's South Terminal Station boasted of its modern amenities, including "almost everything that the traveler needs down to cradles in which the baby may be soothed." An 1882 tourist guide promised readers that they could live on the Pacific Railroad "with as much

true enjoyment as the home drawing room." Its "neat and clean" cars would become "your home. Here you sit and read, play your games, indulge in social conversation." Railcars manufactured by the famous Pullman Company of Chicago set a national standard for taste and elegance. Fitted with rich carpets, upholstery, and woodwork, Pullman's Palace cars and sleeping cars influenced trends in home decor.

The best accommodations, of course, were in first-class cars, whose opulence marked passengers' wealth as well as their desire for domesticity. Part of the appeal of consumer culture, however, was that less affluent Americans could indulge their tastes in new ways. One train conductor noticed, after years of working on the railroads, that the luxuries of a Pullman car were enjoyed most by passengers of modest means. It was grocers' wives, he observed, who were most likely to "sweep . . . into a parlor car as if the very carpet ought to feel highly honored by their tread." First-class and "ladies' cars" also became sites of struggle for African American rights. Before the Supreme Court sanctioned segregation in 1896, blacks often succeeded in securing seats. One African American clubwoman noted, however, "There are few ordeals more nerve-wracking than the one which confronts a colored woman when she tries to secure a Pullman reservation in the South and even in some parts of the North." At the turn of the century, the exclusion of blacks from first-class cars became one of the most public and painful marks of racism.

The purveyors of modern consumer culture designed one popular site specifically for women: the department store. In earlier generations, men had largely controlled the family pocketbook; women's task was to labor at home to produce their families' food and clothing. By the late nineteenth century, especially in towns and cities, women became the chief family shoppers. Department stores attracted middle-class women by offering tearooms, children's play areas, and other welcoming features. Such tactics succeeded so well that New York's department store district became known as Ladies' Mile. Boston department store magnate William Filene called the department store an "Adamless Eden."

From Female Moral Authority to Feminism

Changing expectations about the use of public space reflected a broader expansion of women's public activities, from patriotic work to many types of reform. Starting in the 1880s, women's clubs sprang up in cities and towns across the United States. So many had been formed by 1890 that their leaders created a nationwide umbrella organization, the General Federation of Women's Clubs. Moving from educational and literary topics into reform, women's clubs began to study such problems as pollution, unsafe working conditions, and urban poverty. Such groups frequently justified their work through the ideology of **maternalism**; they appealed to what they saw as women's special talents as mothers, Christians, and moral guides. Maternalism was an intermediate step between domesticity and modern arguments for gender equality. It came in many forms. In dozens of organizations, women undertook "municipal housekeeping" in order to help other women, promote national patriotism, and engage in "race uplift." By the 1890s, humorist Josh Billings looked at all this public activity and joked, "Wimmin is everywhere."

The Woman's Christian Temperance Union One of the first places women sought to reform was the saloon. The Woman's Christian Temperance Union (WCTU) was founded in 1874 and spread rapidly after 1879, when the charismatic Frances Willard became its leader. It became the leading U.S. organization advocating prohibition of liquor. The WCTU, more than any other group of the late nineteenth century, launched women into public reform. Willard knew how to frame political demands in the language of feminine self-sacrifice. She advised her followers: "Womanliness first; afterward, what you will." WCTU members vividly described the plight of hungry, abused wives and children whose husbands and fathers suffered in the grip of alcoholism. Willard's motto was "Home Protection," and though it placed all the blame on alcohol rather than other factors, the WCTU became the first national organization to identify and combat domestic violence.

The prohibitionist movement drew together reformers from many backgrounds. Middle-class city dwellers worried about the link between alcoholism and crime, especially in the growing immigrant wards. They saw a ban on drinking as beneficial to society. Rural citizens equated liquor with big-city sins such as prostitution, political corruption, and public disorder. Methodists, Baptists, Mormons, and members of other denominations condemned drinking for religious reasons. Immigrants passionately disagreed, however: Germans and Irish Catholics enjoyed their Sunday beer and saw no harm in it. Saloons were a centerpiece of working-class leisure and community life, offering free lunches, public toilets, and a place to sit and share neighborhood news. For many immigrants, prohibition was an attack on their ethnic cultures.

The WCTU did not focus solely on prohibition. Investigating alcohol abuse, Willard increasingly confronted a host of related problems. "Do Everything," she urged WCTU members. Across the United States, WCTU chapters founded soup kitchens and free libraries. They introduced a German educational innovation, the kindergarten. They investigated prison conditions. Addressing workers' issues—while Knights of Labor leaders simultaneously endorsed temperance—Willard advocated laws establishing an eight-hour workday and abolishing child labor.

Willard was one of the first mainstream American reformers to call for women's suffrage, lending considerable support to the small, independent women's rights movement that had emerged during Reconstruction. However, Willard avoided any talk of "rights" and spoke instead of "prayerful, persistent pleas for the opportu-

THE TEMPERANCE CRUSADE—WHO WILL WIN?

A Plea for Temperance, 1874

The origins of the Woman's Christian Temperance Union lay in spontaneous prayer meetings held by women outside local saloons, where they appealed for men to stop drinking and liquor sellers to destroy their product. A string of such meetings in Ohio won national attention, as in this image from a popular magazine, the *Daily Graphic*. "Who Will Win?" asked the artist. The answers varied. A few saloon owners, struck with remorse over the damage caused by alcohol abuse, smashed their beer kegs and poured their liquor into the gutters. Far more refused, but in the 1880s, temperance women succeeded in building the largest grassroots movement of their day to build support for outlawing liquor sales.   The Granger Collection, New York.

nity of duty." Controversially, Willard threw the WCTU's influence behind a new political party, the Prohibition Party, which exercised considerable clout in the 1880s. Women worked in the party as stump speakers, convention delegates, and even candidates for local office.

The WCTU and Prohibition Party met formidable obstacles. Liquor was big business, and powerful interests mobilized to block Prohibition Party candidates and antiliquor legislation. In many parts of the country— particularly the growing cities—prohibition simply did not gain majority support. Willard, discouraged by the movement's failure to obtain a national prohibition law, retired to England, where she died in 1898. But the legacy of her work was powerful. After 1900, groups like the Anti-Saloon League took up the banner, and after World War I they finally won a constitutional amendment prohibiting "the manufacture, sale, or transportation of intoxicating liquors." In the meantime, the

WCTU had taught women how to lobby, raise money, and even run for office. Willard wrote that "perhaps the most significant outcome" of the movement she led was women's "knowledge of their own power."

The movement for women's voting rights benefited from the influx of **temperance** support. Though it had split into two rival organizations during Reconstruction, the movement reunited in 1890 in the National American Woman Suffrage Association. Soon afterward, suffragists won two victories in the West: Colorado in 1893 and Idaho in 1896. In the following decade, movement leaders were discouraged by many state-level defeats and by the continued refusal of Congress to take up a constitutional amendment for women's voting rights. But the movement picked up momentum again in 1911 (Map 18.2). By 1913, the majority of women living west of the Mississippi River had the vote. In many other states and localities, women

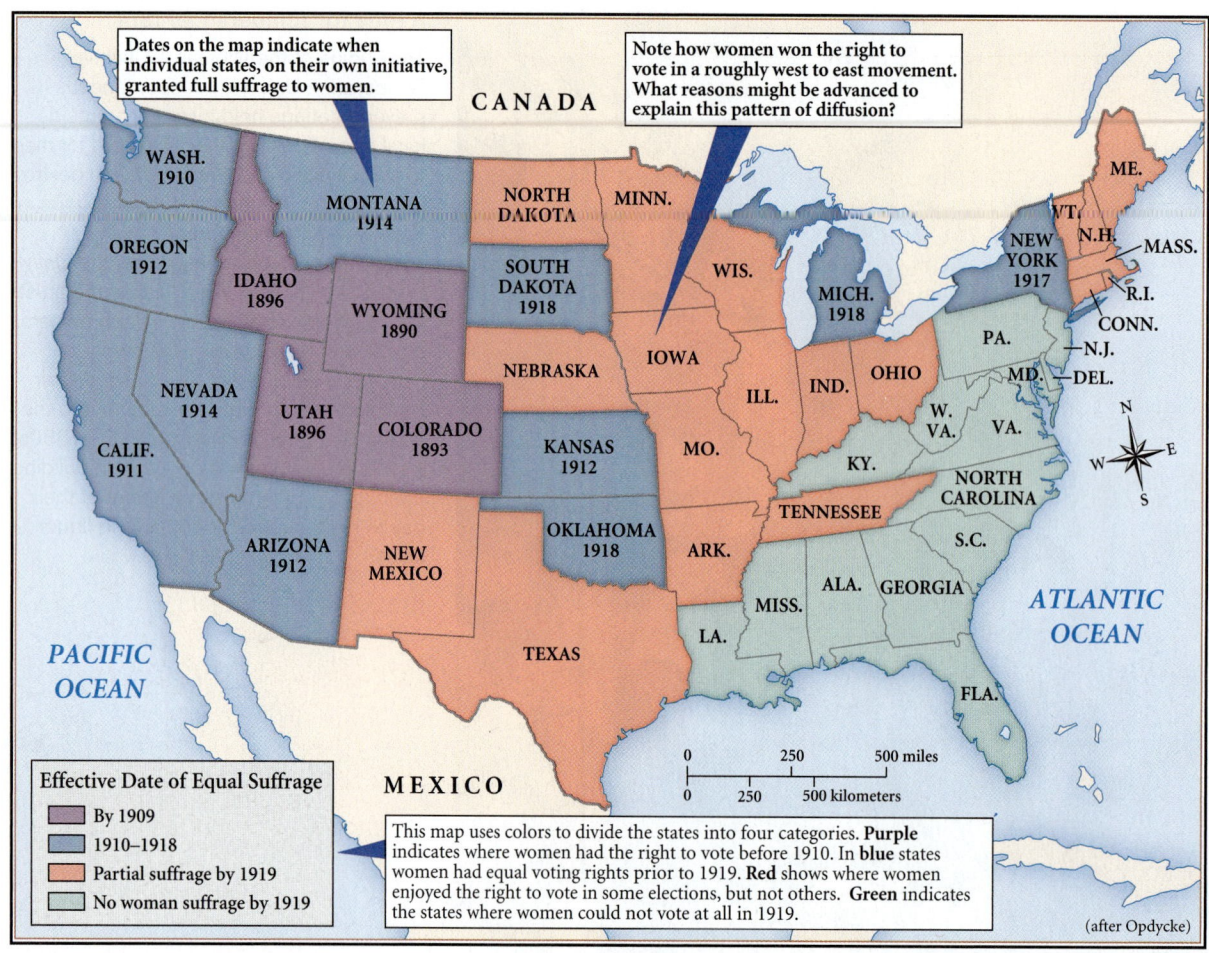

Dates on the map indicate when individual states, on their own initiative, granted full suffrage to women.

Note how women won the right to vote in a roughly west to east movement. What reasons might be advanced to explain this pattern of diffusion?

Effective Date of Equal Suffrage

- By 1909
- 1910–1918
- Partial suffrage by 1919
- No woman suffrage by 1919

This map uses colors to divide the states into four categories. **Purple** indicates where women had the right to vote before 1910. In **blue** states women had equal voting rights prior to 1919. **Red** shows where women enjoyed the right to vote in some elections, but not others. **Green** indicates the states where women could not vote at all in 1919.

(after Opdycke)

MAP 18.2

Woman Suffrage, 1890–1919

By 1909, after more than sixty years of agitation, only four lightly populated western states had granted women full voting rights. A number of other states offered partial suffrage, limited to voting for school boards and such issues as taxes and local referenda on whether or not to permit the sale of liquor licenses (the so-called "local option"). Between 1910 and 1918, as the effort shifted to the struggle for a constitutional amendment, eleven states joined the list granting full suffrage. The West remained the most progressive region in granting women's voting rights; the most stubborn resistance lay in the ex-Confederacy.

had secured voting rights in municipal elections, in school elections, or on liquor licensing questions.

Women, Race, and Patriotism | Like temperance work, patriotic activism became women's special province in the post–Civil War decades. Members of the Daughters of the American Revolution (DAR), founded in 1890, devoted themselves to celebrating the memory of Revolutionary War heroes. Significantly, the DAR excluded African American women, even those who could prove they had descended from soldiers who had fought for U.S. independence. Equally influential was the United Daughters of the Confederacy (UDC), founded in 1894 to celebrate the memory

of the South's "lost cause." The UDC's elite southern members played a central role in shaping Americans' memory of the Civil War by building monuments, distributing Confederate flags, and donating portraits of Robert E. Lee to southern schools. Starting in Georgia in 1896, the UDC also undertook a national campaign to edit U.S. history textbooks. They ensured that such books portrayed the formation of the Confederacy as a noble effort, Reconstruction as a terrible mistake, and former slaves as unfit for citizenship. In the early twentieth century, such work played an important role in maintaining support for segregation and disfranchisement.

African American women did not sit idle in the face of this challenge. By 1896 they created the Na-

Colored Women's League of Washington, D.C.

At a time when black men were being driven out of electoral politics in the South, African American women organized to create an alternative voice of black conscience. Sara Iredell Fleetwood, superintendent of the Freedman's Hospital Training School for Nurses, founded the Colored Women's League of Washington, D.C., in 1892 for purposes of "racial uplift." This picture of league members was taken on the steps of Frederick Douglass's home in Anacostia, Washington. Fleetwood is seated at the far right, third row from the bottom. The notations are by someone seeking to identify the other members, a modest effort to save the names of these women, mostly teachers, for posterity.   Library of Congress.

tional Association of Colored Women, a network of local women's clubs that focused their attention on community support. Black club women arranged for the care of orphans, founded homes for the elderly, worked for temperance, and undertook public health campaigns. Such women shared with white women an abiding faith in domesticity—and a determination to carry it into the public sphere. Black journalist Victoria Earle Matthews hailed the American home as "the foundation upon which nationality rests, the pride of the citizen, and the

glory of the Republic." African American women used the language of domesticity and respectability to seek white women's cooperation in their work.

The largest African American women's group arose within the National Baptist Church (NBC), which by 1906 represented 2.4 million churchgoers. Founded in 1900, the Women's Convention of the NBC promoted and funded night schools, health clinics, kindergartens, day care centers, and outreach programs for men and women in prison. Paralleling the work of white

Christian Missions in Japan, 1909

Through this colorful postcard, Protestant missionaries in Japan demonstrate their success in winning converts (at least a few) and their adaptation of missionary strategies to meet local needs and expectations. Here, outside their headquarters, they demonstrate "preaching by means of banners." The large characters on the vertical banner proclaim the "Association of Christian Gospel Evangelists." The horizontal banner is a Japanese translation of Matthew 11:28, "Come unto me, all ye who labor and are heavy laden, and I will give you rest." © Bettmann/Corbis.

reformers, one convention leader called for women to focus on education for children and youth, and "to extend the number of occupations for women."

Adella Hunt Logan, born in Alabama, exemplified how such work could lead women to demand political rights. Educated at Atlanta University, Logan became a club woman, a teacher at Tuskegee Institute, and an advocate of woman suffrage. "If white American women, with all their mutual and acquired advantage, need the ballot," she declared, "how much more do Black Americans, male and female, need the strong defense of a vote to help secure them their right to life, liberty, and the pursuit of happiness?"

Feminism Despite divisions of race and ethnicity, many women recognized that they shared problems across lines of economic class. Some created new organizations to call attention to the plight of poorly paid female wage-earners and to agitate for better working conditions. The most famous example was the National Trade Union League, founded in New York in 1903. Financed by wealthy supporters, the league trained working-class leaders like Rose Schneiderman, who became a union organizer among garment workers. Although often frustrated by the patronizing ways of their well-to-do sponsors, trade-union women identified their cause with the broader struggle for women's rights. When New York State held suffrage referenda in 1915 and 1917, strong support came from Jewish and Italian precincts where many unionized garment workers lived.

By the early twentieth century, the most radical women took a public stance against women's "separate sphere." A famous site of sexual rebellion was New York's Greenwich Village, where radical intellectuals, including many gays and lesbians, created a vibrant community by the 1910s. Among their many other political activities, women in Greenwich Village founded the Heterodoxy Club (1912), open to any woman who pledged not to be "orthodox in her opinions." The club brought together intellectuals, journalists, and labor organizers. Almost all supported women's voting rights, but they had a more ambitious view of what was needed for women's liberation. Such women began to use the term **feminism** to describe their movement. They articulated broad goals for women's personal development. "I wanted to belong to the human race, not to a ladies' aid society," wrote one divorced journalist who joined Heterodoxy. As women entered the public sphere, feminists argued, they should not just fulfill Victorian expectations of self-sacrifice for others; they should work on their own behalf. Feminist thinker Charlotte Perkins Gilman imagined a transformation in women's private and public lives: "Here she comes, running, out of prison and off the pedestal; chains off, crown off, halo off, just a live woman."

Domesticity and Missions

While few American women fully shared the ideas of the Heterodoxy Club, hundreds of thousands engaged in more widely accepted forms of public activism, through their churches and religious groups. Some sponsored Christian missions in the American West, which eastern women regarded as uncivilized and in need of uplift.

Protestant Missionaries and Chinese Women's Education

Missionary Luella Miner, seated at the desk, presides over student recitations at the North China Union College, founded in 1905. By the late 1890s, about seven thousand young Chinese women attended such schools; a decade later, Chinese reformers used the challenge posed by these schools to persuade the Emperor to authorize government schooling for girls. The vertical banners above the desk are a biblical verse from Psalms 63:8, "My soul clings to you; your right hand upholds me." Luella Miner folder, American Board of Commissioners for Foreign Missions (ABCFM) photographs, Houghton Library, Harvard University.

The Women's National Indian Association, for example, funded missionary work on reservations, arguing that women had a special duty to promote "civilized home life" among Indians. In San Francisco, elite and middle-class white women built a rescue home for Chinese women who had been sold into sexual slavery. The project not only was racially condescending but also generated fierce opposition from white residents who hated Chinese immigration. The home nonetheless fulfilled its mission: It served many Chinese women who managed to reach its doors, escape from prostitution, and in some cases marry and start their own families.

Nowhere was the rhetoric of domesticity more powerful than in the movement for overseas missions, which grew from a modest start in the pre–Civil War period to a peak in the early twentieth century. By 1915, American religious organizations sponsored more than nine thousand overseas missionaries; these workers were supported at home by missionary society volunteers, including more than three million women. The largest number of American Protestant missionaries served in Asia, with smaller numbers posted to Africa and the Middle East. Most saw American-style domesticity as a central part of Christian evangelism. In particular, they sought to uplift foreign women who could, one missionary journal exhorted, "by the grace of God [be] nourished and cultivated into true Christian womanhood."

To accomplish this goal, missionary societies emphasized the importance of sending married couples into the field. Remarkably, by the turn of the century, many unmarried women also went overseas as missionary administrators, teachers, doctors, and nurses (though almost never as ministers). "To American woman, more than to any other on earth," declared one Christian reformer, "is committed the exalted privilege of extending over the world those blessed influences, that are to renovate degraded man."

As this woman's words suggest, missionaries who worked to foster Christianity and domesticity often showed considerable condescension toward their "poor heathen sisters." Potential converts often bristled at missionary assumptions (see Voices from Abroad, "Kinzo Hirai: A Japanese View of American Christianity," p. 578). In many places missionaries won converts, in part by offering medical care and promoting scientific progress and women's education. Some missionaries came to love and respect the people among whom they served. But others became deeply frustrated. One Presbyterian in Syria, who found Muslims uninterested in his gospel message, bitterly denounced all Muslims as "corrupt and immoral" and Muslim women in particular as "profane, slanderous, and capricious." By imposing their views on "heathen races" and criticizing those who did not agree with them, Christian missionaries sometimes ended up justifying and supporting Western imperialism.

- How did America's expanding consumer culture change women's lives?

- What political reform goals did women pursue in this era? Whose interests did these various movements serve? In your view, which of these projects was most beneficial, and to whom?

- How did Protestant missionaries define their goals abroad? What were some of the consequences of their work?

All the nations and people I had hitherto passed through resembled
own in their manners, customs and langu...

Kinzo Hirai
A Japanese View of American Christianity

In 1893, in connection with the Chicago World's Fair, a World's Parliament of Religions met in Chicago. For the first time, representatives of most of the world's prominent religions, ranging from Christianity and Judaism to Taoism and Zoroastrianism, discussed similarities and differences among their faiths. Although English-speaking Protestants dominated the program, several representatives from Asia spoke. One was Kinzo Hirai, a lay Buddhist delegate from Japan. In his speech, Hirai set out to explain persistent opposition to Christianity in his country. He reviewed Japan's experience of contact with the United States since Commodore Matthew C. Perry arrived to "open" the country in 1853. By the time Hirai spoke, Japan's leaders had undertaken a program of rapid modernization and Japan was asserting its military might in the Pacific.

I do not understand why the Christian lands have ignored the rights and advantages of forty million souls of Japan for forty years since the stipulations of the [1854 Treaty of Kanagawa]. One of the excuses offered by foreign nations is that our country is not yet civilized. Is it the principle of civilized law that the rights of and profits of the so-called uncivilized, or the weaker, should be sacrificed? As I understand it, the spirit and necessity of law is to protect the rights and profits of the weaker against the aggression of the stronger; but I have never learned in my shallow study of law that the weaker should be sacrificed for the stronger.

Another kind of apology comes from the religious source, and the claim is made that the Japanese are idolaters and heathen. . . . [A]dmitting for the sake of argument that we are idolaters and heathen, is it Christian morality to trample upon the rights and advantages of a non-Christian nation, coloring all their natural happiness with the dark stain of injustice? . . .

You send your missionaries to Japan and they advise us to be moral and believe Christianity. We like to be moral, we know that Christianity is good; and we are very thankful for this kindness. But at the same time our people are rather perplexed and very much in doubt of about their advice.

For when we think that the treaty stipulated in the time of feudalism, when were yet in our youth, is still clung to by the powerful nations of Christendom; when we find that every year a good many western vessels of seal fishery are smuggled into our seas; when legal cases are always decided by the foreign authorities in Japan unfavorably to us; when some years ago a Japanese was not allowed to enter a university on the Pacific coast of American because of his being of a different race; when a few months ago the school board in San Francisco enacted a regulation that no Japanese should be allowed to enter the public school there; when last year the Japanese were driven out in wholesale from one of the territories of the United States; when our business men in San Francisco were compelled by some union not to employ Japanese assistants and laborers, but the Americans; when there are some in the same city who speak on the platform against those of us who are already here; when there are many who go in procession hoisting lanterns marked "Japs must go"; when the Japanese in the Hawaiian Islands were deprived of their suffrage; when we see some western people in Japan who erect before the entrance to their houses a special post upon which is the notice, "No Japanese is allowed to enter here"—just like a board upon which is written, "No dogs allowed"; when we are in such a situation, notwithstanding the kindness of the western nations from one point of view, who send their missionaries to us, that we unintelligent heathens are embarrassed and hesitate to swallow the sweet and warm liquid of the heaven of Christianity, will not be unreasonable.

Source: *The World's Parliament of Religions*, ed. John Henry Barrows (Chicago: Parliament Publishing Co., 1893), 444–450.

ANALYZING THE EVIDENCE

- How would you characterize Hirai's attitude toward Christianity and American Christians?

- What events does Hirai mention that are taking place in the United States, not in Japan? How might he have learned of such events? How does his awareness of what is going on in the United States shape his view of American Christian missions in Japan?

- How do you think American delegates to the Parliament—especially Protestant missionaries— might have responded to Hirai's criticisms?

Science and Faith

As the activities of missionaries showed, the United States continued to be a deeply religious nation. However, the late nineteenth century brought increasing public attention to another kind of belief: faith in science. Before the Civil War, most Americans had believed the world was about six thousand years old. No one knew what lay beyond the solar system. By 1900, however, paleontologists had traced the rise and fall of the dinosaurs, and many scientists—as well as ordinary Americans—accepted the theory of evolution. By the 1910s, astronomers had identified distant galaxies and scientists could measure the speed of light.

It is hardly surprising, amid these staggering achievements, that "fact worship" became a central feature of American intellectual life. Researchers in many fields became converts to scientific methods, arguing that one could rely only on hard facts and observable phenomena. In their enthusiasm, some economists and sociologsts rejected all reform efforts as romantic and sentimental. American fiction writers and artists kept a more humane emphasis, but they made use of similar methods—close observation and attention to real-life experience—to create works of literary and artistic realism. Other Americans sought to reconcile scientific discoveries with their religious faith, setting the stage for intellectual and political conflicts over Darwinism and evolution.

Darwinism and Its Critics

Evolution—the idea that species are not fixed, but ever changing—was not a simple idea on which all scientists agreed in the late nineteenth century. The idea was widely associated with British naturalist Charles Darwin and his immensely influential book *On the Origin of Species* (1859), which proposed the theory of **natural selection**. In nature, Darwin argued, all creatures struggle to survive. When individual members of a species are born with random genetic mutations that better fit them for their particular environment—for example, camouflage coloring for a bird or butterfly—these survival characteristics, since they are genetically transmissible, become dominant in future generations.

Darwin himself disapproved of the word *evolution* (which does not appear in his book) because it implied upward progression. In his view, natural selection was blind: environments changed randomly, and so did plants' and animals' adaptations. But other people were less scrupulous than Darwin about drawing sweeping conclusions from his work. British philosopher Herbert Spencer spun out an elaborate theory of how human society had advanced through competition and "survival of the fittest." **Social Darwinism**, as Spencer's idea became known, found its American champion in William Graham Sumner, a sociology professor at Yale. Competition, said Sumner, is a law of nature that "can no more be done away with than gravitation." Who were the fittest? "Millionaires," Sumner declared; their success showed they were "naturally selected." Sumner argued that industrialists "live in luxury, but the bargain is a good one for society."

Even in the heyday of Social Darwinism, Sumner's views were controversial (see Comparing American Voices, "Three Interpretations of Social Darwinism," pp. 580–581). Many scientists accepted evolutionary ideas but rejected Darwin's theory of natural selection. They followed a line of thinking laid out by French biologist Jean Baptiste Lamarck, who argued, unlike Darwin, that individual animals or plants could acquire transmittable traits within a single lifetime. A rhinoceros that fought fiercely, in Lamarck's view, could build up a stronger horn; its offspring would then be born with that trait. If Lamarck's ideas were true, then "evolution" had a very different meaning for humans: People who acquired education or good habits could pass these on genetically to their children. Other thinkers rejected the whole notion of applying evolutionary ideas to the realm of society and government. They pointed out that Lamarck's and Darwin's theories applied to finch and tortoise species, over thousands of years, and not to human relationships. Social Darwinism, they argued, was simply an excuse for the worst excesses of industrialization. By the early twentieth century, American intellectuals were in full revolt against Sumner and his allies.

Meanwhile, though, the most dubious applications of evolutionary ideas were codified into new reproductive laws. Some Americans embraced **eugenics**, a so-called science of human breeding. Eugenicists argued that mentally deficient people should be prevented from reproducing. They proposed sterilizing those deemed "unfit," especially residents of state asylums for the insane or mentally disabled. In early-twentieth-century America, almost half of the states enacted eugenics laws. By the time belief in eugenics subsided in the 1930s, about twenty thousand people had been sterilized, with California and Virginia taking the lead. Eugenicists also had a broader impact on public policy. Because they associated mental unfitness with "lower races"—including people of African, Asian, and Native American descent—their arguments bolstered segregation and racial discrimination. By warning that immigrants from Eastern and Southern Europe would dilute white

Thus I have given you, I think, the Substance of the Arguments on both sides of that great and important Question

Three Interpretations of Social Darwinism

Between the Civil War and World War I, the idea that human society advanced through the "survival of the fittest" was a popular doctrine in America. It was widely referred to as "Social Darwinism," though Charles Darwin himself rejected the idea that natural selection applied to human society. Many Americans agreed with Harvard sociologist William Graham Sumner, who argued that the poor and weak were a "burden," a "dead-weight on the society in all its struggles to realize any better things." Such views prompted many responses, ranging from enthusiastic endorsement to uneasy accommodation to impassioned opposition.

Theodore Dreiser

The Financier

Theodore Dreiser (1871–1945) was an American literary naturalist. His novel *The Financier* (1912) traces the rise of Frank Cowperwood, a young man who, during the last years of the nineteenth century, becomes a powerful banker. Dreiser loosely based Cowperwood's character on that of real-life financier and streetcar magnate Charles Yerkes. In the following excerpt, the narrator describes a transformative moment in Cowperwood's youth.

[Cowperwood] could not figure out how this thing he had come into — this life — was organized. How did all these people get into the world? What were they doing here? Who started things, anyhow? His mother told him the story of Adam and Eve, but he didn't believe it. . . .

One day he saw a squid and a lobster put in [a] tank, and in connection with them was witness to a tragedy which stayed with him all his life and cleared things up considerably intellectually. The lobster, it appeared from the talk of the idle bystanders, was offered no food, as the squid was considered his rightful prey. He lay at the bottom of the clear glass tank . . . apparently seeing nothing — you could not tell in which way his beady, black buttons of eyes were looking — but apparently they were never off the body of the squid. The latter, pale and waxy in texture, looking very much like pork fat or jade, moved about in torpedo fashion; but his movements were apparently never out of the eyes of his enemy, for by degrees small portions of his body began to disappear, snapped off by the relentless claws of his pursuer. . . .

[One day] only a portion of the squid remained. . . . In the corner of the tank sat the lobster, poised apparently for action. The boy stayed as long as he could, the bitter struggle fascinating him. Now, maybe, or in an hour or a day, the squid might die, slain by the lobster, and the lobster would eat him. He looked again at the greenish-copperish engine of destruction in the corner and wondered when this would be. . . .

He returned that night, and lo! the expected had happened. There was a little crowd around the tank. The lobster was in the corner. Before him was the squid cut in two and partially devoured. . . .

The incident made a great impression on him. It answered in a rough way that riddle which had been annoying him so much in the past: "How is life organized?" Things lived on each other — that was it. Lobsters lived on squids and other things. What lived on lobsters? Men, of course! . . . And what lived on men? he asked himself. Was it other men? Wild animals lived on men. And there were Indians and cannibals. And some men were killed by storms and accidents. He wasn't so sure about men living on men; but men did kill each other. How about wars and street fights and mobs? . . .

Frank thought of this and of the life he was tossed into, for he was already pondering on what he should be in this world, and how he should get along. From seeing his father count money, he was sure that he would like banking; and Third Street, where his father's office was, seemed to him the cleanest, most fascinating street in the world.

Source: Theodore Dreiser, *The Financier* (New York: Harper and Brothers, 1912), 10–15.

Lyman Abbott

The Evolution of Christianity

The liberal Congregationalist minister Lyman Abbott (1835–1922) was a noted advocate of the Social Gospel — the belief that people of faith should work in the world, by taking up reform causes such as temperance and antipoverty. In *The Evolution of Christianity* (1896), Abbott sought to reconcile the theory of evolution with the development of Christianity.

The doctrine of evolution is not a doctrine of harmonious and uninterrupted progress. The most common, if not the most accurate formula of evolution is "struggle for existence, survival of the fittest." The doctrine of evolution assumes that there are forces in the world seemingly hostile to progress, that life is a perpetual battle and progress a perpetual victory.

The Christian evolutionist will then expect to find Christianity a warfare—in church, in society, in the individual. . . . He will remember that the divine life is resident in undivine humanity. He will not be surprised to find the waters of the stream disturbed; for he will reflect that the divine purity has come into a turbid stream, and that it can purify only by being itself indistinguishably combined with the impure. When he is told that modern Christianity is only a "civilized paganism," he will reply, "That is exactly what I supposed it to be; and it will continue to be a civilized paganism until civilization has entirely eliminated paganism." He will not be surprised to find pagan ceremonies in the ritual, ignorance and superstition in the church, and even errors and partialisms in the Bible. For he will remember that the divine life, which is bringing all life into harmony with itself, is a life resident in man. He will remember that the Bible does not claim to be the absolute Word of God; that, on the contrary . . . it claims to be the Word of God . . . as spoken to men, and understood and interpreted by men, which saw it in part as we still see it, and reflected it as from a mirror in enigmas.

He will remember that the Church is not yet the bride of Christ, but the plebeian daughter whom Christ is educating to be his bride. He will remember that Christianity is not the absolutely divine, but the divine in humanity, the divine force resident in man and transforming man into the likeness of the divine. Christianity is the light struggling with the darkness, life battling with death, the spiritual overcoming the animal. We judge Christianity as the scientist judges the embryo, as the gardener the bud, as the teacher the pupil,—not by what it is, but by what it promises to be.

Source: Lyman Abbott, *The Evolution of Christianity* (Boston: Houghton, Mifflin and Company), 8–10.

Lester Frank Ward

Glimpses of the Cosmos

Sociologist Lester Frank Ward (1841–1913) did much to establish his scholarly field in the United States. Following the French philosopher Auguste Comte, Ward held that the social sciences must develop methods of improving society. In his autobiography *Glimpses of the Cosmos* (1913–1918), Ward rejected the Social Darwinism of men like Sumner.

How shall we distinguish this human, or anthropic, method from the method of nature? Simply by reversing all the definitions. Art is the antithesis of nature. If we call one the natural method, we must call the other the artificial method. If nature's process is rightly named natural selection, man's

process is artificial selection. The survival of the fittest is simply the survival of the strong, which implies, and might as well be called, the destruction of the weak. And if nature progresses through the destruction of the weak, man progresses through the *protection* of the weak. . . .

. . . Man, through his intelligence, has labored successfully to resist the law of nature. His success is conclusively demonstrated by a comparison of his condition with that of other species of animals. No other cause can be assigned for his superiority. How can the naturalistic philosophers shut their eyes to such obvious facts? Yet, what is their attitude? They condemn all attempts to protect the weak, whether by private of public methods. They claim that it deteriorates the race by enabling the unfit to survive and transmit their inferiority. . . . Nothing is easier than to show that the unrestricted competition of nature does not secure the survival of the fittest possible, but only of the actually fittest, and in every attempt man makes to obtain something fitter than this actual fittest he succeeds, as witness improved breeds of animals and grafts of fruits. Now, the human method of protecting the weak deals in such way with men. It not only increases the number but improves the quality.

Source: Lester Frank Ward, *Glimpses of the Cosmos* (New York: Harper and Brothers), 371, 374.

ANALYZING THE EVIDENCE

- What meaning does the death of the squid have for Dreiser's Frank Cowperwood? Why does he find this more persuasive than the story of Adam and Eve?
- How did Lyman Abbott describe Christianity as "evolving"? To what extent does he draw upon the idea of "survival of the fittest," and to what extent does he reject it?
- How does Lester Frank Ward reinterpret the Social Darwinist doctrine of "survival of the fittest"?
- Imagine Abbott and Ward reading *The Financier*. How do you think they would have responded to Cowperwood's conclusions about the squid's death? Why?

Americans' racial purity, eugenicists helped win passage of immigration restriction in the 1920s.

Realism in the Arts

Inspired by the quest for facts, American authors rebelled against the nineteenth century's most important artistic movement—Romanticism—and what they saw as its unfortunate product, Victorian sentimentality. Instead, they took up literary **realism**. In the 1880s, William Dean Howells, one of the country's leading editors and novelists, began to call for writers "to picture the daily life in the most exact terms possible." Howells put his ideas into practice in novels such as *The Rise of Silas Lapham* (1885). By the 1890s, a younger generation of writers took up the call. Theodore Dreiser dismissed "professional optimists" who always arrived "at a happy ending." Stephen Crane's *Maggie: A Girl of the Streets* (1893), privately printed because no publisher would touch it, described the seduction, abandonment, and death of a slum girl. In *Main-Travelled Roads* (1891), a collection of stories based on his family's struggle to farm in Iowa and South Dakota, writer Hamlin Garland turned the same unsparing eye on the hardships of rural life.

Some authors believed that realism did not go far enough to overturn Victorian morality. Jack London spent his teenage years as a factory worker, sailor, and tramp. In stories such as "The Law of Life" (1901) and "To Build a Fire" (1908), London dramatized what he saw as the harsh reality of an uncaring universe. American society, he remarked, was "a jungle wherein wild beasts eat and are eaten." Similarly, Stephen Crane said that his fiction tried to capture "a world full of fists." London and Crane helped create literary **naturalism**. They suggested that human beings were not so much rational agents and shapers of their own destinies, but blind victims of forces beyond their control—including their own subconscious impulses and desires.

America's most famous fiction writer, Samuel Langhorne Clemens, who took the pen name of Mark Twain, came to take an equally bleak view. Though he achieved success with such lighthearted books as *The Innocents Abroad* (1869) and *The Adventures of Tom Sawyer* (1876), Clemens created controversy with his satirical *Adventures of Huckleberry Finn* (1884)—especially in its indictment of slavery and racism. Soon afterward, Clemens was devastated by the loss of his wife and two daughters, as well as by failed investments and bankruptcy. Starting with his novel *A Connecticut Yankee in King Arthur's Court* (1889), which ends with a bloody, technology-driven slaughter of Arthur's knights,

Mark Twain became one of the bitterest voices criticizing America's idea of progress. He became an outspoken critic of imperialism and foreign missions, and he parodied the biblical story of Adam and Eve in his hilarious *Letters from the Earth* (1908). *The Mysterious Stranger*, published posthumously in 1916, denounced Christianity itself as a hypocritical delusion. Like his friend the industrialist Andrew Carnegie, Samuel Langhorne Clemens "got rid of theology."

By the time Clemens died in 1910, realist and naturalist writers had laid the groundwork for literary **modernism**. Modernists rejected traditional canons of literary taste. They tended to be religious skeptics or atheists. Questioning the whole idea of progress and order, they focused their attention on the subconscious and "primitive" mind. Above all, they sought to overturn convention and tradition; the poet Ezra Pound exhorted, "Make it new!" Modernism became the first great literary and artistic movement of the twentieth century—one that remains influential, even today.

In the visual arts, technological changes helped introduce a new aesthetic. By 1900, some photographers argued that the rise of photography made painting obsolete. But painters invented their own form of realism. The Nebraska-born artist Robert Henri became fascinated with life in the burgeoning eastern cities. "The backs of tenement houses are living documents," he declared, and he set out to put them on canvas. Henri and his followers, notably John Sloan, called themselves the New York Realists. Critics derided them as the "Ash Can School," because they chose subjects that were not uplifting or conventionally beautiful.

In 1913, New York Realists participated in one of the most controversial events in American art history, the Armory Show. Housed in an enormous National Guard building in New York, the Armory Show introduced America to modern art. Some painters whose work appeared at the show were experimenting with such styles as cubism, characterized by abstract, geometric forms. Along with works by Henri and Sloan, organizers featured paintings by European rebels such as Marcel Duchamp and Pablo Picasso. America's academic art world was shocked. One critic called cubism "the total destruction of the art of painting." The *New York Times* denounced the Armory Show paintings as "revolting in their inhumanity." But the exhibition went on to Boston and Chicago, and more than 250,000 people crowded to see it. The Armory Show transformed American art. It was another marker of the shift from Romanticism to various forms of realism, and then to modernism in its starkest forms.

**John French Sloan,
A Woman's Work, 1912**
The subject of this painting—
a woman hanging out laundry
behind a city apartment building—
is typical of the subjects chosen
by American artist John Sloan
(1871–1951). Sloan and a group
of his allies became famous as
realists; critics derided them as
the "Ash Can School" because
they did not paint rural landscapes, still lifes, or other conventional subjects considered
worthy subject matter for a painting. Sloan, though, warned against
seeing his paintings as simple
representations of reality, even if
he described his work as based
on "a creative impulse derived out
of a consciousness of life." "'Looks
like' is not the test of a good
painting," he wrote: "Even the
scientist is interested in effects
only as phenomena from which
to deduce order in life." Cleveland
Museum of Art. Gift of Amelia Elizabeth
White.

A striking feature of both realism and modernism, as they developed, was that many of the movement's leading writers and artists were men. They denounced nineteenth-century culture as hopelessly feminized and ridiculed popular sentimental novels, especially those written for women. In making their work strong and modern, these men also wanted to make it masculine. Stephen Crane called for "virility" in literature. Jack London described himself as a "man's man" who was "lustfully roving and conquering by sheer superiority and strength." The artist Robert Henri urged his students to be "fighters"; he banned small brushes because they were "too feminine." In their own ways, these writers and artists contributed to a broad movement to masculinize American culture.

Religion: Diversity and Innovation

By the turn of the twentieth century, new scientific, literary, and artistic ideas posed a significant challenge to religious faith. Some Americans argued that science would sweep away religion altogether. "The old superstitions which connected unusual sickness with the wrath of offended Deity," decreed one Michigan doctor, "have faded in the light of science." Nonetheless, American religious practice remained vibrant. Protestants

Arthur B. Davies, *Dancers*, 1914

Artist Arthur Davies (1862–1928) was one of the primary organizers of New York's 1913 Armory Show, which introduced Americans to modernist art. An associate of John Sloan and other New York realists, Davies experimented with an array of painting styles, as well as printmaking and tapestry making. This painting dates from a three-year period, just after the Armory Show, in which Davies experimented with Cubist techniques.   *Dancers*, 1914–1915 (oil on canvas), Arthur Bowen Davies (1862–1928) / Detroit Institute of Arts, USA / Gift of Ralph Harman Booth / The Bridgeman Art Library.

developed creative new responses to the challenges of industrialization, while millions of newcomers built their own institutions for worship and religious education. In fact, this very trend horrified some Protestants. By 1920, almost two million children attended Catholic elementary schools instead of public schools, and Catholic dioceses across the country operated more than fifteen hundred high schools. The era of mass immigration and the rise of great cities was marked by both religious innovation and tensions among people of different faiths.

Immigrant Faiths | Arriving in the United States in large numbers, and facing the dominant assumptions and beliefs of Protestants, Catholics and Jews wrestled with many similar questions. To what degree should they adapt their faith to American society? Should children attend religious or public schools? What happened if they married outside the faith? Should the education of clergy be changed? Among Catholic leaders, Bishop John Ireland of St. Paul, Minnesota, felt that "the principles of the Church are in harmony with the interests of the Republic." But traditionalists, led by Archbishop Michael A. Corrigan of New York, denied the possibility of such harmony and sought to insulate the church from the pluralistic American environment. Many pointed to the same threats that frightened Protestants: On the one hand, industrial poverty and overwork kept working-class people away from worship services; on the other hand, new consumer pleasures offered somewhere else to go. Like Protestants, many Catholics and Jews succumbed to these new conditions and fell away from religious practice.

Those immigrant Catholics who remained faithful to the church were anxious to preserve what they had known in Europe, and they generally supported the church's traditional wing. But they also wanted religious life to express their ethnic identities. Italians,

FOR FURTHER EXPLORATION

On family life and education see Andrea Tone, *Devices and Desires* (2001); Jane Hunter, *How Young Ladies Became Girls* (2003); Joseph F. Kett, *Rites of Passage* (1977); Kim Townsend, *Manhood at Harvard* (1996); and Barbara M. Solomon, *In the Company of Educated Women* (1985). Cindy Aron traces the rise of vacations in *Working at Play* (1999). On athletics see Thomas Winter, *Making Men, Making Class* (2002); Clifford Putney, *Muscular Christianity* (2001); and Neil Lanctot, *Negro League Baseball* (2004). Stephen Fox covers environmentalism in *The American Conservation Movement* (1985). See also Mark David Spence, *Dispossessing the Wilderness* (1999), and Karl Jacoby, *Crimes Against Nature* (2001).

On domesticity and the railroad see Barbara Young Welke, *Recasting American Liberty* (2001), and Amy Richter, *Home on the Rails* (2005). On women's public work see Ruth Bordin, *Woman and Temperance* (1981); Evelyn Brooks Higginbotham, *Righteous Discontent* (1993); Sharon Wood, *The Freedom of the Streets* (2005); Peggy Pascoe, *Relations of Rescue* (1990); Glenda Gilmore, *Gender and Jim Crow* (1996); Francesca Morgan, *Women and Patriotism in Jim Crow America* (2005); and Karen L. Cox, *Dixie's Daughters* (2003). On missions see Patricia Hill, *The World Their Household* (1985).

On culture see Alan Trachtenberg, *The Incorporation of America* (1983); David Shi, *Facing Facts* (1994); and Richard Hofstadter, *Social Darwinism in American Thought* (1944). For religion, see Patrick W. Carey, *The Roman Catholics in America* (1996); Jonathan Sarna, *American Judaism* (2004); and on the Salvation Army, Diane Winston, *Red-Hot and Righteous* (1999).

TEST YOUR KNOWLEDGE

To assess your command of the material in this chapter, see the Online Study Guide at **bedfordstmartins.com/henretta**.

For Web sites, images, and documents related to topics and places in this chapter, visit **bedfordstmartins.com/makehistory**.

TIMELINE

1872	First national park established at Yellowstone
1873	Association for the Advancement of Women founded
1874	Woman's Christian Temperance Union founded
1876	Baseball's National League founded Appalachian Mountain Club founded
1879	Salvation Army established in the United States
1881	Tuskegee Institute founded
1885	Mississippi State College for Women founded
1890	National American Woman Suffrage Organization and Daughters of the American Revolution founded
1892	Elizabeth Cady Stanton delivers "solitude of self" speech to Congress John Muir founds Sierra Club
1893	World's Parliament of Religions meets in Chicago
1896	National Association of Colored Women founded Charles Sheldon publishes *In His Steps*
1903	First World Series First National Wildlife Refuge established at Pelican Island, Florida
1906	Lacey Act passed
1913	Armory Show of modern art held in New York City
1916	National Park Service created

CHAPTER 19

"Civilization's Inferno": The Rise and Reform of Industrial Cities, 1880–1917

Clarence Darrow, a successful lawyer from Ashtabula, Ohio, felt isolated and overwhelmed when he moved to Chicago in the 1880s. "There is no place so lonely to a young man as a great city where he has no intimates or companions," Darrow later wrote. "When I walked along the street I scanned every face I met to see if I could not perchance discover someone from Ohio." Instead he saw "a solid, surging sea of human units, each intent upon hurrying by." At one point, Darrow felt "gloom amounting almost to despair. If it had been possible I would have gone back to Ohio; but I didn't want to borrow the money, and I dreaded to confess defeat."

In the era of industrialization, more and more Americans had experiences like Darrow's. In 1860, the United States was a rural country: Less than 20 percent of Americans lived in an urban location, defined by census takers as a place with more than 2,500 inhabitants. By 1910, more Americans lived in cities (42.1 million) than had lived in the *entire* United States on the eve of the Civil War (31.4 million). Most striking was the growth of giant urban centers. In 1860, only three cities—New York, Brooklyn (then considered separate from New York), and Philadelphia—had populations over 250,000. By 1910, nineteen cities fit that definition. The largest, New York, had almost 5 million inhabitants. Though the Northeast remained by far the most urbanized region, cities in the industrial Midwest and the West were beginning to catch up. Even the predominantly rural South boasted of such thriving cities as Atlanta and Birmingham.

Cities became the locus for vibrant economic and cultural experimentation. Here skyscrapers rose and immigrant neighborhoods grew. Here emerged new sites of working-class leisure and pleasure like the dance hall and the amusement park, along with a thriving intellectual world of artists, writers, and critics. As journalist Frederic C. Howe declared in 1905, "Man has entered on an urban age." Americans had long feared cities as centers of vice and sin, where saloons and brothels flourished and hucksters fleeced unwitting

Mulberry Street, New York City, c. 1900

The influx of immigrants—especially southern and eastern Europeans—in the late nineteenth century created densely populated ghettos in the heart of New York City and other major American cities. This view is of Mulberry Street in New York's "Little Italy," a thoroughfare famous for its pushcarts, street peddlers, and bustling traffic. The inhabitants are mostly Italians; some of them, noticing the photographer preparing his camera, have gathered to be in the picture. Library of Congress.

newcomers. Industrialization added more perceived dangers: slums, pollution, disease, and corrupt political machines. In particular, cities were places where the extravagantly wealthy bumped up against the homeless and destitute. As one African American observer put it, the city was "Civilization's Inferno." As a consequence of their urgent problems, industrial cities became important sites of political innovation and reform

The New Metropolis

Mark Twain, arriving in New York in 1867, remarked that it was "too large. . . . You cannot accomplish anything in the way of business, you cannot even pay a friendly call without devoting a whole day to it. . . . [The] distances are too great." At that time, technologies like the steam engine and streetcar were already starting to allow engineers and planners to reorganize big cities like New York. Over the next fifty years, such cities developed a new geography. Their specialized districts included not only areas for finance, manufacturing, wholesaling, and warehousing but also immigrant neighborhoods, affluent suburbs, shopping districts, and business-oriented downtowns. It was an exciting and bewildering new world.

The Shape of the Industrial City

Before the Civil War, cities served the needs of commerce and finance, not industry. Early manufacturing sprang up mostly in the countryside, where mill owners could draw waterpower from streams, find plentiful fuel and raw materials, and recruit workers from farms and villages. The nation's largest cities were seaports, and most urban areas were places where merchants and traders bought and sold goods for distribution into the interior or to world markets.

As industrialization developed, cities became sites for manufacturing as well as finance and trade. Steam engines played a central role in this change: With them, mill operators no longer had to depend on less reliable water-driven power. Quick to make use of new railroad links, iron makers gravitated to Pittsburgh because of its access to coal and ore fields. Chicago, midway between western livestock suppliers and eastern markets, became a great meatpacking center. Steam power also vastly increased the scale of industry. In some places, a plant that employed thousands of workers instantly created a small city, in the form of a company town like Aliquippa, Pennsylvania, which belonged body and soul

to the Jones and Laughlin Steel Company. Older commercial cities also became more industrial. Warehouse districts could readily convert to small-scale manufacturing; a distribution network was right at hand. In addition, port cities that served as immigrant gateways offered abundant cheap labor, an essential element in the industrial economy.

Mass Transit and the Suburb New technologies helped residents and visitors negotiate the large distances of the industrial city. Steam-driven cable cars appeared in the 1870s. By 1887, engineer Frank Sprague designed an electric trolley system for Richmond, Virginia. It used electricity from a central generating plant, fed to the trolleys through overhead power lines, which each trolley touched with a long pole mounted on the top of its roof. The trolley quickly became the primary mode of transportation in most American cities. Congestion and frequent accidents, however, led to demands that trolley lines be moved off streets. The "el"—the elevated railroad, built as early as 1879 in New York City—became a safer alternative. Chicago developed elevated transit most fully. Other urban planners built down, not up. Boston opened a short underground line in 1897; by 1904, completion of a subway running the length of Manhattan demonstrated the full potential of high-speed underground trains.

Even before the Civil War, the arrival of railroads led to the growth of **suburbs**, outlying residential districts for the well-to-do. The high cost of transportation effectively segregated these affluent districts, and most working-class residents remained near the city center, where they could walk to work. In the late nineteenth century this trend accelerated. Businessmen and professionals built homes on large, beautifully landscaped lots in outlying towns such as Riverside, Illinois, and Tuxedo Park, New York. In the suburbs, affluent wives and children enjoyed refuge from the pollution and perceived dangers of the city. As men traveled daily from home to work and back, they became commuters, a word widely recognized by the early 1900s.

Chicago's El

Elevated railroads quickly became a familiar sight to city dwellers. Most urban transit networks were operated by private companies, and tensions over expensive fares ran high in many cities. Nonetheless, such transit systems helped people negotiate the great distances of the new metropolis.   Jazz Age Chicago.

Los Angeles entrepreneur Henry Huntington, nephew of a wealthy Southern Pacific Railroad magnate, expanded the suburban ideal as he pitched the benefits of southern California sunshine. Huntington invested his family fortune in Los Angeles real estate and transportation. Along his trolley lines, he subdivided property into lots and built rows of bungalows, planting the tidy yards with lush trees and tropical fruits. Middle-class buyers flocked to purchase Huntington's houses. One new resident exclaimed, "I have apparently found a Paradise on Earth." Anticipating twentieth-century Americans' love for single-family homes in the suburbs, Huntington had invented southern California sprawl.

The rise of the suburb was abetted by another invention, Alexander Graham Bell's telephone (1876). Originally intended for business use on local exchanges, telephones were eagerly adopted by residential customers. By the 1890s, switchboards in most major cities and towns allowed suburban wives and urban businessmen to stay in touch during the workday. In 1893, two-thirds of the nation's telephones belonged to businesses; over the next fifteen years, residential users expanded by a factor of ten. Overall, by 1907, the nation had more than three million telephone customers.

Skyscrapers By the 1880s, the invention of steel girders, durable plate glass, and passenger elevators began to revolutionize downtown building methods. Architects invented the skyscraper, a building that was supported by its steel skeleton while its walls bore little weight, serving instead as curtains to enclose the structure. The skyscraper was an expensive form of construction, but it enabled downtown landowners to leverage the cost of a small plot of land. By investing in a skyscraper, a landlord could collect rent for ten or even twenty floors of space. Large corporations also favored skyscrapers as symbols of business prowess and centralized corporate authority.

The first skyscraper built on the new design principles was William Le Baron Jenney's ten-story Home Insurance Building (1885) in Chicago. Although unremarkable in appearance—it looked just like other downtown buildings—Jenney's steel-girder building inspired the creativity of American architects. A Chicago school sprang up, dedicated to the design of buildings whose form expressed, rather than masked, their structure and function. The presiding genius of this school was architect Louis Sullivan, who developed a "vertical aesthetic" of set-back windows and strong columns that not only gave skyscrapers a "proud and soaring" presence but

Woolworth Building, New York City

Under construction in this photograph, taken between 1910 and 1913, the headquarters of the nationwide Woolworth's five-and-dime chain became a dominant feature of the New York skyline. Manhattan soon had more skyscrapers than any other city in the world. Library of Congress.

also offered plenty of natural light for workers inside. Chicago pioneered skyscraper construction, but New York, with its unrelenting demand for prime downtown space, took the lead by the late 1890s. The fifty-five-story Woolworth Building, completed in 1913, marked the beginning of the modern Manhattan skyline.

The Electric City For ordinary citizens, one of the most dramatic urban amenities was electric light. Gaslight, produced from coal gas, had been employed for residential light since the early nineteenth century, but gas lamps were too dim to brighten streets and public spaces. In the 1870s, as generating technology became commercially viable, the first use of electricity was for better urban lighting. Charles F. Brush's electric arc lamps, installed in Wanamaker's department store in Philadelphia in 1878, created a sensation with their brilliant illumination. Electric streetlights soon replaced gaslights on city streets across the country. Electric lighting also entered the American home, thanks to Thomas Edison's invention of a serviceable incandescent bulb in 1879.

Before it had a significant effect on industry, electricity gave the city its modern tempo. It lifted elevators, illuminated department store windows, and powered streetcars and subway trains. Most of all, it turned night into day. Electric streetlights made residents feel safer; as one magazine put it in 1912, "A light is as good as a policeman." Electricity also made nightlife more appealing. One journalist described Broadway in 1894 as a place where "all the shop fronts are lighted, and the entrances to the theaters blaze out on the sidewalk like open fireplaces." At the end of a long working day, city dwellers flocked to this free entertainment. Nothing, declared an observer, matched the "festive panorama" of Broadway "when the lights are on."

Newcomers and Neighborhoods

The explosive growth of America's urban population made cities a world of newcomers, including millions of immigrants from overseas. Most numerous in Boston were the Irish; in Minneapolis, Swedes; in most other northern cities, Germans. Arriving in the metropolis, immigrants confronted many difficulties. One Polish man, who had lost the address of his American cousins, felt utterly alone upon his arrival at Ellis Island. Then he heard someone speaking in Polish. "From sheer joy," he recalled, "tears welled up in my eyes to hear my native tongue." He was relieved to get help from a kindly Polish American couple. Such experiences suggest why most immigrants moved in well-defined networks, relying on relatives and friends to become oriented and find jobs. A high degree of ethnic clustering resulted, even within a single factory. At the Jones and Laughlin steelworks in Pittsburgh, for example, the carpentry shop was German, the hammer shop Polish, and the blooming mill Serbian. "My people . . . stick together," observed the son of an immigrant couple from Ukraine. "They attend their own churches." But, he added, "we who are born

Lighting Up Minneapolis, 1883
Like other American cities, Minneapolis at night had been lit by dim gaslight until the advent of Charles F. Brush's electric arc lamps. This photograph marks the opening day, February 28, 1883, of Minneapolis's new era: the first lighting of a 257-foot tower topped by a ring of electric arc lamps. The electric poles on the right, connecting the tower to a power station, would soon proliferate into a blizzard of poles and overhead wires, as Minneapolis became an electric city.
© Minnesota Historical Society/CORBIS.

in this country . . . are different from those born in the old country. We feel this country is our home."

Patterns of settlement varied by ethnic group. Many Italians, recruited by padroni, or labor bosses, found work in northeastern and Mid-Atlantic cities. Their urban concentration was especially marked after the 1880s, as more and more immigrants—especially men—arrived from southern Italy. The attraction of America was obvious to one young man, who had grown up as the third of nine children in a poor southern Italian

farm family. "I had never gotten any wages of any kind before," he reported after settling with his uncle in Newark, New Jersey. "The work here was just as hard as that on the farm; but I didn't mind it much because I would receive what seemed to me like a lot." A substantial number of Italians settled on the Pacific coast. Amadeo Peter Giannini, who started off as a produce merchant in San Francisco, soon turned to banking. After the San Francisco earthquake in 1906, his Banca d'Italia was the first financial institution to reopen in the Bay area. Expanding steadily across the West, it eventually became Bank of America.

Like Giannini's bank, institutions of many kinds sprang up to serve ethnic urban communities. Immigrants throughout America avidly read the newspaper *Il Progresso Italo-Americano* and the Yiddish-language *Jewish Daily Forward*, both published in New York. Bohemians gathered in singing societies, while New York Jews patronized a lively Yiddish theater. By 1903, Italians in Chicago had sixty-six mutual aid societies, mostly comprised of people from particular provinces or towns. These societies collected dues from members and paid

support in case of death or disability on the job. Mutual benefit societies also functioned as fraternal and political clubs. "We are strangers in a strange country," explained one member of a Chinese *tong*, or communal order, in Chicago. "We must have an organization (*tong*) to control our country fellows and develop our friendship."

Sharply defined ethnic neighborhoods—such as San Francisco's Chinatown, Italian North Beach, and Jewish Hayes Valley—grew up in every major city, driven both by discrimination and by immigrants' desire to stick together (Map 19.1). In addition to patterns

MAP 19.1

The Lower East Side, New York City, 1900

As this map shows, the Jewish immigrants dominating Manhattan's Lower East Side preferred to live in neighborhoods populated by those from their home regions of Eastern Europe. Their sense of a common identity made for a remarkable flowering of educational, cultural, and social institutions on the Jewish East Side. Ethnic neighborhoods became a feature of almost every American city.

The Cherry Family, 1906

Wiley and Fannie Cherry migrated in 1893 from North Carolina to Chicago, settling in the small African American community that had established itself on the city's West Side. The Cherrys apparently prospered. By 1906, when this family portrait was taken, they had entered the black middle class. When migration intensified after 1900, longer-settled urban blacks like the Cherrys often became uncomfortable, and relations with needy rural newcomers were sometimes tense.   Collection of Lorraine Heflin.

of ethnic and racial segregation, the residential districts of almost all industrial cities were divided along lines of economic class. In Los Angeles, Mexican neighborhoods around the central plaza became ethnically diverse, incorporating Italians and Jews. Later, as the plaza became a site for business and tourism, immigrants were pushed into working-class neighborhoods like Belvedere and Boyle Heights, which sprang up to the east. Though ethnically diverse, East Los Angeles was resolutely working-class, while middle-class white neighborhoods grew up predominantly in West Los Angeles.

Along with immigrants, African Americans also sought urban opportunities. At the turn of the twentieth century, 90 percent of American blacks still lived in the South, but increasing numbers moved to urban areas such as Baton Rouge, Jacksonville, Montgomery, and Charleston, all of whose populations were more than 50 percent African American. Blacks also settled in northern cities, albeit not in the numbers that would arrive during the Great Migration of World War I. Though African Americans constituted only 2 percent of New York City's population in 1910, they already numbered more than 90,000. These newcomers to the city confronted conditions that were even worse than those for foreign-born immigrants. Relentlessly turned away from manufacturing jobs, most black men and women took up work in the service sector, becoming porters, laundrywomen, and domestic servants.

Blacks faced another urban danger: the race riot, an attack by white mobs triggered by street altercations

Le Petit Journal

SUPPLÉMENT ILLUSTRÉ

DIMANCHE 7 OCTOBRE 1906

LES « LYNCHAGES » AUX ÉTATS-UNIS
Massacre de nègres à Atlanta (Georgie)

The Atlanta Race Riot – Seen from France

The cover of this Paris newsmagazine depicts the Atlanta race riot of 1906. While the artist had almost certainly never visited Atlanta, his dramatic illustration shows that, from this early date, racial violence could be a source of embarrassment to the United States in its relations with other countries.   Picture Research Consultants & Archives.

or rumors of crime. One of the most virulent episodes occurred in Atlanta, Georgia, in 1906. This set of events, which came to be known as the Atlanta race riot, was fueled by a nasty political campaign that generated sensational false charges of "negro crime." Roaming bands of white men attacked black Atlantans, even invading middle-class black neighborhoods and in one case lynching two barbers after seizing them in their shop. The rioters killed at least twenty-four blacks and wounded more than a hundred. The disease of race hatred was not limited to the South. Race riots similar to the one in Atlanta broke out in New York City's Tenderloin district in 1900; in Evansville, Indiana, in 1903; and in Springfield, Illinois, in 1908. By that year, one journalist observed, "in every important Northern city, a distinct race-problem already exists which must, in a few years, assume serious proportions."

Whether they arrived from the rural South or from Europe, Mexico, or Asia, working-class city residents needed cheap housing near their jobs (Map 19.2). They faced grim choices. As urban land values climbed, speculators tore down older houses that had been vacated by middle-class families moving to the suburbs. In their

place, they erected five- or six-story tenements, buildings that housed twenty or more families in cramped, airless apartments (Figure 19.1). In tenements, disease was rampant and infant mortality horrific. In New York's Eleventh Ward, an average of 986 persons occupied each acre, a density exceeded only in Bombay, India. One investigator in Philadelphia described twenty-six people living in nine rooms of a tenement. "The bathroom at the rear of the house was used as a kitchen," she reported. "One privy compartment in the yard was the sole toilet accommodation for the five families living in the house." African Americans often suffered most. A study of Albany, Syracuse, and Troy in New York noted, "The colored people are relegated to the least healthful buildings."

Denouncing these conditions, some reformers called for model tenements financed by public-spirited citizens willing to accept a limited return on their investment. When private philanthropy failed to make a dent, cities turned to housing codes. The most advanced was New York's Tenement House Law of 1901, which required interior courts, indoor toilets, and fire safeguards for new structures. The law, however, had

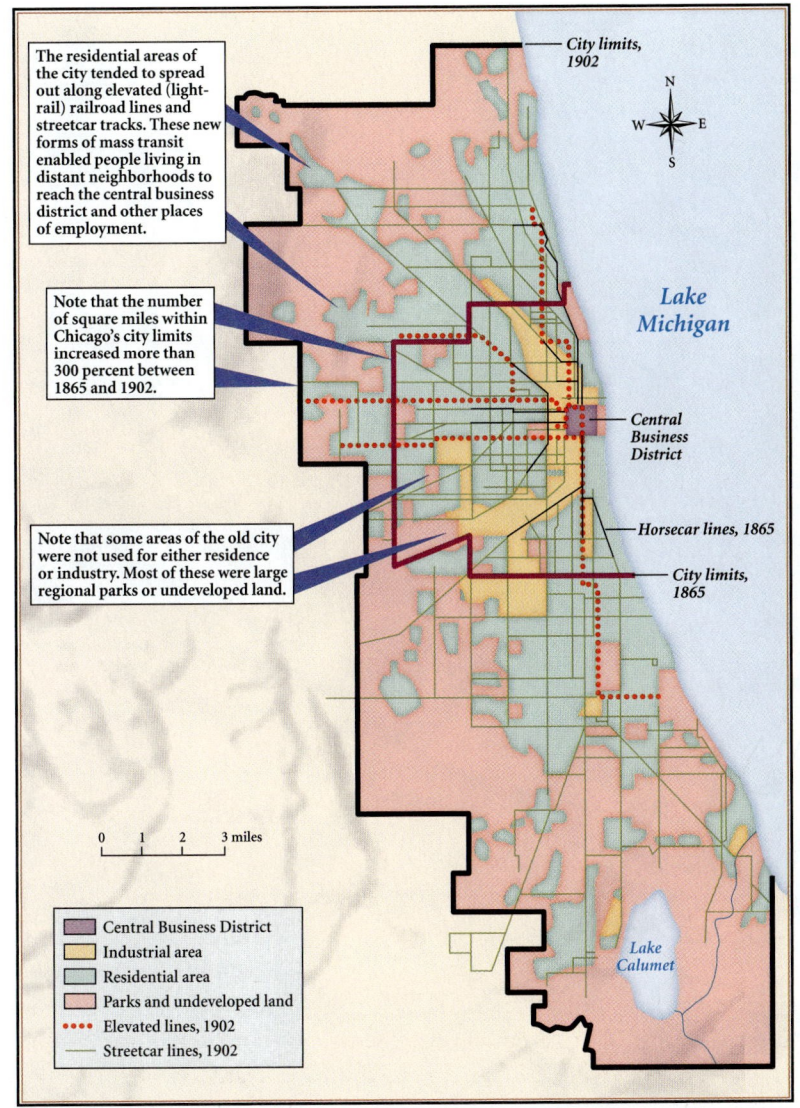

The residential areas of the city tended to spread out along elevated (light-rail) railroad lines and streetcar tracks. These new forms of mass transit enabled people living in distant neighborhoods to reach the central business district and other places of employment.

Note that the number of square miles within Chicago's city limits increased more than 300 percent between 1865 and 1902.

Note that some areas of the old city were not used for either residence or industry. Most of these were large regional parks or undeveloped land.

City limits, 1902

Lake Michigan

Central Business District

Horsecar lines, 1865

City limits, 1865

Lake Calumet

0 1 2 3 miles

■ Central Business District
■ Industrial area
■ Residential area
■ Parks and undeveloped land
••• Elevated lines, 1902
— Streetcar lines, 1902

MAP 19.2

The Expansion of Chicago, 1865–1902

In 1865, Chicagoans depended on horsecar lines to get around town. By 1900, the city limits had expanded enormously and so had the streetcar service, which was by then electrified. Elevated trains eased the congestion on downtown streets. Ongoing extension of the streetcar lines, some beyond the city limits, ensured that suburban development would continue as well.

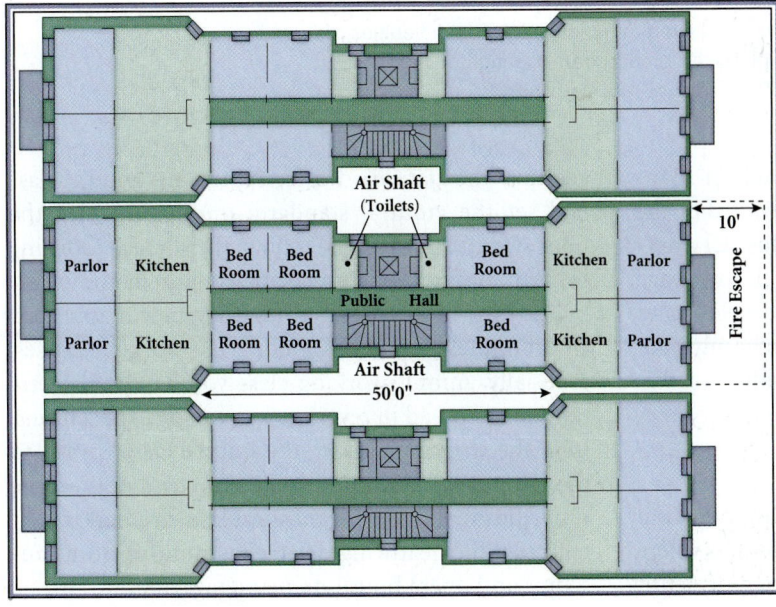

Air Shaft (Toilets)

Parlor | Kitchen | Bed Room | Bed Room | Bed Room | Kitchen | Parlor

Public Hall

Parlor | Kitchen | Bed Room | Bed Room | Bed Room | Kitchen | Parlor

Air Shaft

50'0"

Fire Escape

10'

FIGURE 19.1

Floor Plan of a Dumbbell Tenement

In a contest for a design that met an 1879 requirement for every room to have a window, the dumbbell tenement won. The interior indentation, which created an airshaft between adjoining buildings, gave the tenement its "dumbbell" shape. But what was touted as a model tenement demonstrated instead the futility of trying to reconcile maximum land usage with decent housing. Each floor contained four apartments of three or four rooms, the largest only 10 by 11 feet. The two toilets in the hall became filthy or broke down under daily use by forty or more people. The narrow airshaft provided almost no light for the interior rooms and served mainly as a dumping ground for garbage. So deplorable were these tenements that they became the stimulus for the next wave of New York housing reform.

City Garbage

"How to get rid of the garbage?" was a question that bedeviled every American city. The difficulties of keeping up are all too clear in this ground-level photograph by the great urban investigator Jacob Riis, looking down Tammany Street in New York City circa 1890.   Museum of the City of New York.

no effect on 44,000 tenements already built in Manhattan and the Bronx. Reformers were thwarted by the economic facts of urban development. Industrial workers could not afford transportation to their low-wage jobs and had to live nearby; commercial development pushed up land values. Only high-density, cheaply built housing earned landlords a significant profit.

City Cultures

Despite their many dangers and problems, industrial cities could also be exciting places to live—places where people could challenge older mores. In the nineteenth century, the nation's white, Protestant middle class had set the cultural standard; immigrants and the poor were expected to follow their cues, working toward "uplift" and respectability. But in the cities, by the turn of the twentieth century, new mass-based entertainments emerged among the working classes, especially among working-class youth. These entertainments spread in reverse of prevailing expectations, *from* the working class *to* the middle class (much to the distress of many middle-class parents). At the same time, the great cities proved stimulating centers for intellectual life, featuring diverse institutions from museums and opera houses to newsmagazines.

Amusement Park, Long Beach, California

The origins of the roller coaster go back to LaMarcus Thompson's Switchback Railway, installed at New York's Coney Island in 1884 and featuring gentle dips and curves. By 1900, when the Jack Rabbit Race was constructed at Long Beach, California, the goal was to create the biggest possible thrill. Angelenos journeyed out by trolley to Long Beach not only to take a dip in the ocean but also to ride the new roller coaster. The airplane ride in the foreground is a further wrinkle on the peculiarly modern notion that the way to have fun is to be scared to death.   © Curt Teich Postcard Archives, Lake County Museum.

Urban Amusements One enticing attraction for city dwellers was **vaudeville**, which arose in the 1880s and 1890s. Vaudeville theaters invited customers to walk in anytime and watch a continuous sequence of musical acts, skits, juggling, magic shows, and other entertainment. First popular among the working class, vaudeville quickly broadened its appeal to include middle-class audiences. By the early 1900s, vaudeville faced growing competition from early movie theaters, or nickelodeons, which offered audiences the chance to see short films for a nickel entry fee. One reporter described the audience at a typical movie theater as "workingmen," "mothers of bawling infants," and "newsboys, bootblacks, and smudgy urchins." By the 1910s, even working girls who refrained from less respectable amusements might indulge in a movie once or twice a week.

Even more spectacular were the great amusement parks that appeared around 1900, most famously at New York's Coney Island (see Voices from Abroad, "José Martí: Coney Island, 1881," p. 602). These parks had their origins in World's Fairs, whose free educational exhibits proved less popular than their paid entertainment areas. Fairgoers flocked to ride giant Ferris wheels, take camel rides through "a street in Cairo," and watch exotic Middle Eastern dances. Entrepreneurs found that such attractions were big business. Between 1895 and 1904, they installed them permanently at a group of rival amusement parks near Coney Island's popular beaches. The parks offered millions a chance to come over by ferry, escape the hot city, and enjoy roller coasters, "shoot-the-chute" lagoon plunges, and "hootchykootchy" dance shows. Amusement parks soon offered similar fun at sites near Chicago, Kansas City, and other large cities. By the summer of 1903, Philadelphia's Willow Grove Park counted three million visitors annually; so did two amusement parks outside of Los Angeles.

Ragtime Popular music also became a booming business in the industrial city. By the 1890s, Tin Pan Alley, the nickname for New York City's song-publishing district, produced such national hit tunes as "A Bicycle Built for Two" and "My Wild Irish Rose." The most famous sold more than a million copies of sheet music, as well as audio recordings on newly invented phonograph cylinders. To find out what would sell, publishers had musicians play their compositions at New York's working-class beer gardens, saloons, and dance halls. One publishing agent, who visited "sixty joints a week" to test new songs, declared later that "the best songs came from the gutter."

African American musicians brought a syncopated beat that, by the 1890s, began to work its way into mainstream hits like "A Hot Time in the Old Town Tonight." Black performers soon became stars in their own right with the rise of ragtime music. Ragtime was apparently named for its "ragged rhythm," which combined a steady beat in the bass (played with the left hand on the piano) and syncopated, off-beat rhythms in the treble (played with the right). Ragtime became wildly popular among audiences of all classes and races who heard, in its infectious rhythms, something exciting and modern—a decisive break with Victorian hymns and parlor songs.

For the master of the genre, composer Scott Joplin, ragtime was serious music. Joplin, the son of former slaves, grew up along the Texas-Arkansas border and took piano lessons as a boy from a German teacher. He and other traveling performers first introduced ragtime

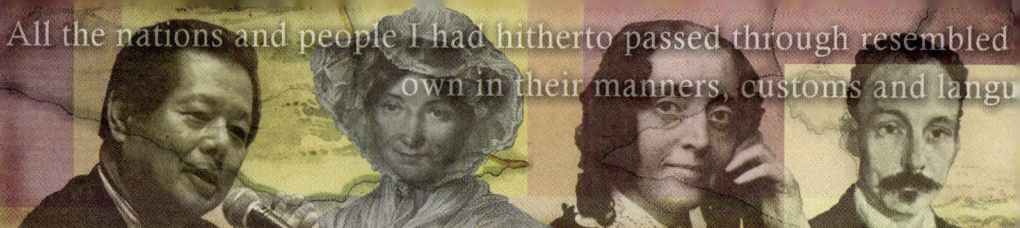
VOICES FROM ABROAD

José Martí
Coney Island, 1881

José Martí, a Cuban patriot and poet, was a journalist by profession. In exile from Cuba between 1880 and 1895, due to his revolutionary activities in opposition to Spanish rule, he spent most of his time in New York City, writing articles in support of his cause and reporting to Latin American readers on the customs of the Yankees. Martí took special—one might say perverse—pleasure in observing Americans at play. As you read his account of Coney Island, bear in mind that Martí was writing from a cultural perspective that was self-consciously different from that of native-born North Americans.

From all parts of the United States, legions of intrepid ladies and Sunday-best farmers arrive to admire the splendid sights, the unexampled wealth, the dizzying variety, the herculean surge, the striking appearance of Coney Island, the now famous island, four years ago an abandoned sand bank, that today is a spacious amusement area providing relaxation and recreation for hundreds of thousands of New Yorkers who throng to its pleasant beaches every day. . . .

Other nations—ourselves among them—live devoured by a sublime demon within that drives us to the tireless pursuit of an ideal of love or glory. . . . Not so with these tranquil souls, stimulated only by a desire for gain. One scans those shimmering beaches . . . one views the throngs seated in comfortable chairs along the seashore, filling their lungs with the fresh, invigorating air. But it is said that those from our lands who remain here long are overcome with melancholy . . . because this great nation is void of spirit.

But what coming and going! What torrents of money! What facilities for every pleasure! What absolute absence of any outward sadness or poverty! Everything in the open air: the animated groups, the immense dining rooms, the peculiar courtship of North Americans, which is virtually devoid of the elements that compose the shy, tender, elevated love in our lands, the theatre, the photographers' booth, the bathhouses! Some weigh themselves, for North Americans are greatly elated, or really concerned, if they find they have gained or lost a pound. . . .

This spending, this uproar, these crowds, the activity of this amazing ant hill never slackens from June to October, from morning 'til night. . . . Then, like a monster that vomits its contents into the hungry maw of another monster, that colossal crowd, that straining, crushing mass, forces its way onto the trains, which speed across wastes, groaning under their burden, until they surrender it to the tremendous steamers, enlivened by the sound of harps and violins, convey it to the piers, and debouch the weary merrymakers into the thousand trolleys that pursue the thousand tracks that spread through slumbering New York like veins of steel.

Source: Juan de Onís, trans., *The America of José Martí: Selected Writings* (New York: Noonday Press, 1954), 103–110.

ANALYZING THE EVIDENCE

- When Martí says America is "devoid of spirit," what does he mean? Why would such a thought be prompted by his observation of people having fun at Coney Island?

- In the final paragraph, Martí describes what might be considered a technological marvel—the capacity of New York's transportation system to move many thousands of revelers from Coney Island back to their homes in a few hours. But consider how Martí characterizes this—"a monster that vomits its contents into the hungry maw of another monster." Does Martí's distaste negate the value of his account as a historical source about city mass transit?

- Suppose you hadn't read the text's treatment of urban leisure. What would you gain from reading Martí's account? Having read the text's discussion, do you find that Martí's account adds new insights, or changes your view?

to national audiences at the Chicago World's Fair in 1893. Seeking to elevate African American music and secure a broad national audience, Joplin warned pianists, "It is never right to play 'Ragtime' fast." But his instructions were widely ignored. Young Americans embraced ragtime as dance music—and thus a way to embrace one another.

Ragtime ushered in an urban dance craze. By 1910, New York alone had more than five hundred dance halls. In Kansas City, shocked moral reformers counted 16,500 dancers on the floor on a Saturday night; Chicago had 86,000. Some young Polish and Slovak women chose restaurant jobs rather than domestic service so that they would have the free time to visit dance halls, one investigator reported, "several nights a week." New dances like the Bunny Hug and Grizzly Bear were overtly sexual: They called for close body contact and plenty of hip movement. In fact, many of these dances originated in brothels. Despite widespread denunciations, dance mania soon spread from the urban working classes to rural and middle-class youth.

By the 1910s, black music was achieving a central place in American popular culture. African American trumpet player and bandleader W. C. Handy, born in Alabama, electrified national audiences by performing music drawn from the cotton fields of the Mississippi Delta. This music became known as the blues. The blues featured banjo or guitar and a rasping vocal style, with instrument and voice following each other in a "call and response" drawn from traditional African American folk music. In its themes, blues music spoke of hard work and heartbreak, as in Handy's popular hit "St. Louis Blues" (1914):

> Got de St. Louis Blues jes blue as ah can be,
> Dat man got a heart lak a rock cast in the sea,
> Or else he wouldn't gone so far from me.

Though it first emerged in the rural South, blues music won fame in the city. It spoke to the emotional lives of young people who were far from home, experiencing dislocation, loneliness, and bitter disappointment along with the thrills of urban life. Like Coney Island amusements, ragtime and blues helped forge new collective experiences in a world of strangers.

Like other mass commercial amusements, ragtime dance music lacked educational or "uplifting" content; its purpose was sheer pleasure. It spread quickly and had a profound influence on twentieth-century American culture. By the time Handy published "St. Louis Blues," composer Irving Berlin, a Russian Jewish immigrant, was introducing altered ragtime pieces into musical theater—versions that eventually transferred to radio and the movies. The new music often featured sexual innuendo, as in the title of Berlin's hit song "If You Don't Want My Peaches (You'd Better Stop Shaking My Tree)." The popularity of such music showed that a modern youth culture was arriving on the scene. Its enduring features included "crossover" music that originated in the black working class—ragtime and jazz at first, rock and hip-hop in later decades—and a commercial music industry that brazenly appropriated such black musical styles.

Sex and the City In the city, many young people found parental oversight weaker than it had been in previous generations. Amusement parks and dance halls helped foster the new custom of "dating," which like many other cultural innovations emerged first among the working class. Gradually, it became more acceptable for a young man to escort a young woman out on the town for commercial entertainments rather than spending the evening at home under a chaperone's watchful eye. For young people, dating opened a new world of pleasure, sexual adventure, and danger. Young women sometimes headed to dance halls alone to "pick up" men; the term *gold digger* came into use to describe a woman who wanted a man's money more than the man himself.

But it was young women, not men, who proved most vulnerable in the new system of dating. Having less money to spend than men did, because they earned half or less of men's wages, working-class girls relied on the "treat." Some tried to maintain strict standards of respectability, keenly aware that their prospects for marriage depended—much more than young men's did—on a virtuous reputation. But others became so-called charity girls, eager for a good time. Such young women, one investigator reported, "offer themselves to strangers, not for money, but for presents, attention and pleasure, and, most important, a yielding to sex desire." For some women, sexual favors could look like a matter of practical necessity. "If I did not have a man," declared one waitress, "I could not get along on my wages." In the anonymous city, there was not always a clear line between working-class treats and casual prostitution.

Dating and casual sex were hallmarks of an urban world in which large numbers of residents were young and single. Seeking jobs, greater personal freedom, or both, young unmarried women moved to urban areas in large numbers. The 1900 census found that more than 30 percent of women in St. Paul and Minneapolis, Minnesota, lived as boarders and lodgers, not in family units; the percentage topped 20 percent in Detroit,

Philadelphia, and Boston. Single men also found opportunities in the city. One historian has labeled the late nineteenth century the Age of the Bachelor, a time when being an unattached male lost its social stigma. With its boardinghouses, restaurants, and abundant personal services, the city afforded bachelors all the comforts of home and, on top of that, an array of men's clubs, saloons, and sporting events.

In addition to informal and casual heterosexual relationships, many industrial cities developed robust gay subcultures. A gay world flourished in New York, for example, including an array of drinking and meeting places, as well as underground gay clubs and drag balls. Middle-class men, both straight and gay, frequented such venues for entertainment or to find companionship. One medical student remembered being taken to a ball at which he was startled to find five hundred gay and lesbian couples "waltzing to the music of a good band." By the 1910s, the word *queer* had come into use as slang for *homosexual*. Though episodes of harassment were frequent, and reformers like Anthony Comstock issued regular denunciations of "degeneracy," arrests were few. Gay sex shows and saloons were lucrative for those who ran them (and for police, who took bribes to look the other way, just as they did for brothels). The exuberant gay urban subculture offered a dramatic challenge to Victorian ideals.

Urban High Culture   For elites, the rise of great cities offered an opportunity to build museums, libraries, and other cultural institutions that could flourish only in major metropolitan centers. Millionaires patronized the arts partly to advance themselves socially but also out of a sense of civic duty and national pride. As early as the 1870s, symphony orchestras emerged in Boston and New York. National tours by leading orchestras planted the seeds for orchestral societies in many other cities. Composers and conductors embraced new musical forms. By the 1890s, the Metropolitan Opera drew enthusiastic crowds to hear the work of Richard Wagner. In 1907, the Met shocked audiences by presenting Richard Strauss's musically innovative and sexually scandalous opera *Salome*.

As the ferment of urban life overturned older cultural norms, some artists began to question the whole concept of "high culture." American composers began looking to folk music for inspiration. Edward McDowell, for example, called on American artists to free themselves from "the restraint that an almost unlimited deference to European thought and prejudice has imposed upon us." He called for "manly" music that

represented Americans' "undaunted tenacity of spirit." Seeking authenticity, McDowell incorporated Native American musical themes into works like his *Indian Suite* (1896).

Art museums and natural history museums also emerged as prominent new institutions in this era. The nation's first major art museum, the Corcoran Gallery of Art, opened in Washington, D.C., in 1869, while New York's Metropolitan Museum of Art settled into its permanent home in 1880. In the same decades, public libraries grew from modest collections into major urban institutions. The greatest library benefactor was steel magnate Andrew Carnegie, who announced in 1881 that he would build a library in any town or city that was prepared to maintain it. By 1907, Carnegie had spent more than $32.7 million to establish about a thousand libraries throughout the United States.

Investigative Journalism   Patrons of Carnegie's libraries could read not only books but also an increasing array of mass-market newspapers. Joseph Pulitzer, owner of the *St. Louis Post-Dispatch* and, after 1883, the *New York Journal*, led the way in building his sales base with sensational investigations, human-interest stories, and targeted sections covering sports, fashion, and high society. By the 1890s, Pulitzer faced a vigorous challenge from William Randolph Hearst, who transformed himself from the pampered son of a California silver king into one of the nation's leading news barons. Starting with the *San Francisco Examiner* and then adding the *New York World*, Hearst went toe-to-toe with Pulitzer as advertising increased, newsstand prices dropped, and newspaper circulation escalated rapidly (Table 19.1).

The arrival of Sunday color comics, such as F. G. Outcault's *The Yellow Kid* (1894), lent their name to *yellow journalism*, a derogatory term used for mass-market newspapers. Disapproving commentators dis-

TABLE 19.1

Newspaper Circulation, 1870–1909

Year	Total Circulation
1870	2,602,000
1880	3,566,000
1890	8,387,000
1900	15,102,000
1909	24,212,000

SOURCE: *Historical Statistics of the United States*, 2 vols. (Washington, DC: U.S. Bureau of the Census, 1975), 2: 810.

Who Said Muck Rake?
The Smile That Won't Come Off.)

Who Said Muck Rake?

A popular biographer in the 1890s, Ida Tarbell turned her journalistic talents to investigative journalism, or muckraking. The first installment of what would become her book *The History of the Standard Oil Company* appeared in *McClure's Magazine* in November 1902. The serial was a bombshell, with its exposure of the ruthless machinations used by John D. Rockefeller in building up his fabulous petroleum fortune. In this cartoon, Tarbell appears as a respectable lady—but note her threatening muck rake and, further in the background, a cowering President Theodore Roosevelt. That Roosevelt was paying attention, the cartoon suggests, is apparent in the headline of the newspaper she is reading.   Drake Oil Well Museum.

liked these papers for their flagrant reliance on murders, scandals, sob stories, and anything that might arouse what Hearst's editor called "the gee-whiz emotion." Hearst's and Pulitzer's sensational coverage was often irresponsible, and in the late 1890s their papers helped whip up a nationwide frenzy for the United States to go to war against Spain. But Hearst and Pulitzer also exposed many scandals and injustices. They believed their papers should challenge the powerful by speaking for, and to, ordinary Americans.

Some of Hearst's and Pulitzer's best reporters played a role in the emerging field of investigative journalism. As early as the 1870s and 1880s, news reporters and independent investigators drew attention to corrupt city governments, the abuse of power by large corporations, and threats to public health. Researcher Helen Campbell reported on tenement conditions in such exposés as *Prisoners of Poverty* (1887). Making innovative use of the invention of flash photography, Danish-born journalist Jacob Riis included photographs of tenement interiors in his famous book *How the Other Half*

Lives (see Reading American Pictures, "Jacob Riis Captures Tenement Life," p. 606). Riis had a profound influence on Theodore Roosevelt when the future president served as New York City's police commissioner. Roosevelt asked Riis to give him tours around the city, to help him better understand the problems of poverty, disease, and crime.

By 1900, new magazines such as *Collier's* and *McClure's* introduced middle-class readers to the work of such reporters as Ida Tarbell, who exposed the machinations of John D. Rockefeller, and David Graham Phillips, whose "Treason of the Senate," published in *Cosmopolitan* in 1906, documented the deference of U.S. senators—especially Republicans—to wealthy corporate interests. Such journalists usually lived and worked in big cities, where their magazines were published. President Roosevelt dismissed them as **muckrakers** who focused too much on the negative side of American life. But their influence was profound. They inspired thousands of readers to get involved in reform movements and tackle the problems caused by industrialization.

Jacob Riis Captures Tenement Life

Jacob Riis was not the first journalist to investigate American slums. But he found a visual form that powerfully represented the lives of the poor to middle America. Riis used newly invented flash photography in his famous exposé *How the Other Half Lives* (1890). Adopting this technology as a tool of investigative journalism, Riis photographed the inhabitants of tenement houses, sometimes in their most vulnerable moments. He accompanied the images with dramatic, sometimes lurid descriptions of tenement life. Consider the photograph shown here—one of Riis's most famous. What does the image convey to the viewer about tenement life, and to what purpose?

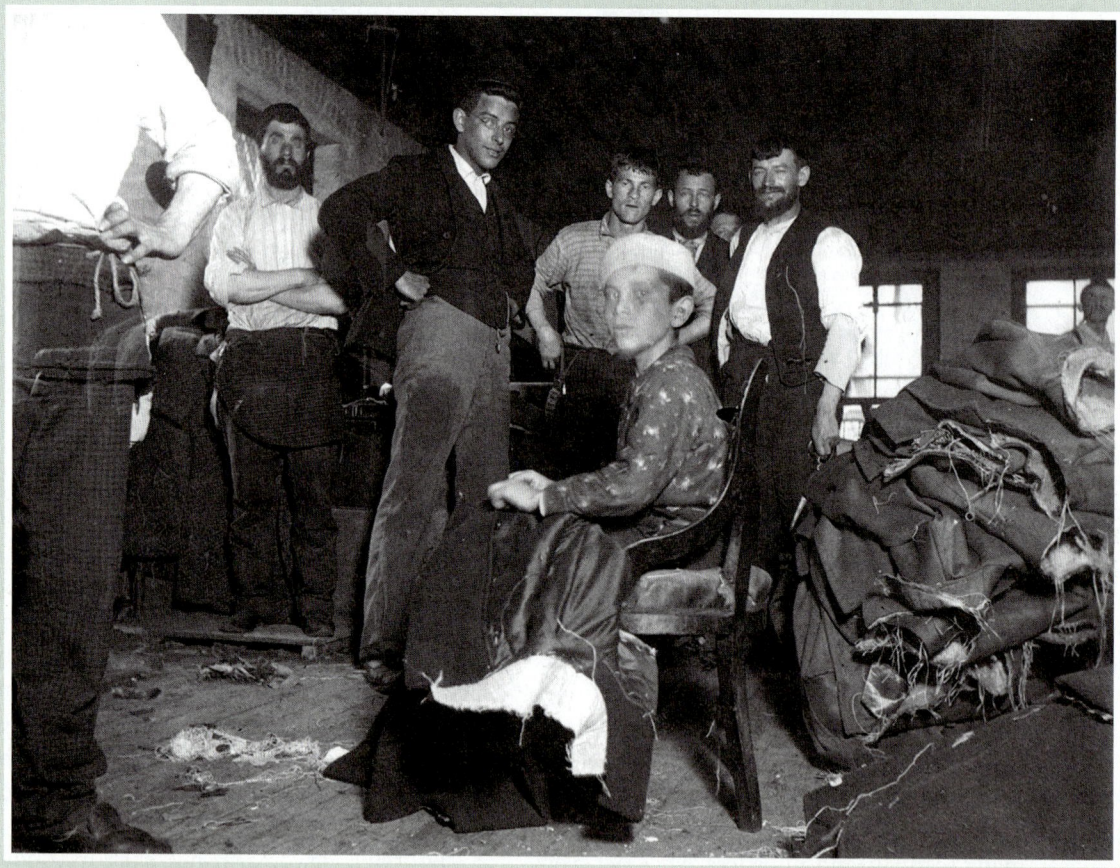

"Twelve-year-old boy (who had sworn he was sixteen) pulling threads in a sweat shop, about 1889." Museum of the City of New York.

ANALYZING THE EVIDENCE

- The photograph centers on the boy. Why do you think Riis was drawn to photograph him? What does Riis want the viewer to notice?

- The title of the photo calls attention to the boy, but what about the men in the background? What do you think was Riis's purpose in including them? Why do you think they agreed to be included in the picture?

- What audience might Riis have been trying to reach with this picture? What reactions might he have hoped to elicit?

- What economic and technological factors shaped the development of cities and urban life after 1860? How were the new cities different from the typical city before 1860?

- What conditions of life did immigrants and other newcomers face in cities during this period?

- What forms of elite and popular culture developed in urban areas? How did they challenge prevailing traditions and values?

Governing the Great City

One of the most famous muckraking journalists was Lincoln Steffens, whose book *The Shame of the Cities* (1904), first published serially in *McClure's*, denounced the corruption afflicting America's urban governments. Steffens used dramatic language to expose "swindling" politicians. He described, for example, how the mayor of Minneapolis turned his city over to "outlaws." In St. Louis, "bribery was a joke," while Pittsburgh's Democratic Party operated a private company that handled almost all the city's street-paving projects, at a hefty profit. Historians now believe that Steffens and other middle-class crusaders took a rather extreme view of urban politics; the reality was more complex. But charges of corruption could hardly be denied. As industrial cities grew with breathtaking speed, they posed a serious problem of governance.

Urban Machines

In the United States, cities relied largely on private developers to build streetcar lines and provide urgently needed water, gas, and electricity. This preference for business solutions gave birth to what one urban historian calls the "private city"—a place shaped by individuals, all pursuing their own goals and bent on making money. The lure of profit, Americans believed, spurred great innovations—trolley cars, electric lighting, skyscrapers—and drove urban real estate development. Investment opportunities looked so tempting, in fact, that new cities sprang up almost overnight from the ruins of a catastrophic Chicago fire in 1871 and a major San Francisco earthquake in 1906. Real estate interests were often instrumental in pushing streetcar lines outward from the central districts. When contractors sought city business, or saloonkeepers needed licenses, they turned to the **political machine**.

Machines were party organizations—like New York's infamous Tammany Society, referred to more often by the name of its meeting place, Tammany Hall—that remained in office, year after year, on the strength of their political clout and popularity among urban voters. To middle-class Americans, machines were corrupt, in part, because they relied on the support of recent immigrants. To serve these grassroots constituents, machines recruited layers of functionaries—precinct captains, ward bosses, aldermen—whose main job was to be accessible and, as best they could, serve the needs of the party faithful. The machine acted as a rough-and-ready social service agency, providing jobs for the jobless or a helping hand for a bereaved family. Tammany ward boss George Washington Plunkitt, for example, reported that he arranged housing for families after their apartments burned, "fix[ing] them up until they get things runnin' again. It's philanthropy, but it's politics, too—mighty good politics." Plunkitt was an Irishman, and so were most Tammany Hall leaders. But by the 1890s, Plunkitt's Fifteenth District was filling up with Italians and Russian Jews. On a given day (as recorded in his diary) he might attend an Italian funeral in the afternoon and a Jewish wedding in the evening.

The favors dispensed by men like Plunkitt came via a system of boss control that was, as Lincoln Steffens charged, corrupt. Though rural, state, and national politics were hardly immune to such problems, cities offered the most flagrant opportunities for bribes and kickbacks. The level of corruption, as Plunkitt put it, rose "accordin' to the opportunities." When politicians made contracts for city services, some of the money ended up in their pockets. In the 1860s, William Marcy Tweed, known commonly as Boss Tweed, had made Tammany Hall a byword for corruption, until he was brought down in 1871 by flagrant overpricing in the contracts for a lavish city courthouse. Thereafter, machine corruption became more surreptitious. Plunkitt declared that he had no need for outright bribes. He favored what he called "honest graft," the easy profits that came to savvy insiders. Plunkitt made most of his money building wharves on Manhattan's waterfront.

Middle-class reformers condemned immigrants for supporting machines. But urban voters believed that few middle-class Americans cared about the plight of poor city folk like themselves. Machines were hardly perfect, but immigrants could rely on them for jobs, emergency aid, and the only public services they could hope to obtain. Astute commentators saw that bosses dominated city government because they provided what was needed, with no moralistic lectures. As one put it, machines offered "neighborly kindness instead of annual political sermons."

Despite breakneck urban development and widespread corruption, machine-style governments achieved notable successes. They built extensive public parks and markets; paved streets; and supplied streetcars, clean water, gaslight, and sewage removal. As early as 1866, at the moment when Boss Tweed was divvying up tax money with his cronies, the very same Tammany Hall machine helped oversee a triumph of public health. When the arrival of a German ship with infected passengers threatened to spread cholera, political leaders sprang into action, keenly aware that a similar outbreak in 1849 had killed more than five thousand New Yorkers. This time, by appointing an expert board of health with the authority to clean streets, disinfect buildings, and impose quarantines, the city soon brought the epidemic under control.

In the following decades, city governance improved impressively. Though by no means free of corruption, municipal agencies became far better organized and more expansive in the functions they undertook. Nowhere in the world were there more massive public projects—aqueducts, sewage systems, bridges, and spacious parks—than in American cities. The nature of this achievement can be grasped by comparing Chicago, Illinois, with Berlin, the capital of Germany, in 1900. At that time, Chicago's waterworks pumped 500 million gallons of water a day, providing 139 gallons per resident; Berliners had to make do with 18 gallons each. Flush toilets, a rarity in Berlin, could be found in 60 percent of Chicago homes. Chicago lit its streets with electricity, while Berlin still relied mostly on gaslight. Chicago had twice as many parks as the German capital, and it had just completed an ambitious sanitation project that reversed the course of the Chicago River, carrying sewage into Lake Michigan, away from city residents.

Chicago's achievement was especially remarkable because American municipal governments labored under severe political constraints. Judges did grant cities some authority: In 1897, the State Supreme Court ruled that New York City was entirely within its rights to operate a municipally owned subway. The use of private land was also subject to whatever regulations the city might impose. But, starting with an 1868 ruling in Iowa, the American legal system largely classified the city as a "corporate entity" subject to state control. In contrast to state governments, cities had only a limited police power, which they could use, for example, to stop crime, but not to pass more ambitious measures for public welfare. States, not cities, also held most taxation power

and received most public revenues. Machines and their private allies flourished, in part, because cities were starved for legitimate cash.

As cities continued to expand, the limits of machine government became increasingly clear. In addition to the problem of corruption, even the hardest-working ward boss could help individuals only on a local level, in limited ways. A city like New York might manage to ward off cholera. But Tammany Hall could not achieve systemic solutions to poverty, pollution, and unemployment, all of which were direct consequences of industrialization. Money talked; powerful economic interests warped city government. Working-class voters—even those who saw no alternative to the machine—knew that the cleanest sidewalks, newest electric lights, and most convenient trolley lines served affluent neighborhoods and suburbs, where citizens had the most clout. Hilda Satt, a Polish immigrant who moved into a poor Chicago neighborhood in 1893, recalled garbage-strewn streets and filthy backyard privies. "The streets were paved with wooden blocks," she later wrote, "and after a heavy rainfall the blocks would become loose and float about in the street." She remembered that on one such occasion, local pranksters posted a sign saying "The Mayor and the Aldermen are Invited to Swim Here."

The Limits of Machine Government

Even a casual observer could see that American cities were finding it difficult to cope with extremely rapid growth, and that some urban politicians (like their counterparts elsewhere) preferred personal gain to public welfare. The results were dramatically evident during the depression of the 1890s, when the working-class unemployment rate reached a staggering 25 percent in some cities. Homelessness and hunger were rampant. To make matters worse, most cities had abolished the early-nineteenth-century system of "outdoor relief," which provided public support for the indigent. Arguing that this promoted laziness among the poor, middle-class reformers insisted on private, not public, charity. Even cities that did continue to provide outdoor relief in the 1890s were overwhelmed by the magnitude of the crisis. Flooded with "tramps," police stations were forced to end the long-standing practice of allowing homeless individuals to sleep inside.

The crisis of the 1890s radicalized many urban voters, who proved none too loyal to the machines when better alternatives arose. Cleveland, Ohio, for example, experienced eighty-three labor strikes between 1893 and 1898; much frustration centered on the private businesses that provided urban services such as streetcar transportation. The city's Central Labor Union, dissatisfied with Democrats' failure to address their concerns, worked with middle-class allies to build a thriving local branch of the People's Party. Their demands for stronger government measures, especially to curb corporate power, culminated in citywide protests in 1899, during a strike against the hated streetcar company. That year, more than eight thousand workers participated in the city's annual Labor Day parade. As they passed the mayor's reviewing stand, each band fell silent, and the unions furled their flags in a solemn protest against the mayor's failure to support their cause.

To recapture support from working-class Clevelanders, Democrats made a dramatic change in 1901, nominating Tom Johnson for mayor. Johnson, a reform-minded businessman, advocated municipal ownership of utilities and a tax system in which "monopoly and privilege" bore the main burdens. (Johnson once thanked Cleveland's city appraisers for raising taxes on his own mansion.) Johnson's comfortable victory transformed Democrats into Cleveland's chief reform party. While the new mayor did not fulfill the whole agenda of the Central Labor Union and its allies, he became an advocate of publicly owned utilities, and one of the nation's most famous and innovative reformers.

Like Johnson, other reform mayors began to oust machines and launch ambitious programs. Some modeled their municipal governments on those of Glasgow, Scotland; Düsseldorf, Germany; and other European cities on the cutting edge of innovation. In Boston, Mayor Josiah Quincy built public baths, gyms, swimming pools, and playgrounds and provided free public concerts. Like other mayors, he battled streetcar companies to bring down fares. The scope of such projects varied. In 1912, San Francisco managed to open one short municipally owned streetcar line to compete with private companies. Milwaukee, Wisconsin, on the other hand, elected Socialists who experimented with a sweeping array of measures, including publicly subsidized medical care and housing.

Republican Hazen Pingree, mayor of Detroit from 1890 to 1897, was a particularly notable reformer who worked for better streets and public transportation. During the 1890s, Pingree opened a network of vacant city-owned lots as community vegetable gardens. "Pingree's Potato Patches" helped feed thousands of Detroit's working people during the harsh depression years. By 1901, a coalition of reformers who campaigned against New York's Tammany Hall began to borrow ideas from Pingree and other mayors. In the wealthier wards of New York, they promised to reduce crime and save taxpayer dollars. In working-class neighborhoods,

they promised to provide affordable housing and municipal ownership of gas and electricity. They defeated Tammany's candidates, and though they did not fulfill all of their promises, they did provide more funding for overcrowded public schools.

Reformers also experimented with new ways of organizing municipal government itself. After a devastating hurricane killed an estimated 6,000 people in Galveston, Texas, in 1900, and destroyed much of the city, rebuilders adopted a commission system that became a nationwide model for efficient government. Leaders of the National Municipal League advised cities to elect small councils and hire professional city managers who would direct operations like a corporate executive. The league had great difficulty persuading politicians to adopt its business-oriented model; it won its greatest victories in young, small cities like Phoenix, Arizona, where the professional classes held political power. Other cities chose, instead, to enhance democratic participation. As part of the "Oregon System," which called for direct voting on key political questions, Portland voters participated in 129 municipal referendum votes between 1905 and 1913.

- **What role did political machines play in city government? Do you think they served the goals of representative democracy? Why, or why not?**

- **What factors limited the effectiveness of machine government? How did reformers try to address these limits? To what extent did they succeed?**

Cities as Crucibles of Reform

As experiments in city government showed, the challenges that arose in the industrial city presented rich opportunities for experimentation and reform. Thus it is not surprising that progressivism (see Chapter 20) — an overlapping set of movements to combat the ills of industrialization — had a powerful urban basis. In the slums and tenements of the giant metropolis, grassroots reformers invented new forms of civic participation that soon shaped national politics.

Public Health

One of the most urgent problems of the big city was disease. In the late nineteenth century, scientists in Europe came to understand the role of germs and bacteria. Though researchers could not yet cure epidemic diseases, they could recommend effective measures for

A HINT TO BOARDS OF HEALTH—HOW OUR CITIES INVITE THE CHOLERA.

A Hint to Boards of Health

In 1884, *Frank Leslie's Illustrated Newspaper* urged municipal and state boards of health to work harder to protect urban children. When this cartoon appeared, New Yorkers were reading shocking reports of milk dealers who diluted milk with borax and other chemicals. Note the range of health threats that the cartoonist identifies. Rutherford B. Hayes Presidential Center.

prevention. Following up on New York City's victory against cholera in 1866, city and state officials began to champion more public health projects. With a major clean-water initiative for its industrial cities in the late nineteenth century, Massachusetts demonstrated that it could largely eliminate typhoid fever. Memphis, Tennessee, after a horrific yellow fever epidemic in 1878 that killed perhaps 12 percent of the population, invested in state-of-the-art sewage and drainage. Though the new system did not eliminate yellow fever, it unexpectedly cut death rates from typhoid and cholera, as well as infant deaths from waterborne disease. Other cities followed suit. By 1913, a nationwide survey of 198 cities found that they were spending an average of $1.28 per resident for public health measures.

The public health movement became one of the era's most visible and influential reforms. In cities, the impact of pollution was more obvious than it was in rural areas. Children played on piles of garbage, breathed toxic air, and consumed poisoned food, milk, and water. Infant mortality rates were shocking. In the early 1900s, a baby born to a Slavic woman in an American city had a one-in-three chance of dying in infancy. Outraged, urban reformers mobilized to demand safe water and better garbage collection. Hygiene reformers taught hand-washing and other techniques to fight the spread of tuberculosis.

Rising fears of unsafe food and drugs also led to government action to improve food and drug safety. At the end of the Civil War, federal and state governments provided no regulation of food or medical products. In 1904, a riveting series of articles in *Collier's* exposed many popular pharmaceutical products as "undiluted frauds." Two years later, journalist Upton Sinclair published his novel *The Jungle*, an exposé of labor exploitation in Chicago meatpacking plants. What caught the nation's attention was not Sinclair's account of workers' plight, but his descriptions of rotten meat and filthy packing conditions. With constituents up in arms, Congress passed the Pure Food and Drug Act and created the Food and Drug Administration (1906) to oversee compliance with the new law.

Hull House Playground, Chicago, 1906

When this postcard was made, the City of Chicago's Small Parks Commission had just taken over management of the playground from settlement workers at Hull House, who had created it. In a pattern repeated in many cities, social settlements introduced new institutions and ideas—such as safe places for urban children to play—and inspired municipal authorities to assume responsibility and control. Private Collection.

Reformers worked in other ways to make cities healthier and more beautiful to live in. Many municipalities adopted smoke-abatement laws, though they had limited success with enforcement until the post–World War I adoption of natural gas, which burned cleaner than coal. Recreation also received attention. Even before the Civil War, urban planners had established sanctuaries, like New York's Central Park, where city people could stroll, rest, and contemplate natural landscapes. By the turn of the twentieth century, the "City Beautiful" movement arose to advocate more and better urban park spaces. Though most parks still featured flower gardens and tree-lined paths, they also made room for skating rinks, tennis courts, baseball fields, and swimming pools. Many included play areas with swing sets and seesaws, promoted by the National Playground Association as a way to keep urban children safe and healthy.

Campaigns against Urban Prostitution

Distressed by the commercialization of sex in American cities, reformers also launched a nationwide campaign against prostitution. They warned, in dramatic language, of the perils of "white slavery," alleging (in spite of considerable evidence to the contrary) that young white women were being kidnapped and forced into prosti-

tution. In *The City's Perils* (1910), author Leona Prall Groetzinger wrote that young women arrived in the city "burning with high hope and filled with great resolves, but the remorseless city takes them, grinds them, crushes them, and at last deposits them in unknown graves."

Practical investigators found a more complex reality: Women entered prostitution as a result of many factors, including low-wage jobs, economic desperation, abandonment, and often sexual and domestic abuse. Some workingwomen—even working-class housewives—undertook occasional, casual prostitution to make ends meet. Women who bore a child out of wedlock were often shunned by their families and forced into prostitution. For decades, female reformers had tried to "rescue" such women and retrain them for more respectable employment. Results were, at best, mixed. Efforts to curb demand—that is, to focus on arresting and punishing men who employed prostitutes—proved unpopular with voters.

Nonetheless, with public concern mounting over "white slavery" and the payoffs that machine bosses exacted from brothel keepers, many cities appointed vice commissions in the early 1900s. A wave of brothel closings crested between 1909 and 1912, as police shut down red-light districts in cities nationwide. Meanwhile, Congress passed the Mann Act (1910) to prohibit the transportation of prostitutes across state lines.

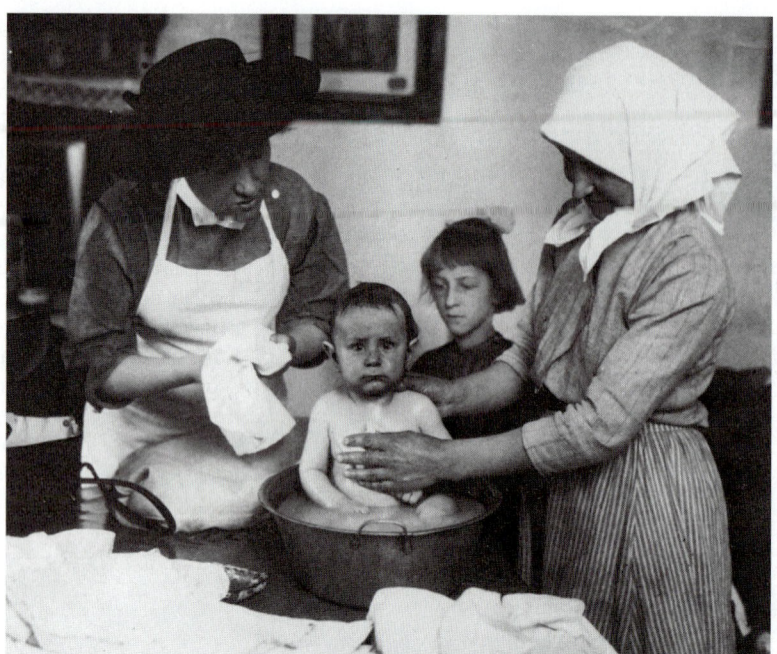

Saving the Children

In the early years at Hull House, Jane Addams recalled, toddlers sometimes arrived for kindergarten tipsy from a breakfast of bread soaked in wine. To settlement-house workers, the answer to such harmful practices lay in education, and so began the program of sending visiting nurses into immigrant homes. Nurses taught mothers the proper methods of caring for children — including, as this photograph shows, the daily infant bath, given in a dishpan if necessary.   Chicago Historical Society.

The crusade against prostitution accomplished its main goal — closing brothels — but in the long term it worsened the conditions under which many prostitutes worked. Though conditions in some brothels were horrific, sex workers who catered to wealthy clients made high wages and were relatively protected by madams, many of whom set strict rules for clients and provided medical care for their workers. In the wake of brothel closings, such women lost control of the prostitution trade. Instead, almost all sex workers became "streetwalkers" or "call girls," more vulnerable to violence and often earning lower wages than they had in earlier years.

The Movement for Social Settlements

The most celebrated urban reform institution of the industrial era, and one of the most effective, emerged out of Christian urban missions, educational and social welfare centers that were founded in the 1870s and 1880s. Some of these, like the Hampton Institute, sprang up to aid former slaves in Southern cities during Reconstruction; others, like Grace Baptist Temple and Samaritan Hospital in Philadelphia, served northern working-class and immigrant populations. To meet the needs of urban residents, missions offered such services as employment counseling, medical clinics, day care, and sometimes an athletic facility in cooperation with the Young Men's Christian Association (YMCA).

At the same time, other reformers were focusing on the plight of urban working-class women, tackling such problems as low wages and lack of day care for working mothers. Some groups created cooperative exchanges through which women could support themselves by selling needlework and crafts. In the 1880s, heiress Grace Dodge founded a network of working girls' clubs in New York City that featured housekeeping and self-improvement classes. In Davenport, Iowa, professional women and dozens of female clerks and wageworkers joined together to create the Working Women's Lend a Hand Club. The club rented a comfortable suite in the downtown business district where its members could rest, change clothes, or share lunch.

Such projects soon evolved into a far more ambitious project: the **social settlement**. The most famous of these was Hull House on Chicago's West Side, founded in 1889 by Jane Addams and her close companion Ellen Gates Starr. The project was an idea they had borrowed not only from American missions but also from Toynbee Hall, a London settlement they had visited while touring Europe. The dilapidated mansion they called Hull House, flanked by saloons in a neighborhood of mainly Italian immigrants, served as a community center and a spark plug for neighborhood betterment and political reform.

Jane Addams, a daughter of the middle class, first expected that Hull House would offer art classes and "cultural uplift" to the poor. But Addams's views quickly changed as she got to know her new neighbors and struggled to keep Hull House open during the depression of the 1890s. Addams's views were also reshaped

The Crusade against "White Slavery"

With the growth of large cities, prostitution was a major cause of concern in the Progressive Era. Though the number of prostitutes per capita in the United States was probably declining by 1900, the presence of red light districts was obvious; thousands of young women (as well as a smaller number of young men) were exploited in the sex trade. This image appeared in *The Great War on White Slavery*, published by the American Purity Foundation in 1911. It illustrates how immigrant women could be ensnared in the sex trade by alleged "friends" who offered them work. Reformers' denunciations of "white slavery" show an overt racial bias: While anti-prostitution campaigners reported on the exploitation of Asian and African American women, the victimization of white women received the greatest emphasis and most effectively grabbed the attention of prosperous, middle-class Americans. From *The Great War on White Slavery*, by Clifford G. Roe, 1911. Courtesy Vassar College Special Collections.

"FRIENDS" MEETING EMIGRANT GIRL AT THE DOCK
"The girl was met at New York by two 'friends' who took her in charge. These 'friends' were two of the most brutal of all the white slave traders who are in the traffic."
—U. S. Dist. Attorney Edwin W. Sims
Foreign girls are more helplessly at the mercy of white slave hunters than girls at home. Every year thousands of girls arriving in America from Italy, Sweden, Germany, etc., are never heard of again.

by her conversations with fellow Hull House worker Florence Kelley, who had studied in Europe and returned to the United States as a committed socialist. Dr. Alice Hamilton, who opened a pediatric clinic at Hull House, wrote that Addams "looked upon Hull House as a bridge between the classes. . . . She always held that this bridge was as much of a help to the well-to-do as to the poor." Settlements offered idealistic young people "a place where they could live as neighbors and give as much as they could of what they had."

Addams and her colleagues came to believe that immigrants already *knew* what they needed. What they lacked were the resources to fulfill those needs, as well as a strong political voice. These, settlement workers tried to provide. Hull House was typical in offering a bathhouse, a playground, a kindergarten, and a day care center. Hamilton soon investigated lead poisoning and other health threats at local factories. Addams, mean-

while, encouraged local women to inspect the neighborhood and bring back a list of dangers to health and safety. Together, they prepared a complaint to city council. The women, Addams wrote, had shown "both civic enterprise and moral conviction" in carrying out the project themselves, with her aid.

In the early twentieth century, social settlements sprang up all over the United States. They engaged in an array of public activities and took many forms. Some attached themselves to preexisting missions and African American colleges. Others were founded by energetic graduates of Smith, Vassar, and other women's colleges. The St. Elizabeth Center in St. Louis was run by Catholics; Boston's Hebrew Industrial School was Jewish. Whatever their origins, social settlements sought to serve poor urban neighborhoods. In the words of Jane Addams, they were "an experimental effort to aid in the solution of the social and industrial problems which are engendered by the modern condition of life in a great city."

Social settlements used their resources and influence in many ways. They opened libraries and gymnasiums for working men and women. They operated employment bureaus, penny savings banks, and cooperative kitchens where tired families could purchase a meal at the end of the day. (Addams humbly closed her Hull House kitchen when she found that her bland New England cooking had little appeal for Italians, who were accustomed to spicier food. Her coworker, Alice Hamilton, became a convert to the health benefits of garlic.) In cities across the country, settlement workers fought city hall to get better schools and factory safety laws. At the Henry Street Settlement in New York, Lillian Wald developed a system of visiting nurses to improve health in tenement wards. Mary McDowell, head of the University of Chicago Settlement, operated a citizenship school for recent immigrants.

Settlement work served as a springboard for other projects. Hull House worker Julia Lathrop, for example, investigated the plight of teenagers caught in the criminal justice system. She drafted a proposal for separate juvenile courts and persuaded Chicago to adopt it. Pressuring the city to experiment with better rehabilitation strategies for juveniles convicted of crime, Lathrop created a model for juvenile court systems across the United States. Other settlement workers went on to prominent national reform careers. Jane Addams and Florence Kelley of Hull House became two of America's most famous advocates for children, labor, women's rights, and international peace.

Settlements were an early, crucial proving ground for the emerging profession of social work, which transformed the provision of public welfare. Social workers rejected the older model of private Christian charity, dispensed by well-meaning middle-class people to those in need. Instead, social workers defined themselves as caseworkers who served as advocates of social justice. Like many reformers of their era, they allied themselves with the new social sciences, such as sociology and economics, and undertook statistical surveys and other systematic methods for gathering facts. Social work proved to be an excellent opportunity for educated women who sought professional careers. By 1920, women made up 62 percent of U.S. social workers.

Cities and National Politics

Despite the work of reformers, the problems of the industrial city grew more rapidly than remedies for them could be found. To overcome the ills of industri-

alization—which wrought transformations at the national and even global level—city governments needed allies in state and national politics. That urgent need was made clear in New York City by a shocking event on March 25, 1911. On that Saturday afternoon, just before quitting time, a fire broke out at the Triangle Shirtwaist Company. It quickly spread through the three floors the company occupied at the top of a ten-story building. Panicked workers discovered that, despite fire safety laws, employers had locked the emergency doors to prevent theft. Dozens of Triangle workers, mostly young immigrant women, were trapped in the flames. Many leaped to their deaths; the rest never reached the windows. The average age of the 146 people who died was just nineteen (see Comparing American Voices, "'These Dead Bodies Were the Answer': The Triangle Fire," pp. 616–617).

Shocked by this horrific event, New Yorkers responded across lines of class, religion, and ethnicity. Many remembered that, only a year earlier, shirtwaist workers had walked off the job to protest abysmal safety and working conditions—and that the owners of Triangle, among other employers, had broken the strike. Facing public demands for action, New York State appointed a factory commission that developed a remarkable program of labor reform: fifty-six laws dealing with such issues as fire hazards, unsafe machines, and wages and working hours for women and children. The chairman and vice chairman of the commission were Robert F. Wagner and Alfred E. Smith, both Tammany Hall politicians then serving in the state legislature. They established the commission, participated fully in its work, and marshaled party regulars to pass the proposals into law—all with the approval of Tammany. The labor code that resulted was the most advanced in the United States. Tammany's response to the Triangle fire showed that it was conceding to reform: the social and economic problems of the industrial city had outgrown the power of party machines. Only stronger state and national laws could bar industrial firetraps, alleviate sweatshop conditions, and improve slums. Machine politicians like Wagner and Smith saw that Tammany had to change or die.

The political aftermath of the Triangle fire demonstrated how challenges posed by industrial cities pushed politics in new directions, not only by transforming urban government but also by helping to build broader movements for reform. At the end of the Civil War, the nation's political and cultural standard had been set by native-born, rural, Protestant, and middle-class Americans. Over the decades that followed, people had thronged to the great cities from rural areas and from

The Triangle Fire

Artist John Sloan's drawing captures better than any photograph the horror of the 1911 Triangle fire. According to observers, a number of young workers, having no other way to escape the flames, chose to fall to their deaths in each other's arms. The fireman who cannot bear to watch may be a product of Sloan's imagination, but the anguish he felt is true enough: When the fire trucks arrived, they did not have the equipment to save anyone. Not only were the ladders too short, but the safety nets were too weak—the bodies simply shot right through to the ground.   *Harper's Weekly*, May 8, 1915.

countries around the world. They helped build America into a global industrial power. In the process, they created an electorate that was far more ethnically, racially, and religiously diverse then ever before. This diversity was most obvious in the cities.

In the era of industrialization, some rural and native-born commentators warned that immigrants were "inferior breeds" who would "mongrelize" American culture. But urban political leaders defended cultural pluralism, expressing their appreciation—even admiration—for Southern and Eastern European immigrants, Catholics and Jews who sought a better life in the United States. At the same time, urban reformers worked to improve the conditions of work, housing, and daily living for the diverse residents of American cities. It is not surprising, then, that cities played a pivotal role in national efforts to remedy the ills of industrialization. City problems, and the innovative solutions proposed by urban leaders, held a central place in the national consciousness as Americans turned to the task of progressive reform.

- If you had lived in a large American city in the post–Civil War decades, might you have joined any of the reform movements working to improve public health, morals, and welfare? If not, why not? If so, which ones, and why?

- What were the goals of the founders of social settlements? How did those goals evolve, and what roles did settlements play in their communities?

- What effect did the Triangle fire have on politics? Why do you think its impact was so wide-ranging?

SUMMARY

After 1865, American cities grew at an unprecedented rate, and urban populations swelled with workers from rural areas and abroad. To move burgeoning populations around the city, cities pioneered innovative forms of mass transit. Skyscrapers came to mark urban skylines, and new electric lighting systems encouraged nightlife. Neighborhoods divided along class and ethnic lines, with white middle-class people moving out to new suburban communities. Working-class city dwellers lived in crowded, shoddily built tenements. Immigrants developed new ethnic cultures in their neighborhoods, while racism followed African American migrants from country to city. At the same time, new forms of popular urban culture bridged class and ethnic lines, challenging traditional sexual norms and gender roles. Popular journalism rose to prominence and helped build rising sympathy for reform.

Industrial cities confronted a variety of new political challenges. Despite notable achievements, established machine governments could not address urban problems through traditional means. Forward-looking politicians took the initiative and implemented a range of political, labor, and social reforms. Urban reformers also

"These Dead Bodies Were the Answer": The Triangle Fire

Entire books have been written about the catastrophic 1911 fire at the Triangle Shirtwaist Company in New York City. The following excerpts are from documents by four contemporaries who in various ways played a part in the Triangle tragedy and its aftermath. Note the different audiences that these speakers and authors were addressing, and the lessons that each one draws from this horrific event.

William G. Shepherd, Reporter

William G. Shepherd's eyewitness account appeared in newspapers across the country. Working for the United Press, Shepherd phoned the story to his editor as he watched the unfolding tragedy.

I was walking through Washington Square when a puff of smoke issuing from a factory building caught my eye. I reached the building before the alarm was turned in. I saw every feature of the tragedy visible from outside the building. I learned a new sound—a more horrible sound than description can picture. It was the thud of a speeding, living body on a stone sidewalk. . . .

I looked up—saw that there were scores of girls at the windows. The flames from the floor below were beating in their faces. Somehow I knew that they, too, must come down, and something within me—something I didn't know was there—steeled me.

I even watched one girl falling. Waving her arms, trying to keep her body upright until the very instant she struck the sidewalk, she was trying to balance herself. Then came the thud—then a silent, unmoving pile of clothing and twisted, broken limbs. . . .

On the sidewalk lay heaps of broken bodies. A policeman later went about with tags, which he fastened with wire to the wrists of the dead girls, numbering each with a lead pencil, and I saw him fasten tag no. 54 to the wrist of a girl who wore an engagement ring. . . .

The floods of water from the firemen's hose that ran into the gutter were actually stained red with blood. I looked upon the heap of dead bodies and I remembered these girls were the shirtwaist makers. I remembered their great strike of last year in which these same girls had demanded more sanitary conditions and more safety precautions in the shops. These dead bodies were the answer.

Stephen S. Wise, Rabbi

A week after the fire, on April 2, 1911, a memorial meeting was held at the Metropolitan Opera House. One of the speakers, Rabbi Stephen S. Wise, a prominent figure in New York reform circles, made the following remarks.

This was not an inevitable disaster which man could neither foresee nor control. We might have foreseen it, and some of us did; we might have controlled it, but we chose not to do so. . . . It is not a question of enforcement of law nor of inadequacy of law. We have the wrong kind of laws and the wrong kind of enforcement. Before insisting upon inspection and enforcement, let us lift up the industrial standards so as to make conditions worth inspecting, and, if inspected, certain to afford security to workers. . . . And when we go before the legislature of the state, and demand increased appropriations in order to ensure the possibility of a sufficient number of inspectors, we will not forever be put off with the answer: We have no money.

The lesson of the hour is that while property is good, life is better; that while possessions are valuable, life is priceless. The meaning of the hour is that the life of the lowliest worker in the nation is sacred and inviolable, and, if that sacred human right be violated, we shall stand adjudged and condemned before the tribunal of God and history.

Rose Schneiderman, Trade Unionist

Rose Schneiderman also spoke at the Metropolitan Opera House meeting. At age thirteen, she had gone to work in a garment factory like Triangle Shirtwaist's and, under the tutelage of the Women's Trade Union League, had become a labor organizer. The strike she mentions in her speech was popularly known as the Uprising of the 30,000, a nearly spontaneous walkout in 1909 that launched the union movement in the women's garment trades.

I would be a traitor to these poor burned bodies if I came here to talk good fellowship. We have tried you good people of the public and we have found you wanting. The old Inquisition had its rack and its thumbscrews and its instruments of torture with iron teeth. We know what these things are today; the iron teeth are our necessities, the thumbscrews are the high-powered and swift machinery close to which we must work, and the rack is here in the firetrap structures that will destroy us the minute they catch on fire.

This is not the first time girls have been burned alive in the city. . . . Every year thousands of us are maimed. The life of men and women is so cheap and property is so sacred. There are so many of us for one job it matters little if 146 of us are burned to death.

We have tried you citizens; we are trying you now, and you have a couple of dollars for the sorrowing mothers, brothers, and sisters by way of a charity gift. But every time the workers come out in the only way they know to protest against conditions which are unbearable the strong hand of the law is allowed to press down heavily upon us . . . [and] beats us back, when we rise, into the conditions that make life unbearable.

I can't talk fellowship to you who are gathered here. Too much blood has been spilled. I know from my experience it is up to the working people to save themselves. The only way they can save themselves is by a strong working-class movement.

Max D. Steuer, Lawyer

After finding physical evidence of the locked door that had blocked escape from the fire, New York's district attorney brought manslaughter charges against the Triangle proprietors, Max Blanck and Isaac Harris, who hired in their defense the best, highest-priced trial attorney in town, Max D. Steuer. In this talk, delivered some time later to a rapt audience of lawyers, Steuer described how he undermined the testimony of the key witness for the prosecution, by suggesting that she had been coached to recite her answer. The trial judge instructed the jury that they could only convict Blanck and Harris if it was *certain* they had known the emergency exits were locked; as Steuer notes, the jury voted to acquit.

There are many times, many times when a witness has given evidence very hurtful to your cause and you say, "No questions," and dismiss him or her in the hope that the jury will dismiss the evidence too. [*Laughter.*] But can you do that when the jury is weeping, and the little girl witness is weeping too? [*Laughter.*] . . . There is one [rule] that commands what not to do. Do not attack the witness. Suavely, politely, genially, toy with the story.

In the instant case, about half an hour was consumed by the examiner [Steuer]. . . . Very little progress was made; but the tears had stopped. And then [the witness] was asked, "Now, Rose, in your own words, and in your own way will you tell the jury everything you did, everything

you said, and everything you saw from the moment you first saw flames."

The question was put in precisely the same words that the District Attorney had put it, and little Rose started her answer with exactly the same word that she had started it to the District Attorney . . . and the only change in her recital was that Rose left out one word. And then Rose was asked, "Didn't you leave out a word that you put in when you answered it before?" . . . So Rose started to repeat to herself the answer [*laughter*], and as she came to the missing word she said, "Oh, yes!" and supplied it; and thereupon the examiner went on to an entirely different subject. . . . [W]hen again he [asked her to repeat her story] . . . Rose started with the same word and finished with the same word, her recital being identical with her first reply to the same question.

The jurymen were not weeping. Rose had not hurt the case, and the defendants were acquitted; there was not a word of reflection at any time during that trial upon poor little Rose.

Source: Leon Stein, ed., *Out of the Sweatshop* (New York: Quadrangle Books, 1977), 188–198.

ANALYZING THE EVIDENCE

- **The hardest task of the historian is to conjure up the reality of the past — to say, "This is what it was really like." That's where eyewitness evidence like the reporter Shepherd's comes in. What is there in his account that you could only obtain from an eyewitness?**

- **Both Rabbi Wise and Rose Schneiderman were incensed at the Triangle carnage, yet their speeches are quite different. In what ways? What conclusions do you draw about the different motivations and arguments that led to reform?**

- **Max Steuer and Rose Schneiderman came from remarkably similar backgrounds. They were roughly the same age, grew up in poverty on the Lower East Side, and started out as child workers in the garment factories. The differences in their adult lives speak to the varieties of immigrant experience in America. Does anything in their statements help to account for their differing life paths? What might have happened if Rose Schneiderman, rather than "little Rose," had faced Max Steuer on the witness stand?**

launched campaigns to address public health, morals, and welfare. They did so through a variety of innovative institutions, most notably social settlements, which brought affluent Americans into working-class neighborhoods to learn, cooperate, and advocate on behalf of their neighborhoods. Such projects began to increase Americans' acceptance of urban diversity and their confidence in government's ability to solve the problems of industrialization.

CHAPTER REVIEW QUESTIONS

- What were the major features of industrial cities that arose in the United States in the late nineteenth and early twentieth centuries? What institutions and innovations helped make urban life distinctive?

- What were the limitations and the achievements of urban governments run by ethnic political machines?

- Why did so many reform initiatives of the early twentieth century emerge in large cities? What were some of those initiatives, and what was their political impact?

FOR FURTHER EXPLORATION

On industrial cities see Sam Bass Warner, *Streetcar Suburbs* (1962); Carl Condit, *Rise of the New York Skyscraper* (1996); and Harold L. Platt, *The Electric City* (1991). On urban life see Gunther Barth, *City People* (1982); David Nasaw, *Going Out* (1993); Joanne Meyerowitz, *Women Adrift* (1988); Howard P. Chudacoff, *The Age of the Bachelor* (1999); Kathy Peiss, *Cheap Amusements* (1986); Tera Hunter, *To 'Joy My Freedom* (1997); and George Chauncey, *Gay New York* (1994). On popular music, see Richard Crawford, *America's Musical Life* (2001). Among many books on immigrant life see Susan Glenn, *Daughters of the Shtetl* (1990), and George Sanchez, *Becoming Mexican American* (1993).

On urban Progressivism see Maureen A. Flanagan, *America Reformed* (2007), John Buenker, *Urban Liberalism and Progressive Reform* (1973), and Eric Rauchway's *Blessed Among Nations* (2006). On the settlement movement, Jane Addams's *Twenty Years at Hull House* (1910) is a must; see also Allen Davis, *Spearheads for Reform* (1984); Elisabeth Lasch-Quinn, *Black Neighbors* (1993); Robert Handy, *The Social Gospel in America* (1966); and Ralph Luker, *The Social Gospel in Black and White* (1991).

On prostitution and campaigns against it, see Ruth Rosen, *The Lost Sisterhood* (1982). On the Triangle fire see David von Drehle, *Triangle: The Fire That Changed America* (2003), and Leon Stein, *The Triangle Fire* (1962).

TEST YOUR KNOWLEDGE

To assess your command of the material in this chapter, see the Online Study Guide at **bedfordstmartins.com/henretta**.

For Web sites, images, and documents related to topics and places in this chapter, visit **bedfordstmartins.com/makehistory**.

TIMELINE

1866	New York City contains cholera epidemic
1876	Alexander Graham Bell invents telephone
1878	Yellow fever epidemic in Memphis, Tennessee
1879	First elevated railroad opened in Chicago Edison invents incandescent light bulb
1885	First skyscraper completed in Chicago
1887	First electric trolley system built in Richmond, Virginia
1889	Jane Addams and Ellen Gates Starr found Hull House in Chicago
1893	Ragtime introduced to national audience at Chicago World's Fair
1897	First subway line opened in Boston
1903	National Trade Union League founded
1904	Subway running the length of Manhattan completed
1906	Food and Drug Administration established
1910	Mann Act prohibits transportation of prostitutes across state lines
1911	National Urban League founded Triangle Shirtwaist Company fire in New York
1913	Fifty-five-story Woolworth Building completed in New York

CHAPTER 20

Whose Government? Politics, Populists, and Progressives, 1880–1917

"We are living in a grand and wonderful time," declared Kansas political organizer Mary E. Lease in 1891. "Men, women and children are in commotion, discussing the mighty problems of the day." She declared this "movement among the masses" to be based on the words of Jesus: "Whatsoever ye would that men should do unto you, do ye even so unto them." Between the 1880s and the 1910s, thousands of reformers like Lease confronted the problems of an industrializing nation. Lease herself stumped not only for the People's Party, which sought more government regulation of the economy, but also for the Knights of Labor, the Woman's Christian Temperance Union, and the woman suffrage movement. In addition, she advocated new initiatives in education and public health.

Between the end of Reconstruction and the start of World War I, prominent political reform movements focused on four main goals: making politics more effective, limiting the power of big business, ameliorating poverty, and promoting social justice. In the 1880s and 1890s, labor unions and farm radicals took the lead in critiquing the new industrial order and demanding change. Over time, more and more middle-class and elite Americans also took up the call, eventually earning the name **progressives**. On the whole, middle-class progressives proposed more limited measures than farmer and labor advocates did, but since they wielded more political clout, they often had greater success in winning passage of new laws. Thus, while their goals and tactics differed, both radicals and progressives played important roles in advancing reform.

Although historians call this era of political agitation and innovation the Progressive Era, no single group led the way. On the contrary, prominent reformers took opposing views on such questions as immigration policy, racial justice, women's rights, and imperialism. Most middle-class progressives were initially hostile to the sweeping critiques of capitalism advanced by farmer-labor movements and by socialists, but over time some adopted more radical

Coxey's Army on the March, 1894

During the severe depression of the 1890s, Ohio businessman Jacob Coxey organized unemployed men for a peaceful march to the U.S. Capitol, to plead for an emergency jobs program. They called themselves the Commonweal of Christ but won the nickname "Coxey's Army." Though it failed to win sympathy from Congress, the army's march on Washington — one of the nation's first — inspired similar groups to set out from many cities. Here, Coxey's group nears Washington, D.C. The man on horseback is Carl Browne, one of the group's leaders and a flamboyant publicist. As the marchers entered Washington, Coxey's seventeen-year-old daughter Mamie, dressed as the "Goddess of Peace," led the procession on a white Arabian horse. Library of Congress.

ideas themselves. Dramatic changes in national politics also shaped the course of reform. Close party competition early in the era gave way to Republican control between 1894 and 1910, followed by a period of Democrat-led progressivism during the presidency of Woodrow Wilson (1913–1919). Progressives gave their era its name, not because they acted as a unified force, but because they engaged in diverse, energetic movements to improve American life.

Reform Visions, 1880–1892

In the 1880s, radical farmers' groups and the Knights of Labor provided the most urgent, powerful challenge to industrialization (see Chapter 17). At the same time, groups like the Woman's Christian Temperance Union began to lay the groundwork for middle-class progressivism, especially among women (see Chapter 18). Though they had different goals, these groups confronted similar dilemmas as they entered the political arena. Should they work through existing political parties, or create new ones? Or should they instead generate pressure from the outside, through nonpartisan organizations? At different times, reformers tried all these strategies as they wrestled with the realities of post-Reconstruction politics.

Electoral Politics after Reconstruction

The collapse of Reconstruction ushered in a period of high voter turnout and fierce partisan conflict. Republicans and Democrats traded control of the Senate three times between 1880 and 1894, and control of the House five times (Table 20.1). The causes of this up-

TABLE 20.1		
Composition and Control of Congress, 1869–1897		
Congress	**Senate/House** **Seats**	**Entry of States and Shifts in Partisan Control**
41st; 1869–1871	68 / 226	1870: Last ex-Confederate states reenter Union
42nd; 1871–1873	74 / 243	
43rd; 1873–1875	74 / 292	1874 election: House control shifts to Democrats
		1876: Colorado enters Union
44th, 45th; 1875–1879	76 / 293	1878 election: Senate control shifts to Democrats
46th; 1879–1881	76 / 293	1880 election: House control shifts to Republicans
47th; 1881–1883	76 / 293	1882 election: Senate control shifts to Republicans
48th; 1883–1885	76 / 325	1884 election: House control shifts to Democrats
49th; 1885–1887	76 / 325	
50th; 1887–1889	76 / 325	1888 election: House control shifts to Republicans
		1889: Montana, North and South Dakota, and Washington enter Union
		1890: Idaho and Wyoming enter Union
51st; 1889–1891	88 / 332	1890 election: House control shifts to Democrats
52nd; 1891–1893	88 / 332	1892 election: Senate control shifts to Democrats
53rd; 1896–1895	88 / 356	1894 election: Control of both houses shifts to Republicans
		1896: Utah enters Union
54th; 1895–1897	90 / 357	

Republicans and Democrats traded control of both the Senate and the House of Representatives several times during the tumultuous era of Reconstruction and its aftermath. Equally striking were changes in the size of Congress, based on the nation's geographic expansion and rapid population growth. Note how the entry of new Western states, as well as adjustments after each census (implemented soon after 1870, 1880, and 1890), increased the numbers of senators and representatives.

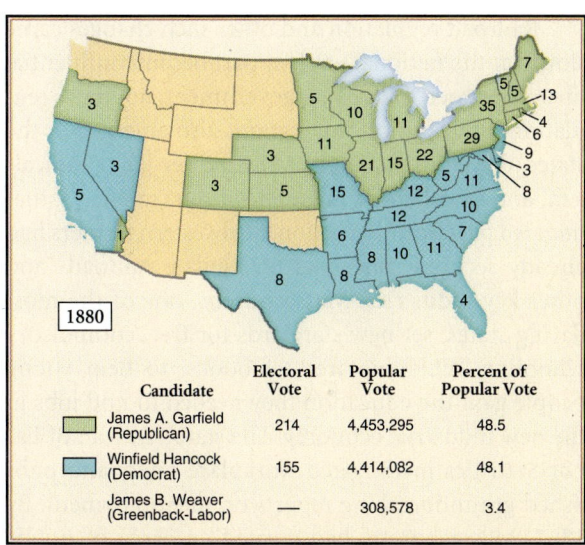

Candidate	Electoral Vote	Popular Vote	Percent of Popular Vote
James A. Garfield (Republican)	214	4,453,295	48.5
Winfield Hancock (Democrat)	155	4,414,082	48.1
James B. Weaver (Greenback-Labor)	—	308,578	3.4

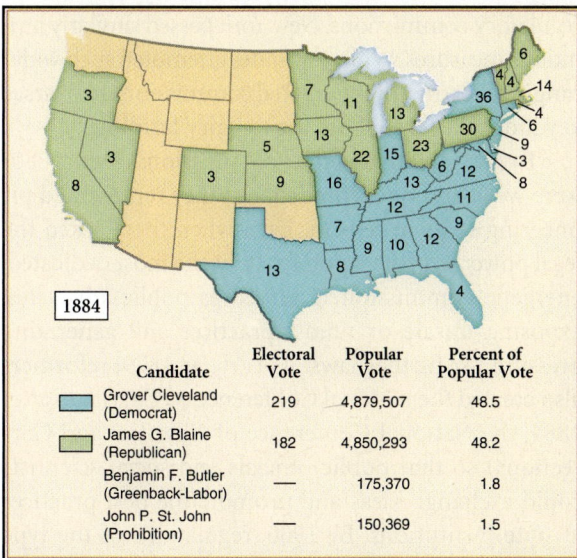

Candidate	Electoral Vote	Popular Vote	Percent of Popular Vote
Grover Cleveland (Democrat)	219	4,879,507	48.5
James G. Blaine (Republican)	182	4,850,293	48.2
Benjamin F. Butler (Greenback-Labor)	—	175,370	1.8
John P. St. John (Prohibition)	—	150,369	1.5

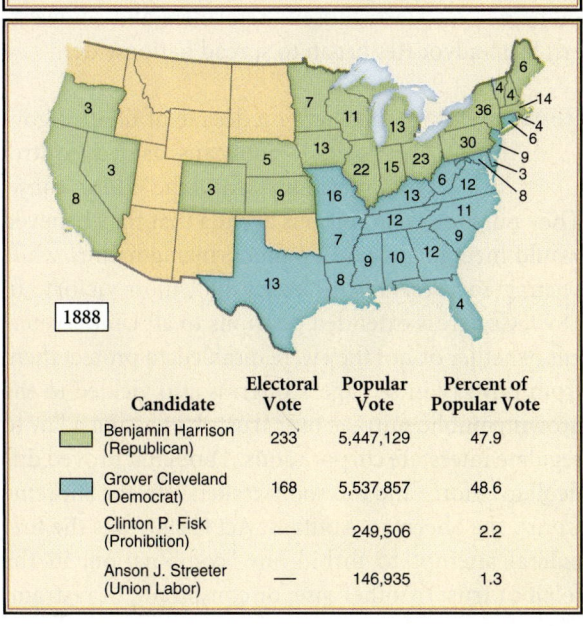

Candidate	Electoral Vote	Popular Vote	Percent of Popular Vote
Benjamin Harrison (Republican)	233	5,447,129	47.9
Grover Cleveland (Democrat)	168	5,537,857	48.6
Clinton P. Fisk (Prohibition)	—	249,506	2.2
Anson J. Streeter (Union Labor)	—	146,935	1.3

MAP 20.1

The Presidential Elections of 1880, 1884, and 1888

The anatomy of hard-fought, narrowly won presidential campaigns is evident in this trio of electoral maps of the 1880s. First, note the equal division of the popular vote between Republicans and Democrats. Second, note the persistent pattern of electoral votes, as states overwhelmingly went to the same party in all three elections. Here, we can identify who determined the outcomes—"swing" states, such as New York and Indiana, whose vote shifted every four years and always in favor of the winning candidate.

heaval included northerners' disillusionment with Reconstruction and the resurgence of ex-Confederates, who regained a strong base in Congress. Dizzying population growth and the entry of new western states also changed the size and shape of Congress, contributing to political uncertainty.

Heated party competition drew Americans into the fray: Proportionately more voters turned out in presidential elections from 1876 to 1892 than at any other time in American history. The presidents of this era—Rutherford B. Hayes, James Garfield, Chester Arthur, Grover Cleveland, and Benjamin Harrison—are often remembered as colorless and ineffective. But they had limited room to maneuver in a period of extremely tight competition. Hayes and Harrison both won in the electoral college but lost the popular vote. In 1880, Garfield won the popular vote by a margin of less than 0.5 percent. Four years later, Cleveland won only 29,214 more votes than his opponent, James Blaine, while almost half a million voters rejected both major candidates (Map 20.1). With key states decided by razor-thin margins, both Republicans and Democrats engaged in vote buying, ballot-box stuffing, and other forms of fraud.

Close elections inspired fierce party loyalty among many voters. As early as the 1880s, though, other Americans became frustrated with electoral politics. Republicans had enacted Emancipation and other major achievements, but after Reconstruction ended they gradually became defenders of the economic status quo. National leaders of the Democratic Party, meanwhile, at first resisted the idea that industrialization might signal the need to use government power in new ways. Disillusioned with both Republicans and Democrats, some reformers created new parties. For a brief moment in the early 1890s, it appeared that the new People's Party might displace Republicans in the South or Democrats in the West and become a major party in its own right. Though third-party strategies ultimately failed, they made for lively politics in the 1880s and 1890s. By putting important policy ideas on the table, new parties helped build national momentum for reform.

New Initiatives in the 1880s

One of the first federal reforms enacted in the post-Reconstruction years resulted from tragedy. On July 2, 1881, only four months after entering the White House, President James Garfield was shot. After lingering for several agonizing months, he died. Most historians now believe the assassin, Charles Guiteau, suffered from mental illness. But reformers at the time blamed the **spoils system**, arguing that Guiteau had killed Garfield out of disappointment in the scramble for **patronage**, the granting of government jobs to loyal party supporters. In the wake of Garfield's death, Congress passed the Pendleton Act (1883), establishing the nonpartisan Civil Service Commission to fill federal jobs by examination. Initially, civil service applied to only 10 percent of such jobs, but the act laid the groundwork for a sweeping transformation of public employment. By the 1910s, Congress extended the act to cover most federal positions, and cities and states across the country enacted similar laws, dramatically reducing the power of political parties to control government office holding.

Leaders of the civil service movement included many proponents of classical liberalism. At the time, the word *liberal* was used very differently than it is today. It described those Americans, especially former Republicans, who became disillusioned with Reconstruction and advocated more limited and professionalized government. Many had opposed President Ulysses S. Grant's reelection in 1872. In 1884, they again left the Republican Party because they could not stomach its scandal-tainted candidate, James Blaine. Liberal Republicans—ridiculed by their enemies as Mugwumps (fence-sitters who had their "mugs" on one side of the fence and their "wumps" on the other)—threw their support to Democrat Grover Cleveland. They believed Cleveland shared their vision of smaller government. After he entered the White House, Cleveland showed that to a large extent he did share their views. But in 1887, responding to pressure from farmer-labor advocates in the Democratic Party, he signed the Hatch Act and the Interstate Commerce Act (see Chapter 17), two major bills that expanded federal power. The Interstate Commerce Act, by establishing a national commission to investigate and regulate railroad shipping rates, set an important precedent for later regulation.

Railroad regulation and other such changes came slowly at the national level, in part because influential liberals pressed for smaller government, not more regulation. But political innovations also emerged in the states, driven in some places by farmer-labor radicalism, and in others by Republican reform energy that lingered past Reconstruction. Midwestern farmers had already secured state laws to regulate railroads and other key industries. Massachusetts, one of the most daring states, set new standards for free, compulsory schooling, including free textbooks, to help young people gain the education they needed to find jobs in the new industrial economy. The state's Bureau of Labor Statistics investigated workplace safety and published groundbreaking reports on unemployment. By 1887, Massachusetts had created an array of public regulatory commissions. New York passed similarly ambitious measures. While few states attempted such wide-ranging reforms, many created commissions to oversee key industries from banking to dairy farming.

By later standards, state commissions of the 1880s were weak and underfunded, but they represented pioneering steps in reform. Even when they lacked the legal power to protect public safety, the most dedicated, energetic commissioners served as public advocates, exposing unsafe or unjust practices and generating pressure for further laws. As early as 1879, reformers also created the national Conference of Charities (after 1884, the National Conference of Charities and Corrections) so that public officials and social scientists could exchange ideas and promote the best practices at state institutions. By 1900, regulations of the type pioneered by Massachusetts reformers and Midwestern farm advocates began to spread nationwide.

Republican Activism   In 1888, after a decade of divided government, Republicans gained control of both Congress and the White House. They pursued an ambitious agenda that they believed would meet the needs of a modernizing nation, while seeking to preserve the legacy of Union victory. In 1890, Congress extended pensions to all Union veterans, whether or not they were disabled, to protect them from poverty in old age. Congress also yielded to the growing public outrage over trusts by passing a law to regulate interstate corporations. Though it proved difficult to enforce and was soon weakened by the Supreme Court, the Sherman Antitrust Act (1890) was the first federal attempt to forbid any "combination, in the form of trust or otherwise, or conspiracy, in restraint of trade."

BILLION-DOLLARISM 'HOLE

Harrison and the Billion-Dollar Congress

President Benjamin Harrison and Republican congressional leaders embarked on ambitious initiatives in 1890. These included an expanded pension program for Union veterans, new steel-hulled battleships for the U.S. Navy, and other expensive programs, prompting critics to dub this the "Billion-Dollar Congress." This cartoon represents a classical liberal perspective – it praises former President Grover Cleveland for his fiscal restraint and criticizes his successor, Benjamin Harrison, for increased federal spending. Unfriendly cartoonists often illustrated Harrison in a very large hat – a sly suggestion that the hat of Benjamin's grandfather, President William Henry Harrison, was too large for the grandson to wear (that is, William Henry Harrison was a political giant and his grandson was of lesser stature). Cartoonists for *Puck* drew the hat larger and larger, and Benjamin Harrison smaller and smaller, until he was defeated for reelection. Then the hat remained, but Harrison vanished completely.   Library of Congress.

President Benjamin Harrison also sought to protect black voting rights in the South. Warned during his campaign that the issue was politically risky, Harrison vowed that he would not "purchase the presidency by a compact of silence upon this question." He found allies in Congress. Massachusetts representative Henry Cabot Lodge drafted a bill to create a bipartisan federal elections board. Whenever 100 citizens, in any district or city of 20,000 or more, appealed for intervention, the board would investigate. If it found sufficient evidence of fraud or disenfranchisement, the board could work with federal courts to seat the rightful winner. Despite cries of outrage from southern Democrats—who warned that this so-called force bill meant "Negro supremacy"—the House passed the measure.

But the bill met deep resistance in the Senate. Northern liberals, who wanted the "best men" to rule through professional expertise, thought it provided for too much democracy. Urban machine bosses denounced the threat of federal interference in the cities. Southerners threatened to boycott northern products if the law went into effect, frightening manufacturers. Most damaging of all was the opposition of Republicans from the trans-Mississippi West. With the entry of ten new states since 1863, and thus twenty new U.S. senators, westerners had gained enormous clout. Senator William Stewart of Nevada, who had southern family ties, claimed that Lodge's proposal would bring "monarchy or revolution." He and his allies killed the bill by a single vote.

The defeat was a devastating blow to those who sought to defend black voting rights. In the verdict of one furious Republican leader who supported Lodge's proposal, the episode marked the demise of the party of Emancipation. "Think of it," he fumed. "Nevada, barely a respectable *county*, furnished two senators to betray the Republican Party and the rights of citizenship." In fact, many of the Republicans' 1890 programs—including Lodge's bill, even though it never became law—proved unpopular. In a sweeping repudiation of Republican policies, Democrats took control of the House in the 1890 elections. Two years later, by the largest margin seen in twenty years, they reelected Grover Cleveland to the presidency for his nonconsecutive second term. Congress abandoned all further attempts to enforce fair elections in the South.

The Populist Program

When Democrats took power in Washington, they faced rising pressure from rural voters in the South and West who had organized the Farmers' Alliance. Some savvy politicians responded quickly, as they had done in passing the Interstate Commerce Act. Iowa Democrats, for example, took up some of farmers' demands, forestalling the creation of a separate farmer-labor party in that state. But other politicians listened to Alliance pleas and did nothing. It was a response they came to regret.

In Kansas, a state chock-full of Union veterans and railroad boosters, Republicans dominated the political

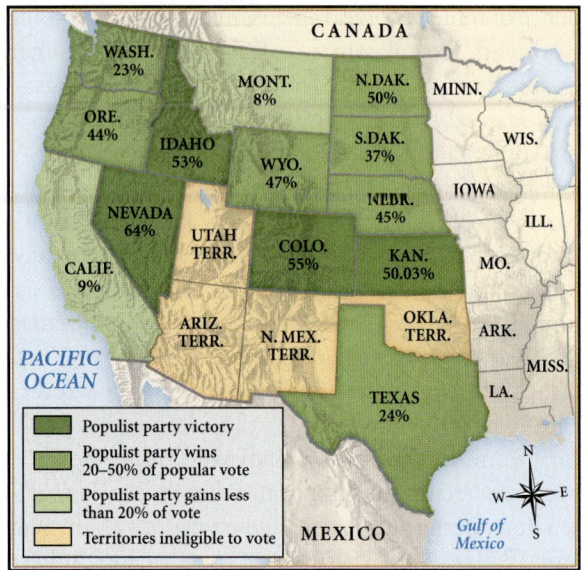

MAP 20.2

The Heyday of Western Populism, 1892

This map shows the percentage of the popular vote won by James B. Weaver, the People's Party candidate, in the presidential election of 1892. Except in California and Montana, the Populists won broad support across the West and genuinely threatened the established parties in that region.

scene. They treated the Kansas Farmers' Alliance with contempt. In a breakthrough election in 1890, the alliance joined with the state Knights of Labor and created the People's Party. They stunned the nation by capturing four-fifths of the lower house of the Kansas legislature and most of the state's congressional seats. The victory electrified Knights of Labor and Farmers' Alliance members across the country. In July 1892, after conferences in Cincinnati and St. Louis, delegates from these groups met at Omaha, Nebraska, and formally created the national People's Party. They nominated former Union general and Greenback-Labor leader James B. Weaver for president. In November, the Populists, as they became known, captured a million votes and carried four western states (Map 20.2).

In recognizing an "irrepressible conflict between capital and labor," the Populists split from the mainstream parties, calling for a stronger state that would adopt new measures to protect ordinary Americans. "We believe," declared their Omaha Platform in 1892, "that the power of government—in other words, of the people—should be expanded as rapidly and as far as the good sense of an intelligent people and the teachings of experience shall justify, to the end that oppression, injustice and poverty should eventually cease in the land." Populists called for public ownership of railroad and telegraph systems, protection of land and natural resources from monopoly and foreign ownership, a federal income tax on the highest incomes, and a looser monetary policy to help borrowers.

Riding to a Populist Rally, Dickinson County, Kansas, 1890s

Farm families in wagons carry their banners to a local meeting of the People's Party. Men, women, and children often traveled together to campaign events, which included not only stump speeches but also picnics, glee club music, and other family entertainments.   Kansas State Historical Society.

Though farmers' votes were its chief instrument of victory, the People's Party attracted support from other groups. Labor planks won the movement a strong base among such groups as Alabama steelworkers and Rocky Mountain miners. Antiliquor and woman suffrage leaders, including Frances Willard and Elizabeth Cady Stanton, attended the party's organizing conferences in 1891 and 1892, hoping that Populists would adopt their causes, but they were disappointed. In addition to divisions among reformers with different goals and priorities, the bitter legacies of the Civil War also hampered the party. Southern Democrats warned that the Populists were Radical Republicans in disguise; northeastern Republicans claimed that southern "Pops" were ex-Confederates plotting another round of treason. In the midst of these heated debates, the Populists and their opponents suddenly confronted a national economic crisis.

- **What factors shaped party politics after the end of Reconstruction? In the 1880s, what important measures did federal and state governments implement?**

- **What were the origins of the People's Party? How did it exemplify dissatisfaction with the two established parties?**

The Political Earthquakes of the 1890s

Hitting in 1893 and lingering almost to the turn of the century, the severe depression of the 1890s transformed American politics. In 1894 and 1896, voters outside the South voted overwhelmingly for Republicans who promised safety and prosperity. These elections destroyed the rising People's Party and ended the era of close party competition in national elections. The shift shaped politics for decades to come, creating both opportunities and challenges for reformers. In the South, meanwhile, Democrats moved from being the leading political party to becoming virtually the *only* political party. The resulting formal disenfranchisement and segregation of African Americans left a bitter legacy that lasted for generations.

Depression and Reaction

At the time of Grover Cleveland's inauguration in March 1893, farm foreclosures and railroad bankruptcies were signaling economic trouble, as hard times in Europe caused investors there to pull money out of the United States. Only a few weeks after Cleveland entered the White House, the Pennsylvania and Reading Railroad went bankrupt, followed soon afterward by the National Cordage Company. Investors panicked, and the stock market crashed. Europeans who had invested in the United States called back their money. By July, major banks had drained their reserves and "suspended," unable to give depositors access to their money. By year's end, 500 banks and thousands of other businesses went under. "Boston," one observer remembered, "grew suddenly old, haggard, and thin." The unemployment rate quickly soared above 20 percent.

For Americans who had lived through the terrible 1870s, the depression looked grimly familiar. Even fresher in the public mind were recent labor uprisings, including the 1886 Haymarket bombing and the 1892 showdown at Homestead — followed, during the depression's first year, by a massive Pennsylvania coal strike and a Pullman railroad boycott that ended with bloody clashes between angry crowds and the U.S. Army. Prosperous Americans were terrified of a nationwide uprising of workers making a desperate stand for survival. They also feared the farmer-labor movement that had organized its political revolt through the People's Party. Would the United States hold together amid the crisis?

In the summer of 1894, another protest jolted Americans. Radical reformer Jacob Coxey of Ohio proposed that the U.S. government hire the unemployed to fix the nation's roads. In 1894, he organized hundreds of jobless men — nicknamed "Coxey's Army" — to carry out a peaceful march to Washington to appeal for the program. Though public works of the kind Coxey proposed would become a central part of the New Deal in the 1930s, in the 1890s many Americans viewed Coxey as a dangerous extremist. Public alarm grew when other spontaneous marches followed the one led by Coxey (Map 20.3). In some towns and cities, marchers found warm support and offers of aid. In others, police and property owners drove the marchers away at gunpoint. Coxey was stunned by what happened on May 1, when his group reached Capitol Hill: He was arrested and jailed for trespassing on the grass. Coxey's marchers went home hungry.

The public blamed hard times and political upheaval not only on radicals like Coxey but also on the Democrats who held power. Any president would have been hard-pressed to cope, but Grover Cleveland made a particularly bad hash of it. Cleveland was out of step with his party on a major issue: expansion of federal coinage to include silver as well as gold. Advocates of

MAP 20.3

Routes of the Industrial Armies of 1894

The march of "Coxey's Army" inspired many groups of desperate, unemployed men to appeal for government aid. Various peaceful "armies"—some seeking federal funds for irrigation projects in the West, as well as emergency public employment programs—organized in many cities and started east for the national capital, usually walking, but sometimes commandeering trains or boats to ease their way. As the armies marched through, residents of some towns and cities met them with food, shelter, and support; others, terrified, met them with loaded guns and barred their entry. Many of the armies gave up after Coxey's initial group met hostility and defeat. Those who made it to Washington ended up in makeshift campgrounds in Maryland and Virginia that Coxey's followers had created, eventually dispersing to seek other ways to survive.
Source: Carlos. A. Schwantes, *Coxey's Army: An American Odyssey* (Lincoln: University of Nebraska Press, 1985).

"free silver" ("free" because, under this plan, the U.S. Mint would not charge a fee for minting silver coins) believed the policy would expand the U.S. money supply, encourage borrowing, and stimulate industry. But Cleveland was a firm advocate of the gold standard; the money supply should not be expanded, he believed, but should remain tied solely to the nation's reserves of gold. After 1893, neither collapsing prices nor a groundswell of free-silver sentiment in his own party budged Cleveland. With gold reserves dwindling, in 1895 he made a secret arrangement with a syndicate of bankers led by John Pierpont Morgan to arrange gold purchases to replenish the Treasury. Morgan helped maintain America's gold supply—preserving the gold standard—and in doing so turned a tidy profit. Cleveland's deal, once

discovered, enraged his fellow Democrats. South Carolina orator Ben Tillman vowed to go to Washington and "poke old Grover with a pitchfork," thus earning him the nickname "Pitchfork Ben."

As the 1894 midterm elections loomed, Democrats tried to distance themselves from Cleveland. But on Election Day, large numbers of voters chose the Republicans, who promised to support business, put down social unrest, and bring back prosperity. In western states, voters turned Populists out of office. In the Midwest and Mid-Atlantic states, voters handed the Democrats crushing defeats. In the next congressional session, Republicans controlled the House by a margin of 245 to 105. The election began sixteen years of Republican dominance in national politics.

Democrats and the "Solid South"

In the South, the only region where Democrats gained strength in the 1890s, the People's Party met defeat for distinctive reasons. After the rollback of Reconstruction, while some states adopted poll taxes and other measures to limit voting, African Americans in other states had continued to vote in significant numbers. As long as Democrats competed for (and sometimes bought) black votes, the possibility remained that other parties could win African Americans' loyalty. The People's Party proposed new measures to help farmers and wage earners—an appealing message for poverty-stricken people of both races. Some white Populists went out of their way to forge cross-racial ties. "The accident of color can make no difference in the interest of farmers, croppers, and laborers," argued Georgia Populist Tom Watson. "You are kept apart that you may be separately fleeced of your earnings."

Such Populist appeals threatened the foundations of elite southern politics. As ex-Confederates had done during Reconstruction, Democrats struck back, calling themselves the "white man's party" and denouncing Populists for promoting "Negro rule." From Georgia to Texas, many white farmers, tenants, and wage earners ignored such appeals and continued to support the Populists in large numbers. Democrats found they could put down the Populist threat only through fraud and violence. "We had to do it!" one Georgia Democrat later explained, admitting that he had stuffed ballot boxes and threatened black voters. "Those damned Populists would have ruined the country."

Having suppressed the political revolt, Democrats vowed that white supremacy was non-negotiable— but they looked for new ways to enforce it. As early as 1890, a state constitutional convention in Mississippi adopted a key innovation: an "understanding clause" that required would-be voters who appeared at registrars' offices to interpret a clause of the state constitution, with local Democratic officials deciding who met the standard. After the Populist uprising, such measures spread to other southern states. Louisiana's **grandfather clause**, which denied the vote to any man whose grandfather, in slavery days, had been unable to vote, was struck down by the U.S. Supreme Court. But in *Williams v. Mississippi* (1898), the Court allowed poll taxes and **literacy tests** to stand. By 1908, every southern state had adopted such measures.

The impact of disenfranchisement can hardly be overstated (Map 20.4). In most of the South, voter turnout plunged, from above 70 percent to 34 percent or even lower. Not only blacks but also many poor whites ceased to vote. Since Democrats faced virtually no opposition, political activity shifted to the "white primaries," where Democratic candidates competed for party nominations. Some former Populists joined the Democrats in openly advocating white supremacy (see Comparing American Voices, "Negro Domination!" pp. 630–631). The racial climate hardened. Segregation laws proliferated, barring blacks not only from white schools and railroad cars but also from hotels, parks, and public drinking fountains. Lynchings of African Americans increasingly occurred in broad daylight, with crowds of thousands gathering to watch.

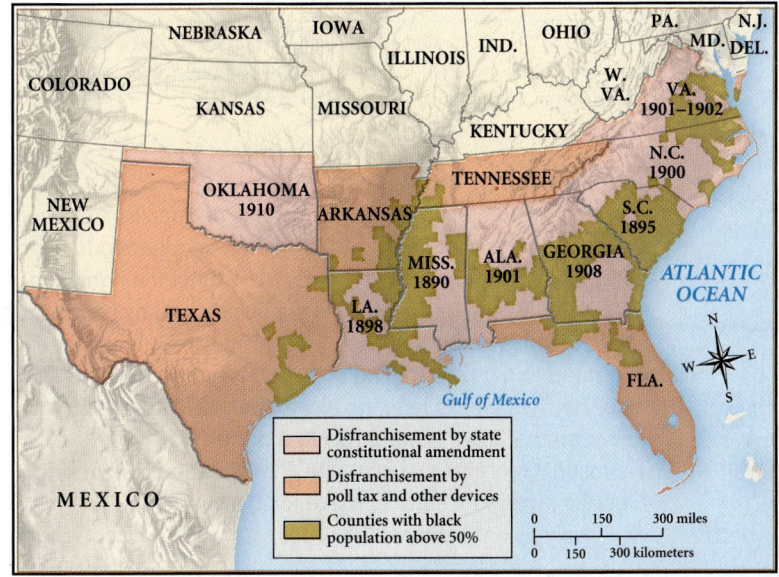

MAP 20.4

Disenfranchisement in the New South

In the midst of the Populist challenge to Democratic one-party rule in the South, a movement to deprive blacks of the right to vote spread from Mississippi across the South. By 1910, every state in the region except Tennessee, Arkansas, Texas, and Florida had made constitutional changes designed to prevent blacks from voting, and these four states accomplished much the same result through poll taxes and other exclusionary methods. For the next half century, the political process in the South would be for whites only.

COMPARING AMERICAN VOICES

"Negro Domination!"

The title of this feature – Comparing American Voices – does not always mean comparing what different Americans have said. It's also possible, taking a chronological approach, to compare what a single individual said at different times. The two documents that follow were both written by Tom Watson, a fiery Georgia Populist. In both, he was addressing the "everlasting and overshadowing Negro Question" that he thought distinguished the South and obstructed the radical, class-based politics he advocated. The two documents offer diametrically opposite answers and thereby illuminate how it came to be that the race-obsessed South disenfranchised its black population.

Tom Watson: 1892

In 1892, when Watson wrote the following essay, he had recently been elected to Congress on a third-party ticket and had high hopes that Populism would break the grip of the conservative Democrats and bring a new day for the South's oppressed tenant farmers, black and white.

The white tenant lives adjoining the colored tenant. Their houses are almost equally destitute of comforts. Their living is confined to bare necessities. . . . They pay the same enormous prices for farm supplies. Christmas finds them both without any satisfactory return for a year's toil. Dull and heavy and unhappy, they both start the plows again when "New Year's" passes.

Now the People's Party says to these two men, "You are kept apart that you may be separately fleeced of your earnings. You are made to hate each other because upon that hatred is rested the keystone of the arch of financial despotism which enslaves you both. You are deceived and blinded that you may not see how this race antagonism perpetuates a monetary system which beggars both." This is so obviously true it is no wonder both these unhappy laborers stop to listen. No wonder they begin to realize that no change of law can benefit the white tenant which does not benefit the black one likewise; that no system which now does injustice to one of them can fail to injure both. Their every material interest is identical. The moment this becomes a conviction, mere selfishness, the mere desire to better their conditions, escape onerous taxes, avoid usurious charges, lighten their rents, or change their precarious tenements into smiling, happy homes, will drive these two men together, just as their mutual inflamed prejudices now drive them apart.

. . . Why should the colored man always be taught that the white man of his neighborhood hates him, while a Northern man, who taxes every rag on his back, loves him?

Why should not my tenant come to regard me as his friend rather than the manufacturer who plunders us both?

Why should we perpetuate a policy which drives the black man into the arms of the Northern politician?

. . . To the emasculated individual who cries "Negro supremacy!" there is little to be said. . . . Not being prepared to make any such admission in favor of any race the sun ever shone on, I have no words which can portray my contempt for the white men, Anglo-Saxons, who can knock their knees together, and through their chattering teeth and pale lips admit they are afraid the Negroes will "dominate us." The question of social equality does not enter into the calculation at all. That is a thing each citizen decides for himself. No statute ever yet drew the latch of the humblest home — or ever will. Each citizen regulates his visiting list — and always will.

The conclusion, then, seems to me this: They will become political allies, and neither can injure the one without weakening both. It will be in the interest of both that each should have justice. And on these broad lines of mutual interest, mutual forbearance, and mutual support the present will be made the stepping-stone to future peace and prosperity.

Source: "The Negro Question in the South," *Arena*, vol. 6 (1892), in *A More Perfect Union: Documents in U.S. History*, 2 vols., ed. Paul F. Boller and Ronald Story (Boston: Houghton Mifflin, 1984), 2: 83–85.

Tom Watson: 1904

After the 1896 election and the collapse of Populism, Watson withdrew from politics. In 1904, however, he returned to head a Populist presidential ticket, in part to protest the rightward drift of the Democratic Party. He was chagrined by his poor showing in his native state (only 117,000 votes), which he attributed to the race-baiting of the conservative Democratic machine. Two weeks later, on November 19, 1904, he delivered the following address to a partisan crowd in Thomson, Georgia. (In 1907–1908, with Watson's backing, Georgia enacted a state constitutional amendment that effectively disenfranchised blacks.)

There never was a time when the greedy corporations, the soulless combinations of sordid wealth, has so nearly got the industrial world by the throat. . . . There never was a time when the avarice of the few so monopolized the wealth created by the laborers of this republic as to-day. . . .

The time has come when we must act for the best interests for our homes and firesides. Negroes may call themselves Republicans, or call themselves Democrats, or call themselves Methodists, or call themselves Baptists, but when you touch them on any subject that concerns their color they are all just negroes. They run together, they stand as one man representing the colored race. So with the whites in the South. . . . When any question comes up in the South that concerns us as a race then every distinction falls down and we stand together. . . . Every man ought to know that; every man does know it.

And yet we allow these small politicians [to frighten] us, year after year, into voting for men whom we know nothing about and for a platform we utterly detest. . . . Our task from the beginning has been peculiarly difficult in the South because of the belief if the white people divide the negro would be the balance of power and would rule the South. That has been our stumbling block. . . . Now, no Southern man wanted negro domination . . . no Anglo-Saxon man anywhere ever wanted it. No. The white race has made civilization what it is, and the white race intends to keep it what it is. We told those colored people whenever we spoke to them that "when we took hold of you, you were savages from Africa; we taught you everything you know. . . . You have had the best example of civilization and to the extent that you have copied it you have become good citizens, farmers, carpenters, black-smiths — Christians, because our God has become your God." And we said to those people, "Follow us and we will guarantee you" — what? Social equality? No. Political equality? — No. We said, "We will give you equality as a citizen, under the law that will protect your life, your limb, your property, your home and your fire-side, just as it protects ours." That is as far as we ever went, and I am willing to go that far to-day. [Applause.] And the man who does not believe in going that far is not a man who believes in Jeffersonian democracy. [Applause.]

But the Democrats said, "You will divide the white people and the negro will have the balance of power. We will have negro domination." . . . We wept; and bowed down in sack-cloth and ashes. That is all we could do. Our Party was swept out of existence. Then what? The Southern states began to disfranchise the negro, and in almost every state the negro has been taken out of politics. And why hasn't he been taken out of politics in Georgia? . . . [The Democrats] were using the fear of negro domination to hold your votes. . . . Now what? What! They were afraid of the negro, weren't they? They were afraid of the negro and negro domination (They say) and here they had had almost a generation to put him out but he is in as big as life. The negro is an old sinner 364 days of the year, but the 365th, which is on election day, he is "sugar in the gourd." [Applause, laughter and cheers.]

At the very opening of this campaign, I threw at their feet the challenge — "If you are earnest in what you say, if you are afraid of the negro, if you are really afraid of the negro, you miserable coward [applause], if you really mean it, then we are ready to help you out of your scrape, you pusillanimous political coward, we will come up and help you pass any kind of law that you yourself say was necessary to keep the white man on top." [Applause and cheers.]

Source: "Speech of Hon. Thomas E. Watson, Delivered at Thomson, Ga., November 19th, 1904," unpublished ms., Watson Papers, University of North Carolina. Printed by permission.

ANALYZING THE EVIDENCE

- In what ways did Watson's views change between 1892 and 1904? Can you identify any ways in which his views did *not* change — any reasons why audiences in 1904 might have said, "yes, that's the same old Tom Watson we've always known"?

- Why do you think Watson changed his arguments? In what ways did this reflect broader changes in electoral politics, and in race relations, between 1892 and 1904?

- How might a disenfranchised African American voter have responded to Watson's 1904 speech?

Disenfranchisement

This political illustration from the July 30, 1892, issue of *Judge* magazine shows the Ku Klux Klan barring black voters from the polls. Violence, however, was giving way to legally sanctioned disenfranchisement. Though literacy tests and poll taxes presented blacks with less physical menace than the Klan, they increased the likelihood that states would evade the constitutional requirement (note the sign behind the Klansmen) under the Fifteenth Amendment that the right to vote not be denied "on account of race, color, or previous condition of servitude."   Museum of American Political Life.

The nature of this political counterrevolution can be illustrated by events in Grimes County, a cotton-growing area in eastern Texas where African Americans comprised more than half of the population. African American voters kept the local Republican Party going after Reconstruction and regularly sent black representatives to the Texas legislature. Many local white Populists proved immune to Democrats' taunts of "negro supremacy," and a Populist-Republican coalition swept the county elections in 1896 and 1898. But after their 1898 defeat, Democrats in Grimes County organized a secret brotherhood. They forcibly prevented African Americans from voting in town elections, shooting two black leaders in cold blood. The Populist sheriff proved unable to bring the murderers to justice. Reconstituted in 1900 as the White Man's Party, Democrats carried Grimes County by an overwhelming margin. Gunmen then laid siege to the Populist sheriff's office, killed his brother and a friend, and drove the wounded sheriff out of the county. The White Man's Party ruled Grimes County for the next fifty years.

The Election of 1896 and Its Aftermath

After their crushing defeats outside the South in 1894, Democrats astonished the country by embracing parts of the radical farmer-labor program in the presidential election of 1896. They nominated young free-silver advocate William Jennings Bryan of Nebraska, who sealed his nomination with a passionate defense of farmers and an attack on the gold standard. "Burn down your cities and leave our farms," Bryan declared, "and your cities will spring up again as if by magic; but destroy our farms and the grass will grow in the streets of every city in the country." He ended with a vow: "You shall not crucify mankind on a cross of gold." Cheering

Lynching in Texas

Lynchings peaked between 1890 and 1910; while most common in the South, they occurred in almost every state, from Oregon to Minnesota to New York. After many lynchings — such as this one in the town of Center, Texas, in 1920 — crowds posed to have their pictures taken. Commercial photographers often, as in this case, produced photographic postcards to sell as souvenirs. What do we make of these gruesome rituals? Who is in the crowd, and who is not? What do we learn from the fact that this group of white men, some of whom may have been responsible for the lynching, felt comfortable having their photographs recorded with the body? The victim in this photograph, a young man named Lige Daniels, was seized from the local jail by a mob that broke down the prison door to kidnap and kill him. The inscription on the back of the postcard includes information about the killing, along with the instructions "Give this to Bud From Aunt Myrtle." Private Collection.

delegates nominated Bryan on a platform that advocated free silver and a federal income tax on the wealthy that would replace **tariffs** as a source of revenue. The national Democratic Party, which had long defended **states' rights** and limited government, was moving toward a more activist stance.

Populists, reeling from their recent defeats, endorsed Bryan for president. But their power was waning. Bryan ignored them, running as a straight Democrat without ever acknowledging the People's Party nomination. Populist leader Tom Watson, who had wanted a separate, more radical program, observed that Democrats had cast the Populists as "Jonah while they play whale." The Populists never recovered from their electoral losses in 1894 or from Democrats' ruthless opposition in the South. By 1900, the party had largely faded. Rural voters pursued their reform efforts elsewhere, particularly through the newly energized Bryan wing of the Democrats.

Republicans' brilliant manager, Ohio manufacturer Mark Hanna, orchestrated an unprecedented fundraising campaign in 1896 among corporate leaders. Republicans denounced Bryan's supporters as "revolutionary and anarchistic." Under Hanna's guidance, the party backed away from moral issues such as prohibition of liquor and reached out to invite new immigrants to join them. The Republican candidate William McKinley won handily, with 271 electoral votes to Bryan's 176 (Map 20.5). McKinley had persuaded the nation that he would bring prosperity.

Nationwide, as in the South, the 1894–1896 realignment prompted a wave of political changes — but they were the kind of "reforms" that excluded voters rather than increasing democratic participation. As in the South, many northern states imposed literacy tests and restrictions on voting by new immigrants. Leaders of both major parties worked to shut out future threats from new movements like the Populists, making it more

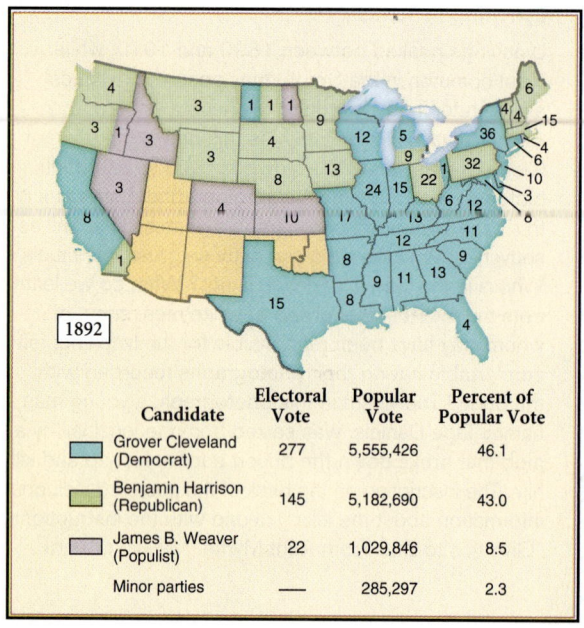

Candidate	Electoral Vote	Popular Vote	Percent of Popular Vote
Grover Cleveland (Democrat)	277	5,555,426	46.1
Benjamin Harrison (Republican)	145	5,182,690	43.0
James B. Weaver (Populist)	22	1,029,846	8.5
Minor parties	—	285,297	2.3

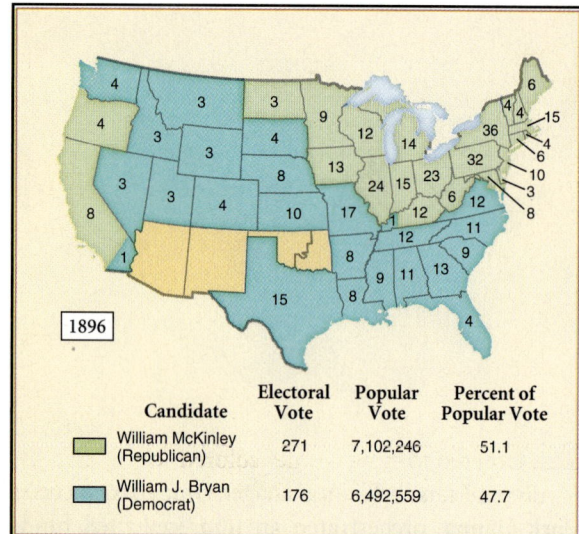

Candidate	Electoral Vote	Popular Vote	Percent of Popular Vote
William McKinley (Republican)	271	7,102,246	51.1
William J. Bryan (Democrat)	176	6,492,559	47.7

MAP 20.5

The Presidential Elections of 1892 and 1896

In the 1890s, the age of political stalemate came to an end. Students should compare the 1892 map with Map 20.1 (p. 623) and note especially Cleveland's breakthrough in the normally Republican states of the upper Midwest. In 1896, the pendulum swung in the opposite direction, with McKinley's consolidation of Republican control over the Northeast and Midwest far overbalancing the Democratic advances in the thinly populated western states. The 1896 election marked the beginning of sixteen years of Republican dominance in national politics.

difficult for new parties to get their candidates listed on the ballot. In the wake of such laws, voter turnout declined. In all parts of the United States, the electorate narrowed in ways that favored the native born and wealthy.

Antidemocratic restrictions on voting helped, paradoxically, to foster democratic innovations. Having excluded or reduced the number of poor, African American, and immigrant voters, elite and middle-class reformers felt far more comfortable increasing the power of the voters who remained. Both major parties increasingly turned to the **direct primary**, asking voters (in most states, registered party members) rather than party leaders to choose nominees. Another measure that enhanced democratic participation was the Seventeenth Amendment to the Constitution (1913), which required that U.S. senators be chosen not by the state legislatures, but by popular vote. Though many states had already adopted the practice, southern states had resisted, since Democrats feared that it might give more power to their political foes. After disenfranchisement, such objections faded and the measure passed. Thus a gross injustice—disenfranchisement of blacks—helped pave the way for a measure that today enhances the direct voting power of all Americans. Such were the ironies of political reform in the wake of the upheaval of the 1890s.

The Courts Reject Reform

While the major political parties restricted suffrage, federal courts invalidated many of the regulatory laws that states had passed to protect workers and promote public welfare. As early as 1882, in the case of *In re Jacobs*, the New York State Court of Appeals struck down a public-health law that prohibited cigar manufacturing in tenements, arguing that such regulation exceeded the state's police powers. In *Lochner v. New York* (1905), the U.S. Supreme Court told New York State that it could not limit bakers' workdays to ten hours because that violated bakers' rights to make contracts. Judges found support for such rulings in the Fourteenth Amendment to the Constitution (1868), which prohibited states from depriving "any person of life, liberty, or property, without due process of law." The due process clause had been intended to protect the rights of former slaves, but the courts used it to shield contract rights. Judges argued that they were protecting workers' freedom *from* government regulation. Interpreted in this way, the Fourteenth Amendment became a powerful obstacle to state laws regulating private business.

Farmer and labor advocates, along with some urban progressives who supported stronger regulation of the

THE SACRILEGIOUS CANDIDATE.

No man who drags into the dust the most sacred symbols of the Christian world is fit to be president of the United States.

The Cross of Gold

William Jennings Bryan's "Cross of Gold" speech was one of the great orations in American political history. Republican critics, however, were not so keen on it and did their best to puncture its Christian aura. In this cartoon by Grant Hamilton, Bryan is accused of cynically using the cross and crown of thorns for political purposes. The cartoon suggests that what Bryan was really up to was revolution; hence in the background are a pillaged city and a man dressed as a figure from the French Revolution and waving an "Anarchy" flag.   Library of Congress.

economy, vehemently disagreed with such rulings. They believed judges, not state legislators, were overreaching their power. While courts treated employers and employees as equal parties, critics dismissed this as a "legal fiction." "Modern industry has reduced 'freedom of contract' to a paper privilege," declared one labor advocate, "a mere figure of rhetoric." Supreme Court Justice Oliver Wendell Holmes Jr., dissenting in the *Lochner* decision, agreed. If the choice was between working and starving, he observed, how could bakers "choose" their hours of work? Employers set the rules, and employees' only alternatives were to work the specified hours or lose their jobs. Holmes's view, known as legal realism, eventually won judicial favor, but it only did so after years of progressive and labor activism.

Meanwhile, in its landmark decision in *Plessy v. Ferguson* (1896), the Supreme Court put the nation's stamp of approval on racial discrimination. The case was brought by civil rights advocates on behalf of Homer Plessy, a New Orleans resident who was one-eighth

black. Ordered to move to the "colored" car of a Louisiana train, Plessy refused and was arrested. Advocates hoped to challenge the growing number of southern **Jim Crow** laws, which segregated whites and blacks in hotels, trains, streetcars, and even cemeteries. The Court ruled that such segregation did not violate the Fourteenth Amendment as long as blacks had access to accommodations equal to those of whites. This "separate but equal" doctrine—like the Court's ruling on bakers' work hours—protected theoretical rights while ignoring reality. Segregated facilities in the South were flagrantly unequal; state funding for African American schools, for example, lagged far behind that for whites. Segregation was clearly discriminatory, but the Court allowed it to stand. Of all the decisions of the 1890s, *Plessy* had perhaps the most powerful and long-lasting impact. Though the Supreme Court became friendlier to economic regulation after 1900, *Plessy* remained in place until 1954, when the *Brown v. Topeka Board of Education* ruling finally struck down segregation.

The U.S. Supreme Court, 1894

During the 1890s, the Supreme Court struck down a number of pieces of progressive legislation, including a progressive federal income tax that had been signed into law by Congress and the president. In the Knight Sugar Case (*United States v. E. C. Knight Co.*), the Court ruled that the federal government had limited power over interstate commerce when a company did most of its manufacturing in a single state. In another 1894 decision, *In re Debs*, manufacturers were allowed free use of injunctions to shut down strikes. Two years later, in *Plessy v. Ferguson*, the Court gave national sanction to racial segregation. In the front row, from left to right, are justices Horace Gray, Stephen J. Field, Chief Justice Melville W. Fuller, John Marshall Harlan I, and David J. Brewer. Standing in the back row, left to right, are justices Howell Jackson, Henry B. Brown, George Shiras, and Edward Douglas White.   C.M. Bell, Collection of the Supreme Court of the United States.

- **What were the political consequences of the economic crisis of the 1890s?**

- **What was the impact of measures, both in the South and elsewhere, to restrict the vote?**

- **What role did the federal courts play in the political transformations of the 1890s?**

Reform Reshaped, 1901–1917

William McKinley was a powerful presence in the White House, but he was no reformer. He won the 1896 campaign on a promise to restore order and prosperity, and many affluent Americans greeted his victory with profound relief. Amid the crisis of the 1890s, the nation's leading journals dismissed labor unions as "wild-eyed radicals" and Populists as ignorant "hayseeds." McKinley's victory was widely understood as a triumph for business, especially for industrial titans who had contributed heavily to his campaign.

But the depession of the 1890s, by subjecting millions of ordinary Americans to severe hardship, had dramatically illustrated the problems industrialization had created. By the turn of the twentieth century, more and more prosperous citizens acknowledged that government needed to play a more active role in the economy. At the same time, the very success of McKinley's campaign managers—who spent more than $3.5 million, versus Bryan's $300,000—raised unsettling questions about the power of corporations and the use of money in politics. Once the crisis of the 1890s passed, middle-class Americans proved increasingly willing to embrace progressive ideas. This process accelerated after a shocking assassination brought a reformer to the presidency.

Theodore Roosevelt in the White House

In 1900, William McKinley easily won his second political face-off against Democrat William Jennings Bryan. Only six months into his second term, however, on September 14, 1901, the president was shot as he attended the Pan-American Exposition in Buffalo, New York. He died eight days later. The murderer, Leon Czolgosz, was influenced by anarchist thinkers and inspired by recent assassinations in Europe. McKinley's violent death was another warning, many Americans felt, of the threat posed by radical immigrants (even though Czolgosz was American-born). As the nation mourned its third murdered president in less than four decades, Vice President Theodore Roosevelt was sworn in as McKinley's replacement.

Roosevelt, born into a prominent family, had chosen an unconventional path. After graduating from Harvard, he plunged into politics, winning a seat as a New York assemblyman. In 1884, Roosevelt had joined Mugwump Republicans in opposing James Blaine's nomination. Disillusioned by the group's failure to steer the party in a reform direction, Roosevelt left politics and moved to a North Dakota ranch, creating a "frontier" persona that later served him well. But Roosevelt's cattle herd was wiped out in the blizzards of 1887. He returned east, winning appointments as a U.S. Civil Service commissioner, head of the New York City Police Commission, and McKinley's assistant secretary of the navy. An energetic presence in all these jobs, Roosevelt gained broad knowledge of the problems America faced at the municipal, state, and federal levels.

Roosevelt became a popular hero when he enlisted in the army during the War of 1898. Elected as New York's governor soon afterward, he asserted his faith in government's capacity to improve the lives of ordinary people. As governor, Roosevelt pushed through civil service reform and a tax on corporations. In an effort to neutralize this rising (and rather unpredictable) political star, Republican bosses chose Roosevelt as McKinley's running mate in 1900, hoping the vice presidency would be a political dead end. Instead, they suddenly found Roosevelt in the White House.

Roosevelt did not prove to be quite the rebel his critics feared. He was, after all, a Republican who had denounced the "extreme" views of Populists, and he blended reform with the needs of private enterprise. Roosevelt won fame as an environmentalist, for example, but many of his conservation policies had a strong pro-business bent. He increased the amount of land held in federal forest reserves and turned their management over to the new, independent U.S. Forest Service. But Roosevelt's forestry chief, Gifford Pinchot, insisted on fire suppression to maximize logging potential. In addition, Roosevelt lent his support to the Newlands Reclamation Act (1902), which had much in common with earlier Republican policies to promote economic development in the West. Under the Newlands Act, the federal government sold public lands to raise money for irrigation projects that expanded agriculture on arid lands. In funding such projects, however, Roosevelt not only met business needs but also fulfilled one of the demands of the unemployed men who had marched with Coxey's Army.

Antitrust Legislation | Despite his generally supportive attitude toward business, Roosevelt undertook some marked departures from his predecessors. During a bitter 1902 coal strike, he threatened to nationalize the big coal companies if their owners refused to negotiate with the miners' union. The owners hastily came to the table. Roosevelt also sought better enforcement of the Interstate Commerce Act and the Sherman Antitrust Act. In 1903, he pushed through the Elkins Act, which prohibited discriminatory railway rates that favored powerful customers. That same year, he created

Teddy Roosevelt and the "Square Deal"

When William McKinley ran for president in 1896, he sat on his front porch in Canton, Ohio, and received delegations of voters. That was not Theodore Roosevelt's way. He was a vigorous campaigner, and used the office of the presidency brilliantly to mobilize public opinion and to assert his leadership. The preeminence of the presidency in American public life began with Roosevelt's administration. Here, at the height of his crusading power, Roosevelt stumps from a train in the 1904 election.   Library of Congress.

Reining in Big Business

This 1904 cartoon from *Puck* shows Theodore Roosevelt as a tiny figure with a sword marked "public service," taking on railroad developer Jay Gould, financier John Pierpont Morgan, and other Wall Street titans. The figure at the top right is oil magnate John D. Rockefeller. In its reference to the folktale "Jack the Giant Killer," the cartoon suggests how difficult it will be for the president to limit the power of globally connected bankers and financiers.   Library of Congress.

trusts. He regarded large-scale enterprise as the natural tendency of modern industry, but he hoped to identify and punish "malefactors of great wealth" who abused their power. In 1906, after much wrangling in Congress, Roosevelt won a major victory with the passage of the Hepburn Act, which enabled the Interstate Commerce Commission to set shipping rates (see Reading American Pictures, "Theodore Roosevelt and the Hepburn Act," p. 639).

At the time Roosevelt acted, trusts had partially protected themselves with the help of two friendly state legislatures. New Jersey and then Delaware had loosened their regulations, inviting trusts to incorporate under new state laws. As anticipated, dozens of large companies took up the offer and established headquarters in these states. With its Northern Securities ruling, however, the Supreme Court began to recognize federal authority to dissolve the most egregious monopolies. After 1908, Roosevelt left a powerful legacy to his successor, William Howard Taft. In its *Standard Oil* decision in 1911, the Supreme Court agreed with Taft's Justice Department that John D. Rockefeller's massive oil monopoly should be broken up into several competing companies. After this ruling, Taft's attorney general undertook antitrust actions against other giant companies.

Theodore Roosevelt was a man of contradictions whose presidency left a mixed legacy. An unabashed believer in what he called "Anglo-Saxon" superiority, Roosevelt nonetheless invited Booker T. Washington to dine at the White House, earning fierce criticism from white supremacists. Similarly, Roosevelt was an advocate of elite rule who called for the "best men" to enter politics, but he also defended the dignity of labor. Later in his public career, Roosevelt read and recommended works written by European socialists. This complex mix of condescension and social-justice activism was characteristic of many elite and middle-class progressives.

Grassroots Progressive Movements

In part, President Roosevelt provided reform leadership because he faced increasing pressure for government action. At the grassroots, farmer and labor leaders continued to demand stronger remedies for dangerous working conditions, low pay, and concentrated corporate power. Building on earlier movements such as civil service reform and the antiliquor cause, elite and middle-class progressives were also mobilizing for change. They concentrated on cleaning up government, protecting public health and safety, and launching crusades against the vice industry and political machines. Some toured

the Bureau of Corporations, empowered to investigate business practices and bolster the Justice Department's capacity to mount antitrust suits. The department had already filed such a suit against the Northern Securities Company, a combine of the railroad systems of the northwestern part of the country. In a landmark decision in 1904, the Supreme Court ordered Northern Securities dissolved.

That year, calling for every American to get what he called a "Square Deal," Roosevelt handily defeated a weak Democratic candidate, Alton B. Parker. Now president in his own right, Roosevelt stepped up his attack on the

Theodore Roosevelt and the Hepburn Act

Theodore Roosevelt's bold antitrust initiatives drew the fury of corporate interests and their legislative supporters, as well as the acclaim of those who advocated greater regulation of the national economy. Both sides used the power of the illustrated press, circulating satirical cartoons that either vilified or lauded the activist president. During the months leading up to passage of the Hepburn Act (1906), Roosevelt struggled with Congress over whether the federal government should gain the power to set railroad shipping rates. The cartoon below, based on the biblical story of Samson and Delilah, offers one perspective on the controversy.

ANALYZING THE EVIDENCE

- What clues does the cartoon give to its biblical source? What do those clues suggest about the assumptions of the cartoonist regarding his audience?

- Roosevelt worked hard to cultivate a powerfully masculine public persona. Does his role in the cartoon as Delilah undermine that persona? Why, or why not?

- What does the cartoon suggest about the relationship between presidential and congressional power during Roosevelt's administration?

- What overall attitude toward Roosevelt's antitrust policy does the cartoon suggest?

"The American Samson." *Puck*, December 13, 1905.

other parts of the world, exchanging ideas with peers (see Voices from Abroad, "Henry Demarest Lloyd: A Progressive Report from New Zealand," p. 641).

Women and Reform | As they had since the 1880s, women played prominent roles in reform. Justifying their work through maternalism—the claim that women should expand their motherly role in the public sphere—they focused on the welfare of working-class women and children. The National Congress of Mothers, founded in 1897, promoted better child-rearing techniques. Women also served as leaders in The National Child Labor Committee, created in 1907. The committee hired photographer Lewis Hine to record brutal conditions in mines and mills where children worked (see Hine's photograph on p. 542). Impressed with the committee's work, Theodore Roosevelt sponsored the White House Conference on Dependent Children, bringing national attention to child welfare. In 1912, momentum from the conference resulted in the creation of the Children's Bureau in the U.S. Labor Department.

As the bureau's creation showed, progressives were partly inspired by the emerging fields of social work and social science. Social scientists focused special attention on the plight of the urban poor. They argued that unemployment and crowded slums were not caused by individual laziness and ignorance, as elite Americans had long believed. Instead, wrote journalist Robert Hunter in his landmark study, *Poverty* (1904), such problems resulted from "miserable and unjust social conditions." A reform leader in Boston agreed. "How vain to waste our energies on single cases of relief," he declared, "when *society* should aim at removing the prolific sources of all the woe."

No one exemplified this new attitude more than Josephine Shaw Lowell, a Civil War widow from a prominent family. After years of struggling to aid poverty-stricken individuals in New York City, Lowell concluded that charity was not enough. In 1890, she helped found the New York Consumers' League, to improve the wages and working conditions of female clerks in the city's stores. The league encouraged shoppers to patronize only stores on the "White List" they issued, where wages and working conditions were known to be fair. The organization spread to other cities and by 1899 had become the National Consumers' League (NCL). At its head stood the outspoken Florence Kelley, a Hull House worker and, for a brief time, chief factory inspector of Illinois. Kelley believed that only government oversight could protect exploited workers. Under her crusading leadership,

the NCL became a powerful advocate for protective legislation.

One of the NCL's greatest triumphs was the Supreme Court's decision in *Muller v. Oregon* (1908), which upheld an Oregon law limiting the workday to ten hours for women. To win the case, the NCL recruited Louis Brandeis, a son of Jewish immigrants, who was widely known as "the people's lawyer" for his eagerness to take on vested interests. Brandeis's legal brief in the *Muller* case devoted only two pages to the constitutional issue of state "police powers." Instead, Brandeis rested his arguments on data gathered by the NCL describing the toll that long hours took on women's health. The "Brandeis brief" cleared the way for use of social-science research and other expert testimony in legal decisions.

By approving an expansive welfare role for the states, the *Muller* decision encouraged women's organizations to lobby for further reforms. Their achievements included the first law providing public assistance for single mothers with dependent children (Illinois, 1911) and the first minimum wage law for women (Massachusetts, 1912). The NCL, working with the National Child Labor Committee, also played a role in creation of the Children's Bureau, and later the Women's Bureau, in the U.S. Department of Labor.

But the *Muller* decision had significant drawbacks both for labor and for women's rights. Though critics noted that men as well as women suffered from long work hours, the *Muller* case did not protect men. Brandeis's brief treated all women as potential mothers, focusing on the state's interest in protecting their future children. Brandeis and his allies hoped this strategy would open the door to broader regulation of working hours. In its ruling, however, the Supreme Court seized on motherhood as the critical issue. It asserted that the female worker, because of her maternal function, was "properly placed in a class by herself, and legislation for her protection may be sustained, even when like legislation is not necessary for men and could not be sustained." This conclusion dismayed labor advocates and divided female reformers. In the 1920s, while some women's rights advocates continued to fight for more laws to protect working women, others protested against any "discrimination or restriction based upon sex."

Civil Rights | In the wake of the *Plessy* decision and southern disenfranchisement, African American leaders grappled with a distinct set of political challenges. Faced with the obvious deterioration of African American rights—and the indifference or hostility of most whites—a new generation of black leaders challenged the leadership of Tuskegee educator

VOICES FROM ABROAD

Henry Demarest Lloyd
A Progressive Report from New Zealand

In most chapters, the Voices from Abroad feature records the impressions of a foreign visitor to the United States. In this case, however, we examine the views of an American who traveled overseas. Henry Demarest Lloyd, a reform journalist who had written extensively on politics and advocated greater social and economic justice, undertook a study tour of New Zealand in 1899. Such tours were appealing to many reformers—especially radicals discouraged by the defeat of Populism in the United States. Lloyd was enthusiastic about New Zealand's sudden burst of reform legislation, which had stemmed from a great industrial strike in 1890 and a subsequent election that swept the Labor Party into office. As Lloyd recounts, a host of major reforms followed over the next few years.

Lloyd was one of many reformers who looked overseas for progressive reform ideas. Jane Addams, for example, partly got the idea for Hull House from a London settlement project. Many American cities and states, in addition to the federal government, learned from Progressive initiatives in other parts of the industrializing world. Such borrowed ideas ranged from municipal ownership of utilities to scientific forest management to workmen's compensation laws.

New Zealand democracy is the talk of the world to-day. It has made itself the policeman and partner of industry to an extent unknown elsewhere. It is the "experiment station" of advanced legislation. Reforms that others have been only talking about, New Zealand has done. . . .

Instead of escaping from the evils of the social order by going to a new country, the Englishmen who settled New Zealand found that they had brought all its problems with them, as if these were their shadows, as they were. . . . The best acres were in the hands of monopolists. . . . The little farmer, forced by unjust and deliberately contrived laws to pay his own and his rich neighbor's taxes, had to sell out his little homestead to that neighbor for what he could get. The workingman, able to get neither land nor work, had to become a tramp. . . . The blood of the people was the vintage of the rich.

Here is the record of ten years [of progressive legislation to address these injustices]:

. . . The rich man, because rich, is made to pay more. . . .

By compulsory arbitration the public gets for the guidance of public opinion all the facts as to disputes between labor and capital, [and] puts an end to strikes and lock-outs. . . . For the unemployed the nation makes itself a labor bureau. It brings them and the employers together. It reorganizes its public works and land system so as to give land to the landless and work to the workless. . . . The state itself insures the working people against accident.

. . . The nation's railroads are used to redistribute unemployed labour, to rebuild industry shattered by calamity, to stimulate production by special rates to and from farms and factories, to give health and education to the school and factory population and the people generally by cheap excursions.

. . . Women are enfranchised. . . . On election day one can see the baby-carriage standing in front of the polls while the father and mother go in and vote—against each other if they choose.

Last of all, pensions are given to the aged poor.

. . . We are exhorted to take "one step at a time," and are assured that this is the evolutionary method. This theory does not fit the New Zealand evolution. . . . It was, one of its leaders said, "a substitute for a French revolution." But it was a revolution. It was not merely a change in parties; it was a change in principles and institutions that amounted to nothing less than a social right-about-face. It was a New Zealand revolution, one which without destruction passed at once to the tasks of construction.

Source: Henry Demarest Lloyd, *Newest England* (New York: Doubleday, 1901), 1, 364–374.

ANALYZING THE EVIDENCE

- What specific reforms has New Zealand enacted that the author admires? What problems did these reforms solve, according to Lloyd?

- New Zealand had a population of about 1 million in 1890, the vast majority immigrants from the British Isles, or their descendants, along with a much smaller number of native Maori people. New Zealand's population was roughly half rural and half urban. Can you think of reasons why reform might have been easier to achieve there than in the United States?

Ida B. Wells

In 1887, Ida Wells (Wells-Barnett after she married in 1895) was thrown bodily from a train in Tennessee for refusing to vacate her seat in a section reserved for whites, launching her into a lifelong crusade for racial justice. Her mission was to expose the evil of lynching in the South. This image is the title page of a pamphlet she published in 1892.   Schomburg Center for Research in Black Culture, New York Public Library.

Booker T. Washington. Harvard-educated sociologist W. E. B. Du Bois called for a "talented tenth" of educated blacks to develop new strategies. "The policy of compromise has failed," wrote William Monroe Trotter, pugnacious editor of the *Boston Guardian*. "The policy of resistance and aggression deserves a trial." Ida Wells-Barnett, a fearless journalist who undertook a one-woman crusade against lynching, joined the call for new ideas.

In 1905, Du Bois and Trotter called a meeting at Niagara Falls — on the Canadian side, because no hotel on the U.S. side would admit blacks. The resulting Niagara Movement had a broad impact. The group's Niagara Principles called for full voting rights; an end to segregation; equal treatment in the justice system; and equal opportunity in education, jobs, health care, and military service. These principles, based on black pride and an uncompromising demand for full equality, guided the civil rights movement throughout the twentieth century.

Not long after the Niagara conference, a shocking atrocity brought public attention to the civil rights cause. In 1908, a bloody race riot broke out in Springfield, Illinois, hometown of Abraham Lincoln. Appalled by the violence against blacks, New York settlement worker Mary White Ovington called together a small group of sympathetic progressives. Their meeting led in 1909 to the creation of the National Association for the Advancement of Colored People (NAACP). Most leaders of the Niagara Movement soon joined, and W. E. B. Du Bois became editor of the NAACP journal, *The Crisis*. The fledgling NAACP found allies in the black churches and the National Association of Colored Women's Clubs. It also cooperated with the National Urban League (1911), a union of agencies that assisted black migrants in the North. Over the coming decades, these groups grew into a powerful force for racial justice.

Innovation in the States   As reform emerged at the local level, some states served as important seedbeds. Theodore Roosevelt dubbed Wisconsin a "laboratory of democracy" under energetic Republican governor Robert La Follette (1901–1905). La Follette promoted what he called the "Wisconsin Idea" — greater government intervention in the economy. To promote this goal, he relied heavily on experts at the University of Wisconsin, particularly economists, for policy recommendations. La Follette combined respect for experts with a strong commitment to democracy. He won battles to restrict lobbying and give Wisconsin citizens the right of **recall** (voting to remove unpopular politicians from office) and **referendum** (voting directly on a proposed policy measure, rather than leaving it in the hands of elected legislators). Going on to a long career in the U.S. Senate, La Follette, like Roosevelt, advocated increasingly aggressive measures to protect workers and rein in corporate power.

Labor reforms also advanced steadily through state initiatives, most notably workmen's compensation laws. The U.S. industrial workplace was incredibly dangerous; coal miners, for example, died from cave-ins and explosions at a rate 50 percent higher than in German mines. Between 1910 and 1917, all the industrial states

W. E. B. Du Bois

W. E. B. Du Bois was born in western Massachusetts in 1868, the son of a barber and a domestic worker. He received an excellent local education and went on to earn his B.A. and Ph.D. at Harvard, as well as to study with cutting-edge social scientists in Germany. By 1900, Du Bois had become a national civil rights leader and America's leading black intellectual. Famous for his sociological and historical studies, including *The Souls of Black Folk* (1903), Du Bois helped found the National Association for the Advancement of Colored People (NAACP) and edited the organization's journal, *The Crisis*. Between 1900 and 1945 he helped organize Pan-African conferences in locations around the world. Toward the end of his life Du Bois pursued this Pan-African ideal by moving to Ghana, the first modern African nation formed after the end of European colonialism. He died there in 1963.   Special Collections and Archives, W. E. B. Du Bois Library, University of Massachusetts at Amherst.

Robert M. La Follette

La Follette was transformed into a political reformer when, in 1891, a Wisconsin Republican boss attempted to bribe him to influence a judge in a railway case. As he described it in his autobiography, "Out of this awful ordeal came understanding; and out of understanding came resolution. I determined that the power of this corrupt influence . . . should be broken." This photograph captures him at the top of his form, expounding his progressive vision to a rapt audience of Wisconsin citizens at an impromptu street gathering.   Library of Congress.

enacted insurance laws covering on-the-job accidents, so that workers' families would not starve if a breadwinner was injured or killed. Some states also experimented with so-called mothers' pensions or widows' pensions, which provided state assistance after a breadwinner's desertion or death. Mothers, however, were subjected to home visits to determine whether they were "deserving" of government aid; injured workmen were not, a pattern of gender discrimination that reflected the broader impulse to protect women, while treating them differently from men. Although mothers' pensions reached relatively small numbers of women, they laid the foundations for federal Aid to Dependent Children, an important component of the Social Security Act of 1935.

While federalism gave states considerable freedom to innovate, it hampered national reforms. In some states, for example, opponents of child labor won laws that barred young children from factory work and strictly regulated the hours and conditions of older children's labor. In the South, however, and in some industrial states like Pennsylvania, manufacturers fiercely resisted such laws—as did many working-class parents who relied on children's income to keep the family fed. A proposed U.S. constitutional amendment to abolish child labor won ratification in only four states. Tens of thousands of children continued to work in low-wage jobs, especially in the South. The same decentralized power that permitted innovation in Wisconsin also hampered the creation of national minimum standards for pay and conditions of work.

The Problem of Labor   The failure to pass labor laws reflected both Republican political control and unions' reluctance to engage in electoral politics. Leaders of the nation's dominant union, the American Federation of Labor, had long preached that workers should improve wages and working conditions through self-help. **Voluntarism**, as trade unionists called this doctrine, centered on strikes and direct negotiations with employers, not political action. But voluntarism began to weaken by the 1910s. As muckraking journalists exposed the plight of workers and progressive reformers came forward with solutions, labor leaders in state after state began to join the cause.

At the same time, the nation confronted a daring wave of labor militancy. In 1905, the Western Federation of Miners (WFM), led by fiery leaders like William D. "Big Bill" Haywood, joined with other radicals to create a new movement, the Industrial Workers of the World (IWW). The Wobblies, as they were called, were fervent supporters of the Marxist class struggle. As **syndical-**

ists, they believed that by resisting in the workplace and ultimately launching a **general strike**, workers could overthrow capitalism. A new society would emerge, run directly by workers. At its height, around 1916, the IWW had about 100,000 members. Though divided by internal conflicts, the group helped spark a number of local protests during the 1910s, including strikes of railcar builders in Pennsylvania; textile operatives in Lawrence, Massachusetts; rubber workers in Ohio; and miners in northern Minnesota.

Meanwhile, after midnight on October 1, 1910, an explosion ripped through the *Los Angeles Times* headquarters, killing twenty employees and wrecking the building. It turned out that John J. McNamara, a high official of the American Federation of Labor's Bridge and Structural Iron Workers Union, had planned the bombing against the fiercely anti-union *Times*. McNamara's brother and another union member had carried out the attack. The bombing created a sensation, as did the terrible Triangle Shirtwaist fire (see Chapter 19) and the IWW's high-profile strikes. What should be done? As the election of 1912 approached, the "labor question" moved high on the nation's agenda.

Taft and the Election of 1912

In 1908, President Theodore Roosevelt chose to retire. He bequeathed the Republican nomination to William Howard Taft, a talented administrator. Taft portrayed himself as "Roosevelt's man," though he maintained a closer relationship than his predecessor had with pro-business Republicans in Congress. Taft's Democratic opponent in 1908 was William Jennings Bryan. Eloquent as ever, Bryan attacked Republicans as the party of "plutocrats," men who used their wealth to buy political influence. He outdid Taft in urging tougher antitrust and pro-labor legislation, but Taft won comfortably.

In the wake of Taft's victory, however, rising pressure for national reform initiatives began to divide Republicans. Conservatives dug in against further reforms, while militant progressives within the party thought Roosevelt and his successor had not gone far enough. Reconciling these conflicting forces was a daunting task. For Taft it spelled disaster. Through various incidents he found himself on the opposite side of progressive Republicans, who began to call themselves Insurgents and plot their own path.

Returning from a yearlong safari in Africa, Roosevelt yearned to reenter the political fray. Taft's dispute with the Insurgents gave the former president the reason he needed. In a speech in Osawatomie, Kansas, in August 1910, Roosevelt made the case for what he

JUNE. 1914 10 CENTS

The MASSES

IN THIS ISSUE

CLASS WAR IN COLORADO—Max Eastman
WHAT ABOUT MEXICO ?—John Reed

The Ludlow Massacre, 1914

Like his drawing of the Triangle Shirtwaist fire victims on page 615, this cover illustration for the popular socialist magazine *The Masses* is another demonstration of John Sloan's outrage at social injustice in progressive America. The drawing memorializes a tragic episode during a coal miners' strike at Ludlow, Colorado—the asphyxiation of women and children when the state militia torched the tent city of evicted miners—and the aftermath, an armed revolt by enraged miners. *The Masses*, June 1914.

called the New Nationalism. In modern America, he argued, property had to be controlled "to whatever degree the public welfare may require it." With this formulation, Roosevelt took up social justice issues, proposing a federal child labor law, more recognition of labor rights, and a national minimum wage for women. Pressed by friends like Jane Addams, Roosevelt also endorsed women's voting rights. Most radical was his attack on the legal system. Insisting that courts stood in the way of reform, Roosevelt proposed sharp curbs on their powers, even raising the possibility of popular recall of court decisions.

Early in 1912, Roosevelt announced himself as a Republican candidate for president, sweeping Insurgents into his camp. A bitter battle within the party ensued. Roosevelt won the states that held primary elections, but Taft controlled party caucuses elsewhere. Dominated by regulars, the Republican convention chose Taft. Roosevelt led his followers into what became known

as the Progressive Party, offering his New Nationalism directly to the people. Though she harbored private doubts (especially about Roosevelt's mania for battleships), Jane Addams called the new party "the American exponent of a world-wide movement for juster social conditions." In a nod to Roosevelt's combative stance, the Progressive Party won the nickname "Bull Moose Party."

Roosevelt was not the only rebel on the ballot in 1912. The major parties also faced a challenge from charismatic socialist Eugene V. Debs. In the 1890s, Debs had founded the American Railway Union (ARU), a broad-based union that included both skilled and unskilled workers. In 1894, amid the upheavals of depression and popular protest, the ARU had boycotted luxury Pullman sleeping cars, in support of a strike by workers at the Pullman Company. Railroad managers, claiming that the strike obstructed the U.S. mail, persuaded Grover Cleveland's administration to intervene

On to the White House

At the 1912 Democratic convention, Woodrow Wilson only narrowly defeated the front-runner, Champ Clark of Missouri. *Harper's Weekly* depicted Wilson immediately after his nomination—the scholar turned politician triumphantly riding off on the Democratic donkey, with his running mate, Thomas R. Marshall, hanging on behind. The magazine's editor, George Harvey, had identified Wilson as presidential timber back in 1906—long before the Princeton president had thought of politics—and had worked on his behalf from then on.   *Harper's Weekly*, June 13, 1912.

against the union. The strike failed. Along with other ARU leaders, Debs served time in prison. The experience radicalized him, and in 1901 he launched the Socialist Party of America. Debs translated socialism into an American idiom, emphasizing the democratic process as a means to defeat capitalism. By the early 1910s, his party had secured a minor but persistent role in politics.

Both the Progressive and Socialist Parties drew strength from the West, a region with vigorous urban reform movements and a legacy of farmer-labor activism. The Progressive Party tapped California's reform governor, Hiram Johnson, as Roosevelt's running mate on the Progressive ticket. Watching the threats posed by the insurgent Progressive and Socialist Parties, Democrats were also keen to build on dramatic gains they

had made in the 1910 midterm elections. Among their new generation of leaders was Virginia-born Woodrow Wilson, a political scientist who had served as president of Princeton University. As governor of New Jersey, Wilson had compiled an impressive reform record, including passage of a direct primary, workers' compensation, and utility regulation. In 1912, he won the Democratic presidential nomination.

Wilson possessed, to a fault, the moral certainty that characterized many elite progressives. Only gradually did he hammer out a coherent reform program, calling it the New Freedom. Wilson had much in common with Roosevelt. "The old time of individual competition is probably gone by," Wilson admitted, and he agreed on the need for more federal measures to restrict big business. But his program appeared less sweeping than Roosevelt's. "If America is not to have free enterprise," Wilson warned, "then she can have freedom of no sort whatever." He claimed that Roosevelt's program represented collectivism, whereas the New Freedom would preserve political and economic liberty.

With four candidates in the field — Taft, Roosevelt, Wilson, and Debs — the 1912 campaign generated intense excitement. But the division of former Republicans between Taft and Roosevelt made the results fairly easy to predict. Wilson won, though he received only 42 percent of the popular vote, and almost certainly would have lost if Roosevelt had not been in the race (Map 20.6). With his defense of free enterprise and his markedly southern racial views, Wilson appeared to be a rather old-fashioned choice. But with labor protests reaching new peaks of visibility and middle-class progressives gathering public support, Wilson faced intense pressure to act.

Wilson and the New Freedom

In his inaugural address, Wilson acknowledged that industrialization had precipitated a crisis. "There can be no equality or opportunity, the first essential of justice in the body politic," he said, "if men and women and children be not shielded . . . from the consequences of great industrial and social processes which they cannot alter, control, or singly cope with." Wilson was a Democrat, and labor interests and farmers made up important components of his party's base. Thus, though the Greenback-Labor and People's Parties had faded away, rural Democrats played a central role in the reforms achieved under Wilson. In an era of rising corporate power, such Democrats had come to believe that workers needed stronger government to intervene on their behalf.

Democrats continued to have an enormous blind spot: their opposition to African American rights, a position to which the national party adhered until 1948, and to which southern Democrats clung even longer. There was no hope, for example, that Democrats would pass federal antilynching legislation. But Republicans, who had had plentiful opportunities, had also conspicuously failed to pass such a law. In 1912, the Progressive Party had refused to seat southern black delegates or take a stand for racial equality. While African Americans had no reason to vote for Democrats, they found few reasons to vote for Republicans or Progressives, either.

In other ways, Democrats were transforming themselves into a modern, state-building party. The Wilson administration achieved a series of landmark economic

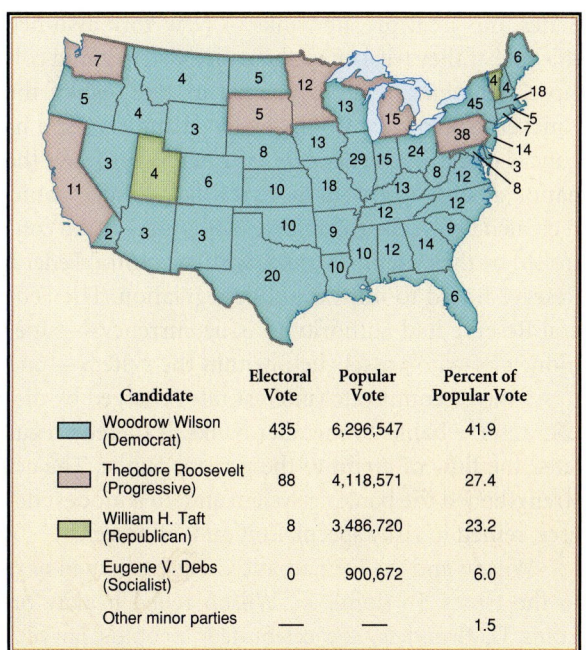

Candidate	Electoral Vote	Popular Vote	Percent of Popular Vote
Woodrow Wilson (Democrat)	435	6,296,547	41.9
Theodore Roosevelt (Progressive)	88	4,118,571	27.4
William H. Taft (Republican)	8	3,486,720	23.2
Eugene V. Debs (Socialist)	0	900,672	6.0
Other minor parties	—	—	1.5

MAP 20.6

The Presidential Election of 1912

The 1912 election reveals why the two-party system is so strongly rooted in American politics – especially in presidential elections. The Democrats, though a minority party, won an electoral landslide because the Republicans divided their vote between Roosevelt and Taft. This result indicates what is at stake when major parties splinter. The Socialist Party candidate, Eugene V. Debs, despite a record vote of 900,000, received no electoral votes.

reforms. The most enduring was the federal income tax. This long-sought tax required a federal constitutional amendment, which was ratified by the states in February 1913. The next year, Congress used this new power to enact an income tax of 1 to 7 percent on Americans who had annual incomes of $4,000 or more. At a time when white male wageworkers might expect to make $800 per year, the tax affected less than 5 percent of households. Three years later, Congress followed it with an inheritance tax. These measures created an entirely new way to fund the federal government; they replaced Republicans' high tariff as the chief source of revenue, and tariff reduction benefited ordinary consumers. Over subsequent decades, especially between the 1930s and the 1970s, the income tax system markedly reduced America's extremes of wealth and poverty.

The new president also reorganized the nation's financial system to address problems caused by the absence of a central bank. The main function of central banks at the time was to back up commercial banks in case they could not meet their obligations. In the United

States, the great private banks of New York assumed this role; if they weakened, the entire system could collapse. This had nearly happened in 1907, when the Knickerbocker Trust Company failed and caused a financial panic. The Federal Reserve Act of 1913 gave the nation a banking system more resistant to such panic. It created twelve district reserve banks funded and controlled by their member banks, with the central Federal Reserve Board to impose public regulation. The Federal Reserve had authority to issue currency—paper money based on assets held within the system—and to set the discount rate (interest rate) charged by district reserve banks to member banks. It thereby regulated the flow of credit to the general public. The act strengthened the banking system and, to a modest degree, reined in risky speculation on Wall Street.

Wilson and the Democratic Congress turned next to the trusts. In doing so, Wilson relied heavily on Louis D. Brandeis, the celebrated "people's lawyer." Brandeis denied that monopoly meant efficiency. On the contrary, he believed vigorous competition in a free market was most efficient. The trick was to prevent trusts from unfairly using their power to curb such competition. In the Clayton Antitrust Act of 1914, which amended the Sherman Act, the definition of illegal practices was left flexible, subject to the test of whether an action "substantially lessen[ed] competition or tend[ed] to create a monopoly." The new Federal Trade Commission received broad powers to decide what was fair, investigating companies and issuing "cease and desist" orders against anticompetitive practices.

Equally important was Wilson's appointment of the blue-ribbon U.S. Commission on Industrial Relations, charged with investigating the conditions of labor. In its majority report, the commission summed up the impact of industrialization on low-skilled workers. Many earned $10 or less a week and endured regular episodes of unemployment. Some faced long-term poverty and hardship, and they held "an almost universal conviction" that they were "denied justice." The commission concluded that the core reason for industrial violence was the ruthless anti-unionism of American employers. In its most important recommendation, the majority report called for federal laws protecting workers' right to organize and engage in collective bargaining. Though such laws were, in 1915, too radical to win passage, the commission's report helped set a new national agenda for labor rights that would come to fruition in the 1930s.

Guided by the revelations of this commission, President Wilson warmed up to labor. In 1915 and 1916, he championed a host of bills to benefit American workers. They included the Adamson Act, which established an eight-hour day for railroad workers; the Seamen's Act, which eliminated age-old abuses of merchant sailors; and a workmen's compensation law for federal employees. Wilson, despite his initial modest goals, had presided over a major expansion of federal authority, reflected in the steady growth of U.S. government offices during his term (Figure 20.1).

Progressive Legacies

In the post–Civil War era, millions of Americans understood that the political system needed to adjust to new industrial conditions. In the 1880s, radical farmer and labor advocates proposed sweeping limitations on industrial capitalism; though they exerted substantial pressure, especially within the Democratic Party after 1896, only a portion of their vision was fulfilled. By the turn of the twentieth century, economic reform gained increasing support from middle-class and elite pro-

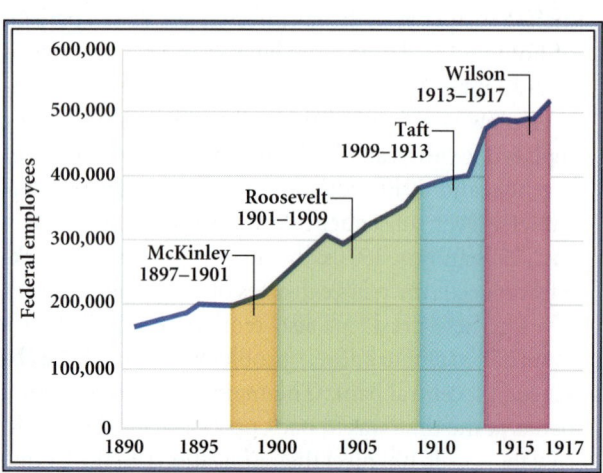

FIGURE 20.1

The Federal Bureaucracy, 1890–1917

The surge in federal employment after 1900 mirrored the surge in government authority. Progressive initiatives at the local and state levels, along with pressure from grassroots reformers, led to new federal departments and bureaus, designed to oversee and regulate the economy and protect public welfare.   Source: Wallace S. Sayre, ed., *The Federal Government Service* (Englewood Cliffs, NJ: Prentice-Hall, 1965).

gressives, especially in the cities. They tended to propose more modest measures, often shying away from democratic solutions in favor of expert commissions and political management by the "best men." But they held substantial clout.

Whether they were rural, working-class, or middle-class, reformers faced fierce opposition from powerful business interests. Whenever reformers managed, at last, to win a key regulatory law, they often found it struck down by hostile courts. Thus, the Progressive Era in the United States should be understood partly by its limitations. Racial prejudice and increasing elitism warped the cause of reform; African Americans, their plight ignored by many white reformers, faced segregation and violence, and along with some immigrants and poor whites, they found themselves disenfranchised. Meanwhile, federal courts slowed down the progress of key reforms like state protections for labor. Divided power in a federalist system blocked the passage of uniform national laws on such key issues as child labor. Urgently needed social welfare programs, including national health insurance and old-age pensions—which became popular in Europe during these decades—scarcely made it onto the American agenda until the New Deal of the 1930s.

An international perspective suggests several reasons for the U.S. resistance to social welfare programs. Business interests in the United States were exceptionally successful and powerful, flush with recent expansion. And in general, during the era of industrialization, voters in countries with older, more native-born populations supported more robust government regulation and social welfare spending than did voters in countries with younger populations and large numbers of immigrants. Younger voters, understandably, seem to have been less concerned than older voters about health insurance and security in old age. Divisions within the American working class also played a role. Black, immigrant, and native-born white laborers often viewed one another as enemies or strangers rather than as members of a unified class with common interests. This helps explain why the Socialist Party drew, at its peak, less than 6 percent of the U.S. vote at a time when its counterparts in Finland, Germany, and France drew 40 percent or more. Lack of pressure from a strong, self-conscious workingmen's party led to more limited results in the United States.

But it would be wrong to underestimate the achievements of Progressive Era reformers. Over the course of several decades, they persuaded more and more comfortable, prosperous Americans that the industrial economy required stronger government regulation. Even the most cautious, elite progressives recognized that the United States had entered a new era. Giant multinational corporations overshadowed small businesses; with immigrants and farmers' children crowding into vast cities, ties of kin and village melted away. Outdated political methods—from the "spoils system" to corrupt urban machines—would no longer do. Walter Lippman, a founding editor of the progressive magazine *The New Republic*, observed in 1914 that Americans found themselves with "no precedents to guide us, no wisdom that wasn't made for a simpler age." Progressives created new wisdom. Between 1883 and 1917, they drew the blueprints for a modern American state, one whose powers began to suit the needs of an industrial era. At the same time, a stronger, more assertive United States began to exercise new influence on the world stage.

- What types of progressive legislation passed in the early 1900s? How might results have been different if William McKinley had survived the assassination attempt and remained as president?

- What grassroots reform movements emerged during this period? What were their goals, and how successfully did they realize them?

- What factors account for Woodrow Wilson's victory in 1912? How did the reforms achieved under Wilson differ from those passed during Theodore Roosevelt's presidency?

- What factors explain the limits of progressive reform during this period?

SUMMARY

The Progressive Era emerged from the political turmoil of the 1880s and 1890s. In the 1880s, despite the limits imposed by close elections, federal and state governments managed to achieve important administrative and economic reforms. After 1888, Republican leaders undertook more sweeping efforts, including the Sherman Antitrust Act, but failed in a quest to protect black voting rights. In the South and West, the People's Party called for much stronger government intervention in the economy, but its radical program drew bitter Republican and Democratic resistance.

The depression of the 1890s brought a wave of political reaction. Labor unrest threw the nation into crisis, and Cleveland's intransigence over the gold standard cost the Democrats dearly in the 1894 and 1896 elections. While Republicans took over the federal government, southern Democrats restricted voting rights to build the "Solid South." Meanwhile, federal courts struck down regulatory laws and supported southern racial discrimination.

After McKinley's assassination, Roosevelt launched a program that balanced reform and private enterprise. At both the federal and state levels, Progressive reformers made extensive use of elite expertise. At the grassroots level, black and white reformers battled racial discrimination; women reformers worked on issues ranging from public health to women's working conditions; and labor activists tried to address the conditions that fueled persistent labor unrest. The election of 1912 split the Republicans, giving victory to Woodrow Wilson, who launched a Democratic program of economic and labor reform. Despite the limits of the Progressive Era, the reforms of this period laid the foundation for a modern American state.

CHAPTER REVIEW QUESTIONS

- Reformers in the Progressive Era came from different backgrounds and represented several distinct interests. What were some of those backgrounds and interests? How did their goals differ?

- How did the economic crisis of the 1890s shape American politics?

- Compare the reform legislation passed during Theodore Roosevelt's presidency (1901–1909) with that during Woodrow Wilson's first term in the White House (1913–1917). How were these goals and achievements shaped by the broader agenda of the party that held power (Republicans, in Roosevelt's case, and Democrats, in Wilson's)?

- Historians generally call the decades from the 1880s to the 1910s the "Progressive Era." Given the limitations and new problems that emerged during this time, as well as the achievements of progressive reform, do you think the name is warranted? What other names might we suggest for this era?

FOR FURTHER EXPLORATION

On post-Reconstruction politics see H. Wayne Morgan, *From Hayes to McKinley* (1969) and Charles Calhoun, *Conceiving a New Republic* (2006). On liberals see Nancy Cohen, *The Reconstruction of American Liberalism* (2002). On rural reformers and labor see Elizabeth Sanders, *Roots of Reform* (1999) and Michael Kazin's biography of William Jennings Bryan, *A Godly Hero* (2006). On Populism, see Robert C. McMath's *American Populism* (1993) and Charles Postel's *The Populist Vision* (2007). Alexander Keyssar, *The Right to Vote* (2000), explores assaults on popular politics. On southern politics, the seminal book is C. Vann Woodward, *Origins of the New South, 1877–1913* (1951); a recent revision is Edward Ayers, *The Promise of the New South* (1992). On disenfranchisement see Michael Perman, *Struggle for Mastery* (2001), and J. Morgan Kousser, *The Shaping of Southern Politics* (1974).

On the crisis of the 1890s see Henry May, *Protestant Churches and Industrial America* (1949), R. Hal Williams, *Years of Decision* (1978), and Carlos Schwantes, *Coxey's Army* (1985). For the impact on labor, see William Forbath, *Law and the Shaping of the American Labor Movement* (1991). Bedford has issued helpful treatments of key Supreme Court decisions: *Plessy v. Ferguson*, ed. Brook Thomas (1997), and *Muller v. Oregon*, ed. Nancy Woloch (1996).

The literature on progressivism is voluminous. See Maureen Flanagan, *America Reformed* (2007); Robert D. Johnson, *The Radical Middle Class* (2003); Kathryn Kish Sklar, *Florence Kelley and the Nation's Work* (1995); Alan Dawley, *Changing the World* (2003); and Daniel Rogers, *Atlantic Crossings* (1998). A comparative treatment of Roosevelt and Wilson is John Milton Cooper's *The Warrior and the Priest* (1983).

TEST YOUR KNOWLEDGE

To assess your command of the material in this chapter, see the Online Study Guide at **bedfordstmartins.com/henretta**.

For Web sites, images, and documents related to topics and places in this chapter, visit **bedfordstmartins.com/makehistory**.

TIMELINE

1881	President James Garfield assassinated
1883	Pendleton Act establishes the Civil Service Commission
1890	Sherman Antitrust Act People's Party created in Kansas
1893	Economic depression begins
1894	Coxey's Army marches on Washington, D.C.
1895	John Pierpont Morgan arranges gold purchases to rescue U.S. Treasury
1896	William McKinley wins presidency *Plessy v. Ferguson* establishes "separate but equal" doctrine
1899	National Consumers' League founded
1901	Eugene Debs founds the Socialist Party of America McKinley assassinated; Theodore Roosevelt assumes presidency
1902	Newlands Reclamation Act
1903	Elkins Act
1905	Industrial Workers of the World founded
1906	Hepburn Act
1908	*Muller v. Oregon* limits women's work hours
1912	Three-way election gives presidency to Woodrow Wilson
1913	Seventeenth Amendment Graduated income tax introduced Federal Reserve Act
1914	Clayton Antitrust Act

An Emerging World Power, 1877–1918

When he accepted the Democratic presidential nomination in 1900, William Jennings Bryan delivered a famous speech denouncing U.S. military occupation of overseas territories. "God Himself," Bryan declared, "placed in every human heart the love of liberty. . . . He never made a race of people so low in the scale of civilization or intelligence that it would welcome a foreign master." Two years earlier, the United States had helped Cuban rebels liberate their island from Spanish rule. Bryan and other Democrats had supported that cause, believing the United States was helping create an independent Cuba. By 1900, however, the political landscape had shifted. Republican president William McKinley was leading the United States in an ambitious plan of overseas expansion, which proved popular at home. McKinley's administration had asserted control over much of the Caribbean, claimed Hawaii as a territory, and sought to annex the Philippines. Bryan failed to convince a majority of the public that **imperialism** (the exercise of military, political, and economic power overseas) was the wrong path for the United States to take. He lost the 1900 election by a landslide, and the reelected McKinley moved forward with Philippine annexation.

In the longer run, however, Bryan's views were in some ways more influential than McKinley's. That became clear in the 1910s, when, despite initial efforts to remain neutral as European alliances battled each other in World War I, the United States became caught up in the catastrophic conflict. By the end of this horrific war, European nations' grip on their colonial empires was weakening. The United States ceased acquiring overseas territories and pursued a different path. It developed an "informal empire," based on business interests rather than administrative control. President Woodrow Wilson, who in 1913 appointed Bryan as his first secretary of state, believed the United States should steer a middle course between revolutionary socialism and European-style imperialism. In Wilson's phrase, America would "make the world safe for democracy," while unapologetically working to foster global capitalism and advance U.S. economic interests. Critics argued that these goals constituted another form of imperialism, grounded in economic rather than administrative power. Advocates, however, established the dual goal of spreading democracy and capitalism as an enduring basis for American foreign policy.

American Soldiers on a French Battlefield, 1918

As the United States asserted its power on the world stage, American soldiers found themselves fighting on foreign battlefields. This 1918 photograph shows a few of the 1 million U.S. soldiers who joined French and British troops fighting on the brutal Western Front to defeat Germany in the Great War. Over 26,000 American soldiers lost their lives on the battlefield during World War I, and 95,000 were wounded. Library of Congress.

From Expansion to Imperialism

Historians used to describe turn-of-the-twentieth-century U.S. imperialism as something new. Now they emphasize continuities between foreign policy in this era and the nation's relentless earlier expansion across the North American continent. Wars against native peoples had occurred almost continuously since the nation's founding; in the 1840s, the United States had taken one-third of Mexico. The United States never administered a large colonial empire, as did European powers like Spain, England, Belgium, and Germany, partly because the United States had a plentiful supply of natural resources in the American West. But policymakers went on a determined quest for global markets. Industrialization and a modern navy gave the United States muscle; the economic crisis of the 1890s provided a spur.

Foundations of Empire

As they embarked on empire-building around 1900, American policymakers fulfilled a vision laid out three decades earlier by William Seward (secretary of state under presidents Abraham Lincoln and Andrew Johnson), who emphasized access to global markets as the key to power. Seward's ideas had won only limited support in the wake of the Civil War, but the severe economic depression of 1893 (see Chapter 20) brought Republicans into power and Seward's ideas back into vogue. Confronting high unemployment and mass protests, policymakers feared that American workers would embrace socialism or communism. The alternative, they believed, was to manufacture products for overseas markets in order to create jobs and prosperity at home.

Intellectual trends also favored imperialism. As early as 1885, in his popular book *Our Country*, Congregationalist minister Josiah Strong urged Protestants to proselytize overseas. He predicted that the American "Anglo-Saxon race"—"the representative, let us hope, of the largest liberty, the purest Christianity, the highest civilization, having developed particularly aggressive traits calculated to impress its institutions upon mankind"—would "spread itself over the earth." Such arguments were grounded in **American exceptionalism**, the idea that the United States had a destiny unique among nations to foster democracy and civilization.

As Strong's exhortation suggested, imperialists also drew on increasingly popular racial theories, which claimed that people of "Anglo-Saxon" descent—English and often German—were superior to all other peoples. "Anglo-Saxon" rule over foreign people of color made sense in an era when, at home, the Supreme Court sanctioned racial segregation, and many whites believed that native peoples were vanishing and black voters should be disenfranchised. Imperialists often linked white Americans' conquest of the North American continent with the drive for overseas power. Responding to critics of U.S. occupation of the Philippines, Theodore Roosevelt scoffed: If America ought to return the Philippines to Filipinos, he declared, then it was "morally bound to return Arizona to the Apaches." Imperialists also justified their views through racialized Social Darwinism. Josiah Strong, for example, predicted that with the lands of the globe fully occupied, a "competition of races" would ensue, based on "survival of the fittest."

Fear of ruthless competition drove the United States, like European nations, to invest in the latest weapons. American policymakers saw that the European powers were amassing steel-plated battleships and carving up Africa and Asia among themselves. In his book *The Influence of Sea Power upon History* (1890), U.S. naval officer Alfred T. Mahan urged the United States to enter the fray, observing that naval power had been essential to the growth of past empires. In 1890, Congress appropriated funds for three battleships. President Grover Cleveland continued this naval program.

Cleveland's secretary of state, Richard Olney, turned rising imperial interests into direct confrontation when he warned European powers away from Latin America, which he saw as the United States' rightful sphere of influence. Without consulting the nation of Venezuela, Olney suddenly demanded in July 1895 that Britain resolve a long-standing border dispute between Venezuela and Britain's neighboring colony, British Guiana. Invoking the Monroe Doctrine, which stated that the Western Hemisphere was off-limits to further European colonization, Olney warned that the United States would brook no challenge to its interests. Startled, Britain agreed to arbitrate. American power was on the ascent.

The War of 1898

While Olney was intervening in Venezuela, events were unfolding in the Caribbean that would present the United States with a far greater opportunity to wield power. In February 1895, Cuban patriots mounted a major guerrilla war against Spain, which had lost most of its New World territories but had managed to hold on to the island of Cuba. The Spanish commander responded by rounding up Cuban civilians into concentration camps, where as many as 200,000 died of starvation, exposure, or dysentery. In the United States, William Randolph Hearst turned their plight into a cause célèbre. Hearst's campaign fed a surge of nationalism, especially among those who feared that American men were losing strength and courage amid the conditions of industrial society. The government should not pass up this opportunity, said Indiana senator Albert Beveridge, to "manufacture manhood." Congress called for Cuban independence.

President Cleveland had no interest in supporting the Cuban rebellion, but he worried over Spain's failure to end it. The war was disrupting trade and damaging American-owned sugar plantations on the island. An unstable Cuba was incompatible with America's strategic interests, which included a proposed canal whose Caribbean approaches would have to be safeguarded. Taking office in 1897, President William McKinley was inclined to take a tougher stance than Cleveland had. In September, the U.S. minister in Madrid informed Spain that it must ensure an "early and certain peace" or the United States would step in. At first, this hard line seemed to work: Spain's conservative regime fell, and a liberal government, taking office in October 1897, offered Cuba limited self-rule. But Spanish loyalists in Havana rioted against the proposal, while Cuban rebels held out for full independence.

On February 9, 1898, Hearst's *New York Journal* published a private letter in which Dupuy de Lôme, Spanish minister to the United States, belittled the McKinley administration. De Lôme resigned, but exposure of the letter intensified Americans' indignation toward Spain. The next week brought shocking news: The U.S. battle cruiser *Maine* had exploded and sunk in Havana harbor, with 260 seamen lost. "Whole Country Thrills with the War Fever," proclaimed the *New York Journal.* "Remember the *Maine* and to hell with Spain," became the chant across the country. Popular passions were now a major factor in the march toward war.

McKinley assumed that the sinking of the *Maine* had been accidental. Improbably, though, a U.S. naval board of inquiry blamed a mine, fueling public outrage. (Later investigators disagreed: The more likely cause was a faulty ship design that placed explosive munitions too close to coal bunkers, which were prone to fire.) No evidence linked Spain to the purported mine. But if a mine sank the ship, then Spain was responsible for not protecting the American vessel.

Hesitant business leaders now became impatient, believing that war was preferable to an unending Cuban crisis. On March 27, McKinley cabled an ultimatum to Madrid: an immediate ceasefire in Cuba for six months and, with the United States as mediator, peace negotiations with the rebels. Spain, though desperate to avoid war, balked at McKinley's added demand that mediation must result in Cuban independence. On April 11, McKinley asked Congress for authority to intervene in Cuba "in the name of humanity, in the name of civilization, [and] in behalf of endangered American interests."

Historians long referred to the ensuing fight as the Spanish-American War, but that name ignores the central role of Cuban revolutionaries, who had started the war and hoped to achieve national independence. Therefore, many historians now call the three-way conflict the War of 1898. At the time, Americans widely admired Cuban rebels' aspirations for freedom; even so, the McKinley administration defeated a congressional attempt to recognize the rebel government. In response, Senator Henry M. Teller of Colorado added an amendment to the war bill, disclaiming any intention by the United States to occupy Cuba. The Teller Amendment reassured Americans that their country would uphold democracy abroad as well as at home. McKinley's expectations differed, however. He wrote privately, "While we are conducting war and until its conclusion, we must keep all we get; when the war is over we must keep what we want."

On April 24, 1898, Spain declared war on the United States. The news provoked full-blown war fever. Across America, young men enlisted for the fight. Theodore Roosevelt accepted a commission as lieutenant colonel of a cavalry regiment. Recruits poured into makeshift bases around Tampa, Florida, where confusion reigned. Rifles did not arrive; food was bad, sanitation worse. No provision had been made for getting troops to Cuba, so the government hastily collected a fleet of yachts and commercial boats. Fortunately, the small regular army was a disciplined, professional force, and its 28,000 seasoned troops provided a nucleus for the 200,000 volunteers. The navy was in better shape: Spain had nothing to match America's seven battleships and armored cruisers. The Spanish admiral bitterly predicted that his fleet would "like Don Quixote go out to fight windmills and come back with a broken head."

The first, decisive military engagement took place in the Pacific. This was the handiwork of Theodore Roosevelt, who, while still in the Navy Department, had gotten intrepid Commodore George Dewey appointed

Cutting Sugar Cane, Hawaii.

Sugarcane Plantation, Hawaii

More than 300,000 Asians from China, Japan, Korea, and the Philippines came to work in the Hawaiian sugarcane fields between 1850 and 1920. The hardships they endured are reflected in plantation work songs, such as this one by Japanese laborers:

But when I came what I saw was Hell
The boss was Satan
The *lunas* [overseers] his helpers.

© Curt Teich Postcard Archives, Lake County Museum.

commander of the Pacific fleet. In the event of war, Dewey had instructions to sail immediately for the Spanish-owned Philippines. When war was declared, Roosevelt confronted his surprised superior and pressured him into validating Dewey's instructions. On May 1, 1898, American ships cornered the Spanish fleet in Manila Bay and destroyed it. Manila, the Philippine capital, fell on August 13. Dewey's victory was critical. "We must on no account let the [Philippines] go," declared Senator Henry Cabot Lodge. McKinley and his advisors agreed. The United States now had a major foothold in the western Pacific.

Dewey's victory instantly directed policymakers' attention to the Hawaiian Islands. Nominally an independent nation, Hawaii had long been under American dominance, since its climate had attracted a horde of American sugarcane planters. An 1876 treaty between the United States and the island's monarch gave Hawaiian sugar tariff-free access to the American market, with Hawaii pledging to sign no such agreement with any other power. In 1887, Hawaii also granted a long-coveted lease for a U.S. naval base at Pearl Harbor. When Hawaii's access to the U.S. market was canceled by a new tariff in 1890, sugar planters revolted against the islands' ruler, Queen Liliuokalani, and negotiated a treaty of annexation. But Grover Cleveland rejected the treaty when he entered office. He declared that it would violate America's "unbroken tradition" against acquiring territory overseas.

Dewey's victory delivered what the planters wanted: Hawaii acquired strategic value as a halfway station to the Philippines. In July 1898, Congress authorized the annexation of Hawaii. Further annexations then took on their own logic. The navy pressed for another coal-ing base in the central Pacific; that meant Guam, a Spanish island in the Marianas. A strategic base was needed in the Caribbean; that meant Puerto Rico. By early summer, before U.S. troops had fired a shot in Cuba, McKinley's broader war aims were crystallizing.

In Cuba, Spanish forces were depleted by the long guerrilla war. Though poorly trained and equipped, American forces had the advantages of a demoralized foe and knowledgeable Cuban allies. The main battle occurred on July 1 at San Juan Hill, near Santiago, where the Spanish fleet was anchored (Map 21.1). Roosevelt's Rough Riders took the lead, but four African American regiments bore the brunt of the fighting. White observers credited much of the victory to the "superb gallantry" of these soldiers. Spanish troops retreated to a well-fortified second line, but U.S. forces were spared the test of a second assault. On July 3, the Spanish fleet in Santiago harbor tried a desperate run through the American blockade and was destroyed. Days later, Spanish forces surrendered. American combat casualties had been few; most U.S. soldiers' deaths had resulted from malaria and yellow fever.

The Spoils of War

The United States and Spain quickly signed a preliminary peace agreement in which Spain agreed to liberate Cuba and cede Puerto Rico and Guam to the United States. But what would the United States do with the Philippines, an immense archipelago that lay more than 5,000 miles from California? Initially, the United States aimed to keep only Manila, because of its fine harbor. Manila was not defensible, however, without the whole of Luzon, the large island on which the city was located.

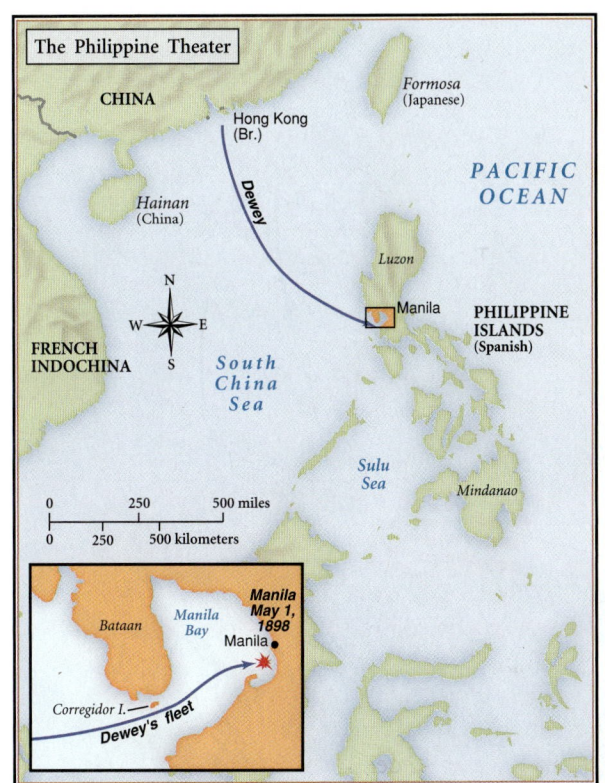

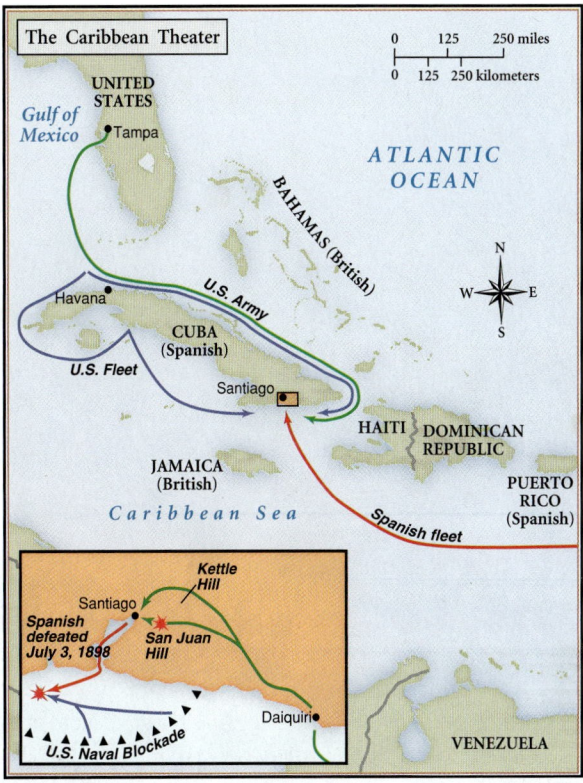

MAP 21.1

The War of 1898

America's swift victory against Spain in the War of 1898 resulted from overwhelming naval superiority. Dewey's destruction of the Spanish fleet in Manila harbor doomed the Spaniards in the Philippines. In Cuba, the ill-equipped and poorly supplied American ground forces won a hard victory on San Juan Hill. With the United States in control of the seas, the Spaniards saw no choice but to give up the battle for Cuba and the Philippines.

After some deliberation, McKinley found a justification for annexing the whole Philippines. He decided that "we could not leave [the Filipinos] to themselves — they were unfit for self-rule."

This declaration provoked heated debate. Under the Constitution, argued Republican senator George F. Hoar, "no power is given to the Federal Government to acquire territory to be held and governed permanently as colonies" or "to conquer alien people and hold them in subjugation." Leading citizens and peace advocates, including Jane Addams and Mark Twain, enlisted in the anti-imperialist cause. Steel king Andrew Carnegie offered $20 million to purchase Philippine independence. Labor leader Samuel Gompers warned union members about the threat of competition from Filipinos working for low wages. Anti-imperialists, however, were a diverse lot. Some argued that Filipinos were perfectly capable of self-rule; others warned about the dangers of annexing 8 million Filipinos of an "inferior race." "No matter whether they are fit to govern themselves or not," declared one Missouri congressman, "they are not fit to govern us."

Beginning in late 1898, Anti-Imperialist Leagues sprang up around the country, but they never sparked a mass movement. McKinley's "splendid little war" was, in fact, immensely popular. Confronted with that political reality, Democrats waffled in their opposition. Their standard-bearer, William Jennings Bryan, decided not to stake his party's future on opposition to a policy that he believed to be irreversible. He threw his party into turmoil by declaring last-minute support for McKinley's proposed treaty. Having met military defeat, Spanish representatives had little choice. In the Treaty of Paris, Spain ceded the Philippines to the United States for a payment of $20 million.

But annexation was not as simple as U.S. policymakers had expected. On February 4, 1899 — two days before the Senate ratified the treaty — fighting broke out between American and Filipino patrols on the edge of Manila. Confronted by annexation, rebel leader

The Battle of San Juan Hill

On July 1, 1898, the key battle for Cuba took place on heights overlooking Santiago. African American troops bore the brunt of the fighting. Although generally overlooked, black soldiers' role in the San Juan battle is done justice in this contemporary lithograph, without the demeaning stereotypes by which blacks were normally depicted in an age of intensifying racism. Note, however, that as in the Civil War, blacks enlisted as foot soldiers; their officers were white.   Library of Congress.

Emilio Aguinaldo asserted his nation's independence and turned his guns on occupying American forces. Though Aguinaldo found it difficult to organize a mass-based resistance movement, the ensuing conflict between Filipino nationalists and U.S. troops far exceeded in length and ferocity the war just concluded with Spain. Fighting tenacious guerrillas, the U.S. Army resorted to the same tactics Spain had employed in Cuba: burning crops and villages and rounding up civilians. Atrocities became commonplace on both sides. In three years of warfare, 4,200 Americans and an estimated 200,000 Filipinos died; many of the latter were dislocated civil-ians, particularly children, who succumbed to malnu-trition and disease.

McKinley's convincing victory over William Jennings Bryan in 1900 suggested popular satisfaction with America's overseas adventure, even in the face of dogged Filipino resistance to U.S. rule. The fighting ended in 1902, and William Howard Taft, appointed as governor-general of the Philippines, sought to make the territory a model of road building and sanitary engi-neering. Yet misgivings lingered as Americans con-fronted the brutality of the war. Philosopher William James noted that the United States had destroyed "these

Emilio Aguinaldo

At the start of the War of 1898, U.S. military leaders brought Filipino patriot Emilio Aguinaldo back from Singapore (where he had been living in exile) to foment a popular uprising that would help defeat the Spaniards. Aguinaldo came because he thought the Americans favored an independent Philippines. While it has remained a matter of dispute what assurances Aguinaldo received from the United States, differing intentions were the root cause of the Filipino insurrection against U.S. occupation, which proved far costlier in American and Filipino lives than the U.S. war with Spain that preceded it.   © Bettmann/Corbis.

islanders by the thousands, their villages and cities. . . . Could there be any more damning indictment," he asked, "of that whole bloated ideal termed 'modern civilization'?" (see Comparing American Voices, "Debating the Philippines," pp. 660–661).

Constitutional issues also remained unresolved. The treaty, while guaranteeing freedom of religion to inhabitants of ceded Spanish territories, withheld any promise of citizenship. It was up to Congress to decide Filipinos' "civil rights and political status." In 1901, the Supreme Court upheld this provision in a set of decisions known as the Insular Cases. The Constitution, declared the court, did not automatically extend citizenship to people in acquired territories; Congress could decide. Puerto Rico, Guam, and the Philippines were thus marked as colonies, not future states. In accordance with a special commission set up by McKinley, the Jones Act of 1916 eventually committed the United States to Philippine independence but set no date. (The Philippines at last achieved independence in 1946.) Though the war's carnage had rubbed off some of the moralizing gloss, America's global aspirations remained intact (Map 21.2).

- **What economic and intellectual factors promoted U.S. imperialism in the late nineteenth century?**

- **What factors combined to precipitate the U.S. war with Spain in 1898, and then with Filipinos who resisted U.S. rule of their islands? What controversies at home did the war provoke?**

Thus I have given you, I think, the Substance of the Arguments o
both sides of that great and important Questi

Debating the Philippines

As President McKinley privately acknowledged in writing – "when the war is over we must keep what we want" – seizing the Philippines was an act of national self-interest. Of the alternatives, it was the one that seemed best calculated to serve America's strategic aims in Asia. But McKinley's geopolitical decision had unintended consequences. For one, it provoked a bloody insurrection. For another, it challenged the nation's democratic principles. As these consequences hit home, a divided Senate set up a special committee and held closed hearings. Congressional testimony is a source much prized by historians. Though some of it is prepared, once questioning begins, testimony becomes unscripted, and can be especially revealing. The following documents are taken from the 1902 testimony before the Senate Committee on the Philippines.

Ideals

General Arthur MacArthur (1845–1912) was in on the action in the Philippines almost from the start. He commanded one of the first units to arrive there in 1898 and in 1900 was reassigned as the islands' military governor and general commander of the troops. His standing as a military man – holder of the Congressional Medal of Honor from the Civil War – was matched later by his more famous son, Douglas MacArthur, who fought in the Pacific during World War II. Here the elder MacArthur explains in prepared testimony his vision of America's mission to the Philippines.

At the time I returned to Manila [May 1900] to assume the supreme command it seemed to me that . . . our occupation of the island was simply one of the necessary consequences in logical sequence of our great prosperity, and to doubt the wisdom of [occupation] was simply to doubt the stability of our own institutions and in effect to declare that a self-governing nation was incapable of successfully resisting strains arising naturally from its own productive energy. It seemed to me that our conception of right, justice, freedom, and personal liberty was the precious fruit of centuries of strife . . . [and that] we must regard ourselves simply as the custodians of imperishable ideas held in trust for the general benefit of mankind. In other words, I felt that we had attained a moral and intellectual height from which we were bound to proclaim to all as the occasion arose the true message of humanity as embodied in the principles of our own institutions. . . .

All other governments that have gone to the East have simply planted trading establishments; they have not materially affected the conditions of the people. . . . There is not a single establishment, in my judgment, in Asia to-day that would survive five years if the original power which planted it was withdrawn therefrom.

The contrasting idea with our idea is this: In planting our ideas we plant something that can not be destroyed. To my mind the archipelago is a fertile soil upon which to plant republicanism. . . . We are planting the best traditions, the best characteristics of Americanism in such a way that they can never be removed from that soil. That in itself seems to me a most inspiring thought. It encouraged me during all my efforts in those lands, even when conditions seemed most disappointing, when the people themselves, not appreciating precisely what the remote consequences of our efforts were going to be, mistrusted us; but that fact was always before me — that going deep down into that fertile soil were the indispensable ideas of Americanism.

Skepticism

At this point, the general was interrupted by Colorado senator Thomas Patterson, a Populist-Democrat and a vocal anti-imperialist.

Sen. Patterson: Do you mean that imperishable idea of which you speak is the right of self-government?

Gen. MacArthur: Precisely so; self-government regulated by law as I understand it in this Republic.

Sen. Patterson: Of course you do not mean self-government regulated by some foreign and superior power?

Gen. MacArthur: Well, that is a matter of evolution, Senator. We are putting these institutions there so they will evolve themselves just as here and everywhere else where freedom has flourished. . . .

Sen. Patterson [after the General concluded his statement]: Do I understand your claim of right and duty to retain the Philippine Islands is based upon the proposition that they have come to us upon the basis of our morals, honorable dealing, and unassailable international integrity?

Gen. MacArthur: That proposition is not questioned by anybody in the world, excepting a few people in the United States. . . . We will be benefited, and the Filipino people will be benefited, and that is what I meant by the original proposition—

Sen. Patterson: Do you mean the Filipino people that are left alive?

Gen. MacArthur: I mean the Filipino people. . . .

Sen. Patterson: You mean those left alive after they have been subjugated?

Gen. MacArthur: I do not admit that there has been any unusual destruction of life in the Philippine Islands. The destruction is simply the incident of war, and of course it embraces only a very small percentage of the total population.

. . . I doubt if any war—either international or civil, any war on earth—has been conducted with as much humanity, with as much careful consideration, with as much self-restraint, as have been the American operations in the Philippine Archipelago. . . .

Realities

Brigadier General Robert P. Hughes, a military district commander, testified as follows.

Q: In burning towns, what would you do? Would the entire town be destroyed by fire or would only the offending portions of the town be burned?

Gen. Hughes: I do not know that we ever had a case of burning what you would call a town in this country, but probably a barrio or a sitio; probably half a dozen houses, native shacks, where the insurrectos would go in and be concealed, and if they caught a detachment passing they would kill some of them.

Q: What did I understand you to say would be the consequences of that?

Gen. Hughes: They usually burned the village.

Q: All of the houses in the village?

Gen. Hughes: Yes, every one of them.

Q: What would become of the inhabitants?

Gen. Hughes: That was their lookout.

Q: If these shacks were of no consequence what was the utility of their destruction?

Gen. Hughes: The destruction was as a punishment. They permitted these people to come in there and conceal themselves. . . .

Q: The punishment in that case would fall, not upon the men, who could go elsewhere, but mainly upon the women and little children.

Gen. Hughes: The women and children are part of the family, and where you wish to inflict a punishment you can punish the man probably worse in that way than in any other.

Q: But is that within the ordinary rules of civilized warfare? . . .

Gen. Hughes: These people are not civilized.

Cruelties

Daniel J. Evans, Twelfth Infantry, describes the "water cure."

Q: The committee would like to hear . . . whether you were the witness to any cruelties inflicted upon the natives of the Philippine Islands; and if so, under what circumstances.

Evans: The case I had reference to was where they gave the water cure to a native in the Ilicano Province at Ilocos Norte . . . about the month of August 1900. There were two native scouts with the American forces. They went out and brought in a couple of insurgents. . . . They tried to get from this insurgent . . . where the rest of the insurgents were at that time. . . . The first thing one of the Americans— I mean one of the scouts for the Americans—grabbed one of the men by the head and jerked his head back, and then they took a tomato can and poured water down his throat until he could hold no more. . . . Then they forced a gag into his mouth; they stood him up . . . against a post and fastened him so that he could not move. Then one man, an American soldier, who was over six feet tall, and who was very strong, too, struck this native in the pit of the stomach as hard as he could. . . . They kept that operation up for quite a time, and finally I thought the fellow was about to die, but I don't believe he was as bad as that, because finally he told them he would tell, and from that day on he was taken away, and I saw no more of him.

Source: Henry F. Graff, ed., *American Imperialism and the Philippine Insurrection* (Boston: Little, Brown, 1969), 64–65, 80–81, 137–139, 144–145.

ANALYZING THE EVIDENCE

- **The text of this chapter offers the U.S. reasons for holding on to the Philippines. In what ways does General MacArthur's testimony confirm, add to, or contradict the text account?**

- **The chapter text also describes the anti-imperialist movement. What does Senator Patterson's cross-examination of General MacArthur reveal about the anti-imperialists' beliefs?**

- **Does the clash of ideas in these excerpts remain relevant to our own time? How does it compare to what you might read or hear about in a news source today?**

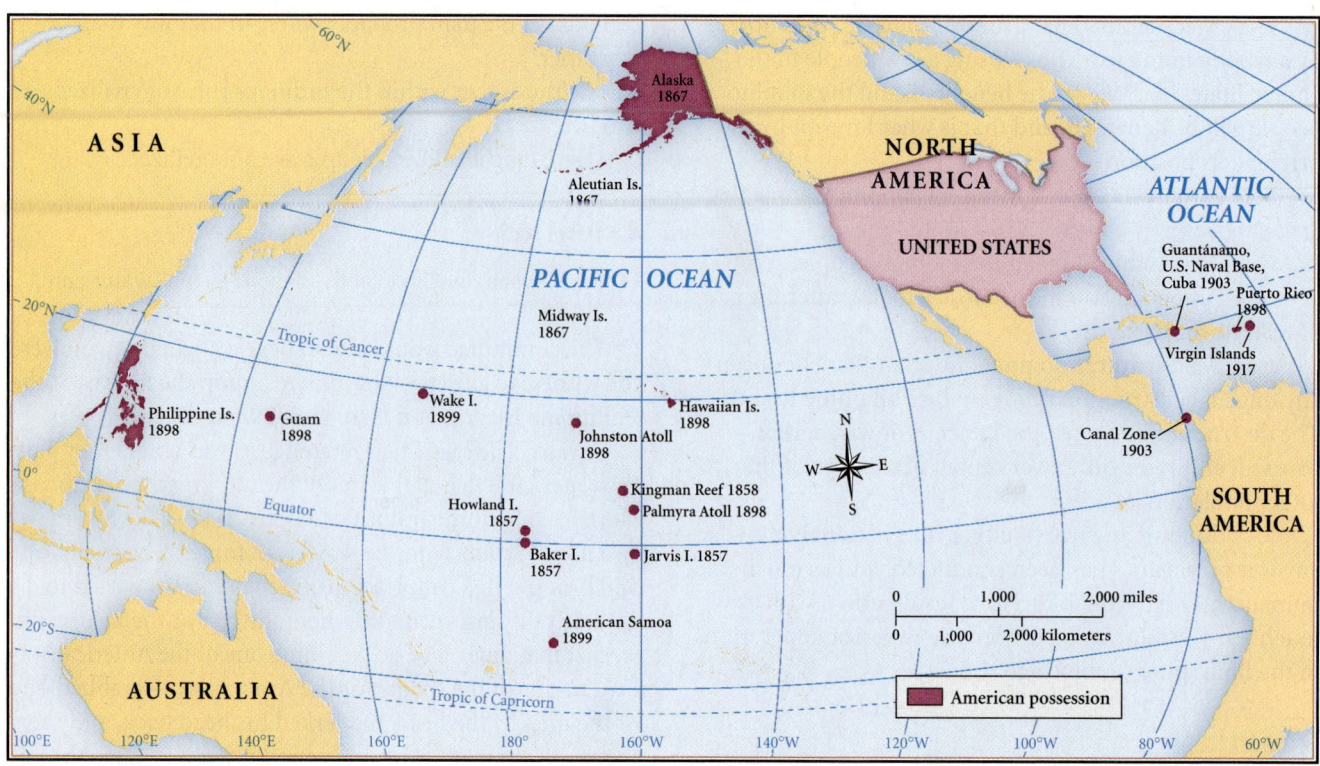

MAP 21.2

The American Empire, 1917

In 1890, Alfred T. Mahan wrote that the United States should regard the oceans as "a great highway" across which America would carry on world trade. That was precisely what resulted from the empire the United States acquired after the War of 1898. The Caribbean possessions; the strategically located Pacific islands; and, in 1903, the Panama Canal Zone gave the United States commercial and naval access to a wider world.

A Power among Powers

No one appreciated America's emerging influence more than the man who, after the assassination of William McKinley, became president in 1901. Theodore Roosevelt was an avid student of world affairs who called on "all the civilized and orderly powers to insist on the proper policing of the world." He meant, in part, directing the affairs of "backward peoples." For Roosevelt, imperialism went hand in hand with domestic progressivism. He argued that a strong federal government, asserting itself both at home and abroad, would enhance economic stability and political order. Overseas, Roosevelt sought to arbitrate disputes and maintain a global balance of power, but also to assert U.S. interests.

The Open Door in Asia

American policymakers and business leaders had a burning interest in East Asian markets, but they were entering a crowded field (Map 21.3). In the late 1890s, following Japan's victory in the Sino-Japanese War of 1894–1895, Japan, Russia, Germany, France, and Britain divided coastal China into spheres of influence. Fearful of being shut out, U.S. Secretary of State John Hay sent these powers a note in 1899, claiming the right of equal trade access—an "open door"—for all nations seeking to do business in China. The United States lacked leverage in Asia, and Hay's note elicited only noncommittal responses. But he chose to interpret this as acceptance of his position.

When a secret society of Chinese nationalists, known outside China as Boxers because of their pugnacious political stance, rebelled against foreign occupation in 1900, the United States sent 5,000 troops to join a multinational campaign to break the Boxers' siege of European government offices in Beijing. Hay took this opportunity to assert a second principle of the open door: China must be preserved as a "territorial and administrative entity." As long as the legal fiction of an

MAP 21.3

The Great Powers in East Asia, 1898–1910

European powers established dominance over China by way of "treaty ports," where the powers based their naval forces, and through "spheres of influence" that extended from the ports into the hinterland. This map reveals why the United States had a weak hand: It lacked a presence on this colonized terrain. The Boxer Rebellion in 1900, by bringing an American expeditionary force to Peking (Beijing), gave the United States a chance to insert itself on the Chinese mainland, and American diplomats made the most of the opportunity to defend U.S. commercial interests in China. As noted in the key, all place names in this map are those in use in 1910: Modern *Beijing*, for example is shown as *Peking*.

independent China survived, American could claim equal access to that market.

In the same years, Europe and the United States were startled by an unexpected development: Japan emerged as East Asia's dominant power. A decade after its victory over China in the Sino-Japanese War of 1895, Japan responded to Russian rivalry for control of both the Korean Peninsula and Manchuria, in northern China, by attacking the czar's fleet at Russia's leased Chinese port. In a series of brilliant victories, the Japanese smashed the Russian forces. Westerners were shocked: For the first time, a European power had been defeated by a nation that was non-Western and non-white. Conveying both admiration and alarm, American cartoonists sketched Japan as a rising sun and as a martial artist knocking down the Russian giant. Roosevelt mediated a settlement in 1905.

Though he was contemptuous of other Asians, Roosevelt respected the Japanese, whom he called "a wonderful and civilized people." More important, he understood Japan's rising military might, and he aligned himself with the mighty. The United States approved Japan's "protectorate" over Korea in 1905 and, six years later, its seizure of full control. (Japan's victory over Russia prompted quite different responses from peoples subjected to European imperialism: It helped inspire nationalist uprisings in Iran, Turkey, and China, while in India and Indonesia, respectively, the British and Dutch faced new pressure from their colonial subjects for self-determination.) With Japan asserting harsh authority over Manchuria, the energetic Chinese diplomat Yüan Shih-k'ai tried to encourage the United States to intervene as a counterweight. But Roosevelt reviewed America's weak position in the Pacific and declined. He conceded that Japan had "a paramount interest in what surrounds the Yellow Sea." In 1908, the United States and Japan signed the Root-Takahira Agreement, confirming principles of free oceanic commerce and recognizing Japan's authority over Manchuria.

William Howard Taft entered the White House in 1909 convinced that the United States had been short-changed in Asia. He pressed for a larger role for American investors, especially in Chinese railroad construction. Eager to promote U.S. business interests abroad, he hoped that infusions of American capital would offset Japanese power. When the Chinese Revolution of 1911

The Panama Canal: Excavating the Culebra Cut

The United States acquired the narrow Canal Zone on the Isthmus of Panama by dubious means, but the building of the Panama Canal itself—which required 35,000 workers and eight years—was a triumph of American ingenuity. Dr. William C. Gorgas cleaned out the malarial mosquitoes that had stymied an earlier, French canal-building effort. Under the direction of Colonel George W. Goethals, the U.S. Army accomplished a mighty feat of engineering. The 51-mile-long canal includes seven sets of locks that can raise and lower 50 large ships in a twenty-four-hour period. This 1904 photograph shows the December excavation of the Culebra Cut, an 8-mile-long, 300-foot-wide artificial valley large enough for oceangoing ships to pass through the canal.   © Bettmann/Corbis.

toppled the Manchu dynasty, Taft supported the victorious Nationalists, who wanted to modernize their country and liberate it from Japanese domination. The United States had entangled itself in China and entered a long-term rivalry with Japan for power in the Pacific, a competition that would culminate thirty years later in World War II.

The United States in the Caribbean

Closer to home, European powers conceded Roosevelt's argument that the United States had a "paramount interest" in the Caribbean. In 1900, the United States consulted with Britain on building a canal across Central America. Britain—facing a rising military chal-

lenge from Germany, and entangled in a bloody war against Afrikaners in South Africa—welcomed a closer alliance with the United States and proved willing to give up some of its Latin American claims. In the Hay-Pauncefote Treaty (1901), Britain recognized the United States' sole right to build and fortify a Central American canal. Two years later, Britain helped resolve the last remaining U.S.-Canadian border disputes. No formal alliance emerged, but Anglo-American friendship was so firm that the British Admiralty designed its war plans on the assumption that America was "a kindred state." Roosevelt heartily agreed.

In facing rivals, Roosevelt famously argued that the United States should "speak softly and carry a big stick." By "big stick" he meant most of all naval power, and rapid access to two oceans required a canal. Freed by Britain's surrender of canal rights, Roosevelt persuaded Congress to authorize $10 million, plus future payments of $250,000 per year, to purchase from Colombia a six-mile strip of land across Panama, a Colombian province. Furious when Colombia rejected this proposal, Roosevelt contemplated outright seizure of Panama but settled on a more roundabout solution. Panamanians, long separated from Colombia by miles of remote jungle, chafed under Colombian rule. The United States lent covert assistance to an independence movement, triggering a bloodless revolution. On November 6, 1903, the United States recognized the new nation of Panama; two weeks later, it obtained a perpetually renewable lease on a canal zone. Roosevelt never regretted the venture, though in 1922 the United States paid Colombia $25 million as a kind of conscience money. To build the canal, the U.S. Army Corps of Engineers hired thousands of laborers, who cleared vast swamps, excavated 240 million cubic yards of earth, and constructed a series of immense locks. The project, a great engineering feat, took eight years. Opened in 1914, the Panama Canal gave the United States a commanding position in the Western Hemisphere.

Roosevelt was already working in other ways to strengthen U.S. control of the Caribbean. As a condition for its withdrawal from Cuba in 1902, for example, the United States forced the newly independent island nation to accept a proviso in its constitution called the Platt Amendment. This blocked Cuba from making a treaty with any country except the United States and gave the United States the right to intervene in Cuban affairs if it saw fit. Cuba also granted the United States a lease on Guantánamo Bay (still in effect), where the U.S. Navy built a large base. It was a bitter pill for Cubans, who found that their hard-fought independence was stillborn.

Claiming that instability invited European intervention, Roosevelt announced in 1904 that the United States would police all parts of the Caribbean (Map 21.4). This so-called Roosevelt Corollary to the Monroe Doctrine actually turned that doctrine upside down: Instead of guaranteeing that the United States would protect its Latin American neighbors from European powers and help preserve their independence, it asserted the United States' unrestricted right to regulate Caribbean affairs. The Roosevelt Corollary was not a treaty; it was a unilateral declaration sanctioned only

MAP 21.4

Policeman of the Caribbean

After the War of 1898, the United States vigorously asserted its interest in the affairs of its neighbors to the south. As the record of interventions shows, the United States truly became the "policeman" of the Caribbean.

Pancho Villa, 1914

This photograph captures Mexican general Pancho Villa at the height of his power, at the head of Venustiano Carranza's northern army in 1914. The next year, he broke with Carranza and, among other desperate tactics, began to attack Americans. Though he had been much admired in the United States, Villa instantly became America's foremost enemy. He evaded General John J. Pershing's punitive expedition of 1916, however, demonstrating the difficulties even modern armies could have against a guerrilla foe who knows his home terrain and can melt away into a sympathetic population.   Brown Brothers.

by America's military and economic might. Citing the corollary, the United States intervened regularly in Caribbean states over the next three decades.

Wilson and Mexico

Democratic president Woodrow Wilson criticized his predecessors' foreign policy decisions. In a speech soon after he took office in 1913, Wilson promised that the United States would "never again seek one additional foot of territory by conquest," but instead would advance "human rights, national integrity, and opportu-

nity" abroad. This stance appealed to anti-imperialists in the Democratic base, including longtime supporters of William Jennings Bryan. But the new president soon showed that, when American interests called for it, his actions were not so different from those of Roosevelt and Taft.

Since the 1870s, Mexican dictator Porfirio Díaz had created a friendly climate for American investors who purchased Mexican railroads, plantations, mines, and much-coveted oil fields. By the early 1900s, however, Díaz feared the extraordinary power of these economic interests and began to nationalize—reclaim—key resources. Powerful American investors who faced the loss of their Mexican holdings began to back Francisco Madero, an advocate of constitutional government who was friendly to U.S. interests. In 1911, Madero forced Díaz to resign and proclaimed himself president. The revolution prompted thousands of poor Mexicans to mobilize rural armies and demand more radical change. At the same time, Madero's position was weak, and several strongmen sought to overthrow him. In February 1913, leading general Victoriano Huerta deposed and murdered Madero.

The Wilson administration became increasingly fearful that the unrest in Mexico threatened U.S. interests. Over the strong protests of Venustiano Carranza, the Mexican leader whom Wilson most favored, the United States threw its own forces into the emerging Mexican Revolution. On the pretext of a minor insult to the U.S. Navy, Wilson ordered U.S. occupation of the port of Veracruz on April 21, 1914, at the cost of 19 American and 126 Mexican lives. The Huerta regime crumbled. Carranza's forces, after nearly engaging the Americans themselves, entered Mexico City in triumph in August 1914. But despite Wilson's support of Carranza, his heavy-handed interference caused lasting mistrust.

Carranza's victory did not subdue all revolutionary activity in Mexico. In 1916, General Pancho Villa stirred up trouble on the U.S.-Mexico border, killing sixteen American civilians and raiding the town of Columbus, New Mexico. Wilson sent 11,000 troops under General John J. Pershing across the border after Villa. Soon Pershing's force resembled an army of occupation. Mexican public opinion demanded withdrawal, and armed clashes broke out between U.S. and Mexican troops. At the brink of war, both governments backed off, and U.S. forces withdrew. The following year, Carranza's government finally received official recognition from Washington. But U.S. policymakers had shown their intention to police not only the Caribbean and Central America but also Mexico when they deemed it necessary. The Caribbean Sea, as one commentator quipped, had become an "American lake."

- How did Japan challenge the influence of European powers and the United States in Asia? How did U.S. policymakers respond?

- How did U.S. policymakers justify their policies in the Caribbean, and how did the United States achieve control of the region?

- How did Wilson's policies toward Mexico evolve amid the Mexican Revolution? What were the consequences of Wilson's policy?

The United States in World War I

While competing imperial claims fostered conflicts around the globe, a war of unprecedented scale was brewing in Europe. Germany, a rising power, had humiliated France in the Franco-Prussian War of 1870; its subsequent military buildup terrified its neighbors. To the east, the disintegrating Ottoman Empire was losing its grip on the Balkans, while European powers jockeyed to claim and defend their colonies in Africa, the Middle East, and Asia. Out of these conflicts, two rival power blocs emerged: the Triple Alliance (Germany, Austria-Hungary, and Italy) and the Triple Entente (Britain, France, and Russia). Within each alliance, national governments pursued their own interests but were bound to one another by both public and secret treaties.

Americans had no obvious stake in these developments. In 1905, when Germany suddenly challenged French control of Morocco, Theodore Roosevelt arranged an international conference to defuse the crisis. Germany got a few concessions, but France—with British backing—retained control of Morocco. At the time, the conference seemed a diplomatic triumph. One U.S. official boasted that America had kept peace by "the power of our detachment." Such optimism proved wildly off the mark. A war was about to begin that would cause untold suffering and transform global power relations—and the United States would not remain detached.

The Great War Begins, 1914–1917

The spark that ignited World War I came in the Balkans, where Austria-Hungary and Russia competed for control. Austria's 1908 seizure of the Ottoman provinces of Bosnia and Herzegovina, with their substantial Slavic populations, angered Russia and its ally, the independent Slavic state of Serbia. In response, Serbian revolutionaries recruited Bosnian Slavs, including university student Gavrilo Princip, to resist Austrian rule. In June 1914, in the city of Sarajevo, Princip assassinated Archduke Franz Ferdinand, heir to the Austro-Hungarian throne.

Like dominos falling, the system of European alliances rapidly pushed all the powers into war. Austria-Hungary blamed Serbia for the assassination and declared war on July 28. Russia, tied by secret treaty to Serbia, mobilized its armies against Austria-Hungary.

Flying Aces
As millions of men suffered and died in the trenches during the Great War, a few hundred pilots did battle in the sky. America's best-known ace pilot was Eddie Rickenbacker (middle) of the Ninety-fourth Aero Pursuit Squadron—a pilot who was credited with shooting down twenty-six enemy aircraft. The Ninety-fourth was known as the hat-in-the-ring squadron, after the American custom by which a combatant threw his hat into the ring as an invitation to fight. Note the hat insignia on the plane.   © Bettman/Corbis.

Russia's move prompted Germany to declare war on Russia and its ally France. As a preparation for attacking France, Germany launched a brutal invasion of the neutral country of Belgium, which caused Great Britain to declare war on Germany. By August 4, most of Europe was at war. The Allies—Great Britain, France, and Russia—confronted the Central Powers of Germany and Austria-Hungary, joined in November by the Ottoman Empire.

Two major war zones emerged. Germany battled the British and French on the Western Front. Assisted by Austrians and Hungarians, Germany also fought Russia on the Eastern Front. Because most of the warring nations held colonial empires, the conflict spread to the Middle East, Africa, and China, throwing the future of those areas into question. Hoping to secure valuable colonies, Italy and Japan soon joined the Allied side, while Bulgaria linked up with the Central Powers.

The so-called Great War wreaked terrible devastation. New technology, some of it devised in the United States, made warfare deadlier than ever before. Every soldier carried a long-range, high-velocity rifle that could hit a target at 1,000 yards—a vast technical advancement over the 300-yard range of the rifles used in the U.S. Civil War. The machine gun was even more deadly. Its American-born inventor, Hiram Maxim, had moved to Great Britain in the 1880s to follow a friend's advice: "If you want to make your fortune, invent something which will allow those fool Europeans to kill each other more quickly."

These technological developments gave a tremendous advantage to soldiers in defensive positions. Once the German advance ran into French fortifications, it stalled. For four bloody years, millions of soldiers fought a **war of attrition** in heavily fortified trenches that cut across a narrow swath of Belgium and northeastern France. Soldiers hunkered in wet trenches for months on end. One side and then the other mounted attacks across the no-man's-land that lay between them, only to be mangled by barbed wire or mowed down by machine guns. Struggling to break the stalemate, Germany launched an attack at the Belgian city of Ypres in April 1915 that introduced a new nightmare: poison gas. As the Germans tried to break through French lines at Verdun between February and December 1916, they suffered 450,000 casualties. The French fared even worse, with 550,000 dead or wounded soldiers. It was all to no avail. From 1914 to 1918, the Western Front barely moved.

From Neutrality to War

At the outbreak of the Great War, President Woodrow Wilson called on Americans to be "neutral in fact as well as in name, impartial in thought as well as in action." If he kept the United States out of the conflict, Wilson reasoned, he could influence the postwar settlement, much as President Theodore Roosevelt had helped arbitrate the Russo-Japanese War in 1905. Even if Wilson had wanted to unite Americans behind the Allies, that would have been nearly impossible in 1914. Many Irish Americans viewed Britain as an enemy, resenting its continued occupation of Ireland. Millions of German Americans maintained ties to their homeland. Progressive-minded Republicans such as Senator Robert La Follette of Wisconsin vehemently opposed taking sides in a European fight, as did Socialists who condemned the war as a conflict among greedy capitalist empires. Two giants of American industry, Andrew Carnegie and Henry Ford, opposed the war. In December 1915, Ford sent a hundred men and women to Europe on a "peace ship" to urge an end to the conflict. "It would be folly," declared the *New York Sun*, "for the country to sacrifice itself to . . . the clash of ancient hatreds which is urging the Old World to destruction."

The Struggle to Remain Neutral | The United States, wishing to trade with all the warring nations, might have remained neutral if Britain had not held commanding power at sea. In September 1914, the British imposed a naval blockade on the Central Powers to cut off vital supplies of food and military equipment. The Wilson administration protested this infringement of the rights of neutral carriers but did not take action. Profit was one reason: A spectacular increase in U.S. trade with the Allies more than made up for lost commerce with Germany and Austria. Trade with Britain and France grew fourfold over the next two years, from $824 million to $3.2 billion in 1916; moreover, by 1917, U.S. banks had lent the Allies $2.5 billion. In contrast, American trade and loans to Germany stood then at a mere $56 million. This imbalance undercut U.S. neutrality, tying America's economic health to Allied victory. If Germany won and Britain and France defaulted on their debts, American companies would suffer catastrophic losses.

To challenge the British navy, Germany launched a devastating new weapon, the U-boat (short for *Unterseeboot*, "undersea boat," or submarine). In April 1915, the German embassy in Washington issued a warning that all ships flying the flags of Britain or its allies were liable to destruction. A few weeks later, a U-boat torpedoed the British luxury liner *Lusitania* off the coast of Ireland, killing 1,198 people, including 128 Americans. The attack on the passenger ship (which was later revealed to have been carrying munitions) incensed Americans. President Wilson sent strongly worded protests to Germany, but tensions had subsided by September, when Germany announced that U-boats would no longer attack passenger vessels without warning. Nonetheless, the *Lusitania* crisis prompted Wilson to reconsider his options. He quietly tried to mediate an end to the European conflict. Finding neither side seriously interested in peace, Wilson endorsed a $1 billion buildup of the U.S. Army and Navy in the fall of 1915.

American public opinion still ran strongly against entering the war, a fact that shaped the election of 1916. The reunited Republican Party rejected the belligerently prowar Theodore Roosevelt in favor of Supreme Court justice Charles Evans Hughes, a progressive former governor of New York. Democrats renominated Wilson, who campaigned on his domestic record and as the president who "kept us out of war." Wilson eked out a narrow victory; winning California by a mere 4,000 votes, he secured a slim majority in the electoral college.

America Enters the War | Despite Wilson's campaign slogan, events pushed him toward war. On February 1, 1917, Germany resumed unrestricted submarine warfare, a decision dictated by the impasse on the Western Front. In response, Wilson broke off diplomatic relations with Germany. A few weeks later, newspapers published an intercepted dispatch from the German foreign secretary, Arthur Zimmermann, to his minister in Mexico City. The note urged Mexico to join the Central Powers; Zimmermann promised that if the United States entered the war, Germany would help Mexico recover "the lost territory of Texas, New Mexico, and Arizona." With Pancho Villa's border raids still fresh in the public mind, this threat jolted American opinion. Meanwhile, German U-boats attacked American ships without warning, sinking three on March 18 alone.

On April 2, 1917, Wilson asked Congress for a declaration of war. He argued that Germany had trampled on American rights and imperiled its trade and citizens' lives. "We desire no conquest, no dominion," Wilson declared, "no material compensation for the sacrifices we shall freely make." Rather, reflecting his Protestant zeal and progressive idealism, Wilson promised that American involvement would make the world "safe for democracy." On April 6, the United States declared war on Germany. Reflecting the nation's divided views, the vote was far from unanimous. Six senators and fifty members of the House voted against entry, including Representative Jeannette Rankin of Montana, the first woman elected to Congress. "You can no more win a war than you can win an earthquake," Rankin said. "I want to stand by my country, but I cannot vote for war."

"Over There"

To Americans, Europe seemed a great distance away — "over there," in the lyrics of a popular song by George M. Cohan. Many assumed that the United States would simply provide munitions and economic aid. "Good

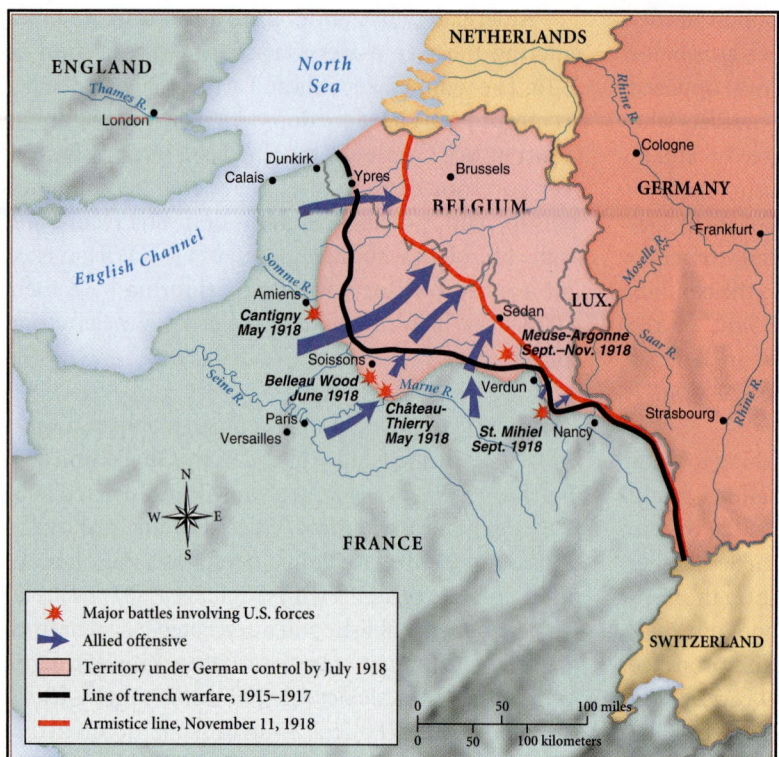

MAP 21.5

U.S. Participation on the Western Front, 1918

When American troops reached the European front in significant numbers in 1918, the Allied and Central Powers had been fighting a deadly war of attrition for almost four years. The influx of American troops and supplies helped to break the stalemate. Successful offensive maneuvers by the American Expeditionary Force included those at Belleau Wood and Château-Thierry and the Meuse-Argonne campaign.

Lord," exclaimed one U.S. senator to a Wilson administration official, "You're not going to send soldiers over there, are you?" But when General John J. Pershing asked how the United States could best support the Allies, the French commander put it bluntly: "Men, men, and more men."

In 1917, the U.S. Army numbered fewer than 200,000 soldiers. To field a fighting force, Congress instituted a military draft in May 1917. In contrast to the Civil War, when resistance was common, conscription went smoothly, partly because local, civilian-run draft boards played a central role in the new system. Still, draft registration demonstrated government's increasing power over ordinary citizens. On a single day — June 5, 1917 — more than 9.5 million men between the ages of twenty-one and thirty registered at their local voting precincts for possible military service.

President Wilson chose General Pershing to head the American Expeditionary Force (AEF), which had to be trained, outfitted, and carried across the submarine-infested Atlantic. Thus, the nation's first significant contribution to the war effort was safer shipping. When the United States entered the war, German U-boats were sinking 900,000 tons of Allied ships each month. By sending merchant and troop ships in armed convoys, the U.S. Navy cut that monthly rate to 400,000 tons by the end of 1917. With trench warfare grinding on, Al-

lied commanders pleaded for American soldiers to fill their depleted units, but Pershing waited until the AEF reached full strength. As late as May 1918, the brunt of the fighting fell to the French and British.

The Allies' burden increased when the Eastern Front collapsed following the Bolshevik (Communist) Revolution in Russia in November 1917. To consolidate its power at home, the new Bolshevik government, led by Vladimir Ilych Lenin, sought peace with the Central Powers. In the Treaty of Brest-Litovsk, signed on March 3, 1918, Russia surrendered its sovereignty over vast parts of central Europe — including Russian Poland, Ukraine, and the Baltic provinces — in exchange for peace. Released from the fight against Germany, the Bolsheviks turned their attention to struggles against their domestic enemies, including supporters of the ousted tsar. Japan and several Allied countries, including the United States, sent troops into Russian ports to fight the Bolsheviks. But after a four-year civil war, Lenin's forces established full control over Russia and reclaimed Ukraine, the Caucasus, and other former Russian possessions. In 1922, the Communists created the Union of Soviet Socialist Republics (USSR), or Soviet Union.

Peace with Russia freed Germany to launch a major offensive on the Western Front. By May 1918, German troops advanced to within 50 miles of Paris. As Allied leaders called desperately for U.S. troops, Pershing at last committed about 60,000 men to help the French in the battles of Château-Thierry and Belleau Wood. With American soldiers arriving in massive numbers, Allied forces brought the German offensive to a halt in July; by September, they had forced a German retreat. Then Pershing pitted more than 1 million American soldiers against an outnumbered and exhausted German army in the Argonne forest. By early November, this attack had broken the German defense of a crucial rail hub at Sedan. The cost was high: 26,000 Americans killed and 95,000 wounded (Map 21.5). But the flood of American troops and supplies turned the tide. Recognizing the inevitability of defeat and facing popular uprisings at home, the German government signed an armistice on November 11, 1918. The Great War was over.

The American Fighting Force By the end of World War I, almost 4 million American men—popularly known as "doughboys"—wore U.S. uniforms, as did several thousand female nurses. The recruits reflected America's heterogeneity: One-fifth had been born outside the United States, and soldiers spoke forty-nine different languages. Though ethnic diversity worried some observers, most predicted that military service would promote immigrants' Americanization.

More than 400,000 African American men enlisted, accounting for 13 percent of the armed forces. Their wartime experiences were often grim. They served in segregated units and were given the most menial tasks.

Racial discrimination disrupted military efficiency and erupted in violence at several camps. The worst incident occurred in August 1917, when, after suffering a string of racial attacks, black members of the Twenty-fourth Infantry's Third Battalion rioted in Houston, killing 15 white civilians and police officers. The army tried 118 of the soldiers in military courts for mutiny and riot, hanged 19, and sentenced 63 to life in prison.

Unlike African Americans, Native Americans served in integrated combat units. Racial stereotypes about Native Americans' prowess as warriors enhanced their military reputations, but it also prompted officers to assign them hazardous duties as scouts, messengers, and snipers. Approximately 13,000, or 25 percent, of the United States' adult male Native American population served during the war. Roughly 5 percent of these soldiers died, compared to 2 percent for the military as a whole.

About two-thirds of American soldiers in France saw military action, but most escaped the horrors of sustained trench warfare. Still, during the brief period of American participation, 53,000 servicemen died in action. Another 63,000 died from disease, mainly the devastating influenza pandemic that began early in 1918 and, over the next two years, killed 50 million people worldwide. The nation's military deaths, though substantial, were only a tenth as many as those of the 500,000 American civilians who died of this terrible epidemic—not to mention the staggering 8 million soldiers lost by the Allies and Central Powers.

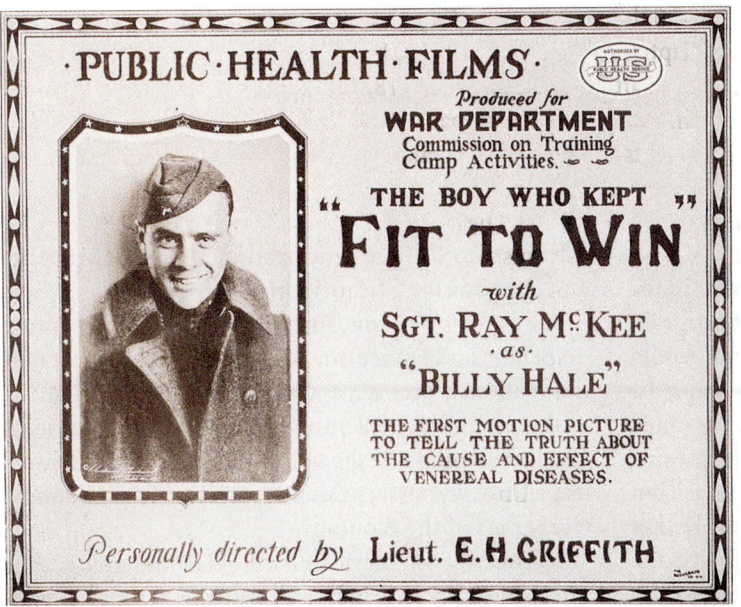

Safe Sex, Vintage 1919

To teach young American men how to avoid venereal diseases, the War Department used posters, pep talks, and films. There were no effective treatments for venereal infections until 1928, when Alexander Fleming discovered penicillin, and so the army urged soldiers to refrain from visiting prostitutes or to use condoms. *Fit to Win* starred handsome Ray McKee, who had already appeared in eighty films, and was directed by E. H. Griffith, who would go on to direct sixty Hollywood films between 1920 and 1946. Social Welfare History Archives Center, University of Minnesota/Picture Research Consultants & Archives.

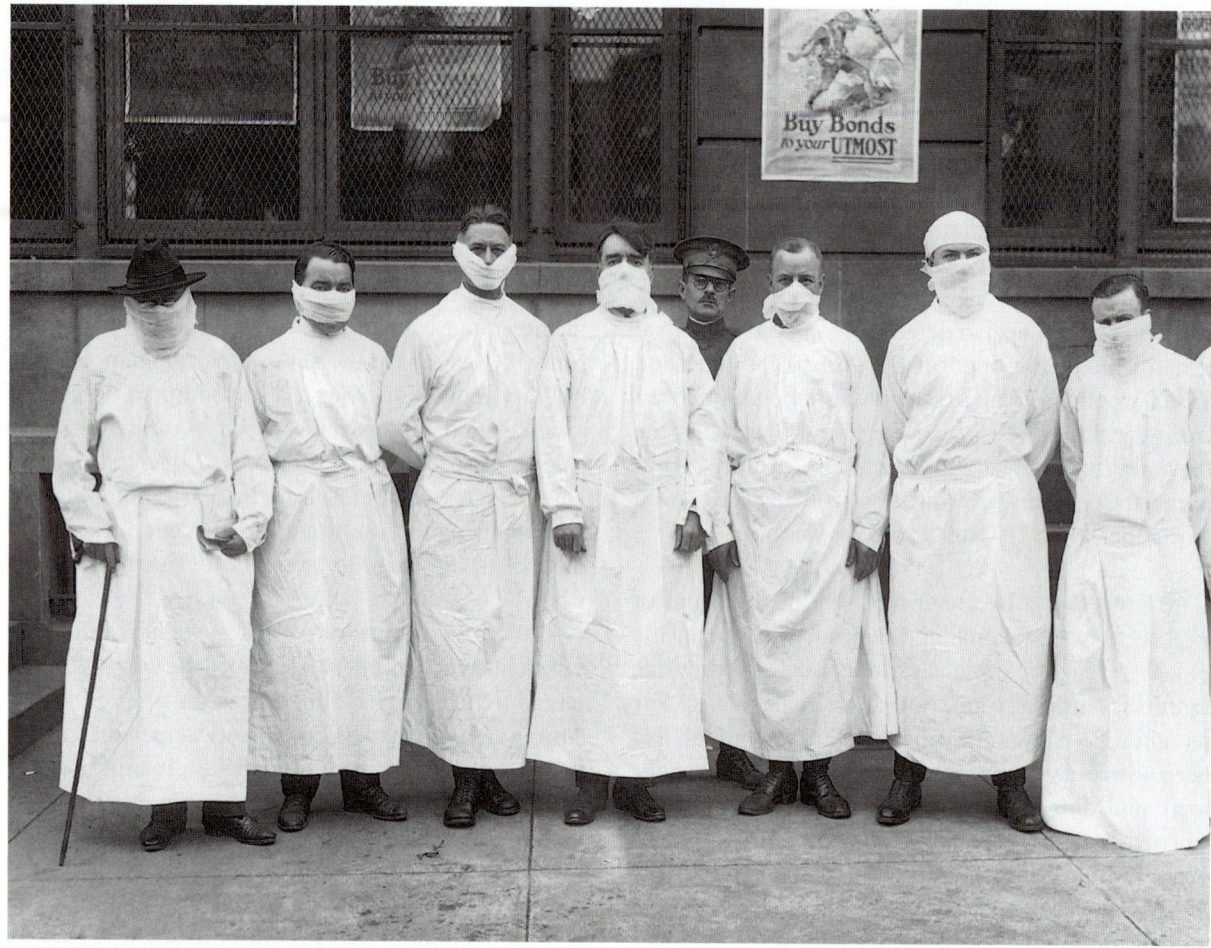

Fighting the Flu

Influenza traversed the globe in 1918–1919, becoming a pandemic that killed as many as 50 million people. According to recent research, the flu began as a virus native to wild birds and then mutated into a form that passed easily from one human to another. In the United States, one-fifth of the population was infected and more than 500,000 civilians died—ten times the number of American soldiers who died in combat during World War I. In the United States, the flu virus spread with frightening speed, and the epidemic strained the resources of a public health system already fully mobilized for the war effort. In October 1918 alone, 200,000 Americans died. This photo shows doctors, army officers, and reporters who donned surgical masks and gowns before touring hospitals that treated influenza patients. ©Bettman/Corbis.

War on the Home Front

In the United States, opponents of the war were in the minority. Most progressives hoped that Wilson's ideals, along with wartime demands for national unity, would renew Americans' attention to reform. Supporting the Allies did trigger an economic boom that benefited farmers and working people, and the federal government built an array of new agencies and programs. But the results bitterly disappointed progressives. Rather than enhancing democracy, World War I chilled the political climate as government agencies tried to enforce "100 percent loyalty."

Mobilizing the Economy American businesses made big bucks from World War I. As grain, weapons, and manufactured goods flowed to Britain and France, the United States became a creditor nation. Moreover, as the war drained British financial reserves, U.S. banks provided capital for investments around the globe. At the same time, government powers expanded, with new federal agencies overseeing almost every part of the economy.

The War Industries Board (WIB), established in July 1917, directed military production. After a fumbling start that showed the limits of voluntarism, the

Wilson administration reorganized the board and placed Bernard Baruch, a Wall Street financier, at its head. Baruch was a superb administrator. Under his direction, the WIB allocated scarce resources among industries, ordered factories to convert to war production, set prices, and standardized procedures. Although he could compel compliance, Baruch preferred to win voluntary cooperation from industry. A man of immense charm, he usually succeeded — helped by the lucrative military contracts at his disposal. Despite higher taxes, corporate profits soared, as military production sustained a boom that continued until 1920.

Some federal agencies took dramatic measures. The Fuel Administration, for example, introduced daylight saving time to conserve coal and oil. The War Finance Corporation lent $1 billion to companies that converted to war production. In December 1917, the Railroad Administration seized control of the nation's chaotic hodgepodge of private railroads, seeking to facilitate rapid movement of troops and equipment — an experiment that had, at best, mixed results. To reassure railroads' stock and bond holders, the Railroad Administration guaranteed them a "standard return" and promised to return railroads to private control at war's end.

Perhaps the most successful wartime agency was the Food Administration, created in August 1917 and led by engineer Herbert Hoover. With the slogan "Food will win the war," Hoover convinced farmers to almost double their acreage of grain. This allowed a threefold rise in food exports to Europe. Among citizens, the Food Administration mobilized a "spirit of self-denial and self-sacrifice" rather than mandatory rationing. Female volunteers went from door to door to persuade housekeepers to observe "Wheatless" Mondays and "Porkless" Thursdays. Hoover, a Republican, emerged from the war as one of the nation's most admired public figures.

"Remember Your First Thrill of American Liberty"

Once the United States entered the Great War, government officials were eager to enlist all Americans in the battle against the Central Powers. They carefully crafted patriotic advertising campaigns that urged Americans to buy bonds, conserve food, enlist in the military, and join in the war effort in countless other ways. This poster targeted recent immigrants to the United States, reminding them that "American Liberty" carried with it the "Duty" to buy war bonds. Library of Congress.

Promoting National Unity During the war, suppressing dissent became a near obsession for President Wilson. In April 1917, Wilson formed the Committee on Public Information (CPI), a government propaganda agency headed by journalist George Creel. Professing lofty goals — educating citizens about democracy, assimilating immigrants, and ending the isolation of rural life — the committee set out to mold Americans into "one white-hot mass" of war patriotism. The CPI touched the lives of practically every civilian. It distributed seventy-five million pieces of literature and enlisted thousands of volunteers — "Four Minute Men" — to deliver short prowar speeches at movie theaters.

The CPI urged recent immigrants and long-established ethnic groups to become "One Hundred Percent Americans." German Americans bore the brunt of this campaign. Concert halls banned music by Beethoven, Bach, and other German composers. School districts shut down German-language programs. Hamburgers were renamed "liberty sandwiches." With posters exhorting citizens to root out German spies, a spirit of conformity pervaded the home front. A quasi-vigilante group, the American Protective League, mobilized about 250,000 self-appointed "agents," furnished them with badges issued by the Justice Department, and trained them to spy on neighbors and coworkers. In 1918, members of the league led violent raids against draft evaders

Jacob Lawrence: The Labor Agent in the South

This evocative painting shows how many African American workers found a route to opportunity: Northern manufacturers, facing severe wartime labor shortages, sent agents to the South to recruit workers. Agents often arranged loans to pay for train fare and other travel expenses; once laborers were settled and employed in the North, they repaid the loans from their wages. Here, a line of men waits for the agent to record their names in his open ledger. This panel, from the famous "Great Migration" series by African American painter Jacob Lawrence, was created in 1940. The bare tree in the background suggests the barrenness of economic prospects for impoverished rural blacks in the South; it also hints at the threat of lynching and racial violence.   Digital Image © The Museum of Modern Art / Licensed by SCALA / Art Resource, NY.

and peace activists. Government propaganda helped fuel public mistrust of "hyphenated Americans"—a new term embracing Irish, Polish, Italian, and Jewish Americans—and helped rouse a nativist hysteria that would linger in the 1920s.

During the war, Congress passed two new laws to curb dissent. The Espionage Act of 1917 imposed stiff penalties for antiwar activities. The Sedition Act of 1918 prohibited any words or behavior that might "incite, provoke, or encourage resistance to the United States, or promote the cause of its enemies." Because these acts defined treason and sedition loosely, they led to the conviction of more than a thousand people. The Justice Department prosecuted members of the Industrial Workers of the World (IWW), whose opposition to militarism threatened to disrupt war production of lumber and copper. When a Quaker pacifist teacher in New York City refused to teach a prowar curriculum, she was fired for "conduct unbecoming a teacher." Socialist Party leader Eugene V. Debs was sentenced to ten years in jail for arguing that wealthy capitalists had started the conflict but forced workers to fight the battles.

Federal courts mostly supported the acts. In *Schenck v. United States* (1919), the Supreme Court upheld the conviction of a socialist who was jailed for circulating pamphlets that urged army draftees to resist induction. The justices followed this with a similar decision in *Abrams v. United States* (1919), stating that authorities could prosecute speech that they believed to pose "a clear and present danger to the safety of the country." In an important dissent, however, Justices Oliver Wendell Holmes Jr. and Louis Brandeis objected to the *Abrams* decision. Though Holmes denied that he was changing his position on "clear and present danger," his questions about the definition of that phrase helped launch twentieth-century legal battles over free speech and civil liberties.

Great Migrations | World War I created new economic opportunities at home. Jobs in war industries drew thousands of people to the cities, including immigrants (see Voices from Abroad, "Jesús Colón: A Puerto Rican in New York," p. 675). For the first time, with so many men in uniform, jobs in heavy industry opened to African Americans. Well before the war, some southern blacks had moved to the North; wartime jobs accelerated the pace. During World War I, more than 400,000 African Americans moved to such cities as St. Louis, Chicago, New York, and Detroit, in what became known as the Great Migration. The rewards were great, and taking war jobs could be a source of patriotic pride. "If it hadn't been for the negro at that time," a Carnegie Steel manager later recalled, "we could hardly have carried on our operations."

Blacks in the North encountered considerable discrimination in jobs, housing, and education. But in the first flush of opportunity, most celebrated their escape from the repressive racism and low pay of the South. "It

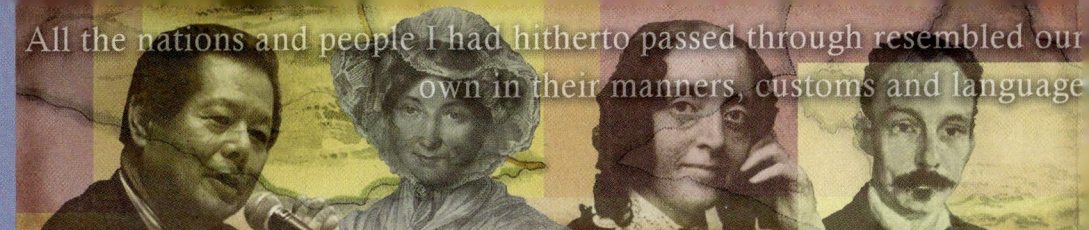
VOICES FROM ABROAD

Jesús Colón
A Puerto Rican in New York

Born in 1901 in Cayey, Puerto Rico, Jesús Colón grew up in the aftermath of the War of 1898. The American Tobacco Company controlled much of the island's tobacco production; at the cigar factory near his house, Colón received an informal education from workers. In 1917, Colón stowed away on a ship to New York City. There he lived with family, working on the dock and in factories.

As a Puerto Rican, Colón was of course an American — an identity, this reading suggests, that strongly appealed to him. But before he even left Puerto Rico, he saw signs that he did not count as a real American. Colón became a leader in the Puerto Rican nationalist movement seeking the island's independence from U.S. control. Though Colón remained in New York until his death in 1974, his ashes were scattered, as he had requested, on the La Plata River in Cayey.

I still remember the day [as a child, when] the school gave me that fat history book: *A History of the United States. . . .* Almost by accident I came to discover a phrase in one of the documents at the end of the book. . . . That phrase stuck with me all day like one of those musical phrases of a nameless song that keeps coming up in the sound of your whistling again and again, sometimes for hours. That phrase was: "We the people of the United States. . . ."

I went home from school with that phrase on my lips. Repeating it over and over again. — "We the people of the United States." And I accented the phrase with the pounding of my feet over the centuries-old cobblestones of the streets of old San Juan. We-the-people-of-the-United-States.

My 8th grade teacher was a six-foot Montanan. Mr. Whole was his name. A fading smile was always on his lips. One day he was sitting on the wide porch of the YMCA. For construction of this building we in school were politely obliged to bring in a quarter as a contribution. Mr. Whole hailed me from the porch. He invited me to play a game of checkers. I sat in front of him, the checker board between us, ready to start the game. Out came somebody in authority. He informed Mr. Whole that I could not play there with him as I did not belong to the white race. Mr. Whole said not a word and the game, not yet started, ended. . . .

The workers and the cigar makers taught me — they gave me pamphlets and papers to read — they told me that we were a colony — a sort of storage house for cheap labor and a market for "seconds" (cheap industrial goods). That we Puerto Ricans were a part of a great colonialism system. And that not until colonialism was wiped out and full independence given to Puerto Rico would the conditions under which we were living be remedied. I suddenly realized that there was no future for a young man in Puerto Rico, but the future of the sugar cane field, with starvation wages. . . .

[After coming to New York City I worked] in a factory with my brother in Brooklyn during the First World War. The shop manufactured woolen leggings and caps for the army. . . . There were about one hundred men and women making leggings and caps where we were working. Every item was supposed to be thoroughly examined by government examiners. Nothing that was the least bit defective was going to be sent to the boys in France. But the opposite was the customary thing to do. Rotten old woolen material was used in the manufacture of this indispensible woolen apparel for the soldiers in France. The government examiners okayed everything, stamping their seal of approval on all that was sent to the soldiers in the front line. Why did the examiners do it? I will let you take one guess. It seemed to my innocent young mind that on pay day the government examiners were happier than usual. . . .

I came to New York to poor pay, long hours, terrible working conditions, discrimination even in the slums and in the poor paying factories where the bosses very dexterously pitted Italians against Puerto Ricans and Puerto Ricans against American Negroes and the Jews. Somehow in New York, I did not seem to find the pot of gold at the end of the rainbow that I expected to find.

Source: Jesús Colón, *A Puerto Rican in New York and Other Sketches* (New York: Mainstream, 1961), 197–198, 46–47, 200.

ANALYZING THE EVIDENCE

- Consider Colón's account of his first encounter with American ideals. How do they come to have meaning for him? What experiences in his own life seemed to contradict those ideals?
- What conditions of work does Colón describe in New York City during World War I? Why does the factory in which he works send substandard products to U.S. soldiers fighting in France?

is a matter of a dollar with me and I feel that God made the path and I am walking therein," one woman reported to her sister back home. "Tell your husband work is plentiful here." "I just begin to feel like a man," wrote another migrant to a friend in Mississippi. "My children are going to the same school with the whites. . . . Will vote the next election and there isnt any 'yes sir' and 'no sir'—its all yes and no and Sam and Bill."

Wartime labor shortages also prompted Mexican Americans in California, Texas, New Mexico, and Arizona to leave farm labor for industrial jobs in rapidly growing southwestern cities. At the same time, continuing political instability in Mexico, combined with increased demand for farm workers in the United States, encouraged more Mexicans to move across the border. Between 1917 and 1920, at least 100,000 Mexicans entered the United States, and despite discrimination, large numbers stayed. If asked why, many might have echoed the words of an African American man who left New Orleans for Chicago: They were going "north for a better chance."

Women were the largest group to take advantage of wartime employment opportunities (see Reading American Pictures, "'Over Here': Women's Wartime Opportunities," p. 677). About 1 million women joined the paid labor force for the first time, while another 8 million gave up low-wage service jobs for higher paying industrial work. Americans soon got used to the sight of female streetcar conductors, train engineers, and defense workers. Though most people expected these jobs to return to men in peacetime, the war created a new comfort level with women's work outside the home.

Women's Voting Rights

One of World War I's enduring legacies was woman suffrage. When the United States entered the war, the National American Woman Suffrage Association (NAWSA) threw the support of its 2 million members behind Wilson. Its president, Carrie Chapman Catt, declared that women had to prove their patriotism to advance

Wagon Decorated for the Labor Day Parade, San Diego, California, 1910

As the woman suffrage movement grew stronger in the years before and during World War I, working-class women played increasingly prominent and visible roles in its leadership. This Labor Day parade float, created by the Women's Union Label League of San Diego, showed that activists championed equal pay for women in the workplace as well as women's voting rights. "Union Label Leagues" urged middle-class shoppers to purchase only clothing with a union label, certifying that the item had been manufactured under safe conditions and the workers who made it had received a fair wage.   San Diego Historical Society, Title Insurance Trust Collection.

"Over Here": Women's Wartime Opportunities

Women took on new jobs during World War I—as mail carriers, police officers, heavy machinery operators, and farm laborers attached to the Women's Land Army. African American women, who were customarily limited to employment as domestic servants or agricultural laborers, found that the war opened up new opportunities and better wages in industry. When the war ended, black and white women alike usually lost jobs deemed to be men's work. However, in 1919, when an anonymous photographer took this picture, these women riveters were still hard at work at the Puget Sound Navy Yard near Seattle, Washington.

Working Women at the Puget Sound Navy Yard, Washington, 1919. National Archives.

ANALYZING THE EVIDENCE

- Look carefully at the picture. What had the women been doing when asked by the photographer to pose for this shot? What clues indicate their work?

- Why do you imagine that the photograph was taken? If this photograph had been published in a Seattle newspaper, how might viewers have responded to it?

- Although the women are posed, the men in the background seem to be acting in a spontaneous fashion. How might we interpret their behavior?

- What does the photograph suggest about the women's attitude toward their work as shipbuilders?

- The presence of black women indicates diversity in the wartime Seattle workforce. Does anything in the photo tell us about the relationship between white and black women in the shipyards?

the cause of suffrage. NAWSA members in thousands of communities promoted food conservation, aided war workers, and distributed emergency relief through organizations such as the Red Cross.

Alice Paul and the National Woman's Party (NWP) took a more confrontational approach. Paul was a Quaker who had worked in the settlement movement and earned a PhD in political science. As a lobbyist for NAWSA, Paul found her cause dismissed by congressmen, and in 1916 she founded the NWP. Inspired by militant British suffragists, the party began picketing the White House in July 1917. Standing as "Silent Sentinels" with suffrage banners, Paul and other NWP activists faced arrest for obstructing traffic and were sentenced to seven months in jail. They protested by going on a hunger strike, which prison authorities met with forced feeding. Public shock at the women's treatment put pressure on Wilson and drew attention to the suffrage cause.

Impressed by NAWSA's patriotism and worried by the NWP's militancy, the antisuffrage Wilson reversed his position. In January 1918, he urged support for woman suffrage as a "war measure." The constitutional amendment quickly passed the House of Representatives; it took eighteen months to get through the Senate and another year to win ratification by the states. On August 26, 1920, Tennessee gave the Nineteenth Amendment the last vote it needed, becoming the only ex-Confederate state to ratify it. Seventy-two years after the women's rights convention at Seneca Falls, American women finally had full voting rights.

In explaining why suffragists achieved victory, historians have debated the relative effectiveness of Catt's patriotic strategy and Paul's militant protests. Both played a role in persuading Wilson and Congress to act, but neither might have worked without the extraordinary impact of the Great War. Across the globe, before 1914, the only places where women had full suffrage were New Zealand, Australia, Finland, and Norway. After World War I, many nations moved to enfranchise women. The new Soviet Union acted first, in 1917, with Great Britain and Canada following in 1918; by 1920, the measure had passed in Germany, Austria, Poland, Czechoslovakia, and Hungary as well as the United States. Major exceptions were France and Italy, where women did not gain voting rights until after World War II, and Switzerland, which held out until 1971. Thus, while World War I introduced modern horrors on the battlefield—machine guns and poison gas—it brought more positive forms of modernization at home: new economic opportunities, urban growth, and women's political participation.

- What were the causes of World War I, and how did the war progress on the Western Front?
- What role did the United States hope to play as a neutral power? What factors undercut that neutrality? Why did it finally enter the war?
- How did U.S. involvement affect the course of the war?
- In what ways did the war transform the economy, society, and politics of the United States?

The Treaty of Versailles

In January 1917, the idealistic Wilson had proposed "peace without victory," arguing that only "peace among equals" could last. Having achieved victory at an incredible price, Britain and France showed absolutely no interest in such a plan. But the immense devastation wrought by the war created popular pressure for an outcome that was just and enduring. Wilson scored a diplomatic victory at the Paris Peace Conference, held at Versailles in January 1919, when the Allies chose to base the negotiations on his Fourteen Points—a blueprint for peace that he had first presented a year earlier in a speech to the U.S. Congress.

Wilson's Fourteen Points embodied one important strand in American progressivism. They called for open diplomacy; "absolute freedom of navigation upon the seas"; arms reduction; removal of trade barriers; and national self-determination for peoples in the Austro-Hungarian, Russian, and German empires. Essential to Wilson's vision was the founding of an international regulatory body, eventually called the League of Nations, that would guarantee "independence and territorial integrity to great and small States alike." The League would mediate disputes, supervise arms reduction, and—according to the crucial Article X of its covenant—curb aggressor nations through collective military action. Wilson hoped the League would "end all wars." But Wilson's idealism had marked limitations—and at the negotiating table, his proposals met harsh realities.

The Fate of Wilson's Ideas

Though the conference at Versailles included ten thousand representatives from around the globe, leaders of France, Britain, and the United States dominated the proceedings. When the Japanese delegation proposed a declaration that all races be treated equally, the Allies rejected it. Similarly, they ignored a global Pan-African

The Peace at Versailles

This painting by Sir William Orpen of the signing of the peace treaty in the Hall of Mirrors at Versailles in June 1919 captures the solemnity and grandeur of the occasion. U.S. president Woodrow Wilson holds a copy of the treaty, with British prime minister David Lloyd George to his right and French premier Georges Clemenceau to his left. Though many nations and peoples had fought in the Great War and suffered from its impact, a handful of powerful negotiators largely determined the treaty results. Imperial War Museum, London.

Congress, organized by W. E. B. Du Bois and other black leaders, and they snubbed Arab representatives — even those who had been military allies during the war. Distrustful of the new Communist regime in Russia, the Allies deliberately excluded its representatives. Even Italy's prime minister, Vittorio Orlando — at first included among the influential "Big Four" — eventually withdrew from the conference, aggrieved at the way British and French leaders had marginalized him. Meanwhile, the Allies entirely barred Germany from the conference, choosing to impose conditions on their defeated foe. For Wilson's proposed "peace among equals," it was not a hopeful start.

European Allied leaders — most notably Prime Minister David Lloyd George of Great Britain and Premier Georges Clemenceau of France — imposed harsh punishments on Germany. Unbeknownst to the world at the time, Britain and France had already made secret agreements to divide up Germany's African colonies

and take them as spoils of war. At Versailles, they also forced the defeated nation to pay $33 billion in reparations and to give up coal supplies, merchant ships, valuable patents, and even part of its territory along the French border. These requirements caused keen resentment and economic hardship in Germany. Over the following two decades they helped lead to World War II.

Given these conditions, it is a tribute to Wilson that he influenced the Treaty of Versailles as much as he did. He intervened repeatedly to soften harsh demands against Germany. Moreover, in accordance with the Fourteen Points, he worked with Clemenceau, Lloyd George, and Italy's Orlando to fashion nine new independent states. This string of nations, stretching from the Baltic Sea to the Mediterranean, was intended as a buffer to protect Western Europe from the new Communist Soviet Union; the plan also embodied Wilson's principle of self-determination for European states.

MAP 21.6

Europe and the Middle East after World War I

World War I and its aftermath dramatically altered the landscape of Europe and the Middle East. In central Europe, the collapse of the German, Russian, and Austro-Hungarian empires brought the reconstitution of Poland and the creation of a string of new states based on the principle of national (ethnic) self-determination. The demise of the Ottoman Empire resulted in the appearance of the quasi-independent territories of Iraq, Syria, Lebanon, and Palestine, whose affairs were supervised by one of the Allied powers under a mandate of the League of Nations.

In other parts of the world, however, the Allies dismantled the Central Powers' colonial empires but did not create independent states; instead, they assigned themselves colonies to administer as "mandates" (Map 21.6). Because the war finished off the Ottoman Empire, France and England laid claim to Ottoman and German colonies in Africa and the Middle East. Japan took Germany's possessions in East Asia. France refused to give up its longstanding occupation of Indochina. Clemenceau's snub of future Vietnamese leader Ho Chi Minh, who sought representation at Versailles, had grave long-term consequences for both France and the United States.

The establishment of a British mandate, rather than an independent nation, in Palestine (now Israel) also proved crucial. During the war, British foreign secretary Sir Arthur Balfour had stated that his country would work to establish there a "national home for the Jewish people," with the condition that "nothing shall be done which may prejudice the civil and religious rights of existing non-Jewish communities in Palestine." Under the British mandate, thousands of Jews moved to Palestine and purchased land, in some cases evicting Palestinian tenants. As early as 1920, riots erupted between Jews and Palestinians—a situation that escalated, over the next two decades, far beyond British control.

Given these results, the Versailles treaty must be judged one of history's greatest catastrophes. Not only in Europe itself, but also in places as far-flung as Palestine and Indochina, it created the conditions for horrific future bloodshed. Balfour astutely described Clemenceau, Lloyd George, and Wilson as "three all-powerful, all-ignorant men, sitting there and carving up continents." Remarkably, however, Wilson remained optimistic as he returned to the United States—even though his health was beginning to fail. The president hoped the new League of Nations, authorized by the treaty, would moderate the terms of the settlement and secure a peaceful resolution of other disputes. For this to occur, American participation in the League was crucial. So Wilson set out to persuade the Senate to ratify the Treaty of Versailles.

Congress Rejects the Treaty

The outlook was not promising. Though major opinion makers and religious denominations supported the treaty, the Republican Party was openly hostile, and it held a majority in the Senate. One group, called the "irreconcilables," consisted of western Republicans, such as Hiram Johnson of California and Robert La Follette of Wisconsin, who opposed U.S. involvement in European affairs. Another group of Republicans, led by Senator Henry Cabot Lodge of Massachusetts, worried that Article X—the provision for collective security—would prevent the United States from pursuing an independent foreign policy. Was the nation, Lodge asked, "willing to have the youth of America ordered to war" by an international body? Wilson refused to accept any amendments, especially to placate Lodge, a hated political rival. "I shall consent to nothing," the president told the French ambassador. "The Senate must take its medicine."

To mobilize support for the treaty, Wilson embarked on an exhausting speaking tour. His impassioned defense of the League of Nations brought large audiences to tears, but the strain proved too much for the president. In Pueblo, Colorado, in September 1919, Wilson collapsed. A week later, back in Washington, he suffered a severe stroke that left one side of his body paralyzed. Wilson still urged Democratic senators to reject all Republican amendments. When the treaty came up for a vote in November 1919, it failed to win the required two-thirds majority; a second attempt, in March 1920, fell seven votes short.

The treaty was dead, and so was Wilson's leadership. The president never fully recovered from his stroke. During the final eighteen months of his administration, the government drifted as Wilson's physician, his wife, and various cabinet heads secretly took charge of routine work. The United States never ratified the Versailles treaty or joined the League of Nations. In turn, the weak League failed to do what Wilson had hoped. When Wilson died in 1924, his dream of a just and peaceful international order lay in ruins.

The impact of World War I on international politics can hardly be overstated. When the conflict began in 1914, European powers dominated the globe, but four brutal years of warfare shattered Europe's imperial supremacy. By 1918, the United States was no longer just a regional power; it was a major participant in world affairs. The war, and Wilson's energetic vision, forced Americans to confront big questions. How would the United States advance its interests? Could it serve as an independent force for peace—as William Jennings Bryan had put it, an "accepted arbiter of the world's disputes"? Having rejected the Versailles treaty, the United States appeared to turn its back on the world. But in laying claim to Hawaii and the Philippines, exerting its power in Latin America, and intervening in East Asia, the United States had already entangled itself deeply in imperial politics. The nation had gained too much economic control and diplomatic clout for isolation to be a realistic option. In the long term, World War I set the conditions for the United States to become a dominant twentieth-century power.

On the home front, the effect of World War I was no less dramatic. Wartime jobs and prosperity ushered in an era of exuberant consumerism, while the achievements of women's voting rights seemed to presage a new era of reform. But as peace returned, it became clear that the war would not further political reform. An ominous signal was Wilson's rejection of a plan by the War Industries Board to stabilize the economy during demobilization. This was a harbinger of things to come. Rather than embracing government activism, Americans of the 1920s proved eager to relinquish it. The war introduced, instead, a decade of political nativism, racism, and anticommunism.

- **How did World War I affect the U.S. economy, society, and politics?**

- **What were the flaws of the Treaty of Versailles? To what extent did Wilson succeed in influencing the development of the treaty?**

- **What factors led to the treaty's rejection by the U.S. Senate?**

- **On balance, do you think U.S. entry into World War I had beneficial results that outweighed the costs? Why or why not?**

SUMMARY

Between 1877 and 1918, the United States rose as a major economic and military power. Justifications for overseas expansion emphasized access to global markets, the importance of sea power, and the need to police international misconduct and trade. These justifications shaped U.S. policy toward European powers in Latin America, and victory in the War of 1898 enabled the United States to take control of former Spanish colonies in the Caribbean and Pacific. Victory, however, also led to a bloody conflict in the Philippines as the United States struggled to suppress Filipino resistance to American rule.

After 1899, the United States aggressively asserted its interests in Asia and Latin America. In China, the United States used the Boxer Rebellion to make good its claim to an "open door" to Chinese markets. Later, President Theodore Roosevelt strengthened relations with Japan, and his successor, William Howard Taft, supported U.S. business interests in China. In the Caribbean, the United States constructed the Panama Canal and regularly exercised the "right," claimed under the Roosevelt Corollary, to intervene in the affairs of states in the region. President Woodrow Wilson publicly disparaged the imperialism of his predecessors but repeatedly used the U.S. military to "police" Mexico.

At the outbreak of World War I, the United States asserted neutrality, but its economic ties to the Allies rapidly undercut that claim. In 1917, German submarine attacks drew the United States into the war on the side of England and France. Involvement in the war profoundly transformed the economy, politics, and society of the nation, resulting in an economic boom, mass migrations of workers to industrial centers, and the achievement of national voting rights. At the Paris Peace Conference, Wilson attempted to implement his Fourteen Points. However, the designs of the Allies in Europe undermined the Treaty of Versailles, while Republican resistance at home prevented ratification of the treaty. Although Wilson's dream of a just international order failed, the United States had taken its place as a major world power.

CHAPTER REVIEW QUESTIONS

- Historians sometimes engage in "counterfactual" reasoning: They imagine that historical events unfolded differently, in order to gain insight into the events that really *did* happen. Using this approach, answer the following questions: What would have happened if the United States had *not* gone to war against Spain in 1898, and had *not* annexed Hawaii or the Philippines? If the United States had remained neutral and never entered World War I? Alternatively, what might have happened if the United States, after helping the Allies win the Great War, had ratified the Treaty of Versailles and joined the League of Nations?

- How do your answers to these questions help explain the significance of the events that actually occurred?

FOR FURTHER EXPLORATION

Walter LaFeber's *The American Search for Opportunity, 1865–1913* (1993) is an excellent, up-to-date synthesis. LaFeber's influential *The New Empire* (1963) initiated scholarly debate on the quest for overseas markets as a driving force behind U.S. imperialism. Helpful on the Spanish-Cuban-American-Philippine conflict are Louis Pérez Jr., *The War of 1898* (1998); Stuart Creighton Miller, *"Benevolent Assimilation"* (1982); Paul Kramer, *The Blood of Government* (2006); and Kristin Hoganson, *Fighting for American Manhood* (1998). On U.S. involvement in the Caribbean, see César Ayala, *American Sugar Kingdom* (1999); on the United States and Mexico, see John S. D. Eisenhower, *Intervention!* (1993); and on the Panama Canal, see Julie Greene, *The Canal Builders* (2009).

On World War I, see Hew Strachan, *The First World War* (2004), and visit **www.pbs.org/greatwar/index .html**. Frank Freidel's *Over There* (1990) offers soldiers' vivid firsthand accounts, while the home front is captured in Meirion Harries and Susie Harries, *The Last Days of Innocence* (1997), and David M. Kennedy, *Over Here* (1990). On the Great Migration, see James R. Grossman, *Land of Hope* (1999), and Joe William Trotter Jr., ed., *The Great Migration in Historical Perspective* (1991). On woman suffrage, see the essays in Jean H. Baker, ed., *Votes for Women* (2002); and on its consequences, see Nancy Cott, *The Grounding of Modern Feminism* (1987). On the influenza epidemic of 1918, see **www.archives.gov/exhibits/influenza-epidemic/ index.html** and **www.pbs.org/wgbh/amex/influenza**.

TEST YOUR KNOWLEDGE

To assess your command of the material in this chapter, see the Online Study Guide at **bedfordstmartins.com/henretta**.

For Web sites, images, and documents related to topics and places in this chapter, visit **bedfordstmartins.com/makehistory**.

TIMELINE

1890	Congress appropriates funds for construction of modern battleships
1895	United States arbitrates border dispute between Britain and Venezuela Guerrilla war against Spanish rule begins in Cuba
1898	War between United States and Spain United States annexes territories in the Caribbean and Pacific 1899–1902 Philippine War; United States pursues open-door policy in China
1900	United States helps suppress Boxer Rebellion
1901	Hay-Pauncefote Treaty
1902	Platt Amendment
1903	U.S. recognition of Panama's independence
1905	Russo-Japanese War; Roosevelt mediates peace
1908	Root-Takahira Agreement
1914	Panama Canal opens U.S. military actions in Mexico World War I begins in Europe
1916	Jones Act commits United States to Philippine independence
1917	United States declares war on Germany and its allies; creates new agencies to mobilize economy and promote national unity
1918	Sedition Act World War I ends
1919	*Schenck v. United States* *Abrams v. United States* Wilson introduces his Fourteen Points Senate rejects the Treaty of Versailles
1920	Nineteenth Amendment grants women suffrage Senate again rejects the Treaty of Versailles

Wrestling with Modernity, 1918-1929

Margaret Sanger, a nurse who moved with her family to New York in 1911, immersed herself in the city's exciting political scene. She joined labor protests and the Socialist Party and volunteered in the immigrant wards of the Lower East Side. Horrified by women's suffering from constant pregnancies – and remembering her devout Catholic mother, who had died young after bearing eleven children – Sanger launched a crusade for what she called "birth control." Her column in the *New York Call*, "What Every Girl Should Know," soon garnered an indictment for violating obscenity laws. Sanger fled to England, where she spent fourteen months talking with sex radicals and economists studying overpopulation. After returning to the United States, Sanger opened the nation's first birth control clinic in Brooklyn, in 1916. Authorities shut it down, and Sanger spent a month in jail.

Sanger was in many ways a quintessential progressive reformer. She championed women's rights and believed birth control could solve urgent problems of industrialization and poverty. By the eve of World War I, she had launched a grassroots movement. Letters flooded in from across the country – some hostile, others begging for help. "Please send me one of your Papers on birth control, I have seven children and cannot afford any more," pleaded one woman. "Tell me how it is," demanded another, "that the wealthier class of people can get information like that and those that really need it, can't?" Allies set up clinics in St. Paul, Minnesota, and Ann Arbor, Michigan.

Yet, like many progressives, Sanger found herself on the defensive after World War I. Amid a postwar Red Scare that targeted the political left, Sanger's alliance with Socialists collapsed. Critics charged that birth control represented the most sinful and dangerous trends of modern society. Sanger had to respond to new political realities. To attract middle-class support, she emphasized expert, scientific approaches to birth control. Though she had previously advocated woman-to-woman educational networks, she now argued that only medical personnel should dispense contraception. Her new American Birth Control League cultivated support from eugenicists, who called for sterilization of the "unfit" and warned that darker races were reproducing more quickly than whites. Sanger herself was eventually forced out of the league by leaders seeking to make the cause respectable.

In the 1920s, debates over Sanger's work mirrored larger struggles between tradition and modernity, faith and secularism, and rural and urban ways

Celebrating the Fourth of July, 1926

This *Life* magazine cover celebrates two famous symbols of the 1920s: jazz music and the "flapper," in her droopy tights and scandalously short skirt, who loves to dance to its rhythms. The flags at the top record the latest slang expressions, including "so's your old man" and "step on it" ("it" being the accelerator of an automobile, in a decade when cars were America's hottest commodity). If you examine the bottom of the picture, you will also find a note of protest: While July 4, 1926, marked the 150th anniversary of the Declaration of Independence, *Life* says that Americans have had only "143 years of liberty" – followed by "seven years of Prohibition." Picture Research Consultants & Archives.

of life. World War I placed new emphasis on centralized planning and expert control, not grassroots democracy. After the war, political leaders abandoned two decades of trust busting and regulation and deferred to business interests. Political initiative shifted to groups that sought to keep out immigrants and preserve America's "racial purity." Millions turned their attention to radio shows, movies, cars, and other products of a thriving consumer culture. Americans wanted prosperity, not progressivism—at least until 1929, when the nation met up with the consequences of economic instability and excessive debt, through the shock of the Great Depression.

Conflicted Legacies of World War I

"The World War has accentuated all our differences," a journalist in the magazine *World's Work* observed. "It has not created those differences, but it has revealed and emphasized them." In the aftermath of the war, thousands of strikes revealed continuing class tensions. Violent race riots exposed determined white resistance to the rising expectations of African Americans, while an obsessive hunt for foreign radicals showed that ethnic pluralism would not win easy acceptance.

Racial Strife

African Americans emerged from World War I determined to insist on citizenship rights. Millions had loyally supported the war effort; 350,000 had served their country in uniform. The black man, one observer wrote, "realized that he was part and parcel of the great army of democracy. . . . With this realization came the consciousness of pride in himself as a man, and an American citizen." The Great Migration also drew hundreds of thousands of blacks from the South to Northern industrial cities, where they secured good wartime jobs and found they could vote, advocate for political reforms, and use their new economic clout to build community institutions and work for racial justice.

Across the United States, these trends sparked white violence. In the South, the number of lynchings rose from 48 in 1917 to 78 in 1919, including several murders of returning black soldiers in their military uniforms. Such incidents continued through the 1920s. A brutal lynching in the quiet railroad town of Rosewood, Florida, in 1921 prompted black residents to arm for self-defense. Mobs of furious whites responded by torching houses and hunting down black residents.

Police and state authorities refused to intervene; completely destroyed, the town of Rosewood vanished from the map.

In northern and midwestern cities, the arrival of thousands of southern blacks deepened existing racial tensions. Blacks competed with whites—including recent immigrants—for scarce housing and jobs. Unionized white workers resented blacks who served as strikebreakers. Racism turned such economic and political conflicts into violent confrontations. Attacks on African Americans broke out in more than twenty-five cities. One of the deadliest riots occurred in 1917 in East St. Louis, Illinois, where nine whites and more than forty blacks died. Chicago endured five days of rioting in July 1919. By that September, the national death toll from racial violence had reached 120.

The oil boom town of Tulsa, Oklahoma, was the site of a particularly horrific incident in June 1921. Sensational, false news reports of an alleged rape helped incite white mobs who resented increasing black prosperity. Anger focused on the 8,000 residents of Tulsa's prosperous Greenwood district, locally known as "the black Wall Street." The white mob—helped by National Guardsmen, who arrested any residents who resisted—burned thirty-five blocks of Greenwood and killed several dozen African Americans. The city's leading paper acknowledged that "semi-organized bands of white men systematically applied the torch, while others shot on sight men of color." It took a decade for black residents, who refused to be driven out, to slowly rebuild Greenwood.

Erosion of Labor Rights

African Americans were not the only ones who faced challenges to hard-won recent gains. The war effort, overseen by a Democratic administration sympathetic to labor, had temporarily increased the size and power of

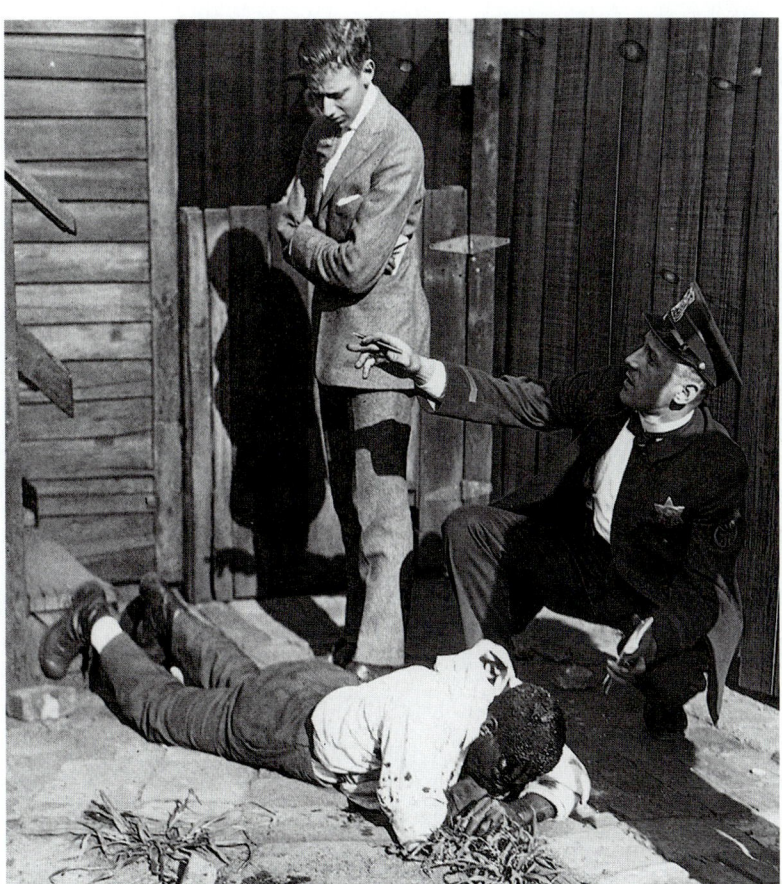

Chicago Race Riot

When racial violence exploded in Chicago during the summer of 1919, *Chicago Evening Post* photographer Jun Fujita was on the scene to capture it. As one of the few Japanese immigrants in Chicago at the time, Fujita was probably no stranger to racism, and it took personal courage to put himself in the midst of the escalating violence. When the riot finally ended, thirty-eight people were dead and more than five hundred were injured.   Chicago Historical Society/ Photo by Jun Fujita.

labor unions. The National War Labor Board (NWLB), formed in April 1918, established an eight-hour day for war workers, with time-and-a-half pay for overtime, and endorsed equal pay for women. In return for a no-strike pledge, the NWLB also supported workers' right to organize. Membership in the American Federation of Labor (AFL) grew by a third, reaching more than 3 million by war's end. Workers' expectations rose as the war economy brought higher pay and better working conditions.

But when workers tried to maintain these standards after the war, employers cut wages and rooted out unions. These developments prompted a massive confrontation. In 1919, more than 4 million wage laborers—one in every five—went on strike, a proportion never since equaled. A walkout of shipyard workers in Seattle sparked a general strike that shut down the city. Another major strike disrupted the steel industry, as 350,000 workers demanded union recognition and an end to twelve-hour shifts. Elbert H. Gary, the head of United States Steel Corporation, refused to negotiate; he hired Mexican and African American strikebreakers and eventually broke the strike. Meanwhile, business leaders in rising

industries, such as automobile manufacturing, resolutely resisted unions, leading to the creation of more and more non-unionized industrial jobs.

Public employees fared no better. Late in 1919, Boston's police force shocked many Americans by demanding a union and going on strike to get it. Massachusetts governor Calvin Coolidge won national fame by declaring, "There is no right to strike against the public safety by anybody, anywhere, anytime." Coolidge fired the entire police force, and the strike failed. A majority of the public supported the governor, and Republicans rewarded Coolidge by nominating him for the vice presidency in 1920.

Antilabor decisions by the Supreme Court were an important factor in unions' decline. In *Coronado Coal Company v. United Mine Workers* (1925), the Court ruled that a striking union could be penalized for illegal restraint of trade. The Court also struck down federal legislation regulating child labor; in *Adkins v. Children's Hospital* (1923), it voided a minimum wage for women workers in the District of Columbia, reversing many of the gains that had been achieved before World War I through the groundbreaking decision

General Strike in Seattle

Seattle was a strong union town, and the participation of 110 local unions in a general strike in 1919 paralyzed the city. Although the strike was peaceful, city officials deputized local citizens for police duty, such as this ragtag group of volunteers being issued guns. Museum of History and Industry, Seattle, Washington.

in *Muller v. Oregon* (see Chapter 20). Such decisions, along with aggressive anti-union campaigns, caused membership in labor unions to fall from 5.1 million in 1920 to 3.6 million in 1929 — only 10 percent of the nonagricultural workforce.

In place of unions, the 1920s marked the heyday of **welfare capitalism**, a system of labor relations that stressed management's responsibility for employees' well-being. Employers hoped this would build a loyal workforce and head off strikes and labor unrest. At a time when government unemployment compensation and Social Security did not exist, General Electric, U.S. Steel, and other large corporations offered workers health insurance and old-age pensions. But such plans covered only about 5 percent of the industrial workforce. In the tangible benefits that it offered workers, welfare capitalism had serious limitations.

The Red Scare

Many prosperous Americans sided with management in the upheavals of the postwar years. They blamed workers for the rapidly rising cost of living, which jumped nearly 80 percent between 1917 and 1919. The socialist outlook of some recent immigrants frightened native-born citizens, and the communist **ideology** of the Russian Bolsheviks terrified them. When Bolsheviks founded the Third International (or Comintern) in 1919, an organization intended to foster revolutions, some Americans began to fear that dangerous radicals were hiding everywhere. Hatred of Germans (disparaged as "Huns") was replaced by hostility toward Bolsheviks (labeled "Reds," after the color of Communist party badges and flags). Ironically, Communists remained few in number and had little political influence. Of the 50 million adults in the United States in 1920, no more than 70,000 belonged to either the fledgling U.S. Communist Party or the Communist Labor Party. The Industrial Workers of the World (IWW) had been weakened by wartime repression and internal dissent. Yet the public and the press blamed labor unrest on alien radicals.

In 1919, tensions mounted amid a series of threats and bombings. In April, alert postal workers discovered and defused thirty-four mail bombs addressed to government officials. In June, a bomb detonated outside the Washington townhouse of recently appointed attorney general A. Mitchell Palmer. Palmer escaped unharmed, but he used the incident to fan public fears. With President Woodrow Wilson incapacitated by stroke, Palmer had a free hand. He set up an antiradicalism division in the Justice Department and appointed his assistant J. Edgar Hoover to direct it; shortly afterward, it became the Federal Bureau of Investigation (FBI). Then, in November 1919, Palmer's agents stormed the headquarters of radical organizations. The dragnet captured thousands of aliens who had committed no crimes but who held anarchist or revolutionary beliefs. Lacking the protection of U.S. citizenship, many were deported without formal indictment or trial.

The Passion of Sacco and Vanzetti, by Ben Shahn (1931–1932)

Ben Shahn (1898–1969) came to the United States from Lithuania as a child and achieved fame as a social realist painter and photographer. Shahn used his art to advance his belief in social justice. In this painting, Sacco and Vanzetti lie dead and pale, hovered over by three distinguished Massachusetts citizens. These grim-faced men – holding lilies, a symbol of death – are Harvard University president A. Lawrence Lowell and the two other members of a commission appointed by the governor in 1927 to review the case. The commission concluded that the men were guilty, a finding that led to their execution. Judge Webster Thayer, who presided at the original trial in 1921, stands in the window in the background. Copyright Geoffrey Clements/Corbis, Copyright Estate of Ben Shahn/VAGA, New York.

The "Palmer raids" peaked on a notorious night in January 1920, when federal agents invaded homes and meeting halls, arrested six thousand citizens and aliens, and denied the prisoners access to legal counsel. Then Palmer, ambitious for the presidency, overreached. He predicted that on May 1 a radical conspiracy would attempt to overthrow the U.S. government. State militia units and police went on twenty-four-hour alert to guard the nation against the alleged threat, but not a single incident occurred. As the summer of 1920 passed without major strikes or renewed bombings, the Red Scare began to abate.

Like other postwar legacies, however, antiradicalism persisted through the next decade. In May 1920, at the height of the Red Scare, police arrested Nicola Sacco, a shoemaker, and Bartolomeo Vanzetti, a fish peddler, for the murder of two men during a robbery of a shoe company in South Braintree, Massachusetts. Sacco and Vanzetti were Italian aliens and self-proclaimed anarchists who had evaded the draft. Convicted of the murders, Sacco and Vanzetti sat in jail for six years while supporters appealed their verdicts. In 1927, Judge Webster Thayer denied a motion for a new trial and sentenced them to death. Scholars still debate Sacco and Vanzetti's guilt or innocence. But it was clear that their trial was biased by prosecutors' emphasis on their ties to radical groups. The execution of Sacco and Vanzetti was one of the ugly scars left by the ethnic and political hostilities of the Great War.

- What factors contributed to racial and labor violence after the war?

- What factors, both international and domestic, contributed to the emergence of the Red Scare?

Politics in the 1920s

As the plight of labor suggested, the 1920s were a tough decade for the progressives who had gained ground before World War I. After a few early victories for reform, including the achievement of national woman suffrage, the dominant motif of the 1920s was limited government. At the grass roots, native-born white Protestants rallied against what they saw as big-city values and advocated such goals as immigration restriction. A series of Republican presidents placed responsibility for the nation's well-being in the hands of business interests. President Calvin Coolidge solemnly declared, "The man who builds a factory builds a temple. The man who works there worships there." The same theme prevailed in continued interventions in Latin America and elsewhere: The United States sought to reshape other nations' economies and finances to enhance American business needs.

Women in Politics

At the start of the 1920s, many progressive women hoped that the attainment of full voting rights would offer women new leverage to tackle industrial poverty. They created organizations like the Women's Joint Congressional Committee, a Washington-based advocacy group. The committee's greatest accomplishment was the first federally funded health-care legislation, the

The League of Women Voters

The League of Women Voters was the brainchild of Carrie Chapman Catt, president of the National American Woman Suffrage Association. Formed in 1920, as the Nineteenth Amendment was about to give women the vote, the league undertook to educate Americans in responsible citizenship and to win enactment of legislation favorable to women. The league helped secure passage of the Sheppard-Towner Act of 1921, which provided federal aid for maternal and child-care programs. In the 1930s, members campaigned for the enactment of Social Security and other social welfare legislation.   Library of Congress.

Sheppard-Towner Federal Maternity and Infancy Act (1921). Sheppard-Towner provided federal funds to subsidize medical clinics, prenatal education programs, and visiting nurses. Though opponents warned that the act would lead to socialized medicine, Sheppard-Towner improved health care for the poor and significantly lowered infant mortality rates. It also marked the first time that Congress designated federal funds to the states and encouraged them to administer a social welfare program.

Moved by the immense scale of suffering caused by World War I, some women joined the growing international peace movement. While diplomats conducted negotiations at Versailles, women peace advocates from around the world convened in Zurich and called on all nations to use their resources to end hunger and promote human welfare. The treaty negotiators in Paris ignored them, but the women activists organized for sustained opposition to war. In 1919, they created the Women's International League for Peace and Freedom (WILPF), whose leading members included Jane Addams. Through the 1920s and beyond, members of WILPF denounced imperialism, stressed the suffering caused by militarism, and proposed social justice measures.

Despite such work, women's activism suffered major setbacks in the 1920s. The WILPF came under fierce attack during the Red Scare because of the presence of Socialist women among its ranks. And though women proved to be effective lobbyists, they had difficulty gaining access to posts in the Republican and Democratic parties. Finding that women did not vote as a bloc, politicians in both parties began to take their votes for granted. New reforms failed to gain support, and a key achievement was rolled back. Many congressmen had initially supported the Sheppard-Towner Act because they feared the voting power of women, but Congress ended the program in the late 1920s.

Republican "Normalcy"

With President Wilson ailing in 1920, Democrats nominated Ohio governor James M. Cox for president, on a platform calling for U.S. participation in the League of Nations and continuation of Wilson's progressivism. Republicans, led by their probusiness wing, tapped genial Ohio senator Warren G. Harding. In a dig at Wilson's sweeping idealism, Harding promised "not nostrums but normalcy." On Election Day he won in a landslide, beginning an era of Republican dominance that lasted until 1932.

Harding's most energetic appointee was Secretary of Commerce Herbert Hoover, well-known head of the wartime Food Administration. Under Hoover's direction, the Commerce Department helped create two thousand trade associations representing companies in almost every major industry. Government officials worked closely with the associations, providing statistical research, suggesting industry-wide standards, and promoting stable prices and wages. Hoover hoped that through voluntary business cooperation with government—an "associated state"—he could achieve what progressive reformers had sought through governmental regulation.

But more sinister links between government and corporate interests were soon revealed. When President Harding died suddenly of a heart attack in August 1923, evidence was just coming to light that parts of his administration were riddled with corruption. The worst scandal concerned the secret leasing of government oil reserves in Teapot Dome, Wyoming, and Elk Hills, California, to private companies. Secretary of the Interior Albert Fall was eventually convicted of taking $300,000 in bribes and became the first cabinet officer in U.S. history to serve a prison sentence.

Vice President Calvin Coolidge ascended to the presidency upon Harding's death. He maintained Republican dominance while offering, with his austere Yankee morality, a contrast to his predecessor's cronyism. Campaigning for election in his own right in 1924, Coolidge called for limited government, isolationism in foreign policy, and tax cuts for business. Rural and urban Democrats, deeply divided over such issues as prohibition and immigration restriction, deadlocked at their national convention; delegates cast 102 ballots before finally choosing John W. Davis, a Wall Street lawyer. Coolidge easily defeated Davis and staved off a challenge by Senator Robert M. La Follette of Wisconsin, who tried to resuscitate the Progressive Party. In the end, Coolidge received 15.7 million votes to Davis's 8.4 million and La Follette's 4.9 million.

For the most part, Republicans declined to carry forward progressive initiatives from the prewar years. The Republican-dominated Federal Trade Commission (FTC) failed to enforce antitrust laws. The Supreme Court, now headed by former Republican president William Howard Taft, refused to break up the mammoth U.S. Steel Corporation, despite evidence of its near-monopoly power. With the agricultural sector facing hardship, Congress sought to aid farmers with the McNary-Haugen bills of 1927 and 1928, which proposed a system of federal price supports for major crops. But President Coolidge opposed the bills as special-interest legislation and vetoed them both. While some state and municipal leaders continued to pursue ambitious agendas, they were shut out of power at the federal level.

Dollar Diplomacy

Political campaigns emphasized domestic issues in the 1920s, but the United States nonetheless remained deeply engaged in foreign affairs. Republican presidential administrations sought to advance U.S. business interests, especially by encouraging private banks to make foreign loans. Policymakers hoped such loans would stimulate growth and increase demand for U.S. products in developing markets. Bankers, though, wanted government assurance of repayment in countries that they perceived as weak or unstable.

U.S. officials acted to provide such assurance. In 1922, for example, when American banks offered an immense loan to Bolivia (at a hefty profit), State Department officials pressured the South American nation to accept it. The diplomats also forced Bolivia to agree to financial oversight by a commission under the banks' control. A similar arrangement was reached with El Salvador's government in 1923, though efforts to broker such deals in Honduras and Guatemala fell through. Where stronger action was needed, the United States intervened militarily, often to force repayment of debt. The U.S. Marines occupied Nicaragua almost continuously from 1912 to 1933, the Dominican Republic from 1916 to 1924, and Haiti from 1915 to 1934.

In these lengthy military deployments Americans came to think of the occupied countries as essentially U.S. possessions, much like Puerto Rico and the Philippines. Sensational memoirs by marines who had served in Haiti popularized the island as the "American Africa." White Americans became fascinated by *vodou* (voodoo) and other Haitian religious customs, reinforcing their view of Haitians as either dangerous savages or child-like people who needed U.S. guidance and supervision. One commander testified that his troops saw themselves as "trustees of a huge estate that belonged to minors. . . . The Haitians were our wards."

At home, critics denounced loan guarantees and military interventions as **dollar diplomacy**. The term was coined in 1924 by Samuel Guy Inman, a Disciples of Christ missionary who had toured U.S.-occupied Haiti and the Dominican Republic. "The United States," Inman declared, "cannot go on destroying with impunity the sovereignty of other peoples, however weak." African American leaders also denounced the Haitian occupation. On behalf of the Women's International League for Peace and Freedom and the International Council of Women of the Darker Races, a delegation conducted a fact-finding tour of Haiti in 1926. Their report exposed, among other things, the sexual exploitation of Haitian women by U.S. soldiers.

By the late 1920s, dollar diplomacy was on the defensive, in keeping with a broader mood of isolationism and disgust with international affairs. At the same time, political leaders became frustrated with their poor results. Dollar diplomacy usually managed to get loans repaid, securing bankers' profits. But the loans often ended up in the pockets of local elites; U.S. policies failed to build broad-based prosperity overseas. Military intervention could have even more dire results. In Haiti, the marines crushed peasant protests and helped the Haitian elite consolidate its power. U.S. occupation thus helped create the conditions for harsh dictatorships that Haitians endured through the rest of the twentieth century.

Culture Wars

By 1929, ninety-three U.S. cities had populations of more than 100,000. New York City's population exceeded 7 million, and Los Angeles's had exploded to 1.2 million. The lives and beliefs of urban Americans—including millions of recent immigrants—often differed dramatically from those in small towns and farming areas. Native-born rural Protestants, faced with a dire perceived threat, rallied in the 1920s to protect what they saw as American values.

Religion in Politics | Rural and native-born Protestants started the decade with the achievement of a longtime goal: national prohibition of liquor (see Chapter 18). Wartime anti-German prejudice was a major spur. Since major breweries like Pabst and Busch were owned by German Americans, many citizens decided it was unpatriotic to drink beer. Mobilizing the economy for war, Congress also limited brewers' and distillers' use of barley, hops, and other scarce grains, causing consumption to decline. The nation's decades-long prohibition campaign culminated with Congress's passage of the Eighteenth Amendment in 1917. Ratified in 1919 by nearly every state and effective in January 1920, the amendment prohibited the "manufacture, sale, or transportation of intoxicating liquors" anywhere in the United States. Though widely circumvented in urban speakeasies and other illegal drinking sites, the amendment remained in force until its repeal in 1933. Defenders hailed the Eighteenth Amendment as a victory for health, morals, and Christian values.

At the state and local levels, controversy erupted as fundamentalist Protestants sought to mandate school curricula based on the biblical account of creation. In 1925, Tennessee's legislature outlawed the teaching of "any theory that denies the story of the Divine creation of man as taught in the Bible, [and teaches] instead that man has descended from a lower order of animals." The American Civil Liberties Union (ACLU), which had been formed during the Red Scare to protect free speech rights, challenged the Tennessee law's constitutionality. The ACLU intervened in the trial of John T. Scopes, a high school biology teacher who taught

Defining *Beer*

The Eighteenth Amendment banned the manufacture, sale, and transportation of "intoxicating liquors." Over the strong objections of the beer industry, the Volstead Act of 1919 outlawed beverages with an alcoholic content of more than 0.5 percent. As support for prohibition declined in the early 1930s, former brewery owners and workers campaigned for the legalization of beer, as in this march. In March 1933, nine months before the repeal of the Eighteenth Amendment, Congress amended the Volstead Act to allow the manufacture of beer with an alcoholic content of 3.2 percent.   Library of Congress.

the theory of evolution to his class and faced a jail sentence for doing so. The case attracted national attention because Clarence Darrow, a famous criminal lawyer, defended Scopes, while William Jennings Bryan, the three-time Democratic presidential candidate, spoke for the prosecution.

Journalists dubbed the Scopes case "the monkey trial." This label referred both to Darwin's argument that human beings and other primates share a common ancestor and to the circus atmosphere at the trial, which was broadcast live over a Chicago radio station. (Proving that sophisticated urbanites had their own bitter prejudices, acerbic critic H. L. Mencken dismissed anti-evolutionists as "gaping primates of the upland valleys," implying that they had not evolved.) The jury took

only eight minutes to deliver its verdict: guilty. Though the Tennessee Supreme Court later overturned Scopes's conviction, the controversial law remained on the books for more than thirty years.

Nativism | Many native-born Protestants saw unrestricted immigration as the primary cause of cultural and religious disputes. A nation of 105 million people had added more than 23 million immigrants over the previous four decades. The newcomers included many Catholics and Jews from Southern and Eastern Europe, whom one Maryland congressman referred to as "indigestible lumps" in the "national stomach." Such **nativism**, which recalled hostility toward the Irish and Germans in the 1840s and 1850s, was widely shared.

Resurgent nativism fueled a momentous shift in immigration policy. "America must be kept American," President Coolidge declared in 1924. Congress had banned Chinese immigration in 1882, and Theodore Roosevelt had negotiated a so-called gentleman's agreement that limited Japanese immigration in 1907. Now nativists charged that there were also too many European immigrants, some of whom undermined Protestantism and imported anarchism, socialism, and other radical doctrines. Responding to these concerns, Congress passed emergency immigration restrictions in 1921 and a permanent measure three years later. The National Origins Act (1924) used thirty-four-year-old census data to establish a baseline: in the future, annual immigration from each country could not exceed 2 percent of that nationality's U.S. population as it had stood in 1890. Since only small numbers of Italians, Greeks, Poles, Russians, and other Southern and Eastern European immigrants had arrived before 1890, the law drastically limited immigration from those places. In 1929, Congress imposed even more restrictive quotas, setting a cap of 150,000 immigrants per year from Europe and continuing to ban most immigrants from Asia.

The new laws, however, permitted unrestricted immigration from the Western Hemisphere. Latin Americans arrived in increasing numbers, finding jobs in the West that had gone to Asian immigrants before exclusion. More than 1 million Mexicans entered the United States between 1900 and 1930, including many during World War I. Nativists lobbied Congress to cut this flow; so did labor leaders, who argued that impoverished migrants lowered wages for other American workers. But Congress heeded the pleas of employers, especially farmers in Texas and California, who wanted cheap labor. Only the coming of the Great Depression cut off migration from Mexico (see Reading American Pictures, "Patrolling the Texas Border," p. 695).

Other expressions of nativism emerged at the state level. In 1913, by an overwhelming majority, California's legislature had passed a law declaring that "aliens ineligible to citizenship" could not own "real property." The law aimed to exclude Asians, especially Japanese immigrants, from owning land, though some had lived in the state for decades and built up prosperous farms. In the wake of World War I, California tightened these laws, making it increasingly difficult for Asian immigrant families to establish themselves. California, Washington, and Hawaii also severely restricted schools that taught Japanese language, history, and culture to young Japanese Americans. California, for example, passed a law forbidding any Japanese school from operating more than one hour per day; textbooks could make no references to samurai warriors, emperors, or other "controversial" elements of Japanese history. Relentless hostility, which denied Asians both citizenship and land rights, left Japanese Americans in a vulnerable position at the outbreak of World War II, when anti-Japanese hysteria swept the United States.

The Klan Revived

The 1920s also brought a nationwide rebirth of the Ku Klux Klan (KKK), the white supremacist group formed in the post–Civil War South. Soon after the premiere of *Birth of a Nation* (1915), a popular film that glorified the Reconstruction-era Klan, a group of southerners gathered on Georgia's Stone Mountain to revive the group. With its blunt motto, "Native, white, Protestant supremacy," the Klan recruited supporters across the country. KKK members did not limit their harassment to blacks but targeted Catholics and Jews as well, with physical intimidation, arson, and economic boycotts. The KKK also turned to politics, and hundreds of Klansmen won election to local offices and state legislatures (Map 22.1).

At the height of its power, the Klan wielded considerable political clout and counted more than three million members, including many women. The Klan's mainstream appeal was illustrated by President Woodrow Wilson's public praise for *Birth of a Nation*. Though it declined nationally after 1925, robbed of a potent issue by passage of the anti-immigration bill, the Klan remained strong in the South, and pockets of KKK activity persisted in all parts of the country. Klan activism also lent a menacing cast to other political issues. Some local Klansmen, for example, cooperated with members of the Anti-Saloon League to enforce prohibition laws through threats and violent attacks.

The Election of 1928

Conflicts over race, religion, and ethnicity created the climate for a stormy presidential election in 1928. Democrats had traditionally drawn strength from white voters in the South and immigrants in the North. In the 1920s, however, these groups divided over prohibition, immigration restriction, and the Klan. By 1928, the northern urban wing gained firm control. Democrats nominated Governor Al Smith of New York, the first presidential candidate to reflect the aspirations of the urban working class. The grandson of Irish peasants, Smith had risen through New York City's Democratic machine and had become a dynamic reformer. But Smith offended many small-town and rural Americans. He spoke in a heavy New York accent and sported a brown derby that highlighted his ethnic working-class origins. Middle-class reformers questioned his ties to

Patrolling the Texas Border

In 1926, San Antonio photographer Eugene Omar Goldbeck took this photograph of U.S. Border Patrol officers in Laredo, Texas. Since 1917, Mexicans, like other immigrants, had been subject to a head tax and a literacy test. However, because of pressure from southwestern employers eager for cheap Mexican labor, the U.S. government had not enforced these provisions and migrant laborers moved back and forth across the border. Following the passage of the National Origins Act of 1924, the federal government established the Border Patrol to prevent Europeans from entering the United States illegally through Canada and Mexico. The Border Patrol focused its enforcement efforts on the Southwest and then mainly on stemming the tide of Mexican immigration. In addition to the Border Patrol, new procedures, including bathing, delousing, and medical inspections at key points of entry, "hardened" the border and ended the casual movement of Mexican workers in and out of the United States.

The U.S. Border Patrol, Laredo, Texas, 1926. Nettie Lee Benson Latin American Collection, University of Texas at Austin General Libraries.

ANALYZING THE EVIDENCE

- Goldbeck's photograph is obviously posed. What do you suppose was the intent of presenting the Border Patrol in this fashion?

- Look carefully at the officers' clothes. Do all the hats have badges? How many patrol members are dressed as civilians (including one with a bowtie)? What might this signify?

- If you were an immigrant worker, how might you read this image?

Ku Klux Klan Women Parade in Washington, D.C.
During the 1920s, the antiblack and anti-Catholic Ku Klux Klan was a powerful force in American life. Perhaps as many as 500,000 women joined the Women of the Ku Klux Klan (WKKK), including these women who paraded down Pennsylvania Avenue in Washington, D.C., in 1928. The organization was so deeply rooted in the daily lives of many southern and midwestern white Protestants that one woman from rural Indiana remembered her time in the KKK as "just a celebration . . . a way of growing up." National Archives at College Park, Maryland.

Tammany Hall; temperance advocates opposed him as a "wet." The governor's greatest handicap was his religion. Although Smith insisted that his Catholic beliefs would not affect his duties as president, many Protestant leaders opposed him. "No Governor can kiss the papal ring and get within gunshot of the White House," vowed a Methodist bishop from Buffalo.

Smith proved no match for the Republican nominee, Secretary of Commerce Herbert Hoover, an outstanding administrator who embodied the technological promise of the modern age. Women who had mobilized for Hoover's food conservation campaigns during World War I enlisted as "Hoover Hostesses," inviting friends to their homes to hear the candidate's radio speeches.

Enjoying the benefit of eight years of Republican prosperity, Hoover promised voters that individualism and cooperative endeavors would banish poverty. He won a major victory, receiving 58 percent of the popular vote to Smith's 41 percent and an overwhelming 444 electoral votes to Smith's 87 (Map 22.2). Because many southern Protestants refused to vote for a Catholic, Hoover carried five ex-Confederate states, breaking the Democratic "Solid South" for the first time since Reconstruction. Despite his resounding defeat, though, Smith carried the industrialized states of Massachusetts and Rhode Island. He also carried the nation's twelve largest cities — suggesting that urban voters were moving into the Democratic camp.

MAP 22.1

Ku Klux Klan Politics and Violence in the 1920s

Unlike the Reconstruction-era Klan, the Klan of the 1920s was geographically dispersed and had substantial strength in the West and Midwest as well as in the South. Although the Klan is often thought of as a rural movement, some of the strongest "klaverns" were in Chicago, Los Angeles, Atlanta, Detroit, and other large cities. The organization's members operated as vigilantes in areas where they were strong; elsewhere, their aggressive tactics triggered riots between Klansmen and their ethnic and religious targets.

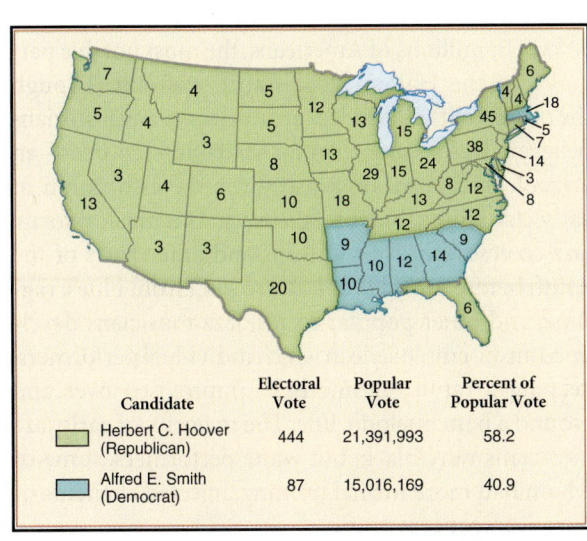

MAP 22.2

The Presidential Election of 1928

Historians still debate the extent to which 1928 was a critical election—an election that produced a significant realignment in voting behavior. Although the Republican Herbert Hoover swept the popular and the electoral votes, Democrat Alfred E. Smith won majorities not only in the South, his party's traditional stronghold, but also in Rhode Island, Massachusetts, and (although it is not evident on this map) all of the large cities of the North and Midwest. In subsequent elections, the Democrats won even more votes among African American and European ethnic groups and, until 1980, were the nation's dominant political party.

- What activist movements did women reformers undertake in the 1920s, and how successful were these?

- To what extent was Republicans' foreign policy during the 1920s consistent with their domestic agenda?

- How did grassroots conflicts over race, religion, and immigration shape politics in the 1920s?

Intellectual Modernism

Before World War I, dramatic forms of modernism had emerged in art and literature. In the 1920s, these became—like political campaigns—sites of struggle between modernity and tradition, secularism and faith. The horrors of the war prompted many American intellectuals, like their European counterparts, to question long-standing assumptions about civilization, progress, and the alleged superiority of Western cultures over so-called primitive ways of life. Some of these intellectual movements—such as the Harlem Renaissance—emerged from the social and economic upheavals that the Great War had wrought at home.

Harlem in Vogue

As the Great Migration tripled New York's black population in the decade after 1910, Harlem stood as "the symbol of liberty and the Promised Land to Negroes everywhere," as one black minister put it. Talented black artists and writers flocked to the district, where they broke with genteel traditions and asserted ties to Africa. Poet Langston Hughes drew on African American music in *The Weary Blues* (1926), a groundbreaking collection of poems. He captured the upbeat spirit of the Harlem Renaissance when he asserted, "I am a Negro—and beautiful."

Like Hughes, other writers and artists of the Harlem Renaissance championed race pride. Claude McKay, Jean Toomer, and Jessie Fauset explored the black experience and represented in fiction what philosopher Alain Locke called the "New Negro." Painter Jacob Lawrence, who had grown up in crowded tenement districts of the urban North, used bold shapes and vivid colors to portray the daily life, aspirations, and suppressed anger of African Americans. Author Zora Neale Hurston spent a decade collecting folklore in the South and the Caribbean and incorporated that material into short stories and novels. This creative work embodied the ongoing struggle to find a way, as the influential

The Harlem Renaissance

The Crisis, edited by the leading black intellectual W. E. B. Du Bois, was the magazine of the National Association for the Advancement of Colored People (NAACP). With its dramatic use of modern architecture and art, this cover from 1929 suggests the cultural and political awakenings associated with the Harlem Renaissance.   Henry Lee Moon Library and Civil Rights Archive, NAACP, Washington, D.C.

black intellectual W. E. B. Du Bois explained, "to be both a Negro and an American."

Jazz | To millions of Americans, the most notable part of the Harlem Renaissance was jazz. Though the origins of the word *jazz* are unclear, many historians believe it was a slang term for sexual intercourse—an etymology that makes sense, given the association of early jazz with urban vice districts. As a musical form, jazz coalesced in New Orleans and other parts of the South before World War I. Borrowing from blues, ragtime, and other popular forms, jazz musicians developed an ensemble style in which individual performers, keeping a rapid ragtime beat, improvised over and around a basic melodic line. The majority of early jazz musicians were black, but white performers, some of whom had more formal training, injected elements of European concert music.

CRAZY BLUES

By PERRY BRADFORD

MAMIE SMITH AND HER JAZZ HOUNDS

Get this number for your phonograph on Okeh Record No. 4169

PUBLISHED BY
PERRY BRADFORD
MUSIC PUB. CO.
1547 BROADWAY, N. Y. C.

All That Jazz

The phonograph machine dramatically expanded the popularity of jazz music, which Americans could now hear at home as well as in a city jazz joint. The success of "Crazy Blues" by Mamie Smith and her Jazz Hounds, which sold a million records in 1920, convinced record companies that there was an African American market for what were called "race records." Composer Perry Bradford plays the piano; Bradford was also the composer of "Keep a Knockin'," which Little Richard made into a major rock 'n' roll hit in 1957. Division of Political History, Smithsonian Institution, Washington, D.C.

In the 1920s, as jazz spread nationwide, musicians developed its signature mode of performance, the improvised solo. The key figure in this development was cornetist and trumpeter Louis Armstrong. A native of New Orleans, Armstrong learned his craft while playing in the saloons and brothels of Storyville, the city's vice district. Armstrong showed an inexhaustible capacity for melodic invention. His dazzling solos inspired other musicians to try solos. The white trumpeter Bix Beiderbecke, for example, pioneered an influential bright-toned style. By the late 1920s, soloists had become the celebrities of jazz, thrilling audiences with their improvisational skills (see Voices from Abroad, "Patrick 'Spike' Hughes and Leo Vauchant: Europeans Encounter American Jazz," p. 700).

As jazz spread, it generally followed the routes of the Great Migration from the South to northern and western cities, where it met consumers primed to receive it. Before World War I, ragtime and other forms of dance music had created broad, enthusiastic audiences for African American music. Most cities had plentiful venues where jazz could be featured. By the 1920s, radio also helped popularize jazz, as the emerging record industry churned out records of the latest tunes. New York became the hub of this commercially lucrative jazz. While the New Orleans style persisted in Chicago, attracting enthusiasts across racial lines, New York's jazz, which featured less syncopation and fewer blues inflections, had more mainstream appeal. White listeners flocked to theaters, ballrooms, and expensive clubs to hear the "Harlem sound" from the orchestras of Duke Ellington and other stars. Yet those who hailed "primitive" black music rarely suspended their racial condescension: Visiting a mixed-race club became known as "slumming."

VOICES FROM ABROAD

Patrick "Spike" Hughes and Leo Vauchant

Europeans Encounter American Jazz

U.S. involvement in World War I carried American jazz to Europe. After the war ended, some discharged African American soldiers remained in France. Many of these veterans were musicians who quickly found work in Parisian nightclubs, performing for war-weary audiences ready for the pleasures of the new music. Soon, forward-looking European musicians adopted the form and introduced it to cities across the continent. Below, two Europeans comment on their experience of jazz during the 1920s.

Patrick "Spike" Hughes was a British musician, composer, and journalist. In 1926 he saw the all-black revue Blackbirds, *which featured an American jazz orchestra led by Pike Davies.*

I was hearing, for the first time, Negro music played with all its characteristic colorfulness and vitality. The initial impact of the orchestra was rather strange; here was a group of wind and percussion players using familiar instruments such as trumpets, trombones, saxophones, clarinet, piano and the rest, who played tunes with the most elementary harmonic sequence, who yet succeeded in sounding entirely new. . . .

Whereas the European convention demands that brass instruments should be used in orchestras only for festive or solemn moments in music, here was a band which used them for gay, farcical and sentimental purposes so that the lions we knew could roar could also coo gently as any sucking dove.

Above all things, though, I learned from the Blackbirds orchestra that the music which cathedral organists and ill-informed writers of letters to the newspapers described as "barbaric," "undisciplined," "crude," and "atavistic," was in fact based on a remarkable technical precision of execution in ensemble passages, and a strict, unalterable set of rules governing all improvised playing.

Born Leo Arnaud, French drummer and trombonist Leo Vauchant became a noted jazz musician in Paris. He also studied classical composition and later, after emigrating to the United States, wrote Hollywood film scores. Here he recalls the Parisian jazz scene as he experienced it after World War I.

[On Sunday evenings in Paris, after playing an afternoon show] there was nothing to do. So I'd go somewhere to jam. I'd go to the Abbaye Thélème or Zelli's—anywhere. I knew all the musicians so I could go where I wanted. Most of the trombone players were guys that sat there and played from the stocks. So I could go anywhere and be welcome. I wouldn't go to the big places. I'd go to the little clubs and sometimes there'd be black Americans and we'd play till about five o'clock in the morning.

I was always especially glad to play with the black guys. It was always better to play with them. In the first place I liked to speak English. Talking about jazz in French always seemed to me to be ridiculous. It didn't ring true. "Hey, stay in B flat for the first ending." That meant something. The language has a lot to do with it. In America, even today, musicians dress differently, talk differently, they even shake hands differently. . . . I wanted to come to America so much, you've no idea.

To the blacks, life in Europe was like heaven, I can tell you, . . . being able to go any place, and live where they wanted. Also they were looked up to as stars. And that must have been pretty pleasant after life in the States. A lot of French guys resented the blacks going off with their women. But every guy I knew found himself a white broad— Montmartre women mostly. . . . They met them as hostesses who danced with them and they got a tip as an escort.

Source: Chris Goddard, *Jazz Away from Home* (New York: Paddington Press, 1979), 85, 17, 274, 262.

ANALYZING THE EVIDENCE

- What do Hughes's and Vauchant's comments suggest about why so many discharged African American soldiers chose to remain in France after the war?

- What do Hughes and Vauchant view as truly innovative in jazz? What do their remarks suggest about the broader critical reception of jazz in Europe?

- In America, jazz was popularly associated with the "primitive." How do you think these European observers would have responded to that association?

Through jazz, the recording industry began to develop products specifically aimed at urban working-class blacks. The breakthrough came in 1920, when Otto K. E. Heinemann, a producer who sold immigrant records in Yiddish, Swedish, and other languages, recorded singer Mamie Smith performing "Crazy Blues." This smash hit prompted big recording labels like Columbia and Paramount to develop "race records" for black audiences. Yet, while its marketing reflected the segregation of American society at large, jazz brought black music to the center stage of American culture. It became the era's signature music, so much so that novelist F. Scott Fitzgerald dubbed the 1920s the "Jazz Age."

Marcus Garvey and the UNIA | Harlem produced not only a tremendous burst of artistic creativity but also broad political aspirations. It was no accident that the Universal Negro Improvement Association (UNIA), which arose in the 1920s to mobilize African American workers, was based in Harlem. The UNIA's charismatic leader, Jamaican-born Marcus Garvey, championed black separatism. Garvey urged followers to move to Africa, arguing that peoples of African descent would never be treated justly in white-run countries.

The UNIA grew rapidly in the early 1920s and soon claimed four million followers, including many recent migrants to northern industrial centers. It published a newspaper, *Negro World*, opened "liberty halls" in northern cities, and solicited funds for the Black Star Line steamship company, which Garvey intended to trade with the West Indies and carry American blacks back to Africa. But the UNIA declined as quickly as it had risen. In 1925, Garvey was imprisoned for mail fraud because of his solicitations for the Black Star Line. President Coolidge commuted his sentence but ordered his deportation to Jamaica. Without Garvey's leadership, the movement collapsed.

The UNIA left a legacy of activism, however, especially among working-class blacks. Garvey and his followers represented an emerging **pan-Africanism**: They argued that people of African descent, in all parts of the world, had a common destiny and should cooperate in political action. Black men's military service in Europe during World War I, the Pan-African Congress that had sought representation at the treaty table, protests against the U.S. occupation of Haiti, and modernist experiments in literature and the arts all contributed to this emerging transnational consciousness. One African American historian wrote in 1927: "The grandiose schemes of Marcus Garvey gave to the race a consciousness such as it had never possessed before. The dream

Augusta Fells Savage, African American Sculptor
Born in Florida in 1892, Augusta Fells Savage arrived in New York to study in 1921 and remained to take part in the Harlem Renaissance. Widowed at a young age, and struggling to support her parents and young daughter, Savage faced both racism and poverty. Much of her work has been lost, because she sculpted in clay and could not afford to cast in bronze. Savage began to speak out for racial justice after she was denied, on the basis of her race, a fellowship to study in Paris. In 1923, she married a close associate of UNIA leader Marcus Garvey.   Archives of American Art/ Smithsonian Institution.

of a united Africa, not less than a trip to France, challenged the imagination, and the soul of the Negro experienced a new sense of freedom."

Critiquing American Life

Paralleling the defiant creativity of Harlem, other artists and intellectuals of the 1920s registered various types of dissent. Some had experienced firsthand the shock and devastation of World War I, an experience so searing that American writer Gertrude Stein dubbed those who survived it the "Lost Generation." Novelist John Dos Passos railed at the obscenity of "Mr. Wilson's war" in *The Three Soldiers* (1921). Ernest Hemingway's novels *The Sun Also Rises* (1926) and *A Farewell to Arms* (1929) portrayed the futility and dehumanizing consequences of war. Such work linked American writers to European counterparts such as Siegfried Sassoon,

Rebecca West, and Erich Maria Remarque, who explored the devastating impact of trench warfare. In a broad sense, the cataclysm of World War I challenged intellectuals' belief in progress. In his influential poem *The Waste Land* (1922), American expatriate T. S. Eliot, living in Britain, evoked the shattered fragments of a civilization in ruins.

The war also accelerated a literary trend of exploring the dark side of the human psyche. In such dramas as *Desire Under the Elms* (1924), for example, playwright Eugene O'Neill offered a Freudian view of humans' raw, ungovernable sexual impulses. O'Neill first made his mark with *The Emperor Jones* (1920), which appealed to Americans' fascination with Haiti. Telling the story of a black dictator driven from power by an uprising of his people, *The Emperor Jones* offered an ambiguous message. The drama's black protagonist was played not by the customary white actors made up in blackface, but by African Americans who won acclaim for their performances. W. E. B. Du Bois called the popular Broadway drama "a splendid tragedy." But many blacks were dissatisfied with the play's primitivism; one actor who played Emperor Jones altered the script to omit the offensive word *nigger*. The white crowds who made *The Emperor Jones* a hit, much like those who flocked to Harlem's jazz clubs, indulged their fascination with "primitive" sexuality while projecting those traits onto people of African descent.

In a decade of conflict between traditional and modern worldviews, many writers exposed what they saw as the hypocrisy of small-town and rural life (see Comparing American Voices, "Urban Writers Describe Small-Town America," pp. 704–705). The most savage critic of conformity was Sinclair Lewis, whose novel *Babbitt* (1922) depicted the disillusionment of an ordinary small-town salesman. *Babbitt* was widely denounced as un-American; *Elmer Gantry* (1927), a satire about a greedy evangelical minister on the make, provoked even greater outrage. But critics found Lewis's work superb, and in 1930 he became the first American to win the Nobel Prize for literature. Even more famous was F. Scott Fitzgerald's *The Great Gatsby* (1925), which offered a scathing indictment of Americans' mindless pursuit of pleasure and material wealth.

- In what ways did the Harlem Renaissance and pan-Africanism reflect changes in African American experience?

- What were the origins of jazz, and what role did it play in the culture of the 1920s?

- What criticisms of mainstream culture did modernist American writers offer in the 1920s?

From Boom to Bust

Spurred by rapid expansion during the war, American business thrived in the 1920s. Corporations expanded more and more into overseas markets, while at home the decade brought the flowering of a national consumer culture that emphasized leisure and amusement. But some sectors of the economy, notably agriculture, never recovered from a sharp recession in the wake of World War I. Meanwhile, close observers worried over the rapid economic growth and easy credit that fueled the "Roaring Twenties." Their fears proved well-founded. In 1929, these factors helped trigger the Great Depression.

Business after the War

By the 1920s, large-scale corporations headed by chief executive officers (CEOs) had replaced individual- or family-run enterprises as the major form of American business organization. Through successive waves of consolidation, the two hundred largest businesses came to control almost half of the country's nonbanking corporate wealth by 1929. The greatest number of mergers occurred in rising industries such as chemicals (with DuPont emerging as the leader) and electrical appliances (General Electric). Rarely did any single corporation monopolize an entire field; rather, an **oligopoly** of a few major producers tended to dominate each market. At the same time, mergers between Wall Street banks enhanced the role of New York City as the financial center of the United States and, increasingly, the world. U.S. companies exercised growing international power. Seeking cheaper livestock, giant American meatpackers opened plants in Argentina. The United Fruit Company developed plantations in Costa Rica, Honduras, and Guatemala. General Electric set up production facilities in Latin America, Asia, and Australia. Republican "dollar diplomats" in Washington worked to support such enterprises.

Immediately after World War I, however, the United States experienced a series of economic shocks. They began with rampant inflation, as prices jumped by one-third in 1919 alone. Then came a sharp two-year recession that raised unemployment to 10 percent. Finally, the economy began to grow smoothly and more Americans began to benefit from the success of corporate enterprise. Between 1922 and 1929, the gross domestic product grew from $74 billion to $103 billion; in the same years, national per capita income rose an impressive 24 percent. Consumer goods, particularly the automobile, sparked this expansion. Not only did the

products themselves create growth, but manufacturing cars and refrigerators required huge quantities of steel, chemicals, and oil.

Despite the boom, the U.S. economy had areas of significant weakness throughout the 1920s. Agriculture, which still employed one-fourth of all American workers, never fully recovered from the postwar recession. Once Europe's economy revived, its farmers flooded world markets with grain and other farm products, causing agricultural prices to fall. Other industries, including coal and textiles, languished for similar reasons. As a consequence, many rural Americans shared little of the decade's prosperity. The bottom 40 percent of American families earned an average annual income of only $725 (about $9,100 today). Many, especially rural tenants and sharecroppers, languished in conditions of poverty and malnutrition.

Consumer Culture

In homes across the country, middle-class Americans during the 1920s sat down to a breakfast of Kellogg's corn flakes. They got into Ford Model Ts to go to work or to shop at Safeway. In the evening, families gathered around their radios to listen to such popular programs as *Great Moments in History*; on weekends, they might go to see the newest Charlie Chaplin film at the local theater. By 1929, 40 percent of American households owned a radio. At the same time, electric refrigerators and vacuum cleaners came into use in affluent homes. If one judged from the advertisements in *Good House-keeping*, *The Saturday Evening Post*, and other popular magazines, all Americans wore fashionable clothes and drove the latest model cars. That, of course, was not true, but the advertising industry reached new levels

Urban Writers Describe Small-Town America

In the early twentieth century, the United States was becoming an urban society. By 1920, life outside the metropolis seemed sufficiently remarkable to warrant sociological investigation—or at least, city people thought so. Presented here are three views of rural and small-town America, all published during the 1920s. Though cities had become the wellspring of American intellectual life, urban writers juxtaposed their own experiences with those of people they thought of as living in "Middletown, U.S.A."

Sinclair Lewis

Main Street

In his novel *Main Street* (1920), Sinclair Lewis portrayed the fictional midwestern town of Gopher Prairie. In the first two excerpts below, Lewis's narrator describes the reactions of young, urban Carol Kennicott, wife of the town's new doctor, and Bea Sorenson, a Swedish American farm girl.

When Carol had walked for thirty-two minutes she had completely covered the town, east and west, north and south; and she stood at the corner of Main Street and Washington Avenue and despaired.

Main Street with its two-story brick shops, its story-and-a-half wooden residences, its muddy expanse from concrete walk to walk, its huddle of Fords and lumber-wagons, was too small to absorb her. The broad, straight, unenticing gashes of the streets let in the grasping prairie on every side. She realized the vastness and the emptiness of the land. The skeleton iron windmill on the farm a few blocks away, at the north end of Main Street, was like the ribs of a dead cow. She thought of the coming of the Northern winter, when the unprotected houses would crouch together in terror of storms galloping out of that wild waste. They were so small and weak, the little brown houses. They were shelters for sparrows. . . .

She wanted to run, fleeing from the encroaching prairie, demanding the security of a great city. Her dreams of creating a beautiful town were ludicrous. Oozing out from every drab wall, she felt a forbidding spirit which she could never conquer.

She trailed down the street on one side, back on the other, glancing into the cross streets. It was a private Seeing Main Street tour. She was within ten minutes beholding not only the heart of a place called Gopher Prairie, but ten thousand towns from Albany to San Diego.

Dyer's Drug Store, a corner building of regular and unreal blocks of artificial stone. Inside the store, a greasy marble soda-fountain with an electric lamp of red and green and curdled-yellow mosaic shade. Pawed-over heaps of toothbrushes and combs and packages of shaving-soap.

Shelves of soap-cartons, teething-rings, garden-seeds, and patent medicines in yellow packages—nostrums for consumption, for "women's diseases"—notorious mixtures of opium and alcohol, in the very shop to which her husband sent patients for the filling of prescriptions.

The train which brought Carol to Gopher Prairie also brought Miss Bea Sorenson.

Miss Bea was a stalwart, corn-colored, laughing young woman, and she was bored by farm-work. She desired the excitements of city-life, and the way to enjoy city-life was, she had decided, to "go get a yob as a hired girl in Gopher Prairie." . . .

Bea had never before been in a town larger than Scandia Crossing, which has sixty-seven inhabitants.

As she marched up the street she was meditating that it didn't hardly seem like it was possible there could be so many folks all in one place at the same time. My! It would take years to get acquainted with them all. And swell people, too! A fine big gentleman in a new pink shirt with a diamond, and not no washed-out blue denim working-shirt. A lovely lady in a longery dress (but it must be an awful hard dress to wash). And the stores! . . . A drug store with a soda fountain that was just huge, awful long, and all lovely marble . . . and the soda spouts, they were silver, and they came right out of the bottom of the lamp-stand! Behind the fountain there were glass shelves, and bottles of new kinds of soft drinks, that nobody ever heard of. Suppose a fella took you *there*!

Source: Sinclair Lewis, *Main Street* (New York: Harcourt, Brace and Company, 1920), 38–39.

Anzia Yezierska

Bread Givers

A child of Jewish immigrants from Eastern Europe, Anzia Yezierska grew up on the Lower East Side of New York City. In her autobiographical novel *Bread Givers* (1925), Yezierska described her arrival in the Ohio town where she attended college.

Before this, New York was all of America to me. But now I came to a town of quiet streets, shaded with green trees. No crowds, no tenements. No hurrying noise to beat the race of the hours. Only a leisured quietness whispered in the air: Peace. . . .

Each house had its own green grass in front, its own free space all around, and it faced the street with the calm security of being owned for generations, and not rented by the month from a landlord. In the early twilight, it was like a picture out of fairyland to see people sitting on their porches, lazily swinging in their hammocks, or watering their own growing flowers.

So these are the real Americans, I thought, thrilled by the lean, straight bearing of the passers-by. They had none of that terrible fight for bread and rent that I always saw in the New York people's eyes. . . . All the young people I had ever seen were shut up in factories. But here were young girls and young men enjoying life, free from the worry for a living. . . . The spick-and-span cleanliness of these people! It smelled from them, the soap and the bathing. Their fingernails so white and pink. . . . What a feast of happenings each day of college was to those other students. Societies, dances, letters from home, packages of food, midnight spreads and even birthday parties. I never knew that there were people glad enough of life to celebrate the day they were born.

Source: Anzia Yezierska, *Bread Givers* (New York: Doubleday, 1925), 210–212, 218.

Robert S. Lynd and Helen Merrell Lynd

Middletown

In 1929, sociologists Robert S. Lynd and Helen Merrell Lynd published *Middletown*, a study of life in a small midwestern city. Middletown was not a single community but a composite of several communities studied by the Lynds.

The first real automobile appeared in Middletown in 1900. . . . At the close of 1923 there were 6,221 passenger cars in the city, one for every 6.1 persons, or roughly two for every three families. . . . As, at the turn of the century, business class people began to feel apologetic if they did not have a telephone, so ownership of an automobile has now reached the point of being an accepted essential of normal living. . . .

According to an officer of a Middletown automobile financing company, 75 to 90 percent of the cars purchased locally are bought on time payment, and a working man earning $35.00 a week frequently plans to use one week's pay each month as payment for his car. The automobile has apparently unsettled the habit of careful saving for some

families. . . . "I'll go without food before I'll see us give up the car," said one woman emphatically. . . .

Many families feel that an automobile is justified as an agency holding the family group together. . . . [But] the fact that 348 boys and 382 girls in the three upper years of the high school placed "use of the automobile" fifth and fourth respectively in a list of twelve possible sources of disagreement between them and their parents suggests that this may be an increasing decentralizing agent. . . .

If the automobile touches the rest of Middletown's living at many points, it has revolutionized its leisure . . . making leisure-time enjoyment a regularly expected part of every day and week rather than an occasional event. . . . The frequency of movie attendance of high school boys and girls is about equal, business class families tend to go more often than do working class families, and children of both groups attend more often without their parents than do all the individuals or combinations of family members put together. . . . It is probable that time formerly spent in lodges, saloons, and unions is now being spent in part at the movies, at least occasionally with other members of the family. Like the automobile and radio, the movies [break] up leisure time into an individual, family, or small group affair.

Source: Robert S. Lynd and Helen Merrell Lynd, *Middletown: A Study in American Culture* (New York: Harcourt, Brace and Company, 1929), 253, 255–258, 260, 264–265.

ANALYZING THE EVIDENCE

- What attitudes toward the small town and big city does *Main Street* represent? Why do you think Lewis includes views as different as Carol's and Bea's?

- How does the urban experience of Yezierska's narrator shape her reaction to life in an Ohio town? How might small-town residents have reacted to her description of them as "the real Americans"? How might Lewis have responded to Yezierska's description?

- How do the two novelists (Lewis and Yezierska) differ from the sociologists (the Lynds) in the issues they emphasize, and in their tone and point of view? What features of small-town life does each text emphasize?

of ambition and sophistication, entering what one historian calls the era of the "aggressive hard sell." The 1920s gave birth, for example, to fashion modeling and style consulting. "Sell them their dreams," one radio announcer urged advertisers in 1923. "People don't buy things to have things. . . . They buy hope—hope of what your merchandise will do for them."

In practice, the question of who participated in consumer culture was contested. It was no accident that white mobs in the Tulsa race riot plundered radios and phonograph players from the homes of prosperous African Americans: The clear message was that whites deserved such items and blacks did not. But neither prosperity nor poverty was limited by race. Surrounded by exhortations to indulge in luxuries, millions of working-class Americans—white, black, Latino, immigrant, or native-born—barely squeaked by, with wives and mothers often taking paid work to provide basic necessities. In times of crisis, some families sold all their furniture, starting with pianos and phonograph players and continuing, if necessary, with dining tables and beds. In the Los Angeles suburb of South Gate, white working-class men secured jobs in the steel, automobile, and tire industries, but urban prices were high and families often found it difficult to make ends meet. Self-help was the watchword as husbands and wives pinched pennies, bartered with neighbors, and used their yards to raise large vegetable gardens, rabbits, and chickens.

When every dollar counted, the lure of consumer culture often created friction. Married women resented husbands who spent discretionary cash at the ballpark and expected wives to make do. Generational conflicts emerged, especially when wage-earning children challenged the long-standing expectation that their pay should go "all to mother." In St. Louis, a Czech-born woman was exasperated when her son and daughter stopped contributing to their room and board and pooled their wages to buy a car. In Los Angeles, one fifteen-year-old girl spent her summer earning $2 a day sorting tiles at a local factory. Planning to enroll in business school, she spent the resulting $75 on "a black coat with a red fox collar, costing $40," as well as shoes and other ready-made clothes. Her brother reported that "Mom is angry at her for 'squandering' so much money."

Poor and affluent families often had one thing in common: They stretched their incomes by taking advantage of new forms of borrowing, such as auto loans and installment plans. "Buy now, pay later," said the ads, and millions did—a factor that contributed to the country's broad economic overextension in the 1920s. Anyone, no matter how rich, could get into debt, but consumer credit was particularly perilous for those living on the economic margins. In Chicago, one Lithuanian man casually described his neighbor's financial situation: "She ain't got no money. Sure she buys on credit, clothes for the children and everything." Such borrowing turned out to be a contributing factor to the bust in 1929.

The Automobile

No possession typified national consumer culture more than the automobile, a showpiece of modern consumer capitalism that revolutionized American economic and social life. Mass production of cars played a major role in the boom of the 1920s. In a single year, 1929, Americans spent $2.58 billion on automobiles. By the end of the decade, they owned 23 million cars—about 80 percent of the world's automobiles—or an average of one car for every six people.

The exuberant expansion of the auto industry rippled through the economy, with both positive and negative results. It stimulated the steel, petroleum, chemical, rubber, and glass industries and, directly or indirectly, provided jobs for 3.7 million workers. Highway construction became a billion-dollar-a-year enterprise, financed by federal subsidies and state gasoline taxes. Car ownership spurred the growth of suburbs and, in 1924, the first suburban shopping center: Country Club Plaza outside Kansas City, Missouri. But cars were expensive, and most Americans bought them on credit. This created risks not only for buyers but for the whole economy. Borrowers who could not pay off car loans lost their entire investment in their cars, and if they defaulted, banks were left holding unpaid loans. Amid the boom of the 1920s, however, such a scenario seemed remote.

Cars changed the way Americans spent their leisure time, as proud drivers took their machines on the road. An infrastructure of gas stations, motels, and drive-in restaurants soon catered to drivers. Cars also changed the dating patterns of young Americans. A Model T offered more privacy than did the family living room or front porch and contributed to increased sexual experimentation among the young. Though early cars were hardly comfortable places for sex, manufacturers learned to accommodate the market. The suggestive Playboy car was advertised, in 1923, as designed for the woman who "can do with eleven hundred pounds of steel and action when he's going high, wide and handsome." The Jewett, introduced in 1925, even had a fold-down bed—for camping on the road, or for other pleasures.

Railroad travel began to falter as automobiles became central to tourism. The American Automobile

Automobiles at Jacksonville Beach, Florida, 1923

The automobile transformed Americans' leisure pursuits. As proud car owners took to the road in ever-larger numbers, the "vacation" became a summer staple. Auto travel created a booming business in gas stations, roadside motels, campgrounds, and sightseeing destinations. A Florida vacation—once reserved for wealthy northeasterners who had traveled to Miami's exclusive hotels by first-class railcar—became an attainable luxury for middle-class and even some working-class families.   © Curt Teich Postcard Archives, Lake County Museum.

Association, founded in 1902, estimated that in 1929 almost a third of the population took vacations by car, patronizing "autocamps" and cabins. Already, by 1923, there were 247 autocamps in Colorado alone. "I had a few days after I got my wheat cut," reported one Kansas farmer, "so I just loaded my family . . . and lit out." One elite Californian complained that automobile travel was no longer "aristocratic and exclusive." "All the mechanics, the clerks and their wives and sweethearts," observed a reporter, "driving through the Wisconsin lake

Burlington Farm Machinery Company, Wisconsin, 1926

The appeal of the internal combustion engine ranged far beyond urban consumers. In this Wisconsin showroom, farmers could view the latest combines and trucks for use on the farm. Farmers invested heavily in such equipment during the 1920s, where they could afford to do so. More and more rural laborers (along with horses and mules) were displaced by modern machines which did the work of planting and harvest. Wisconsin Historical Society.

country, camping at Niagara, scattering tin cans and pop bottles over the Rockies, made those places taboo for bankers and chairmen of the board."

In rural areas, cars contributed to a consolidation of churches, schools, and post offices: These could now be reached over longer distances, so fewer were needed. The automobile also stimulated intercommunity leagues for softball and other activities—as well as an insatiable interest in movies and other commercial pleasures. It was hard to find any corner of the United States untouched by the automobile. Rural southern blacks, if they could get use of a car, found they could travel three counties away and secure a loan that white bankers in their own county might be reluctant to offer. Whites in South Dakota were "amazed to see Sioux Indians whirl into town in family automobiles." An anthropologist in California found, to his surprise, that men among the Pit River Achumawi people were well prepared to disassemble and repair the engine on his Model T.

Hollywood | Movies, which had their roots in the short silent films shown in turn-of-the-century nickelodeons, formed a second centerpiece of consumer culture in the 1920s. By 1910, the moviemaking industry had moved to southern California to take advantage of cheap land, sunshine, and varied scenery within easy reach. The large studios—United Artists, Paramount, and Metro-Goldwyn-Mayer—were run mainly by Eastern European Jewish immigrants. Adolph Zukor, for example, arrived in the United States from a Hungarian Jewish shtetl in the 1880s. Starting in Chicago with fur sales, Zukor and a partner set up five-cent theaters in Manhattan. "I spent a good deal of time watching the faces of the audience," Zukor recalled. "With a little experience I could see, hear, and 'feel' the reaction to each melodrama and comedy." Founding Paramount Pictures, Zukor sought to produce high-quality, feature-length films. He succeeded, in part, by signing famous rising stars.

The Appeal of the Movies, 1921

Advertising in *Ladies' Home Journal* in May 1921, Paramount Pictures suggested that the local movie theater could bring families closer together. Eager to make the show, father and son help the women of the family clean up after supper so they can drive together to the theater.   Picture Research Consultants & Archives.

By the end of World War I, Hollywood reigned as movie capital of the world, producing nearly 90 percent of all films. New feature-length movies, exhibited in large, ornate theaters, attracted middle-class as well as working-class audiences. Early stars such as Charlie Chaplin, Mary Pickford, and Douglas Fairbanks became idols who set national trends in clothing and hairstyles. In Chicago, young Mexican American men sported sideburns like those of screen star Rudolph Valentino; they called each other "sheik," a reference to one of Valentino's famous roles. Thousands of young women followed the lead of actress Clara Bow, Hollywood's famous flapper, who flaunted her boyish figure. Decked out in knee-length skirts, flappers shocked the older generation by smoking and wearing makeup.

Flappers represented only a tiny minority of women, but thanks to the movies and advertising, they became an influential symbol of women's sexual and social emancipation. In cities, young immigrant women eagerly bought American makeup and the latest flapper fashions and went dancing to jazz. Jazz stars helped popularize the style among working-class African Americans. Mexican American teenagers joined the trend, though they usually found themselves under the watchful eyes of *la dueña*, the chaperone. One *corrido* (ballad) commented sarcastically on the results:

> The girls of San Antonio
> Are lazy at the *metate*.
> They want to walk out bobbed-haired,
> With straw hats on.
> The harvesting is finished,
> So is the cotton;
> The flappers stroll out now
> For a good time.

American radio and film had an immediate global impact, and politicians grasped the potential benefits for the United States. In 1919, with government support, General Electric spearheaded the creation of Radio Corporation of America (RCA), to expand U.S. presence in foreign radio markets. During the 1920s, RCA—which had a federal appointee on its board of directors—emerged as a major provider of radio transmission in Latin America and East Asia. Meanwhile, by 1925, American films made up 95 percent of the movies screened in Britain, 80 percent in Latin America, and 70 percent in France. When Britain and Germany instituted quotas, requiring that the number of imported films not exceed the number of domestic ones, Hollywood studios set up European subsidiaries to churn out hundreds of "quota quickies," allowing the flow of imports to continue unchecked.

Charlie Chaplin and Jackie Coogan

Charlie Chaplin (left) and Jackie Coogan starred together in *The Kid* (1921), a silent comedy that also included sentimental and dramatic moments, promising viewers "a smile . . . and perhaps a tear." Chaplin, born in London in 1889, moved to the United States in 1912 and over the next two decades reigned as one of Hollywood's most famous silent film stars. In 1919, he joined with D. W. Griffith, Mary Pickford, and other American directors and stars to create the independent studio United Artists. *The Kid* made the Los Angeles–born Coogan—discovered by Chaplin on the vaudeville stage—into America's first child star. Library of Congress.

As European and Latin American audiences embraced the American movie industry, critics understood it as a serious cultural challenge. Protestant missionaries with "pious brochures," one Frenchman noted gloomily, had been replaced by their "more cheerful offspring," who now deluged the world with "blond movie stars." But, he added, both groups were "equally devoted to spreading the American way of life." As early as 1920, movie stars Douglas Fairbanks and Mary Pickford were greeted by immense crowds when they visited London and Paris on their honeymoon. The State Department, tracking their trip, arranged for the couple to gain extra publicity by meeting with European royalty. The United States was experimenting with what historians call **soft power**—the exercise of popular cultural influence—as radio and movies exuberantly celebrated the American Dream.

The Coming of the Great Depression

Toward the end of the decade, strains on the economy began to show. By 1927, consumer lending had become the tenth-largest business in the country, topping $7 billion a year. Increasing numbers of Americans also bought into the stock market, often with unrealistic expectations. One Yale professor proclaimed that stocks had reached a "permanently high plateau"; a General Motors executive assured readers of *Ladies' Home Journal* that if they saved $15 a month and bought stocks, in two decades they would have $80,000. Corporate profits were so high that some companies, fully invested in their own operations, plowed excess earnings into the stock market. Other market players compounded risk by purchasing on margin. This meant, for example, that an investor spent $20 of his own money and borrowed $80 to buy a $100 share of stock, expecting to pay back the loan as the stock rose rapidly in value. Such a strategy raked in gains as long as the economy grew, jobs were plentiful, and the stock market climbed. But those conditions did not last.

Yet even when the stock market crashed, in a series of plunges between October 25 and November 13, 1929, few onlookers understood the magnitude of the crisis. Deep, cyclical depressions had been a familiar part of the industrializing economy since at least the panic of the 1830s; in a **business cycle** such depressions tended to follow periods of rapid growth and speculation. A sharp downturn had occurred recently, in 1921, without triggering long-term disaster. The market rose again in late 1929 and early 1930, and while a great deal of money had been lost, most Americans hoped the aftermath of the crash would be brief. In fact, the nation had entered the Great Depression. Over the next four years, industrial production fell by 37 percent, and construction plunged by 78 percent. Prices for crops and other raw materials, already low, fell by half. By 1932, unemployment had reached a staggering 24 percent (Figure 22.1).

A precipitous drop in consumer spending helped deepen the crisis. Having bought on credit, and now facing hard times, consumers cut back dramatically, creating a vicious cycle of falling demand and forfeited loans. In late 1930, several major banks went under,

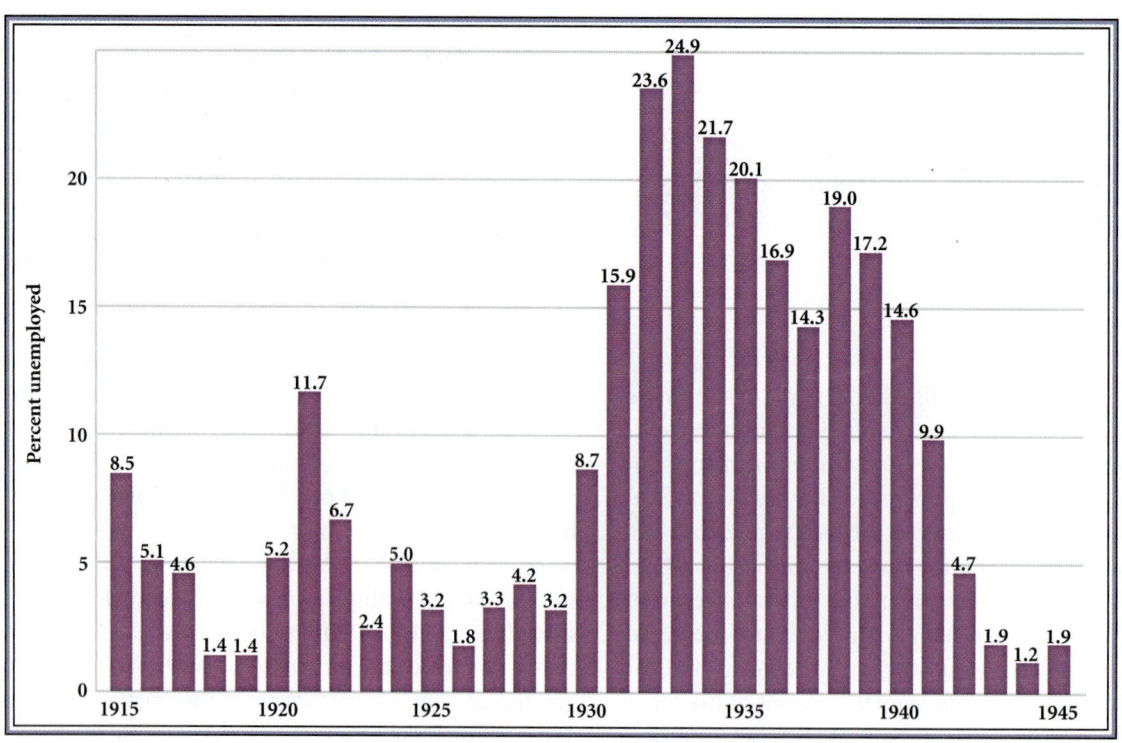

FIGURE 22.1

Unemployment, 1915–1945

During the 1920s, business prosperity and low rates of immigration resulted in historically low unemployment levels. The Great Depression threw millions of people out of work; by 1933 one in four American workers was unemployed, and the rate remained high until 1941, when the nation mobilized for World War II.

victims of overextended credit and reckless management. As industrial production slowed, a much larger wave of bank failures occurred in 1931. These bank failures caused an even more severe shock. Since the government did not insure bank deposits, savings in failed banks simply vanished. Some people with steady jobs and comfortable savings suddenly found themselves unemployed and penniless.

The Great Depression was, in part, a global crisis that emerged from the aftermath of World War I. By shattering Europe politically and economically, the war had destabilized international systems of trade and finance. Britain's central bank had long played a key role in managing the international financial system; the heavy cost of the war prevented it from resuming that role. In addition, the war disrupted the international gold standard. The United States and most European nations had long tied the value of their currencies to gold. This system had worked fairly well before the crisis of World War I, but it was vulnerable during economic downturns, when foreign financiers withdrew their investments and demanded gold payments.

While many factors caused the Great Depression, adherence to the gold standard was a major factor in its length and severity in the United States. Faced with economic catastrophe, both Britain and Germany abandoned the gold standard in 1931; when they did so, their economies began a modest recovery. A similar pattern held for other industrialized and developing countries. But the Hoover administration argued that such a move would cause irreparable damage to trade and the value of the dollar. Thus the Federal Reserve, the central banking system that had been created in 1913, was forced to do two contradictory things at once: try to revive the economy and protect the nation's gold supply. The United States finally left the gold standard in 1933, under Franklin D. Roosevelt's administration. This, and Roosevelt's resuscitation of banks, stimulated a partial recovery between 1933 and 1937. But by that time, the crisis had achieved catastrophic dimensions. Billions had been lost in bank and business failures, and the economy had stalled completely. Partial recovery brought unemployment down from 25 to a "mere" 14 percent.

Adhering to their long-standing faith in high protective tariffs, Republicans not only protected the gold standard but also enacted the Smoot-Hawley Tariff of 1930, hoping to stimulate domestic manufacturing. Historians are divided on whether the tariff worsened the depression, but it certainly did not help. It triggered retaliatory tariffs in other countries, as governments worldwide struggled to protect their own industries. Adopting a more helpful measure, in 1932, President Hoover created the Reconstruction Finance Corporation to provide loans to banks, railroads, and utilities. The administration also slashed taxes, and Hoover exhorted state and local governments to employ the jobless on public projects (though he and Congress proved unwilling to enact such measures at the federal level). Overall, though, Republicans clung to the belief that depressions were healthy and self-regulating. Treasury Secretary Andrew Mellon suggested that the downturn would help Americans "work harder" and "live a more moral life."

Thus, while the Great Depression began mere months after Hoover took office, the conditions that worsened it unfolded gradually over his presidential term. By the early 1930s, comprehending the magnitude of the crisis, Americans looked back wistfully on the previous decade of prosperity. In the 1920s, business had boomed and politics had been so placid that people chuckled when President Coolidge disappeared on extended fishing trips. In the following decade, Americans still flocked to the movies when they could afford it, eager to see lighthearted comedies that would help them forget their woes. But they now wanted bold action in Washington. In 1932, voters replaced Herbert Hoover with Democrat Franklin D. Roosevelt. Republicans, who had held solid majorities in both houses of Congress as late as 1931, found themselves swept out of power. Faced with the cataclysm of the Great Depression, Americans transformed their government and created a modern welfare state.

- **How did the automobile exemplify both the opportunities and the risks of 1920s consumer culture?**

- **What domestic and global factors triggered the Great Depression? What accounted for its length and severity? What steps did Hoover take to address the crisis?**

SUMMARY

Although involvement in the Great War (World War I) strengthened the United States economically and diplomatically, it also left the nation profoundly unsettled. Racial tensions exploded after the war as African Americans sought to pursue new opportunities and assert their rights. Meanwhile, labor unrest grew as employers cut wages and sought to break unions. Labor's power declined sharply in the war's aftermath, while anxieties over radicalism and immigration also prompted the nationwide Red Scare.

The politics of the 1920s brought a backlash against prewar progressivism. The efforts of women reformers to advance a reform agenda met very limited success. Republican administrations pursued pro-business "normalcy" at home and "dollar diplomacy" abroad. Prohibition and the Scopes trial demonstrated the influence religion could exert on public policy, while rising nativism fueled a resurgent Ku Klux Klan and led to sweeping new restrictions on immigration.

Postwar alienation found artistic expression in new forms of modernism, which denounced the dehumanizing effects of the war and criticized American materialism and hypocrisy. Spreading throughout the nation from New Orleans, jazz appealed to elite and popular audiences alike. Black artists and intellectuals of the Harlem Renaissance, including many who were inspired by pan-African ideas, explored the complexities of African American life.

During the 1920s, business thrived and a booming consumer culture, exemplified by the automobile and Hollywood films, created new forms of leisure, influencing daily life and challenging older sexual norms.

However, the risky speculation and easy credit of the period undermined the foundations of the economy. After the 1929 crash, these factors, along with a range of interconnected global conditions, plunged the United States into the Great Depression.

CHAPTER REVIEW QUESTIONS

- What was the Republican vision of "normalcy," and how did the Coolidge and Harding administrations seek to realize it?

- Along what lines did Americans find themselves divided in the 1920s? How did those conflicts get expressed in politics? In culture and intellectual life?

- Why did the 1920s end with a severe economic crisis? What factors that drove economic growth and consumer spending, in the years of prosperity that preceded 1929, contribute to the crash that followed?

FOR FURTHER EXPLORATION

Lynn Dumenil, *The Modern Temper* (1995), offers a good overview of the 1920s; see also Michael Parris, *Anxious Decades* (1992). On Margaret Sanger see Linda Gordon, *The Moral Property of Women* (2002); on race riots, Scott Ellsworth, *Death in a Promised Land* (1982), and Michael D'Orso, *Like Judgement Day* (1996). On nativism see David M. Reimers, *Unwelcome Strangers* (1998), and Noriko Asato, *Teaching Mikadoism* (2006).

For politics, consult Ellis Hawley, *The Great War and the Search for a Modern Order* (1979), and Lee Nash, ed., *Understanding Herbert Hoover* (1987). Emily S. Rosenberg covers foreign relations in *Spreading the American Dream* (1982) and *Financial Missionaries to the World* (2003). On U.S. involvement in Haiti, see Mary A. Renda, *Taking Haiti* (2001). On the Harlem Renaissance see David Levering Lewis, *When Harlem Was in Vogue* (1979), and on Marcus Garvey, **www.pbs.org/wgbh/amex/garvey**.

An overview of consumer credit is Martha L. Olney, *Buy Now, Pay Later* (1991). On working-class and immigrant families see Susan Porter Benson, *Household Accounts* (2007), Becky Nicolaides, *My Blue Heaven* (2002), Vicki Ruíz, *From Out of the Shadows* (1998), and Gabriela Arredondo, *Mexican Chicago* (2008). On the impact of cars see James J. Flink, *The Automobile Age* (1988), and Michael L. Berger, *The Devil Wagon in God's Country* (1979). On the coming of the Great Depression a groundbreaking book is Barry Eichengreen, *Golden Fetters* (1992). For a broad view of the crash see **www.pbs.org/wgbh/amex/crash**.

TEST YOUR KNOWLEDGE

To assess your command of the material in this chapter, see the Online Study Guide at **bedfordstmartins.com/henretta**.

For Web sites, images, and documents related to topics and places in this chapter, visit **bedfordstmartins.com/makehistory**.

TIMELINE

1912	United States occupies Nicaragua
1913	Henry Ford introduces moving assembly line
1915	New Ku Klux Klan founded United States occupies Haiti
1916	United States occupies Dominican Republic
1917	Race riot in East St. Louis, Illinois
1919	Race riot in Chicago Boston police strike Palmer raids Women's International Committee for Peace founded
1920	Height of Red Scare Sacco and Vanzetti arrested Eighteenth Amendment takes effect Warren Harding wins presidency Eugene O'Neill's *The Emperor Jones*
1921	Race riots in Rosewood, Florida, and Tulsa, Oklahoma Sheppard-Towner Federal Maternity and Infancy Act
1923	*Adkins v. Children's Hospital* President Harding dies; Calvin Coolidge assumes presidency
1924	National Origins Act Coolidge wins presidential election First suburban shopping center opens in Kansas City, Missouri
1925	*Coronado Coal Company v. United Mine Workers* Scopes "monkey trial" Height of new Ku Klux Klan's power Marcus Garvey deported F. Scott Fitzgerald's *The Great Gatsby*
1927	Sacco and Vanzetti executed
1928	Herbert Hoover wins presidency
1929	Stock market crashes precipitate Great Depression
1930	Smoot-Hawley Tariff
1932	Franklin D. Roosevelt elected president
1933	United States abandons gold standard

PART

6

THE MODERN STATE AND THE AGE OF LIBERALISM, 1929–1973

"What Rome was to the ancient world," proclaimed the influential journalist Walter Lippmann in 1945, "America is for the world of tomorrow." Lippmann believed that the United States, having emerged from World War II triumphant, was poised to play a leading role in world affairs. What Lippman underestimated were the challenges, global and domestic, confronting the postwar United States. In this Part 6, covering the years 1929–1973, we track how the United States responded to the depression by creating a modern welfare state, enlarged that state to fight a war on three continents, and then entered a prolonged period of international tension and conflict known as the Cold War. These developments were intertwined with the predominance of liberalism in American politics. One might think of an "age of liberalism" in this era, encompassing the social welfare liberalism of the New Deal and the rights liberalism of the 1960s—inspired by the modern civil rights movement—both of which fell under the larger umbrella of Cold War liberalism.

ECONOMY

The New Deal expanded federal responsibility for the welfare of ordinary citizens

Era of the Middle Class and Social Welfare

In response to the Great Depression, President Franklin Roosevelt's New Deal expanded federal responsibility for the welfare of ordinary citizens, sweeping away much of the laissez-faire individualism that dominated earlier eras. Wartime measures went even further, as the government mobilized the entire economy and tens of millions of citizens to fight the Axis Powers. After the war, prodded by liberal ideas about the good that government can do, legislators from both political parties helped create the largest middle class in the nation's history, through such measures as the GI Bill, subsidies for suburban homeownership, and educational initiatives. More than ever, the American economy was driven by mass consumption and the accompanying process of suburbanization. Poverty, however, affected nearly one-third of Americans in the 1960s. The lack of economic opportunity became a driving force in the civil rights movement and in the Great Society under President Lyndon Johnson.

DIPLOMACY

The United States extended ... political and military reach onto every continent

The Cold War and Third World Revolution

Faced with the rise of fascist powers in Europe and Japan and of isolationist sentiment at home, the Roosevelt administration steered a middle course. In the late 1930s, it began to send aid to its traditional ally Great Britain without committing U.S. military forces. This strategy kept the nation out of the brewing wars in Europe and the Pacific until late 1941. When the United States officially joined World War II, it entered into a "Grand Alliance" with England and the Soviet Union. That alliance proved impossible to sustain after 1945, as the United States and the Soviet Union became competitors to shape postwar Europe, Asia, and the developing world. The resulting Cold War lasted four decades, during which the United States extended an unprecedented political and military reach onto every continent.

Cold War liberalism ... rejected radicalisms of both the left and the right

A defining characteristic ... was the growth of the American middle class

The advertising industry ... create[d] consumer desire and shape[d] purchasing habits

Rise and Fall of the Liberal Consensus

The New Deal set the tone for American politics throughout this period. Though Democrats and Republicans differed over key issues—such as the power of the labor movement—there was broad agreement that a modern welfare state was necessary to regulate the economy and provide a basic safety net for the nation's citizens. Anti-communism was another unifying force. Political leaders from both parties sought to contain communism abroad and isolate "subversives" at home. The result was "Cold War liberalism," a centrist politics that rejected radicalisms of both the left and the right. By the late 1960s, however, Cold War liberalism was under attack from the antiwar and civil rights movements on the left and new conservative groups on the right. The liberal coalition fractured and split, and by the 1970s a new conservative age had dawned.

Social Movements and the Rights Revolution

A defining characteristic of the "age of liberalism" was the growth of the American middle class. Rising wages, increasing access to higher education, and the availability of suburban homeownership raised living standards and allowed more Americans than ever to afford consumer goods. Suburbanization transformed the nation's cities, and the Sunbelt led the nation in population growth. But the new prosperity had mixed results. Cities declined and new racial and ethnic ghettoes formed. These conditions, alongside continued southern segregation, helped to fuel the civil rights movement, a decades-long effort to ensure equal opportunity for African Americans. Adopting the civil rights model, women, Mexican Americans and other Latino groups, Native Americans, and gays and lesbians helped spawn a "rights" revolution.

Consumer Culture and Its Critics

Two powerful forces shaped American culture in this era: the advent of television and the youth-centered baby boom. By the mid-1950s, nearly every household in the country had a television. Americans increasingly experienced defining events—the Cuban Missile Crisis, the assassination of President Kennedy, and the Vietnam War, for instance—through television. Through this new medium, the advertising industry attained an unprecedented power to create consumer desire and shape purchasing habits. Meanwhile, baby boom children embraced new musical forms (rock 'n roll, rhythm and blues, and the folk revival, especially), experimented with countercultural sexual values, and forged a "youth culture" that remains influential to this day.

THE MODERN STATE AND THE AGE OF LIBERALISM, 1929–1973

	ECONOMY	DIPLOMACY	POLITICS	SOCIETY	CULTURE
1929	• Great Depression, 1929–1941 • WPA aids development • Rise of CIO and organized labor	• Rise of European fascist powers • Spanish Civil War (1936–1939) • Japan invades China (1937) • Atlantic Charter (1941) • United States enters World War II (1941)	• Franklin Roosevelt elected president (1932) • First New Deal (1933) • Second New Deal (1935) • Social welfare liberalism	• Bonus Army (1932) • Social Security created (1935) • Rural electrification • Federal Housing Authority (1937)	• Documentary impulse in arts • WPA assists artists
1945	• War spending ends depression • Married women enter workforce • Bretton Woods system established: World Bank, IMF	• Atomic bombing of Japan (1945) • Marshall Plan (1947) • Containment strategy emerges	• Truman's Fair Deal • Loyalty-Security Program • Taft-Hartley Act (1947) • Truman reelected	• Imprisonment of Japanese Americans • Segregation in armed services • Rural blacks and whites migrate to cities for war jobs • Early civil rights organizing	• Film industry aids war effort • Rationing curbs consumer spending
1950	• Rise of military-industrial complex • Real wages increase • Economy based on consumption • Government stimulates growth	• NATO created (1949) • Permanent mobilization: NSC-68 • Korean War (1950–1953) • United States in Iran, Guatemala, Vietnam	• Cold War liberalism • McCarthyism and Red Scare • Eisenhower's liberal Republicanism	• Treaty of Detroit (1950) • *Brown v. Board of Education* (1954) • Montgomery bus boycott (1955)	• Growth of suburbia and sunbelt • Height of baby boom • Jazz, Bebop, the Beats • Youth culture develops
1960	• Economic boom • Government spending on Vietnam and Great Society	• Cuban missile crisis (1962) • Vietnam War escalates (1965) • Tet Offensive (1968); peace talks begin	• Kennedy's New Frontier • Kennedy assassinated (1963) • War on Poverty; Great Society • Nixon elected (1968)	• March on Washington (1963) • Civil Rights legislation (1964, 1965) • Student and antiwar activism • Black Power	• Shopping malls and fast food • Baby boomers swell college enrollment • Hippie counter-culture
1970	• Inflation	• Nixon invades Cambodia (1971)	• Nixon landslide (1972)	• Revival of women's movement • Conservative resurgence	• Consumer-safety movement

The Great Depression and the New Deal, 1929–1939

In his inaugural address in March 1933, President Franklin Delano Roosevelt did not hide the country's precarious condition. "A host of unemployed citizens face the grim problem of existence," he said, "and an equally great number toil with little return. Only a foolish optimist can deny the dark realities of the moment." Roosevelt, his demeanor sincere and purposeful, saw both despair and determination as he looked out over the country. "This nation asks for action, and action now." From Congress he would request "broad Executive power to wage a war against the emergency, as great as the power that would be given to me if we were in fact invaded by a foreign foe." With these words, Roosevelt launched a program of federal activism—which he called the New Deal—that would change the nature of American government.

The New Deal represented a new form of liberalism, a fresh interpretation of the ideology of individual rights that had long shaped the character of American society and politics. Classical nineteenth-century liberals believed that, to protect those rights, government should be small and relatively powerless. However, the "regulatory" liberals of the early twentieth century had safeguarded individual freedom and opportunity by strengthening state and federal control over large businesses and monopolies. New Deal activists went much further: Their **social-welfare liberalism** expanded individual rights to include minimum standards of economic security. Beginning in the 1930s and continuing through the 1960s, they increased the responsibility of the national government for the welfare of ordinary citizens. Their efforts did not go unchallenged. Conservative critics of the New Deal charged that its program of "big government" and "social welfare" was both paternalistic and dangerous—a threat to individual responsibility and personal freedom. This division between the advocates and the critics of the New Deal shaped American politics for the next half century.

Before Roosevelt became president, between the onset of the depression in 1929 and the election of 1932, the "dark realities of the moment" wore down American society. Rising unemployment, shuttered businesses, failing banks, and home foreclosures tore at the nation's social fabric. As crisis piled upon crisis, and the federal government's initiatives under President Hoover proved weak and ineffectual, Americans had to reconsider more than the role of government in economic life: They had to rethink many of the principles of individualism and free enterprise that had guided so much of the nation's history.

The New Deal

This Federal Arts Project poster from 1936 captured the spirit of the New Deal under President Franklin Roosevelt. Roosevelt and other "New Dealers" hoped to get people working again during the depths of the Great Depression, raise their spirits, and help rebuild the national infrastructure. Library of Congress.

The Early Years of the Depression, 1929–1932

The American economy went rapidly downhill between 1929 and 1932. U.S. gross domestic product fell almost by half, from $103.1 billion to $58 billion. Consumption dropped by 18 percent, construction by 78 percent, and private investment by 88 percent. Nearly 9,000 banks closed their doors, and 100,000 businesses failed. Corporate profits fell from $10 billion to $1 billion. Most tellingly, unemployment rose to 25 percent. Fifteen million people were out of work by 1933, and many who had jobs took wage cuts. "Hoover made a souphound outa me!" sang jobless harvest hands in the Southwest.

Down and Out: Life in the Great Depression

Not all Americans were devastated by the depression; the middle class did not disappear, and the rich lived in their accustomed luxury. But more Americans than ever were without gainful employment or means of support. Incomes plummeted among workers in the cities and among farmers in rural areas. In September 1931, with unemployment hovering around 17 percent, Salt Lake City ran out of money. Barbers traded haircuts for onions and Idaho potatoes. Laborers put in a day's work for payment in eggs, peaches, or pork. The depression years are filled with such stories. The down and out did what they could to survive. "We do not dare to use even a little soap," wrote a jobless Oregonian, "when it will pay for an extra egg, a few more carrots for our children." "I would be only too glad to dig ditches to keep my family from going hungry," wrote a North Carolina man. By almost any standard, the depression was the worst national crisis since the Civil War.

Where did people turn in these years? The first line of defense was private charity, especially churches and synagogues. But by the winter of 1931, these institutions were overwhelmed, unable to keep pace with the extraordinary need. Only eight states provided any unemployment insurance, and it was minimal. There was no public support for the aged—the elderly, statistically among the poorest citizens, relied on their grown children. Few Americans had any retirement savings. Soup kitchens, bread lines, and the helping hands of neighbors were appreciated, but they could not permanently lift the millions whom the depression had wiped out.

Even if they fell short of being wiped out, Americans had to adapt to depression conditions. Couples delayed marriage and reduced the number of children they conceived. As a consequence, the marriage rate fell to a historical low, and the birthrate dropped from 97 births per 1,000 women to 75 by 1933. Limiting reproduction was a couple's decision, but often the responsibility for birth control fell to women. It "was one of the worst problems of women whose husbands were out of work," one Californian told a reporter. Women also endured additional burdens. Campaigns against hiring married women were common, on the theory that available jobs should go to male breadwinners. Three-quarters of the school districts in the country banned married women from being hired as teachers. Despite such restrictions, female employment increased during the decade of the 1930s, as women expanded their financial contributions to their families in the face of hard times.

Depression conditions respected no national or regional boundaries, though the severity of economic contraction varied from place to place. Germany had preceded the United States into depression in 1928, and its economy, burdened by World War I reparation payments, had been brought to its knees by 1929. France, Britain, Argentina, Poland, and Canada were hard hit as well (see Voices from Abroad, "Denis W. Brogan: A British Historian Looks at the Great Depression," p. 722). Within the United States, there were regional variations. Southern states generally fared better, having fewer manufacturing establishments than northern states—although agricultural wages plummeted in the South. Bank failures tended to be concentrated in farming states in the Midwest and Plains. Regions dependent on timber, mining, and other resource extraction industries experienced a steeper downturn than regions with more mixed economies. In northern industrial cities and the southern states, the unemployment rate among African American men was double that of white men. Among African American women it was triple that of white women. The depression, and the lives the crisis changed, touched every corner of the country.

Herbert Hoover Responds

President Hoover responded to the downturn by drawing on two powerful American traditions. The first was the belief that economic outcomes were the product of individual character. Success went to those who deserved it. People's fate was in their own hands, not in the workings of the market. The second tradition held that through voluntary action, the business community could regulate itself. Reflecting these ideologies, Hoover asked Americans to tighten their belts and

FDR

Franklin Delano Roosevelt was a successful politician partly because he loved to mix with a crowd. Despite Roosevelt's upper-class background, he had a knack for relating easily to those from all occupations. Although a well-dressed crowd turned out to greet him in Elm Grove, West Virginia, as he campaigned for the presidency in 1932, Roosevelt took care to be photographed shaking hands with coal miner Zeno Santinello.   Courtesy of the Franklin D. Roosevelt Library.

work hard. Following the stock market crash, he cut federal taxes in an attempt to boost private spending and corporate investment. "Any lack of confidence in the economic future or the strength of business in the United States is foolish," Hoover assured the country in late 1929.

But the president recognized that voluntarism might not be enough, given the depth of the crisis, and he proposed government action as well. He called on state and local governments to provide jobs by investing in public projects. And in 1931, he secured an unprecedented increase of $700 million in federal spending for public works. Hoover's most innovative program was the Reconstruction Finance Corporation (RFC), which stimulated economic activity by providing federal loans to railroads, banks, and other businesses. This plan might have worked, but the RFC lent money too cautiously. By the end of 1932, after a year in operation, it had loaned out only 20 percent of its $1.5 billion in funds. Like most federal initiatives under Hoover, the RFC was not nearly aggressive enough given the severity of the depression.

Hoover was as unlucky as any American president. Few chief executives could have survived the downward economic spiral of 1929–1932, but Hoover's reluctance to break with the philosophy of limited government and his insistence that recovery was always just around the corner contributed to his unpopularity. Unemployment during the depression was simply too massive for private charities and local governments to handle. By 1932, Americans perceived Hoover, despite his many accomplishments, as insensitive to the depth of the country's economic woes. The nation had come a long way since the depressions of the 1870s and 1890s, when no one except the most radical figures, such as Jacob Coxey, called for direct federal aid to the unemployed (see Chapter 20). Compared with previous chief executives—and in contrast to his popular image as a "do-nothing" president—Hoover had responded to the national emergency with government action on an unprecedented scale. But the nation's needs were even more unprecedented, and Hoover's programs failed to meet them.

Rising Discontent

As the depression deepened, the American vocabulary now included "Hoovervilles" (shantytowns where people lived in packing crates) and "Hoover blankets" (newspapers). Bankrupt farmers banded together to resist the bank agents and sheriffs who tried to evict them from their land. To protest low prices for their goods, thousands of farmers joined the Farm Holiday Association, which cut off supplies to urban areas by barricading roads and dumping milk, vegetables, and other foodstuffs onto the roadways.

Layoffs and wage cuts led to violent industrial strikes. When coal miners in Harlan County, Kentucky, went on strike over a 10 percent wage cut in 1931, the mine owners called in the state's National Guard, which

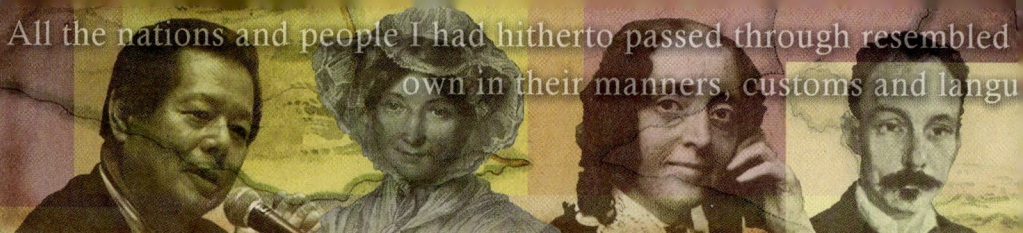

All the nations and people I had hitherto passed through resembled
own in their manners, customs and langu

Denis W. Brogan
A British Historian Looks at the Great Depression

Denis Brogan, a professor at Cambridge University in England, was a noted critic of the United States. In a book written in the 1950s, Brogan looked back at the descent into the Great Depression between 1929 and 1932 and explained the significance of Franklin Roosevelt's election from a European perspective. A frequent visitor to the United States, Brogan had a disdain for certain American characteristics shared by many members of the British upper class and was deeply invested in European superiority.

It is now nearly thirty-five years since I first visited the United States, and in that time I have returned repeatedly. . . . In the course of these visits I have been more than once in every region of the country, and have lived stretches of time in all of them except the Deep South. Thus my view of the promise, achievements, and limitations of American life has changed continually over the past generation or more, as the United States itself has changed. . . .

My opinion (a representative one I think) was that American society, except in the field of economic production, had a great deal to learn from Europe, while, except in that field, we had little to learn from America.

The success of the United States was limited, so the critics thought, to the more crude forms of material advancement, to central heating, a car in every garage, the creation of a mass market supplied by crude if popular artifacts like the Model T Ford. The life that was satisfied by these material achievements was drab and spiritually uninteresting. . . .

Then came the great debacle. No event . . . has so colored the European view of the United States as "the Depression." The first news of the crash of 1929 was not ill received. There was not only a marked feeling of *Schaden-freude* at the snub that destiny had given to the overconfident masters of the new world, but also a widespread belief that the extravagant gambling of the New York market was one of the chief causes of our ills. A sharp purge of America's dangerous economic humors and the discovery of new sources of gold to induce some sage inflation were popular panaceas between 1926 and 1929. But as the extent, depth, and duration of the American depression began to be appreciated, as its impact on all the world, especially on the dangerously unstable political and economic *status quo* of Germany and Austria, became more evident, as the old wound of unemployment was made to bleed more deeply in Britain, the tendency to blame the United States became overwhelming. Gone were the illusions about the "secret of high wages." If ever found, it had now been lost.

In the depression years more people fled America than entered it. The emigrants were embittered, disillusioned. Their stories of bread lines, of apple sellers, of the savagery

of the police (including Ford's muscle men), of the cruelties of the primitive social services, revived all the old suspicions of a country in which the rich, ruthless, callous, savage, ruled. The belief that it was American bankers' pressure that brought down the second British Labour government; the French belief that all Mr. Hoover's moves were designed to save the assets of American investors in Germany; the decline in the American demand for European exports; the defiance of European needs and rational policy that marked the Smoot-Hawley tariff—all were taken as proofs of the unfitness of the American people, above all their leaders, for the role in which history had miscast them.

American politics was seen as not only sterile but positively immoral and dangerous. . . . American business and its political arm, the Republican Party, had been tried in the balance and found wanting. And it is safe to say that the election of F. D. Roosevelt was welcomed in every country of Europe as good news almost overshadowing the nomination of Adolf Hitler as Chancellor of the German Reich.

Nothing was known, it is true, of the President-elect. Nothing but that he was not Mr. Hoover. Nothing was known about the Democrats but that they were not the Republicans. The "New Deal" started in the minds of most British observers with these two great advantages.

Source: Denis W. Brogan, "From England," in *As Others See Us: The United States Through Foreign Eyes*, ed. Franz M. Joseph (Princeton, NJ: Princeton Univeristy Press, 1959), 3–10.

ANALYZING THE EVIDENCE

- Why would Brogan call the United States "overconfident masters of the new world"? What are his criticisms of U.S. economic policy?

- Brogan writes that Europeans imagined the United States to be a "country in which the rich, ruthless, callous, savage, ruled." What does he mean?

- Why does Brogan distrust that Americans could manage the Great Depression?

crushed the union. A 1932 confrontation between workers and security forces at the Ford Motor Company's giant River Rouge factory outside Detroit left five workers dead and fifty with serious injuries. A photographer had his camera shot from his hands, and fifteen policemen were clubbed or stoned. Such examples abounded.

Veterans staged the most publicized—and most tragic—protest. In the summer of 1932, the so-called Bonus Army, a determined group of 15,000 unemployed World War I veterans, hitchhiked to Washington to demand immediate payment of pension awards that were due to be paid in 1945. "We were heroes in 1917, but we're bums now," one veteran complained bitterly. While their leaders unsuccessfully lobbied Congress, the Bonus Army set up camps near the Capitol building. Hoover called out regular army troops under the command of General Douglas MacArthur. MacArthur forcefully evicted the marchers and burned their main encampment to the ground. When newsreel footage showing the U.S. Army attacking and injuring veterans reached movie theaters across the nation, Hoover's popularity plunged. In another measure of how the country had changed since the 1890s, what Americans had applauded when done to Coxey in 1894 was condemned in 1932.

The 1932 Election

Despite rising discontent, the national mood was mixed as the 1932 election approached. Many Americans had internalized the ideal of the self-made man and blamed themselves for their economic hardships. Despair, not anger, characterized their mood. Others, out of work for a year or more, perhaps homeless, felt the deeper stirrings of frustration and rage. Regardless of their circumstances, most Americans believed that something altogether *new* had to be tried—whatever that might be. The Republicans, reluctant to dump an incumbent president, unenthusiastically renominated Hoover. The Democrats turned to New York governor Franklin Delano Roosevelt, whose state had initiated innovative relief and unemployment programs.

Roosevelt, born into a wealthy New York family, was a distant cousin to former president Theodore Roosevelt, whose career he emulated. After attending Harvard College and Columbia University, Franklin Roosevelt served as assistant secretary of the navy during World War I (as Theodore Roosevelt had done before the War of 1898). Then, in 1921, a crippling attack of polio left both of his legs paralyzed for life. Strongly supported by his wife, Eleanor, he slowly returned to public life and campaigned successfully for the governorship of New York in 1928 and again in 1930. In campaigning for the presidency in 1932, Roosevelt pledged vigorous action but gave no indication as to what that might be, arguing simply that "the country needs and, unless I mistake its temper, the country demands bold, persistent experimentation." He won easily, receiving 22.8 million votes to Hoover's 15.7 million.

Elected in November, Roosevelt would not begin his presidency until March 1933. (The Twentieth Amendment, ratified in 1933, set subsequent inaugurations for January 20.) Meanwhile, Americans suffered through the worst winter of the depression. Unemployment continued to climb, and in three major industrial cities in Ohio, it was staggering: 50 percent in Cleveland, 60 percent in Akron, and 80 percent in Toledo. Private charities and public relief agencies reached only a fraction of the needy. The nation's banking system was so close to collapse that many state governors closed banks temporarily to avoid further withdrawals. By March 1933, the nation had hit rock bottom.

- **How did President Hoover respond to the economic emergency? Why did he choose the course of action he did?**

- **What problems in the economy and society of the United States were exposed by the Great Depression?**

The New Deal Arrives, 1933–1935

Ironically, the ideological differences between Herbert Hoover and Franklin Roosevelt were not vast. Both leaders wished to maintain the nation's economic institutions and social values, to save capitalism while easing its worst downturns. Both believed in a balanced government budget and extolled the values of hard work, cooperation, and sacrifice. But Roosevelt's personal charm, political savvy, and willingness to experiment made him immensely popular and far more effective than Hoover. Most Americans felt a kinship with their new president, calling him simply "FDR." His New Deal programs put people to work and restored hope for the nation's future. "The New Deal was so abruptly different it was startling," remarked a seasoned Washington journalist.

Roosevelt and the First Hundred Days

A wealthy aristocrat from a patrician family, Roosevelt was an unlikely figure to inspire millions of ordinary Americans. But inspire them he did. His close rapport with the American people was critical to his political success. More than 450,000 letters poured into the White House in the week after his inauguration. The president's masterful use of the new medium of radio, especially his "fireside chats," made him an intimate presence in people's lives. Thousands of citizens felt a personal relationship with FDR, saying, "He gave me a job" or "He saved my home" (see Comparing American Voices, "Ordinary People Respond to the New Deal," pp. 726–727).

Roosevelt's charisma, coupled with the national economic emergency, allowed him to broaden further the presidential powers that Theodore Roosevelt and Woodrow Wilson had expanded previously. To draft legislation and policy, he relied heavily on financier Bernard Baruch and a "Brains Trust" of professors from Columbia, Harvard, and other leading universities. Roosevelt turned as well to his talented cabinet, which included Harold L. Ickes, secretary of the interior; Frances Perkins at the Labor Department; Henry A. Wallace at Agriculture; and Henry Morgenthau Jr., secretary of the Treasury. These intellectuals and administrators attracted hundreds of highly qualified recruits to Washington. Inspired by the idealism of the New Deal, many of them would devote their lives to public service and the principles of social-welfare liberalism.

Roosevelt could have done little, however, without a sympathetic Congress. The 1932 election had swept Democratic majorities into both the House and Senate, giving the new president the lawmaking allies he needed. The political tide had turned against the Republicans in full. The first months of FDR's administration produced a whirlwind of activity on Capitol Hill. In a legendary session, known as the "Hundred Days," Congress enacted fifteen major bills that focused primarily on four problems: banking failures, agricultural overproduction, the business slump, and soaring unemployment. Derided by opponents as an "alphabet soup" because of the many abbreviations they spawned (CCC, WPA, AAA, etc.), the new policies and agencies were more than bureaucracies: They represented the first blush of a new American state.

Banking Reform   The weak banking system placed a drag on the entire economy, curtailing consumer spending and business investment. Widespread bank failures had cut into the savings of nearly nine million families, and panicked account holders raced to withdraw their funds. On March 5, 1933, the day after his inauguration, FDR declared a national "bank holiday"—closing all the banks—and called Congress into special session. Four days later, Congress passed the Emergency Banking Act, which permitted banks to reopen if a Treasury Department inspection showed that they had sufficient cash reserves.

In his first Sunday night fireside chat, to a radio audience of sixty million, the president reassured citizens of the safety of their money. When the banking system reopened on March 13, deposits exceeded withdrawals, restoring stability to the nation's basic financial institutions. "Capitalism was saved in eight days," quipped Roosevelt's advisor Raymond Moley. Four thousand banks had collapsed in the months prior to Roosevelt's inauguration; only sixty-one closed their doors in all of 1934 (Table 23.1). A second banking law, the Glass-Steagall Act, further restored public confidence by creating the Federal Deposit Insurance Corporation (FDIC), which insured deposits up to $2,500 (and now insures them up to $250,000) and prohibited banks from making risky, unsecured investments. And in a move with profound symbolic importance, Roosevelt removed the U.S. Treasury from the gold standard, which allowed the Federal Reserve to lower interest rates—it had been *raising* rates since 1931, which had only deepened the downturn.

Agriculture and Manufacturing   Roosevelt and the New Deal Congress next turned to agriculture and manufacturing. The national government had long assisted farmers through cheap prices for land, Department of Agriculture programs, and low-interest loans. But the Agricultural Adjustment

---

TABLE 23.1

American Banks and Bank Failures, 1920–1940

Year	Total Number of Banks	Total Assets ($ billion)	Bank Failures
1920	30,909	53.1	168
1929	25,568	72.3	659
1931	22,242	70.1	2,294
1933	14,771	51.4	4,004
1934	15,913	55.9	61
1940	15,076	79.7	48

SOURCE: *Historical Statistics of the United States: Colonial Times to 1970* (Washington, D.C: U.S. Government Printing Office, 1975), 1019, 1038–1039.

Selling the NRA in Chinatown

To mobilize support for its program, the National Recovery Administration (NRA) distributed millions of posters to businesses and families, urging them to display its symbol, the Blue Eagle, in shops, factories, and homes. Here Constance King and Mae Chinn of the Chinese YMCA affix a poster (and a Chinese translation) to a shop in San Francisco that is complying with the NRA codes.   © Copyright Bettmann / Corbis.

Act (AAA) began direct governmental regulation of the farm economy. To solve the problem of overproduction, which lowered prices, the AAA provided cash subsidies to farmers who cut production of seven major commodities: wheat, cotton, corn, hogs, rice, tobacco, and dairy products. The hope was that farm prices would rise as production fell.

By dumping cash in farmers' hands, the AAA briefly stabilized the farm economy. But the act's benefits were not evenly distributed. Subsidies went primar-ily to the owners of large- and medium-sized farms, who often cut production by reducing the amount of land they rented to tenants and sharecroppers. In Mississippi, one plantation owner received $26,000 from the federal government, while thousands of black share-croppers living in the same county received only a few dollars in relief payments.

In manufacturing, the New Deal attacked declining production with the National Industrial Recovery Act. A new government agency, the National Recovery

Ordinary People Respond to the New Deal

Franklin Roosevelt's fireside chats and his relief programs prompted thousands of ordinary Americans to write directly to the president and his wife Eleanor. Taken together, their letters offer a vivid portrait of depression-era America that includes popular support for, and opposition to, the New Deal.

Mrs. M. H. A.

Mrs. M. H. A. worked in the County Court House in Eureka, California.

June 14, 1934

Dear Mrs. Roosevelt:

I know you are overburdened with requests for help and if my plea cannot be recognized, I'll understand it is because you have so many others, all of them worthy. . . .

My husband and I are a young couple of very simple, almost poor families. We married eight years ago on the proverbial shoe-string but with a wealth of love. . . . We managed to build our home and furnish it comfortably. . . . Then came the depression. My work has continued and my salary alone has just been sufficient to make our monthly payments on the house and keep our bills paid. . . . But with the exception of two and one-half months work with the U.S. Coast and Geodetic Survey under the C.W.A. [Civil Works Administration], my husband has not had work since August, 1932.

My salary could continue to keep us going, but I am to have a baby. . . . I can get a leave of absence from my job for a year. But can't you, won't you do something so my husband can have a job, at least during that year? . . .

As I said before, if it were only ourselves, or if there were something we could do about it, we would never ask for help.

We have always stood on our own feet and been proud and happy. But you are a mother and you'll understand this crisis.

Very sincerely yours,

Mrs. M. H. A.

Unsigned Letter

This unsigned letter came from a factory worker in Paris, Texas.

November 23, 1936

Dear President,

[N]ow that we have had a land Slide [in the election of 1936] and done just what was best for our country . . . I do believe you Will Strain a point to help the ones who helped you mostly & that is the Working Class of People I am not smart or I would be in a different line of work & better up in ever way yet I will know you are the one & only President that ever helped a Working Class of People. . . .

I am a White Man American age, 47 married wife 2 children in high School am a Finishing room foreman I mean a Working foreman & am in a furniture Factory here in Paris Texas where thaire is 175 to 200 Working & when the NRA [National Recovery Administration] came in I was Proud to See my fellow workmen Rec 30 Per hour in Place of 8 cents to 20 cents Per hour. . . .

I can't see for my life President why a man must toil & work his life out in Such factories 10 long hours ever day except Sunday for a small sum of 15 cents to 35 cents per hour & pay the high cost of honest & deason living expences. . . .

please see if something can be done to help this one Class of Working People the factories are a man killer not venelated or kept up just a bunch of Republickins Grafters 90/100 of them Please help us some way I Pray to God for relief. I am a Christian . . . and a truthful man & have not told you wrong & am for you to the end.

[not signed]

R. A.

R. A. was sixty-nine years old and an architect and builder in Lincoln, Nebraska.

May 19/34

Dear Mrs Roosevelt:

In the Presidents inaugral address delivered from the capitol steps the afternoon of his inauguration he made mention of The Forgotten Man, and I with thousands of others am wondering if the folk who was borned here in America some 60 or 70 years a go are this Forgotten Man, the President had in mind, if we are this Forgotten Man then we are still Forgotten.

We who have tried to be diligent in our support of this most wonderful nation of ours boath social and other wise, we in our younger days tried to do our duty without complaining. . . .

And now a great calamity has come upon us and seemingly no cause of our own it has swept away what little savings we had accumulated and we are left in a condition that is imposible for us to correct, for two very prominent reasons if no more.

First we have grown to what is termed Old Age, this befalls every man.

Second, . . . we are confronted on every hand with the young generation, taking our places, this of corse is what we have looked forward to in training our children. But with the extra ordinary crisese which left us helpless and placed us in the position that our fathers did not have to contend with. . . .

We have been honorable citizens all along our journey, calamity and old age has forced its self upon us please do not send us to the Poor Farm but instead allow us the small pension of $40.00 per month. . . .

Mrs. Roosevelt I am asking a personal favor of you as it seems to be the only means through which I may be able to reach the President, some evening very soon, as you and Mr. Roosevelt are having dinner together privately will you ask him to read this. And we American citizens will ever remember your kindness.

Yours very truly.

R. A.

M. A.

M. A. was a woman who held a low-level salaried position in a corporation.

Jan. 18, 1937

[Dear Mrs. Roosevelt:]

I . . . was simply astounded to think that anyone could be nitwit enough to wish to be included in the so called social security act if they could possibly avoid it. Call it by any name you wish it, in my opinion, (and that of many people I know) [it] is nothing but downright stealing. . . .

I am not an "economic royalist," just an ordinary white collar worker at $1600 per [year—about $23,600 in 2009]. Please show this to the president and ask him to remember the wishes of the forgotten man, that is, the one who dared to vote against him. We expect to be tramped on but we do wish the stepping would be a little less hard.

Security at the price of freedom is never desired by intelligent people.

M. A.

M. A. H.

M. A. H. was a widow who ran a small farm in Columbus, Indiana.

December 14, 1937

Mrs. Roosevelt:

I suppose from your point of view the work relief, old age pensions, slum clearance and all the rest seems like a perfect remedy for all the ills of this country, but I would like for you to see the results, as the other half see them.

We have always had a shiftless, never-do-well class of people whose one and only aim in life is to live without work. I have been rubbing elbows with this class for nearly sixty years and have tried to help some of the most promising and have seen others try to help them, but it can't be done. We cannot help those who will not try to help themselves and if they do try a square deal is all they need, . . . let each one paddle their own canoe, or sink. . . .

I live alone on a farm and have not raised any crops for the last two years as there was no help to be had. I am feeding the stock and have been cutting the wood to keep my home fires burning. There are several relievers around here now who have been kicked off relief but they refuse to work unless they can get relief hours and wages, but they are so worthless no one can afford to hire them. . . . They are just a fair sample of the class of people on whom so much of our hard earned tax-money is being squandered and on whom so much sympathy is being wasted. . . .

You people who have plenty of this worlds goods and whose money comes easy have no idea of the heart-breaking toil and self-denial which is the lot of the working people who are trying to make an honest living, and then to have to shoulder all these unjust burdens seems like the last straw. . . . No one should have the right to vote theirself a living at the expense of the tax payers. . . .

M. A. H.

Sources (in order): Robert S. McElvaine, *Down and Out in the Great Depression* (Chapel Hill: University of North Carolina Press, 1983), 54–55; Gerald Markowitz and David Rosner, eds., *"Slaves of the Depression": Worker's Letters about Life on the Job* (Ithaca, NY: Cornell University Press, 1987); Robert S. McElvaine, *Down and Out in the Great Depression* (Chapel Hill: University of North Carolina Press, 1983), 97, 147, 143.

ANALYZING THE EVIDENCE

- **How do you explain the personal, almost intimate, tone of these letters to the Roosevelts?**

- **How have specific New Deal programs helped or hurt the authors of these letters?**

- **What are the basic values of the authors? Do they differ between those who support and oppose the New Deal?**

Administration (NRA), set up separate self-governing private associations in six hundred industries. Each industry—ranging from large corporations producing coal, cotton textiles, and steel to small businesses making pet food and costume jewelry—regulated itself by agreeing on a code of prices and production quotas. Because large companies usually ran these associations, the NRA solidified its power at the expense of smaller enterprises and consumer interests.

The AAA and the NRA were designed to rescue the nation's productive industries and stabilize the economy. The measures had positive effects in some regions, but most historians agree that, overall, they did little to end the depression.

Unemployment Relief | The Roosevelt administration next addressed the problems of massive unemployment. By 1933, local governments and private charities had exhausted their resources and were looking to Washington for assistance. Although Roosevelt wanted to avoid a budget deficit, he asked Congress to provide relief for millions of unemployed Americans. In May, Congress established the Federal Emergency Relief Administration (FERA). Directed by Harry Hopkins, a hard-driving social worker from New York, the FERA provided federal funds for state relief programs.

Roosevelt and Hopkins had strong reservations about the "dole," the nickname for government welfare payments. As Hopkins put it, "I don't think anybody can go year after year, month after month, accepting relief without affecting his character." To support the traditional values of individualism, the New Deal put people to work. Early in 1933, Congress established the Public Works Administration (PWA), a construction program, and several months later, Roosevelt created the Civil Works Administration (CWA) and named Hopkins its head. Within thirty days, Hopkins had put 2.6 million men and women to work; at its peak in 1934, the CWA provided jobs for 4 million Americans repairing bridges, building highways, and constructing public buildings. A stopgap measure to get the country through the winter of 1933–1934, the CWA lapsed in the spring, when Republican opposition compelled New Dealers to abandon it. A more long-term program, the Civilian Conservation Corps (CCC), mobilized 250,000 young men to do reforestation and conservation work. Over the course of the 1930s, the "CCC boys" built thousands of bridges, roads, trails, and other structures in state and national parks, bolstering the national infrastructure (Map 23.1).

Housing Crisis | Millions of Americans also faced the devastating prospect of losing their homes. The 1920s' economic expansion had produced the largest inflationary housing bubble in American history to that point. In the early 1930s, as home prices collapsed and banks closed, homeowners were dragged down with them. More than half a million Americans lost their homes between 1930 and 1932, and in cities such as Cleveland and Indianapolis, half of all home mortgage holders faced possible foreclosure. In response, Congress created the Home Owners Loan Corporation (HOLC) to refinance home mortgages. In just two years of operation, the HOLC helped more than a million Americans retain their homes. The Federal Housing Act of 1934 would extend this program under a new agency, the Federal Housing Administration (FHA). Together, the HOLC, the FHA, and the subsequent Housing Act of 1937 permanently changed the mortgage system and set the foundation for the broad expansion of homeownership in the post–World War II decades (see Chapter 25).

When an exhausted Congress recessed in June 1933, at the end of the Hundred Days, it had enacted Roosevelt's agenda: banking reform, recovery programs for agriculture and industry, public works, and unemployment relief. Few presidents had won the passage of so many measures in so short a time. The new agencies established in Washington were far from perfect and had their critics on both the radical left and the conservative right. But the vigorous actions taken by Roosevelt and Congress had halted the downward psychological spiral of the Hoover years, stabilized the financial sector, and sent a message of hope from the nation's political leaders. For all that, however, they did not break the grip of the depression.

The New Deal under Attack

As New Dealers waited anxiously for the economy to revive, Roosevelt turned his attention to the reform of Wall Street, where reckless speculation and overleveraged buying of stocks had helped trigger the financial panic of 1929. In 1934, Congress established the Securities and Exchange Commission (SEC) to regulate the stock market. The commission had broad powers to determine how stocks and bonds were sold to the public, to set rules for margin (credit) transactions, and to prevent stock sales by those with inside information about corporate plans. The Banking Act of 1935 authorized the president to appoint a new Board of Governors of the Federal Reserve System, placing control of

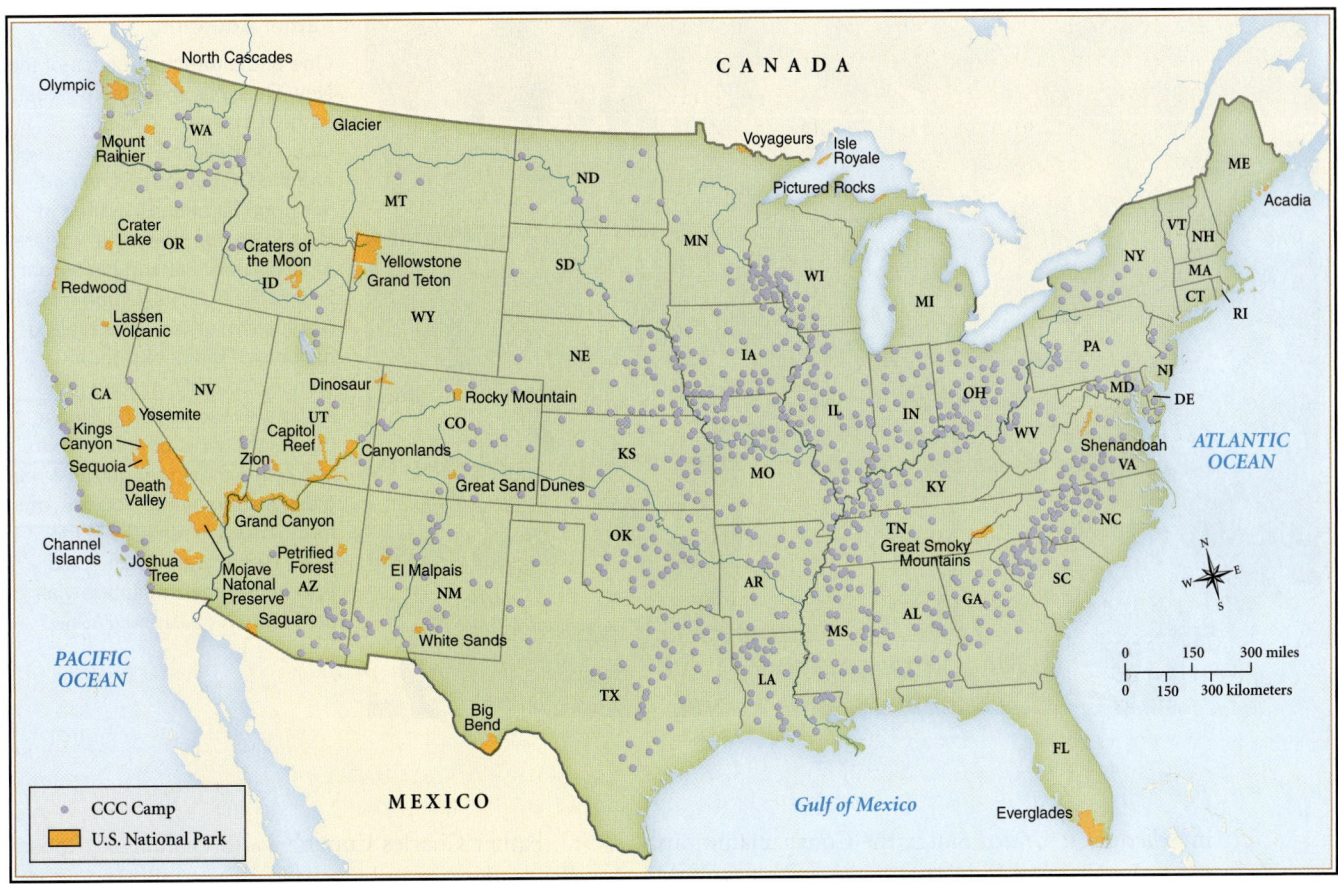

MAP 23.1

Civilian Conservation Corps Camps

The Civilian Conservation Corps (CCC) gave hope to unemployed young men during the Great Depression. The first camp opened in Big Meadows, Virginia, in July 1933, and by the end of the decade CCC camps had appeared across the length of the country, located in rural, mountainous, and forested regions alike. Young men constructed bridges and roads, built hiking trails, erected public campgrounds, and performed other improvements. By the early 1940s, the CCC had planted 3 billion trees, among its many other contributions to the national infrastructure.

interest rates and other money-market policies in a federal agency rather than in the hands of private bankers.

Critics on the Right Such measures exposed the New Deal to attack from economic conservatives— also known as the political right. A man of wealth, Roosevelt saw himself as the savior of American capitalism, declaring simply, "To preserve we had to reform." Many bankers and business executives disagreed. To them, FDR became "That Man," a traitor to his class. In 1934, Republican business leaders joined with conservative Democrats in the Liberty League to fight the "reckless spending" and "socialist" reforms of the New Deal. Reflecting their outlook, Herbert Hoover condemned the NRA as a "state-controlled or state-directed social or economic system." That, declared the former president, was "tyranny, not liberalism."

More important than the Liberty League in opposing the New Deal, because its influence would stretch far into the post–World War II decades, was the National Association of Manufacturers (NAM). Sparked by a new generation of business leaders who believed that a publicity campaign was needed to "serve the purposes of business salvation," the NAM was producing radio programs, motion pictures, billboards, and direct mail by the late 1930s. In response to what many conservatives perceived as Roosevelt's antibusiness policies, the NAM promoted free enterprise and unfettered capitalism. After World War II, the NAM would emerge as one of the staunchest critics of liberalism and would forge alliances with influential postwar conservative politicians such as Barry Goldwater and Ronald Reagan.

For its part, the Supreme Court repudiated many of the cornerstones of the early New Deal. In May 1935,

Father Coughlin

One of the foremost critics of the New Deal was the "Radio Priest," Father Charles E. Coughlin. Coughlin believed that Roosevelt and the Democratic Party had not gone far enough in their efforts to ensure the social welfare of all citizens. He and his organization, the National Union for Social Justice, urged Roosevelt to nationalize the banks, for instance. Coughlin, whose radio audience reached 30 million at the height of his popularity, was one of the most recognizable religious leaders in the country. Unfortunately, his remarks in the early 1930s were often laced with anti-Semitism (anti-Jewish sentiment).   © Bettmann/Corbis.

in *Schechter v. United States*, the Court unanimously ruled the National Industrial Recovery Act unconstitutional because it delegated Congress's power to make laws to the executive branch and extended federal authority to intrastate (in contrast to interstate) commerce. Roosevelt protested but watched helplessly as the Court struck down more New Deal legislation: the Agricultural Adjustment Act, the Railroad Retirement Act, and the Frazier-Lemke Act (intended to provide debt relief).

Critics on the Populist Left   If business leaders and the Supreme Court thought that the New Deal had gone too far, many ordinary Americans believed it had not gone far enough. Among these were public figures who, in the tradition of American populism, sought to place government on the side of ordinary citizens against corporations and the wealthy. Francis Townsend, a doctor from Long Beach, California, spoke for the nation's elderly, most of whom had no pensions and feared poverty in their old age. In 1933, Townsend proposed the Old Age Revolving Pension Plan, which would give the considerable sum of $200 a month (about $3,300 today) to citizens over the age of sixty. To receive payments, the elderly would have to retire from their jobs, opening their positions to younger workers. Townsend Clubs sprang up across the country, mobilizing mass support for old-age pensions.

Father Charles Coughlin also challenged Roosevelt's leadership and attracted a large following, especially in the Midwest. A Catholic priest in Detroit, Coughlin had turned to the radio in the mid-1920s to enlarge his pastorate. By 1933, an astonishing 40 million Americans listened regularly to his broadcasts. Coughlin, known as the "Radio Priest," initially supported the New Deal but turned against it when Roosevelt refused to nationalize the banking system and expand the money supply. To promote his own ideas on money and banking, Coughlin organized the National Union for Social Justice.

The most direct political threat to Roosevelt came from Louisiana senator Huey Long. As the Democratic governor of Louisiana from 1928 to 1932, the flamboyant Long had achieved stunning popularity. He increased taxes on corporations, lowered the utility bills of consumers, and built new highways, hospitals, and schools. To push through these measures, Long seized almost dictatorial control of the state government. Now a U.S. Senator, Long broke with the New Deal in 1934 and, like Townsend and Coughlin, established a national movement. His Share Our Wealth Society maintained that because wealth was so unequally distributed, millions of ordinary families lacked the funds to buy goods and thereby keep the factories humming. Long's society advocated a tax of 100 percent on all income

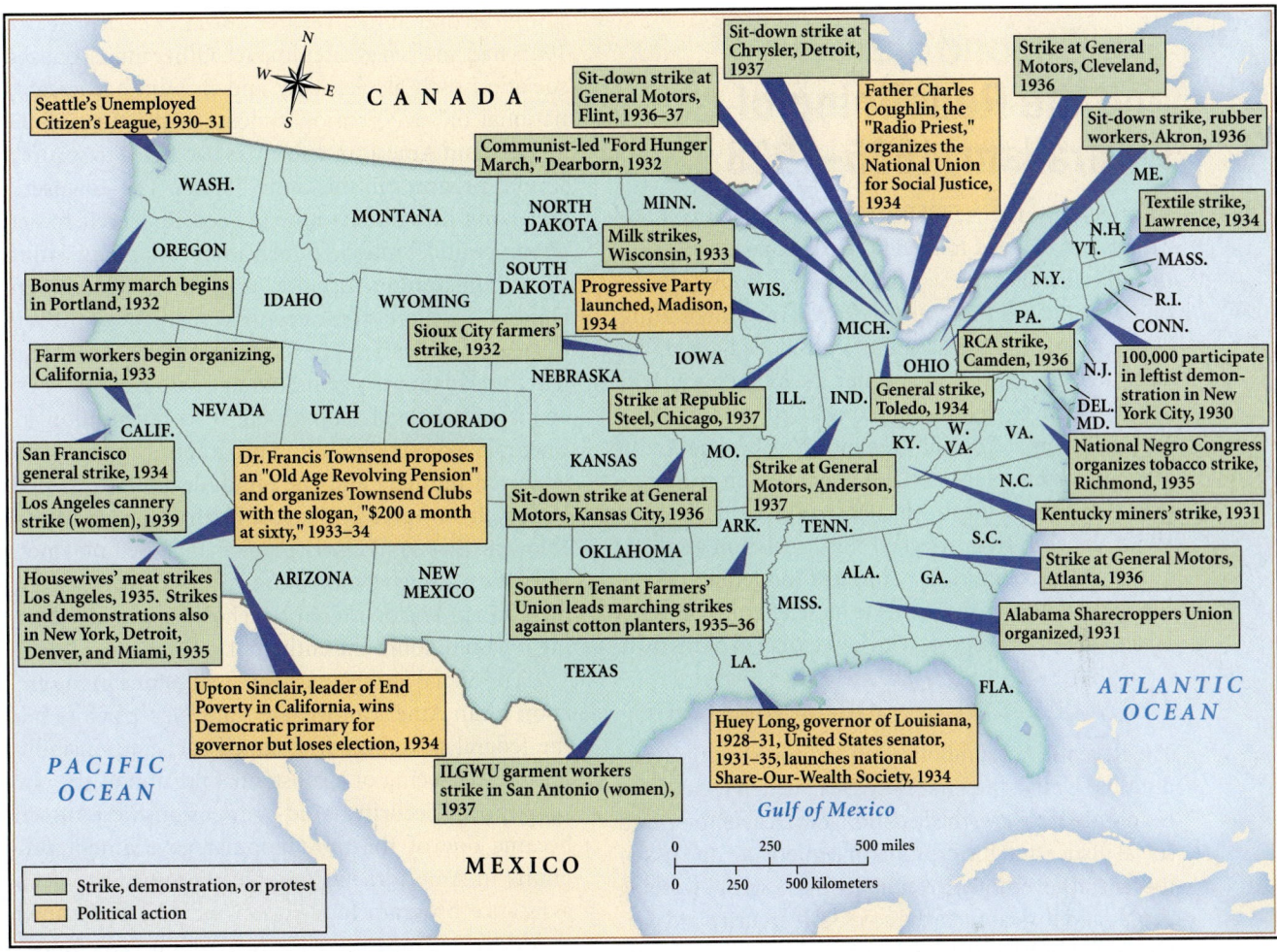

Seattle's Unemployed Citizen's League, 1930–31

Sit-down strike at General Motors, Flint, 1936–37

Communist-led "Ford Hunger March," Dearborn, 1932

Sit-down strike at Chrysler, Detroit, 1937

Father Charles Coughlin, the "Radio Priest," organizes the National Union for Social Justice, 1934

Strike at General Motors, Cleveland, 1936

Sit-down strike, rubber workers, Akron, 1936

Textile strike, Lawrence, 1934

Bonus Army march begins in Portland, 1932

Milk strikes, Wisconsin, 1933

Progressive Party launched, Madison, 1934

Sioux City farmers' strike, 1932

RCA strike, Camden, 1936

100,000 participate in leftist demonstration in New York City, 1930

Farm workers begin organizing, California, 1933

Strike at Republic Steel, Chicago, 1937

General strike, Toledo, 1934

National Negro Congress organizes tobacco strike, Richmond, 1935

San Francisco general strike, 1934

Dr. Francis Townsend proposes an "Old Age Revolving Pension" and organizes Townsend Clubs with the slogan, "$200 a month at sixty," 1933–34

Sit-down strike at General Motors, Kansas City, 1936

Strike at General Motors, Anderson, 1937

Kentucky miners' strike, 1931

Los Angeles cannery strike (women), 1939

Strike at General Motors, Atlanta, 1936

Housewives' meat strikes Los Angeles, 1935. Strikes and demonstrations also in New York, Detroit, Denver, and Miami, 1935

Southern Tenant Farmers' Union leads marching strikes against cotton planters, 1935–36

Alabama Sharecroppers Union organized, 1931

Upton Sinclair, leader of End Poverty in California, wins Democratic primary for governor but loses election, 1934

ILGWU garment workers strike in San Antonio (women), 1937

Huey Long, governor of Louisiana, 1928–31, United States senator, 1931–35, launches national Share-Our-Wealth Society, 1934

☐ Strike, demonstration, or protest
☐ Political action

MAP 23.2

Popular Protest in the Great Depression, 1933–1939

The depression forced Americans to look closely at their society, and many of them did not like what they saw. Some citizens expressed their discontent through popular movements, and this map suggests the geography of discontent. The industrial Midwest witnessed union movements, strikes, and Radio Priest Charles Coughlin's demands for social reform. Simultaneously, farmers' movements—tenants in the South, smallholders in the agricultural Midwest—engaged in strikes and dumping campaigns, and rallied behind the ideas of progressives in Wisconsin and Huey Long in the South. Protests took diverse forms in California, which was home to strikes by farmworkers, women, and—in San Francisco—all wageworkers. The West was also the seedbed of two important reform proposals: Upton Sinclair's End Poverty in California (EPIC) movement and Francis Townsend's Old Age Revolving Pension clubs.

over $1 million and on all inheritances over $5 million. He hoped that this populist program would carry him into the White House.

That prospect encouraged conservatives, who hoped that a split between New Dealers and populist reformers might return the Republican Party, and its ideology of limited government and free enterprise, to political power. In fact, Roosevelt feared that Townsend, Coughlin, and Long might join forces to form a third party. He had to respond or risk the political unity of the country's liberal forces (Map 23.2).

● What were the main programs of the New Deal's Hundred Days? What were their goals? How were they different from reforms in the early decades of the century?

● Who were the New Deal's major critics, and what were their alternative programs?

The Second New Deal and the Redefining of Liberalism, 1935–1938

As attacks on the New Deal increased, Roosevelt and his advisors moved to the left. Historians have labeled this shift in policy the Second New Deal. Roosevelt now openly criticized the "money classes," proudly stating, "We have earned the hatred of entrenched greed." He also moved decisively to counter the rising popularity of Townsend, Coughlin, and Long by adopting parts of their programs. The administration's Revenue Act of 1935 proposed a substantial tax increase on corporate profits and higher income and estate taxes on the wealthy. When conservatives attacked this legislation as an attempt to "soak the rich," Congress moderated its tax rates. But FDR was satisfied. He had met the Share Our Wealth Society's proposal with a wealth plan of his own.

The Welfare State Comes into Being

The Revenue Act symbolized the administration's new outlook. Unlike the First New Deal, which focused on economic recovery, the Second New Deal emphasized social justice and the creation of a safety net: the use of the federal government to enhance the power of working people and to guarantee the economic security and welfare of the old, the disabled, and the unemployed. The resulting welfare state—a term applied to industrial democracies that adopted some form of government-guaranteed social safety net—fundamentally changed American society.

The Wagner Act and Social Security The first beneficiary of Roosevelt's move to the left was the labor movement. Section 7(a) of the National Industrial Recovery Act (NIRA) had given workers the right to organize unions, producing a dramatic growth in rank-and-file militancy and leading to a strike wave in 1934. When the Supreme Court voided the NIRA in 1935, labor unions called for new legislation that would allow workers to organize and bargain collectively with employers. Named for its sponsor, Senator Robert F. Wagner of New York, the Wagner Act (1935) upheld the right of industrial workers to join unions. The act outlawed many practices that employers had used to suppress unions, such as firing workers for organizing activities. It established the National Labor Relations Board (NLRB), a federal agency with the authority to protect workers from employer coercion and to guarantee collective bargaining.

A second initiative, the Social Security Act of 1935, had an even greater impact. Other industrialized societies, such as Germany and Britain, had created national old-age pension systems at the turn of the century, but American reformers had failed to secure a similar program in the United States. The Townsend and Long movements now pressed Roosevelt to act, giving political muscle to pension proponents within the administration. Also pressuring the president were children's welfare advocates concerned about the fate of fatherless families. The resulting Social Security Act had three main provisions: old-age pensions for workers; a joint federal-state system of compensation for unemployed workers; and a program of payments to widowed mothers and the blind, deaf, and disabled. Roosevelt, however, limited the reach of the legislation. Knowing that compulsory pension and unemployment legislation alone would be controversial, he refused to include a provision for national health insurance, fearing it would doom the entire bill.

The Social Security Act was a milestone in the creation of an American welfare state. Never before had the federal government assumed such responsibility for the well-being of a substantial portion of the citizenry. Social Security, as old-age pensions were known, became one of the most popular government programs in American history. On the other hand, the assistance program for widows and children known as Aid to Dependent Children (ADC) became one of its most controversial measures. ADC covered only 700,000 youngsters in 1939; by 1994, its successor, Aid to Families with Dependent Children (AFDC), enrolled 14.1 million Americans. A minor program during the New Deal, AFDC grew enormously in the 1960s and remained a cornerstone of the welfare state, if a contentious and controversial one, until it was eliminated under President Clinton in 1996.

New Deal Liberalism The Second New Deal created what historians call New Deal liberalism. Classical liberalism held individual liberty to be the foundation of a democratic society, and the word *liberal* had traditionally denoted support for free-market policies and weak government. Roosevelt and his advisors, along with intellectuals such as education reformer John Dewey and economist John Maynard Keynes, disagreed. They countered that, to preserve individual liberty, government must assist the needy and guarantee the basic welfare of citizens. This liberal welfare state was opposed by inheritors of the nineteenth-century ideology of laissez-faire capitalism, who gradually became known as conservatives.

Labor on the March

Trade unions were among the most active and vocal organizations of the 1930s. Organized labor led a number of major strikes between 1934 and 1936 in various industries. None was more important to the future of trade unions than the sit-down strike at General Motors in Flint, Michigan, in 1936. It was this strike that compelled GM to recognize the United Auto Workers (UAW). After this strike had spread to Chevrolet, more than 75 women (workers and the wives of workers) clashed with company police. © Bettmann/Corbis.

These two visions of liberty and government — with liberals on one side and conservatives (as classical liberals came to be known) on the other — would shape American politics for the next half century.

From the outset, however, New Dealers wrestled with potentially fatal racial politics. Franklin Roosevelt and the Democratic Party depended heavily on white voters in the South, who were determined to keep African Americans poor and powerless. But many Democrats in the North and West — centers of New Deal liberalism — opposed racial discrimination. This meant, ironically, that the nation's most liberal political forces and some of its most conservative political forces existed side by side in the same political party.

From Reform to Stalemate

Roosevelt's first term had seen an extraordinary expansion of the federal state. The great burst of government action between 1933 and 1935 was unequaled in the nation's history (and would be matched only by Congress and President Lyndon Johnson in 1965–1966 — see Chapter 28). Roosevelt's second term, however, was characterized by a series of political entanglements and economic bad news that stifled further reform.

The 1936 Election   FDR was never enthusiastic about public relief programs. But with the election of 1936 on the horizon and 10 million Americans still out of work, he won funding for the Works Progress Administration (WPA). Under the energetic direction of Harry Hopkins, the WPA employed 8.5 million Americans between 1935 and 1943. The agency's workers constructed or repaired 651,087 miles of road, 124,087 bridges, 125,110 public buildings, 8,192 parks, and 853 airports. Although the WPA was an extravagant operation by 1930s standards, it reached only about one-third of the nation's unemployed.

As the 1936 election approached, new voters joined the Democratic Party. Many had personally benefited from New Deal programs such as the WPA or knew people who had (Table 23.2). One was Jack Reagan, a down-on-his-luck shoe salesman (and the father of future president Ronald Reagan), who took a job as a federal relief administrator in Dixon, Illinois, and became a strong supporter of the New Deal. In addition to voters such as Reagan, Roosevelt could count on a powerful coalition of organized labor, midwestern farmers, white ethnic groups, northern blacks, and middle-class families concerned about unemployment and old-age security. He also commanded the support of intellectuals and progressive Republicans. With difficulty, the Democrats held on to the votes of their white southern constituency as well.

Republicans recognized that the New Deal was too popular to oppose directly, so they chose as their candidate the progressive governor of Kansas, Alfred M. Landon. Landon accepted the legitimacy of many New Deal programs but stridently criticized their inefficiency and expense. He also pointed to authoritarian regimes in Italy and Germany, directed by Benito Mussolini and Adolph Hitler, respectively, and hinted that FDR harbored similar dictatorial ambitions. These charges fell on deaf ears. Roosevelt's victory in 1936 was one of the biggest landslides in American history. The assassination of Huey Long by a Louisiana political rival in September 1935 had eliminated the threat of a serious third-party challenge. Roosevelt received 60 percent of the popular vote and carried every state except Maine and Vermont. Organized labor, in particular, mobilized on behalf of FDR, donating money, canvassing door-to-door, and registering hundreds of thousands of new voters. The *New Republic*, a liberal publication, boasted that "it was the greatest revolution in our political history." The New Deal was at high tide.

"I see one-third of a nation ill-housed, ill-clad, ill-nourished," the president declared in his second inaugural address in January 1937. But any hopes that FDR had for expanding the liberal welfare state were quickly dashed. Within a year, staunch opposition to Roosevelt's initiatives arose in Congress, and a sharp recession undermined confidence in his economic leadership.

TABLE 23.2	
Major New Deal Legislation	
Agriculture	
1933	Agricultural Adjustment Act (AAA)
1935	Resettlement Administration (RA)
	Rural Electrification Administration
1937	Farm Security Administration (FSA)
1938	Agricultural Adjustment Act of 1938
Finance and Industry	
1933	Emergency Banking Act
	Glass-Steagall Act (created the FDIC)
	National Industrial Recovery Act (NIRA)
1934	Securities and Exchange Commission (SEC)
1935	Banking Act of 1935
	Revenue Act (wealth tax)
Conservation and the Environment	
1933	Tennessee Valley Authority (TVA)
	Civilian Conservation Corps (CCC)
	Soil Conservation and Domestic Allotment Act
Labor and Social Welfare	
1933	Section 7(a) of NIRA
1935	National Labor Relations Act (Wagner Act)
	National Labor Relations Board (NLRB)
	Social Security Act
1937	National Housing Act
1938	Fair Labor Standards Act (FLSA)
Relief and Reconstruction	
1933	Federal Emergency Relief Administration (FERA)
	Civil Works Administration (CWA)
	Public Works Administration (PWA)
1935	Works Progress Administration (WPA)
	National Youth Administration (NYA)

Court Battle and Economic Recession   Roosevelt's first setback came when he surprised the nation by asking for fundamental changes to the Supreme Court. In 1935, the Court had struck down a series of New Deal measures by the narrow margin of 5 to 4. With the Wagner Act, the Tennessee Valley Authority, and Social Security all coming up on appeal with the Court, the future of the New Deal slate of programs rested in the hands of a few elderly, conservative-minded judges. To diminish their influence, the president proposed adding a new justice to the Court for every member over the age of seventy. Roosevelt's opponents protested that he was trying to "pack" the Court. After a bitter, months-long debate, Congress rejected this blatant attempt to alter the judiciary to the president's advantage.

If Roosevelt lost the battle, he went on to win the war. Swayed in part by the president's overwhelming electoral victory in the 1936 election, the Court upheld the Wagner and Social Security Acts. Moreover, a series of timely resignations allowed Roosevelt to reshape the Supreme Court after all. His new appointees—who included the liberal-leaning and generally pro–New Deal Hugo Black, Felix Frankfurter, and William O. Douglas—viewed the Constitution as a "living document" that had to be interpreted in the light of present conditions.

The so-called Roosevelt recession of 1937–1938 dealt another blow to the president. From 1933 to 1937, gross domestic product had grown at a yearly rate of about 10 percent, bringing industrial output and real income back to 1929 levels. Unemployment had declined from 25 percent to 14 percent. "The emergency has passed," declared Senator James F. Byrnes of South Carolina. Acting on this assumption, Roosevelt slashed the federal budget. Following the president's lead, Congress cut the WPA's funding in half, causing layoffs of about 1.5 million workers, and the Federal Reserve, fearing inflation, raised interest rates. These measures halted recovery. The stock market responded by dropping sharply, and unemployment jumped to 19 percent. Quickly reversing course, Roosevelt began once again to spend his way out of the recession by boosting funding for the WPA and resuming public works projects.

Although improvised, this spending program accorded with the theories of John Maynard Keynes, a visionary British economist of the first part of the twentieth century. Keynes transformed economic policymaking in capitalist societies by arguing that government intervention could smooth out the highs and lows of the business cycle through **deficit spending** and the manipulation of interest rates, which determined the money supply. Though it had been sharply criticized by Republicans and conservative Democrats in the 1930s, **Keynesian economics** gradually won wider acceptance as defense spending during World War II finally ended the Great Depression.

A reformer rather than a revolutionary, Roosevelt had preserved capitalism and liberal individualism—even as he transformed them in significant ways. He had met the challenge to American capitalism and democratic institutions posed by the Great Depression. At the same time, conservatives had reclaimed a measure of power in Congress, and those who believed the New Deal had created an intrusive federal bureaucracy kept reform in check after 1937. Throughout Roosevelt's second term, a conservative coalition composed of southern Democrats, rural Republicans, and industrial interests in both parties worked to block or impede social legislation. By 1939, the era of change was over.

- How did the Second New Deal differ from the first? What were FDR's reasons for changing course?
- Describe Keynesian economic policies. How important were they to the programs of the New Deal?

The New Deal's Impact on Society

Whatever the limits of the New Deal, it had a tremendous impact. Its ideology of social-welfare liberalism fundamentally altered Americans' relationship to their government and provided assistance to a wide range of ordinary people: the unemployed, the elderly, workers, and racial minorities. In doing so, New Dealers created a sizable federal bureaucracy: The number of civilian federal employees increased by 80 percent between 1929 and 1940, reaching a total of 1 million. The expenditures—and deficits—of the federal government grew at an even faster rate. In 1930, the Hoover administration spent $3.1 billion and had a surplus of almost $1 billion; in 1939, New Dealers expended $9.4 billion and ran a deficit of nearly $3 billion (still small by later standards). But the New Deal represented more than figures on a balance sheet. Across the country, the new era in government inspired democratic visions among ordinary citizens.

A People's Democracy

In 1939, writer John La Touche and musician Earl Robinson produced "Ballad for Americans." A patriotic song, it called for uniting "everybody who's nobody . . . Irish, Negro, Jewish, Italian, French, and English, Spanish, Russian, Chinese, Polish, Scotch, Hungarian, Litvak, Swedish, Finnish, Canadian, Greek, and Turk, and Czech and double Czech American." The song captured the democratic aspirations that the New Deal had awakened. Millions of ordinary people believed that the nation could, and should, become more egalitarian. Influenced by the liberal spirit of the New Deal, Americans from all walks of life seized the opportunity to push for change in the nation's social and political institutions.

A First Lady without Precedent

Reflecting Eleanor Roosevelt's tendency to turn up in odd places, a famous 1933 *New Yorker* cartoon shows two workers in a coal mine, one saying to another, "For gosh sakes, here comes Mrs. Roosevelt." Life soon imitated art. In this photograph from 1935, the first lady emerges from a coal mine in Dellaire, Ohio, still carrying her miner's cap in her left hand and talking to mine supervisor Joseph Bainbridge.   AP Images.

Organized Labor Demoralized and shrinking during the 1920s, labor unions increased their numbers and clout during the New Deal, thanks to the Wagner Act. "The era of privilege and predatory individuals is over," labor leader John L. Lewis declared. By the end of the decade, the number of unionized workers had tripled to 23 percent of the nonagricultural workforce. A new union movement, led by the Congress of Industrial Organizations (CIO), promoted "industrial unionism"—organizing all the workers in an industry, from skilled machinists to unskilled janitors, into a single union. American Federation of Labor (AFL), representing the other major group of unions, favored organizing workers on a craft-by-craft basis. Both federations dramatically increased their membership in the second half of the 1930s.

Labor's new vitality translated into political action and a long-lasting alliance with the Democratic Party. The CIO helped fund Democratic campaigns in 1936, and its political action committee became a major Dem-

ocratic contributor during the 1940s. These successes were real but limited. The labor movement did not become the dominant force in the United States that it was in Europe, and unions never enrolled a majority of American wageworkers. Employer groups such as the National Association of Manufacturers and the Chamber of Commerce, vehemently anti-union, remained powerful forces in American business life. After a decade of gains, organized labor remained an important, but secondary, force in American industry.

Women and the New Deal The New Deal did not directly challenge gender inequities. The high point of first-wave feminism, the ratification of the Nineteenth Amendment in 1920, had long passed. Women's advocates struggled for the attention of policymakers, who saw the depression primarily as a crisis of male breadwinners. New Deal measures generally enhanced women's welfare, but few addressed their needs and concerns directly. The

Roosevelt administration did welcome women into the higher ranks of government. Frances Perkins, the first woman named to a cabinet post, served as secretary of labor throughout Roosevelt's presidency. While relatively few, female appointees often worked to open up other opportunities in government for talented women.

The most prominent woman in American politics was the president's wife, Eleanor Roosevelt. In the 1920s, she had worked to expand positions for women in political parties, labor unions, and education. A tireless advocate for women's rights, during her years in the White House, Mrs. Roosevelt emerged as an independent public figure and the most influential First Lady in the nation's history. Descending deep into coal mines to view working conditions, meeting with African Americans seeking antilynching laws, and talking to people on breadlines, she became the conscience of the New Deal, pushing her husband to do more for the disadvantaged. "I sometimes acted as a spur," Mrs. Roosevelt later reflected, "even though the spurring was not always wanted or welcome."

Without the intervention of Eleanor Roosevelt, Frances Perkins, and other prominent women, New Deal policymakers would have largely ignored the needs of women. A fourth of the National Recovery Act codes set a lower minimum wage for women than for men performing the same jobs, and only 7 percent of the workers hired by the Civil Works Administration were female. The Civilian Conservation Corps excluded women entirely. Women fared better under the Works Progress Administration; at its peak, 405,000 women were on the payroll. Most Americans agreed with such policies. When Gallup pollsters in 1936 asked people whether wives should work outside the home when their husbands had jobs, 82 percent said no. Such sentiment reflected a persistent belief in women's secondary status in public life.

African Americans under the New Deal

Across the nation, but especially in the South, African Americans held the lowest-paying jobs and faced harsh social and political discrimination. Though FDR did not fundamentally change this fact, he was the most popular president among black Americans since Abraham Lincoln. African Americans held 18 percent of WPA jobs, although they constituted 10 percent of the population. The Resettlement Administration, established in 1935 to help small farmers and tenants buy land, actively protected the rights of black tenant farmers. Black involvement in the New Deal, however, could not undo centuries of

Mary McLeod Bethune

This 1943 painting by Betsy Graves Reyneau captures the strength and dignity of one of the twentieth century's most important African Americans. Behind Bethune is a picture of the first building at the Daytona Literary and Industrial School for Training Negro Girls, which in 1924 became Bethune-Cookman College (and in 2007 became Bethune-Cookman University). National Portrait Gallery, Smithsonian Institution / Art Resource, NY.

racial subordination, nor could it change the overwhelming power of southern whites in the Democratic Party.

Nevertheless, black Americans received significant benefits from New Deal relief programs. Help from New Deal agencies and a belief that the White House cared about their plight caused a momentous shift in African Americans' political allegiance. Since the Civil War, African Americans had staunchly supported the Republican Party, the party of Abraham Lincoln, the Great Emancipator. Even in the Depression year of 1932, they overwhelmingly supported Republican candidates. But in 1936, as part of the tidal wave of national support for FDR, northern blacks gave Roosevelt 71 percent of their votes. African American voters have remained solidly Democratic ever since.

African Americans supported the New Deal partly because the Roosevelt administration appointed a number of black people to federal office, and an informal "black cabinet" of prominent African American intellectuals advised New Deal agencies. Among the most important appointees was Mary McLeod Bethune. Born in 1875 in South Carolina to former slaves, Bethune founded Bethune-Cookman College and served during the 1920s as president of the National Association of Colored Women. She joined the New Deal in 1935, confiding to a friend that she "believed in the democratic and humane program" of FDR. Americans, Bethune observed, had to become "accustomed to seeing Negroes in high places." Bethune had access to the White House and pushed continually for New Deal programs to help African Americans.

But there were sharp limits on the New Deal in regard to race. Roosevelt did not go further in support of black rights, because of both his own racial blinders and his need for the votes of the white southern Democrats in Congress. Most New Deal programs reflected prevailing racial attitudes. Civilian Conservation Corps camps segregated blacks, and most NRA codes did not protect black workers from discrimination. Both Social Security and the Wagner Act explicitly excluded domestic and agricultural workers, the two categories where most African Americans labored in the 1930s. Roosevelt also refused to support legislation making lynching a federal crime, which was one of the most pressing demands of African Americans in the 1930s. Between 1882 and 1930, more than 2,500 African Americans were lynched by white mobs in the southern states; statistically, one man, woman, or child was murdered every week for fifty years. But despite pleas from black leaders, and from Mrs. Roosevelt herself, FDR feared that southern white Democrats would block his other reforms in retaliation for such legislation.

If lynching embodied southern lawlessness, southern law was not much better. In an infamous 1931 case in Scottsboro, Alabama, nine young black men were accused of rape by two white women hitching a ride on a freight train. The women's stories contained many inconsistencies, but within weeks a white jury had convicted all nine defendants; eight received the death sentence. After the U.S. Supreme Court overturned the sentences because the defendants had been denied adequate legal counsel, five of the men were again convicted and sentenced to long prison terms. Across the country, the Scottsboro Boys, as they were known, inspired solidarity within African American communities. Among whites, the Communist Party took the lead in publicizing the case—and was one of the only white organizations to do so—helping to support the Scottsboro Defense Committee, which raised money for legal efforts on the defendants' behalf.

In southern agriculture, where many sharecroppers were black while landowners and government administrators were white, the Agricultural Adjustment Act hurt rather than helped the poorest African Americans. White landowners collected government subsidy checks but refused to distribute payments to their sharecroppers. Such practices forced 200,000 black families off the land. Some black farmers tried to protect themselves by joining the Southern Tenant Farmers Union (STFU), a biracial organization founded in 1934. "The same chain that holds you hold my people, too," an elderly black farmer reminded his white neighbors. But landowners had such economic power and such support from local sheriffs that the STFU could do little.

The biggest obstacle to fundamental change, however, was political. In the South, Democrats had a monopoly on power, and they remained wedded to white supremacy. They resisted any government action that would overturn racial segregation. As a result, Roosevelt and other New Dealers had to trim their proposals of measures that would substantially benefit African Americans. FDR could not afford to lose the support of powerful southern senators, many of whom held influential committee posts in Congress. A generation of African American leaders came of age inspired by the New Deal's democratic promise. But it remained just a promise. Another thirty years would pass before black Americans would gain an opportunity to reform U.S. racial laws and practices.

Indian Policy New Deal reformers seized the opportunity to implement their vision for the future of Native Americans. The results were decidedly mixed. Indian peoples had long been one of the nation's most disadvantaged and powerless groups. In 1934, the average individual Indian income was only $48 per year, and the Native American unemployment rate was three times the national average. The plight of Native Americans won the attention of the commissioner of the Bureau of Indian Affairs (BIA), John Collier, a progressive intellectual and staunch critic of the past practices of the BIA. Collier understood what Indian peoples had long known: that the government's decades-long policy of forced assimilation, prohibition of Indian religions, and the taking of Indian lands had left most tribes poor, isolated, and without basic self-determination.

Collier helped to write and push through Congress the Indian Reorganization Act of 1934, sometimes called the Indian New Deal. On the positive side, the law reversed the Dawes Act of 1887 (see Chapter 16)

Scottsboro Defendants

The 1931 trial in Scottsboro, Alabama, of nine black youths accused of raping two white women became a symbol of the injustices African Americans faced in the South's legal system. Denied access to an attorney, the defendants were found guilty after a three-day trial, and eight were sentenced to death. When the U.S. Supreme Court overturned their convictions in 1932, the International Labor Defense organization hired noted criminal attorney Samuel Leibowitz to argue the case. Leibowitz eventually won the acquittal of four defendants and jail sentences for the rest. This 1933 photograph, taken in a Decatur jail, shows Leibowitz conferring with Haywood Patterson, in front of the other eight defendants.
Brown Brothers.

by promoting Indian self-government through formal constitutions and democratically elected tribal councils. A majority of Indian peoples—some 181 tribes—accepted the reorganization policy, but 77 declined to participate, primarily because they preferred the traditional way of making decisions by consensus rather than majority vote. Through the new law, Indians won a greater degree of religious freedom, and tribal governments regained their status as semisovereign dependent nations. When the latter policy was upheld by the courts, Indian people gained a measure of leverage that would have major implications for native rights in the second half of the twentieth century.

Like so many other federal Indian policies, however, the "Indian New Deal" was far from an uncomplicated blessing. For some peoples, the model of self-government the act imposed proved incompatible with tribal traditions and languages. The Papagos of southern Arizona, for instance, had no words for *budget* or *representative*, and made no linguistic distinctions among *law*, *rule*, *charter*, and *constitution*. In another case, the nation's largest tribe, the Navajos, rejected the BIA's new policy, in large part because the government was simultaneously reducing Navajo livestock to protect the Boulder Dam project. In theory, the new policy gave Indians a much greater degree of self-determination. In practice, however, although some tribes did benefit, the BIA and Congress did not stop interfering in internal Indian affairs and retained financial control of reservation governments.

Struggles in the West | By the 1920s, agriculture in California had become a big business—intensive, diversified, and export-oriented. Large-scale corporate-owned farms produced specialty crops—lettuce, tomatoes, peaches, grapes, and cotton—whose staggered harvests allowed the use of transient laborers. Thousands of workers, immigrants from Mexico and Asia and white migrants from the midwestern states, trooped from farm to farm and from crop to crop

Indian New Deal

Commissioner of Indian Affairs John Collier poses with chiefs of the Blackfoot Indian tribe in 1934. Collier helped reform the way the U.S. federal government treated Native Americans. As part of what many called the Indian New Deal, Collier lobbied Congress to pass the Indian Reorganization Act. The act gave Indian tribes greater control over their own affairs and ended many of the most atrocious federal practices, such as forcing Indian children into white-run boarding schools and dividing up and selling reservation land. The legislation's long-term results were mixed, but it signaled the beginning of greater autonomy for Indian tribes across the country.   © Bettmann/Corbis.

during the long picking season. Some migrants settled in the rapidly growing cities along the West Coast, especially the sprawling metropolis of Los Angeles.

Under both Hoover and FDR, the federal government promoted the "repatriation" of Mexican citizens — their deportation to Mexico. Between 1929 and 1937, approximately half a million people of Mexican descent were deported. But historians estimate that more than 60 percent of these were legal U.S. citizens, making the government's actions constitutionally questionable. Many Mexican farm laborers left voluntarily as the depression deepened. They knew that most local officials would not provide them with relief assistance. Virtually every immigrant Mexican family in the United States in the early 1930s confronted the decision of whether to leave or stay.

Despite the deportations, many Mexican Americans benefited from the New Deal and generally held Roosevelt and the Democratic Party in high regard. People of Mexican descent, like other Americans, took jobs with the WPA and the CCC, or received relief in

the worst years of the depression. The National Youth Administration (NYA), which employed young people from families on relief and sponsored a variety of school programs, was especially important in southwestern cities. In California, the Mexican American Movement (MAM), a youth-focused organization, received assistance from liberal New Dealers. New Deal programs did not improve the migrant farm labor system under which so many people of Mexican descent labored, but Mexicans joined the New Deal coalition in large numbers because of the Democrats' commitment to ordinary Americans. "Franklin D. Roosevelt's name was the spark that started thousands of Spanish-speaking persons to the polls," noted Los Angeles activist Beatrice Griffith.

Men and women of Asian descent — mostly from China, Japan, and the Philippines — formed a small minority of the American population but were a significant presence in some western cities and towns. Immigrants from Japan and China had long faced discrimination. A California law of 1913 prohibited them from owning land. Japanese farmers, who specialized in

THE GOVERNOR SENDS
"AID TO PIXLEY"
24 DEPUTY SHERIFFS
11 HIGHWAY PATROLMEN

WE WANT FOOD!

Mexican American Farm Workers

Among the most hard-pressed workers during the Great Depression where those who labored in the nation's agricultural field, orchards, and processing plants. Agriculture was a big-time corporate business by the 1930s, and in California and other parts of the Southwest it employed hundreds of thousands of poor Mexican Americans and Mexican immigrants. Seizing on the spirit of social protest sweeping the country in the early 1930s, many of these workers went on strike for better wages and working conditions. Here, women from Mexican American communities are heading to the cotton fields near Corcoran, California, to urge workers to join a major strike of cotton pickers. Though the workers in Corcoran won some wage improvements in this 1933 strike, the fierce battle between employers and workers in American agriculture was far from over and continues to this day.   Library of Congress.

fruit and vegetable crops, circumvented this restriction by putting land titles in the names of their American-born children. As the depression cut farm prices and racial discrimination excluded young Japanese Americans from nonfarm jobs, about 20 percent of the immigrants returned to Japan.

Chinese Americans were less prosperous than their Japanese counterparts. Only 3 percent of Chinese Americans worked in professional and technical positions, and discrimination barred them from most industrial jobs. In San Francisco, most Chinese worked in small businesses: restaurants, laundries, and firms that imported textiles and ceramics. During the depression, they turned for assistance to Chinese social organizations such as *huiguan* (district associations) and to the city government; in 1931, about one-sixth of San Francisco's Chinese population was receiving public aid. But few Chinese benefited from the New Deal. Until the repeal of the Exclusion Act in 1943, Chinese immigrants

were classified as "aliens ineligible for citizenship" and therefore were excluded from most federal programs.

Because Filipino immigrants came from a U.S. territory, they were not affected by the ban on Asian immigration enacted in 1924. During the 1920s, their numbers swelled to about 50,000, many of whom worked as laborers on large corporate-owned farms. As the depression cut wages, Filipino immigration slowed to a trickle, and it was virtually cut off by the Tydings-McDuffie Act of 1934. The act granted independence to the Philippines (which since 1898 had been an American colony), classified all Filipinos in the United States as aliens, and restricted immigration from the Philippines to fifty people per year.

Reshaping the Environment

Attention to the land and natural resources was a dominant motif of the New Deal, and the shaping of

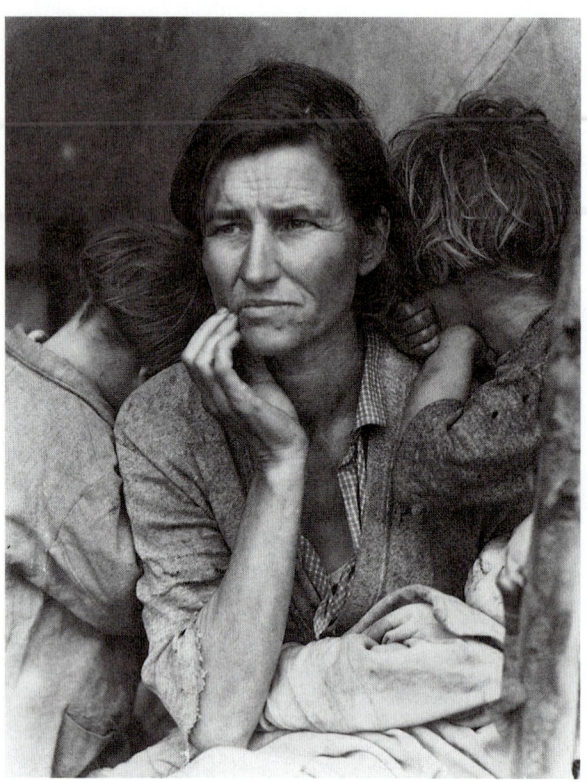

The Human Face of the Great Depression

Migrant Mother by Dorothea Lange is one of the most famous documentary photographs of the 1930s. On assignment for the Resettlement Administration, Lange spent only ten minutes in a pea-pickers' camp in Nipomo, California. There she captured this image (though not the name) of the woman whose despair and resignation she so powerfully recorded. In the 1970s the woman was identified as Florence Thompson, a full-blooded Cherokee from Oklahoma, who disagreed with Lange's recollections of the circumstances of the taking of the photograph. Thompson and her family had left Nipomo, however, by the time the publication of this image sparked a large relief effort directed at the camp's migrant workers. Library of Congress.

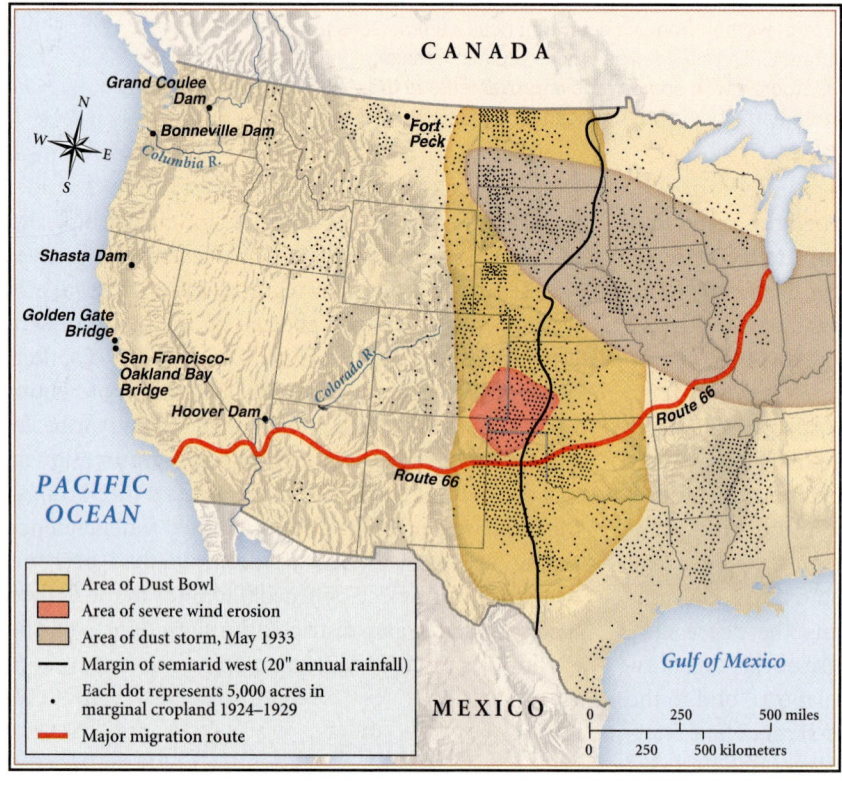

MAP 23.3

The Dust Bowl and Federal Building Projects in the West, 1930–1941

A U.S. Weather Bureau scientist called the drought of the 1930s "the worst in the climatological history of the country." Conditions were especially severe in the southern plains, where farming on marginal land threatened the environment even before the drought struck. As farm families migrated west on U.S. Route 66, the federal government began a series of massive building projects that provided flood control, irrigation, electric power, and transportation facilities to residents of the states of the Far West.

Drought Refugees

Like the fictional Joad family in John Steinbeck's powerful novel *The Grapes of Wrath* (1939), many thousands of poor people hit hard by the drought, dust, and debt of farm life in the Great Plains loaded their possessions into pickup trucks and hoped for brighter futures in the West. This 1937 photograph by Dorothea Lange shows a Missouri family of five, drought refugees on Highway 99 near Tracy, California. Lange titled another photograph of this family with the quote "Broke, baby sick, car trouble." Library of Congress.

the landscape was among its most visible legacies. Franklin Roosevelt and Interior Secretary Harold Ickes saw themselves as conservationists in the tradition of FDR's cousin, Theodore Roosevelt. In an era before environmentalism, FDR practiced what he called the "gospel of conservation." The president cared first and foremost about making the land—and other natural resources, such as trees and water—better serve human needs. National policy stressed scientific management of the land and ecological balance. Preserving wildlife and wilderness were of secondary importance. Under Roosevelt, the federal government both responded to acute environmental crises and aggressively reshaped how natural resources, especially water, were used in the United States.

The Dust Bowl Among the most hard-pressed citizens during the depression were farmers fleeing the "dust bowl" of the Great Plains. Their land had taken a beating. Between 1930 and 1941, a severe drought afflicted the semiarid states of Oklahoma, Texas, New Mexico, Colorado, Arkansas, and Kansas. Farmers in these areas had stripped the land of its native vegetation, which destroyed the delicate ecology of the plains. To grow wheat and other crops, they had pushed agriculture beyond the natural limits of the soil and climate, making their land vulnerable, in times of drought, to wind erosion of the topsoil (Map 23.3). When the winds came, huge clouds of thick dust rolled over the land, turning the day into night. This ecological disaster prompted a mass exodus. At least 350,000 "Okies" (so called whether or not they were from Oklahoma) loaded their belongings into cars and trucks and headed to California. John Steinbeck's novel *The Grapes of Wrath* (1939) immortalized them, and New Deal photographer Dorothea Lange's haunting images of California migrant camps made them the public face of the depression's human toll.

Poor land practices, Roosevelt and Ickes believed, made for poor people. Under their direction, government agencies tackled the dust bowl's human causes. Agents from the newly created Soil Conservation Service, for instance, taught farmers to prevent soil erosion by tilling hillsides along the contours of the land. They also encouraged (and sometimes paid) farmers to take certain commercial crops out of production and plant soil-preserving grasses instead. One of the U.S. Forest Service's most widely publicized programs was the Shelterbelts, the planting of 220 million trees running north along the 99th meridian from Abilene, Texas, to the Canadian border. Planted as a windbreak, the trees also prevented soil erosion. Ultimately, agencies from the CCC to the U.S. Department of Agriculture lent their expertise to establishing sound farming practices in the plains.

Tennessee Valley Authority | The most extensive New Deal environmental undertaking was the Tennessee Valley Authority (TVA), which Roosevelt imagined as the first step in modernizing the South. Funded by Congress in 1933, the TVA integrated flood control, reforestation, inexpensive electricity generation, and agricultural and industrial development, including the production of chemical fertilizers. The dams and their hydroelectric plants provided cheap electric power for homes and factories as well as ample recreational opportunities for the valley's residents. The massive project won praise around the world (Map 23.4).

The TVA was an integral part of the Roosevelt administration's effort to keep farmers on the land by enhancing the quality of rural life. The Rural Electrification Administration (REA), established in 1935, was also central to that goal. Fewer than one-tenth of the nation's 6.8 million farms had electricity. The REA addressed this problem by promoting nonprofit farm cooperatives that offered loans to farmers to install power lines. By 1940, 40 percent of the nation's farms had electricity; a decade later, 90 percent did. Electricity brought relief from the drudgery and isolation of farm life. Electric irons, vacuum cleaners, and washing machines eased women's burdens, and radios brightened the lives of the entire family. Along with the automobile and the movies, electricity broke down the barriers between urban and rural life.

Grand Coulee | As the nation's least populated but fastest-growing region, the West benefited enormously from the New Deal's attention to the environment. With the largest number of state and federal parks in the country, the West gained countless trails, bridges, cabins, and other recreational facilities, laying the groundwork for the post–World War II expansion of western tourism. On the Colorado River, Boulder Dam (later renamed Hoover Dam) was completed in 1935 with Public Works Administration funds; the dam generated power for the region's growing cities such as Las Vegas, Los Angeles, and Phoenix.

The largest project in the West, however, took shape in an obscure corner of Washington State, where the PWA and the Bureau of Reclamation built the Grand Coulee Dam on the Columbia River. When it was completed in 1941, Grand Coulee was the largest electricity-producing structure in the world, and its 150-mile lake provided irrigation for the state's major crops: apples, cherries, pears, potatoes, and wheat. Inspired by the dam and the modernizing spirit of the New Deal, folk singer Woody Guthrie wrote a song about the Columbia. "Your power is turning our darkness to dawn," he sang, "so roll on, Columbia, roll on!"

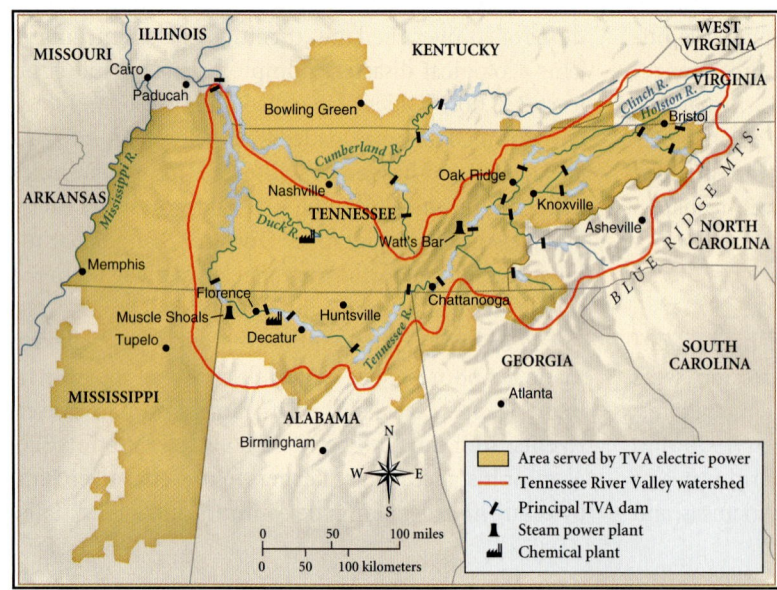

MAP 23.4

The Tennessee Valley Authority, 1933–1952

The Tennessee Valley Authority was one of the New Deal's most far-reaching environmental projects. Between 1933 and 1952, the TVA built twenty dams and improved five others, taming the flood-prone Tennessee River and its main tributaries. The cheap hydroelectric power generated by the dams brought electricity to industries as well as hundreds of thousands of area residents, and artificial lakes provided extensive recreational facilities. Widely praised at the time, the TVA came under attack in the 1970s for its practice of strip mining and the pollution caused by its power plants and chemical factories.

Grand Coulee Dam

This extraordinary photo from a *Life* magazine essay shows workers hitching a ride on a 13-ton conduit as it is lowered into place on the Grand Coulee Dam in Washington State. Dozens of dams were constructed across the country under the auspices of various New Deal programs, but none were more majestic than two in the West: Boulder Dam (renamed Hoover Dam in 1947) and Grand Coulee. Built to harness the awesome power of the Columbia River as it rushed to the Pacific, Grand Coulee would ultimately provide electric power to Seattle, Portland, and other West Coast cities and new irrigation waters for Washington's apple and cherry orchards, among many other crops.   Library of Congress.

New Deal projects that enhanced people's enjoyment of the natural environment can be seen today throughout the country. CCC and WPA workers built the famous Blue Ridge Parkway, which connects the Shenandoah National Park in Virginia with the Great Smoky Mountains National Park in North Carolina. In the West, government workers built the San Francisco Zoo, Berkeley's Tilden Park, and the canals of San Antonio. The Civilian Conservation Corps helped to complete the East Coast's Appalachian Trail and the West Coast's Pacific Crest Trail through the Sierra Nevada.

In state parks across the country, cabins, shelters, picnic areas, lodges, and observation towers stand as monuments to the New Deal ethos of recreation coexisting with nature.

The New Deal and the Arts

In response to the Great Depression, many American writers and artists redefined their relationship to society. Never had there been a decade, critic Malcolm Cowley suggested in 1939, "when literary events followed so closely on the flying coat-tails of social events." New Deal administrators encouraged artists to create projects that would be of interest to the entire community, not just the cultured elite. "Art for the millions" became a popular New Deal slogan and encouraged the painting of murals in hundreds of public buildings (see Reading American Pictures, "Interpreting the Public Art of the New Deal," p. 747).

The Federal Art Project, an arm of the WPA, gave work to many young artists who would become the twentieth century's leading painters, muralists, and sculptors. Jackson Pollock, Alice Neel, Willem de Kooning, and Louise Nevelson all received support. The Federal Music Project and Federal Writers' Project (FWP) employed 15,000 musicians and 5,000 writers, respectively. Among the latter were Saul Bellow, Ralph Ellison, and John Cheever, future novelists of great stature. The FWP collected oral histories, including two thousand narratives by former slaves. The black folklorist and novelist Zora Neale Hurston finished three novels while in the Florida FWP, among them *Their Eyes Were Watching God* (1937). Richard Wright won the 1938 *Story* magazine prize for the best tale by a WPA writer and went on to complete *Native Son* (1940), a searing novel about white racism. Similarly, the Federal Theatre Project (FTP) nurtured such talented directors, actors, and playwrights as Orson Welles, John Huston, and Arthur Miller.

The WPA arts projects reflected a broad cultural trend known as the "documentary impulse." Documentary artists focused on actual events that were relevant to people's lives and presented them in ways that engaged the interest and emotions of the audience. This trend influenced practically every aspect of American culture: literature, photography, art, music, film, dance, theater, and radio. It is evident in novels such as John Steinbeck's *The Grapes of Wrath* and in John Dos Passos's *USA* trilogy (1930–1936), which used actual newspaper clippings and headlines in its fictional story. New photojournalism magazines, including *Life* and *Look*, carried this documentary approach into millions of living rooms.

The Legacies of the New Deal

The New Deal addressed the Great Depression by restoring hope and promising security. FDR and Congress created a powerful social-welfare state that took unprecedented responsibility for the well-being of American citizens. During the 1930s, millions of people began to pay taxes directly to the Social Security Administration, and more than one-third of the population received direct government assistance from federal programs, including old-age pensions, unemployment compensation, farm loans, relief work, and mortgage guarantees. New legislation regulated the stock market, reformed the Federal Reserve System, and subjected business corporations to federal regulation. The New Deal's pattern of government involvement in social life would persist for the rest of the twentieth century. In the 1960s, Lyndon Johnson and the "Great Society" Congress dramatically expanded social-welfare programs, most of which remained intact in the wake of the "Reagan Revolution" of the 1980s.

Like all other major social transformations, the New Deal was criticized both by those who thought it did too much and by those who believed it did too little. Conservatives, who prioritized limited government and individual freedom, pointed out that the New Deal state intruded deeply into the personal and financial lives of the citizenry. Conversely, advocates of social-welfare liberalism complained that the New Deal's safety net had many holes: no national health-care system, welfare programs that excluded domestic workers and farm laborers, and the fact that state governments often limited the benefits distributed under New Deal programs.

Whatever the merits of its critics, there is no question that the New Deal transformed the American political landscape. From 1896 to 1932, the Republican Party had commanded the votes of a majority of Americans. That changed as Franklin Roosevelt's magnetic personality and innovative programs brought millions of voters into the Democratic fold. Democratic recruits included first- and second-generation immigrants from southern and central Europe—Italians, Poles, Slovaks, and Jews—as well as African American migrants to northern cities. Organized labor aligned itself with a Democratic administration that had recognized unions as a legitimate force in modern industrial life. The elderly and the unemployed, assisted by the Social Security Act, likewise supported FDR. This New Deal coalition of ethnic groups, city dwellers, organized labor, blacks, and a cross-section of the middle class formed the nucleus of the northern Democratic Party and supported additional liberal reforms in the decades to come.

- What was the impact of the New Deal on organized labor, women, and racial and ethnic minorities? How would you explain its success and failures in reaching these groups?

- What was the New Deal's long-term legacy?

Interpreting the Public Art of the New Deal

Murals are perhaps the most pervasive artistic legacy of the New Deal. They decorate federal buildings throughout the nation today. The goals of the agencies that commissioned the murals were to give employment to artists, bring art to the masses, and celebrate the American people and their nation. New Deal murals were realistic in style, and many embodied the decade's emphasis on regionalism by depicting the history of a locality and its people at work and play. The image shown here comes from a large three-panel mural by well-known artist Ben Shahn that adorns a public school in Roosevelt, New Jersey. Originally called the Jersey Homesteads, the town of Roosevelt was created by the Farm Security Administration as a planned community for poor immigrant Jewish garment workers from New York City. The first two panels of the mural depict Jewish immigrants and their work. The third panel, pictured here, features in the left corner a teacher instructing workers about the history of unions. Seated at the right are New Deal planners and labor leaders. The figures behind them are the prospective residents of the new community. For the full mural, visit www2.scc.rutgers.edu/njh/Homesteads/art.php.

Ben Shahn, *The Promise of the New Deal* (1938). Roosevelt Arts Project.

ANALYZING THE EVIDENCE

- What does this third panel of Shahn's mural tell us about the character and the goals of the New Deal?
- Note the blueprint of the street plan and the houses depicted on the mural (top center). Then turn to the photo in Chapter 26 (p. 830) that depicts a suburban housing development built by a private corporation in the 1950s. What does a comparison of those two images suggest?
- How does Shahn's mural fit with the discussion of the documentary impulse discussed in this chapter?

SUMMARY

We have seen how Franklin Delano Roosevelt's First New Deal focused on stimulating recovery, providing relief to the unemployed, and regulating banks and other financial institutions. The Second New Deal was different. Influenced by the persistence of the depression and the growing popularity of Huey Long's Share the Wealth proposals, Roosevelt promoted social-welfare legislation that provided Americans with economic security.

We also explored the impact of the New Deal on various groups of citizens, especially African Americans, women, and unionized workers. Our survey paid particular attention to the lives of the Mexicans, Asians, and Okies who worked in the farms and factories of California. Because of New Deal assistance, the members of those groups gravitated toward the Democratic Party. The party's coalition of ethnic workers, African Americans, farmers, parts of the middle classes, and white southerners gave FDR and other Democrats a landslide victory in 1936.

Finally, we examined the accomplishments of the New Deal. In 1933, New Deal programs resolved the banking crisis while preserving capitalist institutions. Subsequently, these programs expanded the federal government and, through the Social Security system, farm subsidy programs, and public works projects, launched federal policies that were important to nearly every American. Great dams and electricity projects sponsored by the Tennessee Valley Authority, the Works Progress Administration in the West, and the Rural Electrification Administration permanently improved the quality of life for the nation's citizens.

CHAPTER REVIEW QUESTIONS

- Some historians have seen the New Deal as an evolution of the reform initiated by progressives earlier in the century, but others have argued that it represented a revolution in social values and government institutions. What do you think? Provide evidence for your argument.

- What changes took place during the depression era with respect to the lives of women, workers, and racial and ethnic minority groups? What role did the New Deal play in helping those groups of Americans?

- In what ways did the New Deal coalition and the social programs it developed change the character of American politics? Why did Republicans oppose the Democratic initiatives?

FOR FURTHER EXPLORATION

Robert S. McElvaine, *The Great Depression* (1984), and Amity Shlaes, *The Forgotten Man: A New History of the Great Depression* (2007), provide a general treatment of the Great Depression and New Deal. Katie Louchheim, ed., *The Making of the New Deal: The Insiders Speak* (1983), portrays important New Dealers. Robert S. McElvaine's *Down and Out in the Great Depression* (1983) contains letters written by ordinary people. For audio versions of Studs Terkel's interviews, visit the Chicago Historical Society Web site at **www.studsterkel .org/index.html**. John Steinbeck, *The Grapes of Wrath* (1939); Josephine Herbst, *Pity Is Not Enough* (1933); and Richard Wright, *Native Son* (1940), are classic Depression-era novels. On African Americans in the depression, see Harvard Sitkoff, *A New Deal for Blacks: The Emergence of Civil Rights as a National Issue* (1978). For two extensive collections of 1930s materials, see the "New Deal Network" at **newdeal.feri.org** and "America in the 1930s" at **xroads.virginia.edu/~1930s/home _1.html**, which includes clips from radio programs. A good all-around New Deal site for teachers is **newdeal .feri.org/classrm/a.htm**. Also, the wonderful collection of government-commissioned art at **www.archives .gov/exhibits/new_deal_for_the_arts**. The Library of Congress multimedia presentation "Voices from the Dust Bowl" can be viewed at **memory.loc.gov/ammem/ afctshtml/tshome.html**; a superb collection of photographs covering the years 1935–1945 can be found at **lcweb2.loc.gov/ammem/fsowhome.html** and **memory.loc.gov/ammem/fsahtml/fahome.html**. The slave narratives collected by the Federal Writer's Project can be found at **memory.loc.gov/ammem/ snhtml**.

TEST YOUR KNOWLEDGE

To assess your command of the material in this chapter, see the Online Study Guide at **bedfordstmartins.com/henretta**.

For Web sites, images, and documents related to topics and places in this chapter, visit **bedfordstmartins.com/makehistory**.

TIMELINE

1931–1937	Scottsboro case: trials and appeals
1932	Bonus Army marches on Washington, D.C.
	Franklin Delano Roosevelt elected president
1933	FDR's inaugural address and first fireside chats
	Emergency Banking Act begins the Hundred Days
	Civilian Conservation Corps (CCC) created
	Agricultural Adjustment Act (AAA)
	National Industrial Recovery Act (NIRA)
	Tennessee Valley Authority (TVA) established
	Townsend Clubs promote Old Age Revolving Pension Plan
	Twenty-first Amendment repeals Prohibition
1934	Securities and Exchange Commission (SEC) created
	Tenant Farmers Union (STFU) founded
	Indian Reorganization Act
	Senator Huey Long promotes Share Our Wealth Society
	Father Charles Coughlin founds National Union for Social Justice
1935	Supreme Court voids NRA in *Schechter v. United States*
	National Labor Relations (Wagner) Act
	Social Security Act creates old-age pension system
	Works Progress Administration (WPA) created
	Huey Long assassinated
	Rural Electrification Administration (REA) established
	Supreme Court voids Agricultural Adjustment Act
	Congress of Industrial Organizations (CIO) formed
1936	General Motors sit-down strike
	Landslide reelection of FDR marks peak of New Deal power
1937	FDR's Supreme Court plan fails
1937–1938	"Roosevelt recession" raises unemployment
1938	Fair Labor Standards Act (FLSA)
1939	Federal Theatre Project terminated

CHAPTER 24

The World at War, 1937–1945

The Second World War was the defining international event of the twentieth century. Battles raged across six of the world's seven continents and all of its oceans. It killed 50 million human beings and left hundreds of millions of others wounded. When it was over, the industrial economies and much of the infrastructure of Europe and East Asia lay in ruins. Waged with both technologically advanced weapons and massive armies, the war involved every industrialized power in Europe, North America, and Asia, as well as dozens of smaller nations, many of them colonies of the industrialized countries.

The military conflict began on two continents: in Asia with Japan's 1937 invasion of China across the Sea of Japan, and in Europe with the 1939 blitzkrieg (lightning war) conducted by superbly engineered German tanks across the plains of Poland. It ended in 1945 after American planes dropped two atomic bombs, the product of stunning yet ominous scientific breakthroughs, on the Japanese cities of Hiroshima and Nagasaki. In between these demonstrations of technological prowess and devastating power, huge armies confronted and destroyed one another in the fields of France, the forests and steppes of Russia, the river valleys of China, the volcanic islands of the Pacific, and the sandy deserts of North Africa.

"Armed defense of democratic existence is now being gallantly waged in four continents," President Franklin Delano Roosevelt told the nation in January 1941. After remaining on the sidelines for several years, the United States would soon commit to that "armed defense." Both FDR and British prime minister Winston Churchill came to see the war as a defense of democratic values from the threat posed by German, Italian, and Japanese fascism. For them, the brutal conflict was the "good war." When the grim reality of the Jewish Holocaust came to light, U.S. participation in the war seemed even more just. But there was another side to the war. As much as it represented a struggle between democracy and fascism, it was also inescapably a war to maintain British, French, and Dutch control of colonies in Africa, India, the Middle East, and Southeast Asia. By 1945, democracy in the industrialized world had been preserved, and a new Euro-American alliance had taken hold; the future of the vast European colonial empires, however, remained unresolved.

On the U.S. domestic front, World War II brought an end to the Great Depression, hastened profound social changes, and expanded the scope and authority of the federal government. Race relations and gender roles shifted under the weight of wartime protest, migration, and labor shortages.

One City (and Island) at a Time

By late 1944, the victory of the United States and its allies was nearly certain, but Japanese and German troops continued to fight with great courage and determination. Many European cities and every Pacific island had to be taken foot by foot. Here, American troops from the 325th Regiment of the 82nd Airborne Division advance slowly through the rubble-filled street of a German city in early 1945. Collection of Jeff Ethell.

The pace of urbanization increased as millions of Americans uprooted themselves and moved hundreds or thousands of miles to join the military or to take a war job. These developments, which were accelerations of social transformations already under way, would have repercussions far into the postwar decades.

At the same time, federal laws and practices established during the war—universal taxation of incomes, a huge military establishment, and multibillion-dollar budgets, to name but a few—became part of American life. So, too, did the active participation of the United States in international politics and alliances, an engagement intensified by the unresolved issues of the wartime alliance with the Soviet Union and the postwar fate of colonized nations. A robust American state, the product of a long, hard-fought war, would remain in place to fight an even longer, more expensive, and potentially more dangerous Cold War.

The Road to War

The Great Depression disrupted economic life around the world and brought the collapse of traditional political institutions. In response, an antidemocratic movement known as fascism, which had originated in Italy during the 1920s, developed in Germany, Spain, and Japan. By the mid-1930s, these nations had instituted authoritarian, militaristic governments led by powerful dictators: Benito Mussolini in Italy, Adolf Hitler in Nazi Germany, Francisco Franco in Spain, and, after 1940, Hideki Tojo in Japan. As early as 1936, President Roosevelt warned that other peoples had "sold their heritage of freedom" and urged Americans to work for "the survival of democracy" both at home and abroad. Hampered at first by strong isolationist sentiment, by 1939 FDR was leading the nation toward war against the fascist powers.

Fascism was sharply at odds with the capitalist democracies of Europe and the United States, as well as with the communist Soviet Union. Fascism, as established in Germany by Hitler, combined a centralized, authoritarian state, a doctrine of Aryan racial supremacy, and intense nationalism in a call for the spiritual reawakening of the German people. Fascist leaders worldwide disparaged parliamentary government, independent labor movements, and individual rights. They opposed both the economic collectivism of the Soviet Union—where, in theory, the state managed the economy to ensure social equality—and the competitive capitalist economies of the United States and Western Europe. Fascist movements arose around the world in the 1930s—the closest in the United States was the

Ku Klux Klan—but managed to achieve power in only a handful of countries. Those countries were at the center of global war making in the 1930s.

The Rise of Fascism

World War II had its roots in the settlement of World War I (see Chapter 21). Germany struggled under the harsh terms of the Treaty of Versailles, and Japan and Italy had their dreams of overseas empires thwarted by the treaty makers. Faced with the expansive ambitions and deep resentments of those countries, the League of Nations, the collective security system established at Versailles, proved unable to maintain the existing international order.

Japan and Italy   The first challenge came from Japan. To become an industrial power, Japan required raw materials and overseas markets. Like the Western European powers and the United States before it, Japan embarked on a program of military expansion in pursuit of colonial possessions. In 1931, its troops occupied Manchuria, an industrialized province in northern China, and in 1937, the Japanese launched a full-scale invasion of China. In both instances, the League of Nations condemned Japan's actions but did nothing to stop them.

Japan's defiance of the League encouraged a fascist leader half a world away: Italy's Benito Mussolini, who had come to power in 1922. Il Duce (The Leader), as Mussolini was known, had long denounced the Versailles treaty, which denied Italy's claim on German and Turkish colonies in Africa and the Middle East. As

Adolf Hitler

Adolf Hitler salutes German troops during a parade at the Nazi Party's annual congress at Nuremberg. German fascism reveled in great public spectacles, such as the famous Nuremberg rallies held every year between the early 1920s and the late 1930s. Hitler used these mass rallies, at which tens and sometimes hundreds of thousands of soldiers and civilians gathered, to build wide support for his policies of aggressive militarism abroad and suppression of Jews and other minorities at home.   Getty Images.

in Japan, the Italian fascists desired overseas colonies for raw materials, markets, and national prestige. In 1935, Mussolini invaded Ethiopia, one of the few remaining independent countries in Africa. Ethiopian emperor Haile Selassie appealed to the League of Nations, but the League's verbal condemnation and limited sanctions did not stop Italy's forces, which took control of Ethiopia in 1936.

Hitler's Germany   It was Germany that posed the gravest threat to the existing world order. Huge World War I reparation payments, economic depression, fear of communism, labor unrest, and rising unemployment fueled the ascent of Adolf Hitler and his National Socialist (Nazi) Party. When Hitler became chancellor of Germany in 1933, the Reichstag (the German legislature) granted him dictatorial powers to deal with the economic crisis. Using that emergency authority, Hitler outlawed other political parties, arrested many of his political rivals, and took the title of *führer* (leader). Now under unchallenged Nazi control, the Reichstag invested all legislative power in Hitler's hands.

Hitler's goal was nothing short of European domination and world power, as he had made clear in his book *Mein Kampf* (*My Struggle*), first published in 1925. His writings outlined his plans to overturn the territorial settlements of the Versailles treaty, unite Germans living throughout central Europe in a great German fatherland, and annex large areas of Eastern Europe. The "inferior races" who lived in these regions—Jews, Gypsies, and Slavs—would be removed or subordinated to the German "master race." A virulent anti-Semite, Hitler had long blamed Jews for Germany's problems. Once in power, he began a sustained and brutal persecution of Jews, which expanded into a campaign of extermination in the early 1940s.

Hitler's strategy for restoring Germany's military power and lost territories was to escalate his objectives in a series of small steps, daring Britain and France to go to war to stop him each time. In 1935, Hitler began to rearm Germany, in violation of the Versailles treaty. No one stopped him. In 1936, he sent troops into the Rhineland, a demilitarized zone under the terms of Versailles. Once again, France and Britain took no action. Later that year, Hitler and Mussolini formed the Rome-Berlin Axis, a political and military alliance between the two fascist nations. Also in 1936, Germany signed a pact to create a military alliance with Japan against the Soviet Union.

Isolationists versus Interventionists

As Hitler pushed his initiatives in Europe, which was mired in economic depression as deeply as the United States, the Roosevelt administration faced widespread isolationist sentiment at home. In part, this desire to avoid European entanglements reflected disillusion with American participation in World War I. In 1934, Gerald P. Nye, a progressive Republican senator from North Dakota, launched an investigation into the profits of munitions makers during that war. Nye's committee concluded that arms manufacturers (popularly labeled "merchants of death") had maneuvered President Wilson into World War I.

Although Nye's committee failed to prove its charge against weapon makers, its factual findings prompted Congress to pass a series of acts to prevent the nation from being drawn into another overseas war. The Neutrality Act of 1935 imposed an embargo on selling arms to warring countries and declared that Americans traveling on the ships of belligerent nations did so at their own risk. In 1936, Congress banned loans to belligerents, and in 1937 it imposed a "cash-and-carry" requirement: If a warring country wanted to purchase nonmilitary goods from the United States, it had to pay cash and carry them in its own ships, keeping the United States out of potentially dangerous naval warfare.

Among the general public, there was little enthusiasm for war. Isolationist sentiment was vocalized by a wide variety of different groups. Many isolationists looked to Ohio senator Robert Taft, who despised and distrusted Roosevelt. Taft believed that overseas entanglements would draw the United States closer to Europe, which he viewed as a decadent society unworthy of emulation. Another conservative group, the National Legion of Mothers of America, combined isolationism with anticommunism, Christian morality, and even anti-Semitism. Most isolationists came from among conservatives, but some progressives (or liberals) opposed America's potential involvement in the war on pacifist or moral grounds. Whatever their philosophies, ardent isolationists and a disinterested public forced Roosevelt to be cautious in his approach to the brewing war.

The Popular Front | Other Americans, notably writers, intellectuals, and liberal social activists, responded to the rise of fascism in Europe by advocating U.S. intervention. Some joined the American Communist Party, which had taken the lead in opposing fascism and had increased its membership as the depression revealed flaws in the capitalist system. Between 1935 and 1938, Communist Party membership peaked at about 100,000 in the United States, drawn from a wide range of social groups, including African American civil rights activists and even a few New Deal administrators. Many intellectuals did not join the party but considered themselves "fellow travelers." They sympathized with the party's objectives and supported various left-wing groups and causes.

The courting of intellectuals, union members, and liberals reflected a shift in the strategy of the Communist Party. Fearful of German and Japanese aggression, the Soviet leaders instructed Communists in Western Europe and the United States to join in a coalition of opponents to fascism known as the Popular Front. The Popular Front threw its support behind various international causes—supporting the Loyalists in their fight against fascist leader Francisco Franco in the Spanish Civil War (1936–1939), for example, even as the United States, France, and Britain remained neutral. In time, however, many supporters in the United States grew uneasy with the Popular Front because of the rigidity of its Communist associates and the cynical brutality and political repression under Soviet leader Joseph Stalin. Nevertheless, Popular Front activists were among a small but vocal group of Americans encouraging Roosevelt to take a more determined stand against European fascism.

The Failure of Appeasement | Encouraged by the weak worldwide response to the invasions of China, Ethiopia, and the Rhineland, and emboldened by British and French neutrality during the Spanish Civil War, Hitler grew more aggressive in 1938. He sent troops to annex German-speaking Austria while making clear his intention to seize part of Czechoslovakia. Because Czechoslovakia had an alliance with France, war seemed imminent. But at the Munich Conference in September 1938, Britain and France again capitulated, agreeing to let Germany annex the Sudetenland—a German-speaking border area of Czechoslovakia—in return for Hitler's pledge to seek no more territory. The agreement, declared British prime minister Neville Chamberlain, guaranteed "peace for our time." Hitler drew a different conclusion, telling his generals: "Our enemies are small fry. I saw them in Munich."

Within six months, Hitler's forces had overrun the rest of Czechoslovakia and were threatening to march into Poland. Realizing that their policy of appeasement—capitulating to Hitler's demands—had been disastrous, Britain and France warned Hitler that further expansion meant war. Then, in August 1939, Hitler and Stalin shocked the world by signing a mutual nonaggression pact. For Hitler, this pact was crucial, as it meant that

Charles Lindbergh

Charles Lindbergh, the first person to fly solo nonstop across the Atlantic Ocean, was an American hero in the 1930s. In 1941, he was also the public face of the America First Committee, which was determined the keep the United States from entering the wars raging in Europe and Asia. Here, he is seen greeting an enthusiastic audience at an America First rally in New York's Madison Square Garden in late October 1941. Less than a month and a half later, Japan attacked Pearl Harbor, and isolationist sentiment all but disappeared in the United States.   © Bettmann/ Corbis.

Germany would not have to wage a two-front war against Britain and France in the west and Russia in the east. On September 1, 1939, Hitler launched a blitzkrieg against Poland. Two days later, Britain and France declared war on Germany. World War II had officially begun.

Two days after the European war started, the United States declared its neutrality. But President Roosevelt made no secret of his sympathies. When war broke out in 1914, Woodrow Wilson had told Americans to be neutral "in thought as well as in action." FDR, by contrast, said: "This nation will remain a neutral nation, but I cannot ask that every American remain neutral in thought as well." The overwhelming majority of Americans—some 84 percent, according to a poll in 1939—supported Britain and France rather than Germany, but most did not want to be drawn into another European war.

At first, the need for U.S. intervention seemed remote. After the German conquest of Poland in September 1939, calm settled over Europe. Then, on April 9, 1940, German forces invaded Denmark and Norway. In May, the Netherlands, Belgium, Luxembourg, and France were invaded. On June 14, German troops occupied Paris, and Hitler's armies marched along the Champs-Élysées. The final shock came on June 22, 1940, when France surrendered. Britain stood alone against Hitler's plans for domination of Europe.

War Arrives | What *Time* magazine would later call America's "thousand-step road to war" had already begun. After a bitter battle in Congress in 1939, Roosevelt won a change in the neutrality laws to allow the Allies to buy arms as well as nonmilitary goods on a cash-and-carry basis. Interventionists, led by journalist William Allen White and his Committee to Defend America by Aiding the Allies, became increasingly vocal. In response, in 1940 isolationists formed the America First Committee (AFC), with well-respected figures such as the aviator Charles Lindbergh and Senator Gerald Nye speaking on the AFC's behalf, to keep the nation out of the war.

Because of the efforts of America Firsters, Roosevelt continued to act cautiously in 1940 as he moved the United States closer to involvement. The president did not want war, but he believed that most Americans "greatly underestimate the serious implications to our own future," as he confided to William Allen White. In May, Roosevelt created the National Defense Advisory Commission and brought two prominent Republicans, Henry Stimson and Frank Knox, into his cabinet as secretaries of war and the navy, respectively. During the summer, the president traded fifty World War I destroyers to Great Britain in exchange for the right to build military bases on British possessions in the Atlantic, circumventing neutrality laws by using an executive order to complete the deal. In October, a bipartisan vote in Congress approved a large increase in defense spending and instituted the first peacetime draft in American history. "We must be the great arsenal of democracy," FDR declared.

As the war in Europe and the Pacific expanded, the United States was preparing for the 1940 presidential election. The crisis had convinced Roosevelt that he should seek an unprecedented third term. The Republicans nominated Wendell Willkie of Indiana, a former Democrat who supported many New Deal policies. The two parties' platforms differed only slightly. Both pledged aid to the Allies, and both candidates promised not to "send an American boy into the shambles of a European war," as Willkie put it. Willkie's spirited campaign resulted in a closer election than those of 1932 or 1936; nonetheless, Roosevelt won 55 percent of the popular vote.

Having been reelected, Roosevelt now undertook to persuade Congress to increase aid to Britain, whose survival he viewed as key to American security. In January 1941, he delivered one of the most important speeches of his career. Defining "four essential human freedoms"— freedom of speech, freedom of religion, freedom from want, and freedom from fear—Roosevelt cast the war as a noble defense of democratic societies. He then linked the fate of democratic regimes in Western Europe with the new welfare state at home. Sounding a decidedly New Deal note, Roosevelt pledged to end "special privileges for the few" and to preserve "civil liberties for all." Americans, Roosevelt suggested, must continue to democratize their own society while steadfastly supporting Britain. His words inspired people far beyond the shores of the United States: in Africa, India, and Asia. Like President Wilson's speech championing national self-determination at the close of World War I, Roosevelt's "Four Freedoms" speech outlined a liberal international order with appeal well beyond its intended European and American audiences.

Two months later, in March 1941, with Britain no longer able to pay cash for arms, Roosevelt convinced Congress to pass the Lend-Lease Act. The legislation authorized the president to "lease, lend, or otherwise dispose of" arms and equipment to Britain or any other country whose defense was considered vital to the security of the United States. When Hitler abandoned his nonaggression pact with Stalin and invaded the Soviet Union in June 1941, the United States promptly extended lend-lease to the Soviets. The implementation of lend-lease marked the unofficial entrance of the United States into the European war.

Roosevelt underlined his support for the Allied cause by meeting in August 1941 with British prime minister Winston Churchill (who had succeeded Chamberlain in 1940). Their joint press release, which became known as the Atlantic Charter, provided the ideological foundation of the Western cause. Drawing from Wilson's Fourteen Points and Roosevelt's Four Freedoms, the charter called for economic collaboration, national self-determination, and guarantees of political stability after the war to ensure "that all men in all the lands may live out their lives in freedom from fear and want." It would become the basis for a new American-led transatlantic alliance after the war's conclusion.

In the fall of 1941, the reality of U.S. involvement in the war drew closer. By September, Nazi U-boats and the American Navy were exchanging fire in the Atlantic, though the conflict remained largely unknown to the American public (Map 24.1). With isolationists still a potent force, Roosevelt hesitated to declare war and insisted that the United States would defend itself only against a direct attack. But behind the scenes, the president openly discussed American involvement with close advisors and considered war inevitable.

The Attack on Pearl Harbor

The crucial provocation came not from Germany but from Japan. After Japan invaded China in 1937, Roosevelt had denounced "the present reign of terror and international lawlessness" and suggested that aggressors be "quarantined" by peace-loving nations. Despite such rhetoric, the United States refused to intervene when Japanese troops sacked the city of Nanjing, massacred 300,000 Chinese residents, and raped thousands of women.

Without a counterweight, the imperial ambitions of Japan's military officers expanded. In 1940, General Hideki Tojo became war minister. After concluding a formal military alliance with Germany and Italy, Tojo dispatched Japanese troops to occupy the northern section of the French colony of Indochina (present-day Vietnam, Cambodia, and Laos). Tojo's goal, supported by Emperor Hirohito, was to create a "Greater East Asia Co-Prosperity Sphere," run by Japan and stretching from the Korean Peninsula south to Indonesia. Like Germany and Italy, Japan sought to match the overseas empires of Britain, France, Holland, and the United States.

The United States responded to the invasion of Indochina by restricting trade with Japan, especially aviation-grade gasoline and scrap metal. Roosevelt

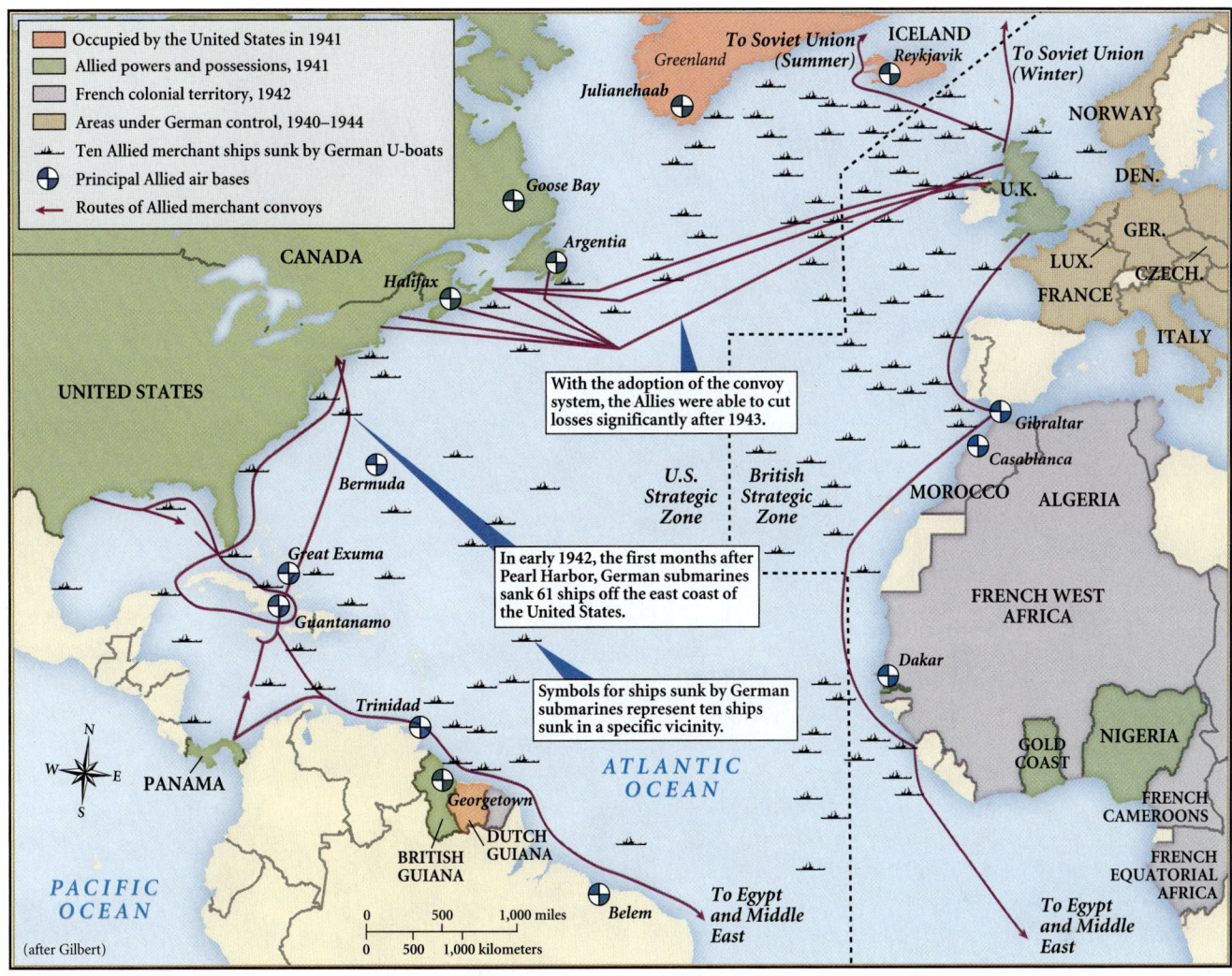

MAP 24.1

World War II in the North Atlantic, 1939–1943

After the start of the war in Europe in September 1939, Germany escalated its submarine attacks on Allied and American merchant shipping in the Atlantic. Continued German advances spurred Congress to pass the Lend-Lease Act in March 1941 and President Roosevelt and Prime Minister Churchill to issue the Atlantic Charter in August. A pivotal factor in the Allied victory in Europe would be countering the U-boat threat in the Atlantic. With the establishment of the convoy system — the protection of merchant vessels with destroyers armed with sonar and anti-submarine depth charges — the Atlantic shipping lanes became safer, allowing the transport of troops and materials to Great Britain and North Africa.

hoped that these economic sanctions would deter Japanese aggression. But in July 1941, Japanese troops occupied the remainder of Indochina. Roosevelt then froze Japanese assets in the United States and instituted an embargo on all trade with Japan, including vital oil shipments that accounted for almost 80 percent of Japanese consumption.

Meanwhile, in October 1941, General Tojo had become prime minister and had accelerated secret preparations for war against the United States. By November,

American military intelligence knew that Japan was planning an attack but did not know where it would occur. Early on Sunday morning, December 7, 1941, Japanese bombers attacked Pearl Harbor in Hawaii, killing more than 2,400 Americans. They destroyed or heavily damaged eight battleships, three cruisers, three destroyers, and almost two hundred airplanes.

Although the assault was devastating, it united the American people. Calling December 7 "a date which will live in infamy," President Roosevelt asked Congress

Pearl Harbor, December 7, 1941

Sailors at the Ford Island Naval Air Station in Pearl Harbor stare in disbelief as a huge explosion rocks the destroyer USS *Shaw*, in drydock across the channel. The Japanese bombed both the American fleet and the nearby military airfields to prevent a counterattack against the aircraft carriers that had launched the strike.   U.S. Naval Historical Foundation.

for a declaration of war against Japan. The Senate voted unanimously for war, and the House concurred by a vote of 388 to 1. The lone dissenter was Jeannette Rankin of Montana, a committed pacifist—she also voted against entry into World War I—and the first female member of Congress. Three days later, Germany and Italy declared war on the United States, which in turn declared war on the Axis powers. The long shadows of two wars, one in Europe and one in Asia, had at long last converged over the United States.

- Why did the United States wait until 1941, after nearly every European nation had fallen to Germany, to enter World War II? What were the sources of American political isolationism?

- Did Roosevelt maneuver the nation into war? Could war have been avoided? At what possible price?

Organizing for Victory

The task of fighting on a global scale brought a dramatic increase in the power of the federal government. Coordinating the changeover from civilian to military production, raising an army, and assembling the necessary workforce required a huge expansion in government authority and bureaucracy. When Congress passed the War Powers Act in December 1941, it gave President Roosevelt unprecedented control over all aspects of the war effort. This act marked the beginning of what historians call the **imperial presidency**: the far-reaching use (and sometimes abuse) of executive authority during the latter part of the twentieth century.

Financing the War

A prominent British economic historian has argued that "the Great Depression was without doubt the most important macroeconomic [large-scale structural] event of the twentieth century; the mobilization of the American economy in World War II is a close second." Defense mobilization ended the Great Depression. Between 1940 and 1945, the annual gross national product doubled, after-tax profits of American businesses nearly doubled, and farm output grew by one-third. Federal spending on war production powered this advance. By late 1943, two-thirds of the economy was directly involved in the war effort (Figure 24.1). The government paid for these military expenditures by raising taxes and borrowing money. The Revenue Act of 1942 expanded the number of people paying income taxes from 3.9 million to 42.6 million. Taxes on personal incomes and business profits paid half the cost of the war. The government borrowed the rest, both from wealthy Americans and from ordinary citizens, who invested in long-term Treasury bonds (war bonds).

Financing and coordinating the war effort required far-reaching cooperation between government and private business. The number of civilians employed by the government increased almost fourfold, to 3.8 million—a far higher rate of growth than that during the New Deal. The powerful War Production Board (WPB) awarded defense contracts, allocated scarce resources—such as rubber, copper, and oil—for military uses, and persuaded businesses to convert to military production. For example, it encouraged Ford and General Motors to build tanks rather than cars by granting generous tax write-offs for re-equipping existing factories and building new ones. In other instances, the board approved "cost-plus" contracts, which guaranteed a profit, and allowed corporations to keep new steel mills, factories, and shipyards after the war. Such government subsidies of defense industries would intensify during the Cold War and continue to this day.

To secure maximum production, the WPB preferred to deal with major corporations rather than with small businesses. The nation's fifty-six largest corporations received three-fourths of the war contracts; the top ten received one-third. The best-known contractor was Henry J. Kaiser. Already highly successful from building roads in California and the Hoover and Grand Coulee dams, Kaiser went from government construction work to navy shipbuilding. At his shipyard in Richmond, California, he revolutionized ship construction by applying Henry Ford's techniques of mass production. To meet wartime production schedules, Kaiser broke the work process down into small, specialized tasks that newly trained workers could do easily. Soon, each of his work crews was building a "Liberty Ship," a large vessel to carry cargo and troops to the war zone, every two weeks. The press dubbed him the "Miracle Man."

Central to Kaiser's success were his close ties to federal agencies. The government financed the great dams that he built during the depression, and the Reconstruction Finance Corporation lent him $300 million to build shipyards and manufacturing plants during the war. Working together in this way, American business and government turned out a prodigious supply of military hardware: 86,000 tanks; 296,000 airplanes; 15 million rifles and machine guns; 64,000 landing craft; and 6,500 cargo ships and naval vessels. The sheer productivity of the U.S. economy, as much as or more than its troops, proved the decisive factor in the war's outcome. The system of allotting contracts, along with

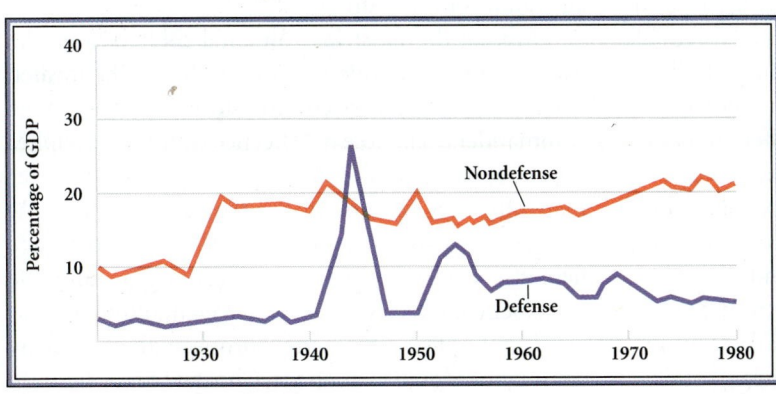

FIGURE 24.1

Government Military and Civilian Spending as a Percentage of GDP, 1920–1980

Government military spending was about 3 percent of the gross domestic product (GDP) in the 1920s and 1930s, but it ballooned to more than 25 percent during World War II, to 13 percent during the Korean War, and to nearly 10 percent during the Vietnam War. Federal government spending for civilian purposes doubled during the New Deal and has remained at about 17 to 20 percent of GDP ever since.

Shipyards in Wartime

The shipyard workers shown here are laying the keel of the *Joseph N. Teal*, a 10,500-ton "Liberty" freighter bound for the war in the Pacific in 1942. Amidst scaffolding, tools, and wires, these workers at Henry J. Kaiser's shipyard in Portland, Oregon, constructed the entire ship in just ten days after the keel was laid, to shatter all previous shipbuilding records. Kaiser was the king of shipbuilding on the West Coast, with massive yards in Portland and the San Francisco Bay Area. In all, Kaiser's workers built nearly 1,500 ships in three years, one-quarter of the total constructed during the war.   © Bettmann/Corbis.

the suspension of antitrust prosecutions during the war, created huge corporate enterprises. By 1945, the largest one hundred American companies produced 70 percent of the nation's industrial output. These same corporations would form the core of what came to be known as the nation's "military-industrial complex" in the Cold War era (see Chapter 25).

Mobilizing the American Fighting Force

The expanding federal bureaucracy also had a human face. To fight the war, the government began to mobilize tens of millions of soldiers, civilians, and workers—coordinated on a scale unprecedented in U.S. history. During World War II, the armed forces of the United States enlisted more than fifteen million men and women. In no other military conflict have so many American citizens, from such different backgrounds, served in the armed services. They came from every region and economic station: black sharecroppers from Alabama; white farmers' sons from the Midwest; the sons and daughters of European, Mexican, and Caribbean immigrants; native men from Navajo and Choctaw reservations and other tribal communities; women from every state in the nation; and Holly-

wood celebrities. From urban, rural, and suburban areas, from working-class and middle-class backgrounds—they all served in the military.

In contrast to its otherwise democratic character, the American army segregated the nearly one million African Americans in uniform. The National Association for the Advancement of Colored People (NAACP) and other civil rights groups reprimanded the government, saying "A Jim Crow army cannot fight for a free world," but the military continued to separate African Americans and assign them menial duties. In contrast, Native Americans and Mexican Americans were never officially segregated; they rubbed elbows with the sons of European immigrants and native-born soldiers from all regions of the country.

Among the most instrumental soldiers were the Native American "code talkers." In the Pacific theater, native Navajo speakers communicated orders to fleet commanders. Japanese intelligence could not decipher the code, based on the Navajo language, which fewer than fifty non-Navajos in the world understood. At the battle of Iwo Jima, for instance—one of the war's fiercest—Navajo code talkers, working around the clock, sent and received more than eight hundred messages without error. In the European theater, army commanders used Comanche, Choctaw, and Cherokee speakers to thwart the Nazis and pass crucial military commands back and forth on the battlefield. No Axis nation ever broke the codes devised by Native Americans.

Approximately 350,000 American women enlisted in the armed services. About 140,000 served in the Women's Army Corps (WAC), and 100,000 served in the navy's Women Accepted for Volunteer Emergency Service (WAVES). One-third of the nation's registered nurses, almost 75,000 overall, volunteered for military duty. In addition, about 1,000 Women's Airforce Service Pilots (WASPs) ferried planes and supplies in noncombat areas. The armed forces limited the duties assigned to women, however. Female officers could not command men, and WACs and WAVES were barred from combat duty, although nurses of both sexes served close to the front lines, risking capture or death. Most of the jobs that women did in the military—clerical work, communications, and health care—resembled women's jobs in civilian life.

These Americans from dramatically different walks of life were viewed by an admiring nation as citizen-soldiers. Dating from the War of Independence, the citizen-soldier ideal held that citizens, especially adult men, owed a military obligation to community and country. Soldiers fought to preserve the nation. While in combat, however, soldiers also fought for more personal, less abstract reasons: for their comrades and their loved ones, and simply to survive and return home.

After visiting troops, the actor Alan Ladd revealed that soldiers preferred movies with "street scenes, normal people on the streets, women who look like their mothers, wives, sweethearts." Why? Because they "bring them near home," Ladd said.

Workers and the War Effort

As millions of working-age citizens joined the military, the nation faced a critical labor shortage. As a result, substantial numbers of women and African Americans joined the industrial workforce, taking jobs unavailable to them prior to the conflict. Unions, benefiting from the demand for labor, negotiated higher wages and improved conditions for America's workers. By 1943, with the economy operating at full capacity, the breadlines and double-digit unemployment of the 1930s were a memory.

Rosie the Riveter | Government officials and corporate recruiters urged women to take jobs in defense industries, creating a new image of working women. "Longing won't bring him back sooner . . . GET A WAR JOB!" one poster urged, while artist Norman Rockwell's famous "Rosie the Riveter" illustration beckoned to women from the cover of the *Saturday Evening Post*. The government directed its publicity at housewives, but many working women gladly

Rosie the Riveter
Women workers install fixtures and assemblies to a tail fuselage section of a B-17 bomber at the Douglas Aircraft Company plant in Long Beach, California. To entice women to become war workers, the War Manpower Commission created the image of "Rosie the Riveter," later immortalized in posters and by a Norman Rockwell illustration on the cover of the *Saturday Evening Post*. A popular 1942 song celebrating Rosie went: "Rosie's got a boyfriend, Charlie/Charlie, he's a marine/Rosie is protecting Charlie/Working overtime on the riveting machine." Even as women joined the industrial workforce in huge numbers (half a million in the aircraft industry alone), they were understood as fulfilling a nurturing, protective role.   Library of Congress.

abandoned low-paying "women's jobs" as domestic servants or secretaries for higher-paying work in the defense industry. Suddenly, the nation's factories were full of women working as airplane riveters, ship welders, and drill-press operators (see Comparing American Voices, "Women in the Wartime Workplace," pp. 764–765). Women made up 36 percent of the labor force in 1945, compared with 24 percent at the beginning of the war. War work did not free women from traditional expectations and limitations, however. Women often faced sexual harassment on the job and usually received lower wages than men did. In shipyards, women with the most seniority and responsibility earned $6.95 a day, whereas the top men made as much as $22.

Wartime work thus remained bittersweet for women. The majority remained clustered in low-wage service jobs. Child care was hard to come by, despite the largest government-sponsored child care program in history. When the men came home from war, Rosie the Riveter was usually out of a job. Government propaganda, which during the war years had badgered women to "take a war job," now reversed course and encouraged them back into the home — where, it was implied, their true calling lay in raising families and standing behind the returning soldiers. But many married women refused, or could not afford, to put on aprons and stay home. Women's participation in the paid labor force rebounded by the late 1940s and continued to rise over the rest of the twentieth century, bringing major changes in family life (see Chapter 26).

Wartime Civil Rights | Among African Americans, a new mood of militancy prevailed during the war. Pointing to parallels between anti-Semitism in Germany and racial discrimination in the United States, black leaders waged the Double V campaign: victories over Nazism abroad and racism at home. "This is a war for freedom. Whose freedom?" the renowned black leader W. E. B. Du Bois asked. If it meant "the freedom of Negroes in the Southern United States," Du Bois answered, "my gun is on my shoulder."

Even before Pearl Harbor, black labor activism was on the rise. In 1940, only 240 of the nation's 100,000 aircraft workers were black, and most of them were janitors. African American leaders demanded that the government require defense contractors to hire more blacks. When Washington took no action, A. Philip Randolph, head of the Brotherhood of Sleeping Car Porters, the largest black labor union in the country, announced plans for a march on Washington in the summer of 1941.

Roosevelt was not a strong supporter of civil rights, but he wanted to avoid public protest and a disruption of the nation's war preparations. So the president made a deal: He issued Executive Order 8802, and in June 1941 Randolph canceled the march. The order prohibited "discrimination in the employment of workers in defense industries or government because of race, creed, color, or national origin" and established the Fair Employment Practices Commission (FEPC). Mary McLeod Bethune called the wartime FEPC "a refreshing shower in a thirsty land." This federal commitment to black employment rights was unprecedented but limited: It did not affect segregation in the armed forces, and the FEPC could not enforce compliance with its orders.

Nevertheless, wartime developments laid the groundwork for the civil rights revolution of the 1960s. The NAACP grew ninefold, to 450,000 members, by 1945. In Chicago, James Farmer helped to found the Congress of Racial Equality (CORE) in 1942, a group that would become known nationwide in the 1960s for its direct-action protests such as sit-ins. The FEPC inspired black organizing against employment discrimination in hundreds of cities and workplaces. This combination of government action and black militancy was the framework within which the civil rights movement advanced on multiple fronts in the postwar years.

Mexican Americans, too, challenged long-standing practices of discrimination and exclusion. Throughout much of the Southwest, it was still common to see signs reading "No Mexicans Allowed," and Mexican American workers were confined to menial, low-paying jobs. There was no single Mexican American counterpart to the NAACP, but several organizations, including the League of United Latin American Citizens (LULAC) and the Congress of Spanish Speaking Peoples, pressed the government and private employers to end anti-Mexican discrimination. Workers themselves, often in Congress of Industrial Organization (CIO) unions such as the Cannery Workers and Shipyard Workers, also led efforts to enforce the equal employment mandate of the FEPC.

Exploitation persisted, however. To meet wartime labor demands, the U.S. government brought tens of thousands of Mexican contract laborers into the United States under the Bracero Program. Paid little and treated poorly, the braceros (who took their name from the Spanish *brazo*, "arm") highlighted the oppressive conditions of farm labor in the United States. After the war, the federal government continued to be a willing participant in labor exploitation, bringing hundreds of thousands of Mexicans into the United States to perform low-wage work in agriculture. Future Mexican Ameri-

Wartime Civil Rights

Fighting fascism abroad while battling racism at home was the approach taken by black communities across the country during World War II. Securing democracy in Europe and Asia while not enjoying it in the United States did not seem just. Jobs were plentiful as the wartime economy hummed along at a fevered pitch. But when employers and unions kept Jim Crow hiring policies in place, African Americans did not hesitate to protest. Here picketers rally for defense jobs outside the Glenn Martin Plant in Omaha, Nebraska, in the early 1940s. Schomburg Center for Research in Black Culture, New York Public Library/Art Resource, NY.

can civil rights leaders Dolores Huerta and Cesar Chavez began to fight this labor system in the 1940s.

Organized Labor   During the war, unions solidified their position as the most powerful national voice on behalf of American workers, an extension of their gains under the New Deal. By 1945, almost 15 million workers belonged to a union, up from 9 million in 1939. Representatives of the major unions made a no-strike pledge for the duration of the war, and Roosevelt rewarded them by creating the National War Labor Board (NWLB), composed of representatives of labor, management, and the public. The NWLB established wages, hours, and working conditions and had the authority to seize manufacturing plants that did not comply.

Despite these arrangements, many Americans felt cheated as consumer prices rose and corporate profits soared. In 1943, John L. Lewis led more than half a million United Mine Workers out on strike, demanding a higher wage increase than that recommended by the NWLB. Congress responded by passing (over Roosevelt's veto) the Smith-Connally Labor Act of 1943, which allowed the president to prohibit strikes in defense industries and forbade political contributions by unions. Congressional hostility would continue to hamper the union movement in the postwar years. Organized labor would emerge from World War II more powerful than at any time in U.S. history. But its business and corporate opponents, too, would emerge from the war with new strength.

Politics in Wartime

In one of his most farsighted speeches—his 1944 State of the Union address—FDR called for a second Bill of Rights, one that would guarantee all Americans access to education and jobs, adequate food and clothing, and decent housing and medical care. Like his Four Freedoms speech, this was a call to extend the New Deal by broadening the rights to individual security and welfare guaranteed by the government. The answer to his call, however, would have to wait for the war's conclusion. Congress created new government benefits only for military veterans, known as GIs (short for "government issue"). The Servicemen's Readjustment Act (1944), an extraordinarily influential program popularly known as the "GI Bill of Rights," provided education, job training, medical care, pensions, and mortgage loans for men and women who had served in the armed forces.

The president's call for social legislation sought to reinvigorate the New Deal political coalition. In the election of 1944, Roosevelt once again headed the Democratic ticket. But party leaders, aware of FDR's health

Women in the Wartime Workplace

During World War II, millions of men served in the armed forces and millions of women worked in war-related industries. A generation later, some of these women workers recounted their wartime experiences to historians in oral interviews.

Evelyn Gotzion

Becoming a Union Activist

Evelyn Gotzion went to work at Rayovac, a battery company in Madison, Wisconsin, in 1935; she retired in 1978. While at Rayovac, Gotzion and her working husband raised three children.

I had all kinds of jobs. [During the war] we had one line, a big line, where you'd work ten hours and you'd stand in one spot or sit in one spot. It got terrible, all day long. So I suggested to my foreman, the general foreman, that we take turns of learning everybody's job and switching every half hour. Well, they [the management] didn't like it, but we were on the side, every once in a while, learning each other's job and learning how to do it, so eventually most all of us got so we could do all the jobs, [of] which there were probably fifteen or twenty on the line. We could do every job so we could go up and down the line and rotate. And then they found out that that was really a pretty good thing to do because it made the people happier. . . .

One day I was the steward, and they wouldn't listen to me. They cut our rates, so I shut off the line, and the boss came up and he said, "What are you doing?" I said, "Well, I have asked everybody that I know why we have gotten a cut in pay and why we're doing exactly the same amount of work as we did. . . . So, anyhow, we wrote up a big grievance and they all signed it and then I called the president of the union and then we had a meeting. . . . At that point the president decided that I should be added to the bargaining committee so that I would go in and argue our case, because I could do it better than any of the rest of them because I knew what it was. . . . We finally got it straightened out, and we got our back pay, too. From then on I was on the bargaining committee all the years that I worked at Rayovac.

Source: Michael E. Stevens and Ellen D. Goldlust, eds., *Women Remember the War, 1941–1945* (Madison: State Historical Society of Wisconsin Press, 1993), 26–29.

Fanny Christina (Tina) Hill

War Work: Social and Racial Mobility

After migrating to California from Texas and working as a domestic servant, Tina Hill, an African American, got a wartime job at North American Aircraft. After time off for a pregnancy in 1945, Hill worked there until 1980.

Most of the men was gone, and . . . most of the women was in my bracket, five or six years younger or older. I was twenty-four. There was a black girl that hired in with me. I went to work the next day, sixty cents an hour. . . . I could see where they made a difference in placing you in certain jobs. They had fifteen or twenty departments, but all the Negroes went to Department 17 because there was nothing but shooting and bucking rivets. You stood on one side of the panel and your partner stood on this side and he would shoot the rivets with a gun and you'd buck them with the bar. That was about the size of it. I just didn't like it . . . went over to the union and they told me what to do. I went back inside and they sent me to another department where you did bench work and I liked that much better. . . .

Some weeks I brought home twenty-six dollars . . . then it gradually went up to thirty dollars [about $420 in 2010]. . . . Whatever you make you're supposed to save some. I was also getting that fifty dollars a month from my husband and that was just saved right away. I was planning on buying a home and a car. . . . My husband came back [from the war, and] . . . looked for a job in the cleaning and pressing place, which was just plentiful. . . . That's why he didn't bother to go out to North American. But what we both weren't thinking about was that they [North American] have better benefits because they did have an insurance plan and a union to back you up. Later he did come to work there, in 1951 or 1952. . . .

When North American called me back [after I left to have a baby,] was I a happy soul! . . . It made me live better. It really did. We always say that Lincoln took the bale off of the Negroes. I think there is a statue up there in Washington,

D.C., where he's lifting something off the Negro. Well, my sister always said—that's why you can't interview her because she's so radical—"Hitler was the one that got us out of the white folks' kitchen."

Source: Excerpted from Sherna B. Gluck, *Rosie the Riveter Revisited* (Boston: G. K. Hall & Co., 1987), 37–42.

Peggy Terry

War: Wider Horizons and Personal Tragedies

Peggy Terry was born in Oklahoma; grew up in Paducah, Kentucky; and worked in defense plants in Kentucky and Michigan before settling in Chicago.

The first work I had after the Depression was at a shell-loading plant in Viola, Kentucky. It is between Paducah and Mayfield. They were large shells: anti-aircraft, incendiaries, and tracers. . . . We made the fabulous sum of thirty-two dollars a week [about $465 in 2010]. To us it was just an absolute miracle. Before that, we made nothing.

You won't believe how incredibly ignorant I was. I knew vaguely that a war had started, but I had no idea what it meant. . . . I was eighteen. My husband was nineteen. We were living day to day. When you are involved in stayin' alive, you don't think about big things like a war. It didn't occur to us that we were making these shells to kill people. It never entered my head. . . . We were just a bunch of hill-billy women laughin' and talkin' . . . .

I worked in building number 11. I pulled a lot of gadgets on a machine. The shell slid under and powder went into it.

Another lever you pulled tamped it down. Then it moved on a conveyer belt to another building where the detonator was dropped in. You did this over and over.

Tetryl was one of the ingredients and it turned us orange. Just as orange as an orange. Our hair was streaked orange. Our hands, our face, our neck just turned orange, even our eyeballs. We never questioned. None of us ever asked, What is this? Is this harmful? . . . The only thing we worried about was other women thinking we had dyed our hair. Back then it was a disgrace if you dyed your hair. . . .

I think of how little we knew of human rights, union rights. We knew Daddy had been a hell-raiser in the mine workers' union, but at that point it hadn't rubbed off on any of us women. Coca-Cola and Dr. Pepper were allowed in every building, but not a drop of water. You could only get a drink of water if you went to the cafeteria, which was about two city blocks away. Of course you couldn't leave your machine long enough to go get a drink. . . .

The war just widened my world. Especially after I came up to Michigan. . . . We made ninety dollars a week [about $1,050 in 2010]. We did some kind of testing for airplane radios. Ohh, I met all those wonderful Polacks. They were the first people I'd ever known that were any different from me. A whole new world just opened up. I learned to drink beer like crazy with 'em. They were all very union-conscious. I learned a lot of things that I didn't even know existed. . . .

My husband was a paratrooper in the war, in the 101st Airborne Division. He made twenty-six drops in France, North Africa, and Germany. . . . Until the war he never drank. He never even smoked. When he came back he was an absolute drunkard. And he used to have the most awful nightmares. He'd get up in the middle of the night and start screaming. I'd just sit for hours and hold him while he just shook. We'd go to the movies, and if they'd have films with a lot of shooting in it, he'd just start to shake and have to get up and leave. He started slapping me around and slapped the kids around. He became a brute.

Source: Studs Terkel, *"The Good War": An Oral History of World War II* (New York: Pantheon, 1984), 102–111.

ANALYZING THE EVIDENCE

- **What common themes appear in the working lives of these three women? For example, how did labor unions affect their conditions of employment?**
- **How did the war change the lives of these women?**
- **These interviews occurred long after the events they describe. How might that long interval have affected the women's accounts of those years?**

problems and anxious to find a middle-of-the-road successor, dropped Vice President Henry Wallace from the ticket. They feared that Wallace's outspoken support for labor, civil rights, and domestic reform would alienate southern Democrats. In his place they chose Senator Harry S. Truman of Missouri. A straight-talking, no-nonsense politician, Truman was a product of the Democratic machine in Kansas City.

The Republicans nominated Governor Thomas E. Dewey of New York. Dewey accepted the general principles of welfare state liberalism domestically and favored internationalism in foreign affairs, and so attracted some of Roosevelt's supporters. But a majority of voters preferred political continuity. Roosevelt received 53.5 percent of the nationwide vote and 60 percent in cities of more than 100,000 people, where labor unions and working-class voters of all backgrounds strongly supported Democratic candidates. The Democratic coalition retained its hold on government power, and the era of Republican political dominance (1896–1932) slipped further into the past.

- **In what ways did World War II contribute to the growth of the federal government? How did it foster what historians now call the military-industrial complex?**

- **What impact did war mobilization have on women, racial minorities, and organized labor?**

Life on the Home Front

The United States escaped the physical devastation that ravaged Europe and East Asia, but the war profoundly changed the country. Americans welcomed wartime prosperity but shuddered when they saw a Western Union boy on his bicycle, fearing that he carried a War Department telegram reporting the death of someone's son, husband, or father. Citizens also grumbled about annoying wartime regulations and rationing but accepted that their lives would be different "for the duration."

"For the Duration"

People on the home front took on wartime responsibilities. They worked on civilian defense committees, recycled old newspapers and scrap material, and served on local rationing and draft boards. About twenty million backyard "victory gardens" produced 40 percent of the nation's vegetables. Various federal agencies encour-

aged these efforts, especially the Office of War Information (OWI), which disseminated news and promoted patriotism. The OWI urged advertising agencies to link their clients' products to the war effort, arguing that patriotic ads would not only sell goods but also "invigorate, instruct and inspire" the citizenry (see Reading American Pictures, "U.S. Political Propaganda on the Home Front during World War II," p. 767).

Popular culture, especially the movies, reinforced connections between the home front and the war effort. Hollywood producers, directors, and actors offered their talents to the War Department. Director Frank Capra created a documentary series titled *Why We Fight* to explain war aims to conscripted soldiers. Movie stars such as John Wayne, Anthony Quinn, and Spencer Tracy portrayed the heroism of American fighting men in numerous films, such as *Guadalcanal Diary* (1943) and *Thirty Seconds over Tokyo* (1945). Demand was so great that many theaters operated around the clock to accommodate defense workers on the swing and night shifts. In this pre-television era, newsreels accompanying the feature films kept the public up-to-date on the war, as did on-the-spot radio broadcasts by Edward R. Murrow and other well-known commentators.

For many Americans, the major inconvenience during the war years was the shortage of consumer goods. Federal agencies subjected almost everything Americans ate, wore, or used to rationing or regulation. The first major scarcity was rubber. The Japanese conquest of Malaysia and Dutch Indonesia cut off 97 percent of America's imports of that essential raw material. To conserve rubber for the war effort, the government rationed tires, so many of the nation's 30 million car owners put their cars up on blocks. As more people walked, they wore out their shoes. In 1944, shoes were rationed to two pairs per person a year, half the prewar usage. By 1943, the government was regulating the amount of meat, butter, sugar, and other foods Americans could buy. Most citizens cooperated with the complicated rationing and coupon system, but at least one-quarter of the population bought items on the black market, especially meat, gasoline, cigarettes, and nylon stockings.

One thing not in short supply was money. Workers earned higher take-home pay, despite wage freezes, than at any point since the 1920s. "Money came easy, and they spent it easy," one worker observed. Much of it was earned as overtime, with shipyards and other manufacturers running operations around the clock. "There were no more weekends or nights. It was just twenty-four hours a day, seven days a week," a California shipyard worker explained.

U.S. Political Propaganda on the Home Front during World War II

In times of war, governments use visual imagery to motivate the public and frame the meaning of the war both at home and abroad. During World War II the U.S. government made every effort to convince the American people to understand and support the war. But what can visual imagery tell us about the nature of World War II? These two posters—produced in the United States during the war—provide some answers. The first is a 1942 lithograph by two artists, Karl Koehler and Victor Ancona, depicting a Nazi officer. The second is a poster of train travelers produced by the Office of Defense Transportation.

Karl Koehler and Victor Ancona, *This is the Enemy*.
Smithsonian American Art Museum, Washington, D.C./Art Resource NY.

U.S. Office of Defense Transportation, *Is Your Trip Necessary?* Picture Research Consultants & Archives.

ANALYZING THE EVIDENCE

- How might these images affect a viewer? What visual cues or elements did the image makers employ to create an impact? List some of these items and compare them across the two images. Is one image more convincing than the other? Why?

- What kind of message does each image convey? Are these messages consistent with each other? Can you combine the messages into a larger statement explaining the U.S. perspective on fighting the war?

767

A Family Effort

After migrating from the Midwest to Portland, Oregon, fifteen members of the family of John R. Brauckmiller (sixth from left) found jobs at Henry Kaiser's Swan Island shipyard. From 1943 to 1945, the shipyard turned out 152 T-2 Tankers, mostly for use by the U.S. Navy to carry fuel oil. A local newspaper pronounced the Brauckmillers as "the shipbuildingest family in America," and because of the importance of shipbuilding to the war effort, *Life* magazine featured the family in its issue of August 16, 1943.   Ralph Vincent, *The Journal*, Portland, OR.

Migration and the Wartime City

The war determined where people lived. When husbands entered the armed services, their families often followed them to training bases or points of debarkation. Civilians moved to take high-paying defense jobs. About 15 million Americans changed residences during the war years, half of them moving to another state. One of them was Peggy Terry, who grew up in Paducah, Kentucky; worked in a shell-loading plant in nearby Viola; and then moved to a defense plant in Michigan. There, she recalled, "I met all those wonderful Polacks [Polish Americans]. They were the first people I'd ever

known that were any different from me. A whole new world just opened up."

As the center of defense production for the Pacific war, California experienced the largest share of wartime migration. The state welcomed nearly three million new residents and grew by 53 percent during the war. "The Second Gold Rush Hits the West," announced the *San Francisco Chronicle* in 1943. One-tenth of all federal dollars flowed into California, and the state's factories turned out one-sixth of all war materials. People went where the defense jobs were: to Los Angeles, San Diego, and cities around San Francisco Bay. Some towns grew practically overnight; within two years of the opening

Zoot-Suit Youth in Los Angeles
During a four-day riot in June 1943, servicemen in Los Angeles attacked young Latino men wearing distinctive zoot suits, which were widely viewed as emblems of gang membership and a delinquent youth culture. The police response was to arrest scores of zoot-suiters. Here, a group of handcuffed young Latino men is about to board a Los Angeles County Sheriff's bus to make a court appearance. Note the wide-legged pants that taper at the ankle, a hallmark of the zoot suit. The so-called "zoot-suit riot" was evidence of cracks in wartime unity on the home front.   Library of Congress.

of the huge Kaiser Corporation shipyard in Richmond, California, the town's population had quadrupled. Other industrial states—notably New York, Illinois, Michigan, and Ohio—also attracted both federal dollars and migrants on a large scale.

The growth of war industries accelerated patterns of rural-urban migration. Cities across the country grew by leaps and bounds, as factories, shipyards, and other defense work drew millions of citizens from small towns and rural areas. This newfound mobility, coupled with people's distance from their hometowns, loosened the authority of traditional institutions and made wartime cities vibrant and exciting. Around-the-clock work shifts kept people on the streets night and day, and jazz clubs, dance halls, and nightclubs proliferated, fed by the ready cash of war workers.

Racial Conflict | Migration and the relaxing of social boundaries meant that people of different racial and ethnic groups rubbed elbows in the booming cities. More than one million African Americans left the rural South for California, Illinois, Michigan, Ohio, and Pennsylvania—a continuation of the Great Migration earlier in the century (see Chapter 21). As blacks and whites competed for jobs and housing, racial conflicts broke out in more than a hundred cities during 1943. The worst violence took place in Detroit. In June 1943, a riot incited by southern-born whites and

Polish Americans against African Americans left thirty-four people dead and hundreds injured.

Racial conflict struck the West as well. In Los Angeles, male Hispanic teenagers formed pachuco (youth) gangs. Many dressed in "zoot suits"—broad-brimmed felt hats, thigh-length jackets with wide lapels and padded shoulders, pegged trousers, and clunky shoes; they wore their long hair slicked down and carried pocket knives on gold chains. Pachucas (young women) favored long coats, huarache sandals, and pompadour hairdos. Other working-class teenagers in Los Angeles and elsewhere took up the zoot-suit style to underline their rejection of middle-class values. To many adults, the zoot suit symbolized juvenile delinquency. Rumors circulating in Los Angeles in July 1943 that a pachuco gang had beaten an Anglo (white) sailor set off a four-day riot. Anglo servicemen roamed through Mexican American neighborhoods and attacked zoot-suiters, taking special pleasure in slashing their pegged pants.

Gay and Lesbian Community Formation | Wartime migration to urban centers created new opportunities for gay men and women to establish communities. Widespread hostility toward and suspicion of gays and lesbians kept the majority of them silent and their sexuality hidden. Religious morality and social convention prevented the recognition of homosexuality as normal and natural.

New Urban Communities

Folk singer Pete Seeger performs at the opening of the Washington, D.C., labor canteen in 1944, sponsored by the Congress of Industrial Organizations (CIO). Wartime migration brought people from across the country to centers of industry and military operations. Migration opened new possibilities for urban communities. African American neighborhoods grew dramatically; urban populations grew younger and more mobile; and gay and lesbian communities began to flourish and become more visible. The Granger Collection, New York.

During the war, however, cities such as New York, San Francisco, Los Angeles, Chicago, and even Kansas City, Buffalo, and Dallas developed vibrant gay neighborhoods, sustained in part by a sudden influx of migrants and the relatively open wartime atmosphere. These communities became centers of the gay rights movement of the 1960s and 1970s (see Chapter 29).

The military tried to screen out homosexuals but had little success. Once in the services, homosexuals found opportunities to participate in a gay culture often more extensive than that in civilian life. In the last twenty years, historians have documented extensive communities of gay and lesbian soldiers in the World War II military. Some "came out under fire," as one historian put it, but most kept their sexuality hidden from authorities, because army officers, doctors, and psychiatrists treated homosexuality as a psychological disorder that was grounds for dishonorable discharge.

Japanese Removal

Unlike World War I, which evoked widespread harassment of German Americans, World War II produced relatively little condemnation of Euro-Americans. Fed-

eral officials held about 5,000 potentially dangerous German and Italian aliens during the war. Despite the presence of small but vocal groups of Nazi sympathizers and Mussolini supporters, German American and Italian American communities were largely left in peace during the war. The relocation and temporary imprisonment of Japanese immigrants and Japanese American citizens was a glaring exception to this otherwise tolerant record on the home front. Immediately after the attack on Pearl Harbor, the West Coast remained calm. Then, as residents began to fear spies, sabotage, and further attacks, California's long history of racial animosity toward Asian immigrants surfaced. Local politicians and newspapers whipped up hysteria against Japanese Americans, who numbered only about 112,000, had no political power, and lived primarily in small enclaves in the Pacific coast states.

Early in 1942, President Roosevelt responded to anti-Japanese fears by issuing Executive Order 9066, which gave the War Department the authority to force Japanese Americans from their West Coast homes and hold them in relocation camps for the rest of the war. Although there was no disloyal or seditious activity among the evacuees, few public leaders opposed the

Behind Barbed Wire

As part of the forced relocation of 112,000 Japanese Americans, Los Angeles photographer Toyo Miyatake and his family were sent to Manzanar, a camp in the California desert east of the Sierra Nevada. Miyatake secretly began shooting photographs of the camp with a handmade camera. Eventually, Miyatake received permission from the authorities to document life in the camp—its births, weddings, deaths, and high school graduations. To communicate the injustice of internment, he also took staged photographs, such as this image of three young boys behind barbed wire with a watchtower in the distance. For Miyatake, the image gave new meaning to the phrase "prisoners of war." Toyo Miyatake.

plan. "A Jap's a Jap," snapped General John DeWitt, the officer charged with defense of the West Coast. "It makes no difference whether he is an American citizen or not."

The relocation plan shocked Japanese Americans, more than two-thirds of whom were Nisei; that is, their parents were immigrants, but they were native-born American citizens. Army officials gave families only a few days to dispose of their property. Businesses that had taken a lifetime to build were liquidated overnight (see Voices from Abroad, "Monica Itoi Sone: Japanese Relocation," p. 772). The War Relocation Authority moved

the prisoners to hastily built camps in desolate areas in California, Arizona, Utah, Colorado, Wyoming, Idaho, and Arkansas (Map 24.2). Ironically, the Japanese Americans who made up one-third of the population of Hawaii, and presumably posed a greater threat because of their numbers and proximity to Japan, were not imprisoned. They provided much of the unskilled labor in the island territory, and the Hawaiian economy could not have functioned without them.

Cracks soon appeared in the relocation policy. A labor shortage in farming led the government to furlough

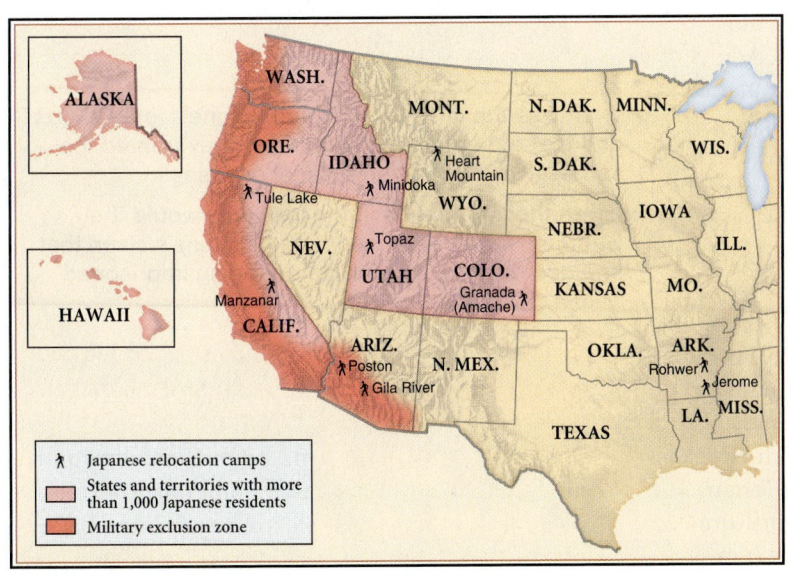

MAP 24.2

Japanese Relocation Camps

In 1942, the government ordered 112,000 Japanese Americans living on the West Coast into internment camps in the nation's interior because of their supposed threat to public safety. Some of the camps were as far away as Arkansas. The federal government rescinded the mass evacuation order in December 1944, but 44,000 people still remained in the camps when the war ended in August 1945.

Monica Itoi Sone
Japanese Relocation

As Monica Itoi Sone discovered, her legal status as an American citizen did not keep her from being treated like an unwelcome foreigner. Her autobiography, *Nisei Daughter* (1953), tells the story of the relocation and internment of Japanese Americans during World War II. In 1942 Sone was a young woman who had been born and raised in Seattle; she saw herself as an American. In this selection, Sone ponders the question of national identity as she describes the Itoi family's forced evacuation by the U.S. Army. Her family spent the entire war in an internment camp in Idaho, but in 1943 Sone was allowed to attend college in Indiana.

We felt fortunate to be assigned to a room at the end of the barracks because we had just one neighbor to worry about. The partition wall separating the rooms was only seven feet high with an opening of four feet at the top, so at night, Mrs. Funai next door could tell when Sumi was still sitting up in bed in the dark, putting her hair up. "Mah, Sumi-chan," Mrs. Funai would say through the plank wall, "are you curling your hair tonight again? Do you put it up every night?" Sumi would put her hands on her hips and glare defiantly at the wall.

The block monitor, an impressive Nisei who looked like a star tackle with his crouching walk, came around the first night to tell us that we must all be inside our room by nine o'clock every night. At ten o'clock, he rapped at the door again, yelling, "Lights out!" and Mother rushed to turn the light off not a second later.

Throughout the barracks, there were a medley of creaking cots, whimpering infants and explosive night coughs. Our attention was riveted on the intense little wood stove which glowed so violently I feared it would melt right down to the floor. We soon learned that this condition lasted for only a short time, after which it suddenly turned into a deep freeze. Henry and Father took turns at the stove to produce the harrowing blast which all but singed our army blankets, but did not penetrate through them. As it grew quieter in the barracks, I could hear the light patter of rain. Soon I felt the "splat! splat!" of raindrops digging holes into my face. The dampness on my pillow spread like a mortal bleeding, and I finally had to get out and haul my cot toward the center of the room. In a short while Henry was up. "I've got multiple leaks, too. Have to complain to the landlord first thing in the morning."

All through the night I heard people getting up, dragging cots around. I stared at our little window, unable to sleep. I was glad Mother had put up a makeshift curtain on the window for I noticed a powerful beam of light sweeping across it every few seconds. The lights came from high towers placed around the camp where guards with Tommy guns kept a twenty-four hour vigil. I remembered the wire fence encircling us, and a knot of anger tightened in my breast. What was I doing behind a fence like a criminal? If there were accusations to be made, why hadn't I been given a fair trial? Maybe I wasn't considered an American anymore. My citizenship wasn't real, after all. Then what was I?

I was certainly not a citizen of Japan as my parents were. On second thought, even Father and Mother were more alien residents of the United States than Japanese nationals for they had little tie with their mother country. In their twenty-five years in America, they had worked and paid their taxes to their adopted government as any other citizen.

Of one thing I was sure. The wire fence was real. I no longer had the right to walk out of it. It was because I had Japanese ancestors. It was also because some people had little faith in the ideas and ideals of democracy. They said that after all these were but words and could not possibly insure loyalty. New laws and camps were surer devices. I finally buried my face in my pillow to wipe out burning thoughts and snatch what sleep I could.

Source: Monica Itoi Sone, *Nisei Daughter* (Boston: Little, Brown & Co., 1953), 176–178.

ANALYZING THE EVIDENCE

- What was the difference between Sone's legal status and that of her parents? Why were they treated the same, given their different legal statuses?

- Given the information in the text, how would the Supreme Court have responded to Sone's claim that she deserved a "fair trial" before being imprisoned "like a criminal"?

seasonal agricultural workers from the camps as early as 1942. About 4,300 students were allowed to attend colleges outside the West Coast military zone. Another route out of the camps was enlistment in the armed services. The 442nd Regimental Combat Team, a unit composed almost entirely of Nisei volunteers, served with distinction in Europe.

Gordon Hirabayashi was among the Nisei who actively resisted incarceration. A student at the University of Washington, Hirabayashi was a religious pacifist who had registered with his draft board as a conscientious objector. He refused to report for evacuation and turned himself in to the FBI. "I wanted to uphold the principles of the Constitution," Hirabayashi later stated, "and the curfew and evacuation orders which singled out a group on the basis of ethnicity violated them." Tried and convicted in 1942, he appealed his case to the Supreme Court in *Hirabayashi v. United States* (1943). In that case and in *Korematsu v. United States* (1944), the Court allowed the removal of Japanese Americans from the West Coast on the basis of "military necessity" but avoided ruling on the constitutionality of the incarceration program. The Court's refusal to rule directly on the relocation program underscored the fragility of civil liberties in wartime. Congress issued a public apology in 1988 and awarded $20,000 to each of the eighty thousand surviving Japanese Americans who had once been internees.

- What was the impact of World War II on the everyday life of the majority of Americans?

- How do you explain the decision to temporarily hold virtually all Americans of Japanese birth or ancestry?

Fighting and Winning the War

World War II was a war for control of the world. Had the Axis powers triumphed, Germany would have dominated, either directly or indirectly, all of Europe and much of Africa and the Middle East; Japan would have controlled most of East and Southeast Asia. To prevent this outcome, which would have crippled democracy in Europe and restricted American power to the Western Hemisphere, the Roosevelt administration took the United States to war. American intervention, the extraordinary endurance of Britain, and the profound civilian and military sacrifices of the Soviet Union decided the outcome of the conflict and shaped the character of the postwar world.

Wartime Aims and Tensions

Great Britain, the United States, and the Soviet Union were the key actors in the Allied coalition. China, France, and other nations played crucial but smaller roles. The leaders who came to be known as the Big Three — President Franklin Roosevelt, Prime Minister Winston Churchill of Great Britain, and Premier Joseph Stalin of the Soviet Union — set military strategy. However, Stalin was not a party to the Atlantic Charter, which Churchill and Roosevelt had signed in August 1941, and disagreed fundamentally with some of its precepts, such as a capitalist-run international trading system. Another major disagreement among the Allies related to military strategy and timing. The Big Three made defeating Germany (rather than Japan) the top military priority, but differed over how best to do it. In 1941, a massive German force had invaded the Soviet Union and advanced to the outskirts of Leningrad, Moscow, and Stalingrad before being halted in early 1942 by hard-pressed Russian troops. To relieve pressure on the Soviet Army, Stalin wanted the British and Americans to open a second front with a major invasion of Germany through France.

Roosevelt informally assured Stalin that the Allies would comply in 1942, but the British opposed an early invasion, and American war production was not yet sufficient to support it. For eighteen months, Stalin's pleas went unanswered, and the Soviet Union bore the brunt of the fighting — in the 1943 Battle of Kursk alone, the Soviet Army suffered 860,000 casualties, several times what the Allies would suffer for the first two months of the European campaign after D-Day. Then, at a conference of the Big Three in Tehran, Iran, in November 1943, Churchill and Roosevelt agreed to open a second front in France within six months in return for Stalin's promise to join the fight against Japan. Both sides adhered to this agreement, but the long delay angered Stalin, who became increasingly suspicious of American and British intentions.

The War in Europe

Throughout 1942, the Allies suffered one defeat after another. German armies pushed deep into Soviet territory, advancing through the wheat fields of the Ukraine and the rich oil fields of the Caucasus. Simultaneously, German forces began an offensive in North Africa aimed at seizing the Suez Canal. In the Atlantic,

U-boats relentlessly devastated American convoys carrying oil and other vital supplies to Britain and the Soviet Union.

Over the winter of 1942–1943, however, the tide began to turn in favor of the Allies. In the epic Battle of Stalingrad, Soviet forces not only decisively halted the German advance, but allowed the Russian army to push westward (Map 24.3). By early 1944, Stalin's troops had driven the German army out of the Soviet Union. Meanwhile, as Churchill's temporary substitute for a second front in France, the Allies launched a major counteroffensive in North Africa. Between November 1942 and May 1943, Allied troops under the leadership of General

Dwight D. Eisenhower and General George S. Patton defeated the German Afrika Korps, led by General Erwin Rommel.

From Africa, the Allied command followed Churchill's strategy of attacking the Axis through its "soft underbelly": Sicily and the Italian peninsula. Faced with an Allied invasion, the Italian king ousted Benito Mussolini's fascist regime in July 1943. But German troops, which far outmatched the Allies in skill and organization, took control of Italy and strenuously resisted the Allied invasion. American and British divisions took Rome only in June 1944 and were still fighting German forces in northern Italy when the European war ended

MAP 24.3

World War II in Europe, 1941–1943

Hitler's Germany reached its greatest extent in 1942, by which time Nazi forces had occupied Norway, France, North Africa, central Europe, and much of western Russia. The tide of battle turned in late 1942 when the German advance stalled at Leningrad and Stalingrad. By early 1943, the Soviet Army had launched a massive counterattack at Stalingrad, and Allied forces had driven the Germans from North Africa and launched an invasion of Sicily and the Italian mainland.

in May 1945 (Map 24.4). Churchill's southern strategy proved a time-consuming and costly mistake.

D-Day | The long-promised invasion of France came on D-Day, June 6, 1944. That morning, the largest armada ever assembled moved across the English Channel under the command of General Eisenhower. When American, British, and Canadian soldiers hit the beaches of Normandy, they suffered terrible casualties but secured a beachhead. Over the next few days, more than 1.5 million soldiers and thousands of tons of military supplies and equipment flowed into France. Much to the Allies' advantage, they never faced more than one-

third of Hitler's Wehrmacht (armed forces), because the Soviet Union continued to hold down the Germans on the eastern front. In August, Allied troops liberated Paris; by September, they had driven the Germans out of most of France and Belgium. Meanwhile, long-range Allied bombers attacked German cities such as Hamburg and Dresden as well as military and industrial targets. The air campaign killed some 305,000 civilians and soldiers, and injured another 780,000 — a grisly reminder of the war's human brutality.

The Germans were not yet ready to give up, however. In December 1944, they mounted a final offensive in Belgium, the so-called Battle of the Bulge, before

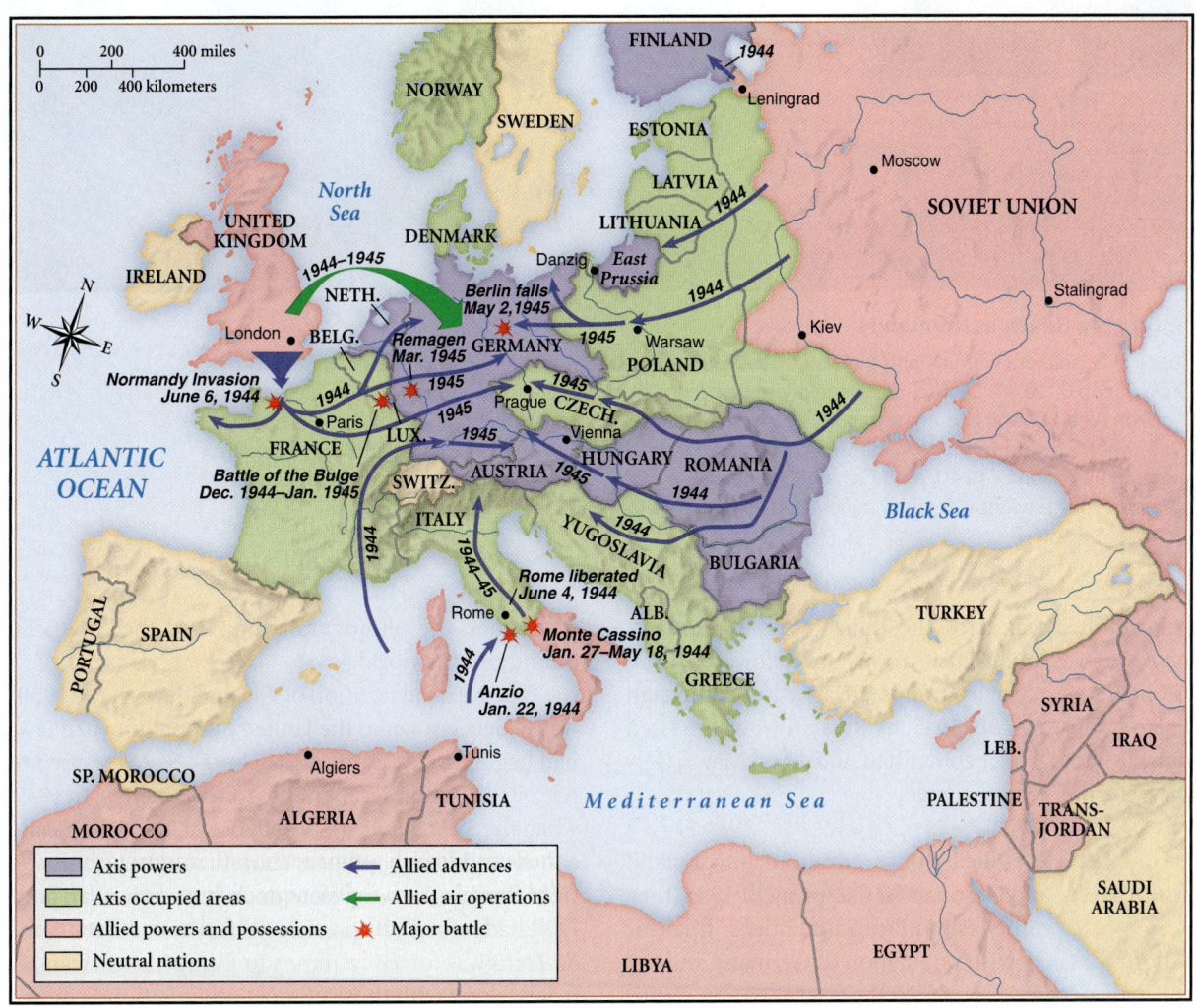

MAP 24.4

World War II in Europe, 1944–1945

By the end of 1943, the Russian Army had nearly pushed the Germans out of the Soviet Union, and by June 1944, when the British and Americans finally invaded France, the Russians had liberated eastern Poland and most of southeastern Europe. By the end of 1944, British and American forces were ready to invade Germany from the west, and the Russians were poised to do the same from the east. Germany surrendered on May 7, 1945.

Hitting the Beach at Normandy

These U.S. soldiers were among the 156,000 Allied troops who stormed the beaches of Normandy on D-Day, June 6, 1944: On that day alone, more than 10,000 were killed or wounded. Within a month, 1 million Allied troops had come ashore. Most Americans learned of the invasion at 3:30 A.M. Eastern Time, when Edward R. Murrow, the well-known radio journalist whose reports from war-torn London had gripped the nation in 1940, read General Eisenhower's statement to the troops. "The eyes of the world are upon you," Eisenhower told the men as they prepared to invade the European mainland.   Library of Congress.

being pushed back across the Rhine River into Germany. As American and British troops drove toward Berlin from the west, Soviet troops advanced east through Poland. On April 30, 1945, as Russian troops massed outside Berlin, Hitler committed suicide; on May 7, Germany formally surrendered.

The Holocaust As Allied troops advanced into Poland and Germany in the spring of 1945, they came face-to-face with Hitler's "final solution" for the Jewish population of Germany and the German-occupied countries: the extermination camps in which 6 million Jews had been put to death, along with another 6 million Poles, Slavs, Gypsies, homosexuals, and others deemed "undesirables." Photographs of the Nazi death camps at Buchenwald, Dachau, and Auschwitz showed bodies stacked like cordwood and survivors so emaciated that they were barely alive. Quickly published in *Life* and other mass-circulation

magazines, the photographs horrified the American public and the world.

The Nazi persecution of German Jews in the 1930s was widely known in the United States. But when Jews had begun to flee Europe, the United States refused to relax its strict immigration laws to take them in. In 1939, when the SS *St. Louis*, a German ocean liner with nearly a thousand Jewish refugees aboard, sought permission from President Roosevelt to dock at an American port, FDR had refused. Its passengers' futures uncertain, the *St. Louis* was forced to return to Europe. American officials, along with those of most other nations, continued this exclusionist policy during World War II as the Nazi regime extended its control over millions of Eastern European Jews.

Among the various factors that inhibited American action, the most important was widespread anti-Semitism: in the State Department, Christian churches, and the public at large. The legacy of the immigration

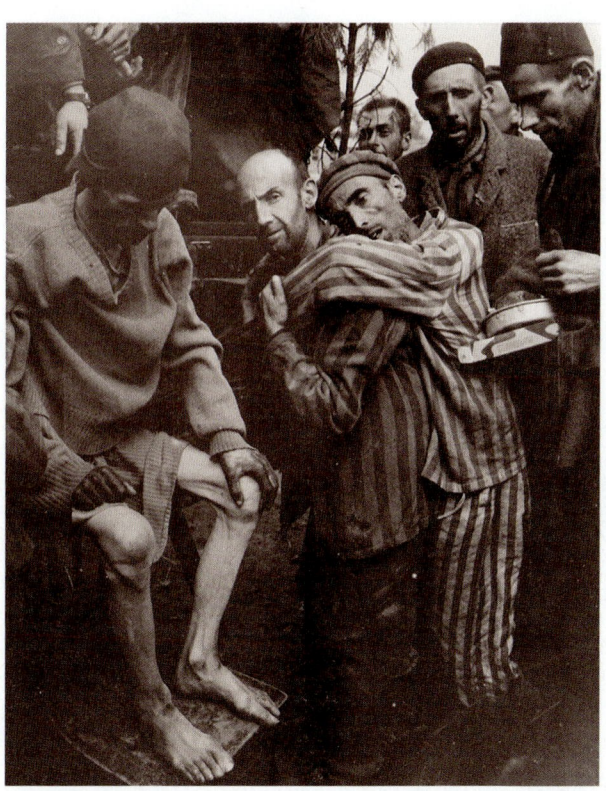

The Living Dead

When Allied troops advanced into Germany in the spring of 1945, they discovered the existence of what had long been rumored—concentration camps, Adolf Hitler's "final solution" for the Jews of Nazi-dominated Europe. In this picture from the Wöbbelin concentration camp—liberated by the 82nd Airborne Division and 8th Infantry Division of the U.S. Army—emaciated inmates are being taken to a hospital. In the days before the Allied troops reached the camp, one thousand of the five thousand prisoners had been allowed to starve to death. National Archives.

restriction legislation of the 1920s and the isolationist attitudes of the 1930s also discouraged policymakers from assuming responsibility for the fate of the refugees. Taking a narrow view of the national interest, the State Department allowed only 21,000 Jewish refugees to enter the United States during the war. But the War Refugee Board, which President Roosevelt established in 1944 at the behest of Secretary of the Treasury Henry Morgenthau, helped move 200,000 European Jews to safe havens in other countries.

The War in the Pacific

Winning the war against Japan was every bit as arduous as waging the campaign against Germany. After crippling the American battle fleet at Pearl Harbor, the Japanese quickly expanded into the South Pacific, with seaborne invasions of Hong Kong, Wake Island, and Guam. Japanese forces then advanced into Southeast Asia, conquering the Solomon Islands, Burma, and Malaya and threatening Australia and India. By May 1942, they had forced the surrender of U.S. forces in the Philippine Islands and, in the Bataan "death march," caused the deaths of 10,000 American prisoners of war.

At that dire moment, American naval forces scored two crucial victories. These were possible because the attack on Pearl Harbor had crippled American battleships but left all aircraft carriers unscathed. In the Battle of the Coral Sea, off southern New Guinea in May 1942, they halted the Japanese offensive against Australia. Then, in June, at the Battle of Midway Island, the American navy inflicted serious damage on the Japanese fleet. In both battles, dive-bombers launched from American aircraft carriers provided the margin of victory. The U.S. military command, led by General Douglas MacArthur and Admiral Chester W. Nimitz, now took the offensive in the Pacific (Map 24.5). For the next eighteen months, American forces advanced slowly toward Japan, taking one island after another in the face of determined Japanese resistance. In October 1944, MacArthur and Nimitz began the reconquest of the Philippines by winning the Battle of Leyte Gulf, a massive naval encounter in which the Japanese lost practically their entire fleet (Map 24.6).

By early 1945, victory over Japan was in sight. Japanese military forces had suffered devastating losses, and American bombing of the Japanese homeland had killed 330,000 civilians and crippled the nation's economy. The bloodletting on both sides was horrendous. On the small islands of Iwo Jima and Okinawa, tens of thousands of Japanese soldiers fought to the death, killing 13,000 U.S. Marines and wounding 46,000 more.

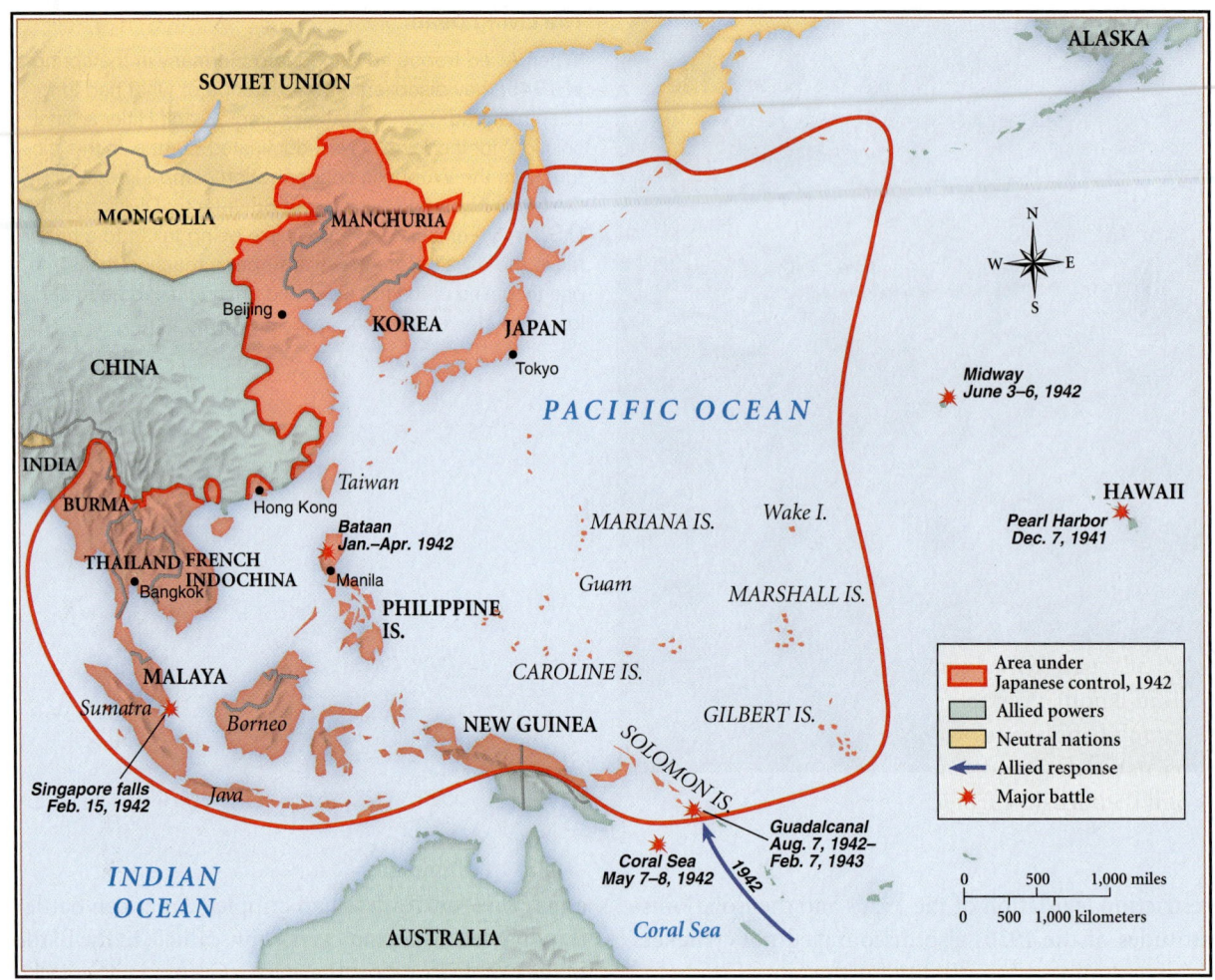

MAP 24.5

World War II in the Pacific, 1941–1942

After the attacks on Pearl Harbor in December 1941, the Japanese rapidly extended their domination in the Pacific. The Japanese flag soon flew as far east as the Marshall and Gilbert islands and as far south as the Solomon Islands and parts of New Guinea. Japan also controlled the Philippines, much of Southeast Asia, and parts of China, including Hong Kong. By mid-1942, American naval victories at the Coral Sea and Midway stopped further Japanese expansion.

Desperate to halt the American advance and short on ammunition, Japanese pilots flew suicidal kamikaze missions, crashing their bomb-laden planes into American ships.

Among the grim realities of war in the Pacific was the conflict's racial overtones. The long tradition of anti-Asian sentiment in the United States was reawakened by the attack on Pearl Harbor. In the eyes of many Americans, the Japanese were "yellow monkeys," an inferior race whose humanity deserved minimal respect. Racism was evident among the Japanese as well. Their brutal attacks on China (including the rape of Nanjing), their forcing of Korean "comfort women" to have sex with soldiers, and their treatment of American prisoners in the Philippines flowed from their own sense of racial superiority. Anti-Japanese attitudes in the United States would subside in the 1950s as the island nation became a trusted ally. But racism would again play a major role in the U.S. war in Vietnam in the 1960s.

As the American Navy advanced on Japan in the late winter of 1945, President Roosevelt returned to the United States from a meeting of the Big Three at Yalta, a resort in southern Ukraine on the Black Sea. The sixty-three-year-old president was a sick man, visibly exhausted by his 14,000-mile trip and suffering from heart failure and high blood pressure. On April 12, 1945,

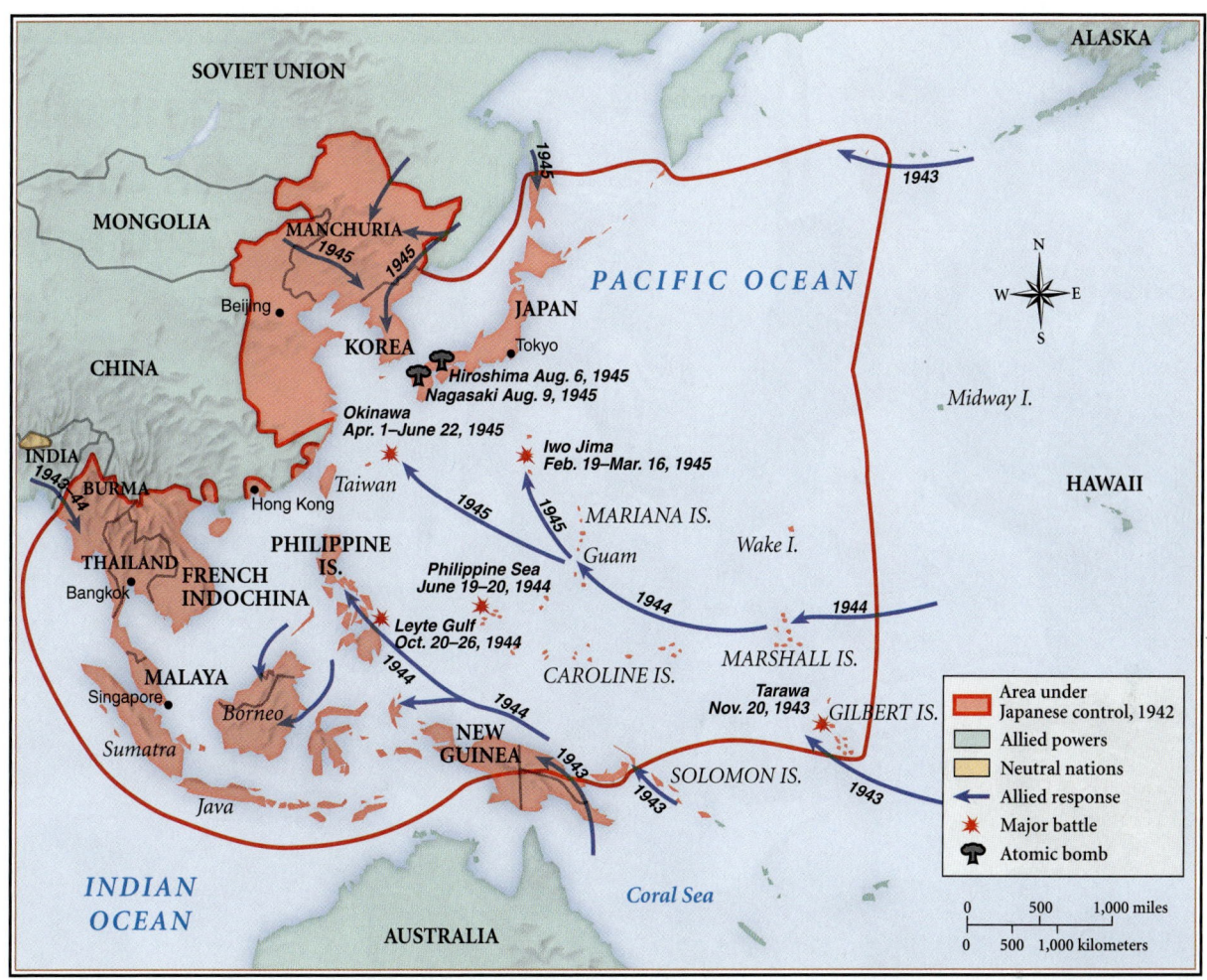

MAP 24.6

World War II in the Pacific, 1943–1945

Allied forces retook the islands of the central Pacific in 1943 and 1944 and ousted the Japanese from the Philippines early in 1945. Carrier-launched planes had started bombing Japan itself in 1942, but the capture of these islands gave U.S. bombers more bases from which to strike Japanese targets. As the Soviet Army invaded Japanese-occupied Manchuria in August 1945, U.S. planes took off from one of the newly captured Mariana Islands to drop the atomic bombs on Hiroshima and Nagasaki. The Japanese offered to surrender on August 10.

during a short visit to his vacation home in Warm Springs, Georgia, Roosevelt suffered a cerebral hemorrhage and died.

The Manhattan Project When Harry Truman assumed the presidency, he learned for the first time about the top-secret Manhattan Project, which was on the verge of testing a new weapon: the atomic bomb. By the 1930s, building on the earlier work of European physicists, scientists theorized that the fission (breaking apart of the nucleus) of highly processed uranium atoms would unleash tre-

mendous amounts of energy. Working at the University of Chicago in December 1942, Enrico Fermi and Leo Szilard, refugees from fascist Italy and Nazi Germany, produced the first controlled atomic chain reaction. With the aid of German-born refugee Albert Einstein, the greatest theorist of modern physics and a scholar at Princeton, they persuaded Franklin Roosevelt to develop an atomic weapon, warning that German scientists were also working on such nuclear reactions.

The Manhattan Project cost $2 billion, employed 120,000 people, and involved the construction of thirty-seven installations in nineteen states—with all of its

The Big Three at Yalta

With victory in Europe at hand, Roosevelt journeyed in February 1945 to Yalta, on the Black Sea, and met for what would be the final time with Churchill and Stalin. The leaders discussed the important and controversial issues of the treatment of Germany, the status of Poland, the creation of the United Nations, and Russian entry into the war against Japan. The Yalta agreements mirrored a new balance of power and set the stage for the Cold War.   Franklin D. Roosevelt Library.

activity hidden from Congress, the American people, and even Vice President Truman. Directed by General Leslie Graves and scientist J. Robert Oppenheimer, the nation's top physicists assembled the first bomb in Los Alamos, New Mexico, and successfully tested it on July 16, 1945. Overwhelmed by its frightening power, as he witnessed the first mushroom cloud, Oppenheimer recalled the words from the *Bhagavad Gita*, one of the great texts of Hindu scripture: "I am become Death, the Destroyer of Worlds."

Three weeks later, President Truman ordered the dropping of atomic bombs on two Japanese cities: Hiroshima on August 6 and Nagasaki on August 9. Why Truman gave this order, and what its implications were,

have long been the subject of scholarly and popular debate. The principal reason was straightforward: Truman and his American advisors, including Secretary of War Henry Stimson and Army Chief of Staff General George Marshall, believed that Japan's military leaders would never surrender unless their country was utterly devastated. Moreover, at the Potsdam Conference in July, the Allies had agreed that only the "unconditional surrender" of Japan was acceptable—the same terms under which Germany and Italy had been defeated. To win such a surrender, it looked as if an invasion of Japan itself would be necessary. Stimson and Marshall told Truman that an invasion of mainland Japan would produce between half a million and a million Allied casualties.

Hiroshima, March 1946

Though the atomic bomb had been dropped on the port city of Hiroshima six months previous to this photo being taken, the devastation is still apparent. The U.S. Army report on the bombing described the immediate effects of the blast: "At 8:15 A.M., the bomb exploded with a blinding flash in the sky, and a great rush of air and a loud rumble of noise extended for many miles around the city; the first blast was soon followed by the sounds of falling buildings and of growing fires, and a great cloud of dust and smoke began to cast a pall of darkness over the city." The only buildings not leveled were those with concrete reinforcement, meant to withstand earthquakes. The human toll of this weapon was unprecedented: Of the estimated population of 350,000, 100,000 were likely killed by the explosion, and many tens of thousands more died slowly of the effects of radiation poisoning. U.S. Air Force.

Before giving the order to drop the atomic bomb, Truman considered other options. His military advisors rejected the most obvious alternative: a nonlethal demonstration of the bomb's awesome power, on a remote island in the Pacific, for instance. If such a demonstration failed—not out of the question, since the bomb had been tested only once—it would embolden Japan further. A detailed advance warning designed to scare Japan into surrender was also rejected as unlikely to succeed. Given the tenacity with which Japan had fought in the Pacific, the Americans simply believed that nothing short of massive devastation or a successful invasion would lead Japan's military leadership to surrender. After all, the deaths of more than 100,000 Japanese civilians in the U.S. fire-bombing of Tokyo and other cities in the spring of 1945 had brought Japan no closer to surrender.

Two final considerations were not lost on Truman's inner circle. The first was Stalin and the Soviet Union.

At Potsdam, Truman had hoped to surprise Stalin with news of "a new weapon of unusual, destructive force" (Truman kept the nature of this weapon secret). However, Stalin's spy network had already informed him of the bomb's successful test, and he showed no shock at this announcement. Disagreements at Yalta had foreshadowed approaching U.S.-Soviet conflict over plans for the postwar world, and Truman hoped that use of the bomb might make Stalin think twice about resisting American initiatives. Second, Stimson, Marshall, and Truman were well aware of the moral implications, both of the bomb's development and of its use against Japan. Historical documents reveal that these discussions took place. Moral objections were not minimized, but they were overruled by the argument that an invasion would spill far more blood, both Allied and Japanese.

In any event, the atomic bombs achieved the immediate goal. The deaths of 100,000 people at Hiroshima and 60,000 at Nagasaki prompted the Japanese government to surrender unconditionally on August 10 and to sign a formal agreement on September 2, 1945. Fascism had been defeated, thanks to a fragile alliance between the capitalist nations of the West and the communist government of the Soviet Union. The coming of peace would strain and then destroy the victorious coalition. Albert Einstein, who had urged Roosevelt to pursue the bomb, found after its use that he was less optimistic. "The unleashed power of the atom has changed everything save our modes of thinking," he wrote in 1946. "And thus we drift toward unparalleled catastrophe."

Planning the Postwar World

As Allied forces neared victory in Europe and advanced toward Japan in the Pacific in February 1945, Roosevelt, Churchill, and Stalin had met in Yalta. Roosevelt focused on maintaining Allied unity, which he saw as the key to postwar peace and stability. But two sets of issues, the fates of the British and French colonial empires, and of the nations of Central and Eastern Europe, divided the Big Three. An independence movement in British India, led by Mohandas K. Gandhi (also known by the honorific Mahatma, "great-souled"), had gathered strength and caused friction between Roosevelt, who favored Indian independence, and Churchill, intent on preserving British rule.

An equally serious conflict was created by Stalin's insistence that Russian national security required pro-Soviet governments in Central and Eastern Europe. Roosevelt pressed for an agreement that guaranteed self-determination and democratic elections in Poland and neighboring countries. However, given the presence of Soviet troops in those nations, FDR had to accept a pledge from Stalin to hold "free and unfettered elections" at a future time. The three leaders agreed to divide Germany into four administrative zones, each controlled by one of the four allied powers (the United States, Great Britain, France, and the Soviet Union), and to similarly partition the capital city, Berlin, which was located in the middle of the Soviet zone.

At Yalta, the Big Three had also agreed to establish an international body to replace the discredited League of Nations. They decided that the new organization, to be known as the United Nations, would have both a General Assembly, in which all nations would be represented, and a Security Council comprised of the five major Allied powers—the United States, Britain, France, China, and the Soviet Union—and six other nations elected on a rotating basis. They determined that the five permanent members of the Security Council should have veto power over decisions of the General Assembly. Roosevelt, Churchill, and Stalin announced that the United Nations would convene in San Francisco on April 25, 1945.

- Evaluate the relative contributions of the Russians and the Americans to the Allied victory. What were the tensions among the Allies over military strategy and postwar territorial issues?

- Explain why the United States used atomic weapons against Japan.

SUMMARY

The rise of fascism in Germany, Italy, and Japan led to the outbreak of World War II. Initially, the American public insisted on noninvolvement. But by 1940, President Roosevelt was mobilizing support for military preparedness and intervention. The Japanese attack on Pearl Harbor in December 1941 brought the nation fully into the conflict. War mobilization dramatically expanded the federal government. It also boosted geographical and social mobility as women, rural whites, and southern blacks took up work in new defense plants in California and elsewhere. Government rules assisted both the labor movement and the African American campaign for civil rights. However, religious and racial animosity caused the exclusion of Jewish refugees and the internment of 112,000 Japanese Americans.

As our account shows, by 1942 Germany and Japan had almost won the war. But in 1943, the Allies took the offensive—with advances by the Soviet Army in Europe and the American Navy in the Pacific—and by the end of 1944, Allied victory was all but certain. The United States emerged from the war with an undamaged homeland, sole possession of the atomic bomb, and a set of unresolved diplomatic disputes with the Soviet Union that would soon lead to the four-decade-long Cold War.

CHAPTER REVIEW QUESTIONS

- World War II has popularly been called the "good war." Do you agree with this assessment? Why do you think it earned that nickname?

- Overall, what sort of impact—positive or negative—did World War II have on women and minority groups in the United States?

- Why was there tension among the Allies during the war, and what long-term impact did it have?

FOR FURTHER EXPLORATION

The standard military history of World War II is Henry Steele Commager's *The Story of World War II*, as expanded and revised by Donald L. Miller (1945; revisions 2001). Fifty-three personal stories of war appear in *War Stories: Remembering World War II* (2002), edited by Elizabeth Mullener. An engaging overview of war on the home front is John Morton Blum, *V Was for Victory* (1976). The National Archives Administration at **www.archives.gov/exhibit_hall/index.html** has two World War II sites: "A People at War" and "Powers of Persuasion: Poster Art from World War II." Powerful novels inspired by the war include John Hersey, *A Bell for Adano* (1944); James Jones, *From Here to Eternity* (1951); and Norman Mailer, *The Naked and the Dead* (1948).

The Library of Congress exhibit "Women Come to the Front: Journalists, Photographers, and Broadcasters During World War II" at **lcweb.loc.gov/exhibits/wcf/wcf0001.html** records the contributions of women during World War II. Sherna B. Gluck, *Rosie the Riveter Revisited* (1988), offers compelling accounts by women war workers. Many sites cover the Japanese internment. For interviews with detainees and thousands of images, go to **www.densho.org/densho.asp**. The Library of Congress site presents "Suffering Under a Great Injustice," a haunting exhibition of Ansel Adams's photographs of the Manzanar camp, at **memory.loc.gov/ammem/aamhtml**. The decision to drop the atomic bomb remains controversial. An excellent site is Lehigh University Professor Edward J. Gallagher's "The *Enola Gay* Controversy: How Do We Remember a War That We Won?" at **www.lehigh.edu/~ineng/enola**.

TEST YOUR KNOWLEDGE

To assess your command of the material in this chapter, see the Online Study Guide at **bedfordstmartins.com/henretta**.

For Web sites, images, and documents related to topics and places in this chapter, visit **bedfordstmartins.com/makehistory**.

TIMELINE

1933	Adolf Hitler becomes chancellor of Germany
1935	Italy invades Ethiopia
1935–1937	U.S. Neutrality Acts
1936	Germany reoccupies Rhineland demilitarized zone Rome-Berlin Axis established Japanese-German pact against the Soviet Union
1937	Japan invades China
1938	Munich conference
1939	German-Soviet nonaggression pact Germany invades Poland Britain and France declare war on Germany
1940	American conscription reinstated Germany, Italy, and Japan form alliance
1941	Roosevelt gives Four Freedoms speech Germany invades Soviet Union Lend-Lease Act passed Fair Employment Practices Commission (FEPC) created Atlantic Charter issued Japanese attack Pearl Harbor (December 7)
1942	Allied defeats in Europe and Asia Executive Order 9066 leads to Japanese internment camps Battles of Coral Sea and Midway halt Japanese advance
1942–1945	Rationing of scarce goods
1943	Race riots in Detroit and Los Angeles Fascism falls in Italy
1944	D-Day: Allied landing in France (June 6) GI Bill of Rights enacted
1945	Yalta Conference (February) Battles of Iwo Jima and Okinawa Harry S. Truman becomes president after Roosevelt's death (April 12) Germany surrenders (May 7) United Nations founded United States drops atomic bombs on Hiroshima and Nagasaki (August 6 and 9) Japan surrenders (August 10)

Cold War America, 1945–1963

In the autumn of 1950, a little-known California congressman named Richard Nixon stood before reporters in Los Angeles. Nixon was running for a U.S. Senate seat. His opponent, Helen Gahagan Douglas, was a Hollywood actress and a New Deal stalwart, having served three terms as a pro-Roosevelt Democrat in the House of Representatives. Nixon looked sternly into the eyes of reporters and told them that Douglas had cast "Communist-leaning" votes and that she was "pink right down to her underwear." Gahagan's voting record was in reality not much different from Nixon's. But the label stuck, and Nixon defeated the "pink lady" with nearly 60 percent of the vote. Tarring her with communism made her seem disloyal and un-American, and as a campaign tactic it worked.

A few months earlier, half a world away, U.S. tanks, planes, and artillery supplies had arrived in a region of Southeast Asia that most of the world knew as French Indochina. A French colony since the nineteenth century, Indochina (present-day Vietnam, Laos, and Cambodia) was home to an independence movement led by Ho Chi Minh and supported by the Soviet Union and China. In the summer of 1950, President Harry S. Truman authorized $15 million worth of military supplies to aid France, which was fighting Ho's army to keep possession of its Indochinese empire. "Neither national independence nor democratic evolution exists in any area dominated by Soviet imperialism," Secretary of State Dean Acheson warned ominously as he announced U.S. support for French imperialism.

Connecting these coincidental historical moments, one domestic and the other international, was a decades-old force in American life that gained renewed strength after World War II: anticommunism. The events in Los Angeles and Vietnam, however different on the surface, were part of the global geopolitical struggle between the United States and the Soviet Union known as the Cold War. Although it did not lead to any direct engagement on the battlefield, the Cold War inaugurated a half century of international tension and proxy wars during which either side, armed with nuclear weapons, might have tipped the entire world into oblivion.

Beginning in Europe before the final shots of World War II had been fired and extending to Asia, Latin America, the Middle East, and Africa by the mid-1950s, the Cold War reshaped international relations across the globe. Imposing a new framework on the centuries-old pattern of rivalry between great powers, it pitted the capitalist, democratic United States against the Communist, authoritarian Soviet Union. In that divided world, the fates of nations and peoples were rendered in stark either/or terms.

The Perils of the Cold War

In this detail of a 1948 Pulitzer Prize–winning cartoon, Rube Goldberg depicts the perilous nature of America's postwar peace—one that was based largely on the threat of nuclear annihilation. The Granger Collection.

In the United States, the Cold War fostered suspicion of "subversives" in government, education, and the media. The arms race that developed between the two superpowers required Congress to boost military expenditures. The resulting **military-industrial complex** enhanced the power of the corporations that built rockets, bombs, planes, munitions, and electronic devices. In politics, the Cold War stifled liberal initiatives as the New Deal coalition tried to advance its domestic agenda in the shadow of anticommunism. In all these ways, the line between the international and the domestic blurred—and that blurred line was an enduring legacy of the Cold War.

Containment in a Divided World

The Cold War began at the close of World War II in 1945 and ended in 1991 with the collapse and dissolution of the Soviet Union. While it lasted, two critical questions stood at the center of global history: Under what conditions, and in whose interest, would the European and Asian balances of political power be maintained? And how would the developing nations (the European colonies in Asia, the Middle East, and Africa) gain their independence and take their places on the world stage? Cold War rivalries framed the possible answers to both questions as they drew the United States into a prolonged engagement with world affairs, unprecedented in the nation's history, that continues to the present day.

The Cold War in Europe, 1945–1946

World War II set the basic conditions for the Cold War. With Germany and Japan defeated and Britain and France exhausted, only two superpowers remained standing in 1945. Even had nothing else divided them, the United States and the Soviet Union would have jostled each other as they moved to fill the postwar vacuum of power. But, of course, the two countries were divided—by geography, by history, by ideology, and by strategic interest. President Franklin Roosevelt understood that maintaining the U.S.-Soviet alliance was an essential condition for postwar global stability. But he also believed that permanent peace and long-term U.S. interests depended on the Wilsonian principles of collective security, self-determination, and free trade (see Chapter 21).

Yalta At the Yalta Conference of February 1945, Roosevelt, British prime minister Winston Churchill, and Soviet premier Joseph Stalin faced the challenge of reconciling Wilsonian principles with U.S.-Soviet power realities. The Big Three agreed there to proceed with the United Nations, on the condition that the United States and the Soviet Union (along with Great Britain, France, and China) receive permanent seats, with veto rights, on the Security Council. The paramount problem at Yalta, however, was Eastern Europe. At the first meeting of the Big Three, at Tehran in 1943, Stalin had agreed to follow the British and American strategy to defeat Hitler, in exchange for assurances that he could reshape the Soviet border with Poland. At Yalta, Roosevelt and Churchill agreed that Poland and its neighbors would fall under the Soviet "sphere of influence," thus meeting Stalin's demand for secure eastern borders. In Stalin's view, Soviet wartime sacrifices and the threat of future invasions through Europe entitled him to a buffer of client states on the USSR's western border — Russia had been invaded three times through Poland (by France once and Germany twice). But the Yalta agreement also called for "free and unfettered" elections to uphold the principle of democratic self-determination.

Such elections eventually took place in Finland, Hungary, Bulgaria, and Czechoslovakia, with varying degrees of democratic openness. This was not the case in Poland and Romania, where Stalin was determined to establish Communist governments and to punish wartime collaborators. As the largest Eastern European nation, Poland was "the big apple in the barrel," according to Roosevelt's secretary of state, Edward Stettinius. Because Stalin's armies occupied both Poland and Romania at the time of the Yalta Conference, Roosevelt and Churchill had little bargaining room. Stalin got the client regimes he desired there and would soon exert near-

East Meets West

With an "East Meets West" placard providing inspiration, Private Frank B. Huff of Virginia (on the right) and a Russian soldier shake hands. Huff was one of the first four Americans to contact the Russians when the two armies met at the River Elbe (seen in the background of this photo) in eastern Germany, on April 25, 1945. The goodwill in evidence in the spring of 1945, as Americans and Russians alike celebrated the defeat of Nazi Germany, would within two short years be replaced by Cold War suspicion and hostility.
© Bettmann/Corbis

complete control over Bulgaria, Czechoslovakia, and Hungary as well. Stalin's unwillingness to honor self-determination for nations in Eastern Europe was, from the American point of view, the precipitating event of the Cold War.

Truman Steps In Historians doubt that even the resourceful Roosevelt, had he lived, could have preserved the alliance with the Soviet Union. With Harry Truman as president, such a possibility grew ever more remote. Truman, who succeeded to the presidency in April 1945, was inexperienced in foreign affairs. Lacking Roosevelt's history of negotiating with the Soviet leader, Truman acted on blunt instinct to stand up to Stalin. "Unless Russia is faced with an iron fist and strong language," he said, "another war is in the making." At a meeting held shortly after he took office, the fledgling president berated the Soviet foreign minister, Vyacheslav Mikhaylovich Molotov, over the Soviets' failure to honor their Yalta agreements. Truman's tough talk may not have been diplomatic, but it pleased many Western European leaders, who feared Stalin nearly as much as they had Hitler.

Truman used what he called "tough methods" again that July at the Potsdam Conference, which had been called to take up postwar planning. After learning of the successful test of America's atomic bomb, Truman "told the Russians just where they got off and generally bossed the whole meeting," recalled Churchill. In the presidency only a few months, Truman had raised Cold War tensions another notch. Stalin, who secretly knew of the Manhattan Project, refused to back down and his suspicion of the West deepened when Truman failed to reveal the bomb's existence, saying only that the United States possessed "a new weapon of unusual, destructive force." On the American side, the bomb encouraged a certain swagger. It was unwise, warned the U.S. secretary of war, Henry L. Stimson, for the United States to try to negotiate with "this weapon rather ostentatiously on our hip."

Germany Germany represented the biggest challenge of all. American officials believed that rebuilding the German economy was essential to the prosperity of democratic regimes throughout Western Europe—and to keeping ordinary Germans from

Postwar Devastation

Berlin, Germany, was reduced to rubble during World War II. Allied bombing, followed by brutal fighting in April 1945 when Soviet troops entered Berlin, devastated the impressive capital city. Here, in a telling statement about the collapse of Hitler's Third Reich, German refugees walk in front of what was once Goebbels's Propaganda Ministry. U.S. policymakers feared that the economic disorder following this type of destruction would make many areas of postwar Europe vulnerable to Communist influence.   National Archives.

turning again to Nazism. Stalin hoped merely to extract reparations from Germany in the form of industrial machines and goods. Unlike in Eastern Europe, in Germany the Americans, British, and French had troops on the ground and could force the compromise on Stalin of dividing Germany into zones of occupation (British, French, American, and Russian) with minimal reparations for the Soviet Union (Map 25.1). Stalin did not like it, but circumstances forced him to accept the compromise, which sharpened his resentment against the West.

The cities and fields of Europe had barely ceased to run with the blood of World War II before they were menaced again by the tense standoff between the Soviet Union and the United States. With Stalin intent on establishing a protective barrier of client states in Eastern

Europe and the United States equally intent on reviving Germany and ensuring collective security throughout Europe, the points of agreement were few and far between.

The Containment Strategy

By 1947, the West had developed a clear strategy toward the Soviet Union that would become known as **containment**. The Soviet Union was expanding its reach: stationing troops in northern Iran, pressing Turkey for access to the Mediterranean, and supporting Communist forces in a guerrilla war in Greece. To counter, the West would seek to contain Soviet expansion, limiting Stalin's influence to Eastern Europe while reconstituting industrial capitalism and democratic governments

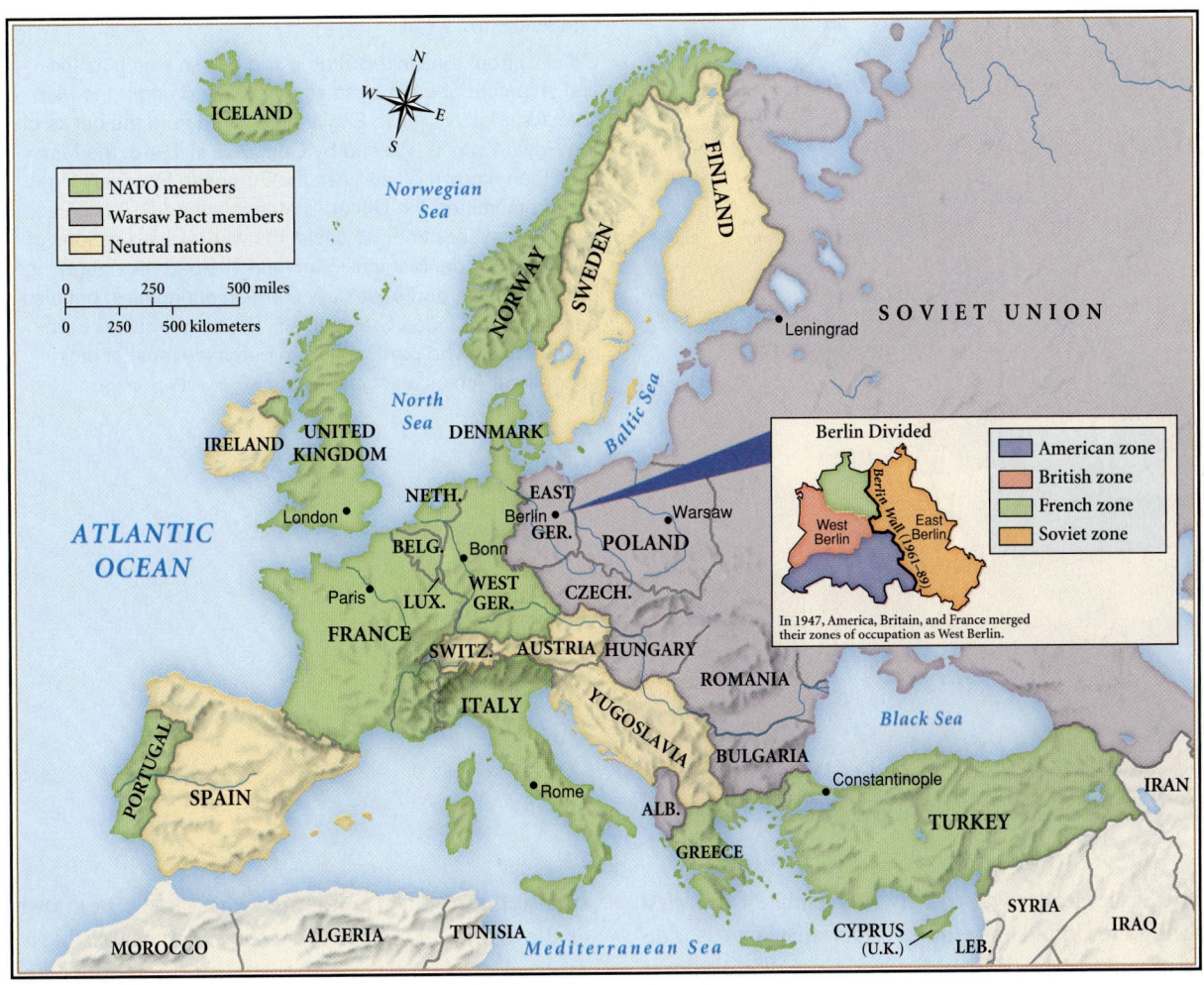

MAP 25.1

Cold War in Europe, 1955

This map vividly shows the Cold War division of Europe. The NATO countries (colored green) are allies of the United States; the Warsaw Pact countries (in purple) are allied to the USSR. At that point, West Germany had just been admitted to NATO, completing Europe's stabilization into two rival camps. But Berlin remained divided, and one can see from its location deep in East Germany why the former capital was always a flash point in Cold War controversies.

in Western Europe. The United States was wedded to the notion—dating to the Wilson administration—that communism and capitalism were incompatible on the world stage.

Toward an Uneasy Peace American thinking was significantly advanced in February 1946 by American diplomat George F. Kennan, in an 8,000-word cable dubbed the "Long Telegram," sent from his post at the U.S. embassy in Moscow. Kennan argued that the Soviet Union was an "Oriental despotism" and that communism was just the "fig-leaf" justifying its aggression. The West's only recourse, Kennan wrote a year later in a famous *Foreign Affairs* article, was

to meet the Soviets "with unalterable counter-force at every point where they show signs of encroaching upon the interests of a peaceful and stable world." Kennan called for "long-term, patient but firm and vigilant containment of Russian expansive tendencies." *Containment*, the key word, came to define America's evolving strategic stance toward the Soviet Union.

Kennan was confident that the Soviet system was inherently unstable and would—not in Stalin's lifetime, but eventually—collapse. Containment would work, Kennan believed, as long as the United States and its allies opposed Soviet expansion in all parts of the world. Kennan's attentive readers included Stalin himself, who quickly obtained a copy of the classified Long Telegram.

The Marshall Plan

Officials from the United States and Britain watch as the first shipment of Caribbean sugar provided under the Marshall Aid Plan arrives in England, lowered from the decks of the *Royal Victoria*. Passed by Congress in 1948, the Marshall Plan (known officially as the European Recovery Program) committed the United States to spend $17 billion over a four-year period to assist the war-ravaged nations of Western Europe. Marshall Plan funds helped the struggling British, French, and especially German economies, but also benefited the United States itself: The plan required European nations who participated to purchase most of their goods from American companies.   Keystone/Getty Images.

The Soviet leader was equally suspicious of the West, seeing the United States as an imperialist aggressor determined to replace Great Britain as the world's dominant capitalist power. Just as Kennan thought that the Soviet system was despotic and unsustainable, Stalin believed that the West suffered from its own fatal weaknesses. Neither side completely understood or trusted the other, and each projected its worst fears onto the other.

In fact, Britain's influence in the world was declining. Exhausted by the war, facing enormous deficits and a collapsing economy at home, and confronted with determined independence movements in India and Egypt, Britain was on the wane as a global power. "The reins of world leadership are fast slipping from Britain's competent but now very weak hands," read a U.S. State Department report. "These reins will be picked up either by the United States or by Russia."

It did not take long for the reality of Britain's decline to resonate across the Atlantic. In February 1947, London informed Truman that it could no longer afford to support the anticommunists in Greece, where a bitter civil war had split the country. If the Communists won in Greece, Truman worried, that would lead to Soviet domination of the eastern Mediterranean and embolden Communist parties in France and Italy. In re-

sponse, the president announced what came to be known as the Truman Doctrine. In a speech on March 12, he asserted an American responsibility "to support free peoples who are resisting attempted subjugation by armed minorities or by outside pressures." To that end, Truman proposed large-scale assistance for Greece and Turkey (then involved in a dispute with the Soviet Union over the Dardanelles, a strait connecting the Aegean Sea and the Sea of Marmara). "If we falter in our leadership, we may endanger the peace of the world," Truman declared. Despite the open-endedness of this military commitment, Congress quickly approved Truman's request for $300 million in aid to Greece and $100 million for Turkey.

Soviet expansionism was not the entire story. Europe was sliding into economic chaos. Already devastated by the war, in 1947 the continent was hit by the worst winter in memory. People were starving, credit was nonexistent, wages were stagnant, and the consumer market had collapsed. For both humanitarian and practical reasons, Truman's advisors believed something had to be done. A global depression might ensue if the European economy, the largest foreign market for American goods, did not recover. Worse, unemployed and dispirited Western Europeans might fill the ranks of the Communist Party, threatening political stability and the legitimacy of the United States. At Secretary of State George C. Marshall's behest, Kennan came up with a remarkable proposal: a massive infusion of American capital to help get the European economy back on its feet. Speaking at the Harvard University commencement in June 1947, Marshall urged the nations of Europe to work out a comprehensive recovery program based on U.S. aid.

This pledge of financial aid met significant opposition in Congress. Republicans castigated the Marshall Plan as a huge "international W.P.A." But in the midst of the congressional stalemate, on February 25, 1948, Stalin ordered a political coup in Czechoslovakia. In response, Congress rallied and voted overwhelmingly to approve funds for the Marshall Plan. Over the next four years, the United States contributed nearly $13 billion to a highly successful recovery effort that benefited both Western Europe and the United States (see Voices from Abroad, "Jean Monnet: Truman's Generous Proposal," p. 792). European industrial production increased by 64 percent, and the appeal of Communist parties waned in the West. Markets for American goods grew stronger and helped foster an economic interdependence between Europe and the United States. Notably, however, the Marshall Plan intensified Cold War tensions. U.S. officials invited the Soviets to participate but insisted on certain restrictions that would virtually guarantee Stalin's refusal. When Stalin did refuse, ordering Soviet client states to do so as well, the onus of dividing Europe appeared to fall on the Soviet leader and deprived his threadbare partners of assistance they sorely needed.

East and West in the New Europe

The flash point for a hot war remained Germany, the most important industrial economy and most strategic land mass in Europe. When no agreement could be reached to unify the four zones of occupation into a single state, the Western allies consolidated their three zones in 1947. They then prepared to establish an independent federal German republic. Marshall Plan funds would jump-start economic recovery. Some of those funds were slated for West Berlin, in hopes of making the city a capitalist showplace 100 miles deep inside the Soviet zone.

Stung by the West's intention to create a German republic without Soviet input, in June 1948 Stalin blockaded all Allied traffic to West Berlin, which he perceived as an indefensible Western outpost. Instead of giving way, as Stalin had expected, Truman and the British were galvanized into action. "We are going to stay, period," Truman said plainly. For nearly a year, American and British pilots, who had been dropping bombs on Berlin only four years earlier, improvised an airlift that flew 2.5 million tons of food and fuel into the Western zones of the city—nearly a ton for each resident. The Berlin crisis was the closest the two sides came to actual war. Military officials reported to Truman that General Lucius D. Clay, the American commander in Berlin, was "drawn as tight as a steel spring." But Stalin backed down: On May 12, 1949, he lifted the blockade. West Berlin became a symbol of resistance to communism.

The crisis in Berlin persuaded Western European nations to forge a collective security pact with the United States. In April 1949, for the first time since the end of

The Berlin Airlift

For 321 days U.S. planes like this one flew missions to bring food and other supplies to Berlin after the Soviet Union had blocked all surface routes into the former German capital. The blockade was finally lifted on May 12, 1949, after the Soviets conceded that it had been a failure. AP Images.

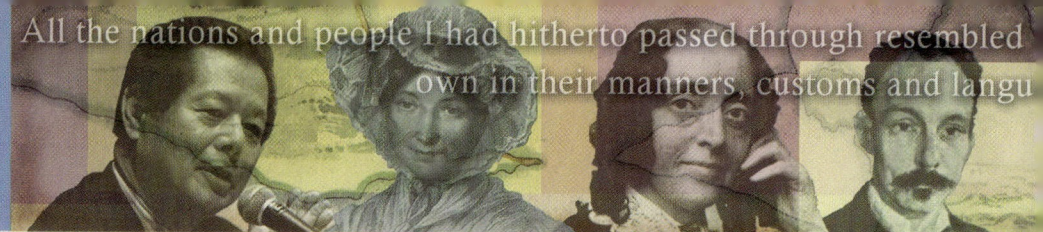
VOICES FROM ABROAD

Jean Monnet
Truman's Generous Proposal

Jean Monnet was an eminent French statesman and a tireless promoter of postwar European union. As head of a French postwar planning commission, he helped oversee the dispersal of Marshall Plan funds, the importance of which he describes in his memoirs.

So we had at last concerted our efforts to halt France's economic decline; but now, once more, everything seemed to be at risk. Two years earlier [1947], we thought that we had plumbed the depths of material poverty. Now we were threatened with the loss of even basic essentials. . . . Our dollar resources were melting away at an alarming rate, because we were having to buy American wheat to replace the crops we had lost during the winter. . . . A further American loan was soon exhausted.

Nor was this grim situation confined to France. Britain too had come to the end of her resources. In February 1947 she had abruptly cancelled her aid to Greece and Turkey, whose burdens she had seemed able to assume in 1945. Overnight, this abrupt abdication gave the United States direct responsibility for part of Europe. Truman did not hesitate for a moment: with the decisiveness that was to mark his actions as President, he at once asked for credits and arms for both Turkey and Greece. . . . [Soon after], he announced the Truman Doctrine of March 12, 1947. Its significance was general: it meant that the United States would prevent Europe from becoming a depressed area at the mercy of Communist advance. On the very same day, the Four-Power Conference began in Moscow. There, for a whole month, George Marshall, Ernest Bevin, and Georges Bidault argued with Vyacheslav Molotov about all the problems of the peace, and above all about Germany.

When Marshall returned to Washington, he knew that for a long time there would be no further genuine dialogue with Stalin's Russia. The "Cold War," as it was soon to be known, had begun. . . . Information from a number of sources convinced Marshall and his Under-Secretary Dean Acheson that once again, as in 1941, the United States had a great historic duty. And once again there took place what I had witnessed in Washington a few years earlier: a small group of men brought to rapid maturity an idea which, when the Executive gave the word, turned into vigorous action. This time, it was done by five or six people, in total secrecy and at lightning speed. Marshall, Acheson, [William] Clayton, Averell Harriman, and George Kennan worked out a proposal of unprecedented scope and generosity. It took us all by surprise when we read the speech that George Marshall made at Harvard on June 5, 1947. Chance had led him to choose the University's Commencement Day to launch something new in international relations: helping others to help themselves.

Source: Jean Monnet, *Memoirs*, trans. Richard Mayne (New York: Doubleday, 1978), 264–266.

ANALYZING THE EVIDENCE

- Why, according to Monnet, did Europe need massive economic assistance, and fast?

- Monnet was writing as an embattled Frenchman about the Marshall Plan. Compare his account with that given in the text. What is missing from Monnet's account?

- Can you explain, on the basis of Monnet's account of the Marshall Plan, why the North Atlantic Treaty Organization, which was established the following year, proved so durable?

the American Revolution, the United States entered into a peacetime military alliance, the North Atlantic Treaty Organization (NATO). Under the NATO pact, twelve nations—Belgium, Canada, Denmark, France, Great Britain, Iceland, Italy, Luxembourg, the Netherlands, Norway, Portugal, and the United States—agreed that "an armed attack against one or more of them in Europe or North America shall be considered an attack against them all." In May 1949, those nations also agreed to the creation of the Federal Republic of Germany (West Germany), which joined NATO in 1955. In response, the Soviet Union set up the German Democratic Republic (East Germany); the Council for Mutual Economic Assistance (COMECON); and, in 1955, the Warsaw Pact, a military alliance for Eastern Europe whose members included Albania, Bulgaria, Czechoslovakia, East Germany, Hungary, Poland, Romania, and the Soviet Union. In these parallel steps, the two superpowers had institutionalized the Cold War through a massive division of the continent.

By the early 1950s, *West* and *East* were the stark markers of the new Europe. As Churchill had observed in 1946, the line dividing the two stretched "from Stettin in the Baltic to Trieste in the Adriatic," cutting off tens of millions of Eastern Europeans—and the ancient capitals Berlin, Belgrade, Bucharest, Budapest, Prague, Sofia, and Warsaw—from the rest of the continent. Stalin's tactics had been dictatorial and often ruthless, but they were not without reason. The Soviets acted out of the sort of self-interest that had long defined powerful nations—ensuring a defensive perimeter of friendly allies, seeking access to raw materials, and pressing the advantage that victory in war allowed.

Nuclear Diplomacy | The final stage in the foundational years of the Cold War came in September 1949, when the Soviet Union detonated an atomic bomb. With America's brief tenure as sole nuclear power over, Truman turned to the U.S. National Security Council (NSC), established by the

Testing the Bomb

After World War II, the development of nuclear weapons went on apace, requiring frequent testing of the more advanced weapons. This photograph shows scientists and government officials viewing the mushroom cloud from one such A-bomb test at the Atomic Energy Commission's proving grounds at Yucca Flats in Nevada, on March 19, 1952. Finally acknowledging the dangers to the atmosphere (and to the people in the vicinity or downwind), the United States and the Soviet Union signed a treaty in 1963 banning aboveground testing. *J. R. Eyerman/Time Life Pictures/ Getty Images.*

Communist China

People in Beijing raise their clenched fists in a welcoming salute for Chinese Communist forces entering the city after the Nationalists surrendered on January 31, 1949. The center portrait behind them is of General Mao Zedong, the leader of the Communist Party of China. Mao's victory in the civil war (1946–1950) meant that from East Germany to the Pacific Ocean, much of the Eurasian land mass (including eastern Europe, the Soviet Union, and China) was ruled by Communist governments.   AP Images.

National Security Act of 1947, for a strategic reassessment. In April 1950, the NSC delivered its report, known as NSC-68. Bristling with alarmist rhetoric, the document urged a crash program to maintain America's nuclear edge, including the development of a hydrogen bomb, a thermonuclear device that used atomic fission to fuse atoms, and which was a thousand times more destructive than the atomic bombs dropped on Japan. The United States exploded the first hydrogen bomb in 1954, but the Soviet Union exploded their own soon thereafter. Paradoxically, with the advent of the hydrogen bomb, the utility of nuclear devices as actual weapons shrank to zero. No political objective could possibly be worth the destructiveness of a thermonuclear exchange.

The "balance of terror" that now prevailed magnified the importance of conventional forces. Having demobilized its wartime army, the United States had treated the atomic bomb as the equalizer against the vast Soviet Army. Now the only credible deterrent was a stronger conventional military. To that end, NSC-68 called for increased taxes to finance "a bold and massive program of rebuilding the West's defensive potential to surpass that of the Soviet world." Truman was reluctant to commit to a major defense buildup, fearing that it would overburden the national budget. But shortly after NSC-68 was completed, events in Asia led him to reverse course.

Containment in Asia

In Asia, U.S. attention centered on Japan. As with Germany, American officials had come to believe that restoring Japan's economy, while limiting its military influence, was key to ensuring prosperity and containing communism in East Asia. After dismantling Japan's military, American occupation forces under General Douglas MacArthur drafted a democratic constitution and paved the way for the restoration of Japanese sovereignty in 1951. Considering the scorched-earth war that had just ended, this was a remarkable achievement, thanks partly to the imperious MacArthur but mainly to the Japanese, who embraced peace and accepted U.S. military protection. However, events on the mainland proved much more difficult for the United States to shape to its advantage.

Civil War in China A civil war had been raging in China since the 1930s as Communist forces led by Mao Zedong (Mao Tse-tung) contended for power with Nationalist forces under Jiang Jieshi (Chiang Kai-shek). Fearing a Communist victory, between 1945 and 1949 the United States provided $2 billion to Jiang's army. Pressing Truman to "save" China, conservative Ohio Republican senator Robert A. Taft predicted that "the Far East is ultimately even more important to our future peace than is Europe." By 1949, Mao's forces held

The Korean War

As a result of President Truman's 1948 Executive Order 9981, for the first time in the nation's history, all troops in the Korean War served in racially integrated combat units. This photo taken during the Battle of Ch'ongch'on in 1950 shows a sergeant and his men of the Second Infantry Division.   National Archives.

the advantage. Truman reasoned that to save Jiang, the United States would have to intervene militarily, something the president was unwilling to do. He cut off aid and left the Nationalists to their fate. The People's Republic of China was formally established under Mao on October 1, 1949, and the remnants of Jiang's forces fled to Taiwan.

Both Stalin and Truman expected Mao to take an independent line, as the Communist leader Tito had just done in Yugoslavia. Mao, however, aligned himself with the Soviet Union, partly out of fear that the United States would re-arm the Nationalists and invade the mainland. As attitudes hardened, many Americans viewed Mao's success as a defeat for the United States. A pro-Nationalist "China lobby" accused Truman's State Department of being responsible for the "loss" of China. Sensitive to these charges, the Truman administration refused to recognize "Red China" and blocked China's admission to the United Nations. But the United States pointedly refused to guarantee Taiwan's independence, and in fact accepted the outcome on the mainland. (Since 1982, however, the United States has recognized Taiwanese sovereignty.)

The Korean War | The United States took a stronger stance in Korea, the narrow peninsula between China and the west coast of Japan. The United States and the Soviet Union had agreed at the close of World War II to occupy Korea jointly, temporarily dividing the former Japanese colony at the 38th parallel. As tensions rose in Europe, the 38th parallel hardened into a permanent demarcation line. The Soviets supported a Communist government, led by Kim Il Sung, in North Korea; the United States backed a right-wing Nationalist, Syngman Rhee, in South Korea. The two sides had waged low-level war since 1945, and both leaders were spoiling for a more definitive fight. However, neither Kim nor Rhee could launch an all-out offensive without the backing of his sponsor. Washington repeatedly said no, and so did Moscow. But Kim continued to press Stalin to permit him to reunify the nation. Convinced by the North Koreans that victory would be swift, the Soviet leader finally relented in the late spring of 1950.

On June 25, 1950, the North Koreans launched a surprise attack across the 38th parallel (Map 25.2). Truman immediately asked the U.N. Security Council

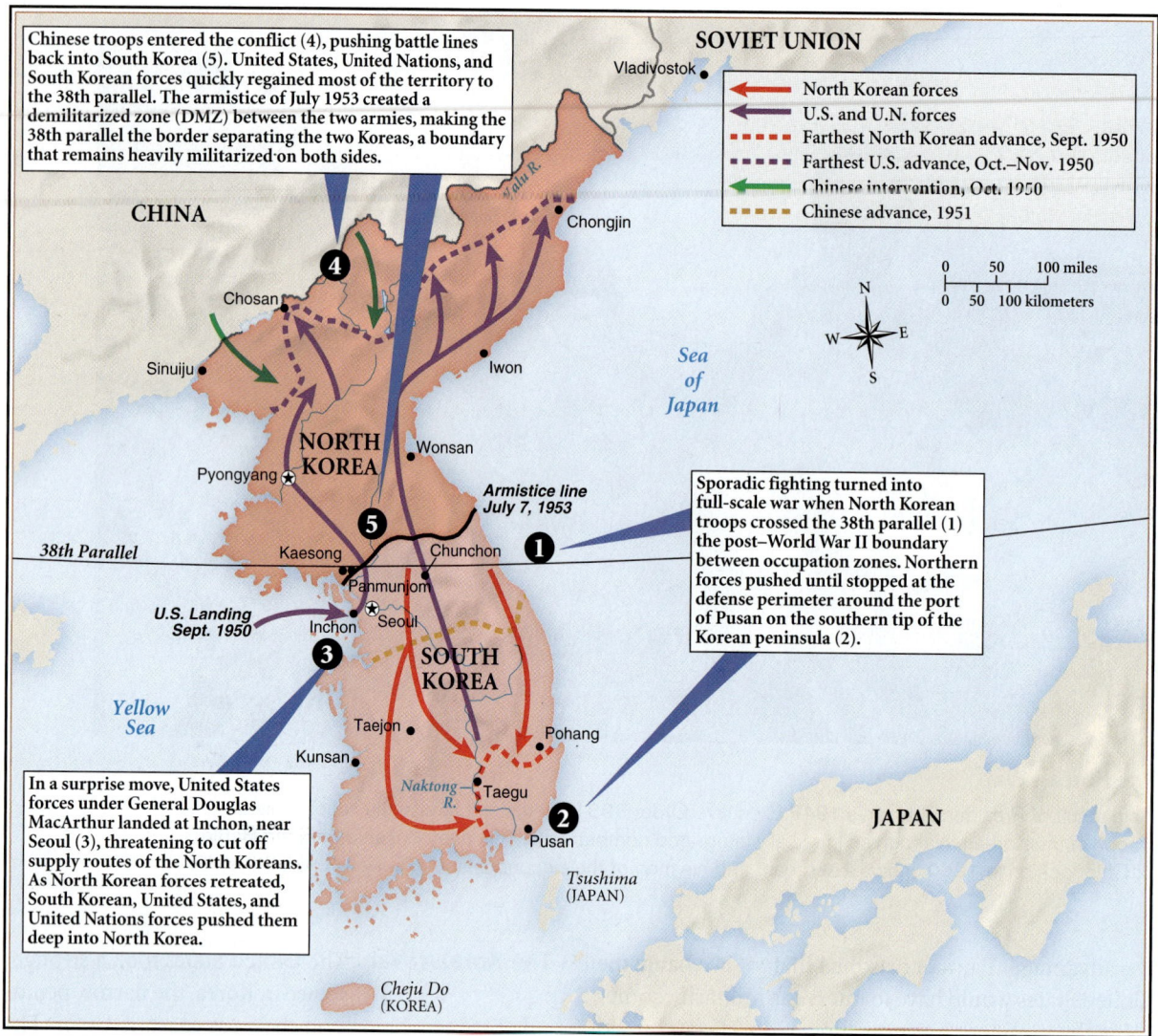

Chinese troops entered the conflict (4), pushing battle lines back into South Korea (5). United States, United Nations, and South Korean forces quickly regained most of the territory to the 38th parallel. The armistice of July 1953 created a demilitarized zone (DMZ) between the two armies, making the 38th parallel the border separating the two Koreas, a boundary that remains heavily militarized on both sides.

North Korean forces
U.S. and U.N. forces
Farthest North Korean advance, Sept. 1950
Farthest U.S. advance, Oct.–Nov. 1950
Chinese intervention, Oct. 1950
Chinese advance, 1951

Sporadic fighting turned into full-scale war when North Korean troops crossed the 38th parallel (1) the post–World War II boundary between occupation zones. Northern forces pushed until stopped at the defense perimeter around the port of Pusan on the southern tip of the Korean peninsula (2).

In a surprise move, United States forces under General Douglas MacArthur landed at Inchon, near Seoul (3), threatening to cut off supply routes of the North Koreans. As North Korean forces retreated, South Korean, United States, and United Nations forces pushed them deep into North Korea.

MAP 25.2

The Korean War, 1950–1953

The Korean War, which the United Nations officially deemed a "police action," lasted three years and cost the lives of more than 36,000 U.S. troops. South and North Korean deaths were estimated at more than 900,000. Although hostilities ceased in 1953, the South Korean Military (with U.S. military assistance) and the North Korean Army continue to face each other across the demilitarized zone, more than fifty years later.

to authorize a "police action" against the invaders. The Soviet Union was boycotting the Security Council to protest China's exclusion from the United Nations and could not veto Truman's request. With the Security Council's approval of a "peacekeeping force," Truman ordered U.S. troops to Korea. The rapidly assembled U.N. army in Korea was overwhelmingly American, with General Douglas MacArthur in command. At first, the North Koreans held a distinct advantage, occupying the entire peninsula except for the southeast corner around Pusan. But on September 15, 1950, MacArthur

launched a surprise amphibious attack at Inchon, far behind the North Korean lines. Within two weeks, the U.N. forces controlled Seoul, the South Korean capital, and almost all the territory up to the 38th parallel.

The impetuous MacArthur ordered his troops across the 38th parallel and led them all the way to the Chinese border at the Yalu River. It was a major blunder, certain to draw China into the war. Sure enough, just after Thanksgiving, a massive Chinese counterattack forced MacArthur's forces into headlong retreat back down the Korean peninsula. Two months later, the

American forces and their allies counterattacked, and pushed back to the 38th parallel. Then stalemate set in. With weak public support for the war in the United States, Truman and his advisors decided to work for a negotiated peace. MacArthur disagreed. In an inflammatory letter to the House minority leader, Republican Joseph J. Martin of Massachusetts, MacArthur denounced the Korean stalemate, declaring, "There is no substitute for victory." On April 11, 1951, Truman relieved MacArthur of his command. Truman's decision was highly unpopular, especially among conservative Republicans, but he had likely saved the nation from years of costly warfare with China.

Notwithstanding MacArthur's dismissal, the war dragged on for more than two years. An armistice in July 1953, pushed by the newly elected president, Dwight D. Eisenhower, left Korea divided at the original demarcation line. North Korea remained firmly allied with the Soviet Union; South Korea signed a mutual defense treaty with the United States. It had been the first major proxy battle of the Cold War, in which the Soviet Union and United States took sides in a civil conflict. It would not be the last.

The Korean War had far-reaching consequences. Truman's decision to commit troops without congressional approval set a precedent for future undeclared wars. His refusal to unleash atomic bombs, even when American forces were reeling under a massive Chinese attack, set ground rules for Cold War conflict. The war also expanded American involvement in Asia, transforming containment into a truly global policy. Finally, the Korean War ended Truman's resistance to a major military buildup. Defense expenditures grew from $13 billion in 1950, roughly one-third of the federal budget, to $50 billion in 1953, nearly two-thirds of the budget (Map 25.3). American foreign policy had become more global, more militarized, and more expensive (Figure 25.1). Even in times of peace, the United States now functioned in a state of permanent military mobilization.

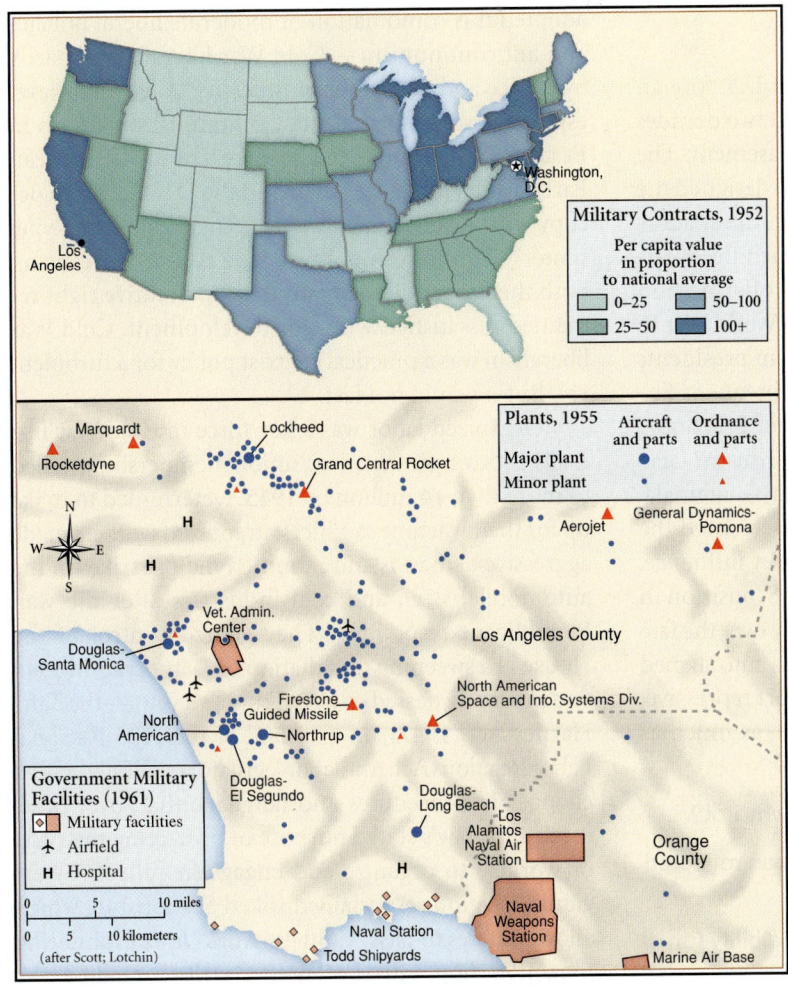

MAP 25.3

The Military-Industrial Complex

Defense spending gave a big boost to the Cold War economy, but, as the upper map suggests, the benefits were by no means equally distributed. The big winners were the Middle Atlantic states, the industrialized Upper Midwest, Washington State (with its aircraft and nuclear plants), and California. The epicenter of California's military-industrial complex was Los Angeles, which, as is evident in the lower map, was studded with military facilities and major defense contractors like Douglas Aircraft, Lockheed, and General Dynamics. There was work aplenty for engineers and rocket scientists.

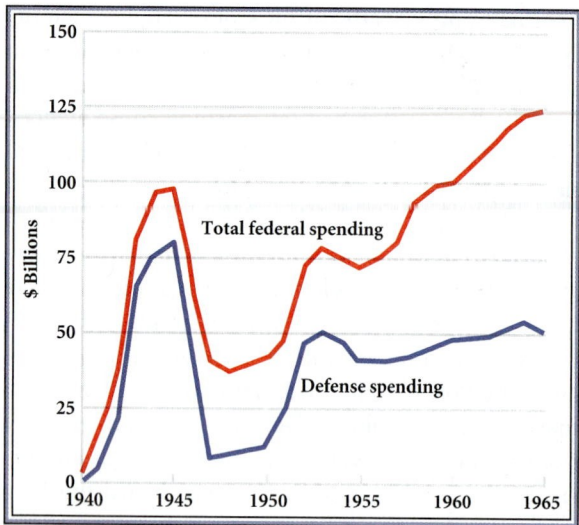

FIGURE 25.1

National Defense Spending, 1940–1965

In 1950, the U.S. defense budget was $13 billion, less than a third of total federal outlays. In 1961, U.S. defense spending reached $47 billion, fully half of the federal budget and almost 10 percent of the gross domestic product.

The Munich Analogy | Behind much of U.S. foreign policy in the first two decades of the Cold War lay the memory of appeasement. The generation of politicians and officials who designed the containment strategy had come of age in the shadow of Munich, the conference in 1938 at which the Western democracies had appeased Hitler by offering him part of Czechoslovakia, paving the road to World War II. Applying the lessons of Munich, American presidents believed that "appeasing" Stalin (and subsequent Soviet rulers Nikita Khrushchev and Leonid Brezhnev) would have the same result: wider war. Thus in Germany, Greece, and Korea, and later in Iran, Guatemala, and Vietnam, the United States staunchly resisted the Soviets — or what it perceived to be Soviet influence. The Munich analogy strengthened the U.S. position in a number of strategic conflicts, particularly over the fate of Germany. But it also drew Americans into armed conflicts — and convinced them to support repressive, right-wing regimes — that compromised, as much as supported, stated American principles.

- Was the Cold War inevitable? Why or why not?

- How were the ideas of George F. Kennan reflected in Truman's Cold War policies?

- How would you assess overall responsibility for the origins of the Cold War?

Cold War Liberalism

Harry Truman never intended to be a caretaker executive and never wanted to be a Cold War president. He had big plans. In September 1945, just fourteen days after Japan surrendered, Truman called for a dramatic expansion of the New Deal, fulfilling the "second Bill of Rights" that Roosevelt had proclaimed in his State of the Union Address in 1944 (see Chapter 24). Truman phrased his proposals in just that way, as rights expected by all Americans — the right to a "useful and remunerative" job, good housing, "adequate medical care," "protection from the economic fears of old age," and a "good education." In the end, his high hopes were crushed, and Truman went down in history not as a New Dealer, but as a Cold Warrior.

Truman and the Democratic Party of the late 1940s and early 1950s forged what historians call Cold War liberalism. They preserved the core programs of the New Deal welfare state, developed the containment policy to oppose Soviet influence throughout the world, and fought so-called subversives at home. But there would be no second act for the New Deal. The Democrats adopted this combination of moderate liberal policies and anticommunism — Cold War liberalism — partly by choice and partly out of necessity. A few high-level espionage scandals and the Communist outcomes in Eastern Europe and China reenergized the Republican Party, which forced Truman and the Democrats to occupy what historian Arthur Schlesinger called the "vital center" of American politics. However, Americans on both the progressive left and the conservative right remained dissatisfied with this development. Cold War liberalism was a practical centrist policy for a turbulent era. But it would not last.

Organized labor was a key force in Cold War liberalism. Stronger than ever, union membership swelled to more than 14 million by 1945. Determined to make up for their wartime sacrifices, unionized workers made aggressive demands and mounted major strikes in the automobile, steel, and coal industries after the war. Republicans responded. They gained control of the House in a sweeping repudiation of Democrats in 1946 and promptly passed — over Truman's veto — the Taft-Hartley Act (1947), an overhaul of the 1935 National Labor Relations Act. Antilabor legislators skillfully crafted changes in procedures and language that, over time, eroded the law's stated purpose of protecting the right of workers to organize and engage in collective bargaining. Unions especially disliked Section 14b, which allowed states to pass "right-to-work" laws prohibiting the union shop. Taft-Hartley effectively "contained" the

Truman Triumphant

In one of the most famous photographs in U.S. political history, Harry S. Truman gloats over an erroneous headline in the November 3 *Chicago Daily Tribune*. Pollsters had predicted an easy victory for Thomas E. Dewey. Their primitive techniques, however, missed the dramatic surge in support for Truman during the last days of the campaign.   © Bettmann/Corbis.

labor movement. Trade unions would continue to support the Democratic Party, but the labor movement would not move into the largely non-union South and would not extend into the many American industries that remained unorganized.

Truman and the End of Reform

By 1947, most observers wouldn't have bet a nickel on Truman's political future. His popularity ratings had plummeted, and "To err is Truman" became a favorite political gibe. Republicans, seeking political advantage in the Cold War, blamed Truman for the Soviet takeover of Eastern Europe. Determined to govern as a Democratic reformer, Truman found his domestic programs stymied and his international efforts questioned and criticized.

The 1948 Election | Democrats would have dumped Truman in 1948 had they found a better candidate. But the party fell into disarray. The left wing split off and formed the Progressive Party, nominating Henry A. Wallace, an avid New Dealer whom Truman had fired as secretary of commerce in 1946 because of his vocal opposition to America's actions in the Cold War. A right-wing challenge came from the South. When northern liberals such as Mayor Hubert H. Humphrey of Minneapolis pushed through

a strong civil rights platform at the Democratic convention, the southern delegations bolted and, calling themselves Dixiecrats, nominated for president South Carolina governor Strom Thurmond, an ardent supporter of racial segregation. The Republicans meanwhile renominated Thomas E. Dewey, the politically moderate governor of New York who had run a strong campaign against FDR in 1944.

Truman surprised everyone. He launched a strenuous cross-country speaking tour and hammered away at the Republicans for opposing progressive legislation and, in general, for running a "do-nothing" Congress. By combining these issues with attacks on the Soviet menace abroad, Truman began to salvage his troubled campaign. At his rallies, enthusiastic listeners shouted, "Give 'em hell, Harry!" Truman won, receiving 49.6 percent of the vote to Dewey's 45.1 percent (Map 25.4).

Close observers could see in this remarkable election a foreshadowing of political turmoil. Truman occupied the center of a sprawling Democratic Party, the New Deal coalition forged under FDR. On his left were progressives, civil rights advocates, and anti–Cold War peace activists. On his right were segregationist white southerners, who opposed civil rights and were allied with Republicans on many economic and foreign policy issues. In 1948, Truman performed a delicate balancing act, largely retaining the support of Jewish and Catholic voters in the big cities, black voters in the

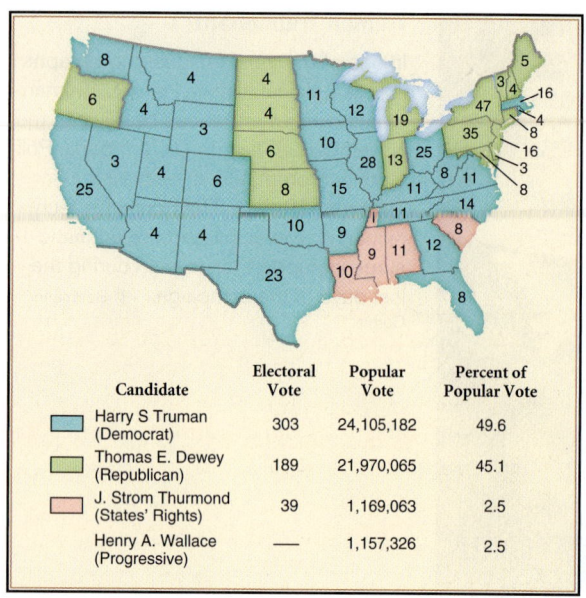

Candidate	Electoral Vote	Popular Vote	Percent of Popular Vote
Harry S Truman (Democrat)	303	24,105,182	49.6
Thomas E. Dewey (Republican)	189	21,970,065	45.1
J. Strom Thurmond (States' Rights)	39	1,169,063	2.5
Henry A. Wallace (Progressive)	—	1,157,326	2.5

MAP 25.4

The Presidential Election of 1948

Truman's electoral strategy in 1948 was to concentrate his campaign in areas where the Democrats had their greatest strength. In an election with a low turnout, Truman held on to enough support from Roosevelt's New Deal coalition of blacks, union members, and farmers to defeat Dewey by more than 2 million votes.

North, and organized labor voters across the country. But Thurmond's strong showing—he carried four states in the Deep South—demonstrated the fragile nature of the Democratic Party's coalition and prefigured the revolt of the party's southern wing in the 1960s. On top of juggling the contending forces in his own party, Truman faced mounting pressure from Republicans to prove his anticommunist credentials and take a tough stand against the Soviet Union.

The Fair Deal | Despite having to perform a balancing act, Truman and progressive Democrats forged ahead. In 1949, reaching ambitiously to extend the New Deal, Truman proposed the Fair Deal: national health insurance, aid to education, a housing program, expansion of Social Security, a higher minimum wage, and a new agricultural program. In its attention to civil rights, the Fair Deal also reflected the growing role of African Americans in the Democratic Party. Congress, however, remained a huge stumbling block, and the Fair Deal fared poorly. The same conservative coalition that had blocked Roosevelt's initiatives in his second term continued the fight against Truman's. Cold War pressure did not help. The nation's

growing paranoia over internal subversion weakened support for bold extensions of the welfare state. Truman's proposal for national health insurance, for instance, was a popular idea, with strong backing from organized labor. But it was denounced as "socialized medicine" by the American Medical Association and the insurance industry. In the end, the Fair Deal's only significant breakthrough, other than improvements to the minimum wage and Social Security, was the National Housing Act of 1949, which authorized the construction of 810,000 low-income units.

Red Scare: The Hunt for Communists

Cold War liberalism was premised on the grave domestic threat posed, many believed, by Communists and Communist sympathizers. Was there any significant Soviet penetration of the American government? Records opened after the 1991 disintegration of the Soviet Union—intelligence files in Moscow and, most important among U.S. sources, the intercepts of Soviet cables collected in a U.S. intelligence project code-named Venona—indicate that there was. Among American suppliers of information to Moscow were FDR's assistant secretary of the treasury, Harry Dexter White; FDR's administrative aide Laughlin Currie; a strategically placed midlevel group in the State Department (including Alger Hiss, who was with FDR at Yalta); and several hundred more, some identified only by code name, working in a range of government departments and agencies.

There have long been competing ways to view this espionage. Many of these enlistees in the Soviet cause had been bright young New Dealers in the mid-1930s, when the Soviet-backed Popular Front suggested that the lines separating liberalism, progressivism, and communism were permeable (see Chapter 24). At that time, the United States was not at war and never expected to be. And when war did come, the Soviet Union was an American ally. For critics of the informants, however, there remained the time between the Nazi-Soviet Pact and the German invasion of the Soviet Union, a nearly two-year period during which cooperation with the Soviet Union could be seen in a less positive light. Moreover, passing secrets to another country, even a wartime ally, was simply indefensible to many Americans. The lines between U.S. and Soviet interests blurred for some; for others, they remained clear and definite.

After World War II, however, most suppliers of information to the Soviets apparently ceased spying. For one thing, the professional apparatus of Soviet spying was dismantled or disrupted by American counterintelligence work. For another, most of the well-connected amateur spies moved on to other careers. The State Department official Alger Hiss, for example, was serving as head of the prestigious Carnegie Endowment for International Peace when he was accused in 1948 by Whittaker Chambers, a Communist-turned-informant, of having passed classified documents to him in the 1930s. Historians have thus developed a healthy skepticism about Soviet espionage in the United States after 1947, but this was not how many Americans saw it at the time. Legitimate suspicions and real fears, along with political opportunism, combined to fuel the national Red Scare, longer and more far-reaching than the one that followed World War I (see Chapter 21).

Loyalty-Security Program | To insulate his administration against charges of Communist infiltration, Truman issued Executive Order 9835 on March 21, 1947, which created the Loyalty-Security Program. The order permitted officials to investigate any employee of the federal government (some 2.5 million people) for "subversive" activities. Representing a profound centralization of power, the order sent shock waves through every federal agency. Truman intended the order to apply principally to actions intended to harm the United States (sabotage, treason, etc.), but it was broad enough to allow anyone to be accused of subversion for the slightest reason — for marching in a Communist-led demonstration in the 1930s, for instance, or signing a petition calling for public housing. Along with suspected political subversives, thousands of gay men and lesbians were dismissed from federal employment in the 1950s, victims of an obsessive search for anyone deemed "unfit" for government work.

Following Truman's lead, many state and local governments, universities, political organizations, churches, and businesses undertook their own antisubversion campaigns, which often included loyalty oaths. In the labor movement, where Communists had served as organizers in the 1930s, charges of Communist domination led to the expulsion of a number of unions by the Congress of Industrial Organizations (CIO) in 1949. Civil rights organizations such as the National Association for the Advancement of Colored People (NAACP) and the National Urban League also expelled Communists and "fellow travelers," or Communist sympathizers. Thus, the Red Scare spread from the federal government to the farthest reaches of American organi-

zational, cultural, and economic life (see Reading American Pictures, "Hollywood and the Cold War," p. 802).

HUAC | The Truman administration had legitimized the vague and malleable concept of "disloyalty." Others proved willing to stretch the concept even further, beginning with the House Un-American Activities Committee (HUAC), which Congressman Martin Dies of Texas and other conservatives had launched in 1938. After the war, HUAC helped spark the Red Scare by holding widely publicized hearings on alleged Communist infiltration in the movie industry. Appearing before HUAC, an actor named Ronald Reagan assured the committee, "I do not believe that the Communists have ever at any time been able to use the motion picture industry." However, a group of writers and directors dubbed the "Hollywood Ten" went to jail for contempt of Congress for refusing to testify about their past associations. Hundreds of other actors, directors, and writers whose names had been mentioned in the HUAC investigation were unable to get work, victims of an unacknowledged but very real blacklist honored by industry executives.

Here, too, however, revelations from the Soviet archives have complicated the picture. Historians have mostly regarded the American Communist Party as a "normal" organization, acting in America's home-grown radical tradition. In some instances, this was the case. Communists were among the most effective trade union organizers in the labor movement, and the American Communist Party promoted black civil rights long before many other organizations did. But Soviet archives have also shown that the American party was not entirely independent — it was taking money and instructions from Moscow. When American Communists joined other organizations, they often pushed Moscow's agenda. Whether this constituted disloyalty or subversion remained a divisive question, easily manipulated for an unknowing public by anticommunist institutions such as HUAC and by determined individuals such as an unknown and undistinguished senator from the Upper Midwest.

McCarthyism | The meteoric career of Senator Joseph McCarthy of Wisconsin marked the finale of the Red Scare. In February 1950, McCarthy delivered a bombshell during a speech in Wheeling, West Virginia: "I have here in my hand a list of 205 . . . a list of names that were made known to the Secretary of State as being members of the Communist Party and who nevertheless are still working and shaping policy

Hollywood and the Cold War

In the 1950s, Hollywood made dozens of horror movies with the theme of "invasion." Notice how these movie posters emphasize a frightened and anxious public threatened by strange creatures from space. Observe the similarities among all four posters (three advertise horror films; the fourth is a drama) and examine them for shared elements. For instance, all four portray individual faces contorted with expressions of deep fear and worry. The color red unites them all as well. These films hit American movie screens at the height of the Cold War, when fear of Communism and the Soviet Union reached its peak. Furthermore, space exploration began in earnest in the 1950s, and the public's anxiety over a potential atomic attack allowed filmmakers to explore the theme of terror descending from the sky.

Invaders from Mars movie poster. © 1955 Twentieth-Fox Film Corp.

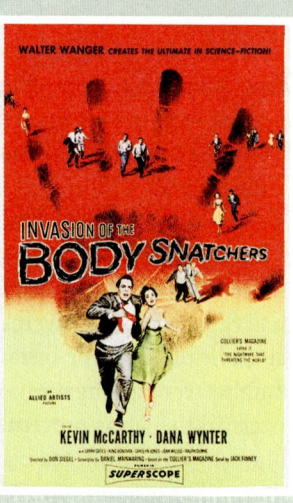

Invasion of the Body Snatchers movie poster. Allied Artists.

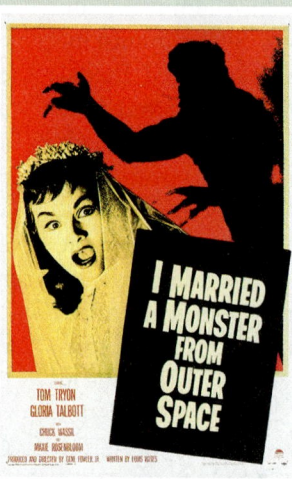

I Married a Monster from Outer Space movie poster. Allied Artists.

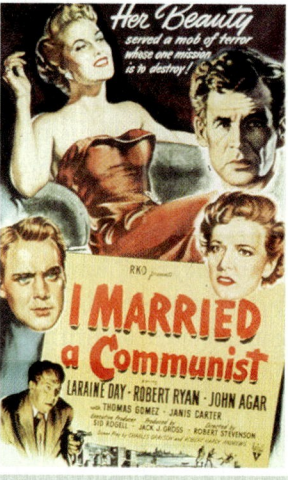

I Married a Communist movie poster. © 1958 Paramount Pictures Corporation/The Michael Barson Collection/Past Perfect.

ANALYZING THE EVIDENCE

- What does the theme of invasion in horror films suggest about Cold War American culture?

- Americans in the 1950s knew little about the Soviet Union, its people, or their daily lives. With this in mind, how might some of the monsters represented on these movie posters be indicative of Americans' perceptions of Communists and Communism?

- What other elements from these posters suggest American worries about the unknown? For instance, Americans would have associated the color red with danger but also with Communism. What does the fear of "marrying a Communist" suggest about how Americans might have imagined the nation's Cold War enemy?

The Army-McCarthy Hearings

These 1954 hearings contributed to the downfall of Senator Joseph McCarthy by exposing his reckless accusations and bullying tactics to the huge television audience that tuned in each day. Some of the most heated exchanges took place between McCarthy (center) and Joseph Welch (seated, left), the lawyer representing the army. When the gentlemanly Welch finally asked, "Have you no sense of decency sir, at long last? Have you left no sense of decency?" he fatally punctured McCarthy's armor. The audience broke into applause because someone had finally had the courage to stand up to the senator from Wisconsin.
© Bettmann/Corbis.

in the State Department." McCarthy later reduced his numbers, gave different figures in different speeches, and never released any names or proof. But he had gained the attention he sought.

For the next four years, from his position as chair of the Senate Permanent Subcommittee on Investigations, he waged a virulent smear campaign. Critics who disagreed with him exposed themselves to charges of being "soft" on communism. Truman called McCarthy's charges "slander, lies, [and] character assassination" but could do nothing to curb him. Republicans, for their part, refrained from publicly challenging their most outspoken senator and, on the whole, were content to reap the political benefits (see Comparing American Voices, "Hunting Communists and Liberals," pp. 804–805). McCarthy's charges almost always targeted Democrats.

In early 1954, McCarthy overreached by launching an investigation into subversive activities in the U.S. Army. When lengthy hearings—the first of their kind broadcast on the new medium of television—brought McCarthy's tactics into the nation's living rooms, support for him plummeted. In December 1954, the Senate

Thus I have given you, I think, the Substance of the Arguments o
both sides of that great and important Questio

Hunting Communists and Liberals

The onset of the Cold War created an opportunity for some conservatives to seize on anticommunism as a weapon to attack the Truman administration. In Senator Joseph McCarthy's case, the charge was that the U.S. government was harboring Soviet spies. There was also a broader, more amorphous attack on people accused not of spying but of having Communist sympathies; such "fellow travelers" were considered "security risks" and thus unsuitable for government positions. The basis of suspicion for this targeted group was generally membership in organizations that either supported policies that overlapped with or seemed similar to policies supported by the Communist Party.

Senator Joseph McCarthy

Speech Delivered in Wheeling, West Virginia, February 9, 1950

Though Senator McCarthy was actually late getting on board the anticommunist rocket ship, this was the speech that launched him into orbit. No one else ever saw the piece of paper he waved about with the names of fifty-seven spies in the State Department. Over time, the numbers he cited fluctuated (in early versions of this speech he claimed to have a list of 205 names), and never materialized into a single indictment for espionage. Still, McCarthy had an extraordinary talent for whipping up anticommunist hysteria. His downfall came in 1954, when the U.S. Senate formally censured him for his conduct; three years later, he died of alcoholism at the age of forty-eight.

Today we are engaged in a final, all-out battle between communistic atheism and Christianity. The modern champions of communism have selected this as the time. And, ladies and gentlemen, the chips are down—they are truly down....

The reason why we find ourselves in a position of impotency is not because our only powerful potential enemy has sent men to invade our shores, but rather because of the traitorous actions of those who have been treated so well by this Nation. It has not been the less fortunate or members of minority groups who have been selling this Nation out, but rather those who have had all the benefits that the wealthiest nation on earth has had to offer—the finest homes, the finest college education, and the finest jobs in Government we can give....

I have in my hand 57 cases of individuals who would appear to be either card carrying members or certainly loyal to the Communist Party, but who nevertheless are still helping to shape our foreign policy.

Fulton Lewis Jr.

Radio Address, January 13, 1949

The groundwork for McCarthy's anticommunist crusade was laid by the House Un-American Activities Committee (HUAC), which had been formed in 1938 by conservative southern Democrats seeking to investigate alleged Communist influence around the country. One of its early targets had been Dr. Frank P. Graham, the distinguished president of the University of North Carolina. A committed southern liberal, Graham was a leading figure in the Southern Conference on Human Welfare, the most prominent southern organization supporting the New Deal, free speech, organized labor, and greater rights for southern blacks—causes that some in the South saw as pathways for Communist subversion. After the war, HUAC stepped up its activities and kept a close eye on Graham. Among Graham's duties was to serve as the head of the Oak Ridge Institute of Nuclear Studies, a consortium of fourteen southern universities designed to undertake joint research with the federal government's atomic energy facility at Oak Ridge, Tennessee. To enable him to carry on his duties, the Atomic Energy Commission (AEC) granted Graham a security clearance, overriding the negative recommendation of the AEC's Security Advisory Board. That was the occasion for the following statement by Fulton Lewis Jr., a conservative radio commentator with a nationwide following.

About Dr. Frank P. Graham, president of the University of North Carolina, and the action of the Atomic Energy Commission giving him complete clearance for all atomic secrets despite the fact that the security officer of the commission flatly rejected him....

President Truman was asked to comment on the matter today at his press and radio conference, and his reply was that he has complete confidence in Dr. Graham.

... The defenders of Dr. Graham today offered the apology that during the time he joined the various subversive and Communist front organizations [like the Southern Conference for Human Welfare] — organizations so listed by the Attorney General of the United States — this country was a co-belligerent with Soviet Russia, and numerous people joined such groups and causes. That argument is going to sound very thin to most American citizens, because the overwhelming majority of us would have no part of any Communist or Communist front connections at any time.

Frank Porter Graham
Telegram to Fulton Lewis Jr., January 13, 1949

One can imagine Graham's shock at hearing himself pilloried on national radio. (He had not even been aware of the AEC's investigation of him.) The following is from his response to Lewis.

In view of your questions and implications I hope you will use my statement to provide for my answers. . . . I have always been opposed to Communism and all totalitarian dictatorships. I opposed both Nazi and Communist aggression against Czechoslovakia and the earlier Russian aggression against Finland and later Communist aggression against other countries. . . .

During the period of my active participation, the overwhelming number of members of the Southern Conference were to my knowledge anti-Communists. There were several isolationist stands of the Conference with which I disagreed. The stands which I supported as the main business of the Conference were such as the following: Federal aid to the states for schools; abolition of freight rate discrimination against Southern commerce, agriculture, and industry; anti–poll tax bill; anti-lynching bill; equal right of qualified Negroes to vote in both primaries and general elections; the unhampered lawful right of labor to organize and bargain collectively in our region; . . . minimum wages and social security in the Southern and American tradition. . . .

I have been called a Communist by some sincere people. I have been called a spokesman of American capitalism by Communists and repeatedly called a tool of imperialism by the radio from Moscow. I shall simply continue to oppose Ku Kluxism, imperialism, fascism, and Communism whether in America . . . or behind the "iron curtain."

House Un-American Activities Committee
Report on Frank Graham, February 4, 1949

Because of the controversy, HUAC released a report on Graham.

A check of the files, records and publications of the Committee on Un-American Activities has revealed the following information: Letterheads dated September 22, 1939, January 17, 1940, and May 26, 1940, as well as the "Daily Worker" of March 18, 1939, . . . reveal that Frank P. Graham was a member of the American Committee for Democracy and Intellectual Freedom. . . . In Report 2277, dated June 25, 1942, the Special Committee on Un-American Activities found that "the line of the American Committee for Democracy and Intellectual Freedom has fluctuated in complete harmony with the line of the Communist Party." The organization was again cited by the Special Committee . . . as a Communist front "which defended Communist teachers." . . .

A letterhead of February 7, 1946, a letterhead of June 4, 1947 . . . and an announcement of the Third Meeting, April 19–21, 1942, at Nashville, Tennessee, reveal that Frank P. Graham was honorary President of the Southern Conference for Human Welfare. . . .

In a report on the Southern Conference for Human Welfare, dated June 16, 1947, the Committee on Un-American Activities found "the most conclusive proof of Communist domination of the Southern Conference for Human Welfare is to be found in the organization's strict and unvarying conformance to the line of the Communist Party in the field of foreign policy. It is also a clear indication of the fact that the real purpose of the organization was not 'human welfare' in the South, but rather to serve as a convenient vehicle in support of the current Communist Party line."

Sources: *Congressional Record*, U.S. Senate, 81st Cong., 2d Sess. (Washington, D.C.: GPO, 1950); Frank Porter Graham Papers, University of North Carolina at Chapel Hill Library.

ANALYZING THE EVIDENCE

- On what grounds did Fulton Lewis Jr. and HUAC assert that Frank Graham was a security risk? Did they charge that he was a Communist? Is there any evidence in these documents that Graham might have been a security risk?

- How does Graham defend himself? Are you persuaded by his defense?

- Do you see any similarity between McCarthy's famous speech at Wheeling, West Virginia, and the suspicions voiced against Graham by Lewis and HUAC a year earlier?

voted 67 to 22 to censure McCarthy for unbecoming conduct. He died from an alcohol-related illness three years later at the age of forty-eight, his name forever attached to a period of political repression of which he was only the most flagrant manifestation.

The Politics of Cold War Liberalism

As Election Day 1952 approached, the nation—just seven years removed from World War II—was embroiled in the tense Cold War with the Soviet Union and fighting a "hot" war in Korea. Though Americans gave the Republicans victory, radical change was not in the offing. The new president, Dwight D. Eisenhower, set the tone for what his supporters called modern Republicanism, an updated GOP approach that aimed at moderating, not dismantling, the New Deal state. Eisenhower and his supporters were more successors of FDR than of Herbert Hoover. Foreign policy revealed a similar continuity. Like their predecessors, Republicans saw the world in Cold War polarities.

Republicans rallied around Eisenhower, the popular former commander of Allied forces in Europe, but they remained deeply divided. On one side, party activists looked to Robert A. Taft of Ohio. The Republican leader in the Senate, Taft was a vehement opponent of the New Deal. A close friend of business, he particularly detested labor unions. Though an ardent anticommunist, the isolationist-minded Taft did not support the aggressive policy of containment pursued by Truman, and he sharply criticized U.S. participation in NATO. Taft ran for president three times, and though he was never the Republican nominee, he won the loyalty of conservative Americans who saw the welfare state as a waste and international affairs as dangerous foreign entanglements.

One the other side, moderate Republicans looked to men like Eisenhower and Nelson Rockefeller, who supported international initiatives such as the Marshall Plan and NATO and were willing to tolerate labor unions and the welfare state. Eisenhower was a man without a political past. Believing that democracy required the military to stand aside, he had never voted. Rockefeller, the scion of one of the richest families in America, was a Cold War internationalist. He served in a variety of capacities under Eisenhower, including as an advisor on foreign affairs. Having made his political name, Rockefeller was elected the governor of New York in 1959 and became the de facto leader of the liberal wing of the Republican party.

For eight years, between 1952 and 1960, Eisenhower steered a precarious course from the middle of the

Dwight Eisenhower

In this photo taken during the 1952 presidential campaign, Dwight D. Eisenhower acknowledges cheers from supporters in Chicago. "Ike" as he was universally known, had been a popular five-star general in World War II (also serving as Supreme Allied Commander in the European theater), and turned to politics in the early 1950s as a member of the Republican Party. However, Eisenhower was a centrist who did little to disrupt the liberal social policies that Democrats had pursued since the 1930s.   © Bettmann/Corbis.

party, with conservative Taft Republicans on one side and liberal Rockefeller Republicans on the other. His popularity temporarily kept the two sides at bay, though staunch conservatives considered him a closet New Dealer. "Ike," as he was widely known, proved willing to work with the mostly Democratic-controlled congresses of those years. He signed bills increasing federal outlays for veterans' benefits, housing, highway construction (see Chapter 26), and Social Security, and increased the minimum wage from 75 cents an hour to $1. He supported the creation of the new Department of Health, Education, and Welfare in 1957. Like Truman, Eisenhower accepted some government responsibility for economic performance, part of a broad liberal consensus in American politics in these years.

America under Eisenhower | The power realities that had called forth containment guided Eisenhower's foreign policy. New developments, however, altered the tone of the Cold War. Stalin's death in March 1953 precipitated an intraparty struggle in the Soviet Union that lasted until 1956, when Nikita Khrushchev emerged as Stalin's successor. Khrushchev soon startled Communists around the world by denouncing Stalin and detailing his crimes and blunders. He also surprised Westerners by calling for "peaceful coexistence" and by dealing more flexibly with dissent in the Communist world. But the new Soviet leader had his limits, and when Hungarians rose up in 1956 to demand independence from Moscow, Khrushchev crushed the incipient revolution.

With no end to the Cold War in sight, Eisenhower turned his attention to limiting the cost of containment. The president hoped to economize by relying on a nuclear arsenal and skimping on expensive conventional forces. Under the "New Look" defense policy, the Eisenhower administration stepped up production of the hydrogen bomb and developed long-range bombing capabilities. The Soviets, however, matched the United States weapon for weapon. By 1958, both nations had intercontinental ballistic missiles. When an American nuclear submarine launched an atomic-tipped Polaris missile in 1960, Soviet engineers raced to produce an equivalent weapon.

Although confident in the international arena, Eisenhower started out a novice in domestic affairs. He did his best to set a less confrontational mood after the rancorous Truman years. He was reluctant to speak out against Joe McCarthy, and he was not a leader on civil rights. His acceptance of the welfare state, however, did not please the more conservative members of the Republican Party. Led by Taft and Arizona senator Barry Goldwater—and supported by the new conservative magazine *National Review*—conservatives began to revolt against liberal and moderate Republicans.

Democrats meanwhile maintained a strong presence in Congress but proved weak in presidential elections in the 1950s. In the two presidential contests of the decade, 1952 and 1956, Eisenhower defeated the admired but politically ineffectual liberal Adlai Stevenson. In the 1952 contest, Stevenson was hampered by the unpopularity of the Truman administration. The deadlocked Korean War and a series of scandals that Republicans dubbed "the mess in Washington" combined to give the war-hero general an easy victory. In 1956, Ike won an even more impressive victory over Stevenson, whose eloquent and learned speeches on liberalism led vice presidential candidate Richard Nixon to call him an "egghead."

During Eisenhower's presidency, new political forces on both the right and the left had begun to stir. But they had not yet fully transformed the party system itself. Particularly at the national level, Democrats and Republicans seemed in broad agreement about the realities of the Cold War and the demands of a modern, industrial economy and welfare state. Indeed, respected commentators in the 1950s declared "the end of ideology" and wondered if the great political clashes that had wracked the 1930s were gone forever. Below the apparent calm of national party politics lay profound differences among Americans over the direction of the nation. Those differences were most pronounced with regard to civil rights for African Americans. But a host of other issues had begun to emerge as controversial subjects that would soon starkly divide the country.

- **What were the components of Cold War liberalism?**
- **How did the Fair Deal differ from the New Deal?**
- **How does recently revealed information about espionage in American government affect how we evaluate McCarthyism?**

Containment in the Postcolonial World

The world scene was changing at a furious pace. New nations were emerging across the Middle East, Africa, and Asia, created in the wake of powerful anticolonial movements whose origins dated to before World War II. Between 1947 and 1962, the British, French, Dutch, and Belgian empires all but disintegrated in a momentous collapse of European global power. FDR had favored the idea of national self-determination, often to the fury of his British and French allies. He expected democracies to be established as new partners in an American-led, free-market world system. But when colonial revolts produced independent- or socialist-minded regimes in the so-called **Third World**, the Truman and Eisenhower administrations often treated them as pawns of the Soviet Union to be opposed at all costs.

The Cold War and Colonial Independence

The Eisenhower administration, concerned less about democracy than about stability, tended to support governments, no matter how repressive, that were overtly anticommunist. Some of America's staunchest allies—the Philippines, South Korea, Iran, Cuba, South Vietnam, and Nicaragua—were governed by dictatorships or right-wing regimes that lacked broad-based support. Moreover, Secretary of State John Foster Dulles often resorted to covert operations against governments that, in his opinion, were too closely aligned with the Soviets.

Believing that these emerging nations had to choose sides, the United States drew them into collective security agreements, with the NATO alliance in Europe as a model. Secretary of State Dulles orchestrated the creation of the Southeast Asia Treaty Organization (SEATO), which in 1954 linked America and its major European allies with Australia, New Zealand, Pakistan, the Philippines, and Thailand. An extensive system of defense alliances eventually tied the United States to more than forty other countries (Map 25.5). The United States also sponsored a strategically valuable defensive alliance between Iraq and Iran, on the southern flank of the Soviet Union.

For covert tasks, Dulles used the newly created (1947) Central Intelligence Agency (CIA), run by his brother, Allen Dulles. When Iran's nationalist premier, Mohammad Mossadegh, seized British oil properties in 1953, CIA agents helped depose him and, eventually, installed the young Mohammad Reza Pahlavi as

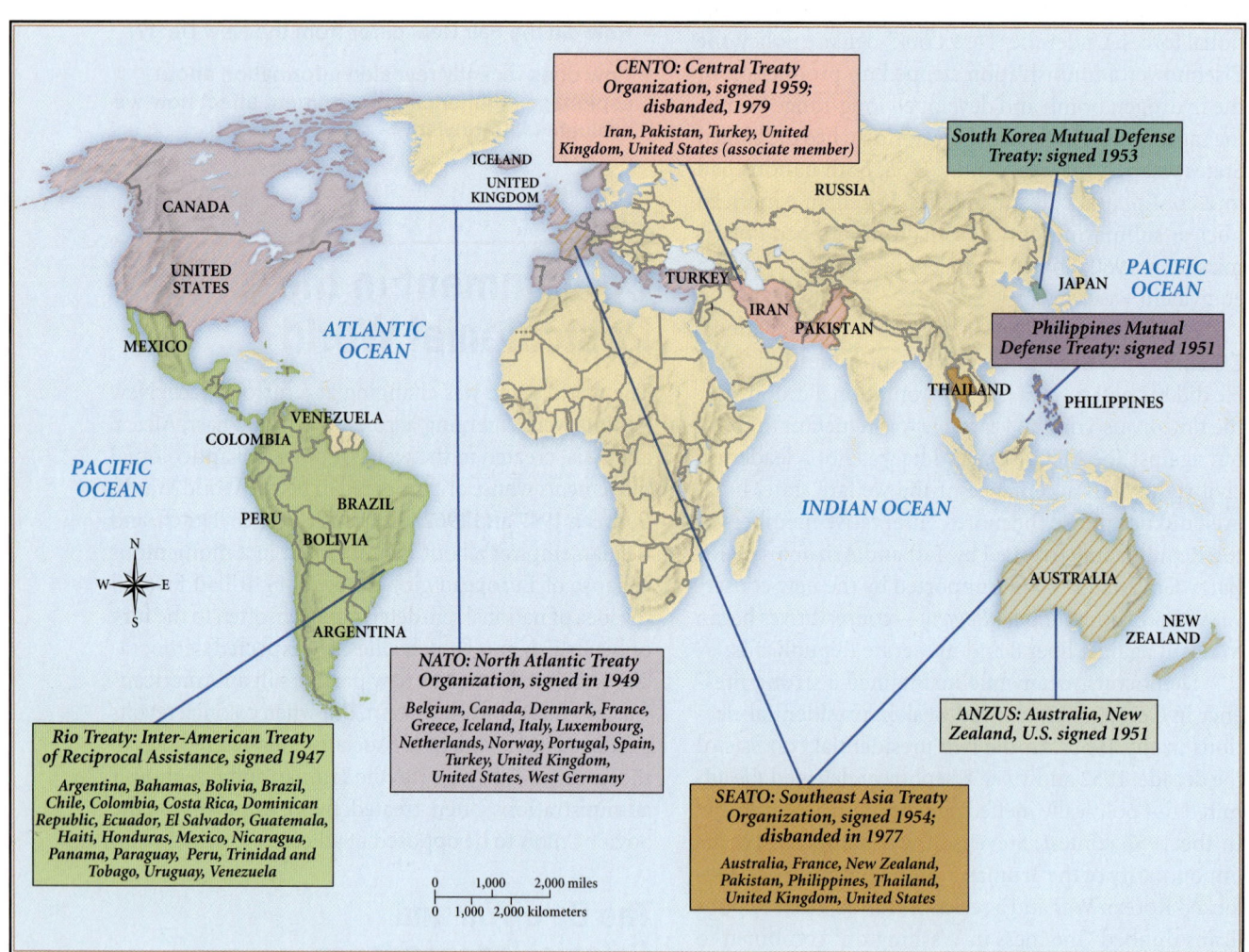

MAP 25.5

American Global Defense Treaties in the Cold War Era

The advent of the Cold War led to a major shift in American foreign policy—the signing of mutual defense treaties. Dating back to George Washington's call "to steer clear of permanent alliances with any portion of the foreign world," the United States had avoided treaty obligations that entailed the defense of other nations. As late as 1919, the U.S. Senate had rejected the principle of "collective security," the centerpiece of the League of Nations established by the Treaty of Versailles that ended World War I. But after World War II, in response to fears of Soviet global expansion, the United States entered defense alliances with much of the non-Communist world.

shah of Iran. Iranian resentment of the 1953 Iranian coup, followed by twenty-five years of U.S. support for the shah, eventually led to the 1979 Iranian Revolution (see Chapter 30). In 1954, the CIA engineered a coup in Guatemala against the democratically elected Jacobo Arbenz Guzmán, who had expropriated land owned by the American-owned United Fruit Company. Eisenhower specifically approved those CIA efforts and expanded the agency's mandate from gathering intelligence to intervening in the affairs of sovereign states.

Vietnam | But when covert operations and coups failed or proved impractical, the American approach to emerging nations could entangle the United States in deeper, more intractable conflicts. Such an instance was already unfolding on a distant stage, in a small country utterly unknown to most Americans: Vietnam. In August 1945, at the close of World War II, the Japanese occupiers of Vietnam surrendered to China in the north and Britain in the south. The Vietminh, the nationalist movement that had led the resistance against the Japanese, seized control in the north. But their leader, Ho Chi Minh, was a Communist, and this single fact outweighed American and British commitment to self-determination. When France moved to restore its control over the country, the United States and Britain sided with their European ally. President Truman rejected Ho's plea to support the Vietnamese struggle for independence. As soon as France returned, in late 1946, the Vietminh resumed their war of national liberation.

Eisenhower picked up where Truman left off. If the French failed, Eisenhower argued, all non-Communist governments in the region would collapse. This so-called "domino theory"—which represented an extension of the containment doctrine—guided U.S. policy in Southeast Asia for the next twenty years. The United States eventually provided most of the financing for the French war, but money was not enough to defeat the determined Vietminh, who were fighting for the liberation of their country. After a fifty-six-day siege in early 1954, the French went down to defeat at the huge fortress of Dien Bien Phu. The result was the 1954 Geneva Accords, which partitioned Vietnam temporarily at the 17th parallel and called for elections within two years to unify the troubled nation.

The United States rejected the Geneva Accords and immediately set about undermining them. With the help of the CIA, a pro-American government took power in South Vietnam in June 1954. Ngo Dinh Diem, an anticommunist Catholic who had been residing in the United States, returned to Vietnam as premier. The next year, in a rigged election, Diem became president of an independent South Vietnam. Facing certain defeat by the popular Ho Chi Minh, Diem called off the scheduled reunification elections. As the last French soldiers left in March 1956, the Eisenhower administration propped up Diem with an average of $200 million a year in aid and a contingent of 675 American military advisors. This support was just the beginning.

The Middle East | If Vietnam was still of minor concern, the same could not be said of the Middle East, an area rich in oil and political complexity. The most volatile area was Palestine, populated by Arabs but also historically the ancient land of Israel and coveted by the Zionist movement as a Jewish national homeland. After World War II, many survivors of the Nazi extermination camps resettled in Palestine, which was still controlled by Britain under a World War I mandate. On November 29, 1947, the U.N. General Assembly voted to partition Palestine between Jewish and Arab sectors. When the British mandate ended, Zionist leaders proclaimed the state of Israel. A coalition of Arab nations known as the Arab League invaded, but Israel survived. Many Palestinians fled or were driven from their homes during the fighting. The Arab defeat left these people permanently stranded in refugee camps. President Truman recognized the new state, winning crucial support from Jewish voters in the 1948 election but alienating the Arab world.

Southeast of Palestine, Egypt gained independence from Britain in 1952. Two years later, Gamal Abdel Nasser emerged as the new Egyptian leader. He proclaimed a pan-Arab socialism designed to end the Middle East's colonial relationship with the West. Caught between the Soviet Union and the United States, Nasser sought an independent route. In 1956, he nationalized the Suez Canal, which was the lifeline for Western Europe's oil. Britain and France, in alliance with Israel, attacked Egypt and seized the canal. Taken by surprise and embarrassed because he had just condemned the Soviet invasion of Hungary, Eisenhower demanded that France and Britain pull back. Egypt reclaimed the Suez Canal and built the Aswan Dam on the Nile with Soviet support.

In early 1957, concerned about Soviet influence in the Middle East, the president announced the Eisenhower Doctrine, which stated that American forces would assist any nation in the region that required aid "against overt armed aggression from any nation controlled by International Communism." Invoking the

The Suez Crisis, 1956

In this photograph, Egyptian president Gamal Abdel Nasser is greeted ecstatically by Cairo crowds after he nationalized the Suez Canal. Nasser's gamble paid off. Thanks to American intervention, military action by Britain, France, and Israel failed, and Nasser emerged as the triumphant voice of Arab nationalism across the Middle East. The popular emotions he unleashed against the West survived his death in 1970 and are more potent today than ever, although now expressed more through Islamic fundamentalism than Nasser's brand of secular nationalism.   Getty Images.

doctrine later that year, Eisenhower helped King Hussein of Jordan put down a Nasser-backed revolt and propped up a pro-American government in Lebanon. The Eisenhower Doctrine was further proof of the global reach of containment, in this instance accentuated by the strategic need to protect the West's access to steady supplies of oil.

John F. Kennedy and the Cold War

Charisma, style, and personality—these, more than platforms and issues, were hallmarks of a new brand of politics in the early 1960s. This was John F. Kennedy's natural environment. Kennedy, a Harvard alumnus,

World War II hero, and senator from Massachusetts, had inherited his love of politics from his grandfathers—colorful, and often ruthless, Irish Catholic politicians in Boston. Ambitious and deeply aware of style, the forty-three-year-old Kennedy made use of his many advantages to become, as novelist Norman Mailer put it, "our leading man." His one disadvantage—that he was Catholic in a country that had never elected a Catholic president—he masterfully neutralized. And thanks to both media advisors and his youthful attractiveness, Kennedy projected a superb television image.

At heart, however, Kennedy was a Cold Warrior who had come of age in the shadow of Munich, Yalta, and the McCarthy hearings. He projected an air of

The Kennedy Magnetism

John F. Kennedy, the 1960 Democratic candidate for president, used his youth and personality (and that of his equally personable and stylish wife) to attract voters. Here the Massachusetts senator draws an enthusiastic crowd on a campaign stop in Elgin, Illinois.   AP Images.

idealism, but his years in the Senate (1953–1960) had proved him to be a conventional Cold War politician. Once elected president, Kennedy would shape the nation's foreign policy by drawing both on his ingenuity and on old-style Cold War power politics.

The Election of 1960 and the New Frontier Kennedy's Republican opponent in the 1960 presidential election, Eisenhower's vice president, Richard M. Nixon, was a seasoned politician and Cold Warrior himself. The great innovation of the 1960 campaign was a series of four nationally televised debates. Nixon, less photogenic than Kennedy, looked sallow and unshaven under the intense studio lights. Polls showed that television swayed political perceptions. Voters who heard the first debate on the radio concluded that Nixon had won, but those who viewed it on television favored Kennedy. Despite the edge Kennedy enjoyed in the debates, he won only the narrowest of electoral victories, receiving 49.7 percent of the popular vote to Nixon's 49.5 percent. Kennedy attracted Catholics, blacks, and the labor vote; his vice-presidential running mate, Texas senator Lyndon Baines Johnson, helped bring in southern Democrats. Yet only 120,000 votes separated the two candidates, and the shift of a few thousand votes in key states would have reversed the outcome.

Kennedy brought to Washington a cadre of young, ambitious newcomers, including Robert McNamara, a renowned systems analyst and former head of Ford Motor Company, as secretary of defense. A host of trusted advisors and academics flocked to Washington to join the New Frontier. Included on the team as attorney general was Kennedy's younger brother Robert, who had made a name as a hard-hitting investigator of organized crime. But not everyone was enchanted. Kennedy's people "may be every bit as intelligent as you say," House Speaker Sam Rayburn told his old friend Lyndon Johnson, "but I'd feel a whole lot better about them if just one of them had run for sheriff once." Sure enough, the new administration immediately got into hot water.

Crises in Cuba and Berlin In January 1961, the Soviet Union announced that it intended to support "wars of national liberation" wherever in the world they occurred. Kennedy took Soviet premier Nikita Khrushchev's words as a challenge, especially as they applied to Cuba, where in 1959 Fidel Castro had overthrown the right-wing dictator Fulgencio Batista and declared a revolution. Determined to keep Cuba out of the Soviet orbit, Kennedy followed through on Eisenhower administration plans to dispatch Cuban exiles to foment an anti-Castro uprising. The invaders, trained by the Central Intelligence Agency, were ill-prepared for their task. On landing at Cuba's Bay of Pigs on April 17, 1961, the force of 1,400 was crushed by Castro's troops. Kennedy had the good sense

MAP 25.6

The United States and Cuba, 1961–1962

Fidel Castro's 1959 Communist takeover of Cuba brought Cold War tensions to the Caribbean. In 1961, the United States tried unsuccessfully to overthrow Castro's regime by sponsoring the Bay of Pigs invasion of Cuban exiles launched from Nicaragua and other points in the Caribbean. In 1962, the United States confronted the Soviet Union over Soviet construction of nuclear missile sites in Cuba. After President Kennedy ordered a naval blockade of the island, the Soviets backed down from the tense standoff and removed the missiles. Despite the 1991 dissolution of the Soviet Union and the official end of the Cold War, the United States continues to view Cuba, still governed in 2010 by Fidel Castro, as an enemy nation.

to reject CIA pleas for a U.S. air strike. Accepting defeat, Kennedy went before the American people and took full responsibility for the fiasco (Map 25.6).

Already strained by the Bay of Pigs incident, U.S.-Soviet relations deteriorated further in June 1961 when Khrushchev stopped movement between Communist-controlled East Berlin and the city's western sector. Kennedy responded by dispatching 40,000 more troops to Europe. The young president further irked Khrushchev by delivering a major speech in Berlin in late June expressing solidarity with the city's residents. *"Ich bin ein Berliner!"* ("I am a Berliner!"), Kennedy pronounced. But in mid-August, to stop the exodus of East Germans, the Communist regime began constructing the Berlin

Wall, policed by border guards under shoot-to-kill orders. Until the 12-foot-high concrete barrier came down in 1989, it served as the supreme symbol of the Cold War.

The climactic Cold War confrontation came in October 1962. In a somber televised address on October 22, Kennedy revealed that U.S. reconnaissance planes had spotted Soviet-built bases for intermediate-range ballistic missiles in Cuba. Some of those weapons had already been installed, and more were on the way. Kennedy announced that the United States would impose a "quarantine on all offensive military equipment" on its way to Cuba. As the world held its breath waiting to see if the conflict would escalate into war, on October 25, ships carrying Soviet missiles turned back. After a week of

The Berlin Wall

A West Berlin resident walks alongside a section of the Berlin Wall in August 1962, a year after its construction. Note the two border guards on the East Berlin side, plus the numerous loudspeakers, which East German Communists used to broadcast propaganda over the barricade that divided the city.
© Bettmann/Corbis.

tense negotiations, both sides made concessions: Kennedy pledged not to invade Cuba, and Khrushchev promised to dismantle the missile bases. Kennedy also secretly ordered U.S. missiles to be removed from Turkey, at Khrushchev's insistence. The risk of nuclear war, greater during the Cuban missile crisis than at any other time in the Cold War, prompted a slight thaw in U.S.-Soviet relations. As national security advisor McGeorge Bundy put it, both sides were chastened by "having come so close to the edge."

Kennedy and the World   Kennedy also launched a series of bold nonmilitary initiatives. One was the Peace Corps, which embodied a call to public service put forth in his inaugural address ("Ask not what your country can do for you, but what you can

do for your country"). Thousands of men and women agreed to devote two or more years as volunteers for projects such as teaching English to Filipino school-children or helping African villagers obtain clean water. Exhibiting the idealism of the early 1960s, the Peace Corps was also a low-cost Cold War weapon intended to show the developing world that there was an alternative to Communism. Kennedy was also keen on space exploration. In a 1962 speech, he proposed that the nation commit itself to landing a man on the moon within the decade. The Soviets had already beaten the United States into space with the 1961 flight of cosmonaut Yuri Gagarin. Capitalizing on America's fascination with space, Kennedy persuaded Congress to increase funding for the National Aeronautics and Space Administration (NASA), enabling the United States to

The Cuban Missile Crisis
During the 1962 Cuban Missile Crisis, President Kennedy meets with U.S. Army officials. Over two tense weeks, the world watched as the United States and the Soviet Union went to the brink of war when it became known that Soviet military officials had begun to construct nuclear weapons bases in Cuba, a mere 90 miles from the southern tip of Florida. Kennedy's threat to intercept Soviet missile shipments with American naval vessels forced the Cold War adversary to back down.   © Corbis

pull ahead of the Soviet Union. Kennedy's ambition was realized when U.S. astronauts arrived on the moon in 1969.

Making a Commitment in Vietnam

Despite slight improvements, U.S.-Soviet relations remained tense and containment the cornerstone of U.S. policy. When Kennedy became president, he inherited Eisenhower's commitment in Vietnam. Kennedy saw Vietnam in Cold War terms, but rather than practicing brinksmanship—threatening nuclear war to stop Communism—Kennedy sought what at the time seemed a more intelligent and realistic approach. He increased the amount of aid sent to the South Vietnamese military and dramatically expanded the role of U.S. Special Forces ("Green Berets") in training the South Vietnamese army in unconventional, small-group warfare tactics.

South Vietnam's corrupt and repressive Diem regime, propped up by Eisenhower since 1954, was losing ground in spite of American aid. By 1961, Diem's

opponents, with backing from North Vietnam, had formed a revolutionary movement known as the National Liberation Front (NLF). NLF guerrilla forces—the Vietcong—found loyalty among peasants alienated by Diem's "strategic hamlet" program, which had uprooted entire villages and moved villagers into barbed-wire compounds. Too, Buddhists charged Diem, a Catholic, with religious persecution. Starting in May 1963, militant Buddhists staged dramatic demonstrations, including self-immolations recorded by American television news crews covering the activities of the 16,000 U.S. military personnel then in Vietnam.

The Buddhist self-immolations, carried by television to an uneasy global audience, powerfully illustrated the dilemmas embedded in U.S. policy in Vietnam. In order to ensure a stable southern government and prevent victory for Ho Chi Minh and the North, the United States had to support Diem's authoritarian regime. But the political repression used by the regime to quell massive opposition to Diem's rule simply made the regime more unpopular. Whether one supported U.S. involvement in Vietnam or not, the elemental

Buddhist Monk's Self-Immolation
One of the most stunning sights of the Vietnam War: the self-immolation of a Buddhist monk in a public square, in the Vietnamese capital city of Saigon. In the summer of 1963, Buddhist monks protested their treatment by Ngo Dinh Diem, the U.S.-backed leader of South Vietnam. Diem, a Catholic, had suppressed Buddhist rituals and favored other Catholics in land distribution and government employment. To dramatize their persecution, more than half a dozen monks committed suicide by lighting themselves on fire in public. AP Images.

paradox remained unchanged: In its efforts to win, the United States brought defeat ever closer.

Nothing proved that paradox more than the events of early November 1963. Having lost patience with Diem, Kennedy let it be known in Saigon that the United States would support a military coup. Kennedy's hope was that if the dictatorial Diem, now reviled throughout the south, could be replaced by a popular general or other military figure, a stable government — one strong enough to repel the NLF — would emerge. But when Diem was overthrown on November 1, the generals went further than Kennedy's team had anticipated and assassinated both Diem and his brother. This made the coup look less like an organic uprising and more like an American plot. South Vietnam fell into a period of chaos marked by a series of coups and defined by the increasing ungovernability of both the cities and countryside. Kennedy himself was assassinated in late November and would not live to see the grim results of Diem's murder: American engagement in a long and costly civil conflict in the name of fighting communism.

- How did America's deepening involvement in the Third World in the 1950s present the nation with a dilemma?

- Why did the United States support right-wing dictatorships?

- In what ways was Kennedy's foreign policy a break with past? In what ways was it not?

SUMMARY

We have seen how the Cold War began as a conflict between the United States and the Soviet Union over Eastern Europe and the fate of Germany. Very early in the conflict, the United States adopted a strategy of containment. Although initially intended only for Europe, the containment strategy quickly expanded to Asia after China became a Communist state under Mao Zedong. The first effect of that expansion was the Korean War, after which, under Dwight D. Eisenhower, containment of communism became America's guiding principle across the developing world — often called the Third World. Cold War tensions relaxed in the late 1950s but erupted again under John F. Kennedy, with the Cuban missile crisis, the building of the Berlin Wall, and major increases in American military assistance to South Vietnam. Cold War imperatives between 1945 and the early 1960s meant a major military buildup, a massive nuclear arms race, and unprecedented entanglements across the globe.

We have also seen how, on the domestic front, Harry S. Truman started out with high hopes for an expanded New Deal, only to be stymied by resistance from Congress and the competing demands of the Cold War. The greatest Cold War–inspired distraction, however, was a climate of fear over internal subversion by Communists that gave rise to McCarthyism. Truman's successor, Eisenhower, brought the Republicans back into power. Although personally conservative,

Eisenhower actually proved a New Dealer in disguise. He declined to cut back on social welfare programs and broke new ground in federal spending on highways, scientific research, and higher education. When Eisenhower left office, and Kennedy became president, it seemed that a "liberal consensus" prevailed, with old-fashioned, **laissez-faire** conservatism mostly marginalized in American political life.

CHAPTER REVIEW QUESTIONS

- What factors gave rise to the Cold War?

- What was the domestic impact of the anticommunist crusade of the late 1940s and 1950s?

- Why did the United States become involved in Vietnam?

FOR FURTHER EXPLORATION

On the Cold War from different perspectives, see John Lewis Gaddis, *The Cold War: A New History* (2005), and Thomas J. McCormick, *America's Half Century: United States Foreign Policy in the Cold War and After* (1989). On the Fair Deal, see Alonzo Hamby, *Beyond the New Deal: Harry S. Truman and American Liberalism* (1973). Jennifer Klein, in *For All These Rights* (2003), explains why the United States failed to develop a national health-care system. On McCarthyism, Ellen Schrecker, *Many Are the Crimes: McCarthyism in America* (1998), is excellent. For analysis of Soviet espionage, see John Earl Haynes and Harvey Klehr, *Venona: Decoding Soviet Espionage in America* (1999). David Halberstam's *The Fifties* (1993) offers a brief but searing account of CIA covert activities in Iran and Guatemala. A good starting point for Kennedy's presidency is W. J. Rorabaugh, *Kennedy and the Promise of the Sixties* (2002).

The Woodrow Wilson International Center has established the Cold War International History Project at **www.wilsoncenter.org/cwihp**. The Center for the Study of the Pacific Northwest's site, "The Cold War and Red Scare in Washington State," at **www.washington.edu/uwired/outreach/cspn/Website/Resources/Curriculum/Cold War/Cold War Main.html**, provides detailed information on how the Red Scare operated in one state. The Truman Library site's "1948 Whistle Stop Tour" feature is at **www.trumanlibrary.org/whistlestop/TruWhisTour/coverpge.htm**. "Korea + 50: No Longer Forgotten" is cosponsored by the Harry S. Truman and Dwight D. Eisenhower Presidential Libraries, at **www.trumanlibrary.org/korea**.

TEST YOUR KNOWLEDGE

To assess your command of the material in this chapter, see the Online Study Guide at **bedfordstmartins.com/henretta**.

For Web sites, images, and documents related to topics and places in this chapter, visit **bedfordstmartins.com/makehistory**.

TIMELINE

1945	Yalta and Potsdam conferences End of World War II Senate approves U.S. participation in United Nations
1946	George F. Kennan outlines containment policy War begins between French and Vietminh over control of Vietnam
1947	Truman Doctrine House Un-American Activities Committee (HUAC) investigates film industry Marshall Plan aids economic recovery in Europe
1948	Communist coup in Czechoslovakia State of Israel created Stalin blockades West Berlin; Berlin airlift begins
1949	North Atlantic Treaty Organization (NATO) founded Soviet Union detonates atomic bomb Mao Zedong establishes People's Republic of China
1950–1953	Korean War
1950	NSC-68 leads to nuclear buildup Joseph McCarthy announces "list" of Communists in government
1952	Dwight D. Eisenhower elected president
1953	Joseph Stalin dies
1954	Army-McCarthy hearings on army subversion French defeat at Dienbienphu in Vietnam Geneva Accords partition Vietnam
1956	Crises in Hungary and at Suez Canal
1958	National Aeronautics and Space Administration (NASA) established
1960	John F. Kennedy elected president
1961	Eisenhower warns nation against military-industrial complex Kennedy orders the first contingent of Special Forces ("Green Berets") to Vietnam
1963	Diem assassinated in South Vietnam

Triumph of the Middle Class, 1945–1963

At the height of the Cold War, in 1959, U.S. vice president Richard Nixon debated Soviet premier Nikita Khrushchev on the merits of Pepsi-Cola, TV dinners, and electric ovens. Face-to-face at the opening of the American National Exhibit in Moscow, Nixon and Khrushchev strolled through a model American home, assembled to demonstrate the consumer products available to the typical citizen of the United States. Nixon explained to Khrushchev that although the Soviet Union may have had superior rockets, the United States was ahead in other areas, such as color television.

This was Cold War politics by other means – a symbolic contest over which country's standard of living was higher. What was so striking about the so-called kitchen debate was Nixon's insistence, to a disbelieving Khrushchev, that a modern home filled with shiny new refrigerators, toasters, televisions, and all manner of other consumer products was, rather than a luxury, accessible to the average American worker. "Any steelworker could buy this house," Nixon told the Soviet leader, who stood with other members of the politburo before cameras and reporters. Ever practical, Khrushchev noted, "Many things you've shown us are interesting but they are not needed in life." He added, condescendingly, "They are merely gadgets."

The kitchen debate settled little in the geopolitical rivalry between the United States and the Soviet Union. But it speaks to us across the decades because it reveals how Americans had come to see themselves by the late 1950s: as homeowners and consumers, as a people for whom the middle-class American dream was a commercial aspiration. The designers of the model home in Moscow, architect Andrew Geller and developer Herbert Sadkin, went on to build suburban developments on the East Coast, including the aptly named Leisurama on New York's Long Island. They were among legions of Americans – including architects, developers, advertising executives, and landscape designers – who created new middle-class tastes in the postwar decades.

The real story of the postwar period was the growing number of Americans who adopted those tastes. In the two decades following the end of World War II, nothing short of a new middle class was born in the United States. *Fortune* magazine estimated that in the 1950s the middle class – defined as families with more than $5,000 in annual earnings after taxes (about $40,000 today) – was increasing at the rate of 1.1 million people per year. Riding a wave of rising incomes, American dominance in the global economy, and Cold War federal spending, the postwar middle class enjoyed the highest standard of living in the world.

The Middle-Class Family Ideal

A family eats breakfast at a campground in Zion National Park, Utah. Americans embraced a middle-class, nuclear family ideal in the postwar decades. Photo by Justin Locke/National Geographic/Getty Images.

However, the success of the middle class could not hide deeper troubles. This was an era of neither universal conformity nor diminishing social strife. Jim Crow laws, contradictions in women's lives, cultural rebelliousness among young people, and changing sexual mores were only the most obvious sources of social tension. Suburban growth came at the expense of cities, hastening inner-city decay and exacerbating racial segregation. Nor was prosperity ever as widespread as the Moscow exhibit implied. The suburban lifestyle was beyond the reach of the working poor, the elderly, immigrants, Mexican Americans, and most African Americans—indeed, the majority of the country.

Economy: From Recovery to Dominance

The United States enjoyed enormous economic advantages at the close of World War II. While the Europeans and Japanese were still clearing the war's rubble, America stood poised to enter a postwar boom. As the only major industrial nation not devastated by war, the United States held an unprecedented global position. The American economy also benefited from an expanding internal market and heavy investment in research and development. Two additional developments stood out: One was that, for the first time in the nation's history, employers generally accepted collective bargaining, which for workers translated into rising wages, expanding benefits, and an increasing rate of home ownership. The other was that the federal government's outlays for military and domestic programs gave a huge boost to the economy.

Engines of Economic Growth

U.S. corporations, banks, and manufacturers so dominated the world economy that the postwar period has been called the Pax Americana (a Latin term meaning "American Peace" and harking back to the Pax Romana of the first and second centuries A.D.). So confident was he in the nation's growing power that during World War II, *Life* magazine publisher Henry Luce had immodestly predicted that the world was witnessing the dawning of the "American century." The preponderance of American economic power in the postwar decades, however, was not simply an artifact of the global war—it was not an inevitable development. Several key elements came together, internationally and at home, to propel three decades of unprecedented economic growth.

The Bretton Woods System American global supremacy rested partly on the economic institutions created at a United Nations conference in Bretton Woods, New Hampshire, in July 1944. The first of those institutions was the World Bank, created to provide loans for the reconstruction of war-torn Europe as well as for the development of former colonized nations—the so-called Third World or developing world. A second institution, the International Monetary Fund (IMF), was set up to stabilize currencies and provide a predictable monetary environment for trade, with the U.S. dollar serving as the benchmark. Third, in 1947, multilateral trade negotiations resulted in the first General Agreement on Tariffs and Trade (GATT), which established an international framework for overseeing trade rules and practices.

The World Bank, the IMF, and GATT formed the cornerstones of the Bretton Woods system, which guided the world economy after the war. The Bretton Woods system served America's conception of an open-market global economy and complemented the nation's ambitious diplomatic aims in the Cold War. Anything less, Secretary of State Dean Acheson told Congress, would lead to "shrinking international trade, lower levels of living, and hostility between nations." The chief idea of the Bretton Woods system was to make American capital available, on cheap terms, to nations that adopted free-trade capitalist economies. Critics charged, rightly, that Bretton Woods favored the United States at the expense of recently independent countries, because the United States could dictate lending terms and stood to benefit as nations purchased more American goods.

The Military-Industrial Complex A second engine of postwar prosperity was defense spending. In his final address to the nation in 1961, President Dwight D. Eisenhower spoke about the power of what he called the military-industrial

The Kitchen Debate

At the American National Exhibition in Moscow in 1959, the United States put on display the technological wonders of American home life. When Vice President Richard Nixon visited, he and Soviet premier Nikita Khrushchev got into a heated debate over the relative merits of their rival systems, with the up-to-date American kitchen as a case in point. This photograph shows the debate in progress. Khrushchev is the bald man pointing his finger at Nixon. To Nixon's left stands Leonid Brezhnev, who would be Khrushchev's successor.   Getty Images.

complex, which by then employed 3.5 million Americans. Even though his administration had fostered this defense establishment, Eisenhower feared its implications: "We must guard against the acquisition of unwarranted influence, whether sought or unsought, by the military-industrial complex," he said. The military-industrial complex that Eisenhower identified had its roots in the business-government partnerships of World War II. After 1945, though the country was nominally at peace, the economy and the government operated in a state of perpetual readiness for war.

Based at the sprawling Pentagon in Arlington, Virginia, the Defense Department evolved into a massive bureaucracy. In the name of national security, defense-related industries entered into long-term relationships with the Pentagon. Some companies did so much business with the government that they in effect became private divisions of the Defense Department. Over 60 percent of the income of Boeing, General Dynamics, and Raytheon, for instance, came from military contracts, and the percentages were even higher for Lockheed and Republic Aviation. In previous peacetime years, military spending had constituted only 1 percent of gross domestic product (GDP); now it represented 10 percent. Economic growth was increasingly dependent on a robust defense sector.

As permanent mobilization took hold, science, industry, and the federal government became intertwined. Cold War competition for military supremacy spawned both an arms race and a space race. The United States and the Soviet Union each sought to de-

velop more explosive bombs and more powerful rockets. Federal spending underwrote 90 percent of the cost of research for aviation and space, 65 percent for electricity and electronics, 42 percent for scientific instruments, and even 24 percent for automobiles. With the government footing the bill, corporations lost little time in transforming new technology into useful products. Backed by the Pentagon, for instance, IBM and Sperry Rand pressed ahead with research on integrated circuits, which later spawned the computer revolution.

When the Soviet Union launched the world's first satellite, *Sputnik*, in 1957, the startled United States went into high gear to catch up in the Cold War space competition. Alarmed that the United States was falling behind in science and technology, Eisenhower persuaded Congress to appropriate additional money for college scholarships and university research. The National Defense Education Act of 1958 funneled millions of dollars into American universities, helping institutions such as the University of California at Berkeley, Stanford University, the Massachusetts Institute of Technology, and the University of Michigan become the leading research centers in the world.

The defense buildup also created jobs—lots of them. Taking into account the additional positions created to serve and support defense workers, perhaps one American in seven owed his or her job to the military-industrial complex by the 1960s. But increased military spending also limited the resources for domestic social needs. Critics calculated the tradeoffs: The money spent

The Military-Industrial Complex

Often, technology developed for military purposes, such as the complex design of jet airplanes, was easily transferred to the consumer market. The Boeing Aircraft Company—their Seattle plant is pictured here in the mid-1950s—became one of the leading commercial airplane manufacturers in the world in the 1960s, boosted in part by tax dollar—financed military contracts. Major American corporations—such as Boeing, McDonnell Douglas, General Electric, General Dynamics, and dozens of others—benefited enormously from military contracts from the Department of Defense in the years after World War II. © Bettmann/Corbis.

for a nuclear aircraft carrier and support ships could have paid for a subway system for Washington, D.C., while the cost of one Huey helicopter could have built sixty-six units of low-income housing.

Corporate Power | For over half a century, the consolidation of economic power into large corporate firms had characterized American capitalism. In the postwar decades, that tendency accelerated. By 1970, the top four U.S. automakers produced 91 percent of all motor vehicles sold in the country; the top four firms in tires produced 72 percent; those in cigarettes, 84 percent; and those in detergents, 70 percent. Eric Johnston, former president of the American Chamber of Commerce, declared that "we have entered a period of accelerating *bigness* in all aspects of American life." Expansion into foreign markets also spurred corporate growth. During the 1950s, U.S. exports nearly doubled, giving the nation a trade surplus of close to

$5 billion in 1960. By the 1970s, such firms as Coca-Cola, Gillette, IBM, and Mobil made more than half their profits abroad.

To staff their bureaucracies, the postwar corporate giants required a huge white-collar army. A new generation of corporate chieftains emerged, operating in a complex environment that demanded long-range forecasting. Companies turned to the universities, which grew explosively after 1945. Postwar corporate culture inspired numerous critics, who argued that the obedience demanded of white-collar workers was stifling creativity and blighting lives. In *The Lonely Crowd* (1950), the sociologist David Riesman mourned a lost masculinity and contrasted the independent businessmen and professionals of earlier years with the managerial class of the postwar world. The sociologist William Whyte painted a somber picture of "organization men" who left the home "spiritually as well as physically to take the vows of organization life." Andrew Hacker, in *The*

Corporation Take-Over (1964), warned that a small handful of such organization men "can draw up an investment program calling for the expenditure of several billions of dollars" and thereby "determine the quality of life for substantial segments of society."

Many of these "investment programs" relied on mechanization, or automation—another important factor in the postwar boom. From 1947 to 1975, worker productivity more than doubled across the whole of the economy. American factories replaced manpower with machines, substituting cheap fossil energy for human muscle. As industries mechanized, they could turn out products more efficiently and at lower cost. Mechanization did not come without social costs, however. Over the course of the postwar decades, millions of high-wage manufacturing jobs were lost as machines replaced workers, affecting entire cities and regions. Corporate leaders approved, but workers and their union representatives were less enthusiastic. "How are you going to sell cars to all of these machines?" wondered Walter Reuther, president of the United Auto Workers (UAW).

The Economic Record The military-industrial complex produced an extraordinary economic record. America's annual GDP jumped from $213 billion in 1945 to more than $500 billion in 1960; by 1970, it exceeded $1 trillion (Figure 26.1). This sustained economic growth meant a 25 percent rise in real income for ordinary Americans between 1946 and 1959. Even better, the new prosperity featured low inflation. After a burst of high prices in the immediate postwar period, inflation slowed to 2 to 3 percent annually, and it stayed low until the escalation of the Vietnam War in the mid-1960s. Low inflation meant stable and predictable prices. Feeling secure about the future, Americans were eager to spend and rightly felt that they were better off than ever before. In 1940, 43 percent of American families owned their homes; by 1960, 62 percent did. In that period, moreover, income inequality dropped sharply. The share of total income going to the top tenth—the richest Americans—declined by nearly one-third from the 45 percent it had been in 1940. American society had become not only more prosperous but also more egalitarian.

However, the picture was not as rosy at the bottom, where tenacious poverty accompanied the economic boom. In *The Affluent Society* (1958), economist John Kenneth Galbraith argued that the poor were only an "afterthought" in the minds of economists and politicians, who largely celebrated the new growth. As Galbraith noted, one in thirteen families at the time earned less than $1,000 a year (about $7,500 in today's

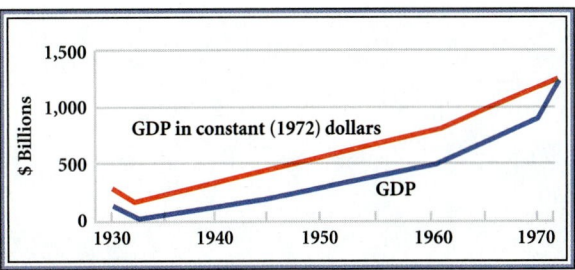

FIGURE 26.1

Gross Domestic Product, 1930–1972

After a sharp dip during the Great Depression, the GDP rose steadily in both real and constant dollars in the postwar period.

dollars). Four years later, in *The Other America* (1962), Michael Harrington chronicled "the economic underworld of American life," and a U.S. government study, echoing a well-known sentence from Franklin Roosevelt's second inaugural address ("I see one-third of a nation ill-housed, ill-clad, ill-nourished"), declared "one-third of the nation" to be poorly paid, poorly educated, and poorly housed. It appeared that in economic terms, as the top and the middle converged, the bottom remained far behind.

A Nation of Consumers

The most breathtaking development in the postwar American economy was the dramatic expansion of the domestic consumer market. The sheer quantity of consumer goods available to the average person was without precedent. In some respects, the postwar decades seemed like the 1920s all over again, with an abundance of new gadgets and appliances, a craze for automobiles, and new types of mass media. Yet there was a significant difference: In the 1950s, consumption became associated with citizenship. Buying things, once a sign of personal indulgence, now meant participating fully in American society and, moreover, fulfilling a social responsibility. What the suburban family consumed, asserted *Life* magazine in a photo essay, would help to ensure "full employment and improved living standards for the rest of the nation."

The GI Bill The new ethic of consumption appealed to the postwar middle class, the driving force behind the expanding domestic market. Middle-class status was more accessible than ever before because of the Serviceman's Readjustment Act of 1944, popularly known as the GI Bill. In the immediate postwar years, more than half of all U.S. college students

College on the GI Bill

In 1947 – the year this photo was taken of a crowded lecture hall at the University of Iowa – more than 6,000 of this university's 10,000 students (60 percent) were veterans whose education was financed by the G.I. Bill. Across the country, American universities were bursting at the seams from the massive enrollment of World War II veterans. Government financing of college education for these vets made the U.S. workforce one of the best educated in the world in the 1950s and 1960s. Margaret Bourke-White/Time Life Pictures/Getty Images.

were veterans attending class on the government's dime. By the middle of the 1950s, 2.2 million veterans had attended college and another 5.6 million had attended trade school with government financing. The son of an Italian immigrant from Queens, New York, said simply: "It was a hell of a gift, an opportunity, and I've never thought of it any other way." Before the GI Bill, commented another, "I looked upon college education as likely as my owning a Rolls-Royce with a chauffeur."

Government financing of education helped make the U.S. workforce the best educated in the world in the 1950s and 1960s. American colleges, universities, and trade schools grew by leaps and bounds to accommodate the flood of students — and expanded again when the children of those students, the baby boomers, reached college age in the 1960s. At Rutgers University, enrollment went from 7,000 before the war to 16,000 in 1947; at the University of Minnesota, from 15,000 to more than 27,000. The GI Bill trained nearly half a million engineers, 200,000 doctors, dentists, and nurses, and 150,000 scientists (among many other professions). Better education meant higher earning power, and higher earning power translated into the consumer spending that drove the postwar economy. One observer of the GI Bill was so impressed with its achievements that he declared it responsible for "the most important educational and social transformation in American history."

The GI Bill stimulated the economy and expanded the middle class in another way: Home ownership increased under its auspices. Between the end of World War II and 1966, one of every five single-family homes built in the United States was financed through a GI Bill mortgage — 2.5 million new homes in all. In cities and suburbs across the country, the Veterans Administration (VA), which helped former soldiers purchase new homes with no down payment, sparked a building boom that created jobs in the construction industry and fueled consumer spending in home appliances and automobiles. Education and home ownership were more than personal triumphs for the families of World War II veterans (and Korean War veterans, after a new GI Bill was passed in 1952). They were concrete financial *assets* that helped lift more Americans than ever before into a mass-consumption-oriented middle class.

Trade Unions Organized labor also expanded the ranks of the middle class. For the first time ever, trade unions and collective bargaining became major factors in the nation's economic life. In the past, organized labor had been confined to a narrow band of craft trades and a few industries, primarily coal mining, railroading, and the building and metal trades. The power balance shifted during the Great Depression, and by the time the dust settled after World

War II, labor unions overwhelmingly represented America's industrial workforce (Figure 26.2). A question then arose: How would labor's power be used?

In late 1945, Walter Reuther of the UAW thought he knew. The youthful Reuther was thinking big, beyond a single company or even a single industry. He aimed at nothing less than a reshaped, high-wage economy. To jump-start it, he demanded a 30 percent wage hike from General Motors (GM) with no price increase for GM cars. When GM said it could not afford such largesse, Reuther demanded that the company "open the books"—a demand that company executives implacably resisted. The company endured a 113-day strike and soundly defeated the UAW. Having made its point, GM laid out its terms for a durable relationship. It would accept the UAW as a bargaining partner and guarantee GM workers an ever-higher living standard. The price was that the UAW abandon its assault on the company's "right to manage." Reuther accepted the company's terms and signed the five-year GM contract of 1950—the Treaty of Detroit, it was called.

The Treaty of Detroit opened the way for a broader "labor-management accord"—not industrial peace, because the country still experienced many strikes, but general acceptance of collective bargaining as the method for setting the terms of employment. For industrial workers, the result was rising real income. The average worker with three dependents gained 18 percent in spendable real income in the 1950s. In addition, unions delivered greater leisure (more paid holidays and longer vacations) and, in a startling departure, a social safety net. In postwar Europe, America's allies were constructing welfare states. But having lost the bruising battle in Washington for national health care during Truman's presidency, American unions turned to the bargaining table. By the end of the 1950s, union contracts commonly provided pension plans and company-paid health insurance. Collective bargaining had become, in effect, the American alternative to the European welfare state and, as Reuther boasted, the passport into the middle class.

The labor-management accord, though impressive, was never as durable or universal as it seemed. Vulnerabilities lurked. For one thing, the sheltered domestic markets—the essential condition for generous contracts—were in fact quite fragile. In certain industries, the lead firms were already losing market share. Second, generally overlooked were the many unorganized workers with no middle-class passport—those consigned to unorganized industries, casual labor, or low-wage jobs in the service sector. A final vulnerabil-

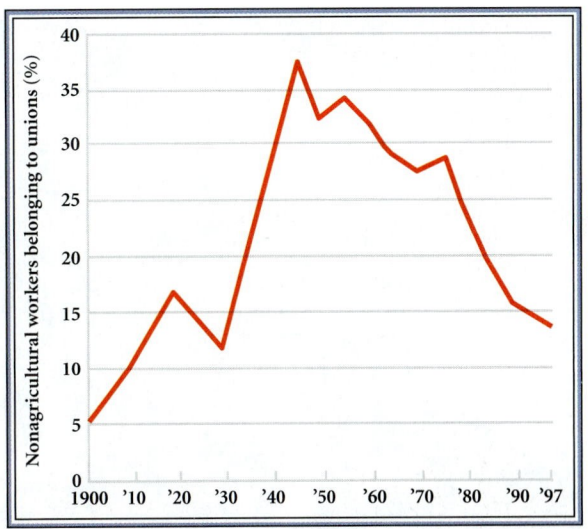

FIGURE 26.2

Labor Union Strength, 1900–1997

Labor unions reached their peak strength immediately after World War II, when they represented close to 40 percent of the nonfarm workforce. Although there was some decline after the mid-1950s, unions still represented nearly 30 percent in 1973. Thereafter, their decline was precipitous.
AFL-CIO Information Bureau, Washington, D.C.

ity was the most basic: the abiding anti-unionism of American employers. At heart, managers regarded the labor-management accord as a negotiated truce, not a permanent peace. It was only a matter of time and the onset of a more competitive environment before the scattered anti-union forays of the 1950s turned into a full-scale counteroffensive. The postwar labor-management accord turned out to be a transitory event, not a permanent condition of American economic life.

Houses, Cars, and Children Increased educational levels, growing home ownership, and higher wages all enabled more Americans than ever before to become what one historian has called members of a "consumer republic." But what did they buy? The postwar emphasis on nuclear families and suburbs provides the answer. In the emerging suburban nation, three elements came together to create patterns of consumption that would endure for decades: houses, cars, and children.

A feature in a 1949 issue of *McCall's*, a magazine targeting middle-class women, illustrates the connections. "I now have three working centers," a typical housewife explains. "The baby center . . . a baking center . . . and a cleaning center." Accompanying illustrations reveal the interior of the brand-new house, stocked with the latest

Teenagers

These teenage girls and boys are being restrained by police outside an Elvis Presley concert in Florida in 1956. Elvis, who introduced the white middle class to rock 'n' roll music in the mid-1950s, was one example of a broader phenomenon: The creation of the "teenager" as a distinct demographic, cultural category, and, perhaps most significantly, consumer group. Beginning in the 1950s, middle-class teenagers had money to spend, and advertisers and other entrepreneurs — such as the music executives who marketed Elvis or the Hollywood executives who invented the "teen film" — sought ways to win their allegiance and their dollars.   Photo by Charles Trainor/Time Life Pictures/Getty Images.

consumer products: accessories for the baby's room; a new stove, oven, and refrigerator; and a washer and dryer, along with cleaning products and other household goods. The article does not mention automobiles, but the photo of the house's exterior makes the point clear: Father drives home from work in a new car.

Consumption for the home, including automobiles, drove the postwar American economy as much as, or more than, the military-industrial complex did. If we think like advertisers and manufacturers, we can see why. Between 1945 and 1970, more than 25 million new houses were built in the United States. Each required its own supply of new appliances, from refrigerators to lawn mowers. In 1955 alone, Americans purchased 4 million new refrigerators, and between 1940 and 1951 the sale of power mowers increased from 35,000 per year to more than 1 million. Moreover, as American industry discovered planned obsolescence — the encouragement of consumers to replace appliances and cars every few years — the home became a site of perpetual consumer desire.

Children also encouraged consumption. The baby boomers born between World War II and the late 1950s

have consistently, throughout every phase of their lives, been the darlings of American advertising and consumption. When they were infants, companies focused on developing new baby products, from disposable diapers to instant formula. When they were toddlers and young children, new television programs, board games, fast food, TV dinners, and thousands of different kinds of toys came to market to supply the rambunctious youth. When they were teenagers, rock music, Hollywood films, and a constantly marketed "teen culture" — with its appropriate clothing, music, hairstyles, and other accessories — bombarded them. Remarkably, in 1956, middle-class American teenagers on average had a weekly income of more than $10, close to the weekly disposable income of an entire family a generation earlier.

Television | The emergence of commercial television in the United States was swift and overwhelming. In the realm of technology, only the automobile and the personal computer were its equal in transforming everyday life in the twentieth century. In 1947, there were 7,000 TV sets in American homes. A year later, the CBS and NBC radio networks began of-

Advertising in the TV Age

Aggressive advertising of new products such as the color television helped fuel the surge in consumer spending during the 1950s. Marketing experts emphasized television's role in promoting family togetherness, while interior designers offered decorating tips that placed the television at the focal point of living rooms and the increasingly popular "family rooms." In this 1951 magazine advertisement, the family is watching a variety program starring singer Dinah Shore, who was the television spokeswoman for Chevrolet cars. Every American probably could hum the tune of the little song she sang in praise of the Chevy.   Courtesy of Motorola Museum © 1951 Motorola, Inc./ Picture Research Consultants & Archives.

fering regular programming, and by 1950 Americans owned 7.3 million sets. Ten years later, 87 percent of American homes had at least one television set. Having conquered the home, television would soon become the principle mediator between the consumer and the marketplace.

Television advertisers mastered the art of creating desire and directing it toward consumption. TV stations, like radio stations before them, depended entirely on advertising for profits. The first television executives understood that as long as they sold viewers to advertisers they would stay on the air. Early corporate-sponsored shows (such as *General Electric Theater* and *U.S. Steel Hour*) and simple product jingles (such as "No matter what the time or place, let's keep up with that happy pace. . . . 7-Up your thirst away!") gave way by the early 1960s to slick advertising campaigns that used popular

music, movie stars, sports figures, and stimulating graphics to captivate viewers.

By creating powerful visual narratives of pleasure and comfort, television revolutionized advertising and changed forever the ways products were sold to American, and global, consumers. On *Queen for a Day*, a show popular in the mid-1950s, women competed to see who could tell the most heartrending story of tragedy and loss. The winner was lavished with household products: refrigerators, toasters, ovens, and the like. In a groundbreaking advertisement for Anacin aspirin, a tiny hammer pounded inside the skull of a headache sufferer. Almost overnight, sales of Anacin increased by 50 percent.

What Americans saw on television, both in the omnipresent commercials and in the programming, was an overwhelmingly white, Anglo-Saxon, Protestant world of nuclear families, suburban homes, and middle-class life. A typical show was *Father Knows Best*, starring Robert Young and Jane Wyatt. Father left home each morning wearing a suit and carrying a briefcase. Mother was a full-time housewife and stereotypical female, prone to bad driving and tears. *The Honeymooners*, starring Jackie Gleason as a Brooklyn bus driver, and *The Life of Riley*, a situation comedy featuring a California aircraft worker, were rare in their treatment of working-class lives. *Beulah*, starring Ethel Waters and then Louise Beavers as the African American maid for a white family, and the comedic *Amos 'n' Andy* were the only shows featuring black actors in major roles. Black characters appeared mainly as sidekicks and servants, as with Rochester on Jack Benny's comedy show. Television was never a showcase for the breadth of American society. It was instead a vehicle for the transmission of a narrow range of middle-class tastes and values.

Religion and the Middle Class

In an age of anxiety about nuclear annihilation and the spread of "godless Communism," Americans yearned for a reaffirmation of faith. Church membership jumped from 49 percent of the population in 1940 to 70 percent in 1960. People flocked to the evangelical Protestant denominations, beneficiaries of a remarkable new crop of preachers. Most eloquent was the young Reverend Billy Graham, who made brilliant use of television, radio, and advertising. His massive 1949 revival in Los Angeles and his 1957 crusade at Madison Square Garden in New York, attended or viewed by hundreds of thousands of Americans, established Graham as the nation's leading evangelical.

Rather than clashing with the new middle-class ethic of consumption, the religious reawakening was designed to mesh with it. Preachers such as Graham and the California-based Robert Schuller told Americans that so long as they lived moral lives, they deserved the material blessings of modern life. No one was more influential in this regard than the author Norman Vincent Peale, whose best-selling book *The Power of Positive Thinking* (1952) embodied the therapeutic use of religion as an antidote to life's trials and tribulations. Peale taught that with faith in God and "positive thinking," anyone could overcome obstacles and become a success. Graham, Schuller, Peale, and other 1950s evangelicals laid the foundation for the rise of the televangelists, who created popular television ministries in the 1970s.

The postwar purveyors of religious faith cast Americans as a righteous people opposed to Communist atheism. When Julius and Ethel Rosenberg were sen-

Billy Graham

Charismatic and inspiring, Billy Graham wore down shoe leather to bring Christian conversion to hundreds of thousands of Americans in the 1940s and 1950s, preaching to large crowds such as this one in Columbia, South Carolina. He also migrated onto the radio and television airwaves, using technology to reach even wider audiences. Graham used the Cold War to sharpen his message, telling Americans that "godless communism" was an inferior system, but that democracy in America required belief in god and a constant struggle against "sin."   Photo by John Dominis/Time Life Pictures/Getty Images.

tenced to death in 1953, the judge criticized them for "devoting themselves to the Russian ideology of denial of God." Cold War imperatives drew Catholics, Protestants, and Jews into an influential ecumenical movement that downplayed doctrinal differences. The phrase "under God" was inserted into the Pledge of Allegiance in 1954, and U.S. coins carried the words "In God We Trust" after 1956. These religious initiatives struck a distinctly moderate tone, however, in comparison with the politicized evangelism that emerged in the wake of the sexual revolution and other developments in the 1960s and 1970s (see Chapter 29).

- How did the American economy benefit from World War II and the Cold War?

- What were the major factors in the expansion of the middle class in these decades?

- What was the relationship between consumer culture and the emphasis on family life in the postwar era?

A Suburban Nation

Prosperity—how much an economy produces, how much people earn—is more easily measured than is quality of life. During the 1950s, however, the American definition of the good life emerged with exceptional distinctness: a high value on consumption, a preference for suburban living, and a devotion to family and domesticity. In this section, we consider the second dimension of that definition: suburbanization. What drove the nation to abandon its cities for the suburbs, and what social and political consequences did this shift have?

The Postwar Housing Boom

Migration to the suburbs had been going on for a hundred years, but never before on the scale that the country experienced after World War II. Within a decade, farmland on the outskirts of cities filled up with tract housing and shopping malls. Entire counties that had once been rural—such as San Mateo, south of San Francisco, or Passaic and Bergen in New Jersey, west of Manhattan—went suburban. By 1960, one-third of Americans lived in suburbs. Home construction, having ground to halt during the Great Depression, surged after the war. One-fourth of the country's entire housing stock in 1960 had not even existed a decade earlier.

William J. Levitt and the FHA Two unique postwar developments remade the national housing market and gave it a distinctly suburban shape. First, an innovative Long Island building contractor, William J. Levitt, revolutionized suburban housing by applying mass-production techniques and turning out new homes at a dizzying speed. Levitt's basic four-room house, complete with kitchen appliances, was priced at $7,990 in 1947 (about $76,000 today). Levitt did not need to advertise; word of mouth brought buyers flocking to his developments (all called Levittown) in New York, Pennsylvania, and New Jersey. Dozens of other developers were soon snapping up cheap farmland and building subdivisions around the country.

Even at $7,990, Levitt's homes would have been beyond the means of most young families had the traditional home-financing standard—half down and ten years to pay off the balance—still prevailed. That is where the second postwar development came in. The Federal Housing Administration (FHA) and the Veterans Administration (VA)—that is, the federal government—made the home mortgage market serve a broader range of Americans than ever before. After the war, the FHA insured thirty-year mortgages with as little as 5 percent

down and interest at 2 or 3 percent. The VA was even more generous, requiring only a token $1 down for qualified ex-GIs. FHA and VA mortgages best explain why, after hovering around 45 percent for the previous half century, home ownership jumped to 60 percent by 1960.

What purchasers of suburban houses got, in addition to a good deal, were homogeneous communities (see Reading American Pictures, "The Suburban Landscape of Cold War America," p. 830). The developments contained few old people or unmarried adults. Even the trees were young. Levitt's company enforced regulations about maintaining lawns and not hanging out laundry on the weekends. Then there was the matter of race. Levitt's houses came with restrictive covenants prohibiting occupancy "by members of other than the Caucasian Race." (Restrictive covenants often applied to Jews and, in California, Asian Americans as well.)

After the war, the National Association for the Advancement of Colored People (NAACP), the Congress of Industrial Organization (CIO), and African American civil rights groups launched an ambitious campaign for open-housing ordinances in cities such as Detroit, New York, Philadelphia, and Oakland. White home owners rebelled, voting for racist politicians who promised to keep neighborhoods white by resisting what they called "Negro invasion." When politics failed, white homeowners took matters into their own hands. In Chicago, Detroit, and other major northern cities, they bombed, set fires, threw bricks through windows, and employed other tactics to force black homebuyers out of certain neighborhoods. One California newspaper reported in 1948 that "faced with the great influx of colored population, [members of] the Caucasian race [would have] to protect their property values."

In *Shelley v. Kraemer* (1948), the Supreme Court outlawed restrictive covenants, but racial discrimination in housing changed little. The practice persisted long after *Shelley*, because the FHA and VA continued the policy of redlining: refusing mortgages to African Americans and members of other minority groups seeking to buy in white neighborhoods. Indeed, no federal law—or even court decisions like *Shelley*—actually prohibited racial discrimination in housing until Congress passed the Fair Housing Act in 1968.

Interstate Highways Without automobiles, suburban growth on such a massive scale would have been impossible. Planners laid out subdivisions on the assumption that everybody would drive. And they did—to get to work, to take the children to Little League, to shop. With gas plentiful and cheap (15 cents

The Suburban Landscape of Cold War America

The photo on the left was captured by Dan Weiner, one of the most cele-brated young photojournalists of the 1950s. His photographs showed Americans at work, at leisure, and in the intimate spaces of kitchens and living rooms. In this 1953 photo, daily commuters arrive from Chicago at the Park Forest, Illinois, train station at the end of a long workday. In the photo on the right, taken in 1958, *Life* magazine photographer Ralph Crane depicts diaper service trucks lined up in a California suburb. Mothers and their children greet the deliveries and mingle on the sidewalk.

Dan Weiner, Image from the *Organization Man*. Dan Weiner, Courtesy Sandra Weiner.

Ralph Crane, *San Fernando, California*. Photo by Ralph Crane/Time Life Pictures/Getty Images.

ANALYZING THE EVIDENCE

- What evidence is there that the suburban development in the photograph on the right is new? Why did Americans seek to live in such communities in increasing numbers after World War II?

- What do you notice about the commuters in the photograph on the left? What characteristics do they share? What do their similari-ties suggest about white-collar workers in the 1950s?

- Using these two photographs, describe how they might tell a story about American society in the 1950s. What do these photos suggest about work, family, gender roles, and the difference between urban and suburban space?

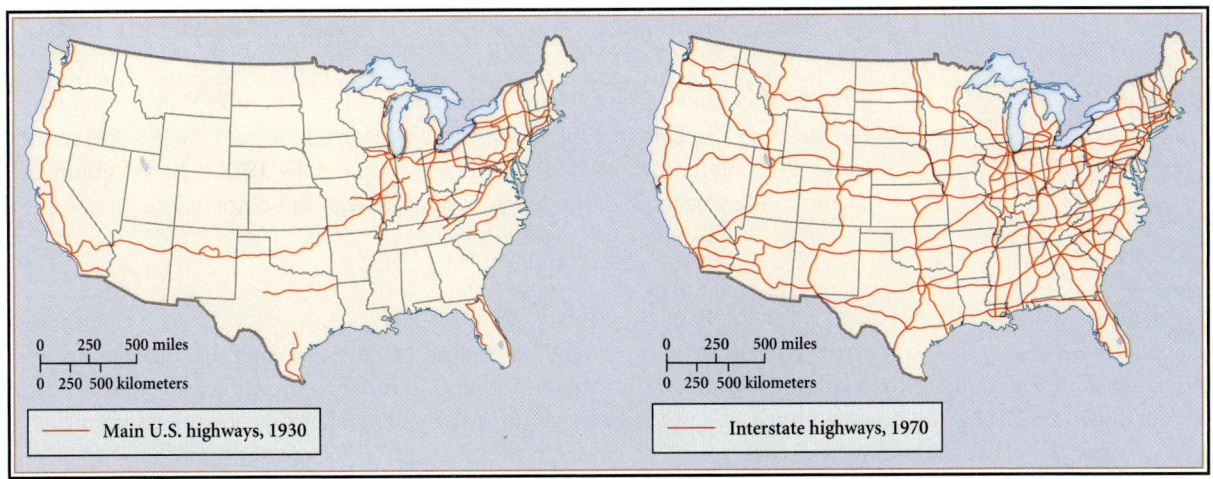

MAP 26.1

Connecting the Nation: The Interstate Highway System, 1930 and 1970

The 1956 Interstate and Defense Highways Act paved the way for an extensive network of federal highways throughout the nation. The act not only pleased American drivers and enhanced their love affair with the automobile but also benefited the petroleum, construction, trucking, real estate, and tourist industries. The new highway system promoted the nation's economic integration, facilitated the growth of suburbs, and contributed to the erosion of America's distinct regional identities.

a gallon), no one cared about the fuel efficiency of their V-8 engines or seemed to mind the elaborate tail fins and chrome that weighed down their cars. In 1945, Americans owned twenty-five million cars; by 1965, just two decades later, the number had *tripled* to seventy-five million (see Voices from Abroad, "Hanoch Bartov: Everyone Has a Car," p. 832). American oil consumption followed, tripling as well between 1949 and 1972.

More cars required more highways, and the federal government obliged. In 1956, in a move that drastically altered America's landscape and driving habits, the National Interstate and Defense Highways Act authorized $26 billion over a ten-year period for the construction of a nationally integrated highway system—42,500 miles (Map 26.1). Cast as a Cold War necessity, because broad highways made evacuating crowded cities easier in the event of a nuclear attack, the law changed American cities forever. An enormous public works program surpassing anything undertaken during the New Deal, federal highways made possible the massive suburbanization of the nation in the 1960s. Interstate highways rerouted traffic away from small towns, bypassed well-traveled main roads such as the cross-country Route 66, and cut wide swaths through old neighborhoods in the cities.

Fast Food and Shopping Malls Americans did not simply fill their new suburban homes with the latest appliances and gadgets; they also pioneered entirely new forms of consumption. Through World War II, downtowns had remained the center of retail sales and restaurant dining with their grand department stores, elegant eateries, and low-cost diners. As suburbanites abandoned big-city centers in the 1950s, ambitious entrepreneurs invented two new commercial forms that would profoundly shape the rest of the century: the shopping mall and the fast-food restaurant.

By the late 1950s, the suburban shopping center had become as much a part of the American landscape as the Levittowns and their imitators. A major developer of shopping malls in the Northeast called them "crystallization points for suburbia's community life." He romanticized the new structures as "today's village green," where "the fountain in the mall has replaced the downtown department clock as the gathering place for young and old alike." Romanticism aside, suburban shopping centers worked perfectly in the world of suburban consumption; they brought "the market to the people instead of people to the market," commented the *New York Times*. In 1939, the suburban share of total metropolitan retail trade in the United States was a paltry 4 percent. By 1961, it was an astonishing 60 percent in the nation's ten largest metropolitan regions.

No one was more influential in creating suburban patterns of consumption than a Chicago-born son of Czech immigrants named Ray Kroc. A former jazz musician and traveling salesman, Kroc found his calling in 1954 when he acquired a single franchise of the little-known McDonald's Restaurant, based in San Bernardino, California. In 1956, Kroc invested in twelve more franchises and by 1958 owned seventy-nine. Three years

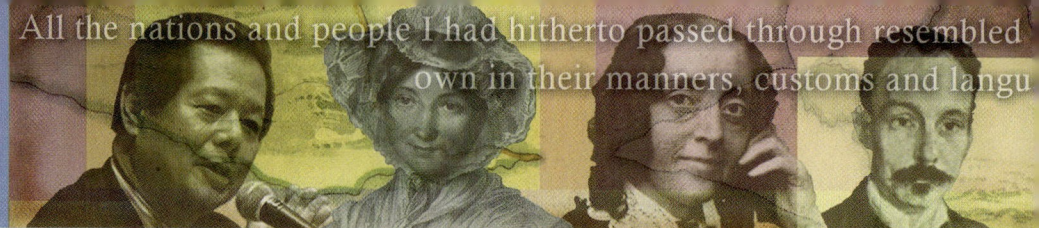
VOICES FROM ABROAD

Hanoch Bartov
Everyone Has a Car

One of Israel's foremost writers and journalists, Hanoch Bartov spent two years in the United States working as a correspondent for the newspaper *Lamerchav*. As a newcomer to Los Angeles in the early 1960s, he was both fascinated and appalled by Americans' love affair with the automobile.

Our immediate decision to buy a car sprang from healthy instincts. Only later did I learn from bitter experience that in California, death was preferable to living without one. Neither the views from the plane nor the weird excursion that first evening hinted at what I would go through that first week.

Very simple—the nearest supermarket was about half a kilometer south of our apartment, the regional primary school two kilometers east, and my son's kindergarten even farther away. A trip to the post office—an undertaking, to the bank—an ordeal, to work—an impossibility.

Truth be told: the Los Angeles municipality . . . does have public transportation. Buses go once an hour along the city's boulevards and avenues, gathering all the wretched of the earth, the poor and the needy, the old ladies forbidden by their grandchildren to drive, and other eccentric types. But few people can depend on buses, even should they swear never to deviate from the fixed routes. . . . There are no tramways. No one thought of a subway. Railroads—not now and not in the future. Why? Because everyone has a car. A man invited me to his house, saying, "We are neighbors, within ten minutes of each other." After walking for an hour and a half I realized what he meant—"ten minute drive within the speed limit." Simply put, he never thought I might interpret his remark to refer to the walking distance. The moment a baby sees the light of day in Los Angeles, a car is registered in his name in Detroit. . . .

At first perhaps people relished the freedom and independence a car provided. You get in, sit down, and grab the steering wheel, your mobility exceeding that of any other generation. No wonder people refuse to live downtown, where they can hear their neighbors, smell their cooking, and suffer frayed nerves as trains pass by bedroom windows. Instead, they get a piece of the desert, far from town, at half price, drag a water hose, grow grass, flowers, and trees, and build their dream house. . . .

The result? A widely scattered city, its houses far apart, its streets stretched in all directions. Olympic Boulevard from west to east, forty kilometers. Sepulveda Boulevard, from Long Beach in the south to the edge of the desert, forty kilometers. Altogether covering 1,200 square kilometers. As of now.

Why "as of now"? Because greater distances mean more commuting, and more commuting leads to more cars. More cars means problems that push people even farther away from the city, which chases after them.

The urban sprawl is only one side effect. Two, some say three, million cars require an array of services. . . .

. . . Why bother parking, getting out, getting in, getting up and sitting down, when you can simply "drive in"? Mailboxes have their slots facing the road, at the level of the driver's hand. That is how dirty laundry is deposited, electricity and water bills paid. That is how love is made, how children are taken to school. That is how the anniversary wreath is laid on the graves of loved ones. There are drive-in movies. And, yes, we saw it with our own eyes: drive-in churches. Only in death is a man separated from his car and buried alone.

Source: Hanoch Bartov, "Measures of Affluence," in Oscar Handlin and Lilian Handlin, eds., *From the Outer World* (Cambridge, MA: Harvard University Press, 1997), 293–296.

ANALYZING THE EVIDENCE

- From Bartov's observations, what are the pluses and minuses of America's car culture? In what ways was the automobile changing American society?
- Why did Bartov find owning a car was necessary, especially in southern California?
- Not everyone, of course, had a car. Who, according to Bartov, used public transportation?

later, Kroc bought the company from the McDonald brothers and proceeded to turn it into the largest chain of restaurants in the world. Based on inexpensive, quickly served hamburgers that hungry families could eat in the restaurant, in their cars, or at home, Kroc's vision transformed the way Americans consumed food.

Rise of the Sunbelt

Suburban living, although a nationwide phenomenon, was most at home in the Sunbelt (the southern and southwestern states), where taxes were low, the climate was mild, and open space allowed for sprawling subdivisions (Map 26.2). Florida added 3.5 million people, many of them retired, between 1940 and 1970. Texas profited from expanding petrochemical and defense industries. Most dramatic was California's growth, spurred especially by the state's booming defense-related aircraft

and electronics industries. By 1970, California contained one-tenth of the nation's population and surpassed New York as the most populous state. At the end of the century, California's economy was among the top ten largest in the world—among *nations*.

A distinctive feature of Sunbelt suburbanization was its close relationship to the military-industrial complex. Building on World War II expansion, military bases proliferated in the South and Southwest in the postwar decades, especially in Florida, Texas, and California. In some instances, entire metropolitan regions—such as San Diego County, California, and the Houston area in Texas—expanded in tandem with nearby military outposts. Moreover, the aerospace, defense, and electronics industries were based largely in Sunbelt metropolitan regions.

Sunbelt suburbanization was best exemplified by Orange County, California. Southwest of Los Angeles,

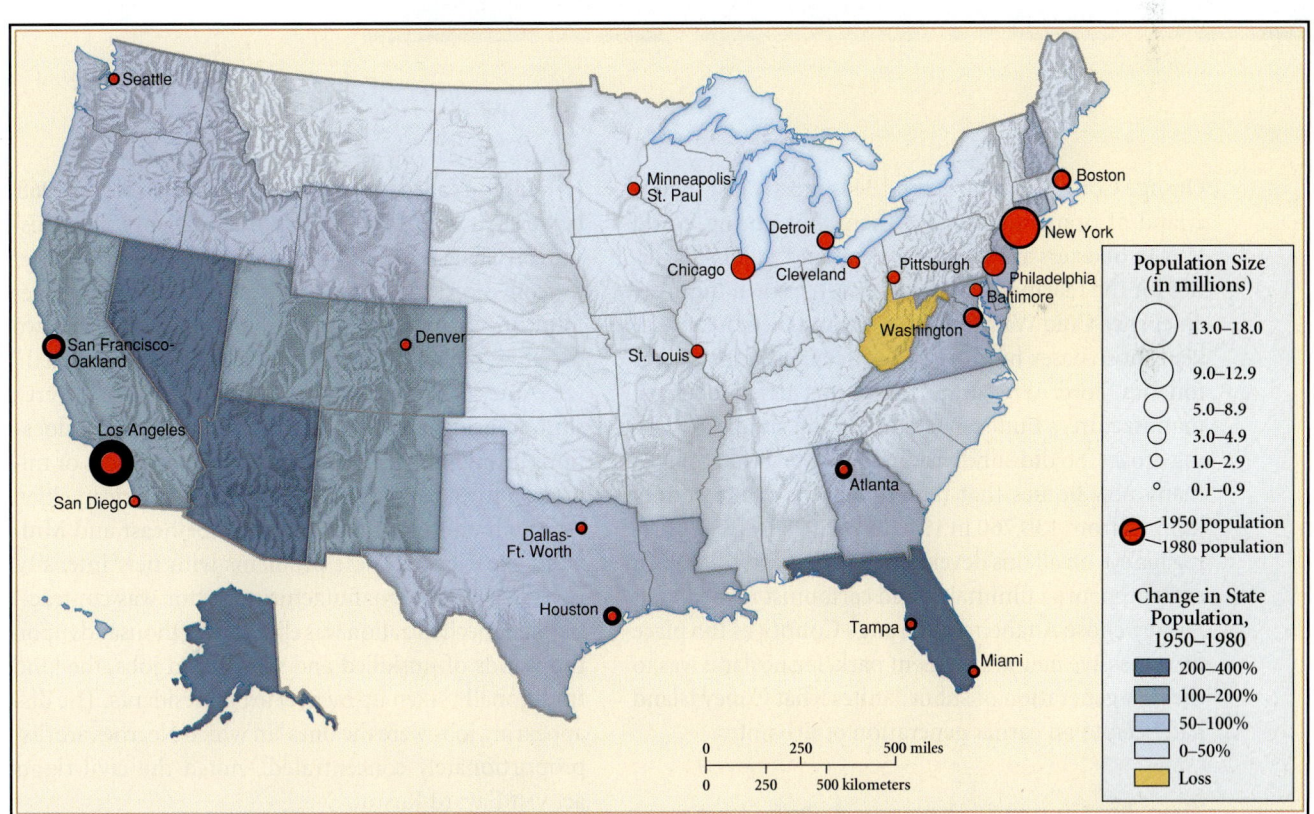

MAP 26.2

Shifting Population Patterns, 1950–1980

This map shows the two major, somewhat overlapping, patterns of population movement between 1950 and 1980. Most striking is the rapid growth of the Sunbelt states. All the states experiencing increases of over 100 percent in that period are in the Southwest, plus Florida. The second pattern involves the growth of metropolitan areas, defined as a central city or urban area and its suburbs. The central cities were themselves mostly not growing, however. The metropolitan growth shown in this map was accounted for by the expanding suburbs. And because Sunbelt growth was primarily suburban growth, that's where we see the most rapid metropolitan growth, with Los Angeles the clear leader.

Fast Food, 1949
The sign atop this suburban Los Angeles restaurant says it all. Suburbanization laid the foundation for a unique postwar phenomenon that would forever change American life: The rise of fast food. Cheap, convenient, and "fast," the food served in the new restaurants, modeled after the industry's pioneer, McDonald's, was not necessarily nutritious, but its chief advantage was portability.   Loomis Dean/Time Life Pictures/Getty Images.

Orange County was until the 1940s mostly just that—a land of oranges, groves of them. But during World War II, boosters attracted new bases and training facilities for the marines, navy, and air force (then the army air corps). Cold War militarization and the Korean War kept those bases humming, and Hughes Aircraft, Autonetics, Ford Aeronautics, and other defense-related manufacturers built new plants in the sunny, sprawling groves. So did subdivision developers, who built so many new homes that the population of the county jumped from 130,760 in 1940 to 703,925 in 1960. Casting his eye on all this development in the early 1950s, an entrepreneurial filmmaker and cartoonist named Walt Disney chose Anaheim in Orange County as the place for a massive new amusement park. Disneyland was to the new generation of suburbanites what Coney Island had been to an earlier generation of urbanites.

Two Nations: Urban and Suburban

While middle-class whites flocked to the suburbs, an opposite stream of working-class migrants, many of them southern African Americans, moved into the cities. In the 1950s, the nation's twelve largest cities lost 3.6 million whites while gaining 4.5 million nonwhites. These urban newcomers inherited a declining economy and a decaying infrastructure. To those enjoying prosperity, the "other America," as the social critic Michael

Harrington called it, remained largely invisible. In 1968, however, a report by the National Advisory Commission on Civil Disorders (informally known as the Kerner Commission), delivered to President Lyndon Baines Johnson, warned that "our nation is moving toward two societies, one black, one white, separate and unequal."

American cities had long been the home of poverty, slum housing, and the hardships and cultural dislocations brought on by immigration from overseas or migration from rural areas. But postwar American cities, especially those in the industrial Northeast and Midwest, experienced these problems with new intensity. By the 1950s, the manufacturing sector was contracting, and mechanization was eliminating thousands upon thousands of unskilled and semiskilled jobs, the kind traditionally taken up by new urban residents. The disappearing jobs were the ones "in which Negroes are disproportionately concentrated," noted the civil rights activist Bayard Rustin.

The Urban Crisis   The intensification of poverty, the deterioration of older housing stock, and the persistence of racial segregation produced what many at the time called the urban crisis. Unwelcome in the shiny new suburbs built by men such as William J. Levitt, blacks found low-paying jobs in the city and lived in aging apartment buildings run by slumlords. Despite a thriving black middle class—indeed,

Urban Crisis

This Pittsburgh neighborhood, photographed in 1955, typified what many came to call the "urban crisis" of the 1950s and 1960s. As suburbanization drew middle-class residents, investment, and jobs away from the core of older cities, those cities began to rot from the inside. Urban neglect left many working-class neighborhoods, increasingly occupied by the nation's poor, with few jobs, little industry, and dilapidated housing.   W. Eugene Smith/Magnum Photos.

larger than ever before—for those without resources, upward mobility remained elusive. Racism in institutional forms frustrated African Americans at every turn: housing restrictions, increasingly segregated schools, and an urban infrastructure that stood underfunded and decaying as whites left for the suburbs.

Housing and job discrimination were compounded by the frenzy of urban renewal that hit black neighborhoods in the 1950s and early 1960s. Seeking to revitalize declining city centers, urban planners, politicians, and real estate developers proposed razing blighted neighborhoods to make way for modern construction projects that would appeal to the fleeing middle class. In Boston, almost one-third of the old city—including the historic West End, a long-established Italian neighborhood—was demolished to make way for a new highway, high-rise housing, and government and commercial buildings. In San Francisco, some 4,000 residents of the Western Addition, a predominantly black neighborhood, lost out to an urban renewal program that built luxury housing,

a shopping center, and an express boulevard. Between 1949 and 1967, urban renewal nationwide demolished almost 400,000 buildings and displaced 1.4 million people.

The urban experts believed they knew what to do with the dislocated: relocate them to federally funded housing projects, an outgrowth of New Deal housing policy, now much expanded and combined with generous funding for slum clearance. However well intended, these grim projects too often took the form of cheap high-rise slums that isolated their inhabitants from surrounding neighborhoods. The impact was felt especially strongly among African Americans, who often found that public housing *increased* racial segregation and concentrated the poor. The Robert Taylor Homes in Chicago, with twenty-eight buildings of sixteen stories each, housed 20,000 residents, almost all of them black. Despite the planners' wish to build decent affordable apartments, the huge complex became a notorious breeding ground for crime and hopelessness.

West Side Story

The influx of Puerto Rican immigrants after World War II inspired the 1957 Broadway hit *West Side Story* (a still from the 1961 film version is shown here). Arthur Laurents's plot recast Shakespeare's *Romeo and Juliet* in a Puerto Rican neighborhood on New York's West Side in the 1950s, with music by Leonard Bernstein and lyrics by Stephen Sondheim. The violent confrontations between two rival youth gangs, one Puerto Rican and the other white (primarily Polish American), were set to highly stylized dance routines. The Kobal Collection.

Urban Immigrants Despite the evident urban crisis, cities continued to attract immigrants from abroad. Since the passage of the National Origins Act of 1924 (see Chapter 22), U.S. immigration policy had aimed mainly at keeping foreigners out. But World War II and the Cold War began slowly to change American policy. The Displaced Persons Act of 1948 permitted the entry of approximately 415,000 Europeans, many of them Jewish refugees. In a gesture to an important war ally, the Chinese Exclusion Act was repealed in 1943. More far-reaching was the 1952 McCarran-Walter Act, which ended the exclusion of Japanese, Koreans, and Southeast Asians.

After the national-origins quota system went into effect in 1924, Mexico replaced Eastern and Southern Europe as the nation's labor reservoir. During World War II, the federal government introduced the Bracero Program to ease wartime labor shortages (see Chapter 24) and then revived it in 1951, during the Korean War. The federal government's ability to force workers to return to

Mexico, however, was strictly limited. The Mexican population continued to grow, and by the time the Bracero Program ended in 1964, many of that group—an estimated 350,000—had settled permanently in the United States. Braceros were joined by other Mexicans from small towns and villages, who immigrated to the United States to escape poverty or to earn money to return home and purchase land for farming.

As generations of immigrants had before them, Mexicans gravitated to major cities. Mostly, they settled in Los Angeles, Long Beach, San Jose, El Paso, and other southwestern cities. But many also went north, augmenting well-established Mexican American communities in Chicago, Detroit, Kansas City, and Denver. Although still important to American agriculture, Mexican Americans were employed in substantial numbers as industrial and service workers by 1960.

Another major group of Spanish-speaking migrants came from Puerto Rico. American citizens since 1917, Puerto Ricans enjoyed an unrestricted right to move to the mainland United States. Migration increased dramatically after World War II, when mechanization of the island's sugarcane agriculture pushed many Puerto Ricans off the land. Airlines began to offer cheap direct flights between San Juan and New York City. With the fare at about $50 (two weeks' wages), Puerto Ricans became America's first immigrants to arrive en masse by air. Most Puerto Ricans went to New York, where they settled first in East ("Spanish") Harlem and then scattered in neighborhoods across the city's five boroughs. This massive migration, which increased the Puerto Rican population to 613,000 by 1960, transformed the ethnic composition of the city. More Puerto Ricans now lived in New York City than in San Juan.

Cuban refugees constituted the third largest group of Spanish-speaking immigrants. In the six years after Fidel Castro's seizure of power in 1959 (see Chapter 25), an estimated 180,000 people fled Cuba for the United States. The Cuban refugee community grew so quickly that it turned Miami into a cosmopolitan, bilingual city almost overnight. Unlike other urban migrants, Miami's Cubans quickly prospered, in large part because they had arrived with money and middle-class skills.

Spanish-speaking immigrants—whether Mexican, Puerto Rican, or Cuban—created huge barrios in major American cities, where bilingualism flourished, the Catholic Church shaped religious life, and families sought to join the economic mainstream. Though distinct from one another, these Spanish-speaking communities remained largely segregated from white, or Anglo, neighborhoods and suburbs as well as from African American districts.

- In what ways did the federal government shape postwar suburbanization?

- How are we to explain the relationship between suburbanization and consumption?

- In what sense was the United States "two nations"?

Gender, Sex, and Family in the Era of Containment

Marriage, family structure, and gender roles had been undergoing significant changes since the turn of the twentieth century (see Chapter 18). Beginning in the nineteenth century, middle-class Americans increasingly saw marriage as "companionate," that is, based on romantic love and a lifetime of shared friendship. Companionate did not mean equal. In the mid-twentieth century, family life remained governed by notions of paternalism, in which men provided economic support and controlled the family's financial resources, while women cared for children and occupied a secondary position in public life.

The resurgent postwar American middle class was preoccupied with paternalism and its virtues. Everyone from professional psychologists to television advertisers and every organization from schools to the popular press celebrated nuclear families. Children were prized, and women's caregiving roles were valorized. This view of family life, and especially its emphasis on female "domesticity," was bolstered by Cold War politics. Americans who deviated from prevailing gender and sexual norms were not only viewed with scorn but were sometimes thought to be subversive and politically dangerous. The word *containment* could apply to the home as easily as to foreign policy. Sex had become politicized by the Cold War.

The model of domesticity so highly esteemed in postwar middle-class morality hid deeper, longer-term changes in the way marriage, gender roles, women's work, and even sex were understood. To comprehend the postwar decades, we have to keep in mind both the value placed on domesticity and the tumultuous changes surging beneath its prescriptions.

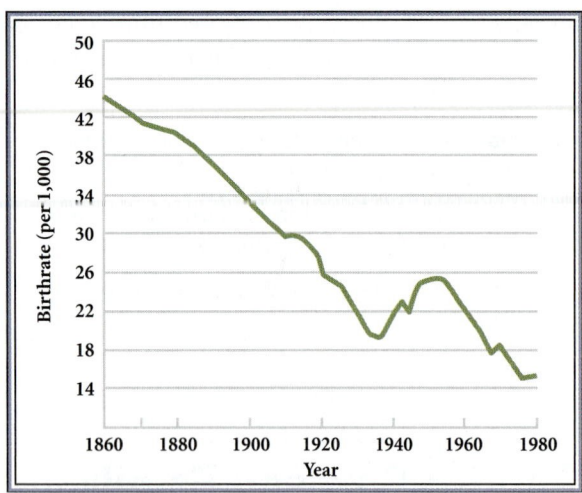

FIGURE 26.3

The American Birthrate, 1860–1980

When birthrates are viewed over more than a century, the postwar baby boom is clearly only a temporary reversal of the long-term downward trend in the American birthrate.

The Baby Boom

A popular 1945 song was called "Gotta Make Up for Lost Time," and Americans did just that. Two things were noteworthy about the families they formed after World War II: First, marriages were remarkably stable. Not until the mid-1960s did the divorce rate begin to rise sharply. Second, married couples were intent on having babies. Everyone expected to have several children — it was part of adulthood, almost a citizen's responsibility. After a century and a half of decline, the birthrate shot up. More babies were born between 1948 and 1953 than in the previous thirty years (Figure 26.3).

One of the reasons for this baby boom was that people were having children at the same time. A second was a drop in the average marriage age — down to twenty-two for men and twenty for women. Younger parents meant a bumper crop of children. Women who came of age in the 1930s averaged 2.4 children; their counterparts in the 1950s averaged 3.2 children. Such a dramatic turnaround reflected couples' decisions during the Great Depression to limit childbearing and couples' contrasting decisions in the postwar years to have more children. The baby boom peaked in 1957 and remained at a high level until the early 1960s. Far from "normal," all of these developments were anomalies, temporary reversals of long-standing demographic trends. From the perspective of the whole of the twen-tieth century, the 1950s and early 1960s stand out as exceptions to declining birthrates, rising divorce rates, and the steadily rising marriage age.

The passage of time revealed the ever-widening impact of the baby boom. When baby boomers competed for jobs during the 1970s, the labor market became tight. When career-oriented baby boomers belatedly began having children in the 1980s, the birthrate jumped. And in our own time, as baby boomers begin retiring, huge funding problems threaten to engulf Social Security and Medicare. The intimate decisions of so many couples after World War II continued to shape American life well into the twenty-first century.

Improving Health and Education   Baby boom children benefited from a host of important advances in public health and medical practice in the postwar years. Formerly serious illnesses became merely routine after the introduction of such "miracle drugs" as penicillin (introduced in 1943), streptomycin (1945), and cortisone (1946). When Dr. Jonas Salk perfected a polio vaccine in 1954, he became a national hero. The free distribution of Salk's vaccine in the nation's schools, followed in 1961 by Dr. Albert Sabin's oral polio vaccine, demonstrated the potential of government-sponsored public health programs.

The baby boom also gave the nation's educational system a boost. Postwar middle-class parents, America's first college-educated generation, placed a high value on education. Suburban parents approved 90 percent of school bond issues during the 1950s. By 1970, school expenditures accounted for 7.2 percent of the gross national product, double the 1950 level. In the 1960s, the baby boom generation swelled college enrollments. State university systems grew in tandem: the pioneering University of California, University of Wisconsin, and State University of New York systems added dozens of new campuses and offered students in their states a low-cost college education.

Dr. Benjamin Spock   To keep baby boom children healthy and happy, middle-class parents increasingly relied on the advice of experts. Dr. Benjamin Spock's *Common Sense Book of Baby and Child Care* sold 1 million copies every year after its publication in 1946. Spock urged mothers to abandon the rigid feeding and baby-care schedules of an earlier generation. New mothers found Spock's common-sense approach liberating. "Your little paperback is still in my

Mom at Home

Middle-class women's lives grew increasingly complicated in the postwar decades. They may have dreamed of a suburban home with a brand-new kitchen, like the one shown in this 1955 photograph, but laboring all day over children, dirty dishes, and a hot stove proved dissatisfying to many. Betty Friedan called the confinement of women's identities to motherhood the "feminine mystique." Elliott Erwitt/Magnum Photos.

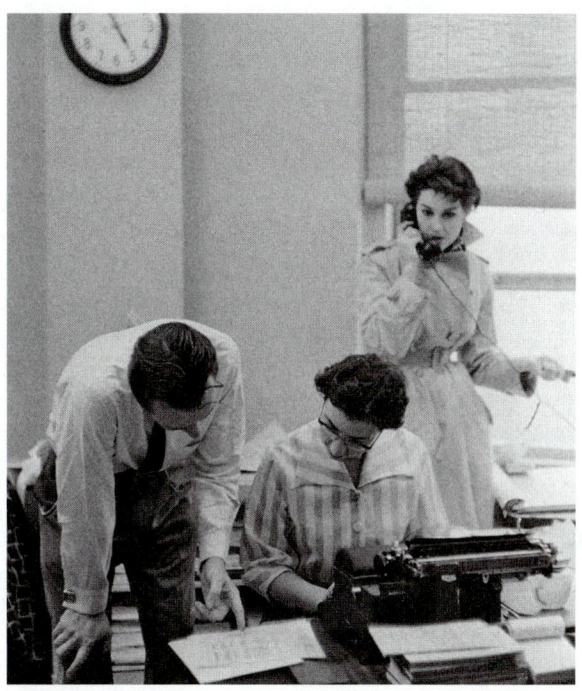

Mom at Work

Did the working woman have it much better? Hardly. Most women in the 1950s and 1960s were confined to low-level secretarial work, waitressing, and other service-sector work—or, worse, factory or domestic labor. By the end of the 1960s, women had begun to crack the "glass ceiling" and enter the professions in larger numbers. But regardless of their occupation, the majority of working women performed the "double day": a full day at work and full day at home. Such were the expectations and double-bind women faced. Inge Morath © The Inge Morath Foundation/Magnum Photos.

cupboard, with loose pages, rather worn from use because I brought up two babies using it as my 'Bible,'" a California housewife wrote to Spock.

Despite his commonsense approach to child-rearing, Spock was part of a generation of psychological experts whose advice often failed to reassure women. If mothers were too protective, Spock and others argued, they might hamper their children's preparation for adult life. On the other hand, mothers who wanted to work outside the home felt guilty because Spock recommended that they be constantly available for their children. As American mothers aimed for the perfection demanded of them seemingly at every turn, many began to question these mixed messages. Some of them

would be inspired by the resurgence of feminism in the 1960s.

Women, Work, and Family

Two powerful forces shaped women's relationships to work and family life in the postwar decades. One was the middle-class domestic ideal, which feminist Betty Friedan would later call the "feminine mystique." "The suburban housewife—she was the dream image of the young American women" in the 1950s, Friedan wrote. "She was healthy, beautiful, educated, concerned only about her husband, her children, her home." The second force was the job market. Most working-class women

Coming of Age in the Postwar Years

At the dawn of the postwar era, Americans faced new opportunities and new anxieties. Many former soldiers attended college on the GI Bill, part of a massive expansion of the nation's educational system. With a college education, veterans found their lives forever changed. Women faced new pressures to realize the ideal role of housewife and mother. And on the horizon, in both reality and in the American imagination, lurked Communism, which Americans feared but little understood. Recorded here are several different reactions to these postwar tensions, distinct experiences of coming of age in the 1940s and 1950s.

Art Buchwald
Studying on the GI Bill

Art Buchwald was one of the best-known humorists in American journalism in the 1950s and 1960s. His column in the *Washington Post* was widely reprinted. But in 1946, he was an ordinary ex-serviceman hoping to use the GI Bill to go to college.

It was time to face up to whether I was serious about attending school. My decision was to go down to the University of Southern California and find out what I should study at night to get into the place. There were at least 4,000 ex-GIs waiting to register. I stood in line with them. Hours later, I arrived at the counter and said, "I would like to . . ." The clerk said, "Fill this out." . . .

Having been accepted as a full-time student under the G.I. Bill, I was entitled to seventy-five dollars a month plus tuition, books, and supplies. . . . Meanwhile, I found a boardinghouse a few blocks from campus, run by a cheery woman who was like a mother to her thirteen boarders. While she liked us very much, she hated blacks, Jews, Hispanics, Orientals, and other minorities—not necessarily in that order. She used to subscribe to a German newspaper with a swastika on the front page. I saw it in her living room when I went to pay my rent. Mrs. Liebschen did not connect her tenants with the races and nationalities she despised. . . .

At the time, just after the Second World War had ended, an undeclared class war was going on at USC. The G.I.s returning home had little use for the fraternity men, since most of the frat boys were not only much younger, but considered very immature.

The G.I.s were intent on getting their educations and starting new lives. Some fraternity people partied, drank, cheated on tests, and tried to take over school politics. In those days, the administration catered to the fraternities, knowing that eventually they would be the big financial supporters of the school, as opposed to the independents, who would probably not be heard from again. . . .

It wasn't my first decision to favor the have-nots over the haves. I had been doing it all my life, and I confess that it may have had something to do with my envy of the haves, starting with their Christmas trees and girlfriends under the clock at the Biltmore.

Source: Art Buchwald, *Leaving Home: A Memoir* (New York: G. P. Putnam's Sons, 1993): 201–205.

Betty Friedan
Living the Feminine Mystique

Like Buchwald, Betty Friedan would one day become famous as a writer—in her case, as a feminist who wrote one of the most widely read books of the 1960s, *The Feminine Mystique*. In the late 1940s, Friedan was not yet a feminist, as she notes, but she was deeply engaged in the politics of the era.

That was the year it really hit, the feminine mystique, though at the time we didn't know what it was. It was just that our lives seemed to have shifted in dimension, in perspective. . . .

And then the boys our age had come back from the war. I was bumped from my job on a small labor news service by a returning veteran, and it wasn't so easy to find another job I really liked. I filled out the applications for Time-Life researcher, which I'd always scorned before. All the girls I knew had jobs like that, but it was official policy that no matter how good, researchers, who were women, could never become writers or editors. They could write the whole article, but the men they were working with would always get the by-line as writer. I was certainly not a feminist then—none of us were a bit interested in women's rights. But I could never bring myself to take that kind of job. . . .

After the war, I had been very political, very involved, consciously radical. Not about women, for heaven's sake! If you were a radical in 1949, you were concerned about the Negroes, and the working class, and World War III, and the Un-American Activities Committee and McCarthy and loyalty oaths, and Communist splits and schisms, Russia,

China and the UN, but you certainly didn't think about being a woman, politically. It was only recently that we had begun to think of ourselves as women at all. But that wasn't political—it was the opposite of politics.

Source: Betty Friedan, *"It Changed My Life": Writings on the Women's Movement* (Cambridge, MA: Harvard University Press, 1976): 6–8.

Susan Allen Toth

Learning About Communism

Toth is a writer and scholar who grew up in Ames, Iowa, a small college town surrounded by cornfields. She writes here about her experience learning just how anxious people could become in the 1950s when the issue of communism was raised.

Of course, we all knew there was Communism. As early as sixth grade our teacher warned us about its dangers. I listened carefully to Mr. Casper describe what Communists wanted, which sounded terrible. World domination. Enslavement. Destruction of our way of life. . . . I hung around school one afternoon hoping to catch Mr. Casper, whom I secretly adored, to ask him why Communism was so bad. He stayed in another teacher's room so late I finally scrawled my question on our blackboard: "Dear Mr. Casper, why is Communism so bad . . . Sue Allen" and went home. Next morning the message was still there. Like a warning from heaven it had galvanized Mr. Casper. He began class with a stern lecture, repeating everything he had said about dangerous Russians and painting a vivid picture of how we would all suffer if the Russians took over the city government in Ames. We certainly wouldn't be able to attend a school like this, he said, where free expression of opinion was allowed. At recess that day one of the boys asked me if I was a "dirty Commie": two of my best friends shied away from me on the playground; I saw Mr. Casper talking low to another teacher and pointing at me. I cried all the way home from school and resolved never to commit myself publicly with a question like that again.

Source: Susan Allen Toth, *Blooming: A Small-Town Girlhood* (Boston: Little, Brown and Company, 1978): 202–203.

ANALYZING THE EVIDENCE

- What do you think Buchwald meant by "an undeclared class war"? Why would the influx of former soldiers into colleges on the GI Bill create conflict?

- Why do you think Friedan "didn't think about being a woman, politically" in the 1940s and 1950s? Did other political issues crowd out women's concerns? Why do you think she was "bumped from" her job by a "returning veteran"?

- What does Toth's experience as a young student suggest about American anxieties during the Cold War? Why could her question so easily become a source of embarrassment and ridicule?

had to earn a paycheck to help their family. Despite their education, middle-class women found that jobs in the professions and business were dominated by men and often closed to them. For both groups, the market offered mostly "women's jobs"—in teaching, nursing, and other areas of the growing service sector—and little room for advancement (see Comparing American Voices, "Coming of Age in the Postwar Years," pp. 840–841).

The idea that a woman's place was in the home was, of course, not new. The feminine mystique of the 1950s and 1960s—the idea that "the highest value and the only commitment for women is the fulfillment of their own femininity"—bore a remarkable similarity to the nineteenth century's notion of domesticity. The updated version drew on new elements of twentieth-century science and culture. Psychologists equated motherhood with "normal" female identity and suggested that career-minded mothers needed therapy. Television shows and movies depicted career women as social misfits. The postwar consumer culture also emphasized women's domestic role as purchasing agents for home and family. "Can a woman ever feel right cooking on a dirty range?" asked one advertisement.

The postwar domestic ideal held that women's principal economic contribution came through consumption—women shopped for the family. In reality, their contributions increasingly took them outside their homes and into the workforce. In 1954, married women made up half of all women workers. Six years later, the 1960 census reported a stunning fact: The number of mothers who worked had increased four times, and over one-third of these women had children between the ages of six and seventeen. In that same year, 30 percent of wives worked, and by 1970, it was 40 percent. For working-class women, in particular, the economic needs of their families demanded that they work outside the home.

Despite rising employment rates, occupational segmentation still haunted women. Until 1964, the classified sections of newspapers separated employment ads into "Help Wanted Male" and "Help Wanted Female." More than 80 percent of all employed women did stereotypical women's work as sales clerks, health-care technicians, waitresses, stewardesses, domestic servants, receptionists, telephone operators, and secretaries. In 1960, only 3 percent of lawyers and 6 percent of physicians were women—on the flip side, 97 percent of nurses and 85 percent of librarians were women. Along with women's jobs went women's pay, which averaged 60 percent of men's pay in 1963.

Contrary to stereotype, however, women's paid work was not merely supplementary. It helped lift families into the middle class. Even in the prosperous 1950s, many men found that their wages could not pay for what middle-class life demanded: cars, houses, vacations, and college education for the children. Many families needed more than one wage earner just to get by. Among married women, the highest rates of labor-force participation in the 1950s were found in families at the lower end of the middle class. Over the course of the postwar decades, from 1945 to 1965, more and more women, including married women, from all class backgrounds, entered the paid workforce.

How could American society steadfastly uphold the domestic ideal when so many wives and mothers were out of the house and at work? In many ways, the contradiction was hidden by the women themselves. Fearing public disapproval, women would explain their work in family-oriented terms—as a way to save money for the children's college education, for instance. Moreover, when women took jobs outside the home, they still bore full responsibility for child care and household management, contributing to the "double day" of paid work and family work. As one overburdened woman noted, she now had "two full-time jobs instead of just one—underpaid clerical worker and unpaid housekeeper." Finally, the pressures of the Cold War made strong nuclear families with breadwinning fathers and domesticated mothers symbols of a healthy nation. Americans wanted to believe this even if it did not perfectly describe the reality of their lives.

Sex and the Middle Class

In many ways, the two decades between 1945 and 1965 were a period of sexual conservatism that reflected the values of domesticity. At the dawn of the 1960s, going steady as a prelude to marriage was the fad in high school. College women had curfews and needed permission to see a male visitor. Americans married young; more than half of those who married in 1963 were under the age of twenty-one. After the birth control pill came on the market in 1960, few doctors prescribed it to unmarried women, and even married women did not enjoy unfettered access to contraception until the Supreme Court ruled it a "privacy" right in the 1965 decision *Griswold v. Connecticut*.

Both women and men were expected to channel their sexual desire strictly toward marriage. Men might temporarily escape such expectations, so long as their sexual adventures occurred prior to marriage and did not interfere with starting a family. Women faced much harsher social sanction, not to mention potential unwanted pregnancies, if they pursued similar adventures.

The Kinsey Reports

Like the woman on the cover of this light-hearted 1953 book of photographs, many Americans reacted with surprise when Alfred Kinsey revealed the country's sexual habits. In his 1948 book about men and his 1953 book about women, Kinsey wrote about American sexual practices in the detached language of science. But it still made for salacious reading. Evangelical minister Billy Graham (see p. 828) warned: "It is impossible to estimate the damage this book will do to the already deteriorated morals of America." Picture Research Consultants & Archives.

Oh! Dr. Kinsey!
PRICE $1.00
A PHOTOGRAPHIC REACTION TO THE KINSEY REPORT
by LAWRENCE LARIAR

Hugh Hefner, who founded *Playboy* magazine in 1953, created a countermorality of bachelorhood, a fictional world populated by "hip" men and sexually available women. Hefner was the exception that proved the rule: Marriage, not swinging bachelorhood, remained the destination for the vast majority of men. Millions of men read *Playboy*, but few adopted its fantasy lifestyle.

Beneath the surface of middle-class sexual morality, Americans were less repressed than confused. On the one hand, men and women were increasingly encouraged to embrace "sexual liberalism," in which sex was valued apart from its role in procreation. On the other hand, the notion of sex as an act of pleasure created anxieties Americans had yet to resolve, resulting in many unanswered questions: Should adults have sex before marriage? When was it appropriate for young men versus women to become sexually active? Should marriage itself define the boundaries of a person's sexual life? Was greater sexual freedom just another means of exploiting women? Should men have sex with, and could they love, other men? Could women?

Alfred Kinsey | Two controversial studies by an unassuming Indiana University zoologist named Alfred Kinsey forced questions about sexuality into the open. Kinsey and his research team published *Sexual Behavior in the Human Male* in 1948 and fol-

lowed it up in 1953 with *Sexual Behavior in the Human Female*—an 842-page book that sold 270,000 copies in the first month after its publication. Taking a scientific, rather than moralistic, approach, Kinsey, who became known as "the sex doctor," documented the full range of sexual experiences of thousands of Americans. He broke numerous taboos, discussing such topics as masturbation, orgasms, homosexuality, and marital infidelity in the detached language of science.

Both studies confirmed that a sexual revolution, although a largely hidden one, had already begun to transform American society by the early 1950s. Kinsey estimated that 85 percent of white men had had sex prior to marriage, that more than 90 percent of men masturbated, and that more than 25 percent of married women had had sex outside of marriage by the age of forty. These were shocking public admissions in the late 1940s and early 1950s, and "hotter than the Kinsey report" became a national figure of speech. Kinsey was criticized by statisticians—because his samples were not randomly selected—and condemned even more fervently by religious leaders, who charged him with encouraging promiscuity and adultery. But his research opened a national conversation with profound implications for the future. Even if Kinsey's numbers were off, he helped Americans learn to talk more openly about sex.

The Homophile Movement | Among the most controversial of Kinsey's claims was that homosexuality was far more prevalent than most Americans believed. Although the American Psychiatric Association would officially define homosexuality as a mental illness in 1952, Kinsey's research found that 37 percent of men had engaged in some form of homosexual activity by early adulthood, as had 13 percent of women. Even more important, Kinsey claimed that 10 percent of American men were *exclusively* homosexual. These claims came as little surprise, but great encouragement, to a group of gay and lesbian activists who called themselves "homophiles." Organized primarily in the Mattachine Society (the first gay rights organization in the country, founded in 1951) and the Daughters of Bilitis (a lesbian organization founded in 1955), homophiles were a tiny but determined collection of activists who sought equal rights for gays and lesbians. "The lesbian is a woman endowed with all the attributes of any other woman," wrote the pioneer lesbian activist Del Martin in 1956. "The salvation of the lesbian lies in her acceptance of herself without guilt or anxiety."

Building on the urban gay and lesbian communities that had coalesced during World War II, homophiles sought to change American attitudes about same-sex love. They faced daunting obstacles, since same-sex sexual relations were illegal in every state and scorned, or feared, by most Americans. To combat prejudice and change the laws, homophile organizations cultivated a respectable, middle-class image. Members were encouraged to avoid bars and nightclubs, to dress in conservative shirts and ties (for men) and modest skirts and blouses (for women), and to seek out professional psychologists who would attest to their "normalcy." Only in the 1960s did homophiles begin to talk about the "homophile vote" and their "rights as citizens," laying the groundwork for the gay rights movement of the 1970s.

Youth Culture

One of the most striking developments in American family life in the postwar decades was the emergence of the teenager as a cultural phenomenon. In 1956, only partly in jest, the CBS radio commentator Eric Sevareid questioned "whether the teenagers will take over the United States lock, stock, living room, and garage." Sevareid was grumbling about American youth culture, a phenomenon first noticed in the 1920s and with its roots in the lengthening years of education, the role of peer groups, and the consumer tastes of teenagers.

Market research revealed a distinct teen market to be exploited. *Newsweek* noted with awe in 1951 that the aggregate of the $3 weekly spending money of the average teenager was enough to buy 190 million candy bars, 130 million soft drinks, and 230 million sticks of gum. Increasingly, advertisers targeted the young, both to capture their spending money and to exploit their influence on family purchases. Note the changing slogans for Pepsi-Cola: "Twice as much for a nickel" (1935), "Be sociable — have a Pepsi" (1948), "Now it's Pepsi for those who think young" (1960), and "the Pepsi Generation" (1965).

Hollywood movies played a large role in fostering a teenage culture. Young people made up the largest audience for motion pictures, and Hollywood studios learned over the course of the 1950s to cater to them. The success of films such as *The Wild One* (1953), starring Marlon Brando; *Blackboard Jungle* (1955), with Sidney Poitier; and *Rebel Without a Cause* (1955), starring James Dean, convinced movie executives that films directed at teenagers were worthy investments. "What are you rebelling against?" Brando is asked in *The Wild One*. "Whattaya got?" he replies. By the early 1960s, Hollywood had retooled its business model, shifting emphasis away from adults and families to teenagers. The "teenpic" soon included multiple genres: horror, rock 'n' roll, dangerous youth, and beach party, among others.

Rock 'n' Roll | What really defined the youth culture, however, was its music. Rejecting the romantic ballads of the 1940s, teenagers discovered rock 'n' roll, which originated in African American rhythm and blues. The Cleveland disc jockey Alan Freed took the lead in introducing white America to the black-created sound by playing what were called "race" records. "If I could find a white man who had the Negro sound and the Negro feel, I could make a billion dollars," a record company owner is quoted as saying. The performer who fit that bill was Elvis Presley, who rocketed into instant celebrity in 1956 with his hit records "Hound Dog" and "Heartbreak Hotel," covers of songs originally recorded by black artists such as Big Momma Thornton. Between 1953 and 1959, record sales increased from $213 million to $603 million, with rock 'n' roll as the driving force.

Many unhappy adults saw in rock 'n' roll music and teen movies an invitation to race mixing, rebellion, and a more flagrant sexuality. The media featured hundreds of stories on problem teens, and in 1955 a Senate subcommittee conducted a high-profile investigation of juvenile delinquency and its origins in the popular media. Denunciations only bounced off the

Motown

Mary Wilson, Diana Ross, and Florence Ballard (from left to right) were the founding members of the Motown singing group the Supremes (shown here in concert, in 1963) that produced twelve number-one singles. Motown, a record label owned by African American entrepreneur Berry Gordy, specialized in so-called "cross-over" acts: black singers who sold records to white audiences. In the era of Jim Crow, Motown represented a small but noteworthy step toward a less racially segregated American culture.   © Steve Schapiro/Corbis.

new youth culture or, if anything, increased its popularity. Both Hollywood and the music industry had learned that youth rebellion sold tickets.

Cultural Dissenters   Youth rebellion was only one aspect of a broader discontent with the sometimes saccharine commercial culture of the 1950s. A great number of artists, jazz musicians, and writers embarked on powerful new experimental projects in a remarkable flowering of intensely personal, introspective art forms. In jazz, for instance, black musicians developed a hard-driving improvisational style known as bebop. Whether the "hot" bebop of saxophonist Charlie Parker or the more subdued "cool" West Coast sound of the trumpeter Miles Davis, postwar jazz was cerebral, intimate, and individualistic. As such, it stood in stark contrast to the commercialized, dance-oriented "swing" bands of the 1930s and 1940s.

Black jazz musicians found eager fans not only in the African American community but also among young white Beats, a group of writers and poets centered in New York and San Francisco who disdained middle-class materialism. In his poem "Howl" (1956), which became a manifesto of the Beat generation, Allen Ginsberg lamented: "I saw the best minds of my generation destroyed by madness, starving hysterical naked, / dragging

themselves through the negro streets at dawn looking for an angry fix." In works such as Jack Kerouac's novel *On the Road* (1957), the Beats glorified spontaneity, sexual adventurism, drug use, and spirituality. The Beats were apolitical, but their cultural rebellion would, in the 1960s, inspire a new generation of young rebels disenchanted with both the political and cultural status quo.

- How would you explain the contradictions in postwar domesticity? What were the benefits of domestic values? The costs?

- What were the cultural expectations of men and women in the 1950s? How had they changed from the 1920s? The 1930s?

SUMMARY

We have explored how, at the same time it became mired in the Cold War, the United States entered an unparalleled era of prosperity in which a new middle class came into being. Indeed, the Cold War was one of the engines of prosperity. The postwar economy was marked by the dominance of big corporations and defense spending.

After years of depression and war-induced insecurity, Americans turned inward toward religion, home, and family. Postwar couples married young, had several children, and—if they were white and middle class—raised their children in a climate of suburban comfort and consumerism. The pro-family orientation of the 1950s celebrated traditional gender roles, even though millions of women entered the workforce in those years. Not everyone, however, shared in the postwar prosperity. Postwar cities increasingly became places of last resort for the nation's poor. Black migrants, unlike earlier immigrants, encountered an urban economy that had little use for them. Without opportunity, and faced by pervasive racism, many of them were on their way to becoming an American underclass, even as sparkling new suburbs emerged outside cities to house the new middle class. Many of the smoldering contradictions of the postwar period—Cold War anxiety in the midst of suburban domesticity, tensions in women's lives, economic and racial inequality—helped spur the protest movements of the 1960s.

CHAPTER REVIEW QUESTIONS

- How do you account for the economic prosperity of the postwar era?

- Why did the suburb achieve paramount significance for Americans in the 1950s?

- Who were the people left out of the postwar boom? How do you account for their exclusion?

FOR FURTHER EXPLORATION

Two engaging introductions to postwar society are Paul Boyer, *Promises to Keep* (1995), and David Halberstam, *The Fifties* (1993). John K. Galbraith, *The Affluent Society* (1958), is an influential contemporary analysis of the postwar economy. Nelson Lichtenstein, *State of the Union: A Century of American Labor* (2002), offers a searching account of the labor-management accord. The best book on consumer culture is Lizabeth Cohen, *A Consumers' Republic: The Politics of Mass Consumption in Postwar America* (2003). Elaine Tyler May, *Homeward Bound* (1988), is the classic introduction to postwar family life. On gender in the 1950s and 1960s, see Susan J. Douglas, *Where the Girls Are: Growing Up Female with the Mass Media* (1994), and James Gilbert, *Men in the Middle: Searching for Masculinity in the 1950s* (2005). A good guide to sex and sexuality in the period is Estelle Freedman and John D'Emilio, *Intimate Matters: A History of Sexuality in America* (1998). A good introduction to the complexity of the homophile movement is Marc Stein, *City of Sisterly and Brotherly Loves: Lesbian and Gay Philadelphia* (2000). For insightful essays on the impact of television, see Karal Ann Marling, *As Seen on TV* (1996). For youth culture, see William Graebner, *Coming of Age in Buffalo* (1990). On the urban crisis, see Thomas J. Sugrue, *The Origins of the Urban Crisis: Race and Inequality in Postwar Detroit* (1996). The Academy of American Poets has a "Brief Guide to the Beat Poets" page (which has links to other "Beat" poetry and prose resources) on their site: **www.poets .org/viewmedia.php/prmMID/5646**.

TIMELINE

1944	Bretton Woods economic conference World Bank and International Monetary Fund (IMF) founded GI Bill (Servicemen's Readjustment Act)
1946	First edition of Dr. Spock's *Baby and Child Care*
1947	First Levittown built
1948	Beginning of network television *Shelley v. Kraemer* Alfred Kinsey's *Sexual Behavior in the Human Male* published
1949	Billy Graham revival in Los Angeles
1950	Treaty of Detroit initiates labor-management accord
1951	Bracero Program revived Mattachine Society founded
1952	McCarran-Walter Act
1953	Kinsey's *Sexual Behavior of the Human Female* published
1954	Ray Kroc buys the first McDonald's franchise
1955	AFL and CIO merge Daughters of Bilitis Founded
1956	National Interstate and Defense Highways Act Elvis Presley's breakthrough records Allen Ginsberg's poem "Howl" published
1957	Peak of postwar baby boom
1965	*Griswold v. Connecticut*

TEST YOUR KNOWLEDGE

To assess your command of the material in this chapter, see the Online Study Guide at **bedfordstmartins.com/henretta**.

For Web sites, images, and documents related to topics and places in this chapter, visit **bedfordstmartins.com/makehistory**.

CHAPTER 27

Walking into Freedom Land: The Civil Rights Movement, 1941-1973

In June 1945, as the war in Europe was coming to a close, Democratic senator James O. Eastland of Mississippi stood on the floor of the U.S. Senate and brashly told his colleagues that "the Negro race is an inferior race." Flailing his arms, his tie askew from vigorous gesturing, Eastland ridiculed black troops. "The Negro soldier was an utter and dismal failure in combat," he said. "They have disgraced the flag of this country."

Eastland's assertions were untrue. Black soldiers had served honorably; many won medals for bravery in combat. All-black units, such as the 761st "Black Panther" Tank Battalion and the famous Tuskegee Airmen, were widely praised by military commanders, including General George Patton. But the fact remained that Eastland, and segregationists who shared his views, were a nearly unassailable force in Congress, able to block civil rights legislation, shape national opinion, and slander African Americans at will.

In the 1940s, two generations after W. E. B. Du Bois penned the indelible statement "The problem of the twentieth century is the problem of the color line," few white Americans believed in racial equality. Racial segregation remained firmly entrenched across the country, South and North. Much of the Deep South, like Eastland's home state of Mississippi, was a "closed society": Black people had no political rights and lived on the margins of white society, impoverished and exploited. Northern cities proved more hospitable to blacks, but schools, neighborhoods, and many businesses remained segregated and unequal in the North as well.

Across the nation, however, winds of change had begun to gather. Between World War II and the 1970s, slowly at first, and then with greater urgency in the 1960s, the civil rights movement swept aside the nationwide system of racial segregation. It could not sweep away racial inequality completely, but the movement constituted a "second Reconstruction" in which African American activism prompted a reshaping of the nation's laws and practices. Civil rights was the paradigmatic social movement of the twentieth century—it provided inspiration for every subsequent social movement. Its model of nonviolent protest and its calls for self-determination inspired the New Left, the rebirth of feminism, the Chicano movement, the gay rights movement, the American Indian movement, and many others. Each of those movements was distinct, with unique goals, but all of them followed in the deep

The March from Selma to Montgomery, 1965

Leading a throng of 25,000 marchers, Martin Luther King Jr. holds the hand of his wife, Coretta Scott King, as they enter downtown Montgomery, Alabama, at the end of the Selma to Montgomery march. Bob Adelman/Magnum Photos, Inc.

footprints left by black civil rights activists and organizations. Born in multiple communities, by the 1960s the movement was pushing for massive changes in American society and governing institutions.

Most important, the black-led civil rights movement, joined at key moments by Latinos, Asian Americans, and Native Americans, redefined *liberalism* amid titanic social upheaval. In the 1930s, New Deal liberalism had established a welfare state to protect citizens from economic hardship. The civil rights movement forged a new "rights liberalism": the notion that individuals require state protection from discrimination. This version of liberalism focused on identities—such as race or sex—rather than general social welfare, and as such would prove to be both a necessary expansion of the nation's ideals *and* a divisive concept that produced political backlash. Indeed, the quest for racial justice would contribute to a crisis of liberalism itself.

The Emerging Civil Rights Struggle, 1941–1957

As it took shape during World War II and the early Cold War, the battle against racial injustice proceeded along two tracks: at the grass roots and in governing institutions—federal courts, state legislatures, and ultimately the U.S. Congress. Labor unions, churches, and protest organizations such as the Congress of Racial Equality (CORE) inspired hundreds of thousands of ordinary citizens to join the movement. But grassroots struggle was not black citizens' only weapon. They also had the Bill of Rights and the Reconstruction amendments to the Constitution. Civil rights lived in those documents—especially in the Fourteenth Amendment, which guaranteed equal protection under the law to all U.S. citizens, and in the Fifteenth, which guaranteed the right to vote regardless of "race, color, or previous condition of servitude"—but had been ignored or violated by whites for nearly a century. The task was to restore the Constitution's legal force. Neither track—grassroots or legal/legislative—was entirely independent of the other. Together, they were the foundation of the fight for racial equality in the postwar decades.

Life under Jim Crow

Racial segregation and economic exploitation defined the lives of the majority of African Americans in the postwar decades. Numbering 15 million in 1950, African Americans were approximately 10 percent of the U.S. population. In the South, however, they constituted between 30 and 50 percent of the population of several states, such as South Carolina and Mississippi. Segregation, commonly known as Jim Crow (see Chapter 20), prevailed in every aspect of southern life. In southern states, where two-thirds of all African Americans lived in 1950, blacks could not eat in restaurants patronized by whites or use the same waiting rooms at bus stations. All forms of public transportation were rigidly segregated by custom or by law. Public parks and libraries were segregated. Even drinking fountains were labeled "White" and "Colored."

This system of segregation underlay economic and political structures that further marginalized and disempowered black citizens. Virtually no African American could work for city or state government, and the best jobs in the private sector were reserved for whites. Blacks worked "in the back," cleaning, cooking, stocking shelves, and loading trucks for the lowest wages. Rural African Americans labored in a sharecropping system that kept them stuck in poverty, often prevented them from obtaining an education, and offered virtually no avenue of escape. Politically, less than 20 percent of eligible black voters were allowed to vote, the result of poll taxes, literacy tests, intimidation, fraud, and the "white primary" (elections in which only whites could vote). This near-total disenfranchisement gave whites power disproportionate to their numbers—black people were one-third of the residents of Mississippi, South Carolina, and Georgia but had virtually no political influence in those states.

In the North, racial segregation in everyday life was less acute but equally tangible. Northern segregation took the form of a spatial system in which whites increasingly lived in suburbs or on the outskirts of cities, while African Americans were concentrated in down-

Jim Crow

As the law of the land in most southern states, racial segregation (known as Jim Crow) required the complete separation of blacks and whites in most public spaces. The "colored waiting room" shown in this 1940 photograph of a bus terminal in Birmingham, Alabama, was typical. Everything from waiting areas to libraries, public parks, schools, drinking fountains, and even cola vending machines were subject to strict racial segregation.   Library of Congress.

town neighborhoods. The result was what many called ghettos: all-black districts characterized by high rents, low wages, and inadequate city services. Employment discrimination and lack of adequate training left many African Americans without any means of support. Few jobs other than the most menial were open to African Americans; journalists, accountants, engineers, and other highly educated men from all-black colleges and universities often labored as railroad porters because jobs commensurate with their skills remained for whites only. These conditions produced a self-perpetuating cycle that kept far too many black citizens trapped on the social margins.

It is customary in history textbooks to contrast Jim Crow racial segregation in the South with the relatively more open racial system of the North. To be certain, African Americans found greater freedom in the North and West. They could vote, participate in politics, and, at least after the early 1960s, enjoy equal access to public accommodations. But we err in thinking that racial segregation was *only* a southern problem or that poverty and racial discrimination were not also deeply entrenched in the North and West. In northern cities

such as Detroit, Chicago, and Philadelphia, for instance, white home owners in the 1950s used various tactics — from police harassment to thrown bricks, burning crosses, bombs, and mob violence — to keep African Americans from living near them. Moreover, as we saw in Chapter 26, Federal Housing Authority (FHA) and bank redlining excluded African American home buyers from the all-white suburbs emerging around major cities. Racial segregation was a national, not regional, problem.

Origins of the Civil Rights Movement

Since racial discrimination had been part of American life for hundreds of years, why did the civil rights movement arise when it did? After all, the National Association for the Advancement of Colored People (NAACP), founded in 1909, had begun challenging racial segregation in a series of court cases in the 1930s. And other organizations, such as Marcus Garvey's United Negro Improvement Association in the 1920s, had attracted significant popular support. These precedents were important, but a series of factors came together in the middle of the twentieth century to make a broad and unique movement possible.

An important influence was World War II. "The Jewish people and the Negro people both know the meaning of Nordic supremacy," wrote the African American poet Langston Hughes in 1945. In the war against fascism, the Allies sought to discredit racist Nazi ideology. Committed to an antiracist ideology abroad, Americans increasingly condemned all forms of racism, even those at home. The Cold War placed added pressure on U.S. officials. "More and more we are learning how closely our democracy is under observation," President Harry S. Truman commented in 1947. To inspire other nations in the global standoff with the Soviet Union, Truman explained, "we must correct the remaining imperfections in our practice of democracy."

Among the most consequential factors was the growth of the urban black middle class. Historically small, the black middle class experienced robust growth after World War II. Its ranks produced most of the civil rights leaders: ministers, teachers, trade union representatives, attorneys, and other professionals. Churches, for centuries a sanctuary for black Americans, were especially important. Moreover, in the 1960s African American college students—part of the largest expansion of college enrollment in U.S. history—joined the movement, adding new energy and fresh ideas (Table 27.1). With access to education, media, and institutions, this new middle class had more resources than ever before. Less dependent on white patronage, and therefore less vulnerable to white retaliation, middle-class African Americans were in a position to lead a movement for change.

Still other influences assisted the movement. Labor leaders were generally more equality-minded than the rank and file, but the United Auto Workers, the United Steel Workers, and the Communication Workers of America, among many other trade unions, were reliable allies at the national level. The new medium of television, too, played a crucial role. When television networks covered early desegregation struggles, such as the 1957 integration of Little Rock High School, Americans across the country saw the violence of white supremacy firsthand. None of these factors alone was decisive. None ensured an easy path. The civil rights movement faced enormous resistance and required dauntless courage and sacrifice from thousands upon thousands of activists for more than three decades. Ultimately, however, the movement changed the nation for the better and improved the lives of millions of Americans.

World War II: The Beginnings

During the war fought "to make the world safe for democracy," America was far from ready to extend full equality to its own black citizens. Black workers faced discrimination in wartime employment, and while more than a million black troops served in World War II, they were placed in segregated units commanded by whites. Both at home and abroad, World War II "immeasurably magnified the Negro's awareness of the disparity between the American profession and practice of democracy," NAACP president Walter White observed.

Executive Order 8802 On the home front, activists pushed two strategies. First, A. Philip Randolph, whose Brotherhood of Sleeping Car Porters was the most prominent black trade union, called for a march on Washington in early 1941. Randolph planned to bring 100,000 protesters to the nation's capital if African Americans were not given equal opportunity in war jobs—then just beginning to expand with President Franklin Roosevelt's pledge to supply the Allies with materiel. To avoid a divisive protest, FDR issued Executive Order 8802, prohibiting racial discrimination in defense industries, and Randolph agreed to cancel the march. The resulting Fair Employment Practices Commission (FEPC) was weak, but it set an important precedent: federal action. Randolph's efforts showed that white leaders and institutions could be swayed by concerted African American action. It would be a critical lesson for the movement.

The Double V Campaign A second strategy jumped from the pages of the *Pittsburgh Courier*, one of the foremost African American newspapers of the era. It was the brainchild of an ordinary cafeteria worker from Kansas. In a 1942 letter to the edi-

TABLE 27.1	

African American College Enrollment

Year	Number of African Americans Enrolled at Colleges and Universities (numbers rounded to nearest thousand)
1940	60,000
1950	110,000
1960	185,000
1970	430,000
1980	1.4 million
1990	3.6 million

Postwar Desegregation

Picketers outside the July 1948 Democratic National Convention demand that the party include equal rights and anti–Jim Crow planks in its official platform and desegregate the armed services. Leading the pickets is A. Philip Randolph, president of the Brotherhood of Sleeping Car Porters. Randolph headed the March on Washington Movement that pressured President Roosevelt to desegregate defense employment during World War II, and led the committee that convinced President Truman to desegregate the armed forces in 1948.   © Bettmann/Corbis.

tor, James G. Thompson urged that "colored Americans adopt the double VV for a double victory"—victory over fascism abroad and victory over racism at home. Edgar Rouzeau, editor of the paper's New York office, agreed: "Black America must fight two wars and win in both." Instantly dubbed the Double V Campaign, Thompson's notion, with Rouzeau's backing, spread like wildfire through black communities across the country. African Americans would demonstrate their love of country by fighting the Axis Powers. But they would also demand, peacefully but emphatically, the defeat of racism at home. "The suffering and privation may be great," Rouzeau told his readers, "but the rewards loom even greater."

The Double V efforts met considerable resistance. In war industries, factories periodically shut down in Chicago, Baltimore, Philadelphia, and other cities because of "hate strikes": the refusal of white workers to labor with black workers. Detroit was especially tense. Referring to racial tension, *Life* magazine reported in 1942 that "Detroit is Dynamite. . . . It can either blow up Hitler or blow up America." In 1943, it nearly did the latter. On a hot summer day, whites from the city's ethnic neighborhoods taunted and beat African Americans in a local park. Three days of rioting ensued in which thirty-four people were killed, twenty-five of them black. Federal troops were called in to restore order.

Despite and because of such incidents, a generation was spurred into action during the war years. In New York City, employment discrimination on the city's transit lines prompted one of the first bus boycotts in the nation's history, led in 1941 by Harlem minister Adam Clayton Powell Jr. In Chicago, James Farmer and three other members of the Fellowship of Reconciliation (FOR), a nonviolent peace organization, founded the Congress of Racial Equality (CORE) in 1942. FOR

Wartime Workers

During World War II, hundreds of thousands of black migrants left the South, bound for large cities in the North and West. There, they found jobs such as the welding work done by these African American women at the Landers, Frary, and Clark plant in New Britain, Connecticut. Fighting employment discrimination during the war represented one of the earliest phases in the long struggle against racial segregation in the United States.   Library of Congress.

Political Influence in the North

Laws, political tactics, and white intimidation kept more than two-thirds of southern blacks from voting in the mid-twentieth century. But migration to northern cities increasingly gave African Americans electoral clout. From New York City's Harlem, Reverend Adam Clayton Powell Jr. was elected to Congress in 1944. Here he talks with friends before taking his seat in the House of Representatives. Black political influence in northern cities, such as New York, would be a major factor in the emerging civil rights revolution.   George Skadding/Time Life Pictures/Getty Images.

and CORE adopted the philosophy of nonviolent disobedience espoused by Mahatma Gandhi. Meanwhile, after the war, hundreds of thousands of African American veterans used the GI Bill to go to college, trade school, or graduate school, placing them in a position to push against segregation. At the war's end, Powell affirmed that "the black man . . . is ready to throw himself into the struggle to make the dream of America become flesh and blood, bread and butter."

Cold War Civil Rights

Demands for justice persisted in the early years of the Cold War. African American efforts were propelled by symbolic victories to be certain—as when Jackie Robinson broke through the color line in major league

baseball by joining the Brooklyn Dodgers in 1947 — but the growing black vote in northern cities proved more decisive. During World War II, more than a million African Americans migrated to northern and western cities, where they joined the Democratic Party of Franklin Roosevelt and the New Deal (Map 27.1). This newfound political leverage awakened northern liberals, who became allies of civil rights advocates. Ultimately, the Cold War produced mixed results, as the nation's commitment to anticommunism opened some avenues for civil rights while closing others.

Civil Rights and the New Deal Coalition African American leaders had high hopes for President Truman, inheritor of the New Deal coalition. Although not opposed to using racist

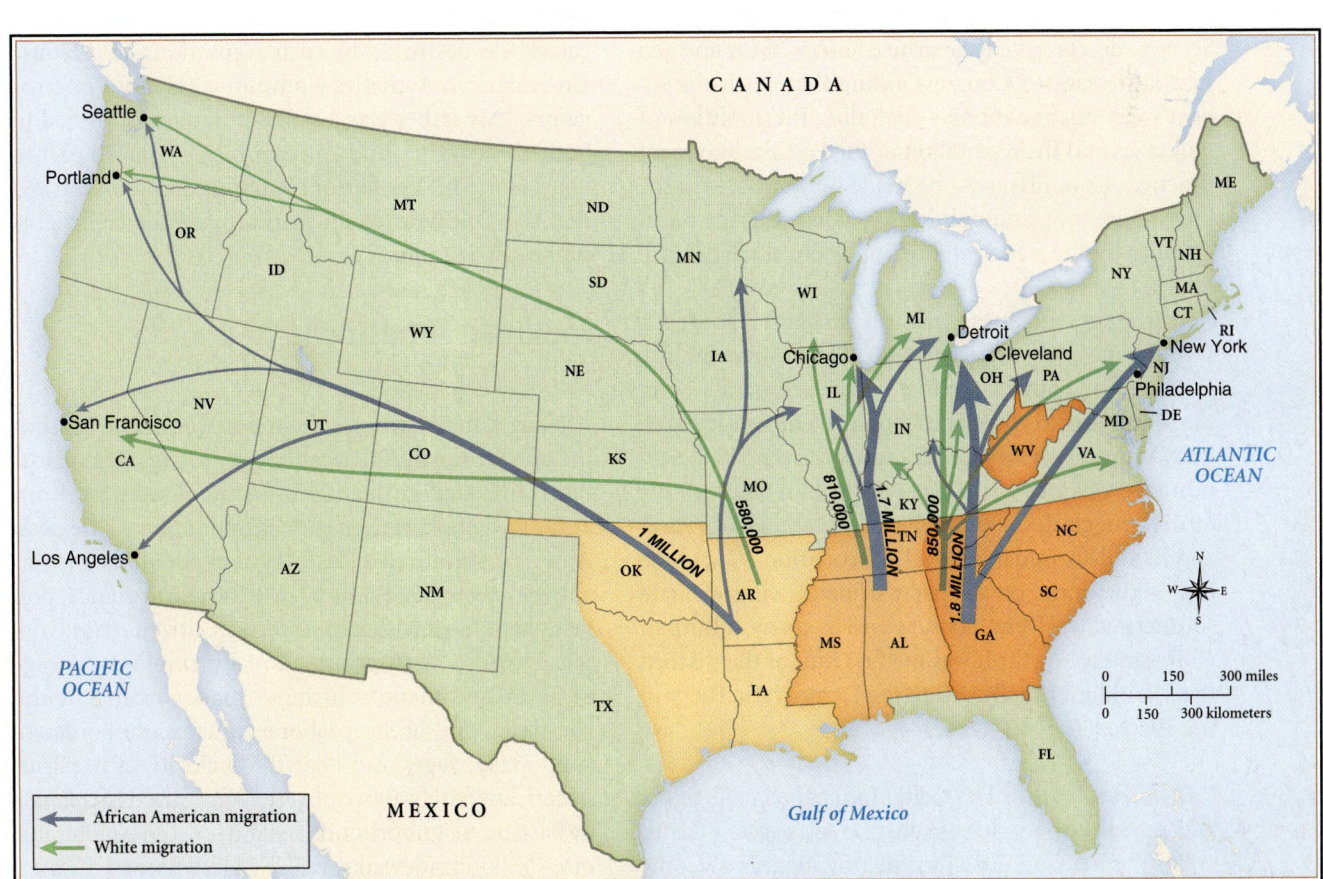

MAP 27.1

Internal Migrations

The migration of African Americans from the South to other regions of the country produced one of the most remarkable demographic shifts of the mid-twentieth century. Between World War I — which marked the start of the Great Migration — and the 1970s, more than 6 million blacks left the South. Where they settled in the North and West, they helped change the politics of entire cities and even states. Seeking black votes, which had become a key to victory in major cities, liberal Democrats and Republicans alike in New York, Illinois, California, and Pennsylvania, for instance, increasingly made civil rights part of their platform. In this way, migration advanced the political cause of black equality.

language himself, Truman supported civil rights on moral grounds. Moreover, he understood the growing importance of the small but often decisive black vote in key northern states such as New York, Illinois, and Michigan. Civil rights activists Randolph and Powell—along with vocal white liberals such as Hubert Humphrey, the mayor of Minneapolis, and members of Americans for Democratic Action (ADA), a liberal organization—pressed Truman to act.

With no support for civil rights in Congress, Truman turned to executive action. In 1946, he appointed the Presidential Committee on Civil Rights, whose 1947 report, "To Secure These Rights," called for robust federal action to ensure equality for African Americans. With the report fresh in his mind, in 1948 Truman issued an executive order desegregating employment in federal agencies and, under pressure from Randolph's Committee Against Jim Crow in Military Service, desegregated the armed forces. Truman then sent a message to Congress asking that all of the report's recommendations—including the abolition of poll taxes and the restoration of the Fair Employment Practices Commission—be made into law. It was the most aggressive, and politically boldest, call for racial equality by the leader of a major political party since Reconstruction.

Truman's boldness was too much for southern Democrats. Under the leadership of Strom Thurmond, governor of South Carolina, white Democrats from the South formed the States' Rights Democratic Party, known popularly as the Dixiecrats, for the 1948 election (see Chapter 25). This brought into focus an internal struggle developing within the Democratic Party and its still-formidable New Deal coalition. Would the civil rights aims of the party's liberal wing alienate southern white Democrats, as well as many suburban whites in the North? It was the first hint of the discord that would eventually divide the Democratic Party in the 1960s.

Race and Anticommunism   The Cold War shaped civil rights in both positive and negative terms. In a time of growing fear of Communist expansionism, Truman worried about America's image in the world. He reminded Americans that when whites and blacks "fail to live together in peace," that failure hurt "the cause of democracy itself in the whole world." Indeed, the Soviet Union used American racism as a means of discrediting the United States abroad. "We cannot escape the fact that our civil rights record has been an issue in world politics," the Committee on Civil Rights wrote. The Soviet Union even

compared the South's treatment of African Americans to the Nazis' treatment of Jews. International tensions between the United States and the Soviet Union thus appeared to strengthen the hand of civil rights leaders, because Americans needed to demonstrate to the rest of the world that its race relations were improving (see Voices from Abroad, "Hailou Wolde-Giorghis: African Encounters with U.S. Racism," p. 857).

The Cold War strengthened one hand while weakening the other. McCarthyism and the hunt for subversives at home held the civil rights movement back. Civil rights opponents charged that racial integration was "communistic," and the NAACP was banned in many southern states as an "anti-American" organization. Black Americans who spoke favorably of the Soviet Union, such as the actor and singer Paul Robeson, or had been "fellow travelers" in the 1930s, such as the pacifist Bayard Rustin, were persecuted. Robeson, whose career was destroyed by such accusations, told House Un-American Activities Committee (HUAC) interrogators, "My father was a slave, and my people died to build this country, and I am going to . . . have a part of it just like you." The fate of people like Robeson showed that the Cold War could work *against* the civil rights cause just as easily as for it.

Mexican Americans and Japanese Americans

African Americans were the most prominent, but not the only, group in American society to organize against racial injustice in the 1940s. In the Southwest, from Texas to California, Mexican immigrants and Mexican Americans endured a "caste" system not unlike the Jim Crow system in the South. In Texas, for instance, poll taxes kept most Mexican American citizens from voting. Decades of discrimination by employers in agriculture and manufacturing—made possible by the constant supply of cheap labor from across the border—suppressed wages and kept the majority of Mexican Americans barely above poverty. Many lived in *colonias* or barrios, neighborhoods separated from Anglos and often lacking sidewalks, reliable electricity and water, and public services.

Developments within the Mexican American community set the stage for fresh challenges to these conditions in the 1940s. Labor activism in the 1930s and 1940s, especially in Congress of Industrial Organizations (CIO) unions with large numbers of Mexican Americans, improved wages and working conditions in some industries and produced a new generation of leaders. Additionally, more than 400,000 Mexican Americans

All the nations and people I had hitherto passed through resembled our own in their manners, customs and language

Hailou Wolde-Giorghis
African Encounters with U.S. Racism

Africans who visited the United States in the postwar era found themselves shocked by racial segregation and the poverty in which the majority of African Americans lived. Many African nations were in the midst of anticolonial struggles to free themselves from European control—a form of imperialism dating to the late nineteenth century. Hailou Wolde-Giorghis was an Ethiopian student who visited the United States at the invitation of the State Department in the early 1960s. Wolde-Giorghis's account of his visit to the United States appeared in a journal in Uganda, which achieved independence from Great Britain in 1962.

"Negroes are dirty," say the whites, but in nearly all restaurants I saw Negro waiters and cooks. "They're lazy": I noticed that it is the Negro who does the hardest manual work. They are said to be uncultivated and are therefore denied access to culture. As George Bernard Shaw said, "The haughty American nation makes the Negro shine its shoes, and then demonstrates his physical and mental inferiority by the fact that he is a shoe-cleaner."

But why should this racism exist? Some will tell you that it's because the white man is ignorant of the Negro: he doesn't know him and has never tried to understand him. Why should the master bother to know his Negro cook? . . . The last and perhaps most important explanation of racism relates to the economy: the white worker is afraid of the competition represented by the Negro. The latter is offered all the degrading work, such as shining shoes and working as porters (at the airport n New York, for instance, I saw only one white porter). When the Negro has other capabilities, he is victimized by discrimination. . . .

When speaking with an ex-racist or quite simply an honest Southerner, I noticed that when I spoke to him of certain injustices or of the white man's exploitation of the Negro, he would immediately ask me about Communism. In the South, for example, all anti-racist demonstrators are accused of being Communist. Therefore, in fighting the Negro the Southerner must also fight this twentieth-century "sickness." Nor is the United Nations exempted; it is "Communist," and if it is successfully to carry out its mission it must first be purged of all Negro nations and all eastern countries. . . .

What is known as integration in the South is the ability of a Negro to enter a shop and buy a record, or the fact that, of ten thousand students enrolled in a university, two of them are Negroes. "A miracle!" they cry. Real integration, however, does not exist, not even in the North, and by real integration I mean interracial communication, complete equality in the strict sense of the word. Still another example drawn from the South: the manager of a television studio told me in frigid terms that he would not hire Negroes; there would be a scandal and all his sponsors would protest.

One of the consequences of this discrimination is obviously the Negro's economic situation; with the exception of a few wealthy Negroes in show business or sports, or businessmen (in Atlanta, for example, some of the most important banks are owned by Negroes), most belong to the lower class. I could talk here a little about the southern slums, which I personally saw, where thousands of Negroes are housed in quasi-military camps. I was told at great length—the way one profusely excuses oneself—that there were whites living in the same conditions. That is very possible, but I did not see any.

There are occasionally completely segregated quarters consisting of old wooden houses, many of them shacks built with soap boxes. In most of them there is neither water nor electricity (and remember this is the United States in the twentieth century); sanitary conditions are frightfully similar to those of many African countries.

Source: Hailou Wolde-Giorghis, "My Encounters with Racism in the United States," in *Views of America*, eds. Alan F. Westin et al. (New York: Harcourt, Brace, and World, 1966): 228–231.

ANALYZING THE EVIDENCE

- Why does Wolde-Giorghis observe the contradictions in the ways whites see African Americans? They are said to be dirty, yet they cook and clean. They are said to be lazy, yet they perform back-breaking labor. What does this reveal about southern white society?
- Why were antiracist activists in the South accused of being Communists?
- Wolde-Giorghis is especially critical of southern "integration." As an African, what kind of perspective would he bring to this question?
- What are the different explanations Wolde-Giorghis gives for the poverty of many African Americans?

Mexican Americans
In the Southwest, Mexican immigrants and many Mexican Americans encountered a caste system not unlike Jim Crow segregation. Most of the hardest, lowest-paying work in states such as Texas, Arizona, and California was performed by people of Mexican descent. Here a group of braceros, migrant Mexican workers allowed into the United States for a limited time, harvest a field of strawberries in California's Salinas Valley. © Bettmann/Corbis.

served in World War II. Having fought for their country, many returned to the United States determined to challenge their second-class citizenship. Indeed, many historians consider World War II to be the seminal event in the emergence of the Mexican American civil rights movement. Additionally, a new Mexican American middle class began to take shape in major cities such as Los Angeles, San Antonio, El Paso, and Chicago, which, like the African American middle class, gave leaders and resources to the cause.

In Texas and California, Mexican Americans created new civil rights organizations in the postwar years. In Corpus Christi, Texas, World War II veterans founded the American GI Forum in 1948 to protest the poor treatment of Mexican American soldiers and veterans. Activists in Los Angeles created the Community Services Organization (CSO) the same year. Both groups arose to address specific local injustices (such as the segregation of military cemeteries), but they quickly broadened their scope to encompass political and economic justice for the larger community. Among the first young activists to work for the CSO were Cesar Chavez and Dolores Huerta, who would later found the United Farm Workers (UFW) and inspire the Chicano movement of the 1960s.

Activists also pushed for legal change. In 1947, five Mexican American fathers in California sued a local school district for placing their children in separate "Mexican" schools. The case, *Mendez v. Westminster School District*, never made it to the U.S. Supreme Court. But the Ninth Circuit Court ruled such segregation unconstitutional, laying the legal groundwork for broader challenges to racial inequality. Among those filing briefs in the case was the NAACP's Thurgood Marshall, who was then developing the legal strategy to strike at racial segregation against African Americans in the South. In another significant legal victory, the Supreme Court ruled in 1954—just two weeks before the landmark *Brown v. Board of Education* decision—that Mexican Americans constituted a "distinct class" that could claim protection from discrimination.

Also on the West Coast, Japanese Americans accelerated their legal challenge to discrimination. Undeterred by rulings in the *Hirabayashi* (1943) and *Korematsu* (1944) cases upholding wartime imprisonment (see Chapter 24), the Japanese American Citizens League (JACL) filed lawsuits in the late 1940s to regain property lost during the war. The JACL also challenged the constitutionality of California's Alien Land Law, which prohibited Japanese immigrants from owning land, and successfully lobbied Congress to enable those same immigrants to become citizens—a right they were denied for fifty years. These efforts by Mexican and Japanese Americans enlarged the scope of civil rights beyond demands by African Americans and laid the foundation for a broader notion of racial equality in the postwar years.

The Legal Strategy and *Brown v. Board of Education*

With civil rights legislation blocked in Congress by southern Democrats throughout the 1950s, activists looked to the federal courts for a breakthrough. In the late 1930s, NAACP lawyers Thurgood Marshall, Charles Hamilton Houston, and William Hastie had begun preparing the legal ground in a series of cases challenging racial discrimination. The key was prodding the U.S. Supreme Court to use the Fourteenth Amendment's "equal protection" clause to overturn its 1898 ruling in

Plessy v. Ferguson, which upheld racial segregation under the "separate but equal" doctrine.

Thurgood Marshall | Marshall was the great-grandson of slaves. Of modest origins, his parents instilled in him a faith in law and the Constitution. After his 1930 graduation from Lincoln University, a prestigious African American institution near Philadelphia, Marshall applied to the University of Maryland Law School. Denied admission because the school did not accept blacks, he enrolled at all-black Howard University. There Marshall met Houston, a law school dean, and the two forged a friendship and intellectual partnership that would change the face of American legal history. Marshall, with Houston's help, would argue most of the NAACP's landmark cases. In the late 1960s, President Johnson appointed Marshall to the Supreme Court—the first African American to have that honor.

Marshall, Houston, Hastie, and six other attorneys filed suit after suit, deliberately selecting each one from

The Legal Strategy

On the steps of the Supreme Court on the day in 1954 that *Brown v. Board of Education of Topeka* was decided, are the architects of the NAACP legal strategy in the *Brown* case and dozens of others. Together, (from left to right) George E. C. Hayes, Thurgood Marshall, and James M. Nabrit pursued cases that undermined the constitutional foundation of racial segregation. Their efforts were not enough to destroy Jim Crow, however—that would take marches, protests, and sacrifices from ordinary citizens.   AP Images.

dozens of possibilities. The strategy was slow and time-consuming, but progress came. In 1936, Marshall and Hamilton won a state case that forced the University of Maryland Law School to admit qualified African Americans—a ruling of obvious significance to Marshall. Eight years later, in *Smith v. Allwright* (1944), Marshall convinced the U.S. Supreme Court that all-white primaries were unconstitutional. In 1950, with Marshall once again arguing the case, the Supreme Court ruled in *McLaurin v. Oklahoma* that universities could not segregate black students from others on campus. None of these cases produced swift or immediate changes in the daily lives of most African Americans, but they confirmed that civil rights attorneys were on the right track.

Brown v. Board of Education | The NAACP's legal strategy achieved its ultimate validation in a case involving Linda Brown, a black pupil in Topeka, Kansas, who had been forced to attend a distant segregated school rather than the nearby white elementary school. In *Brown v. Board of Education of Topeka*, Marshall argued that such segregation was unconstitutional because it denied Linda Brown the "equal protection of the laws" guaranteed by the Fourteenth Amendment (Map 27.2). In a unanimous decision on May 17, 1954, the Supreme Court agreed, overturning the "separate but equal" doctrine at last. Speaking for the Court, the new chief justice, Earl Warren, wrote: "We conclude that in the field of public education the doctrine of 'separate but equal' has no place. Separate educational facilities are inherently unequal." In an implementing 1955 decision known as *Brown II*, the Court declared simply that integration should proceed "with all deliberate speed."

In the South, however, Virginia senator Harry F. Byrd issued a call for "massive resistance." Calling May 17 "Black Monday," the Mississippi segregationist Tom P. Brady invoked the language of the Cold War to discredit the decision, assailing the "totalitarian government" that had rendered the decision in the name of "socialism and communism." That year, half a million

School Desegregation in Little Rock, Arkansas

Less well known than the crisis at Little Rock's Central High School the same year, the circumstances at North Little Rock were nonetheless strikingly similar: white resistance to the enrollment of a handful of black students. In this photograph, white students block the doors of North Little Rock High School, preventing six African American students from entering on September 9, 1957. This photograph is noteworthy because it shows a striking new feature of southern racial politics: the presence of film and television cameras that broadcast these images to the nation and the world.   AP Images.

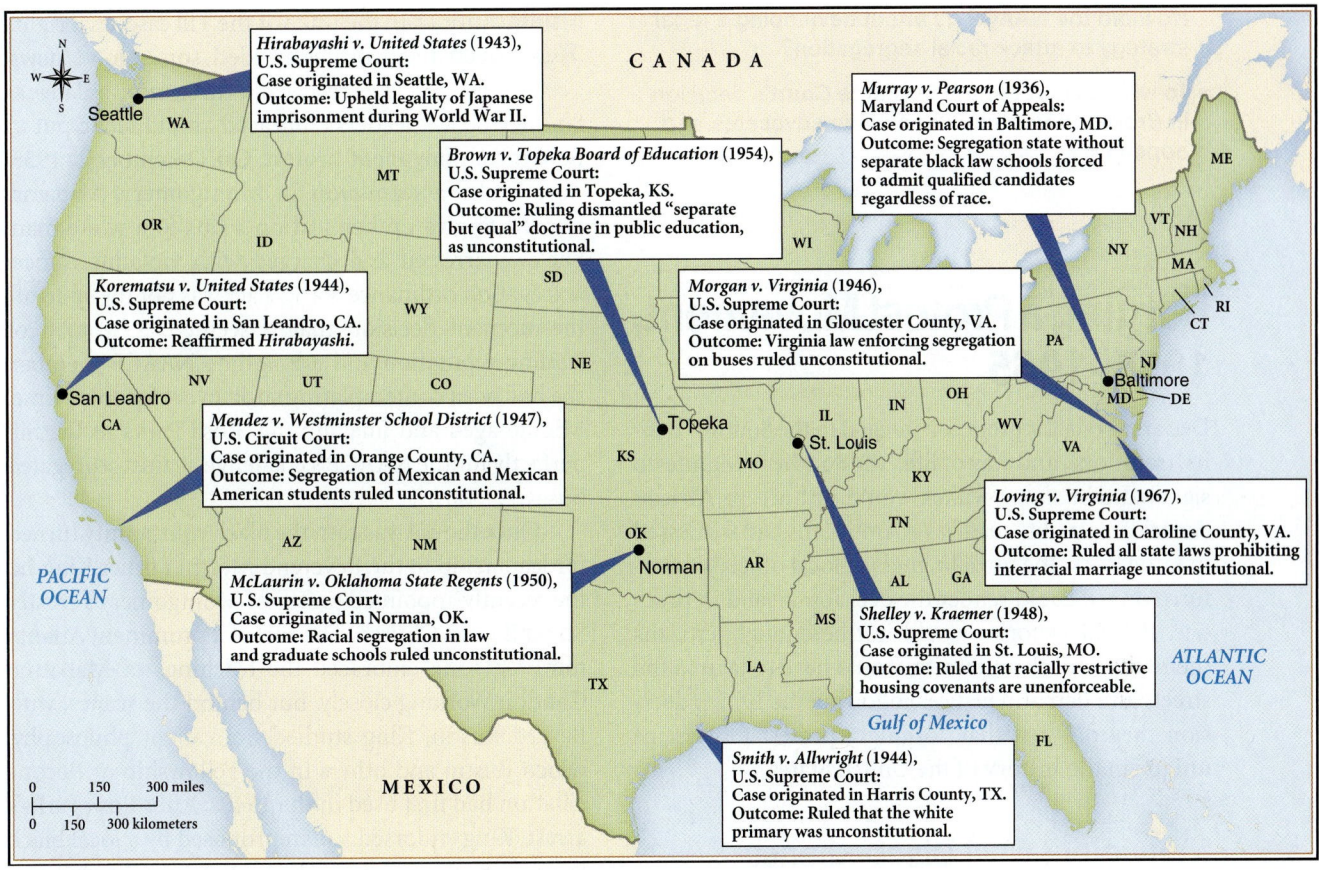

Hirabayashi v. United States (1943), U.S. Supreme Court: Case originated in Seattle, WA. Outcome: Upheld legality of Japanese imprisonment during World War II.

Brown v. Topeka Board of Education (1954), U.S. Supreme Court: Case originated in Topeka, KS. Outcome: Ruling dismantled "separate but equal" doctrine in public education, as unconstitutional.

Murray v. Pearson (1936), Maryland Court of Appeals: Case originated in Baltimore, MD. Outcome: Segregation state without separate black law schools forced to admit qualified candidates regardless of race.

Korematsu v. United States (1944), U.S. Supreme Court: Case originated in San Leandro, CA. Outcome: Reaffirmed Hirabayashi.

Morgan v. Virginia (1946), U.S. Supreme Court: Case originated in Gloucester County, VA. Outcome: Virginia law enforcing segregation on buses ruled unconstitutional.

Mendez v. Westminster School District (1947), U.S. Circuit Court: Case originated in Orange County, CA. Outcome: Segregation of Mexican and Mexican American students ruled unconstitutional.

Loving v. Virginia (1967), U.S. Supreme Court: Case originated in Caroline County, VA. Outcome: Ruled all state laws prohibiting interracial marriage unconstitutional.

McLaurin v. Oklahoma State Regents (1950), U.S. Supreme Court: Case originated in Norman, OK. Outcome: Racial segregation in law and graduate schools ruled unconstitutional.

Shelley v. Kraemer (1948), U.S. Supreme Court: Case originated in St. Louis, MO. Outcome: Ruled that racially restrictive housing covenants are unenforceable.

Smith v. Allwright (1944), U.S. Supreme Court: Case originated in Harris County, TX. Outcome: Ruled that the white primary was unconstitutional.

MAP 27.2

Desegregation Court Cases

Desegregation court battles were not limited to the South. Note the important California cases regarding Mexican Americans and Japanese Americans. Two seminal decisions, the 1948 housing decision in *Shelley v. Kraemer* and the 1954 school decision in *Brown v. Board of Education*, originated in Missouri and Kansas respectively. This map helps show that racial segregation and discrimination were a national, not simply a southern, problem.

southerners joined White Citizens' Councils dedicated to blocking school integration. Some whites revived the old tactics of violence and intimidation, swelling the ranks of the Ku Klux Klan to levels not seen since the 1920s. The "Southern Manifesto," signed in 1956 by 101 members of Congress, denounced the *Brown* decision as "a clear abuse of judicial power" and encouraged local officials to defy it. The white South had declared all-out war on *Brown*.

Enforcement of the Supreme Court's decision was complicated further by Dwight Eisenhower's presence in the White House—the president was no champion of civil rights. Eisenhower accepted the *Brown* decision as the law of the land, but he thought it a mistake. Ike was especially unhappy about the prospect of committing federal power to enforce the decision. A crisis in Little Rock, Arkansas, finally forced his hand. In Sep-

tember 1957, when nine black students attempted to enroll at the all-white Central High School, Governor Orval Faubus called out the National Guard to bar them. Angry white mobs appeared daily to taunt the students, chanting "Go back to the jungle." As the vicious scenes played out on television night after night, Eisenhower finally acted. He sent 1,000 federal troops to Little Rock and nationalized the Arkansas National Guard, ordering them to protect the black students. Eisenhower thus became the first president since Reconstruction to use federal troops to enforce the rights of African Americans. But Little Rock also showed that southern officials had more loyalty to local custom than to the law—a repeated problem in the post-*Brown* era.

● **In what ways did World War II and the Cold War help advance the cause of civil rights?**

- How did the NAACP go about developing a legal strategy to attack racial segregation?

- To what extent did the Supreme Court's decision in *Brown* bring about the change advocates had hoped for?

Forging a Protest Movement, 1955–1965

Declaring racial segregation integral to the South's "habits, traditions, and way of life," the Southern Manifesto signaled that many whites would not accept African American equality readily. As Americans had witnessed in Little Rock, the unwillingness of local officials to enforce *Brown* could render the decision invalid in practice. If legal victories would not be enough, citizens themselves, black and white, would have to take to the streets and demand justice. Following the *Brown* decision they did just that, forging a protest movement unique in the history of the United States.

Nonviolent Civil Disobedience

Brown had been the law of the land for barely a year when a single act of violence struck at the heart of black America. A fourteen-year-old African American from the South Side of Chicago, Emmett Till, was visiting relatives in Mississippi in the summer of 1955. Seen talking to a white woman in a grocery store ("Bye, baby," he reportedly said), Till was tortured and murdered under cover of night. His mutilated body was found at the bottom of a river, tied with barbed wire to a heavy steel cotton gin fan. Photos of Till's body in *Jet* magazine brought national attention to the heinous crime.

Two white men were arrested for Till's murder. During the trial, followed closely in African American communities across the country, the lone witness to Till's kidnapping—his uncle, Mose Wright—identified both killers. Feeling "the blood boil in hundreds of white people as they sat glaring in the courtroom," Wright said, "it was the first time in my life I had the courage to accuse a white man of a crime." Despite Wright's eyewitness testimony, the all-white jury found the defendants innocent. Afterward, *Look* magazine paid the two men $4,000 for their story. Safe from prosecution, they admitted to the murder. This miscarriage of justice—extreme even for the southern legal system—galvanized an entire generation of African Americans; no one who lived through the Till case ever forgot it.

Montgomery Bus Boycott   In the wake of the Till case, civil rights advocates needed some good news. They received it three months later, as Southern black leaders embraced an old tactic put to new ends: nonviolent protest. On December 1, 1955, Rosa Parks, a seamstress in Montgomery, Alabama, refused to give up her seat on a bus to a white man. She was arrested and charged with violating a local segregation ordinance. Parks's act was not the spur-of-the-moment decision that it seemed: A woman of sterling reputation and a longtime NAACP member, she had been contemplating such an act for some time. Middle-aged and unassuming, Rosa Parks fit the bill perfectly for the NAACP's challenge against segregated buses.

Once the die was cast, the black community turned for leadership to the Reverend Martin Luther King Jr., the recently appointed pastor of Montgomery's Dexter Street Baptist Church. The son of a prominent Atlanta minister, King embraced the teachings of Mahatma Gandhi. Working closely, but behind the scenes, with Bayard Rustin, King studied nonviolent philosophy, which Rustin and others in the Fellowship of Reconciliation had first used in the 1940s. After Rosa Parks's arrest, King endorsed a plan proposed by a local black women's organization to boycott Montgomery's bus system. They were inspired by similar boycotts that had taken place in Harlem, New York, in 1941 and Baton Rouge, Louisiana, in 1953.

For the next 381 days, Montgomery's African Americans formed car pools or walked to work. "Darling, it's empty!" Coretta Scott King exclaimed to her husband as a bus normally filled with black riders rolled by their living room window on the first day of the boycott. The transit company neared bankruptcy, and downtown stores complained about the loss of business. But only after the Supreme Court ruled in November 1956 that bus segregation was unconstitutional did the city of Montgomery finally comply. "My feets is tired, but my soul is rested," said one woman boycotter.

The Montgomery bus boycott catapulted King to national prominence. In 1957, along with the Reverend Ralph Abernathy, he founded the Atlanta-based Southern Christian Leadership Conference (SCLC). The black church, long the center of African American social and cultural life, now lent its moral and organizational strength to the civil rights movement. Black churchwomen were a tower of strength, transferring the skills they had honed during years of church work to the fight for civil rights. The SCLC quickly joined the NAACP at the leading edge of the movement for racial justice.

Martin Luther King Jr.

In this 1960 photograph, a young-looking Martin Luther King Jr. addresses the crowd at a Chicago demonstration demanding that the Republican Party adopt a stronger stance on civil rights. Until 1955, King was a little-known minister at Dexter Avenue Baptist Church in Montgomery, Alabama. Over the ensuing decade, however, King would become the most recognizable rights leader in the world, leading the fight against racial segregation and discrimination in the United States and winning the Nobel Peace Prize in 1964.   Photo by Francis Miller/Time Life Pictures/ Getty Images.

Greensboro Sit-Ins   The battle for civil rights entered a new phase in Greensboro, North Carolina, on February 1, 1960, when four black college students took seats at the whites-only lunch counter at the local Woolworth's five-and-dime store. This simple act was entirely the brainchild of the four students, who had discussed it in their dorm rooms over several preceding nights. A New York–based spokesman for Woolworth's said the chain would "abide by local custom," which meant refusing to serve African Americans at the lunch counter. The students were determined to "sit in" until they were served. For three weeks, they took turns sitting at the counters, quietly eating, doing homework, or reading. Taunted by groups of whites, pelted with food and other debris, the black students—often occupying more than sixty of the sixty-six seats—held strong. "I felt as though I had gained my manhood," recalled Franklin McCain, one of the "Greensboro Four." Although many were arrested, the tactic worked: The Woolworth's lunch counter was desegregated, and sit-ins quickly spread to other southern cities (see Comparing American Voices, "Challenging White Supremacy," pp. 864–865).

Ella Baker and SNCC   Inspired by the developments in Greensboro and elsewhere, Ella Baker, an administrator with the SCLC, helped organize the Student Nonviolent Coordinating Committee (SNCC, pronounced "Snick") to facilitate student sit-ins. Rolling like a great wave across the Upper South, from North Carolina into Virginia, Maryland, and Tennessee, by the end of the year sit-ins had been launched in 126 cities. More than 50,000 people participated, and 3,600 were jailed. The sit-ins drew African American college students into the movement in significant numbers for the first time. Northern students formed soli-

Thus I have given you, I think, the Substance of the Arguments o[n]
both sides of that great and important Questi[on]

Challenging White Supremacy

Among the many challenges historians face is figuring out the processes by which long-oppressed ordinary people finally rise up and demand justice. During the 1950s, a liberating process was quietly under way among southern blacks, bursting forth dramatically in the Montgomery bus boycott of 1955 and then, by the end of the decade, emerging across the South. Here are excerpts of the testimony of two individuals who stepped forward and took the lead in those struggles.

Franklin McCain
Desegregating Lunch Counters

Franklin McCain was one of the four African American students at North Carolina A&T College in Greensboro, North Carolina, who sat down at the Woolworth's lunch counter on February 1, 1960, setting off a wave of student sit-ins that rocked the South and helped initiate a national civil rights movement. In the following interview, McCain describes how he and his pals took that momentous step.

The planning process was on a Sunday night, I remember it quite well. I think it was Joseph who said, "It's time that we take some action now. We've been getting together, and we've been, up to this point, still like most people we've talked about for the past few weeks or so—that is, people who talk a lot but, in fact, make very little action." After selecting the technique, then we said, "Let's go down and just ask for service." It certainly wasn't titled a "sit-in" or "sit-down" at that time. "Let's just go down to Woolworth's tomorrow and ask for service, and the tactic is going to be simply this: we'll just stay there."

. . . Once getting there . . . we did make purchases of school supplies and took the patience and time to get receipts for our purchases, and Joseph and myself went over to the counter and asked to be served coffee and doughnuts. As anticipated, the reply was, "I'm sorry, we don't serve you here." And of course we said, "We just beg to disagree with you. We've in fact already been served." . . . The attendant or waitress was a little bit dumbfounded, just didn't know what to say under circumstances like that. . . .

At that point there was a policeman who had walked in off the street, who was pacing the aisle . . . behind us, where we were seated, with his club in his hand, just sort of knocking it in his hand, and just looking mean and red and a little bit upset and a little bit disgusted. And you had the feeling that he didn't know what the hell to do. . . . Usually his defense is offense, and we've provoked him, yes, but we haven't provoked him outwardly enough for him to resort to violence. And I think this is just killing him; you can see it all over him.

If it's possible to know what it means to have your soul cleansed—I felt pretty clean at that time. I probably felt better on that day than I've ever felt in my life. Seems like a lot of feelings of guilt or what-have-you suddenly left me, and I felt as though I had gained my manhood. . . . Not Franklin McCain only as an individual, but I felt as though the manhood of a number of other black persons had been restored and had gotten some respect from just that one day.

The movement started out as a movement of nonviolence and a Christian movement. . . . It was a movement that was seeking justice more than anything else and not a movement to start a war. . . . We knew that probably the most powerful and potent weapon that people have literally no defense for is love, kindness. That is, whip the enemy with something that he doesn't understand. . . . The individual who had probably the most influence on us was Gandhi. . . . Yes, Martin Luther King's name was well-known when the sit-in movement was in effect, but . . . no, he was not the individual we had upmost in mind when we started the sit-in movement.

Source: Howell Raines, *My Soul Is Rested.* Copyright ©1977 by Howell Raines. Originally published by Penguin Putnam, 1977. Reprinted with permission of PFD, Inc.

John McFerren
Demanding the Right to Vote

In this interview, given about ten years after the events he describes, John McFerren tells of the battle he undertook in 1959 to gain the vote for the blacks of Fayette County, Tennessee. By the time of the interview, McFerren had risen in life and become a grocery-store owner and property holder, thanks, he says, to the economic boycott imposed on him by angry whites. Unlike Greensboro, the struggle in Fayette County never made national headlines. It was just one of many local struggles that signaled the beginning of a new day in the South.

My name is John McFerren. I'm forty-six years old. I'm a Negro was born and raised in West Tennessee, the county of Fayette, District 1. My foreparents was brought here from North Carolina five years before the Civil War . . . because the rumor got out among the slaveholders that West Tennessee was still goin to be a slaveholdin state. And my people was brought over here and sold. And after the Civil War my people settled in West Tennessee. That's why Fayette and Haywood counties have a great number of Negroes.

Back in 1957 and '58 there was a Negro man accused of killin a deputy sheriff. This was Burton Dodson. He was brought back after he'd been gone twenty years. J. F. Estes was the lawyer defendin him. Myself and him both was in the army together. And the stimulation from the trial got me interested in the way justice was bein used. The only way to bring justice would be through the ballot box.

In 1959 we got out a charter called the Fayette County Civic and Welfare League. Fourteen of us started out in that charter. We tried to support a white liberal candidate that was named L. T. Redfearn in the sheriff election and the local Democrat party refused to let Negroes vote.

We brought a suit against the Democrat party and I went to Washington for a civil-rights hearing. Myself and Estes and Harpman Jameson made the trip. It took us twenty-two hours steady drivin. . . . I was lookin all up— lotsa big, tall buildins. I had never seen old, tall buildins like that before. After talkin to [John Doar] we come on back to the Justice Department building and we sat out in the hall while he had a meetin inside the attorney general's office. And when they come out they told us they was gonna indict the landowners who kept us from voting. . . .

Just after that, in 1960, in January, we organized a thousand Negroes to line up at the courthouse to register to vote. We started pourin in with big numbers—in this county it was 72 percent Negroes—when we started to register to vote to change the situation.

In the followin . . . October and November they started puttin our people offa the land. Once you registered you had to move. Once you registered they took your job. Then after they done that, in November, we had three hundred people forced to live in tents on Shepard Towles's land. And when we started puttin em in tents, then that's when the White Citizens Council and the Ku Klux Klan started shootin in the tents to run us out.

Tent City was parta an economic squeeze. The local merchants run me outa the stores and said I went to Washington and caused this mess to start. . . . They had a blacklist . . . And they had the list sent around to all merchants. Once you registered you couldn't buy for credit or cash. But the best thing in the world was when they run me outa them stores. It started me thinkin for myself. . . .

The southern white has a slogan: "Keep em niggers happy and keep em singin in the schools." And the biggest mistake of the past is that the Negro has not been taught

economics and the value of a dollar. . . . Back at one time we had a teacher . . . from Mississippi—and he pulled up and left the county because he was teachin the Negroes to buy land, and own land, and work it for hisself, and the county Board of Education didn't want that taught in the county.

And they told him, "Keep em niggers singin and keep em happy and don't teach em nothin." . . . You cannot be free when you're beggin the man for bread. But when you've got the dollar in your pocket and then got the vote in your pocket, that's the only way to be free. . . . And I have been successful and made good progress because I could see the only way I could survive is to stay independent.

. . . The Negro is no longer goin back. He's goin forward.

Source: Stanley I. Kutler, ed., *Looking for America*, 2nd ed., 2 vols. (New York: Norton, 1979), 2:449–453.

ANALYZING THE EVIDENCE

- McCain took a stand on segregated lunch counters. McFerren took a stand on the right to vote. Why did they choose different targets? Does it matter that they did?

- McCain speaks of the sense of "manhood" he felt as he sat at that Woolworth's counter. Would that feeling have been enough to satisfy McFerren?

- Almost certainly, McCain and McFerren never met. Suppose they had. What would they have had in common? Would what they had in common have been more important than what separated them?

- McCain speaks knowingly of the figures and ideas that influenced him. Why do you suppose McFerren is silent about such matters? If he had spoken up, do you suppose he would have—or should have—mentioned Booker T. Washington?

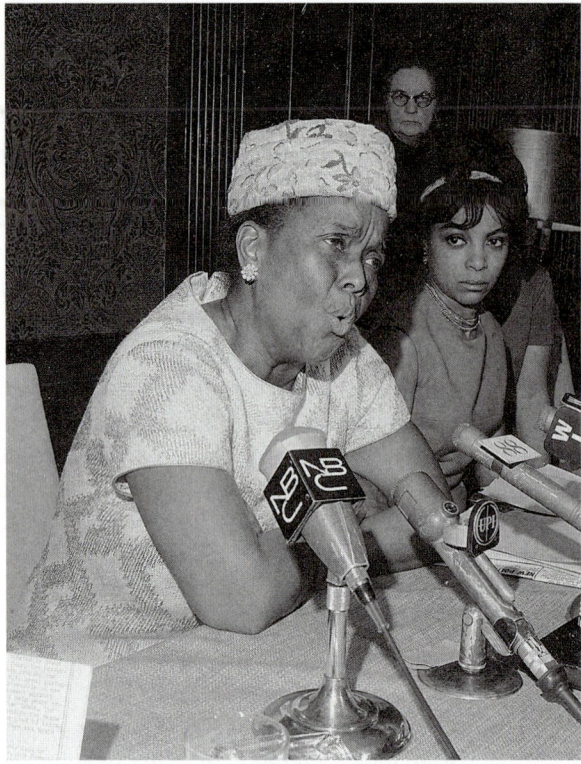

Ella Baker

Born in Virginia and educated at Shaw University in Raleigh, North Carolina, Ella Baker was one of the foremost theorists of grassroots, participatory democracy in the United States. Active all her life in the black freedom movement, in 1960 Baker cofounded the Student Nonviolent Coordinating Committee (SNCC). Her advocacy of leadership by ordinary, non-elite people often led her to disagree with the top-down movement strategy of Martin Luther King Jr. and other ministers of the Southern Christian Leadership Conference (SCLC).   AP Images.

darity committees and raised money for bail. SNCC quickly emerged as the most important student protest organization in the country and inspired a generation of students on college campuses everywhere.

Baker took a special interest in these students, because she found them receptive to her notion of participatory democracy. The granddaughter of slaves, Baker had moved to Harlem in the 1930s, where she worked for New Deal agencies and then the NAACP. She believed in nurturing leaders from the grass roots, encouraging ordinary people to stand up for their rights rather than to depend on charismatic figureheads. "My theory is, strong people don't need strong leaders," she once said. Nonetheless, Baker nurtured a generation of young activists in SNCC, including Stokely Carmichael, Anne Moody, John Lewis, and Diane Nash, who went

on to become some of the most important civil rights leaders in the United States. Decentralized, nonhierarchical, and based on grassroots input and involvement, participatory democracy inspired many of the most vocal social movements of the 1960s.

Freedom Rides | Emboldened by SNCC's sit-in tactics, in 1961 the Congress of Racial Equality (CORE) organized a series of what were called Freedom Rides on interstate bus lines throughout the South. The aim was to call attention to blatant violations of recent Supreme Court rulings against segregation in interstate commerce. The activists who signed on—mostly young, both black and white—knew that they were taking their lives in their hands. They found courage in song, as civil rights activists had begun to do across the country, with lyrics such as "I'm taking a ride on the Greyhound bus line. . . . Hallelujah, I'm traveling down freedom's main line!"

Courage they needed. Club-wielding Klansmen attacked the buses when they stopped in small towns. Outside Anniston, Alabama, one bus was fire-bombed; the Freedom Riders escaped only moments before it exploded. Some riders were then brutally beaten. Freedom Riders and news reporters were also viciously attacked by Klansmen in Birmingham and Montgomery. Despite the violence, state authorities refused to intervene. "I cannot guarantee protection for this bunch of rabble rousers," declared Governor John Patterson of Alabama.

Once again, local officials' refusal to enforce the law left the fate of the Freedom Riders in Washington's hands. The new president, John F. Kennedy, was cautious about civil rights. Despite a campaign commitment, he failed to deliver on a civil rights bill. Elected by a thin margin, Kennedy believed that he could ill afford to lose the support of powerful southern Senators. But civil rights was unlike other domestic issues. Its fate was going to be decided not in the halls of Congress, but on the streets of southern cities. Although President Kennedy discouraged the Freedom Rides, beatings shown on the nightly news forced Attorney General Robert Kennedy to dispatch federal marshals. Civil rights activists thus learned the value of nonviolent protest that provoked violent white resistance.

The victories so far had been limited, but the groundwork had been laid for a civil rights offensive that would transform the nation. The NAACP's legal strategy had been followed closely by the emergence of a major protest movement. And now civil rights leaders focused their gaze on Congress.

Legislating Civil Rights, 1963–1965

The first civil rights law in the nation's history came in 1875 during Reconstruction (see Chapter 15). Its provisions had long been ignored, and for nearly ninety years new civil rights legislation was blocked or filibustered by southern Democrats in Congress. Only a weak, largely symbolic act was passed in 1957 during the Eisenhower administration. But by the early 1960s, with legal precedents in their favor and nonviolent protest awakening the nation, civil rights leaders believed the time had come for a serious civil rights bill. The challenge was getting one through a still-reluctant Congress.

The Battle for Birmingham   The road to such a bill began when Martin Luther King Jr. called for demonstrations in "the most segregated city in the United States": Birmingham, Alabama. King and the SCLC needed a concrete victory in Birmingham to validate their strategy of nonviolent protest. In May 1963, thousands of black marchers tried to picket Birmingham's department stores. Eugene "Bull" Connor, the city's public safety commissioner, ordered the city's police troops to meet the marchers with violent force: snarling dogs, electric cattle prods, and high-pressure fire hoses. Television cameras captured the scene for the evening news.

While serving a jail sentence for leading the march, King, scribbling in pencil on any paper he could find, composed one of the classic documents of nonviolent civil disobedience: "Letter from Birmingham Jail." "Why direct action?" King asked. "There is a type of constructive, nonviolent tension that is necessary for growth." The civil rights movement sought, he continued, "to create such a crisis and establish such a creative tension." Grounding his actions in equal parts Christian brotherhood and democratic liberalism, King argued that

The Battle of Birmingham

One of the hardest-fought desegregation struggles of the early 1960s took place in April and May of 1963, in Birmingham, Alabama. In response to the daily rallies and peaceful protests, authorities cracked down, arresting hundreds. They also employed tactics such as those shown here, turning fire hoses on young, nonviolent student demonstrators, and using police dogs to intimidate peaceful marchers (see Reading American Pictures, p. 874). These protests, led by Martin Luther King Jr. and broadcast on television news, prompted President Kennedy to introduce a civil rights bill in Congress in June 1963.   © Bob Adelman/Corbis.

Americans confronted a moral choice: They could "preserve the evil system of segregation" or take the side of "those great wells of democracy . . . the Constitution and the Declaration of Independence."

Outraged by the brutality in Birmingham and embarrassed by King's imprisonment for leading a nonviolent march, President Kennedy decided that it was time to act. On June 11, 1963, after newly elected Alabama governor George Wallace barred two black students from the state university, Kennedy denounced racism on national television and promised a new civil rights bill. Many black leaders felt Kennedy's action was long overdue, but they nonetheless hailed this "Second Emancipation Proclamation." That night, Medgar Evers, president of the Mississippi chapter of the NAACP, was shot in the back in his driveway in Jackson by a white supremacist. Evers's martyrdom became a spur to further action (Map 27.3).

The March on Washington and the Civil Rights Act To marshal support for Kennedy's bill, civil rights leaders adopted a tactic that A. Philip Randolph had first advanced in 1941: a massive demonstration in Washington. Under the leadership of Randolph and Bayard Rustin, thousands of volunteers across the country coordinated carpools, "freedom buses," and "freedom trains," and on August 28, 1963, delivered a quarter of a million people to the Lincoln Memorial for the officially named March on Washington for Jobs and Freedom. "We are the advance guard of a massive moral revolution for jobs and freedom," Randolph said to open the program.

Although other people primarily did the planning, Martin Luther King Jr. was the public face of the march. It was King's dramatic "I Have a Dream" speech, beginning with his admonition that too many black people lived "on a lonely island of poverty" and ending with the exclamation from a traditional black spiritual—"Free at last! Free at last! Thank God almighty, we are free at last!"—that captured the nation's imagination. The sight of 250,000 blacks and whites marching solemnly together marked the high point of the civil rights movement and confirmed King's position as the leading spokesperson for the cause.

To have any chance of getting the civil rights bill through Congress, King, Randolph, and Rustin knew they had to sustain this broad coalition of blacks and whites. They could afford to alienate no one. Reflecting a younger, more militant set of activists, however, SNCC member John Lewis had prepared a more provocative speech for that afternoon. Lewis wrote, "The time will come when we will not confine our march-

ing to Washington. We will march through the South, through the Heart of Dixie, the way Sherman did." Signaling a growing restlessness among black youth, Lewis warned: "We shall fragment the South into a thousand pieces and put them back together again in the image of democracy." Fearing the speech would alienate white supporters, Rustin and others implored Lewis to tone down his rhetoric. With only minutes to spare before he stepped up to the podium, Lewis agreed. He delivered a more conciliatory speech, but his conflict with march organizers signaled an emerging rift in the movement.

Although the March on Washington galvanized public opinion, it changed few congressional votes. Southern senators continued to block Kennedy's legislation. Georgia senator Richard Russell, a leader of the opposition, refused to support any bill that would "bring about social equality and intermingling and amalgamation of the races." Then, suddenly, tragedies piled up, one on another. In September, white supremacists bombed a Baptist church in Birmingham, killing four black girls in Sunday school. Less than two months later, Kennedy himself lay dead, the victim of assassination.

On assuming the presidency, Lyndon Johnson made passing the civil rights bill a priority. A southerner and former Senate majority leader, Johnson was renowned for his fierce persuasive style and tough political bargaining. Using equal parts moral leverage, the memory of the slain JFK, and his own brand of hardball politics, Johnson overcame the filibuster. In June 1964, Congress approved the most far-reaching civil rights law since Reconstruction. The keystone of the Civil Rights Act, Title VII, outlawed discrimination in employment on the basis of race, religion, national origin, and sex. Another section guaranteed equal access to public accommodations and schools. The law granted new enforcement powers to the U.S. attorney general and established the Equal Employment Opportunity Commission to implement the prohibition against job discrimination.

Freedom Summer The Civil Right Act was a law with real teeth, but it left untouched the obstacles to black voting rights. So protesters went back into the streets. In 1964, in the period that came to be known as Freedom Summer, black organizations mounted a major campaign in Mississippi. The effort drew several thousand volunteers from across the country, including nearly one thousand white college students from the North. Led by the charismatic SNCC activist Robert Moses, the four major civil rights organizations (SNCC, CORE, NAACP, and SCLC) spread out across the state. They established freedom schools for black children

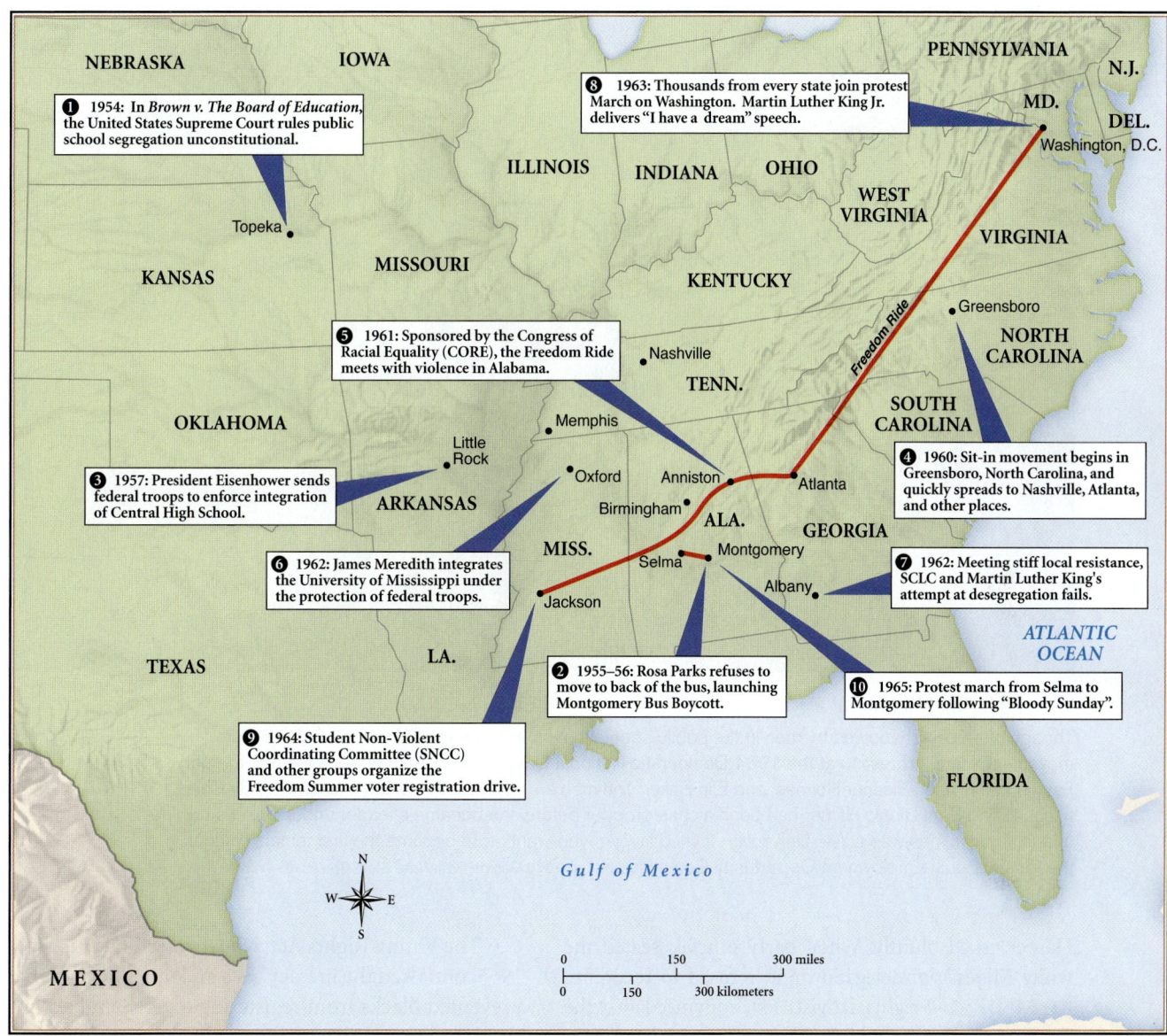

MAP 27.3

The Civil Rights Struggle, 1954–1965

In the postwar battle for black civil rights, the first major victory was the NAACP litigation of *Brown v. Board of Education*, which declared public school segregation unconstitutional. As indicated on this map, the struggle then quickly spread, raising other issues and seeding new organizations. Other organizations quickly joined the battle and shifted the focus away from the courts to mass action and organization. The year 1965 marked the high point, when violence against the Selma, Alabama, marchers spurred the passage of the Voting Rights Act.

and conducted a major voter registration drive. So determined was the opposition that only about twelve hundred black voters were registered that summer, at a cost of four murdered civil rights workers and thirty-seven black churches bombed or burned.

The murders strengthened the resolve of the Mississippi Freedom Democratic Party (MFDP), which had been founded during Freedom Summer. Banned from

the "whites only" Mississippi Democratic Party, MFDP leaders were determined to attend the 1964 Democratic National Convention in Atlantic City, New Jersey, as the legitimate representatives of their state. Inspired by Fannie Lou Hamer, a former sharecropper turned civil rights activist, the MFDP challenged the most powerful figures in the Democratic Party, including Lyndon Johnson, the Democrats' presidential nominee. "Is this America?"

Women in the Movement

Though often overshadowed by men in the public spotlight, women were crucial to the black freedom movement. Here, protesting at the 1964 Democratic National Convention in Atlantic City, are (left to right) Fannie Lou Hamer, Eleanor Holmes, and Ella Baker. The men are (left to right) Emory Harris, Stokely Carmichael, and Sam Block. Hamer had been a sharecropper before she became a leader under Baker's tutelage, and Holmes was a Yale University–trained lawyer who went on to become the first female chair of the federal Equal Employment Opportunity Commission.   © 1976 George Ballis/Take Stock/The Image Works.

Hamer asked bluntly. When party officials seated the white Mississippi delegation and refused to recognize the MFDP, civil rights activists left, convinced that the Democratic Party would not change. Demoralized, Moses told television reporters: "I will have nothing to do with the political system any longer."

Selma and the Voting Rights Act Martin Luther King Jr. and the SCLC did not share Moses's skepticism. They believed that another confrontation with southern injustice could provoke further congressional action. In March 1965, James Bevel of the SCLC called for a march from Selma, Alabama, to the state capital, Montgomery, to protest the murder of a voting-rights activist. As soon as the six hundred marchers left Selma, crossing over the Edmund Pettus Bridge, mounted state troopers attacked them with tear gas and clubs. The scene was shown on national television that night, and the day became known as Bloody Sunday. Calling the episode "an American tragedy," President Johnson went back to Congress.

The Voting Rights Act, which passed on August 6, 1965, outlawed the literacy tests and other devices that prevented blacks from registering to vote, and authorized the attorney general to send federal examiners to register voters in any county where registration was less than 50 percent. Together with the Twenty-fourth Amendment (1964), which outlawed the poll tax in federal elections, the Voting Rights Act enabled millions of blacks to vote for the first time since the Reconstruction era.

In the South, the results were stunning. In 1960, only 20 percent of blacks had been registered to vote; by 1971, registration reached 62 percent (Map 27.4). Moreover, across the nation the number of black elected officials began to climb, quadrupling from 1,400 to 4,900 between 1970 and 1980 and doubling again by the early 1990s. Most of those elected held local offices—from sheriff to county commissioner—but nonetheless embodied a shift in political representation nearly unimaginable a generation earlier. As Hartman Turnbow, a Mississippi farmer who risked

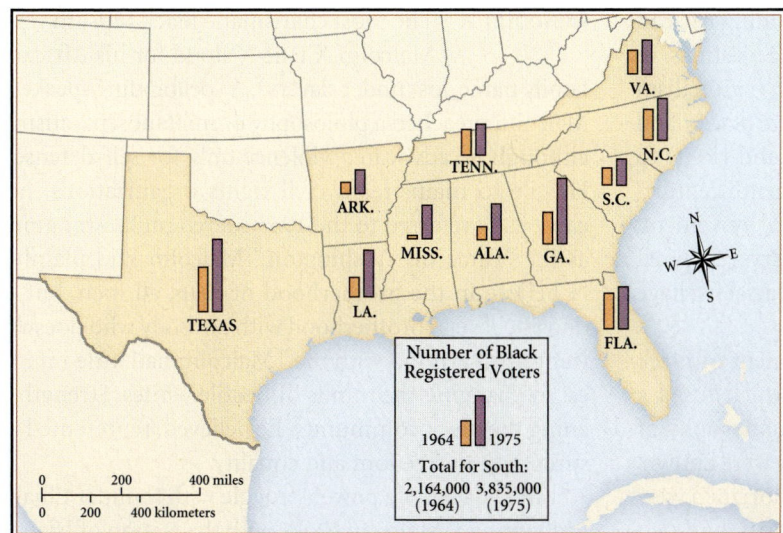

MAP 27.4

Black Voter Registration in the South, 1964 and 1975

After passage of the Voting Rights Act of 1965, black registration in the South increased dramatically. The bars on the map show the number of blacks registered in 1964, before the act was passed, and in 1975, after it had been in effect for ten years. States in the Deep South, such as Mississippi, Alabama, and Georgia, had the biggest increases.

his life to register in 1964, later declared, "It won't never go back where it was."

Something else would never go back either: the liberal New Deal coalition. By the second half of the 1960s, the liberal wing of the Democratic Party had won its battle with the conservative, segregationist wing. Democrats had embraced the civil rights movement and made African American equality a cornerstone of a new "rights" liberalism. But over the next generation, between the 1960s and the 1980s, southern whites and many conservative northern whites would respond by switching to the Republican Party. Strom Thurmond, the segregationist senator from South Carolina, symbolically led the revolt by renouncing the Democrats and becoming a Republican in 1964. The New Deal coalition—which had joined working-class whites, northern African Americans, urban professionals, and white southern segregationists together in a fragile political alliance since the 1930s—was beginning to crumble.

- What factors explain the rise of the civil rights protest movement? Why was nonviolent civil disobedience the chosen tactic?

- In what ways did white resistance hinder the movement? In what ways did it help?

Beyond Civil Rights, 1966–1973

Activists had long known that Supreme Court decisions and new laws do not automatically produce changes in society. But in the mid-1960s, civil rights advocates confronted a more profound issue: Perhaps even *protests* were not enough. In 1965, Bayard Rustin wrote of the need to move "from protest to politics" in order to build institutional black power. Some black leaders, such as the young SNCC activists Stokely Carmichael, Frances Beal, and John Lewis, grew frustrated with the slow pace of reform and the stubborn resistance of whites. Still others believed that addressing black poverty and economic disadvantage remained the most important objective. Neither new laws nor long marches appeared capable of meeting these varied and complex challenges.

The conviction that civil rights alone were incapable of guaranteeing equality took hold in many minority communities in this period. African Americans were joined by Mexican Americans, Puerto Ricans, and American Indians. They came at the problem of inequality from different perspectives, but each group asked a similar question: As crucial as legal equality was, how much did it matter if most people of color remained in or close to poverty, if white society still regarded nonwhites as inferior, and if the major social and political institutions in the country were run by whites? Black leaders and representatives of other nonwhite communities increasingly asked themselves these questions as they searched for ways to build on the significant achievements of the civil rights decade of 1954–1965.

Black Nationalism

Seeking answers to these questions led many African Americans to embrace black nationalism. The philosophy of black nationalism signified many things in the 1960s. It could mean anything from pride in one's community to total separatism, from building African American–owned businesses to wearing dashikis in honor of African traditions. Historically, nationalism had emphasized the differences between blacks and whites as well as black people's power (and right) to shape their own destiny. In the late nineteenth century, nationalists founded the Back to Africa movement, and in the 1920s the nationalist Marcus Garvey inspired African Americans to take pride in their racial heritage (see Chapter 22).

In the early 1960s, the leading exponent of black nationalism was the Nation of Islam, which fused a rejection of Christianity with a strong philosophy of self-improvement. Black Muslims, as they were known, adhered to a strict code of personal behavior; men were recognizable by their dark suits, white shirts, and ties, women by their long dresses and head coverings. Black Muslims preached an apocalyptic brand of Islam, anticipating the day when Allah would banish the white "devils" and give the black nation justice. Although its full converts numbered only about ten thousand, the Nation of Islam had a wide popular following among African Americans in northern cities.

Malcolm X | The most charismatic Black Muslim was Malcolm X (the *X* stood for his African family name, lost under slavery). A spellbinding speaker, Malcolm preached a philosophy of militant separatism, although he advocated violence only for self-defense. Hostile to mainstream civil rights organizations, he caustically referred to the 1963 March on Washington as the "Farce on Washington." Malcolm said plainly, "I believe in the brotherhood of man, all men, but I don't believe in brotherhood with anybody who doesn't want brotherhood with me." Malcolm had little interest in changing the minds of hostile whites. Strengthening the black community, he believed, represented a surer path to freedom and equality.

In 1964, after a power struggle with founder Elijah Muhammad, Malcolm broke with the Nation of Islam. While he remained a black nationalist, he moderated his antiwhite views and began to talk of a class struggle uniting poor whites and blacks. Following an inspiring trip to the Middle East, where he saw Muslims of all races worshipping together, Malcolm formed the Organization of Afro-American Unity to promote black pride and to work with traditional civil rights

Malcolm X

Until his murder in 1965, Malcolm X was the leading proponent of black nationalism in the United States. A brilliant and dynamic orator, Malcolm had been a minister in the Nation of Islam for nearly thirteen years, until he broke with the Nation in 1964. His emphasis on black pride and self-help and his unrelenting criticism of white supremacy made him one of the freedom movement's most inspirational figures, both in life and well after his death. ©Topham/The Image Works.

groups. But he got no further. On February 21, 1965, Malcolm X was assassinated while delivering a speech in Harlem. Three Black Muslims were later convicted of his murder.

Black Power | A more secular brand of black nationalism emerged in 1966 when SNCC and CORE activists, following the lead of Stokely Carmichael, began to call for black self-reliance under the banner of Black Power. Advocates of Black Power asked fundamental questions: If alliances with whites were necessary to achieve racial justice, as King believed they were, did that make African Americans dependent on the good intentions of whites? If so, could black people trust those good intentions in the long run? Increasingly, those inclined toward Black Power believed that African Americans should build economic and political power in their own communities. Such power would translate into a less dependent relationship with white America. "For once," Carmichael wrote, "black people are going to use the words they want to use—not the words whites want to hear."

Spurred by the Black Power slogan, African American activists turned their attention to the poverty and social injustice faced by so many black people. President Johnson had declared the War on Poverty, and black organizers joined, setting up day-care centers, running community job training programs, and working to improve housing and health care in the inner cities. In major cities such as Philadelphia, New York, Chicago, and Pittsburgh, activists sought to open jobs in police and fire departments and in construction and transportation to black workers, who had been excluded from these occupations for decades. Others worked to end police harassment—a major problem in urban black communities—and to help black entrepreneurs to receive small-business loans. CORE leader Floyd McKissick explained, "Black Power is not Black Supremacy; it is a united Black Voice reflecting racial pride."

The attention to racial pride led some African Americans to reject white society and to pursue more authentic cultural forms. In addition to focusing on economic disadvantage, Black Power emphasized black pride and self-determination. Blacks subscribing to these beliefs wore African clothing, chose natural hairstyles, and awakened an interest in black history, art, and literature. The Black Arts movement thrived, and musical tastes shifted from the crossover sounds of Motown to the soul music of Philadelphia, Memphis, and Chicago (see Reading American Pictures, "Civil Rights and Black Power: Protest and the Human Body," p. 874).

Black Panther Party | One of the most radical nationalist groups was the Black Panther Party, founded in Oakland, California, in 1966 by two college students, Huey Newton and Bobby Seale. A militant self-defense organization dedicated to protecting African Americans from police violence, the Panthers took their cue from the slain Malcolm X. They vehemently opposed the Vietnam War and declared their affinity for Third World revolutionary movements and armed struggle (Map 27.5). In their manifesto, "What We Want, What We Believe," the Panthers outlined their Ten Point Program for black liberation.

The Panthers' organization spread to other cities in the late 1960s, where members undertook a wide range of community-organizing projects. Their free breakfast program for children and their testing program for sickle-cell anemia, an inherited disease with a high incidence among African Americans, were especially popular. However, the Panthers' radicalism and belief in armed self-defense resulted in violent clashes with police. Newton was charged with murdering a police officer, several Panthers were killed by police, and dozens went to prison. Moreover, under its domestic counterintelligence program, the Federal Bureau of Investigation (FBI) had begun disrupting party activities.

Young Lords | Among those inspired by the Black Panthers were Puerto Ricans in New York. Their vehicle was the Young Lords Organization (YLO), later renamed the Young Lords Party. Like the Black Panthers, YLO activists sought self-determination for Puerto Ricans, both those in the United States and those on the island in the Caribbean. In practical terms, the YLO focused on improviong neighborhood conditions: City garbage collection was notoriously poor in East Harlem, where most Puerto Ricans lived, and slumlords had allowed the housing to deteriorate to a near-intolerable level. Women in the YLO were especially active, publicizing sterilization campaigns against Puerto Rican women and fighting to improve access to health care. As was true of so many nationalist groups, immediate victories for the YLO were few, but their dedicated community organizing produced a generation of leaders (many of whom later went into politics) and awakened community consciousness.

The New Urban Politics | Black Power also inspired African Americans to work within the political system. By the mid-1960s, black residents neared 50 percent of the population in several major American cities—such as Atlanta, Cleveland, Detroit, and Washington, D.C. Black Power in these

Civil Rights and Black Power: Protest and the Human Body

The civil rights movement produced some of the most recognizable and memorable photographs of the second half of the twentieth century. Here are two examples. On the left, police in Birmingham, Alabama, use trained German shepherds against peaceful African American protesters in 1963. Nonviolent civil disobedience required that protesters remain calm and passive in the face of such violent assaults. On the right, U.S. Olympians Tommie Smith and John Carlos raise their fists in a Black Power salute at the 1968 Olympics in Mexico City. Smith and Carlos, who were part of a movement among black Olympic athletes to dramatize racial discrimination in the United States, earned gold and bronze medals in the 200 meters. The silver medalist, Australian Peter Norman, is wearing an Olympic Project for Human Rights badge to show his support.

Racial Violence in Birmingham. AP Images/Bill Hudson.

Black Power Salute at the 1968 Olympics. AP Images.

ANALYZING THE EVIDENCE

- In what ways does each photograph capture the tenor—the spirit—of the civil rights movement at a particular historical moment? How would you characterize that spirit?

- If we think about the human bodies in the photographs, how would you interpret each: the protester being attacked by the dog and the police officers in the first photograph; the two African American athletes and the Australian in the second? What do these bodies tell us about power in American society? About the nature of different kinds of protest?

- In one photograph, the black figure appears passive, a victim. In the other, the black figures appear triumphant, powerful. In both instances, the African Americans pictured were expressing their desire for equal rights and an end to racism. What emotions does each photograph project? What emotions does each elicit in the viewer?

The Black Panther Party

One of the most radical organizations of the 1960s, the Black Panther Party was founded in 1966 by Bobby Seale and Huey Newton (shown together in the photograph on the left) in Oakland, California. Its members carried weapons, advocated socialism, and fought police brutality in black communities, but they also ran into their own trouble with the law. Nevertheless, the party had great success in reaching ordinary people, often with programs targeted at the poor. On the right, party members distribute free hot dogs to the public in New Haven, Connecticut, in 1969.   LEFT: Bruno Barbey/Magnum Photos. RIGHT: Photo by David Fenton/Getty Images.

cities was not abstract; it counted in real votes. Residents of Gary, Indiana, and Cleveland, Ohio, elected the first black mayors of large cities in 1967. Richard Hatcher in Gary and Carl Stokes in Cleveland helped forge a new urban politics in the United States. Their campaign teams registered thousands of black voters and made alliances with enough whites to create a working majority. Many saw Stokes's victory, in particular, as heralding a new day. One Stokes campaign staffer summed up its importance: "If Carl Stokes could run for mayor in the eighth largest city in America, then maybe who knows. We could be senators. We could be anything we wanted."

Having met with some political success, in 1972 black leaders gathered in Gary for the National Black Political Convention. In a meeting that brought together radicals, liberals, and centrists, debate centered on whether to form a third political party. Hatcher recalled that many in attendance believed "there was going to be a black third party." In the end, however, delegates decided to "give the Democratic Party one more chance." Instead of creating a third party, the convention issued the National Black Political Agenda, which included calls for community control of schools in black neighborhoods, national health insurance, and the elimination of the death penalty.

By the end of the century, black elected offcials had become commonplace in major American cities. There were forty-seven African American big-city mayors by the 1990s, and blacks had led most of the nation's most prominent cities: Atlanta, Chicago, Detroit, Los Angeles, New York, Philadelphia, and Washington, D.C. These politicians had translated black power not into a rejection of white society but into a revitalized liberalism that would remain an indelible feature of urban politics for the rest of the century.

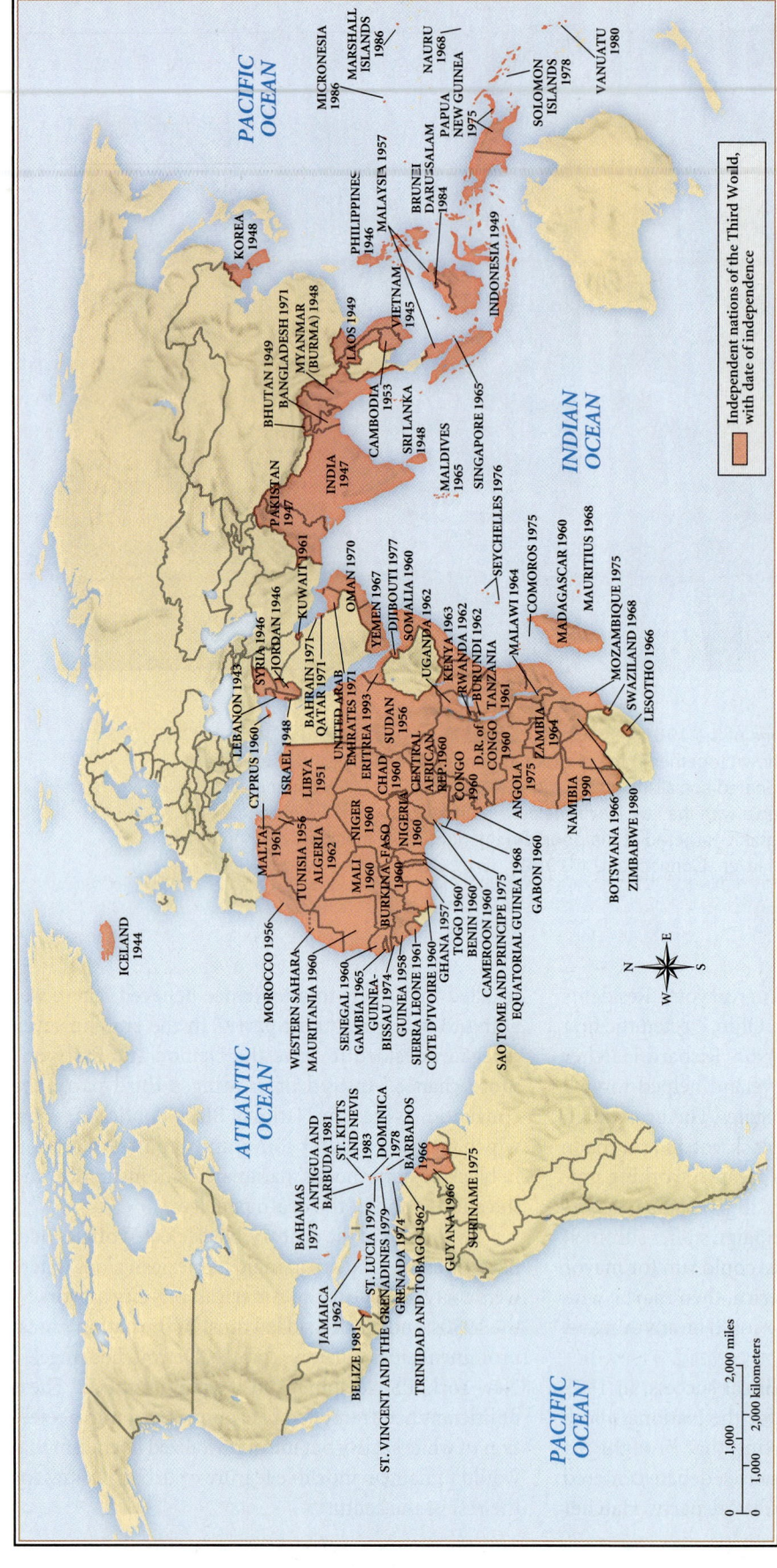

MAP 27.5

Decolonization and the Third World, 1943–1990

In the decades after World War II, African nations threw off the yoke of European colonialism. Some new nations, such as Ghana, the former British colony of Gold Coast, achieved independence rather peacefully. Others, such as Algeria and Mozambique, did so only after bloody anticolonial wars. American civil rights activists watched African decolonization with great enthusiasm, seeing the two struggles as linked. "Sure we identified with the blacks in Africa," civil rights leader John Lewis said. "Here were black people, talking of freedom and liberation and independence thousands of miles away." In 1960 alone, the year that student sit-ins swept across the American South, more than a dozen African nations gained independence.

Poverty and Urban Violence

Black Power was not, fundamentally, a violent political ideology. But violence did play a decisive role in the politics of black liberation in the mid-1960s. Too many Americans, white and black, had little knowledge or understanding of the rage that existed just below the surface in many poor northern black ghettos. That rage boiled over in a wave of riots that struck the nation's cities in mid-decade. The first "long hot summer" began in July 1964 in New York City when police shot a black criminal suspect in Harlem. Angry youths looted and rioted there for a week. Over the next four years, the volatile issue of police brutality set off riots in dozens of cities.

In August 1965, the arrest of a young black motorist in the Watts section of Los Angeles sparked six days of rioting that left thirty-four people dead. "There is a different type of Negro emerging," one riot participant told investigators. "They are not going to wait for the evolutionary process for their rights to be a man." The riots of 1967, however, were the most serious, engulfing twenty-two cities in July and August. Forty-three people were killed in Detroit alone, nearly all of them black, and $50 million worth of property was destroyed. President Johnson called in the National Guard and U.S. Army troops, many of them having just returned from Vietnam, to restore order.

Johnson, who believed that the Civil Rights Act and the Voting Rights Act had immeasurably helped African Americans, was stunned by the rioting. Despondent at the news from Watts, "he refused to look at the cables from Los Angeles," recalled one aide. Virtually all black leaders condemned the rioting, though they understood its origins in poverty and deprivation. At a meeting in Watts, Martin Luther King Jr. admitted that he had "failed to take the civil rights movement to the masses of the people," such as those in the Los Angeles ghetto. His appearance appeased few. "We don't need your dreams; we need jobs!" one heckler shouted at King.

Following the gut-wrenching riots of 1967, Johnson appointed a presidential commission, headed by Illinois governor Otto Kerner, to investigate the causes of the violence. Released in 1968, the Kerner Commission Report was a searing look at race in America, the most honest and forthright government document about race since the Presidential Committee on Civil Rights' 1947 report "To Secure These Rights." "Our nation is moving toward two societies," the Kerner Commission Report concluded, "one black, one white — separate and unequal." The report did not excuse the brick-throwing, fire-bombing, and looting of the previous summers, but

it placed the riots in sociological context. Shut out of white-dominated society, impoverished African Americans felt they had no stake in the social order. Pushed to the margins, many believed that violence was their only way to push back.

Stirred by turmoil in the cities, and seeing the limitations of his civil rights achievements, Martin Luther King Jr. began to expand his vision beyond civil rights to confront the deep-seated problems of poverty and racism in America as a whole. He began to criticize President Johnson and Congress for prioritizing the war in Vietnam over the fight against poverty at home, and he began to plan a massive movement called the Poor People's Campaign to fight economic injustice. To advance that cause, he went to Memphis, Tennessee, to support a strike by predominantly black sanitation workers. There, on April 4, 1968, he was assassinated by escaped white convict James Earl Ray. King's death set off a further round of urban rioting, with major violence breaking out in more than a hundred cities.

Tragically, King was murdered before achieving the transformations he sought: an end to racial injustice and a solution to poverty. The civil rights movement had helped set in motion permanent, indeed revolutionary, changes in American race relations. Jim Crow segregation ended, federal legislation ensured black Americans' most basic civil rights, and the white monopoly on political power in the South was broken. However, by 1968, the fight over civil rights had also divided the nation. The Democratic Party was splitting, and a new conservatism was gaining strength. Many whites felt that the issue of civil rights was receiving too much attention, to the detriment of other national concerns. The riots of 1965, 1967, and 1968 further alienated many whites, who blamed the violence on the inability of Democratic officials to maintain law and order.

Rise of the Chicano Movement

Mexican Americans had something of a counterpart to Martin Luther King: Cesar Chavez. In Chavez's case, however, economic struggle in community organizations and the labor movement had shaped his approach to mobilizing society's disadvantaged. He and Dolores Huerta had worked for the Community Service Organization (CSO), a California group founded in the 1950s to promote Mexican political participation and civil rights. Leaving that organization in 1962, Chavez concentrated on the agricultural region around Delano, California. With Huerta, he organized the United Farm Workers (UFW), a union for migrant workers.

Cesar Chavez

Influenced equally by the Catholic Church and Mahatma Gandhi, Cesar Chavez was one of the leading Mexican American civil rights and social justice activists of the 1960s. With Dolores Huerta, he co-founded the United Farm Workers (UFW), a union of primarily Mexican American agricultural laborers in California. Here he speaks at a rally in support of the grape boycott, an attempt by the UFW to force the nation's grape growers — and, by extension, the larger agriculture industry — to improve wages and working conditions and to bargain in good faith with the union.   ©Jason Laure / The Image Works.

Huerta was a brilliant organizer, but it was the deeply spiritual and ascetic Chavez who embodied the moral force behind what was popularly called La Causa. A 1965 grape pickers' strike led the UFW to call a nationwide boycott of table grapes, bringing Chavez huge publicity and backing from the AFL-CIO. In a bid for attention to the struggle, Chavez staged a hunger strike in 1968, which ended dramatically after twenty-eight days with Senator Robert F. Kennedy at his side to break the fast. Victory came in 1970 when California grape growers signed contracts recognizing the UFW.

Mexican Americans shared some civil rights concerns with African Americans—especially access to jobs—but they also had unique concerns: the status of the Spanish language in schools, for instance, and immigration policy. Mexican Americans had been politically active since the 1940s, aiming to surmount factors that obstructed their political involvement: poverty, language barriers, and discrimination. Their efforts began to pay off in the 1960s, when the Mexican

American Political Association (MAPA) mobilized support for John F. Kennedy and worked successfully with other organizations to elect Mexican American candidates such as Edward Roybal of California and Henry González of Texas to Congress. Two other organizations, the Mexican American Legal Defense Fund (MALDF) and the Southwest Voter Registration and Education Project, carried the fight against discrimination to Washington, D.C., and mobilized Mexican Americans into an increasingly powerful voting bloc.

Younger Mexican Americans grew impatient with civil rights groups such as MAPA and MALDF, however. The barrios of Los Angeles and other western cities produced the militant Brown Berets, modeled on the Black Panthers (who wore black berets). Rejecting their elders' assimilationist approach (i.e., a belief in adapting to Anglo society), fifteen hundred Mexican American students met in Denver in 1969 to hammer out a new political and cultural agenda. They proclaimed a new term, *Chicano* (and its feminine form, *Chicana*), to replace *Mexican American*, and later organized a political party, La Raza Unida (The United Race), to promote Chicano interests. Young Chicana feminists formed a number of organizations, including Las Hijas (The Daughters), which organized women both on college campuses and in the barrios. In California and many southwestern states, students staged demonstrations to press for bilingual education, the hiring of more Chicano teachers, and the creation of Chicano studies programs. By the 1970s, dozens of such programs were offered at universities throughout the region.

The American Indian Movement

American Indians, inspired by the Black Power and Chicano movements, organized to address their unique circumstances. Numbering nearly 800,000 in the 1960s, native people were exceedingly diverse—divided by language, tribal history, region, and degree of integration into American life. As a group, they shared a staggering unemployment rate—ten times the national average—and were the worst off in housing, disease

rates, and access to education. Native people also had an often troubling relationship with the federal government. In the 1960s, the prevailing spirit of protest swept through Indian communities. Young militants challenged their elders in the National Congress of American Indians. Beginning in 1960, the National Indian Youth Council (NIYC), under the slogan "For a Greater Indian America," promoted the notion of all Indian people as a single ethnic group. The effort to both unite Indians and celebrate individual tribal culture proved a difficult balancing act.

The NIYC had substantial influence within tribal communities, but two other organizations, the militant Indians of All Tribes (IAT) and American Indian Movement (AIM), attracted more attention in the larger society. These groups embraced the concept of Red Power, and beginning in 1968 staged escalating protests to draw attention to Indian concerns. In 1969, members of the IAT occupied the deserted federal penitentiary on Alcatraz Island in San Francisco Bay and proclaimed: "We will purchase said Alcatraz Island for twenty-four dollars in glass beads and red cloth, a precedent set by

Native American Activism

In November 1969, a group of Native Americans, united under the name "Indians of all Nations," occupied Alcatraz Island in San Francisco Bay. They claimed the land under a nineteenth-century treaty, but their larger objective was to force the federal government – which owned the island – to address the long-standing grievances of native peoples, including widespread poverty on reservations. Shown here is the view along the gunwale of the boat carrying Tim Williams, a chief of the Klamath River Hurek tribe in full ceremonial regalia, to the island. Ralph Crane/Time Life Pictures/Getty Images.

the white man's purchase of a similar island [Manhattan] about 300 years ago." In 1972, AIM members joined the Trail of Broken Treaties, a march sponsored by a number of Indian groups. When AIM activists seized the headquarters of the hated Bureau of Indian Affairs in Washington, D.C., and ransacked the building, older tribal leaders denounced them.

However, AIM managed to focus national media attention on Native American issues with a siege at Wounded Knee, South Dakota, in February 1973. The site of the infamous 1890 massacre of the Sioux, Wounded Knee was situated on the Pine Ridge reservation, where young AIM activists had cultivated ties to sympathetic elders. For more than two months, AIM members occupied a small collection of buildings, surrounded by a cordon of FBI agents and U.S. marshals. Several gun battles left two dead, and the siege was finally brought to a negotiated end. Although upsetting to many white onlookers and Indian elders alike, AIM protests attracted widespread mainstream media coverage and spurred government action on tribal issues.

- How would you characterize the different forms that the Black Power movement took? How were these forms related to traditions in African American history?

- Many minority groups in the late 1960s and early 1970s called for racial or ethnic pride and independence from white America. What were the advantages and disadvantages of such calls?

SUMMARY

Both African Americans and other people of color who fought for civil rights from World War II through the early 1970s sought equal rights and economic opportunity. For most of the first half of the twentieth century, African Americans faced a harsh Jim Crow system in the South and a segregated, though more open, society in the North. Segregation was held in place by a widespread belief among whites in black inferiority and by a southern political system that denied African Americans the vote. In the Southwest and West, Mexican Americans, Native Americans, and Americans of Asian descent faced discriminatory laws and social practices that marginalized them.

The civil rights movement attacked racial inequality in three ways. First, the movement sought equal standing for all Americans, regardless of race, under the law. This required patient work through the judicial system and the more arduous task of winning congressional legislation, such as the Civil Rights Act of 1964 and the Voting Rights Act of 1965. Second, grassroots activists, using nonviolent protest, pushed all levels of government (from city to federal) to abide by Supreme Court decisions (such as *Brown v. Board of Education*) and civil rights laws. Third, the movement sought to open economic opportunity for minority populations. This was embodied in the 1963 March on Washington for Jobs and Freedom. Ultimately, the civil rights movement was successful in establishing the principle of legal equality, but its participants encountered more considerable odds in ending poverty and creating meaningful, widespread economic opportunity.

Limitations in the civil rights model of social change led black activists—along with Mexican Americans, Native Americans, and others—to adopt a more nationalist stance after 1966. Nationalism stressed creating political and economic power in communities of color themselves, taking pride in one's racial heritage, and refusing to allow whites to define cultural standards.

CHAPTER REVIEW QUESTIONS

- Why did the civil rights movement begin when it did?

- How would you explain the rise of the protest movement after 1955? How did nonviolent tactics help the movement?

- How did the civil rights movement create a crisis in liberalism?

FOR FURTHER EXPLORATION

Historical work on the civil rights movement is rich and broad. For useful overviews, see Thomas J. Sugrue, *Sweet Land of Liberty: The Forgotten Struggle for Civil Rights in the North* (2008), Taylor Branch, *Parting the Waters: America in the King Years, 1954–63* (1988), and Peniel Joseph, *Waiting 'til the Midnight Hour: A Narrative History of Black Power in America* (2006). For powerful biographies of central activists, see John D'Emilio, *Lost Prophet: The Life and Times of Bayard Rustin* (2003); Barbara Ransby, *Ella Baker and the Black Freedom Movement* (2003); and David J. Garrow, *Bearing the Cross: Martin Luther King, Jr., and the Southern Christian Leadership Conference* (1986). For thoughtful case studies, see Charles Payne, *I've Got the Light of Freedom: The Organizing Tradition and the Mississippi Freedom Struggle* (1995), and William Chafe, *Civilities and Civil Rights: Greensboro, North Carolina, and the Black Struggle for Freedom* (1980). On women in the movement, see Bettye Collier-Thomas and V. P. Franklin, eds., *Sisters in the Struggle: African American Women in the Civil Rights–Black Power Movement* (2001). On the Mexican American and Chicano movements, see Ian F. Haney López, *Racism on Trial: The Chicano Fight for Justice* (2003). The Internet offers numerous resources. The Civil Rights in Mississippi Digital Archive, at **www.lib.usm.edu/~spcol/crda**, offers 150 oral histories relating to Mississippi. Audio clips are also included, as are short biographies, photographs, newsletters, FBI documents, and arrest records.

TEST YOUR KNOWLEDGE

To assess your command of the material in this chapter, see the Online Study Guide at **bedfordstmartins.com/henretta**.

For Web sites, images, and documents related to topics and places in this chapter, visit **bedfordstmartins.com/makehistory**.

TIMELINE

1941	A. Philip Randolph proposes march on Washington Roosevelt issues Executive Order 8802
1942	Double V campaign launched
1943	Congress of Racial Equality (CORE) founded
1947	"To Secure These Rights" published Jackie Robinson integrates major league baseball *Mendez v. Westminster School District*
1948	States' Rights Democratic Party (Dixiecrats) founded
1954	*Brown v. Topeka Board of Education*
1955	Emmett Till murdered (August) Montgomery Bus Boycott (December)
1956	"Southern Manifesto" issued against *Brown* ruling
1957	Integration of Little Rock High School Southern Christian Leadership Council (SCLC) founded
1960	Greensboro, North Carolina, sit-ins (February) Student Non-Violent Coordinating Committee (SNCC) founded
1961	Freedom Rides (May)
1963	Demonstrations in Birmingham, Alabama March on Washington for Jobs and Freedom
1964	Civil Rights Act passed by Congress Freedom Summer
1965	Voting Rights Act passed by Congress Malcolm X assassinated (February 21) Riot in Watts neighborhood of Los Angeles (August)
1966	Black Panther Party founded
1967	Riots in Detroit and Newark
1968	Martin Luther King Jr. assassinated (April 4) Fair Housing Act passed by Congress
1969	Young Lords founded Occupation of Alcatraz
1972	National Black Political Convention "Trail of Broken Treaties" protest

CHAPTER 28

Uncivil Wars: Liberal Crisis and Conservative Rebirth, 1964–1972

The civil rights movement stirred American liberals and pushed them to initiate bold new government policies to advance racial equality. That progressive spirit inspired an even broader reform agenda that came to include women's rights, new social programs for the poor and the aged, job training, environmental laws, and a host of educational and other social benefits for the middle class. All told, Congress passed more liberal legislation between 1964 and 1972 than in any period since the 1930s. The great bulk of it came during the 1965–1966 legislative session, one of the most active in American history. Liberalism was at high tide.

It did not stay there long. Liberals quickly came under assault from two directions. First, young activists became frustrated with slow progress on civil rights and rebelled against the Vietnam War. They accused the liberal establishment, represented by President Lyndon Baines Johnson, of imperial overreach in Southeast Asia. At the Democratic National Convention in 1968 in Chicago, police teargassed and clubbed antiwar demonstrators, who screamed (as the TV cameras rolled), "The whole world is watching!" Some of them had been among the idealistic youth exhorted into action by Kennedy's inaugural address and the civil rights movement. Now they detested everything that Cold War liberalism stood for. Inside the convention hall, the proceedings were chaotic, the atmosphere poisonous, the delegates bitterly divided over Vietnam.

A second assault on liberalism came from conservatives, who began to find their footing after being marginalized during the 1950s. Conservatives opposed the dramatic expansion of the federal government under Johnson and disdained the "permissive society" they believed liberalism had unleashed. Advocating law and order, belittling welfare, and resisting key civil rights reforms, conservatives leaped back to political life in the late sixties. Their champion was Barry Goldwater, a Republican senator from Arizona, who warned that "a government big enough to give you everything you want is also big enough to take away everything you have."

The clashing of left, right, and center made the eight years in between the passage of the 1964 Civil Rights Act and the 1972 landslide reelection of Richard Nixon one of the most contentious, complicated, and explosive eras in American history. There were thousands of marches and demonstrations; massive new federal programs aimed at achieving civil rights, ending poverty,

Peace Demonstrators

Antiwar demonstrators wave a red flag bearing the peace sign near the Washington Monument, where thousands gathered on November 15, 1969, for a Moratorium Day rally in the nation's capital. © Bettmann/Corbis.

and extending the welfare state; and new voices among women, blacks, and Latinos demanding to be heard. With heated, vitriolic rhetoric on all sides, these developments overlapped with political assassinations and violence both overseas and at home. All of it coincided in these extraordinary years. Civil rights leader John Lewis captured the urgency of the time when he said, simply, "Wake up, America!"

In this chapter, we undertake to explain how the passionate rekindling of liberal reform under the twin auspices of the civil rights movement and the leadership of President Johnson gave way in short order to a profound liberal crisis and the resurgence of conservatism.

The Great Society: Liberalism at High Tide

In May 1964, Lyndon Johnson, president for barely six months, delivered the commencement address at the University of Michigan. Johnson offered his audience a grand and inspirational vision of a new liberal age. "We have the opportunity to move not only toward the rich society and the powerful society," Johnson continued, "but upward to the Great Society." As the sunbaked graduates listened, Johnson spelled out what he meant: "The Great Society rests on abundance and liberty for all. It demands an end to poverty and racial injustice." Even this, Johnson declared, was just the beginning. He would push to renew American education, rebuild the cities, and restore the natural environment. Ambitious—even audacious—Johnson's vision was a New Deal for a new era. From that day forward, the president would harness his considerable political skills in an effort to make the vision a reality. A tragic irony, however, was that he held the presidency at all.

John F. Kennedy's Promise

In 1961, three years before Johnson's Great Society speech, John F. Kennedy declared at his inauguration: "Let the word go forth from this time and place, to friend and foe alike, that the torch has been passed to a new generation of Americans." He challenged his fellow citizens to "ask what you can do for your country," an inspiring call to service that many Americans took to heart. The British journalist Henry Fairley called Kennedy's activism "the politics of expectation." Over time, the expectations Kennedy embodied, combined with his ability to inspire a younger generation, laid the groundwork for an era of liberal reform.

Tragically, he would not live to see that era. On November 22, 1963, Kennedy went to Texas on a political trip. As he and his wife, Jacqueline, rode in an open car past the Texas School Book Depository in Dallas, he was shot through the head and neck by a sniper. He died within the hour. (The accused killer, Lee Harvey Oswald, a twenty-four-year-old loner, was himself killed while in custody a few days later by an assassin, a Dallas nightclub owner named Jack Ruby.) Before Air Force One left Dallas to take the president's body back to Washington, a grim-faced Lyndon Johnson was sworn in, making the transition from vice president to president.

Kennedy's youthful image, the trauma of his assassination, and the nation's sense of loss contributed to a powerful Kennedy mystique. His canonization after death capped what had been an extraordinarily stage-managed presidency. An admiring country saw in Jack and Jackie Kennedy an ideal American marriage (though JFK was, in fact, an obsessive womanizer); in Kennedy the epitome of robust good health (though he was actually afflicted by Addison's disease); and in the Kennedy White House a glamorous world of high fashion and celebrity. No other presidency ever matched the Kennedy aura, but every president after him embraced the idea that image mattered as much as reality in conducting a politically effective presidency.

Lyndon B. Johnson and the Liberal Resurgence

In many ways, Lyndon Johnson was the opposite of Kennedy. A seasoned Texas politician and longtime Senate leader, Johnson was most at home in the back rooms of power. He was a rough-edged character who had scrambled his way up, without too many scruples, to wealth and political eminence. But he never forgot his

The Great Society
President Lyndon Johnson toured poverty-stricken regions of the country in 1964. Here he visits with Tom Fletcher, a father of eight children in Martin County, Kentucky. Johnson envisioned a dramatic expansion of liberal social programs, both to assist the needy and to strengthen the middle class, that he called the "Great Society."
© Bettmann/Corbis.

modest, hill-country origins or lost his sympathy for the downtrodden. Johnson lacked the Kennedy style, but he capitalized on Kennedy's assassination, applying his astonishing energy and negotiating skills to bring to fruition several of Kennedy's stalled programs and many more of his own, in the ambitious Great Society.

On assuming the presidency, Johnson promptly pushed for civil rights legislation as a memorial to his slain predecessor (see Chapter 27). His motives were complex. As a southerner who had previously opposed civil rights for African Americans, Johnson wished to prove that he was more than a regional figure—he would be the president of all the people. He also wanted to make a mark on history, telling Martin Luther King Jr. and other civil rights leaders to lace up their sneakers because he would move so fast on civil rights they would be running to catch up. Politically, the choice was risky. Johnson would please the Democratic Party's liberal wing, but because most northern blacks already voted Democratic, the party would gain few additional votes. Moreover, southern white Democrats would likely revolt, dividing the party at a time when Johnson's legislative agenda most required unanimity. But Johnson pushed ahead, and the 1964 Civil Rights Act stands, in part, as a testament to the president's political risk-taking.

War on Poverty | More than civil rights, what drove Johnson hardest was his determination to "end poverty in our time." The president called it a national disgrace that in the midst of plenty, one-fifth of all Americans—hidden from most people's sight

in Appalachia, urban ghettos, migrant labor camps, and Indian reservations—lived in poverty. Many had fallen through the cracks and were not served by New Deal–era welfare programs. But, Johnson declared, "for the first time in our history, it is possible to conquer poverty."

The Economic Opportunity Act of 1964, which created a series of programs to reach these Americans, was the president's answer—what he called the War on Poverty. Head Start provided free nursery schools to prepare disadvantaged preschoolers for kindergarten. The Job Corps and Upward Bound provided young people with training and employment. Volunteers in Service to America (VISTA), modeled on the Peace Corps, offered technical assistance to the urban and rural poor. An array of regional development programs aimed at spurring economic growth in impoverished areas.

One of the most controversial features of the War on Poverty was the Community Action Program (CAP), which encouraged the poor to demand a voice in the decisions that affected their lives. CAP organizers, allied with lawyers employed by the federally funded Legal Services Program, pressed city and state governments to expand social programs and devote more resources to impoverished citizens. This often brought them into conflict with Democratic officials in large cities, splitting two constituencies of the New Deal coalition.

The 1964 Election | With the Civil Rights Act passed and his War on Poverty initiatives off the ground, Johnson turned his attention to the upcoming presidential election. Not content to govern in Kennedy's shadow, he wanted a national mandate of his own. Privately, Johnson cast himself less as a copy of Kennedy than as the heir of Franklin Roosevelt and the expansive liberalism of the 1930s. Johnson had come to Congress for the first time in 1937 and had long admired FDR's political skills. He reminded his advisors never to forget "the meek and the humble and the lowly," because "President Roosevelt never did."

In the 1964 election, Johnson faced Republican Barry Goldwater of Arizona. An archconservative, Goldwater ran on an anticommunist, antigovernment platform, offering "a choice, not an echo"—meaning he represented a genuinely conservative alternative to liberalism rather than the echo of liberalism offered by the moderate wing of the Republican Party (see Chapter 25). Goldwater campaigned against the Civil Rights Act of 1964 and promised a more vigorous Cold War foreign policy. Among those supporting him was former actor Ronald Reagan, whose speech on behalf of Goldwater at the Republican convention, called "A Time for Choosing," made him a rising star in the party.

But Goldwater's strident foreign policy alienated voters. "Extremism in the defense of liberty is no vice," he told Republicans at the convention. Moreover, there remained strong national sentiment for Kennedy. Telling Americans that he was running to fulfill Kennedy's legacy, Johnson and his running mate, Hubert H. Humphrey of Minnesota, won in a landslide (Map 28.1). In the long run, Goldwater's candidacy marked the beginning of a grassroots conservative revolt that would eventually transform the Republican Party. In the short run, however, Johnson's sweeping victory gave him a popular mandate and, equally important, the filibuster-proof Senate majority he needed to push the Great Society forward (Table 28.1).

Great Society Initiatives | One of Johnson's first successes was breaking the congressional deadlock on education and health care. Passed in April 1965, the Elementary and Secondary Education Act authorized $1 billion in federal funds for teacher training and other educational programs. Standing in his old Texas schoolhouse, Johnson, a former teacher, said: "I believe no law I have signed or will ever sign means more to the future of America." Six months later, Johnson signed the Higher Education Act, providing federal scholarships for college students. Johnson also had the votes he needed to achieve some form of national health insurance. He proposed two new programs: Medicare, a health plan for the elderly funded by a surcharge on Social Security payroll taxes, and Medicaid,

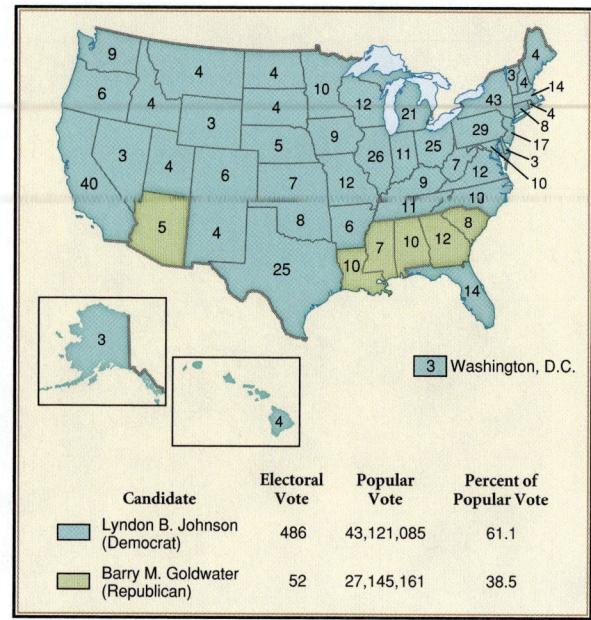

MAP 28.1

The Presidential Election of 1964

This map reveals how one-sided was the victory of Lyndon Johnson over Barry Goldwater in 1964. Except for Arizona, his home state, Goldwater won only five states in the Deep South—not of much immediate consolation to him, but a sure indicator that the South was cutting its historic ties to the Democratic Party. Moreover, although soundly rejected in 1964, Goldwater's Far Right critique of "big government" laid the foundation for a Republican resurgence in the 1980s.

Candidate	Electoral Vote	Popular Vote	Percent of Popular Vote
Lyndon B. Johnson (Democrat)	486	43,121,085	61.1
Barry M. Goldwater (Republican)	52	27,145,161	38.5

a health plan for the poor paid for by general tax revenues and administered by the states.

Also high on the Great Society's agenda was environmental reform. President Johnson pressed for an expanded national park system, improvement of the nation's air and water, protection for endangered species, stronger land-use planning, and highway beautification. Hardly pausing for breath, Johnson oversaw the creation of the Department of Housing and Urban Development (HUD), won funding for hundreds of thousands of units of public housing, made new investments in urban rapid transit such as the new Washington, D.C., Metro and the Bay Area Rapid Transit (BART) system in San Francisco, ushered new child safety and consumer protection laws through Congress, and helped create the National Endowment for the Arts and the National Endowment for the Humanities to support the work of artists, writers, and scholars.

It even became possible, at this moment of reform zeal, to tackle the nation's discriminatory immigration

TABLE 28.1

Major Great Society Legislation

Civil Rights

1964	Twenty-fourth Amendment	Outlawed poll tax in federal elections
	Civil Rights Act	Banned discrimination in employment and public accommodations on the basis of race, religion, sex, or national origin
1965	Voting Rights Act	Outlawed literacy tests for voting; provided federal supervision of registration in historically low-registration areas

Social Welfare

1964	Economic Opportunity Act	Created Office of Economic Opportunity (OEO) to administer War on Poverty programs such as Head Start, Job Corps, and Volunteers in Service to America (VISTA)
1965	Medical Care Act	Provided medical care for the poor (Medicaid) and the elderly (Medicare)
1966	Minimum Wage Act	Raised hourly minimum wage from $1.25 to $1.40 and expanded coverage to new groups

Education

1965	Elementary and Secondary Education Act	Granted federal aid for education of poor children
	National Endowment for the Arts and Humanities	Provided federal funding and support for artists and scholars
	Higher Education Act	Provided federal scholarships for postsecondary education

Housing and Urban Development

1964	Urban Mass Transportation Act	Provided federal aid to urban mass transit
	Omnibus Housing Act	Provided federal funds for public housing and rent subsidies for low-income families
1965	Housing and Urban Development Act	Created Department of Housing and Urban Development (HUD)
1966	Metropolitan Area Redevelopment and Demonstration Cities Acts	Designated 150 "model cities" for combined programs of public housing, social services, and job training

Environment

| 1964 | Wilderness Preservation Act | Designated 9.1 million acres of federal lands as "wilderness areas," barring future roads, buildings, or commercial use |
| 1965 | Air and Water Quality Acts | Set tougher air quality standards; required states to enforce water quality standards for interstate waters |

Miscellaneous

1964	Tax Reduction Act	Reduced personal and corporate income tax rates
1965	Immigration Act	Abandoned national quotas of 1924 law, allowing more non-European immigration
	Appalachian Regional and Development Act	Provided federal funding for roads, health clinics, other public works projects in economically depressed regions

policy. The Immigration Act of 1965 abandoned the quota system that favored northern Europeans, replacing it with numerical limits that did not discriminate among nations. To promote family reunification, the law also stipulated that close relatives of legal residents in the United States could be admitted outside the numerical limits, an exception that especially benefited Asian and Latin American immigrants. Since 1965, Asian and Latin American immigrants have become increasingly visible in American society (see Chapter 31).

The "Johnson Treatment"
Lyndon B. Johnson, a shrewd and adroit politician, learned many of his legislative skills while serving as majority leader of the Senate from 1953 to 1960. He was well-known for "the Treatment" (a combination of physical intimidation and forceful monologue) he used to persuade fellow politicians to his point of view, and in this photo he zeroes in on Senator Theodore Francis Green of Rhode Island. After assuming the presidency, Johnson remarked, "They say Jack Kennedy had style, but I'm the one who got the bills passed." George Tames, *New York Times.*

Assessing the Great Society The Great Society had mixed results. The proportion of Americans living below the poverty line dropped from 20 percent to 13 percent between 1963 and 1968 (Figure 28.1). Medicare and Medicaid, the most enduring of the Great Society programs, helped millions of elderly and poor citizens afford necessary health care. Further, as millions of African Americans moved into the middle class, the black poverty rate fell by half.

Conservatives, however, gave more credit for these changes to the decade's booming economy than to government programs. In the final analysis, the Great Society dramatically improved the financial situation of the elderly, reached millions of children, and increased the racial diversity of American society and workplaces. However, entrenched poverty remained, racial segrega-

tion in the largest cities worsened, and the national distribution of wealth remained highly skewed. In relative terms, the bottom 20 percent remained as far behind as ever. In these arenas, the Great Society made little progress.

The Women's Movement Reborn

The new era of liberal reform reawakened the American women's movement. Inspired by the civil rights movement and legislative advances under the Great Society, but frustrated by the lack of attention both gave to women, feminism sprang back to life as a mass movement. Refusing to allow women's needs to be sidelined, feminists entered the political fray and demanded not simply inclusion, but a rethinking of national priorities.

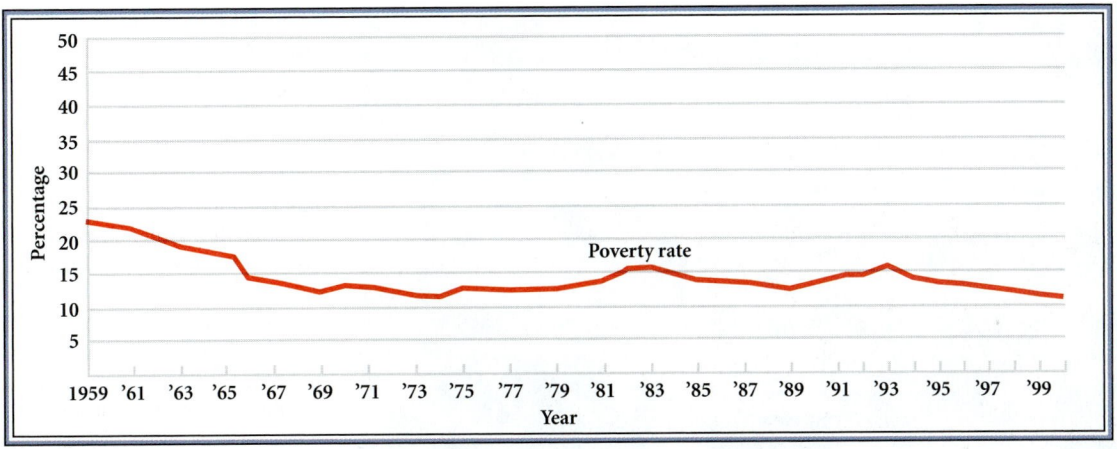

FIGURE 28.1

Americans in Poverty, 1959–2000

Between 1959 and 1973 the poverty rate among American families dropped by more than half—from 23 percent to 11 percent. There was, however, sharp disagreement about the reasons for that notable decline. Liberals credited the War on Poverty, while conservatives favored the high-performing economy, with the significant poverty dip of 1965–1966 caused by military spending, not Johnson's domestic programs.

Labor Feminists The women's movement had not languished entirely in the postwar years. Feminist concerns were kept alive in the 1950s and early 1960s by working women, who campaigned for such things as maternity leave and equal pay for equal work. One historian has called these women "labor feminists," because they belonged to unions and fought for equality and dignity in the workplace. "It became apparent to me why so many employers could legally discriminate against women—because it was written right into the law," said one female labor activist.

Labor feminists were responding to the times. More women—including married women (40 percent by 1970) and mothers with young children (30 percent by 1970)—were working outside the home than ever before. But they encountered a labor market in which their contributions were undervalued. Moreover, most working women faced the "double day": they were expected to earn a paycheck and then return home to do mestic labor. One woman put the problem succinctly: "The working mother has no 'wife' to care for her children."

Betty Friedan and the National Organization for Women When Betty Friedan's indictment of suburban domesticity, *The Feminine Mystique*, appeared in 1963, it targeted a different audience: college-educated, middle-class women who found themselves stifled by their domestic routine. Tens of thousands of women read Friedan's book—in which she identified "the problem that has no name"—and thought, "She's talking about me." *The Feminine Mystique* became a runaway bestseller. Friedan persuaded middle-class women that they needed more than the convenience foods, improved diapers, and better laundry detergents that magazines and television urged them to buy. To live rich and fulfilling lives, they needed education and work outside the home.

Paradoxically, the domesticity described in *The Feminine Mystique* was already crumbling. After the postwar baby boom, women were again having fewer children, aided now by the birth control pill, first marketed in 1960. And as states liberalized divorce laws, more women were divorcing. Educational levels were also rising: By 1970, women made up 42 percent of the college population. All of these changes undermined traditional gender roles and enabled women to embrace *The Feminine Mystique*'s liberating prescriptions.

Government action also made a difference. In 1961, Kennedy appointed the Presidential Commission on the Status of Women, which issued a 1963 report documenting job and educational discrimination. The same year, Congress passed the Equal Pay Act, which established the principle of equal pay for equal work. A bigger breakthrough resulted from sheer happenstance. Hoping to derail the pending Civil Rights Act of 1964, a key conservative congressman added the word *sex* to the categories protected against discrimination. The act passed anyway, and to great national surprise, women suddenly had a powerful legal tool for fighting sex discrimination.

To force compliance with the new act, Friedan and others founded the National Organization for Women (NOW) in 1966. Modeled on the NAACP, NOW intended to be a civil rights organization for women, with the aim of bringing "women into full participation in . . . American society now, exercising all the privileges and responsibilities thereof in truly equal partnership with men." Under Friedan's leadership, membership grew to fifteen thousand by 1971, and NOW became, like the NAACP, a powerful voice for equal rights.

One of the ironies of the 1960s was the enormous strain that all of this liberal activism placed on the New Deal coalition. Faced with often competing demands from the civil rights movement, feminists, the poor, labor unions, conservative southern Democrats, the suburban middle class, and urban political machines, the old Rooseveltian coalition had begun to fray. Johnson hoped that the New Deal coalition was strong enough to negotiate competing demands among its own constituents while simultaneously resisting conservative attacks. In 1965, that still seemed possible. It would not remain so for long.

- **What were the key components of the Great Society?**

- **What accounted for the resurgence of feminism in the 1960s?**

The War in Vietnam, 1963–1968

As the accelerating rights revolution placed strain on the Democratic coalition, the war in Vietnam divided the country. In a CBS interview before his death, Kennedy remarked that it was up to the South Vietnamese whether "their war" would be won or lost. But the young president had already placed the United States on a course that would make retreat difficult. Like other presidents, Kennedy believed that giving up in Vietnam would weaken America's "credibility." Withdrawal "would be a great mistake," he said. It is impossible to know how JFK would have managed Vietnam had he lived. What is known is that when Kennedy gave the approval for the coup that cost president Ngo Dinh Diem his life (see Chapter 25), South Vietnam tumbled into political chaos.

Escalation under Johnson

Just as Kennedy had inherited Vietnam from Eisenhower, so Lyndon Johnson inherited Vietnam from Kennedy. Johnson's inheritance was more burdensome, however, for by now, only massive American intervention could prevent the collapse of South Vietnam

(Map 28.2). Johnson, like Kennedy, was a subscriber to the Cold War tenets of global containment. "I am not going to lose Vietnam," he vowed on taking office. "I am not going to be the President who saw Southeast Asia go the way China went."

Gulf of Tonkin It did not take long for Johnson to place his stamp on the war. During the summer of 1964, the president got reports that North Vietnamese torpedo boats had fired on the U.S. destroyer *Maddox* in the Gulf of Tonkin. In the first attack, on August 2, the damage inflicted was limited to a single bullet hole; a second attack, on August 4, later proved to be only misread radar sightings. It didn't matter if it was a real or imagined attack; Johnson believed a wider war was inevitable and issued a call to arms, sending his national approval rating from 42 to 72 percent. In the entire Congress, only two senators voted against his request for authorization to "take all necessary measures to repel any armed attack against the forces of the United States and to prevent further aggression." The Gulf of Tonkin Resolution, as it became known, gave Johnson the freedom to conduct operations in Vietnam as he saw fit.

Despite his mandate, Johnson was initially cautious about revealing his plans to the American people. "I had no choice but to keep my foreign policy in the wings . . . ," Johnson later said. "I knew that the day it exploded into a major debate on the war, that day would be the beginning of the end of the Great Society." So he ran in 1964 on the pledge that there would be no escalation—no American boys fighting Vietnam's fight. Privately, he doubted the pledge could be kept.

The New American Presence With the 1964 election safely behind him, Johnson began an American takeover of the war in Vietnam (see Comparing American Voices, "The Toll of War," pp. 892–893). The escalation, beginning in the early months of 1965, took two forms: deployment of American ground troops, and the intensification of bombing against North Vietnam.

On March 8, 1965, the first marines waded ashore at Da Nang. By 1966, more than 380,000 American soldiers

MAP 28.2

The Vietnam War, 1968

The Vietnam War was a guerrilla war, fought in skirmishes rather than set-piece battles. Despite repeated airstrikes, the United States was never able to halt the flow of North Vietnamese troops and supplies down the Ho Chi Minh Trail, which wound through Laos and Cambodia. In January 1968, Vietcong forces launched the Tet offensive, a surprise attack on cities and provincial centers across South Vietnam. Although the attackers were pushed back with heavy losses, the Tet offensive revealed the futility of American efforts to suppress the Vietcong guerrillas and marked a turning point in the war.

Thus I have given you, I think, the Substance of the Arguments on both sides of that great and important Questi...

The Toll of War

The Vietnam War produced a rich and graphic literature: novels, journalists' reports, interviews, and personal letters. These brief selections suggest the war's profound impact on those Americans who experienced it firsthand.

Donald Whitfield

Donald L. Whitfield was a draftee from Alabama who was interviewed some years after the war.

I'm gonna be honest with you. I had heard some about Vietnam in 1968, but I was a poor fellow and I didn't keep up with it. I was working at a Standard Oil station making eight dollars a day. I pumped gas and tinkered a little with cars. I had a girl I saw every now and then, but I still spent most of my time with a car. When I got my letter from the draft lady, I appealed it on the reason it was just me and my sister at home. We were a poor family and they needed me at home, but it did no good.

My company did a lot of patrolling. We got the roughest damn deal. Shit, I thought I was going to get killed every night. I was terrified the whole time. We didn't have no trouble with the blacks. I saw movies that said we done the blacks wrong, but it wasn't like that where I was. Let's put it like this: they make pretty good soldiers, but they're not what we are. White Americans, can't nobody whip our ass. We're the baddest son of a bitches on the face of this earth. You can take a hundred Russians and twenty-five Americans, and we'll whip their ass. . . .

I fly the Rebel flag because this is the South, Bubba. The American flag represents the whole fifty states. That flag represents the southern part. I'm a Confederate, I'm a Southerner. . . .

I feel cheated about Vietnam, I sure do. Political restrictions—we won every goddamned battle we was in, but didn't win the whole goddamn little country. . . . Before I die, the Democratic-controlled Congress of this country—and I blame it on 'em—they gonna goddamn apologize to the Vietnam veterans.

Source: James R. Wilson, *Landing Zones: Southern Veterans Remember Vietnam* (Durham, NC: Duke University Press, 1990), 203, 204, 207, 209, 210.

George Olsen

George Olsen served in Vietnam from August 1969 to March 1970, when he was killed in action. He wrote this letter to his girlfriend.

31 Aug '69
Dear Red,
Last Monday I went on my first hunter-killer operation. . . . The frightening thing about it all is that it is so very easy to kill in war. There's no remorse, no theatrical "washing of the hands" to get rid of nonexistent blood, not even any regrets. When it happens, you are more afraid than you've ever been in your life—my hands shook so much I had trouble reloading. . . . You're scared, really scared, and there's no thinking about it. You kill because that little SOB is doing his best to kill you and you desperately want to live, to go home, to get drunk or walk down the street on a date again. And suddenly the grenades aren't going off any more, the weapons stop and, unbelievably fast it seems, it's all over. . . .

I have truly come to envy the honest pacifist who honestly believes that no killing is permissible and can, with a clear conscience, stay home and not take part in these conflicts. I wish I could do the same, but I can't see letting another take my place and my risks over here. . . . The only reason pacifists such as the Amish can even live in an orderly society is because someone—be they police or soldiers—is taking risks to keep the wolves away. . . . I guess that's why I'm over here, why I fought so hard to come here, and why, even though I'm scared most of the time, I'm content to be here.

Source: Bernard Edelman, ed., *Dear America: Letters Home from Vietnam* (New York: Pocket Books, 1985), 204–205.

Arthur E. Woodley Jr.

Special Forces Ranger Arthur E. Woodley Jr. gave this interview a decade after his return.

You had to fight to survive where I grew up. Lower east Baltimore. . . . It was a mixed-up neighborhood of Puerto Ricans, Indians, Italians, and blacks. Being that I'm light-skinned, curly hair, I wasn't readily accepted in the black community. I was more accepted by Puerto Ricans and some rednecks. They didn't ask what my race classification was. I went with them to white movies, white restaurants, and so forth. But after I got older, I came to the realization that I was what I am and came to deal with my black peers. . . .

I figured I was just what my country needed. A black patriot who could do any physical job they could come up with. Six feet, one hundred and ninety pounds, and healthy. . . .

I didn't ask no questions about the war. I thought communism was spreading, and as an American citizen, it was my part to do as much as I could to defeat the Communist from coming here. Whatever America states is correct was the tradition that I was brought up in. And I thought the only way I could possibly make it out of the ghetto was to be the best soldier I possibly could. . . .

Then came the second week of February of '69. . . . We recon this area, and we came across this fella, a white guy, who was staked to the ground. His arms and legs tied down to stakes. . . . He had numerous scars on his face where he might have been beaten and mutilated. And he had been peeled from his upper part of chest to down to his waist.

Skinned. Like they slit your skin with a knife. And they take a pair of pliers or a instrument similar, and they just peel the skin off your body and expose it to the elements. . . .

And he start to cryin', beggin' to die.

He said, "I can't go back like this. I can't live like this. I'm dying. You can't leave me here like this dying." . . .

It took me somewhere close to 20 minutes to get my mind together. Not because I was squeamish about killing someone, because I had at that time numerous body counts. Killing someone wasn't the issue. It was killing another American citizen, another GI. . . . We buried him. We buried him. Very deep. Then I cried. . . .

When we first started going into the fields, I would not wear a finger, ear, or mutilate another person's body. Until I had the misfortune to come upon those American soldiers who were castrated. Then it got to be a game between the Communists and ourselves to see how many fingers and ears that we could capture from each other. After a kill we would cut his finger or ear off as a trophy, stuff our unit patch in his mouth, and let him die.

With 89 days left in country, I came out of the field. What I now felt was emptiness. . . . I started seeing the atrocities that we caused each other as human beings. I came to the realization that I was committing crimes against humanity and myself. That I really didn't believe in these things I was doin'. I changed.

Source: Wallace Terry, *Bloods: An Oral History of the Vietnam War by Black Veterans* (New York: Ballantine, 1984), 243–263.

Gayle Smith

Gayle Smith was a nurse in a surgical unit in Vietnam in 1970–1971 and gave this interview a few years later.

I objected to the war and I got the idea into my head of going there to bring people back. I started thinking about it in 1966 and knew that I would eventually go when I felt I was prepared enough. . . .

Boy, I remember how they came in all torn up. It was incredible. The first time a medevac came in, I got right into it. I didn't have a lot of feeling at that time. It was later on that I began to have a lot of feeling about it, after I'd seen it over and over and over again. . . . I turned that pain into anger and hatred and placed it onto the Vietnamese. . . . I did not consider the Vietnamese to be people. They were human, but they weren't people. They weren't like us, so it was okay to kill them. It was okay to hate them. . . .

I would have dreams about putting a .45 to someone's head and see it blow away over and over again. And for a long time I swore that if the Vietnamese ever came to this country I'd kill them.

It was in a Vietnam veterans group that I realized that all my hatred for the Vietnamese and my wanting to kill them was really a reflection of all the pain that I had felt for seeing all those young men die and hurt. . . . I would stand there and look at them and think to myself, "You've just lost your leg for no reason at all." Or "You're going to die and it's for nothing." For nothing. I would never, never say that to them, but they knew it.

Source: Albert Santoli, ed., *Everything We Had* (New York: Random House, 1981), 141–148.

ANALYZING THE EVIDENCE

- Why did these four young people end up in Vietnam?
- How would you describe their experiences there?
- How were they changed by the war? What do their reflections suggest about the war's impact on American society?

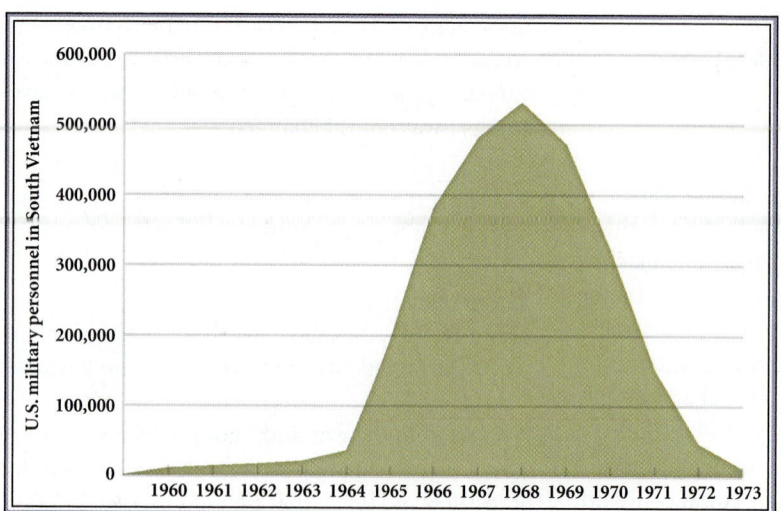

FIGURE 28.2

U.S. Troops in Vietnam, 1960–1973

This figure graphically tracks America's involvement in Vietnam. After Lyndon Johnson decided on escalation in 1964, troop levels jumped from 23,300 to a peak of 543,000 personnel in 1968. Under Richard Nixon's Vietnamization program, beginning in the summer of 1969, levels drastically declined; the last U.S. military forces left South Vietnam on March 29, 1973.

were stationed in Vietnam; by 1967, 485,000; and by 1968, 536,000 (Figure 28.2). The escalating demands of General William Westmoreland, the commander of U.S. forces, and Robert McNamara, the secretary of defense, pushed Johnson to Americanize the ground war in an attempt to stabilize South Vietnam. "I can't run and pull a Chamberlain at Munich," Johnson privately told a reporter in early March 1965, referring to the British prime minister who appeased Hitler in 1938.

In the meantime, Johnson authorized Operation Rolling Thunder, a massive bombing campaign against North Vietnam. Over the entire course of the war, the United States dropped twice as many tons of bombs on Vietnam as the Allies had dropped in both Europe and the Pacific during the whole of World War II. To McNamara's surprise, the bombing had little effect on the Vietcong's ability to wage war in the South. The North Vietnamese quickly rebuilt roads and bridges, and moved munitions plants underground. Instead of destroying the morale of the North Vietnamese, Operation Rolling Thunder hardened their will to fight. The massive commitment of troops and air power devastated Vietnam's countryside, however. After one harsh but not unusual engagement, a commanding officer reported, that "it became necessary to destroy the town in order to save it"—a statement that came to symbolize the terrible logic of the war.

The Johnson administration gambled that American superiority in personnel and weaponry would ultimately triumph. This strategy was inextricably tied to political considerations. For domestic reasons, policymakers searched for an elusive middle ground between all-out invasion of North Vietnam, which included the possibility of war with China, and disengagement.

"In effect, we are fighting a war of attrition," said General Westmoreland. "The only alternative is a war of annihilation."

Public Opinion and the War

Johnson, who remained cautious in 1964, gradually grew more confident that his Vietnam policy had the support of the American people. Both Democrats and Republicans approved Johnson's escalation in Vietnam, and so did public opinion polls in 1965 and 1966. But then opinion began to shift.

Every night, Americans saw on their television screens the carnage of war, including dead and wounded Americans. One such incident occurred in the first months of fighting in 1965. Television reporter Morley Safer witnessed a marine unit burning the village of Cam Ne to the ground. "Today's operation is the frustration of Vietnam in miniature," Safer explained. America can "win a military victory here, but to a Vietnamese peasant whose home is [destroyed] it will take more than presidential promises to convince him that we are on his side."

With such firsthand knowledge of the war, journalists began to write about a "credibility gap." The Johnson administration, they charged, was concealing bad news about the war's progress. In February 1966, television coverage of hearings by the Senate Foreign Relations Committee (chaired by J. William Fulbright, an outspoken critic of the war) raised further questions about the administration's policy. Johnson complained to his staff in 1966 that "our people can't stand firm in the face of heavy losses, and they can bring down the government." Economic problems put Johnson even more on the defensive. The Vietnam War cost taxpayers $27 billion in 1967, pushing the federal deficit from $9.8 billion to $23 billion. By then, military spending had set in motion the inflationary spiral that would plague the U.S. economy throughout the 1970s.

Out of these troubling developments, an antiwar movement began to crystallize. Its core, in addition to long-standing pacifist groups, comprised a new generation of peace activists such as SANE (the National Committee for a Sane Nuclear Policy), which in the 1950s had protested atmospheric nuclear testing. After the escalation in 1965, the activist groups were joined by student groups, clergy, civil rights advocates, even Dr. Benjamin Spock, whose book on child care had helped raise many of the students. Although they were a diverse lot, these opponents of the war shared a skepticism about U.S. policy in Vietnam. They charged variously that intervention was antithetical to American ideals; that an independent, anticommunist South Vietnam was unattainable; and that no American objective justified the suffering that was being inflicted on the Vietnamese people (see Voices from Abroad, "Che Guevara: Vietnam and the World Freedom Struggle," p. 896).

Rise of the Student Movement

College students, many of them inspired by the civil rights movement, helped lead the antiwar movement. In Ann Arbor, Michigan, they founded Students for a Democratic Society (SDS) in 1960. Two years later, forty students from Big Ten and Ivy League universities held the first national SDS convention in Port Huron, Michigan. Tom Hayden penned a manifesto, the Port Huron Statement, expressing students' disillusionment with the nation's consumer culture and the gulf between rich and poor. "We are people of this generation," Hayden wrote, "bred in at least modest comfort, housed now in universities, looking uncomfortably to the world we inherit." These students rejected Cold War foreign policy, including but not limited to the Vietnam conflict.

The New Left | The founders of SDS referred to their movement as the New Left to distinguish themselves from the Old Left—Communists and Socialists of the 1930s and 1940s. As New Left influence spread, it hit major university towns first—places such as Ann Arbor, Michigan; Madison, Wisconsin; and Berkeley, California. One of the first major demonstrations erupted in the fall of 1964 at the University of California at Berkeley after administrators banned student political activity on university property. In protest,

Free Speech at Berkeley, 1964

Students at the University of California's Berkeley campus protested the administration's decision to ban political activity in the school plaza. Free speech demonstrators, many of them active in the civil rights movement, relied on the tactics and arguments that they learned during that struggle. University of California at Berkeley, Bancroft Library.

student organizations formed the Free Speech Movement and organized a sit-in at the administration building. Some students had just returned from Freedom Summer in Mississippi, radicalized by their experience. Mario Savio spoke for many when he compared the conflict in Berkeley to the civil rights struggle in the South: "The same rights are at stake in both places—the right to participate as citizens in a democratic society and to struggle against the same enemy." Emboldened by the Berkeley movement, students across the nation were soon protesting their universities' academic policies and then, more passionately, the Vietnam War.

One spur to student protest was the military's Selective Service System, which in 1967 abolished automatic student deferments. To avoid the draft, some young men enlisted in the National Guard or applied for conscientious objector status; others dodged the draft by leaving the country, most often for Canada or Sweden. In public demonstrations, opponents of the war burned their draft cards, picketed induction centers, and on a few occasions broke into Selective Service offices and destroyed records. Antiwar demonstrators numbered in the tens or, at most, hundreds of thousands—a small fraction of American youth—but they were vocal, visible, and determined.

Che Guevara
Vietnam and the World Freedom Struggle

Ernesto "Che" Guevara was a middle-class, medically trained Argentinian who enlisted in Castro's Cuban Revolution and became a world icon of guerrilla resistance. In 1965, he left Cuba in order to foment revolutionary struggle in Africa and Latin America. Two years later, he was captured in Bolivia and executed. Between his departure from Cuba and his death in Bolivia in 1967, he made only one public statement, which he titled "Vietnam and the World Freedom Struggle."

This is the painful reality: Vietnam, a nation representing the aspirations and the hopes for victory of the entire world of the disinherited, is tragically alone. . . .

And—what grandeur has been shown by this people! What stoicism and valor in this people! And what a lesson for the world their struggle holds!

It will be a long time before we know if President Johnson ever seriously thought of initiating some of the popular reforms necessary to soften the sharpness of the class contradictions that are appearing with explosive force and more and more frequently.

What is certain is that the improvements announced under the pompous label of the Great Society have gone down the drain in Vietnam.

The greatest of the imperialist powers feels in its own heart the drain caused by a poor, backward country; and its fabulous economy feels the effect of the war. . . .

And for us, the exploited of the world, what should our role be in this? . . .

Our part, the responsibility of the exploited and backward areas of the world, is to eliminate the bases sustaining imperialism—our oppressed peoples, from whom capital, raw materials, technicians and cheap labor are extracted, and to whom new capital, means of domination, arms and all kinds of goods are exported, submerging us in absolute dependence.

The fundamental element of this strategic goal will be, then, the real liberation of the peoples, a liberation that will be obtained through armed struggle in the majority of cases, and which, in the Americas, will have almost unfailingly the property of becoming converted into a socialist revolution.

In focusing on the destruction of imperialism, it is necessary to identify its head, which is none other than the United States of North America. . . .

The adversary must not be underestimated; the North American soldier has technical ability and is backed by means of such magnitude as to make him formidable. He lacks the essential ideological motivation which his most

hated rivals of today have to the highest degree—the Vietnamese soldiers. . . .

Over there, the imperialist troops encounter the discomforts of those accustomed to the standard of living which the North American nation boasts. They have to confront a hostile land, the insecurity of those who cannot move without feeling that they are walking on enemy territory; death for those who go outside of fortified redoubts; the permanent hostility of the entire population.

All this continues to provoke repercussions inside the United States; it is going to arouse a factor that was attenuated in the days of the full vigor of imperialism—the class struggle inside its own territory.

Source: Ernesto Guevara, *Che Guevara Speaks* (New York: Pathfinder Press, 1967), 144–159.

ANALYZING THE EVIDENCE

- Guevara was a Latin American. He had never been to Southeast Asia. Why was he interested in Vietnam?
- How does Guevara define the struggle going on in Vietnam?
- How does he describe the two warring sides? Can you see, on the basis of those descriptions, why Guevara was confident the United States couldn't win the Vietnam War?
- Why would Guevara have bothered to speak about Johnson's Great Society program?
- Can you explain, based on this document, why Guevara was an inspirational figure to many student antiwar protesters?

Students were on the front lines as the campaign against the war escalated. The 1967 Mobilization to End the War brought 100,000 protesters into the streets of San Francisco, while more than a quarter million followed Martin Luther King Jr. from Central Park to the United Nations in New York. Another 100,000 marched on the Pentagon. President Johnson absorbed the blows and counterpunched—"The enemy's hope for victory . . . is in our division, our weariness, our uncertainty," he proclaimed—but it had become clear that Johnson's war, as many began calling it, was no longer uniting the country.

Young Americans for Freedom The New Left was not the only political force on college campuses. Conservative students were less noisy but more numerous. For them, the 1960s was not about protesting the war, staging student strikes, and idolizing Black Power. Inspired by the group Young Americans for Freedom (YAF), conservative students asserted their faith in "God-given free will" and their fear that the federal government "accumulates power which tends to diminish order and liberty." The YAF, the largest student political organization in the country, defended free enterprise and supported the war in Vietnam. Its founding principles were outlined in "The Sharon Statement," drafted (in Sharon, Connecticut) two years before the SDS was formed, and inspired young conservatives who would play important roles in the Reagan administration in the 1980s.

The Counterculture While the New Left organized against the political and economic system and the YAF defended it, many other young Americans embarked on a general revolt against authority and middle-class respectabil-ity. The "hippie"—identified by ragged blue jeans or army fatigues, tie-dyed T-shirts, beads, and long unkempt hair—symbolized the new counterculture. With roots in the 1950s Beat culture of New York's Greenwich Village and San Francisco's North Beach, the 1960s counterculture initially turned to folk music for its inspiration. Pete Seeger set the tone for the era's idealism with songs such as the 1961 antiwar ballad "Where Have All the Flowers Gone?" In 1963, the year of the civil rights demonstrations in Birmingham and President Kennedy's assassination, Bob Dylan's "Blowin' in the Wind" reflected the impatience of people whose faith in America was wearing thin. Joan Baez emerged alongside Dylan and pioneered a folk sound that inspired a generation of female musicians.

By the mid-1960s, other winds of change in popular music came from the Beatles, four working-class Brits whose awe-inspiring music—by turns lyrical and driving—spawned a commercial and cultural phenomenon known as Beatlemania. American youths' embrace of the Beatles—as well as even more rebellious bands such as the Rolling Stones, the Who, and the Doors—deepened the generational divide between young people and their elders. So did the recreational use of drugs—especially marijuana and the hallucinogen popularly known as LSD or acid—which was celebrated in popular music.

For a brief time, adherents of the counterculture believed that a new age was dawning. In 1967, the "world's first Human Be-In" drew 20,000 people to Golden Gate Park in San Francisco. That summer—called the Summer of Love—San Francisco's Haight-Ashbury, New York's East Village, and Chicago's Uptown neighborhoods swelled with young dropouts, drifters, and teenage runaways whom the media dubbed "flower children." Although most young people had little interest

Jimi Hendrix at Woodstock

The three-day outdoor Woodstock concert in August 1969 was a defining moment in the rise of the counterculture. The event attracted 400,000 young people to Bethel, New York, for a weekend of music, drugs, and sex. Jimi Hendrix closed the show early Sunday morning with an electrified version of "The Star-Spangled Banner." More overtly political than most counterculture music, Hendrix's solo guitar rendition featured sound effects that seemed to evoke the violence of the Vietnam War. Michael Wadleigh, who directed the 1970 documentary *Woodstock*, called Hendrix's performance "his challenge to American foreign policy." Allan Koss/The Image Works.

in all-out revolt, media coverage made it seem as though all of American youth was rejecting the nation's social and cultural norms.

- What difficulties did the United States face in fighting a war against North Vietnam and the Vietcong in South Vietnam?

- Why did President Johnson suffer a "credibility gap" over Vietnam?

- Contrast the positions taken by SDS, the YAF, and the counterculture. How can we account for the differences?

Days of Rage, 1968–1972

By 1968, a sense of crisis gripped the country. Riots in the cities, campus unrest, and a nose-thumbing counterculture escalated into a general youth rebellion that seemed on the verge of tearing America apart. Calling 1968 "the watershed year for a generation," SDS founder Tom Hayden wrote that it "started with legendary events, then raised hopes, only to end by immersing innocence in tragedy." It was perhaps the most shocking year in the postwar decades. Violent clashes both in Vietnam and back home in the United States combined with political assassinations to produce a palpable sense of despair and hopelessness.

Blood in the Streets

President Johnson had gambled in 1965 on a quick victory in Vietnam, before the political cost of escalation came due. But there was no quick victory. North Vietnamese and Vietcong forces fought on, the South Vietnamese government repeatedly collapsed, and American casualties mounted. By early 1968, the death rate of U.S. troops had reached several hundred a week. Johnson and his generals kept insisting that there was "light at the end of the tunnel." Facts on the ground showed otherwise.

The Tet Offensive On January 30, 1968, the Vietcong unleashed a massive, well-coordinated assault in South Vietnam. Timed to coincide with Tet, the Vietnamese new year, the offensive struck thirty-six provincial capitals and five of the six major cities, including Saigon, where the Vietcong nearly overran the U.S. embassy. In strictly military terms, the Tet offensive was a failure, with very heavy Vietcong losses.

But psychologically, the effect was devastating. Television brought into American homes shocking live images: the American embassy under siege, and the Saigon police chief placing a pistol to the head of a Vietcong suspect and executing him.

The Tet offensive made a mockery of official pronouncements that the United States was winning the war. How could an enemy on the run manage such a large-scale, complex, and coordinated attack? Just before Tet, a Gallup poll found that 56 percent of Americans considered themselves "hawks" (supporters of the war), while only 28 percent identified with the "doves" (war opponents). Three months later, doves outnumbered hawks 42 to 41 percent. Without embracing the peace movement, many Americans simply concluded that the war was unwinnable. The Tet offensive undermined Johnson and discredited his war policies. When the 1968 presidential primary season got under way in March, antiwar senators Eugene McCarthy of Minnesota and Robert Kennedy of New York, JFK's brother, challenged Johnson for the Democratic nomination. Discouraged, perhaps even physically exhausted, on March 31 Johnson stunned the nation by announcing that he would not seek reelection.

Political Assassinations Americans had barely adjusted to the news that a sitting president would not stand for reelection when, on April 4, James Earl Ray's bullet felled Martin Luther King Jr. in Memphis. Riots erupted in more than a hundred cities. The worst of them, in Baltimore, Chicago, and Washington, D.C., left dozens dead and hundreds of millions of dollars in property damaged or destroyed. The violence on the streets of Saigon had found an eerie parallel on the streets of the United States.

One city that did not erupt was Indianapolis. There, Robert Kennedy, in town campaigning in the Indiana primary, gave a quiet, somber speech to the black community on the night of King's assassination. Americans could continue to move toward "greater polarization," Kennedy said, "black people amongst blacks, white amongst whites," or "we can replace that violence . . . with an effort to understand, compassion and love." Kennedy sympathized with African Americans' outrage at whites, but he begged them not to strike back in retribution. Impromptu and heartfelt, Kennedy's speech was a plea to follow King's nonviolent example, even as the nation descended into greater violence.

But two months later, having emerged as the frontrunner for the Democratic nomination, Kennedy, too, would be gone. On June 5, as he was celebrating his vic-

Robert Kennedy
After the assassination of Martin Luther King Jr. and with President Johnson out of the presidential race, Robert Kennedy emerged in 1968 as the leading liberal figure in the nation. A critic of the Vietnam War, a strong supporter of civil rights, and committed to fighting poverty, Kennedy (the brother of the late President John Kennedy) ran a progressive campaign for president. In this photograph he is shown shaking hands with supporters in Detroit in May 1968. However, less than three weeks after this picture was taken, Kennedy, too, was dead, the victim of yet another assassination.
Andrew Sacks/Getty Images.

tory in the California primary over Eugene McCarthy, Kennedy was shot dead by a young Palestinian named Sirhan Sirhan. Amid the national mourning for yet another political murder, one newspaper columnist declared that "the country does not work anymore." *Newsweek* asked, "Has violence become a way of life?" Kennedy's assassination was a calamity for the Democratic Party because only he had seemed able to surmount the party's fissures over Vietnam. In the space of eight weeks, American liberals had lost two of their most important national figures, King and Kennedy. A third, Johnson, was unpopular and politically damaged. Without these unifying leaders, the crisis of liberalism had become unmanageable.

The Antiwar Movement and the 1968 Election

Before their deaths, Martin Luther King Jr. and Robert Kennedy had spoken eloquently against the Vietnam War. To antiwar activists, however, bold speeches and marches had not produced the desired effect. "We are no longer interested in merely protesting the war," declared one. "We are out to stop it." They sought nothing short of an immediate American withdrawal. Their anger at Johnson and the Democratic Party—fueled

by news of the Tet offensive, the murders of King and Kennedy, and the general youth rebellion—had radicalized the movement.

Democratic Convention In August, at the Democratic National Convention in Chicago, the political divisions generated by the war consumed the party. Thousands of protesters descended on the city. The most visible group, led by Jerry Rubin and Abbie Hoffman, a remarkable pair of troublemakers, claimed to represent the Youth International Party. To mock those inside the convention hall, these "Yippies" nominated a pig, Pigasus, for president. Their stunts were geared toward maximum media exposure, but a far more numerous and serious group of activists had come to Chicago to demonstrate against the war—they staged what many came to call the Siege of Chicago.

Democratic mayor Richard J. Daley ordered the police to break up the demonstrations. Several nights of skirmishes between protesters and police culminated on the evening of the nominations. In what an official report later described as a "police riot," police officers attacked protesters with tear gas and clubs. As the nominating speeches proceeded, television networks broadcast scenes of the riot, cementing a popular impression of the Democrats as the party of disorder. "They are going to be spending the next four years picking up the pieces," one Republican said gleefully. Inside the hall, the party dispiritedly nominated Hubert H. Humphrey, Johnson's vice president. The delegates approved a middle-of-the-road platform that endorsed continued fighting in Vietnam while urging a diplomatic solution to the conflict.

Richard Nixon | On the Republican side, Richard Nixon had engineered a remarkable political comeback. After losing the presidential campaign in 1960 and the California gubernatorial race in 1962, he won the Republican presidential nomination in 1968. Sensing Democratic weakness, Nixon and his advisors believed there were two groups of voters ready to switch sides: northern working-class voters and southern whites.

Tired of the antiwar movement, the counterculture, and urban riots, northern blue-collar voters, especially Catholics, had drifted away from the Democratic Party. Growing up in the Great Depression, these families were admirers of FDR and perhaps even had his picture on their living-room wall. But times had changed over three decades. To show how much they had changed, the social scientists Ben J. Wattenberg and Richard Scammon profiled blue-collar workers in their study *The Real Majority* (1970). Consider, Wattenberg and Scammon asked their readers, a forty-seven-year-old machinist's wife from Dayton, Ohio: "[She] is afraid to walk the streets alone at night . . . She has a mixed view about blacks and civil rights." Moreover, they wrote, "she is deeply distressed that her son is going to a community junior college where LSD was found on campus." Such northern blue-collar families were once reliable Democratic voters, but their political loyalties were increasingly up for grabs—a fact Republicans knew well.

George Wallace | Working-class anxieties over student protests and urban riots were first exploited by the outlandish governor of Alabama, George C. Wallace. Running in 1968 as a third-party presidential candidate, Wallace traded on his fame as a segregationist governor. He had tried to stop the federal government from desegregating the University of Alabama in 1963, and he was equally obstructive during the Selma crisis of 1965. Appealing to whites in both the North and the South, Wallace called for "law and order" and claimed that mothers on public assistance were, thanks to Johnson's Great Society, "breeding children as a cash crop."

Wallace's hope was that by carrying the South, he could deny a major candidate an electoral majority and force the election into the House of Representatives. That strategy failed, as Wallace finished with just 13.5 percent of the popular vote. But he had defined hot-button issues—liberal elitism, welfare policies, and law and order—that became hallmarks among the next generation of mainstream conservatives.

George Wallace

George Wallace had become famous as the segregationist governor who stood "in the schoolhouse door" to prevent black students from enrolling at the University of Alabama in 1963 (though after being confronted by federal marshals, he stepped aside). In 1968, he campaigned for the Democratic presidential nomination on a populist "law and order" platform that appealed to many blue-collar voters concerned about antiwar protests, urban riots, and the rise of the counterculture. In this 1968 photograph, Wallace greets supporters on the campaign trail. Lee Balterman/Time Life Pictures/Getty Images.

The Southern Strategy Nixon offered a subtler version of Wallace's populism. He adopted what his advisers called the "southern strategy," which aimed at attracting southern white voters still smarting over the civil rights gains by blacks. Nixon won over the key southerner, Democrat-turned-Republican senator Strom Thurmond of South Carolina, the 1948 Dixiecrat presidential nominee. Nixon informed Thurmond that while formally he had to support civil rights, his administration would go easy on enforcement. He also campaigned against the antiwar movement. He pledged to represent the "quiet voice" of the "great majority of Americans, the forgotten Americans, the nonshouters, the nondemonstrators."

These strategies worked. Nixon received 43.4 percent of the vote to Humphrey's 42.7 percent, defeating him by a scant 500,000 votes out of the 73 million that were cast (Map 28.3). But the numerical closeness of the race could not disguise the devastating blow to the Democrats. Humphrey received almost 12 million fewer votes than had Johnson in 1964. The white South largely abandoned the Democratic Party, an exodus that would accelerate in the 1970s. In the North, Nixon and Wallace made significant inroads among traditionally Democratic voters. New Deal Democrats lost the unity of purpose that had served them for thirty years. A nation exhausted by months of turmoil and violence had chosen a new direction. Nixon's victory in 1968 foreshadowed—and helped propel—a national electoral realignment in the coming decade.

The Nationalist Turn

Vietnam and the increasingly radical youth rebellion intersected with the turn toward nationalism by young African American and Chicano activists. As we saw in Chapter 27, the Black Power and Chicano movements broke with the liberal "rights" politics of an older generation of leaders. These new activists expressed fury at the poverty and white racism that were beyond the reach of civil rights laws; they also saw Vietnam as an unjust war against other people of color.

In this spirit, the Chicano Moratorium Committee organized demonstrations against the war. Chanting "Viva la Raza, Afuera Vietnam" ("Long live the Chicano people, Get out of Vietnam!"), 20,000 Mexican Americans marched in Los Angeles in August of 1970. At another rally, Cesar Chavez said: "For the poor it is a terrible irony that they should rise out of their misery to do battle against other poor people." He and other Mexican American activists charged that the draft was biased against the poor—like most wars in history, Vietnam was, in the words of one retired army colonel, "a poor boy's fight."

Among African Americans, the Black Panther Party and the National Black Antiwar Antidraft League spoke out against the war. "Black Americans are considered to be the world's biggest fools," Eldridge Cleaver of the Black Panther Party wrote in his typically acerbic style, "to go to another country to fight for something they don't have for themselves." Muhammad Ali, the most famous boxer in the world, refused to be inducted in the army. Sentenced to prison, Ali was eventually acquitted on appeal. But his action cost him his heavyweight title, and for years he was not allowed to box in the United States.

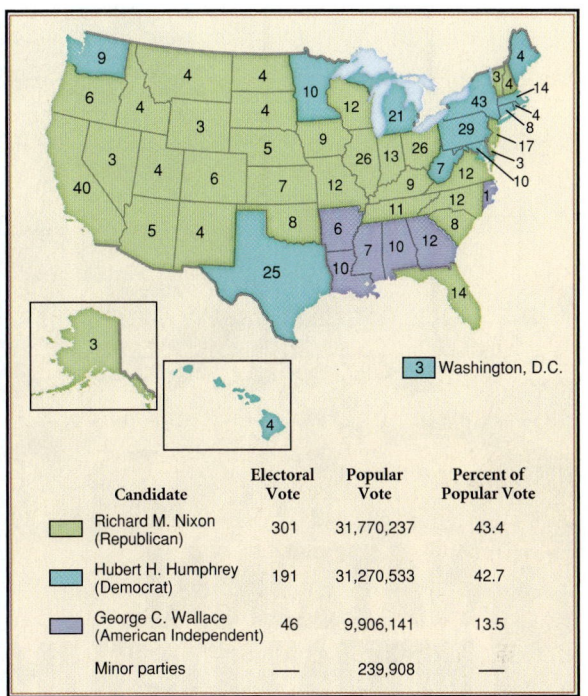

Candidate	Electoral Vote	Popular Vote	Percent of Popular Vote
Richard M. Nixon (Republican)	301	31,770,237	43.4
Hubert H. Humphrey (Democrat)	191	31,270,533	42.7
George C. Wallace (American Independent)	46	9,906,141	13.5
Minor parties	—	239,908	

MAP 28.3

The Presidential Election of 1968

With Lyndon B. Johnson's surprise withdrawal and the assassination of the party's most charismatic contender, Robert Kennedy, the Democrats faced the election of 1968 in disarray. Governor George Wallace of Alabama, who left the Democrats to run as a third-party candidate, campaigned on the backlash against the civil rights movement. As late as mid-September Wallace held the support of 21 percent of the voters. But in November he received only 13.5 percent of the vote, winning five southern states. Republican Richard M. Nixon, who like Wallace emphasized "law and order" in his campaign, defeated Hubert H. Humphrey with only 43.4 percent of the popular vote, but it was now clear, given that Wallace's southern support would otherwise have gone to Nixon, that the South had shifted decisively to the Republican side.

Chicano Moratorium

Between 1969 and 1970, Mexican American activists—who increasingly used the term *Chicano* to describe themselves—held a series of antiwar rallies in California. Known as the Chicano Moratorium
(meaning a moratorium on war), the protests were galvanizing events in the emergence of the Chicano
movement. On August 29, 1970, when 30,000 people marched in East Los Angeles, confrontations
with the police led to violence—four marchers were killed, including the journalist Ruben Salazar.
Los Angeles Public Library.

Women's Liberation

Among women, 1968 also marked a break with the
past. The late 1960s spawned a new brand of feminism:
women's liberation. These feminists were primarily
younger, college-educated women fresh from the New
Left, antiwar, and civil rights movements. Those movements' male leaders, they discovered, considered women
little more than pretty helpers who typed memos and
fetched coffee. Women who tried to raise feminist issues at civil rights and antiwar events were shouted off
the platform with jeers such as "Move on, little girl, we
have more important issues to talk about here than
women's liberation."

Fed up with second-class status, and well versed in
the tactics of organization and protest, women radicals
broke away and organized on their own. Unlike the Na-

tional Organization for Women (NOW), the women's
liberation movement was loosely structured, comprising an alliance of collectives in New York, San Francisco, Boston, and other big cities and college towns.
"Women's lib," as it was dubbed by a skeptical media,
went public in 1968 at the Miss America pageant. Demonstrators carried posters of women's bodies labeled
as slabs of beef—implying that society treated them
as meat. Mirroring the identity politics of Black Power
activists and the self-dramatization of the coun+cul-
ture, women's liberation sought an end to the denigra-
tion and exploitation of women (see Reading American
Pictures, "American Women: Images and Identities in
the Era of the Women's Movement," p. 904). "Sisterhood
is powerful!" read one women's liberationist manifesto. The national Women's Strike for Equality in August 1970 brought hundreds of thousands of women

Muhammad Ali Refuses Army Induction

On April 28, 1967, heavyweight champion boxer Muhammad Ali refused to be drafted into the U.S. Army, claiming that the war in Vietnam was immoral and that as a member of the Nation of Islam he was a conscientious objector. In this photograph, Ali stands outside the U.S. Army induction center in Houston, Texas. Ali's refusal, which was applauded by the antiwar movement, led to a five-year prison sentence. Though that conviction was overturned in 1971 after numerous appeals, Ali's stand against the war cost him his heavyweight boxing title. © Bettmann/Corbis.

into the streets of the nation's cities for marches and demonstrations.

By that year, new terms such as *sexism* and *male chauvinism* had become part of the national vocabulary. As converts flooded in, the two branches of the women's movement began to converge. Radical women realized that key feminist goals—child care, equal pay, and reproduction rights—could best be achieved in the political arena. At the same time, more traditional activists, exemplified by Betty Friedan, developed a broader view of women's oppression. They came to understand

that women required more than equal opportunity: The culture that regarded women as nothing more than sexual objects and helpmates to men had to change as well. Although still largely white and middle class, feminists began to think of themselves as part of a broad social crusade.

"Sisterhood" did not unite all women, however. Rather than joining white-led women's liberation organizations, African American and Latina women continued to work within the larger framework of the civil rights movement. New groups such as the Combahee

Women's Liberation

Arguing that beauty contests were degrading to women, members of the National Women's Liberation Party staged a protest against the Miss America pageant held in Atlantic City, New Jersey, in September 1968. AP Images.

American Women: Images and Identities in the Era of the Women's Movement

Women have long confronted powerful stereotypes about how they should dress and appear in public. In particular, what one historian has called the "beauty myth" created expectations in the early and middle decades of the twentieth century that women conform to a certain image of their bodies, of their clothing, of their looks and behavior — to appeal to men. In the 1960s and 1970s, however, women's liberationists challenged these expectations and criticized their effect on women's *own* self-conception. On the left is a photograph of a fashionably dressed woman in a typical 1960s-style miniskirt. On the right is a photo of a woman taken in 1968 at the Drop City "hippie" commune in New Mexico, one of the first rural communes in the United States, which had been founded in Colorado in 1965.

Woman in a shop doorway. © / Heritage-Images/The Image Works.

"Drop City" Hippie commune. 1968 New Mexico. © Eve Arnold/Magnum Photos.

ANALYZING THE EVIDENCE

- In what ways would you describe the woman on the left as dressed in a "typically" feminine way? What assumptions about femininity underlie your observations?

- How would you describe the appearance of the woman on the right? Is her appearance "feminine"? "Masculine"? Think less about your own expectations than about the expectations of men and women in the 1960s.

- Why would the appearance of the woman on the right represent a challenge to 1960s gender norms? Would the same be true of a similarly dressed woman today?

U.S. Women's Lightweight Crew

Crew was one of those muscle sports from which college women had traditionally been excluded until Title IX came along and opened the sport to women. Some of the best of that first generation of college rowers ended up on the U.S. women's team competing in the Royal Canadian Henley Regatta in 1982, shown at left.   Private collection.

River Collective and the National Black Feminist Organization arose to speak for the concerns of African American women. They criticized sexism but were reluctant to break completely with black men and the struggle for racial equality. Chicana feminists came from Catholic backgrounds in which motherhood and family were held in high regard. "We want to walk hand in hand with the Chicano brothers, with our children, our *viejitos* [elders], our Familia de la Raza," one Chicana feminist wrote. Black and Chicana feminists embraced the larger movement for women's rights but carried on their own struggles to address specific needs in their communities.

One of the most important contributions of women's liberation was to raise awareness about what feminist Kate Millett called "sexual politics." Liberationists argued that unless women had control over their own bodies, they could not freely shape their destinies. They campaigned for reproductive rights, especially access to abortion, and railed against a culture that blamed women in cases of sexual assault and turned a blind eye to sexual harassment in the workplace.

Meanwhile, women's opportunities expanded dramatically in higher education. Dozens of formerly all-male bastions such as Yale, Princeton, and the U.S. military academies admitted women undergraduates for the first time. Hundreds of colleges started women's studies programs, and the proportion of women attending graduate and professional schools rose markedly. With the adoption of Title IX in 1972, Congress broadened the 1964 Civil Rights Act to include educational

institutions, prohibiting colleges and universities that received federal funds from discriminating on the basis of sex. By requiring comparable funding for sports programs, Title IX made women's athletics a real presence on college campuses.

Women also became increasingly visible in public life. Congresswomen Bella Abzug and Shirley Chisholm joined Betty Friedan and Gloria Steinem, the founder of *Ms.* magazine, to create the National Women's Political Caucus in 1971. Abzug and Chisholm, both from New York, joined Congresswomen Patsy Mink from Hawaii and Martha Griffiths from Michigan to sponsor equal rights legislation. Congress authorized child-care tax deductions for working parents in 1972 and in 1974 passed the Equal Credit Opportunity Act, which enabled married women to get credit, including credit cards and mortgages, in their own names.

Antiwar activists, black and Chicano nationalists, and women's liberationists had each challenged the Cold War liberalism of the Democratic Party. In doing so, they helped build on the "rights liberalism" forged first by the African American–led civil rights movement. But they also created rifts among competing parts of the former liberal consensus. Many Catholics, for instance, opposed abortion rights and other freedoms sought by women's liberationists. "Traditional Catholics simply do not accept that abortion is a simple matter to be left between a woman and her doctor," one Texas priest explained. Still other Democrats, many of them blue-collar trade unionists, believed that antiwar protesters were unpatriotic and that supporting one's government in time of war was a citizen's duty. The antiwar movement and the evolving rights liberalism of the sixties had made the old Democratic coalition increasingly unworkable. Women's liberationists introduced the new term *sexual politics* to the protest movements of the late 1960s.

Stonewall and Gay Liberation

The liberationist impulse transformed the gay rights movement as well. Homophile activists in the 1960s (see Chapter 26) had pursued rights by protesting, but they adopted the respectable dress and behavior they knew straight society demanded. Meanwhile, the vast majority of gay men and lesbians remained "in the closet." So many were closeted because homosexuality was illegal in the vast majority of states — sodomy statutes outlawed same-sex relations, and police used other morals laws to harass and arrest gay men and lesbians. In the late 1960s, however, inspired by the Black Power and women's movements, gay activists increasingly demanded immediate and unconditional recognition of their rights. A gay newspaper in New York bore the title *Come Out!*

The new gay liberation found multiple expressions in major cities across the country, but a defining event occurred in New York's Greenwich Village. Police had raided gay bars for decades, making arrests, publicizing the names of patrons, and harassing customers simply for being gay. When a local gay bar called the Stonewall Inn was raided by police in the summer of 1969, however, its patrons — including gay men, lesbians, transvestites, and transsexuals — rioted for two days, burning the bar and battling with police in the narrow streets of the Village. Decades of repression by police had taken their toll. Few commentators excused the violence, and the Stonewall riots were not repeated, but activists celebrated them as a symbolic demand for full citizenship. The gay liberation movement grew quickly after Stonewall. Local gay and lesbian organizations proliferated, and activists began pushing for nondiscrimination ordinances and consensual sex laws at the state level. By 1975, the National Gay Task Force and other national organizations lobbied Congress, served as media watchdogs, and advanced suits in the courts. Despite all the activity, progress was slow; in most arenas of American life, gays and lesbians did not enjoy the same legal protections and rights as other Americans.

- In what ways did 1968 represent a turning point in postwar history? In what ways did it represent a continuation of the status quo?

- How did Black Power, Chicano, women's liberation, and gay liberation groups break with earlier liberal politics?

Richard Nixon and the Politics of the Silent Majority

Lyndon Johnson and the Democratic Party proved ill equipped to navigate Vietnam abroad and the antiwar movement and the counterculture at home. Richard Nixon, in contrast, showed himself to be an effective manipulator of the nation's unrest through carefully timed speeches and strategic displays of moral outrage. A centrist by nature and temperament, Nixon was not part of the conservative Goldwater wing of the Republican Party. Although his presidency ultimately ended ignobly, he laid the groundwork for the conservative resurgence of the 1980s.

In late 1969, following a massive antiwar rally in Washington, President Nixon gave a televised speech in which he referred to his supporters as the "silent majority." It was classic Nixonian rhetoric. In a single phrase, he summed up a generational and cultural struggle, placing himself on the side of ordinary Americans against the rabble-rousers and troublemakers. It was an oversimplification, but the label *silent majority* stuck, and Nixon had defined a political phenomenon. For the remainder of his presidency, Nixon cultivated the impression that he was the defender of a reasonable middle ground under assault from the radical left.

Nixon's War in Vietnam

When it came to Vietnam, Nixon picked up where Johnson had left off. Abandoning Vietnam, Nixon insisted, would damage America's "credibility" and make the country seem "a pitiful, helpless giant." Nixon wanted peace, but only "peace with honor." The North Vietnamese were not about to oblige him. The only outcome acceptable to them was a unified Vietnam under their control.

Vietnamization and Cambodia To neutralize criticism at home, Nixon began delegating the ground fighting to the South Vietnamese. Under this new policy of "Vietnamization," American troop levels dropped from 543,000 in 1968 to 334,000 in 1971 to barely 24,000 by early 1973. American casualties dropped correspondingly. But the killing in Vietnam continued. As Ellsworth Bunker, the U.S. ambassador to Vietnam, noted cynically, it was just a matter of changing "the color of the bodies."

Richard Nixon
Richard Nixon completed one of the more remarkable political rehabilitations in modern times. He had lost the 1960 presidential election and the 1962 California gubernatorial election. But he came back strong in 1968 to ride—and help direct—a growing wave of reaction among conservative Americans against Great Society liberalism, the antiwar movement, civil rights, and the counterculture. In this photograph, President Nixon greets supporters in June 1969, just a few months after his inauguration. © Wally McNamee/CORBIS.

Far from abating, however, the antiwar movement intensified. In November 1969, half a million demonstrators staged a huge protest in Washington. On April 30, 1970, as part of a secret bombing campaign against Vietminh (Vietnamese liberation army) supply lines, American troops destroyed enemy bases in neutral Cambodia. When news of the invasion of Cambodia came out, American campuses exploded in outrage— and, for the first time, students died. On May 4, 1970, at Kent State University in Ohio, panicky National Guardsmen fired into an antiwar rally, wounding eleven students and killing four. At Jackson State College in Mississippi, Guardsmen stormed a dormitory, killing two black students. More than 450 colleges closed in protest. Across the country, the spring semester was essentially canceled.

My Lai Massacre | Meanwhile, one of the worst atrocities of the war had become public. In 1968, U.S. Army troops had executed nearly five hundred people in the South Vietnamese village of My

Lai, including a large number of women and children. The massacre was known only within the military until 1969, when journalist Seymour Hersh broke the story and photos of the massacre appeared in *Life* magazine, discrediting the United States around the world. Americans, *Time* observed, "must stand in the larger dock of guilt and human conscience." Despite the involvement of high-ranking officers in the My Lai massacre and its cover-up, only one soldier, a low-ranking enlisted man named William Calley, was convicted.

Believing that Calley had been made a fall guy for official U.S. policies that inevitably brought death to innocent civilians, a group called Vietnam Veterans Against the War publicized other atrocities committed by U.S. troops. In a controversial protest in 1971, they turned in their combat medals at demonstrations outside the U.S. Capitol. "Here's my merit badge for murder," one vet said. Supporters of the war called the veterans cowards and un-American, but their heartfelt protest exposed the deep personal torment that the war had caused many soldiers.

Pro-War Rally

Under a sea of American flags, construction workers in New York City march in support of the Vietnam War. Wearing hard hats, tens of thousands of marchers jammed Broadway for four blocks opposite City Hall, and the overflow crammed the side streets. Working-class patriotism became a main source of support for Nixon's war.   Paul Fusco/Magnum Photos, Inc.

Détente As protests continued at home, Nixon pursued two strategies to achieve his declared "peace with honor," one diplomatic and the other brutal. First, he sought détente (a lessening of tensions) with the Soviet Union and a new openness with China. In a series of meetings between 1970 and 1972, Nixon and Soviet premier Leonid Brezhnev resolved tensions over Cuba and Berlin and signed the first Strategic Arms Limitation Treaty (SALT I), the latter a symbolic step toward ending the Cold War arms race. Heavily influenced by his national security advisor, the Harvard professor Henry Kissinger, Nixon believed that he could break the Cold War impasse that had kept the United States from productive dialogue with the Soviet Union.

Then, in 1972, Nixon visited China, becoming the first sitting U.S. president to do so. In a televised week-

long trip, the president pledged better relations with China and declared that the two nations — one capitalist, the other Communist — could peacefully coexist. This was the man who had risen to prominence in the 1950s by railing against the Democrats for "losing" China and by hounding Communists and fellow travelers. The president's impeccable anticommunist credentials gave him the political cover to travel to Beijing. He remarked genially to Mao: "Those on the right can do what those on the left only talk about." Praised for his efforts to lessen Cold War tensions, Nixon also had tactical objectives in mind. He hoped that by befriending both the Soviet Union and China, he could play one against the other and strike a better deal over Vietnam at the ongoing peace talks in Paris. His second strategy, however, would prove less praiseworthy and cost more lives.

Exit America   In April 1972, in an attempt to strengthen his negotiating position, Nixon ordered B-52 bombing raids against North Vietnam. A month later, he approved the mining of North Vietnamese ports, something Johnson had never dared to do. The North Vietnamese were not isolated, however: Supplies from China and the Soviet Union continued, and the Vietcong fought on.

With the 1972 election approaching, Nixon sent Henry Kissinger back to the Paris peace talks, initiated under Johnson. In a key concession, Kissinger accepted the presence of North Vietnamese troops in South Vietnam. North Vietnam then agreed to an interim arrangement whereby the Saigon government would stay in power while a special commission arranged a final settlement. With Kissinger's announcement that "peace is at hand," Nixon got the election lift he wanted, but the agreement was then sabotaged by General Nguyen Van Thieu, the South Vietnamese president. So Nixon, in one final spasm of bloodletting, unleashed the two-week "Christmas bombing," the most savage of the entire war. On January 27, 1973, the two sides signed the Paris Peace Accords.

Nixon hoped that with massive U.S. aid, the Thieu regime might survive. But Congress was in revolt. It refused appropriations for bombing Cambodia after August 15, 1973, and gradually cut back aid to South Vietnam. In March 1975, North Vietnamese forces launched a final offensive, and on April 30, Vietnam was reunited. Saigon, the South Vietnamese capital, was renamed Ho Chi Minh City, after the founding father of the Communist regime.

The collapse of South Vietnam in 1975 embodied a powerful, and tragic, historical irony. The Paris Peace Accords produced an outcome little different from what would likely have resulted from the unification vote in 1954 (see Chapter 25). In other words, America's most disastrous military adventure of the twentieth century barely altered the geopolitical realities in Southeast Asia. The Hanoi regime called itself Communist but never

The Fall of Saigon

After the 1973 U.S. withdrawal from Vietnam, the South Vietnamese government lasted another two years. In March 1975, the North Vietnamese forces launched a final offensive; by April, they had surrounded the capital, Saigon. As seen here, many Vietnamese, some of them associated with the fallen South Vietnamese regime, sought sanctuary at the U.S. embassy compound. Thousands of Vietnamese and Americans were evacuated before the last helicopter left the embassy on April 30.   Nik Wheeler/Sipa Press/AP Images.

intended to be a satellite of any country, least of all China, Vietnam's ancient enemy.

Many paid a steep price for the Vietnam War. America's Vietnamese friends lost jobs and property, spent years in "reeducation" camps, or had to flee the country. Millions of Vietnamese had died in a decade of war, which included some of the most intensive aerial bombing of the twentieth century. In next-door Cambodia, the maniacal Khmer Rouge, followers of Cambodia's ruling Communist Party, took over and murdered 1.7 million people in bloody purges. And in the United States, more than 58,000 Americans had sacrificed their lives, and 300,000 had been wounded. On top of the war's $150 billion price tag, slow-to-heal internal wounds divided the country, and Americans increasingly lost confidence in their political leaders.

The 1972 Election

Political realignments have been infrequent in American history. One occurred between 1932 and 1936, when many Republicans, despairing over the Great Depression, had switched sides and voted for FDR. The years between 1968 and 1972 were another such pivotal moment. This time, it was Democrats who abandoned their party.

After the 1968 elections, the Democrats fell into disarray. Bent on sweeping away the party's old guard, reformers took over, adopting new rules that granted women, blacks, and young people delegate seats "in reasonable relation to their presence in the population." In the past, an alliance of urban machines, labor unions, and ethnic groups—the heart of the New Deal coalition—dominated the nominating process. But at the 1972 convention, few of the party faithful qualified as delegates under the changed rules. The crowning insult came when the convention rejected the credentials of Chicago mayor Richard Daley and his delegation, seating instead an Illinois delegation led by Jesse Jackson, a firebrand young black minister and former aide to Martin Luther King Jr.

Capturing the party was one thing; beating the Republicans was quite another. Party reforms opened the door for George McGovern, a left-liberal South Dakota senator and favorite of the antiwar and women's movements, to capture the nomination. But McGovern took a number of missteps, including failing to mollify key party backers such as the AFL-CIO, which, for the first time in memory, refused to endorse the Democratic ticket. A weak campaigner, McGovern was also no match for Nixon, who pulled out all the stops. Using the advantages of incumbency, Nixon gave the economy a well-timed lift and proclaimed (prematurely) a cease-fire in Vietnam. Nixon's appeal to the "silent majority"—people who "care about a strong United States, about patriotism, about moral and spiritual values"—was by now well honed. Court decisions mandating the busing of white students to desegregate public schools in major cities fueled resentment among white parents and thus gave Nixon another populist campaign issue.

Nixon won in a landslide, receiving nearly 61 percent of the popular vote and carrying every state except Massachusetts and the District of Columbia (Map 28.4). The returns revealed how fractured traditional Democratic voting blocs had become. McGovern received only 38 percent of the big-city Catholic vote and lost 42 percent of self-identified Democrats overall. The 1972 election marked a pivotal moment in the country's shift to the right. The full effect of that shift was delayed, however, by the president's soon-to-be-discovered self-inflicted wounds.

Watergate and the Fall of a President

On June 17, 1972, something strange happened at Washington's Watergate office/apartment/hotel complex. Early that morning, five men carrying wiretapping equipment were apprehended there while they were breaking into the headquarters of the Democratic National Committee (DNC). Queried by the press, a White House spokesman dismissed the episode as "a third-rate burglary attempt." Pressed further, Nixon himself denied any White House involvement in "this very bizarre incident." In fact, the two masterminds of the break-in, G. Gordon Liddy and E. Howard Hunt, were former FBI and CIA agents currently working for Nixon's Committee to Re-elect the President (CREEP).

The Watergate burglary was no isolated incident. It was part of a broad pattern of abuse of power by a White House obsessed with its enemies. Liddy and Hunt, CREEP operatives on the White House payroll, were part of a clandestine squad, known as the "plumbers," that Nixon had established to plug administration "leaks" and do other nasty jobs. The two plumbers were soon arranging illegal wiretaps at DNC headquarters, part of a campaign of "dirty tricks" against the Democrats. Nixon's siege mentality best explains his fatal misstep. He could have dissociated himself from the break-in by firing his guilty aides or even just by letting justice take its course. But it was election time, and Nixon did not trust his political future to such a strategy. Instead, he arranged hush money for the burglars and instructed the CIA to stop an FBI investigation into the affair. This was obstruction of justice, a criminal offense.

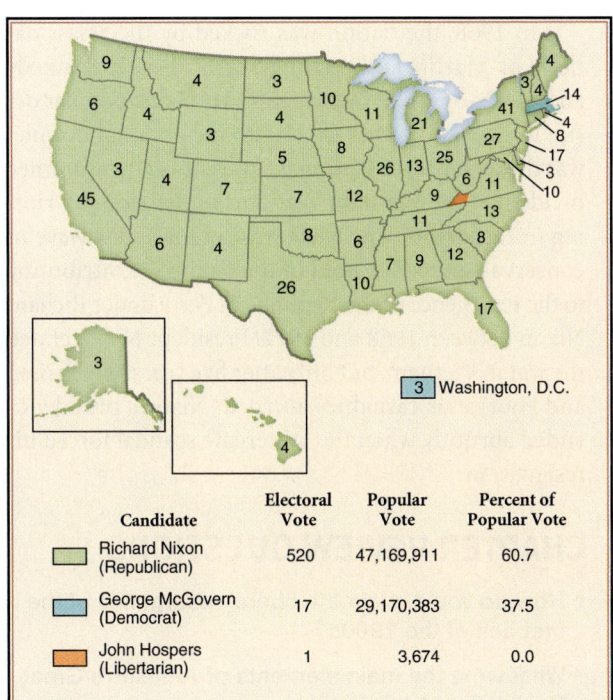

MAP 28.4

The Presidential Election of 1972

In one of the most lopsided presidential elections of the twentieth century, Republican Richard Nixon defeated Democrat George McGovern in a landslide in 1972. It was a reversal of the 1964 election, just eight years before, in which Republican Barry Goldwater had been defeated by a similar margin. Nixon hoped that his victory signaled what Kevin Phillips called "the emerging Republican majority," but the president's missteps and criminal actions in the Watergate scandal would soon bring an end to his tenure in office.

| 3 | Washington, D.C. |

Candidate	Electoral Vote	Popular Vote	Percent of Popular Vote
Richard Nixon (Republican)	520	47,169,911	60.7
George McGovern (Democrat)	17	29,170,383	37.5
John Hospers (Libertarian)	1	3,674	0.0

Nixon kept the lid on until after the election, but in early 1973, one of the Watergate burglars, the security chief for CREEP, began to talk. In the meantime, two reporters at the *Washington Post*, Carl Bernstein and Bob Woodward, uncovered CREEP's illegal slush fund and its links to key White House aides. In May 1973, a Senate investigating committee began holding nationally televised hearings, at which Assistant Secretary of Commerce Jeb Magruder confessed his guilt and implicated former attorney general John Mitchell, White House counsel John Dean, and others. Dean, in turn, implicated Nixon. Just as startling, a former White House aide revealed that Nixon had installed a secret taping system in the Oval Office.

Under enormous pressure, Nixon eventually released some of the tapes, but there was a highly suspicious eighteen-minute gap in one of them. Finally, on June 23, 1974, the Supreme Court ordered Nixon to release the unexpurgated tapes. Lawyers found in them incontrovertible evidence that the president had ordered the cover-up. By then, the House Judiciary Committee was already considering articles of impeachment. Certain of being convicted by the Senate, Nixon became, on August 9, 1974, the first U.S. president to resign his office. The next day, Vice President Gerald Ford was sworn in as president. Ford, the Republican minority leader in the House of Representatives, had replaced Vice President Spiro Agnew, who had himself resigned in 1973 for accepting kickbacks while governor of Maryland. A month after he took office, Ford stunned the nation by granting Nixon a "full, free, and absolute" pardon.

Congress pushed back, passing a raft of laws against the abuses of the Nixon administration: the War Powers Act (1973), which reined in the president's ability to deploy U.S. forces without congressional approval; amendments strengthening the Freedom of Information Act (1974), which gave citizens access to federal records; the Ethics in Government Act (1978); and the Foreign Intelligence Surveillance Act (1978), which prohibited domestic wiretapping without a warrant. However, it can be said that these measures curbed the growth of presidential powers, and of secret sectors of the federal government largely beyond public control, only in the short run.

- **How was President Nixon's Vietnam policy different from President Johnson's? What were the consequences—to Vietnam and to the United States—of the war lasting another four years under Nixon?**

- **What laws and values were at stake in the Watergate scandal? Were Nixon's actions the product of an "imperial presidency" as much as an individual president?**

SUMMARY

In this chapter, we saw how, under the combined pressures of the Vietnam War and racial and cultural conflict, the New Deal coalition fractured and split. Following John Kennedy's assassination in 1963, Lyndon Johnson advanced the most ambitious liberal reform program since the New Deal, securing not only civil rights legislation but also an array of programs in education, medical care, transportation, environmental protection, and, above all, his War on Poverty. But the Great Society fell short of its promise as Johnson escalated the American involvement in Vietnam.

The war bitterly divided Americans. Galvanized by the carnage of war and the draft, the antiwar movement spread rapidly among young people, and the spirit of rebellion spilled beyond the war. The New Left challenged the corporate dominance of society, while the more apolitical counterculture preached personal liberation through sex, drugs, music, and personal transformation. Women's liberationists broke from the New Left and raised a new set of concerns about society's sexism.

In 1968, the nation was rocked by the assassinations of Martin Luther King and Robert F. Kennedy and a wave of urban riots, fueling a growing popular desire for law and order. Adding to the national disquiet was the Democratic National Convention that summer, divided by the Vietnam War and under siege by rioting in the streets. The stage was set for a new wave of conservatism to take hold of the country, contributing to the resurgence of the Republican Party under Richard Nixon between 1968 and 1972. President Nixon ended the war in Vietnam, but only after five years had elapsed and enormous casualties accrued. Nixon's presidency ended abruptly when the Watergate scandal forced his resignation.

CHAPTER REVIEW QUESTIONS

- How do you explain the liberal resurgence of the first half of the 1960s?
- What were the main elements of Johnson's Great Society?
- Why is the Vietnam War so often called a quagmire?

FOR FURTHER EXPLORATION

A good starting point for understanding Lyndon Johnson is Robert Dallek, *Flawed Giant* (1998). On the Great Society, see G. Calvin Mackenzie and Robert Weisbrot, *The Liberal Hour: Washington and the Politics of Change in the 1960s* (2008). On Vietnam, the basic history is Marilyn Young, *The Vietnam Wars, 1945–1990* (1991). A terrific collection of analysis and documents is in Marvin E. Gettleman et al., eds., *Vietnam and America: A Documented History* (1995). A vivid account of dissent in the 1960s is Maurice Isserman and Michael Kazin, *America Divided: The Civil War of the 1960s* (1999). On the women's movement, see Ruth Rosen, *The World Split Open* (2000), and Kimberly Springer, *Living for the Revolution* (2005). *Takin' It to the Streets* (1995), edited by Alexander Bloom and Wini Breines, offers an array of documents that encompass the war, counterculture, civil rights, feminism, and gay liberation. Memoirs of Vietnam are numerous. Phillip Caputo's *A Rumor of War* (1977) and Ron Kovic's *Born on the Fourth of July* (1976) are powerful examples. On President Nixon and political realignment, see Bruce Schulman, *The Seventies* (2001), and for a fascinating look at Watergate, see Michael Schudson, *Watergate in American Memory* (1992). The John F. Kennedy Library and Museum's site at **www.jfklibrary.org** provides a large collection of records from Kennedy's presidency, including transcripts and recordings of JFK's speeches, a database of his executive orders, and a number of other resources. A useful Vietnam site that includes state papers and official correspondence from 1941 to the fall of Saigon in 1975 is at **www.mtholyoke.edu/acad/intrel/vietnam.htm**.

TEST YOUR KNOWLEDGE

To assess your command of the material in this chapter, see the Online Study Guide at **bedfordstmartins.com/henretta**.

For Web sites, images, and documents related to topics and places in this chapter, visit **bedfordstmartins.com/makehistory**.

TIMELINE

1963	John F. Kennedy assassinated; Lyndon B. Johnson assumes presidency
1964	Civil Rights Act
	Economic Opportunity Act inaugurates War on Poverty
	Free Speech Movement at Berkeley
	Gulf of Tonkin Resolution
1965	Immigration Act abolishes national quota system
	Voting Rights Act
	Medicare and Medicaid programs established
	Operation Rolling Thunder escalates bombing campaign (March)
	First U.S. combat troops arrive in Vietnam
1967	Hippie counterculture's "Summer of Love"
	100,000 march in antiwar protest in Washington, D.C. (October)
1968	Tet offensive begins (January)
	Martin Luther King Jr. and Robert F. Kennedy assassinated
	Women's liberation protest at Miss America pageant
	Riot at Democratic National Convention in Chicago (August)
	Richard Nixon elected president
1969	Stonewall riot (June)
1970	National Women's Strike for Equality
1972	Watergate break-in (June 17)
	Nixon wins a second term (November 7)
1973	Senate Watergate hearings
1974	Nixon resigns presidency (August 9)

PART

7

GLOBAL CAPITALISM AND THE END OF THE AMERICAN CENTURY, 1973-2011

For historians, the recent past can be a challenge to evaluate and assess. Insufficient time has passed for scholars to weigh the significance of events and to determine which developments will have a lasting effect and which are more fleeting. Nevertheless, the period between the early 1970s and our own day has begun to emerge in the minds of historians with some clarity. Scholars generally agree on the era's three most significant developments: the resurgence of political conservatism, the end of the Cold War, and the globalization of communications and the economy. What Henry Luce had named the "American Century"—in his call for the United States to assume global leadership in the decades after World War—came decisively to an end in the last quarter of the twentieth century and the first decade of the twenty-first. The United States lost its role as the world's dominant economy, faced rising competition from a united Europe and a surging China, and experienced a wide-ranging and divisive internal debate over its own values and priorities. Part 7 remains necessarily a work-in-progress, because events continue to unfold, but through equal parts conflict, struggle, and ingenuity, Americans collectively created a new era in national history after the 1960s.

POLITICS

Conservative agenda . . . shrinking the welfare state . . . and expanding the military

DIPLOMACY

Global struggle known as the Cold War came to a stunning halt

Conservative Ascendancy

The 1970s constituted a crucial transitional period between the aggressive liberalism of Lyndon Johnson's Great Society and the forthright conservatism of the Reagan era. Under Ronald Reagan, elected president in 1980, the conservative agenda combined reducing the regulatory power of the federal government, shrinking the welfare state created by liberal Democrats during the New Deal and Great Society, and expanding the military. Evangelical Christians and conservative lawmakers challenged abortion rights, feminism, and gay rights, and brought other social issues into the political arena, setting off controversies that sharply divided the American people and produced what many called a "culture war."

End of the Cold War and Rising Conflict in the Middle East

Between 1989 and 1991, the four-decade Cold War came to a stunning halt. The Soviet Union and its satellite communist regimes in Eastern Europe collapsed. The result was, in the words of President George H. W. Bush, a "new world order." Without a credible rival, the United States emerged in the 1990s as the lone military "superpower" in the world. In the absence of a clear Cold War enemy, the United States intervened in civil wars, worked to disrupt terrorist activities, and provided humanitarian aid—but on a case-by-case basis, guided more by pragmatism than principle. The foremost region that occupied U.S. attention was the Middle East, where strategic interest in oil supplies remained paramount. Between 1991 and 2011, U.S. armed forces fought three wars in the region—two in Iraq and one in Afghanistan—and became even more deeply embedded in its politics.

Global expansion of capitalism

Globalization and Increasing Social Inequality

The long post–World War II expansion of the American economy came to an end in the early 1970s. Deindustrialization eliminated much of the nation's manufacturing base. Wages stagnated. Inflation skyrocketed. In the 1980s and 1990s, however, productivity increased, military spending boosted production, and new industries—such as computer technology—emerged. These developments led to renewed economic growth for much of the last two decades of the twentieth century. More and more, though, the economy produced *services* rather than *goods*. Americans increasingly bought products manufactured overseas, in China, Southeast Asia, and Latin America. The end of the Cold War had made possible this global expansion of capitalism, as multinational corporations moved production to low-wage countries.

American society grew increasingly heterogeneous

Increasing Diversity and Culture Wars

American society grew increasingly heterogeneous in this era. Immigrants from Latin America, Asia, and Africa contributed to a new racial and national diversity—the impact of changes in immigration law made in 1965. In the wake of the civil rights and women's and gay rights movements, American workplaces and educational institutions grew more diverse. These changes did not come without controversy, however. Some Americans believed that what they considered traditional culture and the family were under assault. Even as it grew more diverse, American society became more economically unequal. Conservative tax policies, deindustrialization, the decline of unions, and globalization all contributed to a widening inequality between the wealthiest Americans and the middle class and poor.

Boosted economic productivity and . . . the globalization of commerce and trade

The Information and Digital Revolutions

Americans experienced radical changes in their day-to-day lives because of developments in science and technology. In just over three decades, computers, cell phones, satellite and cable television, and the Internet revolutionized everyday life. These dramatic changes boosted economic productivity in the United States and around the world and made the globalization of commerce and trade possible. With new technologies came new questions and challenges: Would the Internet facilitate the export of middle-class jobs? Would enhanced surveillance techniques allow the government to monitor the activities of ordinary people? Would cell phones and computers allow terrorist networks to organize complex operations? The new world of technology altered virtually every aspect of American life.

GLOBAL CAPITALISM AND THE END OF THE AMERICAN CENTURY, 1973–2011

	POLITICS	DIPLOMACY	ECONOMY	SOCIETY	TECHNOLOGY AND SCIENCE
1972	• Arab oil embargo (1973–1974) • Inflation surges, while economy stagnates (stagflation) • New York City nears bankruptcy (1975) • Chrysler bankruptcy averted by federal bailout (1979)	• Paris Peace Accords end Vietnam War (1973) • Camp David Accords between Egypt and Israel (1978) • Iranian Revolution (1979); hostage crisis (1979–1981)	• Endangered Species Act (1973) • Watergate scandal; Nixon resigns (1974) • Jimmy Carter elected president (1976) • Tax revolt in California (1978)	• *Roe v. Wade* (1973) • STOP ERA fights Equal Rights Amendment • *Bakke v. University of California* limits affirmative action (1978) • Harvey Milk assassinated (1978)	• Microsoft founded by Bill Gates and Paul Allen (1975) • Apple Computers founded (1976)
1980	• National debt begins to rise • Revival of military-industrial complex with military buildup • Recession (1981–1982) followed by strong growth (1982–1987)	• Reagan begins arms buildup • Intermediate Nuclear Forces Treaty (1988) • Berlin Wall comes down (1989)	• New Right helps elect Ronald Reagan president (1980) • Reagan tax cut (1981) • Reagan reduces government regulation • G. H. W. Bush elected president (1988)	• Rise in Latino and Asian immigration • AIDS epidemic begins (1981) • Renewed emphasis on material success and the "rich and famous" • *Webster v. Reproductive Health Services* (1989)	• Cable News Network (CNN) founded (1980) • Apple IIe personal computer introduced (1983) • Compact discs and cell phones invented
1990	• Recession (1990–1991) • Debt reduction and new technology spark economic growth and productivity rise • NAFTA ratified (1993)	• Persian Gulf War (1990) • USSR breaks apart; end of Cold War • Al Qaeda bombs World Trade Center (1993) • U.S. peacekeeping forces in Bosnia (1995)	• Bill Clinton elected (1992) • Republican resurgence (1994) • Welfare reform (1996) • Clinton impeached and acquitted (1998–1999)	• Pat Buchanan declares "cultural war" (1992) • Battles over homosexuality and abortion • Defense of Marriage Act (1998)	• Internet gains in popularity • Popularization of e-mail • Biotech revolution • Telecommunications Act deregulates media • Google founded (1998)
2000	• Bush tax cuts • China purchases increasing amounts of U.S. debt • Stock market and housing bubbles • Great Recession (2007–2010)	• Al Qaeda attacks World Trade Center and Pentagon (2001) • United States and allies oust Taliban from Afghanistan (2002) • U.S. invasion of Iraq (2004) • North Korea tests a nuclear weapon; stalemate with Iran over nuclear program	• George W. Bush narrowly elected president (2000) • USA Patriot Act (2002) • Barack Obama elected first African American president (2008) • Health care reform passed (2010) • Tea Party movement (2009–2010)	• More than a dozen states ban gay marriage • Baby boomer retirements begin; crisis forecast in Social Security • Unemployment exceeds 10 percent	• Broadband and wireless access grows • iPod introduced (2001) • Global warming becomes a scientific consensus

CHAPTER 29

The Search for Order in an Era of Limits, 1973-1980

Early in 1971, a new fictional character appeared on national television. Archie Bunker was a gruff blue-collar worker who berated his wife and bemoaned his daughter's marriage to a bearded hippie. Prone to bigoted and insensitive remarks, Archie and his wife Edith sang "Those Were the Days" at the opening of each episode of *All in the Family*, a half-hour situation comedy. The song celebrated a bygone era, when "girls were girls and men were men." Disdainful of the liberal social movements of the 1960s, Archie professed a conservative, hardscrabble view of the world.

Archie Bunker became a folk hero to many conservative Americans in the 1970s; he said what they felt. But his significance went beyond his politics. In its first three years on the air, *All in the Family* gave voice to a national search for order. Archie wrestled each week with a changing world. His feminist daughter, liberal-hippie son-in-law, and black neighbors brought that new world into Archie's modest home in Queens, New York. How would Archie, and by implication the viewer at home, make sense of the changing times? Not all Americans were as resistant to change as Archie. Most were ordinary, middle-of-the-road people confronting the aftermath of the tumultuous late 1960s and early 1970s. The liberal "rights revolution" of those years challenged Americans to think in new ways about race, gender roles, sexual morality, and the family. Vietnam and Watergate had compounded matters by producing a crisis of political authority. Something like an "old order" had seemingly collapsed. But what would take its place was not yet clear. There were as many questions as answers.

Alongside cultural dislocation and political alienation, the country confronted a series of distressing economic setbacks in the 1970s and early 1980s. In 1973, inflation began to climb at a pace unprecedented in the post–World War II decades, and economic growth slowed. An energy crisis, aggravated by American foreign policy in the Middle East, produced fuel shortages. Foreign competition in manufacturing brought less expensive, and often more reliable, goods into the U.S. market from nations such as Japan and West Germany. Both developments helped set off a round of plant closings and deindustrialization. The great economic ride enjoyed by the United States since World War II was over.

What distinguishes the period between the energy crisis and the beginning of President Nixon's second term (1973) and the election of Ronald

No Gas

During the energy crisis of 1973, American motorists faced widespread gasoline shortages for the first time since World War II. Although gas was not rationed, gas stations were closed on Sundays, and some communities instituted further restrictions such as creating systems by which motorists with license plates ending in even numbers could purchase gas on certain days, with alternate days being reserved for odd numbers. Tom Ebenhoh/Black Star/Stockphoto.com.

Reagan to the presidency (1980) is the collective national search for order in the midst of economic crisis, political realignment, and rapid social change. Virtually all of the verities and touchstones of the postwar decades — Cold War liberalism, rising living standards, the nuclear family, sexual conservatism — had come under question, and most agreed on the urgency to act. For some, this search demanded new forms of liberal experimentation. For many others, it led instead to the conservatism of the emerging New Right.

An Era of Limits

Americans were deeply unsettled by the economic downturn of the early 1970s. Every major economic indicator — employment, productivity, growth — turned negative, and by 1973 the economy was in a tailspin. Inflation, brought on in part by military spending in Vietnam, proved especially difficult to control. When a Middle East embargo cut oil supplies in 1973, prices climbed even more. Unemployment remained high and productivity growth low until 1982. Overall, the 1970s represented the worst economic decade of the postwar period — what California governor Jerry Brown called an "era of limits." In this time of distress, Americans were forced to consider other limits to the growth and expansion that had long been markers of national progress. The environmental movement brought attention to the toxic effects of modern industrial capitalism on the natural world. As the urban crisis grew worse, several major cities verged on bankruptcy. Finally, political limits were reached as well: None of the presidents of the 1970s could reverse the nation's economic slide, though each spent years trying.

Energy Crisis

Modern economies run on oil. If the oil supply is drastically reduced, woe follows. Something like that happened to the United States in the 1970s. Once the world's leading oil producer, the United States had become heavily dependent on inexpensive imported oil, mostly from the Persian Gulf (Figure 29.1). American and European oil companies had discovered and developed the Middle Eastern fields early in the twentieth century, when much of the region was ruled by the British and French empires. When Middle Eastern states threw off the remnants of European colonialism, they demanded concessions for access to the fields. Foreign companies still extracted the oil, but now they did so under profit-sharing agreements with the Persian Gulf

states. In 1960, these nations and other oil-rich developing countries formed a cartel (a business association formed to control prices), the Organization of Petroleum Exporting Countries (OPEC).

Conflict between Israel and the neighboring Arab states of Egypt, Syria, and Jordan politicized OPEC between 1967 and 1973. Following Israel's victory in the 1967 Six-Day War, Israeli-Arab tensions in the region grew closer to boiling over with each passing year. In the 1973 Yom Kippur War, Egypt and Syria invaded Israel to regain territory lost in the 1967 conflict. Israel prevailed, but only after being resupplied by an emergency American airlift. Resentful of U.S. support for Israel, the Arab states in OPEC declared an oil embargo in October 1973. Gas prices in the United States quickly jumped by 40 percent, and heating oil prices by 30 percent. Demand outpaced supply, and Americans found themselves parked for hours in mile-long lines at gasoline stations for much of the winter of 1973–1974. Oil had become a political weapon, and the West's vulnerability stood revealed.

The United States scrambled to meet its energy needs in the face of the oil shortage. Just two months after the OPEC embargo began, Congress imposed a national speed limit of 55 miles per hour to conserve fuel. Americans began to buy smaller, more fuel-efficient cars such as Volkswagens, Toyotas, and Datsuns (later Nissans) — while sales of Detroit-made cars (now nicknamed "gas guzzlers") slumped. With one of every six jobs in the country generated directly or indirectly by the auto industry, the effects rippled across the economy. Compounding the distress was the raging inflation set off by the oil shortage; prices of basic necessities, such as bread, milk, and canned goods, rose by nearly 20 percent in 1974 alone. "THINGS WILL GET WORSE," one newspaper headline warned, "BEFORE THEY GET WORSE."

Environmentalism

The energy crisis drove home the realization that the earth's resources are not limitless. Such a notion was also

FIGURE 29.1

U.S. Energy Consumption, 1900–2000

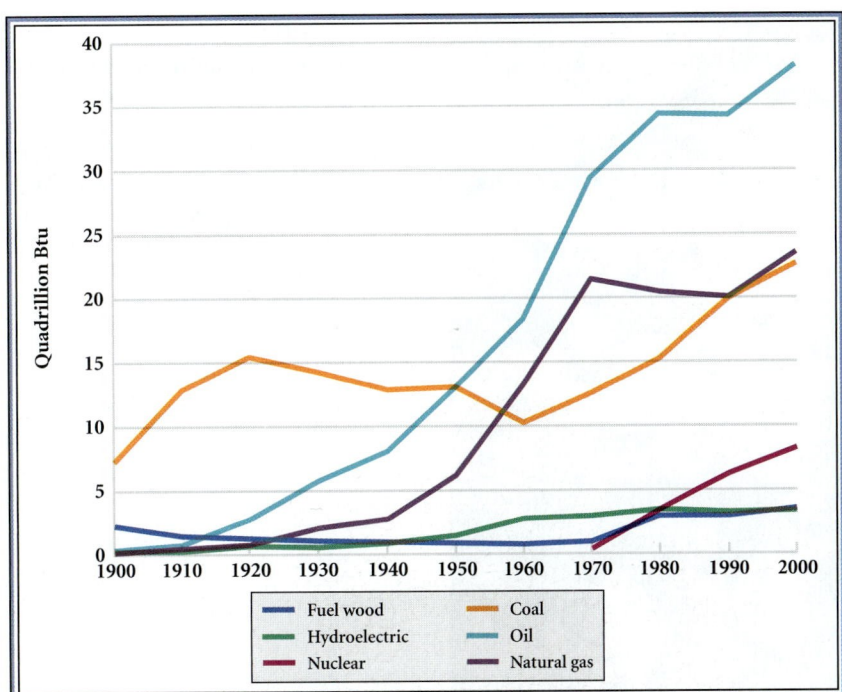

Coal was the nation's primary source of energy until the 1950s, when it was surpassed by oil and natural gas. The revival of coal consumption after 1960 stemmed from new open-pit mining in the West that provided cheaper fuel for power plants. The decline in oil consumption in 1980 reflects the nation's response to the oil crisis of the 1970s, including, most notably, fuel-efficient automobiles. Nuclear energy became an important new fuel source, but after 1990 its contribution leveled off as a result of the safety concerns triggered by the Three Mile Island incident (see p. 922). Source: *World Almanac 2002.*

at the heart of the era's revival of environmentalism. The environmental movement was an offshoot of sixties activism, but it had numerous historical precedents: the preservationist, conservationist, and wilderness movements of the late nineteenth century; the conservationist ethos of the New Deal; and anxiety about nuclear weapons and overpopulation in the 1940s. Three of the nation's leading environmental organizations — the Sierra Club, the Wilderness Society, and the Natural Resources Council — were founded in 1892, 1935, and 1942, respectively. Environmental activists in the 1970s extended the movement's deep roots through renewed efforts to ensure a healthy environment and access to unspoiled nature (see "Reading American Pictures: The Environmental Movement: Reimagining the Human-Earth Relationship," p. 923).

The movement had received a hefty push back in 1962 when biologist Rachel Carson published *Silent Spring*, a stunning analysis of the pesticide DDT's toxic impact on the human and natural food chains. A succession of galvanizing issues followed in the late 1960s. The Sierra Club successfully fought two dams in 1966 that would have flooded the Grand Canyon. And in 1969, there were three major developments: An offshore drilling rig spilled millions of gallons of oil off the coast of Santa Barbara; the Cuyahoga River near Cleveland burst into flames because of the accumulation of flammable chemicals on its surface; and Friends of the Everglades opposed an airport that threatened plants and wildlife in Florida. With these events serving as catalysts, environmentalism became a certifiable mass movement on the first Earth Day, April 22, 1970, when 20 million citizens gathered in communities across the country to express their support for a cleaner, healthier planet.

Environmental Protection Agency Earlier that year, on the heels of the Santa Barbara oil spill, Congress passed the National Environmental Policy Act, which created the Environmental Protection Agency (EPA). A bipartisan bill with broad support, including that of President Nixon, the law required developers to file environmental impact statements assessing the effect of their projects on ecosystems. A spate of new laws followed: the Clean Air Act (1970), the Occupational Health and Safety Act (1970), the Water Pollution Control Act (1972), and the Endangered Species Act (1973).

The Democratic majority in Congress and the Republican president generally found common ground on these issues, and *Time* magazine wondered if the environment was "the gut issue that can unify a polarized nation." Despite the broad popularity of the movement, however, *Time*'s prediction was not borne out. Corporations resented environmental regulations, as did many of their workers, who believed that tightened standards threatened their jobs. "IF YOU'RE HUNGRY

Earth Day, 1970

No single event better encapsulated the growing environmental awareness of Americans than the nationwide celebration of the first Earth Day on April 22, 1970. In this photograph, young people in Dallas, Texas, have just hoisted their placard on a heap of garbage swept up from the city streets.   Time Life Pictures /Getty Images.

AND OUT OF WORK, EAT AN ENVIRONMENTALIST," read one labor union's bumper sticker. By the 1980s, environmentalism starkly divided Americans, with proponents of unfettered economic growth on one side and environmental activists preaching limits on the other.

Nuclear Power   An early foreshadowing of those divisions came in the brewing controversy over nuclear power. Electricity from the atom—what could be better? That was how Americans had greeted the arrival of power-generating nuclear technology in the 1950s. By 1974, U.S. utility companies were operating forty-two nuclear power plants, with a hundred more planned. Given the oil crisis, nuclear energy might have seemed a godsend; unlike coal- or oil-driven plants, nuclear operations produced no air pollutants.

Environmentalists, however, publicized the dangers of nuclear power plants: A reactor meltdown would be catastrophic, and so, in slow motion, would the dumping of the plants' radioactive waste, which would generate toxic levels of radioactivity for hundreds of years. These fears seemed to be confirmed in March 1979, when the reactor core at the Three Mile Island nuclear plant near Harrisburg, Pennsylvania, came close to meltdown. More than 100,000 people fled their homes. A prompt shutdown saved the plant, but the near-catastrophe enabled environmentalists to win the battle over nuclear energy. After the incident at Three Mile

The Environmental Movement: Reimagining the Human-Earth Relationship

The photo on the left was taken by *Apollo 8* crewmember Bill Anders on December 24, 1968, as the *Apollo* spacecraft orbited the moon. It was not until the U.S. space program began sending human beings into orbit, and eventually to land on the moon itself, that such photos of the Earth were possible. The advent of these photographs in the late 1960s revealed a tiny, seemingly fragile island of life in a vast universe. It provoked awareness of the earth itself as finite. That consciousness helped spark the environmental movement of the 1970s. On the right sits an American family, alongside the amount of waste produced by a typical family in the course of a year.

"Earthrise" over the Moon's surface. NASA.

Waste Produced by a Typical Family in a Year.
© Martyn Goddard/CORBIS.

ANALYZING THE EVIDENCE

- What do you make of this juxtaposition of photographs? One shows the planet in the vastness of space; the other shows a mountain of trash. What does the view of Earth from space have to do with the waste produced by a typical family?

- Photographs appeal to the visual sense, but they also evoke emotional responses. What kinds of emotions do you imagine people felt in 1968, in response to this view of Earth? What kinds of emotions do you think the photographer of the waste was attempting to elicit?

- Much of the environmental movement's activism questioned Americans' consumption habits. As a political and social movement to change both public policy and popular attitudes, how was environmentalism like other social movements of the era? How was it dissimilar? How could these two photographs have furthered the environmental cause?

Island, no new nuclear plants were authorized, though a handful with existing authorization were built in the 1980s. Today, nuclear reactors account for 20 percent of all U.S. power generation—substantially less than several European nations, but still fourth in the world.

Economic Transformation

In addition to the energy crisis, the economy was beset by a host of longer-term problems. Government spending on the Vietnam War and the Great Society made for a growing federal deficit and spiraling inflation. In the industrial sector, the country faced more robust competition from West Germany and Japan. America's share of world trade dropped from 32 percent in 1955 to 18 percent in 1970 and was headed downward. As a result, in a blow to national pride, nine Western European countries had surpassed the United States in per capita gross domestic product (GDP) by 1980. Many of these economic woes highlighted a broader, multigenerational transformation in the United States: from an industrial-manufacturing economy to a postindustrial-service one. That transformation, which continues to this day, meant that the United States began to produce fewer automobiles, appliances, and televisions and more financial services, health care services, and management

consulting services—not to mention many millions of low-paying jobs in the restaurant, retail, and tourist industries.

In the 1970s, the U.S. economy was hit simultaneously by unemployment, stagnant consumer demand, and inflation—a combination called stagflation—which contradicted a basic principle taught by economists: Prices were not supposed to rise in a stagnant economy (Figure 29.2). For ordinary Americans, the reality of stagflation was a noticeable decline in the standard of living, as discretionary income per worker dropped 18 percent between 1973 and 1982. None of the three presidents of the decade—Richard Nixon, Gerald Ford, and Jimmy Carter—had much luck tackling stagflation. Nixon's New Economic Policy was perhaps the most radical attempt. Nixon imposed temporary price and wage controls in 1971 in an effort to curb inflation. Then he took an even bolder step: removing the United States from the gold standard, which allowed the dollar to float in international currency markets and effectively ended the Bretton Woods monetary system established after World War II. The underlying weaknesses in the U.S. economy remained, however. Ford, too, had little luck. His Whip Inflation Now (WIN) campaign urged Americans to cut food waste and do more with less, a noble idea but deeply unpopular among the

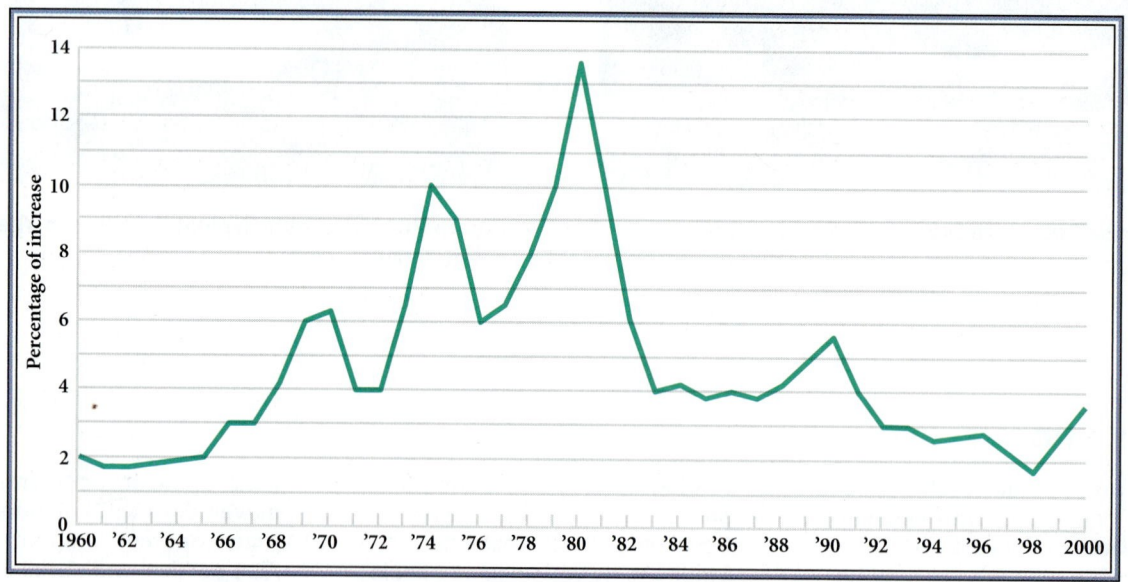

FIGURE 29.2

The Inflation Rate, 1960–2000

The impact of the oil crisis of 1973 on the inflation rate appears all too graphically in Figure 29.2. The dip in 1974 reflects the sharp recession that began that year, after which the inflation rate zoomed up to a staggering 14 percent in 1980. The return to normal levels after 1980 stemmed from very harsh measures by the Federal Reserve Board, which, while they succeeded, came at the cost of a painful slowdown in the economy.   Source: *Statistical Abstract of the United States, 2000.*

Deindustrialization

Increasing economic competition from overseas created hard times for American industry in the 1970s and 1980s. Many of the nation's once-proud core industries, such as steel, declined precipitously in these decades. This photo shows a steel factory in Youngstown, Ohio, that closed in 1980. The result of these closures was the creation of the so-called "rust belt" in the Northeast and Midwest (see Map 29.1).   Richard Kalvar/Magnum Photos.

American public. Carter's policies, considered in a subsequent section of this chapter, were similarly ineffective. The fruitless search for a new economic order was a hallmark of 1970s politics.

Deindustrialization   America's economic woes struck hardest at the industrial sector, which suddenly—shockingly—began to be dismantled. Worst hit was the steel industry, which for seventy-five years had been the economy's crown jewel. Unscathed by World War II, U.S. steel producers had enjoyed an open, hugely profitable field. But lack of serious competition left them without incentives to replace outdated plants and equipment. When the West German and Japanese steel industries rebuilt, they incorporated the latest technology. Foreign steel flooded into the United States during the 1970s, and the American industry was simply overwhelmed. Formerly titanic steel companies began a massive dismantling; virtually the entire Pittsburgh region, once a national hub of steel production, lost its heavy industry in a single generation. By the mid-1980s, downsizing, automation,

and investment in new technologies made the American steel industry competitive again—but it was a shadow of its former self, and it continues to struggle to this day.

The steel industry was the prime example of what became known as **deindustrialization**. The country was in the throes of an economic transformation that left it largely stripped of its industrial base. Steel was hardly alone. A swath of the Northeast and Midwest, the country's manufacturing heartland, became the nation's "Rust Belt" (Map 29.1), strewn with abandoned plants and distressed communities. The automobile, tire, textile, and other consumer durable industries (appliances, electronics, furniture, and the like) all started shrinking in the 1970s. In 1980, *Business Week* bemoaned "plant closings across the continent" and insisted on the "*re*industrialization of America."

Organized Labor in Decline   Deindustrialization threw many tens of thousands of blue-collar workers out of well-paid union jobs. One study followed 4,100 steelworkers left jobless by the 1977 shutdown of the Campbell Works of the

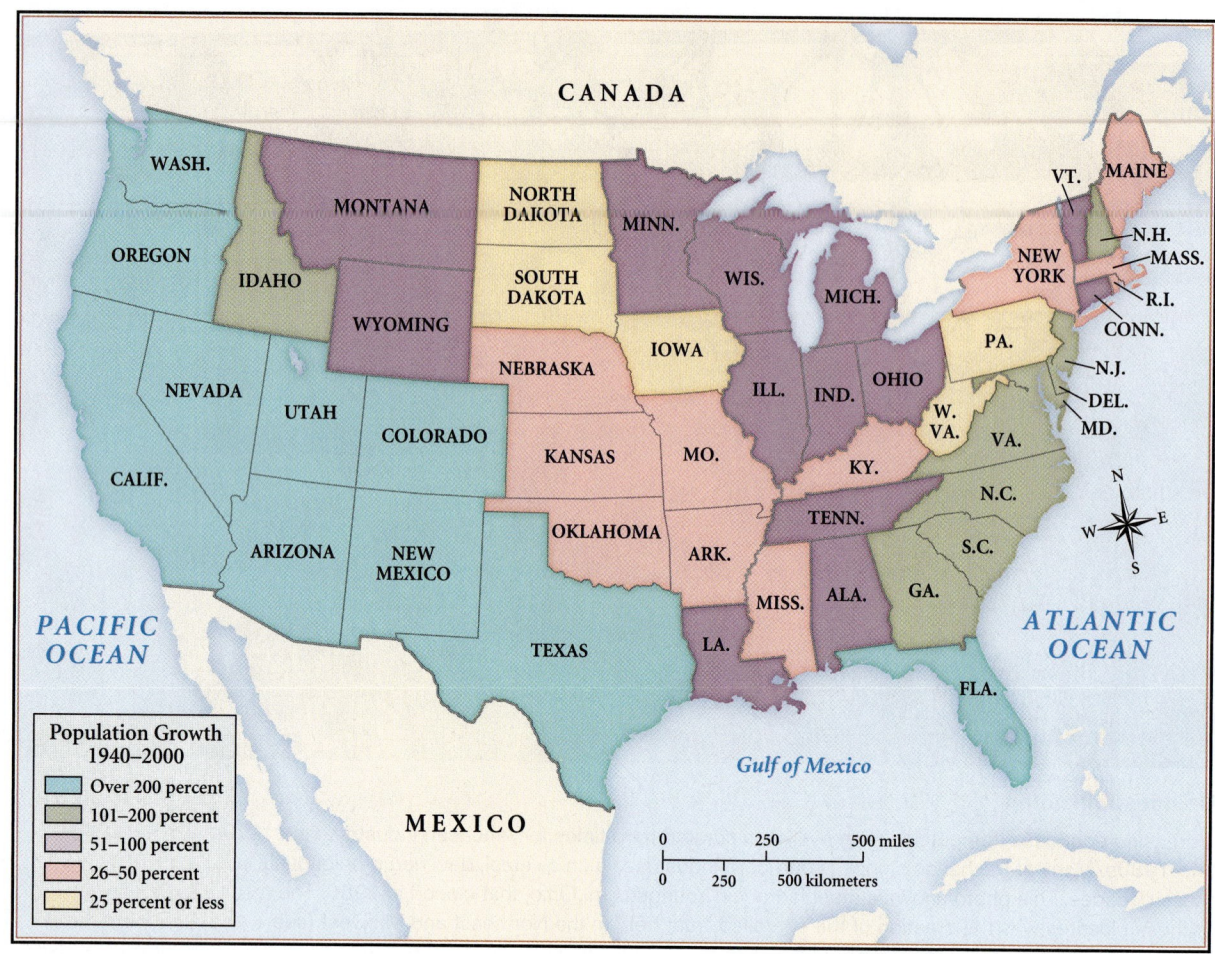

MAP 29.1

From Rust Belt to Sun Belt, 1940–2000

One of the most significant developments of the post–World War II era was the growth of the Sun Belt. Sparked by federal spending for military bases, the defense industry, and the space program, states of the South and Southwest experienced an economic boom in the 1950s. This growth was further enhanced in the 1970s, as the heavily industrialized regions of the Northeast and Midwest declined, and migrants from what was quickly dubbed the "Rust Belt" headed to the South and West in search of jobs.

Youngstown Sheet & Tube Co. Two years later, 35 percent had retired early at half pay; 10 percent had moved; 15 percent were still jobless, with unemployment benefits long gone; and 40 percent had found local work, but mostly in low-paying, service-sector jobs. In another instance, between 1978 and 1981, eight Los Angeles companies—including such giants as Ford, Uniroyal, and U.S. Steel—closed factories employing 18,000 workers. These Ohio and California workers, like hundreds of thousands of their counterparts across the nation, had fallen from their perch in the middle class.

Deindustrialization dealt an especially harsh blow to the labor movement, which had facilitated the postwar expansion of that middle class. In the early 1970s, as inflation hit, the number of strikes surged; 2.4 million workers participated in work stoppages in 1970 alone. However, industry argued that it could no longer afford union demands, and labor's bargaining power produced fewer and fewer concrete results. In these hard years, the much-vaunted labor-management accord of the 1950s, which raised profits and wages by passing costs on to consumers, went bust. Instead of seeking higher wages, unions now mainly fought to save jobs. Union membership went into steep decline, and by the mid-1980s organized labor represented less than 18 percent of American workers, the lowest level since the 1920s. The impact on liberal politics was huge. With labor's decline, a main buttress of the New Deal coalition was coming undone.

Ford to City: "Drop Dead"

In the summer of 1975, New York City nearly went bankrupt. When Mayor Abraham Beame appealed to President Gerald Ford for assistance, these newspaper headlines captured the chief executive's response. Though it was ultimately saved from financial ruin, the city's brush with insolvency symbolized the larger problems facing the nation: economic stagnation, high inflation, and unemployment. Hard times had seemingly spared no one. AP Images.

Urban Crisis Revisited The economic downturn pushed already struggling American cities to the brink of fiscal collapse. Middle-class flight to the suburbs continued apace, and the "urban crisis" of the 1960s spilled into the "era of limits." Facing huge price inflation and mounting piles of debt — to finance social services for the poor and to replace disappearing tax revenue — nearly every major American city struggled to pay its bills in the 1970s. Surrounded by prosperous postwar suburbs, central cities seemingly could not catch a break.

New York, the nation's financial capital and its largest city, fared the worst. Its annual budget was in the billions, larger than that of most states. Unable to borrow on the tightening international bond market, New York neared collapse in the summer of 1975; bankruptcy was a real possibility. When Mayor Abraham Beame appealed to the federal government for assistance, President Ford refused. "Ford to City: Drop Dead" read the headline in the *New York Daily News*. Fresh appeals ultimately produced a solution: the federal government would lend New York money, and banks would declare a three-year moratorium on municipal debt. The arrangement saved the city from defaulting, but the mayor was forced to cut city services, freeze wages, and lay off workers. One pessimistic observer declared that "the banks have been saved, and the city has been condemned."

Cities faced declining fortunes in these years for many reasons, but one key was the continued loss of residents and businesses to nearby suburbs. In the 1970s alone, 13 million people (6 percent of the total U.S. population) moved to the suburbs. New suburban shopping centers opened weekly across the country, and other businesses — such as banks, insurance companies, and technology firms — increasingly sought suburban locations. More and more, people lived *and* worked in suburbs. In the San Francisco Bay area, 75 percent of all daily commutes were suburb-to-suburb, and 78 percent of New York's suburban residents worked in the suburbs. The 1950s "organization man," commuting downtown from his suburban home, had been replaced by the engineer, teacher, nurse, student, and carpenter who lived in one suburb and worked in another.

Tax Revolt and Economic Inequality Suburbanization and the economic crisis combined powerfully in what became known as the "tax revolt," a dramatic reversal of the postwar spirit of generous public investment. The premier example was California. Stagflation pushed real estate values upward, and property taxes skyrocketed. Hardest hit were suburban property-owners, along with retirees and others on fixed incomes, who suddenly faced unaffordable tax bills. Into this dire situation stepped

Howard Jarvis, a conservative anti–New Dealer and a genius at mobilizing grassroots discontent. In 1978, Jarvis proposed Proposition 13, an initiative that would roll back property taxes, cap future increases for present owners, and require that all tax measures have a two-thirds majority in the legislature. Despite opposition by virtually the entire state leadership, including politicians from both parties, Californians voted overwhelmingly for Jarvis's measure.

Proposition 13 hobbled public spending in the nation's most populous state. Per capita funding of California public schools, once the envy of the nation, plunged from the top tier to the bottom, where it was second only to Mississippi. Moreover, Proposition 13's complicated formula benefited middle-class and wealthy homeowners at the expense of less-well-off citizens, especially those who depended heavily on public services. Businesses, too, came out ahead, because commercial property got the same protection as residential property. More broadly, Proposition 13 inspired tax revolts across the country and helped conservatives define an enduring issue: low taxes.

In addition to public investment, another cardinal marker of New Deal liberalism had been a remarkable decline in income inequality. In the 1970s, that trend reversed, and the wealthiest Americans, those among the top 10 percent, began to pull ahead again. As corporations restructured to boost profits during the 1970s slump, they increasingly laid off high-wage workers, paid the remaining workers less, and relocated overseas. Thus, upper-class Americans benefited, while blue-collar families who had been lifted into the middle class during the postwar boom increasingly lost out. An unmistakable trend was apparent by the end of the 1970s. The U.S. labor market was dividing in two: a vast, low-wage market at the bottom and a much narrower high-wage market at the top, with the middle squeezed smaller and smaller.

Politics in Flux, 1974–1980

A search for order characterized national politics in the 1970s as well. Liberals were in retreat, but conservatives had not yet put forth a clear alternative. Popular disdain for politicians, evident in declining voter turnout, deepened with Nixon's resignation in 1974. "Don't vote," read one bumper sticker in 1976. "It only encourages them." Watergate not only damaged short-term Republican prospects but also shifted the party's balance to the right. Despite mastering the populist appeal to the "silent majority," Nixon was never beloved by conservatives. His relaxation of tensions with the So-

viet Union and his visit to communist China, in particular, won him no friends on the right. His disgraceful exit proved a boon to conservative Republicans, who proceeded to reshape the party in their image.

As for the Democrats, Watergate granted them a reprieve, a second chance at recapturing their eroding base. Backed by a public deeply disenchanted with politicians, especially scandal-tainted Republicans, congressional Democrats had an opportunity to repair the party's image. But any high-minded Democratic program that did not halt the nation's economic slide would not reverse the party's weakened position. The years in between Nixon's resignation and the election of Ronald Reagan in 1980 are thus best understood as a transitional period — the aggressive liberalism of the 1960s was losing national support, but nothing distinctly different had yet replaced it.

Watergate Babies Less than a month into his presidency, which began when Nixon resigned on August 9, 1974, Gerald Ford did something unexpected: He officially pardoned Nixon. The decision saved the nation a prolonged and agonizing trial, which was Ford's rationale, but it was decidedly unpopular among the public. Pollster Louis Harris remarked that should a politician "defend that pardon in any part of this country, North or South, [he] is almost literally going to have his head handed to him." Democratic candidates in the 1974 midterm elections made Watergate and Ford's pardon their top issues. It worked. Seventy-five new Democratic members of the House came to Washington in 1975, many of them under the age of forty-five, and the press dubbed them "Watergate babies."

Young and reform-minded, the Watergate babies solidified huge Democratic majorities in both houses of Congress and quickly set to work. They eliminated the House Un-American Activities Committee (HUAC), which had investigated alleged Communists in the 1940s and 1950s and antiwar activists in the 1960s. In the Senate, Democrats reduced the number of votes needed to end a filibuster from 67 to 60 — a move intended to weaken the power of the minority to block legislation. In both houses, Democrats dismantled the existing committee structure, which had entrenched power in the hands of a few elite committee chairs. And in 1978, they passed the Ethics in Government Act, which forced political candidates to disclose financial contributions and limited the lobbying activities of former elected officials. Overall, the Watergate babies helped to decentralize power in Washington and bring greater transparency to American government.

In one of the great ironies of American political history, however, the post-Watergate reforms made government *less* efficient and *more* susceptible to special interests—the opposite of what had been intended. Under the new committee structure, smaller subcommittees proliferated, and the size of the congressional staff doubled to more than 20,000. A diffuse power structure actually gave lobbyists more places to exert influence. As the power of committee chairs weakened, influence shifted to party leaders, such as the Speaker of the House and the Senate majority leader. With little incentive to compromise, the parties grew more rigid, and bipartisanship became rare. Finally, filibustering, a seldom-used tactic largely employed by anti–civil rights southerners, increased in frequency. The Congress that we have come to know today—with its partisan rancor, its army of lobbyists, and its slow-moving response to public needs—came into being in the 1970s.

Political Realignment | Despite Democratic gains in 1974, the electoral realignment that had begun with Richard Nixon's presidential victories in 1968 and 1972 continued. As liberalism proved unable to stop runaway inflation or speed up economic growth, conservatism gained greater traction with the public. The postwar liberal economic formula—sometimes known as the Keynesian consensus—consisted of micro-adjustments to the money supply coupled with federal spending. When that formula failed to restart the economy in the mid-1970s, conservatives in Congress used this opening to articulate alternatives, especially economic deregulation and tax cuts.

On a grander scale, deindustrialization in the Northeast and Midwest and continued population growth in the Sunbelt was changing the political geography of the country. Power was shifting, incrementally but perceptibly, toward the West and South (Table 29.1). As states with strong trade unions at the center of the postwar liberal political coalition—such as New York, Illinois, and Michigan—lost industry, jobs, and people, states with traditions of libertarian conservatism—such as California, Arizona, Florida, and Texas—gained greater political clout. The full impact of this shifting political geography would not be felt until the 1980s and 1990s, but its effects had become apparent by the mid-1970s.

Jimmy Carter: The Outsider as President | "Jimmy who?" was how journalists first responded when James Earl Carter, who had in turn been a naval officer, a peanut farmer, and the governor of Georgia, emerged from the pack to win the

TABLE 29.1

Political Realignment: Congressional Seats

State	1940 Apportionment	1990 Apportionment
Rust Belt		
Massachusetts	14	10
Connecticut	6	6
New York	45	31
New Jersey	14	13
Pennsylvania	33	21
Ohio	23	19
Illinois	26	20
Indiana	11	10
Michigan	17	16
Wisconsin	10	9
Total	199	155
Sun Belt		
California	23	52
Arizona	2	6
Nevada	1	2
Colorado	4	6
New Mexico	2	3
Texas	21	30
Georgia	10	11
North Carolina	12	12
Virginia	9	11
Florida	6	23
Total	90	156

In the fifty years between 1940 and 1990, the Rust Belt states lost political clout, while the Sun Belt states gained it—measured here in congressional seats (which are apportioned based on population). Sun Belt states gained 66 seats, with the Rust Belt losing 44. This shifting political geography helped undermine the liberal coalition, which was strongest in industrial states with large labor unions, and paved the way for the rise of the conservative coalition, which was strongest in southern and Bible Belt states, as well as California. Source: Office of the Clerk of the House, http://clerk.house.gov/art_history/house_history/congApp/bystate.html.

Democratic presidential nomination in 1976. When Carter told his mother that he intended to run for president, she had asked, "President of what?" Trading on Watergate and his down-home image, Carter pledged to restore morality to the White House. "I will never lie to you," he promised voters. Carter played up his credentials as a Washington outsider, although he selected Senator Walter F. Mondale of Minnesota as his running

Jimmy Carter
President Jimmy Carter leans across the roof of his car to shake hands during a parade through Bardstown, Kentucky, in July 1979. The president needed all the support he could get. Inflation in 1979 was 11 percent, one of the highest annual rates in the postwar decades. A thoughtful man and a born-again Christian, Carter proved unable to solve the complex economic problems and international challenges of the late 1970s.   Bob Daugherty/AP Images.

mate, to ensure his ties to traditional Democratic voting blocs. Ford still might have prevailed, but his pardon of Nixon likely cost him enough votes in key states to swing the election to the Democratic candidate. Carter won with 50 percent of the popular vote to Ford's 48 percent.

For a time, Carter got some mileage as an outsider— the common man who walked to the White House after the inauguration and delivered fireside chats in a cardigan sweater. The fact that he was a born-again Christian also played well. But Carter's inexperience began to show. He made strange blunders, such as telling *Playboy* magazine that he had "looked upon a lot of women with lust." Most consequentially, his outsider strategy made for chilly relations with congressional leaders. Disdainful of the Democratic establishment, Carter relied heavily on inexperienced advisors from Georgia. And as a detail-oriented micromanager, he exhausted himself over the fine points of policy better left to his aides.

On the domestic front, Carter's big challenge was managing the economy. The problems that he faced defied easy solution. Most confounding was stagflation. If the government focused on inflation—forcing prices down by raising interest rates—unemployment became worse. If the government tried to stimulate employment, inflation became worse. None of the levers of government economic policy seemed to work. At heart, Carter was an economic conservative. He toyed with the idea

of an "industrial policy" to bail out the ailing manufacturing sector, but he moved instead in a free-market direction by lifting the New Deal–era regulation of the airline, trucking, and railroad industries. Deregulation stimulated competition and cut prices, but it also drove firms out of business and hurt unionized workers.

The president's efforts proved ineffective at reigniting economic growth. Then, the Iranian Revolution curtailed oil supplies, and gas prices jumped again. In a major TV address, Carter lectured Americans about the nation's "crisis of the spirit." He called energy conservation "the moral equivalent of war"—or, in the media's shorthand, "MEOW," which aptly captured the nation's assessment of Carter's sermonizing. By then, his approval rating had fallen below 30 percent. And it was no wonder, given an inflation rate over 11 percent, failing industries, and long lines at the pumps. It seemed the worst of all possible economic worlds, and the first-term president could not help but worry about the political costs to him and his party (see Voices from Abroad, "Fei Xiaotong: America's Crisis of Faith," p. 931).

- Why did the United States enter an energy crisis in the 1970s?

- Why did the environmental movement prove so divisive? Whose interests were threatened?

- What were the causes and effects of deindustrialization?

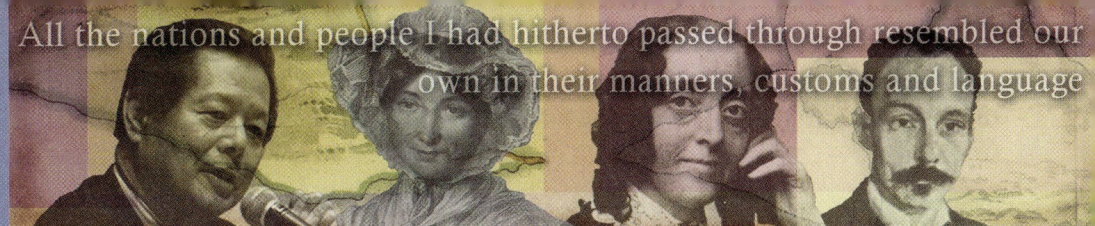
Fei Xiaotong
America's Crisis of Faith

Fei Xiaotong, a Chinese anthropologist and sociologist, wrote influential books on the United States during World War II and the 1950s. Despite his criticism of U.S. foreign policy, his often sympathetic treatment of America contributed to his twenty years of political ostracism in China. Regaining prominence in the late 1970s, he joined an official delegation to the United States in 1979. When he returned to China, Fei wrote a series of essays entitled "Glimpses of America." In this passage, he responds to President Jimmy Carter's assertion in his famous "malaise" speech of 1979 that Americans faced a spiritual crisis.

I read in the newspaper that the energy crisis in the United States is getting worse and worse. I hear that after spending several days of quiet thought in his mountain retreat, President Carter decided that America's real problem is not the energy crisis but a "crisis of faith." The way it is told is that vast numbers of people have lost their faith in the present government and in the political system, and do not believe that the people in the government working with current government methods can solve the present series of crises. Even more serious, he believes that the masses have come to have doubts about traditional American values, and if this continues, in his opinion, the future of America is terrible to imagine. He made a sad and worried speech. I have not had an opportunity to read the text of his speech, but if he has truly realized that the present American social system has lost popular support, that should be considered a good thing because at least it shows that the old method of just treating the symptoms will no longer work.

In fact, loss of faith in the present social system on the part of the broad masses of the American people did not begin with the energy crisis. The spectacular advances in science and technology in America in the last decade or two and the unceasing rise in the forces of production are good. But the social system remains unchanged, and the relations of production are basically the same old capitalism. This contradiction between the forces of production and the relations of production has not lessened but become deeper. The ruling class, to be sure, still has the power to keep on finding ways of dealing with the endless series of crises, but the masses of people are coming increasingly to feel that they have fallen unwittingly into a situation where their fate is controlled by others, like a moth in a spiderweb, unable to struggle free. Not only the blacks of Harlem — who are clearly able to earn their own living but still have to rely on welfare to support themselves without dignity — but even well-off families in gardenlike suburban residences worry all day that some accident may suddenly rob them of everything. As the dependence of individuals on others grows heavier and heavier, each person feels in his heart that this society is no longer to be relied on. . . . No wonder people complain that civilization was created by humans, but humans have been enslaved by it. Such a feeling is natural in a society like America's. Carter is right to call this feeling of helplessness a "crisis of faith," for it is a doubting of the present culture. Only he should realize that the present crisis has been long in the making and is already deep. . . .

These "Glimpses of America" essays may be brought to a close here, but to end with the crisis of faith does violence to my original intention. History is a stream that flows on and cannot be stopped. Words must be cut off, but history goes bubbling on. It is inconceivable that America will come to a standstill at any crisis point. I have full faith in the great American people and hope that they will continue to make even greater contributions to the progress of mankind.

Source: R. David Arkush and Leo O. Lee, trans. and eds., *Land Without Ghosts: Chinese Impressions of America from the Mid-Nineteenth Century to the Present* (Berkeley: University of California Press, 1989), 271–280.

ANALYZING THE EVIDENCE

- Fei is writing about America as someone schooled in Marxist (or Communist) analysis. Can you point to elements in his essay that indicate that perspective?

- Fei agrees with Carter that America's problem is not the energy crisis, but a "crisis of faith." Does that mean he agrees with the president about the nature of the crisis?

- What value, if any, do you think a historian would find in Fei's essay as a historical document?

Reform and Reaction in the 1970s

Having lived through a decade of profound social and political upheaval—the Vietnam War, protests, riots, Watergate, recession—many Americans were exhausted and cynical by the mid-1970s. But while some retreated to private concerns, others took reform in new directions. Civil rights battles continued, the women's movement achieved some of its most far-reaching aims, and gay rights blossomed. These movements pushed the "rights revolution" of the 1960s deeper into American life. Others, however, pushed back. Social conservatives responded by forming their own organizations and resisting the emergence of what they saw as a permissive society.

Civil Rights in a New Era

When Congress banned job discrimination in the 1964 Civil Rights Act, the law required only that employers hire without regard to "race, color, religion, sex, or national origin." But after centuries of slavery and decades of segregation, would nondiscrimination bring African Americans into the economic mainstream? Many liberals thought not. They believed that government, universities, and private employers needed to take positive steps to open their doors to a wider, more diverse range of Americans—including other minority groups and women.

Affirmative Action   Among the most significant efforts to address the legacy of exclusion was affirmative action—procedures designed to take into account the disadvantaged position of minority groups after centuries of discrimination. First advanced by the Kennedy administration in 1961, affirmative action received a boost under President Lyndon Johnson, whose Labor Department fashioned a series of plans in the late 1960s to encourage government contractors to recruit underrepresented racial minorities. Women were added under the last of these plans, when pressure from the women's movement highlighted the problem of sex discrimination. By the early 1970s, affirmative action had been refined by court rulings that identified acceptable procedures: hiring and enrollment goals, special recruitment and training programs, and set-asides (specially reserved slots) for both racial minority groups and women.

March for Affirmative Action

Following the Supreme Court's 1978 *Bakke* decision, Americans grew even more divided over the policy of affirmative action. For many people, such as African Americans and Latinos, affirmative action promised that groups who faced historical discrimination would have equal opportunity in jobs and education. For many whites, affirmative action looked like "reverse discrimination," and they fought its implementation.   AP Images.

Affirmative action, however, did not please many whites, who felt that the deck was being stacked against them. Much of the dissent came from conservative groups that had opposed civil rights all along. They charged affirmative action advocates with "reverse discrimination." Referring to Puerto Ricans and African Americans in an episode of *All in the Family*, Archie Bunker said that if they "want their rightful share of the American dream, let 'em go and hustle for it like I done," a common, if crudely stated, objection to affirmative action. Some liberal groups sought a middle position. In a widely publicized 1972 letter, Jewish organizations, seared by the memory of quotas that once kept Jewish students out of elite colleges, came out against all racial quotas but nonetheless endorsed "rectifying the imbalances resulting from past discrimination."

A major shift in affirmative action policy came in 1978. Allan Bakke, a white man, sued the University of California at Davis Medical School for rejecting him in favor of less-qualified minority-group candidates. Headlines across the country sparked anti–affirmative action protest marches on college campuses and vigorous discussion on television, radio, and in the White House. Ultimately, the Supreme Court rejected the medical school's quota system, which set aside 16 of 100 places for "disadvantaged" students. The Court ordered Bakke admitted but indicated that a more flexible affirmative action plan, in which race could be considered along with other factors, would still pass constitutional muster. *Bakke v. University of California* thus upheld affirmative action but, by rejecting a quota system, also called it into question. Future court rulings and state referenda, in the 1990s and 2000s, would further limit the scope of affirmative action. In particular, California voters passed Proposition 209 in 1996, prohibiting public institutions from using affirmative action to increase diversity in employment and education.

Busing   Another major civil rights objective—desegregating schools—produced even more controversy and fireworks. For fifteen years, southern states, by a variety of stratagems, had fended off court directives that they desegregate "with all deliberate speed." In 1968, only about one-third of all black children in the South attended schools with whites. At that point, the federal courts got serious and, in a series of stiff decisions, ordered an end to "dual school systems." Where schools remained highly segregated, the courts increasingly endorsed the strategy of busing students to achieve integration. Plans differed across the country. In some states, black children rode buses from their neighborhoods to attend previously all-white schools. In others, white children were bused to black or Latino neighborhoods. In an important 1971 decision, the Supreme Court upheld a countywide busing plan for Charlotte-Mecklenburg, a North Carolina school district. Despite local opposition, desegregation proceeded, and many cities in the South followed suit. By the mid-1970s, 86 percent of southern black children were attending school with whites. (In recent years, this trend has reversed.)

In the North, where segregated schooling was also a fact of life—arising from suburban residential patterns—busing orders proved less effective. Detroit dramatized the problem. To integrate Detroit schools would have required merging city and suburban school districts. A lower court ordered just such a merger in 1971, but in *Milliken v. Bradley* (1974), the Supreme Court reversed the ruling, requiring busing plans to remain within the boundaries of a single school district.

Without including the largely white suburbs in busing efforts, however, achieving racial balance in Detroit, and other major northern cities, was all but impossible. Postwar suburbanization had produced in the North what law had mandated in the South: entrenched racial segregation of schools.

The Women's Movement and Gay Rights

Unlike the civil rights movement, whose signal achievements came in the 1960s, the women's and gay rights movements flourished in the 1970s. With three influential wings — radical, liberal, and "Third World" — the women's movement inspired both grassroots activism and legislative action across the nation. For their part, gay activists had further to go: They needed to convince Americans that same-sex relationships were natural and that gay men and lesbians deserved the same protection of the law as all other citizens. Neither movement achieved all of its aims in this era, but each laid a strong foundation for the future.

Women's Liberation In the first half of the 1970s, the women's liberation movement reached its historic peak. Taking a dizzying array of forms — from lobbying legislatures to marching in the streets and establishing all-female collectives — women's liberation produced activism on the scale of the earlier black-led civil rights movement. Women's centers, as well as women-run child-care facilities, began to spring up in cities and towns. A feminist art and poetry movement flourished. Women challenged the admissions policies of all-male colleges and universities — opening such prestigious universities as Yale and Columbia and nearly bringing an end to male-only institutions of higher education. Female scholars began to transform higher education: by studying women's history, by increasing the number of women on college and university faculties, and by founding women's studies programs.

Much of women's liberation activism focused on the female body. Inspired by the Boston collective that first published *Our Bodies, Ourselves* — a groundbreaking book on women's health — the women's health movement founded dozens of medical clinics, encouraged women to become physicians, and educated millions of women about their bodies. To reform anti-abortion laws, activists pushed for remedies in more than thirty state legislatures. Women's liberationists founded the antirape movement, established rape crisis centers around the nation, and lobbied state legislatures and Congress to reform rape laws. Many of these endeavors

Phyllis Schlafly

Phyllis Schlafly, leader of the organization STOP ERA, talks with reporters during a rally at the Illinois State Capitol on March 4, 1975, at a time when the state legislature was considering whether to ratify the Equal Rights Amendment. Schlafly described herself as a housewife and called her strenuous political career a "hobby."
© Bettmann/Corbis.

and movements began as shoestring operations in living rooms and kitchens: *Our Bodies, Ourselves* was first published as a 35-cent mimeographed booklet, and the antirape movement began in small consciousness-raising groups that met in churches and community centers. By the end of the decade, however, all of these causes had national organizations and touched the lives of millions of American women.

Equal Rights Amendment Buoyed by this flourishing of activism, the women's movement renewed the fight for an Equal Rights Amendment (ERA) to the Constitution. First introduced in 1923, the ERA stated, in its entirety, "Equality of rights under the law shall not be denied or abridged by the United States or any State on the basis of sex." Vocal congressional women, such as Patsy Mink (D-HI), Bella

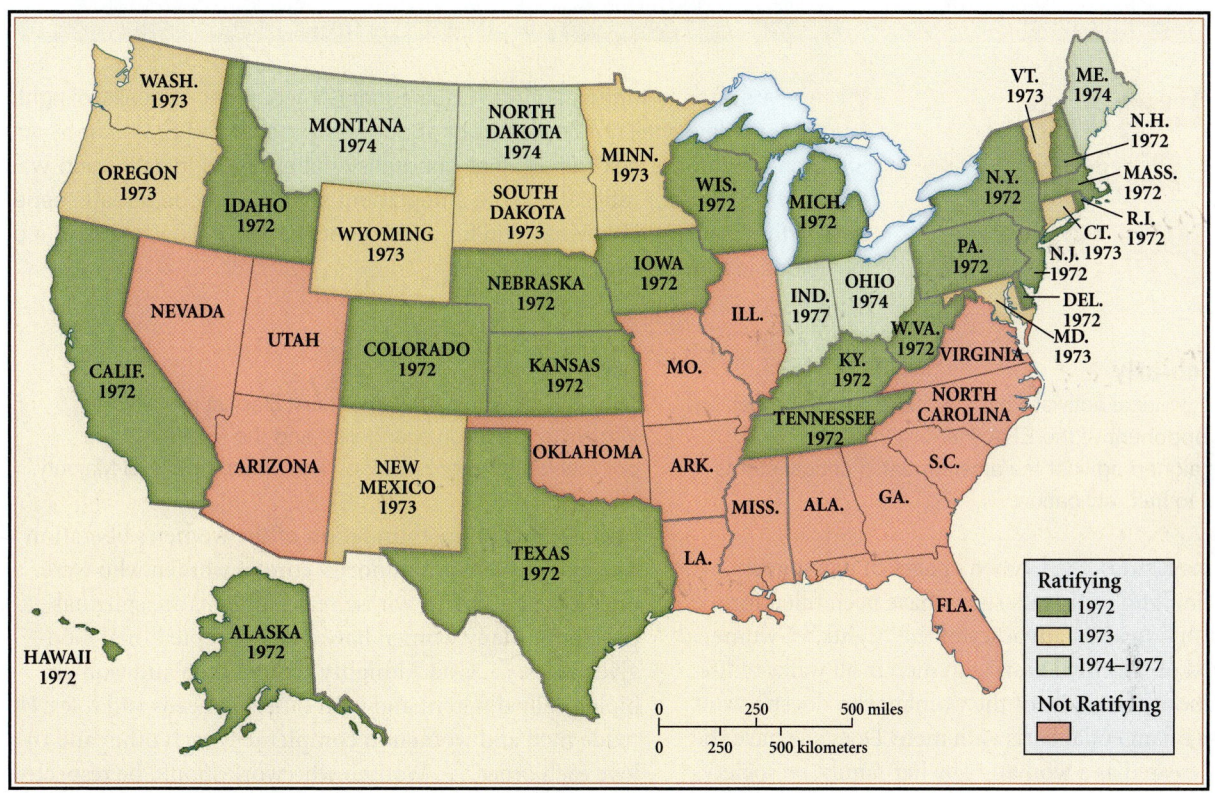

MAP 29.2

States Ratifying the Equal Rights Amendment, 1972–1977

The ratifying process for the Equal Rights Amendment (ERA) went smoothly in 1972 and 1973 but then stalled. The turning point came in 1976, when ERA advocates lobbied extensively, particularly in Florida, North Carolina, and Illinois, but failed to sway the conservative legislatures in those states. After Indiana ratified in 1977, the amendment still lacked three votes toward the three-fourths majority needed for adoption. Efforts to revive the ERA in the 1980s were unsuccessful, and it became a dead issue.

Abzug (D-NY), and Shirley Chisholm (D-NY), found enthusiastic male allies—among both Democrats and Republicans—and Congress adopted the amendment in 1972. Within just two years, thirty-four of the necessary thirty-eight states had ratified it, and the ERA appeared headed for adoption. But then, progress abruptly halted (Map 29.2).

Credit for putting the brakes on ERA ratification goes chiefly to a remarkable woman: Phyllis Schlafly, a lawyer long active in conservative causes. Despite her own flourishing career, Schlafly advocated traditional roles for women. The ERA, she proclaimed, would create an unnatural "unisex society," with women drafted into the army and forced to use single-sex toilets. Abortion, she alleged, could never be prohibited by law. Led by Schlafly's organization, STOP ERA, thousands of women mobilized, showing up at statehouses with home-baked bread and apple pies. As labels on baked goods at one anti-ERA rally expressed it: "My heart and hand went into this dough / For the sake of the family

please vote no." It was a message that resonated widely, especially among those troubled by the rapid pace of social change (see Comparing American Voices, "Debating the Equal Rights Amendment," pp. 936–937). The ERA never was ratified, despite a congressional extension of the deadline to June 30, 1982.

Roe v. Wade | In addition to the ERA, the women's movement had identified another major goal: winning reproductive rights. Activists pursued two tracks: legislative and judicial. In the early 1960s, abortion was illegal in virtually every state. A decade later, thanks to intensive lobbying by women's organizations, liberal ministers, and physicians, a handful of states, such as New York, Hawaii, California, and Colorado, adopted laws making legal abortions easier to obtain. But progress after that was slow, and women's advocates turned to the courts. There was reason to be optimistic. The Supreme Court had first addressed reproductive rights in a 1965 case, *Griswold v. Connecticut*.

Thus I have given you, I think, the Substance of the Arguments o both sides of that great and important Questi

Debating the Equal Rights Amendment

Fifty years after its introduction, the Equal Rights Amendment ("Equality of rights under the law shall not be denied or abridged by the United States or by any State on account of sex") finally met congressional approval in 1972 and was sent to the states for ratification. The amendment set off a furious debate, especially in the South and Midwest, and fell short of ratification. Following are four of the voices in that debate.

Phyllis Schlafly

Lawyer and political activist Phyllis Schlafly was the most prominent opponent of the ERA. Her organization, STOP ERA, campaigned against the amendment in critical states and helped to halt ratification.

Women's magazines, the women's pages of newspapers, and television and radio talk shows have been filled for months with a strident advocacy of the "rights" of women to be treated on an equal basis with men in all walks of life. But what about the rights of the woman who doesn't want to compete on an equal basis with men? Does she have the right to be treated as a woman—by her family, by society, and by the law? . . .

The laws of every one of our 50 states now guarantee the right to be a woman—protected and provided for in her career as a woman, wife, and mother. The proposed Equal Rights Amendment will wipe out all our laws which—through rights, benefits, and exemptions—guarantee this right to be a woman. . . . Is this what American women want? Is this what American men want?

The laws of every one of the 50 states now require the *husband* to support his wife and children—and to provide a home for them to live in. In other words, the law protects a woman's right to be a full-time wife and mother, her right *not* to take a job outside the home, her right to care for her own baby in her own home while being financially supported by her husband. . . .

There are two very different types of women lobbying for the Equal Rights Amendment. One group is the women's liberationists. Their motive is totally radical. They hate men, marriage, and children. They are out to destroy morality and the family. . . . There is another type of woman supporting the Equal Rights Amendment from the most sincere motives. It is easy to see why the business and professional women are supporting the Equal Rights Amendment—many of them have felt the keen edge of discrimination in their employment.

Source: *The Phyllis Schlafly Report*, November 1972, 1–4.

Jerry Falwell

Jerry Falwell was a fundamentalist Baptist preacher in Virginia, a television evangelist, and the founder of the political lobbying organization known as the Moral Majority.

I believe that at the foundation of the women's liberation movement there is a minority core of women who were once bored with life, whose real problems are spiritual problems. Many women have never accepted their God-given roles. . . . God Almighty created men and women biologically different and with differing needs and roles. He made men and women to complement each other and to love each other. . . . Women who work should be respected and accorded dignity and equal rewards for equal work. But this is not what the present feminist movement and equal rights movement are all about.

The Equal Rights Amendment is a delusion. I believe that women deserve more than equal rights. And, in families and in nations where the Bible is believed, Christian women are honored above men. Only in places where the Bible is believed and practiced do women receive more than equal rights. Men and women have differing strengths. The Equal Rights Amendment can never do for women what needs to be done for them. Women need to know Jesus Christ as their Lord and Savior and be under His Lordship. They need a man who knows Jesus Christ as his Lord and Savior, and they need to be part of a home where their husband is a godly leader and where there is a Christian family. . . .

ERA is not merely a political issue, but a moral issue as well. A definite violation of holy Scripture, ERA defies the mandate that "the husband is the head of the wife, even as Christ is the head of the church" (Ep. 5:23). In 1 Peter 3:7 we read that husbands are to give their wives honor as unto the weaker vessel, that they are both heirs together of the grace of life. Because a woman is weaker does not mean that she is less important.

Source: Jerry Falwell, *Listen America* (New York: Doubleday, 1980), 150–151.

Elizabeth Duncan Koontz

Elizabeth Duncan Koontz was a distinguished educator, and the first black woman to head the National Education Association and the U.S. Women's Bureau. At the time she made this statement at state legislative hearings on the ERA in 1977, she was assistant state superintendent for public instruction in North Carolina.

A short time ago I had the misfortune to break my foot. . . . The pain . . . did not hurt me as much as when I went into the emergency room and the young woman upon asking me my name, the nature of my ailment, then asked me for my husband's social security number and his hospitalization number. I asked her what did that have to do with my emergency.

And she said, "We have to be sure of who is going to pay your bill." I said, "Suppose I'm not married, then." And she said, "Then give me your father's name." I did not go through that twenty years ago when I was denied the use of that emergency room because of my color.

I went through that because there is an underlying assumption that all women in our society are protected, dependent, cared for by somebody who's got a social security number and hospitalization insurance. Never once did she assume I might be a woman who might be caring for my husband, instead of him by me, because of some illness. She did not take into account the fact that one out of almost eight women heading families in poverty today [is] in the same condition as men in families and poverty. . . .

My greater concern is that so many women today . . . oppose the passage of the ERA very sincerely and . . . tell you without batting an eye, "I don't want to see women treated that way." And I speak up, "What way is that?" . . . Women themselves have been a bit misguided. We have mistaken present practice for law, and women have . . . assumed too many times that their present condition cannot change. The rate of divorce, the rate of desertion, the rate of separation, and the death rate of male supporters is enough for us to say: "Let us remove all legal barriers to women and girls making their choices—this state cannot afford it."

Source: William A. Link and Marjorie Spruill Wheeler, eds. *The South in the History of the Nation* (Boston: Bedford/St. Martin's, 1999), 295–296.

Caroline Bird

Caroline Bird was the lead author of *What Women Want*, a report produced by women's rights advocates following the 1977 National Women's Conference, held in Houston, Texas.

The Declaration of Independence, signed in 1776, stated that "all Men are created equal" and that governments derive their powers "from the Consent of the Governed." Women were not included in either concept. The original American Constitution of 1787 was founded on English common law, which did not recognize women as citizens or as individuals with legal rights. A woman was expected to obey her husband or nearest male kin, and if she was married her person and her property were owned by her husband. . . .

It has been argued that the ERA is not necessary because the Fourteenth Amendment, passed after the Civil War, guarantees that no state shall deny to "any person within its jurisdiction the equal protection of the laws." . . .

Aside from the fact that women have been subjected to varying, inconsistent, and often unfavorable decisions under the Fourteenth Amendment, the Equal Rights Amendment is a more immediate and effective remedy to sex discrimination in Federal and State laws than case-by-case interpretation under the Fourteenth Amendment could ever be.

Source: Caroline Bird, *What Women Want* (New York: Simon & Schuster, 1978), 120–121.

ANALYZING THE EVIDENCE

- Schlafly and Koontz have different notions of what it means to be a woman. Explain what these differences are and how they inform the authors' distinct views of the ERA.

- Why does Schlafly believe that women will be harmed by the ERA?

- Schlafly and Falwell argue that women need the protection and support of men. Are they right? What would Koontz likely say in response?

- How do each of the four authors define women's roles and responsibilities in society?

Harvey Milk

In November 1977, Harvey Milk became the first openly gay man to be elected to public office in the United States, when he won a seat on the San Francisco Board of Supervisors. Shockingly, almost exactly a year from the day of his election, Milk was assassinated. © Bettmann/Corbis.

Griswold struck down an 1879 state law prohibiting the possession of contraception as a violation of married couples' constitutional "right of privacy." Following the logic articulated in *Griswold*, the Court gradually expanded the right of privacy in a series of cases in the late 1960s and early 1970s.

Those cases culminated in *Roe v. Wade* (1973). In that landmark decision, the justices nullified a Texas law that prohibited abortion under any circumstances, even when the woman's health was at risk, and laid out a new national standard: Abortions performed during the first trimester were protected by the right of privacy. At the time and afterward, some legal authorities questioned whether the Constitution recognized any such privacy right and criticized the Court's seemingly arbitrary first-trimester timeline. Nevertheless, the Supreme Court chose to move forward, transforming a traditionally state-regulated policy into a national, constitutionally protected right.

For the women's movement, *Roe v. Wade* represented a triumph. For evangelical and fundamentalist Christians, Catholics, and conservatives generally, it was a bitter pill. In their view, abortion was, unequivocally, murder. These Americans, represented by groups such as the National Right to Life Committee, did not believe that something they regarded as immoral and sinful could be the basis for women's equality. Women's advocates responded that illegal abortions — common prior to *Roe* — were often unsafe procedures, which resulted in physical harm to women and even death. *Roe* polarized what was already a sharply divided public and mobilized conservatives to seek a Supreme Court reversal or, short of that, to pursue legislation that would strictly limit the conditions under which abortions could be performed. In 1976, they convinced Congress to deny Medicaid funds for abortions, an opening round in a campaign against *Roe v. Wade* that continues today.

Harvey Milk The gay rights movement had achieved notable victories as well. These, too, proved controversial. More than a dozen cities had passed gay rights ordinances by the mid-1970s, protecting gay men and lesbians from employment and housing discrimination. One such ordinance in Dade County (Miami), Florida, sparked a protest led by Anita Bryant, a conservative Baptist and a television celebrity. Her "Save Our Children" campaign in 1977, which garnered national media attention, resulted in the repeal of the ordinance and symbolized the emergence of a conservative religious movement opposed to gay rights.

Across the country from Miami, developments in San Francisco looked promising for gay rights advocates, then turned tragic. No one embodied the combination of gay liberation and hard-nosed politics better than a San Francisco camera-shop owner named Harvey Milk. A closeted businessman in New York until he was forty, Milk arrived in San Francisco in 1972 and threw himself into city politics. Fiercely independent, he refused to work through the established channels of gay leadership in the city, believing that their behind-the-scenes style did more harm than good to the movement. Milk ran as an openly gay candidate for city supervisor (city council) twice and the state assembly once, both times unsuccessfully.

By mobilizing the "gay vote" into a powerful bloc, Milk finally won a supervisor seat in 1977. He was not the first openly gay elected official in the country—Kathy Kozachenko of Michigan and Elaine Noble of Massachusetts share that distinction—but he became a national symbol of emerging gay political power. Tragically, after he helped to win passage of a gay rights ordinance in San Francisco, he was assassinated—along with the city's mayor, George Moscone—by a disgruntled former supervisor named Dan White. When White was convicted of manslaughter rather than murder, five thousand gays and lesbians in San Francisco marched on city hall.

The Supreme Court and the Rights Revolution

The rights revolution found an ally in an unexpected place: the U.S. Supreme Court. The decision that stood as a landmark in the civil rights movement, *Brown v. Board of Education* (1954), triggered a larger judicial revolution. Following *Brown*, the Court increasingly agreed to hear human rights and civil liberties cases—as opposed to its previous focus on property-related suits. Surprisingly, this shift was led by the man whom President Dwight Eisenhower had appointed chief justice in 1953: Earl Warren. A popular Republican governor of California, Warren surprised many, including Eisenhower himself, with his robust advocacy of civil rights and civil liberties. The Warren Court lasted from 1954 until 1969 and established some of the most far-reaching liberal jurisprudence in U.S. history.

Law and Order and the Warren Court | Right-wing activists in the 1970s came to detest the Warren Court, which they accused of "legislating from the bench" and contributing to social breakdown. They pointed, for instance, to the Court's rulings that people who are arrested have a constitutional right to counsel (1963, 1964) and, in *Miranda v. Arizona* (1966), that arrestees have to be informed by police of their right to remain silent. Compounding conservatives' frustration was a series of decisions that liberalized restrictions on pornography. Trying to walk the fine line between censorship and obscenity, the Court ruled in *Roth v. United States* (1957) that obscene material had to be "utterly without redeeming social importance" to be banned. The "social importance" test, however, proved nearly impossible to define and left wide latitude for pornography to flourish. That measure was finally abandoned in 1972, when the Court ruled in *Miller v. California* that "contemporary community standards" were the rightful measure of obscenity. But *Miller*, too, had little effect on the pornographic magazines, films, and peep shows proliferating in the 1970s. Conservatives found these decisions especially distasteful, since the Court had also ruled that religious ritual of any kind in public schools—including prayers and Bible reading—violated the constitutional separation of church and state. To many religious Americans, the Court had taken the side of immorality over Christian values.

Supreme Court critics blamed rising crime rates and social breakdown on the Warren Court's liberal judicial record. Every category of crime was up in the 1970s, but especially disconcerting was the doubling of the murder rate since the 1950s and the 76 percent increase in burglary and theft between 1967 and 1976. Sensational crimes had always grabbed headlines, but now "crime" itself preoccupied politicians, the media, and the public. However, no one could establish a direct causal link between increases in crime and Supreme Court decisions, given a myriad of other social factors, including drugs, income inequality, enhanced statistical record-keeping, and the proliferation of guns. But when many Americans looked at their cities in the 1970s, they saw pornographic theaters, X-rated bookstores, and rising crime rates. Where, they wondered, was law and order?

The Burger Court | In response to what conservatives considered the liberal judicial revolution under the Warren Court, President Nixon came into the presidency promising to appoint "strict constructionists" (conservative-minded justices) to the bench. In three short years, between 1969 and 1972, he was able to appoint four new justices to the Supreme Court, including the new chief justice, Warren Burger. Surprisingly, despite the conservative credentials of its new members, the Burger Court refused to scale back the liberal precedents set under Warren. Most prominently, in *Roe v. Wade* (1973) the Burger Court extended the "right of privacy" developed under Warren to include women's access to abortion. Few Supreme Court decisions in the twentieth century have disappointed conservatives more.

In a variety of cases, the Burger Court either confirmed previous liberal rulings or chose a centrist course.

In 1972, for instance, the Court deepened its intervention in criminal procedure by striking down all existing capital punishment laws, in *Furman v. Georgia*. In response, Los Angeles police chief Ed Davis accused the Court of establishing a "legal oligarchy" that had ignored the "perspective of the average citizen." He and other conservatives vowed a nationwide campaign to bring back the death penalty—which was in fact shortly restored, in *Gregg v. Georgia* (1976). Other decisions advanced women's rights. In 1976, the Court ruled that arbitrary distinctions based on sex in the workplace and other arenas were unconstitutional, and in 1986 that sexual harassment violated the Civil Rights Act. These rulings helped women break employment barriers in the subsequent decades.

In all of their rulings on privacy rights, however, both the Warren and Burger Courts confined their decisions to heterosexuals. The justices were reluctant to move ahead of public attitudes toward homosexuality. Gay men and lesbians still had no legal recourse if state laws prohibited same-sex relations. In a controversial 1986 case, *Bowers v. Hardwick*, the Supreme Court upheld a Georgia sodomy statute that criminalized same-sex sexual acts. The majority opinion held that homosexuality was contrary to "ordered liberty" and that extending sexual privacy to gays and lesbians "would be to cast aside millennia of moral teaching." Not until 2003 (*Lawrence v. Texas*) would the court overturn that decision, recognizing for all Americans the right to sexual privacy.

- How did the idea of civil rights expand during the 1970s?
- How did the U.S. Supreme Court affect the extension or restriction of rights during the 1970s?

The American Family on Trial

In 1973, the Public Broadcasting System (PBS) aired a twelve-part television series that followed the life of a real American family. Producers wanted the show, called simply *An American Family*, to document how a middle-class white family coped with the stresses of a changing society. They did not anticipate that the family would dissolve in front of their cameras. Tensions and arguments raged, and in the final episode, Bill, the husband and father (who had had numerous extramarital affairs), moved out. By the time the show aired, the couple was divorced and Pat, the former wife, had become a single working mother with two sons.

An American Family captured a traumatic moment in the twentieth-century history of the family. Between 1965 and 1985, the divorce rate doubled, and children born in the 1970s had a 40 percent chance of spending part of their youth in a single-parent household. Moreover, as wages stagnated and inflation pushed prices up, more and more families depended on two incomes for survival. Furthermore, the women's movement and the

Blue-Collar Blues

Unemployment in the 1970s affected blue-collar workers most, with many factories closing, and new construction at a standstill. In many cities, joblessness among construction workers stood between 20 and 30 percent. In this 1976 photo, an unemployed carpenter in Cleveland, Ohio, files for unemployment insurance. The "blue-collar blues" caused by long unemployment lines, high inflation, and difficult economic times hit American workers hard in the late 1970s. © 1976 Settle/The New York Times Company. Reprinted with Permission.

counterculture had called into question traditional sex roles—father as provider and mother as homemaker—and middle-class baby boomers rebelled against what they saw as the puritanical sexual values of their parents' generation. In the midst of such rapid change, where did the family stand?

Working Families in the Age of Deindustrialization

One of the most striking developments of the 1970s and 1980s was the relative stagnation of wages. After World War II, hourly wages had grown steadily ahead of inflation, giving workers more buying power with each passing decade. By 1973, that trend had stopped in its tracks. The decline of organized labor, the loss of manufacturing jobs, and runaway inflation all played a role in the reversal. Hardest hit were blue-collar and pink-collar workers and those without college degrees.

Millions of wives and mothers had worked for wages for decades. But many Americans still believed in the "family wage": a breadwinner income, earned by men, sufficient to support a family. After 1973, fewer and fewer Americans had access to that luxury. Between 1973 and the early 1990s, every major income group except the top 10 percent saw their real earnings (accounting for inflation) either remain the same or decline. Over this period, the typical worker saw a 10 percent drop in real wages. To keep their families from falling behind, women streamed into the workforce. Between 1950 and 1994, the proportion of women ages 25 to 54 working for pay increased from 37 to 75 percent. Much of that increase occurred in the 1970s. Americans were fast becoming dependent on the two-income household (Figure 29.3).

The numbers tell two different stories of American life in these decades. On the one hand, the trends unmistakably show that women, especially in blue-collar and pink-collar families, *had* to work for wages to sustain their family's standard of living: to buy a car, pay for college, afford medical bills, support an aging parent, or simply pay the rent. Moreover, the number of single women raising children nearly doubled between 1965 and 1990. Women's paid labor was making up for the declining earning power or the absence of men in American households. On the other hand, women's real income overall grew during the same period. This increase reflected the opening of professional and skilled jobs to educated baby-boomer women. As older barriers began to fall, women poured into law and medicine, business and government, the sciences and engineering. Beneficiaries of feminism, these women pursued careers of which their mothers had only dreamed.

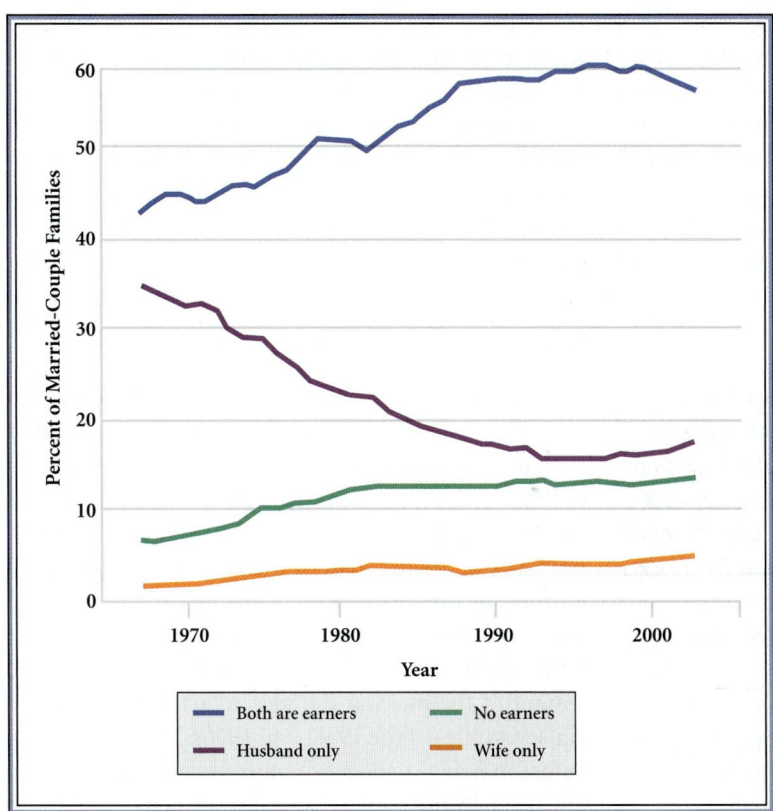

FIGURE 29.3

The Increase in Two-Worker Families

In 1968, about 43 percent of married couples sent both the husband and the wife into the workforce; thirty years later, 60 percent were two-earner families. The percentage of families in which the wife alone worked increased from 3 to 5 percent during these years, while those with no earners (welfare recipients and, increasingly, retired couples) rose from 8 to 13 percent. Because these figures do not include unmarried persons and most illegal immigrants, they do not give a complete picture of the American workplace. But there is no doubt that women now play a major role in the workforce.

Good Times

The popular 1970s sitcom *Good Times* examined how the "blue-collar blues" affected a working-class black family struggling to make ends meet in tough economic times. The show's theme song spoke of "temporary layoffs . . . easy credit ripoffs . . . scratchin' and surviving." Its actors, many of them classically trained, brought a realistic portrait of working-class African American life to television. © Bettmann/Corbis.

Workers in the National Spotlight For a brief period in the 1970s, the trials of working men and women made a distinct imprint on national culture. Reporters wrote of the "blue-collar blues" associated with plant closings and the hard-fought strikes of the decade. A 1972 strike at the Lordstown, Ohio, General Motors plant captivated the nation. Holding out not for higher wages but for better working conditions—the plant had the most complex assembly line in the nation—Lordstown strikers spoke out against what they saw as an inhumane industrial system. Across the nation, the number of union-led strikes surged, even as the number of Americans in the labor movement continued to decline. In Lordstown and most other sites of strikes and industrial conflict, workers won a measure of public attention but typically gained little economic ground.

When Americans turned on their televisions in the mid-1970s, the most popular shows reflected the "blue collar blues" of struggling families. *All in the Family* was joined by *The Waltons*, set during the Great Depression. *Good Times*, *Welcome Back Kotter*, and *Sanford and Son* dealt with poverty in the inner city. *The Jeffersons* featured an upwardly mobile black couple. *Laverne and Shirley* focused on young working women in the 1950s and *One Day at a Time* on working women in the 1970s making do after divorce. The most-watched television series of the decade, 1977's eight-part *Roots*, explored the history of slavery and the survival of African American culture and family roots despite the oppressive labor system. Not since the 1930s had American culture paid such close attention to working-class life.

The decade also saw the rise of musicians such as Bruce Springsteen, Johnny Paycheck, and John Cougar (Mellencamp), who became stars by turning the hardscrabble lives of people in small towns and working-class communities into rock anthems that filled arenas. Springsteen wrote songs about characters who "sweat it out in the streets of a runaway American dream," and, to the delight of his audience, Paycheck famously sang, "Take this job and shove it!" Meanwhile, on the streets of Harlem and the South Bronx in New York, young working-class African American men experimenting with dance and musical forms invented break dancing and rap music—styles that expressed both the hardship and the creativity of working-class black life in the deindustrialized American city.

Navigating the Sexual Revolution

The economic downturn was not the only force that placed stress on American families in this era. Another such force was what many came to call the "sexual revolution." Hardly revolutionary, sexual attitudes in the 1970s were, in many ways, a logical evolution of developments in the first half of the twentieth century. Beginning in the 1920s, Americans increasingly viewed sex as a component of personal happiness, distinct from reproduction. Attitudes toward sex grew even more lenient in the postwar decades, a fact reflected in the Kinsey studies of the 1940s and 1950s. By the 1960s, sex before marriage had grown more socially acceptable—an especially profound change for women—and frank discussions of sex in the media and popular culture had grown more common.

In that decade, three developments dramatically accelerated this process: the introduction of the birth control pill, the rise of the baby-boomer-led counterculture, and the influence of feminism. First made available in the United States in 1960, the birth control pill gave women an unprecedented degree of control over reproduction. By 1965, more than 6 million American women were taking advantage of this pharmaceutical advance. Rapid shifts in attitude accompanied the technological breakthrough. Middle-class baby boomers embraced a sexual ethic of greater freedom and, in many cases, a more casual approach to sex outside marriage. "I just feel I am expressing myself the way I feel at that moment in the most natural way," a female California college student, explaining her sex life, told a reporter in 1966. The rebellious counterculture encouraged this attitudinal shift by associating a puritanical view of sex with their parents' generation.

Finally, women's rights activists reacted to the new emphasis on sexual freedom in at least two distinct ways. For many feminists, the emphasis on casual sex seemed to perpetuate male privilege. They argued that while men could now freely explore numerous sexual relationships without social sanction, women remained trapped by a culture that still required them to be "innocent" and not to "sleep around"—the old double standard. Moreover, sexual harassment was all too common in the workplace, and the proliferation of pornography continued to commercialize women as sex objects. On the one hand, many feminists argued that the sexual revolution was by and for men. On the other hand, they remained optimistic that the new sexual ethic could free women from those older moral constraints. They called for a revolution in sexual *values*, not simply behavior, that would end exploitation and grant women the freedom to explore their sexuality on equal terms with men.

Sex and Popular Culture   In the 1970s, popular culture was suffused with discussions of the sexual revolution. Mass-market books with titles such as *Everything You Always Wanted to Know About Sex*, *Human Sexual Response*, and *The Sensuous Man* shot up the best-seller list. William Masters and Virginia Johnson became the most famous sex researchers since Alfred Kinsey by studying couples in the act of lovemaking. In 1972, English physician Alex Comfort published *The Joy of Sex*, a guidebook for couples that became one of the most popular books of the decade. Comfort made certain to distinguish his writing from pornographic

Sexual Revolution at the Movies

In the mid-1970s, the movie industry embraced the "sexual revolution" and pushed the boundaries of middle-class taste. Movies such as *Shampoo* (1975)—starring Hollywood's leading ladies' man, Warren Beatty—were part of a larger shift in American culture in which frank sexual discussions and the portrayal of sexual situations in various media grew more acceptable.   Columbia Pictures.

exploitation. "Sex is the one place where we today can learn to treat people as people," he wrote.

Hollywood took advantage of the new sexual ethic by making films with explicit erotic content that pushed the boundaries of middle-class taste. Films such as *Midnight Cowboy* (1969), *Carnal Knowledge* (1971), and *Shampoo* (1974), the latter starring Hollywood's leading ladies' man, Warren Beatty, led the way. Throughout the decade, and into the 1980s, the Motion Picture Association of America (MPAA) scrambled to keep its guide for parents—the system of rating pictures G, PG, R, and X (and, after 1984, PG-13)—in tune with Hollywood's advancing sexual revolution.

On television, the popularity of social problem shows, such as *All in the Family*, and the fear of losing advertising revenue moderated the portrayal of sex in the early 1970s. However, in the second half of the decade networks both exploited and criticized the new sexual ethic. In frivolous, lighthearted shows such as the popular *Charlie's Angels*, *Three's Company*, and *The Love Boat*, heterosexual couples explored the often confusing, and usually comical, landscape of sexual morality. At the same time, between 1974 and 1981, the major networks produced more than a dozen made-for-TV movies about children in sexual danger—a sensationalized warning to parents of the potential threats to children posed by a less strict sexual morality.

Middle-Class Marriage Many Americans worried that the sexual revolution threatened marriage itself. The notion of marriage as romantic companionship had defined middle-class norms since the early nineteenth century. It was also quite common throughout most of the twentieth century for Americans to see sexual satisfaction as a healthy part of the marriage bond. But what defined a healthy marriage in an age of rising divorce rates, changing sexual values, and feminist critiques of the nuclear family? Only a small minority of Americans rejected marriage outright; most continued to create monogamous relationships codified in marriage. But many came to believe that they needed help as marriage came under a variety of stresses—economic, psychological, and sexual.

A therapeutic industry arose in response. Churches and secular groups alike established marriage seminars and counseling services to assist couples in sustaining a healthy marriage. A popular form of 1960s psychotherapy, the "encounter group," was adapted to marriage counseling: Couples met in large groups to explore new methods of communicating. One of the most successful of these organizations, Marriage Encounter, was founded by the Catholic Church. It expanded into Protestant and Jewish communities in the 1970s and became one of the nation's largest counseling organizations. Such groups embodied another long-term shift in how middle-class Americans understood marriage. Spurred by both feminism and psychotherapeutic models that stressed self-improvement, Americans increasingly defined marriage not simply by companionship and sexual fidelity but also by the deeply felt emotional connection between two people.

Religion in the 1970s: The Fourth Great Awakening

For three centuries, American society has been punctuated by intense periods of religious revival—what historians have called "Great Awakenings" (see Chapters 4 and 8). These periods have seen rising church membership, the appearance of charismatic religious leaders, and the increasing influence of religion, usually

of the evangelical variety, on society and politics. One such awakening, the fourth in U.S. history, took shape in the 1970s and 1980s. It had many elements, but one of its central features was a growing concern with the family.

In the 1950s and 1960s, many mainstream Protestants had embraced the reform spirit of the age. Some of the most visible Protestant leaders were social activists who condemned racism and opposed the Vietnam War. Organizations such as the National Council of Churches—along with many progressive Catholics and Jews—joined with Martin Luther King Jr. and other African American ministers in the long battle for civil rights. Many mainline Protestant churches, among them the Episcopal, Methodist, and Congregationalist denominations, practiced a version of the "Social Gospel," the reform-minded Christianity of the early twentieth century.

Evangelical Resurgence Meanwhile, evangelical Protestantism survived at the grass roots. Evangelical churches emphasized an intimate, *personal* salvation (being "born again"); focused on a literal interpretation of the Bible; and regarded the death and resurrection of Jesus as the central message of Christianity. These tenets distinguished evangelicals from mainline Protestants as well as from Catholics and Jews, and they flourished in a handful of evangelical colleges, Bible schools, and seminaries in the postwar decades.

No one did more to keep the evangelical fire burning than Billy Graham. A graduate of the evangelical Wheaton College in Illinois, Graham cofounded Youth for Christ in 1945 and then toured the United States and Europe preaching the gospel. Following a stunning 1949 tent revival in Los Angeles that lasted eight weeks, Graham shot to national fame. His success in Los Angeles led to a popular radio program, but he continued to travel relentlessly, conducting old-fashioned revival meetings he called "crusades." A massive sixteen-week 1957 crusade held in New York City's Madison Square Garden made Graham, along with the conservative Catholic priest Fulton Sheen one of the nation's most visible religious leaders.

Graham and other evangelicals in the 1950s and 1960s laid the groundwork for the Fourth Great Awakening. But it was the secular liberalism of the late 1960s and early 1970s that sparked the countervailing evangelical revival. Many Americans regarded feminism, the counterculture, sexual freedom, homosexuality, pornography, divorce, and legalized abortion not as distinct issues, but as a collective sign of moral decay in society. To seek answers and find order, more and more people

Televangelism

Television minister ("televangelist") and conservative political activist Pat Robertson, shown here in the control room of his *700 Club* TV show, was a leading figure in the resurgence of evangelical Christianity in the 1970s and 1980s. Reaching millions of viewers through their television ministries, men such as Robertson built huge churches and large popular followings.   © Wally McNamee/CORBIS

turned to evangelical ministries, especially Southern Baptist, Pentecostal, and Assemblies of God churches. Numbers tell part of the story. As mainline churches lost about 15 percent of their membership between 1970 and 1985, evangelical church membership soared. The Southern Baptist Convention, the largest Protestant denomination, grew by 23 percent, while the Assemblies of God grew by an astounding 300 percent. *Newsweek* magazine declared 1976 "The Year of the Evangelical," and that November the nation made Jimmy Carter the nation's first evangelical president. In a national Gallup poll, 34 percent of Americans answered yes when asked, "Would you describe yourself as a 'born again' or evangelical Christian?"

Much of this astonishing growth came from the creative use of television. Graham had pounded the pavement and worn out shoe leather to reach his converts. But a new generation of preachers brought religious conversion directly into Americans' living rooms through television. These so-called televangelists built huge media empires through small donations from millions of avid viewers—not to mention advertising. Jerry Falwell's *Old Time Gospel Hour*, Pat Robertson's *700 Club*, and Jim and Tammy Bakker's *PTL (Praise the Lord) Club* were the leading pioneers in this televised race for American souls, but another half dozen—including Oral Roberts and Jimmy Swaggart—followed them onto the airwaves. Together, they made the 1970s and 1980s the era of Christian broadcasting.

Religion and the Family   Of primary concern to evangelical Christians was the family. Drawing on selected Bible passages, evangelicals believed that the nuclear family, and not the individual, represented the fundamental unit of society. The family itself was organized along paternalist lines: Father was breadwinner and disciplinarian; mother was nurturer and supporter. "Motherhood is the highest form of femininity," the evangelical author Beverly LaHaye wrote in an influential book on Christian women. Another popular Christian author declared, "A church, a family, a nation is only as strong as its men."

Evangelicals spread their message about the Christian family through more than the pulpit and television. They founded publishing houses, wrote books, established foundations, and offered seminars. Helen B. Andelin, for instance, a California housewife, produced a homemade book called *Fascinating Womanhood* that eventually sold more than 2 million copies. She used the book as the basis for her classes, which by the early 1970s had been attended by 400,000 women and boasted 11,000 trained teachers. *Fascinating Womanhood* was an evangelical response to the women's movement. Where the latter encouraged women to be independent and to seek equality with men, Andelin taught that "submissiveness will bring a strange but righteous power over your man." Andelin was but one of dozens of evangelical authors and educators who encouraged women to defer to men.

Evangelical Christians held that strict gender roles in the family would ward off the influences of an immoral society. Christian activists were especially concerned with sex education in public schools, the proliferation of pornography, legalized abortion, and the rising divorce rate. For them, the answer was to strengthen what they called "traditional" family structures. By the early 1980s, Christians could choose from among hundreds of evangelical books, take classes on how to save a marriage or how to be a Christian parent, attend evangelical churches and Bible study courses, watch evangelical ministers on television, and donate to foundations that promoted "Christian values" in state legislatures and the U.S. Congress.

Wherever one looked in the 1970s and early 1980s, American families were under strain. Nearly everyone agreed that the waves of social liberalism and economic transformation that swept over the nation in the 1960s and 1970s had destabilized society and, especially, family relationships. But Americans did not agree about how to *re*stabilize families. Indeed, different approaches to the family would further divide the country in the 1980s and 1990s, as the New Right would increasingly make "family values" a political issue.

- In what ways were American families tested in the 1970s? Why was there so much concern about the future of the family?

- How did evangelical Christianity influence American society in the 1970s and 1980s?

SUMMARY

For much of the 1970s, Americans struggled with economic problems, including inflation, energy shortages, income stagnation, and deindustrialization. These challenges highlighted the limits of postwar prosperity and forced Americans to consider lowering their economic expectations. In the midst of this gloomy economic climate, they also sought political and cultural resolutions to the upheavals of the 1960s. A movement for environmental protection, widely supported, led to new laws and an awareness of nature's limits. Meanwhile, the battle for civil rights entered a second stage, expanding to encompass women's rights and gay rights, the rights of alleged criminals and prisoners, and, in the realm of racial justice, focusing on the problem of producing concrete results rather than legislation. Many liberals cheered these developments, but another effect was to strengthen a new, more conservative social mood that began to challenge liberal values in politics and society more generally. Finally, we considered the multiple challenges faced by the American family in the 1970s and how a perception that the family was in trouble helped to spur an evangelical religious revival that would shape American society for decades to come.

CHAPTER REVIEW QUESTIONS

- Why did the U.S. economy struggle in the 1970s? How was the period after 1973 different from 1945–1972?

- How was the "rights liberalism" of this era different from the "welfare liberalism" of the 1930s and 1940s?

- How was the American family of the 1970s different from that of the 1950s? Without romanticizing either period, how would you account for the differences?

FOR FURTHER EXPLORATION

Excellent overviews of the era include Rick Perlstein, *Nixonland: The Rise of a President and the Fracturing of America* (2008), and Bruce Schulman, *The Seventies: The Great Shift in American Culture, Society, and Politics* (2001). For documents on the Carter presidency, see Daniel Horowitz, *Jimmy Carter and the Energy Crisis of the 1970s* (2005). On the American environmental movement, see Kirkpatrick Sale, *The Green Revolution: The American Environmental Movement, 1962–1992* (1993). J. Anthony Lukas, *Common Ground* (1985), tells the story of the Boston busing crisis through the biographies of three families. Barbara Ehrenreich examines the backlash against feminism in *Hearts of Men* (1984). A sweeping treatment of *Roe v. Wade* is N. E. H. Hull and Peter Charles Hoffer, *Roe v. Wade: The Abortion Rights Controversy in American History* (2001). For a thought-provoking analysis of Christian broadcasting, see Jeffrey Hadden and Anson Shupe, *Televangelism: Power and Politics on God's Frontier* (1988).

The Oyez Project at Northwestern University, at **www.oyez.org/oyez/frontpage**, is an invaluable resource for more than one thousand Supreme Court cases, with audio transcripts, voting records, and summaries. For this period, see, for example, its materials on *Roe v. Wade*, *Bakke v. University of California*, and *Griswold v. Connecticut*. Documents from the Women's Liberation Movement, culled from the Duke University Special Collections Library, emphasize the women's movement of the late 1960s and early 1970s. This searchable site, at **scriptorium.lib.duke.edu/wlm**, includes books, pamphlets, and other written materials.

TEST YOUR KNOWLEDGE

To assess your command of the material in this chapter, see the Online Study Guide at **bedfordstmartins.com/henretta**.

For Web sites, images, and documents related to topics and places in this chapter, visit **bedfordstmartins.com/makehistory**.

TIMELINE

1970	Earth Day first observed Environmental Protection Agency established
1971	*Swan v. Charlotte-Mecklenburg* approves countywide busing First U.S. trade deficit in twentieth century
1972	Equal Rights Amendment passed by Congress Phyllis Schlafly founds STOP ERA *Furman v. Georgia* outlaws death penalty
1973	*Roe v. Wade* legalizes abortion Endangered Species Act Arab oil embargo; gas shortages Period of high inflation begins *San Antonio School District v. Rodriguez* rules property tax funding of schools constitutional
1974	Nixon resigns over Watergate Busing controversy in Boston *Milliken v. Bradley* limits busing to school district boundaries Congress imposes 55 miles-per-hour speed limit
1975	New York nears bankruptcy "Watergate babies" begin congressional reform
1976	Jimmy Carter elected president
1978	Proposition 13 reduces California property taxes *Bakke v. University of California* limits affirmative action Harvey Milk assassinated in San Francisco
1979	Three Mile Island nuclear accident Chrysler saved from bankruptcy by federal bailout
1980	"Superfund" created to clean up toxic land sites

Conservative America Ascendant, 1973–1991

The decade of the 1970s saw Americans divided by the Vietnam War, wearied by social unrest, and unmoored by economic drift. As a result, many ordinary citizens developed a deep distrust of the muscular Great Society liberalism of the 1960s. Seizing political advantage amid the trauma and divisions, a revived Republican Party, led by the New Right, offered the nation a fresh way forward: economic deregulation, low taxes, Christian morality, and a re-energized Cold War foreign policy. The election of President Ronald Reagan in 1980 symbolized the ascendance of this new political formula, and the president himself helped define the era.

The New Right's rise was part of a larger development in the West in the 1980s. President Reagan in the United States and Prime Minister Margaret Thatcher in England, after decades of largely liberal government policies in both countries, asserted a renewed confidence in "free markets" and called for a smaller government role in economic regulation and social welfare. Reagan famously said, "Government is not the solution to our problem; government *is* the problem." Like the New Right generally, Reagan was profoundly skeptical of the liberal ideology that had informed American public policy since Franklin D. Roosevelt's New Deal. His presidency combined an economically conservative domestic agenda with aggressive anticommunism abroad. Reagan's foreign policy brought an end to **détente** – a lessening of tensions – with the Soviet Union (which had begun with Richard Nixon) and then, unexpectedly, a sudden thawing of U.S.-Soviet relations, laying the groundwork for the end of the Cold War.

Reagan defined the conservative ascendancy of the 1980s, but he did not create the New Right groundswell that brought him into office. Grassroots conservative activists in the 1960s and 1970s built a formidable right-wing movement that awaited an opportune political moment to challenge for national power. That moment came in 1980, when Democratic president Jimmy Carter's popularity plummeted as a result of his mismanagement of two national crises. Raging inflation and the Iranian seizure of U.S. hostages in Tehran undid Carter and provided an opening for the New Right, which would shape the nation's politics for the remainder of the twentieth century and the first decade of the twenty-first.

The Wall Comes Down

As the Communist government of East Germany collapsed, West Berliners showed their contempt for the wall dividing the city by defacing it with graffiti. Then, in November 1989, East and West Berliners destroyed huge sections of the wall with sledgehammers, an act of psychic liberation that symbolized the end of the Cold War. Alexandria Avakian/Woodfin Camp & Associates.

The Rise of the New Right

The Great Depression and World War II discredited the traditional conservative program of limited government at home and diplomatic isolationism abroad. Nevertheless, a right-wing faction survived within the Republican Party. Its adherents continued to oppose the New Deal but reversed their earlier isolationism. Conservatives pushed for military interventions against communism in Europe, Asia, and the developing world while calling for the broadest possible investigation of subversives at home. Heroes of the American right in the 1950s included J. Edgar Hoover, the head of the Federal Bureau of Investigation (FBI) and an outspoken anticommunist; General Douglas MacArthur, who advocated full-scale war with China; and Republican senator Robert A. Taft of Ohio, who accused the New Deal of "socialistic control of all property and income."

However, conservatives failed to devise policies that could win the allegiance of American voters in the two decades after World War II. Republicans by and large continued to favor party moderates, such as Dwight Eisenhower, Thomas Dewey, and Nelson Rockefeller. These were politicians, often called liberal Republicans, who supported much of the New Deal, endorsed the containment policy overseas, and generally steered a middle course through the volatile social and political changes of the postwar era. The conservative faction held out hope, however, that it might one day win the loyalty of a majority of Republicans and remake the party in its image. In the 1960s and 1970s, these conservatives invested their hopes for national resurgence in two dynamic figures: Barry Goldwater and Ronald Reagan. Together, the two carried the conservative banner until the national mood grew more receptive to right-wing appeals.

Barry Goldwater and Ronald Reagan: Champions of the Right

The personal odyssey of Ronald Reagan embodies the story of New Right Republican conservatism. Before World War II, Reagan was a well-known movie actor as well as a New Deal Democrat and admirer of Roosevelt. However, he turned away from liberalism, partly from self-interest (he disliked paying high taxes) and partly on principle. As head of the Screen Actors Guild from 1947 to 1952, Reagan had to deal with its Communist members, who formed the extreme left wing of the American labor movement. Dismayed by their hard-line

Barry Goldwater

Barry Goldwater was a three-term senator from Arizona before he ran for the presidency in 1964 (this photo was taken during the campaign). Goldwater's conservative influence on the Republican Party was considerable, and laid the political groundwork for the rise of Ronald Reagan a decade and a half later.   © Bettmann/Corbis.

tactics and goals, he became a militant anticommunist. After nearly a decade as a spokesperson for the General Electric Corporation, Reagan joined the Republican Party in the early 1960s and began speaking for conservative causes and candidates.

One of those candidates was archconservative Barry Goldwater, a Republican senator from Arizona. Confident in their power, centrist Republicans did not anticipate that grassroots conservatives could challenge the party's old guard and nominate one of their own for president: Goldwater himself. Understanding how they did so in 1964 brings us closer to comprehending the forces that propelled Reagan to the presidency a decade and a half later. Indeed, Reagan the politician came to national attention in 1964 with a televised speech at the Republican convention supporting Goldwater for the presidency. Reagan's address, titled "A Time for Choosing," secured his political future. Striking a dramatic tone, Reagan warned that if we "trade our freedom for the soup kitchen of the welfare state," the nation would "take the first step into a thousand years of darkness."

The Conscience of a Conservative | Like Reagan, Goldwater came from the Sunbelt, where citizens widely celebrated a libertarian spirit of limited government and great personal freedom. His 1960 book, *The Conscience of a Conservative*, set forth an uncompromising conservatism. In direct and accessible prose, Goldwater attacked the New Deal state, arguing that "the natural tendency of government [is] to expand in the direction of absolutism." The problem with the Republican Party, as he saw it, was that Eisenhower had been too accommodating to liberalism. When Ike told reporters that he was "liberal when it comes to human problems," Goldwater privately fumed.

After the appearance of *The Conscience of a Conservative*, a grassroots movement in support of Goldwater emerged in the Republican Party. By distributing his book widely and mobilizing activists at state party conventions, conservatives hoped to create such a groundswell of support that Goldwater could be "drafted" to run for president in 1964, something he reportedly did not wish to do. Meanwhile, Goldwater further enchanted conservatives with another book, *Why Not Victory?*, in which he criticized the containment policy — the strategy of preventing the spread of communism followed by both Democrats and Republicans since 1947 — as weak and defensive. It was, he complained, a policy of "timidly refusing to draw our own lines against aggression . . . unmarked by pride or the prospect of victory." Here was a politician saying exactly what conservatives wanted to hear.

Grassroots Conservatives | Because moderates controlled the Republican Party, winning the 1964 nomination for Goldwater required conservative activists to build their campaign from the bottom up. They found thousands upon thousands of Americans willing to wear down shoe leather for their political hero. Organizations such as the John Birch Society, Young Americans for Freedom, and the Liberty Lobby supplied an army of eager volunteers. They came from such conservative strongholds as Orange County, California, and the fast-growing suburbs of Phoenix, Dallas, Houston, Atlanta, and other Sunbelt cities. A critical boost came in the early spring of 1964, when conservatives outmaneuvered moderates at the state convention of the California Republican Party, which then enthusiastically endorsed Goldwater. The fight had been bruising, and one moderate Republican warned

that "sinister forces are at work to take over the whole Republican apparatus in California."

Another spur to Goldwater backers was the appearance of a book by Phyllis Schlafly, who was then a relatively unknown conservative activist from the Midwest. Like Goldwater's own book, Schlafly's *A Choice Not an Echo* accused moderate Republicans of being Democrats in disguise (that is, an "echo" of Democrats). Schlafly, who reappeared in the national spotlight in the early 1970s to help halt the ratification of the Equal Rights Amendment, denounced the "Rockefeller Republicans" of the Northeast and encouraged the party to embrace a defiant conservatism. Contrasting Goldwater's "grassroots Republicans" with Rockefeller's "kingmakers," Schlafly hoped to "forestall another defeat like 1940, 1944, 1948, and 1960," Democratic victories all.

The conservative groundswell won the Republican nomination for Goldwater. However, his strident tone and militarist foreign policy were too much for a nation mourning the death of John F. Kennedy and still committed to liberalism. Democrat Lyndon B. Johnson defeated Goldwater in a historic landslide (see Chapter 28). Many believed that Goldwater conservatism would wither and die, but instead the nearly four million volunteers who had campaigned for the Arizona senator swung their support to Ronald Reagan. Skilled conservative political operatives such as Richard Viguerie, a Louisiana-born Catholic and antiabortion activist, applied new computer technology to political campaigning. Viguerie took a list of 12,000 Goldwater contributors and used computerized mailing lists to solicit campaign funds, drum up support for conservative causes, and get out the vote on election day. Conservatism was down but not out.

Backed financially by wealthy southern Californians and supported at the grass roots by Goldwaterites, Reagan won California's governorship in 1966 and again in 1970. His impassioned rhetoric supporting limited government and law and order — he vowed to "clean up the mess in Berkeley," referring to campus radicals — won broad support among citizens of the nation's most populous state. More significantly, it made him a force in national politics. His supporters believed that he was in line to succeed Nixon as the next Republican president. The Watergate scandal intervened, however, discrediting Nixon and making Gerald Ford the incumbent. After narrowly losing a campaign against Ford for the Republican presidential nomination in 1976, Reagan was forced to bide his time. When Ford lost to Carter in that year's election, Reagan was the party's brightest star and a near-lock to be the nominee in 1980.

Free-Market Economics and Religious Conservatism

The last phase of Reagan's rise was the product of several additional developments within the New Right. The burgeoning conservative movement increasingly resembled a three-legged stool. Each leg represented an ideological position and a popular constituency: anticommunism, free-market economics, and religious moralism. Uniting all three in a political coalition was no easy feat. Religious moralists demanded strong government action to implement their faith-based agenda, while economic conservatives favored limited government and free markets. Both groups, however, were ardent anticommunists—free marketeers loathed the state-directed Soviet economy, and religious conservatives despised the "godless" secularism of the Soviet state. In the end, the success of the New Right would come to depend on balancing the interests of economic and moral conservatives.

Since the 1950s, William F. Buckley, the founder and editor of the *National Review*, and Milton Friedman, the Nobel Prize–winning economist at the University of Chicago, had been the most prominent conservative intellectuals. Buckley famously wrote that his *National Review* "stands athwart history yelling Stop," meaning it opposed what he called "Liberal orthodoxy." Convinced that "the growth of government must be fought relentlessly," Buckley used the magazine to criticize liberal policy. For his part, Friedman became a national conservative icon with the publication of *Capitalism and Freedom* (1962), in which he argued that "economic freedom is . . . an indispensable means toward the achievement of political freedom." Friedman's free-market ideology, along with that of Friedrich von Hayek, another University of Chicago economist, was taken up by wealthy conservatives, who funded think tanks to disseminate market-based public policy ideas. The Heritage Foundation, the American Enterprise Institute, and the Cato Institute issued policy proposals and attacked liberal legislation and the permissive culture they claimed it had spawned. Followers of Buckley and Friedman envisioned themselves as crusaders, working against what one conservative called "the despotic aspects of egalitarianism."

The most striking addition to the conservative coalition was the Religious Right. Until the 1970s, most fundamentalist and evangelical Protestants worried about saving their souls and preparing for the Second Coming of Christ. Politics was an earthly concern of secondary interest. But the perception that American society had become immoral, combined with the influ-

Jerry Falwell

The resurgence of evangelical religion in the 1970s was accompanied by a conservative movement in politics known as the Religious Right. Founded in 1979 by televangelist Jerry Falwell, the Moral Majority was one of the earliest Religious Right groups, committed to promoting "family values" and (as the title to the record album he is holding in this photo suggests) patriotism in American society and politics.   Wally McNamee/Corbis.

ence of a new generation of popular ministers, made politics relevant. Conservative Protestants and Catholics joined together in a tentative alliance, as the Religious Right condemned divorce, abortion, premarital sex, and feminism. The route to a moral life and to "peace, pardon, purpose, and power," as one evangelical activist said, was "to plug yourself into the One, the Only One [God]."

Charismatic televangelists such as Pat Robertson and Jerry Falwell emerged as the champions of a morality-based political agenda during the late 1970s. Falwell, founder of Liberty University and host of the *Old Time Gospel Hour* television program, established the Moral Majority in 1979. Backed by behind-the-scenes conservative strategists such as Paul Weyrich, the Moral Majority boasted 400,000 members and $1.5 million in contributions in its first year. It would be the organizational vehicle for transforming the Fourth Great

Awakening into a religious political movement. Falwell made no secret of his views: "If you want to know where I am politically," he told reporters, "I thought Goldwater was too liberal." Falwell was not alone. Phyllis Schlafly's STOP ERA, which became Eagle Forum in 1975, continued to advocate for conservative public policy; Focus on the Family was founded in 1977; and a succession of conservative organizations would emerge in the 1980s, including the Family Research Council.

The conservative message preached by Barry Goldwater and Ronald Reagan had appealed to few American voters in 1964. Then came the series of events that undermined support for the liberal agenda of the Democratic Party: the failed war in Vietnam; a judiciary that legalized abortion and pornography, enforced school busing, and curtailed public expression of religion; urban riots; and a stagnating economy. By the late 1970s, the New Right had developed a conservative message that commanded much greater popular support than Goldwater's program had. Religious and free-market conservatives joined with traditional anticommunist hard-liners—alongside whites opposed to black civil rights, affirmative action, and busing—in a broad coalition that attacked welfare-state liberalism, social permissiveness, and an allegedly weak and defensive foreign policy. Ronald Reagan expertly appealed to all of these conservative constituencies and captured the Republican presidential nomination in 1980 (see Comparing American Voices, "Christianity and Public Life," pp. 954–955). It had taken almost two decades, but the New Right appeared on the verge of winning the presidency.

The Carter Presidential Interregnum

First, the Republican Party had to defeat incumbent president Jimmy Carter. Carter's outsider status and his disdain for professional politicians had made him the ideal post-Watergate president. But his ineffectiveness as an executive also made him the perfect foil for Ronald Reagan. Indeed, Reagan and his New Right supporters could not have asked for a better predecessor: Carter's missteps opened the door for Reagan's election.

Carter had an idealistic vision of American leadership in world affairs. He presented himself as the anti-Nixon, a world leader who rejected Henry Kissinger's "realism" in favor of human rights and peacemaking. "Human rights is the soul of our foreign policy," Carter asserted, "because human rights is the very soul of our sense of nationhood." He established the Office of Human Rights in the State Department and withdrew economic and military aid from repressive regimes in Argentina, Uruguay, and Ethiopia—although, in real-

ist fashion, he still funded equally repressive U.S. allies such as the Philippines and South Africa. In Latin America, Carter eliminated a decades-old symbol of Yankee imperialism by signing a treaty on September 7, 1977, turning control of the Panama Canal over to Panama (effective December 31, 1999). Carter's most important efforts came in forging an enduring, although in retrospect limited, peace in the intractable Arab-Israeli conflict. In 1978, he invited Israeli prime minister Menachem Begin and Egyptian president Anwar el-Sadat to Camp David, where they crafted a "framework for peace," under which Egypt recognized Israel and received back the Sinai Peninsula, which Israel had occupied since 1967.

Carter deplored what he called the "inordinate fear of Communism," but his efforts at improving relations with the Soviet Union foundered. His criticism of the Kremlin's record on human rights offended Soviet leader Leonid Brezhnev and slowed arms reduction negotiations. When, in 1979, Carter finally signed the second Strategic Arms Limitations Treaty (SALT II), limiting bombers and missiles, Senate hawks objected. Then, when the Soviet Union invaded Afghanistan that December, Carter suddenly endorsed the hawks' position and treated the invasion as a major crisis; he called it the "gravest threat to world peace since World War II." After ordering an embargo on wheat shipments to the Soviet Union and withdrawing SALT II from Senate consideration, Carter called for increased defense spending and declared an American boycott of the 1980 Summer Olympics in Moscow. In a fateful decision, he and Congress began providing covert assistance to anti-Soviet fighters in Afghanistan, some of whom, including Osama bin Laden, would metamorphose into anti-American Islamic radicals decades later.

Hostage Crisis | Carter's ultimate undoing came in Iran, however. The United States had long counted Iran as a faithful ally, a bulwark against Soviet expansion into the Middle East and a steady source of oil. Since the 1940s, Iran had been ruled by Mohammad Reza Shah Pahlavi. Ousted by a democratically elected parliament in the early 1950s, the shah (king) sought and received the assistance of the U.S. Central Intelligence Agency (CIA), which helped him reclaim power in 1953. American intervention soured Iranian views of the United States for decades. Notwithstanding his fine words, Carter followed the same path in relations with Iran as his Cold War predecessors had, overlooking the crimes of Iran's CIA-trained secret police and ignoring mounting popular enmity toward the United States inside Iran. Early in 1979, a revolution drove the shah into exile and brought a

Thus I have given you, I think, the Substance of the Arguments o
both sides of that great and important Questi

Christianity and Public Life

Modern social-welfare liberalism embodies an ethic of moral pluralism and favors the separation of church and state. Conservative Christians challenge the legitimacy of pluralism and secularism and seek, through political agitation and legal action, to make religion an integral part of public life.

President Ronald Reagan

"The Rule of Law under God"

Reagan's candidacy was strongly supported by Christian conservatives. He delivered these remarks to the National Association of American Evangelicals in 1983.

I want you to know that this administration is motivated by a political philosophy that sees the greatness of America in you, her people, and in your families, churches, neighborhoods, communities—the institutions that foster and nourish values like concern for others and respect for the rule of law under God.

Now, I don't have to tell you that this puts us in opposition to, or at least out of step with, a prevailing attitude of many who have turned to a modern-day secularism, discarding the tried and time-tested values upon which our very civilization is based. No matter how well intentioned, their value system is radically different from that of most Americans. And while they proclaim that they're freeing us from superstitions of the past, they've taken upon themselves the job of superintending us by government rule and regulation. Sometimes their voices are louder than ours, but they are not yet a majority. . . .

Freedom prospers when religion is vibrant and the rule of law under God is acknowledged. When our Founding Fathers passed the First Amendment, they sought to protect churches from government interference. They never intended to construct a wall of hostility between government and the concept of religious belief itself.

Last year, I sent the Congress a constitutional amendment to restore prayer to public schools. Already this session, there's growing bipartisan support for the amendment, and I am calling on the Congress to act speedily to pass it and to let our children pray.

Source: Ronald Reagan, *Speaking My Mind: Selected Speeches* (New York: Simon & Schuster, 1989), 169–180.

Donald E. Wildmon

Network Television as a Moral Danger

Wildmon is a Christian minister and a grassroots religious activist, and the founder of the American Family Association.

One night during the Christmas holidays of 1976, I decided to watch television with my family. . . . Not far into the program was a scene of adultery. I reacted to the situation in the manner as I had been taught. I asked one of the children to change channels. Getting involved in the second program, we were shocked with some crude profanity. . . .

As I sat in my den that night, I became angry. I had been disturbed by the deterioration of morals I had witnessed in the media and society during the previous twenty-five years.

This was accompanied by a dramatic rise in crime, a proliferation of pornography, increasingly explicit sexual lyrics in music, increasing numbers of broken homes, a rise in drug and alcohol use among the youth, and various other negative factors. . . .

Realizing that these changes were being brought into the sanctity of my home, I decided I could and would no longer remain silent. . . .

This great struggle is one of values, particularly which ones will be the standard for our society and a base for our system of justice in the years to come. For 200 years our country has based its morals, its sense of right and wrong, on the Christian view of man. The Ten Commandments and the Sermon on the Mount have been our solid foundation . . .

Television is the most pervasive and persuasive medium we have. At times it is larger than life. It is our only true national medium. Network television is the greatest educator we have. . . .

It is teaching that adultery is an acceptable and approved lifestyle. . . . It is teaching that hardly anyone goes to church, that very few people in our society are Christian or live by Christian principles. How? By simply censoring Christian characters, Christian values, and Christian culture from the programs.

Source: Donald E. Wildmon, *The Home Invaders* (Elgin, IL: Victor Books, 1985), 3–7.

A. Bartlett Giamatti

The Moral Majority as a Threat to Liberty

A. Bartlett Giamatti was the president of Yale University (1978–1986) and subsequently commissioner of Major League Baseball. He offered these remarks to the entering class of Yale undergraduates in 1981.

A self-proclaimed "Moral Majority," and its satellite or client groups, cunning in the use of a native blend of old intimidation and new technology, threaten the values [of pluralism and freedom]. . . .

From the maw of this "morality" come those who presume to know what justice for all is; come those who presume to know which books are fit to read, which television programs are fit to watch. . . . From the maw of this "morality" rise the tax-exempt Savonarolas who believe they, and they alone, possess the "truth." There is no debate, no discussion, no dissent. They know. . . . What nonsense.

What dangerous, malicious nonsense. . . .

We should be concerned that so much of our political and religious leadership acts intimidated for the moment and will not say with clarity that this most recent denial of the legitimacy of differentness is a radical assault on the very pluralism of peoples, political beliefs, values, forms of merit and systems of religion our country was founded to welcome and foster.

Liberty protects the person from unwarranted government intrusions into a dwelling or other private places. In our tradition the State is not omnipresent in the home. And there are other spheres of our lives and existence, outside the home, where the State should not be a dominant presence.

Freedom extends beyond spatial bounds. Liberty presumes an autonomy of self that includes freedom of thought, belief, expression, and certain intimate conduct.

Source: Yale University Archives.

Anthony Kennedy

The Constitution Protects Privacy

Kennedy, a Roman Catholic, was named to the Supreme Court by Ronald Reagan in 1988. In *Lawrence v. Texas* (2003), which challenged a state antisodomy law, he wrote the opinion for five of the six justices in the majority; Sandra Day O'Connor wrote a concurring opinion.

The question before the Court is the validity of a Texas statute making it a crime for two persons of the same sex to engage in certain intimate sexual conduct.

In Houston, Texas, officers of the Harris County Police Department were dispatched to a private residence in re-

sponse to a reported weapons disturbance. They entered an apartment where one of the petitioners, John Geddes Lawrence, resided. . . . The officers observed Lawrence and another man, Tyron Garner, engaging in a sexual act. The two petitioners were arrested, held in custody over night, and charged and convicted before a Justice of the Peace.

The complaints described their crime as "deviate sexual intercourse, namely anal sex, with a member of the same sex (man)." . . .

We conclude the case should be resolved by determining whether the petitioners were free as adults to engage in the private conduct in the exercise of their liberty under the Due Process Clause of the Fourteenth Amendment to the Constitution.

[The Texas statute in question seeks] to control a personal relationship that, whether or not entitled to formal recognition in the law, is within the liberty of persons to choose without being punished as criminals. . . . The liberty protected by the Constitution allows homosexual persons the right to make this choice. . . .

. . . The petitioners are entitled to respect for their private lives. The State cannot demean their existence or control their destiny by making their private sexual conduct a crime. Their right to liberty under the Due Process Clause gives them the full right to engage in their conduct without intervention of the government. "It is a promise of the Constitution that there is a realm of personal liberty which the government may not enter."

Source: *Lawrence v. Texas*, 539 U.S. 558, 562–563, 567, 571, 579 (2003).

ANALYZING THE EVIDENCE

- What would Ronald Reagan think of the opinion written by Justice Kennedy, his appointee? Would he agree with it, given his condemnation of those intent on "subordinating us to government rule and regulation"?
- According to Wildmon, what should be shown on television, and who should make those decisions? How would Giamatti answer that same question?
- When should the government police private conduct?

Afghanistan, 1980

Afghani fighters stand in triumph on a destroyed Soviet helicopter. The weapon that brought it down might well have been a shoulder-launched missile from the American-supplied arsenal, courtesy of the CIA. When the defeated Soviets left Afghanistan, the CIA congratulated itself on its smart moves, only to experience what experts call blowback, as empowered mujahideen (Islamic guerrilla fighters) such as those depicted here, turned on the United States and made Afghanistan under the Taliban a haven for Al Qaeda. As for those shoulder-launched missiles, they have become a major headache for the West in the battle against Islamic terrorism.   © Alain DeJean/Sygma/Corbis.

fundamentalist Shiite cleric, the Ayatollah Ruhollah Khomeini, to power (Shiites represent one branch of Islam, Sunnis the other). When the United States admitted the deposed shah into the country for cancer treatment, Iranian students seized the U.S. embassy in Tehran, taking sixty-six Americans hostages. The captors demanded that the shah be returned to Iran for trial. Carter refused. Instead, he suspended arms sales to Iran and froze Iranian assets in American banks.

For the next fourteen months, the hostage crisis paralyzed Carter's presidency. Night after night, humiliating pictures of blindfolded American hostages appeared on television newscasts. An attempt to mount a military rescue in April 1980 had to be aborted because of equipment failures in the desert. Several months later, however, a stunning development changed the calculus on both sides: Iraq, led by Saddam Hussein, invaded

Iran, officially because of a dispute over deep-water ports but also to prevent the Shiite-led Iranian Revolution from spreading across the border into Sunni-run Iraq. Desperate to focus his nation's attention on Iraq's invasion, Khomeini began to talk with the United States about releasing the hostages. Difficult negotiations dragged on past the American presidential election in November 1980, and the hostages were finally released the day after Carter left office—a final indignity endured by a well-intentioned but ineffectual president.

The Election of 1980   President Carter's sinking popularity hurt his bid for reelection. When the Democrats barely renominated him over his liberal challenger, Edward (Ted) Kennedy of Massachusetts, Carter's approval rating was historically low: A mere 21 percent of Americans believed that he

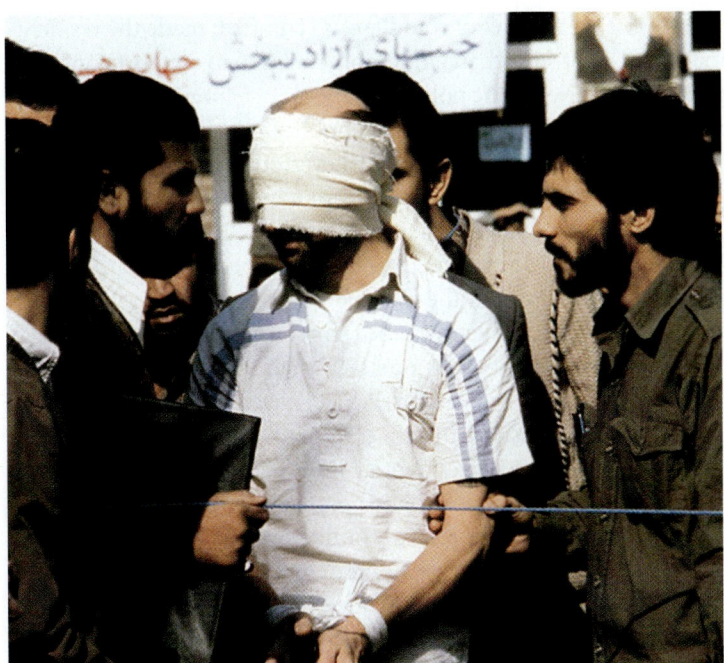

American Hostages in Iran

Images of blindfolded, handcuffed American hostages seized by Iranian militants at the U.S. Embassy in Tehran in November 1979 shocked the nation and created a foreign-policy crisis that eventually cost President Carter his chance for reelection.   Alain Mingam/Gamma/Zuma Press.

was an effective president. The reasons were clear: Economically, millions of citizens were feeling the pinch from stagnant wages, high inflation, crippling mortgage rates, and an unemployment rate of nearly 8 percent. In international affairs, the nation blamed Carter for his weak response to Soviet expansion and the Iranians' seizure of American diplomats.

With Carter on the defensive, Reagan remained upbeat and decisive. "This is the greatest country in the world," Reagan reassured the nation in his warm baritone voice. "We have the talent, we have the drive. . . . All we need is the leadership." To emphasize his intention to be a formidable international leader, Reagan hinted that he would take strong action to win the hostages' return. To signal his rejection of liberal policies, he declared his opposition to affirmative action and forced busing and promised to "get the government off our backs." Most important, Reagan effectively appealed to the many Americans who felt financially insecure. In a televised debate with Carter, Reagan emphasized the hardships facing working- and middle-class Americans in an era of stagflation and asked them: "Are you better off today than you were four years ago?"

In November, the voters gave a clear answer. They repudiated Carter, giving him only 41.0 percent of the vote. Independent candidate John Anderson garnered 6.6 percent (with a few minor candidates receiving fractions of a percent), and Reagan won with 50.7 percent of the popular vote (Map 30.1). Moreover, the Republicans elected thirty-three new members of the House

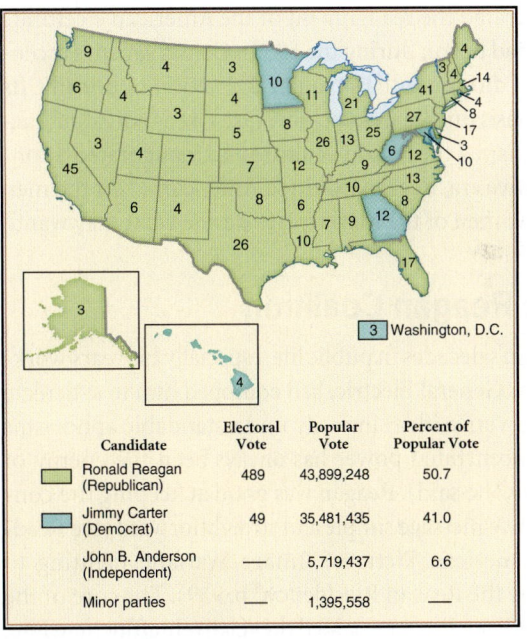

Candidate	Electoral Vote	Popular Vote	Percent of Popular Vote
Ronald Reagan (Republican)	489	43,899,248	50.7
Jimmy Carter (Democrat)	49	35,481,435	41.0
John B. Anderson (Independent)	—	5,719,437	6.6
Minor parties	—	1,395,558	—

MAP 30.1

The Presidential Election of 1980

Ronald Reagan easily defeated Democratic incumbent Jimmy Carter, taking 50.7 percent of the popular vote to Carter's 41.0 percent and winning the electoral vote in all but six states and the District of Columbia. Reagan cut deeply into the traditional Democratic coalition by wooing many southern whites, urban ethnics, and blue-collar workers. More than five million Americans expressed their discontent with Carter's ineffectiveness and Reagan's conservatism by voting for Independent candidate John Anderson, a long-time Republican member of the House of Representatives.

of Representatives and twelve new senators, which gave them control of the U.S. Senate for the first time since 1954. The New Right's long road to national power had culminated in an election victory that signaled a new political alignment in the country.

- Which were the key groups of the new Republican coalition? Were their goals complementary? Contradictory?

- In what ways was the New Right "reactive," responding to liberalism, and in what ways was it "proactive," asserting its own agenda?

The Dawning of the Conservative Age

By the time Ronald Reagan took office in 1981, conservatism commanded wider popular support than at any time since the 1920s. As the New Deal Democratic coalition continued to fragment, the Republican Party accelerated the realignment of the American electorate that had begun during the 1960s. Conservatism's ascendancy did more than realign the nation politically. Its emphasis on free markets, low taxes, and individual success shaped the nation's culture and inaugurated a conservative era. Reagan exhorted Americans, "Let the men and women of the marketplace decide what they want."

The Reagan Coalition

Reagan's decades in public life, especially his years working for General Electric, had equipped him to articulate conservative ideas in easily understandable aphorisms ("Concentrated power has always been the enemy of liberty," he said). Reagan was good at keeping the conservative message simple and straightforward (see Reading American Pictures, "Image Warfare: Fighting to Define the Reagan Presidency," p. 959). The core of the Republican Party remained the relatively affluent, white, Protestant voters who supported balanced budgets, opposed government activism, feared crime and communism, and believed in a strong national defense. Reagan Republicanism also attracted middle-class suburbanites and migrants to the Sunbelt states who endorsed the conservative agenda of combating crime and limiting social welfare spending. Suburban growth in particular, a phenomenon that reshaped metropolitan areas across the country in the 1960s and 1970s, benefited conservatives politically. Suburban traditions of privatization and racial homogeneity, combined with the

amenities of middle-class comfort, made the residents of suburban cities more inclined to support conservative public policies.

This emerging Republican coalition was joined by a large and electorally key group of former Democrats that had been gradually moving toward the Republican Party since 1964: southern whites. Reagan capitalized on the "Southern Strategy" developed by Richard Nixon's advisors in the late 1960s. Many southern whites had lost confidence in the Democratic Party for a wide range of reasons, but one factor stood out: the party's support for civil rights. When Reagan came to Philadelphia, Mississippi, to deliver his first official speech as the Republican presidential nominee, his ringing endorsement of "states' rights" sent a clear message: He validated twenty-five years of southern opposition to federal civil rights legislation. Some of Reagan's advisors had warned him not to go to Philadelphia, the site of the tragic murder of three civil rights workers in 1964, but Reagan believed the opportunity to launch his campaign on a "states' rights" note too important. After 1980, southern whites would remain a cornerstone of the Republican coalition.

The Religious Right proved crucial to the Republican victory as well. Falwell's Moral Majority claimed that it had registered two million new voters for the 1980 election, and the Republican Party's platform reflected its influence. That platform called for a constitutional ban on abortion, voluntary prayer in public schools, and a mandatory death penalty for certain crimes. Republicans also demanded an end to court-mandated busing to achieve racial integration in schools, and, for the first time in forty years, opposed the Equal Rights Amendment. Within the Republican Party, conservatism had triumphed.

Reagan's broad coalition attracted the allegiance of another group dissatisfied with the direction of liberalism in the 1970s: blue-collar Catholics alarmed by antiwar protesters and rising welfare expenditures and hostile to feminist demands. Some observers saw these voters, which many called "Reagan Democrats," as coming from the "silent majority" that Nixon had swung into the Republican fold in 1968 and 1972. They lived in heavily industrialized midwestern states such as Michigan, Ohio, and Illinois, and had been a core part of the Democratic coalition for three decades. Reagan's victory in the 1980s thus hinged on both a revival of right-wing conservative activism and broad dissatisfaction with liberal Democrats—a dissatisfaction that had been building since 1968 but had been interrupted by the post-Watergate backlash against the Republican Party.

Image Warfare: Fighting to Define the Reagan Presidency

As might be expected, U.S. presidents and their staffs attempt to project a positive image of the chief executive and the administration's policies. But contradictions often arise between the image and values cultivated by a president and the actual policies pursued by the White House. The presidency of Ronald Reagan is a case in point. As the text points out, Reagan helped stimulate a conservative movement in American politics and society during the 1980s. Images of Reagan quickly became vital for the White House to deliver its message of conservative reform to the American people. As the cartoon published by the *Arkansas Gazette* illustrates, powerful imagery could also be wielded by Reagan's political opponents.

ANALYZING THE EVIDENCE

- Examine the photo of Reagan at his ranch in California. This image was taken by a White House photographer. What message does the image convey about Reagan as a person? How does this message reinforce the policies created by Reagan that you read about in the text?

- What message does the cartoon convey about Reagan's policies? How does this differ from the official White House message expressed in the photo of Reagan?

- Together, what do these two images tell us about the image and reality of the Reagan presidency? Do you think that cartoons or photographs are a more accurate source of information for understanding the historical meaning of a particular president and his administration? Why or why not?

President Reagan at His Ranch in Southern California.
Ronald Reagan Presidential Library.

Presidential Landscaping. Courtesy *Arkansas Gazette*, 1984.

Conservatives in Power

The new president kept his political message clear and simple. "What I want to see above all," he remarked, "is that this country remains a country where someone can always get rich." Standing in the way, Reagan believed, was government. In his first year in office, Reagan and his chief advisor, James A. Baker III, quickly set new governmental priorities. To roll back the expanded liberal state, they launched a three-pronged assault on federal taxes, social welfare spending, and the regulatory bureaucracy. To prosecute the Cold War, they advocated a vast increase in defense spending and an end to détente with the Soviet Union. And to match the resurgent economies of Germany and Japan, they set out to restore American leadership of the world's capitalist societies and to inspire renewed faith in "free markets."

Reaganomics | To achieve its economic objectives, the new administration advanced a set of policies, quickly dubbed "Reaganomics," to increase the production (and thus the supply) of goods. The theory underlying supply-side economics, as this approach was called, emphasized investment in productive enterprises. According to supply-side theorists, the best way to bolster investment was to reduce the taxes paid by corporations and wealthy Americans, who could then use these funds to expand production. Supply-siders maintained that the resulting economic expansion would increase government revenues and offset the loss of tax dollars stemming from the original tax cuts. Meanwhile, the increasing supply would generate its own demand, as consumers stepped forward to buy ever more goods. Supply-side theory presumed—in fact, gambled—that future tax revenues would make up for present tax cuts. The idea had a growing list of supporters in Congress, led by an ex-professional football player from Buffalo named Jack Kemp. Kemp praised supply-side economics as "an alternative to the slow-growth, recession-oriented policies of the [Carter] administration."

Reagan took advantage of Republican control of the Senate, as well as high-profile allies such as Kemp, to win congressional approval of the 1981 Economic Recovery Tax Act (ERTA), a massive tax cut that embodied supply-side principles. The act reduced income tax rates for most Americans by 23 percent over three years. For the wealthiest Americans—those with millions to invest—the highest marginal tax rate dropped from 70 to 50 percent. The act also slashed estate taxes, levies on inheritances instituted during the Progressive Era to prevent the transmission of huge fortunes from one generation to the next. Finally, the new legislation trimmed the taxes paid by business corporations by $150 billion over a period of five years. As a result of ERTA, by 1986 the annual revenue of the federal government had been cut by $200 billion (nearly half a trillion in 2010 dollars).

David Stockman, Reagan's budget director, hoped to match this reduction in tax revenue with a comparable cutback in federal expenditures. To meet this ambitious goal, he proposed substantial cuts in Social Security and Medicare. But Congress, and even the president himself, rejected his idea; they were not willing to antagonize middle-class and elderly voters who viewed these government entitlements as sacred. As conservative columnist George Will noted ironically, "Americans are conservative. What they want to conserve is the New Deal." After defense spending, Social Security and Medicare were by far the nation's largest budget items; reductions in other programs would not achieve the savings the administration desired. This contradiction between New Right Republican ideology and political reality would continue to frustrate the party into the twenty-first century.

A more immediate embarrassment confronted conservatives, however. In a 1982 *Atlantic* article, Stockman admitted that supply-side theory was based on faith, not economics. To produce optimistic projections of higher tax revenue in future years, Stockman had manipulated the figures. Worse, Stockman told the *Atlantic* reporter candidly that supply-side theory was based on a long-discredited idea: the "trickle-down" notion that helping the rich would eventually benefit the lower and middle classes. Stockman had drawn back the curtain, much to Republicans' consternation, on the flawed reasoning of supply-side theory. But it was too late. The plan had passed Congress, and since Stockman could not cut major programs such as Social Security and Medicare, he had few options to balance the budget.

As the administration's spending cuts fell short, the federal budget deficit increased dramatically. Military spending contributed a large share of the growing **national debt.** But President Reagan remained undaunted. "Defense is not a budget item," he declared. "You spend what you need." To "make America number one again," Reagan and Defense Secretary Caspar Weinberger pushed through Congress a five-year, $1.2 trillion military spending program. During Reagan's presidency, military spending accounted for one-fourth of all federal expenditures and contributed to rising annual budget deficits (the amount overspent by the government in a single year) and a skyrocketing national debt (the cumulative *total* of all budget deficits).

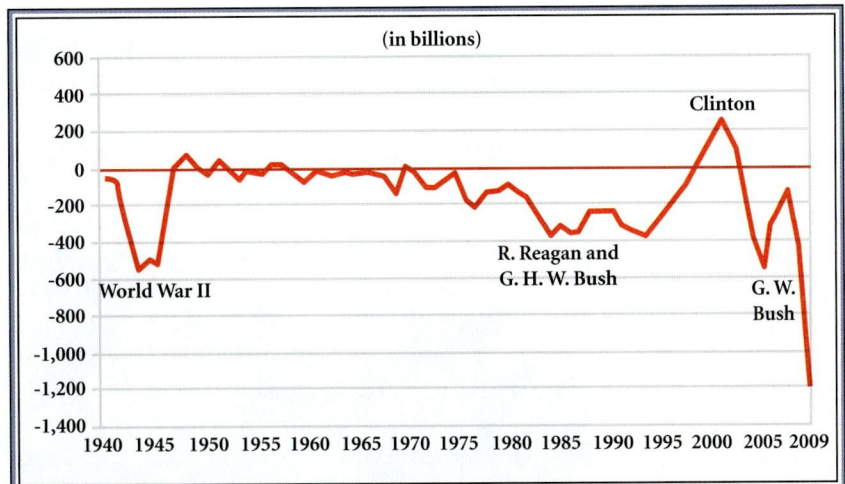

FIGURE 30.1

The Annual Federal Budget Deficit (or Surplus), 1940–2009

During World War II, the federal government incurred an enormous budget deficit. But between 1946 and 1965, it ran either an annual budget surplus or incurred a relatively small debt. The annual deficits rose significantly during the Vietnam War and the stagflation of the 1970s, but they really exploded between 1982 and 1994, in the budgets devised by the Ronald Reagan and George H. W. Bush administrations, and again between 2002 and 2005, in those prepared by George W. Bush. The Republican presidents increased military spending while cutting taxes, an enjoy-it-now philosophy that transferred costs to future generations of Americans.   Source: National Priorities Project. See also *U.S. Budget for Fiscal Year 2010*, Historical Tables, Table 15.6.

By the time Reagan left office, the total federal debt had tripled, rising from $930 billion in 1981 to $2.8 trillion in 1989. The rising annual deficits of the 1980s contradicted Reagan's pledge of fiscal conservatism (Figure 30.1).

Deregulation | Advocates of Reaganomics believed that excessive regulation by federal agencies impeded economic growth. Deregulation of prices in the trucking, airline, and railroad industries had begun under President Carter in the late 1970s, but Reagan expanded the mandate to include cutting back on government protections of consumers, workers, and the environment. Some of the targeted federal bureaucracies, such as the U.S. Department of Labor, had risen to prominence during the New Deal; others, such as the Environmental Protection Agency (EPA) and the Occupational Safety and Health Administration (OSHA), had been created during the Johnson and Nixon administrations. Although these agencies provided many services to business corporations, they also increased their costs—by protecting the rights of workers, mandating safety improvements in factories, and requiring expensive equipment to limit the release of toxic chemicals into the environment. To reduce the reach of federal regulatory agencies, the Reagan administration cut their budgets, by an average of 12 percent.

Reagan also rendered regulatory agencies less effective by staffing them with leaders who were hostile to the agencies' missions. James Watt, an outspoken conservative who headed the Department of the Interior, attacked environmentalism as "a left-wing cult." Acting

on his free-enterprise principles, Watt opened public lands for use by private businesses—oil and coal corporations, large-scale ranchers, and timber companies. Anne Gorsuch Burford, whom Reagan appointed to head the EPA, likewise disparaged environmentalists and refused to cooperate with Congress to clean up toxic waste sites under a program known as the Superfund. The Sierra Club and other environmental groups aroused enough public outrage about these appointees that the administration changed its position. During President Reagan's second term, he significantly increased the EPA's budget and added acreage to the National Wilderness Preservation System and animals and plants to the endangered species lists.

Ultimately, as these adjustments demonstrate, politics in the United States remained "the art of the possible." Savvy politicians know when to advance and when to retreat. Having attained two of his prime goals—a major tax cut and a dramatic increase in defense spending—Reagan did not seriously attempt to scale back big government and the welfare state. When he left office in 1989, federal spending stood at 22.1 percent of the gross domestic product (GDP) and federal taxes at 19 percent of GDP, both virtually the same as in 1981. In the meantime, though, the federal debt had tripled in size and the number of government workers had increased from 2.9 to 3.1 million. This outcome—so different from the president's rhetoric about balancing budgets and downsizing government—elicited harsh criticism from some conservative commentators. "There was no Reagan Revolution," one conservative noted. A former Reagan aide offered a more balanced assessment: "Ronald Reagan did far less than he had hoped . . . and a hell of a lot more than people thought he would."

Remaking the Judiciary | Historians continue to debate whether there was a "Reagan Revolution." Even if he did not achieve everything many of his supporters desired, however, Reagan left an indelible imprint on politics, public policy, and American culture. One place this imprint was felt in far-reaching ways was the judiciary, where Reagan and his attorney general, Edwin Meese, aimed at reversing the liberal judicial philosophy that had prevailed since the late 1950s. During his two terms, Reagan appointed 368 federal court judges—most of them with conservative credentials—and three Supreme Court justices: Antonin Scalia, Sandra Day O'Connor, and Anthony Kennedy. Ironically, the latter two turned out to be far less devoted to New Right conservatism than Reagan and his supporters imagined. O'Connor, the first woman to serve on the Court, shaped its decision making as a swing vote between liberals and conservatives. Kennedy also emerged as a judicial moderate, leaving Scalia as Reagan's only genuinely conservative appointee.

But Reagan also elevated Justice William Rehnquist, a conservative Nixon appointee, to the position of chief justice. Under Rehnquist's leadership (1986–2005), the Court's conservatives took an activist stance, limiting the reach of federal laws, ending court-ordered busing, and endorsing constitutional protection of property rights. However, on controversial issues such as individual liberties, abortion rights, affirmative action, and the rights of criminal defendants, the presence of O'Connor enabled the Court to resist the rightward drift and to maintain a moderate position. As a result, the justices scaled back, but did not usually overturn, the liberal rulings of the Warren and Burger Courts. In the controversial *Webster v. Reproductive Health Services* (1989), for instance, Scalia pushed for the justices to overturn the abortion-rights decision in *Roe v. Wade* (1973). O'Connor refused, but she nonetheless approved the constitutional validity of state laws that limited the use of public funds and facilities for abortions. A more conservative federal judiciary would remain a significant institutional legacy of the Reagan presidency.

AIDS | Another conservative legacy was the slow national response to one of the worst disease epidemics of the postwar decades. The human immunodeficiency virus (HIV), a deadly (though slow-acting) pathogen, developed in Africa when a chimpanzee virus jumped to humans; immigrants carried it to Haiti and

Another Barrier Falls

In 1981, Sandra Day O'Connor, shown here with Chief Justice Warren Burger, was appointed to the Supreme Court by President Ronald Reagan, the first woman to serve on that body. In 1993, she was joined by Ruth Bader Ginsburg, an appointee of President Bill Clinton. O'Connor emerged as a leader of the moderate bloc on the Court during the 1990s; she retired in 2006.   Fred Ward/Black Star/Stockphoto.com.

then to the United States during the 1970s. In 1981, American physicians identified HIV as a new virus—one that caused a disease known as acquired immunodeficiency syndrome (AIDS). Hundreds of gay men, who were prominent among the earliest carriers of the virus, were dying of AIDS. Within two decades, HIV had spread worldwide, infected more than 50 million people of both sexes, and killed more than 20 million.

Within the United States, AIDS took nearly a hundred thousand lives in the 1980s—more than were lost in the Korean and Vietnam Wars combined. However, because its most prominent early victims were gay men, President Reagan, emboldened by New Right conservatives, hesitated in declaring a national health emergency. Some of Reagan's advisors asserted that this "gay disease" might even be God's punishment of homosexuals. Between 1981 and 1986, as the epidemic spread, the Reagan administration took little action—worse, it prevented the surgeon general, C. Everett Koop, from speaking forthrightly to the nation about the disease. Pressed by gay activists and prominent health officials from across the country, in Reagan's last years in office the administration finally began to devote federal re-

HIV/AIDS

The HIV/AIDS epidemic hit the United States in the early 1980s and remained a major social and political issue throughout the decade. Here, AIDS patients and their supporters participate in the 1987 March on Washington for Gay and Lesbian Rights, demanding that the Reagan administration commit more federal resources to finding a cure for the deadly disease.   © Bettmann/Corbis.

sources to treatment for HIV and AIDS patients and research into possible vaccines. But the delay had proved costly, inhumane, and embarrassing.

Morning in America

During his first run for governor of California in 1966, Reagan held a revelatory conversation with a campaign consultant. "Politics is just like the movies," Reagan told him. "You have a hell of an opening, coast for a while, and then have a hell of a close." Reagan indeed had a "hell of an opening": one of the most lavish and expensive presidential inaugurations in American history in 1981 (and another in 1985). While some conservatives, including Goldwater, growled at the ostentatious display, Reagan showed that he was unafraid to celebrate wealth, luxury, and opulence, even with millions of American out of work. Moreover, the rest of Reagan's presidency closely corresponded to the simple formula he outlined in 1966.

Following his spectacular inauguration, Reagan quickly won passage of his tax reduction bill and launched his plan to bolster the Pentagon. But then a long "coasting" period descended on his presidency, during which he retreated on tax cuts and navigated a

major foreign policy scandal. Finally, toward the end of his two-term presidency, Reagan found his "hell of a close," leaving office as major reforms — which he encouraged from afar — had begun to tear apart the Soviet Union and bring an end to the Cold War. Through all the ups and downs, Reagan remained a master of the politics of symbolism, championing a resurgent American economy and reassuring the country that the pursuit of wealth was noble and that he had the reins of the nation firmly in hand.

Reagan's tax cuts had barely taken effect when he was forced to reverse course. High interest rates set by the Federal Reserve Board had cut the runaway inflation of the Carter years. But these rates — as high as 18 percent — sent the economy into a recession in 1981–1982 that put 10 million Americans out of work and shuttered 17,000 businesses. Unemployment neared 10 percent, the highest rate since the Great Depression. These troubles, combined with the booming deficit, forced Reagan to negotiate a tax *increase* with Congress in 1982 — to the loud complaints of supply-side diehards. The president's job rating plummeted, and in the 1982 midterm elections Democrats picked up twenty-six seats in the House of Representatives and seven state governorships.

Election of 1984 | Fortunately for Reagan, the economy had recovered by 1983, restoring the president's job approval rating just in time for the 1984 presidential election. During the campaign, Reagan emphasized the economic resurgence, touring the country promoting his tax policies and the nation's new prosperity. The Democrats nominated former vice president Walter Mondale of Minnesota. With strong ties to labor unions, ethnic and racial minority groups, and party leaders, Mondale epitomized the New Deal coalition. He selected Representative Geraldine Ferraro of New York as his running mate — the first woman to run on the presidential ticket of a major political party. Neither Ferraro's presence nor Mondale's credentials made a difference, however: Reagan won a landslide victory, losing only Minnesota and the District of Columbia. Still, Democrats retained their majority in the House and, in 1986, regained control of the Senate.

Reagan's 1984 campaign slogan, "It's Morning in America," projected the image of a new day dawning on a confident people. In Reagan mythology, the United States was an optimistic nation of small towns, close-knit families, and kindly neighbors. "The success story of America," he once said, "is neighbor helping neighbor." The mythology may not have reflected the *actual* nation — which was overwhelmingly urban and suburban, and in which the hard knocks of capitalism held down more than opportunity elevated — but that mattered little. Reagan's remarkable ability to produce positive associations and feelings, alongside robust economic growth after the 1981–1982 recession, helped make the 1980s a decade characterized both by both backward-looking nostalgia and aggressive capitalism.

Return to Prosperity | Between 1945 and the 1970s, the United States was the world's leading exporter of agricultural products, manufactured goods, and investment capital. Then American manufacturers lost market share, undercut by cheaper and better-designed products from Germany and Japan. By 1985, for the first time since 1915, the United States registered a negative balance of international payments. It now imported more goods and capital than it exported. The country became a debtor (rather than a creditor) nation. The rapid ascent of the Japanese economy to become the world's second largest was a key factor in this historic reversal (see Voices from Abroad, "Yoichi Funabashi: Japan and America, Global Partners," p. 965). More than one-third of the American annual trade deficit of $138 billion in the 1980s was from trade with Japan, whose corporations exported huge quantities of electronic goods and made nearly one-quarter of all cars bought in the United States. Reflecting these profits, Japan's Nikkei stock index tripled in value between 1965 and 1975 and then tripled again by 1985.

Meanwhile, American businesses grappled with a worrisome decline in productivity. Between 1973 and 1992, American productivity (the amount of goods or services per hour of work) grew at the meager rate of 1 percent a year — a far cry from the post–World War II rate of 3 percent. Because managers wanted to cut costs, the wages of most employees stagnated. Further, because of foreign competition, the number of high-paying, union-protected manufacturing jobs shrank. By 1985, more people in the United States worked for McDonald's slinging Big Macs than rolled out rails, girders, and sheet steel in the nation's steel industry. Middle-class Americans, baby boomers included, also found themselves with less economic security as corporations reduced the number, pay, and pensions of middle-level managers and accountants.

A brief return to competitiveness in the second half of the 1980s masked the steady long-term transformation of the economy that had begun in the 1970s. The nation's heavy industries — steel, autos, chemicals — continued to lose market share to global competitors. Nevertheless, the U.S. economy grew at the impressive average rate of 2 to 3 percent per year for much of the late 1980s and 1990s (with a short recession in 1990–1991). What had changed was the direction of growth and its beneficiaries. Increasingly, financial services, medical services, computer technology — *service* industries, broadly speaking — were the leading sectors of growth. This shift in the underlying foundation of the American economy, from manufacturing to service, from making *things* to producing *services*, would have long-term consequences for the global competitiveness of U.S. industries and the value of the dollar.

Culture of Success | The economic growth of the second half of the 1980s popularized the materialistic values championed by the free marketeers. Every era has its capitalist heroes, but Americans in the 1980s celebrated wealth accumulation in ways unseen since the 1920s. When the president christened self-made entrepreneurs "the heroes for the eighties," he probably had people like Lee Iacocca in mind. Born to Italian immigrants and trained as an engineer, Iacocca rose through the ranks to become president of the Ford Motor Corporation. In 1978, he took over the ailing Chrysler Corporation and made it profitable again — by securing a crucial $1.5 billion loan from the U.S.

All the nations and people I had hitherto passed through resembled our own in their manners, customs and language

Yoichi Funabashi
Japan and America: Global Partners

Yoichi Funabashi is a prize-winning Japanese journalist who writes regularly in both English and Japanese. Educated at the University of Tokyo and Keio University, Funabashi specializes in the U.S.-Japan economic relationship. During the 1980s, he lived in the United States as a columnist (and later bureau chief) for the *Asahi Shimbun*, one of Japan's most important daily newspapers.

As Japan struggled to rebuild itself after World War II, the charismatic Shigeru Yoshida, prime minister during the critical years of 1948 to 1952, called on the country to be a good loser. The Japanese have lost the war, he said, but they must not lose heart. Japan must cooperate with the United States, and pull itself out of misery and disgrace. The Japanese did indeed cooperate willingly with the Allied occupation—with the American (and British) "devils" whom they had been taught for years to despise to the very core of their souls. . . .

Postwar Japan went on to prove that it could indeed be a good loser. Under the new constitution promulgated under the guidance of the occupation, it has developed into a democratic country with a relatively moderate disparity between rich and poor and a stable, smoothly functioning political system. Egalitarianism and stability in turn made possible sustained growth and economic development. . . .

The Japanese-U.S. relationship has thus come to occupy a truly unique position in world history. Never before has a multiethnic, contract-based society and a homogenous, traditional society joined together to form such a powerful team. As global powers, Japan and the United Sates combined have a decisive impact on world politics. . . .

Potential sources of bilateral friction are as numerous as ever: the trade imbalance, market liberalization, growing Japanese investment in the United States, heavy U.S. dependence on Japanese technology, and so on. Occasional outbursts of economic nationalism, or "revisionist" thinking are probably inevitable as the debate over these issues unfolds. . . .

Before they can build a strong bilateral relationship, Americans and Japanese must outgrow their obsession with being Number One. This psychological adjustment is absolutely necessary for both peoples. Projecting the nature of its own hierarchical society, Japan tends to view the rest of the world, it is said, in terms of ranking. This inclination fosters behavior patterns that are oriented more toward what to *be* than what to *do*. Japan is also overly conscious of itself as a late-starter, having entered modern international society only in the mid-nineteenth century, and this history has made catching up with and outpacing other countries a sort of national pastime. Japanese must realize that this proclivity can destabilize relations not only with America but with other countries as well. It may be even more difficult for the United States, which dominated the free world during the Cold War, to make the psychological adjustments required to enter into a partnership with Japan that is truly equal. Equal cooperation will be required in every project, and there will be no other way than to learn global partnership "on the job," so to speak, as Americans and Japanese work together on specific undertakings. . . .

Both sides should also explore more thoroughly their "sharing edge" in areas where the two countries can mobilize their respective strengths to help each other grow. The merits of Japanese elementary education, for example, might be used in reinvigorating American schools, while the strengths of American higher education could be harnessed to help reform Japan's universities. Other candidates for the sharing edge include social infrastructure and science. Japanese know-how in the field of vocational training and public transportation, and America's accumulated excellence in biotechnology and airport construction, for instance, should be shared and used. The exchange of strong points of American basic science and Japanese applied science should also be promoted.

Source: Yoichi Funabashi, "Japan and America: Global Partners," *Foreign Policy* 86 (Spring 1992): 24–39.

ANALYZING THE EVIDENCE

- What does Funabashi mean when he writes that after World War II Japan was a "good loser"?
- Among the "sources of bilateral friction" Funabashi lists the trade imbalance and Japanese investment in the United States. Why would these cause friction?
- How had the U.S.-Japanese relationship changed between 1945 and the 1980s?

government, pushing the development of new cars, and selling them on TV. His patriotic commercials in the 1980s echoed Reagan's rhetoric: "Let's make American mean something again." Iacocca's restoration would not endure, however: In 2009, Chrysler declared bankruptcy and was forced to sell a majority stake to the Italian company Fiat.

If Iacocca symbolized a resurgent corporate America, high-profile financial wheeler-dealers also captured Americans' imagination. One was Ivan Boesky, a white-collar criminal convicted of insider trading (buying or selling stock based on information from corporate insiders). "I think greed is healthy," Boesky told a business school graduating class. Boesky inspired the fictional film character Gordon Gekko, who proclaimed "Greed is good!" in 1987's *Wall Street*. A new generation of Wall Street executives, of which Boesky was one example, pioneered the leveraged buyout (LBO). In a typical LBO, a financier used heavily leveraged (borrowed) capital to buy a company, quickly restructured that company to make it appear spectacularly profitable, and then sold it at a higher price.

Americans had not set aside the traditional work ethic, but the Reagan-era public was fascinated with money and celebrity. (The documentary television show *Lifestyles of the Rich and Famous* began its run in 1984.) One of the most fascinating of money moguls was Donald Trump, a real estate developer who craved publicity. In 1983, the flamboyant Trump built the equally flamboyant Trump Towers in New York City. At the entrance of the $200 million apartment building stood two enormous bronze *T*'s, a display of self-promotion reinforced by the media. Calling him "The Donald," a nickname used by Trump's first wife, TV reporters and magazines commented relentlessly on his marriages, divorces, and glitzy lifestyle.

The Computer Revolution While Trump grabbed headlines and made splashy real estate investments, a handful of quieter, less flashy entrepreneurs was busy changing the face of the American economy. Bill Gates, Paul Allen, Steve Jobs, and Steve Wozniak were four entrepreneurs who pioneered the computer revolution in the late 1970s and 1980s. They took a technology that had been used exclusively for large-scale enterprises — the military and multinational corporations — and made it accessible to individual consumers. Scientists had devised the first computers for military purposes during World War II. Cold War military research subsequently funded the construction of large mainframe computers. But government and private-sector first-generation computers were bulky, cumbersome machines that had to be placed in large air-conditioned rooms.

Between the 1950s and the 1970s, concluding with the development of the microprocessor in 1971, each generation of computers grew faster and smaller. By the mid-1970s, a few microchips the size of the letter *O* on this page provided as much processing power as a World War II–era computer. The day of the personal computer (PC) had arrived. Working in the San Francisco Bay Area, Jobs and Wozniak founded Apple Computers in 1976 and within a year were producing small, individual computers that could be easily used by a single person. When Apple enjoyed success, other companies scrambled to get into the market. International Business Machines (IBM) offered its first personal computer in 1981, but Apple Corporation's 1984 Macintosh computer (later shortened to "Mac") became the first runaway commercial success for a personal computer.

Meanwhile, two former high school classmates, Gates, age nineteen, and Allen, age twenty-one, had set a goal in the early 1970s of putting "a personal computer on every desk and in every home." They recognized that software was the key. In 1975, they founded the Microsoft Corporation, whose MS-DOS and Windows operating systems soon dominated the software industry. By 2000, the company's products ran nine out of every ten personal computers in the United States and a majority of those around the world. Gates and Allen became billionaires, and Microsoft exploded into a huge company with 57,000 employees and annual revenues of $38 billion. In three decades, the computer had moved from a few military research centers to thousands of corporate offices and then to millions of peoples' homes. Ironically, in an age that celebrated free-market capitalism, government research and government funding had played an enormous role in the development of the most important technology since television.

- **What were the key elements of Reagan's domestic policy? How did that policy reflect conservative ideology?**

- **What limits did Reagan face in promoting his policies? What were his successes and failures?**

The End of the Cold War

Ronald Reagan entered office determined to confront the Soviet Union diplomatically and militarily. Backed by Republican and Democratic hard-liners alike, Reagan unleashed some of the harshest Cold War rhetoric since the 1950s, labeling the Soviet Union an "evil empire" and vowing that it would end up "on the ash heap of history." In a remarkable turnaround, however, by his second term Reagan had decided that this goal would be best achieved by actively cooperating with Mikhail Gorbachev, the reform-minded Russian Communist leader. The downfall of the Soviet Union in 1991 ended the nearly fifty-year-long Cold War, but a new set of foreign challenges quickly emerged.

U.S.-Soviet Relations in a New Era

When Reagan assumed the presidency in 1981, he broke with his immediate predecessors—Richard Nixon, Gerald Ford, and Jimmy Carter—in Cold War strategy. Nixon regarded himself as a "realist" in foreign affairs. That meant, above all, advancing the national interest without regard to ideology. Nixon's policy of détente with the Soviet Union and China embodied this realist view. President Carter endorsed détente and continued to push for relaxing Cold War tensions. This worked for a time, but the Soviet invasion of Afghanistan empowered hard-liners in the U.S. Congress and forced Carter to take a tougher line—which he did with the Olympic boycott and grain embargo. This was the relationship Reagan inherited in 1981: a decade of détente that had produced a noticeable relaxation of tensions with the Communist world, followed by a year of

tense standoffs over Soviet advances into Central Asia, which threatened U.S. interests in the Middle East.

Reagan's Cold War Revival   Conservatives did not believe in détente. Neither did they believe in the containment policy that had guided U.S. Cold War strategy since 1947. Reagan and his advisors wanted to *defeat* the Soviet Union. His administration pursued a two-pronged strategy toward that end. First, it abandoned détente and set about rearming America. This buildup in American military strength, reasoned Secretary of Defense Caspar Weinberger, would force the Soviets into an arms race that would strain their economy and cause domestic unrest. Second, the president supported CIA initiatives to roll back Soviet influence in the developing world by funding anticommunist movements in Angola, Mozambique, Afghanistan, and Central America.

To accomplish this objective, Reagan supported repressive, right-wing regimes. Nowhere was this more conspicuous in the 1980s than in the Central American countries of Guatemala, Nicaragua, and El Salvador. Conditions were unique in each country but held to a pattern: The United States sided with military dictatorships and oligarchies if democratically elected governments or left-wing movements sought support from the Soviet Union. In Guatemala, this approach produced a brutal military rule—thousands of opponents of the

Iran-Contra

The 1987 Iran-Contra congressional hearings, which lasted more than a month and were broadcast on live television, helped to uncover a secret and illegal White House scheme to provide arms to the Nicaraguan Contras. Though Lt. Col. Oliver North (shown here during his testimony before Congress) concocted much of the scheme and was convicted of three felonies, he never served prison time and emerged from the hearings as a populist hero among American conservatives, who saw him as a patriot. © Bettmann/Corbis.

government were executed or kidnapped. In Nicaragua, Reagan actively encouraged a coup against the left-wing Sandinista government, which had overthrown the U.S.-backed strongman Anastasio Somoza. And in El Salvador, the U.S.-backed government maintained secret "death squads," which murdered members of the opposition. In each case, Reagan blocked Soviet influence, but the damage done to local communities and to the international reputation of the United States, as in Vietnam, was great.

Iran-Contra | Reagan's determination to oppose left-wing movements in Central America engulfed his administration in a major scandal during the president's second term. For years, Reagan had de-

nounced Iran as an "outlaw state" and a supporter of terrorism. But in 1985, he wanted its help. To win Iran's assistance in freeing two dozen American hostages held by Hezbollah, a pro-Iranian Shiite group in Lebanon, the administration sold arms to Iran without public or congressional knowledge. While this secret arms deal was diplomatically and politically controversial, the use of the resulting profits in Nicaragua was explicitly illegal. To overthrow the democratically elected Sandinistas, which the president accused of threatening U.S. business interests, Reagan ordered the CIA to assist an armed opposition group called the Contras (Map 30.2). Although Reagan praised the Contras as "freedom fighters," Congress worried that the president and other executive branch agencies were assuming

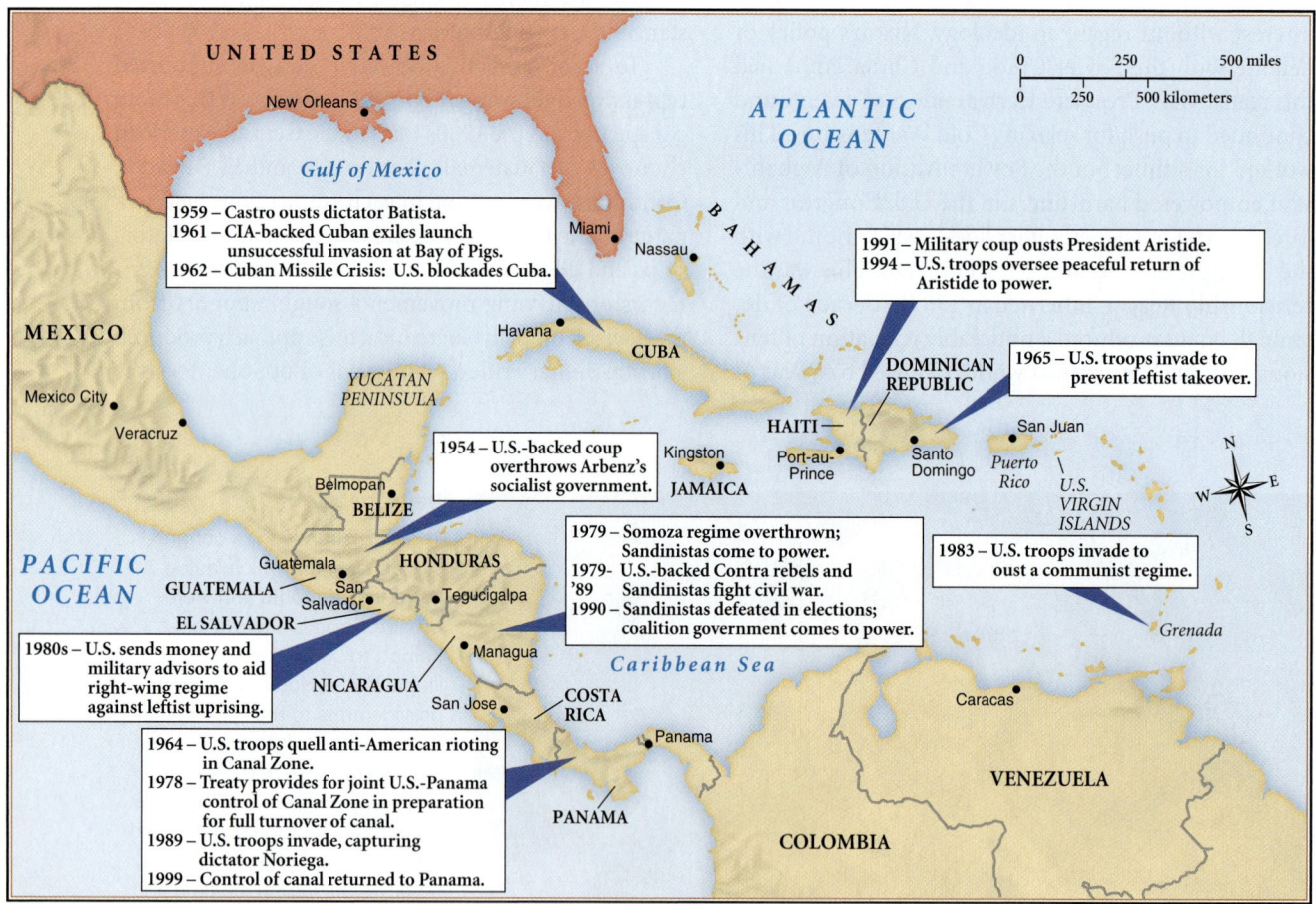

MAP 30.2

U.S. Involvement in Latin America and the Caribbean, 1954–2000

Ever since the Monroe Doctrine (1823), the United States has claimed a special interest in Latin America. During the Cold War, U.S. foreign policy throughout Latin America focused on containing instability and the appeal of communism in a region plagued by poverty and military dictatorships. Providing foreign aid was one approach to addressing social and economic needs, but the United States frequently intervened with military forces (or by supporting military coups) to remove unfriendly or socialist governments. The Reagan administration's support of the Contra rebels in Nicaragua, some of which was contrary to U.S. law, was one of those interventions.

Reagan and Gorbachev: Fellow Political Revolutionaries

Both Ronald Reagan and Mikhail Gorbachev changed the political outlook of their nations. As Reagan undermined social-welfare liberalism in the United States, Gorbachev challenged the rigidity of the Communist Party and state socialism in the Soviet Union. Although they remained ideological adversaries, by the mid-1980s the two leaders had established a personal rapport, which helped facilitate agreement on a series of arms reduction measures. © Bettmann/Corbis.

war-making powers that the Constitution reserved to the legislature. In 1984, Congress banned the CIA and all other government agencies from providing any military support to the Contras.

Oliver North, a lieutenant colonel in the U.S. Marines and an aide to the National Security Council, defied that ban. With the tacit or explicit consent of high-ranking administration officials, including the president, North used the profits from the Iranian arms deal to assist the Contras. When asked whether he knew of North's illegal actions, Reagan replied, "I don't remember." Still swayed by Reagan's charm, the public accepted his convenient loss of memory. Nonetheless, the Iran-Contra affair not only resulted in the prosecution of North and several other officials but also jeopardized the president's reputation. The Iran-Contra scandal weakened Reagan domestically—he proposed no bold domestic policy initiatives in his last two years. But the president remained steadfastly engaged in in-

ternational affairs, where events were unfolding that would bring a dramatic close to the Cold War.

Gorbachev and Soviet Reform The Soviet system of state socialism and central economic planning had transformed Russia from an agricultural to an industrial society between 1917 and the 1950s. But it had done so inefficiently. Lacking the incentives of a market economy, most enterprises hoarded raw materials, employed too many workers, and did not develop new products. Except in military weaponry and space technology, the Russian economy fell further and further behind those of capitalist societies, and most people in the Soviet bloc endured a low standard of living. Moreover, the Soviet invasion of Afghanistan in 1979, like the American war in Vietnam, turned out to be major blunder—an unwinnable war that cost vast amounts of money, destroyed military morale, and undermined popular support of the government.

Pope John Paul II in Poland, 1979

Polish-born Karol Joseph Wojtyla (1920–2005) was named a cardinal of the Roman Catholic Church in 1967 and was selected as pope in 1978. The following year he visited Poland, where he reiterated his opposition to communist rule. His visit sparked the formation of the Solidarity workers' movement and, as its founder Lech Walesa put it, "started this chain of events that led to the end of communism." Martin Athenstaedt/DPA/Corbis.

Mikhail Gorbachev, a relatively young Russian leader who became general secretary of the Communist Party in 1985, recognized the need for internal economic reform and an end to the war in Afghanistan. An iconoclast in Soviet terms, Gorbachev introduced policies of *glasnost* (openness) and *perestroika* (economic restructuring), which encouraged widespread criticism of the rigid institutions and authoritarian controls of the Communist regime. To lessen tensions with the United States, Gorbachev met with Reagan in 1985, and the two leaders established a warm personal rapport. By 1987, they had agreed to eliminate all intermediate-range nuclear missiles based in Europe. A year later, Gorbachev ordered Soviet troops out of Afghanistan, and Reagan replaced many of his hard-line advisors with policymakers who favored a renewal of détente. Reagan's sudden reversal with regard to the Soviet Union remains one of the most intriguing aspects of his presidency. Many conservatives worried that their cowboy-hero president had been duped by a duplicitous Gorbachev, but Reagan's gamble paid off: The easing of tensions with the United States allowed the Soviet leader to press forward with his domestic reforms.

As Gorbachev's efforts revealed the flaws of the Soviet system, the peoples of eastern and central Europe demanded the ouster of their Communist governments. In Poland, the Roman Catholic Church and its pope — Polish-born John Paul II — joined with Solidarity, the trade union movement, to overthrow the pro-Soviet regime. In 1956 and 1964, Russian troops had quashed similar popular uprisings in Hungary and East Germany. Now they did not intervene, and a series of peaceful uprisings—"Velvet Revolutions"—created a new political order throughout the region. The destruction of the Berlin Wall in 1989 symbolized the end of Communist rule in Central Europe. Millions of television viewers worldwide watched jubilant Germans knock down the hated wall. The cement and barbed-wire barrier, which had divided the city since 1961, was a vivid symbol of Communist repression and the Cold War division of Europe. Now East and West Berliners, young and old, danced on the remains of the forbidding wall. A new geopolitical order in Europe was in the making.

Alarmed by the reforms, Soviet military leaders seized power in August 1991 and arrested Gorbachev. But widespread popular opposition led by Boris Yeltsin, the president of the Russian Republic, thwarted their efforts to oust Gorbachev from office. This failure broke the dominance of the Communist Party. On December 25, 1991, the Union of Soviet Socialist Republics formally dissolved to make way for an eleven-member Commonwealth of Independent States (CIS). The Russian Republic assumed leadership of the CIS, but the Soviet Union was no more (Map 30.3). The collapse of the Soviet Union was the result of internal weaknesses of the Communist economy. External pressure from the United States played an important, though secondary, role.

"Nobody—no country, no party, no person—'won' the cold war," concluded George Kennan, the architect in 1947 of the American policy of containment. The Cold War's cost was enormous, and both sides benefited greatly from its end. In 1956, Nikita Khrushchev had told the United States, "We will bury you." For more than forty years, the United States had fought a bitter economic and ideological battle against that Communist foe, a struggle that exerted an enormous impact on American society. Taxpayers had spent some $4 trillion on nuclear weapons and trillions more on conventional arms, placing the United States

MAP 30.3

The Collapse of the Soviet Union and the Creation of Independent States, 1989–1991

The collapse of Soviet communism dramatically altered the political landscape of Central Europe and Central Asia. The Warsaw Pact, the USSR's answer to NATO, vanished. West and East Germany reunited, and the nations created by the Versailles treaty of 1919—Estonia, Latvia, Lithuania, Poland, Czechoslovakia, Hungary, and Yugoslavia—reasserted their independence or split into smaller, ethnically defined nations. The Soviet republics bordering Russia, from Belarus in the west to Kyrgyzstan in the east, also became independent states, while remaining loosely bound with Russia in the Commonwealth of Independent States (CIS).

on a permanent war footing and creating a massive military-industrial complex. The physical and psychological costs were equally high: radiation from atomic weapons tests, anticommunist witch hunts, and—most pervasive of all—a constant fear of nuclear annihilation. Of course, most Americans had no qualms about proclaiming victory, and advocates of free-market capitalism, particularly conservative Republicans, celebrated the outcome. The collapse of communism in Eastern Europe and the disintegration of the Soviet Union itself, they argued, demonstrated that they had been right all along.

A New Political Order at Home and Abroad

Ronald Reagan's role in facilitating the end of the Cold War was probably his most important achievement. Otherwise, his presidency left a mixed legacy. Despite his pledge to get the federal government "off our backs," he could not ultimately reduce its size or scope. Social Security and other entitlement programs remained untouched, and enormous military spending outweighed cuts in other programs. Determined not to divide the country, Reagan did not actively push controversial policies espoused by the Religious Right. He called for tax credits for private religious schools, restrictions on abortions, and a constitutional amendment to permit prayer in public schools, but he did not expend his political capital to secure these measures.

While Reagan failed to roll back the social welfare and regulatory state of the New Deal–Great Society era, he changed the dynamic of American politics. The Reagan presidency restored popular belief that America—and individual Americans—could enjoy increasing prosperity. And his antigovernment rhetoric won many adherents, as did his bold and fiscally dangerous tax cuts. One historian has summed up Reagan's domestic legacy as follows: "For the next twenty years at least, American policies would focus on retrenchment and cost-savings, budget cuts and tax cuts, deregulation and policy redefinitions." Social welfare liberalism, ascendant since 1933, remained intact but was now on the defensive—conservatives had changed the political conversation.

Election of 1988 | George H. W. Bush, Reagan's vice president and successor, was not beloved by conservatives, who did not see him as one of their own. But he possessed an insider's familiarity with government and a long list of powerful allies, ac-

cumulated over three decades of public service. Bush's route to the White House reflected the post-Reagan alignments in American politics. In the primaries, he faced a spirited challenge from Pat Robertson, the arch-conservative televangelist whose influence and profile had grown during Reagan's two terms. After securing the presidential nomination, which he won largely because of his fierce loyalty to Reagan, Bush felt compelled to select as his vice-presidential running mate an unknown and inexperienced Indiana senator, Dan Quayle. Bush hoped that Quayle would help secure the Christian "family values" vote. Robertson's challenge and Quayle's selection showed that the Religious Right had become a major force in Republican politics.

On the Democratic side, Jesse Jackson became the first African American to challenge for a major-party nomination, winning eleven states in primary and caucus voting. However, the much less charismatic Massachusetts governor, Michael Dukakis, emerged as the Democratic nominee. Dukakis, a liberal from the Northeast, proved unable to win back the constituencies Democrats had lost in the 1970s: southern whites, midwestern blue-collar Catholics, and middle-class suburbanites. Indeed, Bush's campaign manager, Lee Atwater, baited Dukakis by calling him a "card-carrying liberal," a not-so-subtle reference to J. Edgar Hoover's 1958 phrase "card-carrying communist." Bush won with 53 percent of the vote, a larger margin of victory than Reagan's in 1980. The election confirmed a new pattern in presidential politics that would last through the turn of the twenty-first century: Every four years, Americans would refight the battles of the 1960s, with liberals on one side and conservatives on the other.

Middle East | The end of the Cold War left the United States as the world's only military superpower and raised the prospect of a "new world order" dominated by the United States and its European and Asian allies. But American officials and diplomats now confronted an array of regional, religious, and ethnic conflicts that defied easy solutions. None were more pressing or more complex than those in the Middle East—the oil-rich lands stretching from Iran to Algeria. Middle Eastern conflicts would dominate the foreign policy of the United States for the next two decades, replacing the Cold War at the center of American geopolitics.

After Carter's success negotiating the 1979 Egypt-Israel treaty at Camp David, there were few bright spots in U.S. Middle Eastern diplomacy. In 1982, the Reagan administration supported Israel's invasion of Lebanon,

Men – and Women – at War
Women played visible roles in the Persian Gulf War, comprising approximately 10 percent of the American troops. In the last decades of the twentieth century, increasing numbers of women chose military careers and, although prohibited from most fighting roles, were increasingly assigned to combat zones.   Luc Delahaye/ Sipa Press.

a military operation intended to destroy the Palestine Liberation Organization (PLO). But when Lebanese militants, angered at U.S. intervention on behalf of Israel, killed 241 American marines, Reagan abruptly withdrew the forces. Three years later, Palestinians living in the Gaza Strip and along the West Bank of the Jordan River — territories occupied by Israel since 1967 — mounted an intifada, a civilian uprising against Israeli authority. In response, American diplomats stepped up their efforts to persuade the PLO and Arab nations to accept the legitimacy of Israel and to convince the Israelis to allow the creation of a Palestinian state. Neither initiative met with much success. Unable, or unwilling, to solve the region's most intractable problems and burdened by a history of support for undemocratic regimes in Middle Eastern countries, the United States was not seen by residents of the region as an honest broker.

Persian Gulf War | American interest in a reliable supply of oil from the region led the United States into a short but consequential war in the Persian Gulf in the early 1990s. Ten years earlier, in September 1980, the revolutionary Shiite Islamic nation of Iran, headed by Ayatollah Khomeini, came un-

der attack from Iraq, a secular state headed by the ruthless dictator Saddam Hussein. The fighting was intense and long lasting — a war of attrition that claimed a million casualties. Reagan supported Hussein with military intelligence and other aid — in order to maintain supplies of Iraqi oil, undermine Iran, and preserve a balance of power in the Middle East. Finally, in 1988, an armistice ended the inconclusive war, with both sides still claiming the territory that sparked the conflict.

Two years later, in August 1990, Hussein went to war to expand Iraq's boundaries and oil supply. Believing (erroneously) that he still had the support of the United States, Hussein sent in troops and quickly conquered Kuwait, Iraq's small, oil-rich neighbor, and threatened Saudi Arabia, the site of one-fifth of the world's known oil reserves and an informal ally of the United States. To preserve Western access to oil, President George H. W. Bush sponsored a series of resolutions in the United Nations Security Council calling for Iraq to withdraw from Kuwait. When Hussein refused, Bush successfully prodded the UN to authorize the use of force, and the president organized a military coalition of thirty-four nations. Dividing mostly along party lines, the Republican-led House of Representatives authorized American participation by a vote of 252 to

182, and the Democratic-led Senate agreed by the close margin of 52 to 47.

The coalition forces led by the United States quickly won the war for the "liberation of Kuwait." To avoid a protracted struggle and retain French and Russian support for the UN coalition, Bush wisely decided against occupying Iraq and removing Saddam Hussein from power. Instead, he won passage of UN Resolution 687, which imposed economic sanctions against Iraq unless it allowed unfettered inspection of its weapons systems, destroyed all biological and chemical arms, and unconditionally pledged not to develop nuclear weapons. The military victory, the low incidence of American casualties, and the quick withdrawal produced a euphoric reaction at home. "By God, we've kicked the Vietnam syndrome once and for all," Bush gloated, and his approval rating shot up precipitously. But the president spoke too soon. Saddam Hussein remained a formidable power in the region. The dictator's alleged ambitions were one factor that, in March 2003, would cause Bush's son, President George W. Bush, to initiate another war in Iraq — one that would be much more protracted, expensive, and bloody for Americans and Iraqis alike.

Thus, the end of the Cold War brought not peace, but American militarism in the Middle East. For half a century, the United States and the Soviet Union had tried to divide the world into two rival economic and ideological blocs: communist and capitalist. The next decades promised a new set of struggles, one of them between a Western-led agenda of economic and cultural globalization and an anti-Western ideology of Muslim and Arab regionalism. Still more post–Cold War shifts were coming into view as well. One was the spectacular emergence of the European Union as a massive united trading bloc, economic engine, and global political force. Another was the equally spectacular economic growth in China, which was just beginning to take off in the early 1990s. The post–Cold War world promised to be a *multi*polar one, with great centers of power in Europe, the United States, and East Asia, and seemingly intractable conflict in the Middle East.

- What factors led to the end of the Cold War?

- Why did the United States intervene in the conflicts between Iraq and Iran, and between Iraq and Kuwait? What were the American goals in each case?

SUMMARY

This chapter examined two central developments of the years 1973–1991: the rise of the New Right in U.S. politics and the end of the Cold War. Each development set the stage for a new era in American life, one that stretches to our own day. Domestically, the New Right, which had been building in strength since the mid-1960s, criticized the "excessive" liberalism of the Great Society and the permissiveness conservative activists associated with feminism and the sexual revolution. Shifting their allegiance from Barry Goldwater to Ronald Reagan, right-wing Americans built a conservative movement from the ground up and in 1980 elected Reagan president. Advocating free-market economics, lower taxes, and fewer government regulations, Reagan became a champion of the New Right. His record as president was more mixed than his rhetoric would suggest, however. Reagan's initial tax cuts were followed by tax hikes. Moreover, he frequently dismayed the Christian Right by not pursuing their interests forcefully enough — especially regarding abortion and school prayer.

Reagan played a role in the ending of the Cold War. His massive military buildup in the early 1980s strained an already overstretched Soviet economy, which struggled to keep pace. Reagan then agreed to meet with Soviet leader Mikhail Gorbachev in several summits between 1985 and 1987. More important than Reagan's actions, however, were inefficiencies and contradictions in the Soviet economic structure itself. Combined with the forced military buildup and the disastrous war in Afghanistan, these strains led Gorbachev to institute the first significant reforms in Soviet society in half a century. The reforms stirred popular criticism of the Soviet Union, which formally collapsed in 1991.

CHAPTER REVIEW QUESTIONS

- What was the "three-legged stool" of New Right conservatism? In what ways were the three components compatible? Incompatible?

- How would you assess the historical importance of Ronald Reagan? What were his most significant legacies, domestically and internationally? Why?

- Why did the Cold War come to an end when it did? What were the contributing factors?

FOR FURTHER EXPLORATION

James T. Patterson, *Restless Giant: The United States from Watergate to Bush v. Gore* (2005), provides a solid analysis of the 1980s and 1990s. For evangelical politics, see Frances FitzGerald, *Cities on a Hill* (1986), which has a section on Jerry Falwell and the Moral Majority; and William Martin, *With God on Our Side: The Rise of the Religious Right in America* (1996). On the rise of the New Right, see Lisa McGirr, *Suburban Warriors: The Origins of the New American Right* (2001). Two valuable overviews of the Reagan presidency are Lou Cannon, *President Reagan: The Role of a Lifetime* (2000), and Haynes Johnson, *Sleepwalking through History: America in the Reagan Years* (1992). John Greene, *The Presidency of George Bush* (2000), discusses the policies of the senior Bush.

On foreign policy, consult Richard A. Melanson, *American Foreign Policy Since the Vietnam War* (2005) and Raymond Garthoff, *The Great Transition: American-Soviet Relations and the End of the Cold War* (1994). Two fine Web sites that document various Cold War incidents are the National Security Archive, at **www.gwu.edu/~nsarchiv**, and the Cold War International History Project, at **www.wilsoncenter.org/index.cfm?fuseaction=topics.home&topic_id=1409**. For the Gulf War, see Michael Gordon and Bernard Trainor, *The Generals' War: The Inside Story of the Conflict in the Gulf* (1995), and **www.pbs.org/wgbh/pages/frontline/gulf**, a site with maps, documents, and interviews with decision makers and soldiers.

TEST YOUR KNOWLEDGE

To assess your command of the material in this chapter, see the Online Study Guide at **bedfordstmartins.com/henretta**.

For Web sites, images, and documents related to topics and places in this chapter, visit **bedfordstmartins.com/makehistory**.

TIMELINE

1981	Ronald Reagan becomes president Republicans gain control of Senate Economic Recovery Tax Act (ERTA) cuts taxes Military expenditures increase sharply Reagan cuts budgets of regulatory agencies Sandra Day O'Connor appointed to the Supreme Court
1981–1989	National debt triples Emergence of New Right think tanks: Heritage Foundation, American Enterprise Institute, and the Cato Institute United States assists Iraq in war against Iran (1980–1988)
1985	Mikhail Gorbachev takes power in Soviet Union
1986	Iran-Contra scandal weakens Reagan presidency William Rehnquist named chief justice
1987	United States and USSR agree to limit missiles in Europe
1988	George H. W. Bush elected president
1989	Destruction of Berlin Wall "Velvet Revolutions" in Eastern Europe *Webster v. Reproductive Health Services* limits abortion services
1990–1991	Persian Gulf War
1991	Dissolution of Soviet Union ends Cold War

CHAPTER 31

National Dilemmas in a Global Society, 1989-2011

On the morning of September 11, 2001, two commercial airliners were deliberately flown into the World Trade Center in lower Manhattan, causing raging fires and bringing the towers to the ground. Millions of Americans, and many more people worldwide, watched live on television and the Internet as the towers collapsed. Simultaneously, a third plane was crashed into the Pentagon, and though passengers gained control of a fourth plane, it went down in rural western Pennsylvania. It took Federal Bureau of Investigation officials only a few hours to determine the identity of most of the hijackers, as well as the organization behind the murderous attacks — Al Qaeda. As elements of the shocking crime became clearer over the subsequent days, it was evident that the attacks had been directed from Al Qaeda bases in Afghanistan, where Osama bin Laden, a wealthy exile from Saudi Arabia, and Khalid Sheikh Mohammed, an American-educated jihadist originally from Kuwait, were protected by the Afghan government.

The attacks of September 11 symbolized the emergence of an anti-Western radical Islamic movement across much of the Middle East. But, tellingly, the attacks were made possible by the new era of globalization. Of the nineteen terrorists involved in the hijackings, fifteen were from Saudi Arabia, two were from the United Arab Emirates, one was from Egypt, and one was from Lebanon. Many had trained in Afghanistan, in guerrilla warfare camps operated by bin Laden. Four had gone to flight school in the United States itself. Several had lived and studied in Germany. They communicated with one another and with planners in Afghanistan through e-mail, Web sites, and cell phones. Al Qaeda sympathizers could be found among Muslims from Indonesia to Algeria. The most conspicuous crime of the twenty-first century, which left 2,900 people dead and sent waves of shock and anxiety through the American public, would have been impossible without the openness and interconnectivity that are central features of globalization.

The response, too, was global. Messages of sympathy and support poured into the United States from nearly every nation. Citizens of fifty-three different countries had perished in the World Trade Center, itself a symbol of the global financial and insurance industries. The world, quite literally, stood in shock. The emergence in the Middle East of a radical Muslim movement willing to use terrorism to inflict major damage on the United States and the West testified to the altered realities of global politics. The simple Cold War duality — communism versus capitalism — had for decades obscured regional, ethnic,

A Poignant Symbol

This striking photograph captures one of the nation's most revered symbols, the Statue of Liberty, against a backdrop of smoke from New York City's World Trade Center following the terrorist attacks of September 11, 2001. Daniel Hulshizer/AP Images.

and religious loyalties and conflicts. Those loyalties and conflicts moved to center stage in an era of globalization.

Globalization saw the rapid spread of capitalism around the world, huge increases in global trade and commerce, and a diffusion of communications technology, including the Internet, that linked the world's people to one another in ways unimaginable a generation earlier. Suddenly, the United States faced a dizzying array of opportunities and challenges, both at home and abroad. "Profound and powerful forces are shaking and remaking our world," said a young President Bill Clinton in his first inaugural address in 1993. He continued: "The urgent question of our time is whether we can make change our friend and not our enemy."

For Americans, the period between the Cold War (which devolved between 1989 and 1991) and our own day has been defined by twin dilemmas. The first relates to globalization. How should the United States engage in global trade and commerce? How should it relate diplomatically to emerging nations? How can it best confront radical Islamic terrorists? As the lone military superpower in a post–Cold War world of energetic capitalism, the United States has found it difficult to answer these vital questions. The second dilemma relates to domestic politics and the economy. In an era of conservative political dominance, how would the nation manage its cultural conflicts and ensure both economic opportunity and economic security for its citizens? As "profound and powerful forces" shook the world, these were, as the chapter title suggests, Americans' national dilemmas in a global society.

America in the Global Economy

On November 30, 1999, nearly 50,000 protesters took to the streets of Seattle, Washington. For much of the morning and afternoon, sometimes in pouring rain, they immobilized a wide swath of the city's downtown. Police, armed with pepper spray and arrayed in riot gear, worked feverishly to clear the clogged streets, get traffic moving, and usher well-dressed government ministers from around the world into a conference hall. Protesters jeered, chanted, and held hundreds of signs and banners aloft. A radical contingent joined the otherwise peaceful march, and a handful of them began breaking the windows of the chain stores they saw as symbols of global capitalism: Starbucks, Gap, Old Navy.

What had aroused such passion in the so-called Battle of Seattle? Globalization. The vast majority of Americans never surged into the streets, as had the Seattle protesters who tried to shut down this 1999 meeting of the World Trade Organization (WTO), but no American by the late 1990s could deny that developments in the global economy reverberated at home. In that decade, Americans rediscovered a long-standing truth: The United States was not an island, but was linked in countless different ways to a global economy and society. Economic prosperity in the post–World War II decades had obscured for Americans this fundamental reality (Figure 31.1).

A question remained, however. In whose interest was the global economy structured? Many of the Seattle activists took inspiration from the five-point "Declaration for Global Democracy," issued by the nonprofit human rights organization Global Exchange during the WTO's Seattle meeting. "Global trade and investment," the declaration demanded, "must not be ends in themselves but rather the instruments for achieving equitable and sustainable development, including protections for workers and the environment." The declaration addressed other issues, such as inequality among nations, which called attention not to the mere *fact* of globalization but to the disparate *impact* of globalized trade and investment. Who benefited from globalization and who did not—such as the many impoverished citizens

WTO Demonstration, Seattle, 1999

In November 1999, an estimated 75,000 people from many states and foreign nations staged an effective protest at a World Trade Organization (WTO) meeting in Seattle. The goals of the protesters were diffuse; many feared that the trend toward a system of free (capitalist-run) trade would primarily benefit multinational corporations and would hurt both developing nations and the working classes in the industrialized world. Protests have continued at subsequent meetings of the WTO and the World Bank.   Hector Mata/ AFP/Getty Images.

of the Middle East who turned to radical Islam for answers—were important questions in the new era.

The Rise of the European Union and China

During the Cold War, from 1945 through the late 1980s, the United States and the Soviet Union dominated the global balance of power. These two superpowers oversaw what observers called a bipolar world—two powerful poles, one capitalist and the other communist, around which global geopolitics were organized. Since the early 1990s, however, a multipolar world has emerged—with centers of power in Europe, Japan, China, and the United States, along with rising regional powers such as India and Brazil.

In 1992, the nations of Western Europe created the European Union (EU) and moved toward the creation of a single federal state, somewhat like the United States. By the end of the 1990s, the European Union embraced more than twenty countries and 450 million people—the third largest population in the world, behind China and India—and accounted for a fifth of all global imports and exports. In 2002, the EU introduced a single currency, the euro, which soon rivaled the dollar and the Japanese yen as a major international currency (Map 31.1). Militarily, however, the EU remained a secondary power. European countries preferred social programs to armies and posed no military challenge to the United States. An economic juggernaut and trading rival with a suspicion of warfare, the EU presented a number of new dilemmas for American officials.

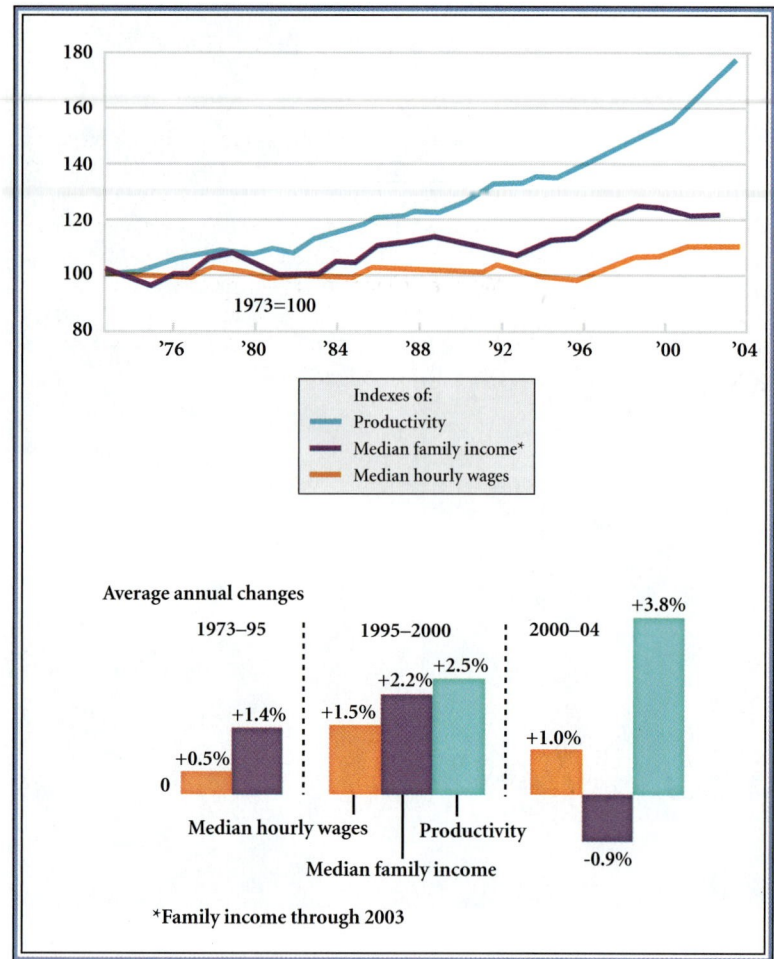

FIGURE 31.1

Productivity, Family Income, and Wages, 1970–2004

This chart tells a complex and not altogether happy story. The median hourly wages of American workers (adjusted for inflation) stagnated between 1970 and 1995. The rise in median family income reflected the increasing proportion of two-earner families, as more married women entered the workforce. The dramatic increases in productivity did not lead to higher wages for workers. Rather, businesses used those gains either to cut prices to compete in the global marketplace or to reward owners, shareholders, and, particularly, corporate executives.

So did China, a vast nation of 1.3 billion people that was the world's fastest-rising economic power in the first decade of the twenty-first century. Between 2000 and 2008, China *quadrupled* its gross domestic product (GDP). Economic growth rates during those years were consistently near 10 percent—higher than the United States achieved during its periods of furious economic growth in the 1950s and 1960s. The irony is that China could hardly have put up such impressive numbers without its symbiotic relationship with American consumers. Although still governed by the Communist Party, China embraced capitalism, and its factories produced inexpensive products for export, which Americans eagerly purchased—everything from children's toys and television sets to clothing, household appliances, and video games. Such a relationship is possible because China has deliberately kept its currency weak against the American dollar, ensuring that its exports remain cheap in the United States.

Beneficial to American consumers in the short run, the implications of this relationship for the future may be less promising. Two such implications stand out. First, as more and more goods that Americans buy are produced in China, the manufacturing base in the United States continues to shrink, costing jobs and adversely affecting communities. Second, China has kept its currency low against the dollar primarily by purchasing American debt. China now owns nearly 25 percent of total U.S. debt, more than any other nation. Many economists believe that it is unwise to allow a single country to wield so much influence over the U.S. currency supply. Should this relationship continue unchanged, Americans may find their manufacturing sector contracting even more severely in the coming decades.

An Era of Globalization

Over the centuries, Americans have depended on foreign markets to which they export their tobacco, cotton, wheat, and industrial goods, and have long received imported products and immigrants from other coun-

MAP 31.1

Growth of the European Community, 1951–2005

The European Community (EU) began in the 1950s as a loose organization of Western European nations. Over the course of the following decades, it created stronger common institutions, such as the European Parliament in Strasbourg, the EU Commission in Brussels, and the Court of Justice in Luxembourg. With the collapse of communism, the EU has expanded to include the nations of Eastern and Central Europe. It now includes twenty-five nations and 450 million people.

Map legend:
- Original members of the European Economic Union
- Became members 1973–1995
- Became members in 2004
- Applying for membership

tries. But the *intensity* of international exchange has varied over time, as has Americans' awareness of that exchange. In the 1990s, both intensity and awareness were on the upswing. The end of the Cold War shattered barriers that had restrained international trade and impeded capitalist development of vast areas of the world. New communications systems—satellites, fiber-optic cables, global positioning networks—were shrinking the world's physical spaces to a degree unimaginable at the beginning of the twentieth century. Perhaps most important, global financial markets became integrated to an unprecedented extent, allowing investment capital to "flow" into and out of nations and around the world in a matter of moments. The global economy was entering a new phase.

International Organizations and Corporations International organizations, many of them created in the wake of World War II, set the rules for capitalism's worldwide expansion. During the final decades of the Cold War, the leading capitalist industrial nations formed the Group of Seven (G7) to manage global economic policy. Russia joined in 1997, creating the Group of Eight (G8). The G8 nations—the United States, Britain, Germany,

France, Italy, Japan, Canada, and Russia—largely controlled the major international financial organizations: the World Bank, the International Monetary Fund (IMF), and the General Agreement on Trades and Tariffs (GATT). In 1995, GATT evolved into the World Trade Organization (WTO), with nearly 150 participating nations.

As globalization accelerated, so did the integration of regional economies. To offset the economic clout of the European bloc, in 1993 the United States, Canada, and Mexico signed the North American Free Trade Agreement (NAFTA). This treaty, as ratified by the U.S. Congress, envisioned the eventual creation of a free-trade zone covering all of North America. In East Asia, the capitalist nations of Japan, South Korea, Taiwan, and Singapore consulted on economic policy; as China developed a quasi-capitalist economy and became a major exporter of manufactures, its Communist-led government joined their deliberations.

International organizations set the rules, but globalization was made possible by the proliferation of multinational corporations (MNCs). In 1970, there were 7,000 corporations with offices and factories in multiple countries; by 2000, the number had exploded to 63,000. Many of the most powerful MNCs were, and

A Nike Factory in China

In 2005, Nike produced its shoes and sportswear at 124 plants in China; additional factories were located in other low-wage countries. Most of the Chinese plants were run by subcontractors, who housed the workers—mostly women between the ages of sixteen to twenty-five—in crowded dormitories. The wages were low, about $3 a day, but more than the women could earn if they remained in their rural villages. AP Images.

continue to be, American-based. Walmart, the biggest retailer in the United States, is also the world's largest corporation, with 1,200 stores in other nations and $32 billion in foreign sales. The McDonald's restaurant chain had 1,000 outlets outside the United States in 1980; twenty years later, there were nearly 13,000, and "McWorld" had become a popular shorthand term for globalization.

Globalization was driven by more than a quest for new markets. Corporations also sought ever-cheaper sources of labor. Many American MNCs closed their factories in the United States and outsourced manufacturing jobs to plants in Mexico, Eastern Europe, and especially Asia. The athletic sportswear firm Nike was a prime example. The company established manufacturing plants for its shoes and apparel in Communist Vietnam and China as well as in capitalist Indonesia. By the mid-1990s, Nike had 150 factories in Asia that em-

ployed more than 450,000 workers, most of whom received low wages, endured harsh working conditions, and had no health or pension benefits. Highly skilled jobs were outsourced as well.

Financial Deregulation   As trade restrictions among nations began to fall in the 1980s and 1990s, so did restrictions on investment. One of the principal differences between this new era of globalization and previous eras has been the opening of national financial and currency markets to investment from around the world. Global financial integration has been a hallmark of our time. The United States and Britain led the way. Both countries came under the sway of powerful political forces in the 1980s calling for the total deregulation of banks, brokerage houses, investment firms, and financial markets—letting the free market replace government oversight. Together, the

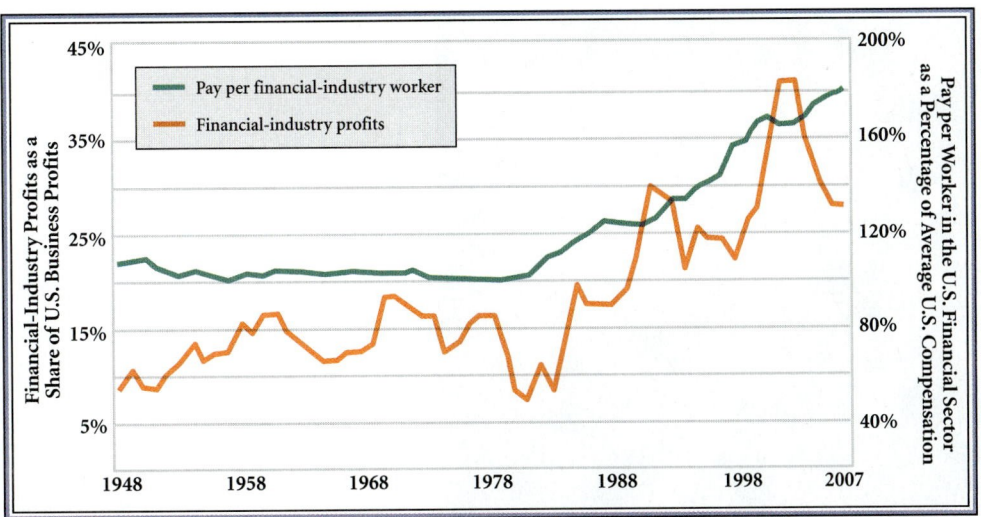

FIGURE 31.2

Financial-Industry Profits and Compensation

From the end of World War II until the late 1970s, financial markets (largely securities trading) accounted for less than 20 percent of the overall American economy. Since the 1970s, however, the financial industry has nearly doubled its share of economic activity, accounting for more than 40 percent of all U.S. business profits by the late 1990s. Financial sector salaries increased proportionally. Many economists doubt the wisdom of allowing securities trading to account for such a large share of economic activity, especially since U.S. manufacturing declined precipitously over these same decades.

United States and Britain led a quiet revolution in which investment markets around the world were gradually set free.

Financial deregulation led to spectacular profits for investors but produced a more fragile, crash-prone global economy. On the profit side, financial-industry profits in the United States rose from less than 10 percent of total business profits in the 1950s to more than 40 percent in the 1990s (Figure 31.2). But the costs were becoming clear as well: the bankruptcy of the American savings and loan industry in the 1980s; the "lost decade" in Japan in the 1990s; the near-bankruptcy of Russia in the late 1990s and of Argentina in 2001; the 1997 Asian financial crisis, centered in Thailand and Indonesia; and the collapse of nearly the entire global economy in 2008. These and other episodes dramatized the extraordinary risks that financial globalization has introduced.

The New Technology

The technological advances of the 1980s and 1990s changed the character of everyday life for millions of Americans, linking them with a global information and media environment unprecedented in world history. Not since television was introduced to American homes in the years following World War II had tech-

nology so profoundly changed the way people lived their lives. Personal computers, cell phones and smartphones, the Internet and the World Wide Web, the iPod, and other electronic devices and systems altered work, leisure, and access to knowledge in stunning ways. Like unimpeded trade, these advances in communications and personal technologies enhanced globalization.

During the 1990s, personal computers, which had emerged in the late 1970s, grew even more significant with the spread of the Internet and the World Wide Web. Like the computer itself, the Internet was the product of military-based research. During the late 1960s, the U.S. Department of Defense, in conjunction with the Massachusetts Institute of Technology, began developing a decentralized computer network, the Advanced Research Projects Agency Network (ARPANET). The Internet, which grew out of the ARPANET, was soon used by government scientists, academic specialists, and military contractors to exchange data, information, and electronic mail (e-mail). By the 1980s, the Internet had spread to universities, businesses, and the general public.

The debut in 1991 of the graphics-based World Wide Web—a collection of servers that allowed access to millions of documents, pictures, and other materials—enhanced the popular appeal and commercial possibilities of the Internet. By 2009, 75 percent of all Americans

Akio Morita and the Sony Corporation

In 1946, Akio Morita and Masaru Ibuka founded the Tokyo Telecommunications Engineering Corporation, which evolved into the Sony Corporation. Its first great sales success came in the mid-1950s with a pocket-sized transistor radio. Other innovative products followed in subsequent decades: in the 1960s, the popular Trinitron TV; in the 1970s, the Betamax video recorder and the Walkman radio; in the 1980s, the compact disc, the 3.5-inch diskette, and, shown here in a picture of Morita in 1985, the Handycam. In the 1990s, Sony devised the PlayStation, the memory stick, and many more electronic products. In 2005, Sony employed 150,000 workers and sold goods worth $18 billion in the United States and $67 billion worldwide.   Photo by Bill Pierce/Time Life Pictures/Getty Images.

Internet versus Newspapers

Between 2000 and 2010, dozens of large and medium-sized newspapers went out of business, their once-robust readership drained away by the convenience of news available for free on the Internet. In 2009, the *Seattle Post-Intelligencer* newspaper ceased print publication and became an online-only news source. In this photo, the paper's news-boxes sit empty, an ominous sign of the struggling newspaper business in the early 2000s.   © Bettmann/Corbis.

FIGURE 31.3

Boom and Bust in the Stock Market

In late 1999, the stock market took off. As the line in this figure indicates, the rise in the index of stocks listed on the NASDAQ exchange (which includes about 3,700 companies) was particularly rapid because of the NASDAQ's heavy emphasis on technology companies. In little more than a year, the NASDAQ index tripled in value. Its descent was equally quick. By mid-2002, the index was back where it started, and it continued to fall until early 2003. As in all booms and busts, fortunes were made—and lost—overnight.

and more than one billion people worldwide used the Internet to send messages and view information. Businesses used the World Wide Web to sell their products and services; e-commerce transactions totaled $114 billion in 2003, $172 billion in 2005, and well over $200 billion by 2008. The Web proved instantly democratic, providing ordinary people with easy access to knowledge. For nearly two centuries, local public libraries had served that function; now, more and more material in libraries was instantly available in a home or an office.

Advances in electronic technology resulted in the rapid creation of new leisure and business products. The 1980s saw the introduction of videocassette recorders (VCRs), compact disc (CD) players, and inexpensive fax machines. By 2000, cameras took digital pictures that could be stored and transmitted on computers, and digital video discs (DVDs) had become the newest technology for viewing movies. Cellular telephones (cell phones), which also became available in the 1980s, ignited a communications revolution. By 2010, more than 80 percent of American adults carried one of these portable devices.

By the first decade of the twenty-first century, Americans had come to live in a world saturated with instantaneous electronic information. This total media environment left one of the most significant forms of media of the last four centuries struggling to survive: newspapers. As more and more Americans began to get their news from television and the Internet, advertising revenue migrated accordingly and newspapers suffered calamitously. Across the country, newspaper subscriptions were in freefall between 2000 and 2010, declining between 25 and 50 percent in various cities. Hundreds of newspapers—from small-town weeklies to major big-city dailies such as the *Rocky Mountain News* and the *Seattle Post-Intelligencer*—closed their doors in that decade. The printed newspaper, around since the 1660s, was expected to survive in some form, but few observers could predict what its rapid demise would mean in coming decades.

- **What were the most important factors in globalization? How would you evaluate or rank their importance in reshaping the world?**

- **In what ways has the United States benefited from globalization? In what ways has it not?**

Politics and Partisanship in a New Era

Standing at the podium at the 1992 Republican National Convention, his supporters cheering by the thousands, Patrick Buchanan did not mince words. He had lost the nomination for president, but he still hoped to shape the party's message to voters. Buchanan was a former speechwriter for President Richard Nixon and a White House aide to President Ronald Reagan, and he remained a fiery opponent of the liberal social movements of the 1960s and 1970s. This election, he told the audience—including millions watching on television— "is about what we stand for as Americans." Citing Democratic support for abortion rights and the rights of lesbians and gay men, Buchanan claimed there was "a religious war going on in our country for the soul of America." It was, he emphasized, "a cultural war."

To Buchanan and other conservatives, the success of rights liberalism in the previous decades led to this "cultural war." For them, racial pluralism and "family values"—which was their term for issues related primarily to abortion and the status of women and gay Americans—remained hot-button concerns that could reliably energize conservative voters. Buchanan's war was another name for a long-standing political struggle, dating to the 1920s, between religious traditionalists and secular liberals (see Chapter 22). This time, however, Americans struggled over these questions in the long shadow of the sixties, which had taken on an exaggerated meaning in the nation's politics. Against the backdrop of globalization, American politics in the 1990s and early 2000s remained caught in a cycle of battles over the consequences of social upheaval during the

sixties. The era's politics careened back and forth between contests over divisive social issues and concern over the nation's economic future.

An Increasingly Plural Society

Exact estimates vary, but demographers predict that at some point between 2040 and 2050 the United States will become a "majority-minority" nation: No single ethnic or racial group will be in the numerical majority. This is already the case in California, where in 2010 African Americans, Latinos, and Asians together constituted a majority of the state's residents. As this unmistakable trend became apparent in the 1990s, it fueled renewed debates over ethnic and racial identity and over public policies such as affirmative action.

New Immigrants | According to the Census Bureau, the population of the United States grew from 203 million in 1970 to 280 million in 2000 (see Comparing American Voices, "Cheap Labor: Immigration and Globalization," pp. 988–989). Of that 77-million-person increase, immigrants accounted for 28 million, with legal entrants numbering 21 million and illegal entrants adding another 7 million (Figure 31.4). As a result, by 2000, 26 percent of California's population was foreign-born, as was 20 percent of New York's

New Immigrants

In the early years of the 2000s, more immigrants lived in the United States than at any time since the first decades of the twentieth century. Most came from Asia, Latin America, and Africa. Many, like those pictured here, started small businesses that helped revive the economies of urban and suburban neighborhoods across the country.
© Bettmann/Corbis.

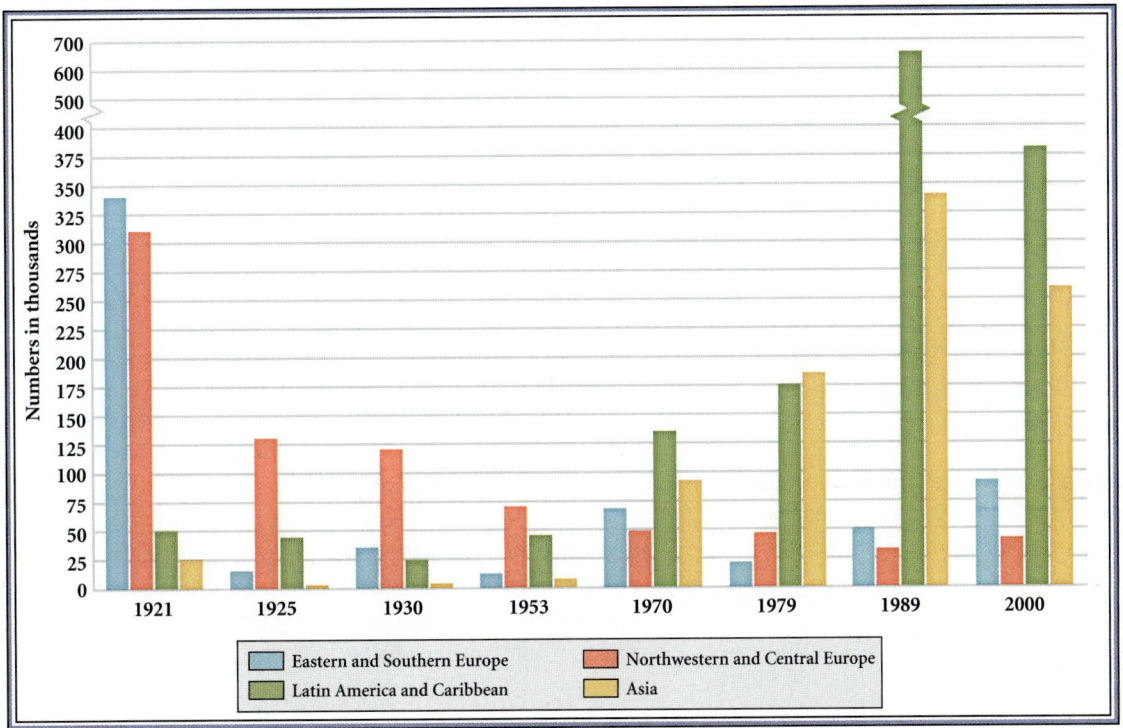

FIGURE 31.4

American Immigration, 1920–2000

Legislation inspired by nativism slowed the influx of immigrants after 1920, as did the dislocations brought on by economic depression and war in the 1930s and 1940s. Note the high rate of non-European immigration since the 1970s, the result of new eligibility rules in the Immigration Act of 1965 (see Chapter 28). The dramatic increase since 1980 in the number of migrants from Latin America and Asia reflects American economic prosperity, traditionally a magnet for migrants, and the rapid acceleration of illegal immigration.

and 17 percent each of New Jersey's and Florida's. Relatively few immigrants came from Europe, which had dominated immigration to the United States between 1880 and 1924. The overwhelming majority—some 25 million—now came from Latin America (16 million) and East Asia (9 million) (Map 31.2).

This extraordinary inflow of immigrants was the unintended result of the Immigration and Nationality Act of 1965, one of the less well-known but most influential pieces of Great Society legislation. Known as the Hart-Celler Act, the legislation eliminated the 1924 quota system, which had favored Northern Europe. In its place Congress created a more equal playing field among nations and a slightly higher total limit on immigration. The legislation also included provisions that eased the entry of immigrants who were professionals, scientists, and artists "of exceptional ability," or who possessed skills in high demand in the United States. Finally, a provision with far-reaching implications was included in the new law: Immediate family members of those already legally resident in the United States were admitted outside of the total numerical limit. President Johnson signed the law at the base of the Statue of Liberty and said simply that immigrants would be admitted "on the basis of their skills and their close relationship to those already here."

American residents from Latin America and the Caribbean were best positioned to take advantage of the family provision. Millions of Mexicans came to the United States to join their families, and U.S. residents from El Salvador and Guatemala—tens of thousands of whom had arrived seeking sanctuary or asylum during the civil wars of the 1980s—and the Dominican Republic now brought their families to join them. Nationally, there were now more Latinos than African Americans. Many of these immigrants profoundly shaped the emerging global economy by sending substantial portions of their earnings, called remittances, back to family members in their home countries. In 2006, for instance, workers in the United States sent $23 billion to Mexico, a massive remittance flow that constituted Mexico's third-largest source of foreign exchange. Another $3 billion went to the Dominican Republic.

Cheap Labor: Immigration and Globalization

Immigrants have long populated the United States, and they continue to remake it. But for whose benefit? Under what conditions? And at whose expense? Those are three of the questions raised by the following testimonials from men and women employed in agricultural production, janitorial services, and garment manufacturing.

George Stith and Juanita Garcia

"Local farm workers could not get jobs at all."

George Stith and Juanita Garcia were farmworkers and union members. In 1952, they testified before a congressional committee considering whether to expand or restrict the Mexican Bracero Program.

STITH: Mr. Chairman and members of the committee, My name is George Stith. My address is Star Route Box 5, Gould, Ark. All my life I have worked on cotton plantations. When I was 4 years old my family moved to southern Illinois, near Cairo. We picked cotton in southeast Missouri, and west Tennessee nearly every year. We later moved across the river into Missouri and share-cropped. In 1930 we moved back to Arkansas. I don't know whether I am a migratory worker or not, but we certainly did a lot of migrating.

In 1936 when I was share cropping in Woodruff County, Ark. I joined the union which was then called the Southern Tenant Farmers Union. It is now the National Farm Labor Union, A. F. of L. I have been a member of the union ever since. . . .

For a long time I had heard about labor shortages in the West and how Mexican workers were being imported. I was sure that no people would be imported from Mexico to work on farms in Arkansas. There were too many people living in the little towns and cities who go out to chop and pick cotton. . . .

The importation of Mexican nationals into Arkansas did not begin until the fall of 1949. Cotton-picking wages in my section were good. We were getting $4 per 100 pounds for picking. As soon as the Mexicans were brought in the wages started falling. Wages were cut to $3.25 and $3 per 100 pounds. In many cases local farm workers could not get jobs at all. . . . The cotton plantation owners kept the Mexicans at work and would not employ Negro and white pickers. . . .

GARCIA: My name is Juanita Garcia. I live in Brawley, Calif. I work in the field and in the packing sheds. I lost my job in a packing shed about 2 weeks ago. I was fired because

I belonged to the National Farm Labor Union. . . . My father, my brothers, and sisters also work on the farms. For poor people like us who are field laborers, making a living has always been hard. Why? Because the ranchers and companies have always taken over. . . .

In the Imperial Valley we have a hard time. It so happens that the local people who are American citizens cannot get work. . . . The wetbacks [illegal immigrants] and nationals from Mexico have the whole Imperial Valley. . . . The nationals and wetbacks take any wages the ranchers offer to pay them. The wages get worse every year. . . .

Last year they fired some people from the shed because they had nationals to take their jobs. There was a strike. . . . They took the nationals from the camps to break our strike. They had 5,000 scabs that were nationals. We told the Mexican consul about this. We told the Labor Department. They were supposed to take the nationals out of the strike. They never did take them away.

Source: Migratory Labor, Hearings before Subcommittee on Labor and Labor-Management Relations, 82nd Congress, 2nd Session (Washington, D.C., Government Printing Office, 1952), 89–90, 93–94.

Trong and Thanh Nguyen

"We're political refugees. . . . We spend our money here."

Trong and Thanh Nguyen fled from Communist Vietnam in the mid-1970s.

TRONG: When my wife and I came to Chicago, our major concern was to feed our five small children. We had Vietnamese pride and did not want to take public aid. We wanted the American community and authorities to respect us.

Just trying to begin a new life here, we had so many difficulties. When I worked as a janitor at Water Tower Place, a co-worker told me, "Trong, do you know that America is overpopulated? We have more than two hundred million people. We don't need you. Go back where you belong." I was shocked to hear people trying to chase us out. . . .

THANH: When we first came to Chicago, I cried a lot. In the factory where I worked, there weren't many Americans. Most were Mexicans, some legal, but also many illegal aliens. . . .

They cursed our people. Some Mexicans said, "You come here and take our jobs. Go back wherever you came from." . . . "You come here to make money, then go back home and live like kings." That was too much. I couldn't hold it in any more.

I told them in a very soft voice, "We are Vietnamese people. You don't have enough education to know where our country is. Vietnam is a small country, but we did not come to America to look for jobs. We're political refugees. We can't go back home." I didn't call them bad names or anything, but I said, "You are the ones who come here to make money to bring back to your country. We spend our money here." After that, they didn't bother us very much.

Source: Paul S. Boyer, ed., *Enduring Voices*, 3rd ed. (Boston: Houghton Mifflin, 1996), 408–409.

Petra Mata and Feiyi Chen

"Garment workers . . . made a decent living before free trade."

Petra Mata and Feiyi Chen are immigrants from low-wage countries who were "insourced"; on coming to the United States, they worked as low-paid garment workers. Then, their jobs were outsourced – sent abroad to workers paid even less, as a result of free trade and globalization.

MATA: My name is Petra Mata. I was born in Mexico. I have completed no more than the sixth grade in school. In 1969, my husband and I came to the U.S. believing we would find better opportunities for our children and ourselves. We first arrived without documents, then became legal, and finally became citizens. For years I moved from job to job until I was employed in 1976 by the most popular company in the market, Levi Strauss & Company. I earned $9.73 an hour and also had vacation and sick leave. Levi's provided me and my family with a stable situation, and in return I was a loyal employee and worked there for fourteen years.

On January 16, 1990, Levi's closed its plant in San Antonio, Texas, where I had been working, leaving 1,150 workers unemployed, a majority of whom were Mexican-American women. The company moved its factory to Costa Rica. . . .

As a result of being laid off, I personally lost my house, my method of transportation, and the tranquility of my home. My family and I had to face new problems. My husband was forced to look for a second job on top of the one he already had. He worked from seven in the morning to six at night. Our reality was very difficult. At that time, I had not the slightest idea what free trade was or meant. . . .

Our governments make agreements behind closed doors without participation from the working persons who are most affected by these decisions—decisions that to my knowledge only benefit large corporations and those in positions of power. . . .

CHEN: My name is Feiyi Chen. I immigrated to the United States in December 1998 from China. I began my working career as a seamstress in a garment factory because I did not speak English and the garment manufacturing industry was one of the few employment opportunities available to me. I typically worked ten hours a day, six days a week, at a backbreaking pace. Most garment bosses know that new immigrants have few choices when it comes to work and so they take advantage by paying workers less than the minimum wage with no overtime pay. . . . I learned from some of the older garment workers that garment workers in San Francisco actually made a decent living before free trade lured many of the better-paying garment factories over to other countries and forced the smaller and rule-abiding factories to shut down because they could not compete with the low cost of production from neighboring countries. . . .

Working as a seamstress and an assembly worker has always been hard, but with so many of the factories leaving the country in search of cheaper labor, life for immigrant workers like myself is getting worse. For example, many garment workers who were paid one dollar for sewing a piece of clothing are now only making fifty cents for the same amount of work. There are a lot of garment workers who still work ten hours a day but make less than thirty dollars a day.

Source: Christine Ahn, *Shafted: Free Trade and America's Working Poor* (Oakland, CA: Food First Books, 2003), 32–38.

ANALYZING THE EVIDENCE

- Describe the experiences of the workers as related in their statements. What generalizations can you make about the impact of immigration on wages? On the relations among ethnic groups in the United States?

- How does globalization, a major focus of this chapter, affect the lives of these workers? Provide some specific examples from the documents that show its impact.

- What role would these workers like the federal government to play? According to the discussion in this chapter, what is American policy with respect to globalization?

- Who benefits from immigration, legal or illegal? How does immigration affect working conditions? What are the costs, and who pays those costs?

MAP 31.2

Hispanic and Asian Populations, 2000

In 2000, people of Hispanic descent made up more than 11 percent of the American population, and now outnumber African Americans as the largest minority group. Asian Americans accounted for an additional 4 percent of the population. Demographers predict that by the year 2050 only about half of the U.S. population will be composed of non-Hispanic whites. Note the high percentage of Hispanics and Asians in California and certain other states.

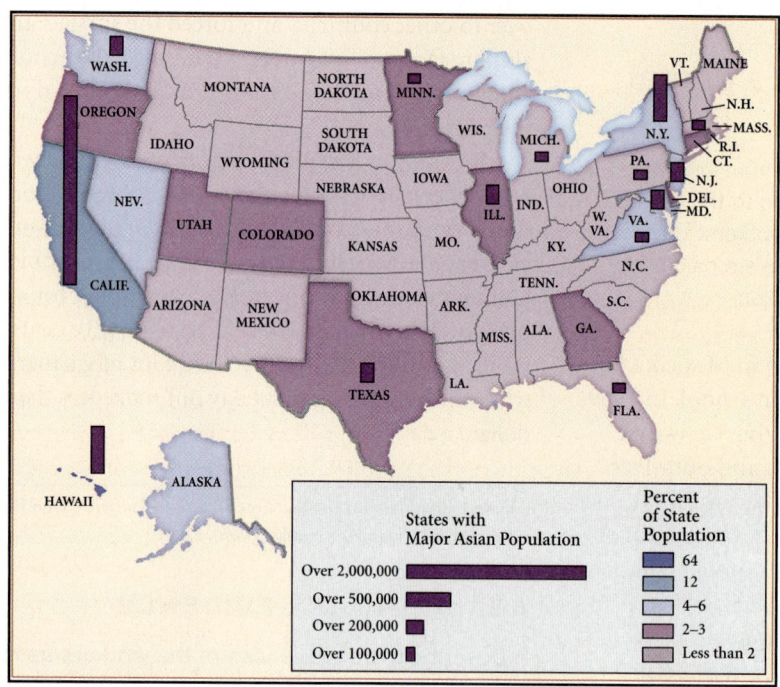

Asian immigrants came largely from China, the Philippines, South Korea, India, and Pakistan. In addition, 700,000 refugees came to the United States from Southeast Asia (Vietnam, Laos, and Cambodia) after the Vietnam War. This immigration signaled more than new flows of people into the United States. Throughout much of its history, the United States had oriented itself toward the Atlantic. Indeed, at the end of the nineteenth century, American secretary of state John Hay observed, "The Mediterranean is the ocean of the past; the Atlantic the ocean of the present." He added, presciently, "The Pacific [is] the ocean of the future." By the last decades of the twentieth century, Hay's future had arrived. As immigration from Asia increased, as Japan and China grew more influential economically, and as more and more transnational trade crossed the Pacific, commentators on both sides of the ocean began speaking of the Pacific Rim as an important new region.

English Only

Not everyone was pleased with the new influx of immigrants. Anti-immigrant movements arose in various states, especially those along the Mexican border. In 1998, conservative activist Ron Unz sponsored Proposition 227 in California. The measure, which banned bilingual education in public schools, passed by a wide margin. In this photo, Unz delivers a speech supporting Proposition 227 to an audience in Los Angeles.   AP Images.

Multiculturalism and Its Critics

Most new immigrants arrived under the terms of the 1965 law. But those who did not—and who thus became known as illegal aliens—stirred political controversy. In 1992, Patrick Buchanan, then campaigning for the Republican presidential nomination, warned Americans that their country was "undergoing the greatest invasion in its history, a migration of millions of illegal aliens a year from Mexico." Significantly, state governments led the efforts to deal with illegal immigration. In 1986, California voters overwhelmingly supported Proposition 63, which established English as the state's official language; seventeen other states followed suit. Eight years later, Californians approved Proposition 187, a ballot initiative forthrightly named "Save Our State," which barred illegal aliens from public schools, nonemergency care at public health clinics, and all other state social services. When a federal judge ruled that Proposition 187 was unconstitutional, supporters of the measure demanded that Congress take action to curtail legal immigration and expel illegal aliens—action that has yet to materialize.

Debates over post-1965 immigration looked a great deal like conflicts in the early decades of the century. Then, many native-born white Protestants worried that the largely Jewish and Catholic immigrants from Southern and Eastern Europe, along with African American migrants leaving the South, could not assimilate and threatened the "purity" of the nation. Although the conflicts looked the same, the cultural paradigm had shifted. In the earlier era, the melting pot—a term borrowed from the title of a 1908 play—became the metaphor for how American society would accommodate its newfound diversity. Some native-born Americans found solace in the melting-pot concept, because it implied that a single "American" culture would predominate. In the 1990s, however, a different concept, multiculturalism, emerged to define social diversity. Americans, this concept suggested, were not a single people into whom others melted; rather, they comprised a diverse set of ethnic and racial groups living and working together. A shared set of public values held the multicultural society together, even as different groups maintained unique practices and traditions.

Critics, however, charged that multiculturalism perpetuated ethnic chauvinism and conferred preferential treatment on minority groups. Many government policies, as well as a large number of private employers, for instance, continued to support affirmative action programs designed to bring African Americans, Latinos, and women into public- and private-sector jobs and universities in larger numbers. Conservatives argued that such governmental programs were deeply flawed, because they promoted "reverse discrimination" against white men and resulted in the selection and promotion of less-qualified applicants for jobs and educational advancement. Individualism, rather than multiculturalism, ought to prevail, they argued.

California stood at the center of the debate. In 1995, under pressure from Republican governor Pete Wilson, the regents of the University of California scrapped their twenty-year-old policy of affirmative action. A year later, California voters approved Proposition 209, which outlawed affirmative action in state employment and public education. At the height of the 1995 controversy, President Bill Clinton delivered a major speech defending affirmative action. He reminded Americans that Richard Nixon, a Republican president, had endorsed affirmative action, and he concluded by saying the nation should "mend it," not "end it." However, as in the *Bakke* decision of the 1970s (see Chapter 29), it was the U.S. Supreme Court that spoke loudest on the subject. In two parallel 2003 cases, the Court invalidated one affirmative action plan at the University of Michigan but allowed racial preference policies that promoted a "diverse" student body. Thus, diversity became the law of the land, the constitutionally acceptable basis for affirmative action. The policy had been narrowed but preserved.

Additional anxieties about a multicultural nation centered on language. In 1998, Silicon Valley software entrepreneur Ron Unz sponsored a California initiative calling for an end to bilingual education in public schools. Unz argued that bilingual education had failed because it did not adequately prepare Spanish-speaking students to succeed in an English-speaking society. The state's white, Anglo residents, largely approved of the measure; most Mexican American, Asian American, and civil rights organizations opposed it. When Unz's measure, Proposition 227, passed with a healthy 61 percent majority, it seemed to confirm the limits of multiculturalism in the nation's most diverse state.

Clashes over "Family Values"

If the promise of a multicultural nation was one contested political issue, another was the state of American families. New Right conservatives charged that the "abrasive experiments of two liberal decades," as a Reagan administration report put it, had eroded respect for marriage and what they had called, since the 1970s, "family values." They pointed to the 40 percent rate of divorce among whites and the nearly 60 percent rate of out-of-wedlock pregnancies among African Americans. To conservatives, there was a wide range of culprits: legislators who enacted liberal divorce laws, funded child care, and allowed welfare payments to unmarried mothers, as well as judges who condoned abortion and banished religious instruction from public schools.

Abortion | Abortion was central to the battles between feminists and religious conservatives, and a defining issue between Democrats and Republicans. Feminists who described themselves as "pro-choice" viewed the issue from the perspective of the pregnant woman; they argued that the right to a legal, safe abortion was crucial to her control over her body and life. Conversely, religious conservatives, who pronounced themselves "pro-life," viewed abortion from the perspective of the unborn fetus and claimed that its rights trumped those of the living mother. That is where the debate had stood since the U.S. Supreme Court's 1973 decision in *Roe v. Wade* (see Reading American Pictures, "The Abortion Debate Hits the Streets," p. 993). Both ideologies had roots in the American commitment to "life, liberty, and the pursuit of happiness." The questions remained: Whose life? Whose liberty? Whose definition of happiness?

By the 1980s, fundamentalist Protestants had assumed leadership of the antiabortion movement, which became increasingly confrontational and politically powerful. In 1987, the religious activist Randall Terry founded Operation Rescue, which mounted protests outside abortion clinics and harassed their staffs and clients. While such vocal protests took shape outside clinics, antiabortion activists also won state laws that limited public funding for abortions, required parental notification before minors could obtain abortions, and mandated waiting periods before any woman could undergo an abortion procedure. Such laws further restricted women's reproductive choices.

Homosexuality | The issue of homosexuality stirred equally deep passions—on all sides. As more gay men and women came out of the closet in the years after Stonewall (see Chapter 28), they demanded legal protections from discrimination in housing, education, and employment. Public opinion about these demands varied by region, but by the 1990s, many cities and states had indeed banned discrimination on the basis of sexual orientation. Gay rights groups also sought legal rights for same-sex couples—such as the eligibility for workplace health-care coverage—that were akin to those enjoyed by married heterosexuals. Many of the most prominent national gay rights organizations, such as the Human Rights Campaign, focused on full marriage equality: a legal recognition of same-sex marriage that was on par with opposite-sex marriages.

The Religious Right had long condemned homosexuality as morally wrong. Televangelist Pat Robertson, North Carolina senator Jesse Helms, activist Phyllis Schlafly, and other conservatives campaigned vigorously

The Abortion Debate Hits the Streets

Few issues in U.S. history divided late-twentieth-century Americans as profoundly as abortion. Since the Supreme Court's decision in *Roe v. Wade* (1973), protests and counterprotests have continued. As the text suggests, the issue intrudes constantly into the social, cultural, and political history of recent decades (see Chapters 29 and 30). Because the battle involves a seemingly irreconcilable difference between conflicting moral principles, finding common ground for compromise has been difficult. Antiabortion activists sometimes compare their fight with that of the abolitionists in the pre–Civil War era (who argued that slavery was immoral) and liken *Roe v. Wade* to *Dred Scott*—the 1857 Supreme Court decision that protected slave property. Those who support abortion rights often stake their ground on the rights of the individual—a woman's right to control her life and her body—and invoke the Constitution's protection of individual freedom and privacy. The photograph shown here suggests the character of the resulting political confrontation. What do you see?

Divided Women, Divided Public: Protesting in Washington, D.C., 2004. Declan McCullagh.

ANALYZING THE EVIDENCE

- Describe the people marching in the street. Who is protesting on the sidewalk? What does the composition of the two groups say about the abortion controversy?

- Next, look at how the police are positioned. Why might this sort of police deployment be necessary?

- Finally, look at the signs both groups are holding up. What messages do they convey? How do the slogans frame the debate? What principles do they invoke?

- Abortion was a significant political issue in the mid-nineteenth century, when many states first outlawed the practice, and again in the 1960s, when five states repealed antiabortion laws and eleven others reformed their restrictive legislation. Since the late 1970s, abortion has become an important issue in national politics and often divides Democrats and Republicans. From what you've read in the text and see in this picture, how can you explain the political importance of this issue?

Gay/Lesbian Rights

Nothing proved more controversial in the 1990s than lesbian and gay rights. Whether it was President Clinton's initiative to allow lesbians and gays to serve openly in the U.S. military or the state-level marriage equality movement, issues of sexuality were a central part of the decade's furious culture wars. Here, marchers, including the actress Cybill Shepherd, participate in the 1993 Gay Rights March in Washington, D.C.   AP Images.

against measures that would extend rights to gays. Public opinion remained sharply divided. In 1992, Colorado voters approved an amendment to the state constitution that prevented local governments from enacting ordinances protecting gays and lesbians—a measure that the Supreme Court subsequently overturned as unconstitutional. That same year, however, Oregon voters defeated a more radical initiative that would have prevented the state from using any funds "to promote, encourage or facilitate" homosexuality. In 1998, Congress entered the fray by enacting the Defense of Marriage Act, which allowed states to refuse to recognize gay marriages or civil unions formed in other jurisdictions. More recently, gay marriage has been legalized in six states, including Massachusetts, Connecticut, and Vermont.

Culture Wars and the Supreme Court | Divisive rights issues increasingly came before the U.S. Supreme Court. Abortion led the way, with abortion rights activists challenging the constitutionality of the new state laws limiting access to the procedure. In *Webster v. Reproductive Health Services*

(1989), the Supreme Court upheld the authority of state governments to limit the use of public funds and facilities for abortions. Then, in the important case of *Planned Parenthood of Southeastern Pennsylvania v. Casey* (1992), the court upheld a law requiring a twenty-four-hour waiting period prior to an abortion. Surveying these and other decisions, a reporter suggested that 1989 was "the year the Court turned right," with a conservative majority ready and willing to limit or invalidate liberal legislation and legal precedents.

This observation was only partly correct. The Court was not yet firmly conservative. Although the *Casey* decision upheld certain restrictions on abortions, it affirmed the "essential holding" in *Roe v. Wade* (1973) that women had a constitutional right to control their reproduction. Justice David Souter, appointed to the Court by President George H. W. Bush in 1990, voted with Reagan appointees Sandra Day O'Connor and Anthony Kennedy to uphold *Roe*. Souter, like O'Connor, emerged as an ideologically moderate justice on a range of issues. Moreover, in a landmark decision, *Lawrence v. Texas* (2003), the Supreme Court limited the power of states to prohibit private homosexual activity between consenting adults. The Court had crept incrementally, rather than lurched, to the right while signaling its continued desire to remain within the broad mainstream of American public opinion.

The Clinton Presidency, 1993–2001

The culture wars contributed to a new, divisive partisanship in national politics. Rarely in the twentieth century had the two major parties so adamantly refused to work together. Also rare was the vitriolic rhetoric that politicians used to describe their opponents. The fractious partisanship was filtered through—or, many would argue, created by—the new twenty-four-hour cable news television networks, such as Fox News and CNN. Commentators on these channels, finding that nothing drew viewers like aggressive partisanship, increasingly abandoned their roles as conveyors of information and became entertainers and provocateurs.

That divisiveness was a hallmark of the presidency of William Jefferson Clinton. In 1992, Clinton, the governor of Arkansas, styled himself a "New Democrat" who would bring "Reagan Democrats" and middle-class voters back to the party. Only forty-six, he was an energetic, ambitious policy wonk—extraordinarily well informed about the details of public policy. To win the Democratic nomination in 1992, Clinton had to survive charges that he embodied the permissive social values conservatives associated with the 1960s: namely, that he dodged the draft to avoid service in Vietnam, smoked marijuana, and cheated repeatedly on his wife. The charges were damaging, but Clinton adroitly talked his way into the presidential nomination: He had charisma and a way with words. For his running mate, he chose Albert A. Gore, a senator from Tennessee. Gore was about the same age as Clinton, making them the first baby-boom national ticket as well as the nation's first all-southern major-party ticket.

President George H. W. Bush won renomination over his lone opponent, the conservative columnist Pat Buchanan. The Democrats mounted an aggressive campaign that focused on Clinton's domestic agenda: He promised a tax cut for the middle classes, universal health insurance, and a reduction of the huge Republican budget deficit. It was an audacious combination of traditional social-welfare liberalism and fiscal conservatism. For his part, Bush could not overcome voters' discontent with the weak economy and conservatives' disgust at his tax hikes. He received only 38.0 percent of the popular vote as millions of Republicans cast their ballots for independent businessman Ross Perot,

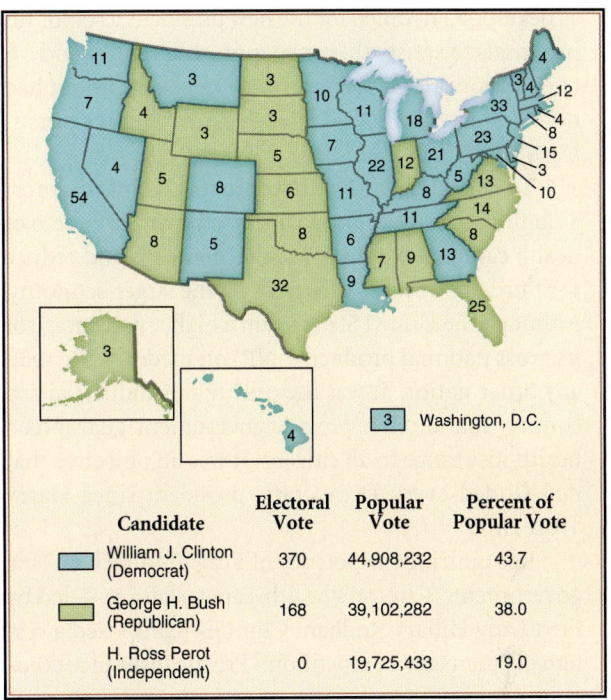

Candidate	Electoral Vote	Popular Vote	Percent of Popular Vote
William J. Clinton (Democrat)	370	44,908,232	43.7
George H. Bush (Republican)	168	39,102,282	38.0
H. Ross Perot (Independent)	0	19,725,433	19.0

MAP 31.3

The Presidential Election of 1992

The first national election after the end of the Cold War focused on the economy, which had fallen into a recession in 1991. The first-ever all-southern Democratic ticket of Bill Clinton (Arkansas) and Al Gore (Tennessee) won support across the country but won the election with only 43.7 percent of the popular vote. The Republican candidate, Vice President George H. W. Bush, ran strongly in his home state of Texas and the South, an emerging Republican stronghold. Independent candidate H. Ross Perot, a wealthy technology entrepreneur, polled an impressive 19.0 percent of the popular vote by capitalizing on voter dissatisfaction with the huge federal deficits of the Reagan-Bush administrations.

who won more votes (19.0 percent) than any independent candidate since Theodore Roosevelt in 1912. With 43.7 percent of the vote, Clinton won the election (Map 31.3). Still, there were reasons for him to worry. Among all post–World War II presidents, only Richard Nixon (in 1969) entered the White House with a comparably small share of the national vote.

New Democrats and Public Policy | As a self-proclaimed New Democrat, Clinton tried to steer a middle course through the nation's increasingly divisive partisanship. On his left was the Democratic Party's weakened but still vocal liberal wing. On his right were party moderates influenced by Reagan-era notions of reducing government regulation and the welfare state. Clinton's "third way," as he dubbed it, called for the new president to tailor his proposals to satisfy these two quite different — and often antagonistic — political constituencies. Clinton had notable successes as well as spectacular failures pursuing this course.

The spectacular failure came first. Clinton's most ambitious social-welfare goal was to provide a system of health care that would cover all Americans and reduce the burden of health-care costs on the larger economy. Although the United States spent a higher percentage of its gross national product (GNP) on medical care than any other nation, it was the only major industrialized country that did not provide government-guaranteed health insurance to all citizens. It was an objective that had eluded every Democratic president since Harry Truman.

Recognizing the potency of Reagan's attack on "big government," Clinton's health-care task force — led by First Lady Hillary Rodham Clinton — proposed a system of "managed competition." Private insurance companies and market forces were to rein in health-care expenditures. The cost of this system would fall heavily on employers, and many smaller businesses campaigned strongly against it. So did the health insurance industry and the American Medical Association, powerful lobbies with considerable influence in Washington. By mid-1994, Democratic leaders in Congress declared that the Clintons' universal health-care proposal was dead. Forty million Americans, or 15 percent of the population, remained without health insurance coverage.

More successful was Clinton's plan to reduce the budget deficits of the Reagan-Bush presidencies. In 1993, Clinton secured a five-year budget package that would reduce the federal deficit by $500 billion. Republicans unanimously opposed the proposal because it raised taxes on corporations and wealthy individuals, and liberal Democrats complained because it limited social spending. But shared sacrifice led to shared rewards. By 1998, Clinton's fiscal policies had balanced the federal budget and begun to pay down the federal debt — at a rate of $156 billion a year between 1999 and 2001. As fiscal sanity returned to Washington, the economy boomed, thanks in part to the low interest rates stemming from deficit reduction.

The Republican Resurgence

But the results of the 1993 budget package lay in the future. More immediately, the midterm election of 1994 confirmed that the Clinton presidency had not produced an electoral realignment: Conservatives still had a working majority. In a well-organized campaign, in which grassroots appeals to the New Right domi-

An Influential First Lady and Senator

Drawing inspiration from Eleanor Roosevelt, Hillary Rodham Clinton hoped the country was ready for a First Lady who actively shaped policy. It wasn't, or at least it wasn't ready for her health-care plan. Subsequently, Hillary Rodham Clinton assumed a less visible role in administration policy-making. In 2000, and again in 2006, she won election to the U.S. Senate from New York. In 2008, she nearly captured the Democratic nomination for president, and in 2009 was appointed secretary of state by the man who defeated her in the Democratic primaries (and who went on to win the presidency), Barack Obama.   Robert Trippet/Sipa Press/AP Images.

nated, Republicans gained fifty-two seats in the House of Representatives, giving them a majority for the first time since 1954. They also retook control of the Senate and captured eleven governorships. Leading the Republican charge was Representative Newt Gingrich of Georgia, who revived calls for significant tax cuts, reductions in welfare programs, anticrime initiatives, and cutbacks in federal regulations. These initiatives had central components of the conservative-backed Reagan Revolution of the 1980s, but Gingrich believed that under the presidency of George H. W. Bush Republicans had not emphasized them enough.

In response to the massive Democratic losses in 1994, Clinton moved to the right. Claiming in 1996 that "the era of big government is over," he avoided expansive social-welfare proposals for the remainder of his presidency and sought Republican support for a centrist New Democrat program. The signal piece of that program was reforming the welfare system, a measure that saved relatively little money but carried a big ideological message. The Aid to Fami-

Bill Clinton
President William (Bill) Clinton returned the Democratic Party to the White House after twelve years under Ronald Reagan and George H. W. Bush. Clinton was best known politically for what he called the "third way," a phrase that described his efforts to craft policies that appealed to both liberals and moderates in his party. Here he signs the Welfare Reform Act of 1996 (officially the Personal Responsibility and Work Opportunity Reconciliation Act), which brought an end to the federal AFDC program that Democrats had created in 1935.   AP Images.

lies with Dependent Children (AFDC) program provided annual payments to needy families. Still, many taxpaying Americans believed—with some supporting evidence—that AFDC perpetuated poverty by encouraging female recipients to remain on welfare rather than seek employment. In August 1996, the federal government abolished AFDC, achieving a long-standing goal of conservatives, when Clinton signed the Personal Responsibility and Work Opportunity Reconciliation Act. Liberals were furious with the president.

Clinton's Impeachment   Even with the concession on welfare, Clinton could not escape an opposition deeply hostile to his presidency. Following a relatively easy victory in the 1996 election, his second term unraveled when a sex scandal led to his impeachment. Clinton denied having had a sexual affair with Monica Lewinsky, a former White House intern. Independent prosecutor Kenneth Starr, a conservative Republican, concluded that Clinton had committed perjury and obstructed justice, and that these actions were grounds for impeachment. Viewed historically, Americans have usually defined "high crimes and misdemeanors"—the constitutional standard for impeachment—as involving a serious abuse of public trust that endangered the republic. In 1998, conservative Republicans favored a much lower standard because they did not accept Clinton's legitimacy as president. They vowed to oust him from office.

On December 19, the House of Representatives narrowly approved two articles of impeachment. Only a minority of Americans supported the House's action; according to a CBS News poll, 38 percent favored impeachment while 58 percent opposed it. Lacking public support, Republicans in the Senate fell well short of the two-thirds majority they needed to remove the president. But like Andrew Johnson, the only other president to be tried by the Senate, Clinton and the Democratic Party paid a high price for his acquittal. Preoccupied with defending himself, the president was unable to fashion a Democratic alternative to the Republicans' domestic agenda. The American public also paid a high price, because the Republicans' vendetta against Clinton drew attention away from pressing national problems.

Post–Cold War Foreign Policy

Politically weakened domestically after 1994, Clinton believed he could nonetheless make a difference on the international stage. There, post–Cold War developments gave him historic opportunities. The 1990s was a decade of stunning change in Europe and Central Asia. A great arc of newly independent states emerged as the Soviet empire collapsed—from Estonia in the far north of Europe, south through Georgia and Armenia in western Asia, and across central Asia to Tajikistan on the border of China. The majority of the 142 million people living in those nations were poor, but the region had a sizable middle class—in countries such as Ukraine, Georgia, and Kazakhstan—and was rich in natural resources, especially oil and natural gas.

Among the challenges for the United States was the question of whether to support the admission of some of the new states, such as Ukraine, Georgia, and Armenia, into the North Atlantic Treaty Organization (NATO). Many observers believed, with some justification, that extending the NATO alliance into Eastern Europe, right up to Russia's western border, would damage U.S.-Russian relations. However, Czechoslovakia, Poland, and Hungary were also eager to become NATO members—an outcome that would draw into the Western alliance three nations that Stalin had decisively placed in the Soviet sphere of influence at the close of World War II. Clinton encouraged NATO admission for those three countries but stopped short of advocating a broader expansion of the alliance during his terms in office. Nonetheless, by 2010, twelve new nations—most of them in Eastern Europe, and ten of them former members of the Warsaw Pact—had been admitted to the NATO alliance.

Two of the new NATO states, Slovenia and Croatia, emerged from an intractable set of conflicts that led to the dissolution of the communist nation of Yugoslavia. In 1992, the heavily Muslim province of Bosnia-Herzegovina declared its independence, but its substantial Serbian population refused to live in a Muslim-run multiethnic state. Slobodan Milosevic, the uncompromising Serbian nationalist, launched a ruthless campaign of "ethnic cleansing" to create a Serbian state. In November 1995, Clinton organized a NATO-led bombing campaign and peacekeeping effort, backed by 20,000 American troops, that ended the Serbs' vicious expansionist drive. Four years later, a new crisis emerged in Kosovo, another province of the Serbian-dominated Federal Republic of Yugoslavia. Again led by the United States, NATO intervened with air strikes and military forces to preserve Kosovo's autonomy. By 2008, seven independent nations had emerged from the wreckage of Yugoslavia (Map 31.4).

MAP 31.4

Ethnic Conflict in the Balkans: The Breakup of Yugoslavia, 1991–1992

The collapse of the Soviet Union spurred the disintegration of the independent communist state of Yugoslavia, a multiethnic and multireligious state held together after 1945 by the near-dictatorial authority of Josip Broz Tito (1892–1980). Fanned by ethnic and religious hatreds, Yugoslavia splintered into warring states. Slovenia and Macedonia won their independence in 1991, but Russian Orthodox Serbia, headed by president Slobodan Milosevic, tried to rule the rest of the Balkan peoples. Roman Catholic Croatia freed itself from Serb rule in 1995, and, after ruthless Serbian aggression against Muslims in Bosnia and later in Kosovo, the United States and NATO intervened militarily to create the separate states of Bosnia-Herzegovina (1995) and Montenegro (2006) and the autonomous Muslim province of Kosovo (1999).

America and The Middle East No post–Cold War development proved more challenging than the emergence of radical Islamic movements in the Middle East. Muslim nations there had a long list of grievances against the West. Colonialism—both British and French—in the early decades of the twentieth century had been ruthless. A U.S.-sponsored overthrow of Iran's government in 1953—and twenty-five years of American support for the Iranian shah—was also a sore point. America's support for Israel in the 1967 Six-Day War and the 1973 Yom Kippur War and its near-unconditional backing of Israel in the 1980s were particularly galling to Muslims. The region's religious and secular moderates complained about these injustices, but many of them had political and economic ties to the West, which constrained their criticism.

This left an opening for radical Islamic fundamentalists to build a movement based on fanatical opposition to Western imperialism and consumer culture. These groups interpreted the American presence in Saudi Ara-

Terrorists Bomb USS *Cole*

On October 12, 2000, a radical Muslim group with ties to Al Qaeda detonated a powerful bomb alongside the USS *Cole*, which was refueling in the port of Aden in Yemen. The explosion tore a large hole in the ship's hull, killing seventeen American sailors and injuring thirty-seven others. After repairs costing $250 million, the USS *Cole* returned to active duty in April 2002.   © Corbis/Sygma.

bia as signaling new U.S. colonial ambitions in the region. Clinton had inherited from President George H. W. Bush a defeated Iraq and a sizable military force—about 4,000 Air Force personnel—in Saudi Arabia. American fighter jets left Saudi Arabian air bases to fly regular missions over Iraq, enforcing a no-fly zone, where Iraqi planes were forbidden, and bombing select targets. Clinton also enforced a UN-sanctioned embargo on all trade with Iraq, a policy designed to constrain Saddam Hussein's military that ultimately denied crucial goods to the civilian population. Angered by the continued U.S. presence in Saudi Arabia, Muslim fundamentalists soon began targeting Americans. In 1993, radical Muslim immigrants set off a bomb in a parking garage beneath the World Trade Center in New York City, killing six people and injuring more than a thousand. Muslim terrorists used truck bombs to blow up U.S. embassies in Kenya and Tanzania in 1998, and they bombed the USS *Cole* in the Yemeni port of Aden in 2000.

The Clinton administration knew these attacks were the work of Al Qaeda, a network of radical Islamic terrorists organized by the wealthy Saudi exile Osama bin Laden. In February 1998, bin Laden had issued a call for holy war—a "*Jihad* against Jews and Crusaders," in which it was said to be the duty of every Muslim to kill Americans and their allies. After the embassy attacks, Clinton ordered air strikes on Al Qaeda bases in Afghanistan, where an estimated 15,000 radical operatives had been trained since 1990. The strikes failed to disrupt this growing terrorist network, and when Clinton left office, the Central Intelligence Agency (CIA), the State Department, and the Pentagon were well aware of the potential threat posed by bin Laden's followers. That was where things stood on September 10, 2001.

● **What were the battle lines in the cultural wars of the 1980s and 1990s? Why were those struggles so intense, and what do they tell us about American politics?**

- What did Clinton mean when he said he was a New Democrat? Why were conservatives still so opposed to his presidency?

Into a New Century

As Americans enter the new century's second decade, they can reflect on two significant developments that have profoundly shaped their own day: the terrorist attack on the United States on September 11, 2001, and the election of the nation's first African American president, Barack Obama, on November 4, 2008. Too little time has passed for us to assess whether either event will be remembered as helping to define the twenty-first century. But both have indelibly marked our present. And both had distinct antecedents and still have profound implications.

The Ascendance of George W. Bush

The 2000 presidential election briefly offered the promise of a break with the intense partisanship of the final Clinton years. The Republican nominee, George W. Bush, the son of President George H. W. Bush, presented himself as an outsider, deploring Washington partisanship and casting himself as a "uniter, not a divider." His opponent, Al Gore—Clinton's vice president—was a liberal policy specialist. The election of 2000 would join those of 1876 and 1960 as the closest and most contested in American history. Gore won the popular vote, amassing 50.9 million votes to Bush's 50.4 million but fell short in the electoral college, 267 to 271. Consumer- and labor-rights activist Ralph Nader ran as the Green Party candidate and drew away precious votes in key states that certainly would have carried Gore to victory.

Late on election night, the vote tally in Florida gave Bush the narrowest of victories. As was their legal prerogative, the Democrats demanded hand recounts in several counties. A month of tumult followed, until the U.S. Supreme Court, voting strictly along conservative/liberal lines, ordered the recount stopped and let Bush's victory stand. Recounting ballots without a consistent standard to determine "voter intent," the Court reasoned, violated the rights of Floridian voters under the Fourteenth Amendment's equal protection clause. As if acknowledging the frailty of this argument, the Court declared that *Bush v. Gore* was not to be regarded as precedent. But by making a transparently partisan decision, Justice John Paul Stevens warned in a dissenting opinion, the conservative majority undermined "the Nation's confidence in the judge as an impartial guardian of the rule of law."

Although Bush had positioned himself as a moderate, countertendencies drove his administration from the start. His vice president, the uncompromising conservative Richard Cheney, became, with Bush's consent, virtually a co-president. Bush also brought into the administration his campaign advisor, Karl Rove, whose advice made for an exceptionally politicized White House. Rove foreclosed the easygoing centrism of Bush the campaigner by arguing that a permanent Republican majority could be built on the party's conservative

The Contested Vote in Florida, 2000

When the vote recount got under way in Palm Beach, Florida, in 2000, both sides brought out supporters to demonstrate outside the Supervisor of Elections Office, in hopes of influencing the officials doing the counting. In this photograph, supporters of George W. Bush clash with supporters of Al Gore after a rally on November 13, 2000, that had been addressed by Jesse Jackson, the dominant African American figure in the Democratic Party.   © Reuters/Corbis.

Colin Powell and Condoleezza Rice

Colin Powell, a distinguished army general, and Condoleezza Rice, a former Stanford academic, were leading figures in the Bush administration and powerful symbols of Bush's efforts at racial inclusiveness. At the time of this photograph (2003), Powell was secretary of state, and Rice national security advisor. In 2005, after Powell resigned, Bush appointed Rice secretary of state. Here they are seated side by side, attending a state dinner at the Grand Palace in Bangkok, Thailand.   Paul J. Richards/AFP/Getty Images.

base. On Capitol Hill, Rove's hard line was reinforced by Tom DeLay, the House majority leader, who in 1995 had declared "all-out war" on the Democrats. To win that war, DeLay pushed congressional Republicans to endorse a fierce partisanship. The Senate, although more collegial, went through a similar hardening process. After 2002, with Republicans in control of both Congress and the White House, bipartisan lawmaking came to an end.

Tax Cuts   The domestic issue that most engaged President Bush, as it had Ronald Reagan, was taxes. Bush's Economic Growth and Tax Relief Act of 2001 had something for everyone. It slashed income tax rates, extended the earned income credit for the poor, and marked the estate tax to be phased out by 2010. A second round of cuts in 2003 targeted dividend income and capital gains. Bush's signature cuts — those favoring big estates and well-to-do owners of stocks and bonds — skewed the distribution of tax benefits upward (Table 31.1). Bush had pushed far beyond any other postwar president, even Reagan, in slashing federal taxes.

Critics warned that such massive tax cuts would plunge the federal government into debt. By 2006, federal expenditures had jumped 33 percent, at a faster clip

than under any president since Lyndon Johnson. Huge increases in health-care costs were the main culprit. Two of the largest federal programs, Medicare and Medicaid — health care for the elderly and the poor, respectively — could not contain runaway medical costs. Midway through Bush's second term, the national debt stood at over $8 trillion — much of it owned by foreign investors, who also financed the nation's huge trade deficit. On top of that, staggering Social Security and Medicare obligations were coming due for retiring baby boomers. It seemed that these burdens would be passed on to future generations (Figure 31.5).

September 11, 2001   How Bush's presidency might have fared in normal times is another of those unanswerable questions of history. As a candidate in 2000, George W. Bush had said little about foreign policy. He had assumed that his administration would rise or fall on his domestic program. But nine months into his presidency, an altogether different political scenario unfolded. On a sunny September morning, nineteen Islamic terrorists from Al Qaeda hijacked four commercial jets and flew two of them into New York City's World Trade Center, destroying its twin towers and killing more than 2,900 people. A third plane crashed into the Pentagon, near Washington, D.C.

TABLE 31.1

Impact of the Bush Tax Cuts, 2001–2003

Income in 2003	Taxpayers	Gross Income	Total Tax Cut	% Change in Tax Bill	Tax Bill	Tax Rate
Less than $50,000	92,093,452	$19,521	$435	−48%	$474	2%
$50,000 to 100,000	26,915,091	70,096	1,656	−21	6,417	9
$100,000 to 200,000	8,878,643	131,797	3,625	−17	18,281	14
$200,000 to 500,000	1,999,061	288,296	7,088	−10	60,464	21
$500,000 to 1,000,000	356,140	677,294	22,479	−12	169,074	25
$1,000,000 to 10,000,000	175,157	2,146,100	84,666	−13	554,286	26
$10,000,000 or more	6,126	25,975,532	1,019,369	−15	5,780,926	22

Source: New York Times, April 5, 2006.

The fourth, presumably headed for the White House or possibly the U.S. Capitol, crashed in Pennsylvania when the passengers fought back and thwarted the hijackers. As an outburst of patriotism swept the United States in the wake of the September 11 attacks, George W. Bush proclaimed a "war on terror" and vowed to carry the battle to Al Qaeda.

Operating out of Afghanistan, where they had been harbored by the fundamentalist Taliban regime, the elusive Al Qaeda briefly offered a clear target. In October 2001, the United States attacked—not with conventional forces, but by deploying military advisors and supplies that bolstered anti-Taliban rebel forces. While Afghani allies carried the ground war, American planes

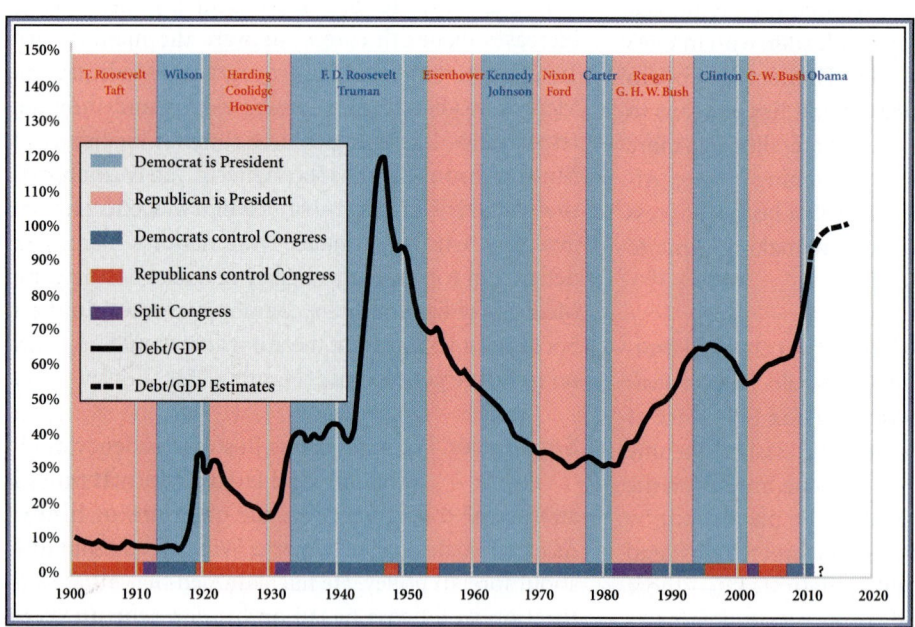

FIGURE 31.5

Gross Federal Debt as a Percentage of Gross Domestic Product

Economists argue that the best measure of a nation's debt is its size relative to the overall economy — that is, its percentage of gross domestic product (GDP). The size of the total U.S. debt declined from its World War II–high until the 1980s, when it increased dramatically under President Reagan. Since then, the debt has consistently increased as a percentage of GDP, aside from a small decline under President Clinton's deficit-reduction plans in the mid-1990s. Source: http://dshort.com.

September 11, 2001

Photographers at the scene after a plane crashed into the north tower of New York City's World Trade Center found themselves recording a defining moment in the nation's history. When a second airliner approached and then slammed into the building's south tower at 9:03 A.M., the nation knew this was no accident. The United States was under attack. Of the 2,843 people killed on September 11, 2,617 died at the World Trade Center.   Robert Clark/AURORA.

rained destruction on the enemy. By early 2002, this lethal combination had ousted the Taliban, destroyed Al Qaeda's training camps, and killed or captured many of its operatives. However, the big potential prize, Al Qaeda leader Osama bin Laden, had retreated to a mountain redoubt. Inexplicably, U.S. Special Operations forces failed to press the attack; bin Laden evidently bought off the local warlords and escaped over the border into Pakistan.

The Invasion of Iraq | Having unseated the Taliban in Afghanistan by early 2002, the Bush administration could have declared victory and relegated the unfinished business—tracking down the Al Qaeda remnants, stabilizing Afghanistan, and shaking up America's security agencies—to a postvictory operational phase. But President Bush had no such inclination. For him, the war on terror was not a metaphor, but the real thing: an open-ended war that required putting aside business as usual.

On the domestic side, Bush declared the terrorist threat too big to be contained by ordinary law-enforcement means. He wanted the government's powers of domestic surveillance placed on a wartime footing. With little debate, Congress passed the USA PATRIOT Act, granting the administration sweeping authority to monitor citizens and apprehend suspected terrorists. On the international front, Bush used the war on terror as the premise for a new policy of preventive war. Under international law, only an imminent threat justified

a nation's right to strike first. Now, under the so-called Bush doctrine, the United States lowered the bar. It reserved for itself the right to act in "anticipatory self-defense." President Bush singled out Iran, North Korea, and Iraq—"an axis of evil"—as the targeted states.

Of the three, Iraq was the preferred mark. Officials in the Pentagon regarded Iraq as unfinished business, left over from the Gulf War of 1991. More grandly, they saw in Iraq an opportunity to unveil America's supposed mission to democratize the world. Iraqis, they believed, would abandon the tyrant Saddam Hussein and embrace democracy if given the chance. The democratizing effect would spread across the Middle East, toppling or reforming other unpopular Arab regimes and stabilizing the region. That, in turn, would secure the Middle East's oil supply, whose fragility Saddam's 1990 invasion of Kuwait had made all too clear. It was the oil, in the end, that was of vital interest to the United States (Map 31.5).

None of these considerations, either singly or together, met Bush's declared threshold for preventive war. So the president reluctantly acceded to the demand by America's anxious European allies that the United States go to the UN Security Council, which demanded that Saddam Hussein allow the return of the UN weapons inspectors expelled in 1998. Saddam surprisingly agreed. Nevertheless, anxious to invade Iraq for its own reasons, the Bush administration geared up for war. Insisting that Iraq constituted a "grave and gathering danger" and ignoring its failure to secure a second, legitimizing UN resolution, Bush invaded in March 2003. America's one

MAP 31.5

U.S. Involvement in the Middle East, 1979–2010

The United States has long played an active role in the Middle East, driven by the strategic importance of that region and, most important, by America's need to ensure a reliable supply of oil from the Persian Gulf states. This map shows the highlights of that troubled involvement, from the Tehran embassy hostage-taking in 1979 to the invasion and current occupation of both Iraq and Afghanistan.

major ally in the rush to war was Great Britain. Relations with France and Germany became poisonous. Even neighboring Mexico and Canada condemned the invasion, and Turkey, a key military ally, refused transit permission, ruining the army's plan for a northern thrust into Iraq. As for the Arab world, it exploded in anti-American demonstrations.

The war began with massive air attacks. Within three weeks, American troops had taken the Iraqi capital. The regime collapsed, and its leaders went into hiding (Saddam Hussein was captured nine months later). Despite meticulous military planning, the Pentagon had made no provision for postconflict operations. Thousands of poor Iraqis looted everything they could get their hands on: stores, shops, museums, industrial plants, government offices, and military arsenals. The looting shattered the infrastructure of Iraq's cities, leaving them without reliable supplies of electricity and water. In the midst of this turmoil, an insurgency began, sparked by Sunni Muslims who had dominated Iraq under Saddam's Baathist regime (see Voices from Abroad, "Abu Musab al-Zarqawi: A Strategy for the Iraq Insurgency," p. 1006).

Iraq's Shiite majority, long oppressed by Saddam, at first welcomed the Americans, but extremist Shiite elements soon turned hostile and U.S. forces found themselves under fire from both sides. With the borders unguarded, Al Qaeda supporters flocked in from all over the Middle East, eager to do battle with the infidel Americans, bringing along a specialty of the jihad: the suicide bomber.

Popular insurgencies are a problem for superpowers. Blinded by their own nationalism, dominant nations tend to underestimate the strength of nationalism in other people. Lyndon Johnson discovered this in Vietnam. Soviet premier Leonid Brezhnev discovered it in Afghanistan. And George W. Bush rediscovered it in Iraq. The intractable fact is that the superpower's troops are invaders. Although it was hard for Americans to believe, that was how Iraqis of all stripes viewed the U.S. forces. Moreover, in a war against insurgents, no occupation force comes out with clean hands. In Iraq, that painful truth burst forth graphically in photographs showing American guards at Baghdad's Abu Ghraib prison abusing and torturing suspected insurgents. The ghastly images shocked the world. For Muslims, they offered final proof of American treachery. At that low point, in 2004, the United States had spent upward of $100 billion. More than 1,000 American soldiers had died, and 10,000 others had been wounded,

Americans, Think!

While incomprehensible to Americans, the murderous attacks of September 11, 2001, were greeted with satisfaction by many in the Muslim world (the anti-American rally shown here was held on September 15, 2001). Their anti-Americanism was based in part on U.S. support for Israel, but also stemmed from their resentment of American wealth and power and of the corrosive effects that they felt Western capitalism and modernity exerted on their societies. In recognition of their global audience, these demonstrators in the Pakistani capital city of Islamabad ask their question in English. B. K. Bangash/AP Images.

many maimed for life. But if the United States pulled out, Iraq would descend into chaos. So, as Bush took to saying, the United States had to "stay the course."

The 2004 Election | As the 2004 presidential election approached, Rove, Bush's top advisor, theorized that stirring the culture wars and emphasizing patriotism and Bush's war on terror would mobilize conservatives and further entrench the Republican Party as the dominant power in Washington. Rove encouraged activists to place antigay initiatives on the ballot in key states to draw conservative voters to the polls; in all, eleven states would pass ballot initiatives that wrote bans on gay marriage equality into state constitutions that year. More conservative voters meant more votes for Bush. The Democratic nominee, Senator John Kerry of Massachusetts, was a Vietnam hero, twice wounded and decorated for bravery—in contrast to the president, who had spent the Vietnam years comfortably in the Texas Air National Guard. But when Kerry returned from service in Vietnam, he had joined the antiwar group Vietnam Veterans Against the War and in 1971 had delivered a blistering critique of the war to the Senate Armed Services Committee. In the logic of the culture wars, this made him vulnerable to charges of being weak and unpatriotic.

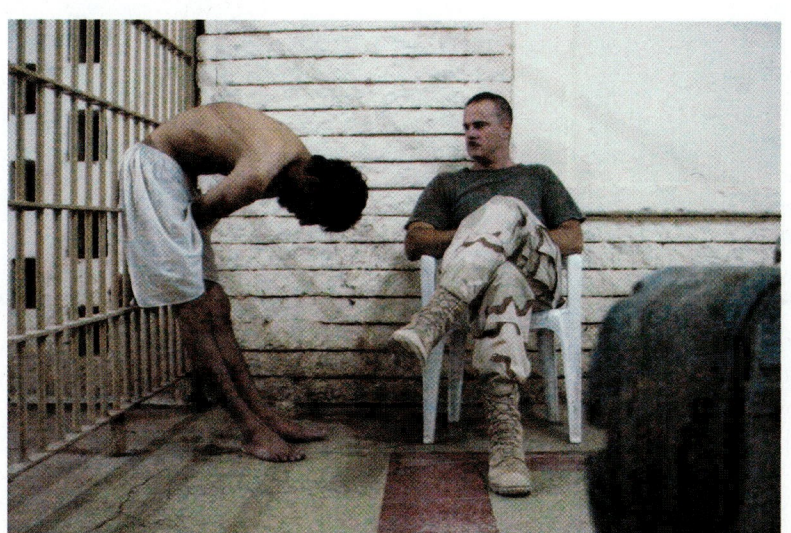

Abu Ghraib

This image of one of the milder forms of torture experienced by inmates at the Abu Ghraib prison was obtained by the Associated Press in 2003. It shows a detainee bent over with his hands through the bars of a cell while being watched by a comfortably seated soldier. This photograph and others showing far worse treatment administered by sometimes jeering military personnel outraged many in the United States and abroad, particularly in the Muslim world. AP Images.

All the nations and people I had hitherto passed through resembled
own in their manners, customs and langu

Abu Musab al-Zarqawi
A Strategy for the Iraq Insurgency

From 2004 to June 2006, when he was killed by American forces, the Jordanian Abu Musab al-Zarqawi led the Al Qaeda–linked insurgency in Iraq. During the 1980s, he had fought as an Islamic jihadist against the Soviet occupation of Afghanistan. Al-Zarqawi then returned to Jordan, where he was imprisoned for conspiring to overthrow the monarchy and establish a caliphate to expel all Western influences from the Islamic world. But al-Zarqawi was also engaged in a struggle within Islam. He was Sunni, and regarded adherents of the other main branch of Islam, Shiites, as heretical enemies as vile as the hated Westerners. Early in 2004, al-Zarqawi wrote the following letter, which outlined his deadly strategy of bombings and sectarian violence. This letter reveals the mind of the figure who, until his death, was most responsible for plunging Iraq into chaos.

God favored the [Islamic] nation with jihad on His behalf in the land of Mesopotamia [the ancient name for Iraq]. . . . The Americans, as you know well, entered Iraq on a contractual basis to create the State of Greater Israel from the Nile to the Euphrates and that this Zionized American Administration believes that accelerating the creation of the State of [Greater] Israel will accelerate the emergence of the Messiah. It came to Iraq with all its people, pride, and haughtiness toward God and his Prophet. It thought that the matter would be somewhat easy. . . . But it collided with a completely different reality. The operations of the brother mujahidin [fighters] began from the first moment. . . . This forced the Americans to conclude a deal with the Shi'a, the most evil of mankind. The deal was concluded on [the basis that] the Shi'a would get two-thirds of the booty for having stood in the ranks of the Crusaders against the mujahidin.

[The Shi'a are] the insurmountable obstacle, the lurking snake, the crafty and malicious scorpion, the spying enemy, and the penetrating venom. . . . History's message is validated by the testimony of the current situation, which informs most clearly that Shi'ism is a religion that has nothing in common with Islam. . . .

[Among the Sunni mujahidin,] jihad here unfortunately [takes the form of] mines planted, rockets launched, and mortars shelling from afar. The Iraqi brothers still prefer safety and returning to the arms of their wives, where nothing frightens them. Sometimes the groups have boasted among themselves that not one of them has been killed or captured. We have told them in our many sessions with them that safety and victory are incompatible . . . that the [Islamic] nation cannot live without the aroma of martyrdom.

America did not come to leave, and it will not leave no matter how numerous its wounds become and how much of its blood is spilled. It is looking to the near future, when it hopes to disappear into its bases secure and at ease and put the battlefields of Iraq into the hands of the foundling government with an army and police that will bring [the

terror] of Saddam . . . back to the people. There is no doubt that the space in which we can move has begun to shrink and that the grip around the throats of the [Arab and Sunni] mujahidin has begun to tighten. . . .

The Shi'a . . . in our opinion are the key to change. I mean that targeting and hitting them in [their] religious, political, and military depth will provoke them to show the Sunnis their rabies . . . If we succeed in dragging them into the arena of sectarian war, it will become possible to awaken the inattentive Sunnis. . . .

I come back and again say that the only solution is for us to strike the religious, military, and other cadres among the Shi'a with blow after blow until they bend to the Sunnis. . . . God's religion is more precious than lives and souls. When the overwhelming majority stands in the ranks of truth, there has to be sacrifice for this religion. Let blood be spilled.

Source: Documents on Terrorist Abu Musab al-Zarqawi, 2004, www.personal
.umich.edu/~jrcole/zarqawi/zarqawi.htm.

ANALYZING THE EVIDENCE

- **According to al-Zarqawi, the Americans invaded Iraq "to create the State of Greater Israel from the Nile to the Euphrates." Why would he make such a fantastic claim?**
- **If the Americans are the occupiers, why is his letter mostly about the Shiites? Why are they his primary target?**
- **By mid-2006, at the time Al-Zarqawi was killed, how successful, based on your reading of the text, was he in fulfilling his stated aims?**

The Democratic convention in August was a tableau of patriotism, filled with waving flags, retired generals, and Kerry's Vietnam buddies. However, a sudden onslaught of slickly produced television ads by a group calling itself Swift Boat Veterans for Truth, falsely charging that Kerry had lied to win his medals, fatally undercut his advantage. Nor did it help that Kerry, as a three-term senator, had a lengthy record that was easily mined for hard-to-explain votes. Republicans tagged him a "flip-flopper," and the accusation, endlessly repeated, stuck. Nearly 60 percent of eligible voters — the highest percentage since 1968 — went to the polls. Bush beat Kerry, with 286 electoral votes to Kerry's 252. In exit polls, Bush did well among voters for whom moral "values" and national security were top concerns. Voters told interviewers that Bush made them feel "safer." Bush was no longer a minority president. He had won a clear, if narrow, popular majority.

Violence Abroad and Economic Collapse at Home

George Bush's second term was defined by crisis management. In 2005, Hurricane Katrina — one of the deadliest hurricanes in the nation's history — devastated New Orleans. Chaos ensued as floodwaters breached earthen barricades surrounding the city and covered low-lying neighborhoods in more than 10 feet of water. Many residents remained without food, drinking water, or shelter for days following the storm, and deaths mounted — the final death toll stood at more than 4,000. Initial emergency responses to the catastrophe by federal and local authorities were uncoordinated and inadequate. Because the hardest-hit parts of the city were poor and African American, Katrina had revealed the poverty and vulnerability at the heart of American cities.

The run of crises did not abate after Katrina. Increasing violence and a rising insurgency in Iraq made the war there even more unpopular in the United States in 2005 and 2006. In 2007, changes in U.S. military strategy helped quell some of the worst violence, but the war dragged into its fifth and sixth years under Bush's watch. A war-weary public grew impatient. Then, in 2008, the American economy began to stumble. By the fall, the Dow Jones Industrial Average had lost half its total value and major banks, insurance companies, and financial institutions were on the verge of collapse. The entire automobile industry was near bankruptcy. Millions of Americans lost their jobs, and the unemployment rate surged to 10 percent. Housing prices dropped by as much as 40 percent in some parts of the country, and millions of Americans defaulted on their mortgages. The United States had entered the worst economic recession since the 1930s, what soon became known as the Great Recession.

The 2008 presidential election took shape in that perilous context. In a historically remarkable primary season, the Democratic nomination was contested between the first woman and the first African American to be viable presidential contenders, Hillary Rodham Clinton and Barack Hussein Obama. In a close-fought contest, Obama had emerged by early summer as the nominee.

Meanwhile, the Bush administration confronted an economy in freefall. In September, less than two months before the election, Secretary of the Treasury Henry Paulson urged Congress to pass the Emergency Economic Stabilization Act, commonly referred to as the "bailout" of the financial sector. Passed in early October, the act dedicated $700 billion to rescuing many of the nation's largest banks and brokerage houses. Between Congress's actions and the independent efforts of the Treasury Department and the Federal Reserve, the U.S. government invested close to $1 trillion in saving the nation's financial system.

The Obama Presidency

During his campaign for the presidency against Republican senator John McCain, Barack Obama, a Democratic senator from Illinois, established himself as a unique figure in American politics. When he was attacked for his relationship with a fiery black minister, Obama gave one of the most honest and insightful speeches about race ever delivered by a major American politician. The son of an African immigrant-student and a young white woman from Kansas, Obama was raised in Hawaii and Indonesia, and he easily connected with an increasingly multiracial and multicultural America. A generation younger than Bill Clinton and George W. Bush, Obama (born in 1961) had not participated in the protests and counterculture of the 1960s and was not enmeshed in the ideological wars that followed. Obama seemed at once a product of the 1960s, especially civil rights gains, and outside its overheated conflicts.

Obama took the oath of office of the presidency on January 21, 2009, amid the deepest economic recession since the Great Depression and with the United States mired in two wars in the Middle East. From the podium, the new president recognized the crises and worried about "a nagging fear that America's decline is inevitable." But like all other presidents at the opening

Barack Obama

In 2008, Barack Obama became the first African American president in U.S. history. Here, presidential candidate Senator Obama shakes hands during the campaign with supporters near Philadelphia, Pennsylvania.　© Bettmann/Corbis.

of their term, Obama hoped to strike an optimistic tone. Americans, he said, must "begin again the work of remaking America."

As the first African American president of the United States, Obama carried more than one immense burden. A nation that a mere two generations ago would not allow black Americans to dine with white Americans had elected a black man to the highest office. Obama himself was less taken with this historic accomplishment — which was also part of his deliberate strategy to downplay race — than with developing a plan to deal with the nation's innumerable challenges, at home and abroad. With explicit comparisons to Franklin Roosevelt, Obama used the "first hundred days" of his presidency to lay out an ambitious agenda: an economic stimulus package of federal spending to invigorate the economy; plans to draw down the war in Iraq and refocus American military efforts in Afghanistan; a reform of the nation's health insurance system; and new federal laws to regulate Wall Street.

Remarkably, the president and the Democratic-controlled Congress accomplished the first three of those objectives within fourteen months of Obama's taking office. In February, Congress passed the American Recovery and Reinvestment Act, an economic stimulus bill that provided $787 billion to state and local governments for schools, hospitals, and transportation projects (roads, bridges, and rail) — one of the largest single packages of government spending in American history. Within weeks of the bill's passage, Obama turned to foreign policy, announcing his plan to withdraw all active combat troops from Iraq by 2010. Then, in December, the president ordered an additional 30,000 American troops to Afghanistan, where the Taliban had regained control of much of the country and Obama had pledged renewed U.S. efforts.

Political debate over the stimulus bill had been heated, with conservatives staunchly opposed. But that battle was a minor skirmish compared to what awaited Obama's health insurance reform proposal. Believing that he had learned from President Clinton's mistake in 1993 — drafting an entire bill in the White House and asking Congress simply to vote it up or down — Obama allowed congressional Democrats to put forth their own proposals. The president, for his part, worked to find Republican allies who might be persuaded to support the first major reform of the nation's health-care system since the introduction of Medicare in 1965. None came forward. Still, conservatives within the president's own party—alongside a lobbying offensive by the insurance industry—ensured that any health-care legislation would not fundamentally alter the private health insurance market. Moreover, as debate dragged on, a set of far-right opposition groups, known collectively as the Tea Party movement, emerged. None of these developments derailed the legislation, but when the president signed the final health care bill (officially called the Patient Protection and Affordable Care Act) into law on March 23, 2010, it contained enough compromises that few could predict its long-term impact.

It remains to be seen how the Obama presidency will affect American politics. From one vantage, Obama looks like the beneficiary of an electoral shift in a liberal direction. Since 1992, Democrats have won the popular vote in four of the five presidential elections, and Obama won a greater share of the popular vote (nearly 53 percent) than either Clinton (who won 43 percent in 1992 and 49 percent in 1996) or Gore (48 percent in 2000). From another vantage, any electoral shift toward liberalism appears contingent and fragile. Even with Democratic majorities in both houses of Congress that rivaled Franklin Roosevelt's in 1937 and Lyndon Johnson's in 1965, Obama was not able to generate political momentum for the kind of legislative advances achieved by those presidential forerunners. The history of his presidency, and of the early twenty-first century more broadly, continues to unfold.

- In what ways was George H. W. Bush a political follower of Ronald Reagan? In what ways was he not?

- How would you compare the Iraq War with previous wars in U.S. history?

- As the nation's first African American president, what kinds of unique challenges has Barack Obama faced?

SUMMARY

This chapter has stressed how globalization—the worldwide flow of capital, goods, and people—entered a new phase after the end of the Cold War. The number of multinational corporations, many of them based in the United States, increased dramatically, and people, goods, and investment capital moved easily across political boundaries. Financial markets, in particular, grew increasingly open and interconnected across the globe. Technological innovations strengthened the American economy and transformed daily life. The computer revolution and the spread of the Internet changed the ways in which Americans shopped, worked, learned, and stayed in touch with family and friends. Globalization facilitated the immigration of millions of Asians and Latin Americans into the United States.

In the decades since 1989, American life has been characterized by the dilemmas presented by the twin issues of globalization and divisive cultural politics. Conservatives spoke out strongly, and with increasing effectiveness, against multiculturalism and what they viewed as serious threats to "family values." Debates over women's rights, access to abortion, affirmative action, and the legal rights of homosexuals intensified. The terrorist attacks of September 11, 2001, temporarily calmed the nation's increasingly bitter partisanship, but that partisanship was revived after President Bush's decision to invade Iraq (a nation not involved in the events of 9/11) in 2003 led to a protracted war. When Barack Obama was elected in 2008, the first African American president in the nation's history, he inherited two wars and the Great Recession, the most significant economic collapse since the 1930s. His, and the nation's, efforts to address these and other pressing issues—including the national debt and global warming—remain ongoing, unfinished business.

CHAPTER REVIEW QUESTIONS

- How has globalization affected American politics? Society? What connections do you see between globalization and the "culture wars" of the 1990s?

- In what ways has the United States' role in the world changed since the end of the Cold War? In what ways has it remained the same?

TIMELINE

1992	Democratic moderate Bill Clinton elected president
	Planned Parenthood of Southeastern Pennsylvania v. Casey
1993	North American Free Trade Agreement (NAFTA)
1994	Clinton fails to win health insurance reform but reduces budget deficit and national debt
	Republicans gain control of Congress
1995	U.S. troops enforce peace in Bosnia
1996	Personal Responsibility and Work Opportunity Act reforms welfare system
1998	Bill Clinton impeached by House of Representatives
	American intervention in Bosnia and Serbia
	Defense of Marriage Act
1999	Clinton acquitted by the Senate
	World Trade Organization (WTO) protests
2000	George W. Bush wins contested presidential election
2001	Bush tax cuts
	September 11, Al Qaeda terrorists attack World Trade Center and Pentagon
	Congress passes USA PATRIOT Act
2002	The United States unseats Taliban in Afghanistan
	President Bush declares Iran, North Korea, and Iraq "an axis of evil"
2003	The United States invades Iraq in March
2004	Torture at Abu Ghraib prison becomes public
	President Bush wins reelection
2007	Great Recession begins
2008	Barack Obama elected president
	American Recovery and Reinvestment Act
2010	Patient Protection and Affordable Care Act

FOR FURTHER EXPLORATION

On globalization, see Alfred Eckes Jr. and Thomas Zeilin, *Globalization and the American Century* (2003). For discussions of recent growth in inequality, see Godfrey Hodgson, *More Equal Than Others* (2004). On American families and the culture wars, see Stephanie Coontz, *The Way We Never Were: American Families and the Nostalgia Trap* (1992); Susan Faludi, *Backlash: The Undeclared War against American Women* (1991); and Gertrude Himmelfarb, *One Nation, Two Cultures* (1999). For the Clinton years, consult William Berman, *From the Center to the Edge: The Politics and Policies of the Clinton Presidency* (2001), and Joe Klein, *The Natural: The Misunderstood Presidency of Bill Clinton* (2002). Richard A. Posner, *An Affair of State: The Investigation, Impeachment, and Trial of President Clinton* (1999), probes the legal aspects of Clinton's impeachment. For online materials on that subject, consult Jurist, the Law Professors' Network, at **jurist.law.pitt.edu/impeach .htm**. Information on all U.S. presidents is available at **www.ipl.org/div/potus**. The literature on the presidency of George W. Bush, the September 11 attacks, and the Iraq War is already vast and growing. A good starting point is Richard A. Clarke, *Against All Enemies: Inside America's War on Terror* (2004), and Michael R. Gordon and Bernard R. Trainor, *Cobra II: The Inside Story of the Invasion and Occupation of Iraq* (2006). See the September 11 Digital Archive at **http://911digitalarchive .org/** for oral histories and both still and moving images from September 11. Barack Obama's first memoir, *Dreams from My Father: A Story of Race and Inheritance* (1995), makes compelling reading.

TEST YOUR KNOWLEDGE

To assess your command of the material in this chapter, see the Online Study Guide at **bedfordstmartins.com/henretta**.

For Web sites, images, and documents related to topics and places in this chapter, visit **bedfordstmartins.com/makehistory**.

Documents

The Declaration of Independence

In Congress, July 4, 1776, The Unanimous Declaration of the Thirteen United States of America

When in the Course of human events, it becomes necessary for one people to dissolve the political bands which have connected them with another, and to assume among the Powers of the earth, the separate and equal station to which the Laws of Nature and of Nature's God entitle them, a decent respect to the opinions of mankind requires that they should declare the causes which impel them to the separation.

We hold these truths to be self-evident, that all men are created equal, that they are endowed by their Creator with certain unalienable rights, that among these are Life, Liberty, and the pursuit of Happiness. That to secure these rights, Governments are instituted among Men, deriving their just powers from the consent of the governed. That whenever any Form of Government becomes destructive of these ends, it is the Right of the People to alter or to abolish it, and to institute new Government, laying its foundation on such principles and organizing its powers in such form, as to them shall seem most likely to effect their Safety and Happiness. Prudence, indeed, will dictate that Governments long established should not be changed for light and transient causes; and accordingly all experience hath shown, that mankind are more disposed to suffer, while evils are sufferable, than to right themselves by abolishing the forms to which they are accustomed. But when a long train of abuses and usurpations, pursuing invariably the same Object evinces a design to reduce them under absolute Despotism, it is their right, it is their duty, to throw off such Government, and to provide new Guards for their future security.— Such has been the patient sufferance of these Colonies; and such is now the necessity which constrains them to alter their former Systems of Government. The history of the present King of Great Britain is a history of repeated injuries and usurpations, all having in direct object the establishment of an absolute Tyranny over these States. To prove this, let Facts be submitted to a candid world.

He has refused his Assent to Laws, the most wholesome and necessary for the public good.

He has forbidden his Governors to pass Laws of immediate and pressing importance, unless suspended in their operation till his Assent should be obtained; and, when so suspended, he has utterly neglected to attend to them.

He has refused to pass other Laws for the accommodation of large districts of people, unless those people would relinquish the right of Representation in the Legislature, a right inestimable to them and formidable to tyrants only.

He has called together legislative bodies at places unusual, uncomfortable, and distant from the depository of their public Records, for the sole purpose of fatiguing them into compliance with his measures.

He has dissolved Representative Houses repeatedly, for opposing with manly firmness his invasions on the rights of the people.

He has refused for a long time, after such dissolutions, to cause others to be elected; whereby the Legislative powers, incapable of Annihilation, have returned to the People at large for their exercise; the State remaining in the mean time exposed to all the dangers of invasion from without and convulsions within.

He has endeavoured to prevent the population of these States; for that purpose obstructing the Laws of Naturalization of Foreigners; refusing to pass others to encourage their migrations hither, and raising the conditions of new Appropriations of Lands.

He has obstructed the Administration of Justice, by refusing his Assent to Laws for establishing Judiciary powers.

He has made Judges dependent on his Will alone, for the tenure of their offices, and the amount and payment of their salaries.

He has erected a multitude of New Offices, and sent hither swarms of Officers to harass our People, and eat out their substance.

He has kept among us, in times of peace, Standing Armies without the Consent of our legislature.

He has combined with others to subject us to a jurisdiction foreign to our constitution, and unacknowledged by our laws; giving his Assent to their Acts of pretended Legislation:

For quartering large bodies of armed troops among us:

For protecting them, by a mock Trial, from Punishment for any Murders which they should commit on the Inhabitants of these States:

For cutting off our Trade with all parts of the world:

For imposing taxes on us without our Consent:

For depriving us, in many cases, of the benefits of Trial by jury:

For transporting us beyond Seas to be tried for pretended offences:

For abolishing the free System of English Laws in a neighbouring Province, establishing therein an Arbitrary government, and enlarging its Boundaries so as to render it at once an example and fit instrument for introducing the same absolute rule into these Colonies:

For taking away our Charters, abolishing our most valuable Laws, and altering fundamentally the Forms of our Governments:

For suspending our own Legislatures, and declaring themselves invested with Power to legislate for us in all cases whatsoever.

He has abdicated Government here, by declaring us out of his Protection and waging War against us.

He has plundered our seas, ravaged our Coasts, burnt our towns, and destroyed the lives of our people.

He is at this time transporting large armies of foreign mercenaries to compleat the works of death, desolation, and tyranny, already begun with circumstances of Cruelty & perfidy scarcely paralleled in the most barbarous ages, and totally unworthy the Head of a civilized nation.

He has constrained our fellow Citizens taken Captive on the high Seas to bear Arms against their Country, to become the executioners of their friends and Brethren, or to fall themselves by their Hands.

He has excited domestic insurrections amongst us, and has endeavoured to bring on the inhabitants of our frontiers, the merciless Indian Savages, whose known rule of warfare, is an undistinguished destruction of all ages, sexes, and conditions.

In every stage of these Oppressions We have Petitioned for Redress in the most humble terms: Our repeated Petitions have been answered only by repeated injury. A Prince, whose character is thus marked by every act which may define a Tyrant, is unfit to be the ruler of a free people.

Nor have We been wanting in attention to our British brethren. We have warned them from time to time of attempts by their legislature to extend an unwarrantable jurisdiction over us. We have reminded them of the circumstances of our emigration and settlement here. We have appealed to their native justice and magnanimity, and we have conjured them by the ties of our common kindred to disavow these usurpations, which would inevitably interrupt our connections and correspondence. They too have been deaf to the voice of justice and of consanguinity. We must, therefore, acquiesce in the necessity, which denounces our Separation, and hold them, as we hold the rest of mankind, Enemies in War, in Peace Friends.

We, therefore, the Representatives of the United States of America, in General Congress, Assembled, appealing to the Supreme Judge of the world for the rectitude of our intentions, do, in the Name, and by Authority of the good People of these Colonies, solemnly publish and declare, That these United Colonies are, and of Right ought to be FREE AND INDEPENDENT STATES; that they are Absolved from all Allegiance to the British Crown, and that all political connection between them and the State of Great Britain, is and ought to be totally dissolved; and that as Free and Independent States, they have full Power to levy War, conclude Peace, contract Alliances, establish Commerce, and to do all other Acts and Things which Independent States may of right do. And for the support of this Declaration, with a firm reliance on the Protection of Divine Providence, we mutually pledge to each other our Lives, our Fortunes, and our sacred Honor.

John Hancock

Button Gwinnett	George Wythe	Geo. Taylor	Abra. Clark
Lyman Hall	Richard Henry Lee	James Wilson	Josiah Bartlett
Geo. Walton	Th. Jefferson	Geo. Ross	Wm. Whipple
Wm. Hooper	Benja. Harrison	Caesar Rodney	Matthew Thornton
Joseph Hewes	Thos. Nelson, Jr.	Geo. Read	Saml. Adams
John Penn	Francis Lightfoot	Thos. M'Kean	John Adams
Edward Rutledge	Lee	Wm. Floyd	Robt. Treat Paine
Thos. Heyward, Junr.	Carter Braxton	Phil. Livingston	Elbridge Gerry
Thomas Lynch, Junr.	Robt. Morris	Frans. Lewis	Step. Hopkins
Arthur Middleton	Benjamin Rush	Lewis Morris	William Ellery
Samuel Chase	Benja. Franklin	Richd. Stockton	Roger Sherman
Wm. Paca	John Morton	John Witherspoon	Sam'el Huntington
Thos. Stone	Geo. Clymer	Fras. Hopkinson	Wm. Williams
Charles Carroll of Carrollton	Jas. Smith	John Hart	Oliver Wolcott

Articles of Confederation and Perpetual Union

Agreed to in Congress, November 15, 1777; Ratified March 1781

BETWEEN THE STATES OF NEW HAMPSHIRE, MASSACHU-SETTS BAY, RHODE ISLAND AND PROVIDENCE PLANTATIONS, CONNECTICUT, NEW YORK, NEW JERSEY, PENNSYLVANIA, DELAWARE, MARYLAND, VIRGINIA, NORTH CAROLINA, SOUTH CAROLINA, GEORGIA.*

Article 1

The stile of this confederacy shall be "The United States of America."

Article 2

Each State retains its sovereignty, freedom and independence, and every power, jurisdiction, and right, which is not by this confederation expressly delegated to the United States, in Congress assembled.

Article 3

The said states hereby severally enter into a firm league of friendship with each other for their common defence, the security of their liberties and their mutual and general welfare; binding themselves to assist each other against all force offered to, or attacks made upon them, or any of them, on account of religion, sovereignty, trade, or any other pretence whatever.

Article 4

The better to secure and perpetuate mutual friendship and intercourse among the people of the different states in this union, the free inhabitants of each of these states, paupers, vagabonds, and fugitives from justice excepted, shall be entitled to all privileges and immunities of free citizens in the several states; and the people of each State shall have free ingress and regress to and from any other State, and shall enjoy therein all the privileges of trade and commerce, subject to the same duties, impositions, and restrictions, as the inhabitants thereof respectively; provided, that such restric-

*This copy of the final draft of the Articles of Confederation is taken from the *Journals*, 9:907–25, November 15, 1777.

tions shall not extend so far as to prevent the removal of property, imported into any State, to any other State of which the owner is an inhabitant; provided also, that no imposition, duties, or restriction, shall be laid by any State on the property of the United States, or either of them.

If any person guilty of, or charged with treason, felony, or other high misdemeanor in any State, shall flee from justice and be found in any of the United States, he shall, upon demand of the governor or executive power of the State from which he fled, be delivered up and removed to the State having jurisdiction of his offence.

Full faith and credit shall be given in each of these states to the records, acts, and judicial proceedings of the courts and magistrates of every other State.

Article 5

For the more convenient management of the general interests of the United States, delegates shall be annually appointed, in such manner as the legislature of each State shall direct, to meet in Congress, on the 1st Monday in November in every year, with a power reserved to each State to recall its delegates, or any of them, at any time within the year, and to send others in their stead for the remainder of the year.

No State shall be represented in Congress by less than two, nor by more than seven members; and no person shall be capable of being a delegate for more than three years in any term of six years; nor shall any person, being a delegate, be capable of holding any office under the United States, for which he, or any other for his benefit, receives any salary, fees, or emolument of any kind.

Each State shall maintain its own delegates in a meeting of the states, and while they act as members of the committee of the states.

In determining questions in the United States, in Congress assembled, each State shall have one vote.

Freedom of speech and debate in Congress shall not be impeached or questioned in any court or place out of Congress: and the members of Congress shall be protected in their persons from arrests and imprisonments, during the time of their going to and from, and attendance on Congress, except for treason, felony, or breach of the peace.

Article 6

No State, without the consent of the United States, in Congress assembled, shall send any embassy to, or receive any embassy from, or enter into any conference, agreement, alliance, or treaty with any king, prince, or state; nor shall any person, holding any office of profit or trust under the United States, or any of them, accept of any present, emolument, office or title, of any kind whatever, from any king, prince, or foreign state; nor shall the United States, in Congress assembled, or any of them, grant any title of nobility.

No two or more states shall enter into any treaty, confederation, or alliance, whatever, between them, without the consent of the United States, in Congress assembled, specifying accurately the purposes for which the same is to be entered into, and how long it shall continue.

No state shall lay any imposts or duties which may interfere with any stipulations in treaties entered into by the United States, in Congress assembled, with any king, prince, or state, in pursuance of any treaties already proposed by Congress to the courts of France and Spain.

No vessels of war shall be kept up in time of peace by any State, except such number only as shall be deemed necessary by the United States, in Congress assembled, for the defence of such State or its trade; nor shall any body of forces be kept up by any State, in time of peace, except such number only as, in the judgment of the United States, in Congress assembled, shall be deemed requisite to garrison the forts necessary for the defence of such State; but every State shall always keep up a well regulated and disciplined militia, sufficiently armed and accoutred, and shall provide, and constantly have ready for use, in public stores, a due number of field pieces and tents, and a proper quantity of arms, ammunition and camp equipage.

No State shall engage in any war without the consent of the United States, in Congress assembled, unless such State be actually invaded by enemies, or shall have received certain advice of a resolution being formed by some nation of Indians to invade such State, and the danger is so imminent as not to admit of a delay till the United States, in Congress assembled, can be consulted; nor shall any State grant commissions to any ships or vessels of war, nor letters of marque or reprisal, except it be after a declaration of war by the United States, in Congress assembled, and then only against the kingdom or state, and the subjects thereof, against which war has been so declared, and under such regulations as shall be established by the United States, in Congress assembled, unless such State be infested by pirates, in which case vessels of war may be fitted out for that occasion, and kept so long as the danger shall continue, or until the United States, in Congress assembled, shall determine otherwise.

Article 7

When land forces are raised by any State for the common defence, all officers of or under the rank of colonel, shall be appointed by the legislature of each State respectively, by whom such forces shall be raised, or in such manner as such State shall direct; and all vacancies shall be filled up by the State which first made the appointment.

Article 8

All charges of war and all other expences, that shall be incurred for the common defence or general welfare, and allowed by the United States, in Congress assembled, shall be defrayed out of a common treasury, which shall be supplied by the several states, in proportion to the value of all land within each State, granted to or surveyed for any person, as such land and the buildings and improvements thereon shall be estimated according to such mode as the United States, in Congress assembled, shall, from time to time, direct and appoint.

The taxes for paying that proportion shall be laid and levied by the authority and direction of the legislatures of the several states, within the time agreed upon by the United States, in Congress assembled.

Article 9

The United States, in Congress assembled, shall have the sole and exclusive right and power of determining on peace and war, except in the cases mentioned in the 6th article; of sending and receiving ambassadors; entering into treaties and alliances, provided that no treaty of commerce shall be made, whereby the legislative power of the respective states shall be restrained from imposing such imposts and duties on foreigners as their own people are subjected to, or from prohibiting the exportation or importation of any species of goods or commodities whatsoever; of establishing rules for deciding, in all cases, what captures on land or water shall be legal, and in what manner prizes, taken by land or naval forces in the service of the United States, shall be divided or appropriated; of granting letters of marque and reprisal in times of peace; appointing courts for the trial of piracies and felonies committed on the high seas, and establishing courts for receiving and determining, finally, appeals in all cases of captures; provided, that no member of Congress shall be appointed a judge of any of the said courts.

The United States, in Congress assembled, shall also be the last resort on appeal in all disputes and differences now subsisting, or that hereafter may arise between two or more states concerning boundary, jurisdiction or any other cause whatever; which authority shall always be exercised in the manner following: whenever the legislative or executive authority, or lawful agent of any State, in controversy with another, shall present a petition to Congress, stating the matter in question, and praying for a hearing, notice thereof shall be given, by order of Congress, to the legislative or executive authority of the other State in controversy, and a day assigned for the appearance of the parties by their lawful agents, who shall then be directed to appoint, by joint consent, commissioners or judges to constitute a court for hearing and determining the matter in question; but, if they cannot agree, Congress shall name three persons out of each of the United States, and from the list of such persons each party shall alternately strike out one, the petitioners beginning, until the number shall be reduced to thirteen; and from that number not less than seven, nor more than nine names, as Congress shall direct, shall, in the presence of Congress, be drawn out by lot; and the persons whose names shall be so drawn, or any five of them, shall be commissioners or judges to hear and finally determine the controversy, so always as a major part of the judges who shall hear the cause shall agree in the determination; and if either party shall neglect to attend at the day appointed, without shewing reasons which Congress shall judge sufficient, or, being present, shall refuse to strike, the Congress shall proceed to nominate three persons out of each State, and the secretary of Congress shall strike in behalf of such party absent or refusing; and the judgment and sentence of the court to be appointed, in the manner before prescribed, shall be final and conclusive; and if any of the parties shall refuse to submit to the authority of such court, or to appear or defend their claim or cause, the court shall nevertheless proceed to pronounce sentence or judgment, which shall, in like manner, be final and decisive, the judgment or sentence and other proceedings begin, in either case, transmitted to Congress, and lodged among the acts of Congress for the security of the parties concerned: provided, that every commissioner, before he sits in judgment, shall take an oath, to be administered by one of the judges of the supreme or superior court of the State where the cause shall be tried, "well and truly to hear and determine the matter in question, according to the best of his judgment, without favour, affection, or hope of reward:" provided, also, that no State shall be deprived of territory for the benefit of the United States.

All controversies concerning the private right of soil, claimed under different grants of two or more states, whose jurisdictions, as they may respect such lands and the states which passed such grants, are adjusted, the said grants, or either of them, being at the same time claimed to have originated antecedent to such settlement of jurisdiction, shall, on the petition of either party to the Congress of the United States, be finally determined, as near as may be, in the same manner as is before prescribed for deciding disputes respecting territorial jurisdiction between different states.

The United States, in Congress assembled, shall also have the sole and exclusive right and power of regulating the alloy and value of coin struck by their own authority, or by that of the respective states; fixing the standard of weights and measures throughout the United States; regulating the trade and managing all affairs with the Indians not mem-

bers of any of the states; provided that the legislative right of any State within its own limits be not infringed or violated; establishing and regulating post offices from one State to another throughout all the United States, and exacting such postage on the papers passing through the same as may be requisite to defray the expences of the said office; appointing all officers of the land forces in the service of the United States, excepting regimental officers; appointing all the officers of the naval forces, and commissioning all officers whatever in the service of the United States; making rules for the government and regulation of the said land and naval forces, and directing their operations.

The United States, in Congress assembled, shall have authority to appoint a committee to sit in the recess of Congress, to be denominated "a Committee of the States," and to consist of one delegate from each State, and to appoint such other committees and civil officers as may be necessary for managing the general affairs of the United States, under their direction; to appoint one of their number to preside; provided that no person be allowed to serve in the office of president more than one year in any term of three years; to ascertain the necessary sums of money to be raised for the service of the United States, and to appropriate and apply the same for defraying the public expences; to borrow money or emit bills on the credit of the United States, transmitting, every half year, to the respective states, an account of the sums of money so borrowed or emitted; to build and equip a navy; to agree upon the number of land forces, and to make requisitions from each State for its quota, in proportion to the number of white inhabitants in such State; which requisitions shall be binding; and thereupon, the legislature of each State shall appoint the regimental officers, raise the men, and cloathe, arm, and equip them in a soldier-like manner, at the expence of the United States; and the officers and men so cloathed, armed, and equipped, shall march to the place appointed and within the time agreed on by the United States, in Congress assembled; but if the United States, in Congress assembled, shall, on consideration of circumstances, judge proper that any State should not raise men, or should raise a smaller number than its quota, and that any other State should raise a greater number of men than the quota thereof, such extra number shall be raised, officered, cloathed, armed, and equipped in the same manner as the quota of such State, unless the legislature of such State shall judge that such extra number cannot be safely spared out of the same, in which case they shall raise, officer, cloathe, arm, and equip as many of such extra number as they judge can be safely spared. And the officers and men so cloathed, armed, and equipped, shall march to the place appointed and within the time agreed on by the United States, in Congress assembled.

The United States, in Congress assembled, shall never engage in a war, nor grant letters of marque and reprisal in time of peace, nor enter into any treaties or alliances, nor coin money, nor regulate the value thereof, nor ascertain the sums and expences necessary for the defence and welfare of the United States, or any of them; nor emit bills, nor borrow money on the credit of the United States, nor appropriate money, nor agree upon the number of vessels of war to be built or purchased, or the number of land or sea forces to be raised, nor appoint a commander in chief of the army or navy, unless nine states assent to the same; nor shall a question on any other point, except for adjourning from day to day, be determined, unless by the votes of a majority of the United States, in Congress assembled.

The Congress of the United States shall have power to adjourn to any time within the year, and to any place within the United States, so that no period of adjournment be for a longer duration than the space of six months, and shall publish the journal of their proceedings monthly, except such parts thereof, relating to treaties, alliances or military operations, as, in their judgment, require secrecy; and the yeas and nays of the delegates of each State on any question shall be entered on the journal, when it is desired by any delegate; and the delegates of a State, or any of them, at his, or their request, shall be furnished with a transcript of the said journal, except such parts as are above excepted, to lay before the legislatures of the several states.

Article 10

The committee of the states, or any nine of them, shall be authorized to execute, in the recess of Congress, such of the powers of Congress as the United States, in Congress assembled, by the consent of nine states, shall, from time to time, think expedient to vest them with; provided, that no power be delegated to the said committee, for the exercise of which, by the articles of confederation, the voice of nine states, in the Congress of the United States assembled, is requisite.

Article 11

Canada acceding to this confederation, and joining in the measures of the United States, shall be admitted into and entitled to all the advantages of this union; but no other colony shall be admitted into the same, unless such admission be agreed to by nine states.

The Constitution of the United States of America

Agreed to by Philadelphia Convention, September 17, 1787
Implemented March 4, 1789

We the People of the United States, in Order to form a more perfect Union, establish Justice, insure domestic Tranquility, provide for the common defence, promote the general Welfare, and secure the Blessings of Liberty to ourselves and our Posterity, do ordain and establish this Constitution for the United States of America.

Article I

Section 1. All legislative Powers herein granted shall be vested in a Congress of the United States, which shall consist of a Senate and a House of Representatives.

Section 2. The House of Representatives shall be composed of Members chosen every second Year by the People of the several States, and the Electors in each State shall have the Qualifications requisite for Electors of the most numerous Branch of the State Legislature.

No Person shall be a Representative who shall not have attained to the Age of twenty-five Years, and been seven Years a Citizen of the United States, and who shall not, when elected, be an Inhabitant of that State in which he shall be chosen.

Representatives and direct Taxes shall be apportioned among the several States which may be included within this Union, according to their respective Numbers, *which shall be determined by adding to the whole Number of free Persons, including those bound to Service for a Term of Years, and excluding Indians not taxed, three fifths of all other Persons.** The actual Enumeration shall be made within three Years after the first Meeting of the Congress of the United States, and within every subsequent Term of ten Years, in such Manner as they shall by Law direct. The Number of Representatives shall not exceed one for every thirty Thousand, but each State shall have at Least one Representative; and *until such enumeration shall be made, the State of New Hampshire shall be entitled to chuse three, Massachusetts eight, Rhode Island and Providence Plantations one, Connecticut five, New York six, New Jersey four, Pennsylvania eight, Delaware one, Maryland six, Virginia ten, North Carolina five, South Carolina five, and Georgia three.*

When vacancies happen in the Representation from any State, the Executive Authority thereof shall issue Writs of Election to fill such Vacancies.

The House of Representatives shall chuse their Speaker and other Officers; and shall have the sole Power of Impeachment.

Section 3. The Senate of the United States shall be composed of two Senators from each State, *chosen by the Legislature thereof,*† for six Years; and each Senator shall have one Vote.

Immediately after they shall be assembled in Consequence of the first Election, they shall be divided as equally as may be into three Classes. The Seats of the Senators of the first Class shall be vacated at the Expiration of the second Year, of the second Class at the Expiration of the fourth Year, and of the third Class at the Expiration of the sixth Year, so that one-third may be chosen every second Year; and if Vacancies happen by Resignation, or otherwise, during the Recess of the Legislature of any State, the Executive thereof may make temporary Appointments until the next Meeting of the Legislature, which shall then fill such Vacancies.‡

No person shall be a Senator who shall not have attained to the Age of thirty Years, and been nine Years a Citizen of the United States, and who shall not, when elected, be an Inhabitant of that State for which he shall be chosen.

The Vice President of the United States shall be President of the Senate, but shall have no Vote, unless they be equally divided.

The Senate shall chuse their other Officers, and also a President pro tempore, in the absence of the Vice President, or when he shall exercise the Office of President of the United States.

The Senate shall have the sole Power to try all Impeachments. When sitting for that Purpose, they shall be on Oath or Affirmation. When the President of the United States is tried, the Chief Justice shall preside: And no Person shall be convicted without the Concurrence of two-thirds of the Members present.

Judgment in Cases of Impeachment shall not extend further than to removal from Office, and disqualification to hold and enjoy any Office of honor, Trust or Profit under the United States: but the Party convicted shall nevertheless be liable and subject to Indictment, Trial, Judgment and Punishment, according to Law.

Note: The Constitution became effective March 4, 1789. Provisions in italics are no longer relevant or have been changed by constitutional amendment.
*Changed by Section 2 of the Fourteenth Amendment.

---

†Changed by Section 1 of the Seventeenth Amendment.
‡Changed by Clause 2 of the Seventeenth Amendment.

Section 4. The Times, Places and Manner of holding Elections for Senators and Representatives, shall be prescribed in each State by the Legislature thereof; but the Congress may at any time by Law make or alter such Regulations, except as to the Places of Chusing Senators.

The Congress shall assemble at least once in every Year, and such Meeting *shall be on the first Monday in December, unless they shall by Law appoint a different Day.**

Section 5. Each House shall be the Judge of the Elections, Returns and Qualifications of its own Members, and a Majority of each shall constitute a Quorum to do Business; but a smaller number may adjourn from day to day, and may be authorized to compel the Attendance of absent Members, in such Manner, and under such Penalties, as each House may provide.

Each House may determine the Rules of its Proceedings, punish its Members for disorderly Behavior, and, with the Concurrence of two-thirds, expel a Member.

Each House shall keep a Journal of its Proceedings, and from time to time publish the same, excepting such Parts as may in their Judgment require Secrecy; and the Yeas and Nays of the Members of either House on any question shall, at the Desire of one-fifth of those Present, be entered on the Journal.

Neither House, during the Session of Congress, shall, without the Consent of the other, adjourn for more than three days, nor to any other Place than that in which the two Houses shall be sitting.

Section 6. The Senators and Representatives shall receive a Compensation for their Services, to be ascertained by Law, and paid out of the Treasury of the United States. They shall in all Cases, except Treason, Felony and Breach of the Peace, be privileged from Arrest during their Attendance at the Session of their respective Houses, and in going to and returning from the same; and for any Speech or Debate in either House, they shall not be questioned in any other Place.

No Senator or Representative shall, during the Time for which he was elected, be appointed to any civil Office under the Authority of the United States, which shall have been created, or the Emoluments whereof shall have been increased, during such time; and no Person holding any Office under the United States, shall be a Member of either House during his Continuance in Office.

Section 7. All Bills for raising Revenue shall originate in the House of Representatives; but the Senate may propose or concur with Amendments as on other Bills.

Every Bill which shall have passed the House of Representatives and the Senate, shall, before it becomes a Law, be presented to the President of the United States; If he approve he shall sign it, but if not he shall return it, with his Objections to that House in which it shall have originated, who shall enter the Objections at large on their Journal, and proceed to reconsider it. If after such Reconsideration two-thirds of that House shall agree to pass the Bill, it shall be sent, together with the Objections, to the other House, by which it shall likewise be reconsidered, and if approved by two-thirds of that House, it shall become a Law. But in all such Cases the Votes of both Houses shall be determined by Yeas and Nays, and the Names of the Persons voting for and against the Bill shall be entered on the Journal of each House respectively. If any Bill shall not be returned by the President within ten Days (Sundays excepted) after it shall have been presented to him, the Same shall be a Law, in like Manner as if he had signed it, unless the Congress by their Adjournment prevent its Return, in which Case it shall not be a Law.

Every Order, Resolution, or Vote to which the Concurrence of the Senate and the House of Representatives may be necessary (except on a question of Adjournment) shall be presented to the President of the United States; and before the Same shall take Effect, shall be approved by him, or being disapproved by him, shall be repassed by two-thirds of the Senate and House of Representatives, according to the Rules and Limitations prescribed in the Case of a Bill.

Section 8. The Congress shall have Power To lay and collect Taxes, Duties, Imposts and Excises, to pay the Debts and provide for the common Defence and general Welfare of the United States; but all Duties, Imposts and Excises shall be uniform throughout the United States;

To borrow money on the credit of the United States;

To regulate Commerce with foreign Nations, and among the several States, and with the Indian Tribes;

To establish an uniform Rule of Naturalization, and uniform Laws on the subject of Bankruptcies throughout the United States;

To coin Money, regulate the Value thereof, and of foreign Coin, and fix the Standard of Weights and Measures;

To provide for the Punishment of counterfeiting the Securities and current Coin of the United States;

To establish Post Offices and post Roads;

To promote the Progress of Science and useful Arts, by securing for limited Times to Authors and Inventors the exclusive Right to their respective Writings and Discoveries;

To constitute Tribunals inferior to the supreme Court;

To define and punish Piracies and Felonies committed on the high Seas, and Offenses against the Law of Nations;

To declare War, grant Letters of Marque and Reprisal, and make Rules concerning Captures on Land and Water;

---

*Changed by Section 2 of the Twentieth Amendment.

To raise and support Armies, but no Appropriation of Money to that Use shall be for a longer Term than two Years;

To provide and maintain a Navy;

To make Rules for the Government and Regulation of the land and naval Forces;

To provide for calling forth the Militia to execute the Laws of the Union, suppress Insurrections and repel Invasions;

To provide for organizing, arming, and disciplining the Militia, and for governing such Part of them as may be employed in the Service of the United States, reserving to the States respectively, the Appointment of the Officers, and the Authority of training the Militia according to the discipline prescribed by Congress;

To exercise exclusive Legislation in all Cases whatsoever, over such District (not exceeding ten Miles square) as may, by Cession of particular States, and the acceptance of Congress, become the Seat of Government of the United States, and to exercise like Authority over all Places purchased by the Consent of the Legislature of the State in which the Same shall be, for the Erection of Forts, Magazines, Arsenals, dock-Yards, and other needful Buildings;—And

To make all Laws which shall be necessary and proper for carrying into Execution the foregoing Powers, and all other Powers vested by this Constitution in the Government of the United States, or in any Department or Officer thereof.

Section 9. The Migration or Importation of such Persons as any of the States now existing shall think proper to admit, shall not be prohibited by the Congress prior to the Year one thousand eight hundred and eight but a tax or duty may be imposed on such Importation, not exceeding ten dollars for each Person.

The privilege of the Writ of Habeas Corpus shall not be suspended, unless when in Cases of Rebellion or Invasion the public Safety may require it.

No Bill of Attainder or ex post facto Law shall be passed.

*No capitation, or other direct, Tax shall be laid, unless in Proportion to the Census or Enumeration herein before directed to be taken.**

No Tax or Duty shall be laid on Articles exported from any State.

No Preference shall be given by any Regulation of Commerce or Revenue to the Ports of one State over those of another: nor shall Vessels bound to, or from, one State, be obliged to enter, clear, or pay Duties in another.

No Money shall be drawn from the Treasury, but in Consequence of Appropriations made by law; and a regular Statement and Account of the Receipts and Expenditures of all public Money shall be published from time to time.

---

*Changed by the Sixteenth Amendment.

No Title of Nobility shall be granted by the United States: And no Person holding any Office of Profit or Trust under them, shall, without the Consent of the Congress, accept of any present, Emolument, Office, or Title, of any kind whatever, from any King, Prince, or foreign State.

Section 10. No State shall enter into any Treaty, Alliance, or Confederation; grant Letters of Marque and Reprisal; coin Money; emit Bills of Credit; make any Thing but gold and silver Coin a Tender in Payment of Debts; pass any Bill of Attainder, ex post facto Law, or Law impairing the Obligation of Contracts, or grant any Title of Nobility.

No State shall, without the Consent of the Congress, lay any Imposts or Duties on Imports or Exports, except what may be absolutely necessary for executing its inspection Laws: and the net Produce of all Duties and Imposts, laid by any State on Imports or Exports, shall be for the Use of the Treasury of the United States; and all such Laws shall be subject to the Revision and Control of the Congress.

No State shall, without the Consent of the Congress, lay any duty of Tonnage, keep Troops, or Ships of War in time of Peace, enter into any Agreement or Compact with another State, or with a foreign Power, or engage in War, unless actually invaded, or in such imminent Danger as will not admit of delay.

Article II

Section 1. The executive Power shall be vested in a President of the United States of America. He shall hold his Office during the Term of four Years, and, together with the Vice President, chosen for the same Term, be elected, as follows:

Each State shall appoint, in such Manner as the Legislature thereof may direct, a Number of Electors, equal to the whole Number of Senators and Representatives to which the State may be entitled in the Congress; but no Senator or Representative, or Person holding an Office of Trust or Profit under the United States, shall be appointed an Elector.

The Electors shall meet in their respective States, and vote by Ballot for two Persons, of whom one at least shall not be an Inhabitant of the same State with themselves. And they shall make a List of all the Persons voted for, and of the Number of Votes for each; which List they shall sign and certify, and transmit sealed to the Seat of the Government of the United States, directed to the President of the Senate. The President of the Senate shall, in the Presence of the Senate and House of Representatives, open all the Certificates, and the Votes shall then be counted. The Person having the greatest Number of Votes shall be the President, if such Number be a Majority of the whole Number of Electors appointed; and if there be more than one who have such Majority, and have an equal Number of Votes, then the House of Representatives shall immediately *chuse by Ballot one of them for President; and if no Person have a Majority, then from the five highest on the List the said House shall in like Manner chuse the President. But in chusing the President, the Votes shall be taken by States, the Representation from each State having one Vote; a quorum for this Purpose shall consist of a Member or Members from two thirds of the States, and a Majority of all the States shall be necessary to a Choice. In every Case, after the Choice of the President, the Person having the greatest Number of Votes of the Electors shall be the Vice President. But if there should remain two or more who have equal Votes, the Senate shall chuse from them by Ballot the Vice President.**

The Congress may determine the Time of chusing the Electors, and the Day on which they shall give their Votes; which Day shall be the same throughout the United States.

No Person except a natural born Citizen, or a Citizen of the United States, at the time of the Adoption of this Constitution, shall be eligible to the Office of President; neither shall any Person be eligible to that Office who shall not have attained to the Age of thirty five Years, and been fourteen Years a Resident within the United States.

In Case of the Removal of the President from Office, or of his Death, Resignation, or Inability to discharge the Powers and Duties of the said Office, the same shall devolve on the Vice President, *and the Congress may by Law provide for the Case of Removal, Death, Resignation, or Inability, both of the President and Vice President, declaring what Officer shall then act as President, and such Officer shall act accordingly, until the Disability be removed, or a President shall be elected.*†

The President shall, at stated Times, receive for his Services a Compensation, which shall neither be increased nor diminished during the Period for which he shall have been elected, and he shall not receive within that Period any other Emolument from the United States, or any of them.

Before he enter on the Execution of his Office, he shall take the following Oath or Affirmation:—"I do solemnly swear (or affirm) that I will faithfully execute the Office of President of the United States, and will to the best of my Ability, preserve, protect and defend the Constitution of the United States."

Section 2. The President shall be Commander in Chief of the Army and Navy of the United States, and of the Militia of the several States, when called into the actual Service of the United States; he may require the Opinion, in writing, of the principal Officer in each of the executive Departments, upon any Subject relating to the Duties of their respective Offices, and he shall have Power to Grant Reprieves and Pardons for Offences against the United States, except in Cases of Impeachment.

He shall have Power, by and with the Advice and Consent of the Senate, to make Treaties, provided two thirds of the Senators present concur; and he shall nominate, and by and with the Advice and Consent of the Senate, shall appoint Ambassadors, other public Ministers and Consuls, Judges of the supreme Court, and all other Officers of the United States, whose Appointments are not herein otherwise provided for, and which shall be established by Law: but the Congress may by Law vest the Appointment of such inferior Officers, as they think proper, in the President alone, in the Courts of Law, or in the Heads of Departments.

The President shall have Power to fill up all Vacancies that may happen during the Recess of the Senate, by granting Commissions which shall expire at the End of their next Session.

Section 3. He shall from time to time give to the Congress Information of the State of the Union, and recommend to their Consideration such Measures as he shall judge necessary and expedient; he may, on extraordinary Occasions, convene both Houses, or either of them, and in Case of Disagreement between them, with Respect to the Time of Adjournment, he may adjourn them to such Time as he shall think proper; he shall receive Ambassadors and other public Ministers; he shall take Care that the Laws be faithfully executed, and shall Commission all the Officers of the United States.

Section 4. The President, Vice President and all civil Officers of the United States, shall be removed from Office on Impeachment for, and Conviction of, Treason, Bribery, or other high Crimes and Misdemeanors.

Article III

Section 1. The judicial Power of the United States, shall be vested in one supreme Court, and in such inferior Courts as the Congress may from time to time ordain and establish. The Judges, both of the supreme and inferior Courts, shall hold their Offices during good Behaviour, and shall, at stated Times, receive for their Services a Compensation, which shall not be diminished during their Continuance in Office.

Section 2. The judicial Power shall extend to all Cases, in Law and Equity, arising under this Constitution, the Laws of the United States, and Treaties made, or which shall be made, under their Authority;—to all Cases affecting Ambas-

---

*Superseded by the Twelfth Amendment.
†Modified by the Twenty-fifth Amendment.

sadors, other public Ministers and Consuls;—to all Cases of admiralty and maritime Jurisdiction;—to Controversies to which the United States shall be a Party;—to Controversies between two or more States;—*between a State and Citizens of another State*;*—between Citizens of different States;—between Citizens of the same State claiming Lands under Grants of different States, and between a State, or the Citizens thereof, and foreign States, Citizens or Subjects.

In all Cases affecting Ambassadors, other public Ministers and Consuls, and those in which a State shall be Party, the supreme Court shall have original Jurisdiction. In all the other Cases before mentioned, the supreme Court shall have appellate Jurisdiction, both as to Law and Fact, with such Exceptions, and under such Regulations as the Congress shall make.

The trial of all Crimes, except in Cases of Impeachment, shall be by Jury; and such Trial shall be held in the State where said Crimes shall have been committed; but when not committed within any State, the Trial shall be at such Place or Places as the Congress may by Law have directed.

Section 3. Treason against the United States, shall consist only in levying War against them, or in adhering to their Enemies, giving them Aid and Comfort. No Person shall be convicted of Treason unless on the Testimony of two Witnesses to the same overt Act, or on Confession in open Court.

The Congress shall have Power to declare the Punishment of Treason, but no Attainder of Treason shall work Corruption of Blood, or Forfeiture except during the Life of the Person attainted.

Article IV

Section 1. Full Faith and Credit shall be given in each State to the public Acts, Records, and judicial Proceedings of every other State. And the Congress may by general Laws prescribe the Manner in which such Acts, Records, and Proceedings shall be proved, and the Effect thereof.

Section 2. The Citizens of each State shall be entitled to all Privileges and Immunities of Citizens in the several States.

A Person charged in any State with Treason, Felony, or other Crime, who shall flee from Justice, and be found in another State, shall on demand of the executive Authority of the State from which he fled, be delivered up, to be removed to the State having Jurisdiction of the Crime.

No Person held to Service or Labour in one State, under the Laws thereof, escaping into another, shall, in Consequence of any Law or Regulation therein, be discharged from such Service or Labour, but shall be delivered up on Claim of the Party to whom such Service or Labour may be due.†

Section 3. New States may be admitted by the Congress into this Union; but no new State shall be formed or erected within the Jurisdiction of any other State; nor any State be formed by the Junction of two or more States, or parts of States, without the Consent of the Legislatures of the States concerned as well as of the Congress.

The Congress shall have Power to dispose of and make all needful Rules and Regulations respecting the Territory or other Property belonging to the United States; and nothing in this Constitution shall be so construed as to Prejudice any Claims of the United States, or of any particular State.

Section 4. The United States shall guarantee to every State in this Union a Republican Form of Government, and shall protect each of them against Invasion; and on Application of the Legislature, or of the Executive (when the Legislature cannot be convened) against domestic Violence.

Article V

The Congress, whenever two-thirds of both Houses shall deem it necessary, shall propose Amendments to this Constitution, or, on the Application of the Legislatures of two-thirds of the several States, shall call a Convention for proposing Amendments, which, in either Case, shall be valid to all Intents and Purposes, as Part of this Constitution, when ratified by the Legislatures of three-fourths of the several States, or by Conventions in three-fourths thereof, as the one or the other Mode of Ratification may be proposed by the Congress; *Provided that no Amendment which may be made prior to the Year One thousand eight hundred and eight shall in any Manner affect the first and fourth Clauses in the Ninth Section of the first Article; and* that no State, without its Consent, shall be deprived of its equal Suffrage in the Senate.

Article VI

All Debts contracted and Engagements entered into, before the Adoption of this Constitution, shall be as valid against the United States under this Constitution, as under the Confederation.

This Constitution, and the Laws of the United States which shall be made in Pursuance thereof; and all Treaties made, or which shall be made, under the Authority of the

---

*Restricted by the Eleventh Amendment.

†Superseded by the Thirteenth Amendment.

United States, shall be the supreme Law of the Land; and the Judges in every State shall be bound thereby, any Thing in the Constitution or Laws of any State to the Contrary notwithstanding.

The Senators and Representatives before mentioned, and the Members of the several State Legislatures, and all executive and judicial Officers, both of the United States and of the several States, shall be bound by Oath or Affirmation, to support this Constitution; but no religious Test shall ever be required as a Qualification to any Office or public Trust under the United States.

Article VII

The Ratification of the Conventions of nine States shall be sufficient for the Establishment of this Constitution between the States so ratifying the Same.

Done in Convention by the Unanimous Consent of the States present the Seventeenth Day of September in the Year of our Lord one thousand seven hundred and Eighty seven and of the Independence of the United States of America the Twelfth. In Witness whereof We have hereunto subscribed our Names.

Go. Washington
President and deputy from Virginia

New Hampshire
John Langdon
Nicholas Gilman

Massachusetts
Nathaniel Gorham
Rufus King

Connecticut
Wm. Saml. Johnson
Roger Sherman

New York
Alexander Hamilton

New Jersey
Wil. Livingston
David Brearley
Wm. Paterson
Jona. Dayton

Pennsylvania
B. Franklin
Thomas Mifflin
Robt. Morris
Geo. Clymer
Thos. FitzSimons
Jared Ingersoll
James Wilson
Gouv. Morris

Delaware
Geo. Read
Gunning Bedford jun
John Dickinson
Richard Bassett
Jaco. Broom

Maryland
James McHenry
Dan. of St. Thos. Jenifer
Danl. Carroll

Virginia
John Blair
James Madison, Jr.

North Carolina
Wm. Blount
Richd. Dobbs Spaight
Hu Williamson

South Carolina
J. Rutledge
Charles Cotesworth Pinckney
Pierce Butler

Georgia
William Few
Abr. Baldwin

Amendments to the Constitution (Including the Six Unratified Amendments)

Amendment I [1791]*

Congress shall make no law respecting an establishment of religion, or prohibiting the free exercise thereof; or abridging the freedom of speech, or of the press; or the right of the people peaceably to assemble, and to petition the Government for a redress of grievances.

Amendment II [1791]

A well regulated Militia, being necessary to the security of a free State, the right of the people to keep and bear Arms shall not be infringed.

Amendment III [1791]

No Soldier shall, in time of peace, be quartered in any house, without the consent of the Owner, nor in time of war, but in a manner to be prescribed by law.

Amendment IV [1791]

The right of the people to be secure in their persons, houses, papers, and effects, against unreasonable searches and seizures, shall not be violated, and no Warrants shall issue, but upon probable cause, supported by Oath or affirmation, and particularly describing the place to be searched, and the persons or things to be seized.

Amendment V [1791]

No person shall be held to answer for a capital or otherwise infamous crime, unless on a presentment or indictment of a Grand Jury, except in cases arising in the land or naval forces, or in the Militia, when in actual service in time of War or public danger; nor shall any person be subject for the same offence to be twice put in jeopardy of life or limb; nor shall be compelled in any criminal case to be a witness against himself, nor be deprived of life, liberty, or property, without due process of law; nor shall private property be taken for public use, without just compensation.

_____
*The dates in brackets indicate when the amendment was ratified.

Amendment VI [1791]

In all criminal prosecutions, the accused shall enjoy the right to a speedy and public trial, by an impartial jury of the State and district wherein the crime shall have been committed, which district shall have been previously ascertained by law, and to be informed of the nature and cause of the accusation; to be confronted with the witnesses against him; to have compulsory process for obtaining witnesses in his favor, and to have the Assistance of Counsel for his defence.

Amendment VII [1791]

In suits at common law, where the value in controversy shall exceed twenty dollars, the right of trial by jury shall be preserved, and no fact tried by a jury, shall be otherwise reexamined in any Court of the United States, than according to the Rules of the common law.

Amendment VIII [1791]

Excessive bail shall not be required, nor excessive fines imposed, nor cruel and unusual punishments inflicted.

Amendment IX [1791]

The enumeration in the Constitution, of certain rights, shall not be construed to deny or disparage others retained by the people.

Amendment X [1791]

The powers not delegated to the United States by the Constitution, nor prohibited by it to the States, are reserved to the States respectively, or to the people.

Unratified Amendment

Reapportionment Amendment (proposed by Congress September 25, 1789, along with the Bill of Rights)

After the first enumeration required by the first article of the Constitution, there shall be one Representative for every thirty thousand, until the number shall amount to one hundred, after which the proportion shall be so regulated by Congress, that there shall be not less than one hundred Representatives, nor less than one Representative for every forty thousand persons, until the number of Representatives shall amount to two hundred; after which the proportion shall be so regulated by Congress, that there shall not be less than two hundred

Representatives, nor more than one Representative for every fifty thousand persons.

Amendment XI [1798]

The Judicial power of the United States shall not be construed to extend to any suit in law or equity, commenced or prosecuted against one of the United States by Citizens of another State, or by Citizens or subjects of any foreign state.

Amendment XII [1804]

The Electors shall meet in their respective States and vote by ballot for President and Vice-President, one of whom, at least, shall not be an inhabitant of the same State with themselves; they shall name in their ballots the person voted for as President, and in distinct ballots the person voted for as Vice-President, and they shall make distinct lists of all persons voted for as President, and of all persons voted for as Vice-President, and of the number of votes for each, which lists they shall sign and certify, and transmit sealed to the seat of government of the United States, directed to the President of the Senate;—the President of the Senate shall, in the presence of the Senate and House of Representatives, open all the certificates and the votes shall then be counted;—The person having the greatest number of votes for President, shall be the President, if such number be a majority of the whole number of Electors appointed; and if no person have such majority, then from the persons having the highest numbers not exceeding three on the list of those voted for as President, the House of Representatives shall choose immediately, by ballot, the President. But in choosing the President, the votes shall be taken by States, the representation from each State having one vote; a quorum for this purpose shall consist of a member or members from two-thirds of the States, and a majority of all the States shall be necessary to a choice. And if the House of Representatives shall not choose a President whenever the right of choice shall devolve upon them, before *the fourth day of March* next following, then the Vice-President shall act as President, as in the case of the death or other constitutional disability of the President.*—The person having the greatest number of votes as Vice-President, shall be the Vice-President, if such number be a majority of the whole number of Electors appointed; and if no person have a majority, then from the two highest numbers on the list, the Senate shall choose the Vice-President; a quorum for the purpose shall consist of two-thirds of the whole number of Senators, and a majority of the whole number shall be necessary to a choice.

*Superseded by Section 3 of the Twentieth Amendment.

But no person constitutionally ineligible to the office of President shall be eligible to that of Vice-President of the United States.

Unratified Amendment

Titles of Nobility Amendment (proposed by Congress May 1, 1810)

If any citizen of the United States shall accept, claim, receive or retain any title of nobility or honor or shall, without the consent of Congress, accept and retain any present, pension, office or emolument of any kind whatever, from any emperor, king, prince or foreign power, such person shall cease to be a citizen of the United States, and shall be incapable of holding any office of trust or profit under them, or either of them.

Unratified Amendment

Corwin Amendment (proposed by Congress March 2, 1861)

No amendment shall be made to the Constitution which will authorize or give to Congress the power to abolish or interfere, within any State, with the domestic institutions thereof, including that of persons held to labor or service by the laws of said State.

Amendment XIII [1865]

Section 1. Neither slavery nor involuntary servitude, except as a punishment for crime whereof the party shall have been duly convicted, shall exist within the United States, or any place subject to their jurisdiction.

Section 2. Congress shall have power to enforce this article by appropriate legislation.

Amendment XIV [1868]

Section 1. All persons born or naturalized in the United States, and subject to the jurisdiction thereof, are citizens of the United States and of the State wherein they reside. No State shall make or enforce any law which shall abridge the privileges or immunities of citizens of the United States; nor shall any State deprive any person of life, liberty, or property, without due process of law; nor deny to any person within its jurisdiction the equal protection of the laws.

Section 2. Representatives shall be apportioned among the several States according to their respective numbers, counting the whole number of persons in each State, excluding Indians not taxed. But when the right to vote at any election for the choice of electors for President and Vice-President of the United States, Representatives in Congress, the Executive and Judicial officers of a State, or the members of the Legislature thereof, is denied to any of the *male* inhabitants of such State, being *twenty-one* years of age and citizens of the United States, or in any way abridged, except for participation in rebellion, or other crime, the basis of representation therein shall be reduced in the proportion which the number of such *male* citizens shall bear to the whole number of *male* citizens *twenty-one* years of age in such State.

Section 3. No person shall be a Senator or Representative in Congress, or Elector of President and Vice-President, or hold any office, civil or military, under the United States, or under any State, who, having previously taken an oath, as a member of Congress, or as an officer of the United States, or as a member of any State legislature, or as an executive or judicial officer of any State, to support the Constitution of the United States, shall have engaged in insurrection or rebellion against the same, or given aid or comfort to the enemies thereof. Congress may, by a vote of two-thirds of each house, remove such disability.

Section 4. The validity of the public debt of the United States, authorized by law, including debts incurred for payment of pensions and bounties for services in suppressing insurrection or rebellion, shall not be questioned. But neither the United States nor any State shall assume or pay any debt or obligation incurred in aid of insurrection or rebellion against the United States, or any claim for the loss or emancipation of any slave; but all such debts, obligations, and claims shall be held illegal and void.

Section 5. The Congress shall have power to enforce, by appropriate legislation, the provisions of this article.

Amendment XV [1870]

Section 1. The right of citizens of the United States to vote shall not be denied or abridged by the United States or by any State on account of race, color, or previous condition of servitude—

Section 2. The Congress shall have power to enforce this article by appropriate legislation.

Amendment XVI [1913]

The Congress shall have power to lay and collect taxes on incomes, from whatever source derived, without apportionment among the several States, and without regard to any census or enumeration.

Amendment XVII [1913]

Section 1. The Senate of the United States shall be composed of two Senators from each State, elected by the people thereof, for six years; and each Senator shall have one vote. The electors in each State shall have the qualifications requisite for electors of [voters for] the most numerous branch of the State legislatures.

Section 2. When vacancies happen in the representation of any State in the Senate, the executive authority of such State shall issue writs of election to fill such vacancies: Provided, that the Legislature of any State may empower the executive thereof to make temporary appointments until the people fill the vacancies by election as the Legislature may direct.

Section 3. *This amendment shall not be so construed as to affect the election or term of any Senator chosen before it becomes valid as part of the Constitution.*

Amendment XVIII [1919; repealed 1933 by Amendment XXI]

Section 1. *After one year from the ratification of this article the manufacture, sale, or transportation of intoxicating liquors within, the importation thereof into, or the exportation thereof from the United States and all territory subject to the jurisdiction thereof, for beverage purposes, is hereby prohibited.*

Section 2. *The Congress and the several States shall have concurrent power to enforce this article by appropriate legislation.*

Section 3. *This article shall be inoperative unless it shall have been ratified as an amendment to the Constitution by the legislatures of the several States, as provided by the Constitution, within seven years from the date of the submission thereof to the States by the Congress.*

Amendment XIX [1920]

Section 1. The right of citizens of the United States to vote shall not be denied or abridged by the United States or by any State on account of sex.

Section 2. Congress shall have the power to enforce this article by appropriate legislation.

Unratified Amendment

Child Labor Amendment
(proposed by Congress June 2, 1924)

Section 1. The Congress shall have power to limit, regulate, and prohibit the labor of persons under eighteen years of age.

Section 2. The power of the several States is unimpaired by this article except that the operation of State laws shall be suspended to the extent necessary to give effect to legislation enacted by Congress.

Amendment XX [1933]

Section 1. The terms of the President and Vice-President shall end at noon on the 20th day of January, and the terms of Senators and Representatives at noon on the 3rd day of January, of the years in which such terms would have ended if this article had not been ratified; and the terms of their successors shall then begin.

Section 2. The Congress shall assemble at least once in every year, and such meeting shall begin at noon on the 3rd day of January, unless they shall by law appoint a different day.

Section 3. If, at the time fixed for the beginning of the term of the President, the President-elect shall have died, the Vice-President-elect shall become President. If a President shall not have been chosen before the time fixed for the beginning of his term, or if the President-elect shall have failed to qualify, then the Vice-President-elect shall act as President until a President shall have qualified; and the Congress may by law provide for the case wherein neither a President-elect nor a Vice-President-elect shall have qualified, declaring who shall then act as President, or the manner in which one who is to act shall be selected, and such person shall act accordingly until a President or Vice-President shall have qualified.

Section 4. The Congress may by law provide for the case of the death of any of the persons from whom the House of Representatives may choose a President whenever the right of choice shall have devolved upon them, and for the case of the death of any of the persons from whom the Senate may choose a Vice-President whenever the right of choice shall have devolved upon them.

Section 5. Sections 1 and 2 shall take effect on the 15th day of October following the ratification of this article.

Section 6. This article shall be inoperative unless it shall have been ratified as an amendment to the Constitution by the Legislatures of three-fourths of the several States within seven years from the date of its submission.

Amendment XXI [1933]

Section 1. The eighteenth article of amendment to the Constitution of the United States is hereby repealed.

Section 2. The transportation or importation into any State, Territory, or Possession of the United States for delivery or use therein of intoxicating liquors, in violation of the laws thereof, is hereby prohibited.

Section 3. This article shall be inoperative unless it shall have been ratified as an amendment to the Constitution by conventions in the several States, as provided in the Constitution, within seven years from the date of the submission thereof to the States by the Congress.

Amendment XXII [1951]

Section 1. No person shall be elected to the office of the President more than twice, and no person who has held the office of President, or acted as President, for more than two years of a term to which some other person was elected President shall be elected to the office of President more than once. But this article shall not apply to any person holding the office of President when this Article was proposed by the Congress, and shall not prevent any person who may be holding the office of President, or acting as President, during the term within which this Article becomes operative from holding the office of President or acting as President during the remainder of such term.

Section 2. This article shall be inoperative unless it shall have been ratified as an amendment to the Constitution by the legislatures of three-fourths of the several States within seven years from the date of its submission to the States by the Congress.

Amendment XXIII [1961]

Section 1. The District constituting the seat of Government of the United States shall appoint in such manner as the Congress may direct: A number of electors of President and Vice-President equal to the whole number of Senators and Representatives in Congress to which the District would be entitled if it were a State, but in no event more than the least populous State; they shall be in addition to those appointed by the States, but they shall be considered for the purposes of the election of President and Vice-President, to be electors appointed by a State; and they shall meet in the District and perform such duties as provided by the twelfth article of amendment.

Section 2. The Congress shall have the power to enforce this article by appropriate legislation.

Amendment XXIV [1964]

Section 1. The right of citizens of the United States to vote in any primary or other election for President or Vice-President, for electors for President or Vice-President, or for Senator or Representative in Congress, shall not be denied or abridged by the United States or any State by reason of failure to pay any poll tax or other tax.

Section 2. The Congress shall have the power to enforce this article by appropriate legislation.

Amendment XXV [1967]

Section 1. In case of the removal of the President from office or of his death or resignation, the Vice-President shall become President.

Section 2. Whenever there is a vacancy in the office of the Vice-President, the President shall nominate a Vice-President who shall take office upon confirmation by a majority vote of both Houses of Congress.

Section 3. Whenever the President transmits to the President pro tempore of the Senate and the Speaker of the House of Representatives his written declaration that he is unable to discharge the powers and duties of his office, and until he transmits to them a written declaration to the contrary, such powers and duties shall be discharged by the Vice-President as Acting President.

Section 4. Whenever the Vice-President and a majority of either the principal officers of the executive departments or of such other body as Congress may by law provide, transmit to the President pro tempore of the Senate and the Speaker of the House of Representatives their written declaration that the President is unable to discharge the powers and duties of his office, the Vice-President shall immediately assume the powers and duties of the office as Acting President.

Thereafter, when the President transmits to the President pro tempore of the Senate and the Speaker of the House of Representatives his written declaration that no inability exists, he shall resume the powers and duties of his office unless the Vice-President and a majority of either the principal officers of the executive department[s] or of such other body as Congress may by law provide, transmit within four days to the President pro tempore of the Senate and the Speaker of the House of Representatives their written declaration that the President is unable to discharge the powers and duties of his office. Thereupon Congress shall decide the issue, assembling within forty-eight hours for that purpose if not in session. If the Congress, within twenty-one days after receipt of the latter written declaration, or, if Congress is not in session, within twenty-one days after Congress is required to assemble, determines by two-thirds vote of both Houses that the President is unable to discharge the powers and duties of his office, the Vice-President shall continue to discharge the same as Acting President; otherwise, the President shall resume the powers and duties of his office.

Amendment XXVI [1971]

Section 1. The right of citizens of the United States, who are eighteen years of age or older, to vote shall not be denied or abridged by the United States or by any State on account of age.

Section 2. The Congress shall have power to enforce this article by appropriate legislation.

Unratified Amendment

Equal Rights Amendment (proposed by Congress March 22, 1972; seven-year deadline for ratification extended to June 30, 1982)

Section 1. *Equality of rights under the law shall not be denied or abridged by the United States or by any State on account of sex.*

Section 2. *The Congress shall have the power to enforce, by appropriate legislation, the provisions of this article.*

Section 3. *This amendment shall take effect two years after the date of ratification.*

Unratified Amendment

District of Columbia Statehood Amendment (proposed by Congress August 22, 1978)

Section 1. *For purposes of representation in the Congress, election of the President and Vice President, and article V of this Constitution, the District constituting the seat of government of the United States shall be treated as though it were a State.*

Section 2. *The exercise of the rights and powers conferred under this article shall be by the people of the District constituting the seat of government, and as shall be provided by Congress.*

Section 3. *The twenty-third article of amendment to the Constitution of the United States is hereby repealed.*

Section 4. *This article shall be inoperative, unless it shall have been ratified as an amendment to the Constitution by* the legislatures of three-fourths of the several states within seven years from the date of its submission.

Amendment XXVII [1992]

No law varying the compensation for the services of the Senators and Representatives, shall take effect, until an election of Representatives shall have intervened.

Appendix

The American Nation

Admission of States into the Union

State	Date of Admission	State	Date of Admission	State	Date of Admission
1. Delaware	December 7, 1787	18. Louisiana	April 30, 1812	35. West Virginia	June 20, 1863
2. Pennsylvania	December 12, 1787	19. Indiana	December 11, 1816	36. Nevada	October 31, 1864
3. New Jersey	December 18, 1787	20. Mississippi	December 10, 1817	37. Nebraska	March 1, 1867
4. Georgia	January 2, 1788	21. Illinois	December 3, 1818	38. Colorado	August 1, 1876
5. Connecticut	January 9, 1788	22. Alabama	December 14, 1819	39. North Dakota	November 2, 1889
6. Massachusetts	February 6, 1788	23. Maine	March 15, 1820	40. South Dakota	November 2, 1889
7. Maryland	April 28, 1788	24. Missouri	August 10, 1821	41. Montana	November 8, 1889
8. South Carolina	May 23, 1788	25. Arkansas	June 15, 1836	42. Washington	November 11, 1889
9. New Hampshire	June 21, 1788	26. Michigan	January 26, 1837	43. Idaho	July 3, 1890
10. Virginia	June 25, 1788	27. Florida	March 3, 1845	44. Wyoming	July 10, 1890
11. New York	July 26, 1788	28. Texas	December 29, 1845	45. Utah	January 4, 1896
12. North Carolina	November 21, 1789	29. Iowa	December 28, 1846	46. Oklahoma	November 16, 1907
13. Rhode Island	May 29, 1790	30. Wisconsin	May 29, 1848	47. New Mexico	January 6, 1912
14. Vermont	March 4, 1791	31. California	September 9, 1850	48. Arizona	February 14, 1912
15. Kentucky	June 1, 1792	32. Minnesota	May 11, 1858	49. Alaska	January 3, 1959
16. Tennessee	June 1, 1796	33. Oregon	February 14, 1859	50. Hawaii	August 21, 1959
17. Ohio	March 1, 1803	34. Kansas	January 29, 1861		

Territorial Expansion

Territory	Date Acquired	Square Miles	How Acquired
Original states and territories	1783	888,685	Treaty of Paris
Louisiana Purchase	1803	827,192	Purchased from France
Florida	1819	72,003	Adams-Onís Treaty
Texas	1845	390,143	Annexation of independent country
Oregon	1846	285,580	Oregon Boundary Treaty
Mexican cession	1848	529,017	Treaty of Guadalupe Hidalgo
Gadsden Purchase	1853	29,640	Purchased from Mexico
Midway Islands	1867	2	Annexation of uninhabited islands
Alaska	1867	589,757	Purchased from Russia
Hawaii	1898	6,450	Annexation of independent country
Wake Island	1898	3	Annexation of uninhabited island
Puerto Rico	1899	3,435	Treaty of Paris
Guam	1899	212	Treaty of Paris
The Philippines	1899–1946	115,600	Treaty of Paris; granted independence

Territory	Date Acquired	Square Miles	How Acquired
American Samoa	1900	76	Treaty with Germany and Great Britain
Panama Canal Zone	1904–1978	553	Hay–Bunau-Varilla Treaty
U.S. Virgin Islands	1917	133	Purchased from Denmark
Trust Territory of the Pacific Islands*	1947–1900	717	United Nations Trusteeship

*A number of these islands have recently been granted independence: Federated States of Micronesia, 1990; Republic of the Marshall Islands, 1991; Republic of Palau, 1994. The Northern Mariana Islands is a commonwealth of the United States.

Presidential Elections

Year	Candidates	Parties	Percentage of Popular Vote*	Electoral Vote	Percentage of Voter Participation
1789	**George Washington**	No party designations		69	
	John Adams†			34	
	Other candidates			35	
1792	**George Washington**	No party designations		132	
	John Adams			77	
	George Clinton			50	
	Other candidates			5	
1796	**John Adams**	Federalist		71	
	Thomas Jefferson	Democratic-Republican		68	
	Thomas Pinckney	Federalist		59	
	Aaron Burr	Democratic-Republican		30	
	Other candidates			48	
1800	**Thomas Jefferson**	Democratic-Republican		73	
	Aaron Burr	Democratic-Republican		73	
	John Adams	Federalist		65	
	Charles C. Pinckney	Federalist		64	
	John Jay	Federalist		1	
1804	**Thomas Jefferson**	Democratic-Republican		162	
	Charles C. Pinckney	Federalist		14	
1808	**James Madison**	Democratic-Republican		122	
	Charles C. Pinckney	Federalist		47	
	George Clinton	Democratic-Republican		6	
1812	**James Madison**	Democratic-Republican		128	
	DeWitt Clinton	Federalist		89	
1816	**James Monroe**	Democratic-Republican		183	
	Rufus King	Federalist		34	
1820	**James Monroe**	Democratic-Republican		231	
	John Quincy Adams	Independent Republican		1	
1824	**John Quincy Adams**	Democratic-Republican	30.5	84	26.9
	Andrew Jackson	Democratic-Republican	43.1	99	
	Henry Clay	Democratic-Republican	13.2	37	
	William H. Crawford	Democratic-Republican	13.1	41	
1828	**Andrew Jackson**	Democratic	56.0	178	57.6
	John Quincy Adams	National Republican	44.0	83	

*Prior to 1824, most presidential electors were chosen by state legislators rather than by popular vote. For elections after 1824, candidates receiving less than 1.0 percent of the popular vote have been omitted from this chart. Hence the popular vote does not total 100 percent for all elections.

†Before the Twelfth Amendment was passed in 1804, the Electoral College voted for two presidential candidates; the runner-up became vice president.

Year	Candidates	Parties	Percentage of Popular Vote	Electoral Vote	Percentage of Voter Participation
1832	**Andrew Jackson**	Democratic	54.5	219	55.4
	Henry Clay	National Republican	37.5	49	
	William Wirt	Anti-Masonic	8.0	7	
	John Floyd	Democratic	‡	11	
1836	**Martin Van Buren**	Democratic	50.9	170	57.8
	William H. Harrison	Whig		73	
	Hugh L. White	Whig		26	
	Daniel Webster	Whig	49.1	14	
	W. P. Mangum	Whig		11	
1840	**William H. Harrison**	Whig	53.1	234	80.2
	Martin Van Buren	Democratic	46.9	60	
1844	**James K. Polk**	Democratic	49.6	170	78.9
	Henry Clay	Whig	48.1	105	
	James G. Birney	Liberty	2.3		
1848	**Zachary Taylor**	Whig	47.4	163	72.7
	Lewis Cass	Democratic	42.5	127	
	Martin Van Buren	Free Soil	10.1		
1852	**Franklin Pierce**	Democratic	50.9	254	69.6
	Winfield Scott	Whig	44.1	42	
	John P. Hale	Free Soil	5.0		
1856	**James Buchanan**	Democratic	45.3	174	78.9
	John C. Frémont	Republican	33.1	114	
	Millard Fillmore	American	21.6	8	
1860	**Abraham Lincoln**	Republican	39.8	180	81.2
	Stephen A. Douglas	Democratic	29.5	12	
	John C. Breckinridge	Democratic	18.1	72	
	John Bell	Constitutional Union	12.6	39	
1864	**Abraham Lincoln**	Republican	55.0	212	73.8
	George B. McClellan	Democratic	45.0	21	
1868	**Ulysses S. Grant**	Republican	52.7	214	78.1
	Horatio Seymour	Democratic	47.3	80	
1872	**Ulysses S. Grant**	Republican	55.6	286	71.3
	Horace Greeley	Democratic	43.9		
1876	**Rutherford B. Hayes**	Republican	48.0	185	81.8
	Samuel J. Tilden	Democratic	51.0	184	
1880	**James A. Garfield**	Republican	48.5	214	79.4
	Winfield S. Hancock	Democratic	48.1	155	
	James B. Weaver	Greenback-Labor	3.4		
1884	**Grover Cleveland**	Democratic	48.5	219	77.5
	James G. Blaine	Republican	48.2	182	
	Benjamin F. Butler	Greenback-Labor	1.8		
	John P. St. John	Prohibition	1.5		
1888	**Benjamin Harrison**	Republican	47.9	233	79.3
	Grover Cleveland	Democratic	48.6	168	
	Clinton P. Fisk	Prohibition	2.2		
	Anson J. Streeter	Union Labor	1.3		
1892	**Grover Cleveland**	Democratic	46.1	277	74.7
	Benjamin Harrison	Republican	43.0	145	
	James B. Weaver	People's	8.5	22	
	John Bidwell	Prohibition	2.2		

‡Independent Democrat John Floyd received the 11 electoral votes of South Carolina; that state's presidential electors were still chosen by its legislature, not by popular vote.

Year	Candidates	Parties	Percentage of Popular Vote	Electoral Vote	Percentage of Voter Participation
1896	**William McKinley**	Republican	51.1	271	79.3
	William J. Bryan	Democratic	47.7	176	
1900	**William McKinley**	Republican	51.7	292	73.2
	William J. Bryan	Democratic; Populist	45.5	155	
	John C. Wooley	Prohibition	1.5		
1904	**Theodore Roosevelt**	Republican	57.4	336	65.2
	Alton B. Parker	Democratic	37.6	140	
	Eugene V. Debs	Socialist	3.0		
	Silas C. Swallow	Prohibition	1.9		
1908	**William H. Taft**	Republican	51.6	321	65.4
	William J. Bryan	Democratic	43.1	162	
	Eugene V. Debs	Socialist	2.8		
	Eugene W. Chafin	Prohibition	1.7		
1912	**Woodrow Wilson**	Democratic	41.9	435	58.8
	Theodore Roosevelt	Progressive	27.4	88	
	William H. Taft	Republican	23.2	8	
	Eugene V. Debs	Socialist	6.0		
	Eugene W. Chafin	Prohibition	1.4		
1916	**Woodrow Wilson**	Democratic	49.4	277	61.6
	Charles E. Hughes	Republican	46.2	254	
	A. L. Benson	Socialist	3.2		
	J. Frank Hanly	Prohibition	1.2		
1920	**Warren G. Harding**	Republican	60.4	404	49.2
	James M. Cox	Democratic	34.2	127	
	Eugene V. Debs	Socialist	3.4		
	P. P. Christensen	Farmer-Labor	1.0		
1924	**Calvin Coolidge**	Republican	54.0	382	48.9
	John W. Davis	Democratic	28.8	136	
	Robert M. La Follette	Progressive	16.6	13	
1928	**Herbert C. Hoover**	Republican	58.2	444	56.9
	Alfred E. Smith	Democratic	40.9	87	
1932	**Franklin D. Roosevelt**	Democratic	57.4	472	56.9
	Herbert C. Hoover	Republican	39.7	59	
	Norman Thomas	Socialist	2.2		
1936	**Franklin D. Roosevelt**	Democratic	60.8	523	61.0
	Alfred M. Landon	Republican	36.5	8	
	William Lemke	Union	1.9		
1940	**Franklin D. Roosevelt**	Democratic	54.8	449	62.5
	Wendell L. Willkie	Republican	44.8	82	
1944	**Franklin D. Roosevelt**	Democratic	53.5	432	55.9
	Thomas E. Dewey	Republican	46.0	99	
1948	**Harry S Truman**	Democratic	49.6	303	53.0
	Thomas E. Dewey	Republican	45.1	189	
	J. Strom Thurmond	States' Rights	2.4		
	Henry Wallace	Progressive	2.4		
1952	**Dwight D. Eisenhower**	Republican	55.1	442	63.3
	Adlai E. Stevenson	Democratic	44.4	89	
1956	**Dwight D. Eisenhower**	Republican	57.6	457	60.6
	Adlai E. Stevenson	Democratic	42.1	73	

Year	Candidates	Parties	Percentage of Popular Vote	Electoral Vote	Percentage of Voter Participation
1960	**John F. Kennedy**	Democratic	49.7	303	62.8
	Richard M. Nixon	Republican	49.5	219	
1964	**Lyndon B. Johnson**	Democratic	61.1	486	61.9
	Barry M. Goldwater	Republican	38.5	52	
1968	**Richard M. Nixon**	Republican	43.4	301	60.8
	Hubert H. Humphrey	Democratic	42.7	191	
	George C. Wallace	American Independent	13.5	46	
1972	**Richard M. Nixon**	Republican	60.7	520	55.2
	George S. McGovern	Democratic	37.5	17	
	John G. Schmitz	American	1.4		
1976	**Jimmy Carter**	Democratic	50.1	297	53.6
	Gerald R. Ford	Republican	48.0	240	
1980	**Ronald W. Reagan**	Republican	50.7	489	52.6
	Jimmy Carter	Democratic	41.0	49	
	John B. Anderson	Independent	6.6	0	
	Ed Clark	Libertarian	1.1		
1984	**Ronald W. Reagan**	Republican	58.4	525	53.1
	Walter F. Mondale	Democratic	41.6	13	
1988	**George H. W. Bush**	Republican	53.4	426	50.2
	Michael Dukakis	Democratic	45.6	111**	
1992	**Bill Clinton**	Democratic	43.7	370	55.2
	George H. W. Bush	Republican	38.0	168	
	H. Ross Perot	Independent	19.0	0	
1996	**Bill Clinton**	Democratic	49	379	49.1
	Robert J. Dole	Republican	41	159	
	H. Ross Perot	Reform	8	0	
2000	**George W. Bush**	Republican	47.8	271	51.3
	Albert Gore	Democratic	48.4	267	
	Ralph Nader	Green	2.7	0	
2004	**George W. Bush**	Republican	50.7	286	55.3
	John Kerry	Democratic	48.3	252	
2008	**Barack Obama**	Democratic	52.9	365	56.8
	John McCain	Republican	45.7	173	

**One Dukakis elector cast a vote for Lloyd Bentsen.

Supreme Court Justices

Name	Terms of Service	Appointed by	Name	Terms of Service	Appointed by
John Jay,* N.Y.	1789–1795	Washington	**Oliver Ellsworth**, Conn.	1796–1800	Washington
James Wilson, Pa.	1789–1798	Washington	Bushrod Washington, Va.	1799–1829	J. Adams
John Rutledge, S.C.	1790–1791	Washington	Alfred Moore, N.C.	1800–1804	J. Adams
William Cushing, Mass.	1790–1810	Washington	**John Marshall**, Va.	1801–1835	J. Adams
John Blair, Va.	1790–1796	Washington	William Johnson, S.C.	1804–1834	Jefferson
James Iredell, N.C.	1790–1799	Washington	Brockholst Livingston, N.Y.	1807–1823	Jefferson
Thomas Johnson, Md.	1792–1793	Washington	Thomas Todd, Ky.	1807–1826	Jefferson
William Paterson, N.J.	1793–1806	Washington	Gabriel Duvall, Md.	1811–1835	Madison
John Rutledge, S.C.	1795	Washington	Joseph Story, Mass.	1812–1845	Madison
Samuel Chase, Md.	1796–1811	Washington	Smith Thompson, N.Y.	1823–1843	Monroe

Name	Terms of Service	Appointed by	Name	Terms of Service	Appointed by
Robert Trimble, Ky.	1826–1828	J. Q. Adams	John H. Clarke, Ohio	1916–1922	Wilson
John McLean, Ohio	1830–1861	Jackson	**William H. Taft**, Conn.	1921–1930	Harding
Henry Baldwin, Pa.	1830–1844	Jackson	George Sutherland, Utah	1922–1938	Harding
James M. Wayne, Ga.	1835–1867	Jackson	Pierce Butler, Minn.	1923–1939	Harding
Roger B. Taney, Md.	1836–1864	Jackson	Edward T. Sanford, Tenn.	1923–1930	Harding
Philip P. Barbour, Va.	1836–1841	Jackson	Harlan F. Stone, N.Y.	1925–1941	Coolidge
John Cartron, Tenn.	1837–1865	Van Buren	**Charles E. Hughes**, N.Y.	1930–1941	Hoover
John McKinley, Ala.	1838–1852	Van Buren	Owen J. Roberts, Pa.	1930–1945	Hoover
Peter V. Daniel, Va.	1842–1860	Van Buren	Benjamin N. Cardozo, N.Y.	1932–1938	Hoover
Samuel Nelson, N.Y.	1845–1872	Tyler	Hugo L. Black, Ala.	1937–1971	F. Roosevelt
Levi Woodbury, N.H.	1845–1851	Polk	Stanley F. Reed, Ky.	1938–1957	F. Roosevelt
Robert C. Grier, Pa.	1846–1870	Polk	Felix Frankfurter, Mass.	1939–1962	F. Roosevelt
Benjamin R. Curtis, Mass.	1851–1857	Fillmore	William O. Douglas, Conn.	1939–1975	F. Roosevelt
John A. Campbell, Ala.	1853–1861	Pierce	Frank Murphy, Mich.	1940–1949	F. Roosevelt
Nathan Clifford, Me.	1858–1881	Buchanan	**Harlan F. Stone**, N.Y.	1941–1946	F. Roosevelt
Noah H. Swayne, Ohio	1862–1881	Lincoln	James R. Byrnes, S.C.	1941–1942	F. Roosevelt
Samuel F. Miller, Iowa	1862–1890	Lincoln	Robert H. Jackson, N.Y.	1941–1954	F. Roosevelt
David Davis, Ill.	1862–1877	Lincoln	Wiley B. Rutledge, Iowa	1943–1949	F. Roosevelt
Stephen J. Field, Cal.	1863–1897	Lincoln	Harold H. Burton, Ohio	1945–1958	Truman
Salmon P. Chase, Ohio	1864–1873	Lincoln	**Frederick M. Vinson**, Ky.	1946–1953	Truman
William Strong, Pa.	1870–1880	Grant	Tom C. Clark, Texas	1949–1967	Truman
Joseph P. Bradley, N.J.	1870–1892	Grant	Sherman Minton, Ind.	1949–1956	Truman
Ward Hunt, N.Y.	1873–1882	Grant	**Earl Warren**, Cal.	1953–1969	Eisenhower
Morrison R. Waite, Ohio	1874–1888	Grant	John Marshall Harlan, N.Y.	1955–1971	Eisenhower
John M. Harlan, Ky.	1877–1911	Hayes	William J. Brennan Jr., N.J.	1956–1990	Eisenhower
William B. Woods, Ga.	1881–1887	Hayes	Charles E. Whittaker, Mo.	1957–1962	Eisenhower
Stanley Matthews, Ohio	1881–1889	Garfield	Potter Stewart, Ohio	1958–1981	Eisenhower
Horace Gray, Mass.	1882–1902	Arthur	Bryon R. White, Colo.	1962–1993	Kennedy
Samuel Blatchford, N.Y.	1882–1893	Arthur	Arthur J. Goldberg, Ill.	1962–1965	Kennedy
Lucius Q. C. Lamar, Miss.	1888–1893	Cleveland	Abe Fortas, Tenn.	1965–1969	Johnson
Melville W. Fuller, Ill.	1888–1910	Cleveland	Thurgood Marshall, Md.	1967–1991	Johnson
David J. Brewer, Kan.	1890–1910	B. Harrison	**Warren E. Burger**, Minn.	1969–1986	Nixon
Henry B. Brown, Mich.	1891–1906	B. Harrison	Harry A. Blackmun, Minn.	1970–1994	Nixon
George Shiras Jr., Pa.	1892–1903	B. Harrison	Lewis F. Powell Jr., Va.	1971–1987	Nixon
Howell E. Jackson, Tenn.	1893–1895	B. Harrison	William H. Rehnquist, Ill.	1971–1986	Nixon
Edward D. White, La.	1894–1910	Cleveland	John Paul Stevens, Ill.	1975–2010	Ford
Rufus W. Peckham, N.Y.	1896–1909	Cleveland	Sandra Day O'Connor, Ariz.	1981–2006	Reagan
Joseph McKenna, Cal.	1898–1925	McKinley	**William H. Rehnquist**, Va.	1986–2005	Reagan
Oliver W. Holmes, Mass.	1902–1932	T. Roosevelt	Antonin Scalia, Va.	1986–	Reagan
William R. Day, Ohio	1903–1922	T. Roosevelt	Anthony M. Kennedy, Cal.	1988–	Reagan
William H. Moody, Mass.	1906–1910	T. Roosevelt	David H. Souter, N.H.	1990–2009	G. H. W. Bush
Horace H. Lurton, Tenn.	1910–1914	Taft	Clarence Thomas, Ga.	1991–	G. H. W. Bush
Charles E. Hughes, N.Y.	1910–1916	Taft	Ruth Bader Ginsburg, N.Y.	1993–	Clinton
Edward D. White, La.	1910–1921	Taft	Stephen G. Breyer, Mass.	1994–	Clinton
Willis Van Devanter, Wy.	1911–1937	Taft	**John G. Roberts, Jr.**, Md.	2005–	G. W. Bush
Joseph R. Lamar, Ga.	1911–1916	Taft	Samuel A. Alito Jr., N.J.	2006–	G. W. Bush
Mahlon Pitney, N.J.	1912–1922	Taft	Sonia Sotomayor, N.Y.	2009–	Obama
James C. McReynolds, Tenn.	1914–1941	Wilson	Elena Kagan, N.Y.	2010–	Obama
Louis D. Brandeis, Mass.	1916–1939	Wilson			

*Chief Justices are printed in bold type.

The American People: a Demographic Survey

A Demographic Profile of the American People

Year	Life Expectancy at Birth White	Life Expectancy at Birth Black	Median Age at First Marriage Men	Median Age at First Marriage Women	Number of Children under 5 (per 1,000 Women Aged 20–44)	Percentage of Persons (age 16+) in Paid Workforce Men	Percentage of Persons (age 16+) in Paid Workforce Women	Percentage of Paid Workers Who Are Women
1820					1,295		6.2	7.3
1830					1,145		6.4	7.4
1840					1,085		8.4	9.6
1850					923		10.1	10.8
1860					929		9.7	10.2
1870					839		13.7	14.8
1880					822		14.7	15.2
1890			26.1	22.0	716	84.3	18.2	17.0
1900	47.6	33.0	25.9	21.9	688	85.7	20.0	18.1
1910	50.3	35.6	25.1	21.6	643	85.1	24.8	20.0
1920	54.9	45.3	24.6	21.2	604	84.6	22.7	20.4
1930	61.4	48.1	24.3	21.3	511	82.1	23.6	21.9
1940	64.2	53.1	24.3	21.5	429	79.1	25.8	24.6
1950	69.1	60.8	22.8	20.3	589	81.6	29.9	27.8
1960	70.6	63.6	22.8	20.3	737	80.4	35.7	32.3
1970	71.7	65.3	22.5	20.6	530	79.7	41.4	38.0
1980	74.4	68.1	24.7	22.0	440	77.4	51.5	42.6
1990	76.1	69.1	26.1	23.9	377	76.4	57.4	45.2
2000	77.6	71.7	26.7	25.1	365	74.8	58.9	46.3
2010*	78.9	73.8	27.7	26.0		73.0	59.5	46.5

SOURCE: U.S. Bureau of the Census, *Historical Statistics of the United States, Colonial Times to 1970* (1975); *Statistical Abstract of the United States, 2001; Statistical Abstract of the United States, 2010.*
*Or latest available data.

Birth Rate, 1820–2010

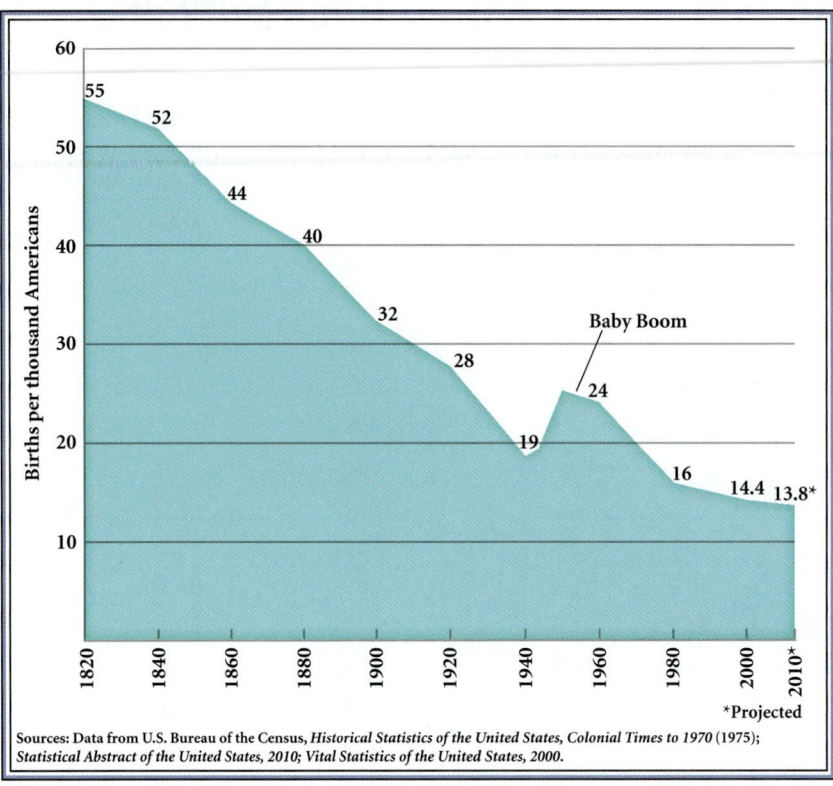

Sources: Data from U.S. Bureau of the Census, *Historical Statistics of the United States, Colonial Times to 1970* (1975); *Statistical Abstract of the United States, 2010; Vital Statistics of the United States, 2000.*

Death Rate, 1900–2010

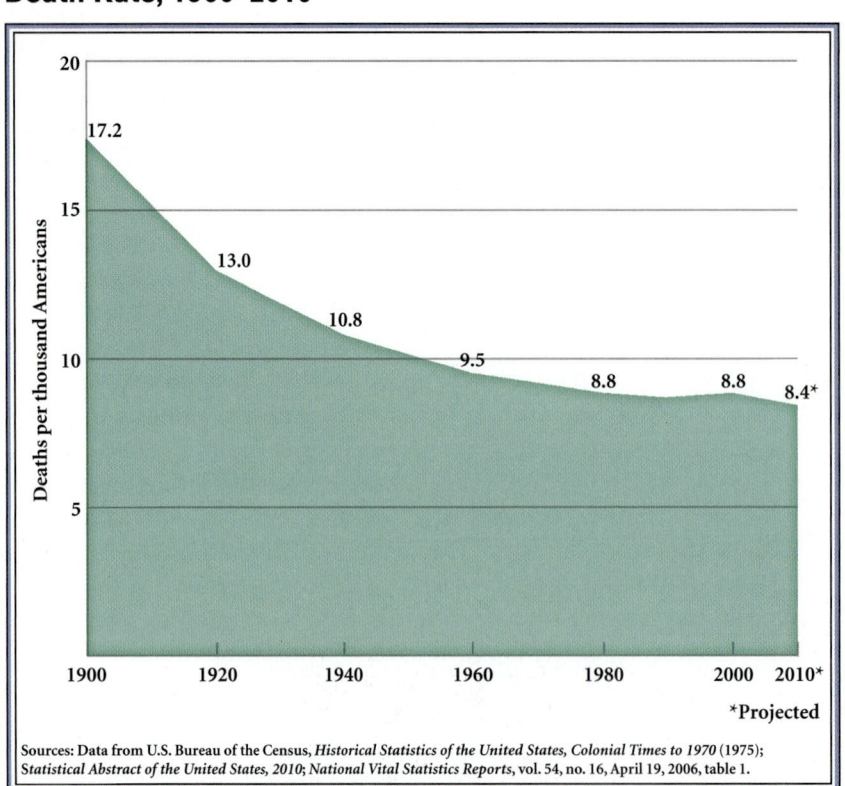

Sources: Data from U.S. Bureau of the Census, *Historical Statistics of the United States, Colonial Times to 1970* (1975); *Statistical Abstract of the United States, 2010; National Vital Statistics Reports,* vol. 54, no. 16, April 19, 2006, table 1.

Life Expectancy (at Birth), 1900–2010

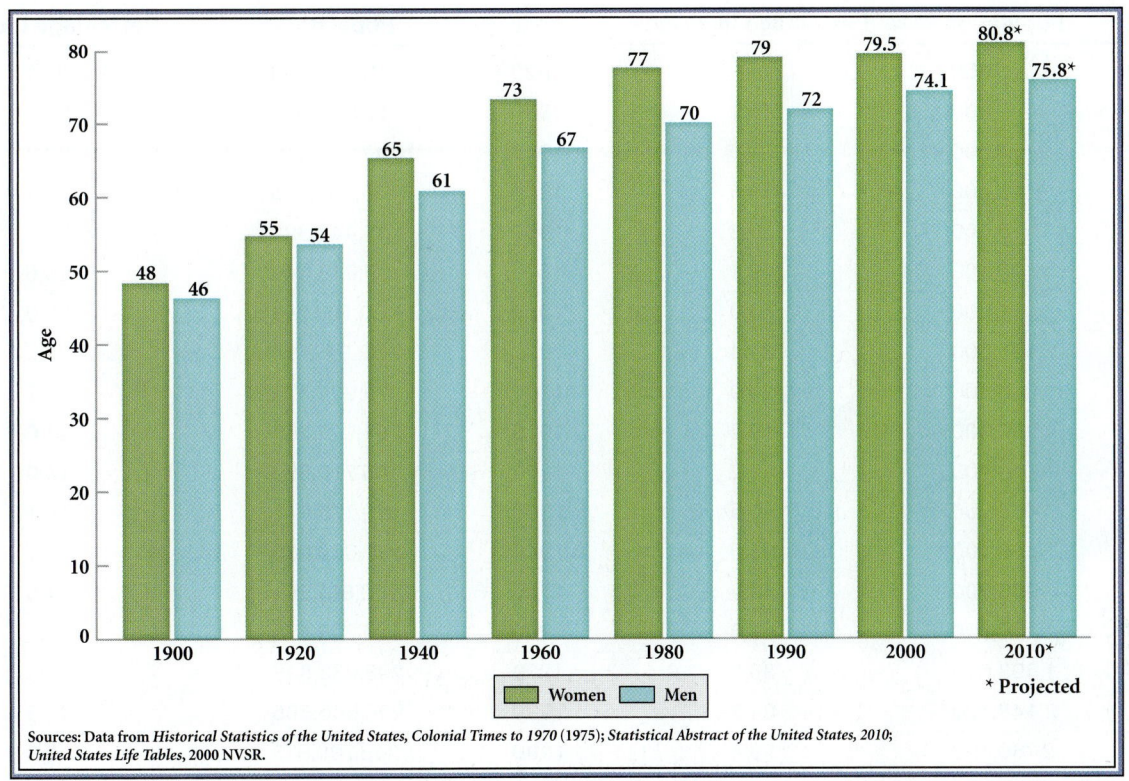

Sources: Data from *Historical Statistics of the United States, Colonial Times to 1970* (1975); *Statistical Abstract of the United States, 2010*; *United States Life Tables*, 2000 NVSR.

The Aging of the U.S. Population, 1850–2010

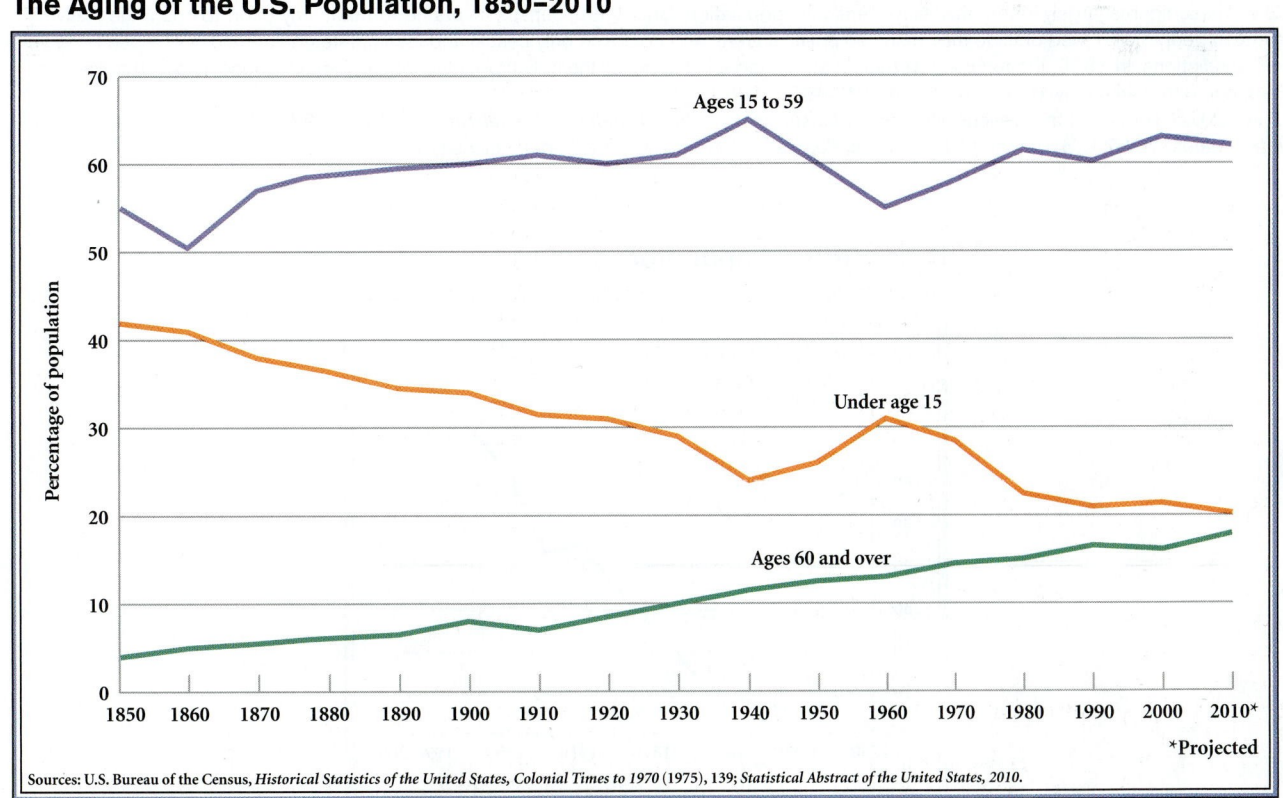

Sources: U.S. Bureau of the Census, *Historical Statistics of the United States, Colonial Times to 1970* (1975), 139; *Statistical Abstract of the United States, 2010*.

Enumerated Population*

Year	Population	Percentage Increase	Year	Population	Percentage Increase
1610	350	–	1820	9,638,453	33.1
1620	2,300	557.1	1830	12,866,020	33.5
1630	4,600	100.0	1840	17,069,453	32.7
1640	26,600	478.3	1850	23,191,876	35.9
1650	50,400	90.8	1860	31,443,321	35.6
1660	75,100	49.0	1870	39,818,449	26.6
1670	111,900	49.0	1880	50,155,783	26.0
1680	151,500	35.4	1890	62,947,714	25.5
1690	210,400	38.9	1900	75,994,575	20.7
1700	250,900	19.2	1910	91,972,266	21.0
1710	331,700	32.2	1920	105,710,620	14.9
1720	466,200	40.5	1930	122,775,046	16.1
1730	629,400	35.0	1940	131,669,275	7.2
1740	905,600	43.9	1950	150,697,361	14.5
1750	1,170,800	29.3	1960	179,323,175	19.0
1760	1,593,600	36.1	1970	203,235,298	13.3
1770	2,148,100	34.8	1980	226,545,805	11.5
1780	2,780,400	29.4	1990	248,709,873	9.8
1790	3,929,214	41.3	2000	281,421,906	13.2
1800	5,308,483	35.1	2010	311,000,000 (proj.)	10.5
1810	7,239,881	36.4			

*Note: These figures largely ignore the Native American population. Until 1890, census takers never made any effort to count the Native American people who lived outside their reserved political areas and compiled only casual and incomplete enumerations of those living within their jurisdictions. In 1890, the federal government attempted a full count of the Indian population: The Census found 125,719 Indians in 1890, compared with only 12,543 in 1870 and 33,985 in 1880.

SOURCES: U.S. Bureau of the Census, *Historical Statistics of the United States, Colonial Times to 1970* (1975); *Statistical Abstract of the United States, 2010*; U.S. Bureau of the Census, Population Finder, http://factfinder.census.gov.

Urban/Rural Population

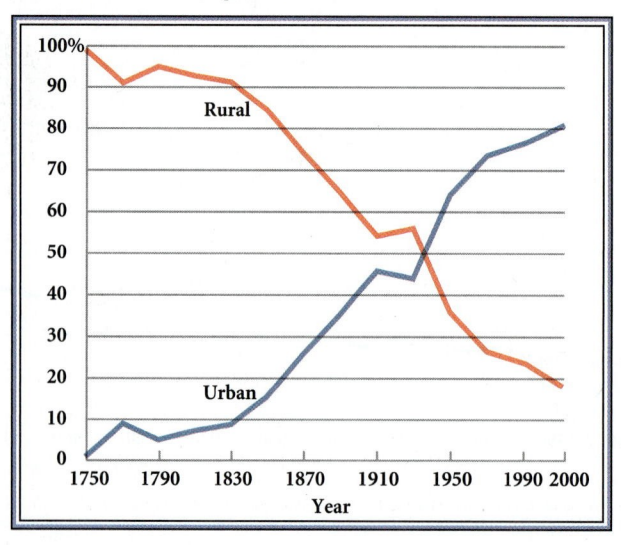

The Ten Largest Cities by Population, 1700–2008

		City	Population			City	Population
1700	1.	Boston	6,700	1930	1.	New York	6,930,446
	2.	New York	4,937*		2.	Chicago	3,376,438
	3.	Philadelphia	4,400†		3.	Philadelphia	1,950,961
1790	1.	Philadelphia	42,520		4.	Detroit	1,568,662
	2.	New York	33,131		5.	Los Angeles	1,238,048
	3.	Boston	18,038		6.	Cleveland	900,429
	4.	Charleston, S.C.	16,359		7.	St. Louis	821,960
	5.	Baltimore	13,503		8.	Baltimore	804,874
	6.	Salem, Mass.	7,921		9.	Boston	781,188
	7.	Newport, R.I.	6,716		10.	Pittsburgh	669,817
	8.	Providence, R.I.	6,380	1950	1.	New York	7,891,957
	9.	Marblehead, Mass.	5,661		2.	Chicago	3,620,962
	10.	Portsmouth, N.H.	4,720		3.	Philadelphia	2,071,605
1830	1.	New York	197,112		4.	Los Angeles	1,970,358
	2.	Philadelphia	161,410		5.	Detroit	1,849,568
	3.	Baltimore	80,620		6.	Baltimore	949,708
	4.	Boston	61,392		7.	Cleveland	914,808
	5.	Charleston, S.C.	30,289		8.	St. Louis	856,796
	6.	New Orleans	29,737		9.	Washington, D.C.	802,178
	7.	Cincinnati	24,831		10.	Boston	801,444
	8.	Albany, N.Y.	24,209	1970	1.	New York	7,895,563
	9.	Brooklyn, N.Y.	20,535		2.	Chicago	3,369,357
	10.	Washington, D.C.	18,826		3.	Los Angeles	2,811,801
1850	1.	New York	515,547		4.	Philadelphia	1,949,996
	2.	Philadelphia	340,045		5.	Detroit	1,514,063
	3.	Baltimore	169,054		6.	Houston	1,233,535
	4.	Boston	136,881		7.	Baltimore	905,787
	5.	New Orleans	116,375		8.	Dallas	844,401
	6.	Cincinnati	115,435		9.	Washington, D.C.	756,668
	7.	Brooklyn, N.Y.	96,838		10.	Cleveland	750,879
	8.	St. Louis	77,860	1990	1.	New York	7,322,564
	9.	Albany, N.Y.	50,763		2.	Los Angeles	3,485,398
	10.	Pittsburgh	46,601		3.	Chicago	2,783,726
1870	1.	New York	942,292		4.	Houston	1,630,553
	2.	Philadelphia	674,022		5.	Philadelphia	1,585,577
	3.	Brooklyn, N.Y.	419,921‡		6.	San Diego	1,110,549
	4.	St. Louis	310,864		7.	Detroit	1,027,974
	5.	Chicago	298,977		8.	Dallas	1,006,877
	6.	Baltimore	267,354		9.	Phoenix	983,403
	7.	Boston	250,526		10.	San Antonio	935,933
	8.	Cincinnati	216,239	2000	1.	New York	8,008,278
	9.	New Orleans	191,418		2.	Los Angeles	3,694,820
	10.	San Francisco	149,473		3.	Chicago	2,896,016
1910	1.	New York	4,766,883		4.	Houston	1,953,631
	2.	Chicago	2,185,283		5.	Philadelphia	1,517,550
	3.	Philadelphia	1,549,008		6.	Phoenix	1,321,045
	4.	St. Louis	687,029		7.	San Diego	1,223,400
	5.	Boston	670,585		8.	Dallas	1,188,580
	6.	Cleveland	560,663		9.	San Antonio	1,144,646
	7.	Baltimore	558,485		10.	Detroit	951,270
	8.	Pittsburgh	533,905	2008	1.	New York	8,364,000
	9.	Detroit	465,766	(est.)	2.	Los Angeles	3,834,000
	10.	Buffalo	423,715		3.	Chicago	2,853,000

*Figure from a census taken in 1698.
†Philadelphia figures include suburbs.
‡Annexed to New York in 1898.

	City	Population			City	Population
4.	Houston	2,242,000		8.	Dallas	1,280,000
5.	Phoenix	1,568,000		9.	San Diego	1,279,000
6.	Philadelphia	1,447,000		10.	San Jose	948,000
7.	San Antonio	1,351,000				

SOURCE: U.S. Census data.

Percentage of Total Population Living in Metropolitan Areas, and in Their Central Cities and Suburbs

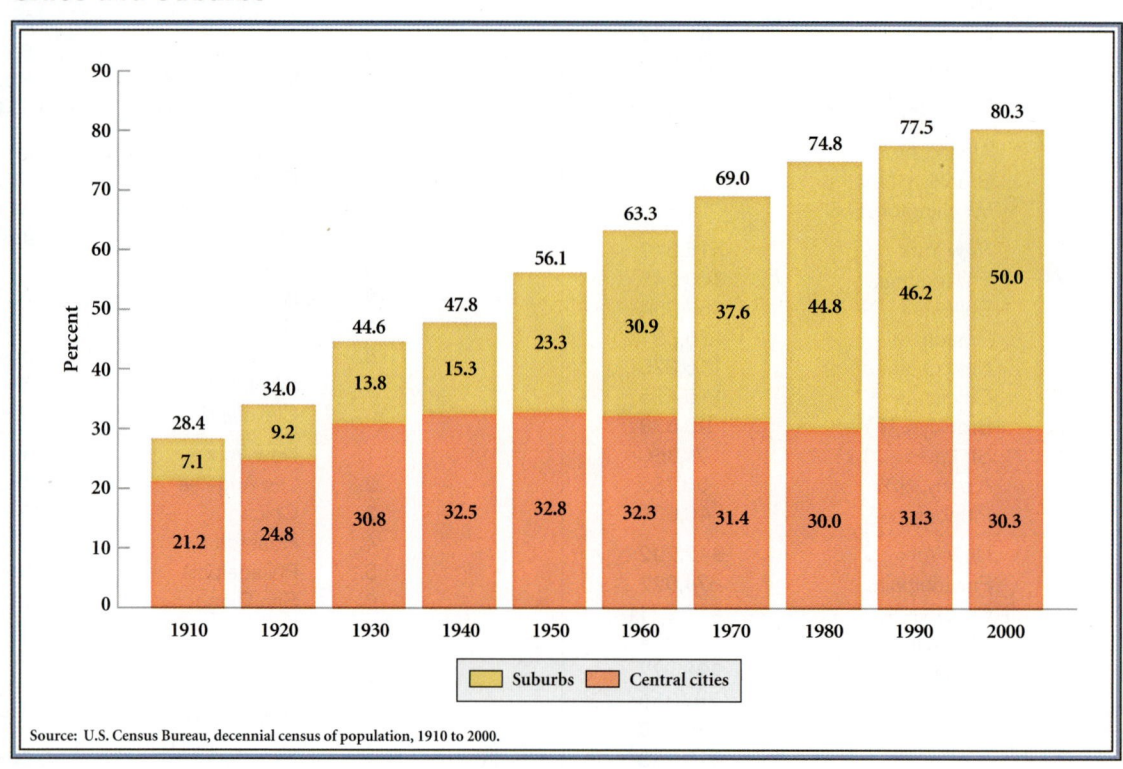

Source: U.S. Census Bureau, decennial census of population, 1910 to 2000.

Immigration by Decade

Year	Number	Immigrants during this Decade as a Percentage of Total Population	Year	Number	Immigrants during this Decade as a Percentage of Total Population
1821–1830	151,824	1.6	1921–1930	4,107,209	3.9
1831–1840	599,125	4.6	1931–1940	528,431	0.4
1841–1850	1,713,251	10.0	1941–1950	1,035,039	0.7
1851–1860	2,598,214	11.2	1951–1960	2,515,479	1.6
1861–1870	2,314,824	7.4	1961–1970	3,321,677	1.8
1871–1880	2,812,191	7.1	1971–1980	4,493,000	2.2
1881–1890	5,246,613	10.5	1981–1990	7,338,000	3.0
1891–1900	3,687,546	5.8	1991–2000	9,095,083	3.7
1901–1910	8,795,386	11.6	**Total**	**32,433,918**	
1911–1920	5,735,811	6.2			
Total	**33,654,785**		**1821–2000**		
			GRAND TOTAL	**66,088,703**	

SOURCES: U.S. Bureau of the Census, *Historical Statistics of the United States, Colonial Times to 1970* (1975), part 1, 105–106; *Statistical Abstract of the United States, 2001.*

Regional Origins

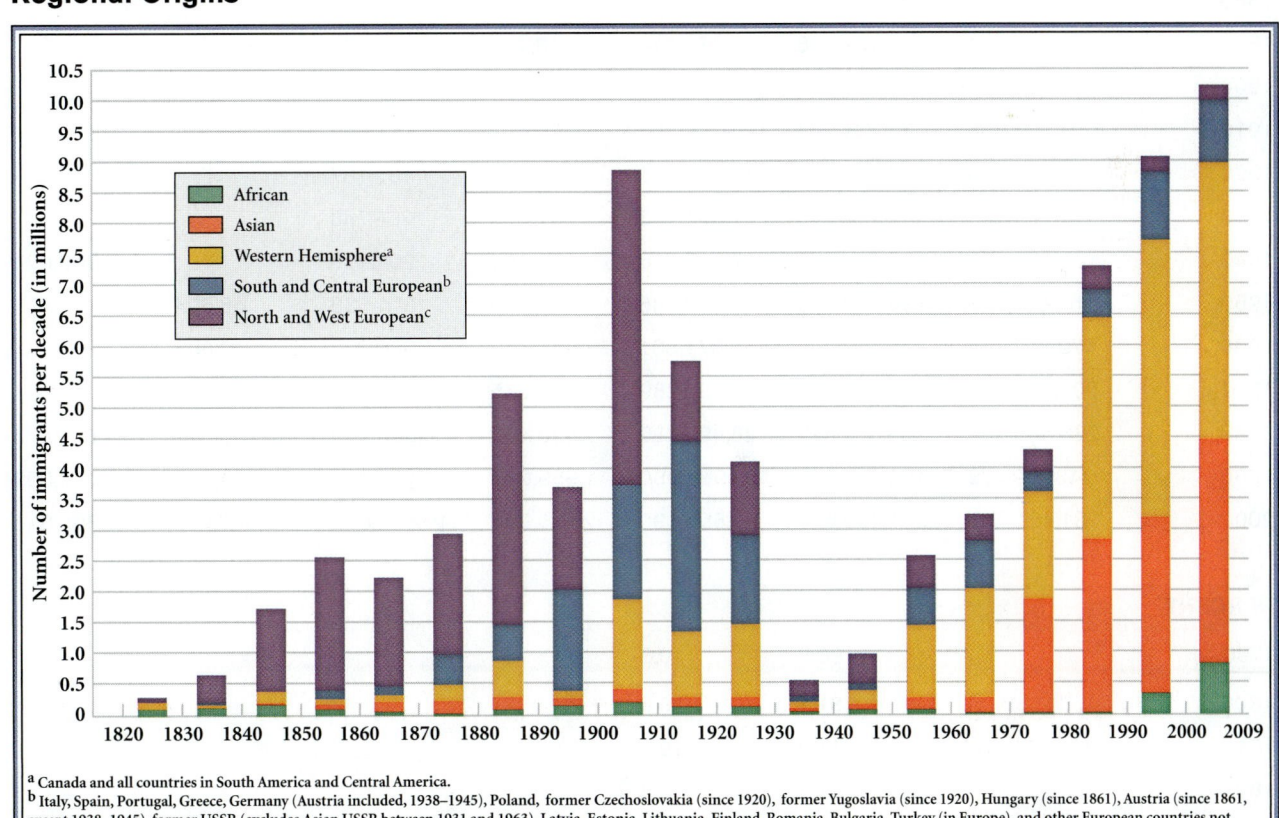

a Canada and all countries in South America and Central America.
b Italy, Spain, Portugal, Greece, Germany (Austria included, 1938–1945), Poland, former Czechoslovakia (since 1920), former Yugoslavia (since 1920), Hungary (since 1861), Austria (since 1861, except 1938–1945), former USSR (excludes Asian USSR between 1931 and 1963), Latvia, Estonia, Lithuania, Finland, Romania, Bulgaria, Turkey (in Europe), and other European countries not classified elsewhere.
c Great Britain, Ireland, Norway, Sweden, Denmark, Iceland, Netherlands, Belgium, Luxembourg, Switzerland, France.
Sources: Stephan Thernstrom, ed., *Harvard Encyclopedia of American Ethnic Groups* (1980), 480; U.S. Bureau of the Census, *Statistical Abstract of the United States, 1991;*
U.S. Department of Homeland Security, *Yearbook of Immigration Statistics, 2009.*

Race in the United States: 1790–2000

Census year	Total population	White	Black (% Free/ Slave)	American Indian, Eskimo, and Aleut	Asian and Pacific Islander	Other Race	Hispanic Origin (of any race)
1790	3,929,214	3,172,006	757,208 (7.9/92.1)				
1800	5,308,483	4,306,446	1,002,037 (10.8/89.2)				
1810	7,239,881	5,862,073	1,377,808 (13.5/86.5)				
1820	9,638,453	7,866,797	1,771,656 (13.2/86.8)				
1830	12,860,702	10,532,060	2,328,642 (13.7/86.3)				
1840	17,063,353	14,189,705	2,873,648 (13.4/86.6)				
1850	23,191,876	19,553,068	3,638,808 (11.9/88.1)				
1860	31,443,321	26,922,537	4,441,830 (11.0/89.0)	44,021	34,933		
1870	38,558,371	33,589,377	4,880,009	25,731	63,254		
1880	50,155,783	43,402,970	6,580,793	66,407	105,613		
1890*	62,947,714	55,101,258	7,488,676	248,253	109,527		
1900	75,994,575	66,809,196	8,833,994	237,196	114,189		
1910	91,972,266	81,731,957	9,827,763	265,683	146,863		
1920	105,710,620	94,820,915	10,463,131	244,437	182,137		
1930	122,775,046	110,286,740	11,891,143	332,397	264,766		
1940	131,669,275	118,214,870	12,865,518	333,969	254,918		1,858,024
1950	150,697,361	134,942,028	15,042,286	343,410	321,033	48,604	
1960	179,323,175	158,831,732	18,871,831	551,669	980,337	87,606	
1970	203,211,926	177,748,975	22,580,289	827,255	1,538,721	516,686	
1980	226,545,805	188,371,622	26,495,025	1,420,400	3,500,439	6,758,319	14,608,673
1990	248,709,873	199,686,070	29,986,060	1,959,234	7,273,662	9,804,847	22,354,059
2000	281,421,906	211,460,626	34,658,190	2,475,956	10,641,833	15,359,073	35,305,818

PERCENT

Census year	Total population	White	Black (% Free/ Slave)	American Indian, Eskimo, and Aleut	Asian and Pacific Islander	Other Race	Hispanic Origin (of any race)
1790		80.7	19.3				
1800		81.1	18.9				
1810		81.0	19.0				
1820		81.6	18.4				
1830		81.9	18.1				
1840		83.2	16.8				

Census year	Total population	Race					
		White	Black (% Free/ Slave)	American Indian, Eskimo, and Aleut	Asian and Pacific Islander	Other Race	Hispanic Origin (of any race)
1850		84.3	15.7				
1860		85.6	14.1	0.1	0.1		
1870		87.1	12.7	0.1	0.2		
1880		86.5	13.1	0.1	0.2		
1890*		87.5	11.9	0.4	0.2		
1900		87.9	11.6	0.3	0.2		
1910		88.9	10.7	0.3	0.2		
1920		89.7	9.9	0.2	0.2		
1930		89.8	9.7	0.3	0.2		
1940		89.8	9.8	0.3	0.2		1.4
1950		89.5	10.0	0.2	0.2		
1960		88.6	10.5	0.3	0.5		
1970		87.5	11.1	0.4	0.8	0.3	
1980		83.1	11.7	0.6	1.5	3.0	6.4
1990		80.3	12.1	0.8	2.9	3.9	9.0
2000		75.1	12.3	0.9	3.78	5.45	12.5

*Includes Indian Territory and Indian reservations.
SOURCE: U.S. Census Bureau

The Labor Force (Thousands of Workers)

Year	Agriculture	Mining	Manufacturing	Construction	Trade	Other	Total
1810	1,950	11	75	–	–	294	2,330
1840	3,570	32	500	290	350	918	5,660
1850	4,520	102	1,200	410	500	1,400	8,250
1860	5,880	176	1,530	520	890	2,114	11,110
1870	6,790	180	2,470	780	1,310	1,400	12,930
1880	8,920	280	3,290	900	1,930	2,070	17,390
1890	9,960	440	4,390	1,510	2,960	4,060	23,320
1900	11,680	637	5,895	1,665	3,970	5,223	29,070
1910	11,770	1,068	8,332	1,949	5,320	9,041	37,480
1920	10,790	1,180	11,190	1,233	5,845	11,372	41,610
1930	10,560	1,009	9,884	1,988	8,122	17,267	48,830
1940	9,575	925	11,309	1,876	9,328	23,277	56,290
1950	7,870	901	15,648	3,029	12,152	25,870	65,470
1960	5,970	709	17,145	3,640	14,051	32,545	74,060
1970	3,463	516	20,746	4,818	15,008	34,127	78,678
1980	3,364	979	21,942	6,215	20,191	46,612	99,303
1990	3,223	724	21,346	7,764	24,622	60,849	118,793
2000	2,464	475	19,644	9,931	15,763	88,260	136,891
2008	2,168	819	15,904	10,974	16,533	98,964	145,362

SOURCES: U.S. Bureau of the Census, *Historical Statistics of the United States, Colonial Times to 1970* (1975), 139; *Statistical Abstract of the United States, 1998*, table 675; *Statistical Abstract of the United States, 2010*.

Changing Labor Patterns

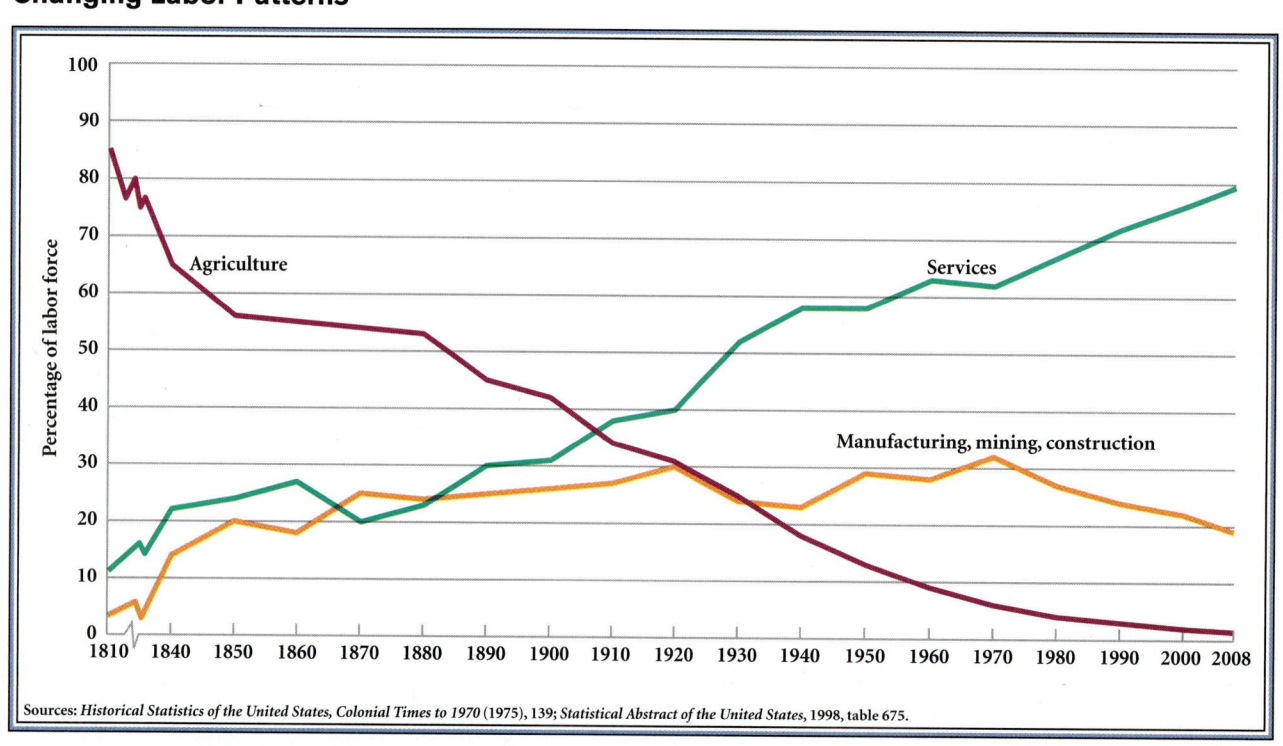

Sources: *Historical Statistics of the United States, Colonial Times to 1970* (1975), 139; *Statistical Abstract of the United States*, 1998, table 675.

Real Gross Domestic Product per Capita, 1790–2010

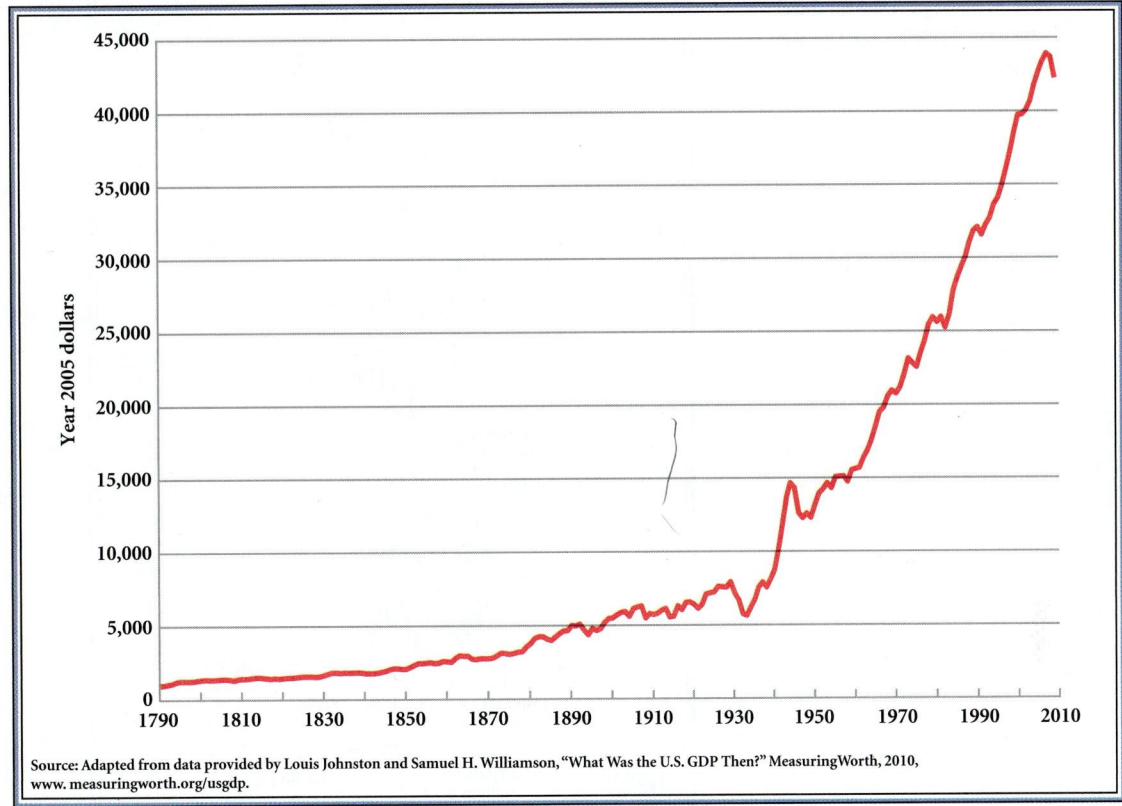

Source: Adapted from data provided by Louis Johnston and Samuel H. Williamson, "What Was the U.S. GDP Then?" MeasuringWorth, 2010, www.measuringworth.org/usgdp.

Main Sectors of the U.S. Economy: 1849, 1899, 1950, 1990, 2001, and 2008

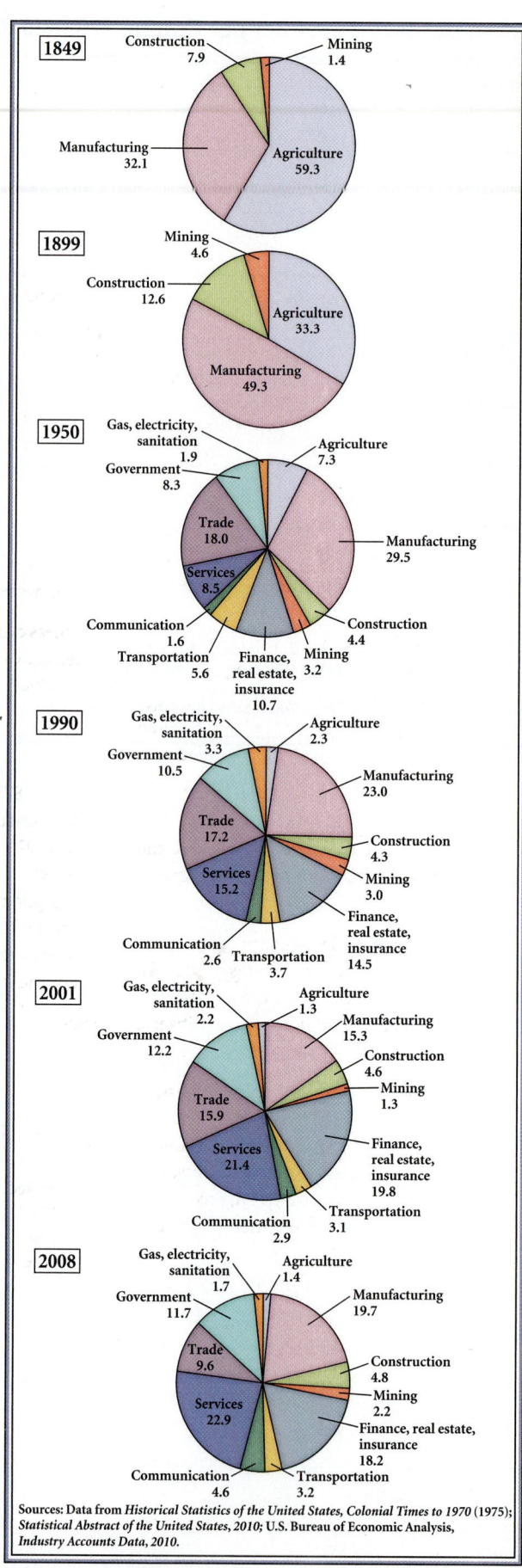

1849
- Construction 7.9
- Mining 1.4
- Agriculture 59.3
- Manufacturing 32.1

1899
- Mining 4.6
- Construction 12.6
- Agriculture 33.3
- Manufacturing 49.3

1950
- Gas, electricity, sanitation 1.9
- Government 8.3
- Trade 18.0
- Services 8.5
- Communication 1.6
- Transportation 5.6
- Finance, real estate, insurance 10.7
- Mining 3.2
- Construction 4.4
- Manufacturing 29.5
- Agriculture 7.3

1990
- Gas, electricity, sanitation 3.3
- Government 10.5
- Trade 17.2
- Services 15.2
- Communication 2.6
- Transportation 3.7
- Finance, real estate, insurance 14.5
- Mining 3.0
- Construction 4.3
- Manufacturing 23.0
- Agriculture 2.3

2001
- Gas, electricity, sanitation 2.2
- Government 12.2
- Trade 15.9
- Services 21.4
- Communication 2.9
- Transportation 3.1
- Finance, real estate, insurance 19.8
- Mining 1.3
- Construction 4.6
- Manufacturing 15.3
- Agriculture 1.3

2008
- Gas, electricity, sanitation 1.7
- Government 11.7
- Trade 9.6
- Services 22.9
- Communication 4.6
- Transportation 3.2
- Finance, real estate, insurance 18.2
- Mining 2.2
- Construction 4.8
- Manufacturing 19.7
- Agriculture 1.4

Sources: Data from *Historical Statistics of the United States, Colonial Times to 1970* (1975); *Statistical Abstract of the United States, 2010*; U.S. Bureau of Economic Analysis, *Industry Accounts Data, 2010.*

Glossary

American exceptionalism The belief that the United States, as the first modern republic, has a mission and destiny distinct from that of all other nations. This belief has often served as the basis for arguments that the United States should influence foreign affairs, in order to encourage other nations and peoples to adopt American institutions and practices. Proponents of American exceptionalism have argued that the United States is uniquely free of class conflict, imperial ambition, and other "Old World" problems. (p. 654)

American Renaissance A burst of American literature during the 1840s, highlighted by the novels of Herman Melville and Nathaniel Hawthorne; the essays of Ralph Waldo Emerson, Henry David Thoreau, and Margaret Fuller; and the poetry of Walt Whitman. (p. 332)

American System The mercantilist system of national economic development advocated by Henry Clay and adopted by John Quincy Adams. It had three interrelated parts: a national bank to manage the nation's financial system; protective tariffs to provide revenue and encourage American industry; and a nationally funded network of roads, canals, and railroads. (p. 305)

anarchism The advocacy of a stateless society achieved by revolutionary means. Feared for their views, anarchists became the scapegoats for the 1886 bombing in Chicago's Haymarket Square. (p. 552)

artisan republicanism An ideology that celebrated small-scale producers, men and women who owned their own shops (or farms). It defined the ideal republican society as one constituted by, and dedicated to the welfare of, independent workers and citizens. (p. 280)

assimilation Efforts by U.S. government agents and Christian missionaries to persuade people of color to adopt white ways. Through assimilation policies, Native Americans, for example, were pressured to abandon their traditional religion, dress, and customs, and adopt Christianity, speak only English, accept U.S. laws concerning private property, and adapt their work and family life to white expectations. (p. 515)

Benevolent Empire A broad-ranging campaign of moral and institutional reforms inspired by evangelical Christian ideals and endorsed by upper-middle-class men and women in the 1820s and 1830s. Ministers who promoted benevolent reform insisted that people who had experienced saving grace should provide moral guidance and charity to the less fortunate. (p. 293)

bills of exchange Credit slips that British manufacturers, West Indian planters, and American merchants used in the eighteenth century in place of currency to settle transactions. (p. 94)

Black Codes Laws passed by southern states after the Civil War that denied ex-slaves the civil rights enjoyed by whites, intending to force blacks back to the plantations. (p. 464)

blacklist A list of people to be excluded from an activity or organization. In the nineteenth century, employers compiled lists of workers affiliated with unions and either fired them or refused to hire them. In the 1950s, governments and private businesses blacklisted alleged communists, denying them positions in government, motion pictures, and many industries and unions. (p. 281)

blue-collar workers Skilled tradesmen who work with their hands, such as carpenters, railroad workers, and industrial factory workers; the nickname came from the blue work shirts that many such men wore on the job. (p. 536)

business cycle The periodic rise and fall of business activity characteristic of market-driven capitalist economies. To increase profits, producers increase output and eventually create a surplus (oversupply); the surplus then prompts a cutback in output, which produces an economic recession. The major periods of pre–World War II economic expansion—1802–1818, 1824–1836, 1846–1856, 1865–1873, 1896–1914, 1922–1928—were followed either by short financial panics or extended depressions (1837–1843, 1873–1896, and 1929–1939). In the postwar period, several short recessions—in 1945, 1949, 1953, 1958, 1961, and 1969—were relatively minor exceptions to steady economic growth. After the steep downturns of 1974–1975 and 1980–1981, there was relatively sustained growth through the 1990s. In 2008, however, the United States experienced its deepest recession since the 1930s. (p. 239)

capitalism A system of economic production based on the private ownership of property and the contractual exchange for profit of goods, labor, and money (capital). Although some elements of capitalism existed in the United States before 1820, a full-scale capitalist economy—and society—emerged only with the Market Revolution (1820–1850). After the Civil War, American capitalism changed in character, as large corporations came to dominate sectors of the economy and state and federal governments increasingly sought to regulate business activity. See *Market Revolution.* (p. 237)

carpetbaggers A derisive name given by southerners to northerners who moved to the South during Reconstruction. (The word derived from the cheap suitcases, known as carpetbags, that held their belongings.) Former Confederates despised these northerners as transient exploiters. Carpetbaggers actually were a varied group that included Union veterans who had served in the South, reformers eager to help former slaves, and others looking for business opportunities. (p. 480)

caste system A form of social organization that divides a society along relatively rigid lines of status based primarily on birth. (p. 32)

caucus A meeting held by a political party to choose candidates, make policies, and enforce party discipline. (p. 305)

chattel slavery A system of bondage in which a slave has the legal status of property and so can be bought and sold like property. (p. 55)

civic humanism The belief that individuals owe a service to their community and its government. During the Renaissance, political theorists argued that selfless service to the polity was of critical importance in a self-governing republic. (p. 21)

clan A group of related families that share a real or legendary common ancestor. Most native peoples north of the Rio Grande organized their societies around clan groups; groups of clans which shared the same language and culture formed a people. (p. 14)

classical liberalism An ideology based on the economic principles of open markets and free competition propounded by Adam Smith and the political ideas of liberty and limited government advanced by John Locke. In the late twentieth century, many economic conservatives embraced the principles of classical liberalism and opposed the principles of social-welfare liberalism. See also *laissez-faire*. (p. 321)

closed shop A workplace in which a job seeker had to be a union member to gain employment. Nineteenth-century craft unions favored closed shops to keep out incompetent and lower-wage workers and to enhance their bargaining position with employers. For that reason, employers strongly opposed closed shops and sought laws to prohibit them. (p. 282)

Columbian Exchange The transfer in the sixteenth century of agricultural products and diseases from the Western Hemisphere to other continents, and those from other continents to the Western Hemisphere. (p. 31)

common law The centuries-old body of English legal customs and procedures that both protected the monarch's subjects against arbitrary acts of the government and resolved private disputes among those subjects. (p. 55)

companionate marriage A marriage based on equality and mutual respect—both republican values. Although husbands in these marriages retained significant legal power, they increasingly came to see their wives as loving partners rather than as inferiors or dependents. (p. 246)

conscience Whigs Whig politicians who opposed the Mexican War (1846–1848) on moral grounds. They argued that the purpose of the war was to expand and perpetuate slavery. They feared that the addition of more slave states would ensure the South's continuing control of the national government and undermine a society of yeomen farmers and "free labor" in the North. (p. 408)

containment The U.S. policy of the late 1940s which sought to contain communism within its existing geographic boundaries, namely the Soviet Union, Eastern Europe, and North Korea (and after 1949, China). Rather than seek to defeat communist governments through military confrontation, the United States would instead "contain" the influence of the communist powers. (p. 788)

cooperatives (co-ops) Organizations through which a group of customers, working together out of common interest, sought to purchase products at wholesale rates, passing on the savings to their members. In the 1880s, rural organizations like the Farmers' Alliance created cooperatives to obtain loans and to purchase farm equipment and an array of consumer products, from cloth and shoes to insurance policies. (p. 553)

craft worker An artisan or other worker who has a specific craft or skill—for example, a mason, a cabinetmaker, a printer, or a weaver. (p. 280)

deficit spending High government spending in excess of tax revenues; the practice is based on the ideas of British economist John Maynard Keynes, who proposed in the 1930s that governments should be prepared to go into debt to stimulate a stagnant economy. (p. 735)

deindustrialization The dismantling of manufacturing—especially in the automobile, steel, and consumer-goods industries—in the decades after World War II, representing a reversal of the process of industrialization that had dominated the American economy from the 1870s through the 1940s. Struck hardest by this were the nation's "Rust Belt" of manufacturing states, which stretched from the Northeast through the Great Lakes region and the Upper Midwest. This long-term process began in the 1950s, but only drew national attention in the 1970s and 1980s. (p. 925)

deism The Enlightenment-influenced belief that the Christian God created the universe and then left it to run according to natural laws. (p. 116)

desegregation The legal requirement that people of all races have equal access to public facilities and services, including public schools, parks, water fountains, railroads, hotels, and restaurants. According to desegregation laws, African Americans in the South, for example, could not be forced to use separate facilities from whites. (p. 483)

détente From the French word for "a relaxation of tension," this term was used to signify the Cold War policy of President Richard Nixon, who sought a reduction of tension and hostility between the United States and the Soviet Union and China in the early 1970s. (p. 949)

direct primary The selection of party candidates by a popular vote rather than by the party convention. The progressive reform that led to the direct primary was especially pressed by Robert La Follette, who viewed it as an instrument for breaking the grip of political machines on the parties. In the South, where it was limited to whites, the direct primary was a means of disenfranchising blacks. (p. 634)

division of labor A system of manufacture that divides production into a series of distinct and repetitive tasks performed by machines or workers. The system took shape in the shoe industry between

1800 and 1830 and soon became the general practice. Although the division of labor improved productivity, it eroded workers' control and sense of achievement. (p. 274)

dollar diplomacy Policy adopted by President Taft connecting U.S. economic and political interests overseas. The benefits of this policy would flow in both directions, as business would gain from diplomatic efforts on its behalf, while the strengthened American economic presence overseas would give added leverage to American diplomacy. (p. 692)

domesticity An ideology of marriage and family life, which called for men to practice self-discipline, temperance, and deference to female moral authority, while women refrained from paid labor in the workplace and devoted themselves to motherhood and family. Though domesticity stressed women's primary role in the home, it also sanctioned women's participation in religious missions and charitable efforts. Grounded in the ideals of republican motherhood and "separate spheres," domesticity was championed particularly by the elite and middle classes. See also *republican motherhood* and *separate spheres*. (p. 473)

dower, dower right A legal right originating in Europe and carried to the American colonies that provided a widow with the use of one-third of the family's land and goods during her lifetime. (p. 18)

economies of scale The reduction of per-unit production and transportation costs (and increased profits) achieved through large-scale production. By developing mass-production techniques, a manufacturer reduces its cost on individual items (for example, from five cents per item to two cents), and can sell more of the product—and for a lower price—than its competitors. (p. 507)

enclosure acts Laws passed in sixteenth-century England that allowed landowners to fence in the open fields that surrounded many villages and use them for grazing sheep. These enclosures deprived peasants of land to cultivate and forced them to work as wage laborers or as wool spinners and weavers. (p. 37)

encomiendas Land grants in Spanish America given in the sixteenth century by the Spanish kings to privileged landholders (*encomenderos*). *Encomiendas* also gave the landholders legal control over native peoples who lived on or near their estates. (p. 31)

established church A church given privileged legal status by the government. Historically, established churches in Europe and America were supported by public taxes, and were often the only legally permitted religious institutions. (p. 258)

ethnocultural politics The practice of voting along ethnic, racial, and religious lines. Ethnocultural allegiances were a prominent feature of American political life in the mid-nineteenth and twentieth centuries. (p. 327)

eugenics The "science" of human breeding, grounded in the Social Darwinist idea that the progress of human evolution is hampered when "unfit" people are permitted to reproduce. Eugenicists lobbied for the forced sterilization of "mental defectives," including the mentally retarded; influenced by contemporary racial and eth-

nic prejudices, they worked particularly to sterilize "unfit" people of color and to restrict immigration from Asia and Eastern and Southern Europe, arguing that new immigrants would dilute the racial purity of Americans descended from Western Europeans. (p. 579)

Exodusters African Americans who left the Deep South in the late 1870s, in the wake of Reconstruction's collapse and the depression of 1873, and sought homesteads on the western frontier. The Exodusters sought better opportunities in states such as Kansas, but like many farmers, they confronted falling crop prices and a harsh Plains environment, which was difficult to farm. (p. 504)

factory A structure first built by manufacturers in the early nineteenth century to concentrate all aspects of production—and the machinery needed to increase output—in one location. (p. 274)

Federalists Supporters of the Constitution of 1787, which created a strong central government; their opponents, the Antifederalists, feared that a strong central government would corrupt the nation's newly won liberty. (p. 198)

feminism Advocates of women's rights adopted this term in the 1910s to describe their belief that women should be equal to men in all areas of life. Earlier women activists and suffragists had accepted the notion of separate spheres for men and women, but feminists sought to overcome all barriers to equality and personal development. (p. 576)

franchise The right to vote. Between 1820 and 1860, most states revised their constitutions to extend the vote to all adult white males. In 1870, the Fifteenth Amendment gave the vote to black men; and in 1920, the Nineteenth Amendment extended the franchise to women. However, malapportionment of the state legislatures meant that some voters had more power than others did. (p. 304)

freehold Land owned in its entirety, without feudal dues or landlord obligations. Freeholders have the legal right to improve, transfer, or sell their landed property. See *leasehold*. (p. 54)

free market A system of economic exchange in which prices of goods, labor, and capital are determined by supply and demand and no producer or consumer dominates the market. The term also refers to markets that are not subject to government regulation. (p. 195)

free-soil movement A political movement of the 1840s that opposed the expansion of slavery. Its members—mostly white yeomen farmers—believed that slavery benefited "aristocratic men." They wanted farm families to settle the western territories and install democratic republican values and institutions there. The short-lived Free-Soil Party (1848–1854) stood for "free soil, free labor, free men," which subsequently became the program of the Republican Party. (p. 408)

fundamentalism An evangelical Protestant religious movement based upon rejection of some tenets of modern science and defense of the literal truth of the Bible. Fundamentalists opposed modernist Protestants, who tried to reconcile Christianity with

Darwin's theory of natural selection and other scientific discoveries. Fundamentalists' promotion of anti-evolution laws for public schools led to the famous Scopes trial of 1925. In recent decades, fundamentalists have organized to support laws that would ban abortions and gay marriages. (p. 586)

gang-labor system A system of work discipline used on southern cotton plantations in the mid-nineteenth century. White overseers or black drivers constantly supervised gangs of enslaved laborers to enforce work norms and achieve greater productivity. (p. 374)

general strike A strike that draws in all the workers in a society, with the intention of shutting the entire system down. Radical groups like the Industrial Workers of the World (IWW), in the early twentieth century, saw the general strike as the means for initiating a social revolution. (p. 644)

gentility A refined style of living and elaborate manners that came to be highly prized among well-to-do English families after 1600. (p. 93)

gentry A class of wealthy English landholders who lacked the social privileges and titles of nobility. During the Price Revolution of the sixteenth century, the wealth and status of the gentry rose while that of the aristocracy fell. (p. 36)

gold standard Monetary system by which a country linked the amount of money circulating, at any given time, to the amount of gold held in its Treasury. Deliberate increases in the money supply, to encourage borrowing and stimulate economic activity, therefore depended not on federal policy decisions (as is the case today, through the Federal Reserve) but on increases in the national and global supply of gold. (p. 496)

grandfather clause A law permitting citizens to register as voters only if their grandfathers had been eligible to vote. Such laws were passed in southern states such as Louisiana, in an attempt to enfranchise all native-born white men and exclude African Americans from the polls, on the grounds that their grandfathers, during slavery times, had not been voters. (p. 629)

Great American Desert The name given to the drought-stricken Great Plains by Euro-Americans in the early nineteenth century. Believing the region unfit for cultivation or agriculture, Congress designated the Great Plains as permanent Indian country in 1834. (p. 504)

greenbacks Paper money issued by the U.S. Treasury during the Civil War to finance the war effort. Greenbacks were legal tender in all public and private transactions. Because it was issued in large amounts and was not backed by gold or silver, the greenback dollar's value fell during the war from $1 to 40 cents. Unlike the Continental dollar issued during the Revolutionary War, which became virtually worthless, the greenback recovered its value as the Union government won the war and reduced its war-related debt. (p. 444)

guild An organization of skilled workers in medieval and early modern Europe that regulated the entry into, and the practice of, a trade. Guilds did not develop in colonial America because artisans generally were in short supply. (p. 21)

habeas corpus Latin for "you have the body," a legal writ forcing government authorities to justify their arrest and detention of an individual. Rooted in English common law, habeas corpus became a formal privilege in the U.S. Constitution (Article 1, Section 9), which also allows its suspension in cases of invasion or insurrection. During the Civil War, Lincoln suspended habeas corpus to stop protests against the draft and other anti-Union activities. The USA PATRIOT Act (2001) likewise suspended this privilege in cases of suspected terrorism. (p. 440)

heresy A religious doctrine inconsistent with the teachings of an established church. Some of the Crusades between 1096 and 1291 targeted groups of Christians whose beliefs the hierarchy of the Roman Catholic Church judged to be heretical. (p. 21)

home rule Self-government by a state within the federal system. After the Civil War, southern Democrats advocated for home rule by painting Reconstruction governments as illegitimate impositions. By 1876, northern Republicans, too, were inclined to accept this claim. (p. 487)

homespun Cloth spun and woven by American women and traditionally worn by poorer colonists. During the boycotts of British goods in the 1760s, wearing homespun clothes became a political act, and even wealthy Patriots began wearing them. Their work making homespun fabrics allowed women to contribute directly to the Patriot movement. (p. 152)

horizontal integration A method employed by companies to raise market share and gain control over prices, by absorbing rival firms. Horizontal integration could be a cooperative process, in which several companies banded together out of common interest. It could also be accomplished through hostile takeovers, when a powerful company pressured or forced competitors to surrender their independence and be absorbed into the structure of the dominant firm. (p. 533)

ideology A systematic philosophy or political theory that purports to explain the character of the social world or to prescribe a set of values or beliefs. (p. 21)

impeachment The first step in the constitutional process for removing the president from office, in which charges of wrongdoing (articles of impeachment) are voted on by the House of Representatives. If the articles pass in the House, the Senate then conducts a trial to determine whether the impeached president is guilty of the charges. (p. 468)

imperialism Imposition of military, political, and economic control over another nation or people. In general, the term *expansion* is used for the imposition of such control over adjacent territories (such as the United States in the American West), while *imperialism* is used for territories overseas (such as the Philippines); in part because the former processes included the expectation of settlement by newcomers, and eventually statehood, while Filipinos did not win representation. Through both expansion and imperialism, however, the United States asserted its control without reference to the wishes of those who already occupied the land, and both processes met the nation's need for new resources, raw materials, and expanded markets. (p. 653)

imperial presidency The far-reaching use (and sometimes abuse) of executive authority during the second half of the twentieth century, especially the centralization of war-making powers, domestic surveillance and overseas espionage, and foreign policy functions in the office of the president. (p. 759)

indenture A contract that required service for a specified period. In the seventeenth century, indentures brought thousands of workers to North America. In exchange for agreeing to work for four or five years without wages, the workers received passage across the Atlantic, room and board, and status as a free person at the end of the contract period. (p. 37)

indulgence A certificate granted by the Catholic Church that claimed to pardon a sinner from punishment in the afterlife. In his *Ninety-five Theses*, written in 1517, Martin Luther condemned the sale of indulgences, a common practice among Catholic clergy. (p. 32)

Industrial Revolution The great transformation in manufacturing goods that began in England about 1750 and spread eventually around the world. It consisted of three interrelated aspects: inanimate power (first from improved water wheels and then from steam engines), advances in machine technology, and disciplined labor working in factories. (p. 273)

injunction A court order that immediately requires or prohibits an activity, either temporarily or permanently. Especially between the 1830s and the 1930s, probusiness judges often issued injunctions to stop workers from picketing or striking. (p. 282)

Jim Crow A term—drawn from a satirical character named "Jim Crow," who appeared in antebellum minstrel shows—used in the age of segregation to describe facilities designated for blacks, such as Jim Crow railway cars. (p. 635)

joint-stock corporation A financial organization devised by English merchants around 1550 that facilitated the colonization of North America. In these companies, a number of investors pooled their capital and received shares of stock in the enterprise in proportion to their share of the total investment. (p. 58)

Keynesian economics The theory, developed by British economist John Maynard Keynes in the 1930s, that purposeful government intervention in the economy (through lowering or raising taxes, interest rates, and government spending) can affect the level of overall economic activity and thereby prevent severe depressions and runaway inflation. (p. 735)

King Cotton A term used to describe the importance of raw cotton in the nineteenth-century economy. More specifically, the Confederate belief during the Civil War that their cotton was so important to the British and French economies that those governments would recognize the South as an independent nation and supply it with loans and arms. (p. 443)

labor theory of value The belief that human labor produces economic value. Adherents argued that the price of a product should be determined not by the market (supply and demand) but by the amount of work required to make it, and that most of the price should be paid to the person who produced it. The idea was advocated in the mid-nineteenth century by many farmers, independent craft workers, and trade unions. (p. 282)

laissez-faire French for "let do" or "leave alone." The principle that the less government does, the better, particularly in reference to the economy. This has been an influential philosophy in the United States. In the nineteenth century, Democrats tended to advocate laissez-faire against state-building Whigs and Republicans. In the twentieth century—especially from the New Deal onward—Republicans have become the main champions of laissez-faire. (p. 321)

land bank An institution, established by a colonial legislature, that printed paper money and lent it to farmers, taking a lien on their land to ensure repayment. (p. 99)

leasehold, leaseholder A piece of land rented out by means of a formal contract for a considerable period of time. The contract specified the obligations of the owner and the lessee. Some leaseholds ran for "three lives"—those of the lessee, his son or heir, and his grandson. See *freehold*. (p. 106)

lien (crop lien) A legal device enabling a creditor to take possession of the property of a borrower, including the right to have it sold in payment of the debt. During Reconstruction, furnishing merchants took such liens on cotton crops as collateral for supplies advanced to sharecroppers during the growing season. This system trapped farmers in a cycle of debt and made them vulnerable to exploitation by the furnishing merchant. (p. 476)

literacy test The requirement that an ability to read be demonstrated as a qualification for the right to vote. This was a device easily used by registrars to prevent blacks from voting, whether they could read or not, and was widely adopted across the South, beginning with Mississippi in 1890. On the prejudicial assumption that illiterate voters were ignorant and could not inform themselves on political questions, and therefore cast illegitimate ballots, literacy tests were adopted in many parts of the United States around 1900. (p. 629)

machine tools Cutting, boring, and drilling machines used to produce standardized metal parts that are then assembled into other machines such as textile looms and sewing machines. The rapid development of machine tools by American inventors in the early nineteenth century was a factor in speeding the spread of industrialization. (p. 279)

Manifest Destiny A term coined by columnist and editor John L. O'Sullivan in 1845 to describe the idea that Euro-Americans were fated by God to settle the entire North American continent. Manifest Destiny implied that the spread of American republican institutions and Protestant churches across the continent was part of God's plan for the world. In the late nineteenth century, the focus of the policy also included overseas expansion. (p. 398)

manorial system A quasi-feudal system of landholding. In the Hudson River Valley of New York, wealthy landlords leased farms to tenants, who paid rent and a quarter the value of all improvements (houses, barns, etc.) if they sold the lease; tenants also owed the landlord a number of days of personal service each year. (p. 74)

manumission From the Latin *manumittere*, "to release from the hand"; the legal act of relinquishing property rights in slaves, thereby allowing them their freedom. In 1782, the Virginia assembly passed an act allowing manumission, and within a decade, planters had freed 10,000 slaves. Worried that a large free black population would threaten the institution of slavery, the assembly repealed the law in 1792. (p. 252)

Market Revolution The dramatic increase between 1820 and 1850 in the exchange of goods and services in market transactions. The Market Revolution reflected the increased output of farms and factories, the entrepreneurial activities of traders and merchants, and the creation of a transportation network of roads, canals, and railroads. (p. 273)

mass production A system of factory production that often combines sophisticated machinery, a disciplined labor force, and assembly lines to turn out vast quantities of identical goods at low cost. In the nineteenth century, the textile and meatpacking industries pioneered mass production, which eventually became the standard mode for making consumer goods from cigarettes to automobiles, telephones, radios, televisions, and computers. (p. 274)

maternalism A justification for women's activism in politics and public life, based on the argument that women, as mothers or potential mothers, have special talents and sympathies. In the late nineteenth and early twentieth centuries, when few Americans believed in women's full equality, maternalism was a particularly effective way for women to defend their political activism. (p. 572)

matrilineal Refers to a system of family organization in which social identity and property descend through the female line. Children are usually raised in their mother's household, and her brother (their uncle) plays a central role in their lives. (p. 15)

mechanic A nineteenth-century term used to refer to a skilled craftsman and inventor who built and improved machinery and machine tools for industry. Mechanics developed a professional identity and established institutes to spread their skills and knowledge. (p. 277)

mercantilism A system of political economy based on government regulation. Beginning in 1650, Britain enacted Navigation Acts that controlled colonial commerce and manufacturing for the enrichment of Britain. After 1790, the United States used tariffs and subsidies to bolster national wealth. Today, many Asian nations—such as Japan, China, and Korea—employ mercantilist policies for a similar purpose. (p. 36)

mestizo A person of mixed blood; specifically, the child of a European and a Native American. (p. 32)

middle class In Europe, the class of traders and townspeople who were not part of either the aristocracy or the peasantry. The term was introduced in America in the early nineteenth century to describe both an economic group (of prosperous farmers, artisans, and traders) and a cultural outlook (of self-discipline, hard work, and social mobility). (p. 243)

Middle Passage The brutal sea voyage from Africa to the Americas in the eighteenth and nineteenth centuries that took the lives of about 1.5 million enslaved Africans. (p. 84)

military-industrial complex A term used by President Dwight D. Eisenhower in his 1961 farewell address to refer to the interlinked government, military, and industrial interests that emerged with the arms buildup of the Cold War. Eisenhower particularly warned against the "unwarranted influence" that the military-industrial complex might exert on public policy. (p. 786)

Minutemen Colonial militiamen who stood ready to mobilize on short notice during the imperial crisis of the 1770s. These volunteers formed the core of the citizens' army that met British troops at Lexington and Concord in April 1775. (p. 163)

modern Of or pertaining to very recent events, rather than the distant past. Though historians describe aspects of many historical periods as "modern," in general they describe modern life as characterized by rapid change, particularly in response to industrialization. Under these circumstances, people found it difficult or undesirable to live as their parents and grandparents did and to maintain traditional assumptions and beliefs. Willingly or not, they responded to radically new conditions by changing their ways of life. (p. 560)

modernism A broad set of literary and artistic movements, extending through the first half of the twentieth century, in which writers and artists rejected traditional rules and conventions and sought new ways to represent reality. The earliest use of the term, by Cuban writer Rubén Dario, appears to date from the 1890s. Modernists often sought to turn nineteenth-century cultural conventions upside down, for example, by critiquing the idea of European and American "civilization" and "progress," and by celebrating artistic forms that had earlier been scorned as "primitive." (p. 582)

muckrakers Journalists in the early twentieth century whose stock-in-trade was exposure of the corruption of big business and government. Theodore Roosevelt gave them the name as a term of reproach. The term comes from *Pilgrim's Progress* (1678), a religious allegory by John Bunyan. (p. 605)

national debt The financial obligations of the U.S. government for money borrowed from its citizens and foreign investors. Alexander Hamilton wanted wealthy Americans to invest in the national debt so that they would support the national government. In recent decades, similar thinking has led the United States to encourage individuals and institutions in crucial foreign nations—for example, Saudi Arabia, Japan, and China—to invest billions of dollars in the American national debt. (p. 206)

nativism Antiforeign sentiment in the United States that fueled anti-immigrant and immigration-restriction policies against the Irish and Germans in the 1840s and 1850s, the Chinese and Japanese in the 1880s and 1890s, migrants from Eastern and Southern Europe in the 1910s and 1920s, and Mexicans in the 1990s and 2000s. Nativism prompted the Chinese Exclusion Act of 1882, the

Immigration Restriction Act of 1924, and the internment of Japanese Americans during World War II. (p. 694)

naturalism A literary movement that arose around 1900 in the United States, influenced by scientific and sociological arguments that described humans' "struggle with nature" and the "survival of the fittest." American naturalist fiction writers such as Theodore Dreiser and Stephen Crane depicted their characters as driven by powerful unconscious desires, as well as by economic and environmental forces beyond their control. Naturalist writers sought to depict their characters' psychological states, and some defied prevailing conventions by writing frankly about sexual desire. Naturalism helped give rise to *modernism* in literature and is itself sometimes viewed as a modernist form. (p. 582)

natural selection The idea, proposed by Charles Darwin, that random genetic mutations occur in animal and plant species, some of which are adaptive and can therefore result in higher survival rates, thus causing species to change (or evolve) over time. For example, in a period of plant scarcity, a longer-necked giraffe has an advantage because it can browse higher branches, and would be more likely to survive and reproduce; over many generations of the same conditions, a longer-necked giraffe species would result. In the late nineteenth and early twentieth centuries, many Americans accepted Darwin's theory of evolution but rejected natural selection as its mechanism, seeing the process as cruel and incompatible with the idea of a benevolent Creator. (p. 579)

nullification The constitutional argument that a state legislature or convention could void a law passed by Congress. The concept of nullification had its origins in the Kentucky and Virginia resolutions of 1798, which were drafted by Thomas Jefferson and James Madison, and was elaborated in John C. Calhoun's *South Carolina Exposition and Protest* (1828) and in the Ordinance of Nullification (1832). (p. 312)

oligopoly In economics, the situation in which a given industry (e.g., steel making, automobile manufacturing) is dominated by a small number of large-scale companies. (p. 702)

outwork A system of manufacturing, also known as *putting out*, used extensively in the English woolen industry in the sixteenth and seventeenth centuries. Merchants provided wool for landless peasants to spin and weave into cloth in their own homes; the merchants then sold the cloth in English and foreign markets. (p. 35)

pagan A person whose spiritual beliefs center on the natural world. Pagans do not worship a supernatural God; instead, they pay homage to spirits and spiritual forces that they believe dwell in the natural world. (p. 19)

pan-Africanism The political argument that people of African descent, in all parts of the world, face related problems—particularly racial discrimination—and share common goals. In the United States, pan-African leaders have urged African Americans to unite with other people of African descent to create movements for self-help and racial justice. (p. 701)

patronage The power of elected officials to grant government jobs and favors to their supporters; also the jobs and favors themselves.

Beginning around 1820, politicians systematically used—and abused—patronage to create and maintain strong party loyalties. After 1870, political reformers gradually introduced merit-based civil service systems in state and federal governments to reduce patronage. (p. 305)

peasant The traditional term for a farmworker in Europe. Some peasants owned land, while others leased or rented small plots from landlords. In some regions, peasants lived in compact communities with strong collective institutions. (p. 17)

peonage (debt peonage) Forced labor, under a pretext of debt. As cotton prices declined during the 1870s, and many sharecroppers fell into permanent debt, merchants often conspired with landowners to make this debt a pretext for the sharecropper's forced labor. (p. 477)

personal-liberty laws Laws enacted in many northern states to protect free blacks and fugitive slaves from southern slave catchers. Early laws required a formal hearing before a local court. When the Supreme Court declared such provisions unconstitutional in *Prigg v. Pennsylvania* (1842), states enacted new laws prohibiting their officers from helping slave catchers. (p. 418)

piecework Unskilled labor, in sewing or other assembly work, for which workers were paid by the piece rather than with an hourly wage. A pieceworker might, for example, sew buttons on men's coats and receive a small payment for each coat she completed. Piecework has frequently been done by women, for very low pay, and often at home. (p. 540)

pocket veto A method by which the U.S. president can kill a piece of legislation without issuing a formal veto: The president "pockets" the bill by simply choosing not to sign it, and letting it expire after Congress adjourns. When congressional Republicans passed the Wade-Davis Bill in 1864, a harsher alternative to President Lincoln's restoration plan, Lincoln used a pocket veto to prevent the bill from being enacted. (p. 464)

political machine Nineteenth-century term for highly organized groups operating within and intending to control political parties. Machines were regarded as antidemocratic by political reformers and were the target especially of Progressive-era leaders such as Robert La Follette. In municipal government, urban machines such as New York's Tammany Hall were often run by ethnic politicians; they won support from immigrant voters, who had few sources of aid in navigating the dangers of city life. Reformers instituted a merit-based civil service and primary elections to limit the power of political machines. (p. 305)

poll tax A tax paid for the privilege of voting, used in the South beginning during Reconstruction to disenfranchise freed blacks. Nationally, the northern states used poll taxes to keep immigrants and others deemed unworthy from voting. (p. 469)

polygamy The practice of marriage to multiple partners, most often, of one husband to multiple wives. Polygamy was customary among some Native American and African peoples; it was also practiced by many Mormons in the United States, particularly between 1840 and 1890. (p. 43)

popular sovereignty The republican principle that ultimate power resides in the hands of the electorate. Popular sovereignty dictates that voters directly (or indirectly through their elected representatives) approve the constitutions and laws of the state and national governments. During the 1850s, the U.S. Congress used the principle of popular sovereignty in devising legislation giving the residents of a western territory the authority to allow or prohibit slavery there. (p. 167)

praying towns Native American settlements in seventeenth-century New England supervised by a Puritan minister. Puritans used these settlements to encourage Indians to adopt Protestant Christianity and English culture. (p. 65)

predatory pricing Temporarily setting the price of a product below the cost of producing it, and accepting the resulting loss of profit, in order to undercut competitors and drive them out of business. Large corporations, which sold their goods all over the United States and sometimes abroad, could afford to use predatory pricing in local markets, against smaller rivals. After driving competitors out of business in a particular market, the corporation could then raise prices to a profitable level. (p. 533)

predestination The Protestant Christian belief that God chooses certain people for salvation before they are born. Sixteenth-century theologian John Calvin was the main proponent of this doctrine, which became a fundamental tenet of Puritan theology. (p. 33)

Price Revolution The high rate of inflation in Europe in the mid-1500s and its consequences. American gold and silver, spent by Spain throughout Europe, doubled the money supply at a time when the population was also increasing. The abrupt rise in prices caused profound social changes—reducing the power of the aristocracy, leaving many peasant families on the brink of poverty, and encouraging substantial migration to America. (p. 36)

primogeniture The practice of passing family land, by will or by custom, to the eldest son. Republic-minded Americans of the Revolutionary era felt this practice was unfair but did not prohibit it. However, most state legislatures eventually passed laws providing that if a father dies without a will, all his children must receive an equal portion of his estate. (p. 18)

probate inventory An accounting of a person's property at the time of death, as recorded by court-appointed officials. Probate inventories list details of personal property, household items, and financial assets and debts, and tell historians a good deal about people's lives. (p. 96)

producerism The argument that real economic wealth is created by people who make their living by physical labor, and that merchants, lawyers, bankers, and other middlemen unfairly gain their wealth from such "producers." In the late nineteenth century, producerism was a popular ideology among farmers, skilled tradesmen, and factory workers. (p. 551)

progressives A loose term for political reformers, used especially during the Progressive Era (1880s–1910s) to describe those working to improve the political system, fight poverty, and increase government involvement in the economy. The term "progressive" was most often applied to urban and middle-class or elite reformers. The work of such reformers, however, was frequently prompted by protests from rural and working-class activists, who tended to propose more radical measures to combat the ills of industrialization. (p. 621)

proprietors Groups of settlers who received land grants from the General Courts of Massachusetts Bay and Connecticut, mostly between 1630 and 1720. The proprietors distributed the land among themselves, usually according to social status and family need. This system encouraged widespread ownership of land in New England. (p. 63)

protective tariff An import duty designed to protect domestic products from cheaper foreign goods. A hot political issue throughout much of U.S. history, protective tariffs became particularly controversial in the 1830s and again between 1880 and 1914, when Whigs and Republicans (for protectionism) and Democrats (for free trade) centered their political campaigns on the issue. (p. 207)

pueblos Multi-story and multi-room stone or mud-brick buildings built as residences by native peoples in the southwestern United States. (p. 12)

Radical Whigs An eighteenth-century faction in the British Parliament that protested political corruption, the growing cost of the empire, and the influence on government of a wealthy class of financiers. (p. 97)

realism A literary and artistic movement, lasting roughly from the 1860s through the 1890s, in which writers and artists strove to offer accurate portrayals of everyday life. American realist writers such as William Dean Howells drew on the ideas of Europeans, particularly French writers Gustave Flaubert and Honoré de Balzac, and also used investigative journalism and nonfiction as models. Rather than giving stories the "right" endings, to prove an appropriate moral point, realists tried to show what might actually happen. In the visual arts, photography's prevalence played a key role in the rise of realism, but the movement also extended to painting: Artists such as John Sloan called for the depiction of everyday scenes—such as a boxing match or life in a city alley—rather than objects of conventional beauty. Realists helped point the way toward the later movements of *naturalism* and *modernism*. (p. 582)

recall A law that permits voters to remove an elected official from his post and elect a replacement, if they are dissatisfied with his or her performance, before the official has completed the full term for which he or she was elected. (p. 642)

reconquista The campaign by Spanish Catholics to drive North African Moors (Muslim Arabs) from the European mainland. After a centuries-long effort to recover their lands, the Spaniards defeated the Moors at Granada in 1492 and secured control of all of Spain. (p. 24)

referendum A direct vote on whether or not to adopt a particular law or government policy. The referendum allows citizens to make policy decisions directly, rather than (or in addition to) choosing elected officials who pledge to carry out specific policies. (p. 642)

republic A state without a monarch or prince that is governed by representatives of the people. During the Renaissance, Italian moneyed elites ruled their city-states as republics. In 1776, Patriot leaders created republics with democratic features in the newly independent American states because they were suspicious of monarchical privilege, moneyed elites, and arbitrary executive power. (p. 21)

republicanism A political ideology that repudiates hereditary rule by kings and princes and celebrates an elected, representative system of government and a virtuous, public-spirited citizenry. Historically, most republics limited active political participation to those with a significant amount of property. After 1800, the United States became a democratic republic with widespread participation by white adult men of all social classes; after 1920, women also became part of the electorate. (p. 183)

republican motherhood The idea that the primary political role of American women was to instill a sense of patriotic duty and republican virtue in their children and mold them into exemplary republican citizens. (p. 246)

revenue tariff A tax on imports levied to raise money for the government. See *protective tariff*. (p. 207)

revival An outburst of religious enthusiasm, often prompted by the preaching of a charismatic Baptist or Methodist minister. The Great Awakening of the 1740s was significant, but it was the revival that swept across the United States between the 1790s and 1850s that imparted a deep religiosity to the culture. Subsequent revivals in the 1880s, 1890s, and late twentieth century helped maintain a strong evangelical Protestant culture in America. (p. 117)

rotten boroughs Tiny electoral districts for Parliament whose voters were controlled by wealthy aristocrats or merchants who used the districts to gain entry to Parliament for themselves or their friends. In the 1760s, Radical Whig John Wilkes called for the elimination of rotten boroughs and greater representation for populous commercial and manufacturing areas. (p. 144)

salutary neglect A term often used to describe British colonial policy during the reigns of George I (r. 1714–1727) and George II (r. 1727–1760). By relaxing their supervision of internal colonial affairs, royal bureaucrats inadvertently assisted the rise of self-government in North America. (p. 97)

scalawags A pejorative term (in fact, an ancient Scots-Irish word for worthless animals) applied to southern whites who joined the Republicans during Reconstruction. Ex-Confederates used this term for ex-Whigs and yeomen farmers who had not supported the Confederacy and who believed that an alliance with the Republicans was the best way to attract northern capital and rebuild the South. (p. 480)

scientific management A system of organizing work, developed by Frederick W. Taylor in the late nineteenth century, designed to both get the maximum productivity from the individual worker and reduce production costs, using methods such as the time-and-motion study. The system was never applied in its totality in any industry, but it contributed to the rise of the "efficiency expert" as well as the field of industrial psychology. (p. 541)

secret ballot Before 1890, most Americans voted in public. That is, voters either announced their votes to a clerk or handed in ballots that had been printed by—and so were recognizable as the work of—a political party. Voting in private or in secret had first been used on a wide scale in Australia, and when the practice was adopted in the United States, it was known as the "Australian ballot." (p. 378)

self-made man A nineteenth-century ideal; an ideology that celebrated men who rose to wealth or social prominence from humble origins through self-discipline, hard work, and temperate habits. (p. 292)

sentimentalism A European cultural movement that emphasized emotions and a physical appreciation of God, nature, and people. Sentimentalism came to the United States in the late eighteenth century and was a factor in the shift to marriages based on love rather than on financial considerations. (p. 245)

separate spheres Term used by contemporaries and historians to describe the nineteenth-century view that men and women have different gender-defined characteristics and, consequently, that the sexes inhabit—and should inhabit—different social worlds. Men should dominate the public sphere of politics and economics, while women should manage the private sphere of home and family. In mid-nineteenth-century America, this cultural understanding was both sharply defined and hotly contested. (p. 354)

severalty Individual ownership of land. The Dawes Severalty Act of 1887 sought to end tribal ownership of land, and grant Indians deeds to individual property holdings; that is, severalty. Policymakers believed that individual landholdings, especially by male household heads, would contribute to Indian assimilation. (p. 516)

sharecropping The labor system by which freedmen agreed to exchange a portion of their harvested crops with the landowner for use of the land, a house, and tools. A compromise between freedmen and white landowners, this system developed in the cash-strapped South because the freedmen wanted to work their own land but lacked the money to buy it, while white landowners needed agricultural laborers but did not have money to pay wages. (p. 476)

Social Darwinism The application of Charles Darwin's biological theory of natural selection to the development of society, this late-nineteenth-century principle encouraged the notion that societies progress as a result of competition and the "survival of the fittest." Intervention by the state in this process was counterproductive because it impeded healthy progress. Social Darwinists justified the increasing inequality of late-nineteenth-century, industrial American society as natural. (p. 579)

Social Gospel A religious movement that called for people of religious faith to engage actively in reform work and public activism. A response to the problems caused by industrialization, the Social Gospel placed particular emphasis on anti-poverty work and urban reform. While the most famous Social Gospel leaders were

Protestants such as Congregationalist minister Washington Gladden, the movement attracted considerable support among reform-minded Catholics and Reform Jews. Generally liberal in theology, Social Gospel advocates encouraged cooperation among people of different faiths. (p. 585)

socialism A theory of social and economic organization based on the common ownership or enjoyment of property and goods. Utopian socialists of the early nineteenth century envisioned small planned self-governing communities; later socialists campaigned for state ownership of railroads and large industries and an end to economic inequality. (p. 336)

social settlement Also sometimes referred to as a "settlement house," the social settlement was an urban institution invented in the late nineteenth century. In a social settlement, well-educated, elite, or middle-class reformers (often women) moved to a poverty-stricken urban neighborhood and established a community center to serve the needs of their own neighbors. Chicago's Hull House, founded by Jane Addams, was America's most famous social settlement. Addams emphasized that the settlement was not a charity organization, but an institution that addressed city problems in a systemic way, while enabling young college graduates to broaden their perspectives and live with a sense of purpose. (p. 612)

social-welfare liberalism The liberal ideology implemented in the United States during the New Deal of the 1930s and the Great Society of the 1960s. It uses the financial and bureaucratic resources of the state and federal governments to provide economic and social security to individual citizens, interest groups, and corporate enterprises. Social welfare programs include old-age pensions, unemployment compensation, subsidies to farmers, mortgage guarantees, and tax breaks for corporations. (p. 719)

soft power In diplomacy, the influence of U.S. cultural institutions, particularly those with broad popular appeal. The eager reception of Hollywood movies and American popular music, for example, may influence public opinion in other countries favorably toward the United States. (p. 709)

Sons of Liberty Patriots—primarily middling merchants and artisans—who banded together to protest the Stamp Act and other imperial reforms of the 1760s. The group originated in Boston in 1765 but soon spread to all the colonies. (p. 148)

spoils system The widespread award of public jobs to political supporters after an electoral victory. In 1829, Andrew Jackson instituted the system on the national level, arguing that the rotation of officeholders was preferable to a permanent group of bureaucrats. The spoils system became a central, and corrupting, element in American political life. (p. 305)

states' rights An interpretation of the Constitution that exalts the sovereignty of the states and circumscribes the authority of the national government. Expressed first by Antifederalists in the debate over the Constitution, and then in the Virginia and Kentucky resolutions of 1798, the ideology of states' rights became especially important in the South. It informed white southerners' resistance to the high tariffs of the 1820s and 1830s, to legislation

to limit the spread of slavery, and to attempts by the national government in the mid-twentieth century to end Jim Crow practices and, more generally, to extend its authority. (p. 211)

suburbs Residential communities adjacent to urban areas that were originally connected to city centers by streetcar or subway lines and later by highways. Early suburbs appealed to the upper and middle classes in particular. By 1910, 25 percent of the population lived in these new communities. The 1990 census revealed that the majority of Americans lived in the suburbs. (p. 592)

suffrage The right to vote. The classical republican ideology current in the United States before 1810 limited suffrage to men who held property and thus had "a stake in society." However, between 1810 and 1860, state constitutions extended the vote to virtually all adult white men and some free black men; subsequently, the Fifteenth (1870) and Nineteenth (1920) amendments to the U.S. Constitution granted the franchise respectively to black men and to women, making adult suffrage nearly universal. (p. 244)

syndicalists Members of a revolutionary movement that, like socialists, believed in the Marxist principle of class struggle and advocated the organization of society on the basis of industrial unionism. The syndicalist approach was advocated by the Industrial Workers of the World (IWW) at the start of the twentieth century. (p. 644)

tariff A tax on imports. *Tariffs for revenue* raise money to pay government expenses; *protective tariffs* also shield domestic products from foreign competition. (p. 207)

temperance, temperance movement A long-term reform movement that encouraged individuals and governments to limit the consumption of alcoholic beverages. Leading temperance groups include the American Temperance Society of the 1830s; the Washingtonian Association of the 1840s; the Women's Christian Temperance Union of the late nineteenth century; and Alcoholics Anonymous, which was founded in the 1930s. (p. 296)

Third World A term that came into use in the post–World War II era to describe developing or ex-colonial nations in Asia, Africa, Latin America, and the Middle East that were not aligned with either the Western capitalist countries led by the United States (the First World) or the socialist states of Eastern Europe led by the Soviet Union (the Second World). (p. 807)

total war A form of warfare, new to the nineteenth and twentieth centuries, that mobilized all of a society's resources—economic, political, and cultural—in support of the military effort. Governments now fielded massive armies of conscripted civilians rather than small forces of professional soldiers. And they attacked civilians and industries that supported the war efforts of their enemies. Witness Sherman's march through Georgia in the Civil War; the massive American bombing of Dresden, Hamburg, and Tokyo during World War II; and the bombing of North Vietnam during the Vietnam War. (p. 439)

town meeting A system of local government in New England in which all male heads of households meet regularly to elect selectmen; levy local taxes; and regulate markets, roads, and schools. (p. 63)

trade unions Organizations of skilled workers, usually limited to men in a specialized field of employment (such as bricklayers, carpenters, or electricians). Trade unions tended to exclude women, and to emphasize direct negotiation with employers, rather than broad-based political action. (p. 549)

transcendentalism A nineteenth-century intellectual movement that posited the importance of an ideal world of mystical knowledge and harmony beyond the world of the senses. As articulated by Ralph Waldo Emerson and Henry David Thoreau, transcendentalism called for the critical examination of society and emphasized individuality, self-reliance, and nonconformity. (p. 332)

trust A legal entity, invented in the 1880s, which enabled a group of companies to combine and operate as a single unit. By doing so, they avoided competing with one another for customers, and were also able to raise market prices and gain near-monopoly power over a given market. To form a trust, each company agreed (sometimes under extreme pressure from a powerful competitor) to deposit stock with a central trustee and submit to the management of a central board of directors. In popular usage, *trust* came to mean any giant corporation that dominated a sector of the economy and wielded monopoly power. (p. 496)

vaudeville A theater that offered audiences a succession of brief singing, dancing, and comedy routines. Vaudeville changed live entertainment from its seedier predecessors like minstrel shows to family entertainment for the urban masses. Vaudeville became popular in the 1880s and 1890s, just before the introduction of movies. (p. 601)

vertical integration A method employed by companies to control the cost of production, by gaining ownership of all parts of the manufacturing process, from raw materials through transportation and marketing. A steel company might, for example, seek to purchase coal and iron mines, and railroad lines that ran between these mines and its factories. A beer manufacturer might seek to own or license a nationwide network of saloons or pubs that sold its beer exclusively. (p. 531)

vice-admiralty court A tribunal presided over by a judge, with no jury. The Sugar Act of 1764 required that offenders be tried in a vice-admiralty court rather than in a common-law tribunal, where a jury decided guilt or innocence. This provision of the act provoked protests from merchant-smugglers accustomed to acquittal by sympathetic colonial juries. (p. 146)

virtual representation A term coined by British politicians in the 1760s in arguing that the interests of the American colonists were adequately represented in Parliament by merchants trading with the colonies and by sugar planters living in England who owned estates in the West Indies. (p. 147)

voluntarism The view that citizens should themselves improve their lives, rather than rely on the efforts of government. Especially favored by Samuel Gompers, voluntarism was a key idea within the labor movement, but one gradually abandoned over the course of the twentieth century. (p. 644)

war of attrition A military strategy of small-scale attacks used, usually by the weaker side, to sap the resources and morale of the stronger side. Examples include the attacks carried out by Patriot militias in the South during the War of Independence, and the guerrilla tactics of the Vietcong and North Vietnamese during the Vietnam War. (p. 181)

welfare capitalism A system of labor relations that stresses management's responsibility for employees' well-being. Originating in the 1920s, welfare capitalism offered such benefits as stock plans, health care, and old-age pensions and was designed to maintain a stable workforce and undercut the growth of trade unions. (p. 688)

Whigs, Whig party An English political party that demanded a constitutional (rather than an absolutist) monarchy. The English Whigs rose to power following the Glorious Revolution of 1688 and governed Britain until the eve of the American Revolution. In 1834, an American political party headed by Henry Clay and Daniel Webster took the name *Whig* to protest the "monarchical" actions of Andrew Jackson, whom they called "King Andrew I." The American Whig party dissolved in the 1850s over the question of whether or not to extend slavery to the territories. See *Radical Whigs* and *conscience Whigs*. (pp. 77, 321)

white-collar workers Middle-class professionals who are salaried workers, as opposed to business owners or wage laborers; they first appeared in large numbers during the industrial expansion of the late nineteenth century. White-collar workers include lawyers, engineers, chemists, salespeople, accountants, and advertising managers. (p. 536)

yeoman In England between 1500 and 1800, a farmer who owned enough land to support his family in reasonable comfort. In America, Thomas Jefferson envisioned a nation of yeomen, that is, politically and financially independent farmers. (p. 36)

Credits

Matthew Pace Andrews, *The Women of the South in War Times* (Baltimore: Norman Remington, 1924); and Rod Gragg, *The Illustrated Confederate Reader* (New York, NY: HarperCollins), 1989.

Voices from Abroad: Excerpts from Ernest Duvergier de Hauranne, "A Frenchman in Lincoln's America" translated by Ralph H. Bowen Copyright © 1974 R.R. Donnelly & Sons Company. Reprinted with permission.

Chapter 15

Voices from Abroad: Allan Nevins (ed.) Excerpts from *America Through British Eyes*. Copyright © 1968 Peter Smith Publishers. Reprinted by permission.

Chapter 16

Voices from Abroad: Excerpts from Oscar Handlin (ed.), *This Was America* (Cambridge, MA: Harvard University Press). Copyright © 1949 Reprinted by permission of the author.

Chapter 17

Comparing American Voices: Reprinted from Mary H. Blewett, *We Will Rise in Our Might: Workingwomen's Voices from Nineteenth-Century New England*. Copyright © 1991 by Cornell University. Used by permission of the publisher, Cornell University Press.

Voices from Abroad: *Land Without Ghosts* by Huang Zunxian. Copyright © 1989 by University of California Press—Books. Reproduced with permission of University of California Press—Books.

Chapter 18

Comparing American Voices: Excerpt from Lyman Abbott, *The Evolution of Christianity*, pages 8–10. Copyright © Reprinted with the permission of Cambridge University Press.

Chapter 19

Comparing American Voices: Excerpts from *Out of the Sweatshop* by Leon Stein, copyright © 1977 by Leo Stein. Used by permission of Quadrangle Books, a Division of Random House, Inc.

Chapter 20

Figure 20.1: From William Sayre (ed.) *Federal Government Services.*

Chapter 21

Comparing American Voices: Henry F. Graff, ed. Pages 64–65, 80–81, 137–139, and 144–145 from *American Imperialism and the Philippine Insurrection*. Copyright © 1969 Reprinted with permission of the author.

Chapter 22

Comparing American Voices: From *Bread Givers* by Anzia Yezierska. Copyright © 1970 by Louise Levitas Henriksen. Reprinted by permission of Persea Books, Inc. New York. Excerpt from

Middletown in Transition by Helen Lynd and Robert S. Lynd, copyright © 1937 by Harcourt, Inc. 1965 by Robert S. Lynd and Helen M. Lynd, reproduced by permission of Houghton Mifflin Harcourt Publishing Company.

Chapter 23

Comparing American Voices: Robert S. McElvaine, *Down and Out in the Great Depression* (Chapel Hill: North Carolina University Press, 1983), 54–55; Michael P. Johnson, ed., *Reading the American Past*, Third Edition, 2 vols. (Boston: Bedford/St. Martin's, 2005), 2: 166–267; Robert D. Marcus and David Burner, eds. *America Firsthand*, Seventh Edition (Boston: Bedford/St. Martin's, 2007), 182–184.

Voices from Abroad: Denis W. Brogan, "From England" In Joseph, Franz M.; *As Others Sees Us* © 1959 Princeton University Press, 1987 renewed PUP Reprinted by permission of Princeton University Press.

Chapter 24

Comparing American Voices: Excerpt from Studs Terkel, *The Good War: An Oral History of World War II*, 102–111. Copyright 1984; Sherna B. Gluck, pp. 37–42 from *Rosie the Riveter Revisited*. Copyright © 1987 Reprinted with permission of the author; and Michael E. Stevens and Ellen D. Goldlust (eds.), excerpt from *Women Remember the War, 1941–1945*. Copyright © 1993 Reprinted with permission of the Wisconsin Historical Society.

Voices from Abroad: From *Nisei Daughter* by Monica Sone. Copyright © 1953 by Monica Sone. Copyright © renewed 1981 by Monica Sone. By permission of Little, Brown & Company.

Chapter 25

Comparing American Voices: Frank Porter Graham Papers, #1819, Southern Historical Collection, Wilson Library, University of North Carolina at Chapel Hill. Reprinted with permission.

Voices from Abroad: Excerpt from Jean Monnet, *Memoirs*, trans. Richard Mayne, pp. 264–266. Copyright 1978.

Chapter 26

Comparing American Voices: Excerpt from *Leaving Home* by Art Buchwald. Copyright © 1993 The Estate of Art Buchwald; Excerpt from *It Changed My Life* by Betty Friedan. Copyright © 1976 Curtis Brown, Ltd.; Susan Allen Toth, Excerpts from *Blooming: A Small-Town Girlhood*. Copyright © 1978 Reprinted with permission.

Voices from Abroad: "Measures of Influence" by Hanoch Bartov (1963) in Chapter 16 from *The Outer World*, edited by Oscar and Lillian Handlin (Cambridge, MA: Harvard University Press). © 1997 Reprinted by permission of Oscar and Lillian Handlin.

Chapter 27

Comparing American Voices: Howell Raines, *My Soul Is Rested* (New York: Penguin/Putnam, 1977) Copyright © 1977 Reprinted by permission of PFD, Inc.; Excerpts from Stanley I. Kutler, *Looking for America*, Second Edition, Volume 2. Copyright © 1979. Reprinted with permission of the author.

Chapter 28

Comparing American Voices: "Donald L. Whitfield" in *Landing Zones*, James R. Wilson, pp. 203–204; 207; 209–210. Copyright © 1990 Duke University Press. All rights reserved. Reprinted by permission of the publisher; Bernard Edelman, Excerpt from *Dear America: Letters Home from Vietnam* (New York: W.W. Norton & Co.) pp. 2–4, 205; From *Bloods* by Wallace Terry, copyright © 1984 by Wallace Terry. Used by permission of Random House, Inc. Al Santoli, Excerpt from *Everything We Had*, Al Santoli, copyright © 1981 by Albert Santoli and Vietnam Veterans of America. Used by permission of Random House.

Voices from Abroad: Ernesto Guevara, excerpts from *Che Guevara Speaks*. Copyright © 1967, 2000 by Pathfinder Press. Reprinted with permission.

Chapter 29

Comparing American Voices: Phyllis Schafly, *The Phyllis Schafly Report* November, 1972, pp. 1–4. Copyright © 1972 Phyllis Schafly. Reprinted by permission of the author; Excerpt from Jerry Falwell, *Listen America* (New York: Doubleday, 1980), pp. 150–151. Copyright © 1980 Reprinted by permission; Excerpt from Caroline Bird, *What Women Want* (New York: Simon & Schuster, 1978), pp. 120–121. Copyright © 1978 Reprinted by permission.

Voices from Abroad: R. David Arkush and Leo O. Lee, trans and eds. *Land Without Ghosts: Chinese Impressions of America From the Mid-Nineteenth Century to the Present.* Copyright © 1989. Reprinted by permission of University of California Press in the formats Text and Other Book via Copyright Clearance Center.

Chapter 30

Comparing American Voices: Reprinted with permission of Simon & Schuster, Inc. from *Speaking My Mind* by Ronald Reagan. Copyright © 1989 Ronald Reagan; Donald E. Wildmon, *Home Invaders* (Elgin, IL: Victor Books, 1985). Copyright © 1985 Reprinted by permission of the author.

Voices from Abroad: Yoichi Funabashi, "Japan and America: Global Partners." *Foreign Policy* 86, Spring, 1992 Copyright © 1992 Reproduced with permission of *Foreign Policy* (Spring, 1992).

Chapter 31

Comparing American Voices: Excerpt from Paul S. Boyer, ed. *Enduring Voices,* Third Edition (Boston: Houghton Mifflin, 1996), pp. 408–409. Copyright © 1996 Reprinted by permission; Christine Ahn, *Shafted: Free Trade and America's Working Poor.* Copyright © 2003 Reprinted by permission.

Voices from Abroad: Reprinted by permission of R. I. Cole.

Fig 31.2: Copyright © 2009 by The Atlantic Monthly. Reproduced with permission of The Atlantic Monthly.

Additional Art Credits

"Voices from Abroad" images (left to right): *Yoichi Funabashi:* Claremont McKenna College. *Frances Trollope:* Miriam and Ira D. Wallach Division of Art, Prints and Photographs, The New York Public Library. Astor, Lenox and Foundations. *Ernestine Rose:* Schlesinger Library, Radcliffe Institute for Advanced Study, Harvard University. *José Martí:* The Granger Collection, New York.

"Comparing American Voices" images (left to right): *Thomas Paine:* Miriam and Ira D. Wallach Division of Art, Prints and Photographs, The New York Public Library. Astor, Lenox and Tilden Foundations. *Emma Hart Willard:* Miriam and Ira D. Wallach Division of Art, Prints and Photographs, The New York Public Library. Astor, Lenox and Tilden Foundations. *Franklin McCain:* © Corbis. All Rights Reserved. *Jesús Colón:* "Biographical Link from the Biographical Dictionary of Hispanic Literature in the United States"; Edited by Nicholas Kanellas; New York: Greenwood Press, 1989.

Part 1 opener credits: Page 2: Old State House, Boston: The Bostonian Society and Old State House Museum. Page 3: Dutch Farmstead painting: New-York State Historical Association; West Indies Sugar Mill: The Granger Collection.

Page 4: Sir William Berkeley: Bridgeman Art Library; Colonial village church procession: *J. Barber's History & Antiquities of N.E., N.Y. , N.J. & Pa./Picture Research Consultants & Archives;* Colleges in Cambridge, MA, 1726: Massachusetts Historical Society.

Part 2 opener credits: Page 136: Pulling down the statue of George III: Library of Congress.

Page 137: Washington Addressing the Constitutional Convention: © Bettmann/Corbis; U.S. Bombardment of Tripoli, 1804: The Granger Collection.

Page 138: Bank of the United States, Philadelphia, 1800: Library Company of Philadelphia; York Pennsylvania Family, 1828: St. Louis Art Museum; *Benjamin Hawkins and the Creek Indians:* Greenville County Museum of Art.

Part 3 opener credits: Page 268: "Tippecanoe and Tyler Too" parade: Franklin D. Roosevelt Library.

Page 269: *Francis Cabot Lowell's mill in Waltham:* Courtesy Gore Place Society, Waltham, MA; *Auction in Chatham Street* by E. Didier: Museum of the City of New York.

Page 270: George Caleb Bingham, *Stump Speaking* (detail): Private Collection/The Bridgeman Art Library Ltd.; Camp Meeting at Eastham, MA, 1851: Library of Congress; "Am I Not a Woman and a Sister?": The Granger Collection, New York.

Part 4 opener credits: Page 392: Military expedition into the Black Hills: National Archives.

Page 393: Captured Sioux Indians in fenced enclosure on Minnesota River: Minnesota Historical Society; *Bombing of Fort Sumter* by Currier & Ives: Anne S. K. Brown Military Collection, Brown University Library.

Index

About the Authors

JAMES A. HENRETTA is a professor emeritus at the University of Maryland, College Park. His publications include *"Salutary Neglect": Colonial Administration under the Duke of Newcastle* (1972); *The Evolution of American Society, 1700–1815: An Interdisciplinary Analysis* (1973); *Evolution and Revolution: American Society, 1600–1820* (1987); *The Origins of American Capitalism* (1991); and an edited volume, *Republicanism and Liberalism in America and the German States, 1750–1850* (2002). His most recent publication is a long article, "Charles Evans Hughes and the Strange Death of Liberal America" (*Law and History Review*, 2006), derived from his ongoing research on the liberal state in America: New York, 1820–1975.

REBECCA EDWARDS is a professor of history at Vassar College. Her research interests focus on the post–Civil War era and include electoral politics, environmental history, and the history of women and gender roles. She is the author of *Angels in the Machinery: Gender in American Party Politics from the Civil War to the Progressive Era* (1997) and *New Spirits: Americans in the "Gilded Age," 1865–1905* (second edition; 2010). She is currently working on a biography of women's rights advocate and People's Party orator Mary E. Lease.

ROBERT O. SELF is an associate professor of history at Brown University. His research focuses on urban history, the history of race and American political culture, post–1945 U.S. society and culture, and gender and sexuality in American politics. His first book, *American Babylon: Race and the Struggle for Postwar Oakland* (2003), won four professional prizes, including the James A. Rawley Prize from the Organization of American Historians (OAH). He is currently at work on a book about gender, sexuality, and political culture in the United States from 1964 to 2004.